"The 2000 presidential election was such a close call— how does that happen? I wonder if it has happened before."

"How am I going to be sure I know all this material for the test? I feel confident now, but..."

"I understand that the Bill of Rights is important, but how is it used in real life?"

mypoliscilab™

Where participation leads to action!

with LongmanParticipate.com 3.0 inside

From **simulations** that place students in the role of campaign manager to **timeline activities**, from **pre- and post-chapter tests** to a fully integrated **Ebook**, MyPoliSciLab brings together an amazing collection of resources for both students and instructors. See a demo now at **www.mypoliscilab.com**!

Here's what's in MyPoliSciLab—

Pre-Test, Post Test, and Chapter Exam.
For each chapter of the text, students will navigate through a pre-test, post-test, and a full chapter exam—all fully integrated with the online Ebook so students can assess, review, and improve their understanding of the material in each chapter.

Ebook.
Matching the exact layout of the printed textbook, the Ebook contains multimedia icons in the margins that launch a wealth of exciting resources.

Chapter Review.
For each chapter, students will find additional resources, such as a complete study guide, learning objectives, a summary, and Web explorations.

Research Navigator™.
This database provides thousands of articles from popular periodicals like *Newsweek* and *USA Today* that give students and professors access to topical content from a variety of sources.

New York Times Online Feed & The New York Times Search by Subject™ Archive.
Both provide free access to the full text of *The New York Times* and articles from the world's leading journalists of the *Times*. The online feed provides students with updated headlines and political news on an hourly basis.

LongmanParticipate.com 3.0
Our well-known and highly respected online tool is now fully updated. Students will find over 100 simulations, interactive timelines, comparative exercises and more—all integrated with the online ebook. Available inside MyPoliSciLab or as a website alone.

LongmanParticipate.com 3.0
Inside!

Go to mypoliscilab.com for a free demo.

GOVERNMENT IN AMERICA

GOVERNMENT IN AMERICA

PEOPLE, POLITICS, AND POLICY

Twelfth Edition

GEORGE C. EDWARDS III
Texas A & M University

MARTIN P. WATTENBERG
University of California, Irvine

ROBERT L. LINEBERRY
University of Houston

New York San Francisco Boston
London Toronto Sydney Tokyo Singapore Madrid
Mexico City Munich Paris Cape Town Hong Kong Montreal

Executive Editor: Eric Stano
Acquisitions Editor: Edward Costello
Development Editor: Karen Helfrich
Senior Marketing Manager: Elizabeth Fogarty
Senior Media Editor: Patrick McCarthy
Media and Supplements Editor: Kristi Olson
Production Manager: Charles Annis
Project Coordination and Electronic Page Makeup: WestWords, Inc.
Cover Design Manager: John Callahan
Cover Designer: Laura Shaw
Cover Images: Courtesy of Corbis, Inc.
Photo Researcher: Photosearch, Inc.
Senior Manufacturing Buyer: Dennis J. Para
Printer and Binder: Quebecor World
Cover Printer: Phoenix Color Corp.

Library of Congress Cataloging-in-Publication Data

Edwards, George C.
    Government in America : people, politics, and policy / George C. Edwards III, Martin P.
Wattenberg, Robert L. Lineberry.—12th ed.
        p. cm.
    ISBN 0–321–29254–5
        1. United States—Politics and government. I. Wattenberg, Martin P., 1956– II.
Lineberry, Robert L. III. Title.

    JK276.E39 2005
    320.473—dc22
                                                                            2004026388

Brief Contents

Detailed Contents

Preface

POLITICS MATTERS. THAT IS THE CORE MESSAGE OF THIS BOOK. The national government provides important services, ranging from retirement security and health care to recreation facilities and weather forecasts. The national government may also send us to war or negotiate peace with our adversaries, expand or restrict our freedom, raise or lower our taxes, and increase or decrease aid to education. In the twenty-first century, decision makers of both political parties are facing difficult questions regarding American democracy and the scope of our government. Students need a framework for understanding these questions.

Focus

We write *Government in America* to provide our readers with a better understanding of our fascinating political system. This twelfth edition of *Government in America* continues to frame its content with a public policy approach to government in the United States. We continually ask—and answer—the question, "What difference does politics make to the policies governments produce?" It is one thing to describe the Madisonian system of checks and balances and separation of powers or the elaborate and unusual federal system of government in the United States; it is something else to ask how these features of our constitutional structure affect the policies governments generate.

We find that this focus engages students' interest. Students, like their instructors, quickly recognize that the principal reason for studying politics is to understand why government produces the policies it does. What many see as "dry" subjects become interesting when they are tied to outcomes that directly affect each of us. Even introductory students feel comfortable asking, "So what?" To reinforce this interest, we have a feature in the margins entitled Why It Matters in which we ask students to think critically about some aspect of our system and how things might be if it worked differently.

We do not discuss policy at the expense of politics, however. We provide extensive coverage of five core subject areas: constitutional foundations, patterns of political behavior, political institutions, public policy outputs, and state and local government, but we try to do so in a more analytically significant—and interesting—manner. We take special pride in introducing students to relevant work from current political scientists, such as the role of PACs or the impact of divided government—something we have found instructors appreciate.

It is not enough to arouse students' interest, however. To be a useful teaching tool, a text must be accessible to students and enjoyable to read. We believe a principal reason for the success of *Government in America* is its high level of readability. To ensure that the material is not only clearly presented but also meaningful, we make special efforts to illustrate points with interesting examples to which students can relate. The ability of Congress to indirectly regulate behavior in the states becomes more meaningful when the power is illustrated with a discussion of raising the drinking age. In addition, this is neither a conservative nor a liberal book. Instead, we make every effort to present material in an evenhanded manner. As a result, over the years we have received many letters in which students have told us how much they enjoyed reading the book. Needless to say, we find this response very gratifying.

Two Themes

To render the policy focus in concrete terms, two important themes appear throughout the book: the nature of democracy and the scope of government. Each chapter begins with a preview of the relevancy of these themes to the chapter's subject, refers to the themes at points within the chapter, and ends with specific sections on the two themes under the heading "Understanding . . ." that show how the themes illuminate the chapter's subject matter.

The first great question central to governing, a question every nation must answer, is *How should we govern?* In the United States, our answer is "democracy." Yet democracy is an evolving and somewhat ambiguous concept. In Chapter 1, we define democracy as a means of selecting policymakers and of organizing government so that policy represents and responds to citizens' preferences. As with previous editions, we continue to incorporate theoretical issues in our discussions of different models of American democracy. We try to encourage students to think analytically about the theories and to develop independent assessments of how well the American system lives up to citizens' expectations of democratic government. To help them do this, in every chapter we raise questions about democracy. For example, does Congress give the American people the policies they want? Is a strong presidency good for democracy? Does our mass media make us more democratic? Are powerful courts that make policy decisions compatible with democracy?

A common complaint about the national government is that it cannot respond to the needs of its citizens, that it suffers from *gridlock*. A subtheme to our discussion of democracy is whether America's diversity and the openness of our political system have the drawback of incapacitating government. The diversity of the American people is reflected in the variety of political interests represented in the political system. This system is so open that many different interests find access to policymakers. In our system of checks and balances, opposition by one set of policymakers can sometimes frustrate the will of the majority. We leave it to the reader to determine whether the difficulty of achieving policy change, be it the Bill Clinton health care reform plan or the George W. Bush tax cut, is a positive feature of our system. Our goal is to promote understanding of the consequences of the American democratic system and to provoke discussion about these consequences. We find that students are especially interested in why government does not "do something."

The second theme, the scope of government, focuses on another great question of governing: *What should government do?* Here we discuss alternative views concerning the proper role and size for American government and how this scope is influenced by the workings of institutions and politics. The government's scope is the core question around which politics revolves in contemporary America, pervading many crucial issues: To what degree should Washington impose national standards such as speed limits on state policies? How high should taxes be? Do elections encourage politicians to promise more governmental services? Questions about the scope of government are policy questions and thus obviously directly related to our policy approach. Since the scope of government is *the* pervasive question in American politics today, students will have little problem finding it relevant to their lives and interests.

A subtheme of the scope of government is the role of *individualism* in American political life. The people who immigrated to America may have been diverse, but many adopted a common dream of America as a place where people could make it on their own without interference from government. Today, individualism remains a powerful influence in the United States. Americans' strong preference for free markets and limited government has important consequences for public policy. For example, it substantially constrains efforts to intervene in the economy, efforts that have long been the norm in other developed democracies.

At the same time, a central contest in American politics has been between two kinds of individualism. Economic individualism embraces the doctrines of capitalism. The purpose of government is to protect the creativity of entrepreneurs and markets, which leads to well being. Democratic individualism appeals to government to redress the social inequalities that result from economic individualism. Puritans, abolitionists, agrarian populists, prohibitionists, civil rights crusaders, feminists, and the contemporary religious right have preached collective purpose against individualism. Thus, we often employ the concept of individualism in our analysis of the scope of government.

We hope that students—long after reading *Government in America*—will employ these perennial questions about the nature of our democracy and the scope of our government when they examine political events. The specifics of policy issues will change, but questions about whether the government is responsive to the people or whether it should expand or contract its scope will always be with us.

Features

Eight features appear throughout *Government in America*: (1) **Issues of the Times;** (2) **You Are the Policymaker/Judge;** (3) **America in Perspective;** (4) **Young People and Politics;** (5) **Making a Difference;** (6) **How You Can Make a Difference;** (7) **Why It Matters;** and (8) **Get Connected.** Each of the features plays a particular role in the text to support our approach to American government.

You Are the Policymaker

We believe students should stay on top of current and enduring issues in American politics and government by reading a newspaper every day. To that end, we introduced in the last edition and have updated in this edition a new feature to each chapter called **Issues of the Times.** This feature presents thought-provoking articles directly from the *New York Times* on important issues in the news along with useful pedagogy that helps students understand and think critically about the issue presented and become comfortable reading politically oriented newspaper articles.

You Are the Judge

We also believe it is important that students recognize and think critically about difficult policy choices they must face as citizens. **You Are the Policymaker** asks students to read arguments on both sides of a specific current issue, such as whether we should prohibit PACs, and then to make a policy decision. In Chapters 4 and 5 (Civil Liberties and Civil Rights), this feature is titled **You Are the Judge** and presents the student with an actual court case. This feature directly supports our policy approach.

America in Perspective

There are many ways to teach lessons, and many instructors find that employing a comparative approach helps them to make their points more effectively. Our **America in Perspective** feature examines how the United States compares to other countries in areas such as tax rates, voter turnout, and the delivery of public services. Through reading these boxes and comparing the United States to other nations, students can obtain a better perspective on the size of our government and the nature of our democracy.

Young People and Politics

One of the greatest challenges to teaching is overcoming student apathy, even in the face of the September 11 attacks and the Iraq War. Students quite naturally want to know how politics impacts them and how their generation is different. As an extension of our central focus on *politics matters*, our new **Young People and Politics** feature illustrates how policies specifically impact young adults, how their political behavior patterns are unique and important, and how their particular policy desires are being met or largely ignored by public officials. These features are also especially useful for instructors, since there is relatively little written on the topic.

How You Can Make a Difference

In **Making a Difference** we focus on an individual who became involved in government and politics and made a difference as a result. Our goal is simple: to show students that individuals, ordinary people, can—and do—make a difference in what government does. This feature nicely complements our increased focus on the relevance of government to our lives.

How You Can Make a Difference provides students with information on how they can get involved with issues in order to influence how government works or what policies are established. This feature is a natural extension of the Making a Difference boxes.

We mentioned earlier our feature that appears several times in each chapter's margins entitled **Why It Matters.** Here we encourage students to think critically about an aspect of government, politics, or policy and ask them to consider the impact—usually on themselves—if things worked differently.

Our **Get Connected** feature gets students involved in the study of politics and government via the Internet. These user-friendly exercises appear at the end of every chapter and have students research a particular topic covered in the chapter by visiting one or more related websites and points out the relevancy of the material presented to their own lives.

To bring some of our new and existing features together and prepare students for making the most of them, we have added a **new section** to the beginning of the book called **Tools for Understanding Government in America.** This "primer" provides helpful guidance on how to read newspapers, study charts and graphs, and understand the Internet.

Each chapter concludes with a contemporary bibliography, a listing of key terms, and Internet resources relevant to the chapter. (The URLs included at the end of each chapter were current when the book went to press. However, changes or updates may have been made to the site at the discretion of the individual site owner or webmaster.)

Finally, as an additional study aid, we also define key terms in the margins of the text when they are first introduced.

Currency

This twelfth edition of *Government in America* is completely up to date and incorporates the best recent scholarship on U.S. government. Our emphasis in each chapter on the scope of government is also very timely, as it remains at the core of debates about taxation, regulating tobacco products, campaign finance, and access to health care. We provide comprehensive coverage of the 2004 presidential, congressional, and state elections—both the campaigns and the results—in Chapters 8–10 and 12–13. We also include the latest Supreme Court decisions from 2004 on federalism, civil liberties, civil rights, and other relevant topics. From the numbers for the 2005 budget to the backgrounds of members of Congress, the text, tables, and figures reflect the most recent available data. Naturally, we devote considerable attention to the Bush administration in Chapter 13 and to the efforts of both the president and Congress to deal with the budget (Chapter 14), which has become central to American politics and policy. Finally, we cover the war on terrorism and the war with Iraq, especially in Chapter 20.

Graphics play an important role in textbooks, and we have substantially upgraded our figures, graphs, tables, and charts in this edition. We have employed more vibrant colors and worked to make all our graphics easier and more interesting to read. We also provide a brief guide to using graphics following this preface.

It is worth noting here that the website for the twelfth edition of *Government in America* (*www.ablongman.com/edwards*) includes a section of updates. These updates provide the latest information on campaign finance, voter turnout, and other matters as soon as the data become available. These allow us to offer the most current information between editions and to provide new links to sources of information useful to both students and faculty.

Appendix

The Appendix continues to include the Constitution and the Declaration of Independence, *Federalist Papers #10* and *#51*, tables on presidents and presidential elections, party control of the presidency and Congress in the twenty-first century, Supreme Court justices serving since 1900, and a glossary of key terms. We continue to provide a list of key terms in Spanish.

Supplements

Instructor Supplements for Qualified College Adopters

MyPoliSciLab and LongmanParticipate.com 3.0 Faculty Teaching Guide Contains chapter-by-chapter detailed summaries for each of the sites' interactive activities, as well as a list of concepts covered, recommendations about how to integrate the sites into coursework, and discussion questions and paper topics for every exercise. Instructors may use the table of contents in the front of the guide to locate information on a given activity icon that appears in the margin of their adopted textbook. This guide also provides faculty with detailed instructions and screen shots showing how to use MyPoliSciLab or LongmanParticipate.com, how to register on the sites, and how to set up and use any available administrative features. The introductory chapter describes the numerous additional resources included on the websites. Written by Scott Furlong of University of Wisconsin.

Instructor's Manual   Written by Jan Leighley of University of Arizona, this comprehensive manual includes a list of pedagogical features, learning objectives, chapter outlines, narrative chapter overviews, key terms and definitions, suggestions for further study, media suggestions, and ideas for class discussion.

Test Bank   This test bank, prepared by Jan Leighley of University of Arizona, has been completely revised and contains thousands of challenging multiple choice, true-false, short answer, and essay questions along with a page-referenced answer key.

TestGen-EQ Computerized Testing System   This flexible, easy-to-use computer test bank includes all the test items in the printed test bank. The software allows professors to edit existing questions and to add their own items. Tests can be printed in several different formats and can include features such as graphs and tables.

PowerPoint® Presentations   PowerPoint® presentations that include a lecture outline of the new edition, along with graphics from the book, are available on the companion website *www.ablongman.com/edwards.*

Transparencies   A set of four-color acetate transparencies includes figures, graphs, and tables from the text.

Digital Media Archive Presentation CD-ROM   This complete multimedia presentation tool provides instructors with the following: a built-in presentation-maker, approximately 100 photos and 150 figures, graphs, and tables from Longman American government textbooks, 40 video clips, and more! All items can be imported into an instructor's existing presentation program, such as PowerPoint®.

Companion Website (CW) www.ablongman.com/edwards   This online course companion provides a wealth of resources for instructors using *Government in America.*

Instructors will have access to lecture outlines, website links, and downloadable visuals from the text.

Longman Political Science Video Program   Qualified adopters can peruse our list of videos for the American government classroom. Contact your local Allyn & Bacon/Longman representative for more information.

Student Supplements for Qualified College Adopters

MyPoliSciLab for American Government with LongmanParticipate.com 3.0 inside! MyPoliSciLab is a state-of-the-art, interactive online solution for your course. Available in CourseCompass, WebCT, or Blackboard, with this text, MyPoliSciLab offers a wealth of simulations, interactive exercises, and assessment tools—all integrated with an online e-book version of this text. For each chapter, students will navigate through a pre-test, post-test, chapter review, and a full chapter exam, allowing them to assess, review, and improve their understanding of key concepts. In addition to the online chapter content, students will have access to LongmanParticipate.com (updated 3.0 version), Longman's best-selling interactive online tool, which offers over 100 exercises for students. These exercises include:

- Simulations putting students in the roll of a political actor.
- Visual Literacy exercises getting students interpreting, manipulating, and applying data.
- Interactive Timelines enabling students to experience the evolution of an aspect of government.
- Participation activities that personalize politics by either getting students involved or exploring their own thoughts and opinions about our system.
- Comparative exercises that have students compare aspects of our system to those of other countries.

Students receive feedback at every step, and instructors can track student work through the gradebook feature. The activities for the site were written and revised by Quentin Kidd, *Christopher Newport University* and William Field, *Temple University*.

Activities and content for previous versions of the sites were written by: James Brent, *San Jose State University*; Laura Roselle, *Elon College*; Denise Scheberle, *University of Wisconsin*; B. Thomas Schuman, *University of New Hampshire*; Sharon Spray, *Elon College*; Cara Strebe, *San Francisco State University*; Ruth Ann Strickland, *Appalachian State University*; Kaare Strøm, *University of California, San Diego*; David Tabb, *San Francisco State University*; Paul Benson, *Tarrant County Community College*; Stephen Sandweiss, *Tacoma Community College*.

LongmanParticipate.com 3.0 is also available as a website alone for instructors who do not wish to use a course management system like CourseCompass.

A free six-month subscription to MyPoliSciLab or LongmanParticipate.com 3.0 is available when access cards to either site are ordered packaged with this text. To find out more about MyPoliSciLab, go to *www.poliscilab.com*. To find out more about LongmanParticipate.com. 3.0, go to *www.longmanparticipate.com*.

SafariX Textbooks Online SafariX Textbooks Online is an exciting new choice for students looking to save money. As an alternative to purchasing the print textbook, students can subscribe to the same content online and save up to 50% off the suggested list price of the print text. With a SafariX WebBook, students can search the text, make notes online, print out reading assignments that incorporate lecture notes, and bookmark important passages for later review. For more information, or to subscribe to the SafariX WebBook, visit www.safarix.com.

Companion Website (CW) www.ablongman.com/edwards This online course companion provides a wealth of resources for students using *Government in America*.

Students will find interactive exercises tied to text material, practice tests, links to related American government sites, updates to the text from the authors, and more.

StudyWizard CD-ROM   This computerized student tutorial program helps students review and master key concepts in the text through practice tests, chapter and topic summaries, and an interactive glossary. Students receive immediate feedback in the form of answer explanations and page references in the text to go to for review.

Study Guide   Written by Charles Matzke of Indiana University Purdue University Indiannapolis, the Study Guide helps students reinforce themes and concepts they encounter in the text. It includes chapter outlines, key terms, multiple choice, fill-in-the-blank, and essay questions, and exercises that help students test their understanding of the material with real-world applications.

Discount Subscription to *The New York Times*   A 10-week subscription for only $20! Contact your local Allyn & Bacon/Longman representative for more information.

Discount Subscription to *Newsweek* Magazine   Students receive 12 issues of *Newsweek* at more than 80% off the regular price. An excellent way for students to keep up with current events.

Culture War? The Myth of a Polarized America   By Morris P. Fiorina, Stanford University, Samuel J. Abrams, Harvard University, and Jeremy C. Pope, Stanford University. The first book in the "Great Questions in Politics" series, *Culture War? The Myth of a Polarized America* combines polling data with a compelling narrative to debunk commonly-believed myths about American politics—particulary the claim that Americans are deeply divided in their fundamental political views.

You Decide! Current Debates in American Politics, 2005 Edition   Edited by John T. Rourke, University of Connecticut, this exciting new debate-style reader examines provocative issues in American politics today. This topics have been selected for their currency, importance, and student interest, and the pieces that argue various sides of a given issue come from recent journals, congressioncal hearings, think tanks, and periodicals. Free when packaged with this text.

Voices of Dissent: Critical Readings in American Politics, Sixth Edition   Edited by William F. Grover, St. Michael's College, and Joseph G. Peschek, Hamline University, this collection of critical essays goes beyond the debate between mainstream liberalism and conservatism to fundamentally challenge the status quo. Available at a discount when ordered packaged with the text.

Ten Things That Every American Government Student Should Read   Edited by Karen O'Connor, American University. We asked American government instructors across the country to vote for the 10 things beyond the text that they believe every student should read, and put them in this brief and useful reader. Free when ordered packaged with the text.

Choices: An American Government Database Reader   This customizable reader allows instructors to choose from a database of over 300 readings to create a reader that exactly matches their course needs. Go to www.pearsoncustom.com/database/choices.html for more information.

Penguin-Longman Value Bundles   Longman offers 25 penguin Putnam titles at more than a 60% discount when packaged with any Longman text. A totally unique offer and a wonderful way to enhance students' understanding of concepts in American government. Please go to *www.ablongman.com/penguin* for more information.

Writing in Political Science, Third Edition   Written by Diane Schmidt, this guide takes students step-by-step through all aspects of writing in political science. Available at a discount when ordered package with any Longman textbook.

Getting Involved: A Guide to Student Citizenship   Written by Mark Kann, Todd Belt, Gabriela Cowperthwaite, and Steven Horn. A unique and practical handbook that guides students through political participation with concrete advice and extensive sample material—letters, telephone scripts, student interviews, and real-life anecdotes—for getting involved and making a difference in their lives and communities.

Texas Politics Supplement, Third Edition   Written by Debra St. John. A 90-page primer on state and local government and issues in Texas. Free when packaged with text.

California Politics Supplement, Fourth Edition   Written by Pamela Fiber. A 70-page primer on state and local government and issues in California. Free when packaged with text.

Florida Politics Supplement   Written by John Bertalan. A 50-page primer on state and local government and issues in Florida. Free when packaged with text.

Acknowledgments

Many, many colleagues have kindly given us comments on the drafts of the twelfth edition of *Government in America*. They are: Ashlyn Kuersten, Western Michigan University; Donald Kent Douglas, Long Beach City College; Jeffrey C. Berry, South Texas Community College; Martin Gruberg, University of Wisconsin; Michael K. Moore, University of Texas at Arlington; Haroon Khan, Henderson State University; Jim Cox, Georgia Perimeter College; Forest Grieves, University of Montana; Donald Aiesi, Furman University; Reed Welch, West Texas A & M University; Dick Hernandez, Orange Coast College; Allison Calhoun-Brown, Georgia State University; Don Cothran, Northern Arizona State University; William R. Thomas, Georgia State University; David Gray Alder, Idaho State University; William Biano, Pennsylvania State University; Richard Bilsker, College of Southern Maryland; Herbert Gooch, California Lutheran University; Martin James, Henderson Sate University; Craig Matthews, Fullerton College; Derrick Moffitt, Georgia Military College; Glen Sussman, Old Dominion University; R. Mark Tiller, Houston Community College-Northwest; John Wood, Oklahoma State University.

A number of editors have provided valuable assistance in the production of this twelfth edition of *Government in America*. Editor Edward Costello provided valuable guidance. Karen Helfrich was a superb developmental editor, coordinating every aspect of the book. Production manager Charles Annis deftly guided the production process. We are grateful to all of them. Finally, we owe a special debt of gratitude to Professor Donald Haider-Markel of the University of Kansas, who did an excellent job drafting Chapter 21, and Professors Paul Fessler of Dordt College and Quentin Kidd of Christopher Newport University, and Dave Rausch of West Texas A & M University for their work on the features Get Connected and How You Can Make a Difference.

George C. Edwards III
Martin P. Wattenberg
Robert L. Lineberry

Tools for Understanding
Government in America

A Student Guide to Reading Charts and Graphs

Information such as voting turnout in the last election, the president's job approval rating, or expenditures on national defense is often presented in quantitative form—that is, through the use of numbers. To help you understand this information, we employ charts and graphs. These figures provide a straightforward, visual representation of quantitative information. Yet charts and graphs can be confusing if you do not understand how to read them.

When you come across one of the charts and graphs in this book, you should ask three questions: First, *what is being measured?* This could be money, public opinion, seats in Congress, or a wide range of other subjects. Second, *what is the unit of measurement?* Is it 50 Americans or 50 percent of Americans? Obviously, it makes a difference. Finally, *what is the purpose of the figure?* Does it show changes over time? Does it compare two or more groups of people or countries? In most instances, captions are provided to explain the purpose of a figure.

After answering these general questions, examine the specific type of figure. This text relies on three main types of figures: pie charts, bar graphs, and line graphs. A *pie chart* is a circle divided into wedge-shaped "slices," or segments. Pie charts show the relative sizes of the segments to one another and to the whole. For example, by glancing at the following chart, you can quickly see that the federal government spends more of its funds on Social Security (21 percent) than on national defense (19 percent). The area of each segment is the same percent of the total circle as the number

The Federal Government Dollar (Fiscal Year 2005 Estimate)

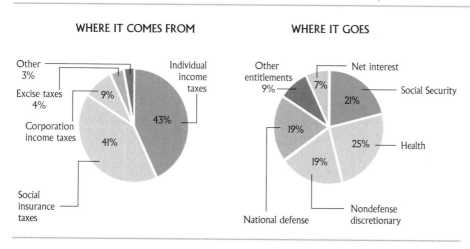

Source: Budget of the United States, Fiscal Year 2005, Historical Tables (Washington, D.C.: U.S. Government Printing Office, 2004), Tables 2.2, 8.3, 16.1.

Poverty Rates for Persons With Selected Characteristics

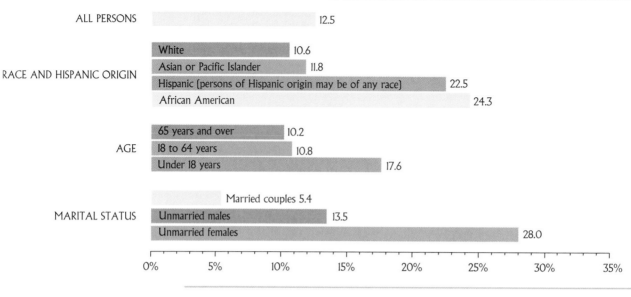

Source: U.S. Census Bureau.

it represents is of the sum of all the numbers in the chart. Since Social Security accounts for 21 percent of federal expenditures, its corresponding segment covers 21 percent of the area of the pie chart.

The second kind of figure, a *bar graph*, displays quantitative information by using rectangles (bars) set within two perpendicular lines, a vertical axis and a horizontal axis. Bar graphs are most frequently used to show and compare the values of multiple entities at a given point in time. Categories (such as groups of people or countries) are set along one axis and a scale (time or numbers, for example) is on the other axis. The length of each bar corresponds to its value on the scale. This makes it easy to visually contrast the values for multiple entities. For example, in the bar graph shown here, which uses a scale measuring poverty rates, you can see that the bars representing persons of African-American origin, young people, and unmarried females are the longest, indicating that they are the most likely to be living in poverty. The characteristics of people are on the vertical axis and on the bars themselves, and the scale representing the percentage of people in poverty is on the horizontal axis.

The third type of figure, a *line graph*, illustrates quantitative information by means of lines. Typically, the vertical axis of a line graph represents a quantitative scale (such as percentages) and the horizontal axis represents a category (such as presidents or a sequence of dates). Specific numbers are represented as points on the graph between the two axes and are connected with a line. Sometimes there is more than one line on a graph, as when numbers are shown for two different sets of information—for example, elections for both the House and Senate, state and federal expenditures, or exports and imports. The two lines can be compared to each other, or, in some cases, the distance between the two lines can be analyzed. In the following line graph, which charts a single set of quantitative information, the percentage of the voting age population that actually voted is shown on the vertical axis, and the horizontal axis represents years of presidential elections. The falling line indicates that turnout has declined since 1892.

By remembering these key features of charts and graphs, you can more accurately assess the information presented in *Government in America*, as well as interpret such figures wherever you encounter them—in other textbooks, in newspapers and magazines, or on the web.

The Decline of Turnout in Presidential Elections, 1892–2004

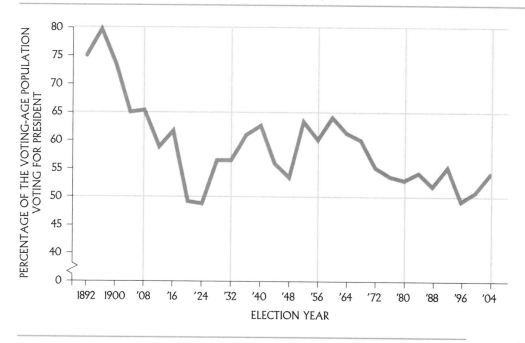

Sources: For data up to 1968, *Historical Statistics of the United States* (Washington, D.C.: Government Printing Office, 1975), part 2, 1,071. For 1972–1988, *Statistical Abstract of the United States, 1990* (Washington, D.C.: Government Printing Office, 1990), 264. Subsequent years from census reports and authors' calculations.

A Student Guide to Reading Newspapers

Although there are a number of good ways to stay on top of what is happening in American government and politics—for example, television and radio news broadcasts— one of the best ways to stay informed is to read a newspaper every day. Newspapers offer more in-depth information on a particular issue than you might get in a 30-second or 1-minute broadcast news story. Here are some guidelines to help you become a better-informed newspaper reader.

Choose your newspaper wisely.   Not all newspapers are the same; they vary greatly in the type and amount of coverage devoted to specific issues. Most newspapers will cover the big stories of the day—terrorist threats, a devastating hurricane, or the presidential campaign. However, they differ when it comes to how much emphasis they give to various stories. For example, a newspaper with a more sensationalistic approach may give front-page coverage to a scandal involving a well-known celebrity and relegate a major story of national interest to page 2 or 3 or even later. A less sensationalistic newspaper would be more likely to feature a national or international news event on the front page and cover the celebrity scandal much further into the newspaper or not at all. Be aware of how your newspaper covers the important stories of the day.

You should also be aware of which newspapers have a more national focus and which are more locally oriented. Many local papers have good national and international coverage. However, there are a few papers that are considered national in scope and that have excellent coverage of national and international affairs. The *New York Times*, the *Washington Post*, the *Wall Street Journal*, the *Christian Science Monitor*, and *USA Today* all fall in this category.

Develop a reading strategy.   Some people prefer to go right to the sports section and work their way back to the national and international news of the day. Others scan the headlines first and then decide which articles they will read. Only you can determine what works best for you. Remember, however, that reading just the gossip and horoscope sections of a newspaper will not do much to promote your understanding of politics and government. This is not to say that you should not read those sections of the paper that most interest you. However, you may want to *first* spend some time reading the national and international news of the day before moving onto other sections of the newspaper.

Most newspapers contain a section called the "op-ed" page (which is short for opinion-editorial). It is also known simply as the editorial page. This section typically contains opinion pieces about current events and issues written by newspaper staff, regular columnists, or other commentators. These pieces can help give you a broad range of opinion and show you the arguments, pro and con, people are making regarding issues in the news. The letters to the editor, which are also usually in the op-ed section, will give the point of view of newspaper readers like yourself. Newspaper editors try to select a range of letters that express a variety of opinions.

Newspapers have a lot of coverage and few people read them cover to cover each day. Develop your own strategy for reading a newspaper regularly and in the time you have available. You can scan the headlines or look at the index or contents page if the newspaper has one in order to see which articles are of interest to you. (The index or contents page often has a brief summary of articles, which can give you a good overview.) If you don't have time to read entire articles, try reading the first four or five paragraphs of those that interest you; that should give you a pretty good grasp of the issue being covered.

Once you have scanned the major stories and read those of interest, try reading or scanning the op-ed page to see what people are saying about those stories. Between reading the key stories and the op-ed pieces about them, you will hone your own critical thinking skills and you can do a better job of forming and supporting your own opinions about the issues of the day.

Be a critical consumer of what you read.   Do not take what you read at face value. Be sure to read between the lines by questioning the sources and data provided in the article. For example, an article on gun control would more than likely include several quotes and data from members of the National Rifle Association along with quotes and data from opposing groups. Neither of these groups are neutral about this issue; they both have a particular agenda to promote. You will need to carefully weigh both sides of the argument before coming to your own conclusions about the issue.

Also, question material that comes from anonymous sources. Ask yourself why a particular person does not want his or her identity noted in the article. Is this a government official attempting to promote a particular agenda? An official who wants to test out public opinion on a particular program? Keep in mind there is always a reason why sources go unidentified.

When you read a column or editorial on the op-ed page, the writer's perspective is usually evident because the writer often states his or her opinion at the outset. Editorials by a newspaper's staff are usually anonymous, and these pieces often reflect the general opinion of the newspaper's management and staff. Thus, as you become familiar with a newspaper's editorials, you will gain a sense of the newspaper's perspective. Editorial pieces by people other than newspaper staff are usually identified, along with the writer's affiliation. You should be aware of the writer's affiliation because it will often give you clues about the writer's opinion and perspective.

Develop your own opinions.   Reading a newspaper every day should not only inform you of what is going on in the world around you, but also help you to develop and expand your own opinions on national and world events based on the material you've read. Do not be a neutral reader; that is, do not just read an article or an editorial and move on to the next one. Take a few minutes to think about the implications of the material you read. For example, you may read an article that challenges your beliefs about a particular group or way of life. Use the material you gleaned from the article to develop and perhaps expand your opinions. Even editorials or columns you do not agree with will help you think about the opinions you hold.

Issues of the Times

To give you experience in critically reading and analyzing a newspaper article, every chapter of *Government in America* includes the feature, Issues of the Times. This feature focuses on articles from the *New York Times* on current and enduring issues in American government and politics. Before you begin each article, pay special attention to The Issue section that precedes it, which will give you valuable background material on the article you are about to read.

The Issue: Affirmative Action

Nearly everyone in America supports equal opportunity for employment, promotion, or admission to universities. Few people believe any group should be at a disadvantage. However, consensus breaks down when the focus turns to equal results in obtaining these jobs or university slots. There is little support for giving some people a special advantage, even if it is to overcome past discrimination.

How do we reconcile these views with the following facts: (1) not everyone has the same chance to take advantage of a theoretical opportunity; (2) discrimination still occurs in some quarters of society; and (3) the nation is becoming more diverse and the legitimacy of institutions requires that they be broadly representative of American society?

As you read the article, pay attention to call-outs within the article that point out different aspects for you to think about.

This decision was affirmative action in its purest, most elemental form. But 25 years of distortion and political warfare over this issue have made it difficult for most people to speak clearly on the subject or even to recognize affirmative action when they see it. Loaded terms such as "quotas" and "reverse discrimination" have made it all but impossible to see affirmative action as a constructive and vitally important policy for the United States.

Loaded terms such as "quotas" and "reverse discrimination" have made it all but impossible to see affirmative action as a constructive and vitally important policy for the United States.

When you finish reading the article, go through each of the Think About It questions and come to your own opinion about the material presented.

Think About It

- Do you support the army's approach to affirmative action?
- Does the army's approach to promotion help get minorities into the army in the first place?
- Can the army's approach to affirmative action be used to rectify the imbalance of minorities in the

nation's leading universities or in the most prestigious and lucrative positions in business? Do most organizations have a similar hierarchy to that in the army?

A Student Guide to Using the Internet

There are a number of ways the Internet can help you understand government in America. You may, for example, go to the Internet to follow up on a specific issue or agency you learned about in class. Or, your instructor may ask you to write a paper on a topic based on material gathered from the Internet and library. In either case, you can find a wealth of information on the Internet. Whether you know just a little about the Internet or you are a sophisticated user, this guide will help you make the most of this electronic research tool.

Finding Information on the Internet

The Internet has changed the way college students work. In addition to using the library, students can now find a wealth of information with just a few keystrokes on a computer keyboard. When looking for information on the Internet, first start with a good search engine. Search engines catalog websites in a series of directories and allow you to do searches by typing in a few key words. There are several good search engines to choose from, for example, Yahoo! (*www.yahoo.com*); AltaVista (*www.altavista.com*); and Lycos (*www.lycos.com*). Many political scientists use the Google search engine (*www.google.com*) because it is fast and helpful in doing research. Use a search engine to research topics when you don't have the name of a particular website. You just type in the particular topic you want to learn about into the search screen. Try to be as precise as possible when performing the search or else you can quickly get information overload. For example, typing in a word like "voting" into the Google search engine will yield over 5 million references to voting! A way to avoid this information overload is to put in a more exact phrase such as "voting trends in the 2002 midterm elections."

Helpful Websites for Studying Government in America

Each chapter of *Government in America* concludes with a list of informative websites focusing on material covered in that chapter. Here is a list of websites that are especially useful in keeping up with government and politics in general.

You can follow politics, government, and policy issues daily through online editions of newspapers. (You may want to make one of these online publications your homepage):

The *New York Times*
www.newyorktimes.com
The *Washington Post*
www.washingtonpost.com

Chicago Tribune
www.chicagotribune.com
USA Today
www.usatoday.com

The cable news networks also maintain great websites for keeping you up-to-date about politics and government:

www.cnn.com
www.msnbc.com

You can locate information on virtually every part of the U.S. government by visiting its official web portal at *www.firstgov.gov*. This site also provides information on state, local, and tribal governments in the United States. Nine times out of ten, you can find a government agency's website by simply entering the name of the agency into a search engine. Or you can use agency initials followed by ".gov." For example, "FBI.gov" will take you to the Federal Bureau of Investigation. "INS.gov" will yield the Immigration and Naturalization Service.

Evaluating Information from the Internet

It is important to carefully evaluate material you get from the Internet. Just because something is printed on a website doesn't mean it is reliable. *Anyone* can publish material on the Internet—your searches can bring up materials published by reliable governmental sources; however, you will also find material published by people who have a particular axe to grind but have no substance or data to back up their claims. Follow these guidelines when evaluating sources:

- *Check the abbreviation that follows the electronic address.* For example, website addresses that end with abbreviations like *.gov* (government body), *.org* (nonprofit organization), and *.edu* (educational institution) are usually reliable places to start your search.
- *Find out who is responsible for the site.* Many websites you'll visit clearly identify who is responsible for maintaining the site. Once you determine who is responsible for the site, you may want to do some further research on the person or group responsible (if it is not a well-known source). If you can't easily find who is responsible for the material on the site or any kind of mission statement for the group, or if what you find doesn't seem credible, be wary of the material posted.
- *Determine the purpose of the site.* Determining the purpose of the sites you visit will help you make better choices about the material presented at the site. Ask yourself the following questions: Does the site communicate information about government and politics from a reliable source? (As noted, check to see who is responsible for the site.) Does the site promote the ideals of a particular interest group? (If so, you should recognize that the material you find usually presents just one side of an issue.) Is the language and material on the site unusually harsh and abrasive? (In this case, you have probably found the site of a political crackpot. Beware of these kinds of sites.)

Get Connected to Government in America

At the end of each chapter in *Government in America*, we introduce an Internet exercise—Get Connected—to help you understand government, politics, and policy. These exercises offer interesting and fun ways to learn about government and politics and will also allow you to practice using some of the guidelines presented in this section. Here is a sample Get Connected exercise from Chapter 7 (The Mass Media and the Political Agenda).

GET CONNECTED

Campaign Advertising

Today's political campaigns rely heavily on campaign advertising to reach voters. Television stations also appear to rely on political campaigns to produce revenue for the station. The Alliance for Better Campaigns found that local television stations increased the prices of candidate ads in the two months before the 2002 elections. How much did candidates in your state spend on political advertising?

Search the Web

Go to the "In Your State" page at the Alliance for Better Campaigns' website at *http://freeairtime.org/docs/index.php?DocID=21*. Look at how much the TV stations you watch earned from political advertising. Compare that amount with the amounts in neighboring states.

Questions To Ask

- How much money did your local television stations earn from campaign advertising?
- How does this compare to the amount of money stations in neighboring states earned? What might explain the differences you find?
- The Alliance for Better Campaigns advocates providing free air time for candidates. You can read about this proposal on the organization's web page. Does it sound like a good idea to provide free air time to candidates?

Why It Matters

In order for voters to make informed decisions in a world with increasingly complicated issues, more detailed information is necessary. Often sound bites don't provide enough information or the right kind of information. The costs of television advertising sometimes cause candidates to end their campaigns and some candidates aren't able to advertise on television. If television is the primary way most voters get political information, it is possible that some candidates' messages may not be heard.

Get Involved

Do you agree or disagree with the Alliance for Better Campaigns' goals? Send them an e-mail to let them know. The Alliance lists their state partner organizations on their web page. Contact these state organizations to find out what they are doing in your state.

To see more Get Connected exercises for Chapter 7, go to www.ablongman.com/edwards.

About the Authors

George C. Edwards III is Distinguished Professor of political science at Texas A & M University and George and Julia Blucher Jordan chair in presidential studies. He has held visiting appointments at the U.S. Military Academy at West Point, Oxford University, Peking University in Beijing, Hebrew University of Jerusalem, the University of London, and the University of Wisconsin in Madison.

When he determined that he was unlikely to become shortstop for the New York Yankees, he turned to political science. Today, he is one of the country's leading scholars of the presidency and has authored dozens of articles and has written or edited 19 books on American politics and public policymaking, including *On Deaf Ears: The Limits of the Bully Pulpit, At the Margins: Presidential Leadership of Congress, Presidential Approval, Presidential Leadership, National Security and the U.S. Constitution, Why the Electoral College Is Bad for America*, and *Implementing Public Policy*.

Professor Edwards has served as president of the Presidency Research Section of the American Political Science Association and on many editorial boards. He has received the Decoration for Distinguished Civilian Service from the U.S. Army, the Pi Sigma Alpha Prize from the Southern Political Science Association, and is a member of the Council on Foreign Relations. He has spoken to more than 150 universities and other groups in the United States and abroad, keynoted numerous national and international conferences, given hundreds of interviews with the national and international press, and can often be heard on National Public Radio. His work has been funded by grants from the National Science Foundation, the Smith-Richardson Foundation, and the Ford Foundation. He serves on the Board of Directors of the Roper Center and the Board of Trustees of the Center for the Study of the Presidency.

Dr. Edwards also applies his scholarship to practical issues of governing, including advising Brazil on its constitution, Russia on building a democratic national party system, and Chinese scholars on democracy, and authoring studies for the 1988 and 2000 U.S. presidential transitions.

When not writing, speaking, or advising, he prefers to spend his time with his wife, Carmella, sailing, skiing, scuba diving, traveling, or attending art auctions.

Martin P. Wattenberg is professor of political science at the University of California, Irvine. His first regular paying job was with the Washington Redskins, from which he moved on to receive a Ph.D. at the University of Michigan.

He is the author of several books published by Harvard University Press: *Where Have All the Voters Gone?* (2002), *The Decline of American Political Parties* (1998), and *The Rise of Candidate-Centered Politics* (1991). In addition, he has contributed many professional articles to journals such as the *American Political Science Review, American Journal of Political Science, American Politics Quarterly*, and *Public Opinion Quarterly*.

Professor Wattenberg has lectured about American politics on all the inhabited continents. His travels have led him to become interested in electoral politics around the world. He recently coedited two books published by Oxford University Press—one on party systems in the advanced industrialized world, and the other on the recent trend toward mixed-member electoral systems.

Robert L. Lineberry   is professor of political science at the University of Houston and has been its senior vice president. He served from 1981 to 1988 as dean of the College of Liberal Arts and Sciences at the University of Kansas in Lawrence.

A native of Oklahoma City, he received a B.A. degree from the University of Oklahoma in 1964 and a Ph.D. in political science from the University of North Carolina in 1968. He taught for seven years at Northwestern University.

Dr. Lineberry has been president of the Policy Studies Section of the American Political Science Association and is currently the editor of *Social Science Quarterly*. He is the author or coauthor of numerous books and articles in political science. In addition, for the past 35 years he has taught regularly the introductory course in American government.

He has been married to Nita Lineberry for 40 years. They have two children, Nikki, who works in Denver, and Keith, who works in Houston. They have five grandchildren—Lee, Hunter, Callie, Arwen, and Elijah.

GOVERNMENT IN AMERICA

Introducing Government in America

1

Chapter Outline

Government

The New York Times **Issues of the Times**

Politics

The Policymaking System

Democracy

The Scope of Government in America

Summary

■ **Politics and government matter**—that is the single most important message of this book. Consider, for example, the following list of ways that government and politics may have already impacted your life:

- Any public schools you attended were prohibited by the federal government from discriminating against females and minorities, and from holding prayer sessions led by school officials. Municipal school boards regulated your education, and the state certified and paid your teachers.
- The ages at which you could get your driver's license, drink alcohol, and vote were all determined by state and federal governments.
- Before you could get a job, the federal government had to issue you a Social Security number and you have been paying Social Security taxes every month that you have been employed. If you worked at a relatively low-paying job, your starting wages were determined by state and federal minimum wage laws.

...ike all Americans, are impacted by governmental policies. Yet, today's generation of young people does ...hat politics matters. The political apathy of today's youth can be seen in low levels of voter turnout, inter-...knowledge of political affairs. This lack of political participation does not mean that this is a generation of ...owever. In fact, their level of volunteerism in community affairs is very high.

...tudent, you may be drawing student ...d by the government. Government ...certain school holidays.
...gasoline prices have recently risen ...deral policy continues to make it pos-...o drive long distances relatively ...ared to citizens in most other coun-...ecause U.S. taxes on gasoline are ...compared to most other advanced ...nations.
...er rented an apartment, federal law ...lords from discriminating against ...of your race or religion.

...mericans—especially young people—...out politics and government. For ...his historic return to space, former ...n Glenn remarked that he worried ...e when we have so many young peo-...athetic and critical and cynical about ...to do with politics. They don't want ...yet politics is literally the personnel ...cracy."[1]

Stereotypes can be mistaken; unfortunately this is one case where widely held impressions are over-whelmingly supported by solid evidence, which will be reviewed briefly here. This is not to say that young people are inactive in American society. As Harvard students Ganesh Sitaraman and Previn Warren write in *Invisible Citizens: Youth Politics After September 11:* "Young people are some of the most active members of their communities and are devoting increasing amounts of their time to direct service work and volunteerism."[2] It is only when it comes to politics that young people seem to express indifference about getting involved. Whether because they feel they can't make a differ-ence, the political system is corrupt, or they just don't care, young Americans are clearly apathetic about public affairs. And while political apathy isn't restricted to young people, a tremendous gap has opened up between the young (defined as under age 25) and the elderly (defined as over 65) on measures of political interest, knowledge, and participation.

3

Figure 1.1   The Political Disengagement of College Students Today

Source: UCLA Higher Education Research Institute.

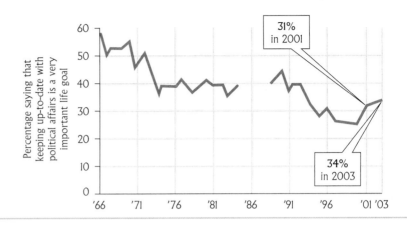

An annual nationwide study of college freshmen found in 2003 that only 34 percent said "keeping up with politics" was an important priority for them. As shown in Figure 1.1, since the terrorist attacks of September 11, there has been some resurgence of political interest among college students, but nevertheless remains far below what researchers found in the 1960s. Furthermore, political interest among young people as a whole is quite low. In 2000, the National Election Study asked a nationwide sample about their general level of interest in politics. Only 26 percent of young people interviewed said they followed politics most or some of the time compared to 73 percent of senior citizens. Yet, there was no generation gap in terms of political interest when 18- to 20-year-olds first became eligible to vote in the early 1970s. Back then, 69 percent of young people expressed at least some interest in politics compared to 65 percent of the elderly.

Because they pay so little attention to public affairs, American youth are less likely to be well informed about politics and government compared to senior citizens. The current pattern of political knowledge increasing with age has become well known in recent years. But it was not always that way. The 1964 and 2000 National Election Studies each contain a substantial battery of political knowledge questions that enable this point to be clearly demonstrated. Figure 1.2 shows the percentage of correct answers to eight questions in 1964 and nine questions in 2000 by age category.[3] In 1964, there was virtually no pattern by age, with those under 30 actually scoring 5 percent higher on this test than senior citizens. By contrast, in 2000 young people provided the correct answer to only one out of every three questions, whereas people over 65 were correct half the time. Regardless of whether the question concerned identifying current political leaders, information about the presidential candidates, or partisan control of the Congress, the result was the same: young people were clearly less knowledgeable than the elderly.

Thomas Jefferson once said that there has never been, nor ever will be, a people who are politically ignorant and free. If this is indeed the case, write Stephen Bennett and Eric Rademacher, then "we can legitimately wonder what the future holds if Xers remain as uninformed as they are about government and public affairs."[4] While this may well be an overreaction, there definitely are important consequences when citizens lack political information. In *What Americans Know About Politics and Why It Matters*, Michael Delli Carpini and Scott Keeter make a strong case for the importance of staying informed about public affairs. Political knowledge, they argue: (1) fosters civic virtues, such as political tolerance; (2) helps citizens to identify what policies would truly benefit them and then incorporate this information in their voting behavior; and (3) promotes active participation in politics.[5] If you've been reading about the debate on health care reform, for example, you'll be able to

Figure 1.2   Age and Political Knowledge: 1964 and 2000 Compared

Note: Entries are based on the percentage of accurate responses to a series of 8 questions in 1964 and 9 questions in 2000. In 1964, respondents were given credit for knowing that Goldwater was from Arizona, Johnson was from Texas, Goldwater and Johnson were Protestants, Democrats had the majority in Congress both before and after the election, Johnson had supported civil rights legislation, and Goldwater had opposed it. In 2000, respondents were given credit for knowing that Bush was from Texas, Gore was from Tennessee, Republicans had the majority in the House and Senate before the election, Lieberman was Jewish, and for identifying William Rehnquist, Tony Blair, Janet Reno, and Trent Lott.

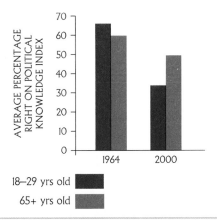

Source: Authors' analysis of 1964 and 2000 National Election Studies.

understand proposed legislation on managed care and patients' rights. This knowledge will then help you identify and vote for candidates whose views agree with yours.

Lacking such information about political issues, however, fewer young Americans are heading to the polls compared to previous generations. This development has pulled the nationwide voter turnout rate down substantially in recent years. In 1996, presidential election turnout fell below the 50 percent mark for the first time since the early 1920s, when women had just received suffrage and not yet begun to use it as frequently as men. Young people have always had the lowest turnout rates, perhaps the reason why there was relatively little opposition in 1971 to lowering the voting age to 18. But even the most pessimistic analysts could not have foreseen the record low participation rates of young people in recent years.

Why does voter turnout matter? As you will see throughout this book, those who participate in the political process are more likely to benefit from government programs and policies. Young people often complain that the elderly have far more political clout than they do—turnout statistics make it clear why this is the case. As shown in Figure 1.3, the voter turnout rate for people under 25 has fallen from 50 percent in 1972 to just 33 percent in 2000. By contrast, turnout among people over 65 has actually gone up slightly over the same period. Political scientists used to write that the frailties of old age led to a decline in turnout after age 60; now such a decline occurs only after 80 years of age. Greater access to medical care provided to today's elderly population because of the passage of Medicare in 1965 must surely be given some of the credit for this change. Who says politics doesn't make a difference?

Of course, today's youth have not had any policy impact them the way that Medicare has benefited their grandparents or that the draft and the Vietnam War affected their parents. However, the cause of young people's political apathy probably runs deeper. A broader reason is that today's youth have grown up in an environment in which public affairs news has not been as readily visible as it has been in the past. It has become particularly difficult to convince a generation that has channel surfed all their lives that politics really does matter.

Major political events were once shared national experiences. Consider how nearly everyone in America was glued to their television to follow the events of

Figure 1.3   Presidential Election Turnout Rates by Age, 1972–2000

Source: U.S. Census Bureau Current Population Surveys. Data can be found at *www.census.gov/population/www/socdemo/voting.html.*

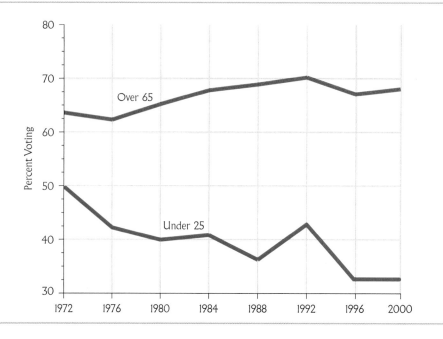

September 11, 2001. For many young people, this was the first time in their lives that they closely followed a major national event along with everyone else. With this lone exception, the current generation of young people has been the first to grow up in a media environment in which there are few such shared experiences. Growing up in a fragmented media environment with dozens of TV channels and thousands of Internet sites has offered today's youth a rich and varied socialization experience, but also one that has enabled them to easily avoid political events.

In contrast, when CBS, NBC, and ABC dominated the airwaves, their blanket coverage of presidential speeches, political conventions, and presidential debates frequently left little else to watch on TV. As channels have proliferated over the last two

🕐 Timeline

Major Technological Innovations that Have Changed the Political Landscape

The narrow 537-vote margin by which George W. Bush carried the state of Florida in 2000 proved the old adage that every vote counts. Here, an election official strains to figure out how to interpret a voter's punch in the tedious process of recounting ballots by hand.

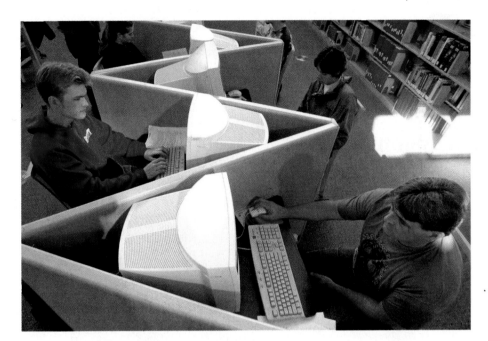

The Internet has opened up a new world of opportunities for computer-savvy young people to learn about politics. But with so many websites for so many specific interests, it remains to be seen whether many people will take advantage of the wide range of political information now available.

decades, though, it has become much easier to avoid exposure to politics altogether by simply grabbing the remote control. Whereas President Nixon got an average rating of 50 for his televised addresses to the nation (meaning that half the population was watching), President Clinton averaged only about 30 in his first term.[6] Political conventions, which once received more TV coverage than the Summer Olympics, have been relegated to an hour per night and draw abysmal ratings. The 2004 presidential debates drew a respectable average rating of 33, but this was only about 60 percent of the typical level of viewers drawn by debates held between 1960 and 1980. In sum, young people have never known a time when most citizens paid attention to major political events. As a result, most of them have yet to get into the habit of following and participating in politics. Initially, there was some hope that September 11 might get more young people to follow national affairs. But to date there has been little evidence of this taking place. For example, a June 2002 Pew Research Center survey revealed that 32 percent of young adults said they enjoyed keeping up with the news compared to 63 percent of senior citizens.

The revolutionary expansion of channels and websites presents both opportunities and challenges for political involvement in the future, especially for today's youth. Some optimistic observers see these developments as offering "the prospect of a revitalized democracy characterized by a more active and informed citizenry."[7] Political junkies will certainly find more political information available than ever before, and electronic communications will make it easier for people to express their political views in various forums and directly to public officials. However, with so many websites for so many specific interests, it will also be extraordinarily easy to avoid the subject of public affairs. Thus, groups that are concerned about low youth turnout are focusing on innovative ways of reaching out to young people to make them more aware of politics. You can read more about various efforts to get young people interested in the 2004 presidential campaign in "Issues of the Times: How Can Young People's Interest in Politics Be Increased?"

It is our hope that after reading this book, you will be persuaded that paying attention to politics and government is important. As noted at the beginning of this chapter, government has a substantial impact on all our lives. But it is also true that we have the opportunity to have a substantial impact on government. In each chapter,

Issues
of the Times

The Issue: How Can Young People's Interest in Politics Be Increased?

As discussed at length in this chapter, the problem of voter apathy—particularly among today's youth—is a matter of much concern to many close observers of American politics. For over a decade now, an organization called Rock the Vote has made appeals to young people to vote by taking advantage of celebrity endorsements, usually by rock stars, and by advertising on MTV and other media young people watch. Up until 2004, the results had been largely disappointing.

In 2004, as discussed in this article, there was much evidence that young people were more interested in the presidential campaign than they had been in quite some time. This article gives several possible explanations why.

Read All About It

Vote Drives Gain Avid Attention of Youth in '04

By Timothy Egan
September 15, 2004

PORTLAND—Four years ago, the presidential election was not even white noise to Marie Reyes. She had bigger concerns, like, um, anything except that whole Social Security lockbox thing that Al Gore and George Bush kept talking about.

"There was nothing in that election that I felt even remotely related to my life," said Ms. Reyes, who is 22.

But now, even with a full college classload, a baby and a part-

time job, she spends nearly 20 hours a week in Albuquerque, her hometown, trying to get other young people to register to vote.

Ms. Reyes is part of the clipboard army scouring malls, public squares, concerts, county fairs and schools this year in search of what campaign managers consider the most malleable of electoral quarry: the young, unregistered voter.

After dismal turnout by young voters in 2000, surveys this year show that interest in the election among the young is near the highest

level it has reached at any time since 18- to 20-year-olds were given the vote in 1972. And state election officials say registration of new young voters is coming in at levels they have not seen in years.

The reason for the registration jump is not just the new mood of the young but also the determined efforts of nonpartisan and partisan groups alike to add to the rolls. Here in Oregon, where the last presidential race was decided by 6,765

Please see Youth   **Page 9**

Youth

Continued from Page 8

votes, it is elbow-to-elbow combat for potential voters.

"If I see anyone else with a clipboard, I run to get the angle," said Alden Goodman, 19, of Portland. "I've followed people onto metro trains, onto buses, and when they finally register, it's because I made it memorable."

In Wisconsin, for example, where the 2000 election was decided by 5,708 votes, more than 74,000 new voters, most of them young, have been added to the rolls by the New Voters Project, a nonpartisan group that is spending nearly $10 million to register new voters in six relatively small states where the outcome was tight in the last election. The project is financed primarily by the Pew Charitable Trusts. The clipboard legions are taking down cellphone numbers and e-mail addresses for a huge follow-through.

Of course, campaigns have tried before to lure the elusive young into active citizenship, only to be disappointed on Election Day.

But this year the tactics for getting the young to turn out have changed, while the level of political engagement is way up, reflecting new concerns of the sons and daughters of baby boomers just coming of age.

Former Gov. Howard Dean of Vermont was the first this year to tap into that group. He had his army of text-messaging and computer-blogging volunteers. Young voter participation was up sharply in the Iowa caucuses, but Dr. Dean still

lost the youth vote to Mr. Kerry. As the Dean campaign flagged, the young fell away as well, and the initial enthusiasm never translated to larger youth turnout through the rest of the primary season, according to surveys of voters leaving the polls.

After failing to increase turnout with rock-star pleas and celebrity robovoice phone nags, the people involved in the major youth vote drives say they have found success

> ## What has changed is not so much that the campaigns have started talking about concerns of young voters as that the issues have come around to topics that this group cares about.

with an old-fashioned strategy—ground troops—while also trying fresh pitches aimed at a "beer and babes" constituency on the Web, in bars and at convenience stores.

Rock the Vote, the big nonprofit youth registration organization that has been criticized as being ineffective despite 14 years of well-financed campaigns, is distributing a million voter registration forms, in English and Spanish, at kiosks in 5,000 convenience stores. Shoppers at 7-Eleven stores can get coupons for soft-drink discounts and voter registration forms at the same stop—"a Big Gulp and a piece of

democracy to go," as Rock the Vote called it.

The group's president, Jehmu Greene, said that more than a half-million people had downloaded registration forms from the group's site.

Another group has gone a step further. The founders of Hot or Not, a popular youth Web site at which people post photographs of themselves that are rated on a "hotness" scale, is holding a sweepstakes that will pay one registered voter $100,000 after the election; another $100,000 will go to the person who helped the winner register for the contest.

Judging by some of the marketing campaigns directed at them, young voters may seem clueless, barely tracking the major political events of a nation. But interviews and surveys showed that the problem was that the young felt disconnected from the national conversation.

"The campaigns would throw up their hands, saying, 'I don't know how to get their vote,' and so the issues agenda was always driven by the reliable interest groups," said Mr. Keeter of the Pew Center.

But what has changed is not so much that the campaigns have started talking about concerns of young voters as that the issues have come around to topics that this group cares about. Education—particularly the rising cost of college—is consistently listed at the top, followed by war and terrorism.

"I have friends and relatives fighting in Iraq, and trying to go to school," Ms. Reyes said. "These things made me think seriously about my future."

Think About It

- What, if anything, do you think particularly interested young people about the 2004 presidential race?
- Do you think the various outreach attempts discussed here really worked to get young people

interested in politics? Are there other ways you can think of that might be effective in getting young people more involved in American politics in the future?

we will present an example of someone whose involvement in politics has made a difference.

Government

government

The institutions and processes through which **public policies** are made for a society.

The institutions that make authoritative decisions for any given society are collectively known as **government.** In our own national government, these institutions are Congress, the president, the courts, and federal administrative agencies ("the bureaucracy"). Thousands of state and local governments also make policies that influence our lives. There are roughly 500,000 elected officials in the United States, which means that policies that affect you are being made almost constantly.

Because government shapes how we live, it is important to understand the process by which decisions are made, as well as what is actually decided. Two fundamental questions about governing will serve as themes throughout this book:

How should we govern? Americans take great pride in calling their government democratic. This chapter examines the workings of democratic government; the chapters that follow will evaluate the way American government actually works compared to the standards of an "ideal" democracy. We will continually ask, "Who holds power and who influences the policies adopted by government?"

What should government do? This text explores the relationship between *how* American government works and *what* it does. In other words, "Does our government do what we want it to do?" Debates over this question concerning the scope of government are among the most important in American political life today. Some people would like to see the government take on more responsibilities; others believe it already takes on too much and that America needs to promote individual responsibility instead.

While citizens often disagree about what their government should do for them, all governments have certain functions in common. National governments throughout the world perform the following functions:

Maintain a national defense. A government protects its national sovereignty, usually by maintaining armed forces. In the nuclear age, some governments possess awesome power to make war through highly sophisticated weapons. The United States currently

In the United States, the transfer of power is achieved through peaceful means. Though the 2000 election was heavily disputed, as evidenced by these protests on Inauguration Day, the transition from Bill Clinton to George W. Bush took place smoothly and without incident on January 20, 2001.

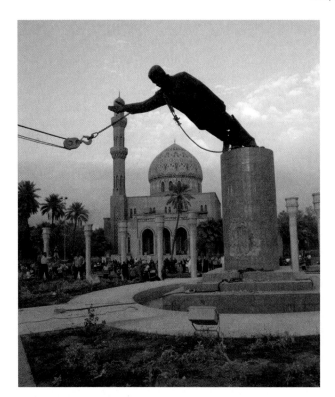

Governments provide a wide range of public services, including providing a national defense. When President George W. Bush judged that the danger of Iraq using weapons of mass destruction was a threat to U.S. security, he ordered an invasion of Iraq to topple the regime of Saddam Hussein. Here we see one symbol of the regime—a giant statue of Saddam in Baghdad—coming down.

spends about $400 billion a year on national defense. Since September 11, the defense budget has been substantially increased in order to cope with the threat of terrorism on U.S. soil.

Provide public services. Governments in this country spend billions of dollars on schools, libraries, weather forecasting, halfway houses, and dozens of other public policies. Some of these services, like highways and public parks, can be shared by everyone and cannot be denied to anyone. These kinds of services are called **public goods.** Other services, such as a college education or medical care, can be restricted to individuals who meet certain criteria, but may be provided by the private sector as well. Governments typically provide these services to make them accessible to people who may not be able to afford privately available services.

public goods

Goods, such as clean air and clean water, that everyone must share.

Preserve order. Every government has some means of maintaining order. When people protest in large numbers, governments may resort to extreme measures to restore order. For example, the National Guard was called in to stop the looting and arson after rioting broke out in Los Angeles after the 1992 Rodney King verdict.

Socialize the young. Most modern governments pay for education and use it to instill national values among the young. School curricula typically offer a course on the theory and practice of the country's government. Rituals like the daily Pledge of Allegiance seek to foster patriotism and love of country.

Collect taxes. Approximately one out of every three dollars earned by an American citizen is used to pay national, state, and local taxes—money that pays for the public goods and services provided by the government.

All these governmental tasks add up to weighty decisions that must be made by our political leaders. For example, how much should we spend on national defense as opposed to education? How high should taxes for Medicare and Social Security be? The way we answer such questions is through politics.

Politics

politics

The process by which we select our governmental leaders and what policies these leaders pursue. Politics produces authoritative decisions about public issues.

Politics determines whom we select as our governmental leaders and what policies these leaders pursue. Political scientists often cite Harold D. Lasswell's famous definition of politics: "Who gets what, when, and how."[8] It is one of the briefest and most useful definitions of politics ever penned. Admittedly, this broad definition covers a lot of ground (office politics, sorority politics, and so on) in which political scientists are not interested. They are interested primarily in politics related to governmental decision-making.

The media usually focus on the *who* of politics. At a minimum, this includes voters, candidates, groups, and parties. *What* refers to the substance of politics and government—benefits, such as medical care for the elderly, and burdens, such as new taxes. *How* people participate in politics is important, too. They get what they want through voting, supporting, compromising, lobbying, and so forth. In this sense, government and politics involve winners and losers.

political participation

All the activities used by citizens to influence the selection of political leaders or the policies they pursue. Voting is the most common but not the only means of political participation in a **democracy**. Other means include **protest** and **civil disobedience**.

The ways in which people get involved in politics make up their **political participation.** Many people judge the health of a government by how widespread political participation is. America does quite poorly when judged by its voter turnout, with one of the lowest rates of voter participation in the world. Low voter turnout has an effect on who holds political power. Because so many people do not show up at the polls, voters are a distorted sample of the public as a whole. Groups such as the elderly benefit by having a high turnout rate, whereas others such as young people lack political clout because of their low likelihood of voting.

single-issue groups

Groups that have a narrow interest, tend to dislike compromise, and often draw membership from people new to politics. These features distinguish them from traditional **interest groups**.

Voting is only one form of political participation. (See Chapter 6 for a discussion of other forms of participation). For a few Americans politics is a vocation rather than an avocation. They run for office, and some even earn their livelihood from holding political office. In addition, there are also many Americans who treat politics as critical to their interests. Many of these people are members of **single-issue groups:** groups so concerned with one issue that members cast their votes on the basis of that issue only, ignoring a politician's stand on everything else. Groups of activists dedi-

Pro-life and pro-choice groups are single-minded and usually uncompromising. Few issues stir up as much passion as whether abortion should be permitted, and if so under what conditions.

cated either to outlawing abortion or to preserving abortion rights are good examples of single-issue groups.

Individual citizens and organized groups get involved in politics because they understand that the public policy choices made by governments affect them in significant ways. Will all those who need student loans receive them? Will everyone have access to medical care? Will people be taken care of in their old age? Is the water safe to drink? These and other questions tie politics to policymaking.

Simulation

How to Satisfy Aunt Martha

The Policymaking System

Americans frequently expect government to do something about their problems. For example, the president and members of Congress are expected to keep the economy humming along; voters will penalize them at the polls if they do not. The **policymaking system** reveals the way our government responds to the priorities of its people. Figure 1.4 shows a skeletal model of this system. The rest of this book will flesh out this model, but for now it will help you understand how government policy comes into being and evolves over time.

People Shape Policy

The policymaking system begins with people. All Americans have interests, problems, and concerns that are touched upon by public policy. Some people may think the government should help train people for jobs in today's new technological environment; others may think that their taxes are too high and that the country would be best served

policymaking system

The process by which policy comes into being and evolves over time. People's interests, problems, and concerns create political issues for government policymakers. These issues shape policy, which in turn impacts people, generating more interests, problems, and concerns.

Figure 1.4 The Policymaking System

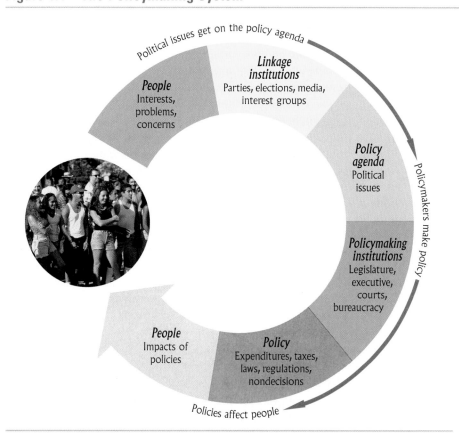

linkage institutions

The political channels through which people's concerns become political issues on the policy agenda. In the United States, linkage institutions include elections, political parties, interest groups, and the media.

policy agenda

The issues that attract the serious attention of public officials and other people actually involved in politics at any given point in time.

political issue

An issue that arises when people disagree about a problem and how to fix it.

policymaking institutions

The branches of government charged with taking action on political issues. The U.S. Constitution established three policymaking institutions—the Congress, the presidency, and the courts. Today, the power of the bureaucracy is so great that most political scientists consider it a fourth policymaking institution.

public policy

A choice that **government** makes in response to a political issue. A policy is a course of action taken with regard to some problem.

by a large tax cut. Some people may expect government to do something to curb domestic violence; others may be concerned about prospects that the government may make it much harder to buy a handgun.

What do people do to express their opinions in a democracy? There are numerous avenues for action, such as voting for candidates who represent their opinions, joining political parties, posting messages to Internet chat groups, and forming interest groups. In this way, people's concerns enter the **linkage institutions** of the policymaking system. Linkage institutions transmit the preferences of Americans to the policymakers in government. Parties and interest groups strive to ensure that their members' concerns receive appropriate political attention. The media investigates social problems and informs people about them. Elections allow citizens the chance to make their opinions heard by choosing their public officials.

All these institutions help to shape the government's **policy agenda,** which consists of the issues that attract the serious attention of public officials and other people actively involved in politics at any given time. Some issues will be considered, and others will not. If politicians want to get elected, they must pay attention to the problems that concern the voters. When you vote, you are partly looking at whether a candidate shares your agenda. If you are worried about rising health care costs and a certain candidate talks only about America's moral decay and ending legalized abortions, you will probably support another candidate.

A government's policy agenda changes regularly. When jobs are scarce and business productivity is falling, economic problems occupy a high position on the government's agenda. If the economy is doing well and trouble spots around the world occupy the headlines, foreign policy questions are bound to dominate the agenda. In general, bad news—particularly about a crisis situation—is more likely than good news to draw sufficient media attention to put a subject on the policy agenda. As they say in journalism schools, "Good news is no news." When unemployment rises sharply it leads the news; when jobs are plentiful, the latest unemployment report is much less of a news story. Thus, the policy agenda responds more to societal failures than successes. The question politicians constantly ask is "How can we as a people do better?"

People, of course, do not always agree on what government should do. Indeed, one group's concerns and interests are often at odds with those of another group. A **political issue** is the result of people disagreeing about a problem or about the public policy needed to fix it. There is never a shortage of political issues; government, however, will not act on any issue until it is high on the policy agenda.

Policymakers stand at the core of the political system, working within the three **policymaking institutions** established by the U.S. Constitution: the Congress, the presidency, and the courts. Policymakers scan the issues on the policy agenda, select those they consider important, and make policies to address them. Today, the power of the bureaucracy is so great that most political scientists consider it a fourth policymaking institution.

Very few policies are made by a single policymaking institution. Environmental policy is a good example. Some presidents have used their influence with Congress to urge clean-air and clean-water policies. When Congress responds by passing legislation to clean up the environment, bureaucracies have to implement the new policies. The bureaucracies, in turn, create extensive volumes of rules and regulations that define how policies are to be implemented. In addition, every law passed and every rule made can be challenged in the courts. Courts make decisions about what the policies mean and whether they conflict with the Constitution.

Policies Impact People

Every decision that government makes—every law it passes, budget it establishes, and ruling it hands down—is **public policy.** There are many types of public policies. Table 1.1 lists some of the most important types.

Table 1.1 Types of Public Policies

TYPE	DEFINITION	EXAMPLE
Congressional statute	Law passed by Congress	Social Security Act
Presidential action	Decision by president	U.S. troops invade Iraq
Court decision	Opinion by Supreme Court or other court	Supreme Court ruling that school segregation is unconstitutional
Budgetary choices	Legislative enactment of taxes and expenditures	The federal budget
Regulation	Agency adoption of regulation	Food and Drug Administration approval of a new drug

Policies can also be established through inaction as well as action. Doing nothing—or nothing different—can prove to be a very consequential governmental decision. Reporter Randy Shilts's book traces the staggering growth in the number of people with AIDS and reveals how governments in Washington and elsewhere did little or debated quietly about what to do.[9] Shilts claims that because politicians initially viewed AIDS as a gay person's disease, they were reluctant to support measures to deal with it, fearful of losing the votes of antigay constituents. The issue thus remained a low priority on the government's policy agenda until infections started to spread to the general population, including celebrities like basketball star Magic Johnson.

Once policies are made and implemented, they affect people. Policy impacts are the effects that a policy has on people and on society's problems. People want policy that addresses their interests, problems, and concerns. A new law, executive order, bureaucratic regulation, or court judgment doesn't mean much if it doesn't work. Environmentalists want an industrial emissions policy that not only claims to prevent air pollution but also does so. Minority groups want a civil rights policy that not only promises them equal treatment but also ensures it.

Having a policy implies a goal. Whether we want to reduce poverty, cut crime, clean the water, or hold down inflation, we have a goal in mind. Policy impact analysts ask how well a policy achieves its goal—and at what cost. The analysis of policy impacts carries the political system back to its point of origin: the concerns of the

AIDS was relatively low on the political agenda until well-known celebrities started to die from the disease. AIDS activists have found, however, that getting the problem on the agenda is only half the political battle. Getting the government to take aggressive action to find and approve new treatments has proved to be at least as difficult.

people. Translating people's desires into effective public policy is crucial to the workings of democracy.

Democracy

In 1848, Karl Marx and Friedrich Engels published *The Communist Manifesto*, one of the most famous political documents ever written. It began with these words: "A specter is haunting Europe. It is the specter of communism." Today one could write, "A specter is haunting the world. It is the specter of democracy."

In recent years, democratic forms of governments have emerged in Eastern European countries that were formerly communist, in Latin American countries that were controlled by military dictatorships, and in South Africa, where apartheid denied basic rights to the Black majority. Yet despite this global move toward democracy, not everyone defines democracy the way Americans do—or think they do.

Defining Democracy

democracy

A system of selecting policymakers and of organizing government so that policy represents and responds to the public's preferences.

Democracy is a means of selecting policymakers and of organizing government so that policy reflects citizens' preferences. Today, the term *democracy* takes its place among terms like *freedom, justice,* and *peace* as a word that seemingly has only positive connotations. Yet the writers of the U.S. Constitution had no fondness for democracy, as many of them doubted the ability of ordinary Americans to make informed judgments about what government should do. Roger Sherman, a delegate to the Constitutional Convention, said the people "should have as little to do as may be with the government." Only much later did Americans come to cherish democracy and believe that all citizens should actively participate in choosing their leaders.

Most Americans would probably say that democracy is "government by the people." This phrase, of course, is part of Abraham Lincoln's famous definition of democracy from his Gettysburg Address: "government of the people, by the people, and for the people." How well each of these aspects of democracy is being met is a matter crucial to evaluating how well our government is working. Certainly, government has always been "of the people" in the United States, for the Constitution forbids the granting of titles of nobility. On the other hand, it is a physical impossibility for government to be "by the people" in a society of 295 million people. Therefore, our democracy involves choosing people from among our midst to govern. Where the serious debate begins is whether political leaders govern "for the people," as there always are significant biases in how the system works. Democratic theorists have elaborated a set of more specific goals for evaluating this crucial question.

Traditional Democratic Theory

Traditional democratic theory rests upon a number of key principles that specify how governmental decisions are made in a democracy. Robert Dahl, one of America's leading theorists, suggests than an ideal democratic process should satisfy the following five criteria:

Equality in voting. The principle of "one person, one vote" is basic to democracy. Voting need not be universal, but it must be representative.

Effective participation. Citizens must have adequate and equal opportunities to express their preferences throughout the decision-making process.

Enlightened understanding. A democratic society must be a marketplace of ideas. A free press and free speech are essential to civic understanding. If one group monopolizes and distorts information, citizens cannot truly understand issues.

Citizen control of the agenda. Citizens should have the collective right to control the government's policy agenda. If wealthy individuals or groups distort the agenda, the people cannot make government address the issues they feel are most important.

Inclusion. The government must include, and extend rights to, all those subject to its laws. Citizenship must be open to all within a nation if the nation is to call itself democratic.[10]

Only by following these principles can a political system be called "democratic." Furthermore, democracies must practice **majority rule,** meaning that in choosing among alternatives, the will of over half the voters should be followed. At the same time, most Americans would not want to give the majority free rein to do anything they can agree on. Restraints on the majority are built into the American system of government in order to protect the minority. Basic principles such as freedom of speech and assembly are inviolable **minority rights,** which the majority cannot infringe upon.

In a society too large to make its decisions in open meetings, a few will have to look after the concerns of the many. The relationship between the few leaders and the many followers is one of **representation.** The literal meaning of representation is to make present once again. In politics, this means that the desires of the people should be replicated in government through the choices of elected officials. The closer the correspondence between representatives and their constituents, the closer the approximation to an ideal democracy. As might be expected for such a crucial question, theorists disagree widely about the extent to which this actually occurs in America.

Three Contemporary Theories of American Democracy

Theories of American democracy are essentially theories about who has power and influence. All, in one way or another, ask the question, "Who really governs in our nation?" Each focuses on a key aspect of politics and government, and each reaches a somewhat different conclusion.

Pluralist Theory. One important theory of American democracy, **pluralist theory,** states that groups with shared interests influence public policy by pressing their concerns through organized efforts.

The National Rifle Association (NRA), the National Organization for Women (NOW), and the United Auto Workers (UAW) are examples of groups of people who share a common interest. Because of open access to various institutions of government and public officials, organized groups can compete with one another for control over policy, and yet no one group or set of groups dominates. Given that power is dispersed in the American form of government, groups that lose in one arena can take their case to another. For example, civil rights groups faced congressional roadblocks in the 1950s but were able to win the action they were seeking from the courts.

Pluralists are generally optimistic that the public interest will eventually prevail in the making of public policy through a complex process of bargaining and compromise. They believe that rather than speaking of majority rule we should speak of groups of minorities working together. Robert Dahl expresses this view well when he writes that in America "all active and legitimate groups in the population can make themselves heard at some crucial stage in the process."[11]

Group politics is certainly as American as apple pie. Writing in the 1830s, Alexis de Tocqueville called us a "nation of joiners," and pointed to the high level of associational activities as one of the crucial reasons for the success of American democracy. The recent explosion of interest group activity can therefore be seen as a very positive development from the perspective of pluralist theory. Interest groups and their lobbyists—the

majority rule

A fundamental principle of **traditional democratic theory.** In a democracy, choosing among alternatives requires that the majority's desire be respected. See also **minority rights.**

minority rights

A principle of **traditional democratic theory** that guarantees rights to those who do not belong to majorities and allows that they might join majorities through persuasion and reasoned argument. See also **majority rule.**

representation

A basic principle of **traditional democratic theory** that describes the relationship between the few leaders and the many followers.

pluralist theory

A theory of government and politics emphasizing that politics is mainly a competition among groups, each one pressing for its own preferred policies. Compare **elite and class theory, hyperpluralism,** and **traditional democratic theory.**

groups' representatives in Washington—have become masters of the technology of politics. Computers, mass mailing lists, sophisticated media advertising, and hard-sell techniques are their stock in trade. As a result, some observers believe that Dahl's pluralist vision that all groups are heard via the American political process is more true now than ever before.

On the other hand, Robert Putnam argues that many of the problems of American democracy today stem from a decline in group-based participation.[12] Putnam theorizes that advanced technology, particularly television, has served to increasingly isolate Americans from one another. He shows that membership in a variety of civic associations, such as Parent-Teacher Associations, the League of Women Voters, the Elks, Shriners, and Jaycees have been declining for decades. Interestingly, Putnam does not interpret the decline of participation in civic groups as meaning that people have become "couch potatoes." Rather, he argues that Americans' activities are becoming less tied to institutions and more self-defined. The most famous example he gives to illustrate this trend is the fact that membership in bowling leagues has dropped sharply at the same time that more people are bowling—indicating that more and more people must be bowling alone. Putnam believes that participation in interest groups today is often like bowling alone. Groups that have mushroomed lately, such as the American Association of Retired Persons (AARP), typically just ask their members to write a check from the comfort of their own home as their participation. If people are indeed participating in politics alone rather than in groups, then pluralist theory is becoming less descriptive of American politics today.

Elite and Class Theory. Critics of pluralism believe that it paints too rosy a picture of American political life. By arguing that almost every group can get a piece of the pie, they say that pluralists miss the larger question of how the pie is distributed. The poor may get their food stamps, but businesses get massive tax deductions worth far more. Some governmental programs may help minorities, but the income gap between African Americans and Whites remains wide.

elite and class theory

A theory of government and politics contending that societies are divided along class lines and that an upper-class elite will rule, regardless of the formal niceties of governmental organization. Compare **hyperpluralism, pluralist theory,** and **traditional democratic theory.**

Elite and class theory contends that our society, like all societies, is divided along class lines and that an upper-class elite pulls the strings of government. Wealth—the holding of assets such as property, stocks, and bonds—is the basis of this power. Over a third of the nation's wealth is currently held by just 1 percent of the population. Elite and class theorists believe that this 1 percent of Americans controls most policy decisions because they can afford to finance election campaigns and control key institutions, such as large corporations. According to elite and class theory, a few powerful Americans do not merely influence policymakers—they *are* the policymakers.

At the center of all theories of elite dominance is big business. No recent president tried harder to help big business than Ronald Reagan, and many elite theorists believe that he succeeded beyond all expectations. As Kevin Phillips wrote in his best-seller *The Politics of Rich and Poor,* "The 1980s were the triumph of upper America—an ostentatious celebration of wealth, the political ascendancy of the richest third of the population and a glorification of capitalism, free markets and finance."[13]

Nothing like this has been written about the Clinton administration. However, journalist Bob Woodward's account of Clinton's first year in office argues that many promises made in Clinton's "Putting People First" program were sacrificed to satisfy the demands of Wall Street.[14] Reflecting on the source of *real* power, Clinton's 1992 campaign manager, James Carville, reportedly told Woodward that, "I used to think if there was reincarnation, I wanted to come back as the president or the pope or a .400 baseball hitter. But now I want to come back as the bond market. You can intimidate everybody."[15]

Elite theorists maintain that who holds office in Washington is of marginal consequence; the corporate giants always have the power. Clearly, most people in politics would disagree with this view, noting that it did make a difference that Bush was elected in 2000 rather than Gore. According to Gore's promises in 2000, for example, the wealthiest Americans would have received no tax cuts had he become president, whereas under President Bush the wealthy and the middle class alike were granted tax cuts.

Hyperpluralism. A third theory, hyperpluralism, offers a different critique of pluralism. Hyperpluralism is pluralism gone sour. In this view, groups are so strong that government is weakened, as the influence of many groups cripples government's ability to make policy. **Hyperpluralism** states that many groups—not just the elite ones—are so strong that government is unable to act.

Whereas pluralism maintains that input from groups is a good thing for the political decision-making process, hyperpluralism asserts that there are *too* many ways for groups to control policy. Our fragmented political system containing governments with overlapping jurisdictions is one major factor that contributes to hyperpluralism. Too many governments can make it hard to coordinate policy implementation. Any policy requiring the cooperation of the national, state, and local levels of government can be hampered by the reluctance of any one of them.

According to hyperpluralists, groups have become sovereign and government is merely their servant. Groups that lose policymaking battles in Congress these days do not give up the battle; they carry it to the courts. Recently, the number of cases brought to state and federal courts has soared. Ecologists use legal procedures to delay construction projects they feel will damage the environment; businesses take federal agencies to court to fight the implementation of regulations that will cost them money; labor unions go to court to secure injunctions against policies they fear will cost them jobs; civil liberties groups go to court to defend the rights of people who are under investigation for possible terrorist activities. The courts have become one more battleground in which policies can be effectively opposed as each group tries to bend policy to suit its own purposes.

These powerful groups divide the government and its authority. Hyperpluralist theory holds that government gives in to every conceivable interest and single-issue group. When politicians try to placate every group, the result is confusing, contradictory, and muddled policy—if politicians manage to make policy at all. Like elite and class theorists, hyperpluralist theorists suggest that the public interest is rarely translated into public policy.

Challenges to Democracy

Regardless of which theory is most convincing, there are a number of continuing challenges to democracy. Many of these challenges apply to American democracy as well as to the fledgling democracies around the world.

Increased Technical Expertise. Traditional democratic theory holds that ordinary citizens have the good sense to reach political judgments and that government has the capacity to act on those judgments. Today, however, we live in a society of experts, whose technical knowledge overshadows the knowledge of the general population. What, after all, does the average citizen—however conscientious—know about eligibility criteria for welfare, agricultural price supports, foreign competition, and the hundreds of other issues that confront government each year? Years ago, the power of the few—the elite—might have been based on property holdings. Today, the elite are likely to be those who command knowledge, the experts. Even the most rigorous democratic theory does not demand that citizens be experts on everything; but as human knowledge has expanded, it has become increasingly difficult for individual citizens to make well-informed decisions.

Limited Participation in Government. When citizens do not seem to take their citizenship seriously, democracy's defenders worry. There is plenty of evidence that Americans know little about who their leaders are, much less about their policy decisions, as we will discuss at length in Chapter 6. Furthermore, Americans do not take full advantage of their opportunities to shape government or select its leaders. Limited

hyperpluralism

A theory of government and politics contending that groups are so strong that government is weakened. Hyperpluralism is an extreme, exaggerated, or perverted form of **pluralism**. Compare **elite and class theory, pluralist theory,** and **traditional democratic theory.**

Many federal employees were furloughed in late 1995 and early 1996 when President Clinton vetoed the budget plans of the Republican Congress. Here, federal employees in Kansas City protest being put in the difficult position of not knowing when they could do their work and receive their next paycheck. Ultimately, such protests led Republican leaders to back down in the confrontation over the budget, as public opinion tended to sympathize with the federal employees and blame the GOP for their plight.

participation in government challenges the foundation of democracy. In particular, because young people represent the country's future, their abysmal voting turnout rates point to an even more serious challenge to democracy on the horizon.

Escalating Campaign Costs. Many political observers worry about the close connection between money and politics, especially in congressional elections. Winning a House seat these days usually requires a campaign war chest of *at least* half a million dollars, and Senate races are even more costly. Candidates have become increasingly dependent on Political Action Committees (PACs) to fund their campaigns because of the escalation of campaign costs. These PACs often represent specific economic interests, and they care little about how members of Congress vote on most issues—just the issues that particularly affect them. Critics charge that when it comes to the issues PACs care about, the members of Congress listen, lest they be denied the money they need for their reelection. When democracy confronts the might of money, the gap between democratic theory and reality widens further.

Diverse Political Interests. The diversity of the American people is reflected in the diversity of interests represented in the political system. As will be shown in this book, this system is so open that interests find it easy to gain access to policymakers. Moreover, the distribution of power within the government is so decentralized that access to a few policymakers may be enough to determine the outcome of public policy battles.

When interests conflict, which they often do, no coalition may be strong enough to form a majority and establish policy. But each interest may use its influence to thwart those whose policy proposals they oppose. In effect, they have a veto over policy, creating what is often referred to as **policy gridlock.** In a big city, gridlock occurs when there are so many cars on the road that no one can move; in politics it occurs when each policy coalition finds its way blocked by others. This political problem is magnified when voters choose a president of one party and congressional majorities of the other party, as has often been the case in recent years.

Democracy is not necessarily an end in itself. For many, evaluations of democracy depend on what democratic government produces. Thus a major challenge to democracy in America is to overcome the diversity of interests and fragmentation of power in order to deliver policies that are responsive to citizens' needs.

policy gridlock

A condition that occurs when no coalition is strong enough to form a majority and establish policy. The result is that nothing may get done.

Preview Questions About Democracy

Throughout *Government in America* you will be asked to evaluate American democracy. The chapters that follow will acquaint you with the development of democracy in the United States. For example, the next chapter will show that the U.S. Constitution was not originally designed to promote democracy but has slowly evolved to its current form. Much of America's move toward greater democracy has centered on the extension of civil liberties and civil rights we review in Chapters 4 and 5. Probably the most important civil right is the right to vote. Upcoming chapters will examine voting behavior and elections and ask the following questions about how people form their opinions and to what extent they express these opinions via elections:

- Are people knowledgeable about matters of public policy?
- Do they apply what knowledge they have to their voting choices?
- Are American elections designed to facilitate public participation?

Linkage institutions, such as interest groups, political parties, and the media, help translate input from the public into output from the policymakers. When you explore these institutions, consider the extent to which they either help or hinder democracy.

- Does the interest group system allow for all points of view to be heard, or do significant biases give advantages to particular groups?
- Do political parties provide voters with clear choices, or do they intentionally obscure their stands on issues in order to get as many votes as possible?
- If there are choices, do the media help citizens understand them?

It is up to public officials to actually make the policy choices because American government is a representative democracy. For democracy to work well, elected officials must be responsive to public opinion.

- Is the Congress representative of American society, and is it capable of reacting to changing times?
- Does the president look after the general welfare of the public, or has the office become too focused on the interests of the elite?

These are some of the crucial questions you will address in discussing the executive and legislative branches of government. In addition, the way our nonelected institutions function—the bureaucracy and the courts—is crucial to evaluating how well American democracy works. These institutions are designed to implement and interpret the law, but bureaucrats and judges often cannot avoid making public policy as well. When they do so, are they violating democratic principles for policy decisions, given that neither institution can be held accountable at the ballot box?

All these questions concerning democracy in America have more than one answer. A goal of *Government in America* is to offer different ways to evaluate and answer these questions. One way to approach the preceding questions is to address one of the most important questions facing modern American democracy: Is the scope of government responsibilities too vast, just about right, or not comprehensive enough?

The Scope of Government in America

In his first presidential address to Congress in 1993, Bill Clinton stated, "I want to talk to you about what government can do because I believe government must do more." Toward this end, President Clinton later proposed a comprehensive government program to require businesses to provide a basic level of health insurance for their employees. Congressional Republicans lined up solidly against Clinton's plan for national health insurance, arguing that government intervention in the affairs of individual citizens and businesses does more harm than good.

NOW, REMEMBER. ONCE THIS TERRORISM PROBLEM IS OVER I WANT YOU RIGHT BACK IN THE LAMP.

SURE! SURE!

BIG GOV.

Belleville News-Democrat
UNIVERSAL PRESS SYNDICATE.
11/2

Those who are inclined to support government involvement in matters such as health care argue that intervention is the only means of achieving important goals in American society. How else, they ask, can we ensure that everyone has enough to eat, clean air and water, and affordable housing? How else can we ensure that the disadvantaged are given opportunities for education and jobs and are not discriminated against? Opponents of widening the scope of government agree that these are worthwhile goals but challenge whether involving the federal government is an effective way to pursue them. Dick Armey, who served as the Republicans' majority leader in the House from 1995 to 2002, expressed this view well when he wrote, "There is more wisdom in millions of individuals making decisions in their own self-interest than there is in even the most enlightened bureaucrat (or congressman) making decisions on their behalf."[16] Or as President George W. Bush regularly told supporters during the 2000 presidential campaign: "Our opponents trust the government; we trust the people."

How Active Is American Government?

gross domestic product

The sum total of the value of all the goods and services produced in a nation.

In terms of dollars spent, government in America is vast. Altogether, our governments—national, state, and local—spend about 29 percent of our **gross domestic product,** the total value of all goods and services produced annually by the United States. Government not only spends large sums of money but also employs large numbers of people. About 18 million Americans work for our government, mostly at the state and local level as teachers, police officers, university professors, and so on. Consider some facts about the size of our national government:

- It spends about $2.4 trillion annually (printed as a number, that's $2,400,000,000,000 a year).
- It employs nearly 2 million people.
- It owns one-third of the land in the United States.
- It occupies 2.6 billion square feet of office space, more than 4 times the office space located in the nation's 10 largest cities.
- It owns and operates over 400,000 nonmilitary vehicles.

How does the American national government spend $2.4 trillion a year? National defense takes about one-sixth of the federal budget, a much smaller percentage than it did three decades ago—even with the recent increase after September 11. Social Security consumes more than one-fifth of the budget. Medicare is another big-ticket item, requiring a little over one-tenth of the budget. State and local governments also get important parts of the federal government's budget. The federal government helps fund highway and airport construction, police departments, school districts, and other state and local functions.

When expenditures grow, tax revenues must grow to pay the additional costs. When taxes do not grow as fast as spending, a budget deficit results. The federal government ran a budget deficit every year from 1969 through 1997. The last few Clinton budgets showed surpluses, but soon after George W. Bush took over the government was running a deficit once again. In fiscal year 2004 the deficit for the year was over $400 billion. No doubt the events of September 11 contributed to the reappearance of deficit spending, due to the negative impact they had on the U.S. economy as well as the added security expenses the government suddenly encountered. But opponents of President Bush have placed much of the blame on the large tax cut the president proposed in the 2000 campaign and then delivered early in his presidency. In any event, years of deficits have left the country with a national debt of about $7 trillion, which will continue to pose a problem for policymakers for decades to come.

Whatever the national problem—pollution, AIDS, earthquake relief, homelessness, hunger, sexism—many people expect Congress and the president to solve it with legislation. Thus, American government certainly matters tremendously in terms of dollars spent, persons employed, and laws passed. Our concern, however, is less about the absolute size of government and more about whether government activity is what we want it to be.

A Comparative Perspective

A useful way to think about political issues, such as the scope of government, is to compare the United States with other countries, especially other democracies with developed economies. For example, it is possible to compare the size of the gross domestic product spent by all levels of government in the United States with similar expenditures in other prosperous nations. Compared to most other economically developed nations, the United States devotes a smaller percentage of its resources to government. As we will see in Chapter 14, the tax burden on Americans is small compared to other democratic nations.

Comparing Political Landscapes

Further, most advanced industrial democracies have a system of national insurance that provides most health care; the United States does not, though Bill Clinton unsuccessfully tried to establish such a system. In other countries, national governments have taken it upon themselves to start up airline, telephone, and communications companies. Governments have built much of the housing in most Western nations, compared to only a small fraction of the housing in America. Thus, in terms of its impact on citizens' everyday lives, government in the United States actually does less than the governments of similar countries.

American Individualism

One reason for the comparatively small scope of American government is the prominence of **individualism**—the belief that people can and should get ahead on their own—in American political thought and practice. The immigrants who founded American society may have been diverse, but many shared a common dream of America as a place where one could make it on one's own without interference from government. Louis Hartz's *The Liberal Tradition in America* is a classic analysis of the

individualism

The belief that individuals should be left on their own by the government. One of the primary reasons for the comparatively small scope of American government is the prominence of this belief in American political thought and practice.

Prime Minister Tony Blair of Great Britain and President George W. Bush worked closely together as allies during the 2003 Iraqi War and formed a close friendship. But the two leaders have extremely different views regarding the proper scope of government in domestic policy. Blair was first elected to the British Parliament as a self-declared socialist, and in his position as prime minister he has strived to strengthen Britain's national health care system. In contrast, President Bush favors free-market policies and opposes the idea of establishing a national health care system in the United States.

dominant political beliefs during America's formative years.[17] Hartz argues that the major force behind limited government in America is that it was settled by people who fled from the feudal and clerical oppressions of the Old World. Once in the New World, they wanted little from government other than for it to leave them alone.

Another explanation for American individualism is the existence of a bountiful frontier—at least up until the start of the twentieth century. Not only did many people come to America to escape from governmental interference, but the frontier allowed them to get away from government almost entirely once they arrived. Frederick Jackson Turner's famous work on the significance of the frontier in American history argues that "the frontier is productive of individualism."[18] According to Turner, being in the wilderness and having to survive on one's own left settlers with an aversion to any control from the outside world—particularly from the government.

The results of these historical influences are evident in American politics today. Individualism remains highly valued in the United States, with the public policy consequences being a strong preference for free markets and limited government. The importance of individualism in American politics will be a recurring topic in our analysis of the scope of government.

What Are American
Civic Values?

Preview Questions About the Scope of Government

Debate over the scope of government is central to contemporary American politics, and it is a theme this text will examine in each chapter. Our goal is not to determine for you the proper role of the national government. Instead, you will explore the implications of the way politics, institutions, and policy in America affect the scope of government. By raising questions such as those listed in the next few paragraphs, you may draw your own conclusions about the appropriate role of government in America. Part 1 of *Government in America* examines the constitutional foundations of American government. A concern with the proper scope of government leads to a series of questions regarding the constitutional structure of American politics, including

- What role did the Constitution's authors foresee for the federal government?
- Does the Constitution favor a government with a broad scope, or is it neutral on this issue?
- Why did the functions of government increase, and why did they increase most at the national rather than the state level?
- Has bigger, more active government constrained freedom, or does the increased scope of government serve to protect civil liberties and civil rights?

Part 2 focuses on those who make demands on government, including the public, political parties, interest groups, and the media. Here you will seek answers to questions such as

- Does the public favor a large, active government?
- Do competing political parties predispose the government to provide more public services?
- Do elections help control the scope of government, or do they legitimize an increasing role for the public sector?
- Are pressures from interest groups necessarily translated into more governmental regulations, bigger budgets, and the like?
- Has media coverage of government enhanced government's status and growth, or have the media been an instrument for controlling government?

Governmental institutions themselves obviously deserve close examination. Part 3 discusses these institutions and asks

- Has the presidency been a driving force behind increasing the scope and power of government (and thus of the president)?
- Can the president control a government with so many programs and responsibilities?
- Is Congress, because it is subject to constant elections, predisposed toward big government?
- Is Congress too responsive to the demands of the public and organized interests?

The nonelected branches of government, which are also discussed in these chapters, are especially interesting when we consider the issue of the scope of government. For instance,

- Are the federal courts too active in policymaking, intruding on the authority and responsibility of other branches and levels of government?
- Is the bureaucracy too acquisitive, constantly seeking to expand its budgets and authority, or is it simply a reflection of the desires of elected officials?
- Is the bureaucracy too large, and thus a wasteful menace to efficient and fair implementation of public policies?

The next 20 chapters will search for answers to these and many other questions regarding the scope of government and why it matters. You will undoubtedly add a few questions of your own as you seek to resolve the issue of the proper scope of government involvement.

Summary

Evidence abounds that young people today are politically apathetic. But they should not be. Politics and government matter a great deal to everyone, and affect many aspects of life. If nothing else, we hope this text will convince you of this.

Government consists of those institutions that make authoritative public policies for society as a whole. In the United States, four key institutions make policy at the national level: Congress, the presidency, the courts, and the bureaucracy. Politics is, very simply, who gets what, when, and how. People engage in politics for a variety of reasons, and all their activities in politics are collectively called political participation. The result of government and politics is public policy. Public policy includes all the decisions and nondecisions made by government.

The first question central to governing is "How should we govern?" Americans are fond of calling their government democratic. Democratic government includes, above all else, a commitment to majority rule and minority rights. This text will help you compare the way American government works with the standards of democracy and will continually address questions about who holds power and who influences the policies adopted by government.

The second fundamental question regarding governing is "What should government do?" One of the most important issues about government in America has to do with its scope. Conservatives often talk about the evils of intrusive government; liberals see the national government as rather modest in comparison both to what it could do and to the functions governments perform in other democratic nations.

KEY TERMS

government	policy agenda	representation
public goods	political issue	pluralist theory
politics	policymaking institutions	elite and class theory
political participation	public policy	hyperpluralism
single-issue groups	democracy	policy gridlock
policymaking system	majority rule	gross domestic product
linkage institutions	minority rights	individualism

INTERNET RESOURCES

www.policyalmanac.org
Contains a discussion of major policy issues of the day and links to resources about them.

thomas.loc.gov/home/histdox/fedpapers.html
The complete collection of The *Federalist Papers.*

www.tocqueville.org
Information and discussion about Tocqueville's classic work, *Democracy in America.*

www.bowlingalone.com
A site designed to accompany Robert Putnam's work, which contains information concerning the data he used and projects he is working on to reinvigorate American communities.

www.yahoo.com/Government
A good place to go to search for information about government and politics.

GET CONNECTED

The Policymaking System

Americans frequently want government to enact specific policies in order to address various problems. However, not all problems are the same. In addition, not all Americans agree on which problems government should solve or on how government should solve them. As Figure 1.4 illustrates, the policymaking system in the United States is complex with many actors and institutions involved. Political parties—one of the many linkage institutions within the policymaking system—play a key role because they bring the people's concerns to the policy agenda. In order to examine this part of the policymaking system up close, let us take a look at a concern shared by many Americans—Social Security insurance and its continued availability—and the proposed policies of key political parties to address this concern.

Search the Web

Go to the websites for the 2004 party platforms of the Green Party *http://www.gp.org/platform.html*,
the Republican Party *http://www.gop.com/GOPAgenda/*,
the Democratic Party *http://www.democrats.org/platform/index.htm*,
and the Libertarian Party *http://www.lp.org/issues/platform/.*

Review the portion of each platform that relates to Social Security. You will need to look under subheadings such as "Tax Justice/Fairness," "Retirement Security," and "Social Security." Get a sense of each party's position on Social Security reform. Write down the key terms and phrases each platform uses.

Questions To Ask

- Based on what you have read, do you think the different political parties have different views on Social Security insurance?
- Which party appears to propose the least significant changes in the Social Security program?
- Which party appears to propose the most significant changes in the Social Security program?
- After reading each party's position, which do you most agree with?

Why It Matters

We all pay Social Security and, hopefully, we will all have a chance to collect it when the time comes. However, there are many proposals to change the Social Security system. Some of the proposals might make it more difficult to collect. Others might make it more costly. Still others might make it possible for citizens to invest part of their Social Security in the stock market. It is important to understand these proposals and to support the party that best reflects your view on what should happen to Social Security insurance.

Get Involved

Go to the web and try to find your major state political party websites. See how each of the parties proposes solving the problems you think are most pressing in your state. For instance, how do the parties propose paying for education or roads? Or, what are their positions on the environment and declining population in rural areas? If you find that you agree with one of them you might want to consider sending an e-mail asking about how you can become involved with that party.

To see more Get Connected exercises for Chapter 1, go to www.ablongman.com/edwards.

FOR FURTHER READING

Bok, Derek. *The State of the Nation: Government and the Quest for a Better Society.* Cambridge, MA: Harvard University Press, 1996. An excellent analysis of how America is doing, compared to other major democracies, on a wide variety of policy aspects.

Dahl, Robert A. *Democracy and Its Critics.* New Haven, CT: Yale University Press, 1982. An excellent work by one of the world's most articulate advocates of pluralist theory.

de Tocqueville, Alexis. *Democracy in America.* New York: Mentor Books, 1956. This classic by a nineteenth-century French aristocrat remains one of the most insightful works on the nature of American society and government.

Hartz, Louis. *The Liberal Tradition in America.* New York: Harcourt, Brace, 1955. A classic analysis of why the scope of American government has been more limited than in other democracies.

Kingdon, John W. *Agendas, Alternatives, and Public Policies,*

2nd ed. New York: HarperCollins, 1995. One of the best efforts by a political scientist to examine the political agenda.

Putnam, Robert. *Bowling Alone: The Collapse and Revival of American Community.* New York: Simon & Schuster, 2000. Putnam's highly influential work shows how Americans have become increasingly disconnected from one another since the early 1960s.

Sitaraman, Ganesh, and Previn Warren. *Invisible Citizens: Youth Politics After September 11.* New York: iUniverse, Inc., 2003. Two Harvard students examine why today's youth demonstrate a commitment to community service while at the same largely neglect involvement in politics.

Stanley, Harold W., and Richard G. Niemi. *Vital Statistics on American Politics, 2003–2004.* Washington, D.C.: Congressional Quarterly Press, 2003. Useful data on government, politics, and policy in the United States.

2

The Constitution

Chapter Outline

The Origins of the Constitution

The Government That Failed: 1776–1787

Making a Constitution: The Philadelphia Convention

The Agenda in Philadelphia

The Madisonian Model

Ratifying the Constitution

Constitutional Change

Understanding the Constitution

The New York Times **Issues of the Times**

Summary

■ Gregory Lee Johnson knew little about the Constitution, but he knew he was upset. He felt that the buildup of nuclear weapons in the world threatened the planet's survival, and he wanted to protest presidential and corporate policies concerning nuclear weapons. Yet, he had no money to hire a lobbyist or to purchase an ad in a newspaper. So he, along with some other demonstrators, marched through the streets of Dallas, chanting political slogans and stopping at several corporate locations to stage "die-ins" intended to dramatize the consequences of nuclear war. The demonstration ended in front of Dallas City Hall, where Gregory doused an American flag with kerosene and set it on fire.

Burning the flag violated the law, and Gregory was convicted of "desecration of a venerated object," sentenced to one year in prison, and fined $2,000. He appealed his conviction, claiming the law that prohibited burning the flag violated his freedom of speech. The U.S. Supreme Court agreed in the case of *Texas v. Gregory Lee Johnson.*

Gregory was pleased with the Court's decision, but he was nearly alone. The public howled its opposition to the decision, and President George

Bush called for a constitutional amendment authorizing punishment of flag desecraters. Many public officials vowed to support the amendment, and organized opposition to the amendment was scarce. However, an amendment to prohibit burning the American flag did not obtain the two-thirds vote in each house of Congress necessary to send a constitutional amendment to the states for ratification.

Instead, Congress passed a law—the Flag Protection Act—that outlawed the desecration of the American flag. The next year, however, in *United States v. Eichman,* the Supreme Court found the act an impermissible infringement on free speech.

After years of political posturing, legislation, and litigation, little has changed. Burning the flag remains a legally protected form of political expression despite the objections of the overwhelming majority of the American public. Gregory Johnson did not prevail because he was especially articulate; nor did he win because he had access to political resources such as money or powerful supporters. He won because of the nature of the Constitution.

Understanding how an unpopular protestor like Gregory Lee Johnson could prevail against the combined forces of the public and its elected officials is central to understanding the American system of government. The Constitution supersedes ordinary law, even when the law represents the wishes of a majority of citizens. The Constitution not only guarantees individual rights but also decentralizes power. Even the president, "the leader of the free world," cannot force Congress to act, as George Bush could not force Congress to start the process of amending the Constitution. Power is not concentrated efficiently in one person's hands, such as the president's. Instead, there are numerous checks on the exercise of power and many obstacles to change. Some complain that this system produces stalemate, while others praise the way it protects minority views. Both positions are correct.

Gregory Johnson's case raises some important questions about government in America. What does democracy mean if the majority does not get its way? Is this how we should be governed? And is it appropriate that the many limits on the scope of government action, both direct and indirect, prevent action desired by most people?

29

constitution

A nation's basic law. It creates political institutions, assigns or divides powers in government, and often provides certain guarantees to citizens. Constitutions can be either written or unwritten. See also **U.S. Constitution.**

A **constitution** is a nation's basic law. It creates political institutions, allocates power within government, and often provides guarantees to citizens. A constitution is also an unwritten accumulation of traditions and precedents that have established acceptable styles of behavior and policy outcomes.

A constitution sets the broad rules of the game of politics, allowing certain types of competition among certain players. *These rules are never neutral*, however. Instead, they give some participants and some policy options advantages over others in the policymaking process. Understanding these rules is vital to understand government and to answer questions about how we are governed and what government does.

The Origins of the Constitution

In the summer of 1776, a small group of men met in Philadelphia and passed a resolution that began an armed rebellion against the government of the most powerful nation on Earth. The resolution was, of course, the Declaration of Independence; the armed rebellion was the American Revolution.

The attempt to overthrow a government forcibly is a serious and unusual act. It is considered treasonous everywhere, including in the United States. Typically, it is punishable by death. A set of compelling ideas drove our forefathers to take such drastic and risky action. It is important to understand these ideas in order to understand the Constitution.

The Road to Revolution

By eighteenth-century standards, life was not bad for most people in America at the time of the Revolution (slaves and indentured servants being major exceptions). In fact, White colonists "were freer, more equal, more prosperous, and less burdened with cumbersome feudal and monarchical restraints than any other part of mankind."[1] Although the colonies were part of the British Empire, the king and Parliament generally confined themselves to governing America's foreign policy and trade. Almost everything else was left to the discretion of individual colonial governments. Although commercial regulations irritated colonial shippers, planters, land speculators, and merchants, these rules had little influence on the vast bulk of the population, who were self-employed farmers or artisans.

As you can see in Figure 2.1, Britain obtained an enormous new territory in North America after the French and Indian War (also known as the Seven Years' War) ended

Figure 2.1   European Claims in North America

Following its victory in the French and Indian War in 1763, Britain obtained an enormous new territory to govern. To raise revenues to defend and administer the territory, it raised taxes on the colonists and tightened enforcement of trade regulations.

in 1763. The cost of defending this territory against foreign adversaries was large, and Parliament reasoned that it was only fair that those who were the primary beneficiaries — the colonists — should contribute to their own defense. Thus, in order to raise revenue for colonial administration and defense, the British legislature passed a series of taxes on newspapers, official documents, paper, glass, paint, and tea. Britain also began tightening enforcement of its trade regulations, which were designed to benefit the mother country, not the colonists.

Colonists resented these taxes, especially because they were imposed while the colonists lacked direct representation in Parliament. They protested, boycotted the taxed goods, and as a symbolic act of disobedience even threw 342 chests of tea into Boston Harbor. Britain reacted by applying economic pressure through a naval blockade of the harbor, further fueling the colonists' anger. The colonists responded by forming the First Continental Congress in September 1774, sending delegates from each colony to Philadelphia to discuss the future of relations with Britain.

Declaring Independence

As colonial discontent with the English festered, the Continental Congress was in almost continuous session during 1775 and 1776. Talk of independence was common among the delegates. Virginia, as it often did in those days, played a leading role at the Philadelphia meeting of the Congress. It sent seven delegates to join the serious discussion of repudiating the rule of King George III. These delegates were joined later by a last-minute substitute for Peyton Randolph, who was needed back in Williamsburg to preside over Virginia's House of Burgesses.

The substitute, Thomas Jefferson, was a young (only 33), well-educated Virginia lawmaker who had just written a resolution in the Virginia legislature objecting to new British policies. Jefferson brought to the Continental Congress his talent as an author and his knowledge of political philosophy. He was not a rabble-rousing pamphleteer like Thomas Paine, whose fiery tract *Common Sense* had appeared in January 1776 and fanned the already hot flames of revolution. Jefferson was steeped in the philosophical writings of European moral philosophers, and his rhetoric matched his reading.[2]

In May and June of 1776, the Continental Congress began debating resolutions about independence. On June 7, Richard Henry Lee of Virginia moved "that these United States are and of right ought to be free and independent states." A committee composed of Thomas Jefferson of Virginia, John Adams of Massachusetts, Benjamin Franklin of Pennsylvania, Roger Sherman of Connecticut, and Robert Livingston of New York was formed to draft a document to justify the inevitable declaration. On July 2, Lee's motion to declare independence from England was formally approved. The famous **Declaration of Independence,** written primarily by Jefferson, was adopted two days later, on July 4.

The Declaration of Independence quickly became one of the most widely quoted and revered documents in America. Filled with fine principles and bold language, it can be read as both a political tract and a philosophical treatise. (It is reprinted in the Appendix of this book.)

Politically, the Declaration was a polemic, announcing and justifying a revolution. Most of the document — 27 of its 32 paragraphs — listed the ways the king had abused the colonies. George III was accused of all sorts of evil deeds, even though he personally had little to do with Parliament's colonial policies. King George was even blamed for inciting the "merciless Indian savages" to make war on the colonists. The king received the blame because the Convention delegates held that Parliament lacked authority over the colonies.

The Declaration's polemical aspects were important because the colonists needed foreign assistance to take on the most powerful nation in the world. France, which was engaged in a war with Britain, was a prime target for the delegates' diplomacy and eventually provided aid that was critical to the success of the Revolution.

Declaration of Independence

The document approved by representatives of the American colonies in 1776 that stated their grievances against the British monarch and declared their independence.

John Adams (from right), Roger Sherman, Robert R. Livingston, Thomas Jefferson, and Benjamin Franklin submit the Declaration of Independence to Continental Congress President John Hancock. Legend has it that Hancock remarked, "We must be unanimous; there must be no pulling different ways; we must hang together," to which Franklin replied, "We must indeed all hang together, or, most assuredly, we shall hang separately."

Today, the Declaration of Independence is studied more as a statement of philosophy than as a political call to arms. In just a few sentences, Jefferson set forth the American democratic creed, the most important and succinct statement of the philosophy underlying American government—as applicable today as it was in 1776.

The English Heritage: The Power of Ideas

Philosophically, the Jeffersonian pen put on paper ideas that were by then common knowledge on both sides of the Atlantic, especially among those people who wished to challenge the power of kings. Franklin, Jefferson, James Madison of Virginia, Robert Morris of Pennsylvania, Alexander Hamilton of New York, and other intellectual leaders in the colonies were learned and widely read men, familiar with the works of English, French, and Scottish political philosophers. These leaders corresponded about the ideas they were reading, quoted philosophers in their debates over the Revolution, and applied those ideas to the new government they formed in the framework of the Constitution.

John Locke was one of the most influential philosophers read by the colonists. His writings, especially *The Second Treatise of Civil Government* (1689), profoundly influenced American political leaders. His work was "the dominant political faith of the American colonies in the second quarter of the eighteenth century. A thousand pulpits thundered with its benevolent principles; a hundred editors filled their pages with its famous slogans."[3]

The foundation upon which Locke built his powerful philosophy was a belief in **natural rights**—rights inherent in human beings, not dependent on governments. Before governments arise, Locke held, people exist in a state of nature in which there are no formal laws or governments. Instead, the laws of nature govern people, laws determined by people's innate moral sense. This natural law brings natural rights, including life, liberty, and property. Natural law can even justify a challenge to the rule of a tyrannical king because it is superior to human law. Government, Locke argued, must be built on the **consent of the governed**; in other words, the people must agree on who their rulers will be. It should also be a **limited government**; that is, there must be clear restrictions on what rulers can do. Indeed, the sole purpose of government, according to Locke, was to protect natural rights. The idea that certain things were beyond the realm of government contrasted sharply with the traditional notion that kings had been divinely granted absolute rights over subjects.

natural rights

Rights inherent in human beings, not dependent on governments, which include life, liberty, and property. The concept of natural rights was central to English philosopher John Locke's theories about government, and was widely accepted among America's Founding Fathers.

consent of the governed

The idea that government derives its authority by sanction of the people.

limited government

The idea that certain restrictions should be placed on government to protect the **natural rights** of citizens.

Two limits on government were particularly important to Locke. First, governments must provide standing laws so that people know in advance whether their acts will be acceptable. Second, and Locke was very forceful on this point, "the supreme power cannot take from any man any part of his property without his consent." To Locke, "the preservation of property was the end of government." The sanctity of property was one of the few ideas absent in Jefferson's draft of the Declaration of Independence. Even though Jefferson borrowed from and even paraphrased Lockean ideas, he altered Locke's phrase "life, liberty, and property" to "life, liberty, and the pursuit of happiness." We shall soon see, though, how the Lockean idea of the sanctity of property figured prominently at the Constitutional Convention. James Madison, the most influential member of that body, directly echoed Locke's view that the preservation of property is the purpose of government.

In an extreme case, said Locke, people have a right to revolt against a government that no longer has their consent. Locke anticipated critics' charges that this right would lead to constant civil disturbances. He emphasized that people should not revolt until injustices become deeply felt. The Declaration of Independence accented the same point, declaring that "governments long established should not be changed for light and transient causes." But when matters went beyond "patient sufferance," severing these ties was not only inevitable but also necessary.

Jefferson's Handiwork: The American Creed

There are some remarkable parallels between Locke's thought and Jefferson's language in the Declaration of Independence (see Table 2.1). Jefferson, like Locke, finessed his way past the issue of how the rebels knew men had rights. Jefferson simply declared that it was "self-evident" that men were equally "endowed by their Creator with certain unalienable rights," including "life, liberty, and the pursuit of happiness." Because it was the purpose of government to "secure" these rights, if it failed to do so, the people could form a new government.[4]

Locke represented only one element of revolutionary thought from which Jefferson borrowed. In the English countryside, there was also a well-established tradition of opposition to the executive power of the Crown and support for recovering the rights of the people. An indigenous American republicanism—stressing moral virtue, patriotism, relations based on natural merit, and the equality of independent citizens— intensified the radicalism of this "country" ideology and linked it with older currents of European thought stretching back to antiquity.

It was in the American colonies that the powerful ideas of European political thinkers took root and grew into what Seymour Martin Lipset has termed the "first new nation."[5] With these revolutionary ideas in mind, Jefferson claimed in the Declaration of Independence that people should have primacy over governments, that they should rule instead of be ruled. Moreover, each person was important as an individual, "created equal" and endowed with "unalienable rights." Consent of the governed, not divine rights or tradition, made the exercise of political power legitimate.

No government had ever been based on these principles. Ever since 1776, Americans have been concerned about fulfilling the high aspirations of the Declaration of Independence.

Winning Independence

The pen may be mightier than the sword, but declaring independence did not win the Revolution—it merely announced its beginning. John Adams wrote to his wife Abigail, "You will think me transported with enthusiasm, but I am not. I am well aware of the toil, blood, and treasure that it will cost us to maintain this Declaration, and support and defend these states." Adams was right. The colonists seemed little match for the finest army in the world, whose size was nearly quadrupled by hired guns from the

Table 2.1   Locke and the Declaration of Independence: Some Parallels

LOCKE	DECLARATION OF INDEPENDENCE
Natural Rights "The state of nature has a law to govern it" "life, liberty, and property"	"Laws of Nature and Nature's God" "life, liberty, and the pursuit of happiness"
Purpose of Government "to preserve himself, his liberty, and property"	"to secure these rights"
Equality "men being by nature all free, equal and independent"	"all men are created equal"
Consent of the Governed "for when any number of men have, by the consent of every individual, made a community, with a power to act as one body, which is only by the will and determination of the majority"	"Governments are instituted among men, deriving their just powers from the consent of the governed."
Limited Government "Absolute arbitrary power, or governing without settled laws, can neither of them consist with the ends of society and government." "As usurpation is the exercise of power which another has a right to, so tyranny is the exercise of power beyond right, which nobody can have a right to."	"The history of the present King of Great Britain is a history of repeated injuries and usurpations."
Right to Revolt "The people shall be the judge. . . . Oppression raises ferments and makes men struggle to cast off an uneasy and tyrannical yoke."	"Prudence, indeed, will dictate that Governments long established should not be changed for light and transient causes. . . . But when a long train of abuses and usurpations, pursuing invariably the same Object evinces a design to reduce them under absolute Despotism, it is their right, it is their duty, to throw off such Government."

German state of Hesse and elsewhere. In 1775, the British had 8,500 men stationed in the colonies and had hired nearly 30,000 mercenaries. Initially, the colonists had only 5,000 men in uniform, and their number waxed and waned as the war progressed. Nevertheless, in 1783, the American colonies won their war of independence. How they eventually won is a story best left to history books. How they formed a new government, however, will be explored in the following sections.

The "Conservative" Revolution

Revolutions such as the 1789 French Revolution, the 1917 Russian Revolution, and the 1978–1979 Iranian Revolution produced great societal change—as well as plenty of bloodshed. The American Revolution was different. Although many people lost their lives during the Revolutionary War, the Revolution itself was essentially a conservative movement that did not drastically alter the colonists' way of life. Its primary goal was to restore rights the colonists felt were already theirs as British subjects.

American colonists did not feel the need for great social, economic, or political upheavals. They "were not oppressed people; they had no crushing imperial shackles to throw off."[6] As a result, the Revolution did not create class conflicts that would split society for generations to come. The colonial leaders' belief that they needed the consent of the governed blessed the new nation with a crucial element of stability—a stability the nation would need.

The Government That Failed: 1776–1787

The Continental Congress that adopted the Declaration of Independence was only a voluntary association of the states. In 1776, the Congress appointed a committee to draw up a plan for a permanent union of the states. That plan, our first constitution, was the **Articles of Confederation.**[7]

The Articles of Confederation

The Articles established a government dominated by the states. The United States, according to the Articles, was a confederation, a "league of friendship and perpetual union" among 13 states. The Articles established a national legislature with one house; states could send as many as seven delegates or as few as two, but each state had only one vote. There was no president and no national court, and the powers of the national legislature—the Congress—were strictly limited. Most authority rested with the state legislatures because the new nation's leaders feared a strong central government would become as tyrannical as British rule.

Because unanimous consent of the states was needed to put the Articles into operation, the Articles adopted by Congress in 1777 did not go into effect until 1781, when laggard Maryland finally ratified them. In the meantime, the Continental Congress barely survived, lurching from crisis to crisis. At one point during the war, some of Washington's troops threatened to create a monarchy with him as king unless Congress paid their overdue wages.

Even after the Articles were ratified, many logistical and political problems plagued the Congress. State delegations attended haphazardly. The Congress had few powers outside maintaining an army and navy—and little money to do even that. It had to request money from the states because it had no power to tax. If states refused to send money (which they often did), Congress did without. In desperation, Congress sold off western lands (land east of the Mississippi and west of the states) to speculators, issued securities that sold for less than their face value, or used its own presses to print money that was virtually worthless. Congress also voted to disband the army, despite continued threats from Britain and Spain.

Congress lacked the power to regulate commerce, which inhibited foreign trade and the development of a strong national economy. It did, however, manage to develop sound policies for the management of the western frontiers, passing the Northwest Ordinance of 1787 that encouraged the development of the Great Lakes region.

In general, the weak and ineffective national government could take little independent action. All government power rested in the states. The national government could not compel the states to do anything, and it had no power to deal directly with individual citizens. The weakness of the national government prevented it from dealing with the hard times that faced the new nation. There was one benefit of the Articles, however: When the nation's leaders began to write a new Constitution, they could look at the provisions of the Articles of Confederation and know some of the things they should avoid.

Articles of Confederation

The first constitution of the United States, adopted by Congress in 1777 and enacted in 1781. The Articles established a national legislature, the Continental Congress, but most authority rested with the state legislatures.

Why It Matters

A Strong National Government
One of the most important features of the Constitution is the creation of a strong national government. If the framers had retained a weak national government, as under the Articles of Confederation, Congress could not create a great national economic market through regulating interstate commerce, the president could not conduct a vigorous foreign policy, federal courts could not issue orders to protect civil rights, and the federal government could not raise the funds to pay for Social Security benefits.

Table 2.2   Power Shift: Economic Status of State Legislators Before and After the Revolutionary War

After the Revolution, power in the state legislatures shifted from the hands of the wealthy to those with more moderate incomes, and from merchants and lawyers to farmers. This trend was especially evident in the northern states.

STATUS OF LEGISLATORS	Three Northern States[a]		Three Southern States[b]	
	PREWAR	POSTWAR	PREWAR	POSTWAR
Wealthy	36%	12%	52%	28%
Well to do	47%	26%	36%	42%
Moderate income	17%	62%	12%	30%
Merchants and lawyers	43%	18%	23%	17%
Farmers	23%	55%	12%	26%

[a]New York, New Jersey, and New Hampshire.
[b]Maryland, Virginia, and South Carolina.
Source: From Jackson Turner Main, "Government by the People: The American Revolution and the Democratization of the Legislatures," *The William and Mary Quarterly,* 3rd ser. 23 (July 1966). Reprinted by permission of the Omohandro Institute of Early American History and Culture.

Changes in the States

What was happening in the states was more important than what was happening in the Congress. The most important change was a dramatic increase in democracy and liberty, at least for White males. Many states adopted bills of rights to protect freedoms, abolished religious qualifications for holding office, and liberalized requirements for voting. Expanded political participation brought a new middle class to power.

This middle class included farmers who owned small homesteads rather than manorial landholders, and artisans instead of lawyers. Before the Revolution, almost all members of New York's assembly were either urban merchants or wealthy landowners. In the 1769 assembly, for example, 25 percent of the legislators were farmers even though nearly 95 percent of New Yorkers were farmers. But after the Revolution, a major power shift occurred. With expanded voting privileges, farmers and craftworkers became a decisive majority, and the old elite of professionals, wealthy merchants, and large landholders saw its power shrink. The same change happened in other states as power shifted from a handful of wealthy individuals to a more broad-based group (see Table 2.2). Democracy was taking hold everywhere.

The structure of government in the states also became more responsive to the people. Power was concentrated in the legislatures because legislators were considered closer to the voters than governors or judges. Governors were often selected by the legislatures and were kept on a short leash, with brief tenures and limited veto and appointment powers. Legislatures overruled court decisions and criticized judges for unpopular decisions.

The idea of equality was driving change throughout the nation. Although the Revolutionary War itself did not transform American society, it unleashed the republican tendencies in American life. Americans were in the process of becoming "the most liberal, the most democratic, the most commercially minded, and the most modern people in the world."[8] Members of the old colonial elite found this turn of affairs quite troublesome because it challenged their hold on power.

Economic Turmoil

After the Revolution, James Madison observed that "the most common and durable source of factions [special interests] has been the various and unequal division of property."[9] The post-Revolutionary legislatures epitomized Madison's argument that economic inequality played an important role in shaping public policy. At the top of the political agenda were economic issues. A postwar depression had left many small farmers unable to pay their debts and threatened them with mortgage foreclosures. Now under control of people more sympathetic to debtors, the state legislatures listened to the demands of small farmers. A few states, notably Rhode Island, demonstrated their support of debtors, passing policies favoring them over creditors. Some printed tons of paper money and passed "force acts" requiring reluctant creditors to accept the almost worthless money. Debtors could thus pay big debts with cheap currency.

Shays' Rebellion

Policies favoring debtors over creditors did not please the economic elite who had once controlled nearly all the state legislatures. They were further shaken when, in 1786, a small band of farmers in western Massachusetts rebelled at losing their land to creditors. Led by Revolutionary War Captain Daniel Shays, this rebellion, called **Shays' Rebellion,** was a series of armed attacks on courthouses to prevent judges from foreclosing on farms. Farmers in other states—though never in large numbers—were also unruly. Jefferson was not distressed at this behavior, calling the attack a "little rebellion," but it remained on the minds of the economic elite. They were scared at the thought that people had taken the law into their own hands and violated the property rights of others. Neither Congress nor the state was able to raise a militia to stop Shays and his followers, and a privately paid force was assembled to do the job, which further fueled dissatisfaction with the weakness of the Articles of Confederation system.

Shays' Rebellion

A series of attacks on courthouses by a small band of farmers led by Revolutionary War Captain Daniel Shays to block foreclosure proceedings.

The Aborted Annapolis Meeting

In September 1786, a handful of leaders assembled at Annapolis, Md., to discuss problems with the Articles of Confederation and suggest solutions. The assembly was an abortive attempt at reform. Only five states—New York, New Jersey, Delaware, Pennsylvania, and Virginia—were represented at the meeting; the 12 delegates were

Shays' Rebellion, in which farmers physically prevented judges from foreclosing on farms, helped spur the birth of the Constitution. News of the small rebellion spread quickly around the country, and some of the Philadelphia delegates thought a full-fledged revolution would result. The event reaffirmed the framers' belief that the new federal government needed to be a strong one.

few enough in number to meet around a dinner table. Called to consider commercial conflicts that had arisen among the states under the Articles of Confederation, the Annapolis delegates decided that a larger meeting and a broader proposal were needed to organize the states. Holding most of their meetings at a local tavern, this small and unofficial band of reformers issued a call for a full-scale meeting of the states in Philadelphia the following May—in retrospect, a rather bold move by so small a group. Their request was granted, however; the Continental Congress called for a meeting of all the states. In May 1787, what we now call the Constitutional Convention got down to business in Philadelphia.

Making a Constitution: The Philadelphia Convention

Representatives from 12 states came to Philadelphia to heed the Continental Congress' call to "take into consideration the situation in the United States." Only Rhode Island, a stronghold of paper-money interests, refused to send delegates. Virginia's Patrick Henry (the colonial firebrand who had declared, "Give me liberty or give me death!"), fearing a centralization of power, also did not attend.

The delegates were ordered to meet "for the sole and express purpose of revising the Articles of Confederation." The Philadelphia delegates did not pay much attention to this order, however, because amending the Articles required the unanimous consent of the states, which they knew would be impossible. Thus, the 55 delegates ignored their instructions and began writing what was to become the **U.S. Constitution.**

U.S. Constitution

The document written in 1787 and ratified in 1788 that sets forth the institutional structure of U.S. government and the tasks these institutions perform. It replaced the Articles of Confederation.

Gentlemen in Philadelphia

Who were these 55 men? They may not have been "demigods," as Jefferson, perhaps sarcastically, called them, but they were certainly a select group of economic and political notables. They were mostly wealthy planters, successful (or once successful) lawyers and merchants, and men of independent wealth. Many were college graduates and most had practical political experience. Most were coastal residents, rather than residents of the expanding western frontiers, and a significant number were urbanites, rather than part of the primarily rural American population.

Philosophy into Action

The delegates in Philadelphia were an uncommon combination of philosophers and shrewd political architects. The debates moved from high principles on the big issues to self-interest on the small ones.[10] The first two weeks were mainly devoted to general debates about the nature of republican government (government in which ultimate power rests with the voters). After that, practical and divisive issues sometimes threatened to dissolve the meeting.

Obviously, these 55 men did not share the same political philosophy. Democratic Benjamin Franklin held very different views from aristocratic Alexander Hamilton, who hardly hid his disgust for democracy. Yet, at the core of their ideas, even those of Franklin and Hamilton, existed a common center. The group agreed on questions of (1) human nature, (2) the causes of political conflict, (3) the objects of government, and (4) the nature of a republican government.

Human Nature. In his famous work entitled *Leviathan* written in 1651, Thomas Hobbes argued that man's natural state was war and that a strong absolute ruler was necessary to restrain man's bestial tendencies. Without a strong government, Hobbes wrote, life would be "solitary, poor, nasty, brutish, and short." The delegates were not convinced of the need for a monarch, but they did hold a cynical view of human nature.

Alexander Hamilton, a New York delegate to the Convention, favored a strong central government; in fact, he favored an elected king. Hamilton was less influential at the Convention than he would be later as an architect of the nation's economic policy.

People, they thought, were self-interested. Franklin and Hamilton, poles apart philosophically, both voiced this sentiment. Said Franklin, "There are two passions which have a powerful influence on the affairs of men: the love of power and the love of money." Hamilton agreed in his characteristically blunt manner: "Men love power." The men at Philadelphia believed that government should play a key role in containing the natural self-interest of people.[11]

Political Conflict. Of all the words written by and about the delegates, none have been more widely quoted than these by James Madison: "The most common and durable source of factions has been the various and unequal distribution of property." In other words, *the distribution of wealth* (land was the main form of wealth in those days) *is the source of political conflict.* "Those who hold and those who are without property," Madison went on, "have ever formed distinct interests in society." Other sources of conflict included religion, views of governing, and attachment to various leaders.[12]

Arising from these sources of conflict are **factions,** which we might call parties or interest groups. A majority faction might well be composed of the many who have little or no property; the minority faction, of those with property. If unchecked, the delegates thought, one of these factions would eventually tyrannize the other. The majority would try to seize the government to reduce the wealth of the minority; the minority would try to seize the government to secure its own gains. Governments that are run by factions, the Founders believed, are prone to instability, tyranny, and even violence. The effects of factions had to be checked.

Objects of Government. To Gouverneur Morris of Pennsylvania, the preservation of property was the "principal object of government." Morris was outspoken and plainly overlooked some other objects of government, including security from invasion, domestic tranquillity, and promotion of the general welfare. However, Morris's remark typifies the philosophy of many of the delegates. John Locke (who was,

factions

Interest groups arising from the unequal distribution of property or wealth that James Madison attacked in **Federalist Paper No. 10.** Today's parties or interest groups are what Madison had in mind when he warned of the instability in government caused by factions.

Pennsylvania delegate Gouverneur Morris was a man of considerable means and, like Hamilton, an extreme anti-Democrat primarily concerned with protecting property holders. He was responsible for the style and wording of the Constitution.

remember, the intellectual patron saint of many of the delegates) had said a century before that "The preservation of property is the end of government." Few of these men would have disagreed. As property holders themselves, these delegates could not imagine a government that did not make its principal objective an economic one: the preservation of individual rights to acquire and hold wealth. A few (like Morris) were intent on shutting out the propertyless altogether. "Give the votes to people who have no property," Morris claimed, "and they will sell them to the rich who will be able to buy them."

Nature of Government. Given their beliefs about human nature, the causes of political conflict, the need to protect property, and the threat of tyranny by a faction, what sort of government did the delegates believe would work? They answered in different ways, but the message was always the same. Power should be set against power, so that no one faction would overwhelm the others. The secret of good government is "balanced" government. They were influenced in their thinking by writings of a French aristocrat, Baron Montesquieu, who advocated separate branches of government with distinct powers and the ability to check the other branches. The Founders agreed, concluding that a limited government would have to contain checks on its own power. So long as no faction could seize the whole of government at once, tyranny could be avoided. A complex network of checks, balances, and separation of powers would be required for a balanced government.

The Agenda in Philadelphia

The delegates in Philadelphia could not merely construct a government from ideas. They wanted to design a government that was consistent with their political philosophy, but they also had to meet head-on some of the thorniest issues confronting the fledgling nation at the time—issues of equality, the economy, and individual rights.

The Equality Issues

The Declaration of Independence states that all men are created equal; the Constitution, however, is silent on equality. Nevertheless, some of the most important issues on the policy agenda in Philadelphia concerned equality. Three issues occupied more attention than almost any others: whether the states were to be equally represented, what to do about slavery, and whether to ensure political equality.

Equality and Representation of the States. One crucial policy issue was how the new Congress would be constituted. The **New Jersey Plan,** proposed by William Paterson of New Jersey, called for each state to be equally represented in the new Congress. The opposing strategy, suggested by Edmund Randolph of Virginia, is usually called the **Virginia Plan.** It called for giving each state representation in Congress based on the state's share of the American population.

The delegates resolved this conflict with a compromise devised by Roger Sherman and William Johnson of Connecticut. The solution proposed by this **Connecticut Compromise** was to create two houses in Congress. One body, the Senate, would have two members from each state (the New Jersey Plan), and the second body, the House of Representatives, would have representation based on population (the Virginia Plan). The U.S. Congress is still organized in exactly the same way. Each state has two senators, and the state's population determines its representation in the House.

Although the Connecticut Compromise was intended to maximize equality between the states, it actually gives more power to people who live in states with small populations than to those who live in more heavily populated states. Every state has two senators and at least one member of the House, no matter how small its population. To take the most extreme case, Wyoming and California have the same number of votes in the Senate (two), although Wyoming has less than 2 percent of California's population. Thus, a citizen of Wyoming has more than 50 *times* the representation in the Senate as does a citizen of California.[13]

Because it is the Senate, not the House, that ratifies treaties, confirms presidential nominations, and hears trials of impeachment, citizens in less populated states have a greater say in these key tasks. In addition, the Electoral College (the body that actually elects the president and is discussed in Chapter 10) gives small states greater weight. If no presidential candidate receives a majority in the Electoral College, the House of Representatives makes the final decision—with each state having one vote. In such a case (which has not occurred since 1824), the votes of citizens of Wyoming would again carry over 50 times as much weight as those of Californians.

Whether representation in the Senate is "fair" is a matter of debate. What is not open to question is that the delegates to the 1787 convention had to accommodate various interests and viewpoints in order to convince all the states to join an untested union.

Slavery. The second equality issue was slavery. The contradictions between slavery and the sentiments of the Declaration of Independence are obvious, but slavery was legal in every state except Massachusetts. It was concentrated in the South, however, where slave labor was commonplace in agriculture. Some delegates, like Gouverneur Morris, denounced slavery in no uncertain terms. But the Convention could not accept Morris's position in the face of powerful Southern opposition led by Charles C. Pinckney of South Carolina. The delegates did agree that Congress could limit *future importing* of slaves (they allowed it to be outlawed after 1808), but they did not forbid slavery itself. The Constitution, in fact, inclines toward recognizing slavery; it stated that persons legally "held to service or labour" (referring to slaves) who escaped to free states had to be returned to their owners.

Another difficult question about slavery arose at the Convention. How should slaves be counted in determining representation in Congress? Southerners were happy

New Jersey Plan

The proposal at the Constitutional Convention that called for equal **representation** of each state in Congress regardless of the state's population.

Virginia Plan

The proposal at the Constitutional Convention that called for **representation** of each state in Congress in proportion to that state's share of the U.S. population.

Connecticut Compromise

The compromise reached at the Constitutional Convention that established two houses of Congress: the House of Representatives, in which **representation** is based on a state's share of the U.S. population, and the Senate, in which each state has two representatives.

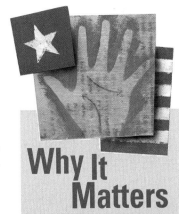

Why It Matters

Representation in the Senate
The Senate both creates a check on the House and over-represents states with small populations. If there were only one house of Congress, governance would be more efficient. If representation were based on population, interests centered in states with small populations would lose an advantage. At the same time, there would be one less important check on government action and perhaps a closer correspondence between public opinion and public policy. Which do you prefer?

DOONESBURY   Garry Trudeau

to see slaves counted toward determining their representation in the House of Representatives (though reluctant to count them for apportionment of taxation). Here the result was the famous *three-fifths compromise*. Representation and taxation were to be based on the "number of free persons," plus three-fifths of the number of "all other persons." Everyone, of course, knew who those other persons were.

Political Equality. The delegates dodged one other issue on equality. A handful of delegates, led by Franklin, suggested that national elections should require universal manhood suffrage (that is, a vote for all free adult males). This still would have left a majority of the population disenfranchised, but for those still smarting from Shays' Rebellion and the fear of mob rule, the suggestion was too democratic. Many delegates wanted to put property qualifications on the right to vote. Ultimately, as the debate

When the Constitution was written, many Northern and Southern delegates assumed that slavery, being relatively unprofitable, would soon die out. A single invention—Eli Whitney's cotton gin—made it profitable again. Although Congress did act to control the growth of slavery, the slave economy became entrenched in the South.

Table 2.3   How Three Issues of Equality Were Resolved: A Summary

PROBLEM	SOLUTION
Equality of the States Should states be represented equally (the New Jersey Plan) or in proportion to their population (the Virginia Plan)?	Both, according to the Connecticut Compromise. States have equal representation in the Senate, but representation in the House is proportionate to population.
Slavery What should be done about slavery?	Although Congress was permitted to stop the importing of slaves after 1808, the Constitution is mostly silent on the issue of slavery.
How should slaves be counted for representation in the House of Representatives?	Count each slave as three-fifths of a person.
Political Equality Should the right to vote be based on universal manhood suffrage, or should it be very restricted?	Finesse the issue. Let the states decide qualifications for voting.

wound down, they decided to leave the issue to the states. People qualified to vote in state elections could also vote in national elections (see Table 2.3).

The Economic Issues

The Philadelphia delegates were deeply concerned about the state of the American economy. Economic issues were high on the Constitution writers' policy agenda. People disagreed (in fact, historians still disagree) as to whether the postcolonial economy was in a shambles. Advocates of the Constitution, called Federalists, stressed the economy's "weaknesses, especially in the commercial sector, and Anti-Federalists (those opposed to a strong national government, and thus opposed to a new constitution) countered with charges of exaggeration."[14] The writers of the Constitution, already committed to a strong national government, charged that the economy was indeed in disarray. Specifically, they claimed that the following problems had to be addressed:

- The states had erected tariffs against products from other states.
- Paper money was virtually worthless in some states, but many state governments, which were controlled by debtor classes, forced it on creditors anyway.
- The Congress was having trouble raising money because the economy was in a recession.

Understanding something about the delegates and their economic interests gives us insight into their views on political economy. They were, by all accounts, the nation's postcolonial economic elite. Some were budding capitalists. Others were creditors whose loans were being wiped out by cheap paper money. Many were merchants who could not even carry on trade with a neighboring state. Virtually all of them thought a strong national government was needed to bring economic stability to the chaotic union of states that existed under the Articles of Confederation.[15]

It is not surprising, then, that the framers of the Constitution would seek to strengthen the economic powers (and thus the scope) of the new national government. One famous historian, Charles A. Beard, claimed that their principal motivation for doing so was to increase their personal wealth. The framers, he said, not only were propertied, upper-class men protecting their interests but also held bonds and investments whose value would increase if the Constitution were adopted. The best evidence, however, indicates that although they were concerned about protecting property rights, the Founders' motivations were in the broad sense of building a strong economy rather than in the narrow sense of increasing their personal wealth.[16]

The delegates made sure that the Constitution clearly spelled out the economic powers of Congress (see Table 2.4). Consistent with the general allocation of power in the Constitution, Congress was to be the chief economic policymaker. It could obtain revenues through taxing and borrowing. These tools, along with the power to appropriate funds, became crucial instruments for influencing the economy (as we will see in Chapter 17). By maintaining sound money and guaranteeing payment for the national debt, Congress was to encourage economic enterprise and investment in the United States. Congress was also given power to build the nation's infrastructure by constructing post offices and roads and to establish standard weights and measures. To protect property rights, Congress was charged with punishing counterfeiters and pirates, ensuring patents and copyrights, and legislating rules for bankruptcy. Equally important (and now a key congressional power, with a wide range of implications for the economy) was Congress' new ability to regulate interstate and foreign commerce. In sum, the Constitution granted Congress the power to create the conditions within which markets could flourish.

In addition, the framers prohibited practices in the states that they viewed as inhibiting economic development, such as maintaining individual state monetary systems, placing duties on imports from other states, and interfering with lawfully contracted debts. Moreover, the states were to respect civil judgments and contracts made in other states, and they were to return runaway slaves to their owners. (This last protection of "property" rights is now, of course, defunct as a result of the Thirteenth Amendment, which outlawed slavery.) To help the states, the national government guaranteed them "a republican form of government" to prevent a recurrence of Shays' Rebellion, in which violence, instead of legislation and the courts, was used to resolve commercial disputes.

The Constitution also obligated the new government to repay all the public debts incurred under the Continental Congress and the Articles of Confederation—debts that totaled $54 million. Although this requirement may seem odd, there was sound economic reason for it. Paying off the debts would ensure from the outset that money would flow into the American economy and would also restore the confidence of investors in the young nation. Even today, people trade in government debt (in the form of bonds) just as they do in the stocks of corporations. Thus, the Constitution helped to spur a capitalist economy.

Table 2.4   Economics in the Constitution

Powers of Congress

1. Levy taxes.
2. Pay debts.
3. Borrow money.
4. Coin money and regulate its value.
5. Regulate interstate and foreign commerce.
6. Establish uniform laws of bankruptcy.

7. Punish piracy.
8. Punish counterfeiting.
9. Create standard weights and measures.
10. Establish post offices and post roads.
11. Protect copyrights and patents.

Prohibitions on the States

1. States cannot pass laws impairing the obligations of contract.
2. States cannot coin money or issue paper money.
3. States cannot require payment of debts in paper money.

4. States cannot tax imports or exports from abroad or from other states.
5. States cannot free runaway slaves from other states (now defunct).

Other Key Provisions

1. The new government assumes the national debt contracted under the Articles of Confederation.
2. The Constitution guarantees a republican form of government.

3. The states must respect civil court judgments and contracts made in other states.

The Individual Rights Issues

There was another major item on the Constitutional Convention agenda; the delegates had to design a system that would preserve individual rights. There was no dispute about the importance of safeguarding individualism, and the Founders believed that this would be relatively easy. After all, they were constructing a limited government that, by design, could not threaten personal freedoms. In addition, they dispersed power among the branches of the national government and between the national and state governments so that each branch or level could restrain the other. Also, most of the delegates believed that the various states were already doing a sufficient job of protecting individual rights.

As a result, the Constitution says little about personal freedoms. The protections it does offer are:

- It prohibits suspension of the **writ of habeas corpus** (except during invasion or rebellion). Such a court order enables persons detained by authorities to secure an immediate inquiry into the causes of their detention. If no proper explanation is offered, a judge may order their release. (Article I, Section 9)
- It prohibits Congress or the states from passing bills of attainder (which punish people without a judicial trial). (Article I, Section 9)
- It prohibits Congress or the states from passing *ex post facto* laws (which punish people or increase the penalties for acts that were not illegal or not as punishable when the act was committed). (Article I, Section 9)
- It prohibits the imposition of religious qualifications for holding office in the national government. (Article VI)
- It narrowly defines and outlines strict rules of evidence for conviction of treason. To be convicted, a person must levy war against the United States or adhere to and aid its enemies during war. Conviction requires confession in open court or the testimony of *two* witnesses to the *same* overt act. The framers of the Constitution would have been executed as traitors if the Revolution had failed, and they were therefore sensitive to treason laws. (Article III, Section 3)
- It upholds the right to trial by jury in criminal cases. (Article III, Section 2)

The delegates were content with their document. When it came time to ratify the Constitution, however, there was widespread criticism of the absence of specific protections of individual rights, such as free expression and the rights of the accused.

writ of habeas corpus

A court order requiring jailers to explain to a judge why they are holding a prisoner in custody.

The Madisonian Model

The framers believed that human nature was self-interested and that inequalities of wealth were the principal source of political conflict. Regardless, they had no desire to remove the divisions in society by converting private property to common ownership; they also believed that protecting private property was a key purpose of government. Their experience with state governments under the Articles of Confederation reinforced their view that democracy was a threat to property. Many of them felt that the nonwealthy majority—an unruly mob—would tyrannize the wealthy minority if given political power. Thus, the delegates to the Constitutional Convention were faced with the dilemma of reconciling economic inequality with political freedom.

Thwarting Tyranny of the Majority

James Madison was the principal architect of the government's final structure, and his work still shapes our policymaking process[17] (see "Making a Difference: James Madison"). He and his colleagues feared both majority and minority factions. Either could take control of the government and use it to their own advantage. Factions of the minority, however, were easy to handle; the majority could simply out-vote them.

Making a Difference

James Madison

James Madison was an unlikely hero. He was not a great orator, nor was he a man of great wealth. He was, however, a careful student of politics and government. Relying on the force of his intellect, he was the preeminent figure at the Constitutional Convention, tirelessly advocating a strong government to a gathering that included Benjamin Franklin, George Washington, and other giants of American history who were many years his senior. As a result, today we celebrate Madison as the father of the Constitution.

Factions of the majority were harder to handle. If the majority united around some policy issue, such as the redistribution of wealth, they could oppress the minority, violating the latter's basic rights.[18]

As Madison would later explain:

> Ambition must be made to counteract ambition . . . . If men were angels, no government would be necessary. If angels were to govern men, neither external nor internal controls would be necessary. In framing a government which is to be administered by men over men, the great difficulty lies in this: you must first enable the government to control the governed; and then in the next place oblige it to control itself.[19]

To prevent the possibility of a tyranny of the majority, Madison proposed the following:

1. Place as much of the government as possible beyond the direct control of the majority.
2. Separate the powers of different institutions.
3. Construct a system of checks and balances.

Limiting Majority Control. Madison believed that to thwart tyranny by the majority, it was essential to keep most of the government beyond their power. His plan placed only one element of government, the House of Representatives, within direct control of the votes of the majority. In contrast, state legislatures were to elect senators and special electors were to select the president; in other words, government officials would be elected by a small minority, not by the people themselves. Judges were to be nominated by the president (see Figure 2.2). If the majority seized control of the House of Representatives, they still could not enact policies without the agreement of the Senate and the president. To further insulate governmental officials from public opinion, judges were given lifetime tenure and senators were given terms of six years, with only one-third elected every two years, compared with the two-year election intervals of all members of the House of Representatives.

separation of powers

A feature of the Constitution that requires each of the three branches of government—executive, legislative, and judicial—to be relatively independent of the others so that one cannot control the others. Power is shared among these three institutions.

Separating Powers. The Madisonian scheme also provided for a **separation of powers.** Each of the three branches of government—executive (the president), legislative (Congress), and judicial (the courts)—would be relatively independent of one another so that no single branch could control the others. The president, Congress,

Figure 2.2   The Constitution and the Electoral Process: The Original Plan

Under Madison's plan, which was incorporated in the Constitution, voters' electoral influence was limited. Only the House of Representatives was directly elected. Senators and presidents were indirectly elected, and judges were nominated by the president. Over the years, Madison's original model has been substantially democratized. The Seventeenth Amendment (1913) established direct election of senators by popular majorities. Today, the Electoral College has become largely a rubber stamp, voting the way the popular majority in each state votes.

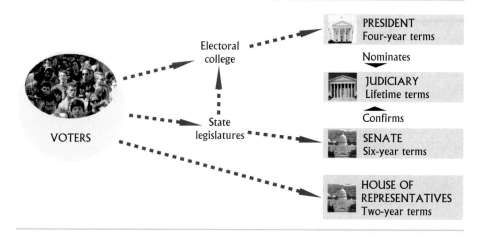

and the courts were all given independent elements of power. Power was not divided absolutely, however; rather, it was *shared* among the three institutions.

Creating Checks and Balances. Because powers were not completely separate, each branch required the consent of the others for many of its actions. This created a system of **checks and balances** that reflected Madison's goal of setting power against power to constrain government actions. He reasoned that if a faction seized one institution, it still could not damage the whole system. The system of checks and balances was an elaborate and delicate creation. The president checks Congress by holding veto power; Congress holds the purse strings of government and must approve presidential appointments.

The courts also figured into the system of checks and balances. Presidents could nominate judges, but their confirmation by the Senate was required. The Supreme Court itself, in *Marbury v. Madison* (1803), asserted its power to check the other branches through judicial review: the right to hold actions of the other two branches unconstitutional. This right, which is not specifically outlined in the Constitution, considerably strengthened the Court's ability to restrain the other branches of government. For a summary of separation of powers and the checks and balances system, see Figure 2.3.

Establishing a Federal System. As we will discuss in detail in Chapter 3, the Founders also established a federal system of government that divided the power of government between a national government and the individual states. Most government activity at the time occurred in the states. The framers of the Constitution anticipated that this would be an additional check on the national government.

checks and balances

Features of the Constitution that limit government's power by requiring that power be balanced among the different governmental institutions. These institutions continually constrain one another's activities.

The American System of Checks and Balances

Figure 2.3   Separation of Powers and Checks and Balances in the Constitution

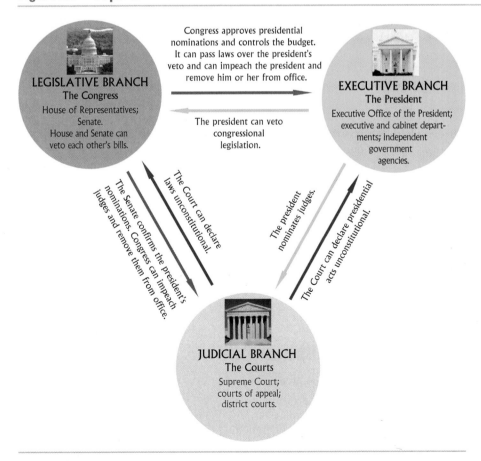

The doctrine of separation of powers allows the three institutions of government to check and balance one another. Judicial review—the power of courts to hold executive and congressional policies unconstitutional—was not explicit in the Constitution, but was asserted by the Supreme Court in *Marbury v. Madison.*

The Constitutional Republic

When asked what kind of government the delegates had produced, Benjamin Franklin is said to have replied, "A republic . . . if you can keep it." Because the Founders did not wish to have the people directly make all decisions (as in a town meeting where everyone has one vote), and because even then the country was far too large for such a proposal to be feasible, they did not choose to create a direct democracy. Their solution was to establish a **republic:** a system based on the consent of the governed in which representatives of the public exercise power. This deliberative democracy required and encouraged reflection and refinement of the public's views through an elaborate decision-making process.

The system of checks and balances and separation of powers favors the status quo. People who desire change must usually have a sizable majority, not just a simple majority of 51 percent. Those opposed to change need only win at one point in the policymaking process—say in obtaining a presidential veto—whereas those who favor change must win *every* battle along the way. Change usually comes slowly, if at all. As a result, the Madisonian system encourages moderation and compromise and slows change. It is difficult for either a minority or a majority to tyrannize; and both property rights and personal freedoms (with only occasional lapses) have survived.

Franklin was correct that such a system is not easy to maintain. It requires careful nurturing and balancing of diverse interests. Some critics argue that the policymaking process lacks efficiency, preventing effective responses to pressing matters. We will examine this issue closely throughout *Government in America*.

The End of the Beginning

On the 109th day of the meetings, in stifling heat made worse because the windows of the Pennsylvania statehouse were closed to ensure secrecy, the final version of the Constitution was read aloud. Then Dr. Franklin rose with a speech he had written, but was so enfeebled he had to ask James Wilson to deliver it. In it, Franklin noted that "There are several parts of this Constitution of which I do not at present approve, but I am not sure that I shall never approve them." He then offered a few political witticisms, defended their handiwork, and concluded by saying, "On the whole, Sir, I cannot help expressing a wish that every member of the Convention who may still have an objection to it, would with me on this occasion, doubt a little of his own infallibility—and make manifest our unanimity, put his name to this instrument."

On Franklin's motion, a vote was taken. Ten states voted yes, and none voted no, but South Carolina's delegates were divided. As the records so quaintly put it, "The Members then proceeded to sign the instrument." Edmund Randolph, Elbridge Gerry, and George Mason of Virginia, however, refused to sign. Franklin then made another short speech, saying that the sun pictured on the chair of convention president George Washington represented the new nation and was rising, not setting. The members then adjourned to a tavern. The experience of the last few hours, when conflict intermingled with consensus, reminded them that implementing this new document would be no small feat.

Ratifying the Constitution

The Constitution did not go into effect once the Constitutional Convention in Philadelphia was over. It had to be ratified by the states. Our awe of the Founders sometimes blinds us to the bitter politics of the day. There is no way of determining the public's feelings about the new document, but as John Marshall (who later became Chief Justice) suggested, "It is scarcely to be doubted that *in some of the adopting states, a majority of the people were in opposition*." (Italics ours.)[20] The Constitution

---

republic

A form of government in which the people select representatives to govern them and make laws.

Why It Matters

Checks and Balances
The checks and balances in the Constitution favor the status quo. They force contending sides to compromise if legislation is going to pass. They also create the potential for gridlock in which no change occurs.

George Washington presides over the signing of the Constitution. "The business being closed," he wrote, "the members adjourned to the City Tavern, dined together and took cordial leave of each other."

itself required that only 9 of the 13 states approve the document before it could be implemented, ignoring the requirement that the Articles of Confederation be amended only by unanimous consent.

Federalists and Anti-Federalists

Throughout the states, a fierce battle erupted between the **Federalists,** who supported the Constitution, and the **Anti-Federalists,** who opposed it. Newspapers were filled with letters and articles, many written under pseudonyms, praising or condemning the document. In praise of the Constitution, three men—James Madison, Alexander Hamilton, and John Jay—wrote a series of articles under the name Publius. These articles, known as the *Federalist Papers,* are second only to the Constitution itself in characterizing the framers.

Beginning on October 27, 1787, barely a month after the Convention ended, the *Federalist Papers* began to appear in New York newspapers as part of the ratification debate in New York. Eighty-five were eventually published. They not only defended the Constitution detail by detail but also represented an important statement of political philosophy. (The essays influenced few of the New York delegates, however, who voted to ratify the Constitution only after New York City threatened to secede from the state if they did not.)

Far from being unpatriotic or un-American, the Anti-Federalists sincerely believed that the new government was an enemy of freedom, the very freedom they had just fought a war to ensure. Adopting names like Aggrippa, Cornelius, and Monteczuma, the Anti-Federalists launched bitter, biting, even brilliant attacks on the Philadelphia document. They frankly questioned the motives of the Constitution writers.

One objection was central to the Anti-Federalists' attacks: The new Constitution was a class-based document, intended to ensure that a particular economic elite controlled the public policies of the national government. The following quotations are from Anti-Federalist critics of the Constitution.

> *Thus, I conceive, a foundation is laid for throwing the whole power of the federal government into the hands of those who are in the mercantile interest; and for the landed, which is the great interest of this country to lie unrepresented, forlorn and without hope.*
> — "Cornelius"

Federalists

Supporters of the **U.S. Constitution** at the time the states were contemplating its adoption.

Anti-Federalists

Opponents of the American Constitution at the time when the states were contemplating its adoption.

Federalist Papers

A collection of 85 articles written by Alexander Hamilton, John Jay, and James Madison under the name "Publius" to defend the Constitution in detail.

As an explanation and defense of the Constitution, the *Federalist Papers* were often discussed at dinner parties and debated in public places. Despite today's high literacy rates, it is doubtful that a similar set of documents, so rich in political philosophy, would be so widely read in modern America.

These lawyers, men of learning, and moneyed men . . . expect to get into Congress themselves . . . so they can get all the power and all the money into their own hands.
—Amos Singletary of Massachusetts[21]

Remember that these charges of conspiracy and elitism were being hurled at the likes of Washington, Madison, Franklin, and Hamilton.

The Anti-Federalists had other fears. Not only would the new government be run by a few, but it would also erode fundamental liberties. James Lincoln was quoted in the records of the South Carolina ratifying convention as saying that he "would be glad to know why, in this Constitution, there is a total silence with regard to the liberty of the press. Was it forgotten? Impossible! Then it must have been purposely omitted; and with what design, good or bad, I leave the world to judge." You can compare the views of the Federalists and Anti-Federalists in Table 2.5.

Table 2.5   Federalists and Anti-Federalists Compared

	ANTI-FEDERALISTS	FEDERALISTS
Backgrounds		
	Small farmers, shopkeepers, laborers	Large landowners, wealthy merchants, professionals
Government Preferred		
	Strong state government	Weaker state governments
	Weak national government	Strong national government
	Direct election of officials	Indirect election of officials
	Shorter terms	Longer terms
	Rule by the common man	Government by the elite
	Strengthened protections for individual liberties	Less concern for individual liberties

These arguments were persuasive. To allay fears that the Constitution would restrict personal freedoms, the Federalists promised to add amendments to the document specifically protecting individual liberties. They kept their word; James Madison introduced 12 constitutional amendments during the First Congress in 1789. Ten were ratified by the states and took effect in 1791. These first 10 amendments to the Constitution, which restrain the national government from limiting personal freedoms, have come to be known as the **Bill of Rights** (see Table 2.6). Another of Madison's original 12 amendments, one dealing with congressional salaries, was ratified 201 years later as the Twenty-seventh Amendment (see the Appendix in this book).

Opponents also feared that the Constitution would weaken the power of the states (which it did). Patrick Henry railed against strengthening the federal government at the expense of the states. "We are come hither," he told his fellow delegates to the Virginia ratifying convention, "to preserve the poor commonwealth of Virginia."[22] Many state political leaders feared that their own power would be diminished as well.

Simulation

You Are James Madison

Bill of Rights

The first ten amendments to the **U.S. Constitution**, drafted in response to some of the **Anti-Federalist** concerns. These amendments define such basic liberties as freedom of religion, speech, and press and guarantee defendants' rights.

Table 2.6   The Bill of Rights (Arranged by Function)

Protection of Free Expression

Amendment 1:	Freedom of speech, press, and assembly Freedom to petition government

Protection of Personal Beliefs

Amendment 1:	No government establishment of religion Freedom to exercise religion

Protection of Privacy

Amendment 3:	No forced quartering of troops in homes during peacetime
Amendment 4:	No unreasonable searches and seizures

Protection of Defendants' Rights

Amendment 5:	Grand jury indictment required for prosecution of serious crime No second prosecution for the same offense No compulsion to testify against oneself No loss of life, liberty, or property without due process of law
Amendment 6:	Right to a speedy and public trial by a local, impartial jury Right to be informed of charges against oneself Right to legal counsel Right to compel the attendance of favorable witnesses Right to cross-examine witnesses
Amendment 7:	Right to jury trial in civil suit where the value of controversy exceeds $20
Amendment 8:	No excessive bail or fines No cruel and unusual punishments

Protection of Other Rights

Amendment 2:	Right to bear arms
Amendment 5:	No taking of private property for public use without just compensation
Amendment 9:	Unlisted rights are not necessarily denied
Amendment 10:	Powers not delegated to the national government or denied to the states are reserved for the states or the people

Finally, not everyone wanted the economy to be placed on a more sound foundation. Creditors opposed the issuance of paper money because it would produce inflation and make the money they received as payment on their loans decline in value. Debtors favored paper money, however. Their debts (such as the mortgages on their farms) would remain constant, but if money became more plentiful, it would be easier for them to pay off their debts.

Ratification

Federalists may not have had the support of the majority, but they made up for it in shrewd politicking. They knew that many members of the legislatures of some states were skeptical of the Constitution and that state legislatures were populated with political leaders who would lose power under the Constitution. Thus, the Federalists specified that the Constitution be ratified by special conventions in each of the states—not by state legislatures.

Delaware was the first to approve, on December 7, 1787. Only six months passed before New Hampshire's approval (the ninth) made the Constitution official. Virginia and New York then voted to join the new union. Two states were holdouts: North Carolina and Rhode Island made the promise of the Bill of Rights their price for joining the other states.

With the Constitution ratified, it was time to select officeholders. The framers of the Constitution assumed that George Washington would be elected the first president of the new government—even giving him the Convention's papers for safekeeping—and they were right. The general was the unanimous choice of the Electoral College for president. He took office on April 30, 1789, in New York City, the first national capital. New Englander John Adams became "His Superfluous Excellence," as Franklin called the vice president.

Constitutional Change

"The Constitution," said Jefferson, "belongs to the living and not to the dead." The U.S. Constitution is frequently—and rightly—referred to as a living document. It is constantly being tested and altered.

Generally, constitutional changes are made either by formal amendments or by a number of informal processes. Formal amendments change the letter of the Constitution. There is also an unwritten body of tradition, practice, and procedure that, when altered, may change the spirit of the Constitution. In fact, not all nations, even those we call democratic, have written constitutions (see "America in Perspective: Democracy *Without* a Constitution?").

The Formal Amending Process

Simulation

You Are Proposing a
Constitutional Amendment

The most explicit means of changing the Constitution is through the formal process of amendment. Article V of the Constitution outlines procedures for formal amendment. There are two stages to the amendment process—proposal and ratification—and each stage has two possible avenues (see Figure 2.4 on page 53). An amendment may be proposed either by a two-thirds vote in each house of Congress or by a national convention called by Congress at the request of two-thirds of the state legislatures. An amendment may be ratified either by the legislatures of three-fourths of the states or by special state conventions called in three-fourths of the states. The president has no formal role in amending the Constitution, although the chief executive may influence the success of proposed amendments.

All but one of the successful amendments to the Constitution have been proposed by Congress and ratified by the state legislatures. The exception was the Twenty-first

America in Perspective

Democracy *Without* a Constitution

Sometimes it is difficult for Americans to understand that constitutions can be both *written* and *unwritten*. They may be surprised to learn that Great Britain—often called the "cradle of democracy"—has no written constitution at all. The unwritten constitution of Britain is a mixture of acts of Parliament, judicial pronouncements, customs, and conventions about the rules of the political game. A number of documents are British constitutional landmarks, including the Magna Carta (the Great Charter), which King John accepted at Runnymeede in 1215 and which limited the power of the monarch. None of these documents, however, outlines Britain's entire gov-

ernmental system, as does the U.S. Constitution for the United States.

Although in theory the British monarch has the power to overrule laws passed by Parliament (the British legislature), the last time the monarch did so was in 1707, when Queen Anne vetoed the Scottish Militia bill. Today, it is unthinkable that the British monarch would veto an act of Parliament. Thus, in Great Britain, there is no way to argue that an act of Parliament is *unconstitutional*, since there is no written constitution to which one can appeal. If Parliament passes a law, it remains a law.

Nevertheless, Britain is undeniably a democracy. The political system allows

free speech, open and free elections, vigorously competing political parties, and all the other characteristics generally associated with democracy. British politicians simply have not had a need to produce a single constitutional document.

Britain has never experienced a sharp break with tradition—as in the American Revolution—forcing politicians to think about the basis of authority and the allocation of power, and then to write down how the country should be governed. As long as there is a basic consensus on how governing should take place, the British system works fine. When such a consensus is lacking, no government, whether it has a written or an unwritten constitution, can endure.

Figure 2.4   How the Constitution Can Be Amended

The Constitution sets up two alternative routes for proposing amendments and two for ratifying them. Only one of the four combinations has been used in every case but one.

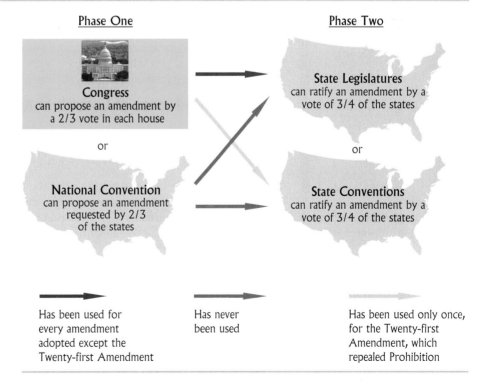

Amendment, which repealed the short-lived Eighteenth Amendment—the prohibition amendment that outlawed the sale and consumption of alcohol. The amendment was ratified by special state conventions rather than by state legislatures. Because proponents of repeal doubted that they could win in conservative legislatures, they persuaded Congress to require that state conventions be called.

Unquestionably, formal amendments have made the Constitution more egalitarian and democratic. The emphasis on economic issues in the original document is now balanced by amendments that emphasize equality and increase the ability of a popular majority to affect government. The amendments are headed by the Bill of Rights (see Table 2.6), which Chapter 4 will discuss in detail. Later amendments, including the Thirteenth Amendment abolishing slavery, have forbidden various political and social inequalities based on race, gender, and age (these amendments will be discussed in Chapter 5). Other amendments, discussed later in this chapter, have democratized the political system, making it easier for voters to influence the government. Only one existing amendment specifically addresses the economy—the Sixteenth, or "income tax," Amendment. Overall, it is clear that the most important effect of these constitutional amendments has been to expand liberty and equality in the United States.

Some amendments have been proposed but not ratified. The best known of these in recent years is the **Equal Rights Amendment**, or **ERA.** First introduced in Congress in 1923 by the nephew of suffragist Susan B. Anthony, the ERA had to wait 49 years—until 1972—before Congress passed it and sent it to the states for ratification. The ERA stated simply that "Equality of rights under the law shall not be denied or abridged by the United States or by any State on account of sex."

This seemingly benign amendment sailed through Congress and the first few state legislatures. The Hawaiian legislature, in fact, arranged for Senator Daniel Inouye's office to signal when the Senate passed the ERA so Hawaii could be the first state to ratify.[23] Public opinion polls showed substantial support for the ERA. Surveys revealed that even people who held traditional views of women's roles still supported it.[24]

Nevertheless, the ERA was not ratified. It failed, in part, because of the system of checks and balances. The ERA had to be approved not by a national majority but by three-fourths of the states. Many conservative Southern states opposed it, thus exercising their veto power despite approval by a majority of Americans.

Proponents of other constitutional amendments have been especially active in recent years. You can consider the issue of frequently amending the Constitution in "You Are the Policymaker: How Frequently Should We Amend the Constitution?"

The Informal Process of Constitutional Change

Think for a moment about all the changes in American government that have taken place without altering a word or a letter of the written document. In fact, there is not a word in the Constitution that would lead us to suspect any of the following developments:

- The United States has the world's oldest two-party system, wherein almost every member of Congress and every president since Washington has declared, "I am a Democrat (or Republican, or Federalist, or Whig, or whatever)."
- Abortions through the second trimester of pregnancy (when the fetus cannot live outside the mother's womb) are legal in the United States.
- Members of the Electoral College consider themselves honor bound (and in some places even legally bound) to follow the preference of their state's electorate.
- Proceedings of both the Senate and the House are on TV; TV influences our political agenda and guides our assessments of candidates and issues.
- Government now taxes and spends about one-third of our gross domestic product, an amount the Convention delegates might have found gargantuan.

None of these things is "unconstitutional." The parties emerged, first technology and then the law permitted abortions, television came to prominence in American

Equal Rights Amendment

A constitutional amendment passed by Congress in 1972 stating that "equality of rights under the law shall not be denied or abridged by the United States or by any state on account of sex." The amendment failed to acquire the necessary support from three-fourths of the state legislatures.

Timeline

The History of Constitutional Amendments

You Are the Policymaker

How Frequently Should We Amend the Constitution?

Since the ratification of the Bill of Rights in 1791, there have been only 17 amendments to the Constitution—an average of one amendment every 13 years. It is now common, however, for political activists—and even political party platforms—to call for amendments. Some recent examples include prohibiting gay marriage, the burning of the American flag, and abortion, permitting prayer in public schools, requiring a balanced national budget, limiting the length of congressional terms, guaranteeing women's rights (the ERA), and protecting victims' rights.

Conservatives have been in the forefront of most recent calls for amendments (the ERA being an exception); many of the proposals for constitutional change are designed to overcome liberal Supreme Court decisions. Liberals, quite naturally, have opposed these amendments. There is a larger question

here than just the particular changes that advocates of amending the Constitution support, however. The big question is: How frequently should we change the fundamental law of the land?

Those who support amending the Constitution argue that the Constitution should reflect the will of the people. If the overwhelming majority of the public wants to prohibit burning the American flag, for example, why shouldn't the Constitution reflect their preference? There is little possibility that a minority or even a narrow majority will be able to impose its will on the people, they argue, because the Constitution requires an extraordinary majority to ratify an amendment. So why should we be reluctant to test the waters of change?

Opponents of changing the Constitution frequently have their own arguments. It is ironic, they say, that

conservatives, who typically wish to preserve the status quo, should be in the forefront of fundamental change. They argue that the Constitution has served the United States very well for more than two centuries with few changes. Why should we risk altering the fundamentals of the political system? And if we do, will we be setting a dangerous precedent that will encourage yet more change in the future? Will such changes undermine the very nature of a constitution that is designed to set the basic rules of the game and be above the political fray?

What do *you* think? Are the arguments simply a reflection of ideologies? Should the Constitution reflect the current sentiment of the public and be changed whenever that opinion changes? Or should we show more caution in amending the Constitution no matter how we feel about a specific amendment?

life—all without having to tinker with the Founders' handiwork. These developments could occur because the Constitution changes *informally* as well as formally. There are several ways in which the Constitution changes informally: through judicial interpretation, through political practice, and as a result of changes in technology and changes in the demands on policymakers.

Judicial Interpretation. Disputes often arise about the meaning of the Constitution. If it is the "supreme law of the land," then someone has to decide how to interpret the Constitution when disputes arise. In 1803, in the famous case of *Marbury v. Madison,* the Supreme Court decided it would be the one to resolve differences of opinion (Chapter 16 discusses this case in detail). It claimed for itself the power of **judicial review.** Implied but never explicitly stated in the Constitution,[25] this power gives courts the right to decide whether the actions of the legislative and executive branches of state and national governments are in accord with the Constitution.

Judicial interpretation can profoundly affect how the Constitution is understood because the Constitution usually means what the Supreme Court says it means. For example, in 1896 the Supreme Court decided that the Constitution allowed racial discrimination despite the presence of the Fourteenth Amendment. Fifty-eight years later it overruled itself and concluded that segregation by law violated the Constitution. In 1973, the Supreme Court decided that the Constitution protected a woman's right to an abortion during the first two trimesters of pregnancy when the fetus is not viable outside the womb—an issue the Founders never imagined. (These cases will be discussed in Chapters 4 and 5.)

Marbury v. Madison

The 1803 case in which Chief Justice John Marshall and his associates first asserted the right of the **Supreme Court** to determine the meaning of the **U.S. Constitution.** The decision established the Court's power of **judicial review** over acts of Congress, in this case the Judiciary Act of 1789.

judicial review

The power of the courts to determine whether acts of Congress, and by implication the executive, are in accord with the **U.S. Constitution.** Judicial review was established by John Marshall and his associates in *Marbury v. Madison.*

How You Can Make a Difference

Amending the Constitution

Today, it's not likely that anyone could have the kind of impact that James Madison had on the Constitution. Nevertheless, there are opportunities for average Americans to influence this enduring but malleable document. If you can't write the original document, you at least have a chance to change it! Every year advocates propose and champion new constitutional amendments. Some never get noticed while others keep percolating year after year. Inevitably, every advocate of a proposed amendment generates a vocal opponent. This is evident in two proposals gaining prominent attention in recent years: the Flag Protection Amendment and the Victims' Rights Amendment.

The drive for the Flag Protection Amendment began in the 1990s after the Supreme Court ruled that state and national laws that prohibited flag desecration were unconstitutional. A constitutional amendment seemed the only alternative to proponents of flag protection. In 1995, 1997, and 2000, only close votes in the Senate prevented the passage of such resolutions. If it passes both the House and the Senate, it appears extremely likely that it would be ratified by the states. Advocates of this amendment like the Citizens Flag Alliance (*www.cfa-inc.org*) argue that the flag deserves to be protected as the nation's most significant and important symbol of unity. Opponents like the ACLU (*www.aclu.org*) counter that this amendment would limit freedom of speech and squelch dissent in America.

The Victims' Rights Amendment, another recent proposal, evokes a similar split in public opinion. This amendment would guarantee victims of crime specific rights, including restitution and an increased role in criminal proceedings. The National Victims' Constitutional Amendment Network (*www.ncvan.org*) claims that this amendment would restore balance to a criminal justice system without restricting the rights due to those accused of crimes. Opponents of this amendment come from a wide spectrum of American political thought. Fears of undermining the Bill of Rights drives the ACLU's opposition to this amendment while the libertarian Cato Institute (*www.cato.org*) argues that the federal government has no responsibility to address criminal problems. Like the Flag Protection Amendment, however, widespread public support within the states make eventual ratification of this amendment a distinct possibility if it ever passes both the House and the Senate.

What you can do:
- Contact the listed organizations and volunteer to help them with their campaigns—perhaps by setting up a table in your student union building or distributing pamphlets.
- Vote for candidates who endorse your views.
- Contact your elected officials and express your views and concerns.

Changing Political Practice. Current political practices also change the Constitution—stretching it, shaping it, and giving it new meaning. Probably no changes are more important than those related to parties and presidential elections.

Political parties as we know them did not exist when the Constitution was written. In fact, its authors would have disliked the idea of parties, which encourage factions. Regardless, by 1800 a party system had developed, and it plays a key role in making policy today. American government would be radically different if there were no political parties, even though the Constitution is silent about them.

Changing political practice has also altered the role of the Electoral College, which has now been reduced to a clerical one in selecting the president. The writers of the Constitution, eager to avoid giving too much power to the uneducated majority, intended that there be no popular vote for the president; instead, state legislatures or the voters (depending on the state) would select wise electors who would then choose a "distinguished character of continental reputation" (as the *Federalist Papers* put it) to be president. These electors formed the Electoral College. Each state would have the same number of electors to vote for the president as it had senators and representatives in Congress.

In 1796, the first election in which George Washington was not a candidate, electors scattered their votes among 13 candidates. By the election of 1800, domestic and foreign policy issues had divided the country into two political parties. To avoid dissipating their support, the parties required electors to pledge in advance to vote for the candidate who won their state's popular vote, leaving electors with a largely clerical function.

Although electors are now rubber stamps for the popular vote, nothing in the Constitution prohibits an elector from voting for any candidate. Every so often, electors have decided to cast votes for their own favorites; some state laws require electors to vote for the candidate chosen by a plurality of their state's citizens, but such laws have never been enforced. The idea that the Electoral College would exercise wisdom independent of the majority of people is now a constitutional anachronism, changed not by formal amendment but by political practice.

Technology. The Constitution has also been changed greatly by technology. The media have always played an important role in politics—questioning governmental policies, supporting candidates, and helping shape citizens' opinions. Modern technology, however, has spurred the development of a *mass* media that can rapidly reach huge audiences, something unimaginable in the eighteenth century. The bureaucracy has grown in importance with the development of computers, which create new potential for bureaucrats to serve the public (such as writing over 40 million Social Security checks each month)—and, at times, create mischief. Electronic communications and the development of atomic weapons have given the president's role as commander in chief added significance, increasing the power of the president in the constitutional system.

Increasing Demands on Policymakers. The significance of the presidency has also grown as a result of increased demands for new policies. The United States' evolution in the realm of international affairs—from an insignificant country that kept to itself to a superpower with an extraordinary range of international obligations—has concentrated additional power in the hands of the chief executive, who is designated to take the lead in foreign affairs. Similarly, the increased demands of domestic policy have positioned the president in a more prominent role in preparing the federal budget and a legislative program.

The Importance of Flexibility

The Constitution, even with all 27 amendments, is a short document containing fewer than 8,000 words. It does not prescribe in detail the structure and functioning of the national government. Regarding the judiciary, Congress is told simply to create a court system as it sees fit. The Supreme Court is the only court required by the Constitution, and even here the number of justices and their qualifications are left up to Congress.

Similarly, many of the governing units we have today—such as the executive departments, the various offices in the White House, the independent regulatory commissions, and the committees of Congress, to name only a few examples—are not mentioned at all in the Constitution.

It is easy to see that the document the framers produced over 200 years ago was not meant to be static, written in stone. Instead, the Constitution's authors created a flexible system of government, one that could adapt to the needs of the times without sacrificing personal freedom. The framers allowed future generations to determine their own needs. As muscle grows on the constitutional skeleton, it inevitably gives new shape and purpose to the government. This flexibility has helped ensure the Constitution's—and the nation's—survival. Although the United States is young compared to other Western nations, it has the oldest functioning Constitution. France, which experienced a revolution in 1789, the same year the Constitution took effect, has had 12 constitutions over the past two centuries. Despite the great diversity of the American population, the enormous size of the country, and the extraordinary changes that have taken place over the nation's history, the U.S. Constitution is still going strong.

Understanding the Constitution

As the body of rules that govern our nation, the Constitution has an impact on our everyday lives. A nation that prides itself on being "democratic" must evaluate the Constitution according to democratic standards. Our theme of the scope of government runs throughout this chapter, which focuses on what the national government can and cannot do. The following section will examine the Constitution in terms of democracy.

The Constitution and Democracy

Comparing Constitutions

Although the United States is often said to be one of the most democratic societies in the world, the Constitution itself is rarely described as democratic. This paradox is hardly surprising, considering the political philosophies of the men who wrote it. Among eighteenth-century upper-class society, democratic government was generally despised. If democracy was a way of permitting the majority's preference to become policy, the Constitution's authors wanted no part of it. The American government was to be a government of the "rich, well-born, and able," as Hamilton said, a government where John Jay's wish that "the people who own the country ought to govern it" would be a reality. Few people today would consider these thoughts democratic.

The Constitution did not, however, create a monarchy or a feudal aristocracy. It created a republic, a representative form of democracy modeled after the Lockean tradition of limited government. Thus, the undemocratic—even antidemocratic—Constitution established a government that permitted substantial movement toward democracy.

One of the central themes of American history is the gradual democratization of the Constitution. What began as a document characterized by numerous restrictions on direct voter participation has slowly become much more democratic. Today, few people share the Founders' fear of democracy. The expansion of voting rights has moved the American political system away from the elitist model of democracy and toward the pluralist model.

The Constitution itself offered no guidelines on voter eligibility, leaving it to each state to decide. As a result, only a small percentage of adults could vote; women and slaves were excluded entirely. Of the 17 constitutional amendments passed since the Bill of Rights, 5 have focused on the expansion of the electorate. The Fifteenth Amendment (1870) prohibited discrimination on the basis of race in determining voter eligibility (although it took the Voting Rights Act of 1965, discussed in Chapter 5, to make the amendment effective). The Nineteenth Amendment (1920) gave women the right to vote (although some states had already done so). The Twenty-third Amendment (1961) accorded the residents of Washington, D.C. the right to vote in presidential elections.

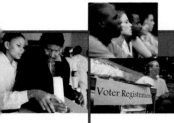

Young People and Politics

Lowering the Voting Age

The 1960s was a tumultuous era, and massive protests by students and other young people regarding the war in Vietnam were common in the last half of the decade. Many young people felt that protesting was the best they could do, because the voting age was 21 in most states— even though 18-year-olds were old enough to marry, work, and pay taxes as others adults did. In the Vietnam War, the average age of U.S. soldiers was 19, and young citizens often asserted that, "If we're old enough to fight, we're old enough to vote."

Majorities in both houses of Congress agreed that the voting age was unfair, and passed the Voting Rights Act of 1970, lowering the voting age to 18 in both federal and state elections. The Supreme Court, however, held that Congress had exceeded its authority and only could set voting ages in national elections.

In 1971, Senator Jennings Randolph, a Democrat from West Virginia, proposed a constitutional amendment to lower the voting age to 18 years: "The right of citizens of the United States, who are eighteen years of age or older, to vote shall not be denied or abridged by the United States or by any State on account of age." Randolph was a warrior for peace and had great faith in young people, arguing that "They possess a great social conscience, are perplexed by the injustices in the world, and are anxious to rectify those ills."

Randolph had introduced legislation lowering the voting age 11 times, beginning in 1942. This time, aided by appreciation of the sacrifices of young soldiers in Vietnam, he was successful. The amendment passed the Senate unanimously, and it passed the House of Representatives by a vote of 400 to 19. It was then sent to the states to be ratified. No state wanted to maintain two sets of voter registration books and go to the expense of running separate election systems for federal elections and for all other elections. Thus, the states were receptive to the proposed amendment, and in just 100 days three-fourths of the states ratified it.

On July 5, the Twenty-sixth Amendment was formally adopted into the Constitution, adding 11 million potential voters to the electorate. Half of these young voters cast their ballots in the 1972 presidential election.

Questions for Discussion
- There are proposals in some states to lower the voting age below 18. What is the appropriate age for voting?
- Would it be appropriate for different states to have different ages for voting?

Three years later, the Twenty-fourth Amendment prohibited poll taxes (which discriminated against the poor). Finally, the Twenty-sixth Amendment (1971) lowered the voter eligibility age to 18 (see "Young People and Politics: Lowering the Voting Age").

Not only are more people eligible to vote, but voters now have more officials to elect. The Seventeenth Amendment (1913) provided for direct election of senators. Presidential elections have been fundamentally altered by the development of political parties. By placing the same candidate on the ballot in all the states and requiring members of the Electoral College to support the candidate who receives the most votes, parties have increased the probability that the candidate for whom most Americans vote will also receive a majority of the Electoral College vote. (For more on the Electoral College, see Chapter 10.) Nevertheless, it is possible for the candidate who receives the most popular votes to lose the election, as occurred in 1824, 1876, 1888, and 2000.

Technology has also diminished the separation of the people from those who exercise power. Officeholders communicate directly with the public through television, radio, and targeted mailings. Air travel makes it easy for members of Congress to commute regularly between Washington and their districts. Similarly, public opinion polls, the telephone, and e-mail enable officials to stay apprised of citizens' opinions on important issues. Even though the American population has grown from fewer than 4 million to more than 290 million people since the first census was taken in 1790, the national government has never been closer to those it serves. (See "Issues of the Times: How Can We Make History Come Alive?")

Issues of the Times

The Issue: How Can We Make History Come Alive?

In this chapter you have learned about the central role of the Declaration of Independence and the Constitution in American government. You have also seen how the unique history of America was critical to both the founding and the development of the nation. If one does not understand from where we have come, it is difficult to understand, much less appreciate, where we are.

Despite the importance of American history and our founding documents, most Americans know little about them. The National Archives, located between the White House and Capitol Hill, has the task of preserving our history and making it come alive to current generations.

Read All About It

Self-Evident Truths, Now More Evident

BY JAMES DAO
September 17, 2003

Despite its imposing architecture and stunning collection, the National Archives has never quite made the A-list of tourist attractions here. Even the city's official convention Web site does not list it on a suggested tour.

But this week the archives will take an important step toward making its building and its precious contents more inviting, not just to history buffs but to the general public.

. . . At the heart of it all is the rotunda's new display for the nation's most cherished documents:

the Declaration of Independence, the Constitution and the Bill of Rights.

The three, known collectively as the Charters of Freedom, have undergone meticulous conservation to repair everything from loosening bits of ink to minuscule insect bites. They are encased in new titanium frames that are larger and placed lower, making them easier to read and more accessible to children and people in wheelchairs.

The new encasements also allow all four pages of the Constitution to be viewed, when previously only the first and fourth pages were displayed. And the ele-

gant rotunda dome, designed by John Russell Pope, the architect for the National Gallery and the Jefferson Memorial, will have improved ambient lighting. . . .

The renovations, which cost a total of $136 million ($114 million is from the government, the rest from private sources) are just the first phase in the archives' ambitious plan. Its ultimate purpose is to reshape its image from that of a fusty repository for the nation's documents to that of a modern, interactive museum, exhibition space and education center.

Please see Archives   Page 61

Archives

Continued from Page 60

A variety of new exhibition areas will open over the next two years. The most important are what the archives calls the Public Vaults, meant to recreate the sensation of strolling through its voluminous stacks. In the archives buildings in the Washington area alone, those stacks contain more than 4 billion pieces of paper, 10 million photographs, 2.6 million maps and charts and 92,000 reels of film.

The six vaults, which will open in fall 2004, will be organized around themes from the preamble to the Constitution, including Form a More Perfect Union, highlighting domestic documents; Provide for the Common Defense, featuring military and diplomatic records; and Promote the General Welfare, cataloging major moments in the nation's history. Each vault will include original documents, letters, photographs, maps and interactive displays.

Visitors, for instance, will be able to pick up telephone receivers and listen to recordings of presidents, from Franklin D. Roosevelt to Richard M. Nixon, conversing in the Oval Office. The Zimmerman Telegram will be displayed under a special viewer that decodes its encrypted message. (The telegram, from the German government to one of its officials in Mexico, urging a Mexican-German alliance, helped draw the United States into World War I after the message was intercepted by the British.)

The vaults will also feature a kaleidoscopic array of documents and images from July 20, 1969, the day Neil Armstrong walked on the moon, ranging from the diary of an American soldier who heard about the event while on patrol in Vietnam

Despite its imposing architecture and stunning collection, the National Archives has never quite made the A-list of tourist attractions . . .

to records detailing the inner workings of the space program. . . .

Work is also under way on a 275-seat theater that will show a 12-minute film about the role of records in a democracy, as well as films and videos from the archives' collection. They will range from documentaries about American life, produced for the United States Information Agency, to World War II recruiting films. The theater, carved out of existing space within the building, is scheduled to open next year.

Within the next two years the archives also plans to open a gallery that will feature exhibits culled not only from the Washington building but also from the 10 presidential libraries and 19 regional components of the National Archives system.

One goal is to make Americans feel more engaged with the vital records of their history. But Mr. Pinkert, who was recruited from the Museum of Science and Industry in Chicago to help redesign the building, acknowledged that this would be no small task. "Documents just sit there," a friend of his warned before he took the job.

But Mr. Pinkert said documents could make the past feel more immediate. "One reason history seems dead is because we read about it in the third person," he observed. "But if you are learning about a battle from a soldier who was there and didn't know the outcome, well, that can be different."

For Catherine Nicholson, a conservationist who did much of the work on the Charters of Freedom, the last two years have provided new insights into the durability of America's most precious documents.

The painstaking restoration involved first removing the documents from 50-year-old glass boxes that had been sealed with lead ribbons and filled with helium to prevent oxidation. The documents, which are printed parchment—lime-treated animal skins—were then humidified to remove small lumps, known as cockles. Every letter on each was scanned with a microscope to locate loose flakes of ink. Tiny drops of adhesive were applied under each flake, and edges damaged by insects were repaired, using special Japanese paper.

The process was nerve-racking, Ms. Nicholson said. No one quite knew what would happen, for example, when the lead seals on the old encasements were broken. "The original boxes didn't exactly come with a book of directions," she said. . . .

Think About It

- Why do you think is it such a challenge to get Americans to take more interest in historic documents such as the Constitution and the Declaration of Independence?
- Can you think of any other ways that the National Archives could make its documents more relevant to the American people?

- The federal government spent over $100 million to restore the National Archives, to, as archivist John W. Carlin says, "help Americans realize that the spirit of America is in these documents." Do you think this expense is worth it?

The Constitution and the Scope of Government

The Constitution created political institutions and the rules for politics and policymaking. Many of these rules limit government action. This limiting function is what the Bill of Rights and related provisions in the Constitution are all about. No matter how large the majority, for example, it is unconstitutional to establish a state-supported church.

Most of these limitations are designed primarily to protect liberty and to open the system to a broad range of participants. The potential range of action for the government is actually quite wide. Thus it is constitutionally permissible, although highly unlikely, for the United States either to abolish Social Security payments to the elderly or to take over ownership of the oil industry or the nation's airlines.

Yet the system of government created by the Constitution has profound implications for what the government does. On one hand, individualism is reinforced at every turn. The separation of powers and the checks and balances established by the Constitution allow almost all groups some place in the political system where their demands for public policy can be heard. Because many institutions share power, groups can usually find at least one sympathetic ear in government. Even if the president opposes the policies a particular group favors, Congress, the courts, or some other institution can help the group achieve its policy goals.

In the early days of the civil rights movement, for example, African Americans found Congress and the president unsympathetic, so they turned to the Supreme Court. Getting their interests on the political agenda would have been much more difficult if the Court had not had important constitutional power.

On the other hand, the Constitution encourages stalemate. By providing effective access for so many interests, the Founders created a system of policymaking in which it is difficult for the government to act. The separation of powers and the system of checks and balances promote the politics of bargaining, compromise, and playing one institution against another. The system of checks and balances implies that one institution is checking another. *Thwarting, blocking,* and *impeding* are synonyms for checking. But if I block you, and you block someone else, and that person blocks me, none of us is going to accomplish anything, and we have gridlock.

Some scholars suggest that so much checking was built into the American political system that effective government is almost impossible. The historian and political scientist James MacGregor Burns has argued that

> We have been too much entranced by the Madisonian model of government . . . The system of checks and balances and interlocked gears of government . . . requires the consensus of many groups and leaders before the nation can act; . . . we underestimate the extent to which our system was designed for deadlock and inaction.[26]

If the president, Congress, and the courts all pull in different directions on policy, the result may be either no policy at all (gridlock) or an inadequate, makeshift policy. The outcome may be nondecisions when hard decisions are needed. If government cannot respond effectively because its policymaking processes are too fragmented, then its performance will be inadequate. Perhaps the Madisonian model has reduced the ability of government to reach effective policy decisions. Certainly, radical departures from the status quo are atypical in American politics.

Summary

The year 1787 was crucial in building the American nation. The 55 men who met in Philadelphia created a policymaking system that responded to a complex policy agenda. Critical conflicts over equality led to key compromises in the New Jersey and Virginia Plans, the three-fifths compromise on slavery, and the decision to leave the issue of voting rights to the states. There was more consensus, however, about the economy. These merchants, lawyers, and large landowners believed that the American economy was in a shambles, and they intended to make the national government an economic stabilizer. The specificity of the powers assigned to Congress left no doubt that Congress was to forge national economic policy. The delegates knew, too, that the global posture of the fledgling nation was pitifully weak. A strong national government would be better able to ensure its own security and that of the nation.

Madison and his colleagues were less clear about the protection of individual rights. Because they believed that the limited government they had constructed would protect freedom, they said little about individual rights in the Constitution. However, the ratification struggle revealed that protection of personal freedoms was much on the public's mind. As a result, the Bill of Rights was proposed. These first ten amendments to the Constitution, along with the Thirteenth and Fourteenth Amendments, provide Americans with protection from governmental restraints on individual freedoms.

It is important to remember that 1787 was not the only year of nation building. The nation's colonial and revolutionary heritage shaped the meetings in Philadelphia. Budding industrialism in a basically agrarian nation put economic issues on the Philadelphia agenda. What Madison was to call an "unequal division of property" made equality an issue, particularly after Shays' Rebellion. The greatest inequality of all, that between slavery and freedom, was so contentious an issue that it was simply avoided at Philadelphia.

Nor did ratification of the Constitution end the nation-building process. Constitutional change—both formal and informal—continues to shape and alter the letter and the spirit of the Madisonian system.

Because that system includes separate institutions sharing power, it results in many checks and balances. Today, some Americans complain that this system has created a government too responsive to too many interests and too fragmented to act. Others praise the way it protects minority views. In Chapter 3, we will look at yet another way in which the Constitution divides governmental power: between the national and the state governments.

KEY TERMS

constitution	U.S. Constitution	republic
Declaration of	factions	Federalists
Independence	New Jersey Plan	Anti-Federalists
natural rights	Virginia Plan	*Federalist Papers*
consent of the governed	Connecticut Compromise	Bill of Rights
limited government	writ of habeas corpus	Equal Rights Amendment
Articles of Confederation	separation of powers	*Marbury v. Madison*
Shays' Rebellion	checks and balances	judicial review

INTERNET RESOURCES

http://www.law.emory.edu/FEDERAL/federalist/
The *Federalist Papers*. Allows you to search the essays using keywords.

www.law.emory.edu/erd/docs/usconst.html
The Constitution. Allows you to search the document using keywords.

www.archives.gov/national_archives_experience/constitution_founding_fathers.html
Biographies of the Founders.

www.earlyamerica.com/earlyamerica/milestones/articles/text.html
The Articles of Confederation. Also provides access to a wide range of documents from the founding period.

GET CONNECTED

Constitutional Change

The Founders did not intend for the Constitution, the rules of our political system, to be static. Instead, they designed the Constitution specifically so that it could be changed—added to or subtracted from—as needed. Figure 2.4 illustrates the ways the Constitution can be changed. Although proposed constitutional changes can originate from national and state conventions, all constitutional changes to date have originated in Congress. So far there have been 27 amendments but there have been many more proposed changes. Even now, there are several proposed changes to the Constitution being debated in the chambers of Congress and in the media. One of the most recent controversial amendment debates defined marriage, and read:

> *Marriage in the United States shall consist only of the union of a man and a woman. Neither this Constitution nor the constitution of any State, nor state or federal law, shall be construed to require that marital status or the legal incidents thereof be conferred upon unmarried couples or groups.*

The proposed amendment failed to pass Congress in Fall 2004.

Search the Web

Go to the websites of a number of groups and people who are on opposite sides of the marriage constitutional amendment debate, including the Alliance for Marriage *http://www.allianceformarriage.org/site/PageServer*, the American Civil Liberties Union *http://www.aclu.org/marriageamendment*, Focus on the Family *http://www.family.org/cforum/fosi/marriage/ssuap/*, the Human Rights Campaign *http://www.hrc.org/marriage*, and the Log Cabin Republicans *http://www.logcabin.org/logcabin/defendconstitution.html*, and review their positions on the proposed constitutional amendment defining marriage. For additional information, review the Guidelines for Constitutional Amendments developed by Citizens for the Constitution *http://www.constitutionproject.org/cai/guidelines/guidelines.pdf* (the guidelines are listed on page 7 of the publication, which requires a pdf reader to view).

Questions To Ask

- Why was the idea of amending a definition of marriage into the U.S. Constitution controversial?
- Which of these groups favored the proposed amendment and what are their reasons for supporting it?
- Which of these groups opposed the amendment and why?
- What is your position on the proposed amendment, and why did you reach that conclusion?
- Did the proposed marriage amendment violate the spirit of the separation of church and state found in the First Amendment?

Why It Matters

Some say the process of amending the Constitution is too difficult and prevents necessary constitutional change. Other observers argue that the obstacles to amending the Constitution are good because they keep proposals like the marriage amendment, on which opinion may change in the next decade, from becoming part of the document. Would our nation be improved if the Constitution were more easily amended? Should constitutional amendments only change governmental structures or should they deal with social issues such as marriage?

Get Involved

The definition of marriage amendment is just one of the many proposals introduced in Congress to amend the Constitution. Can you think of amendments you would like to see added to the Constitution? Make a list of your proposed amendments and compare your list with other students in class.

To see more Get Connected exercises for Chapter 2, go to www.ablongman.com/edwards.

FOR FURTHER READING

Bailyn, Bernard. *The Ideological Origins of the American Revolution.* Cambridge, MA: Harvard University Press, 1967. A leading work on the ideas that spawned the American Revolution.

Becker, Carl L. *The Declaration of Independence: A Study in the History of Political Ideas.* New York: Random House, 1942. Classic work on the meaning of the Declaration.

Dahl, Robert A. *How Democratic Is the American Constitution?*, 2nd ed. New Haven, CT: Yale University Press, 2003.

Hamilton, Alexander, James Madison, and John Jay. *The Federalist Papers.* 2nd ed., Roy P. Fairfield, ed. Baltimore: Johns Hopkins University Press, 1981. Key tracts in the campaign for the Constitution and cornerstones of American political thought.

Higginbotham, A. Leon, Jr. *In the Matter of Color: Race and the American Legal Process, The Colonial Period.* New York: Oxford University Press, 1978. Chronicles how colonial governments established the legal foundations for the enslavement of African Americans.

Jensen, Merrill. *The Articles of Confederation.* Madison: University of Wisconsin Press, 1940. Definitive and balanced treatment of the Articles.

Jillson, Calvin C. *Constitution Making: Conflict and Consensus in the Federal Convention of 1787.* New York: Agathon, 1988. Sophisticated analysis of the drafting of the Constitution.

Lipset, Seymour Martin. *The First New Nation.* New York: Basic Books, 1963. Political sociologist Lipset sees the early American experience as one of nation building.

Maier, Pauline. *American Scripture.* New York: Knopf, 1997. Argues the Declaration was the embodiment of the American mind and historical experience.

McDonald, Forrest B. *Novus Ordo Seclorum: The Intellectual Origins of the Constitution.* Lawrence: University Press of Kansas, 1986. Discusses the ideas behind the Constitution.

Morris, Richard B. *The Forging of the Union, 1781–1789.* New York: Harper & Row, 1987. Written to coincide with the bicentennial of the Constitution, this is an excellent history of the document's making.

Norton, Mary Beth. *Liberty's Daughters.* Boston: Little, Brown, 1980. Examines the role of women during the era of the Revolution and concludes that the Revolution transformed gender roles, setting women on the course to equality.

Rossiter, Clinton. *1787: The Grand Convention.* New York: Macmillan, 1966. A well-written study of the making of the Constitution.

Storing, Herbert J. *What the Anti-Federalists Were For.* Chicago: University of Chicago Press, 1981. Analysis of the political views of those opposed to ratification of the Constitution.

Wood, Gordon S. *The Creation of the American Republic.* Chapel Hill: University of North Carolina Press, 1969. In-depth study of American political thought prior to the Constitutional Convention.

Wood, Gordon S. *The Radicalism of the American Revolution.* New York: Vintage, 1993. Shows how American society and politics were thoroughly transformed in the decades following the Revolution.

Federalism

Chapter Outline

Defining Federalism

The Constitutional Basis of Federalism

Intergovernmental Relations Today

The New York Times **Issues of the Times**

Understanding Federalism

Summary

■ Alfonso Lopez, Jr. was a senior at Edison High School in San Antonio, Texas. One day he arrived at school carrying a concealed .38 caliber handgun. School authorities were alerted by an anonymous tip and confronted Alfonso, who admitted he was carrying the weapon. He was arrested and charged under Texas law with firearm possession on school premises. The next day, the state charges were dismissed after federal agents charged him with violating the Gun-Free School Zones Act of 1990.

A grand jury then indicted Alfonso for violating federal law. Alfonso's lawyers had an ace up their sleeves, however. They moved to dismiss his federal indictment on the grounds that the Gun-Free School Zones Act was unconstitutional because Congress had no power to legislate control over public schools, which are under state control. Congress had relied on its authority to regulate interstate commerce to pass the law, and, Alfonso's lawyers argued, this case had nothing to do with commerce.

Nevertheless, the trial court found Alfonso guilty of violating the law and sentenced him to six months of imprisonment and two years of supervised release. On appeal, Alfonso's lawyers challenged his conviction based on the claim that the law exceeded federal jurisdiction. The court of appeals agreed and reversed Alfonso's conviction. The case then went to the Supreme Court, which ultimately found in *United States v. Lopez* that the Gun-Free School Zones Act did in fact exceed Congress's authority to regulate commerce among the states.

The issue was not whether it was a good idea to prohibit guns in public schools. Almost everyone agreed with that goal. Instead, the issue was establishing boundaries between federal and state—an issue over which America has fought a civil war. The fact that it took the Supreme Court to resolve this seemingly straightforward criminal case illustrates how federalism is at the center of important public policy battles. Indeed, the issue of federalism and the delegation of responsibility to different levels of government is a crucial political

battleground—policymakers' answers to the questions of how we should be governed (in this case, by the states or by the federal government) and what should be the scope of the national government in shaping public policies.

It is important to understand American federalism, the complex relationships between different levels of government in the United States. We will be especially attentive to our themes of democracy and the scope of government. Does federalism, the vertical division of power, enhance democracy in the United States? Does the additional layer of policymakers make government more responsive to public opinion or merely more complicated? Does it enhance the prospects that a national majority of Americans have their way in public policy? And what are the implications of federalism for the scope of the national government's activities? Why has the national government grown so much in relation to state governments, and has this growth been at the expense of the states?

The relationships between governments at the local, state, and national levels often confuse Americans. Neighborhood schools are run by locally elected school boards but also receive state and national funds, and with those funds come state and national rules and regulations. Local airports, sewage systems, pollution control systems, and police departments also receive a mix of local, state, and national funds, so they operate under a complex web of rules and regulations imposed by each level of government.

Sometimes this complex system is almost impossible to understand, especially given the size of the country and the large number of governmental units within it. Even the national government has difficulty keeping track of more than $400 billion in federal aid distributed each year to states and cities. In 1972, when the U.S. Treasury Department first sent revenue-sharing checks to 50 states and 38,000 local governments, some 5,000 checks were returned, marked "addressee unknown," by the Postal Service.[1] If the Postal Service has trouble keeping up with all the governments in America, it's no wonder citizens do, too.

Defining Federalism

Federalism is a rather unusual system for governing, with particular consequences for those who live within it. This section explains the federal system and how it affects Americans living in such a system.

What Is Federalism?

Federalism is a way of organizing a nation so that two or more levels of government have formal authority over the same area and people. It is a system of shared power between units of government. For example, the state of California has formal authority over its inhabitants, but the national government can also pass laws and establish policies that affect Californians. We are subject to the formal authority of both the state and the national governments.

Although federalism is not unique to the United States, it is not a common method of governing. Only 11 of the 190 or so nations of the world have federal systems, and these countries, which include Germany, Mexico, Argentina, Canada, Australia, India, and the United States, share little else (see "America in Perspective: Why Federalism?").

Most governments in the world today are not federal but **unitary governments,** in which all power resides in the central government. If the French Assembly, for instance, wants to redraw the boundaries of local governments or change their forms of government, it can (and has). However, if the U.S. Congress wants to abolish Alabama or Oregon, it cannot.

American states are unitary governments with respect to their local governments. Local governments get their authority from the states; they can be created or abolished by the states. States also have the power to make rules for their own local governments. They can tell them what their speed limits will be, the way in which they should be organized, how they can tax people, what they can spend money on, and so forth. States, however, receive their authority not from the national government, but *directly* from the Constitution.

There is a third form of governmental structure, a *confederation*. The United States began as such, under the Articles of Confederation. In a confederation, the national government is weak and most or all the power is in the hands of its components—for example, the individual states. Today, confederations are rare except in international organizations such as the United Nations (see Chapter 20). Table 3.1 provides a summary of the authority relations in the three systems of government.

The workings of the federal system are sometimes called **intergovernmental relations.** This term refers to the entire set of interactions among national, state, and local governments.[2]

---

federalism

A way of organizing a nation so that two or more levels of government have formal authority over the same land and people. It is a system of shared power between units of government.

---

unitary governments

A way of organizing a nation so that all power resides in the central government. Most national governments today are unitary governments.

Comparing Federal and Unitary Systems

---

intergovernmental relations

The workings of the federal system—the entire set of interactions among national, state, and local governments.

America in Perspective

Why Federalism?

Only 11 countries have federal systems. Trying to determine why these particular nations chose a federal system is an interesting but difficult task. All three North American nations have federal systems, but the trend does not continue in South America, where only two nations have federal systems. Countries large in size—such as Canada and Australia—or large in both size and population—such as India, the United States, Brazil, and Mexico—tend to have federal systems, which decentralize the administration of governmental services. Nevertheless, China and Indonesia—two large and heavily populated countries—have unitary governments, and tiny Malaysia and Switzerland have federal systems.

A nation's diversity may also play a role in the development of a federal system. Brazil, Canada, India, Malaysia, Switzerland, and the United States have large minority ethnic groups that often speak different languages and practice different religions. Many nations with unitary systems, however,

NATION	POPULATION	AREA (THOUSAND) SQUARE MILES	DIVERSITY (ETHNIC, LINGUISTIC, AND RELIGIOUS)
Argentina	38,740,807	1,068	Low
Australia	19,731,984	2,968	Low
Austria	8,188,207	32	Low
Brazil	182,032,604	3,286	Medium
Canada	32,207,113	3,852	High
Germany	82,398,326	138	Low
India	1,049,700,118	1,269	High
Malaysia	23,092,940	127	High
Mexico	104,907,991	762	Low
Switzerland	7,318,638	16	Medium
United States	290,342,554	3,718	Medium

Source: Central Intelligence Agency, *The World Factbook, 2003.*

ranging from Belgium to most African countries, are also replete with ethnic diversity.

Most federal systems are democracies, although most democracies are not federal systems. Authoritarian regimes generally do not wish to disperse power away from the central government. Both the former Soviet Union and the

former Yugoslavia, perhaps reflecting the extraordinary diversity of their populations, had federal systems—of a sort. In both countries, the central government, until recently, retained ultimate power. As democracy swept through these countries, their national governments dissolved and several smaller nations were formed.

Why Is Federalism So Important?

The federal system in America *decentralizes our politics.* Senators are elected as representatives of individual states, not of the entire nation. On Election Day in November, there are actually 51 presidential elections, one in each state and one in Washington, D.C. (see Chapter 10). It is even possible—as happened in 2000—for a candidate who

Table 3.1 Authority Relations in Three Systems of Government

	UNITARY	CONFEDERATE	FEDERAL
Central government	• holds primary authority • regulates activities of states	• limited powers to coordinate state activities	• shares power with states
State government	• few or no powers • duties regulated by central government	• sovereign • allocate some duties to central government	• shares power with central government
Citizens	• vote for central government officials	• vote for state government officials	• vote for both state and central government officials

National campaigns for the presidency actually take place in the states. Candidates must win states rather than the national vote, and they focus their energies on politically competitive states. Here Democrat John Kerry campaigns before the presidential election.

receives the most popular votes in the country to lose the election because of the way the electoral votes are distributed by state.

The federal system decentralizes our politics in more fundamental ways than our electoral system. With more layers of government, more opportunities exist for political participation. With more people wielding power, there are more points of access in government and more opportunities for interests to have their demands for public policies satisfied. With more decisions made in the states, there are fewer sources of conflict at the national level.

As we will see, federalism also enhances judicial power. Dividing government power and responsibilities necessitates umpires to resolve disputes between the two levels of government. In the American system, judges serve as the umpires. Thus, when the national government places prohibitions or requirements on the states, inevitably issues arise for the courts to decide.

The federal system not only decentralizes our politics but also *decentralizes our policies.* The history of the federal system demonstrates the tension between the states and the national government about policy: who controls it and what it should be. In the past, people debated whether the states or the national government should regulate the railroads, pass child labor laws, or adopt minimum-wage legislation. Today, people debate whether the states or the national government should regulate abortions, enforce school desegregation, determine speed limits on highways, or tell 18-year-olds they cannot drink alcohol.[3]

Policies about equality, the economy, the environment, and other matters are subject to both the centralizing force of the national government and the dispersing force of the states. The overlapping powers of the two levels of government mean that most of our public policy debates are also debates about federalism.

States are responsible for most public policies dealing with social, family, and moral issues. The Constitution does not give the national government the power to pass laws that *directly* regulate drinking ages, marriage and divorce, or speed limits. These policy prerogatives belong to the states. They become national issues, however, when aggrieved or angry groups take their cases to Congress or the federal courts in an attempt to use the power of the national government to *influence* states or to get federal courts to find a state's policy unconstitutional. A good example of this process is the federal requirement that states raise their drinking age to 21 in order to receive highway funds (see "Making a Difference: Candy Lightner").

Why It Matters

The Bill of Rights
Your state constitution guarantees you many rights. However, few Americans would feel comfortable with only this protection for their liberties. The Bill of Rights in the U.S. Constitution is the ultimate legal defense of freedom.

The American states have always been policy innovators.[4] The states overflow with reforms, new ideas, and new policies. From clean-air legislation to welfare reform, the states constitute a national laboratory to develop and test public policies and share the results with other states and the national government. Almost every policy the national government has adopted had its beginnings in the states. One or more states pioneered child labor laws, minimum-wage legislation, unemployment compensation, antipollution legislation, civil rights protections, and the income tax. More recently, states have been active in reforming health care, education, and welfare—and the national government is paying close attention to their efforts.

Federalism is an important key to unlocking the secrets of the American political system. Which president is elected, which policy innovations are developed, at what age young men and women can legally drink, and many other issues are profoundly affected by the workings of the federal system.

Making a Difference

Candy Lightner

Candy Lightner was no politician. She was a California real estate broker suffering from the death of her 13-year-old daughter at the hands of a drunk driver. She decided to do something about it and formed Mothers Against Drunk Driving (MADD). MADD lobbied Congress to pass a law withholding federal highway funds from any state that did not raise its drinking age. Today, every state has a legal drinking age of 21.

The Constitutional Basis of Federalism

The word *federalism* is absent from the Constitution, and not much was said about it at the Constitutional Convention. Eighteenth-century Americans had little experience in thinking of themselves as Americans first and state citizens second. In fact, loyalty to state governments was so strong that the Constitution would have been resoundingly defeated had it tried to abolish them. In addition, a central government, working alone,

How You Can Make a Difference

Drinking Age Laws

Do you agree with Candy Lightner's attempts to use the federal government to force states to raise their drinking ages to 21? Although virtually no one would argue against Ms. Lightner's goal of reducing drunk driving, many college-age men and women disagree with the methods advocated by MADD (Mothers Against Drunk Driving) and SADD (Students Against Drunk Driving). Have you ever asked "If I can vote, drive, die for my country and otherwise be considered a legal adult at 18, then what right does the federal government have to restrict my right to drink alcohol until I'm 21?"

If you've pondered this situation, then perhaps you can make a difference in finding a new solution to drunk driving. RALLY (Realistic Alcohol Laws for Legal Youth), a nationwide student-run organization founded in 1995, says the first step should be lowering the drinking age to 18. At the same time, college-age students should become active in promoting alcohol awareness programs in their dorms, schools, cities, and states. Such programs coupled with an emphasis on strong individual responsibility can have a strong impact on reducing alcohol abuse among 18- to 21-year-olds without relying upon discriminatory laws. If you agree with RALLY, then you should start your own chapter on your college campus. Visit their website at *www.rallyusa.org* and get advice and strategy on how to make a direct impact on your college and state.

Finally, however, perhaps you endorse Ms. Lightner's and the federal government's approach to this serious problem. SADD (*www.sadd.org*) strongly believes these laws have saved thousands of lives and averted millions of dollars in property damage. You can also become active in keeping the drinking age at 21 by forming SADD chapters on your own campus or joining existing chapters. SADD and other similar organizations are strongly opposed to RALLY's efforts.

What you can do:
- Contact RALLY and SADD for ways to establish chapters on your campus or join an existing chapter.
- Behave responsibly and hold your friends accountable for their actions.

Table 3.2   The Constitution's Distribution of Powers

TO THE NATIONAL GOVERNMENT	TO BOTH THE NATIONAL AND STATE GOVERNMENTS	TO THE STATE GOVERNMENTS
Some Powers Granted by the Constitution		
Coin money Conduct foreign relations Regulate commerce with foreign nations and among states Provide an army and a navy Declare war Establish courts inferior to the Supreme Court Establish post offices Make laws necessary and proper to carry out the foregoing powers	Tax Borrow money Establish courts Make and enforce laws Charter banks and corporations Spend money for the general welfare Take private property for public purposes, with just compensation	Establish local governments Regulate commerce within a state Conduct elections Ratify amendments to the federal Constitution Take measures for public health, safety, and morals Exert powers the Constitution does not delegate to the national government or prohibit the states from using
Some Powers Denied by the Constitution		
Tax articles exported from one state to another Violate the Bill of Rights Change state boundaries	Grant titles of nobility Permit slavery (Thirteenth Amendment) Deny citizens the right to vote because of race, color, or previous servitude (Fifteenth Amendment) Deny citizens the right to vote because of gender (Nineteenth Amendment)	Tax imports or exports Coin money Enter into treaties Impair obligations of contracts Abridge the privileges or immunities of citizens or deny due process and equal protection of t855he law (Fourteenth Amendment)

would have had difficulty trying to govern eighteenth-century Americans. The people were too widely dispersed, and the country's transportation and communication systems too primitive to allow governing from a central location. There was no other practical choice in 1787 but to create a federal system of government.

The Division of Power

The Constitution's writers carefully defined the powers of state and national governments (see Table 3.2). Although they favored a stronger national government, the framers still made states vital cogs in the machinery of government. The Constitution guaranteed states equal representation in the Senate (and even made this provision unamendable in Article V). It also made states responsible for both state and national elections—an important power. Further, the Constitution virtually guaranteed the continuation of each state; Congress is forbidden to create new states by chopping up old ones, unless a state's legislature approves (an unlikely event).

The Constitution also created obligations of the national government toward the states; it is to protect states against violence and invasion, for example. At times, though, the states find the national government deficient in meeting its obligations, as we will discuss later in this chapter.

supremacy clause

Article VI of the Constitution, which makes the Constitution, national laws, and treaties supreme over state laws when the national government is acting within its constitutional limits.

In Article VI of the Constitution, the framers dealt with what remains a touchy question: In a dispute between the states and the national government, which prevails? The answer that the delegates provided, often referred to as the **supremacy clause,** seems clear enough. They stated that the following three items were the supreme law of the land:

1. the Constitution
2. laws of the national government (when consistent with the Constitution)
3. treaties (which can be made only by the national government)

Judges in every state were specifically told to obey the U.S. Constitution, even if their state constitutions or state laws directly contradicted it. Today, all state executives, legislators, and judges are bound by oath to support the Constitution.

The national government, however, can operate only within its appropriate sphere. It cannot usurp the states' powers. But what are the boundaries of the national government's powers? According to some commentators, the **Tenth Amendment** provides part of the answer. It states that the "powers not delegated to the United States by the Constitution, nor prohibited by it to the states, are reserved to the states respectively, or to the people." To those advocating states' rights, the amendment clearly means that the national government has only those powers specifically assigned to it by the Constitution. The states or people have supreme power over any activity not mentioned there. Despite this interpretation, in 1941 the Supreme Court (in *United States v. Darby*) called the Tenth Amendment a constitutional truism, a mere assertion that the states have independent powers of their own—not a declaration that state powers are superior to those of the national government.

The Court seemed to backtrack on this ruling in favor of national government supremacy in a 1976 case, *National League of Cities v. Usery*, in which it held that extending national minimum-wage and maximum-hours standards to employees of state and local governments was an unconstitutional intrusion of the national government into the domain of the states. In 1985, however (in *Garcia v. San Antonio Metro*), the Court overturned the *National League of Cities* decision. The Court held, in essence, that it was up to Congress, not the courts, to decide which actions of the states should be regulated by the national government. Once again, the Court ruled that the Tenth Amendment did not give states power superior to that of the national government for activities not mentioned in the Constitution.

Occasionally, issues arise in which states challenge the authority of the national government. In the late 1980s, the governors of several states refused to allow their state National Guards to engage in training exercises in Central America. National Guards are state militias, but the Constitution provides that the president can nationalize them. In 1990, the Supreme Court reiterated the power of the national government by siding with the president. Similarly, South Dakota sued the federal government over its efforts to raise states' drinking-age laws and over its efforts to mandate a 55-mph speed limit on highways. The state lost both cases. (In 1995, however, Congress changed the law on speed limits, deciding to leave it up to the states.)

Federal courts can order states to obey the Constitution or federal laws and treaties. However, in deference to the states the *Eleventh Amendment* prohibits individual damage suits against state officials (such as a suit against a police officer for violating one's rights) and protects state governments from being sued against their consent by private parties in federal courts or in state courts[5] or before federal administrative agencies.[6] In 2001, the Court voided the application of the Americans with Disabilities Act to the states, finding it a violation of the Eleventh Amendment (*Board of Trustees of University of Alabama, et al v. Garrett, et al*). Cases arising under the Fourteenth Amendment (usually cases regarding racial discrimination) are an exception.[7] Suits may also be brought by the federal government against states in federal courts, and by individuals against state officials seeking to prohibit future illegal actions.

Recently the Supreme Court has made it easier for citizens to control the behavior of local officials. The Court ruled that a federal law passed in 1871 to protect newly freed slaves permits individuals to sue local governments for damages or seek injunctions against any local official acting in an official capacity who they believe has deprived them of any right secured by the Constitution or by federal law.[8] Such suits are now common in the federal courts.

Tenth Amendment

The constitutional amendment stating that "The powers not delegated to the United States by the Constitution, nor prohibited by it to the states, are reserved to the states respectively, or to the people."

Simulation

You Are a Federal Judge

Establishing National Supremacy

Why is it that the federal government has gained power relative to the states? Four key events have largely settled the issue of how national and state powers are related: (1) the elaboration of the doctrine of implied powers, (2) the definition of the commerce clause, (3) the Civil War, and (4) the long struggle for racial equality.

Implied Powers. As early as 1819, the issue of state versus national power came before the Supreme Court in the case of ***McCulloch v. Maryland.*** The new American government had moved quickly on many economic policies. In 1791, it created a national bank, a government agency empowered to print money, make loans, and engage in many other banking tasks. A darling of Alexander Hamilton and his allies, the bank was hated by those opposed to strengthening the national government's control of the economy. Those opposed—including Thomas Jefferson, farmers, and state legislatures—saw the bank as an instrument of the elite. The First Bank of the United States was allowed to expire, but then the Second Bank was created during James Madison's presidency, fueling a great national debate.

Railing against the "Monster Bank," the state of Maryland passed a law in 1818 taxing the national bank's Baltimore branch $15,000 a year. The Baltimore branch refused to pay, whereupon the state of Maryland sued the cashier, James McCulloch, for payment. When the state courts upheld Maryland's law and its tax, the bank appealed to the U.S. Supreme Court. John Marshall was chief justice when two of the country's most capable lawyers argued the case before the Court.

Daniel Webster, widely regarded as one of the greatest senators in U.S. history, argued for the national bank, and Luther Martin, a delegate to the Constitutional Convention, argued for Maryland. Martin maintained that the Constitution was very clear about the powers of Congress (as outlined in Article I). The power to create a national bank was not among them. Thus, Martin concluded, Congress had exceeded its powers, and Maryland had a right to tax the bank. On behalf of the bank, Webster argued for a broader interpretation of the powers of the national government. The Constitution was not meant to stifle congressional powers, he said, but rather to permit Congress to use all means "necessary and proper" to fulfill its responsibilities.

Marshall, never one to sidestep a big decision, wrote his ruling in favor of the bank before the arguments ended—some said before they even began. He and his colleagues set forth two great constitutional principles in their decision. The first was the *supremacy of the national government over the states.* Marshall wrote that "If any one proposition could command the universal assent of mankind, we might expect it to be this—that the government of the United States, though limited in its power, is supreme within its sphere of action." As long as the national government behaved in accordance with the Constitution, said the Court, its policies took precedence over state policies. Accordingly, federal laws or regulations, such as many civil rights acts and rules regulating hazardous substances, water quality, and clean-air standards, *preempt* state or local laws or regulations and thus preclude their enforcement.

The other key principle of *McCulloch* was that *the national government has certain implied powers that go beyond its enumerated powers.* The Court held that Congress was behaving consistently with the Constitution when it created the national bank. It was true, Marshall admitted, that Congress had certain **enumerated powers,** powers *specifically* listed in Article I, Section 8 of the Constitution. Congress could coin money, regulate its value, impose taxes, and so forth. Creating a bank was not enumerated. But the Constitution added that Congress has the power to "make all laws necessary and proper for carrying into execution the foregoing powers." That, said Marshall, gave Congress certain **implied powers.** It could make economic policy consistent with the Constitution in a number of ways.

Today, the notion of implied powers has become like a rubber band that can be stretched without breaking; the "necessary and proper" clause of the Constitution is

---

McCulloch v. Maryland

An 1819 Supreme Court decision that established the supremacy of the national government over state governments. In deciding this case, Chief Justice John Marshall and his colleagues held that Congress had certain **implied powers** in addition to the **enumerated powers** found in the Constitution.

Federalism and the Supreme Court

---

enumerated powers

Powers of the federal government that are specifically addressed in the Constitution; for Congress, these powers are listed in Article I, Section 8, and include the power to coin money, regulate its value, and impose taxes.

---

implied powers

Powers of the federal government that go beyond those enumerated in the Constitution. The Constitution states that Congress has the power to "make all laws necessary and proper for carrying into execution" the powers enumerated in Article I.

often referred to as the **elastic clause.** Hundreds of congressional policies involve powers not specifically mentioned in the Constitution, especially in the domain of economic policy. Federal policies to regulate food and drugs, build interstate highways, protect consumers, clean up dirty air and water, and do many other things are all justified as implied powers of Congress.

Commerce Power. The Constitution gives Congress the power to regulate interstate and international commerce. American courts have spent many years trying to define commerce. In 1824, the Supreme Court, in deciding the case of *Gibbons v. Ogden,* defined commerce very broadly to encompass virtually every form of commercial activity. Today, commerce covers not only the movement of goods, but also radio signals, electricity, telephone messages, the Internet, insurance transactions, and much more.

The Supreme Court's decisions establishing the national government's implied powers (*McCulloch v. Maryland*) and a broad definition of interstate commerce (*Gibbons v. Ogden*) created a source of national power as long as Congress employed its power for economic development through subsidies and services for business interests. In the latter part of the nineteenth century, however, Congress sought to use these same powers to regulate the economy rather than to promote it. The Court then interpreted the interstate commerce power as giving Congress no constitutional right to regulate local commercial activities such as establishing safe working conditions for laborers or protecting children from working long hours.

When the Great Depression hit, new demands were placed on the national government. Beginning in 1933, the New Deal of President Franklin D. Roosevelt produced an avalanche of regulatory and social welfare legislation, much of which was voided by the Supreme Court (see Chapter 16). But in 1937 the Court reversed itself and ceased trying to restrict the efforts of the national government to regulate commerce at any level. In 1964, Congress prohibited racial discrimination in places of public accommodation such as restaurants, hotels, and movie theaters on the basis of its power to regulate interstate commerce. Thus, regulating commerce is one of the national government's most important sources of power.

In recent years the Supreme Court has scrutinized the use of the commerce power with a skeptical eye, however. As we saw in the opening to this chapter, in 1995 the Court held in *United States v. Lopez* that the federal Gun-Free School Zones Act of 1990, which forbade the possession of firearms in public schools, exceeded Congress' constitutional authority to regulate commerce. Guns in a school zone, the majority said, have nothing to do with commerce. Similarly, in 2000 the Court ruled in *United States v. Morrison* that the power to regulate interstate commerce did not provide Congress with authority to enact the 1994 Violence Against Women Act, which provided a federal civil remedy for the victims of gender-motivated violence. Gender-motivated crimes of violence are not, the Court said, in any sense economic activity.

The Supreme Court announced another limitation on the commerce power in 1996. In *Seminole Tribe of Florida v. Florida*, the Court dealt with the case of a right Congress had given Indian tribes to sue state officials to force good-faith negotiations (in this case over a license to run a casino). Contrary to previous decisions, the Court declared the Eleventh Amendment prohibits Congress from using the interstate commerce power to revoke states' immunity from such lawsuits by private parties. The principal effect of the decision will be to limit suits seeking to enforce rights granted by Congress within its authority under the Commerce Clause (which encompasses much of modern federal regulation).

Several other recent cases have had important implications for federalism. In *Printz v. United States* (1997) and *Mack v. United States* (1997), the Supreme Court voided the congressional mandate in the Brady Handgun Violence Prevention Act that the chief law enforcement officer in each local community conduct background checks on prospective gun purchasers. According to the Court, "The federal government may neither issue directives requiring the states to address particular problems,

elastic clause

The final paragraph of Article I, Section 8, of the Constitution, which authorizes Congress to pass all laws "necessary and proper" to carry out the enumerated powers.

Gibbons v. Ogden

A landmark case decided in 1824 in which the Supreme Court interpreted very broadly the clause in Article I, Section 8, of the Constitution giving Congress the power to regulate interstate commerce, encompassing virtually every form of commercial activity.

In 1963, Alabama Governor George Wallace made a dramatic stand at the University of Alabama to resist integration of the all-White school. Federal marshals won this confrontation, and since then the federal government in general has been able to impose national standards of equal opportunity on the states.

nor commend the states' officers, or those of their political subdivision, to administer or enforce a federal regulatory program."

The Civil War. What *McCulloch* pronounced constitutionally, the Civil War (1861–1865) settled militarily. The Civil War is often thought of mainly as a struggle over slavery; but it was also, and perhaps more important, a struggle between states and the national government. In fact, Abraham Lincoln announced in his 1861 inaugural address that he would willingly support a constitutional amendment guaranteeing slavery if it would save the Union. Instead, it took a bloody civil war for the national government to assert its power over the Southern states' claim of sovereignty.

The Struggle for Racial Equality. A century later, conflict between the states and the national government again erupted over states' rights and national power. In 1954, in *Brown v. Board of Education*, the Supreme Court held that school segregation was unconstitutional. Southern politicians responded with what they called "massive resistance" to the decision. When a federal judge ordered the admission of two African-American students to the University of Alabama in 1963, Governor George Wallace literally blocked the school entrance to prevent federal marshals and the students from entering the admissions office. Despite Wallace's efforts, the students were admitted, and throughout the 1960s the federal government enacted laws and policies to end segregation in schools, housing, public accommodations, voting, and jobs. In 1979 (after African Americans began voting in large numbers in Alabama), George Wallace himself said of his stand in the schoolhouse door: "I was wrong. Those days are over and they ought to be over." The conflict between states and the national government over equality issues was decided in favor of the national government. National standards of racial equality prevailed.

The national government is supreme within its sphere, but the sphere for the states remains a large and important one.

States' Obligations to Each Other

Federalism involves more than relationships between the national government and state and local governments. The states must deal with each other as well, and the Constitution outlines certain obligations that each state has to every other state.

Full Faith and Credit. Suppose that, like millions of other Americans, a person divorces and then remarries. For each marriage this person purchases a marriage license, which registers the marriage with a state. On the honeymoon for the second marriage, the person travels across the country. Is this person married in each state passed through, even though the marriage license is with only one state? Can the person be arrested for bigamy because the divorce occurred in only one state?

The answer, of course, is that a marriage license and a divorce, like a driver's license and a birth certificate, are valid in all states. Article IV of the Constitution requires that states give **full faith and credit** to the public acts, records, and civil judicial proceedings of every other state. This reciprocity is essential to the functioning of society and the economy. Without the full faith and credit clause, people could avoid their obligations, say, to make payments on automobile loans simply by crossing a state boundary. In addition, because contracts between business firms can be enforced across state boundaries, firms incorporated in one state can do business in another.

Usually, the full faith and credit provision in the Constitution poses little controversy. An exception occurred in 1996 when courts in Hawaii recognized same-gender marriages. What would happen in other states that did not recognize Hawaiian marriages between same-gender partners? Congress answered with the Defense of Marriage Act, which permits states to disregard gay marriages, even if they are legal elsewhere in the United States. Hawaii has since overturned recognition of gay marriage, but in 2000 Vermont accorded legal status to gay civil unions. In 2003 the Massachusetts supreme court held that the state constitution guaranteed full marriage rights for gay couples. It remains to be seen whether Congress has the power to make exceptions to the full faith and credit clause, but opponents of gay marriage have focused on amending the Constitution to allow states not to recognize same-gender marriages.

Extradition. What about criminal penalties? Almost all criminal law is state law. If someone robs a store, steals a car, or commits a murder, the chances are that this person is breaking a state, not a federal, law. The Constitution says that states are required to return a person charged with a crime in another state to that state for trial or imprisonment, a practice called **extradition.** Although there is no way to force states to comply, they usually are happy to do so, not wishing to harbor criminals and hoping that other states will reciprocate. Thus, a lawbreaker is prevented from avoiding punishment by simply escaping to another state.

Privileges and Immunities. The most complicated obligation among the states is the requirement that citizens of each state receive all the **privileges and immunities** of any other state in which they happen to be. The goal of this constitutional provision is to prohibit states from discriminating against citizens of other states. If, for example,

full faith and credit

A clause in Article IV, Section 1, of the Constitution requiring each state to recognize the official documents and civil judgments rendered by the courts of other states.

extradition

A legal process whereby an alleged criminal offender is surrendered by the officials of one state to officials of the state in which the crime is alleged to have been committed.

privileges and immunities

A clause in Article IV, Section 2, of the Constitution according citizens of each state most of the privileges of citizens of other states.

Because of the full faith and credit clause of the Constitution, these babies' birth certificates are valid in every state. They are also entitled to most of the benefits—and subject to most of the obligations—of citizenship in any state they visit, thanks to the privileges and immunities clause.

a Texan visits California, the Texan will pay the same sales tax and receive the same police protection as residents of California.

There are many exceptions to the privileges and immunities clause, however. Many of you attend public universities. If you reside in the same state as your university, you generally pay a tuition substantially lower than that paid by your fellow students from out of state. Similarly, only residents of a state can vote in state elections. States often attempt to pass the burdens of financing the state government to those outside the state, such as through taxes on minerals mined in the state but consumed elsewhere or special taxes on hotel rooms rented by tourists.

The Supreme Court has never clarified just which privileges a state must make available to all Americans and which privileges can be limited to its own citizens. In general, the more fundamental the rights—such as owning property or receiving police protection—the less likely it is that a state can discriminate against citizens of another state. In 1999, the Supreme Court held in *Saenz v. Roe* that California could not require a new resident to wait a year before becoming eligible for welfare benefits that exceeded those available in the state from which the new resident came.

Intergovernmental Relations Today

The past two centuries have seen dramatic changes in American federalism. These changes are apparent in two main areas. First, there has been a gradual shift from a dual federalism to a cooperative federalism, which emphasizes power sharing between two levels of government.[9] The second major change has been the rise of fiscal federalism, the elaborate assortment of federal grants-in-aid to the states and localities.

From Dual to Cooperative Federalism

dual federalism

A system of government in which both the states and the national government remain supreme within their own spheres, each responsible for some policies.

One way to understand the changes in American federalism over the past 200 years is to contrast two types of federalism. The first type is called **dual federalism,** in which both the national government and the states remain supreme within their own spheres. The states are responsible for some policies, the national government for others. For example, the national government has exclusive control over foreign and military policy, the postal system, and monetary policy. States are exclusively responsible for schools, law enforcement, and road building. In dual federalism, the powers and policy assignments of the layers of government are distinct, as in a layer cake, and proponents of dual federalism believe that the powers of the national government should be interpreted narrowly.

cooperative federalism

A system of government in which powers and policy assignments are shared between states and the national government. They may also share costs, administration, and even blame for programs that work poorly.

Most politicians and political scientists today argue that dual federalism is outdated. They are more likely to describe the current American federal system as one of **cooperative federalism,** where powers and policy assignments are shared between states and the national government.[10] Instead of a layer cake, they see American federalism as more like a marble cake, with mingled responsibilities and blurred distinctions between the levels of government. After the terrorist attacks on September 11, 2001, the national government asked state and local governments to investigate suspected terrorists and both national and state public health officials dealt with the threat caused by anthrax in the mail in Florida, New York, and Washington, D.C.

Before the national government began to assert its dominance over state governments, the American federal system leaned toward dual federalism. The American system, however, was never neatly separated into purely state and purely national responsibilities. For example, education was usually thought of as being mainly a state and local responsibility, yet even under the Articles of Confederation, Congress set aside land in the Northwest Territory to be used for schools. During the Civil War, the national government adopted a policy to create land grant colleges. Important American universities such as Wisconsin, Texas A&M, Illinois, Ohio State, North Carolina State, and Iowa State owe their origins to this national policy. (To learn more

Cooperative federalism began during the Great Depression of the 1930s. In this photo, Works Progress Administration workers, paid by the federal government, build a local road in New York. In subsequent decades, the entire interstate highway system was constructed with a combination of national and state dollars.

about how federalism affects college education, see "Young People and Politics: Federal Support for Colleges and Universities.")

In the 1950s and 1960s, the national government began supporting public elementary and secondary education. In 1958 Congress passed the National Defense Education Act, largely in response to Soviet success in the space race. The act provided federal grants and loans for college students and financial support for elementary and secondary education in science and foreign languages. In 1965, Congress passed the Elementary and Secondary Education Act, which provided federal aid to numerous schools. Although these policies expanded the national government's role in education, they were not a sharp break with the past.

Today, the federal government's presence is felt in every schoolhouse. Almost all school districts receive some federal assistance. To do so, they must comply with federal rules and regulations. They must, for example, maintain desegregated and nondiscriminatory programs. In addition, as we will see in Chapter 4, federal courts have ordered local schools to implement elaborate desegregation plans and have placed constraints on school prayers.

Highways are another example of the movement toward cooperative federalism. In an earlier era, states and cities were largely responsible for building roads, although the Constitution does authorize Congress to construct "post roads." In 1956, Congress passed an act creating an interstate highway system. Hundreds of red, white, and blue signs were planted at the beginnings of interstate construction projects. The signs announced that the interstate highway program was a joint federal-state project and specified the cost and sharing of funds. In this and many other areas, the federal system has promoted a partnership between the national and state governments.

Cooperative federalism today rests on several standard operating procedures. For hundreds of programs, cooperative federalism involves:

Visual Literacy

Federalism and Regulations

- *Shared costs.* Washington foots part of the bill, but states or cities that want to get their share must pay part of a program's costs. Cities and states can get federal money for airport construction, sewage treatment plants, youth programs, and many other programs, but only if they pay some of the costs.

Young People and Politics

Federal Support for Colleges and Universities

Because most colleges and universities are public institutions created by state and local governments, federalism has direct consequences for the students who attend them. State and local governments provide most of the funding for public colleges and universities, but almost everyone agrees that this funding is inadequate. In response to this problem, the national government has stepped in to support postsecondary education programs.

One could argue that the federal government makes it possible for many students to attend college at all, because it is the primary source of financial aid. The federal government provides more than $17 billion in financial assistance (including grants, loans, and work-study assistance) to more than 8 million postsecondary students each year. Nearly 60 percent of all full-time undergraduates receive some form of financial aid from the federal government, compared to about 52 percent who receive aid from all other sources.

The federal government also provides several billion dollars of direct grants to colleges and universities across the nation. Billions more in federal funds support research in training in certain areas, especially science and engineering—which receive about $20 billion a year. The library, laboratories, and the buildings in most colleges and universities have been assisted by funds from the federal government.

Each year the federal government provides about 11 percent of the revenue for public colleges and universities (10 percent for private schools). Few colleges and universities could withstand an 11 percent budget cut and the loss of most of the financial assistance for its students. Federalism, then, matters quite a lot to college students.

Questions for Discussion
- Why do state institutions of higher education require aid from the federal government? Why don't the states provide adequate funds to run their own colleges and universities?
- Federal aid comes with strings attached. Would it be better to rely completely on state support?

- *Federal guidelines.* Most federal grants to states and cities come with strings attached. Congress spends billions of dollars to support state highway construction, for example, but to get their share, states must adopt and enforce limits on the legal drinking age.
- *Shared administration.* State and local officials implement federal policies, but they have administrative powers of their own. The U.S. Department of Labor, for example, gives billions of dollars to states for job retraining, but states have considerable latitude in spending the money.

The cooperation between the national government and state governments is such an established feature of American federalism that it persists even when the two levels of government are in conflict on certain matters. For example, in the 1950s and 1960s, Southern states cooperated well with Washington in building the interstate highway system, while they clashed with the national government over racial integration.

In his first inaugural address, Ronald Reagan argued that the states had primary responsibility for governing in most policy areas, and he promised to "restore the balance between levels of government." Few officials at either the state or the national level agreed with Reagan about ending the national government's role in domestic programs. However, Reagan's opposition to the national government's spending on domestic policies and the huge federal deficits of the 1980s forced a reduction in federal funds for state and local governments, and shifted some responsibility for policy back to the states. Despite Reagan's move toward a more dual federalism, most Americans embrace a pragmatic view of governmental responsibilities, seeing the national gov-

Table 3.3   A Pragmatic Federalism

The public has a pragmatic view of governmental responsibilities, seeing the national government as more capable of—and thus responsible for—handling some issues, while they view state and local government as better at managing others such as crime, welfare, and education. The Founders did not give much thought to food safety, conservation, or the health care system. Today, Americans frequently turn to Washington for help in dealing with these and other problems, including maintaining a strong economy. These are the results of a 1997 public opinion poll.

Who should be primarily responsible for . . .

	FEDERAL GOVERNMENT	STATE AND LOCAL GOVERNMENT
Ensuring that food and medicines are safe	73%	14%
Managing the economy to prevent another recession or depression	68	13
Ensuring every American has access to affordable health care	58	22
Conserving the country's natural resources	52	21
Providing a decent standard of living for the elderly	46	30
Ensuring that every American can afford to send his or her children to college	35	19
Reducing poverty	34	27
Setting academic standards for public schools	22	50
Promoting greater honesty and stronger morals among people	16	9
Reducing juvenile delinquency	7	31

Source: Pew Research Center, September 25–October 31, 1997.

ernment as more capable of—and thus responsible for—handling some issues, while they view state and local governments as better at managing others (see Table 3.3).

The Republican majorities that captured Congress in 1995 for the first time in four decades have been equally pragmatic in their approach to federalism. The Republicans often referred to a "revolution" in public policy, one aimed primarily at restricting the scope of the national government. They passed bills to give the states more authority over social and environmental programs that have long been in the realm of the national government. An overhaul of welfare policy was designed to allow states to devise innovative ways to lift people out of poverty, while reducing federal spending and cutting some benefits for the poor. Another bill, aimed at making it more difficult to enact new environmental protection legislation, prevented the federal government from imposing requirements on states without providing money to pay for them. Congress also repealed national speed limits and made it more difficult for prisoners to challenge the constitutionality of their sentences in federal court or to appeal to federal officials for relief from poor prison conditions.

At the same time, Republicans found turning to the federal government the most effective way to achieve many of their policy objectives. In an effort to reduce government interference in the marketplace and to protect businesses from a patchwork of state requirements more stringent than federal ones, Republicans designated the federal government the sole regulator of products as diverse as mutual funds and agricultural chemicals. They also nullified state laws that had restricted telecommunications competition and set national standards requiring insurers to cover at least 48 hours of hospitalization for mothers and newborns.

To control immigration, Congress required state and local officials to meet new federal antifraud specifications for birth certificates and driver's licenses. And to combat crime, the legislature extended federal criminal penalties to cover crimes such as stalking, domestic terrorist activities, and rape during carjacking. Congress also threatened to cut off federal grants to states that failed to keep criminals behind bars for about 85 percent of their sentences, or to increase arrests of violent criminals.

In addition, the new welfare bill imposed penalties on states that fail to meet new federal targets for placing welfare recipients in jobs. The states must also meet other requirements, such as creating registries to track child-support orders, or face a considerable loss of federal funds. Similarly, a clean drinking water bill required states to study local drinking water sources, map certain watersheds, and publish annual reports on drinking water violations. Perhaps most importantly, Congress, at President George W. Bush's request, placed significant new requirements on state and local school authorities when it passed the No Child Left Behind Act in 2001.

Fiscal Federalism

fiscal federalism

The pattern of spending, taxing, and providing grants in the federal system; it is the cornerstone of the national government's relations with state and local governments.

The cornerstone of the national government's relations with state and local governments is **fiscal federalism**: the pattern of spending, taxing, and providing grants in the federal system. Subnational governments can influence the national government through local elections for national officials, but the national government has a powerful source of influence over the states—money. Grants-in-aid, federal funds appropriated by Congress for distribution to state and local governments, are the main instrument the national government uses for both aiding and influencing states and localities.

Despite the policy of the Reagan administration to reduce aid to states and cities, federal aid (including loan subsidies) still amounted to more than $400 billion in 2005. Figure 3.1 illustrates the growth in the amount of money spent on federal grants. Federal aid, covering a wide range of policy areas (see Figure 3.2), accounts for about

Figure 3.1   Fiscal Federalism: Federal Grants to State and Local Governments

Federal grants to state and local governments have grown rapidly in recent decades and now amount to more than $400 billion per year.

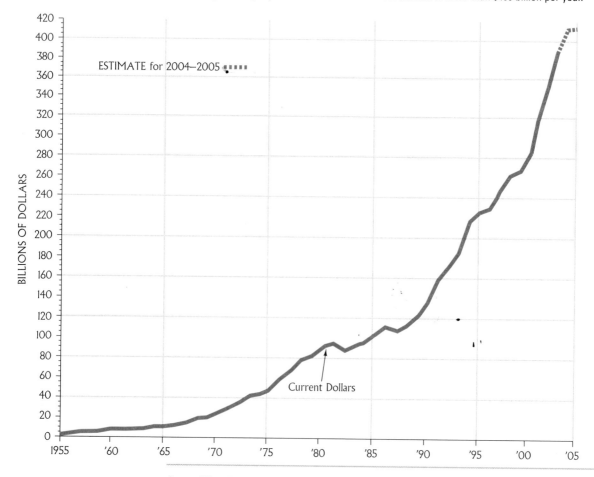

Source: Office of Management and Budget, *Budget of the United States Government, Fiscal Year 2005: Historical Tables* (Washington, D.C.: U.S. Government Printing Office, 2004), Table 12.2.

Figure 3.2   Functions of Federal Grants

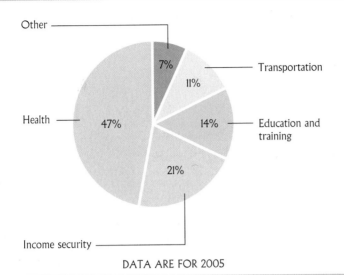

DATA ARE FOR 2005

Other — 7%
Transportation — 11%
Education and training — 14%
Income security — 21%
Health — 47%

Health care receives the largest percentage of federal grants, followed by income security, education and training, and transportation.

Source: Office of Management and Budget, *Budget of the United States Government, Fiscal Year 2005: Historical Tables* (Washington, D.C.: U.S. Government Printing Office, 2004), Table 12.2.

one-fourth of all the funds spent by state and local governments and for about 18 percent of all federal government expenditures in 2004.[11]

The Grant System: Distributing the Federal Pie. The national government regularly publishes the *Catalogue of Federal Domestic Assistance*, a massive volume listing the federal aid programs available to states, cities, and other local governments. The book lists federal programs that support energy assistance for the elderly poor, housing allowances for the poor, drug abuse services, urban rat control efforts, community arts programs, state disaster preparedness programs, and many more.

There are two major types of federal aid for states and localities: categorical grants and block grants. **Categorical grants** are the main source of federal aid to state and local governments. These grants can be used only for one of several hundred specific purposes, or categories, of state and local spending.

Because direct orders from the federal government to the states are rare (an exception is the Equal Opportunity Act of 1982, barring job discrimination by state and local governments), most federal regulation is accomplished in a more indirect manner. Instead of issuing edicts that tell citizens or states what they can and cannot do, Congress attaches conditions to the grants that states receive. The federal government has been especially active in appending restrictions to grants since the 1970s.

One string commonly attached to categorical and other federal grants is a nondiscrimination provision, stating that aid may not be used for purposes that discriminate against minorities, women, or other groups. Another string, a favorite of labor unions, is that federal funds may not support construction projects that pay below the local union wage. Other restrictions may require an environmental impact statement for a federally supported construction project or provisions for community involvement in the planning of the project.

The federal government may also employ *cross-over sanctions*—using federal dollars in one program to influence state and local policy in another, such as when funds are withheld for highway construction unless states raise the drinking age to 21 or establish highway beautification programs.

Cross-cutting requirements occur when a condition on one federal grant is extended to all activities supported by federal funds, regardless of their source. The grandfather of these requirements is Title VI of the 1964 Civil Rights Act (see Chapter 5), which bars discrimination in the use of federal funds because of race, color, national origin, gender, or physical disability. For example, if a university discriminates illegally in one

categorical grants

Federal grants that can be used only for specific purposes, or "categories," of state and local spending. They come with strings attached, such as nondiscrimination provisions. Compare **block grants**.

Why It Matters

Grants-in-Aid
The federal system of grants-in-aid sends revenues from federal taxes to state and local governments. This transfers the burden of paying for services from those who pay state and local taxes, such as taxes on sales and property, to those who pay national taxes, especially the federal income tax.

The federal government often uses grants-in-aid as a carrot and stick for the states. For example, aid has been withheld from some cities until police departments have been racially and sexually integrated.

project grants

Federal **categorical grants** given for specific purposes and awarded on the basis of the merits of applications.

formula grants

Federal **categorical grants** distributed according to a formula specified in legislation or in administrative regulations.

block grants

Federal grants given more or less automatically to states or communities to support broad programs in areas such as community development and social services.

program—such as athletics—it may lose the federal aid it receives for all its programs. There are also cross-cutting requirements dealing with environmental protection, historic preservation, contract wage rates, access to government information, the care of experimental animals, the treatment of human subjects in research projects, and a host of other policies.

There are two types of categorical grants. The most common type is a **project grant.** A project grant is awarded on the basis of competitive applications. National Science Foundation grants obtained by university professors are examples of project grants.

As their name implies, **formula grants** are distributed according to a formula. These formulas vary from grant to grant and may be computed on the basis of population, per capita income, percentage of rural population, or some other factor. A state or local government does not apply for a formula grant; a grant's formula determines how much money the particular government will receive. As a result, Congress is the site of vigorous political battles over the formulas themselves. The most common formula grants are those for Medicaid, child nutrition programs, sewage treatment plant construction, public housing, community development programs, and training and employment programs.

Applications for categorical grants typically arrive in Washington in boxes, not envelopes. Complaints about the cumbersome paperwork and the many strings attached to categorical grants led to the adoption of the other major type of federal aid, **block grants.** These grants are given more or less automatically to states or communities, which then have discretion within broad areas in deciding how to spend the money. First adopted in 1966, block grants are used to support programs in areas like community development and social services. The percentage of federal aid to state and local governments in the form of block grants began increasing in 1995 as the new Republican majority in Congress passed more federal aid in the form of block grants, including grants for welfare programs.

The Scramble for Federal Dollars. With more than $400 billion in federal grants at stake, most states and many cities have established full-time staffs in Washington.[12] Their task is to keep track of what money is available and to help their state or city get some of it. There are many Washington organizations of governments—the U.S. Conference of Mayors and the National League of Cities, for example—that act like other interest groups in lobbying Congress. Senators and representatives regularly go to the voters with stories of their influence in securing federal funds for their constituencies. They need continued support at the polls, they say, so that they will rise in seniority and get key posts to help "bring home the bacon" (see "Issues of the Times: The Distribution of Federal Dollars").

A general rule of federalism is that the more money there is at stake, the more fervently people will argue about its distribution. There are some variations in the amount of money that states give to, and get back from, the national government. On the whole, however, federal grant distribution follows the principle of *universalism*: something for everybody. The vigilance of senators and representatives keeps federal aid reasonably well spread among the states. Indeed, federal aid to states and cities is more equitably distributed than most other things in America, including income, access to education, and taxes.

This equality makes good politics, but it also may undermine public policy. Chapter I of the 1965 Elementary and Secondary Education Act is the federal government's principal endeavor to assist public schools. The primary intent of Chapter I was to give extra help to poor children. Yet the funds are allocated to 95 percent of all the school districts in the country. President Clinton's proposal to concentrate Chapter I funds on the poorest students failed when it ran into predictable opposition in Congress.

The Mandate Blues. States and localities are usually pleased to receive aid from the national government, but there are times when they would just as soon not have it. For example, say Congress decides to extend a program administered by the states and funded, in part, by the national government. It passes a law requiring the states to extend the program if they want to keep receiving aid, which most states do. Requirements that direct states or local governments to comply with federal rules under threat of penalties or as a condition of receipt of a federal grant are called *mandates*. Congress usually (though not always) appropriates some funds to help pay for the new policy, but either way, the states suddenly have to budget more funds for the project just to receive federal grant money.

Medicaid, which provides health care for poor people, is a prime example of a federal grant program that puts states in a difficult situation. Administered by the states, Medicaid receives wide support from both political parties. The national government pays between 50 and 83 percent of the bill, and the states pick up the rest. Since 1984, Congress has moved aggressively to expand Medicaid to specific populations, requiring the states to extend coverage to certain children, pregnant women, and elderly poor. Congress also increased its funding for the program a whopping 146 percent in the 1980s. Increased federal spending for Medicaid has meant increased spending for the states as well, setting priorities for state budgets.

A related problem arises when Congress passes a law creating financial obligations for the states but provides no funds to meet these obligations. For example, in 1990 Congress passed the Americans with Disabilities Act. States were required to make facilities, such as state colleges and universities, accessible to individuals with disabilities but were allocated no funds to implement such a policy. Similarly, the Clean Air Act of 1970 established national air quality standards but requires states to administer them and to appropriate funds for their implementation.

In 1995, the newly elected Republican majorities in Congress made limiting unfunded and underfunded mandates on state and local governments a high priority. Congress passed, and President Clinton signed, a law that requires both chambers to take a separate, majority vote in order to pass any bill that would impose unfunded mandates of more than $50 million on state and local governments. The law also requires the Congressional Budget Office to estimate the costs of all bills that impose such mandates. All antidiscrimination legislation and most legislation requiring state and local governments to take various actions in exchange for continued federal funding (such as grants for transportation) are exempt from this procedure.

State and local governments are the first responders in most emergencies. Their police forces provide most of the nation's internal security, they maintain most of the country's transportation infrastructure (such as highways, mass transit, port facilities,

Issues of the Times

The Issue: The Distribution of Federal Dollars

The federal system decentralizes both politics and policies in the United States, allowing states substantial discretion in providing services for their citizens. In addition, the national government provides substantial funding for state-run programs. Just how much federal money a state receives often depends as much on the political power of the state as it does on the state's need for that funding.

Equal representation in the Senate gives small states an advantage, and they make full use of it. Because the amounts involved in a typical program mean more to the smaller states, they have a greater incentive to hold their ground. Larger states often give up fighting over the money. In addition, allocating funds to small states is often the price the larger states pay to pass a program in the first place.

Yet solving the problem is not as simple as taking money away from a

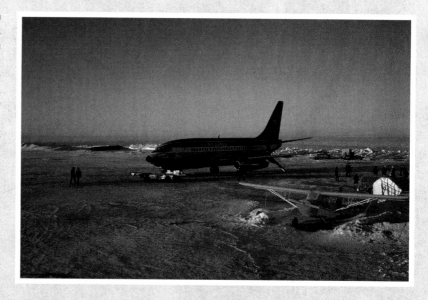

small state and giving it to large states, as some of the most populous states would like. Population, many argue, is an imperfect measure of need.

Read All About It

Security Grants Still Streaming to Rural States

By Dean E. Murphy
October 12, 2004

In the nationwide scramble for domestic security dollars, officials in Alaska are in a predicament that would be the envy of most other states. They must figure out how to spend $2 million in federal money.

The Department of Homeland Security rejected a proposal by Alaska to use the money to buy a jet, but indicated it would be "happy

to entertain" further proposals for the $2 million. Officials are now obliging.

One of the nation's least populous states, Alaska is flush with domestic security grants, on a per-resident basis second only to Wyoming and about three times the amount allocated to New York over the past two years.

Money is so readily available that the Northwest Arctic Borough, a desolate area of 7,300 people that

straddles the Arctic Circle, recently stocked up on $233,000 worth of emergency radio equipment, decontamination tents, headlamps, night vision goggles, bullhorns—even rubber boots.

Alaska's good fortune highlights what many critics say is a serious failing in the way that America is fighting the battle against terrorism at home. While there is consensus

Please see Grants   **Page 87**

Grants

Continued from Page 86

that the threat of an attack should supersede politics as usual, the billions of federal dollars for terrorism preparedness are being doled out to states in much the same way as money for schools, bridges and other routine federal projects. . . .

"No member wants to go home and say my state didn't get any of the money but you are paying for it," said Slade Gorton, a former three-term senator from Washington who was a Republican member of the independent commission that investigated the Sept. 11 attacks. The commission's final report in July harshly criticized the spending pattern, admonishing Congress to "not use this money as a pork barrel." . . .

Alaska, which has 649,000 residents, received nearly $92 per resident in security funds over the last two years, compared with states like New York, which received $32; California, which received $22; and Texas and Florida, $21 each, according to a recent survey by the nonpartisan Congressional Research Service. The survey estimated $8.2 billion was allocated in 2003 and 2004 to state and local governments in so-called first responder domestic security assistance programs by the Departments of Homeland Security and Health and Human Services.

One result is that in the Alaska capital, Juneau, an isolated town of 31,000 that virtually shuts down when the last cruise ship leaves in September, the emergency programs manager says he is awash in federal money. The town has bought or ordered a robot for deactivating

bombs, decontamination equipment, night-vision goggles, pharmaceutical stockpiles and a back-up emergency radio system.

"I don't have to go looking for grants, they are coming to me," said the manager, Michael R. Patterson. "The chief of police said very succinctly, 'I don't need more stuff anymore; I need more people.'"

Richard Ben-Veniste, who was a Democratic member of the 9/11 commission, said distribution of the funds nationwide had lapsed into a "general revenue sharing program" with "political muscle flexing," not terrorism considerations, as the driving force.

> It is the price we pay for the kind of federal system we have. . . . It is nice for Alaska, but from a national perspective it is not justifiable.

"We recognize that it is broken," said Mr. Ben-Veniste, adding that some requests for financing "strain credulity."

In an interview last week, Tom Ridge, the homeland security secretary, said that President Bush recently tried to shift money to higher-risk areas but that it was uncertain how Congress would respond. "We would like to see more of the dollars go toward areas where the population density is greater, where there is more critical infrastructure, and where the threat seems to be higher," Mr. Ridge said.

Political scholars say the problem is as old as Congress itself. Its

origins can be traced to the Constitutional Convention in Philadelphia in 1787, when big states and small states reached the "Great Compromise" on how to apportion Congressional representation.

The deal resulted in a lower house apportioned by population and an upper house that gave the states an equal voice. That system has allowed smaller states to demand a piece of almost everything over the past two centuries, and the latest pot of gold—domestic security dollars— is no exception. . . .

"It is the price we pay for the kind of federal system we have," said Gerald A. McBeath, a professor of political science at the University of Alaska in Fairbanks. "It creates an opportunity that a state like Alaska gets all that it does. It is nice for Alaska, but from a national perspective it is not justifiable." . . .

. . .[S]olving the problem is not as simple as taking money away from Alaska and giving it to California, as some of the most populous states would like. Population, many argue, is an equally imperfect measure of need, because potential threats vary greatly from one urban area to another.

Former Senator Gorton said there were serious concerns that small states would be left vulnerable if money was funneled only to the most threatened. "If you harden some targets, you soften others," he said, suggesting that terrorists would go shopping for targets in states where there was less protection.

That is the argument made in sparsely populated areas of Alaska. Mr. Patterson, the emergency programs manager in Juneau, said it was overly simplistic to assume that rural states were undeserving. . . .

Think About It

- Is it fair that states receive funds for domestic security independent of the threats they face?
- How should the national government allocate grants to states?
- Would it be preferable for states to finance their own programs and not rely on grants from the national government?

Policies of the federal government may have major impacts on core policies of state and local governments like elementary and secondary education and determine how much is spent on these policies. Here President George W. Bush speaks about his "No Child left Behind" education policy in Nashville, Tennessee.

and airports), and they are responsible for protecting the public's health and providing emergency health care. The heightened concern for homeland security since September 11, 2001, has led Congress to impose sizeable new mandates on the states to increase their ability to deal with acts of terrorism, but it has not provided all the resources necessary to increase state and local capabilities. Similarly, the No Child Left Behind Act, passed in 2002, threatens school systems with the loss of federal funds if their schools do not improve student performance. Such improvements cost money, however, and the federal government has only provided a modest increase in funding.

Federal courts also create unfunded mandates for the states. In recent years, federal judges have issued states orders in areas such as prison construction and management, school desegregation, and facilities in mental health hospitals, sometimes even temporarily taking them over. These court orders often require states to spend funds to meet standards imposed by the judge.

A combination of federal regulations and inadequate resources may also put the states in a bind. The national government requires that a local housing authority build or acquire a new low-income housing facility for each one it demolishes. But for years Congress has provided little money for the construction of public housing. As a result, a provision intended to help the poor by ensuring a stable supply of housing actually hurts them because it discourages local governments from demolishing unsafe and inadequate housing.

The federal government may also unintentionally create financial obligations for the states. In 1994, California, New York, Texas, Florida, and other states sued the federal government for reimbursement for the cost of health care, education, prisons, and other public services that the states provide to illegal residents. The states charged that the federal government's failure to control its borders was the source of huge new demands on their treasuries and that Washington, not the states, should pay for the problem. Although the states did not win their cases, their point is a valid one.

Understanding Federalism

The federal system is central to politics, government, and policy in America. The division of powers and responsibilities among different levels of government has implications for both the themes of democracy and the scope of government.

Federalism and Democracy

One of the reasons the Founders established a federal system was to allay the fears of those who believed that a powerful and distant central government would tyrannize the states and limit their voice in government. By decentralizing the political system, federalism was designed to contribute to democracy—or at least to the limited form of democracy supported by the Founders. Has it done so?

Advantages for Democracy. The more levels of government, the more opportunities there are for participation in politics. State governments provide thousands of elected offices for which citizens may vote and/or run.

Additional levels of government also contribute to democracy by increasing access to government. Because different citizens and interest groups will have better access to either state-level governments or the national government, the two levels increase the opportunities for government to be responsive to demands for policies. For example, in the 1950s and 1960s when advocates of civil rights found themselves stymied in Southern states, they turned to the national level for help in achieving racial equality. Business interests, on the other hand, have traditionally found state governments to be more responsive to their demands. Organized labor is not well established in some states, but it can usually depend on some sympathetic officials at the national level who will champion its proposals.

Different economic interests are concentrated in different states: oil in Texas, tobacco farming in Virginia, and copper mining in Montana, for example. The federal system allows an interest concentrated in a state to exercise substantial influence in the election of that state's officials, both local and national. In turn, these officials promote policies advantageous to the interest in both Washington and the state capital. This is a pluralism of interests that James Madison, among others, valued within a large republic.

State and local bases have another advantage. Even if a party loses at the national level, it can rebuild in its areas of strength and develop leaders under its banner at the state and local levels. As a result, losing an election becomes more acceptable, and the peaceful transfer of power is more probable. This was especially important in the early years of the nation before our political norms had become firmly established.

Because the federal system assigns states important responsibilities for public policies, it is possible for the diversity of opinion within the country to be reflected in different public policies among the states. If the citizens of Texas wish to have a death penalty, for example, they can vote for politicians who support it, whereas those in Wisconsin can vote to abolish the death penalty altogether (see "You Are the Policymaker: Should *Whether* You Live Depend on *Where* You Live?"). Similarly, there are large differences in the amounts that states provide for the poor, ranging from $631 per month for a family of three in Alaska to $154 per month in South Carolina (see Figure 3.3).

By handling most disputes over policy at the state and local level, federalism also reduces decision-making and conflict at the national level. If every issue had to be resolved in Washington, the national government would be overwhelmed.

Disadvantages for Democracy. Despite its advantages for democracy, relying on states to supply public services has some drawbacks. States differ in the resources they can devote to services like public education. Thus, the quality of education a child receives is heavily dependent on the state in which the child's parents happen to reside. In 2002, New York state and local governments spent an average of $11,472 for each child in the public schools; in North Dakota the figure was only $4,851 (see Figure 3.4).

Diversity in policy can also discourage states from providing services that would otherwise be available. Political scientists have found that generous welfare benefits can strain a state's treasury by attracting poor people from states with lower benefits. As a result, states may be deterred from providing generous benefits to those in need. A national program with uniform welfare benefits would provide no incentive for welfare recipients to move to another state in search of higher benefits.[13]

You Are the Policymaker

Should *Whether* You Live Depend on *Where* You Live?

Because the federal system allocates major responsibilities for public policy to the states, policies often vary with the different views of the population in different locations. The differences among public policies are especially dramatic in the criminal justice system.

A conviction for first-degree murder in 38 states may well mean the death penalty for the convicted murderer. In 12 other states, first-degree murderers only spend time behind bars. In 17 states, the minimum age for the death penalty is 16; it is 15 in 5 other states, and 16 states have a minimum age of 18.

Some people see diversity in public policy as one of the advantages of federalism. Others may argue that citizens of the same country ought to be subject to uniform penalties. What do you think? Should *whether* you live depend on *where* you live?

Federalism may also have a negative effect on democracy insofar as local interests are able to thwart national majority support of certain policies. As discussed earlier in this chapter, in the 1960s the states—especially those in the South—became battlegrounds when the national government tried to enforce national civil rights laws and court decisions. Federalism complicated and delayed efforts to end racial discrimination because state and local governments were responsible for public education and voting eligibility, for example, and because they had passed most of the laws supporting racial segregation.

Figure 3.3   Diversity in Public Policy: State Welfare Benefits

Because the American federal system allocates major responsibilities for public policy to the states, policies often vary in different locations. This figure shows that for the emotionally charged issue of welfare, different states have adopted quite different policies.

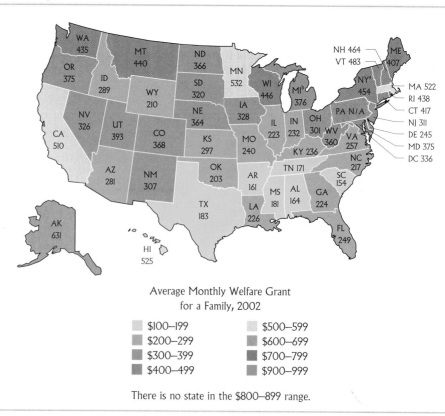

Average Monthly Welfare Grant
for a Family, 2002

$100–199 $500–599
$200–299 $600–699
$300–399 $700–799
$400–499 $900–999

There is no state in the $800–899 range.

Source: House Ways and Means Committee; *2004 Green Book.*

Figure 3.4 The Downside of Diversity: Spending on Public Education

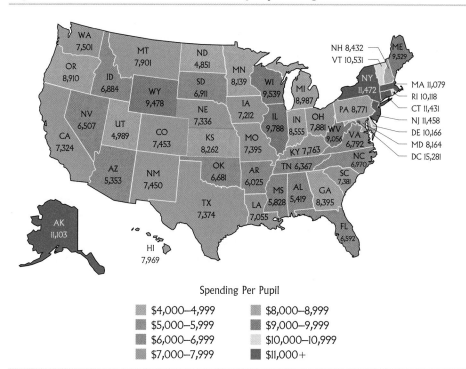

The downside of the public policy diversity fostered by federalism is that states are largely dependent on their own resources for providing public services; these resources vary widely from state to state. This map shows the wide variation among the states in the money spent on each child in the public schools.

Spending Per Pupil

- $4,000–4,999
- $5,000–5,999
- $6,000–6,999
- $7,000–7,999
- $8,000–8,999
- $9,000–9,999
- $10,000–10,999
- $11,000+

Source: U.S. Department of Commerce, *Statistical Abstract of the United States, 2003* (Washington, D.C.: U.S. Government Printing Office, 2004), 169.

Finally, the sheer number of governments in the United States is, at times, as much a burden as a boon to democracy. Program vendors at baseball games say that "You can't tell the players without a scorecard"; unfortunately, scorecards are not available for local governments, where the players are numerous and sometimes seem to be involved in different games. The U.S. Bureau of the Census counts not only people but also governments. Its latest count revealed an astonishing 87,576 American governments (see Table 3.4).

Certainly, 87,000 governments ought to be enough for any country. Are there too many? Americans speak eloquently about their state and local governments as grassroots governments, close to the people. Yet having so many governments makes it difficult to know which governments are doing what. Exercising democratic control over them is even more difficult; voter turnout in local elections is often less than 20 percent.

Participation

Is Federalism Dead and Should It Be?

Table 3.4 The Number of Governments in America

	NUMBER OF GOVERNMENTS
U.S. government	1
States	50
Counties	3,034
Municipalities	19,429
Townships or towns	16,504
School districts	13,506
Special districts	35,052
Total	**87,576**

Source: U.S. Department of Commerce, *Statistical Abstract of the United States, 2003* (Washington, D.C.: U.S. Government Printing Office, 2004), 276.

Federalism and the Scope of the National Government

One of the most persistent questions in American politics has been the scope of the national government relative to that of the states. To understand the relative roles of the two levels of government, we must first understand why the national government grew and then ask whether this growth was at the expense of the states or whether it occurred because of the unique capabilities and responsibilities of the national government.

President Ronald Reagan negotiated quotas on imports of Japanese cars in order to give advantages to the American auto industry, raising the price of all automobiles in the process. At the behest of steel companies, President George Bush exercised his authority to continue Reagan's quotas on the amount of steel that could be imported (thereby making steel products more expensive). In addition, the first major piece of legislation the Bush administration sent to Congress was a bailout plan for the savings and loan industry, which had gotten into financial trouble through a combination of imprudent loans, declining property values, deregulation of banking, incompetence, and corruption. President Clinton proposed that the Pentagon spend nearly $600 million to fund the development of a U.S. industry in "flat-panel displays" used for laptop computers, video games, and advanced instruments. In 2002, President George W. Bush raised tariffs on imported steel—contrary to his position in favor of the open marketplace.

In each of these cases and dozens of others, the national government has involved itself (some might say interfered) in the economic marketplace with quotas and subsidies intended to help American businesses. As Chapter 2 explained, the national government took a direct interest in economic affairs from the very founding of the republic. As the United States changed from an agricultural to an industrial nation, new problems arose and with them new demands for governmental action. The national government responded with a national banking system, subsidies for railroads and airlines, and a host of other policies that dramatically increased its role in the economy.

The industrialization of the country raised other issues as well. With the formation of large corporations in the late nineteenth century—Cornelius Vanderbilt's New York Central Railroad and John D. Rockefeller's Standard Oil Company, for example—came the potential for such abuses as monopoly pricing. If there is only one railroad in town, it can charge farmers inflated prices to ship their grain to market. If a single company distributes most of the gasoline in the country, it can set the price at which gasoline sells. Thus, many interests asked the national government to restrain monopolies and to encourage open competition.

There were additional demands on the national government for new public policies. Farmers sought services such as agricultural research, rural electrification, and price supports. Unions wanted the national government to protect their rights to organize and bargain collectively and to help provide safer working conditions, a minimum wage, and pension protection. Along with other groups, labor unions supported a wide range of social welfare policies, from education to health care. As the country became more urbanized, new problems arose in the areas of housing, welfare, the environment, and transportation. In each case, the relevant interest turned to the national government for help.

Why not turn to the state governments instead? In most cases, the answer is simple: A problem or policy requires the authority and resources of the national government. The Constitution forbids states from having independent defense policies. And even if it did not, how many states would want to take on a responsibility that represents more than half the federal workforce and about one-fifth of federal expenditures?

It is constitutionally permissible, but not sensible, for the states to handle a wide range of other issues. It makes little sense for Louisiana to pass strict controls on polluting the Mississippi River if most of the river's pollution occurs upstream, where Louisiana has no jurisdiction. Rhode Island has no incentive to create an energy policy because no natural energy reserves are located in the state. Similarly, how effectively can a state regulate an international conglomerate such as General Motors? How can each state, acting individually, manage the nation's money supply?

Figure 3.5   Fiscal Federalism: The Public Sector and the Federal System

The federal government's spending increased rapidly during the Great Depression and World War II. In recent years, the role of both federal and state governments has declined slightly.

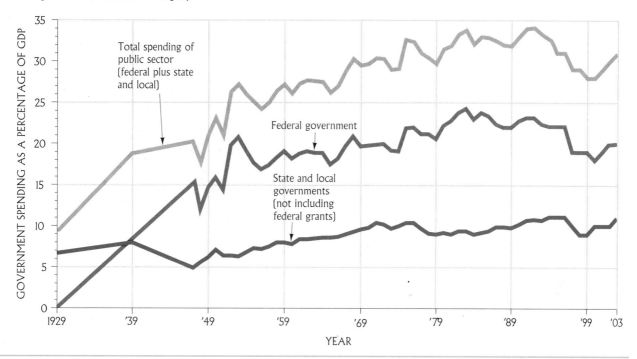

Source: Office of Management and Budget, *Budget of the United States Government, Fiscal Year 2005: Historical Tables* (Washington, D.C.: U.S. Government Printing Office, 2004), Table 15.3.

Each state could have its own space program, but it is much more efficient if the states combine their efforts in one national program. The largest category of federal expenditures is that for economic security, including the Social Security program. Although each state could have its own retirement program, how could state governments determine which state should pay for retirees who move to Florida or Arizona? A national program is the only feasible method of ensuring the incomes of the mobile elderly of today's society.

Figure 3.5 shows that the national government's share of American governmental expenditures has grown rapidly since 1929; most of this growth occurred during the Great Depression. At that time, the national government spent an amount equal to only 2.5 percent of the size of the economy, the gross domestic product (GDP); today, it spends about 20 percent of our GDP (this includes grants to states and localities). The proportion of our GDP spent by state and local governments has grown less rapidly than the national government's share. States and localities spent 7.4 percent of our GDP in 1929; they spend about 11 percent today (not including federal grants).[14]

Figure 3.5 demonstrates that the states have not been supplanted by the national government; indeed, they carry out virtually all the functions they always have. Instead, with the support of the American people (see Table 3.3), the national government has taken on new responsibilities. In addition, the national government has added programs to help the states meet their own responsibilities.

Summary

Federalism is a governmental system in which power is shared between a central government and other governments. Federalism is much less common than are the unitary governments typical of most parliamentary democracies. American federalism consists of 50

Each state could have its own space program, but it is much more efficient for the states to combine their efforts in one national program. The same principle applies to economic security and to a host of other important programs.

state governments joined in an "indestructible union" (as the Supreme Court once called it) under one national government. Today, federal power over the states is indisputable; the Supreme Court cases *McCulloch v. Maryland* and *Gibbons v. Ogden*, the Civil War, and the struggle for racial equality all helped to determine national supremacy. The federal government often uses its fiscal leverage to influence state and local policies.

The United States has moved from a system of dual federalism to one of cooperative federalism, in which the national and state governments share responsibility for public policies. Fiscal federalism is of great help to states. Even after the Reagan administration reductions, the federal government distributes more than $400 billion in federal funds to states and cities each year.

Federalism was instituted largely to enhance democracy in America, and it strengthens democratic government in many ways. At the same time, diverse state policies and the sheer number of local governments cause problems as well. Demands for new policies and the necessity for national policy on certain issues have contributed to the growth of national government relative to state governments. Yet the state governments continue to play a central role in governing the lives of Americans.

Although American federalism concerns state power and national power, it is not a concept removed from most Americans' lives. Federalism affects a vast range of social and economic policies. Slavery, school desegregation, abortion, and teenage drinking have all been debated in terms of federalism.

KEY TERMS

federalism	enumerated powers	dual federalism
unitary governments	implied powers	cooperative federalism
intergovernmental relations	elastic clause	fiscal federalism
	Gibbons v. Ogden	categorical grants
supremacy clause	full faith and credit	project grants
Tenth Amendment	extradition	formula grants
McCulloch v. Maryland	privileges and immunities	block grants

INTERNET RESOURCES

www.cfda.gov
Allows you to search through hundreds of federal grants.

www.ncsl.org/statefed/afipolcy.htm
Information and discussion of issues on federal-state relations.

www.census.gov/statab/www/
The *Statistical Abstract of the United States*, containing a wealth of data on state public policies.

www.statesnews.org
Council of State Governments website with information on states and state public policies.

www.thirteen.org/federalist
Discussions of the *Federalist Papers* and short articles and debates on issues regarding federalism.

GET CONNECTED

Intergovernmental Relations

Even though education, like public safety and public health, is the responsibility of the states, the national government still finds ways to shape education policy. In January 2002, President George W. Bush signed the No Child Left Behind Act into law. This act sets federal standards for education and then makes federal grants available to states that agree to achieve these new national standards. Let us take a closer look at this federal law to determine its impact on federalism.

Search the Web

Reviewing a federal law can be challenging. This review will not be that difficult, however. First, review the Statement of Purposes (just review sec. 1001) of the No Child Left Behind Act *http://www.ed.gov/policy/elsec/leg/esea02/pg1.html#sec1001* so you can gain a basic understanding of the intent of the legislation. Now review the part of the bill that says what the federal government will do for the states (just review sec. 6111 and 6112) *http://www.ed.gov/policy/elsec/leg/esea02/pg87.html#sec6111*. Finally, read what the states must do in order to receive federal money (sec. 1111) *http:// www.ed.gov/policy/elsec/leg/esea02/pg2.html#sec1111*. The National Education Association *http://www.nea.org/esea/memberspeakout1.html* is a critic of No Child Left Behind. The C-SPAN website *http://www.c-span.org/guide/congress/glossary/unfunded.htm* has a definition of "unfunded mandate."

Questions To Ask

- What do states get from the federal government under this act?
- What are some of the things states have to do in order to get the federal money?
- On what does the National Education Association base its criticism of the No Child Left Behind Act?
- Is the No Child Left Behind Act an unfunded mandate?

Why It Matters

Even though the United States is a federal system of governance, increasingly the national government establishes national standards and then encourages states to comply with those standards through a system of spending, taxing, and providing grants—all of which can have a direct effect on you.

Get Involved

Talk to an elementary or high school teacher or a school board member in your community about the No Child Left Behind Act. How does it affect them? How do they think this Act will affect the quality of education in the community?

To see more Get Connected exercises for Chapter 3, go to www.ablongman.com/edwards.

FOR FURTHER READING

Anton, Thomas. *American Federalism and Public Policy.* Philadelphia: Temple University Press, 1989. An overview of how the national, state, and local governments share responsibility for policies.

Beer, Samuel H. *To Make a Nation: The Rediscovery of American Federalism.* Cambridge, MA: Harvard University Press, 1993. An excellent study of the philosophical bases of American federalism.

Conlan, Timothy J. *From New Federalism to Devolution: Twenty-Five Years of Intergovernmental Reform.* Washington, D.C.: Brookings Institution, 1998. An analysis of the efforts to restructure intergovernmental relations since the late 1960s.

Dye, Thomas R. *American Federalism: Competition Among Governments.* Lexington, MA: Lexington Books, 1990. Analyzes competitive federalism, in which states and local governments compete to offer public services at low costs.

Elazar, Daniel J. *American Federalism: A View from the States,* 3rd ed. New York: Harper & Row, 1984. A well-known work surveying federalism from the standpoint of state governments.

Kettl, Donald F. *The Regulation of American Federalism.* Baltimore: Johns Hopkins University Press, 1987. Examines the regulations that the national government imposes on state and local governments.

Peterson, Paul E. *The Price of Federalism.* Washington, D.C.: Brookings Institution, 1995. A good assessment of the costs and benefits of federalism.

Peterson, Paul, Barry G. Rabe, and Kenneth K. Wong. *When Federalism Works.* Washington, D.C.: Brookings Institution, 1986. Examines federal grants-in-aid programs and explains why they are implemented better in some areas than in others.

Walker, David B. *The Rebirth of Federalism,* 2nd ed. Chatham, NJ: Chatham House, 2000. A history of American federalism and an analysis of its current condition.

Wright, Deil S. *Understanding Intergovernmental Relations,* 4th ed. Belmont, CA: Wadsworth, 2003. A review of the relations among the local, state, and national levels of government.

Civil Liberties and Public Policy

■ The Board of Regents of the University of Wisconsin System requires students at the University's Madison campus to pay a segregated activity fee. The fee supports various campus services and extracurricular student activities. In the University's view, such fees enhance students' educational experiences by promoting extracurricular activities, stimulating advocacy and debate on diverse points of view, enabling participation in campus administrative activity, and providing opportunities to develop social skills, all consistent with the University's broad educational mission. Registered student organizations (RSOs) engaging in a number of diverse expressive activities are eligible to receive a portion of the fees, which are administered by the student government subject to the University's approval.

There has been broad agreement that the process for reviewing and approving RSO applications for funding is administered in a viewpoint-neutral fashion. RSOs may also obtain funding through a student referendum. Some students, however, sued the University, alleging that the activity fee violated their First Amendment rights, and that the University

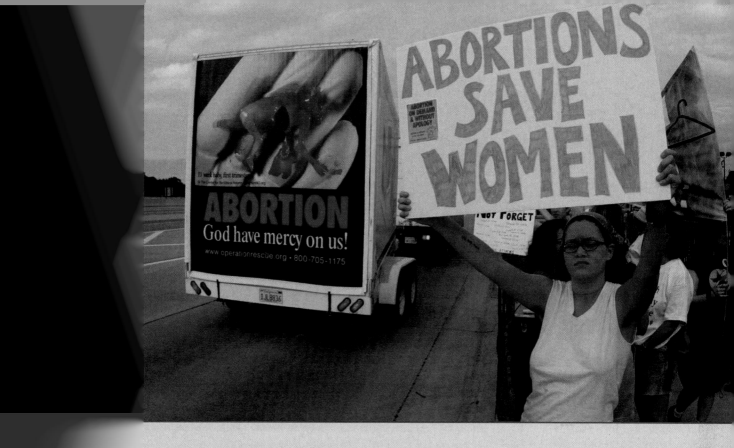

e choice not to fund RSOs that
ind ideological expression offen-
l beliefs.

reme Court held in a unani-
oard of Regents of University of
Southworth that if a university
nission is well served if students
ngage in dynamic discussion on
1es, it may impose a mandatory
lialogue. The Court recognized
evitable that the fees will subsi-
1e students find objectionable or
Court required that a university
:tion to its students' First
ts by requiring viewpoint neutral-
of funding support.

f Wisconsin case is the sort of
y that shapes American civil lib-
it the right to abortion, the right
ihts of criminal defendants, and
nstantly in the news. Some of
m conflicting interests. The
ety against crime often conflicts
o protect the rights of people
ther conflicts derive from strong
n about what is ethical, moral,
nericans, abortion is murder, the
ife. To others, a woman's choice

whether to bear a child, free of governmental intrusion, is a fundamental right. Everyone, however, is
affected by the extent of our civil liberties.

Deciding complex questions about civil liberties
requires balancing competing values, such as maintaining an open system of expression while protecting individuals from the excesses such a system may
produce. As we learned in Chapter 1, civil liberties
are essential to democracy. How could we have free
elections without free speech, for example? But does
it follow that critics of officials should be able to say
whatever they want, no matter how untrue? And
who should decide the extent of our liberty? Should
it be a representative institution such as Congress or
a judicial elite such as the Supreme Court?

The role of the government in resolving civil liberties controversies is also the subject of much
debate. Conservatives usually advocate narrowing
the scope of government, yet many strongly support government-imposed limits on abortion and
government-sanctioned prayers in public schools.
They also want government to be less hindered by
concern for defendants' rights. Liberals, who typically support a broader scope of government, usually
want to limit government's role in prohibiting abortion and encouraging religious activities, and to
place greater constraints on government's freedom of
action in the criminal justice system.

Issues of civil liberties present many vexing problems for the courts to resolve. For example, is burning the American flag desecration of a sacred patriotic symbol, or is it an expression of opposition to government policy protected by the Constitution?

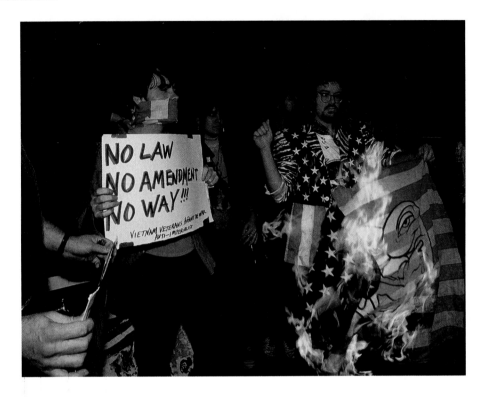

civil liberties

The legal constitutional protections against government. Although our civil liberties are formally set down in the **Bill of Rights**, the courts, police, and legislatures define their meaning.

Bill of Rights

The first ten amendments to the **U.S. Constitution**, which define such basic liberties as freedom of religion, speech, and press and guarantee defendants' rights.

Civil liberties are individual legal and constitutional protections against the government. Americans' civil liberties are set down in the **Bill of Rights,** the first ten amendments to the Constitution. At first glance, many questions about civil liberties look easy. The Bill of Rights' guarantee of a free press seems straightforward; either Americans can write what they choose, or they cannot. In the real world of American law, however, these issues are subtle and complex.

Disputes about civil liberties often end up in court. The Supreme Court of the United States is the final interpreter of the content and scope of our liberties; this ultimate power to interpret the Constitution accounts for the ferocious debate over presidential appointments to the Supreme Court.

Throughout this chapter you will find special features entitled "You Are the Judge." Each feature describes an actual case brought before the courts and asks you to apply your sense of fairness and your standards to arrive at a judgment.

To understand the specifics of American civil liberties, we must first understand the Bill of Rights.

The Bill of Rights—Then and Now

By 1787, all state constitutions had bills of rights, some of which survive, intact, to this day. Although the new U.S. Constitution had no bill of rights, the states made its inclusion a condition of ratification. The Bill of Rights was passed as a group by the First Congress in 1789 and sent to the states for ratification. In 1791, these amendments became part of the Constitution.

The Bill of Rights ensures Americans' basic liberties, such as freedom of speech and religion, and protection against arbitrary searches and being held for long periods without trial (see Table 4.1). The Bill of Rights was passed when British abuses of the colonists' civil liberties were still a fresh and bitter memory. Newspaper editors had been jailed; citizens had been arrested without cause, detained, and forced to confess at gunpoint or worse. Thus, the first ten amendments enjoyed great popular support.

Political scientists have discovered that people are devotees of rights in theory but that their support wavers when it comes time to put those rights into practice.[1] For

Table 4.1 The Bill of Rights

These amendments were passed by Congress on September 25, 1789, and ratified by the states on December 15, 1791.

Amendment I—Religion, Speech, Assembly, Petition
Congress shall make no law respecting an establishment of religion, or prohibiting the free exercise thereof; or abridging the freedom of speech, or of the press; or the right of the people peaceably to assemble, and to petition the Government for a redress of grievances.

Amendment II—Right to Bear Arms
A well-regulated militia, being necessary to the security of a free State, the right of the people to keep and bear arms, shall not be infringed.

Amendment III—Quartering of Soldiers
No Soldier shall, in time of peace be quartered in any house, without the consent of the owner, nor in time of war, but in a manner to be prescribed by law.

Amendment IV—Searches and Seizures
The right of the people to be secure in their persons, houses, papers, and effects, against unreasonable searches and seizures, shall not be violated, and no warrants shall issue, but upon probable cause, supported by oath or affirmation, and particularly describing the place to be searched, and persons or things to be seized.

Amendment V—Grand Juries, Double Jeopardy, Self-Incrimination, Due Process, Eminent Domain
No person shall be held to answer to a capital, or otherwise infamous crime, unless on a presentment or indictment of a Grand Jury, except in cases arising in the land or naval forces, or in the militia, when in actual service in time of war or public danger: nor shall any person be subject for the same offense to be twice put in jeopardy of life or limb; nor shall be compelled in any criminal case to be a witness against himself, nor be deprived of life, liberty, or property, without due process of law; nor shall private property be taken for public use, without just compensation.

Amendment VI—Criminal Court Procedures
In all criminal prosecutions, the accused shall enjoy the right to a speedy and public trial, by an impartial jury of the State and district wherein the crime shall have been committed, which district shall have been previously ascertained by law, and to be informed of the nature and cause of the accusation; to be confronted with the witnesses against him; to have compulsory process for obtaining witnesses in his favor, and to have the assistance of counsel for his defense.

Amendment VII—Trial by Jury in Common-Law Cases
In Suits at common law, where the value in controversy shall exceed twenty dollars, the right of trial by jury shall be preserved, and no fact tried by a jury, shall be otherwise reexamined in any Court of the United States.

Amendment VIII—Bails, Fines, and Punishment
Excessive bail shall not be required, nor excessive fines imposed, nor cruel and unusual punishments inflicted.

Amendment IX—Rights Retained by the People
The enumeration in the Constitution, of certain rights, shall not be construed to deny or disparage others retained by the people.

Amendment X—Rights Reserved to the States
The powers not delegated to the United States by the Constitution, nor prohibited by it to the States, are reserved to the States respectively, or to the people.

example, Americans in general believe in freedom of speech, but many citizens would not let the Ku Klux Klan speak in their neighborhood or allow their public schools to teach about atheism or homosexuality. In addition, Americans seem willing to trade off civil liberties for security when they feel that the nation is threatened, as in the case of terrorism.[2] Few rights are absolute; we cannot avoid the difficult questions of balancing civil liberties and other individual and societal values.

The Bill of Rights and the States

Take another look at the **First Amendment.** Note the first words: "Congress shall make no law . . ." The Bill of Rights was written to restrict the powers of the new national government. In 1791, Americans were comfortable with their state governments; after all, every state constitution had its own bill of rights. Thus, a literal reading of the First Amendment suggests that it does not prohibit a state government from passing a law prohibiting the free exercise of religion, free speech, or freedom of the press.

What happens, however, if a state passes a law violating one of the rights protected by the federal Bill of Rights and the state's constitution does not prohibit this abridgment of freedom? In 1833, the answer to that question was "nothing." The Bill of Rights, said the Court in **Barron v. Baltimore,** restrained only the national government, not states and cities.

First Amendment

The constitutional amendment that establishes the four great liberties: freedom of the press, of speech, of religion, and of assembly.

Barron v. Baltimore

The 1833 Supreme Court decision holding that the **Bill of Rights** restrained only the national government, not the states and cities.

Gitlow v. New York

The 1925 Supreme Court decision holding that freedoms of press and speech are "fundamental personal rights and liberties protected by the **due process clause** of the **Fourteenth Amendment** from impairment by the states" as well as by the federal government. Compare **Barron v. Baltimore.**

Fourteenth Amendment

The constitutional amendment adopted after the Civil War that states, "No State shall make or enforce any law which shall abridge the privileges or immunities of citizens of the United States; nor shall any state deprive any person of life, liberty, or property, without due process of law; nor deny to any person within its jurisdiction the **equal protection** of the laws." See also **due process clause.**

incorporation doctrine

The legal concept under which the **Supreme Court** has nationalized the **Bill of Rights** by making most of its provisions applicable to the states through the **Fourteenth Amendment.**

establishment clause

Part of the **First Amendment** stating that "Congress shall make no law respecting an establishment of religion."

free exercise clause

A **First Amendment** provision that prohibits government from interfering with the practice of religion.

Almost a century later, however, the Court ruled that a state government must respect some First Amendment rights. The 1925 ruling in **Gitlow v. New York** relied not on the First Amendment but on the Fourteenth—the second of three "Civil War Amendments" that ended slavery, gave former slaves legal protection, and ensured their voting rights. Ratified in 1868, the **Fourteenth Amendment** declared:

> No state shall make or enforce any law which shall abridge the privileges or immunities of citizens of the United States nor shall any state deprive any person of life, liberty, or property, without due process of law; nor deny to any person within its jurisdiction the equal protection of the laws.

In *Gitlow*, the Court announced that freedoms of speech and press "were fundamental personal rights and liberties protected by the due process clause of the Fourteenth Amendment from impairment by the states." In effect, the Court interpreted the Fourteenth Amendment to say that states could not abridge the freedoms of expression protected by the First Amendment. This decision began the development of the **incorporation doctrine**, the legal concept under which the Supreme Court has nationalized the Bill of Rights by making most of its provisions applicable to the states through the Fourteenth Amendment. However, not everyone agreed that the Fourteenth Amendment incorporated parts of the Bill of Rights into state laws. For example, Edwin Meese, who served as attorney general under Ronald Reagan, strongly criticized *Gitlow* and called for "disincorporation" of the Bill of Rights.

Initially, only parts of the First Amendment were held binding on the states as a result of *Gitlow*. Gradually, especially during the 1960s when Earl Warren was chief justice, the Supreme Court applied most of the Bill of Rights to the states (see Table 4.2). "One by one," wrote constitutional scholar Samuel Krislov, "the provisions of the Bill of Rights have been held to apply to the states, not in their own right, but as implicit in the Fourteenth Amendment."[3] Many of the court decisions that empowered the Bill of Rights were controversial, but today the Bill of Rights guarantees individual freedoms against infringement by state and local governments as well as by the national government. Only the Second, Third, and Seventh Amendments, the grand jury requirement of the Fifth Amendment, and the prohibition against excessive fines and bail in the Eighth Amendment have not been applied specifically to the states.

Freedom of Religion

The First Amendment contains two elements regarding religion and government. These elements are commonly referred to as the establishment clause and the free exercise clause. The **establishment clause** states that "Congress shall make no law respecting an establishment of religion." The **free exercise clause** prohibits the abridgment of citizens' freedom to worship, or not to worship, as they please. Sometimes these freedoms conflict. The government's practice of providing chaplains on military bases is one example of this conflict; some accuse the government of establishing religion in order to ensure that members of the armed forces can freely practice their religion. Usually, however, establishment clause and free exercise clause cases raise different kinds of conflicts.

The Establishment Clause

Some nations, such as Great Britain, have an established church that is officially supported by the government and recognized as a national institution. A few American colonies had official churches, but the religious persecutions that incited many colonists to move to America discouraged any desire for the First Congress to establish a national church in the United States. Thus, an established national religion is prohibited by the First Amendment.

Table 4.2   The Nationalization of the Bill of Rights

DATE	AMENDMENT	RIGHT	CASE
1925	First	Freedom of speech	*Gitlow v. New York*
1931	First	Freedom of the press	*Near v. Minnesota*
1937	First	Freedom of assembly	*De Jonge v. Oregon*
1940	First	Free exercise of religion	*Cantwell v. Connecticut*
1947	First	Establishment of religion	*Everson v. Board of Education*
1958	First	Freedom of association	*NAACP v. Alabama*
1963	First	Right to petition government	*NAACP v. Button*
	Second	Right to bear arms	Not incorporated[a]
	Third	No quartering of soldiers	Not incorporated[b]
1949	Fourth	No unreasonable searches and seizures	*Wolf v. Colorado*
1961	Fourth	Exclusionary rule	*Mapp v. Ohio*
1897	Fifth	Guarantee of just compensation	*Chicago, Burlington, and Quincy RR v. Chicago*
1964	Fifth	Immunity from self-incrimination	*Mallory v. Hogan*
1969	Fifth	Immunity from double jeopardy	*Benton v. Maryland*
	Fifth	Right to grand jury indictment	Not incorporated
1932	Sixth	Right to counsel in capital cases	*Powell v. Alabama*
1948	Sixth	Right to public trial	*In re Oliver*
1963	Sixth	Right to counsel in felony cases	*Gideon v. Wainwright*
1965	Sixth	Right to confrontation of witnesses	*Pointer v. Texas*
1966	Sixth	Right to impartial jury	*Parker v. Gladden*
1967	Sixth	Right to speedy trial	*Klopfer v. North Carolina*
1967	Sixth	Right to compulsory process for obtaining witnesses	*Washington v. Texas*
1968	Sixth	Right to jury trial for serious crimes	*Duncan v. Louisiana*
1972	Sixth	Right to counsel for all crimes involving jail terms	*Argersinger v. Hamlin*
	Seventh	Right to jury trial in civil cases	Not incorporated
1962	Eighth	Freedom from cruel and unusual punishment	*Robinson v. California*
	Eighth	Freedom from excessive fines or bail	Not incorporated
1965	Ninth	Right of privacy	*Griswold v. Connecticut*

[a]The Supreme Court has upheld limits on the rights of private citizens to bear arms.
[b]The quartering of soldiers has not occurred under the Constitution.

It is much less clear, however, what else the first Congress intended to be included in the establishment clause. Some people argued that it meant only that the government could not favor one religion over another. In contrast, Thomas Jefferson argued that the First Amendment created a "wall of separation" between church and state, forbidding not just favoritism but also any support for religion at all. These interpretations continue to provoke argument, especially when religion is mixed with education.

Debate is especially intense over aid to church-related schools and prayers in public schools. Proponents of *parochiaid* (short for "aid to parochial schools") argue that the aid does not favor any particular religion. Opponents claim that the Roman Catholic Church has by far the largest religious school system in the country and gets most of the aid. It was Protestant Lyndon Baines Johnson who obtained the passage of the first substantial aid to parochial elementary and secondary schools in 1965. He argued that aid went to students, not schools, and thus should go wherever the students were, including parochial schools.

In *Lemon v. Kurtzman* (1971), the Supreme Court declared that aid to church-related schools must

1. Have a secular legislative purpose.
2. Have a primary effect that neither advances nor inhibits religion.
3. Not foster an excessive government "entanglement" with religion.

Lemon v. Kurtzman

The 1971 Supreme Court decision that established that aid to church-related schools must (1) have a secular legislative purpose; (2) have a primary effect that neither advances nor inhibits religion; and (3) not foster excessive government entanglement with religion.

Why It Matters

The Establishment Clause
What if the Constitution did not prohibit the establishment of religion? If a dominant religion received public funds and was in a position to control health care, public education, and other important aspects of public policy, these policies may be quite different from what they are today. In addition, the potential for conflict between followers of the established religion and adherents to other religions would be substantial.

Zelman v. Simmons-Harris

The 2002 Supreme Court decision that upheld a state providing families with vouchers that could be used to pay for tuition at religious schools.

Engel v. Vitale

The 1962 Supreme Court decision holding that state officials violated the **First Amendment** when they wrote a prayer to be recited by New York's schoolchildren.

School District of Abington Township, Pennsylvania v. Schempp

A 1963 Supreme Court decision holding that a Pennsylvania law requiring Bible reading in schools violated the **establishment clause** of the **First Amendment**.

Since that time the Court has had to draw a fine line between aid that is permissible and aid that is not. For instance, the Court has allowed religiously affiliated colleges and universities to use public funds to build buildings. Tax funds may also be used to provide students in parochial schools with textbooks, computers and other instructional equipment, lunches, transportation to and from school, and to administer standardized testing services. Public funds cannot, however, be used to pay teacher salaries or to provide transportation for students on field trips. The theory underlying these decisions is that it is possible to determine that buildings, textbooks, lunches, school buses, and national tests are not used to support sectarian education. However, determining how teachers handle a subject in class or focus a field trip may require complex and constitutionally impermissible regulation of religion.

In an important loosening of its constraints on aid to parochial schools, however, the Supreme Court decided in 1997 in *Agostini v. Felton* that public school systems could send teachers into parochial schools to teach remedial and supplemental classes to needy children. In a landmark decision in 2002, the Court in **Zelman v. Simmons-Harris** upheld a program that provided some families in Cleveland, Ohio, vouchers that could be used to pay tuition at religious schools.

Controversy over aid to schools is not limited to Roman Catholic schools or any other single religion. In 1994, the Supreme Court ruled in *Kiryas Joel v. Grumet* that New York state had gone too far in favoring religion when it created a public school district for the benefit of a village of Hasidic Jews.

At the same time, the Supreme Court has been opening public schools to religious activities. The Court decided that public universities that permit student groups to use their facilities must allow student religious groups on campus to use the facilities for religious worship.[4] In the 1984 Equal Access Act, Congress made it unlawful for any public high school receiving federal funds (almost all of them do) to keep student groups from using school facilities for religious worship if the school opens its facilities for other student meetings.[5] In 2001, this principle was extended to public elementary schools.[6] Similarly, in 1993 the Court required public schools that rent facilities to organizations to do the same for religious groups.[7]

In 1995, the Court held that the University of Virginia was constitutionally required to subsidize a student religious magazine on the same basis as other student publications.[8] However, in 2004 the Court held that the state of Washington was within its rights when it excluded students pursuing a devotional theology degree from its general scholarship program.[9]

The threshold of constitutional acceptability becomes higher when public funds are used in a more direct way to support education. Thus, school authorities may not permit religious instructors to come into public school buildings during the school day to provide religious education,[10] although they may release students from part of the compulsory school day to receive religious instruction elsewhere.[11] In 1980, the Court also prohibited the posting of the Ten Commandments on the walls of public classrooms.[12]

School prayer is perhaps the most controversial religious issue. In 1962 and 1963, the Court aroused the wrath of many Americans by ruling that voluntary recitations of prayers or Bible passages, when done as part of classroom exercises in public schools, violated the establishment clause. In **Engel v. Vitale** and **School District of Abington Township, Pennsylvania v. Schempp** the justices observed that "the place of religion in our society is an exalted one, . . . [but] in the relationship between man and religion, the State is firmly committed to a position of neutrality."

It is *not* unconstitutional, of course, to pray in public schools. Students may pray silently as much as they wish. What the Constitution forbids is the sponsorship or encouragement of prayer, directly or indirectly, by public school authorities. Thus, in 1992 the Court ruled that a school-sponsored prayer at a public-school graduation violated the constitutional separation of church and state.[13] In 2000, the Court held that student-led prayer at football games was also unconstitutional.[14] Three Alabama laws

One of the most controversial issues regarding the First Amendment's prohibition of the establishment of religion is prayers in public schools. Although students may pray on their own, school authorities may not sponsor or encourage prayers.

authorized schools to hold one-minute periods of silence for "meditation or voluntary prayer," but the Court rejected this approach because the state made it clear that the purpose of the statute was to return prayer to the schools. The Court did indicate, however, that a less clumsy approach would pass its scrutiny.[15]

Political scientist Kenneth D. Wald observes that the last few years have been marked by great ferment in the relationship between religion and American political life. Religious issues and controversies have assumed much greater importance in political debate than they commanded before.[16] Much of this new importance is due to fundamentalist religious groups that have spurred their members to political action. Many school districts have simply ignored the Supreme Court's ban on school prayer and continue to allow prayers in their classrooms. Some religious groups and many members of Congress, especially conservative Republicans, have pushed for a constitutional amendment permitting prayer in school. A majority of the public consistently supports school prayer.

Fundamentalist Christian groups have pressed some state legislatures to mandate the teaching of "creation science"—their alternative to Darwinian theories of evolution—in public schools. Louisiana, for example, passed a Balanced Treatment Act requiring schools that taught Darwinian theory to teach creation science, too. Regardless, the Supreme Court ruled in 1987 that this law violated the establishment clause.[17] The Court had already held in a 1968 case that states cannot prohibit Darwin's theory of evolution from being taught in the public schools.[18]

The Supreme Court's struggle to interpret the establishment clause is also evident in areas other than education. For example, displays of religious symbols during the holidays have prompted considerable controversy. In 1984, the Court found that Pawtucket, R.I., could set up a Christmas nativity scene on public property—along with Santa's house and sleigh, Christmas trees, and other symbols of the Christmas season.[19] Five years later, the Court extended the principle to a Hanukkah menorah, placed next to a Christmas tree. The Court concluded that these displays had a secular purpose and provided little or no benefit to religion. At the same time, the Court invalidated display of the nativity scene without secular symbols in a courthouse because, in this context, the county gave the impression of endorsing the display's religious message.[20]

In this case, the Court said the Constitution does not require complete separation of church and state; it mandates accommodation of all religions and forbids hostility toward any. At the same time, the Constitution forbids government endorsement of religious beliefs. Drawing the line between neutrality toward religion and promotion of it is not easy; this dilemma ensures that cases involving the establishment of religion will continue to come before the Court.

The Free Exercise Clause

The First Amendment also guarantees the free exercise of religion. This guarantee seems simple enough. Whether people hold no religious beliefs, practice voodoo, or go to church, temple, or mosque, they should have the right to practice religion as they choose. The matter is, of course, more complicated. Religions sometimes forbid actions that society thinks are necessary; or, conversely, religions may require actions that society finds unacceptable. For example, what if a religion justifies multiple marriages or the use of illegal drugs? Muhammad Ali, the boxing champion, refused induction into the armed services during the Vietnam War because, he said, military service would violate his Muslim faith. Amish parents often refuse to send their children to public schools. Jehovah's Witnesses and Christian Scientists may refuse to accept blood transfusions and certain other kinds of medical treatment for themselves or their children.

Consistently maintaining that people have an inviolable right to *believe* what they want, the courts have been more cautious about the right to *practice* a belief. What if, the Supreme Court once asked, a person "believed that human sacrifices were a necessary part of religious worship?" In *Employment Division v. Smith* (1988), the Court discarded its previous requirement for a *"compelling interest"* before a government could even indirectly limit or prohibit religious practices. In *Smith*, the Court decided that state laws interfering with religious practices but not specifically aimed at religion are constitutional. As long as a law does not single out and ban religious practices because they are engaged in for religious reasons, or only because of the religious belief they display, a general law may be applied to conduct even if the conduct is religiously inspired (denying people unemployment compensation is an exception). In *Smith*, the state of Oregon was allowed to prosecute persons who used the drug peyote as part of their religious rituals.

Even before this decision, the Supreme Court had never permitted religious freedom to be an excuse for any and all behaviors. The Court had upheld laws and regulations forbidding polygamy, outlawing business activities on Sunday as applied to

Cassius Clay was the world heavyweight boxing champion before he converted to Islam, changed his name to Muhammad Ali, and was drafted during the war in Vietnam. Arguing that he opposed war on religious grounds, he refused to join the army. The federal government prosecuted him for draft dodging, and the boxing commission stripped him of his title. In 1971, the Supreme Court overturned his conviction for draft evasion. He is pictured here at the Houston induction center in 1967.

Orthodox Jews, denying tax exemptions to religious schools that discriminate on the basis of race,[21] approving building a road through ground sacred to some Native Americans, and even prohibiting a Jewish air force captain from wearing his yarmulke (Congress later intervened to permit military personnel to wear yarmulkes).

Other religiously motivated practices have been granted protection under the free exercise clause. The Court allowed Amish parents to take their children out of school after the eighth grade. Reasoning that the Amish community was well established and that its children would not burden the state, the Court held that religious freedom took precedence over compulsory education laws.[22] More broadly, although a state can compel parents to send their children to an accredited school, parents have a right to choose religious schools rather than public schools for their children's education. A state may not require Jehovah's Witnesses or members of other religions to participate in public-school flag-saluting ceremonies. Congress has also ruled, and the courts have upheld, that people can become conscientious objectors to war on religious grounds. You can examine another free exercise case in "You Are the Judge: The Case of Animal Sacrifices."

In the Religious Freedom Restoration Act of 1993, Congress attempted to overturn the principle the Court articulated in *Smith*. It conferred on all persons the right to perform their religious rituals unless the government can show that the law or regulation in question is narrowly tailored and in pursuit of a "compelling interest." In 1997, however, the Supreme Court declared this act an unconstitutional intrusion by Congress into the states' prerogatives for regulating the health and welfare of citizens.[23]

Freedom of Expression

A democracy depends on the free expression of ideas. Thoughts that are muffled, speech that is forbidden, and meetings that cannot be held are the enemies of the democratic process. Totalitarian governments know this, which is why they go to enormous trouble to limit expression.

Americans pride themselves on their free and open society. Freedom of conscience is absolute; Americans can *believe* whatever they want. The First Amendment plainly forbids the national government from limiting freedom of *expression*—that is, the right to say or publish what one believes. Is freedom of expression, then, like freedom of conscience, also *absolute?* Supreme Court Justice Hugo Black thought so; he

The free exercise of religious beliefs sometimes clashes with society's other values or laws, as when the Amish—who prefer to lead simple, traditional lives—refused to send their children to public schools. The Supreme Court eventually held in favor of the Amish, arguing that Amish children, living in such a close-knit community, were unlikely to become dependent on the state.

You Are the Judge

The Case of Animal Sacrifices

The church of Lukumi Babalu Aye, in Hialeah, Fla., practiced Santeria, a Caribbean-based mix of African ritual, voodoo, and Catholicism. Central to Santeria is the ritual sacrifice of animals—at birth, marriage, and death rites, as well as at ceremonies to cure the sick and initiate new members.

Offended by these rituals, the city of Hialeah passed ordinances prohibiting animal sacrifices in religious ceremonies. The church challenged the constitutionality of these laws, claiming they violated the free exercise clause of the First Amendment because the ordinances essentially barred the practice of Santeria. The city, the Santerians claimed, was discriminating against a religious minority. Besides, many other forms of killing animals were legal, including fishing, using animals in medical research, selling lobsters to be boiled alive, and feeding live rats to snakes.

You Be the Judge: Do the Santerians have a constitutional right to sacrifice animals in their religious rituals? Does the city's interest in protecting animals outweigh the Santerians' requirement for animal sacrifice?

Answer: In 1993, the Court overturned the Hialeah ordinances that prohibited the use of animal sacrifice in religious ritual. In *Church of the Lukumi Babalu Aye, Inc. v. City of Hialeah*, the justices concluded that governments that permit other forms of killing animals may not then ban sacrifices or ritual killings. In this instance, the Court found no compelling state interest that justified the abridgment of the freedom of religion.

was fond of pointing out that the First Amendment said Congress shall make *no* law. "I read no law abridging to mean no law abridging." In contrast, Justice Oliver Wendell Holmes offered a classic example of impermissible speech in 1919: "The most stringent protection of free speech would not protect a man in falsely shouting 'fire' in a theater and causing a panic."

The courts have been called upon to decide where to draw the line separating permissible from impermissible speech. In doing so, judges have had to balance freedom of expression against competing values like public order, national security, and the right to a fair trial. Currently, one of the most controversial freedom of expression issues surrounds so-called hate speech. Advocates of regulating hate speech, such as Stanford Law Professor Charles R. Lawrence, forcefully argue that racial insults, like fighting words, are "undeserving of First Amendment protection because the perpetrator's intent is not to discover the truth or invite dialogue, but to injure the victim."[24] In contrast, critics of hate speech policy, such as Ira Glasser of the ACLU, argue that "sacrificing free speech rights is too high a price to pay to advance the cause of equality."[25] In 1992, the Supreme Court ruled that legislatures and universities may not single out racial, religious, or sexual insults or threats for prosecution as "hate speech" or "bias crimes."[26] (See "Issues of the Times: Should Universities Regulate Hate Speech?")

The courts have also had to decide what kinds of activities do and do not constitute *speech* (or press) within the meaning of the First Amendment. Holding a political rally to attack an opposing candidate's stand on important issues gets First Amendment protection. Obscenity and libel, which are also expressions, do not. To make things more complicated, certain forms of nonverbal speech, such as picketing, are considered symbolic speech and receive First Amendment protection. Other forms of expression, such as fraud and incitement to violence, are considered action rather than speech. Government can limit action more easily than it can limit expression.

The one thing all freedom of expression cases have in common is the question of whether a certain expression receives the protection of the Constitution.

Prior Restraint

One principle stands out clearly in the complicated history of freedom of expression laws: Time and time again, the Supreme Court has struck down prior restraint on speech and the press. **Prior restraint** refers to a government's actions that prevent

prior restraint

A government preventing material from being published. This is a common method of limiting the press in some nations, but it is usually unconstitutional in the United States, according to the **First Amendment** and as confirmed in the 1931 Supreme Court case of *Near v. Minnesota.*

material from being published; in a word, prior restraint is censorship. In the United States, the First Amendment ensures that even if the government frowns on some material, a person's right to publish it is all but inviolable. A landmark case involving prior restraint is *Near v. Minnesota* (1931). A blunt newspaper editor called local officials a string of names including "grafters" and "Jewish gangsters." The state closed down his business, but the Supreme Court ordered the paper reopened.[27] Of course, the newspaper editor—or anyone else—could later be punished for violating a law or someone's rights *after* publication.

The extent of an individual's or group's freedom from prior restraint does depend in part, however, on who that individual or group is. In 1988, the Supreme Court ruled that a high school newspaper was not a public forum and could be regulated in "any reasonable manner" by school officials.[28]

Restrictions on the right to publish have also been upheld in the name of national security. Wartime often brings censorship to protect classified information. These restrictions often have public support; few would find it unconstitutional if a newspaper, for example, were hauled into court for publishing troop movement plans during a war. Critics of the press during the Persian Gulf War complained that press reporting might have helped to pinpoint locations of SCUD missile attacks, knowledge of which could be used to aim future missiles more precisely. Defenders of the freedom of the press complained that never before had the press been as "managed" as in that conflict: Reporters could get to the field only in the company of official Pentagon press representatives—and some who tried other ways of getting in the field were captured by the Iraqis.

Prior restraint of a different sort was demanded and secured by the national government for books written by former CIA agents Victor Marchetti and Frank Snepp. The government sued Snepp for failing to have his book about Vietnam, *A Decent Interval*, submitted to the agency for censorship, even though the book revealed no classified information.[29] Both men had signed agreements allowing the CIA to clear their future writings about the agency.

Nevertheless, the courts are reluctant to issue injunctions prohibiting the publication of material even in the area of national security. The most famous case involving prior restraint and national security involved the publication of stolen Pentagon papers. We examine this case in "You Are the Judge: The Case of the Purloined Pentagon Papers."

Free Speech and Public Order

Not surprisingly, government has sometimes been a zealous opponent of speech that opposes government policies. In wartime and peacetime, the biggest conflict between press and government has been about the connection between a free press and the need for public order. During World War I, Charles T. Schenck, the secretary of the American Socialist Party, distributed thousands of leaflets urging young men to resist the draft. Schenck was charged with impeding the war effort. The Supreme Court upheld his conviction in 1919 (*Schenck v. United States*). Justice Holmes declared that government could limit speech if it provokes a clear and present danger of substantive evils. Only when such danger exists can government restrain speech. It is difficult to say, of course, when speech becomes dangerous rather than simply inconvenient for the government.

The courts confronted the issue of free speech and public order during the 1950s. In the late 1940s and early 1950s there was widespread fear that communists had infiltrated the government. American anti-communism was a powerful force, and the national government was determined to jail the leaders of the Communist Party. Senator Joseph McCarthy and others in Congress were persecuting people they thought subversive, based on the Smith Act of 1940, which forbade advocating the violent overthrow of the American government. In *Dennis v. United States* (1951), the

Near v. Minnesota

The 1931 Supreme Court decision holding that the **First Amendment** protects newspapers from **prior restraint.**

Timeline

Civil Liberties and National Security

Schenck v. United States

A 1919 decision upholding the conviction of a socialist who had urged young men to resist the draft during World War I. Justice Holmes declared that government can limit speech if the speech provokes a "clear and present danger" of substantive evils.

Issues of the Times

The Issue: Should Universities Regulate Hate Speech?

Traditionally, we expect universities to be forums for full and candid discussion of issues. Limiting or discouraging the expression of a point of view is anathema to most university administrators, professors, and students. But what about speech that is motivated by racial, religious, or other prejudice and that includes offensive—and sometimes shocking—insults to certain categories of people? Advocates of regulating hate speech argue that hateful insults do not deserve protection because the perpetrator's intent is not to discover the truth or invite dialogue, but is to injure the victim. Critics of hate speech policy argue that limiting speech is too high a price to pay.

In 1992, the Supreme Court ruled in *R.A.V. v. St. Paul* that legislatures and universities may not single out racial, religious, or sexual insults or threats for prosecution as "hate speech" or "bias

crimes" (although states may impose longer prison terms on people convicted of "hate crimes"

without violating their rights to free speech). There are other ways to limit speech, however.

Read All About It

Hateful Name-Calling vs. Calling for Hateful Action

BY EDWARD ROTHSTEIN
November 23, 2002

Hate speech is a confused concept. It is impossible to defend crude name-calling and insensitivity, but is it so deserving of special opprobrium? Even ordinary speech, after all, can express hatred. And even the most brutish expression of hatred can be less injurious than

deceitful expressions of good will. What about this approach: if speech offends, let it be freely attacked by opposing speech. If it does more than offend but argues for hateful action—well, that is more serious.

The problem is that these priorities are often inverted. Hate speech tends to be prosecuted as a grievous violation, but arguments that can have far more hateful consequences

tend to be protected as a freedom. Universities are particularly vulnerable to such contrasts, because speech grounded in argument is what a university is all about, so it is ardently defended almost regardless of content.

This leads to strange distinctions. Harvard University's English

Please see Speech   Page 109

Speech

Continued from Page 108

department withdrew its invitation to the poet Tom Paulin to deliver its annual Morris Gray Lecture largely because of mounting protests over what Mr. Paulin had to say about Israel. Mr. Paulin gave an interview to a Cairo-based newspaper, *Al-Ahram Weekly,* in which he said of "Brooklyn born" Jewish settlers on the West Bank: "They should be shot dead. I think they are Nazis, racists, I feel nothing but hatred for them." He also said, "I never believed that Israel had the right to exist at all." Moreover, in a poem published in *The Observer* in 2001, he referred to the Israeli army as "the Zionist SS."

But the English department was soon attacked for its awkward reversal in a new wave of protests. In a letter to *The Harvard Crimson,* Patrick Cavanagh, a Harvard psychology professor who signed a petition urging that Harvard disinvest in Israel called Harvard's president, Lawrence H. Summers, "Ayatollah Summers," accusing him of bigotry for his support of the department's retraction. (Mr. Summers has recently criticized anti-Semitism on American campuses.)

The protestors seemed to suggest that Mr. Paulin wasn't really engaged in hate speech at all. He was actually making arguments— controversial political judgments— that should be protected. The department re-reversed itself.

The confusion over hate speech was also revealed in another recent controversy. The Stanford University Law School invited the lawyer Lynne Stewart to be a Mills Public Interest Mentor in a program the school says is meant "to provide public-interest students the opportunity to meet and learn from practitioners and scholars in public service."

But Ms. Stewart, a political radical who unsuccessfully defended Sheik Omar Abdel Rahman for his

---

Hate speech tends to be prosecuted as a grievous violation, but arguments that can have far more hateful consequences tend to be protected as a freedom.

---

responsibility in the 1993 World Trade Center bombing, was indicted last spring on charges of aiding a terrorist organization and illegally passing messages from the sheik's prison cell. In particular, in June 2000, she publicly confirmed for the sheik's fundamentalist followers in Egypt that he had called for an end to a cease-fire between those followers and the Egyptian government.

Ms. Stewart's assistance in that instance was not out of character.

She said she believes in "violence directed at the institutions which perpetuate capitalism, racism and sexism and at the people who are the appointed guardians of those institutions." In reacting to the civilian deaths of 9/11, she said she was "pretty inured" to the idea that "in an armed struggle, people die."

When some of this became widely known, protests mounted and the dean of the law school stripped Ms. Stewart of the title Mills mentor. But her lectures and mentoring of students took place unhampered.

Yet Ms. Stewart's public service and proclamations may have caused violence (her declaration of the end of that cease-fire was indeed followed by deaths in Egypt) as well as encouraged it against American targets. Presumably, only acts of hate speech would have made her unwelcome at Stanford, but aren't her positions and actions already expressions of a virulent form of hatred?

Not all criticism of Israel is anti-Semitic, but not all criticism of Israel is not anti-Semitic. When standards of justice are applied in profoundly distorted fashion, when those distortions put the literal survival of a society at stake and when murders are taking place and explicitly encouraged, declarations are being made that may even fit university standards for "hate speech." Or perhaps the concept itself should just be retired; it leads to puritanical scrutiny in some cases and is completely ignored in others.

Think About It

- Should your university adopt a policy to limit hate speech?
- If so, how should it define hate speech?
- Is there a danger that a hate speech policy could also limit the expression of important but unpopular views?

- Is there a significant difference between hate speech and arguments advocating policies you find abhorrent?

You Are the Judge

The Case of the Purloined Pentagon Papers

During the Johnson administration, the Department of Defense had amassed an elaborate secret history of American involvement in the Vietnam War. Hundreds of documents, many of them secret cables, memos, and war plans, were included. Many documented American ineptitude and South Vietnamese duplicity. One former Pentagon official, Daniel Ellsberg, who had become disillusioned with the Vietnam War, managed to retain access to a copy of these Pentagon papers. Hoping that revelations of the Vietnam quagmire would help end American involvement, he decided to leak the Pentagon papers to the *New York Times*.

The Nixon administration pulled out all the stops in its effort to embarrass Ellsberg and prevent publication of the Pentagon papers. Nixon's chief domestic affairs advisor, John Ehrlichman, approved a burglary of Ellsberg's psychiatrist's office, hoping to find damaging information on Ellsberg. (The burglary was bungled, and it eventually led to Ehrlichman's conviction and imprisonment.) In the courts, Nixon administration lawyers sought an injunction against the *Times* that would have ordered it to cease publication of the secret documents. Government lawyers argued that national security was being breached and that Ellsberg had stolen the documents from the government. The *Times* argued that its freedom to publish would be violated if an injunction were granted. In 1971 the case of *New York Times v. United States* was decided by the Supreme Court.

You Be the Judge: Did the *Times* have a right to publish secret, stolen Department of Defense documents?

Answer: In a 6-to-3 decision, a majority of the justices agreed that the "no prior restraint" rule prohibited prosecution before the papers were published. The justices also made it clear that if the government brought prosecution for theft, the Court might be sympathetic. No such charges were filed.

Supreme Court upheld prison sentences for several Communist Party leaders for conspiring to advocate the violent overthrow of the government—even in the absence of evidence that they actually urged people to commit specific acts of violence. Although the activities of this tiny, unpopular group resembled yelling "Fire!" in an empty theater rather than a crowded one, the Court ruled that a Communist takeover was so grave a danger that government could squelch their threat. Free-speech advocates were unable to stem the relentless persecution of the 1950s; the Supreme Court, as in the *Dennis* case, valued national security over First Amendment rights at the time.

The prevailing political climate often determines what limits the government will place on free speech. During the early 1950s, Senator Joseph McCarthy's persuasive—if unproven—accusations that many public officials were Communists created an atmosphere in which the courts placed restrictions on freedom of expression—restrictions that would be unacceptable today.

America in Perspective

Civil Liberties in Britain

As discussed in Chapter 2, Great Britain has an unwritten constitution, a set of understood principles that limits governmental power—most of the time. For example, it would be "unconstitutional" to punish someone for an act that is not forbidden by law or for the prime minister to restrict the sovereign's access to government documents. There is no equivalent, however, to the First Amendment to the U.S. Constitution that provides grounds for a lawsuit if someone disapproves of a restriction on freedom of expression. No court in Britain would overturn an act of Parliament for violating someone's freedom of speech.

Freedom of expression is generous in Great Britain, but there are some restrictions there that differ from those in the United States. British libel laws, for instance, are stricter than ours.

In November 1988, the government of Prime Minister Margaret Thatcher imposed a restriction that was too much for many British subjects. It forbade the broadcasting of any radio or television interviews with members of the Irish Republican Army or its legal political organization in Northern Ireland. A group of 200 British journalists, judges, and academics issued a plea for an act of Parliament that would guarantee freedom of expression. No such guarantee has been enacted, however. Of course, the Parliament to which they appealed was led by the same government that had imposed the restrictions.

What would happen if the administration tried something similar in the United States? The Pentagon papers case in 1971 has some similarities to Prime Minister Thatcher's gag rule.

However, the U.S. Supreme Court refused to stop the publication of these classified documents, even though the president said it would harm national security.

The United States has not always been ahead of Britain in permitting free speech and press. Remember the imprisonment of American Communists such as Dennis and his associates in the 1950s. When they used the First Amendment to challenge the Smith Act, the Court ruled in favor of the government. Even where written constitutions exist, judges may rely on their own views of political necessity—which are often shared with the legislative and executive branches that developed the civil liberties policies—to determine the scope of individual rights.

Soon the political climate changed, however, and the Court narrowed the interpretation of the Smith Act, making it more difficult to prosecute dissenters (see "America in Perspective: Civil Liberties in Britain"). In later years, the Court has found that it is permissible to advocate the violent overthrow of the government in the abstract, but not actually to incite anyone to imminent lawless action (*Yates v. United States*, 1957; *Brandenburg v. Ohio*, 1969).

The 1960s brought waves of protest that strained and expanded the constitutional meaning of free speech. Among the unrest over political, economic, racial, and social issues, the Vietnam War was the source of the most bitter controversy. Many people saw military service as a duty and war as an issue that government should decide. Others felt that citizens should not be asked to die or pay for conflicts that they felt were unjust. Organized protests on college and university campuses became common. People burned draft cards, seized university buildings, marched, and demonstrated against the Southeast Asian conflict.

Americans today live in relatively less turbulent times, yet many people still engage in public demonstrations. Courts have been quite supportive of the right to protest, pass out leaflets, or gather signatures on petitions—as long as it is done in public places. Campaign literature may even be distributed anonymously.[30]

Constitutional protections diminish once a person steps on private property, for example, most shopping centers. The Supreme Court has held that federal free-speech guarantees did not apply when a person was on private property.[31] However, it upheld a state's power to include politicking in shopping centers within its own free-speech guarantee,[32] and in 1994, the Supreme Court ruled that cities cannot bar residents from posting signs on their own property.[33]

Comparing Civil Liberties

Free speech sometimes conflicts with public order. The Constitution protects the rights of protestors, such as those pictured here opposing the war with Iraq, to have their say.

Free Press and Fair Trials

The Bill of Rights is an inexhaustible source of potential conflicts among different types of freedoms. One is the conflict between the right of the press to print what it wants and the right to a fair trial. The quantity of press coverage given the 1995 trial (and pretrial hearings) of football star O. J. Simpson, accused of murdering his wife and her friend, surpassed that given the Super Bowl, and little of it was sympathetic to Simpson. The press has also devoted extraordinary coverage to the legal issues of other celebrities such as Kobe Bryant and Martha Stewart. Does such extensive media coverage compromise the fairness of the trial? Defense attorneys argue that such publicity can inflame the community—and potential jurors—against defendants. It may very well. The trouble is that the Constitution's guarantee of freedom of the press entitles journalists to cover every trial.

Fundamental rights are sometimes in conflict. Press coverage of the murder trial of O. J. Simpson, pictured here with one of his lawyers, made it very difficult to impanel a jury whose members had not reached conclusions about his guilt before the trial began.

In addition to arguing that the public has a "right to know," some journalists hope to capitalize on their coverage of lurid crime stories to sell newspapers, gain ratings, or attract advertisers. Those motivations have prompted newspapers to challenge courts' restrictions on media coverage of trials. When a Nebraska judge issued a gag order forbidding the press to report any details of a particularly gory murder (or even to report the gag order itself), the outraged Nebraska Press Association took the case to the Supreme Court. The Court sided with the editors and revoked the gag order.[34] In 1980, the Court reversed a Virginia judge's order to close a murder trial to the public and the press. "The trial of a criminal case," said the Court, "must be open to the public."[35] A pretrial hearing, though, is a different matter. A 1979 case permitted a closed hearing on the grounds that pretrial publicity might compromise the defendant's right to fairness.

Although reporters always want access to trials, they do not always want the courts to have access to their files. Occasionally a reporter withholds some critical evidence that either the prosecution or the defense wants in a criminal case. Reporters argue that "protecting their sources" should exempt them from revealing notes from confidential informants. More than one reporter has gone to jail for this principle, arguing that they had no obligation to produce evidence that might bear on the guilt or innocence of a defendant.

Some states have passed *shield laws* to protect reporters in these situations. In most states, though, reporters have no more rights than other citizens once a case has come to trial. The Supreme Court ruled in *Branzburg v. Hayes* (1972) that in the absence of shield laws, the right of a fair trial preempts the reporter's right to protect sources. This issue came to a head in one celebrated case involving the student newspaper at Stanford University. After a violent confrontation with student protestors, the police got a search warrant and marched off to the *Stanford Daily*, which they believed to have pictures of the scene—from which they could make arrests. The paper argued that its files were protected by the First Amendment, but the decision in **Zurcher v. Stanford Daily** (1978) sided with the police, not the paper.

Zurcher v. Stanford Daily

A 1978 Supreme Court decision holding that a proper **search warrant** could be applied to a newspaper as well as to anyone else without necessarily violating the **First Amendment** rights to freedom of the press.

It is one thing to attempt to obtain the press's cooperation in trials and quite another to limit the press's coverage of judicial proceedings. The balance between a free press and a fair trial is not an even one. The Court has *never* upheld a restriction on the press in the interest of a fair trial. Ultimately, the only feasible measure the judicial system can take against the influence of publicity in high profile cases is to sequester the jury, thereby isolating it from the media and public opinion.

Obscenity

In *The Brethren*, a gossipy portrayal of the Supreme Court, Bob Woodward and Scott Armstrong recount the tale of Justice Thurgood Marshall's lunch with some law clerks. Glancing at his watch at about 1:50 P.M., the story goes, Marshall exclaimed, "My God, I almost forgot. It's movie day, we've got to get back."[36] Movie day at the Court was an annual event when movies brought before the Court on obscenity charges were shown in a basement storeroom.

Several justices boycotted these showings, arguing that obscenity should never be banned and so how "dirty" a movie is has no relevance. In 1957, however, the majority held that "obscenity is not within the area of constitutionally protected speech or press" (**Roth v. United States**). The doctrine set forth in this case still prevails. Deciding what is obscene, though, has never been an easy matter. In a line that would haunt him for the rest of his life, Justice Potter Stewart once remarked that although he could not define obscenity, "I know it when I see it." During the Supreme Court's movie day, law clerks echoed Stewart's line, punctuating particularly racy scenes with cries of "That's it! That's it! I know it when I see it."

Roth v. United States

A 1957 Supreme Court decision ruling that "obscenity is not within the area of constitutionally protected speech or press."

Efforts to define obscenity have perplexed the courts for years. Obviously, public standards vary from time to time, place to place, and person to person. Much of today's

Although the Supreme Court ruled in *Roth v. United States* that obscenity is not protected by the First Amendment, determining just what is obscene has proven difficult. Rapper Eminem has been accused of promoting hate and violence in his song lyrics and performances. Some communities have debated whether they should—or could—ban performances by Eminem and other controversial musicians.

MTV would have been banned a decade or two ago. What might be acceptable in Manhattan's Greenwich Village would shock residents of some other areas of the country. Works that some people call obscene might be good entertainment or even great art to others. At one time or another, the works of Aristophanes, those of Mark Twain, and even the "Tarzan" stories by Edgar Rice Burroughs were banned. The state of Georgia banned the acclaimed film *Carnal Knowledge*—a ban the Supreme Court struck down in 1974.[37]

The Court tried to clarify its doctrine by spelling out what could be classified as obscene and thus outside First Amendment protection in the 1973 case of **Miller v. California.** Then Chief Justice Warren Burger wrote that materials were obscene if:

Miller v. California

A 1973 Supreme Court decision that avoided defining obscenity by holding that community standards be used to determine whether material is obscene in terms of appealing to a "prurient interest" and being "patently offensive" and lacking in value.

1. The work, taken as a whole, appealed "to a prurient interest in sex."
2. The work showed "patently offensive" sexual conduct that was specifically defined by an obscenity law.
3. The work, taken as a whole, lacked "serious literary, artistic, political, or scientific value."

Decisions regarding whether material was obscene, said the Court, should be based on average people (in other words, juries) applying the contemporary standards of local—not national—communities.

The Court did provide "a few plain examples" of what sort of material might fall within this definition of obscenity. Among these examples were "patently offensive representations of ultimate sexual acts, . . . actual or simulated," "patently offensive representations of masturbation or excretory functions," or "lewd exhibition of the genitals." Cities throughout the country duplicated the language of *Miller* in their obscenity ordinances. The difficulty remains in determining what is *lewd* or *offensive.* Laws must satisfy these qualifying adjectives to prevent communities from banning anatomy texts, for example, as obscene.

Another reason why obscenity convictions can be difficult to obtain is that no nationwide consensus exists that offensive material should be banned—at least not when it is restricted to adults. In many communities the laws are lenient regarding pornography, and prosecutors know that they may not get a jury to convict, even when the disputed material is obscene as defined by *Miller.* Thus, obscene material is widely available in adult bookstores, video stores, and movie theaters.

Regulations aimed at keeping obscene material away from the young, who are considered more vulnerable to its harmful influences, are more popular, and courts have consistently ruled that states may protect children from obscenity. The rating scheme of the Motion Picture Association of America is one example, as is the more recent TV ratings system. Equally popular are laws designed to protect the young against pornographic exploitation. It is a violation of federal law to receive sexually explicit photographs of children through the mail or over the Internet, and in 1990 the Supreme Court upheld Ohio's law forbidding the possession of child pornography.[38]

Advances in technology have created a new wrinkle in the obscenity issue. The Internet and the World Wide Web make it easier to distribute obscene material rapidly, and a number of online information services have taken advantage of this opportunity. Congress, especially concerned with protecting minors from exposure to pornography, has recently decided that the Internet is not the electronic equivalent of the printing press and thus does not deserve the free-speech protection of the First Amendment. Instead, it regards the Internet as a broadcast medium, subject to government regulation (discussed later in this chapter).

In 1996, Congress passed the Communications Decency Act, banning obscene material and criminalizing the transmission of indecent speech or images to anyone under 18 years of age. The new law made no exception for material that has serious literary, artistic, political, or scientific merit as outlined in *Miller v. California*. In 1997, the Supreme Court overturned this law as being overly broad and vague and a violation of free speech.[39] In 2002, the Court overturned a law banning virtual child pornography on similar grounds.[40] Apparently the Supreme Court views the Internet similarly to print media, with similar protections against government regulation. In 1999, however, the Court upheld prohibitions on obscene e-mail and faxes.

Despite the Court's best efforts to define obscenity and determine when it can be banned, state and local governments continue to struggle with the application of these rulings. In one famous case, a small New Jersey town tried to get rid of a nude dancing parlor by using its zoning power to ban all live entertainment. The Court held that the measure was too broad and thus unlawful.[41] But the Court has upheld laws banning nude dancing when their effect on overall expression was minimal.[42] Jacksonville, Fla., tried to ban drive-in movies containing nudity. We will examine the Court's reaction in "You Are the Judge: The Case of the Drive-in Theater."

Other attempts to restrict obscenity have been proposed by some women's groups, which claim that pornography degrades and dehumanizes women. Legal scholar Catherine MacKinnon claims that "pornography is an . . . industry of rape and battery and sexual harassment."[43] Some cities, at the urging of an unusual alliance of conservative Christians and feminists, have passed antipornography ordinances on the grounds that pornography harms women. So far, however, courts have struck these ordinances down on First Amendment grounds. No such case has reached the Supreme Court—yet.

Visual Literacy

What Speech Is Protected by the Constitution?

Libel and Slander

Another type of expression not protected by the First Amendment is **libel**: the publication of false statements that are malicious and damage a person's reputation. *Slander* refers to spoken defamation, whereas libel refers to written defamation. Of course, if politicians could collect damages for every untrue thing said about them, the right to criticize the government—which the Supreme Court termed "the central meaning of the First Amendment"—would be stifled. No one would dare be critical for fear of making a factual error.

To encourage public debate, the Supreme Court has held in cases such as **New York Times v. Sullivan** (1964) that statements about public figures are libelous only if made with malice and reckless disregard for the truth. Public figures have to prove to a jury, in effect, that whoever wrote or said untrue statements about them knew that the statements were untrue and intended to harm them. This standard makes libel cases difficult for public figures to win because it is difficult to prove that a publication was intentionally malicious.[44]

libel

The publication of false or malicious statements that damage someone's reputation.

New York Times v. Sullivan

Decided in 1964, this case established the guidelines for determining whether public officials and public figures could win damage suits for libel. To do so, individuals must prove that the defamatory statements were made with "actual malice" and reckless disregard for the truth.

You Are the Judge

The Case of the Drive-in Theater

Almost everyone concedes that *sometimes* obscenity should be banned by public authorities. One instance might be when a person's right to show pornographic movies clashes with another's right to privacy. Presumably, no one wants hard-core pornography shown in public places where schoolchildren might see it. Showing dirty movies in an enclosed theater or in the privacy of your own living room is one thing. Showing them in public is something else. Or is it?

The city of Jacksonville, Fla., wanted to limit the showing of certain kinds of movies at drive-in theaters. Its city council reasoned that drive-ins were public places and that drivers passing by would be involuntarily exposed to movies they might prefer not to see. Some members of the council argued that drivers distracted by steamy scenes might even cause accidents. So the council passed a local ordinance forbidding movies showing nudity (defined in the ordinance as "bare buttocks . . . female bare breasts, or human bare pubic areas") at drive-in theaters.

Arrested for violating the ordinance, a Mr. Erznoznik challenged the constitutionality of the ordinance. He claimed that the law was overly broad and banned nudity, not obscenity. The lawyers for the city insisted that the law could be squared with the First Amendment. The government, they claimed, had a responsibility to forbid a "public nuisance," especially one that might cause a traffic hazard.

You Be the Judge: Did Jacksonville's ban on nudity in movies at drive-ins go too far or was it a constitutional limit on free speech?

Answer: In *Erznoznik v. Jacksonville* (1975) the Supreme Court held that Jacksonville's ordinance was unconstitutionally broad. The city council had gone too far; it could end up banning movies that might not be obscene. The ordinance would, said the Court, ban a film "containing a picture of a baby's buttocks, the nude body of a war victim or scenes from a culture where nudity is indigenous." Said Justice Powell for the Court: "Clearly, all nudity cannot be deemed obscene."

Why It Matters

Libel Law
It is difficult for public figures to win libel cases. Public figures will likely lose even if they can show that the defendant made defamatory falsehoods about them. This may not be fair, but it is essential for people to feel free to criticize public officials. Fear of losing a lawsuit would have a chilling effect on democratic dialogue.

Private individuals have a lower standard to meet for winning libel lawsuits. They need show only that statements made about them were defamatory falsehoods and that the author was negligent. Nevertheless, it is unusual for someone to win a libel case; most people do not wish to draw attention to critical statements about themselves.

Libel cases must balance freedom of expression with respect for individual reputations. If public debate is not free, there can be no democracy. On the other hand, some reputations will be damaged, or at least bruised, in the process. In one widely publicized case, General William Westmoreland, once the commander of American troops in South Vietnam, sued CBS. On January 23, 1982, the network broadcast a documentary called "The Uncounted Enemy." It claimed that American military leaders in Vietnam, including Westmoreland, systematically lied to Washington about their success there to make it appear that the United States was winning the war. All the evidence, including CBS's own internal memoranda, showed that the documentary made errors of fact. Westmoreland sued CBS for libel. Ultimately, the power of the press—in this case, a sloppy, arrogant press—prevailed. Fearing defeat at the trial, Westmoreland settled for a mild apology.[45]

An unusual case that explored the line between parody and libel came before the Supreme Court in 1988, when Reverend Jerry Falwell sued *Hustler* magazine. *Hustler* editor Larry Flynt had printed a parody of a Campari Liquor ad about various celebrities called "First Time" (in which celebrities related the first time they drank Campari, but with an intentional double meaning). When *Hustler* depicted the Reverend Jerry Falwell having had his "first time" in an outhouse with his mother, Falwell sued. He alleged that the ad subjected him to great emotional distress and mental anguish. The case tested the limits to which a publication could go to parody or lampoon a public figure. The Supreme Court ruled that they can go pretty far—all nine justices ruled in favor of the magazine.

Symbolic Speech

Freedom of speech, more broadly interpreted, is a guarantee of freedom of expression. In 1965, Mary Beth Tinker and her brother John were suspended from school in Des Moines, Iowa, when they wore black armbands to protest the Vietnam War. The Supreme Court held that the suspension violated the Tinkers' First Amendment rights. The right to freedom of speech, said the Court, went beyond the spoken word.[46]

When Gregory Johnson set a flag on fire at the 1984 Republican National Convention in Dallas to protest nuclear arms buildup, the Supreme Court decided that the state law prohibiting flag desecration violated the First Amendment (**Texas v. Johnson,** 1989). Burning the flag, the Court said, constituted speech and not just dramatic action.[47] When Massachusetts courts ordered the organizers of the annual St. Patrick's Day parade to include the Irish-American Gay, Lesbian, and Bisexual Group of Boston, the Supreme Court declared that a parade is a form of protected speech and thus the organizers are free to include whomever they want.

Wearing an armband, burning a flag, and marching in a parade are examples of **symbolic speech:** actions that do not consist of speaking or writing but that express an opinion. Court decisions have classified these activities somewhere between pure speech and pure action. The doctrine of symbolic speech is not precise; for example, although burning a flag is protected speech, burning a draft card is not.[48] In 2003, the Court held that states may make it a crime to burn a cross with a purpose to intimidate, as long as the law clearly gives prosecutors the burden of proving that the act was intended as a threat and not as a form of symbolic expression.[49] The relevant cases make it clear, however, that First Amendment rights are not limited by a rigid definition of what constitutes speech.

Texas v. Johnson

A 1989 case in which the Supreme Court struck down a law banning the burning of the American flag on the grounds that such action was **symbolic speech** protected by the **First Amendment.**

symbolic speech

Nonverbal communication, such as burning a flag or wearing an armband. The Supreme Court has accorded some symbolic speech protection under the **First Amendment.**

Commercial Speech

Not all forms of communication receive the full protection of the First Amendment. **Commercial speech,** such as advertising, is restricted far more extensively than expressions of opinion on religious, political, or other matters. The Federal Trade Commission (FTC) decides what kinds of goods may be advertised on radio and television and regulates the content of such advertising. These regulations have responded to changes in social mores and priorities. Thirty years ago, for example, tampons could not be advertised on TV, whereas cigarette commercials were everywhere. Today the situation is just the reverse.

The FTC attempts to ensure that advertisers do not make false claims for their products, but "truth" in advertising does not prevent misleading promises. For example, when ads imply that the right mouthwash or deodorant will improve one's love life, that dubious message is perfectly legal.

Nevertheless, commercial speech on the airwaves is regulated in ways that would clearly be impossible in the political or religious realm—even to the point of forcing a manufacturer to say certain words. For example, the makers of Excedrin pain reliever were forced to add the words "on pain other than headache" in their commercials describing tests that supposedly supported the product's claims of superior effectiveness. (The test results were based on the pain experienced after giving birth.)

Although commercial speech is regulated more rigidly than other types of speech, the courts have been broadening its protection under the Constitution. For years, many states had laws that prohibited advertising for professional services—such as legal and engineering services—and for certain products ranging from eyeglasses and prescription drugs to condoms and abortions. Advocates of these laws claimed that they were designed to protect consumers against misleading claims, while critics charged that the laws prevented price competition. In recent years, the courts have struck down

commercial speech

Communication in the form of advertising. It can be restricted more than many other types of speech but has been receiving increased protection from the Supreme Court.

many such restrictions as violations of freedom of speech. In 1999 the Supreme Court overturned restrictions on advertising casino gambling in states where such gambling is legal.[50] In general, regulation of commercial speech is allowed when the speech concerns unlawful activity or is misleading but otherwise must advance a substantial government interest and be no more extensive than necessary to serve that interest.[51]

Regulation of the Public Airwaves

The Federal Communications Commission (FCC) regulates the content, nature, and very existence of radio and television broadcasting. Although newspapers do not need licenses, radio and television stations do. A licensed station must comply with regulations, including the requirement that they devote a certain percentage of broadcast time to public service, news, children's programming, political candidates, or views other than those its owners support. The rules are more relaxed for cable channels, which can specialize in a particular type of broadcasting because consumers pay for, and thus have more choice about, the service.

This sort of governmental interference would clearly violate the First Amendment if it were imposed on the print media. For example, the state of Florida passed a law requiring newspapers in the state to provide space for political candidates to reply to newspaper criticisms. The Supreme Court, without hesitation, voided this law (**Miami Herald Publishing Company v. Tornillo**, 1974). Earlier, in **Red Lion Broadcasting Company v. Federal Communications Commission** (1969), the Court upheld similar restrictions on radio and television stations, reasoning that such laws were justified because only a limited number of broadcast frequencies were available.

One FCC rule regulating the content of programs restricts the use of obscene words. Comedian George Carlin has a famous routine called "Filthy Words" that could never be said over the airwaves. A New York City radio station tested Carlin's assertion by airing his routine. The ensuing events proved Carlin right. In 1978, the Supreme Court upheld the Commission's policy of barring these words from radio or television when children might hear them.[52]

Similarly, the FCC has twice fined New York disc jockey Howard Stern $600,000 for indecency. It is especially interesting that if Stern's commentaries had been carried by cable or satellite instead of the airwaves, he could have expressed himself with impunity. Technological change has blurred the line between broadcasting and private communications between individuals. With cable television now in most American homes, the Supreme Court is now faced with ruling on the application of free-speech guidelines to cable broadcasting.

Section 505 of the Telecommunications Act of 1996 requires cable television operators providing channels "primarily dedicated to sexually-oriented programming" either to "fully scramble or otherwise fully block" those channels or to limit their transmission to hours when children are unlikely to be viewing, set by administrative regulation as between 10 P.M. and 6 A.M. The Playboy Entertainment Group pointed out that banning transmission restricts sexually oriented programming even to households without children. It challenged the law as an unconstitutional violation of the First Amendment free-speech guarantee, arguing that Congress had less restrictive ways to accomplish its goals.

In 2000 in *United States v. Playboy Entertainment Group*, the Supreme Court agreed. It held that although government had a legitimate right to regulate sexually oriented programming, any such regulation must be narrowly tailored to promote a compelling government interest. If a less restrictive alternative would serve the government's purpose, Congress must use that alternative. The Court concluded that targeted blocking, in which subscribers can ask their cable companies to block a signal to their homes, is less restrictive than banning and is a feasible and effective means of furthering its compelling interests. Thus, the more restrictive option of banning a signal for most of the day cannot be justified.

Miami Herald Publishing Company v. Tornillo

A 1974 case in which the Supreme Court held that a state could not force a newspaper to print replies from candidates it had criticized, illustrating the limited power of government to restrict the **print media**.

Red Lion Broadcasting Company v. Federal Communications Commission

A 1969 case in which the Supreme Court upheld restrictions on radio and television broadcasting. These restrictions on the **broadcast media** are much tighter than those on the **print media** because there are only a limited number of broadcasting frequencies available.

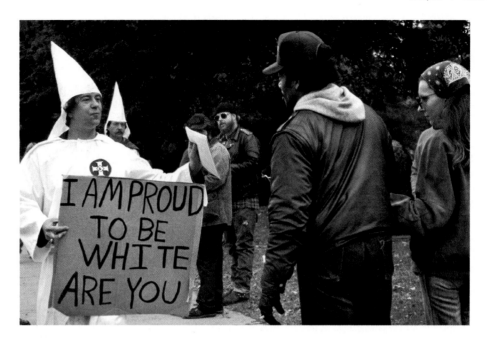

White supremacists and anti-White supremacists square off. The Supreme Court has generally upheld the right of any group, no matter how controversial or offensive, to peaceably assemble, as long as the group's demonstrations remain on public property.

Freedom of Assembly

The last of the great rights guaranteed by the First Amendment is the freedom to "peaceably assemble." This freedom is often neglected alongside the more trumpeted freedoms of speech, press, and religion, yet it is the basis for forming interest groups, political parties, and professional associations, as well as for picketing and protesting.

Right to Assemble. There are two facets of the freedom of assembly. First is the literal right to assemble—that is, to gather together in order to make a statement. This freedom can conflict with other societal values when it disrupts public order, traffic flow, peace and quiet, or bystanders' freedom to go about their business without interference. Within reasonable limits, called *time, place,* and *manner restrictions,* freedom of assembly includes the rights to parade, picket, and protest. Whatever a group's cause, it has the right to demonstrate, but no group can simply hold a spontaneous demonstration anytime, anywhere, and anyway it chooses. Usually, a group must apply to the local city government for a permit and post a bond of a few hundred dollars—a little like making a security deposit on an apartment. The governing body must grant a permit as long as the group pledges to hold its demonstration at a time and place that allows the police to prevent major disruptions. There are virtually no limitations on the content of a group's message. In one important case, the American Nazi Party applied to the local government to march in the streets of Skokie, Ill., a Chicago suburb with a sizable Jewish population, including many survivors of Hitler's death camps. You can examine the Court's response in "You Are the Judge: The Case of the Nazis' March in Skokie."

The balance between freedom and order is tested when protest verges on harassment. Protestors lined up outside abortion clinics have been a common sight. Members of groups such as "Operation Rescue" try to shame clients into staying away and may harass them if they do visit a clinic. Rights are in conflict in such cases: A woman seeking to terminate her pregnancy has the right to obtain an abortion; the demonstrators have the right to protest the very existence of the clinic. The courts have acted to restrain these protestors, setting limits on how close they may come to the clinics and upholding damage claims of clients against the protestors. In one case, pro-life demonstrators in a Milwaukee suburb paraded outside the home of a physician who was reported to perform abortions. The town board forbade future picketing in residential neighborhoods. In 1988, the Supreme Court agreed that the

You Are the Judge

The Case of the Nazis' March in Skokie

Hitler's Nazis slaughtered 6 million Jews in death camps like Bergen-Belsen, Auschwitz, and Dachau. Many of the survivors migrated to the United States, and many settled in Skokie, Ill. Skokie, with 80,000 people, is a suburb just north of Chicago. In its heavily Jewish population are thousands of survivors of German concentration camps.

The American Nazi Party was a rag-tag group of perhaps 25 to 30 members. Their headquarters was a storefront building on the West Side of Chicago, near an area of an expanding African-American population. After being denied a permit to march in an African-American neighborhood of Chicago,

the American Nazis announced their intention to march in Skokie. Skokie's city government required that they post a $300,000 bond to get a parade permit. The Nazis claimed that the high bond was set in order to prevent their march and that it infringed on their freedoms of speech and assembly. The American Civil Liberties Union (ACLU), despite its loathing of the Nazis, defended the Nazis' claim and their right to march. The ACLU lost half its Illinois membership because it took this position.

You Be the Judge: Do Nazis have the right to parade, preach anti-Jewish propaganda, and perhaps provoke vio-

lence in a community peopled with survivors of the Holocaust? What rights or obligations does a community have to maintain order?

Answer: A federal district court ruled that Skokie's ordinance did restrict freedom of assembly and association. No community could use its power to grant parade permits to stifle free expression. In *Collins v. Smith* (Collins was the Nazi leader and Smith was the mayor of Skokie), the Supreme Court let this lower-court decision stand. In fact, the Nazis did not march in Skokie, settling instead for some poorly attended demonstrations in Chicago.

right of residential privacy was a legitimate local concern and upheld the ordinance.[53] In 1994, Congress passed a law enacting broad new penalties against abortion protestors.

Right to Associate. The second facet of freedom of assembly is the right to associate with people who share a common interest, including an interest in political change. In a famous case at the height of the civil rights movement, Alabama tried to harass the state chapter of the National Association for the Advancement of Colored People (NAACP) by requiring it to turn over its membership list. The Court found this demand an unconstitutional restriction on freedom of association (**NAACP v. Alabama**, 1958).

The four freedoms guaranteed by the First Amendment—religion, speech, press, and assembly—are one key part of Americans' civil liberties. When people confront the American legal system as criminal suspects, they also have certain rights under the Constitution. Even suspected and convicted criminals are guaranteed some rights, which regulate how they can be investigated, interrogated, tried, and punished.

NAACP v. Alabama

The Supreme Court protected the right to assemble peaceably in this 1958 case when it decided the NAACP did not have to reveal its membership list and thus subject its members to harassment.

Defendants' Rights

The Bill of Rights contains only 45 words that guarantee the freedoms of religion, speech, press, and assembly. Most of the remaining words concern the rights of people accused of crimes. These rights were originally intended to protect the accused in *political* arrests and trials; British abuse of colonial political leaders was still fresh in the memory of American citizens. Today the protections in the Fourth, Fifth, Sixth, Seventh, and Eighth Amendments are mostly applied in criminal justice cases.

It is useful to think of the stages of the criminal justice system as a series of funnels decreasing in size. Generally speaking, a *crime* is (sometimes) followed by an *arrest*, which is (sometimes) followed by a *prosecution*, which is (sometimes) followed by a *trial*, which (usually) results in a *verdict* of innocence or guilt. The funnels get

Table 4.3 The Constitution and the Stages of the Criminal Justice System

Although our criminal justice system is complex, it can be broken down into stages. The Constitution protects the rights of the accused at every stage.

STAGE	PROTECTIONS
1. Evidence gathered	"Unreasonable search and seizure" forbidden (Fourth Amendment)
2. Suspicion cast	Guarantee that "writ of habeas corpus" will not be suspended, forbidding imprisonment without evidence (Article I, Section 9)
3. Arrest made	Right to have the "assistance of counsel" (Sixth Amendment)
4. Interrogation held	Forced self-incrimination forbidden (Fifth Amendment)
	"Excessive bail" forbidden (Eighth Amendment)
5. Trial held	"Speedy and public trial" by an impartial jury required (Sixth Amendment)
	"Double jeopardy" (being tried twice for the same crime) forbidden (Fifth Amendment)
	Trial by jury required (Article III, Section 2)
	Right to confront witnesses (Sixth Amendment)
6. Punishment imposed	"Cruel and unusual punishment" forbidden (Eighth Amendment)

smaller and smaller, each dripping into the next. Many more crimes occur than are reported; many more crimes are reported than arrests are made (the ratio is about five to one); many more arrests are made than prosecutors prosecute; and many more prosecutions occur than jury trials. At each stage of the criminal justice system, the Constitution protects the rights of the accused (see Table 4.3).

Interpreting Defendants' Rights

The Bill of Rights sets out civil liberties that American citizens have if they are arrested or brought to court. At every stage of the criminal justice system, police, prosecutors, and judges must behave in accordance with the Bill of Rights. Any misstep may invalidate a conviction.

The language of the Bill of Rights comes from the late 1700s and is often vague. For example, just how speedy is a "speedy trial"? How "cruel and unusual" does a punishment have to be in order to violate the Eighth Amendment? The courts continually must rule on the constitutionality of actions by police, prosecutors, judges, and legislatures—actions that a citizen or group could claim violate certain rights. Defendants' rights, just like those rights protected by the First Amendment, are not clearly defined in the Bill of Rights.

One thing is clear, however. The Supreme Court's decisions have extended specific provisions of the Bill of Rights—one by one—to the states as part of the general process of incorporation discussed earlier. Virtually all the rights discussed in the following sections affect the actions of both the national and state authorities.

Searches and Seizures

Police cannot arrest a citizen without reason. They need evidence to arrest, and courts need evidence to convict. Before making an arrest, police need what the courts call **probable cause,** reasonable grounds to believe that someone is guilty of a crime. Often police need to get physical evidence—a car thief's fingerprints, a snatched purse—to use in court. The Fourth Amendment is quite specific in forbidding **unreasonable searches and seizures.** To prevent abuse of police power, the Constitution requires that no court may issue a **search warrant** unless probable cause exists to believe that a crime has occurred or is about to occur. These written warrants must specify the area to be searched and the material sought in the police search.

probable cause

The situation occurring when the police have reason to believe that a person should be arrested. In making the arrest, police are allowed legally to search for and seize incriminating evidence.

unreasonable searches and seizures

Obtaining evidence in a haphazard or random manner, a practice prohibited by the Fourth Amendment. **Probable cause** and/or a **search warrant** are required for a legal and proper search for and seizure of incriminating evidence.

search warrant

A written authorization from a court specifying the area to be searched and what the police are searching for.

One of the most important principles of constitutional law is that defendants in criminal cases have rights. Probable cause and/or a search warrant are required for a legal search for and seizure of incriminating evidence. Here police officers arrest a suspected drug dealer during a raid and read the suspect his rights based on the Supreme Court's decision in *Miranda v. Arizona.*

You Are a Police Officer

A warrant is not a constitutional requirement for a reasonable police search, however. Most searches in this country take place without warrants. Such searches are valid if probable cause exists, if the search is necessary to protect an officer's safety, or if the search is limited to material relevant to the suspected crime or within the suspect's immediate control.

Normally, if police find anything in a search, they find what they have probable cause to believe is there. In two cases involving Fourth Amendment issues, authorities used aerial searches to secure the evidence they needed. The first case involved a marijuana grower named Ciraolo. When police, responding to a tip, went to look at his place, it was surrounded by 10-foot fences. The police then rented a private plane, took pictures of the crop, and secured a conviction. Environmental Protection Agency officials took a similar aerial photo of Dow Chemical's Midland, Mich., plant and located environmental violations. Both Ciraolo and Dow sued, claiming they were the victims of unconstitutional search and seizure. Both lost, however, when their cases came before the Supreme Court. Since then, the Court has also upheld roadside checkpoints in which police randomly examine drivers for signs of intoxication.[54] The Court has, however, voided more general vehicle checkpoints.[55]

exclusionary rule

The rule that evidence, no matter how incriminating, cannot be introduced into a trial if it was not constitutionally obtained. The rule prohibits use of evidence obtained through **unreasonable search and seizure.**

Mapp v. Ohio

The 1961 Supreme Court decision ruling that the Fourth Amendment's protection against **unreasonable searches and seizures** must be extended to the states as well as to the federal government.

Ever since 1914, the Supreme Court has used an **exclusionary rule** to weigh evidence in criminal cases. This rule prevents illegally seized evidence from being introduced in court, but until 1961 the rule applied only to the federal government. The Supreme Court broadened the application in the case of a Cleveland woman named Dollree Mapp, who was under suspicion for illegal gambling activities. The police broke into her home looking for a fugitive, and while there, they searched the house and found a cache of obscene materials. Mapp was convicted of possessing them. She appealed her case to the federal courts, claiming that the exclusionary rule should be made a part of the Fourth Amendment. Since the local police had no probable cause to search for obscene materials—only for materials related to gambling—she argued, the evidence should not be used against her. In an important decision (*Mapp v. Ohio,* 1961), the Supreme Court ruled that the evidence had been seized illegally and the Court reversed Mapp's conviction. Since then, the exclusionary rule has been part of the Fourth Amendment and has been incorporated within the rights that restrict the states, as well as the federal government.

Privacy and Rights of the Accused

Critics of the exclusionary rule, including some Supreme Court justices, argue that its strict application may permit guilty persons to go free because of police care-

You Are the Judge

The Case of Ms. Montoya

Rose Elviro Montoya de Hernandez arrived at the Los Angeles International Airport on Avianca Flight 080 from Bogotá, Colombia. Her first official encounter was with U.S. Customs Inspector Talamantes, who noticed that she spoke no English. Interestingly, Montoya's passport indicated eight recent quick trips from Bogotá to Los Angeles. She had $5,000 in cash but no pocketbook or credit cards.

Talamantes and his fellow customs officers were suspicious. Stationed in Los Angeles, they were hardly unaware of the fact that Colombia was a major drug supplier. They questioned Montoya, who explained that her husband had a store in Bogotá and that she planned to spend the $5,000 at Kmart and JC Penney, stocking up on items for the store.

The inspector, somewhat wary, handed Montoya over to female customs inspectors for a search. These agents noticed what the Supreme Court later referred to delicately as a "firm fullness" in Montoya's abdomen. Suspicions, already high, increased. The agents applied for a court order to conduct pregnancy tests, X rays, and other examinations, and eventually they found 88 balloons containing 80 percent pure cocaine in Montoya's alimentary canal.

Montoya's lawyer argued that this constituted unreasonable search and seizure and that her arrest and conviction should be set aside. There was, he said, no direct evidence that would have led the officials to suspect cocaine smuggling. The government argued that the arrest had followed from a set of odd facts leading to reasonable suspicion that something was amiss.

You Be the Judge: Was Montoya's arrest based on a search-and-seizure incident that violated the Fourth Amendment?

Answer: Justice Rehnquist wrote the majority opinion, holding that U.S. Customs agents were well within their constitutional authority to search Montoya. Even though collection of evidence took the better part of two days, Justice Rehnquist remarked wryly that "the rudimentary knowledge of the human body which judges possess in common with the rest of mankind tells us that alimentary canal smuggling cannot be detected in the amount of time in which other illegal activities may be investigated through brief . . . stops."

lessness or innocent errors. The guilty, they say, should not go free because of a "technicality." Supporters of the exclusionary rule respond that the Constitution is not a technicality and that—because everyone is presumed innocent until proven guilty—defendants' rights protect the *accused*, not the guilty. You can examine one contemporary search-and-seizure case in "You Are the Judge: The Case of Ms. Montoya."

An increasingly conservative Court made some exceptions to the exclusionary rule beginning in the 1980s. The Court allowed the use of illegally obtained evidence when this evidence led police to a discovery that they eventually would have made without it.[56] The justices also decided to establish the good-faith exception to the rule; evidence could be used if the police who seized it mistakenly thought they were operating under a constitutionally valid warrant.[57] In 1995, the Court held that the exclusionary rule does not bar evidence obtained illegally as the result of clerical errors.[58] The Court even allowed evidence illegally obtained from a banker to be used to convict one of his customers.[59]

However, some decisions offer more protection against searches. An Iowa police officer stopped Patrick Knowles for speeding and issued him a citation. The officer then conducted a full search of the car, without either Knowles's consent or probable cause, found marijuana and a "pot pipe," and arrested Knowles. The Supreme Court held that the search of Knowles's car violated the Fourth Amendment. The Court said that although officers may order a driver and passengers out of a car while issuing a traffic citation and may search for weapons to protect themselves from danger, Knowles presented no threat to the officer's safety and thus provided no justification for the intrusion of a search of his car.[60] Similarly, the Supreme Court prohibited highway checkpoints designed to detect ordinary criminal wrongdoing, such as possessing illegal drugs,[61] and it ruled that an anonymous tip that a person is carrying a gun is not sufficient justification for a police officer to stop and frisk that person.[62] In addition, the Court found that police use of a thermal imaging device to detect

Why It Matters

The Exclusionary Rule
The exclusionary rule, in which courts disregard evidence obtained illegally, has been controversial. Although critics view the rule as a technicality that helps criminals to avoid justice, this rule protects defendants (who have *not* been proven guilty) from abuses of police power.

abnormal heat (needed for growing marijuana) in a home violated the Fourth Amendment.[63]

The USA Patriot Act, passed just six weeks after the September 11, 2001, terrorist attacks, gave the government broad new powers for the wiretapping, surveillance, and investigation of terrorism suspects. Attorney General John Ashcroft also eased restrictions on domestic spying in counterterrorism operations, allowing agents to monitor political or religious groups without any connection to a criminal investigation. The Patriot Act gave the federal government the power to examine a terrorist suspect's records held by a third parties such as doctors, libraries, bookstores, universities, and Internet service providers. It also allowed searches of private property without probable cause and without notice to the owner until after the search has been executed, limiting a person's opportunities to challenge a search. Such broad powers have concerned people at both ends of the political spectrum and are sure to invite Supreme Court decisions.

Self-Incrimination

Suppose that evidence has been gathered and suspicion directed toward a particular person, and the police are ready to make an arrest. In the American system, the burden of proof rests on the police and the prosecutors. Suspects cannot be forced to help with their own conviction by, say, blurting out a confession in the stationhouse. The **Fifth Amendment** forbids forced **self-incrimination,** stating that no person "shall be compelled to be a witness against himself." Whether in a congressional hearing, a courtroom, or a police station, suspects need not provide evidence that can later be used against them. Under law, though, the government may guarantee suspects *immunity*—exemption from prosecution in exchange for suspects' testimony regarding their own and others' misdeeds.

You have probably seen television shows in which an arrest is made and the arresting officers recite, often from memory, a set of rights to the arrestee. These rights are authentic and originated from a famous court decision—perhaps the most important modern decision in criminal law—involving an Arizona man named Ernesto Miranda.[64]

Miranda was picked up as a prime suspect in the rape and kidnapping of an 18-year-old girl. Identified by the girl from a police lineup, Miranda was questioned for two hours. During this time, he was told of neither his constitutional right against self-incrimination nor his right to counsel. In fact, it is unlikely that Miranda had even heard of the Fifth Amendment. He said enough to lead eventually to a conviction. The Supreme Court reversed his conviction on appeal, however. In **Miranda v. Arizona** (1966), the Court established guidelines for police questioning. Suspects must be told that:

- they have a constitutional right to remain silent and may stop answering questions at any time;
- what they say can be used against them in a court of law;
- they have a right to have a lawyer present during questioning and that the court will provide an attorney if they cannot afford their own lawyer.

Police departments throughout the country were originally disgruntled by *Miranda*. Officers felt that interrogation was crucial to any investigation. Warning suspects of their rights and letting them call a lawyer were almost certain to silence them. Most departments today, however, seem to take *Miranda* seriously and usually read a *Miranda* card advising suspects of their rights. Ironically, when Ernesto Miranda himself was murdered, the suspect was read his rights from a *Miranda* card.

In the decades since the *Miranda* decision, the Supreme Court has made a number of exceptions to its requirements. In 1991, for example, the Court held that a coerced confession introduced in a trial does not automatically taint a conviction. If

Fifth Amendment

The constitutional amendment designed to protect the rights of persons accused of crimes, including protection against double jeopardy, **self-incrimination,** and punishment without due process of law.

self-incrimination

The situation occurring when an individual accused of a crime is compelled to be a witness against himself or herself in court. The **Fifth Amendment** forbids self-incrimination.

Miranda v. Arizona

The 1966 Supreme Court decision that sets guidelines for police questioning of accused persons to protect them against **self-incrimination** and to protect their right to counsel.

You Are the Judge

The Case of the Dirty Old Man

In 1984, Keith Jacobson, a 56-year-old farmer who supported his elderly father in Nebraska, ordered two magazines and a brochure from a California adult bookstore. He expected nude photographs of adult males, but instead found photographs of nude boys. He ordered no other magazines.

Three months later the federal law was changed to make the receipt of such materials illegal. Finding his name on the mailing list of the California bookstore, two government agencies repeatedly enticed Jacobson through five fictitious organizations and a bogus pen pal with solicitations for sexually explicit photographs of children. After 26 months of enticement, Jacobson finally ordered a magazine and was arrested for violating the Child Protection Act.

He was convicted of receiving child pornography through the mail, which he undoubtedly did. Jacobson claimed, however, that he had been entrapped into committing the crime.

You Be the Judge: Was Jacobson an innocent victim of police entrapment, or was he a dirty old man seeking child pornography?

Answer: The Court agreed with Jacobson. In *Jacobson v. United States* (1992), it ruled that the government had overstepped the line between setting a trap for the "unwary innocent" and the "unwary criminal" and failed to establish that Jacobson was independently predisposed to commit the crime for which he was arrested. Jacobson's conviction was overturned.

other evidence is enough for a conviction, then the coerced confession is a "harmless error" that does not necessitate a new trial.[65] Nevertheless, in 2000 in *Dickerson v. U.S.*, the Court made it clear that it supported the *Miranda* decision and that Congress was not empowered to change it.

The Fifth Amendment prohibits not only coerced confessions but also coerced crimes. The courts have overturned convictions based on *entrapment*—when law enforcement officials encourage persons to commit crimes (such as accepting bribes or purchasing illicit drugs) that they otherwise would not commit. "You Are the Judge: The Case of the Dirty Old Man" addresses this issue.

The Right to Counsel

One of the most important of the *Miranda* rights is the right to secure counsel. Even lawyers who are taken to court hire another lawyer to represent them. (There is an old saying in the legal profession that a lawyer who defends himself has a fool for a client.) Although the **Sixth Amendment** has always ensured the right to counsel in federal courts, this right was not extended to people tried in state courts until the 1960s. Winning this right for poor defendants was a long fight. Until the 1930s, individuals were

Sixth Amendment

The constitutional amendment designed to protect individuals accused of crimes. It includes the right to counsel, the right to confront witnesses, and the right to a speedy and public trial.

THE WIZARD OF ID

Making a Difference

Clarence Gideon

Clarence Earl Gideon was a frail, poorly educated, ex-convict who was arrested for breaking into a poolroom with the intent to rob it. Too poor to hire a lawyer, he conducted his own defense and was found guilty and sentenced to five years in prison. While in prison, he filed a handwritten *pauper's petition* and sent it to the U.S. Supreme Court. Much to his surprise, the Court agreed to hear his case. In *Gideon v. Wainwright* (1963), the Court held that defendants in all felony cases had a right to counsel. Gideon was released, retried (this time with a public defender handling his case), and acquitted. More than a thousand of Gideon's fellow Florida prisoners, plus thousands more who had been convicted in other states without benefit of counsel, were also released.

Gideon v. Wainwright

The 1963 Supreme Court decision holding that anyone accused of a felony where imprisonment may be imposed, however poor he or she might be, has a right to a lawyer. See also **Sixth Amendment**.

plea bargaining

A bargain struck between the defendant's lawyer and the prosecutor to the effect that the defendant will plead guilty to a lesser crime (or fewer crimes) in exchange for the state's promise not to prosecute the defendant for a more serious (or additional) crime.

tried and sometimes convicted for capital offenses (those in which the death penalty could be imposed) without a lawyer. In 1932, the Supreme Court ordered the states to provide an attorney for indigent (poor) defendants accused of a capital crime (*Powell v. Alabama*).

Most crimes are not capital crimes, however, and most crimes are tried in state courts. It was not until 1963, in *Gideon v. Wainwright*,[66] that the Supreme Court extended the right to an attorney for everyone accused of a felony in a state court (see "Making a Difference: Clarence Gideon" for more about this case). Subsequently, the Court went a step further than *Gideon* and held that whenever imprisonment could be imposed, a lawyer must be provided for the accused (*Argersinger v. Hamlin*, 1972).

Trials

Television's portrayal of courts and trials is almost as dramatic as its portrayal of detectives and police officers—both often vary from reality. Highly publicized trials are dramatic, but rare. The murder trial of O. J. Simpson made headlines for months. Cable News Network even carried much of the pretrial and trial live. But in reality, most cases, even ones in which the evidence is solid, do not go to trial.

If you visit a typical American criminal courtroom, you will rarely see a trial complete with judge and jury. In American courts, 90 percent of all cases begin and end with a guilty plea. Most cases are settled through a process called **plea bargaining.** A plea bargain results from a bargain struck between a defendant's lawyer and a prosecutor to the effect that a defendant will plead guilty to a lesser crime (or fewer crimes) in exchange for a state not prosecuting that defendant for a more serious (or additional) crime.

Critics of the plea-bargaining system believe that it permits many criminals to avoid the full punishment they deserve. The process, however, works to the advantage of both sides; it saves the state the time and money that would otherwise be spent on a trial, and it permits defendants who think they might be convicted of a serious charge to plead guilty to a lesser one.

Whether plea bargaining serves the ends of justice is much debated. To its critics, plea bargaining benefits defendants. David Brereton and Jonathan Casper, studying sentencing patterns in three California counties, discovered that a larger proportion of defendants who went to trial (rather than plea bargained) ended up going to prison, compared with those who pleaded guilty and had no trial. In answer to their question "Does it pay to plead guilty?" these authors give a qualified yes.[67] Good or bad, plea bargaining is a practical necessity. Only a vast increase in resources devoted to the court system could cope with a trial for every defendant.

The defendants in the 300,000 cases per year that actually go to trial are entitled to many rights, including the Sixth Amendment's provision for a speedy trial by an impartial jury. These days, defendants (those who can afford it, at least) do not leave jury selection to chance. A sophisticated technology of jury selection has developed. Jury consultants—often psychologists or other social scientists—develop profiles of jurors likely to be sympathetic or hostile to a defendant. Lawyers for both sides spend hours questioning prospective jurors in a major case.

The Constitution does not specify the size of a jury; in principle, it could be anywhere from one to one hundred people. Tradition in England and America has set jury size at 12, although in petty cases 6 jurors are sometimes used. Whereas traditionally a jury had to be unanimous in order to convict, the Supreme Court eroded those traditions, permitting states to use fewer than 12 jurors and to convict with a less than unanimous vote. Federal courts still employ juries of 12 persons and require unanimous votes for a criminal conviction.

In recent years the Supreme Court has aggressively defended the jury's role in the criminal justice process—and limited the discretion of judges in sentencing. In *Apprendi v. New Jersey* (2000) and *Blakely v. Washington* (2004), the Court has held that other than a previous conviction, any fact that increases the penalty for a crime beyond the prescribed statutory maximum or even the ordinary range must be submitted to a jury and proved beyond a reasonable doubt. Both decisions ensure that the judge's authority to sentence derives wholly from the jury's verdict.

The Sixth Amendment (and the protection against the suspension of the writ of habeas corpus) also guarantees that persons who are arrested have a right to be brought before a judge. This occurs at two stages of the judicial process. First, those detained have a right to be informed of the accusations against them. Second, they have a right to a *speedy and public trial*. Normally, these guarantees present few issues. However, in the aftermath of September 11, 2001, terrorist attacks, the FBI detained more than 1,200 persons as possibly dangers to national security. Of these persons, 762 were illegal aliens (mostly Arabs and Muslims), and many of them languished in jail for months until cleared by the FBI.

For the first time in U.S. history, the federal government withheld the names of detainees, reducing their opportunities to exercise their rights for access to the courts and to counsel. The government argued that releasing the names and details of those arrested would give terrorists a window on the terror investigation. In 2004, the Supreme Court refused to consider whether the government properly withheld names and other details about these prisoners. However, in other cases the Court found that detainees held both in the United States and at the naval base at Guantánamo Bay, Cuba, had the right to challenge their detention before a judge or other neutral decision maker (*Hamdi v. Rumsfeld* and *Rasul v. Bush*, 2004).

In addition, defendants have the right to confront the witnesses against them. The Supreme Court has held that testimony cannot be introduced into a trial unless the witness can be cross-examined by the accused (*Crawford v. Washington*, 2004).

Simulation

Balancing Liberation and Security at a Time of War

Cruel and Unusual Punishment

Citizens convicted of a crime can expect punishment ranging from mild to severe, the mildest being some form of probation and the most severe, of course, being the death penalty. The **Eighth Amendment** forbids **cruel and unusual punishment,** although it does not define the phrase. Through the Fourteenth Amendment, this provision of the Bill of Rights applies to the states.

Almost the entire constitutional debate over cruel and unusual punishment has centered on the death penalty (an exception can be found in "You Are the Judge: The Case of the First Offender"). About 3,600 people are currently on death row, about a quarter of them in Florida and Texas. In 1968, the Court overturned a death sentence because opponents of the death penalty had been excluded from the jury at sentencing (*Witherspoon v. Illinois*), a factor that stacked the cards, said the Court, in favor of the extreme penalty.

The Court first confronted the question of whether the death penalty is inherently cruel and unusual punishment in *Furman v. Georgia* (1972). Although *Furman* sent a message, it was a confusing one. Four justices said that the death penalty was not cruel and unusual punishment, yet the Court overturned Georgia's death penalty law because its imposition was "freakish" and "random." Warned by *Furman*, 35 states passed new laws permitting the death penalty. Some states, to prevent arbitrariness in punishment, went to the other extreme, mandating death penalties for some crimes. In *Woodson v. North Carolina* (1976), the Supreme Court ruled against mandatory death penalties.

Eighth Amendment

The constitutional amendment that forbids **cruel and unusual punishment,** although it does not define this phrase. Through the **Fourteenth Amendment**, this **Bill of Rights** provision applies to the states.

cruel and unusual punishment

Court sentences prohibited by the **Eighth Amendment.** Although the Supreme Court has ruled that mandatory death sentences for certain offenses are unconstitutional, it has not held that the death penalty itself constitutes cruel and unusual punishment.

You Are the Judge

The Case of the First Offender

Ronald Harmelin of Detroit was convicted of possessing 672 grams of cocaine (a gram is about one-thirtieth of an ounce). Michigan's mandatory sentencing law required the trial judge to sentence Harmelin, a first-time offender, to life imprisonment without possibility of parole. Harmelin argued that this was cruel and unusual punishment because it was "significantly disproportionate," meaning that, as we might say, the punishment did not fit the crime. Harmelin's lawyers argued that many other crimes more serious than cocaine possession would net similar sentences.

You Be the Judge: Was Harmelin's sentence cruel and unusual punishment?

Answer: The Court upheld Harmelin's conviction in *Harmelin v. Michigan* (1991), spending many pages to explain that severe punishments were quite commonplace, especially when the Bill of Rights was written. Severity alone does not qualify a punishment as "cruel and unusual." The severity of punishment was up to the legislature of Michigan, which, the justices observed, knew better than they the conditions on the streets of Detroit.

Gregg v. Georgia

The 1976 Supreme Court decision that upheld the constitutionality of the death penalty, stating that "It is an extreme sanction, suitable to the most extreme of crimes." The court did not, therefore, believe that the death sentence constitutes **cruel and unusual punishment.**

McCleskey v. Kemp

The 1987 Supreme Court decision that upheld the constitutionality of the death penalty against charges that it violated the **Fourteenth Amendment** because minority defendants were more likely to receive the death penalty than were White defendants.

Race and the Death Penalty

Since then the Court has come down more clearly on the side of the death penalty. Troy Gregg had murdered two hitchhikers and was awaiting execution in Georgia's state prison. Gregg's attorney argued that the death penalty was cruel and unusual punishment. In *Gregg v. Georgia* (1976), the Court disagreed. "Capital punishment," it said, "is an expression of society's outrage at particularly offensive conduct. . . . It is an extreme sanction, suitable to the most extreme of crimes."

A divided Court rebuffed the last major challenge to the death penalty in *McCleskey v. Kemp* (1987) when it refused to rule that the penalty violated the equal protection of the law guaranteed by the Fourteenth Amendment. Although social scientists testified that minority defendants and murderers whose victims were White were disproportionately likely to receive death sentences, the Court insisted that this fact did not violate the Fourteenth Amendment because there was no evidence that juries intended to discriminate on the basis of race. Not everyone is convinced, however.[68] Shortly before retiring from the bench, Justice Harry Blackmun declared that the administration of the death penalty "fails to deliver the fair, consistent and reliable sentences of death required by the Constitution."[69]

Nevertheless, today the death penalty is a part of the American criminal justice system, and more than 900 persons have been executed since the Court's decision in *Gregg v. Georgia*. In 1989, the Court held that it is constitutionally acceptable to execute even 16- or 17-year-olds. The Court has also made it more difficult for death row prisoners to file petitions that would force legal delays and appeals to stave off their appointed executions, and it has allowed "victim impact" statements detailing the character of murder victims and their families' suffering to be used against a defendant. In 2002, however, the Court prohibited executing mentally retarded persons and required that a jury, not just a judge, find an aggravating circumstance necessary for imposition of the death penalty.

On the other hand, Governor George Ryan of Illinois energized the debate over the death penalty when he declared a moratorium on executions in his state after 13 people were released from death row upon proving their innocence. Later, he commuted the death sentences of all prisoners in the state. In addition, attorneys have employed DNA evidence in a number of states to obtain the release of dozens of other prisoners. The debate over the death penalty is likely to continue to be intense (see "Young People and Politics: College Students Help Prevent Wrongful Deaths").

Young People and Politics

College Students Help Prevent Wrongful Deaths

The Center on Wrongful Convictions at Northwestern University investigates possible wrongful convictions and represents imprisoned clients with claims of actual innocence. The young staff, including faculty, cooperating outside attorneys, and Northwestern University law students, pioneered the investigation and litigation of wrongful convictions—including the cases of nine innocent men sentenced to death in Illinois.

Undergraduates as well as law students have been involved in establishing the innocence of men who had been condemned to die. One instance involved the case of a man with an IQ of 51. The Illinois Supreme Court stayed his execution, just 48 hours before it was due to be carried out, because of questions about his mental fitness. This stay provided a professor and students from a Northwestern University investigative journalism class an opportunity to investigate the man's guilt.

They tracked down and reinterviewed witnesses. One eyewitness recanted his testimony, saying that investigators had pressured him into implicating the man. The students found a woman who pointed to her ex-husband as the killer. Then a private investigator interviewed the ex-husband, who made a videotaped statement claiming he killed in self-defense. The students literally helped to save the life of an innocent man.

On January 11, 2003, Governor George H. Ryan of Illinois chose Lincoln Hall at Northwestern University's School of Law to make an historic announcement. He commuted the death sentences of all 167 death row prisoners in Illinois (he also pardoned four others based on innocence the previous day). The governor felt it was fitting to make the announcement there before "the students, teachers, lawyers, and investigators who first shed light on the sorrowful conditions of Illinois' death penalty system."

In addition to saving the lives of wrongfully convicted individuals in Illinois, the Northwestern investigations have also helped trigger a nationwide reexamination of the capital punishment system. To learn more about the Center on Wrongful Convictions visit its website at *http://www.law.northwestern.edu/wrongfulconvictions/*.

Questions for Discussion

- Why do you think college students and others were able to determine the truth about the innocence of condemned men better than the police and prosecutors at the original trials?
- Are there other areas of public life in which students can make important contributions through their investigations?

The Right to Privacy

The members of the First Congress who drafted the Bill of Rights and enshrined American civil liberties would never have imagined that Americans would go to court to argue about wiretapping, surrogate motherhood, abortion, or pornography. New technologies have raised ethical issues unimaginable in the eighteenth century. Today, one of the greatest debates concerning Americans' civil liberties lies in the emerging area of privacy rights.

Is There a Right to Privacy?

Nowhere does the Bill of Rights say that Americans have a **right to privacy.** Clearly, however, the First Congress had the concept of privacy in mind when it crafted the first ten amendments. Freedom of religion implies the right to exercise private beliefs; protections against "unreasonable searches and seizures" make persons secure in their

right to privacy

The right to a private personal life free from the intrusion of government.

How You Can Make a Difference

Internet Privacy

You are sitting in your dorm room cruising the Internet looking for concert tickets, your roommate is online doing research on the construction of the White House, and your friend next door is in a chat room meeting new people. All of you are safe and secure in the knowledge that you have total and complete privacy online. Your college doesn't monitor the Internet sites you visit, or so you think. What you don't know is that if you are using your college's Internet system, your visits to the web aren't as private as you think.

It may come as a surprise that your college has spy software that allows them to make copies of every single online site you visit and know who visited which sites. Where is your privacy? After all, you were only looking for concert tickets or chatting in a chat room, but what if a student is searching online for how to build pipe bombs so he can plant one in your college cafeteria? With the help of spy software, the college could possibly realize that the student poses a threat to the safety of the college campus before it is too late. *Should* you have the right to online privacy and what can you do about it?

Although this debate over Internet privacy has become all the more impor-

tant and relevant in the wake of September 11, it is not new. Public Agenda (*www.publicagenda.org*), a nonpartisan organization dedicated to clearly presenting the various arguments on key political issues, is a good place to start familiarizing yourself with that debate. Do you think that nobody should be able to track your Internet activities unless a warrant is obtained (as telephone conversations are treated)? Then you'd be in favor of mandating the privacy of the Internet with no regulation of its content. Perhaps you think families and individuals should instead use filtering programs to stop pornography and other undesirable content. Or maybe you feel that giving up some of your civil liberties would be an acceptable cost in the war against terrorism. The pros and cons of these various perspectives are clearly outlined at this useful website.

By examining the advocacy groups listed under "First Amendment, Free Speech and the Internet" at *www.politics1.com*, one can see that the debate tends to polarize along lines of civil libertarians advocating firm protection of Internet privacy and those who favor curbing absolute privacy in favor of community standards and security.

Perhaps the preeminent advocacy group in favor of protecting Internet privacy is the Electronic Frontier Foundation (*www.eff.org*)—founded in 1990 at the beginning of the cyberspace era. The EFF encourages you to write your congressional representatives regarding this issue and other key legislation by providing specific form letters on these subjects. In addition, they provide practical advice to protect your anonymity and free speech on the Internet. At the other end of the spectrum, organizations such as the Family Research Council (*www.frc.org*) and Enough Is Enough (*www.enough.org*) emphasize the problems with allowing Internet activity to remain unregulated.

What you can do:
- Visit the websites listed to examine all sides of the issues.
- Get involved by making donations of time or money to those organizations you support.
- Make others aware of the technology available to protect their privacy or protect themselves from pornography and violence.

homes; private property cannot be seized without "due process of law." In 1928, Justice Brandeis hailed privacy as "the right to be left alone—the most comprehensive of the rights and the most valued by civilized men."

The idea that the Constitution guarantees a right to privacy was first enunciated in a 1965 case involving a Connecticut law forbidding the use of contraceptives. It was a little-used law, but a doctor and family planning specialist were arrested for disseminating birth control devices. The state reluctantly brought them to court, and they were convicted. The Supreme Court, in the case of *Griswold v. Connecticut*, wrestled with the privacy issue. Seven justices finally decided that various portions of the Bill of Rights cast "penumbras" (or shadows)—unstated liberties implied by the explicitly stated rights—protecting a right to privacy, including a right to family planning between husband and wife. Supporters of privacy rights argued that this ruling was reasonable enough, for what could be the purpose of the Fourth Amendment, for example, if not to protect privacy? Critics of the ruling—and there were many of them—claimed that the Supreme Court was inventing protections not specified by the Constitution.

The most important application of privacy rights, however, came not in the area of birth control but in the area of abortion. The Supreme Court unleashed a constitutional firestorm in 1973 that has not yet abated.

Controversy over Abortion

In the summer of 1972, Supreme Court Justice Harry Blackmun returned to Minnesota's famous Mayo Clinic, where he had once served as general counsel. The clinic lent him a tiny desk in the corner of a librarian's office, where he worked quietly for two weeks. His research during this short summer vacation focused on the medical aspects of abortion. Blackmun had been assigned the task of writing the majority opinion in one of the most controversial cases ever to come before the Court. The judge was chronically tardy in his opinion writing; this decision was no exception. Later, back in Washington, Blackmun finished his draft opinion and sent it to his impatient colleagues.

The opinion, in **Roe v. Wade** (1973), has been called both radical and temperate. "Jane Roe" was the pseudonym of a Texas woman, Norma McCorvey, who sought an abortion. She argued that the state law allowing the procedure only to save the life of a mother was unconstitutional. Texas argued that states had the power to regulate moral behavior, including abortions.

Blackmun's decision followed medical authorities in dividing pregnancy into three equal trimesters. *Roe* forbade any state control of abortions during the first trimester; it permitted states to allow regulated abortions, but only to protect the mother's health, in the second trimester; and it allowed the states to ban abortion during the third trimester, except when the mother's life or health was in danger. This decision unleashed a storm of protest. The Court's staff needed extra mailboxes to handle the correspondence, some of which contained death threats.[70] Eventually, states adjusted to the new decision, doctors and hospitals cooperated, and, however awkward the reasoning or controversial the result, the decision governed public policy. Since *Roe v. Wade*, about 1.5 million legal abortions have been performed annually.

Yet the furor has never subsided. Congress has passed numerous statutes forbidding the use of federal funds for abortions. Many states have passed similar restrictions. Missouri went as far as any other state, forbidding the use of state funds or state employees to perform abortions. A clinic in St. Louis challenged the law as unconstitutional, but in *Webster v. Reproductive Health Services* (1989), the Court upheld the law. It has also upheld laws requiring minors to notify one or both parents or a judge before obtaining an abortion.

In 1991, the conservative Court went even further in upholding restrictions on abortions. In *Rust v. Sullivan*, the Court found that a Department of Health and Human Services ruling—specifying that family planning services receiving federal funds could not provide women any counseling regarding abortion—was constitutional. This decision was greeted by a public outcry that the rule would deny many poor women abortion counseling and limit the First Amendment right of a medical practitioner to counsel a client. On his third day in office, President Clinton lifted the ban on abortion counseling.

In 1992, in **Planned Parenthood v. Casey**, the Court changed its standard for evaluating restrictions on abortion from one of "strict scrutiny" of any restraints on a "fundamental right" to one of "undue burden" that permits considerably more regulation. The Court upheld a 24-hour waiting period, a parental or judicial consent requirement for minors, and a requirement that doctors present women with information on the risks of the operation. The Court struck down a provision requiring a married woman to tell her husband of her intent to have an abortion. At the same time, the majority also affirmed their commitment to the basic right of a woman to obtain an abortion. In 2000, the Court held in *Sternberg v. Carhart* that Nebraska's prohibition of "partial birth" abortions was unconstitutional because it placed an undue burden on women seeking an abortion by

Roe v. Wade

The 1973 Supreme Court decision holding that a state ban on all abortions was unconstitutional. The decision forbade state control over abortions during the first trimester of pregnancy, permitted states to limit abortions to protect the mother's health in the second trimester, and permitted states to protect the fetus during the third trimester.

Planned Parenthood v. Casey

A 1992 case in which the Supreme Court loosened its standard for evaluating restrictions on abortion from one of "strict scrutiny" of any restraints on a "fundamental right" to one of "undue burden" that permits considerably more regulation.

Figure 4.1   The Abortion Debate

In few areas of public opinion research do scholars find more divided opinion than on abortion. Some people feel very strongly about the matter, enough so that they are "single-issue voters" unwilling to support any candidate who disagrees with them on abortion. Most take a middle position, one that supports the principle of abortion but that also accepts restrictions on access to abortions.

Now, on the issue of abortion: Do you think abortions should be legal under any circumstances, legal only under certain circumstances, or illegal in all circumstances?

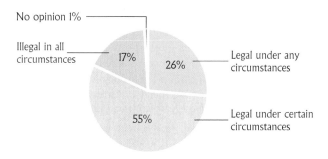

Source: Gallup Poll, October 24–26, 2003.

limiting their options to less safe procedures and because the law provided no exception for cases where the health of the mother was at risk. In 2003, Congress passed a law banning partial birth abortions. It remains to be seen whether the Court will uphold it.

Americans are deeply divided on the issue of abortion (see Figure 4.1). Proponents of choice believe that access to abortion is essential if women are to be fully autonomous human beings. Opponents call themselves pro-life because they believe that the fetus is fully human; therefore, an abortion deprives a fetus of the right to life. These positions are irreconcilable, making abortion a politician's nightmare. Wherever a politician stands on this divisive issue, a large number of voters will be enraged.

Because passions run so strongly on the issue, advocates may take extreme action. In the last decade a number of abortion clinics have been bombed. Opponents of abortion murdered two physicians who performed abortions in Pensacola, Fla.

Efforts to protect women's access to clinics sometimes clash with protesters' rights to free speech and assembly. In 1994, the Court consolidated the right to abortion established in *Roe* with the protection of a woman's right to enter an abortion clinic to exercise that right. Citing the government's interest in preserving order and maintaining women's access to pregnancy services, the Court upheld a state court's order of a 36-foot buffer zone around a clinic in Melbourne, Fla.[71] That same year Congress passed the Freedom of Access to Clinic Entrances Act, which makes it a federal crime to intimidate abortion providers or women seeking abortions. In 2000, it upheld a 100-foot restriction on approaching close to someone at a health care facility to discourage abortions.[72] In another case, the Court decided that abortion clinics could invoke the federal racketeering law to sue violent antiabortion protest groups for damages.[73]

Understanding Civil Liberties

American government is both democratic and constitutional. America is democratic because it is governed by officials who are elected by the people and, as such, are accountable for their actions. The American government is constitutional because it has a fundamental organic law, the Constitution, that limits the things government

Passions sometimes rule in the debate over abortion. Paul Hill went so far as to murder a physician who performed abortions, arguing that he had a right to do so to save the lives of the unborn. The jury did not agree, and Hill was sentenced to death.

may do. By restricting the government, the Constitution limits what the people can empower the government to do. The democratic and constitutional components of government can produce conflicts, but they also reinforce one another.

Civil Liberties and Democracy

The rights ensured by the First Amendment—the freedoms of speech, press, and assembly—are essential to a democracy. If people are to govern themselves, they need access to all available information and opinions in order to make intelligent, responsible, and accountable decisions. If the right to participate in public life is to be open to all, then Americans—in all their diversity—must have the right to express their opinions.

Individual participation and the expression of ideas are crucial components of democracy, but so is majority rule, which can conflict with individual rights. The majority does not have the freedom to decide that there are some ideas it would rather not hear, although at times, the majority tries to enforce its will upon the minority. The conflict is even sharper in relation to the rights guaranteed by the Fourth, Fifth, Sixth, Seventh, and Eighth Amendments. These rights protect all Americans, but they also make it more difficult to punish criminals. It is easy, though misleading, for the majority to view these guarantees as benefits for criminals at the expense of society.

With some notable exceptions, the United States has done a good job in protecting the rights of diverse interests to express themselves. There is little danger that a political or economic elite will muffle dissent. Similarly, the history of the past four decades is one of increased protections for defendants' rights, and defendants are typically not among the elite. Ultimately, the courts have decided what constitutional guarantees mean in practice. Although federal judges, appointed for life, are not directly accountable to popular will,[74] "elitist" courts have often protected civil liberties from the excesses of majority rule.

Civil Liberties and the Scope of Government

Civil liberties in America are both the foundation for and a reflection of our emphasis on individualism. When there is a conflict between an individual or a group attempting to express themselves or worship as they please and an effort by a government to constrain them in some fashion, the individual or group usually wins. If protecting the freedom of an individual or group to express themselves results in inconvenience or even injustice for the public officials they criticize or the populace they wish to reach, so be it. Every nation must choose where to draw the line between freedom and order. In the United States, we generally choose liberty.

Today's government is huge and commands vast, powerful technologies. Americans' Social Security numbers, credit cards, driver's licenses, and school records are all on giant computers to which the government has immediate access. It is virtually impossible to hide from the police, the FBI, the Internal Revenue Service, or any governmental agency. Because Americans can no longer avoid the attention of government, strict limitations on governmental power are essential. The Bill of Rights provides these vital limitations.

Thus, in general, civil liberties limit the scope of government. Yet substantial government efforts are often required to protect the expansion of rights that we have witnessed in this century. Those seeking abortions may need help reaching a clinic; defendants may demand that lawyers be provided them at public expense; advocates of unpopular causes may require police protection; litigants in complex lawsuits over matters of birth or death may rely on judges to resolve their conflicts. It is ironic, but true, that an expansion of freedom may require a simultaneous expansion of government.

Summary

Civil liberties are an individual's protection against the government. The Bill of Rights makes it clear that American government is a constitutional democracy in which individual rights limit government. Disputes about civil liberties are frequent because the issues involved are complex and divisive. Legislatures and courts are constantly defining in practice what the Bill of Rights guarantees in theory.

In a way, the notion that government can protect people from government is contradictory. Thomas Jefferson wrote in the Declaration of Independence that all people "are endowed by their creator with certain unalienable rights." Jefferson's next "self-evident truth" was that "to secure these rights, governments are instituted." People, said Jefferson, do not get their rights from government. Instead, rights precede government, which then gets its power to rule from the people. The Bill of Rights does not give Americans freedom of religion or the right to a fair trial; these amendments merely recognize that these rights exist. People often speak, however, as though rights are things that government gives them.

The First Amendment guarantees freedoms of religion, expression, and assembly. The Bill of Rights also contains protections that are especially important to those accused or convicted of crimes. Together, these rights provide Americans with more liberty than that enjoyed by most other people on Earth.

One task that government must perform is to resolve conflicts between rights. Often, First Amendment rights and rights at the bar of justice exist in uneasy tension; a newspaper's right to inform its readers may conflict with a person's right to a fair trial. Today, most of the rights enjoyed under the U.S. Constitution have been extended to the states.

Today's technologies raise key questions about ethics and the Constitution. Although the Constitution does not specifically mention a right to privacy, the Supreme Court found this right implied by several guarantees in the Bill of Rights. The most controversial application of privacy rights has been in abortion cases.

KEY TERMS

civil liberties
Bill of Rights
First Amendment
Fourteenth Amendment
incorporation doctrine
establishment clause
free exercise clause
prior restraint

libel
symbolic speech
commercial speech
probable cause
unreasonable searches
    and seizures
search warrant
exclusionary rule

Fifth Amendment
self-incrimination
Sixth Amendment
plea bargaining
Eighth Amendment
cruel and unusual punish-
    ment
right to privacy

KEY CASES

Barron v. Baltimore (1833)
Gitlow v. New York (1925)
Lemon v. Kurtzman (1971)
Zelman v. Simmons-Harris (2002)
Engel v. Vitale (1962)
School District of Abington Township, Pennsylvania v. Schempp (1963)
Near v. Minnesota (1931)
Schenck v. United States (1919)
Zurcher v. Stanford Daily (1978)
Roth v. United States (1957)
Miller v. California (1973)
New York Times v. Sullivan (1964)
Texas v. Johnson (1989)
Miami Herald Publishing Company v. Tornillo (1974)
Red Lion Broadcasting Company v. Federal Communications Commission (1969)
NAACP v. Alabama (1958)
Mapp v. Ohio (1961)
Miranda v. Arizona (1966)
Gideon v. Wainwright (1963)
Gregg v. Georgia (1976)
McCleskey v. Kemp (1987)
Roe v. Wade (1973)
Planned Parenthood v. Casey (1992)

INTERNET RESOURCES

www.freedomforum.org
Background information and recent news on First Amendment issues.

www.eff.org
Website concerned with protecting online civil liberties.

www.aclu.org
Homepage of the American Civil Liberties Union offering links to many other sites concerned with civil liberties.

www.firstamendmentcenter.org/rel_liberty/overview.aspx
Overview of freedom of religion in the United States.

www.law.cornell.edu/topics/criminal.html
The text of the landmark cases on criminal justice and background material.

www.law.cornell.edu/topics/first_amendment.html
The text of the landmark cases on freedom of religion, speech, press, and assembly and background material.

www.cc.org/
Christian Coalition homepage containing background information and discussion of current events.

GET CONNECTED

The Bill of Rights and the Pledge of Allegiance

The U.S. Constitution did not originally include basic civil liberties such as those found in the Bill of Rights. In fact, as the text notes, the states made inclusion of the Bill of Rights a condition for ratification of the Constitution. The United States was the first nation to guarantee these basic rights to its citizens. The First Amendment provides that, "Congress shall make no law respecting an establishment of religion, or prohibiting the free exercise thereof; . . ." In its 2003–2004 term, the United States Supreme Court was asked to decide a case, *Elk Grove v. Newdow*, in which a man challenged the inclusion of the words "under God" in the Pledge of Allegiance. The Court ultimately held that the man bringing the case, Dr. Newdow, did not have legal standing to sue, but a similar case is likely in the near future.

Search the Web

After reviewing the U.S. Bill of Rights in the Appendix, visit the Pledge of Allegiance Resource page at the Pew Forum on Religion & Public Life *http://pewforum.org/religion-schools/pledge/*. Read the summary of the case's progress through the federal judicial system, then scroll down to the list of *amicus* briefs. Click on several of the *amicus* briefs in support of the petitioner and several in support of the respondent. The briefs' arguments usually are summarized in the "Interest of Amicus" section near the beginning of each document.

Questions To Ask

- In your opinion, should people, especially children, be forced to repeat a pledge that violates their beliefs? What if the pledge violates their parents' beliefs—or one of their parent's beliefs?
- After reading several of the *amicus* briefs, why did some of the people and groups think "under God" should be removed from the Pledge?
- Why did other groups think "under God" should stay in the Pledge of Allegiance?
- Do the words "under God" in the Pledge of Allegiance violate the First Amendment? Why or why not?

Why It Matters

Any survey of the world shows that religion is a source of intense conflict, often within a single nation. The Bill of Rights guarantees American citizens certain protections from government, including against the establishment of religion. The question is how to prevent the establishment of religion without restricting the free exercise of religion. It is important, but often difficult, to draw the line properly between government neutrality toward religion on the one hand and government support of it on the other.

Get Involved

Examine some of the other religious liberty cases identified on the Pew Forum's Religion and Public Schools Issues page to compare the Pledge case with previous cases.

To see more Get Connected exercises for Chapter 4, go to www.ablongman.com/edwards.

FOR FURTHER READING

Adler, Renata. *Reckless Disregard*. New York: Knopf, 1986. The story of two monumental conflicts between free press and individual reputations.

Baker, Liva. *Miranda: The Crime, the Law, the Politics*. New York: Atheneum, 1983. An excellent book-length treatment of one of the major criminal cases of our time.

Craig, Barbara Hickson, and David M. O'Brien. *Abortion and American Politics*. Chatham, NJ: Chatham House, 1993. Provides a history of the abortion issue since 1973.

Garrow, David J. *Liberty and Sexuality*. New York: Macmillan, 1994. The most thorough treatment of the development of the law on the right to privacy and abortion.

Heymann, Philip B. *Terrorism, Freedom, and Security*. Cambridge, MA: MIT Press, 2004. Thoughtfully balances concerns for freedom with those of safety from terrorism.

Irons, Peter. *The Courage of Their Convictions: Sixteen Americans Who Fought Their Way to the Supreme Court*. New York: Penguin Books, 1990. Accounts of 16 Americans over a period of 50 years who took their cases to the Supreme Court in defense of civil liberties.

Levy, Leonard W. *The Emergence of a Free Press.* New York: Oxford University Press, 1985. A major work on the framers' intentions regarding freedom of expression.

Levy, Leonard W. *The Establishment Clause: Religion and the First Amendment.* New York: Macmillan, 1986. The author argues that it is unconstitutional for government to provide aid to any religion.

Lewis, Anthony. *Make No Law: The Sullivan Case and the First Amendment.* New York: Random House, 1991. A well-written story of the key case regarding American libel law and an excellent case study of a Supreme Court case.

Rosenblatt, Roger. *Life Itself: Abortion in the American Mind.* New York: Random House, 1992. The author seeks to reconcile the clash of absolutes in the abortion controversy with scholarly analysis and interview data.

5

Civil Rights and Public Policy

Chapter Outline

Racial Equality: Two Centuries of Struggle

Race, the Constitution, and Public Policy

Women, the Constitution, and Public Policy

Newly Active Groups Under the Civil Rights Umbrella

Affirmative Action

The New York Times **Issues of the Times**

Understanding Civil Rights and Public Policy

Summary

■ A 42-year-old seamstress named Rosa Parks was riding in the "colored" section of a Montgomery, Ala., city bus on December 1, 1955. A White man got on the bus and found that all the seats in the front, which were reserved for Whites, were taken. He moved on to the equally crowded colored section. J. F. Blake, the bus driver, then ordered all four passengers in the first row of the colored section to surrender their seats because the law prohibited Whites and African Americans from sitting next to or even across from one another.

Three of the African Americans hesitated and then complied with the driver's order. But Rosa Parks, a politically active member of the NAACP, said no. The driver threatened to have her arrested, but she refused to move. He then called the police, and a few minutes later two officers boarded the bus and arrested her.

At this moment the civil rights movement was born. There had been substantial efforts, and some important successes, to use the courts to end racial segregation, but Rosa Parks' refusal to give up her seat led to extensive mobilization of African Americans. Protestors employed a wide range of methods to end segregation, including nonviolent resistance. A new preacher in town, Martin Luther King, Jr. of Atlanta, organized a boycott of the city buses. He was jailed, his house was bombed, and his wife and infant daughter were almost killed, but neither he nor the African-American community wavered. Although they were harassed by the police and went without motor transportation by walking or even riding mules, they persisted in boycotting the buses.

It eventually took the United States Supreme Court to end the boycott. On November 13, 1956, the Court declared that Alabama's state and local laws requiring segregation on buses were illegal. On December 20, federal injunctions were served on the city and bus company officials, forcing them to follow the Supreme Court's ruling.

On December 21, 1956, Rosa Parks boarded a Montgomery city bus for the first time in over a year. She could sit wherever she liked and chose a seat near the front.

Americans have never fully come to terms with equality. Most Americans favor equality in the abstract—a politician who advocated inequality would not attract many votes—yet the concrete struggle for equal rights under the Constitution has been our nation's most bitter battle. It pits person against person, as in the case of Rosa Parks and the nameless White passenger, and group against group.

Those people who enjoy privileged positions in American society have been reluctant to give them up.

Individual liberty is central to democracy. So is a broad notion of equality, such as that implied by the concept of "one person, one vote." Sometimes these values conflict, as when individuals or a majority of the people want to act in a discriminatory fashion. How should we resolve such conflicts between liberty and equality? Can we have a democracy if some citizens do not enjoy basic rights to political participation or suffer discrimination in employment? Can we or should we try to remedy past discrimination against minorities and women?

In addition, many people have called on government to protect the rights of minorities and women, increasing the scope and power of government in the process. Ironically, this increase in government power is often used to *check* government, as when the federal courts restrict the actions of state legislatures. It is equally ironic that society's collective efforts to use government to protect civil rights are designed not to limit individualism but to enhance it, freeing people from suffering and from prejudice. But how far should government go in these efforts? Is an increase in the scope of government to protect some people's rights an unacceptable threat to the rights of yet other citizens?

139

civil rights

Policies designed to protect people against arbitrary or discriminatory treatment by government officials or individuals.

The phrase "all men are created equal" is at the heart of American political culture; yet implementing this principle has proved to be one of our nation's most enduring struggles. Throughout our history, issues involving African Americans, women, and other minorities have raised constitutional questions about slavery, segregation, equal pay, and a host of other issues. Their rallying cry has been **civil rights,** which are policies designed to protect people against arbitrary or discriminatory treatment by government officials or individuals.

The resulting controversies have been fought in the courts, Congress, and the bureaucracy, but the meaning of *equality* remains as elusive as it is divisive. Today's equality debates center on these key types of inequality in America:

- *Racial discrimination.* Two centuries of discrimination against racial minorities have produced historic Supreme Court and congressional policies that seek to eliminate racial discrimination from the constitutional fabric. Issues such as the appropriate role of affirmative action programs have yet to be resolved, however.
- *Gender discrimination.* The role of women in American society has changed substantially since the 1700s. However, equal rights for women have yet to be constitutionally guaranteed. The Equal Rights Amendment was not ratified, and women continue to press for equality and to seek protection from sexual harassment.
- *Discrimination based on age, disability, sexual orientation, and other factors.* As America is "graying," older Americans are demanding a place under the civil rights umbrella. People with disabilities are among the newest claimants for civil rights. Also seeking constitutional protections against discrimination are groups such as gays and lesbians, people with AIDS, and the homeless.

Racial Equality: Two Centuries of Struggle

The struggle for equality has been a persistent theme in our nation's history. Slaves sought freedom, free African Americans fought for the right to vote and to be treated as equals, women pursued equal participation in society, and the economically disadvantaged called for better treatment and economic opportunities. This fight for equality affects all Americans. Philosophically, the struggle involves defining the term *equality.* Constitutionally, it involves interpreting laws. Politically, it often involves power.

Conceptions of Equality

What does *equality* mean? Jefferson's statement in the Declaration of Independence that "all men are created equal" did not mean that he believed everybody was exactly alike or that there were no differences among human beings. Jefferson insisted throughout his long life that African Americans were genetically inferior to Whites. The Declaration went on to speak, however, of "inalienable rights" to which all were equally entitled. A belief in *equal rights* has often led to a belief in *equality of opportunity;* in other words, everyone should have the same chance. What individuals make of that equal chance depends on their abilities and efforts.

American society does not emphasize *equal results* or *equal rewards;* few Americans argue that everyone should earn the same salary or have the same amount of property. In some other countries, such as the Scandinavian nations, for example, the government uses its taxing power to distribute resources much more equally than in the United States. These countries thus have much less poverty. On the other hand, critics of these more egalitarian countries often complain that emphasis on the equal distribution of resources stifles initiative and limits opportunity.

Early American Views of Equality

More than 200 years ago, Virginia lawyer Richard Bland proclaimed, "I am speaking of the rights of a people, rights imply equality." Bland's interpretation of the meaning of the American Revolution was not widely shared. Few colonists were eager to defend slavery, and the delegates to the Constitutional Convention did their best to avoid facing the tension between slavery and the principles of the Declaration of Independence. Women's rights got even less attention than slavery at the Convention. John Adams, for instance, was uncharacteristically hostile to his wife Abigail's feminist opinions. Abigail's claim that "if particular care and attention is not paid to the ladies, we are determined to foment a rebellion" prompted her husband to reply, "I cannot but laugh."[1]

Statements like Bland's were ahead of their times in America but were not unheard of elsewhere. The aspirations of people on this side of the Atlantic were similar to those of people on the other side, such as the French, who were soon to start their own revolution with cries of "liberty, equality, fraternity." Whereas in the French Revolution the king lost his head in the name of equality, in the American Revolution the king lost his colonies in the name of independence.

The Constitution and Inequality

Perhaps the presence of conflicting views of equality in eighteenth-century America explains why the word *equality* does not appear in the original Constitution. In addition, America in 1787 was a place far different from contemporary America, with far different values. The privileged delegates to the Constitutional Convention would have been baffled, if not appalled, at discussions of equal rights for 12-year-old children, deaf students, gay soldiers, or female road dispatchers. The delegates created a plan for government, not guarantees of individual rights.

Not even the Bill of Rights mentions equality. It does, however, have implications for equality in that it does not limit the scope of its guarantees to specified groups within society. It does not say, for example, that only Whites have freedom from compulsory self-incrimination or that only men are entitled to freedom of speech. The First Amendment guarantees of freedom of expression, in particular, are important because they allow those who are discriminated against to work toward achieving equality. This kind of political activism, for instance, led to the constitutional amendment that enacted a guarantee of equality, the Fourteenth Amendment.

The first and only place in which the idea of equality appears in the Constitution is in the **Fourteenth Amendment,** one of the three amendments passed after the Civil War. (The Thirteenth abolishes slavery, and the Fifteenth extends the right to vote to African Americans.) The Fourteenth Amendment forbids the states from denying to anyone "equal protection of the laws." Those five words represent the only reference to the idea of equality in the entire Constitution, yet within them was enough force to begin ensuring equal rights for all Americans. The full force of the amendment was not felt for nearly 100 years, for it was not until the mid-twentieth century that the Fourteenth Amendment was used as an instrument for unshackling disadvantaged groups. Once dismissed as "the traditional last resort of constitutional arguments," the equal protection clause now has few rivals in generating legal business for the Supreme Court.

But what does **equal protection of the laws** mean? The Fourteenth Amendment does not say that "the states must treat everybody exactly alike" or that "every state must promote equality among all its people." Presumably, it means, as one member of Congress said during the debate on the amendment, "equal protection of life, liberty, and property" for all. Thus, a state cannot confiscate an African American's property under the law while letting Whites keep theirs, or otherwise give Whites privileges

Fourteenth Amendment

The constitutional amendment adopted after the Civil War that states, "No State shall make or enforce any law which shall abridge the privileges or immunities of citizens of the United States; nor shall any state deprive any person of life, liberty, or property, without due process of law; nor deny to any person within its jurisdiction the **equal protection of the laws.**" See also **due process clause.**

equal protection of the laws

Part of the **Fourteenth Amendment** emphasizing that the laws must provide equivalent "protection" to all people.

The African-American struggle for equality paved the way for civil rights movements by women and other minorities. Here, civil rights leaders Roy Wilkins, James Farmer, Martin Luther King, Jr., and Whitney Young meet with President Lyndon B. Johnson.

The Struggle for Equal Protection

denied to African Americans. Some members of Congress interpreted the clause to be a much more lavish protection of rights than this interpretation. But shortly after the amendment was ratified in 1868, the narrow interpretation won out in the courts. In *Strauder v. West Virginia* (1880), the Supreme Court invalidated a law barring African Americans from jury service, but the Court refused to extend the amendment to remedy more subtle kinds of discrimination.

Over the last 100 years, however, the equal protection clause has become the vehicle for more expansive constitutional interpretations. In order to determine whether a particular form of discrimination is permissible, the Supreme Court developed three levels of scrutiny, or analysis, called standards of review (see Table 5.1). The Court has ruled that most classifications that are *reasonable*—that bear a rational relationship to some legitimate governmental purpose—are constitutional. The person who challenges these classifications has the burden of proving that they are arbitrary. Thus, for example, the states can restrict the right to vote to people over the age of 18; age is a reasonable classification and hence a permissible basis for determining who may vote. A classification that is arbitrary—a law singling out, say, people with red hair or blue eyes for inferior treatment—is invalid.

The Court has also ruled that racial and ethnic classifications are *inherently suspect*. These classifications are presumed to be invalid and are upheld only if they serve a "compelling public interest" and there is no other way to accomplish the purpose of the law. In this case, the burden of proof is on the state. Classifications by race and ethnicity, such as for college admissions, may be acceptable if they are made in laws seeking to remedy previous discrimination. However, as we will see in our discussion of affirmative action, the future of such laws is in doubt.

Classifications based on gender fit *somewhere between* these two extremes; they are presumed neither to be constitutional nor to be unconstitutional. A law that discriminates on the basis of gender must bear a substantial relationship to an important legislative purpose. If these three levels of judicial scrutiny (reasonable, inherently suspect, and somewhere in between) appear confusing, indeed they are—even judges and legal scholars struggle to interpret these standards.

Today the equal protection clause is interpreted broadly enough to forbid racial segregation in public schools, prohibit job discrimination, reapportion state legisla-

Table 5.1   Supreme Court's Standards for Classifications Under the Equal Protection Clause of the Fourteenth Amendment

BASIS OF CLASSIFICATION	STANDARD OF REVIEW	APPLYING THE TEST
Race	Inherently suspect (difficult to meet)	Is the classification necessary to accomplish a compelling governmental purpose and the least restrictive way to reach the goal?
Gender	Intermediate standard (moderately difficult to meet)	Does the classification bear a substantial relationship to an important governmental goal?
Other (age, wealth, etc.)	Reasonableness (easy to meet)	Does the classification have a rational relationship to a legitimate governmental goal?

tures, and permit court-ordered busing and affirmative action. Conditions for women and minorities would be radically different if it were not for the "equal protection" clause.[2] The next three sections show how equal protection litigation has worked to the advantage of minorities, women, and other groups seeking protection under the civil rights umbrella.

Race, the Constitution, and Public Policy

Throughout American history, African Americans have been the most visible minority group in the United States. These individuals have blazed the constitutional trail for securing equal rights for all Americans. Three eras delineate African Americans' struggle for equality in America: (1) the era of slavery, from the beginnings of colonization until the end of the Civil War in 1865, (2) the era of reconstruction and resegregation, from roughly the end of the Civil War until 1953, and (3) the era of civil rights, roughly from 1954 to the present.

The Era of Slavery

The first African immigrants to America were kidnapped. Most African Americans lived in slavery for the first 250 years of American settlement. Slaves were the property of their masters. They could be bought and sold, and they could neither vote nor own property. The Southern states, whose plantations required large numbers of unpaid workers, were the primary market for slave labor.

During the slavery era, any public policy of the slave states or the federal government had to accommodate the property interests of slave owners, who were often wealthy and enjoyed substantial political influence. The Supreme Court got into the act, too, along with the legislative and executive branches (see Table 5.2). The boldest decision supporting slavery was **Scott v. Sandford** (1857), wherein Chief Justice Taney bluntly announced that a Black man, slave or free, was "chattel" and had no rights under a White man's government and that Congress had no power to ban slavery in the Western territories. This decision invalidated the hard-won Missouri Compromise, which allowed Missouri to become a slave state on the condition that Northern territories would remain free of slavery. As a result, the *Scott* decision was an important milestone on the road to the Civil War.

The Union victory in the Civil War and the ratification of the **Thirteenth Amendment** ended slavery. The promises implicit in this amendment and the other two Civil War amendments introduced the era of reconstruction and resegregation in which these promises were first honored and then broken.

Scott v. Sandford

The 1857 Supreme Court decision ruling that a slave who had escaped to a free state enjoyed no rights as a citizen and that Congress had no authority to ban slavery in the territories.

Thirteenth Amendment

The constitutional amendment ratified after the Civil War that forbade slavery and involuntary servitude.

Table 5.2   Toward Racial Equality: Milestones in the Era of Slavery

1600–1865
Slavery takes hold in the South, comes to characterize almost all relations between African Americans and Whites, is constitutionally justified, and finally abolished.

1619   Slaves from Africa are brought to Jamestown and sold to planters.

1776   The Continental Army enlists African Americans to fight the British after the British offer freedom to slaves who would fight on their side.

1787   The Constitution provides for a slave to be counted as three-fifths of a person in representation and taxation, and permits Congress to forbid the importation of new slaves after 1808.

1808   Congress prohibits importation of slaves.

1857   The *Scott v. Sandford* decision holds that slaves may not gain freedom by escaping to a free state or territory; it upholds the constitutionality of the slave system.

1862   President Lincoln issues the Emancipation Proclamation.

1865   The Thirteenth Amendment abolishes slavery and involuntary servitude.

The Era of Reconstruction and Resegregation

After the Civil War ended, Congress imposed strict conditions on the former confederate states before they could be readmitted to the Union. No one who had served in secessionist state governments or in the Confederate Army could hold state office, the legislatures had to ratify the new amendments, and the military would govern the states like "conquered provinces" until they complied with the tough federal plans for reconstruction. Many African-American men held state and federal offices during the ten years following the war. Some government agencies, such as the Freedmen's Bureau, provided assistance to former slaves who were making the difficult transition to independence.

To ensure his election in 1876, Rutherford Hayes promised to pull the troops out of the South and let the old slave states resume business as usual. This done, Southerners lost little time reclaiming power and imposing a code of *Jim Crow laws*, or segregational laws, on African Americans. ("Jim Crow" was the name of a stereotypical African American in a nineteenth-century minstrel song.) These laws relegated African Americans to separate public facilities, separate school systems, and even separate restrooms. Most Whites lost interest in helping former slaves. And what the Jim Crow laws mandated in the South was also common practice in the North. In this era, racial segregation affected every part of life, from the cradle to the grave. African Americans were delivered by African-American physicians or midwives and buried in African-American cemeteries. Groups such as the Ku Klux Klan terrorized African Americans who violated the norms of segregation, lynching hundreds of them during this era.

Plessy v. Ferguson

An 1896 Supreme Court decision that provided a constitutional justification for segregation by ruling that a Louisiana law requiring "equal but separate accommodations for the White and colored races" was constitutional.

The Supreme Court provided a constitutional justification for segregation in the 1896 case of **Plessy v. Ferguson.** The Louisiana legislature required "equal but separate accommodations for the White and colored races" in railroad transportation. Although Homer Plessy was seven-eighths White, he had been arrested for refusing to leave a railway car reserved for Whites. The Court upheld the law, saying that segregation in public facilities was not unconstitutional as long as the separate facilities were substantially equal. In subsequent decisions, the Court paid more attention to the "separate" than to the "equal" part of this principle. For example, Southern states were allowed to maintain high schools and professional schools for Whites even when there were no such schools for African Americans. A measure of segregation in both the South and the North existed as late as the 1960s; nearly all the African-American physicians in the United States were graduates of two medical schools, Howard University in Washington, D.C. and Meharry Medical College in Tennessee.

Nevertheless, some progress on the long road to racial equality was made in the first half of the twentieth century. The Supreme Court and the president began to prohibit a few of the most egregious practices of segregation (see Table 5.3), paving the way for a new era of civil rights.

The Era of Civil Rights

After searching carefully for the perfect case to challenge legal school segregation, the Legal Defense Fund of the National Association for the Advancement of Colored People (NAACP) selected the case of Linda Brown. Brown was an African-American student in Topeka, Kans., required by Kansas law to attend a segregated school. In Topeka, the visible signs of education—teacher quality, facilities, and so on—were equal between African-American and White schools. Thus, the NAACP chose the case in order to test the *Plessy v. Ferguson* doctrine of "separate but equal." The Court would be forced to rule directly on whether school segregation was inherently unequal and thereby violated the Fourteenth Amendment's requirement that states guarantee "equal protection of the laws."

President Eisenhower had just appointed Chief Justice Earl Warren. So important was the case that the Court had already heard one round of arguments before Warren joined the Court. The justices, after hearing the oral arguments, met in the Supreme Court's conference room. Believing that a unanimous decision would have the most impact, the justices negotiated a broad agreement and then determined that Warren himself should write the opinion.

In ***Brown v. Board of Education*** (1954), the Supreme Court set aside its precedent in *Plessy* and held that school segregation was inherently unconstitutional because it violated the Fourteenth Amendment's guarantee of equal protection. Legal segregation had come to an end.

A year after its decision in *Brown*, the Court ordered lower courts to proceed with "all deliberate speed" to desegregate public schools. Desegregation began, and proceeded slowly in the South, however. A few counties threatened to close their public

Brown v. Board of Education

The 1954 Supreme Court decision holding that school segregation in Topeka, Kans., was inherently unconstitutional because it violated the **Fourteenth Amendment's** guarantee of **equal protection.** This case marked the end of legal segregation in the United States.

Table 5.3   Toward Racial Equality: Milestones in the Era of Reconstruction and Resegregation

1866–1953
Segregation is legally required in the South and sanctioned in the North; lynchings of African Americans occur in the South; civil rights policy begins to appear.

1868   The Fourteenth Amendment makes African Americans U.S. citizens and guarantees "equal protection of the law." This guarantee is widely ignored for nearly a century.

1870   The Fifteenth Amendment forbids racial discrimination in voting, although many states find ways to prevent or discourage African Americans from voting.

1877   End of Reconstruction. African-American gains made in the South (such as antidiscrimination laws) are reversed as former Confederates return to power. Jim Crow laws flourish, making segregation legal.

1883   In the *Civil Rights Cases* the Supreme Court rules that the Fourteenth Amendment does not prohibit discrimination by private businesses and individuals.

1896   The *Plessy v. Ferguson* decision permits "separate but equal" public facilities, providing a constitutional justification for segregation.

1909   The National Association for the Advancement of Colored People (NAACP) is founded by African Americans and Whites.

1915   *Guinn v. United States* bans the grandfather clause that had been used to prevent African Americans from voting.

1941   Executive order forbids racial discrimination in defense industries.

1944   The *Smith v. Allwright* decision bans all-White primaries.

1948   President Truman orders the armed forces desegregated.

1950   *Sweatt v. Painter* finds the "separate but equal" formula generally unacceptable in professional schools.

On September 25, 1957, troops of the 101st Airborne Division escorted nine African-American students to Central High School in Little Rock, Ark. A court had ordered the school's desegregation in response to *Brown v. Board of Education,* but Arkansas Governor Orval Faubus fought the ruling. President Eisenhower used the National Guard to provide continuing protection for the students.

Why It Matters

Brown v. Board of Education
In *Brown v. Board of Education,* the Supreme Court overturned its decision in *Plessy v. Ferguson.* This decision was a major step in changing the face of America. Just imagine what the United States would be like today if we still had segregated public facilities and services like universities and restaurants.

schools; enrollment in private schools by Whites soared. In 1957, President Eisenhower had to send troops to desegregate Central High School in Little Rock, Ark. In 1969, 15 years after its first ruling that school segregation was unconstitutional and in the face of continued massive resistance, the Supreme Court withdrew its earlier grant of time to school authorities and declared that "Delays in desegregating school systems are no longer tolerable" (*Alexander v. Holmes County Board of Education*). In 1964, under the Civil Rights Act, Congress prohibited federal aid to schools that remained segregated. Thus, after nearly a generation of modest progress, Southern schools were suddenly integrated (see Figure 5.1).

The Court found that if schools were legally segregated before, authorities had an obligation to overcome past discrimination. This could include the distribution of students and pupils on a racial basis. Some federal judges ordered the busing of students to achieve racially balanced schools, a practice upheld (but not required) by the Supreme Court in *Swann v. Charlotte-Mecklenberg County Schools* (1971).

Not all racial segregation is what is called *de jure* ("by law") segregation. *De facto* ("in reality") segregation results, for example, when children are assigned to schools near their homes, and those homes are in neighborhoods that are racially segregated for social and economic reasons. Sometimes the distinction between *de jure* and *de facto* segregation has been blurred by past official practices. Because minority groups and federal lawyers demonstrated that Northern schools, too, had purposely drawn district lines to promote segregation, school busing came to the North as well. Denver, Boston, and other cities instituted busing for racial balance, just as Southern cities did.

Busing, one of the least popular remedies for discrimination, has been opposed by majorities of both Whites and African Americans. In recent years, it has become less prominent as a judicial instrument.

Courts do not have the power to order busing between school districts; thus, school districts that are largely composed of minorities must rely on other means to integrate. Kansas City, Mo., spent years and $1.5 billion under federal court orders to attract White students from the city's suburbs, but with limited success. In 1995, in

Figure 5.1   Percentage of Black Students Attending School With Any Whites in Southern States[a]

Despite the Supreme Court's decision in *Brown v. Board of Education* in 1954, school integration proceeded at a snail's pace in the South for a decade. Most Southern African-American children entering the first grade in 1955 never attended school with White children. Things picked up considerably in the late 1960s, however, when the Supreme Court insisted that obstruction of implementation of its decision in *Brown* must come to an end.

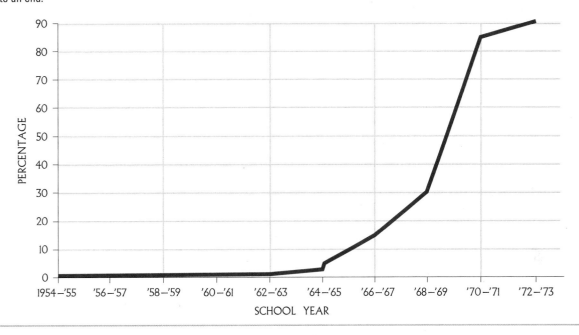

[a]Elementary and secondary students in 11 Southern states, including: Virginia, North Carolina, South Carolina, Georgia, Alabama, Mississippi, Louisiana, Texas, Arkansas, Tennessee, and Florida.

Source: Lawrence Baum, *The Supreme Court,* 8th ed. (Washington, D.C.: Congressional Quarterly, 2004), 199.

Missouri v. Jenkins, the Supreme Court indicated that it would not look favorably on continued federal control of the district.

The civil rights movement organized both African Americans and Whites to end the policies and practices of segregation. As we learned earlier, the movement began in 1955 when Rosa Parks, an African-American woman, refused to give up her seat in a Montgomery, Ala., bus to a White man. This incident prompted a bus boycott led by a local minister, Martin Luther King, Jr., who became the best known civil rights activist.

Sit-ins, marches, and civil disobedience were key strategies of the civil rights movement, which sought to establish equal opportunities in the political and economic sectors and to end policies that put up barriers between people because of race (see "Young People and Politics: Freedom Riders"). The movement's trail was long and sometimes bloody. Its nonviolent marchers were attacked by police dogs in Birmingham, Ala. Other activists were murdered in Meridian, Miss., and Selma, Ala. Fortunately, the goals of the civil rights movement appealed to the national conscience. By the 1970s, overwhelming majorities of White Americans supported racial integration.[3] Today, the principles established in *Brown* have near-universal support.

It was the courts, as much as the national conscience, that put civil rights goals on the nation's policy agenda. *Brown v. Board of Education* was only the beginning of a string of Supreme Court decisions holding various forms of discrimination unconstitutional. *Brown* and these other cases gave the civil rights movement momentum that would grow in the years that followed (see Table 5.4).

As a result of national conscience, the courts, the civil rights movement, and the increased importance of African-American voters, the 1950s and 1960s saw a marked increase in public policies seeking to foster racial equality. These innovations included

Young People and Politics

Freedom Riders

Most political activity is quite safe. There have been occasions, however, when young adults have risked bodily harm and even death to fight for their beliefs. Years after *Brown v. Board of Education (1954)*, segregated transportation continued in some parts of the Deep South. To change this system, the Congress of Racial Equality (CORE) organized Freedom Rides in 1961. Young Black and White volunteers in their teens and early twenties traveled on buses through the Deep South. In Anniston, Ala., one bus was destroyed and riders on another were attacked by men armed with clubs, bricks, iron pipes, and knives. In Birmingham, the passengers were greeted by members of the Ku Klux Klan with further acts of violence. At Montgomery, the state capital, a White mob beat the riders with chains and ax handles.

The Ku Klux Klan hoped that this violent treatment would stop other young people from taking part in freedom rides. It did not. Over the next six months, more than a thousand people took part in freedom rides. A young White man from Madison, Wis., James Zwerg, was badly injured by a mob and left in the road for over an hour. White-run ambulances refused to take him to the hospital. In an interview afterward, he reflected the grim determination of the freedom riders: "Segregation must be stopped. It must be broken down. Those of us on the Freedom Ride will continue. No matter what happens we are dedicated to this. We will take the beatings. We are willing to accept death."

As with the Montgomery Bus Boycott and the conflict at Little Rock, the freedom riders gave worldwide publicity to the racial discrimination suffered by African Americans, and in doing so, helped to bring about change. Attorney General Robert Kennedy petitioned the Interstate Commerce Commission (ICC) to draft regulations to end racial segregation in bus terminals. The ICC was reluctant, but in September 1961 it issued the necessary orders.

The freedom riders did not limit themselves to desegregating buses. During the summer of 1961, they also sat together in segregated restaurants, lunch counters, and hotels. Typically they were refused service, and they were often threatened and sometimes attacked. The sit-in tactic was especially effective when it focused on large companies, who feared boycotts in the North, and who began to desegregate their businesses.

In the end, the courage of young people committed to racial equality prevailed. They helped to change the face of America.

Questions for Discussion
- What are young adults doing to fight racism today?
- Does civil disobedience have a role in contemporary America?

Civil Rights Act of 1964

The law that made racial discrimination against any group in hotels, motels, and restaurants illegal and forbade many forms of job discrimination.

---

policies to promote voting rights, access to public accommodations, open housing, and nondiscrimination in many other areas of social and economic life. The **Civil Rights Act of 1964**:

- made racial discrimination illegal in hotels, motels, restaurants, and other places of public accommodation
- forbade discrimination in employment on the basis of race, color, national origin, religion, or gender[4]
- created the Equal Employment Opportunity Commission (EEOC) to monitor and enforce protections against job discrimination
- provided for withholding federal grants from state and local governments and other institutions that practiced racial discrimination
- strengthened voting rights legislation
- authorized the U.S. Justice Department to initiate lawsuits to desegregate public schools and facilities

The Voting Rights Act of 1965 (discussed next) was the most extensive federal effort to crack century-old barriers to African-American voting in the South. The *Open Housing Act of 1968* took steps to forbid discrimination in the sale or rental of housing.

Table 5.4   Toward Racial Equality: Milestones in the Era of Civil Rights

1954–2005
Integration becomes a widely accepted goal; the civil rights movement grows, followed by urban racial disorders in the 1960s; African-American voting increases; attention shifts to equal results and affirmative action.

1954   *Brown v. Board of Education* holds that segregated schools are inherently unequal and violate the Fourteenth Amendment's equal protection clause.
1955   Martin Luther King, Jr. leads a bus boycott in Montgomery, Ala.
1957   Federal troops enforce desegregation of a Little Rock, Ark., high school.
1963   Civil rights demonstrators numbering 250,000 march on Washington, D.C. Martin Luther King, Jr. delivers "I have a dream . . ." speech.
1964   The Civil Rights Act forbids discrimination in public accommodations and employment.
        The Twenty-fourth Amendment ends the poll tax in federal elections.
1965   The Voting Rights Act sends federal registrars to Southern states and counties to protect African Americans' right to vote and gives registrars the power to impound ballots in order to enforce the act. Executive order requires companies with federal contracts to take affirmative action to ensure equal opportunity. Riots occur in Watts, Calif., and other cities and reappear every summer in various cities for the next five years.
1966   *Harper v. Virginia* holds that the Fourteenth Amendment forbids making payment of a tax a condition of voting in any election.
1967   Cleveland becomes the first major city to elect an African-American mayor (Carl Stokes).
1968   The *Jones v. Mayer* decision and the Civil Rights Act of 1968 make all racial discrimination in the sale or rental of housing illegal. Martin Luther King, Jr. is assassinated.
1971   The *Swann v. Charlotte-Mecklenberg County Schools* decision approves busing as a means of combating state-enforced segregation.
1978   *California Board of Regents v. Bakke* forbids rigid racial quotas for medical school admissions but does not forbid considering race as a factor when deciding admissions.
1979   *United Steelworkers of America v. Weber* permits an affirmative action program to favor African Americans if the program is designed to remedy past discrimination.
        Dayton Board of Education v. Brinkman upholds school busing to remedy Northern school segregation.
1984   Jesse Jackson becomes the first African-American candidate for president to receive substantial support in the primaries.
        Grove City College v. Bell forbids the federal government from withholding all federal funds from a college that refuses to file forms saying that it does not discriminate. (Only a specific program risked its federal funds.)
1988   Congress rewrites the Civil Rights Act to "overturn" the implications of *Grove City College*.
1991   After three years of conflict, Congress enacts the Civil Rights and Women's Equity in Employment Act, which counters the effects of several Supreme Court decisions making it more difficult for workers to bring and win job discrimination suits.
1995   *Adarand Constructors v. Pena* holds that affirmative action programs must undergo strict scrutiny to determine that they are narrowly tailored to serve a compelling governmental interest.
2003   *Grutter v. Bollinger* approves use of race as one factor in college admissions.

So many congressional and judicial policies were instituted after 1954 that virtually every type of segregation was attacked by a legislative or judicial policy. By the 1980s, few, if any, forms of racial discrimination were left to legislate against. Efforts for legislation were successful, in part, because by the mid-1960s federal laws effectively protected the right to vote, in fact as well as on paper. Members of minority groups thus had some power to hold their legislators accountable.

Getting and Using the Right to Vote

When the Constitution was written, no one thought about extending the right to vote to African Americans (most of whom were slaves) or to women. The early Republic limited **suffrage,** the legal right to vote, to a handful of the population—mostly property-holding White males. Only after the Civil War was the right to vote extended, slowly and painfully, to African-American males and then to other minority groups.

suffrage

The legal right to vote, extended to African Americans by the **Fifteenth Amendment,** to women by the **Nineteenth Amendment,** and to people over the age of 18 by the **Twenty-sixth Amendment.**

Fifteenth Amendment

The constitutional amendment adopted in 1870 to extend **suffrage** to African Americans.

poll taxes

Small taxes levied on the right to vote that often fell due at a time of year when poor African-American sharecroppers had the least cash on hand. This method was used by most Southern states to exclude African Americans from voting. Poll taxes were declared void by the **Twenty-fourth Amendment** in 1964.

White primary

One of the means used to discourage African-American voting that permitted political parties in the heavily Democratic South to exclude African Americans from primary elections, thus depriving them of a voice in the real contests. The Supreme Court declared White primaries unconstitutional in 1944.

Twenty-fourth Amendment

The constitutional amendment passed in 1964 that declared **poll taxes** void in federal elections.

Voting Rights Act of 1965

A law designed to help end formal and informal barriers to African-American **suffrage**. Under the law, hundreds of thousands of African Americans were registered and the number of African-American elected officials increased dramatically.

The **Fifteenth Amendment,** adopted in 1870, guaranteed African Americans the right to vote—at least in principle. It said, "The right of citizens to vote shall not be abridged by the United States or by any state on account of race, color, or previous condition of servitude." The gap between these words and their implementation, however, remained wide for a full century. States seemed to outdo one another in developing ingenious methods of circumventing the Fifteenth Amendment.

Many states required potential voters to complete literacy tests before registering to vote. These tests typically required prospective voters to read, write, and understand their state constitution or the U.S. Constitution. In practice, however, the literacy test was rarely administered to Whites, yet the standard of literacy required of Blacks was so high that few were ever able to pass the test. In addition, Oklahoma and other Southern states used a *grandfather clause* that exempted persons whose grandfathers were eligible to vote in 1860 from taking these tests. This exemption did not apply, of course, to the grandchildren of slaves, but did allow illiterate Whites to vote. The law was blatantly unfair; it was also unconstitutional, said the Supreme Court in the 1915 decision *Guinn v. United States.*

To exclude African Americans from registering to vote, most Southern states also relied on **poll taxes,** which were small taxes levied on the right to vote that often fell due at a time of year when poor sharecroppers had the least cash on hand. To render African-American votes ineffective, most Southern states also used the **White primary,** a device that permitted political parties in the heavily Democratic South to exclude African Americans from voting in primary elections, thus depriving them of a voice in the most important contests and letting them vote only when it mattered least. The Supreme Court declared White primaries unconstitutional in 1944 in *Smith v. Allwright.*

The civil rights movement put suffrage high on its political agenda; one by one, the barriers to African-American voting fell during the 1960s. Poll taxes in federal elections were prohibited by the **Twenty-fourth Amendment,** which was ratified in 1964. Two years later, the Supreme Court voided poll taxes in state elections in *Harper v. Virginia State Board of Elections.*

Many areas in the South employed fraudulent or sham voter registration tests—requiring literacy or an understanding of the Constitution, for example—in a discriminatory fashion. Voting registrars would declare literate African Americans to be illiterate and thus ineligible to register to vote, while allowing illiterate Whites to register. The **Voting Rights Act of 1965** prohibited any government from using voting procedures that denied a person the vote on the basis of race or color and abolished the use of literacy requirements for anyone who had completed the sixth grade. Federal election registrars were sent to areas with long histories of discrimination, and these same areas had to submit all proposed changes in their voting laws or practices to a federal official for approval. As a result of these provisions, hundreds of thousands of African Americans registered to vote in Southern states.

The effects of these efforts were swift and certain, as the civil rights movement turned from protest to politics.[5] When the Voting Rights Act passed in 1965, only 70 African Americans held public office in the 11 Southern states. By the early 1980s, more than 2,500 African Americans held elected offices in those states, and the number has continued to grow. There are currently more than 9,000 African-American elected officials in the United States.[6]

The Voting Rights Act of 1965 not only secured the right to vote for African Americans but also ensured that their votes would not be diluted through racial gerrymandering (drawing district boundaries to advantage a specific group). For example, White-majority districts frequently elected members of a city council in at-large seats (in which council members were elected from the entire city) and prevented a geographically concentrated minority from electing a minority council member. When Congress amended the Voting Rights Act in 1982, it further insisted that minorities be

The Voting Rights Act of 1965 produced a major increase in the number of African Americans registered to vote in Southern states. The ability to vote gave African Americans more political clout: In the 20 years following enactment of the law, more than 2,500 African Americans were elected to state and local offices in that region.

able to "elect representatives of their choice" when their numbers and configuration permitted. Thus, redrawing district boundaries was to avoid discriminatory *results* and not just discriminatory *intent*. In 1986, the Supreme Court upheld this principle in *Thornburg v. Gingles*.

Officials in the Justice Department, which was responsible for enforcing the Voting Rights Act, and state legislatures that drew new district lines interpreted these actions as a mandate to create minority-majority districts. Consequently, when congressional district boundaries were redrawn following the 1990 census, several states, including Florida, North Carolina, Texas, Illinois, New York, and Louisiana, created odd-shaped districts that were designed to give minority-group voters a numerical majority. Fourteen new U.S. House districts were drawn specifically to help elect African Americans to Congress, and six districts were drawn to elect new Hispanic members (these efforts worked, as we will see in Chapter 12).

However, in 1993, the Supreme Court heard a challenge to a North Carolina congressional district that in some places was cut no wider than a superhighway to create an African-American majority winding snakeline for 160 miles. In its decision in *Shaw v. Reno*, the Court decried the creation of districts based solely on racial composition, as well as the district drawers' abandonment of traditional redistricting standards such as compactness and contiguity. Thus, the Court gave legal standing to challenges to any congressional map with an oddly shaped minority-majority district that may not be defensible on grounds other than race (such as shared community interest or geographical compactness). The next year, in *Johnson v. DeGrandy*, the Court ruled that a state legislative redistricting plan does not violate the Voting Rights Act if it does not create the greatest possible number of districts in which minority-group votes would make up a majority.

In 1995 in *Miller v. Johnson*, the Court rejected the efforts of the Justice Department to achieve the maximum possible number of minority districts. It held that the use of race as a "predominant factor" in drawing district lines should be presumed to be unconstitutional. The next year, in *Bush v. Vera* and *Shaw v. Hunt*, the Supreme Court voided

Why It Matters

The Voting Rights Act
In passing the Voting Rights Act of 1965, Congress enacted an extraordinarily strong law to protect the rights of minorities to vote. There is little question that officials pay more attention to minorities when they can vote. And many more members of minority groups are now elected to high public office.

You Are Redrawing the
Districts in Your State

three convoluted districts in Texas and one in North Carolina on the grounds that race had been the primary reason for abandoning compact district lines and that the state legislatures had crossed the line into unconstitutional racial gerrymandering.

In yet another turn, in 1999 the Court declared in *Hunt v. Cromartie* that conscious consideration of race is not automatically unconstitutional if the state's primary motivation was potentially political rather than racial. We can expect continued litigation concerning this question over the next few years in the wake of the 2000 census.

Other Minority Groups

As we discuss in Chapter 6, America is heading toward a *minority majority:* a situation in which minority groups will outnumber Caucasians of European descent. As of 2001 African Americans were no longer the largest minority group in the United States. African Americans are not the only racial group that has suffered legally imposed discrimination. Even before the civil rights struggle, Native Americans, Hispanics, and Asians learned how powerless they could become in a society dominated by Whites. The civil rights laws for which African Americans fought have benefited members of these groups as well. In addition, social movements tend to beget new social movements; thus, the African-American civil rights movement of the 1960s spurred other minorities to mobilize to protect their rights.

Native Americans.   The earliest inhabitants of the continent, the American Indians, are, of course, the oldest minority group. Nearly 2 million people identify themselves as Native Americans. The history of poverty, discrimination, and exploitation experienced by American Indians is a long one. For generations, U.S. policy promoted westward expansion at the expense of Native Americans' lands. Native Americans were first isolated on reservations, losing their lands and their rights in the process. After the Dawes Act of 1887, the federal government switched strategies and focused on assimilating Native Americans into mainstream American life. The government sent children to boarding schools off the reservations and banned tribal rituals and languages.

Finally, in 1924 American Indians were made citizens of the United States and given the right to vote, a status that African Americans had achieved a half-century before. Not until 1946 did Congress establish the Indian Claims Act to settle financial disputes arising from lands taken from the American Indians.[7] Today, most Native Americans still live in poverty and ill health, almost half on or near a reservation. American Indians know, perhaps better than any other group, the significance of the gap between public policy and private realization regarding discrimination.

But progress is being made. The civil rights movement of the 1960s created a more favorable climate for Native Americans to secure guaranteed access to the polls, to housing, and to jobs and to reassert their treaty rights. The Indian Bill of Rights was adopted as Title II of the Civil Rights Act of 1968, applying most of the provisions of the Constitution's Bill of Rights to tribal governments. In *Santa Clara Pueblo v. Martinez* (1978), the Supreme Court strengthened the tribal power of individual tribe members and furthered self-government by Indian tribes.

American Indian activists such as Dennis Means of the American Indian Movement (AIM), Vine Deloria, and Dee Brown drew attention to the plight of American Indian tribes. Several Native Americans seized Alcatraz Island in San Francisco Bay in 1969 to protest the loss of Indian lands. In 1973, armed members of AIM seized 11 hostages at Wounded Knee, S.D.—the site of an 1890 massacre of 200 Sioux (Lakota) by U.S. cavalry—and remained there for 71 days until the federal government agreed to examine Indian treaty rights. Ben Nighthorse Campbell was elected a U.S. senator from Colorado in 1992, the first Native American elected to Congress in more than 20 years.

Equally important, Indians began to use the courts to protect their rights. The Native American Rights Fund (NARF), founded in 1970, has won important victories concerning hunting, fishing, and land rights. Native Americans are also retaining access to their sacred places and have had some success in stopping the building of roads and buildings on ancient burial grounds or other sacred spots. Several tribes have won court cases protecting them from taxation of tribal profits.

As in other areas of civil rights, the preservation of Native American culture and the exercise of Native American rights sometimes conflict with the interests of the majority. For example, there is conflict over special rights that some tribes have to fish and even hunt whales. Anglers concerned with the depletion of fishing stock and environmentalists worried about loss of the whale population have voiced protests. Similarly, Native American rights to run businesses denied to others by state law and to avoid taxation on tribal lands have made running gambling casinos a lucrative option for Indians. This has irritated both those who oppose gambling and those who are offended by the tax-free competition.

Hispanic Americans.   Hispanic Americans (or Latinos, as some prefer to be called)—chiefly from Mexico, Puerto Rico, and Cuba but also from El Salvador, Honduras, and other countries in Central America—have displaced African Americans as the largest minority group. Today they compose about 13 percent of the U.S. population.

The first major efforts on behalf of civil rights for Hispanics date only from the mid-1960s. Hispanic leaders drew from the tactics of the African-American civil rights

The growing numbers of Hispanic Americans will soon make them the largest minority group in the United States. Their political power is reflected in Alberto Gonzales's selection for President George W. Bush's cabinet and in the 25 members of the U.S. House of Representatives, such as Loretta and Linda Sanchez of California.

movement and sit-ins, boycotts, marches, and related activities to draw attention to their cause. Inspired by the NAACP's Legal Defense Fund, they also created the Mexican American Legal Defense and Education Fund (MALDEF) in 1968 to help argue their cause in court. In addition, Hispanic groups began mobilizing in other ways to protect their interests. An early prominent example was the United Farm Workers, led by Cesar Chavez, who publicized the plight of migrant workers, a large proportion of whom are Hispanic.

Like Native Americans, Hispanic Americans benefit from the nondiscrimination policies originally passed to protect African Americans. Provisions of the Voting Rights Act of 1965 covered San Antonio, Texas, and thereby permitted Hispanic voters to lend weight to the election of Mayor Henry Cisneros. There are now more than 4,400 elected Hispanic officials in the United States,[8] and Hispanic Americans play a prominent role in the politics of such major cities as Houston, Miami, Los Angeles, and San Diego. In 1973, Hispanics won a victory when the Supreme Court found that multi-member electoral districts (in which more than one person represents a single district) in Texas discriminated against minority groups because they decreased the probability of a minority being elected.[9] Nevertheless, poverty, discrimination, and language barriers continue to depress Hispanic voter registration and turnout.

Asian Americans.   Asian Americans are the fastest growing minority group; their representation in the American population rose from 0.5 percent to 4 percent from 1960 to 2000. Asian Americans suffered discrimination in education, jobs, and housing, as well as restrictions on immigration and naturalization for more than a hundred years prior to the civil rights acts of the 1960s. Discrimination was especially egregious during World War II when the U.S. government, beset by fears of a Japanese invasion of the Pacific Coast, rounded up more than 100,000 Americans of Japanese descent and herded them into encampments. These internment camps were, critics claimed, America's concentration camps. The Supreme Court, however, in **Korematsu v. United States** (1944), upheld the internment as constitutional. Congress has since

Korematsu v. United States

A 1944 Supreme Court decision that upheld as constitutional the internment of more than 100,000 Americans of Japanese descent in encampments during World War II.

One of the low points in the protection of civil rights in the United States occurred during World War II when more than 100,000 Americans of Japanese descent were moved to internment camps.

authorized benefits to the former internees. Today, Americans of Chinese, Japanese, Korean, Vietnamese, and other Asian cultures have assumed prominent positions in U.S. society.

Other Groups.   There are more than 1.2 million persons of Arab ancestry in the United States. Since the terrorist attacks of September 11, 2001, Arab, Muslim, Sikh, and South-Asian Americans, and those perceived to be members of these groups, have been the victims of increased numbers of bias-related assaults, threats, vandalism, and arson. The incidents have consisted of telephone, Internet, mail, and face-to-face threats; minor assaults as well as assaults with dangerous weapons and assaults resulting in serious injury and death; and vandalism, shootings, arson, and bombings directed at homes, businesses, and places of worship. Members of these groups have also been subject to discrimination in employment, housing, education, and access to public accommodations and facilities.

As we saw in Chapter 4, in the wake of the September 11, 2001, terrorist attacks, the FBI detained more than 1,200 persons as possible threats to national security. About two-thirds of these persons were illegal aliens—mostly Arabs and Muslims—and many of them languished in jail for months until cleared by the FBI. This process seemed to violate the right of detainees to be informed of accusations against them found in the Sixth Amendment and the protection against the suspension of the writ of habeas corpus. As we have seen, in 2004 the Supreme Court declared that detainees had the right to challenge their detention before a judge or other neutral decision maker.

The struggle for equal rights has not been limited to racial minorities, however. Political activity on behalf of women has been so energetic and so far-reaching that a separate section is needed to examine this struggle for equality.

Women, the Constitution, and Public Policy

Abigail Adams may have been practically alone in her feminist views in the 1770s, but the next century brought significant feminist activity. The first women's rights activists were products of the abolitionist movement, where they often encountered sexist opposition. Noting that the status of women shared much in common with that of slaves, some leaders resolved to fight for women's rights.

Two of these women, Lucretia Mott and Elizabeth Cady Stanton, organized a meeting at Seneca Falls in upstate New York. They had much to discuss. Not only were women denied the vote, but they were also subjected to patriarchal (male-dominated) family law and denied educational and career opportunities. The legal doctrine known as *coverture* deprived married women of any identity separate from that of their husbands; wives could not sign contracts or dispose of property. Divorce law was heavily biased in favor of husbands. Even abused women found it almost impossible to end their marriages, and men had the legal advantage in securing custody of the children.

The Battle for the Vote

On July 19, 1848, 100 men and women signed the Seneca Falls Declaration of Sentiments and Resolutions. Patterned after the Declaration of Independence, it proclaimed, "The history of mankind is a history of repeated injuries and usurpations on the part of man toward woman, having in direct object the establishment of an absolute tyranny over her." Thus began the movement that would culminate in the ratification of the **Nineteenth Amendment** 72 years later, giving women the vote.

Nineteenth Amendment

The constitutional amendment adopted in 1920 that guarantees women the right to vote. See also **suffrage.**

Charlotte Woodward, 19 years old in 1848, was the only signer of the Seneca Falls Declaration who lived to vote for the president in 1920.

Advocates of women's suffrage hoped that women would be included in the Fifteenth Amendment, but were disappointed when they were excluded from protections accorded to newly freed slaves. Thus, the battle for women's suffrage was fought mostly in the late nineteenth and early twentieth centuries. Leaders like Stanton and Susan B. Anthony were prominent in the cause, which emphasized the vote but also addressed women's other grievances. The suffragists had considerable success in the states, especially in the West. Several states allowed women to vote before the constitutional amendment passed. The feminists lobbied, marched, protested, and even engaged in civil disobedience.[10]

The "Doldrums": 1920–1960

Winning the right to vote did not automatically win equal status for women. In fact, the feminist movement seemed to lose rather than gain momentum after winning the vote, perhaps because the vote was about the only goal on which all feminists agreed. There was considerable division within the movement on other priorities.

Many suffragists accepted the traditional model of the family. Fathers were breadwinners, mothers bread bakers. Although most suffragists thought that women should have the opportunity to pursue any occupation they chose, many also believed that women's primary obligations revolved around the roles of wife and mother. Many suffragists had defended the vote as basically an extension of the maternal role into public life, arguing that a new era of public morality would emerge when women could vote. These *social feminists* were in tune with prevailing attitudes.

Public policy toward women continued to be dominated by protectionism rather than by the principle of equality. Laws protected working women from the burdens of overtime work, long hours on the job, and heavy lifting. The fact that these laws also protected male workers from female competition received little attention. State laws tended to reflect—and reinforce—traditional family roles. These laws concentrated on limiting women's work opportunities outside the home so they could concentrate on their duties within it. In most states, husbands were legally required to support their families (even after a divorce) and to pay child support, though divorced fathers did not always pay. When a marriage ended, mothers almost always got custody of the children, although husbands had the legal advantage in custody battles. Public policy was designed to preserve traditional motherhood and hence, supporters claimed, to protect the family and the country's moral fabric.[11]

Only a minority of feminists challenged these assumptions. Alice Paul, the author of the original **Equal Rights Amendment (ERA),** was one activist who claimed that the real result of protectionist law was to perpetuate gender inequality. Simply worded, the ERA reads, "Equality of rights under the law shall not be denied or abridged by the United States or by any state on account of sex." Most people saw the ERA as a threat to the family when it was introduced in Congress in 1923. It gained little support. In fact, women were less likely to support the amendment than men were.

The Second Feminist Wave

The civil rights movement of the 1950s and 1960s attracted many female activists, some of whom also joined student and antiwar movements. These women often met with the same prejudices as had women abolitionists. Betty Friedan's book *The Feminine Mystique*, published in 1963, encouraged women to question traditional assumptions and to assert their own rights. Groups such as the National Organization for Women (NOW) and the National Women's Political Caucus were organized in the 1960s and 1970s.

Equal Rights Amendment

A constitutional amendment originally introduced in Congress in 1923 and passed by Congress in 1972, stating that "equality of rights under the law shall not be denied or abridged by the United States or by any state on account of sex." Despite public support, the amendment failed to acquire the necessary support from three-fourths of the state legislatures.

Before the advent of the contemporary feminist movement, the Supreme Court upheld virtually any instance of gender-based discrimination. The state and federal governments could discriminate against women—and, indeed, men—as they chose. In the 1970s, the Court began to take a closer look at gender discrimination. In *Reed v. Reed* (1971), the Court ruled that any "arbitrary" gender-based classification violated the equal protection clause of the Fourteenth Amendment (see "Making a Difference: Sally Reed"). This was the first time the Court declared any law unconstitutional on the basis of gender discrimination. Five years later, *Craig v. Boren* established a "medium scrutiny" standard: Gender discrimination would be presumed to be neither valid nor invalid. The courts were to show less deference to gender classifications than to more routine classifications, but more deference than to racial classifications. Nevertheless, the Court has repeatedly said that there must be an "exceedingly persuasive justification" for any government to classify people by gender. Table 5.5 lists important policy milestones on gender equality.

Reed v. Reed

The landmark case in 1971 in which the Supreme Court for the first time upheld a claim of gender discrimination.

Craig v. Boren

In this 1976 ruling, the Supreme Court established the "medium scrutiny" standard for determining gender discrimination.

The Supreme Court has struck down many laws and rules for discriminating on the basis of gender. For example, the Court voided laws giving husbands exclusive control over family property.[12] The Court also voided employers' rules that denied women equal monthly retirement benefits because they live longer than men.[13]

In fact, many of the litigants in cases raising constitutional questions about gender discrimination have been men seeking equality with women in their treatment under the law. For example, the Court has voided laws that

- provided for alimony payments to women only (*Orr v. Orr,* 1979)
- closed a state's nursing school to men (*Mississippi v. Hogan,* 1982)
- set a higher age for drinking for men than for women (*Craig v. Boren,* 1976)
- set a higher age for reaching legal adult status for men than for women (*Stanton v. Stanton,* 1975)

Making a Difference

Sally Reed

An Idaho law enacted in 1864 held that males must be preferred to females in cases where parents otherwise had equal claims (and equal qualifications) to serve as administrator of their child's estate. Sally Reed challenged this law after her 16-year-old son died without a will in 1967. Sally Reed and her estranged husband, Cecil Reed, each filed petitions to be appointed as the administrator of their son's estate. The probate court chose Cecil, and Sally contested the appointment. In 1971, the Supreme Court held in *Reed v. Reed* that the arbitrary preference established in favor of males in the Idaho law violated the Equal Protection Clause of the Fourteenth Amendment— the first time that any law had been voided on the basis of gender discrimination.

Men have not always prevailed in their efforts for equal treatment, however. The Court upheld a statutory rape law applying only to men[14] and the male-only draft, which we will discuss shortly. The Court also allowed a Florida law giving property tax exemptions only to widows, not to widowers.[15]

Contemporary feminists have suffered defeats as well as victories. The ERA was revived when Congress passed it in 1972 and extended the deadline for ratification until 1982. Nevertheless, the ERA was three states short of ratification when time ran out. Paradoxically, the defeat of the ERA had just the opposite effect of that which the 1920 suffrage victory had on feminism. Far from weakening the movement, losing the ERA battle stimulated vigorous feminist activity. Proponents have vowed to keep reintroducing the amendment in Congress and continue to press hard for state and federal action on women's rights.

Women in the Workplace

One reason why feminist activism persists has nothing to do with ideology or other social movements. The family pattern that traditionalists sought to preserve—father at work, mother at home—is becoming a thing of the past. The female civilian labor force amounts to 67 million (as compared to 78 million males), representing 60 percent of adult women. Sixty-one percent of these women are married. There are also

Table 5.5   Toward Gender Equality: Public Policy Milestones

1969–2005

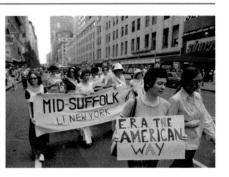

1969	Executive order declares that offering equal opportunities for women at every level of federal service is to be national policy and establishes a program for implementing the policy.
1971	In *Reed v. Reed*, the Supreme Court invalidates a state law preferring men to women in court selection of an estate's administrator.
1972	Provisions of Title VII of the Civil Rights Act of 1964 are extended to cover the faculty and professional staffs of colleges and universities. The Education Act forbids gender discrimination in public schools (with some exceptions for historically single-gender schools). The ERA is proposed by Congress and sent to the states for ratification.
1974	A woman—Ella Grasso of Connecticut—is elected governor for the first time without succeeding her husband to the office.
1975	Congress opens armed services academies to women.
1976	Courts strike down an Oklahoma law setting different legal drinking ages for men and women.
1977	Supreme Court voids arbitrary height and weight requirements for employees in *Dothard v. Rawlinson*.
1978	The deadline for ratification of the ERA is extended. Congress passes the Pregnancy Discrimination Act.
1981	The Supreme Court rules that male-only military draft registration is constitutional. Sandra Day O'Connor becomes the first woman Supreme Court justice.
1982	The ERA ratification deadline passes without ratification of the amendment.
1984	Geraldine Ferraro is nominated as the first woman vice-presidential candidate of a major party.
1988	The Supreme Court unanimously upholds a 1984 New York City law aimed primarily at requiring the admission of women to large, private clubs that play an important role in professional life.
1991	After three years of conflict, Congress enacts the Civil Rights and Women's Equity in Employment Act, which counters the effects of several Supreme Court decisions making it more difficult for workers to bring and win job discrimination suits.
1992	California becomes the first state to be represented by two female U.S. senators.
1993	Supreme Court in *Harris v. Forklift Systems* lowers the threshold for proving sexual harassment in the workplace.
1994	48 women elected to U.S. House and 8 to the Senate, the most in history.
1996	In *United States v. Virginia et al.*, the Supreme Court declares categorical exclusion of women from state-funded colleges unconstitutional.
1997	Madeline Albright appointed secretary of state, the first woman to serve in that role.
2001	Condoleezza Rice appointed national security adviser, the first woman to hold that post.
2002	Representative Nancy Pelosi is elected by her colleagues as House Democratic Leader, becoming the first woman to head her party in Congress.

33 million female-headed households (8 million of which include children), and about two-thirds of American mothers who have children below school age are in the labor force.[16] As conditions have changed, public opinion and public policy demands have changed, too. Protectionism is not dead. Women still assume more duties inside the home than men do, and debates over policies like the "mommy track" (reduced work responsibilities for women workers with children) parental leaves to women reflect this social phenomenon. Demands for equality, however, keep nudging protectionism into the background.

Congress has made some important progress, especially in the area of employment. The Civil Rights Act of 1964 banned gender discrimination in employment. The protection of this law has been expanded several times. For example, in 1972, Congress gave the Equal Employment Opportunity Commission (EEOC) the power to sue employers suspected of illegal discrimination. Title IX of the Education Act of 1972 forbade gender discrimination in federally subsidized education programs, including athletics. The Pregnancy Discrimination Act of 1978 made it illegal for employers to exclude pregnancy and childbirth from their sick leave and health benefits plans. The Civil Rights and Women's Equity in Employment Act of 1991 shifted the burden of proof in justifying hiring and promotion practices to employers, who must show that employment practices are related to job performance and that they are consistent with "business necessity" (an ambiguous term, however).

The Supreme Court also weighed in against gender discrimination in employment and business activity. In 1977, it voided laws and rules barring women from jobs through arbitrary height and weight requirements (*Dothard v. Rawlinson*). Any such prerequisites must be directly related to the duties required in a particular position. Women have also been protected from being required to take mandatory pregnancy leaves from their jobs[17] and from being denied a job because of an employer's concern for harming a developing fetus.[18] Many commercial contacts are made in private business and service clubs, which often have excluded women from membership. The Court has upheld state and city laws that prohibit such discrimination.[19]

Education is closely related to employment. Title IX of the Education Act of 1972 forbids gender discrimination in federally subsidized education programs (which include almost all colleges and universities). But what about single-gender schooling? In 1996, the Supreme Court declared that Virginia's categorical exclusion of women from education opportunities at the state-funded Virginia Military Institute (VMI) violated women's rights to equal protection of the law.[20] A few days later, The Citadel, the nation's only other state-supported all-male college, announced that it would also admit women.

Women have made substantial progress in their quest for equality, but debate continues as Congress considers new laws. Three of the most controversial issues that legislators will continue to face are wage discrimination, the role of women in the military, and sexual harassment.

Wage Discrimination and Comparable Worth

Traditional women's jobs often pay much less than men's jobs that demand comparable skill; a female secretary often earns far less than a male accounts clerk with the same qualifications. Median annual earnings for full-time women workers are only about three-fourths of those of men.[21] In other words, women earn $0.78 for every $1.00 men make.

In 1983, the Washington State Supreme Court ruled that its state government had discriminated against women for years by denying them equal pay for jobs of

Why It Matters

Changes in the Workplace
Laws and Supreme Court decisions striking down barriers to employment for women are not just ornaments. Instead, they have important consequences for employment opportunities for millions of women and have helped them make substantial gains in entering careers formerly occupied almost entirely by men.

As women have become more active in politics, they have begun to assume more leadership roles. Here, Dianne Feinstein and Barbara Boxer celebrate their 1992 victories in the U.S. Senate races in California, marking the first time a state had been represented in the Senate by two female senators.

comparable worth

The issue raised when women who hold traditionally female jobs are paid less than men for working at jobs requiring comparable skill.

comparable worth. The U.S. Supreme Court has remained silent so far on the merits of this issue. The executive branch under Ronald Reagan consistently opposed the idea of comparable worth. The late Clarence Pendleton, Reagan's appointee as head of the U.S. Civil Rights Commission, argued that lawsuits based on comparable worth would interfere with the free market for wages by reducing incentives for women to seek higher-paying, traditionally male jobs. Pendleton called comparable worth "the craziest idea since Looney Tunes." Ridicule has not made this serious dispute go away, however.

Women in the Military

Military service is another controversial aspect of gender equality. Women have served in every branch of the armed services since World War II. Originally, they served in separate units such as the WACS (Women's Army Corps), the WAVES (Women Accepted for Volunteer Emergency Service in the navy), and the Nurse Corps. The military had a 2 percent quota for women (which was never filled) until the 1970s. Now women are part of the regular service. They make up 15 percent of the armed forces (19 percent of the air force), and compete directly with men for promotions. Congress opened all the service academies to women in 1975. Women have done well, including graduating first at the U.S. Naval Academy in Annapolis and serving as first captain of the Corps of Cadets at West Point.

Two important differences between the treatment of men and that of women persist in military service. First, only men must register for the draft when they turn 18 (see "You Are the Judge: Is Male-Only Draft Registration Gender Discrimination?"). Second, statutes and regulations also prohibit women from serving in combat. A breach exists between policy and practice, however, as the Persian Gulf War and the war in Iraq showed. Women piloted helicopters at the front and helped to operate antimissile systems; some were taken as prisoners of war. Women are now permitted to serve as combat pilots in the navy and air force and to serve on navy warships. However, they are still not permitted to serve in ground combat units in the army or marines.

These actions have reopened the debate over whether women should serve in combat. Some experts insist that because women, on average, have less upper-body strength than men, they are less suited for combat. Others argue that men will not be

In the past few years, women have overcome many obstacles to serving in the military, performing well in a variety of nontraditional roles such as piloting helicopters and patrolling in combat vehicles.

You Are the Judge

Is Male-Only Draft Registration Gender Discrimination?

There is no military conscription at present (the United States has had a volunteer force since 1973), but President Jimmy Carter asked Congress to require both men and women to register for the draft after the Soviet Union invaded Afghanistan in 1979. Registration was designed to facilitate any eventual conscription. In 1980, Congress reinstated registration for men only, a policy that was not universally popular. Federal courts ordered registration suspended while several young men filed a suit.

These men argued that the registration requirement was gender-based discrimination that violated the due process clause of the Fifth Amendment.

You Be the Judge: Does requiring only males to register for the draft unconstitutionally discriminate against them?

Answer: The Supreme Court displayed its typical deference to the elected branches in the area of national security when it ruled in 1981 in *Rostker v.* *Goldberg* that male-only registration did not violate the Fifth Amendment. The Court found that male-only registration bore a substantial relationship to Congress' goal of ensuring combat readiness and that Congress acted well within its constitutional authority to raise and regulate armies and navies when it authorized the registration of men and not women. Congress, the Court said, was allowed to focus on the question of military need, rather than "equity."

able to fight effectively beside wounded or dying women. Critics of these views point out that some women surpass some men in upper-body strength and that we do not know how well men and women will fight together. This debate is not only a controversy about ability; it also touches on the question of whether engaging in combat is a burden or a privilege. Clearly some women—and some who would deny them combat duty—take the latter view.

Sexual Harassment

Whether in the military, on the assembly line, or in the office, women for years have voiced concern about sexual harassment which, of course, does not affect only women. In 1986, the Supreme Court articulated this broad principle: Sexual harassment that is so pervasive as to create a hostile or abusive work environment is a form of gender discrimination, which is forbidden by the 1964 Civil Rights Act.[22] In 1993, in *Harris v. Forklift Systems*, the Court reinforced its decision. No single factor, the Court said, is required to win a sexual harassment case under Title VII of the 1964 Civil Rights Act. The law is violated when the workplace environment "would reasonably be perceived, and is perceived, as hostile or abusive." Thus, workers are not required to prove that the workplace environment is so hostile as to cause them "severe psychological injury" or that they are unable to perform their jobs. The protection of federal law comes into play before the harassing conduct leads to psychological difficulty.

In 1998 the Supreme Court again spoke expansively about sexual harassment in the workplace. In *Faragher v. City of Boca Raton* the Court made it clear that employers are responsible for preventing and eliminating harassment at work. They can be held liable for even those harassing acts of supervisory employees that violate clear policies and of which top management has no knowledge. In 2004 in *Pennsylvania State Police v. Suders*, the Court held that if harassment culminates in a tangible action such as a discharge or demotion, an employer is strictly liable if there is no legal defense such as one showing that the employer had set up a system for reporting and correcting sexual harassment but that the employee had unreasonably failed to use that system.

In *Burlington Industries, Inc. v. Ellerth*, the Court found that an employee could sue for sexual harassment even without being able to show job-related harm. Victims must have availed themselves of effective complaint policies and other protection offered by the company first, however. The Court also made it clear that the law also prevents sexual harassment by people of the same gender (*Oncale v. Sundower Offshore Services*).

In 1999, the Court turned its attention to sexual harassment in public schools. It held that school districts can be held liable for sexual harassment in cases of student-on-student harassment where the school district has knowledge of the harassment or is deliberately indifferent to it. The harassment must be so severe, pervasive, and objectively offensive that it can be said to deprive the victims of access to the educational opportunities or benefits provided by the school (*Davis v. Monroe County Board of Education*).

Sexual harassment can occur anywhere but may be especially prevalent in male-dominated occupations such as the military. A 1991 convention of the Tailhook Association, an organization of naval aviators, made the news after reports surfaced of drunken sailors jamming a hotel hallway and sexually assaulting female guests, including naval officers, as they stepped off the elevator. After the much-criticized initial failure of the navy to identify the officers responsible for the assault, heads rolled, including those of several admirals and the secretary of the navy. In 1996 and 1997, a number of army officers and noncommissioned officers had their careers ended, and some went to prison, for sexual harassment of female soldiers in training situations. Behavior that was once viewed as simply male high jinks is now recognized as intolerable. Top officials at the Air Force Academy were removed in 2003 following charges that female cadets were frequently raped by male cadets.

The push for gender equality is a worldwide phenomenon (see "America in Perspective: Mrs. In-the-Back-of-the-House Goes to Parliament"). Many women are asserting their civil rights for the first time.

Comparing Civil Rights

America in Perspective

Mrs. In-the-Back-of-the-House Goes to Parliament

In Japan, married women are often supposed to stay at home to clean the house and raise the children. In fact, the Japanese word for wife means "Mrs. In-the-Back-of-the-House." There are even legal incentives to encourage married women to quit full-time jobs, and a married couple is legally required to use the same last name—almost always the husband's.

Such an environment presents immense obstacles for women to overcome in order to transform themselves into a meaningful force in Japanese politics. Women find it difficult to be taken seriously by voters, facing prejudice such as that reflected in one male candidate's taunt, "Women can't do anything.

They should just shut up." Many of the women who are elected to Parliament are actresses or other celebrities.

Thus, we should not be surprised that in the Japanese Parliament elected in 1996, women composed only 4 percent of the more powerful lower house. Even this low percentage doubled Japanese women's prior representation in Parliament. (In the United States, as we discuss in Chapter 12, women constitute 14 percent of the Senate and 15 percent of the House.) Most of the women who are elected represent opposition parties and thus have little influence.

Despite these cultural barriers, women in Japan are making progress. In the 2000 election, several more

women were elected to the lower house, raising the percentage of women there to over 7 percent. The number of women in local town and county assemblies has also increased over the last decade, bringing attention to issues such as environmental and food safety. It remains to be seen whether the base in local government will be sufficient to propel even more women into positions of power at the national level; however, the trend is promising.

Source: From Sherly WuDunn, "23 Women Break into a Male Citadel," in the *New York Times*, October 26, 1996, p. 4. Updated data from International Parliamentary Union, 2004.

Newly Active Groups Under the Civil Rights Umbrella

Racial and ethnic minorities and women are not the only Americans who can claim civil rights; policies enacted to protect one or two groups can be applied to others. Four recent entrants into the civil rights arena are aging Americans, people with disabilities, and homosexuals. All these groups claim equal rights, as racial minorities and women do, but represent different challenges to mainstream America.

Civil Rights and the Graying of America

America is aging rapidly. People in their 80s make up the fastest growing age group in this country. John Glenn, a 77-year-old senator from Ohio, made history in October 1998 as the oldest person in space when he accompanied a crew of six other astronauts aboard the space shuttle *Discovery*.

When the Social Security program began in the 1930s, 65 was the retirement age. Although this age was apparently chosen arbitrarily, it soon became the mandatory retirement age for many workers. Although many workers might prefer to retire while they are still healthy and active enough to enjoy leisure, not everyone wants or can afford to do so. Social Security is not, and was never meant to be, an adequate income, and not all workers have good pension plans.

Although many elderly people wished to work, employers routinely refused to hire people over a certain age. Graduate and professional schools often rejected applicants in their 30s on the grounds that their professions would get fewer years, and thus less return, out of them. This policy had a severe impact on housewives and veterans who wanted to return to school.

As early as 1967, Congress banned some kinds of age discrimination. In 1975, civil rights law denied federal funds to any institution discriminating against people over the age of 40 because of their age. The Age Discrimination in Employment Act was amended in 1978 to raise the general compulsory retirement age to 70. Now compulsory retirement has been phased out altogether. No one knows what other directions the *gray liberation movement* may take as its members approach the status of a minority majority. In 1976 the Supreme Court, however, declared that it would not place age in the suspect classification category when it upheld a state law requiring police officers to retire at the age of 50. Age classifications would fall under the rational basis test.[23]

Job bias is often hidden, and proving it depends on inference and circumstantial evidence. The Supreme Court made it easier to win cases of job bias in 2000 when it held in *Reeves v. Sanderson* that a plaintiff's evidence of an employer's bias, combined with sufficient evidence to find that the employer's asserted justification is false, may permit juries and judges to conclude that an employer unlawfully discriminated. Thus, employees can win lawsuits without direct evidence of an employer's illegal intent. The impact of the decision is likely to extend beyond questions of age discrimination to the litigation of race and gender discrimination cases brought under Title VII of the Civil Rights Act of 1964 as well as cases brought under the Americans with Disabilities Act.

Civil Rights and People With Disabilities

Americans with disabilities have suffered from both direct and indirect discrimination. They have often been denied rehabilitation services (a kind of affirmative action), education, and jobs. Many people with disabilities have been excluded from the workforce and isolated without overt discrimination. Throughout most of American history, public and private buildings have been hostile to the blind, deaf, and mobility impaired.

Americans with disabilities are among the successors to the 1960s civil rights activists. In the last decade they have been active in demanding government benefits.

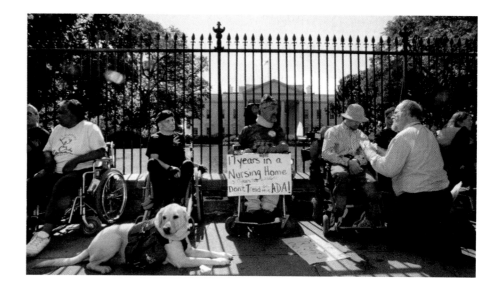

Americans with Disabilities Act of 1990 (ADA)

A law passed in 1990 that requires employers and public facilities to make "reasonable accommodations" for people with disabilities and prohibits discrimination against these individuals in employment.

Stairs, buses, telephones, and other necessities of modern life have been designed in ways that keep these individuals out of offices, stores, and restaurants. As one slogan said, "Once, blacks had to ride at the back of the bus. We can't even get on the bus."

The first rehabilitation laws were passed in the late 1920s, mostly to help veterans of World War I. Accessibility laws had to wait another 50 years. The Rehabilitation Act of 1973 (twice vetoed by Richard Nixon as "too costly") added people with disabilities to the list of Americans protected from discrimination. Because the law defines an inaccessible environment as a form of discrimination, wheelchair ramps, grab bars on toilets, and Braille signs have become common features of American life. The Education of All Handicapped Children Act of 1975 entitled all children to a free public education appropriate to their needs. The **Americans with Disabilities Act of 1990 (ADA)** strengthened these protections, requiring employers and administrators of public facilities to make "reasonable accommodations" and prohibiting employment discrimination against people with disabilities.

Determining who is "disabled" has generated controversy. Are people with Acquired Immune Deficiency Syndrome (AIDS) entitled to protections? In 1998 the Supreme Court answered yes. It ruled that the ADA offered protection against discrimination to people with AIDS.[24] What about people with bad eyesight or high blood pressure? In 1999 the Supreme Court ruled that people with physical impairments who can function normally when they wear glasses or take their medicine cannot be considered disabled and thus do not fall under the ADA's protection against employment discrimination.[25]

Nobody wants to oppose policies beneficial to people with disabilities. After all, people like Helen Keller and Franklin Roosevelt are popular American heroes. Nevertheless, civil rights laws designed to protect the rights of these individuals have met with vehement opposition and, once passed, with sluggish enforcement. The source of this resistance is the same concern that troubled Nixon: cost. Budgeting for such programs is often shortsighted, however. People often forget that changes allowing people with disabilities to become wage earners, spenders, and taxpayers are a gain, rather than drain, on the economy.

Gay and Lesbian Rights

Gay and lesbian activists may face the toughest battle for equality. *Homophobia*—fear and hatred of homosexuals—has many causes; some are very powerful. Some religions, for instance, condemn homosexuality. Such attitudes continue to characterize

Table 5.6   Discrimination Against Homosexuals

Homosexuals face opposition to entering many common occupations from a substantial percentage of the American public, but this opposition seems to be decreasing.

Do you think homosexuals should or should not be hired for each of the following occupations?

	% Saying "Yes, should be hired"				
	1992	1996	1999	2001	2003
Salesperson	82%	90%	90%	91%	92%
Armed forces	57	65	70	72	80
Doctors	53	69	75	78	82
High school teachers	47	60	61	63	67
Clergy	43	53	54	54	56
Elementary school teachers	41	55	54	56	61

Source: Gallup Poll, April 1999, May 2001, May 2003.

a large segment of the American public despite some changes over the past few years (see Table 5.6). Homophobia appeared to be the motive for the brutal 1998 killing of Matthew Shepard, a 21-year-old political science freshman at the University of Wyoming. Shepard was attacked after attending a meeting for Gay Awareness Week events on campus. He was found tied to a fence, where he had been hit in the head with a pistol 18 times and kicked repeatedly in the groin.

Even by conservative estimates, several million Americans are homosexual, representing every social stratum and ethnic group. Gays and lesbians often face discrimination in hiring, education, access to public accommodations, and housing. Of particular concern to the gay community is the AIDS virus, which had an especially devastating effect on male homosexuals when the epidemic struck in the early 1980s.

Civil Rights and Gay Adoption

A notorious incident in a New York City bar in 1969 stimulated the growth of the gay rights movement. The Stonewall bar, frequented by gay men, was raided by the police. Unwarranted violence, arrests, and injury to persons and property resulted. Both gay men and lesbians organized throughout the 1970s and 1980s in an effort to protect their civil rights. During this time, they developed political skills and formed significant interest groups.

The record of gay rights is mixed. In 1986 the Supreme Court, in *Bowers v. Hardwick*, allowed states to ban homosexual relations. In 2000 the Supreme Court held that the Boy Scouts could exclude a gay man from being an adult member because homosexuality violates the organization's principles.[26]

In the summer of 1993, after months of negotiation with the Pentagon and an avalanche of criticism, President Clinton announced a new policy that barred the Pentagon from asking military recruits or service personnel to disclose their sexual orientation. Popularly known as the "don't ask, don't tell" policy, it also reaffirmed the Defense Department's strict prohibition against homosexual conduct. Service members who declare their homosexuality face discharge unless they can prove they will remain celibate, and they are barred from even disclosing to a friend in private conversation that they are gay or bisexual. The policy also requires commanders to have "credible information" that the policy is being violated before launching an investigation.

Gay activists have also won important victories. Seven states, including California, and more than 100 communities have passed laws protecting homosexuals against some forms of discrimination.[27] Most colleges and universities now have gay rights organizations on campus. In 1996, in *Romer v. Evans*, the Supreme Court voided a state constitutional amendment approved by the voters of Colorado that denied homosexuals protection against discrimination. The Court found that the Colorado amendment

When the Massachusetts Supreme Court held that the state's constitution required recognition of gay marriage, the issue became a factor in the 2004 presidential election. Here supporters and opponents of gay marriage protest outside the Massachusetts State House as the legislators considered amending the Massachusetts constitution to overturn the court's decision.

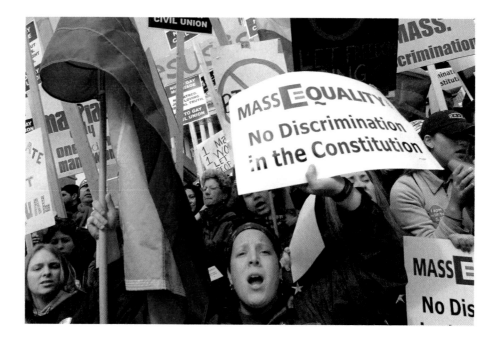

violated the U.S. Constitution's guarantee of equal protection of the law. In 2003, in *Lawrence v. Texas*, the Supreme Court overturned *Bowers v. Hardwick* when it voided a Texas antisodomy law on the grounds that such laws were unconstitutional intrusions of the right to privacy.

The newest issue concerning gay rights is gay marriage. Most states have laws banning same-sex marriage and the recognition of such marriages that occur in other states. However, the state of Vermont recognizes gay "civil unions," and several states provide domestic partnership benefits to same-sex couples. In November 2003, the Massachusetts Supreme Court declared that the state's constitution guaranteed same-sex couples the right to marry. From San Francisco to Boston, gays rushed to the altar, provoking a strong backlash from social conservatives. President Bush called for a constitutional amendment to ban gay marriage.

Amending the Constitution is difficult, and both the public and elected officials are divided on the wisdom of doing so. In the meantime, gays push for benefits associated with marriage, including health insurance, taxes, Social Security payments, hospital visitation rights, and many other aspects of life that most people take for granted.

Affirmative Action

The public policy paths for women and minorities have not been identical. However, they have converged in the debate about affirmative action to overcome the effects of past discrimination. Some people argue that groups that have suffered invidious discrimination require special efforts to provide them access to education and jobs. **Affirmative action** involves efforts to bring about increased employment, promotion, or admission for members of such groups. The goal is to move beyond *equal opportunity* (in which everyone has the same chance of obtaining good jobs, for example) toward *equal results* (in which different groups have the same percentage of success in obtaining those jobs). This goal might be accomplished through special rules in the public and private sectors that recruit or otherwise give preferential treatment to previously disadvantaged groups. Numerical quotas that ensure that a portion of government contracts, law school admissions, or police department promotions go to minorities and women are the strongest and most controversial form of affirmative action.

affirmative action

A policy designed to give special attention to or compensatory treatment for members of some previously disadvantaged group.

The constitutional status of affirmative action is not clear. New state and federal laws have discriminated *in favor of* these previously disadvantaged groups. Some state governments adopted affirmative action programs to increase minority enrollment, job holding, or promotion. Eventually, the federal government mandated that all state and local governments, as well as each institution receiving aid from or contracting with the federal government, adopt an affirmative action program. (See "Issues of the Times: Affirmative Action.")

One such program was introduced at the University of California at Davis. Eager to produce more minority physicians in California, the medical school set aside 16 of 100 places in the entering class for "disadvantaged groups." One White applicant who did not make the freshman class was Allan Bakke. After receiving his rejection letter from Davis for two straight years, Bakke learned that the mean scores on the Medical College Admissions Test of students admitted under the university's program were the 46th percentile on verbal tests and the 35th on science tests. Bakke's scores on the same tests were at the 96th and 97th percentiles, respectively. He sued UC-Davis, claiming that it had denied him equal protection of the laws by discriminating against him because of his race.

The result was an important Supreme Court decision in Bakke's favor, **Regents of the University of California v. Bakke** (1978).[28] The Court ordered Bakke admitted, holding that the UC-Davis Special Admissions Program did discriminate against him because of his race. Yet the Court refused to order UC-Davis never to use race as a criterion for admission. A university could, said the Court, adopt an "admissions program where race or ethnic background is simply one element—to be weighed fairly against other elements—in the selection process." It could *not*, as the UC-Davis Special Admissions Program did, set aside a quota of spots for particular groups.

Although Bakke ended up in medical school, Brian Weber did not get into an apprenticeship program he wanted to enter in Louisiana. In *United Steelworkers of America, AFL-CIO v. Weber* (1979), the Court found that the Kaiser Aluminum Company's special training program, which employed a quota for minorities, was intended to rectify years of past employment discrimination at Kaiser. Thus, said the Court, a voluntary union- and management-sponsored program to take more African Americans than Whites did *not* discriminate against Weber.

Until 1995, the Court was more deferential to Congress than to local government in upholding affirmative action programs. In 1989, the Court found a Richmond, Va., plan that reserved 30 percent of city subcontracts for minority firms to be unconstitutional.[29] In 1980, on the other hand, the Court upheld a federal rule setting aside 10 percent of all federal construction contracts for minority-owned firms.[30] In 1990, the Court agreed that Congress may require preferential treatment for minorities to increase their ownership of broadcast licenses.[31] This event marked the first time the Supreme Court upheld a specific affirmative action program that was not devised to remedy past discrimination.

Things changed in 1995, however. In **Adarand Constructors v. Pena**, the Court overturned the decision regarding broadcast licenses and cast grave doubt on its holding regarding contracts set aside for minority-owned firms. It held that federal programs that classify people by race, even for an ostensibly benign purpose such as expanding opportunities for members of minorities, should be presumed to be unconstitutional. Such programs must be subject to the most searching judicial inquiry and can survive only if they are "narrowly tailored" to accomplish a "compelling governmental interest." In other words, the Court applied criteria for evaluating affirmative action programs similar to those it applies to other racial classifications, the less benign suspect classifications we discussed earlier in the chapter. These are also the same criteria the Court has applied to state affirmative action programs since 1989. Although *Adarand Constructors v. Pena* did not void federal affirmative action programs in general, it certainly limits their potential impact.

On other matters, the Court has approved preferential treatment of minorities in promotions;[32] and it has also ordered quotas for minority union memberships.[33] We

Regents of the University of California v. Bakke

A 1978 Supreme Court decision holding that a state university could not admit less qualified individuals solely because of their race.

Adarand Constructors v. Pena

A 1995 Supreme Court decision holding that federal programs that classify people by race, even for an ostensibly benign purpose such as expanding opportunities for minorities, should be presumed to be unconstitutional.

Issues of the Times

The Issue: Affirmative Action

Nearly everyone in America supports equal opportunity for employment, promotion, or admission to universities. Few people believe any group should be at a disadvantage. However, consensus breaks down when the focus turns to equal results in obtaining these jobs or university slots. There is little support for giving some people a special advantage, even if it is to overcome past discrimination.

How do we reconcile these views with the following facts: (1) not everyone has the same chance to take advantage of a theoretical opportunity; (2) discrimination still occurs in some quarters of society; and (3) the nation is becoming more diverse and the legitimacy of institutions requires that they be broadly representative of American society?

Read All About It

What the United States Army Teaches Us About Affirmative Action

By Brent Staples
January 6, 2003, Monday

The Harvard sociologist Nathan Glazer argued fervently against affirmative action policies during the 1970's but later changed his mind. By the late 1990's, he and many other conservatives had come to see that failing to integrate the institutions that confer wealth and power would threaten the legitimacy of democracy itself.

They may have been looking at California, where the decision to outlaw the use of race in public college admissions in 1996 was initially seen as the death knell for affirmative action. But the disappearance of black and Latino faces from the state's elite public universities, and the threat of a "white out" on campuses nationwide, worried conservatives as well as liberals. Other states began to back away from proposals that would have

killed off affirmative action without leaving a comparable mechanism in its place.

When race-sensitive admissions became an issue in Texas, under Gov. George W. Bush, and in Florida, under his brother Jeb, both states defused an explosive situation with plans that guaranteed admission to fixed percentages of students. As governor, George W. Bush

Please see Action   **Page 169**

Action

Continued from Page 168

kept diversity—and the civic peace—by guaranteeing admission to the top 10 percent of students in each high school.

The core principle behind affirmative action is that excluding black people undermines civic harmony and runs counter to American ideals. This was evident in the case of the United States Army. After years of racial strife and rigorous segregation, it transformed itself into the most fully integrated organization yet seen in this country.

The military during both World Wars consigned most black people to support jobs. The top brass commonly defended discrimination in racist terms, arguing that black men lacked the courage to fight or the intelligence to lead. These bigoted policies shadowed the military long after formal segregation was ended and nearly tore the Army apart during the 1960's and 70's. One of the pivotal figures in the transformation was Clifford Alexander, President Jimmy Carter's secretary of the Army. Early in his tenure, Mr. Alexander put a hold on a list of officers proposed for promotion to general. He was troubled, as he explained in a 1997 Op-Ed article, "because no black colonels had been promoted, even though many had achieved that rank and served with distinction."

The board that handled promotions was ordered to look at the records of eligible black colonels and to determine if they had been given lesser assignments or evaluated negatively by officers who were racially prejudiced. Once race-related blemishes were expunged, black colonels with otherwise sterling records emerged as strong candidates for promotion.

This decision was affirmative action in its purest, most elemental form. But 25 years of distortion and

Loaded terms such as "quotas" and "reverse discrimination" have made it all but impossible to see affirmative action as a constructive and vitally important policy for the United States.

political warfare over this issue have made it difficult for most people to speak clearly on the subject or even to recognize affirmative action when they see it. Loaded terms such as "quotas" and "reverse discrimination" have made it all but impossible to see affirmative action as a constructive and vitally important policy for the United States.

This charged atmosphere has obscured the story of the Army's spectacular transformation. Mr. Alexander, for example, took offense when President Bill Clinton argued that Colin Powell, promoted to brigadier general during Mr. Alexander's tenure, was the product of an affirmative action program. Mr. Alexander viewed the measures he had taken as common-sense fairness but rejected the label "affirmative action." The term, he believed, implied that the black candidates for general had been less qualified than the white candidates or that they had been given some "extra" benefit. The truth, of course, is that the black officers would have been trapped in oblivion but for a strategy that allowed them to escape what were known as "nicks" on their records made by unfair superiors.

The Army also took steps to ensure that race would no longer be an obstacle to promotion. It ensured that all junior officers had a reasonable chance of getting assignments that, if performed well, made them eligible to move up. As the military historians Charles C. Moskos and John Sibley Butler wrote in "All That We Can Be: Black Leadership and Racial Integration the Army Way," the Army is "the only place in American life where whites are routinely bossed around by blacks." Twelve percent of the Army's officers are black.

The typical Army base is far more racially integrated than the average town or college campus. The rest of the country lags behind. Most black and Latino students are still confined to mediocre schools that place even excellent, hard-working students at a disadvantage in terms of standardized test scores.

Think About It

- Do you support the army's approach to affirmative action?
- Does the army's approach to promotion help get minorities into the army in the first place?
- Can the army's approach to affirmative action be used to rectify the imbalance of minorities in the nation's leading universities or in the most prestigious and lucrative positions in business?
- Do most organizations have a similar hierarchy to that in the army?

How You Can Make a Difference

Influencing Affirmative Action

For college students, affirmative action remains an important issue regardless of your race or gender. In one way or another, affirmative action impacts college administration policies, financial aid packages, graduate school prospects, and job opportunities. Emotions can run deep when debating this issue. There is even considerable disagreement over the precise definition of affirmative action. It is possible, however, to get involved in this issue without generating hostility or assailing the character of your opponents.

In the decades following the civil rights movement and the federal intervention in the 1960s and 1970s, the drive for racial and gender equality made big strides. Legal forms of discrimination have all but disappeared as a result of increased government oversight and heightened public awareness. Although few dispute that disparities still remain, there now exists a divide over how to best address these inequalities and ensure civil rights for all in twenty-first-century America. This divide manifests itself most clearly in the debate over affirmative action.

Do you believe that affirmative action is needed to preserve the advances made in civil rights since the 1950s? The NAACP (*www.naacp.org*), Americans United for Affirmative Action (*www.auaa.org*), and the American Association of University Women (*www.aauw.org*) stand out as organizations that can offer you ways to support the policies of affirmative action. Perhaps you believe that affirmative action policies might actually undermine the effort to ensure civil rights for all. If so, you should contact organizations such as Campaign for a Color-Blind America (*www.equalrights.com*), the American Civil Rights Institute (*www.acri.org*), and the Center for Equal Opportunity (*www.ceousa.org*) to see how you can participate in their causes.

Regardless of which view you hold, college students can make a difference in how their university, city, and state respond to affirmative action. You can make your views known through letter and e-mail campaigns, voter registration drives, and even student protests.

What you can do:
- Contact the NAACP, Americans United for Affirmative Action, or the American Association of University Women for more pro-affirmative action information.
- Contact Campaign for a Color-Blind America, the American Civil Rights Institute, or the Center for Equal Opportunity for more information on ending affirmative action.
- Contact school and government officials and express your concerns about affirmative action.
- Educate yourself and others on this issue and publicly advocate your views.

examine a case of a public employer using affirmative action promotions to counter underrepresentation of women and minorities in the workplace in "You Are the Judge: The Case of the Santa Clara Dispatcher."

On the other hand, the Court has ruled that affirmative action does not exempt recently hired minorities from traditional work rules specifying the "last hired, first fired" order of layoffs.[34] In 1986, the Court found unconstitutional an effort to give preference to African-American teachers in layoffs, because this policy punished innocent White teachers and the African-American teachers had not been the actual victims of past discrimination.[35]

Not everyone agrees that affirmative action is a wise or fair policy. There is little support from the general public for programs such as those that set aside jobs or employ quotas for members of minority groups. Opposition is especially strong when people view affirmative action as *reverse discrimination*—as in the case of individuals like Allan Bakke who are themselves blameless—and less qualified individuals are hired or admitted to educational or training programs because of their minority status.

Critics of reverse discrimination argue that any race or gender discrimination is wrong, even when its purpose is to rectify past injustices rather than to reinforce them. After all, Bakke and Johnson could no more help being White and male than Diane Joyce could help being a woman. Opponents of affirmative action believe that merit is the only fair basis for distributing benefits. Bakke and Johnson found that the rules by

You Are the Judge

The Case of the Santa Clara Dispatcher

For four years, Diane Joyce patched asphalt with a Santa Clara county road crew around San Jose, Calif., and its suburbs. She applied for a promotion, hoping to work in the less strenuous and better-paid position of dispatcher. Another applicant for the job was Paul Johnson, a White male who had worked for the agency for 13 years.

Like Diane, Paul did well on the exam given to all applicants; in fact, the two scored among the top six applicants, Diane with a score of 73, and Paul with 75. Knowing that Paul's score was a shade better and his work experience longer, the supervisor decided to hire him. The county's affirmative action officers overruled the supervisor, however, and Diane got the job. Paul decided to get a lawyer.

Paul's lawyer argued that Diane's promotion violated Title VII of the Civil Rights Act of 1964. This law, originally passed to guarantee minority access to jobs and promotions, makes it unlawful for an employer to deprive any individual of employment opportunities because of their race, color, religion, gender, or national origin.

You Be the Judge: Should Diane Joyce have been promoted?

Answer: In *Johnson v. Transportation Agency, Santa Clara County* (1987), the Supreme Court held that public employers may use carefully constructed affirmative action promotion plans, designed to remedy specific past discriminations, to counter women's and minorities' underrepresentation in the workplace. Thus, Diane Joyce kept her job. In a stinging dissent, Justice Scalia complained that the Court was "converting [the law] from a guarantee that race or sex will not be a basis for employment determinations, to a guarantee that it often will."

which institutions operated had suddenly changed—and they suffered as a result. It is easy to sympathize with them.

In 1996, California voters passed Proposition 209, which banned state affirmative action programs based on race, ethnicity, or gender in public hiring, contracting, and educational admissions (Washington state passed a similar ban in 1998). Opponents immediately filed a lawsuit in federal court to block enforcement of the law, claiming that it violated the Fourteenth Amendment but courts upheld the law. There is little question that support for Proposition 209 represents a widespread skepticism about affirmative action programs.

In 2003, the Supreme Court made two important decisions on affirmative action in college admissions. First, the Court agreed that there was a compelling interest in promoting racial diversity on campus. The Court upheld the University of Michigan law school's use of race as one of many factors in admission in *Grutter v. Bollinger* (2003). The Court found that the law school's use of race as a plus in the admissions process was narrowly tailored and that it made individualistic, holistic reviews of applicants in a nonmechanical fashion.

In *Gratz v. Bollinger* (2003), however, the Court struck down the University of Michigan's system of undergraduate admissions in which every applicant from an underrepresented racial or ethnic minority group was automatically awarded 20 points of the 100 needed to guarantee admission. The Court said that the system was tantamount to using a quota, which it outlawed in *Bakke*, because it made the factor of race decisive for virtually every minimally qualified underrepresented minority applicant. The 20 points awarded to minorities were more than the school awarded for some measures of academic excellence, writing ability, or leadership skills.

On the other hand, the case for affirmative action is also persuasive. Proponents of these policies argue that what constitutes merit is highly subjective and can embody prejudices of which the decision maker may be quite unaware. Experts suggest that a man can "look more like" a road dispatcher and thus get a higher rating from interviewers than a woman might. Affirmative action supporters believe that increasing the number of women and minorities in desirable jobs is such an important social goal that

Simulation

You Are the Mayor

it should be considered when determining an individual's qualifications. They claim that what White males lose from affirmative action programs are privileges to which they were never entitled in the first place; after all, nobody has the right to be a doctor or a road dispatcher. Research has found that affirmative action offers significant benefits for women and minorities with relatively small costs for White males.[36]

Understanding Civil Rights and Public Policy

The original Constitution is silent on the issue of equality. The only direct reference is in the Fourteenth Amendment, which forbids the states to deny "equal protection of the laws." Those five words have been the basis for major civil rights statutes and scores of judicial rulings protecting the rights of minorities and women. These laws and decisions, granting people new rights, have empowered groups to seek and gain still more victories. The implications of their success for democracy and the scope of government are substantial.

Civil Rights and Democracy

Equality is a basic principle of democracy. Every citizen has one vote because democratic government presumes that each person's needs, interests, and preferences are neither any more nor any less important than the needs, interests, and preferences of every other person. Individual liberty is an equally important democratic principle, one that can conflict with equality.

Equality tends to favor majority rule. Because under simple majority rule everyone's wishes rank equally, the policy outcome that most people prefer seems to be the fairest choice in cases of conflict. What happens, however, if the majority wants to deprive the minority of certain rights? In situations like these, equality threatens individual liberty. Thus, the principle of equality can invite the denial of minority rights, whereas the principle of liberty condemns such action.[37]

Majority rule is not the only threat to liberty. Politically and socially powerful minorities have suppressed majorities as well as other minorities. Women have long outnumbered men in America, about 53 percent to 47 percent. In the era of segregation, African Americans outnumbered Whites in many Southern states. Inequality persisted, however, because customs that reinforced it were entrenched within the society and because inequality often served the interests of the dominant groups. When slavery and segregation existed in an agrarian economy, Whites could get cheap agricultural labor. When men were breadwinners and women were homemakers, married men had a source of cheap domestic labor.

Both African Americans and women made many gains even when they lacked one essential component of democratic power: the vote. They used other rights—such as their First Amendment freedoms—to fight for equality. When Congress protected the right of African Americans to vote in the 1960s, the nature of Southern politics changed dramatically. The democratic process is a powerful vehicle for disadvantaged groups to press their claims.

Civil Rights and the Scope of Government

Civil rights laws increase the scope and power of government. These laws regulate the behavior of individuals and institutions. Restaurant owners must serve all patrons regardless of race. Professional schools must admit women. Employers must accommodate people with disabilities and make an effort to find minority workers, whether they want to or not. Those who want to reduce the scope of government are uneasy with these laws, if not downright hostile to them.

The Founders might be greatly perturbed if they knew about all the civil rights laws the government has enacted; these policies do not conform to the eighteenth-century idea of limited government. But the Founders would expect the national government to do whatever is necessary to hold the nation together. The Civil War showed that the original Constitution did not adequately deal with issues like slavery that could destroy the society the Constitution's writers had struggled to secure.

However, civil rights, like civil liberties, is an area in which increased government activity in protecting basic rights can lead to greater checks on government by those who benefit from such protections. Remember that much of segregation was *de jure*, established by governments. Moreover, government action in the area of civil rights can be viewed as the protection of individualism. Basic to the notion of civil rights is that individuals are not to be judged according to characteristics they share with a group. Thus, civil rights protect the individual against collective discrimination.

The question of where to draw the line in the government's efforts to protect civil rights has received different answers at different points in American history, but few Americans want to turn back the clock to the days of *Plessy v. Ferguson* and Jim Crow laws or to the exclusion of women from the workplace.

Summary

Racial minorities have struggled for equality since the very beginning of the Republic. In the era of slavery, the Supreme Court upheld the practice and denied slaves any rights. After the Civil War and Reconstruction ended, legal segregation was established. For a time, the Supreme Court sanctioned Jim Crow laws, but in 1954, the *Brown v. Board of Education* case held that *de jure* racial segregation violated equal protection of the laws, which was guaranteed by the Fourteenth Amendment. This event marked the beginning of the era of civil rights. *Brown* inaugurated a movement that succeeded in ending virtually every form of legal discrimination against minorities.

Although feminists have not ignored the courts, the struggle for women's equality has emphasized legislation over litigation. Women won the right to vote in 1920, but the Equal Rights Amendment has not yet been ratified. This defeat did not kill the feminist movement, however. Comparable worth, women's role in the military, sexual harassment, and the balance between work and family are among the many controversial women's issues still being debated.

The interests of women and minorities have converged on the issue of affirmative action—that is, policies requiring special efforts on behalf of disadvantaged groups. In the *Bakke* case and in decisions like *Johnson v. Santa Clara*, the Court ruled that affirmative action plans were both legal and constitutional. However, there is substantial opposition to what many see as reverse discrimination.

The civil rights umbrella is a large one. Increasing numbers of groups seek protection for their rights. Older and younger Americans, people with disabilities, and homosexuals have used the laws to ensure their equality. People with AIDS and other chronically ill people may mount battles yet to be fought in the political arena. It is difficult to predict what controversies the twenty-first century will bring, when minority groups will outnumber the current majority.

KEY TERMS

civil rights
Fourteenth Amendment
equal protection of the
   laws
Thirteenth Amendment
Civil Rights Act of 1964
suffrage

Fifteenth Amendment
poll taxes
White primary
Twenty-fourth
   Amendment
Voting Rights Act of 1965
Nineteenth Amendment

Equal Rights Amendment
comparable worth
Americans with
   Disabilities Act of 1990
affirmative action

KEY CASES

Scott v. Sandford (1857)
Plessy v. Ferguson (1896)
Brown v. Board of Education (1954)
Korematsu v. United States (1944)
Reed v. Reed (1971)
Craig v. Boren (1976)
Regents of the University of California v. Bakke (1978)
Adarand Constructors v. Pena (1995)

INTERNET RESOURCES

www.law.cornell.edu/topics/equal_protection.html
The background material and text of the landmark cases on equal protection.

www.usdoj.gov/crt/
Homepage of the Civil Rights Division of the U.S. Department of Justice containing background information and discussion of current events.

www.usdoj.gov/crt/ada/adahom1.htm
Homepage of the Americans with Disabilities Act of the U.S. Department of Justice containing background information and discussion of current events.

www.naacp.org
Homepage of the NAACP containing background information and discussion of current events.

www.civilrightsproject.harvard.edu/
Homepage of the Civil Rights Project at Harvard University, with background information and other resources on civil rights.

www.usccr.gov/
U.S. Commission on Civil Rights homepage, with news of civil rights issues around the country.

GET CONNECTED

Race, Affirmative Action, and Equal Opportunity

Race is an enduring issue in American politics. Historically, the debate has focused on relations between Blacks and Whites, but demographic trends and immigration is changing the debate. The Hispanic population in the United States is growing, adding to the complexity of race relations. Decision makers have been asked to develop ways to provide for equal opportunities for all races without creating a system of race-based quotas. Let us compare several strategies for implementing affirmative action and/or equal opportunity.

Search the Web

Go the Civil Rights.org web page on affirmative action *http://www.civilrights.org/issues/affirmative/*. You may want to read the information on affirmative action in university admissions decisions more closely. Also visit the Center for Equal Opportunity's website *http://www.ceousa.org/*. You will find some information on affirmative action in university admissions as well.

Questions to Ask

- What is affirmative action? Do the two groups define affirmative action differently?
- What evidence does *civil rights.org* use to defend affirmative action? What evidence does the Center for Equal Opportunity use to oppose affirmative action?
- What do the two groups think should be done to increase access to higher education for all people regardless of race?

Why It Matters

Equality is central to our political culture. One of the most difficult tasks of policymakers is bridging the gap between equality of opportunity and equality of results. It is critical that they integrate all citizens fully into American life, but they must do so in a manner that most citizens perceive to be fair to those who have not suffered from past discrimination.

Get Involved

Look at the other students in the class. How many are of a race different than yours? How many are of the opposite gender? Ask several of those students about racial preferences in college admissions decisions. Are the other students' views about racial preferences different from your own?

To see more Get Connected exercises for Chapter 5, go to www.ablongman.com/edwards.

FOR FURTHER READING

Baer, Judith A. *Women in the Law: The Struggle Toward Equality from the New Deal to the Present*, 2nd ed. New York: Holmes and Meier, 1996. An excellent analysis of women's changing legal status.

Berger, Raoul. *Government by Judiciary: The Transformation of the Fourteenth Amendment.* Cambridge, MA: Harvard University Press, 1977. Berger is not one who favors use of the Fourteenth Amendment to expand equality.

Bergman, Barbara R. *In Defense of Affirmative Action.* New York: Basic Books, 1996. An argument on behalf of affirmative action policies.

Berry, Mary F. *Why ERA Failed.* Bloomington: Indiana University Press, 1986. An excellent account of public policies affecting women, with particular attention to the demise of the Equal Rights Amendment.

Bowen, William G., and Derek Bok. *The Shape of the River: The Long-Term Consequences of Considering Race in College and University Admissions.* Princeton, NJ: Princeton University Press, 1998. Former presidents of Harvard and Princeton discuss affirmative action in higher education.

García, John A. *Latino Politics in America: Community, Culture, and Interests.* Lanham, MD: Rowman & Littlefield, 2003. An insightful view of Latino politics.

Greenberg, Jack. *Crusader in the Courts.* New York: Basic Books, 1994. The story of litigation in the civil rights era as told by one of the chief participants.

Kluger, Richard. *Simple Justice.* New York: Knopf, 1976. The story of the *Brown* case.

Mansbridge, Jane. *Why We Lost the ERA.* Chicago: University of Chicago Press, 1986. The politics of women's rights.

McClain, Paula D., and Joseph Stewart. *"Can't We All Get Along?"*, 3rd ed. Boulder, CO: Westview, 2002. Racial and ethnic minorities in American politics.

McGlen, Nancy, and Karen O'Connor. *Women's Rights: The Struggle for Equality in the Nineteenth and Twentieth Centuries.* New York: Praeger, 1983. A good account of the struggle for equal rights for women.

Nakanishi, Don T., and James S. Lai, eds. *Asian American Politics: Law, Participation, and Policy.* Lanham, MD: Rowman & Littlefield, 2003. Essays focusing on Asian-American politics.

Urofsky, Melvin I. *A Conflict of Rights: The Supreme Court and Affirmative Action.* New York: Scribner's, 1991. A case study of the issues, people, and events surrounding the case of *Joyce v. Johnson.*

Wilkins, David E. *American Indian Politics and the American Political System.* Lanham, MD: Rowman & Littlefield, 2002. Excellent treatment of Native American issues and politics.

Woodward, C. Vann. *The Strange Career of Jim Crow*, 2nd ed. New York: Oxford University Press, 1966. Examines the evolution of Jim Crow laws in the South.

Public Opinion and Political Action

■ American public opinion about the events of September 11, 2001, and the subsequent war in Afghanistan reflected a unanimity that is rarely seen. Normally, analysts find a great diversity of views among the American public, and public opinion surveys usually reveal many conflicting attitudes that frequently reflect ambivalence. But such was not the case in this instance. Hundreds of millions of Americans responded with remarkably near-unanimous opinions. Most everyone agreed that this was an act of war that demanded an immediate response by force. Partisan differences, racial differences, and regional differences mattered little in understanding attitudes about the events of September 11 and the war against terrorism.

A CNN/USA Today poll conducted on September 11, 2001, found that 86 percent felt that the attacks that day had been an act of war. A Washington Post/ABC poll conducted on September 13 found 93 percent favored military action when asked, "If the United States can identify the groups or nations responsible for the attacks, would you support or oppose taking military action against them?" The same poll found that 85 percent favored striking at Afghanistan if Osama Bin Laden was found to be culpable and Afghanistan refused to turn him over. Support for military action dropped a bit when people were asked if it meant innocent civilians might be hurt or killed, and a bit more when posed with the scenario of a long war with large numbers of U.S. troops killed or injured. But 69 percent of the population nevertheless supported the use of force even under the conditions of Afghan civilian casualties and high military costs to the United States.

Not only did the vast majority of the American public immediately give their support for military action, they continued to support such action once hostilities commenced in Afghanistan. At

http://www.pollingreport.com we found reports of 18 different public opinion polls that asked people whether they approved or disapproved of U.S. military action being taken in response to the terrorist attacks. The level of support was consistently high, ranging from 86 to 92 percent. Such support levels exceeded public support levels for the Persian Gulf War in 1991, which is typically thought of as an overwhelmingly supported military operation.

The case of September 11 is clearly an exception to the rule regarding public opinion. Usually, public opinion polls are taken to find out the level of disagreement in the country and what sorts of people favor which actions. As will be seen in this chapter, the degree of unanimity apparent in public opinion immediately after the terrorist attacks is most unusual.

177

Politicians and columnists commonly intone the words "the American people . . ." and then claim their view as that of the citizenry. Yet it would be hard to find a statement about the American people—who they are and what they believe—that is either 100 percent right or 100 percent wrong. The American people are wondrously diverse. There are about 295 million Americans, forming a mosaic of racial, ethnic, and cultural groups. America was founded on the principle of tolerating diversity and individualism, and it remains one of the most diverse countries in the world today. Most Americans view this diversity as one of the most appealing aspects of their society.

public opinion

The distribution of the population's beliefs about politics and policy issues.

The study of American **public opinion** aims to understand the distribution of the population's belief about politics and policy issues. Because there are many groups with a great variety of opinions in the United States, this is an especially complex task. This is not to say that public opinion would be easy to study even if America were a more homogeneous society; as you will see, measuring public opinion involves painstaking interviewing procedures and careful wording of questions. Further complicating the task is the fact that people are often not well informed about the issues. The least informed are also the least likely to participate in the political process, a phenomenon that creates imbalances in who takes part in political action.

For American government to work efficiently and effectively, the diversity of the American public and its opinions must be faithfully channeled through the political process. This chapter reveals just how difficult this task is.

The American People

demography

The science of population changes.

census

A valuable tool for understanding demographic changes. The Constitution requires that the government conduct an "actual enumeration" of the population every ten years.

One way of looking at the American public is through **demography**—the science of human populations. The most valuable tool for understanding demographic changes in America is the **census.** The U.S. Constitution requires that the government conduct an "actual enumeration" of the population every ten years. The first census was conducted in 1790; the most recent census was done in 2000.

The Census Bureau tries to conduct the most accurate count of the population humanly feasible. It isn't an easy job, even with the allocation of billions of federal dollars to the task. After the 1990 Census was completed, the Bureau estimated that 4.7 million people were not counted. Furthermore, they found that members of minority groups were disproportionately undercounted, as they were apparently more suspicious of government and thus less willing to cooperate with census workers. In order to correct for such an undercount in 2000, the Clinton administration approved a plan to scientifically estimate the characteristics of those people who failed to respond to the census forms and follow-up visits from census workers, and then to incorporate this information into the official count. Conservatives maintained that such a procedure would be subject to manipulation, less accurate than a traditional head count, and unconstitutional. In the 1999 case of *Department of Commerce v. U.S. House of Representatives*, the Supreme Court ruled that sampling could not be used to determine the number of congressional districts each state is entitled to. However, the Court left the door open for the use of sampling procedures to adjust the count for other purposes, such as the allocation of federal grants to states. In the end, the Bush administration decided not to use the sampling option.

Changes in the U.S. population, as reflected in census figures, impact our culture and political system in numerous ways, which will be examined in the next few sections.

The Immigrant Society

The United States has always been a nation of immigrants. As John F. Kennedy said, America is "not merely a nation but a nation of nations."[1] All Americans except Native Americans are either descended from immigrants or are immigrants themselves. Today, federal law allows up to 800,000 new immigrants to be legally admitted to the

Responding to criticisms that many minority groups had been undercounted in the previous census, the Census Bureau launched special advertising campaigns to improve cooperation rates in these communities in 2000. Here you can see a poster in Detroit targeted at the large number of Iraqi immigrants in the city.

country every year. This is equivalent to adding a city with the population of Indianapolis every year. And in recent years, illegal immigrants have outnumbered legal immigrants.

There have been three great waves of immigration to the United States.

- Prior to the late nineteenth century, northwestern Europeans (English, Irish, Germans, and Scandinavians) constituted the first wave of immigration.
- During the late nineteenth and early twentieth century, southern and eastern Europeans (Italians, Jews, Poles, Russians, and others) made up much of the second wave. Most of these passed through Ellis Island in New York (now a popular museum) as their first stop in the new world.
- In recent decades, a third wave of immigrants has consisted of Hispanics (from Cuba, Central America, and Mexico) and Asians (from Vietnam, Korea, the Philippines, and elsewhere). The 1980s saw the second largest number of immigrants of any decade in American history, and the 1990s finished not far behind.

Immigrants bring with them their aspirations, as well as their own political beliefs. For example, Cubans in Miami, who nearly constitute a majority of the city's population, first came to America to escape Fidel Castro's Marxist regime and have brought their anti-Communist sentiments with them. Similarly, the Vietnamese came to America after a Communist takeover there. Cubans and Vietnamese are just two recent examples of the many types of immigrants who have come to America over the years to flee an oppressive government. Other examples from previous periods of heavy immigration include the Irish in the first wave and the Russians in the second. Throughout American history, such groups have fostered a great appreciation for individualism in American public policy by their wish to be free of governmental control.

The American Melting Pot

With its long history of immigration, the United States has often been called a **melting pot.** This phrase refers to a mixture of cultures, ideas, and peoples. As the third wave of immigration continues, policymakers have begun to speak of a new **minority majority,** meaning that America will eventually cease to have a White, generally Anglo-Saxon majority. The 2000 census data found an all-time low in the percentage of non-Hispanic White Americans—just over 69 percent of the population. African Americans made up 12 percent of the population, Hispanics 13 percent, Asians 4 percent, and

melting pot

The mixing of cultures, ideas, and peoples that has changed the American nation. The United States, with its history of immigration, has often been called a melting pot.

minority majority

The emergence of a non-Caucasian majority, as compared with a White, generally Anglo-Saxon majority. It is predicted that by about 2060, Hispanic Americans, African Americans, and Asian Americans together will outnumber White Americans.

Figure 6.1   The Coming Minority Majority

Based on the basis of current birth rates and immigration rates, the Census Bureau estimates that the demographics of the country should change as shown in the accompanying graph. Extend the lines a bit beyond the year 2050, and it is clear that the minority groups will soon be in the majority nationwide. Of course, should rates of birth and immigration change, so will these estimates. But already there are 65 congressional districts with a minority majority, about 85 percent of which are represented in the House by an African American, a Hispanic, or an Asian American.

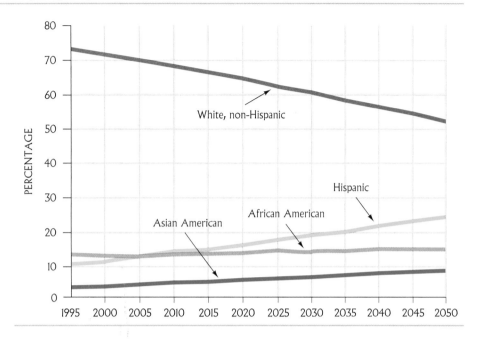

Native Americans slightly less than 1 percent. Between 1980 and 1990, minority populations grew at a much faster rate than the White population. As you can see in Figure 6.1, the Census Bureau estimates that by the middle of the twenty-first century, Whites will represent only 52 percent of the population.

Until recently, the largest minority group in the country has been the African-American population. One in eight Americans is a descendent of these reluctant immigrants: Africans who were brought to America by force as slaves. As discussed in Chapter 5, a legacy of racism and discrimination has left a higher proportion of the African-American population economically and politically disadvantaged than the White population. In 2002, the U.S. Census Bureau found that 24 percent of African Americans lived below the poverty line compared to 10 percent of Whites.

Despite this economic disadvantage, African Americans have recently been exercising a good deal of political power. The number of African-American elected officials has increased by over 500 percent since 1970.[2] African Americans have been elected as mayors of many of the country's biggest cities, including Los Angeles, New York, and Chicago. In 2001, Colin Powell became the first African-American Secretary of State and Condoleezza Rice became the nation's first African-American to serve as the president's National Security Advisor.

The familiar problems of African Americans sometimes obscure the problems of other minority groups, such as Hispanics (composed largely of Mexicans, Cubans, and Puerto Ricans). The 2000 Census reported that for the first time the Hispanic population outnumbered the African-American population. Like African Americans, Hispanics are concentrated in cities. Hispanics are rapidly gaining power in the Southwest, and cities such as San Antonio and Denver have elected mayors of Hispanic heritage. In 2002, the state legislatures of New Mexico, Texas, Arizona, Colorado, Florida, and California all had at least 9 percent Hispanic representation.[3]

An issue of particular concern to the Hispanic community is what to do about the problem of illegal immigration. The Simpson-Mazzoli Act, named after its congressional sponsors, requires that employers document the citizenship of their employees. Whether people are born in Canton, Ohio, or Canton, China, they must prove that they

Just north of San Diego, the problem of illegal immigration from Mexico has taken a dangerous turn. Seeking to make their way around a freeway checkpoint, immigrants sometimes attempt to cross the busy San Diego freeway. After a number of people had been hit by cars, authorities posted signs like these to warn motorists to look out for people crossing the freeway.

are either U.S. citizens or legal immigrants in order to work. Civil and criminal penalties can be assessed against employers who knowingly employ undocumented immigrants. This law has raised concern among leaders of immigrant groups, who worry that employers may simply decline to hire members of such groups rather than take any chances. There has been little evidence of this so far, however. In fact, many believe the provisions of the Simpson-Mazzoli Act have proved to be inadequate in stopping illegal immigration from Mexico. One proposed solution that has been very controversial in recent years involves denying all benefits from government programs to people who cannot prove that they are legal residents of the United States (see "Do We Need to Get Tougher with Illegal Immigrants?").

The Debate Over Immigration

Unlike Hispanics who have come to America to escape poverty, the recent influx of Asians has been driven by a new class of professional workers looking for greater opportunity. Asians who have come to America since the 1965 Immigration Act[4] opened the gate to them make up the most highly skilled immigrant group in American history, as Ronald Takaki documents.[5] Indeed, Asian Americans have often been called

Asian Americans have been labeled as the "superachievers" of the coming minority majority due to their high levels of educational achievement and income. The proportion of Asian-American students currently exceeds 40 percent at some University of California campuses.

You Are the Policymaker

Do We Need to Get Tougher with Illegal Immigrants?

Americans have traditionally welcomed immigrants with open arms. However, some immigrants have recently become less welcome: those who are in the country illegally. In states such as Texas and California, where many illegal immigrants from south of the border reside, there is concern that providing public services to these people is seriously draining state resources. This became the topic of heated debate when Californians voted on Proposition 187 in 1994. Labeled by its proponents as the "save our state initiative," this measure sought to cut illegal immigrants off from public services, such as the right of their children to attend public schools, and medical assistance for people with low incomes. According to its advocates, not only would Proposition 187 save the state treasury, but it would also cut down on the number of illegal immigrants—many of whom, they argued, had come mostly to take advantage of the free goods offered in America.

Opponents replied that although illegal immigration is surely a problem, the idea of cutting off public services could easily do more harm than good. They pointed out the risks to public health of denying illegal immigrants basic health care, such as immunizations that help control communicable diseases. And by throwing the children of illegal immigrants out of school, they argued that many would inevitably turn to crime with nothing to do all day. Besides, though they may be here illegally, these immigrants have to pay sales taxes on everything they buy and pay rent—a portion of which indirectly goes to the state when their landlords pay their property taxes. Given that they contribute to the tax base that pays for public services, opponents of Proposition 187 argued that they should in all fairness be entitled to make use of them.

The proponents of Proposition 187 won at the ballot box. However, so far they have lost in their attempts to get the measure enforced. The courts have consistently ruled that the proposition violated the rights of illegal immigrants as well as national laws concerning eligibility for federally funded benefits. Overall, the proposition was held to be an unconstitutional state scheme to regulate immigration.

Because illegal immigrants continue to stream into the United States, this issue remains a hot one. In 2004, the Republican Party platform advocated "strong workplace enforcement with tough penalties against employees and employers who violate immigration laws." In contrast, the Democratic Party platform proposed that "Undocumented immigrants within our borders who clear a background check, work hard and pay taxes should have a path to earn full participation in America." The Republican platform called such a proposal "amnesty" and argued that this would "have the effect of encouraging illegal immigration and would give an unfair advantage to those who have broken our laws."

What do you think? Do you think a tough approach is the way to go, or do you favor incorporating illegal immigrants who prove themselves worthy into American society? What are the advantages and disadvantages of each approach?

the superachievers of the minority majority. This is especially true in the case of educational attainment—49 percent of Asian Americans over the age of 25 hold a college degree, almost twice the national average. As a result, their median family income has already surpassed that of non-Hispanic Whites. Although still a very small minority group, Asian Americans have had some notable political successes. In 1996, Gary Locke (a Chinese American) was elected governor of Washington and in 2001 Norman Mineta (a Japanese American) was appointed to be Secretary of Transportation.

Whereas Asian Americans are the best off of America's minority groups, by far the worst off is the one indigenous minority, known today as Native Americans. Before Europeans arrived in America, 12 to 15 million Native Americans lived here. War and disease reduced their numbers to a mere 210,000 by 1910. About 4 million Americans currently list themselves as being of Native American heritage. Statistics show that they are the least healthy, the poorest, and the least educated group in the American melting pot. Only a handful of Native Americans have found wealth; even fewer have found power. Some tribes have discovered oil or other minerals on their land and have used these resources successfully. Other tribes have opened profitable casinos on their native lands. Many Native Americans, though, remain economically and politically disadvantaged in American society. In the Dakotas, site of the largest Sioux reservations, census data show that roughly half the Native Americans live below the poverty line.

Americans live in an increasingly multicultural and multilingual society. Yet, regardless of ethnic background most Americans share a common **political culture**— an overall set of values widely shared within a society. For example, there is much agreement among ethnic groups about many basic American values, such as the principle of treating all equally. Yet, not all observers view this most recent wave of immigration without concern. Ellis Cose has written that "racial animosity has proven to be both an enduring American phenomenon and an invaluable political tool." Because America has entered a period of rapid ethnic change, Cose predicts immigration "will be a magnet for conflict and hostility."[6]

The emergence of the minority majority is just one of several major demographic changes that have altered the face of American politics. In addition, the population has been moving and aging.

political culture

An overall set of values widely shared within a society.

Understanding Who We Are

The Regional Shift

For most of American history, the most populous states were concentrated in the states north of the Mason-Dixon line and east of the Mississippi River. As you can see in Figure 6.2, though, over the last 60 years, much of America's population growth has been centered in the West and South. In particular, the populations of Florida, California, and Texas have grown rapidly as people moved to the Sunbelt. From 1990 to 2000, the rate of population growth was 24 percent in Florida, 14 percent in California, and 23 percent in Texas. In contrast, population growth in the Northeast was a scant 5 percent.

Demographic changes are associated with political changes. States gain or lose congressional representation as their population changes, and thus power shifts as well. This **reapportionment** process occurs once a decade, after every census. After each census, the 435 seats in the House of Representatives are reallocated to the states on the basis of population changes. Thus, as California has grown throughout this century, its representation in the House has increased from just 7 in 1900 to 53 as of 2002. New York, on the other hand, has lost about one-third of its delegation over the last 50 years.

reapportionment

The process of reallocating seats in the House of Representatives every ten years on the basis of the results of the census.

The Graying of America

Florida, one of the three megastates, has grown in large part as a result of its attractiveness to senior citizens. Nationwide, the fastest growing age group in America is composed of citizens over 65. Not only are people living longer as a result of medical advances, but the birthrate has dropped substantially. About 60 percent of adult Americans living today grew up in families of four or more children. If the current trend continues, this figure will eventually be cut to 30 percent.[7]

Social Security is structured as a pay-as-you-go system. That means today's workers pay the benefits for today's retirees. In 1940, there were 42 workers per retiree; today there are three. By 2040 there will be only two, which will put tremendous pressure on the Social Security system. Begun under the New Deal, Social Security is exceeded only by national defense as America's most costly public policy. The current group of older Americans and those soon to follow can lay claim to trillions of dollars guaranteed by Social Security. People who have been promised benefits naturally expect to collect them, especially benefits for which they have made monthly contributions. Thus both political parties have long treated Social Security benefits as sacrosanct. Although some politicians have warned about the projected shortfalls in the Social Security system neither major party has yet proposed a plan for how to deal with this looming problem.

Figure 6.2　Shifting Population

These maps paint a population portrait of the United States over the last six decades. The states are drawn to scale on the basis of population. In 1940, the most populous states were concentrated east of the Mississippi River. New York, Pennsylvania, and Illinois stand out. By 2000 the national population picture—and the map—had changed considerably. Today the country's 295 million citizens are scattered more widely, and though large concentrations of population still dominate the East, there has been huge growth on the West Coast, in Texas, and in Florida.

1940

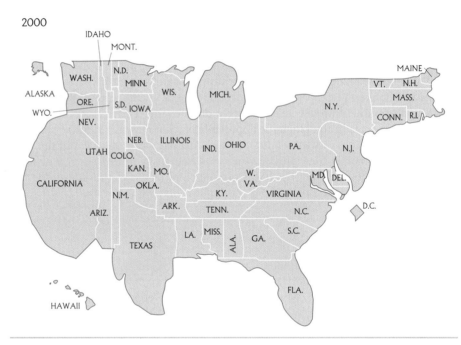

2000

Source: The 1940 map was the work of the National Opinion Research Center, University of Denver, as printed in John Gunther's 1946 book *Inside U.S.A.*

How Americans Learn About Politics: Political Socialization

political socialization

According to Richard Dawson, "the process through which an individual acquires his [or her] particular political orientations—his [or her] knowledge, feelings, and evaluations regarding his [or her] political world."

As the most experienced segment of the population, the elderly have undergone the most **political socialization**. Political socialization is "the process through which an individual acquires his or her particular political orientations—his or her knowledge, feelings, and evaluations regarding his or her political world."[8] As people become more socialized with age, their political orientations grow firmer. It should not be surprising that governments aim their socialization efforts largely at the young, not the elderly. Authoritarian regimes are particularly concerned with indoctrinating their citizens at an early age. For example, youth groups in the former Soviet Union were organized into the Komsomols, the Young Communist League. Membership in these groups was helpful in gaining admission to college and entering certain occupations. In the Komsomols, Soviet youth were taught their government's view of the advantages of communism (though apparently not well enough to keep the system going). In contrast, socialization is a much more subtle process in the United States.

The Process of Political Socialization

Only a small portion of Americans' political learning is formal. Civics or government classes in high school teach citizens some of the nuts and bolts of government—how many senators each state has, what presidents do, and so on. But such formal socialization is only the tip of the iceberg. Americans do most of their political learning without teachers or classes.

Informal learning is really much more important than formal, in-class learning about politics. Most informal socialization is almost accidental. Few parents sit down with their children and say, "Johnny, let us tell you why we're Republicans." Words like *pick up*, *absorb*, and *acquire* perhaps best describe the informal side of socialization. The family, the media, and the schools all serve as important agents of socialization.

The Family.   The family's role in socialization is central because of its monopoly on two crucial resources in the early years: time and emotional commitment. The powerful influence of the family is not easily undermined. Most students in an American government class like to think of themselves as independent thinkers, especially when it comes to politics. Yet one can predict how the majority of young people will vote simply by knowing the political leanings of their parents. Table 6.1 shows how well people's party identification corresponds with that of their parents.

As children approach adult status, though, some degree of adolescent rebellion against parents and their beliefs often takes place. Witnessing the outpouring of youthful rebellion in the late 1960s and early 1970s, many people thought a generation gap was opening up. Radical youth supposedly condemned their backward-thinking parents. Though such a gap did exist in a few families, the overall evidence for it was slim. Eight years after Jennings and Niemi first interviewed a sample of high school seniors and their parents in the mid-1960s, they still found far more agreement than

Table 6.1   How Party Identification Is Passed Down from One Generation to the Next

The National Election Study has sometimes asked respondents whether their parents thought of themselves as Democrats, Independents, or Republicans when they were growing up. In the most recent available data, 87 percent of those who could identify the partisanship of both parents reported that their parents agreed on partisan choice. Here you can see how these respondents have generally followed in their parents' footsteps politically.

	DEMOCRAT	INDEPENDENT	REPUBLICAN	TOTAL
Both parents Democrats	59	29	13	100%
Both parents Independents	17	67	16	100%
Both parents Republicans	12	29	59	100%

Source: Authors' analysis of 1992 National Election Study data.

disagreement across the generational divide. Moving out of the family nest and into adulthood, the offspring did become somewhat less like their parents politically, however.[9] Other socialization agents had apparently exerted influence in the intervening years.

The Mass Media. The mass media are "the new parent" according to many observers. Average grade-school youngsters spend more time each week watching television than they spend at school. And television now displaces parents as the chief source of information as children get older.

Unfortunately, today's generation of young adults is significantly less likely to watch television news and read newspapers than their elders. Many studies have attributed the relative lack of political knowledge of today's youth to their media consumption, or more appropriately, to their lack of it.[10] In 1965, Gallup found virtually no difference between age categories in frequency of following politics through the media. In recent years, however, a considerable age gap has opened up, with older people paying the most attention to the news and young adults the least. In fact, the typical viewer of the major national newscasts is now an astonishing 58 years old.[11] If you have ever turned on the TV news and wondered why so many of the commercials seem to be for various prescription drugs, now you know why.

School. Political socialization is as important to a government as it is to an individual. This is one reason why governments (including America's) often use schools to promote national loyalty and support for its basic values. In most American schools, the day begins with the Pledge of Allegiance. During the 1988 presidential campaign, George Bush argued that teachers should be required to lead students in the Pledge. His opponent, Michael Dukakis, had vetoed a bill to require this in Massachusetts, claiming that it was unconstitutional. Underlying Bush's argument was the assumption that proper socialization in the schools was crucial to the American political system—a position Dukakis disagreed with more in terms of means than in ends.

Governments throughout the world use schools to attempt to raise children committed to the basic values of the system. For years, American children have been successfully educated about the virtues of capitalism and democracy. In the hands of an unscrupulous government, though, educational socialization can sometimes be a dangerous tool. For example, in Nazi Germany, textbooks were used to justify murderous policies. Consider the following example from a Nazi-era math book:

> If a mental patient costs 4 Reichsmarks a day in maintenance, a cripple 5.50, and a criminal 3.50, and about 50,000 of these people are in our institutions, how much does it cost our state at a daily rate of 4 Reichsmarks—and how many marriage loans of 1,000 Reichsmarks per couple could have been given out instead?[12]

One can only imagine how students' constant exposure, to this kind of thinking warped the minds of some young people growing up in Nazi Germany.

Both authoritarian and democratic governments care that students learn the positive features of their political system because it helps ensure that youth will grow up to be supportive citizens. David Easton and Jack Dennis have argued that "those children who begin to develop positive feelings toward the political authorities will grow into adults who will be less easily disenchanted with the system than those children who early acquire negative, hostile sentiments."[13] Of course, this is not always the case. Well-socialized youths of the 1960s led the opposition to the American regime and the war in Vietnam. It could be argued, however, that even these protestors had been positively shaped by the socialization process, for the goal of most activists was to make the system more democratically responsive rather than to change American government radically.

These children—the faces of the coming minority majority population—suggest the unique problem of American political socialization: transforming people of diverse cultural backgrounds and beliefs into participating American citizens.

Today, education is often the issue that people cite as the most important to them, and there is no doubt that educational policy matters a great deal. Most American schools are public schools, financed by the government. Their textbooks are often chosen by the local and state boards, and teachers are certified by the state government. Schooling is perhaps the most obvious intrusion of the government into Americans' socialization. Education exerts a profound influence on a variety of political attitudes and behavior. Better-educated citizens are more likely to vote in elections, they exhibit more knowledge about politics and public policy, and they are more tolerant of opposing (even radical) opinions.

The payoffs of schooling extend beyond better jobs and better pay. Educated citizens also more closely approximate the model of a democratic citizen. A formal civics course may not make much difference, but the whole context of education does. As Albert Einstein once said, "Schools need not preach political doctrine to defend democracy. If they shape men and women capable of critical thought and trained in social attitudes, that is all that is necessary."

Political Learning over a Lifetime

Political learning does not, of course, end when one reaches 18, or even when one graduates from college. Politics is a lifelong activity. Because America is an aging society, it is important to consider the effects of growing older on political learning and behavior.

Aging increases political participation, as well as strength of party attachment. Young adults (those 18 through 25) lack experience with politics. Because political behavior is to some degree learned behavior, there is some learning yet to do. Political participation rises steadily with age until the infirmities of old age make it harder to participate, as can be seen in the data presented in Figure 6.3. Similarly, strength of party identification also increases as one grows older and often develops a pattern for usually voting for one party or another.

Politics, like most other things, is thus a learned behavior. Americans learn to vote, to pick a political party, and to evaluate political events in the world around them. One of the products of all this learning is what is known as public opinion.

Figure 6.3   Turnout by Age, 2000

This graph shows how turnout in the 2000 presidential election was related to age.

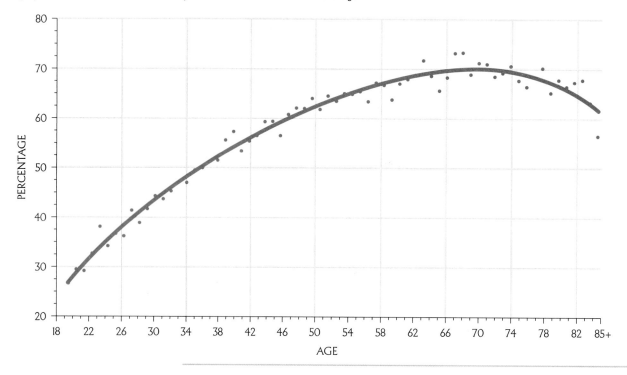

Source: Authors' analysis of 2000 Census Bureau data.

Measuring Public Opinion and Political Information

Before examining the role that public opinion plays in American politics, it is essential to learn about the science of public opinion measurement. How do we really know the approximate answers to questions such as what percentage of young people favor abortion rights, how many Hispanics supported George W. Bush's 2004 campaign, or what percentage of the public favored immediate air strikes against Afghanistan after September 11? Polls provide these answers, but there is much skepticism about polls. Many people wonder how accurately this can be done by only interviewing 1,000 or 1,500 people around the country. This section provides an explanation of how polling works, which will hopefully enable you to become a well-informed consumer of polls.

How Polls Are Conducted

Public opinion polling is a relatively new science. It was first developed by a young man named George Gallup, who initially did some polling for his mother-in-law, a longshot candidate for secretary of state in Iowa in 1932. With the Democratic landslide of that year, she won a stunning victory, thereby further stimulating Gallup's interest in politics. From that little acorn the mighty oak of public opinion polling has grown. The firm that Gallup founded spread throughout the democratic world, and in some languages, *Gallup* is actually the word used for an opinion poll.[14]

It would be prohibitively expensive and time consuming to ask every citizen his or her opinion on a whole range of issues. Instead, polls rely on a **sample** of the population—a relatively small proportion of people who are chosen to represent the

sample

A relatively small proportion of people who are chosen in a survey so as to be representative of the whole.

whole. Herbert Asher draws an analogy to a blood test to illustrate the principle of sampling.[15] Your doctor does not need to drain a gallon of blood from you to determine whether you have mononucleosis, AIDS, or any other disease. Rather, a small sample of blood will reveal its properties.

In public opinion polling, a sample of about 1,000 to 1,500 people can accurately represent the "universe" of potential voters. The key to the accuracy of opinion polls is the technique of **random sampling,** which operates on the principle that everyone should have an equal probability of being selected as part of the sample. Your chance of being asked to be in the poll should therefore be as good as that of anyone else—rich or poor, African American or White, young or old, male or female. If the sample is randomly drawn, about 12 percent of those interviewed will be African American, slightly over 50 percent female, and so forth, matching the population as a whole.

random sampling

The key technique employed by sophisticated survey researchers, which operates on the principle that everyone should have an equal probability of being selected for the sample.

Remember that the science of polling involves estimation; a sample can represent the population with only a certain degree of confidence. The level of confidence is known as the **sampling error,** which depends on the size of the sample. The more people interviewed in a poll, the more confident one can be of the results. A typical poll of about 1,500 to 2,000 respondents has a sampling error of ±3 percent. What this means is that 95 percent of the time the poll results are within 3 percent of what the entire population thinks. If 60 percent of the sample say they approve of the job the president is doing, one can be pretty certain that the true figure is between 57 and 63 percent.

sampling error

The level of confidence in the findings of a public opinion poll. The more people interviewed, the more confident one can be of the results.

In order to obtain results that will usually be within sampling error, researchers must follow proper sampling techniques. In perhaps the most infamous survey ever, a 1936 *Literary Digest* poll underestimated the vote for President Franklin Roosevelt by 19 percent, erroneously predicting a big victory for Republican Alf Landon. The well-established magazine suddenly became a laughingstock and soon went out of business. Although the number of responses the magazine obtained for its poll was a staggering 2,376,000, its polling methods were badly flawed. Trying to reach as many people as possible, the magazine drew names from the biggest lists they could find: telephone books and motor vehicle records. In the midst of the Great Depression, the people on these lists were above the average income level (only 40 percent of the public had telephones then; fewer still owned cars) and were more likely to vote Republican. The moral of the story is this: Accurate representation, not the number of responses, is the most important feature of a public opinion survey. Indeed, as polling techniques have advanced over the last 60 years, typical sample sizes have been getting smaller, not larger.

The newest computer and telephone technology has made surveying less expensive and more commonplace. In the early days of polling, pollsters needed a national network of interviewers to traipse door-to-door in their localities with a clipboard of questions. Now most polling is done on the telephone with samples selected through **random-digit dialing.** Calls are placed to phone numbers within randomly chosen exchanges (for example, 512–471-xxxx) around the country. In this manner, both listed and unlisted numbers are reached at a cost of about one-fifth that of person-to-person interviewing. There are a couple of disadvantages, however. About 7 percent of the population does not have a phone, and people are somewhat less willing to participate over the telephone than in person—it is easier to hang up than to slam the door in someone's face. These are small trade-offs for political candidates running for minor offices, for whom telephone polls are the only affordable method of gauging public opinion. However, in this era of cell phones, many pollsters are starting to worry whether this methodology will continue to work much longer. For an incisive discussion of this issue, see "Issues of the Times: Does Conducting Surveys by Telephone Still Make Sense?" on pages 190–191.

random-digit dialing

A technique used by pollsters to place telephone calls randomly to both listed and unlisted numbers when conducting a survey.

From its modest beginning with George Gallup's 1932 polls for his mother-in-law in Iowa, polling has become a big business. Public opinion polling is one of those American innovations, like soft drinks and fast food restaurants, that has spread throughout the world. From Manhattan to Moscow, from Tulsa to Tokyo, people want to know what other people think.

Simulation

You Are a Polling Consultant

Issues of the Times

The Issue: Does Conducting Surveys by Telephone Still Make Sense?

Polls are important in American democracy because they tell us what Americans think about the issues facing the country. The media regularly reports on poll findings as if they were definitive readings on public opinion. Politicians can, and often do, react to poll findings between elections in order to be responsive to public desires. Both the media and the politicians are quite aware of the margin of error inherent in any poll, as discussed in this chapter.

But what if inaccuracies in polling arise from other sources that cannot easily be measured? The calculations for the margin of error are dependent on the assumption that people who do not respond to the poll are no different from those who do respond. In the days when most people were fairly easy to reach

and were agreeable to being interviewed, this was a fairly reasonable assumption most of the time. However, as the following article notes, this state of affairs has changed due to the proliferation of

cell phones and caller ID. The impact on the polling industry, and our ability to accurately measure what the American public thinks, may well be far-reaching.

Read All About It

Cellphones and Caller ID Are Making Pollsters' Jobs Harder

By Adam Nagourney
November 5, 2002

A rapid rise in the use of cellphones and caller identification technology, along with telemarketing calls that are chasing Americans from their telephones, is making political polling more difficult and increasingly less reliable, pollsters say. A result this Election Day is that it is harder than ever for pollsters to find voters and to get them to say how they intend to vote.

Pollsters say a problem that they first began noting 10 years ago, as

Americans realized that answering machines could be used to screen out unwanted solicitations, is today forcing a re-examination of the methods by which they question voters.

In interviews, several pollsters said they now discussed ways to change how they approached a fundamental procedure in politics that has, over 75 years, moved from the mail to door-to-door canvassing to the telephone.

"At some point, there's going to be a crash between what's happening in the country and what's picked up on the phone," Stanley

Greenberg, President Bill Clinton's pollster in the White House, said yesterday.

Whit Ayres, a veteran Republican pollster, said: "I can't fathom 20 years from now the telephone remaining the primary means of data collection. This industry is in a transition from telephone data collection to Internet data collection."

"In the meantime," Mr. Ayres said, with a note of frustration in his voice, "we've got to get people to answer the phone."

Please see Cellphones Page 191

Cellphones

Continued from Page 190

Pollsters said the increasing difficulty in reaching people was undercutting their efforts to assemble a pool of voters that was scientifically large enough and diverse enough upon which to draw reliable conclusions. While some pollsters said they could compensate for that by staying in the field longer or calling more people, that kind of effort takes time and costs money, two things that are often in short supply at the end of a campaign.

Pollsters said they had tried to respond to the problem with various time-consuming and costly remedies. They have increased the time they spend in the field, employed teams of specialists to methodically call back numbers that are answered by machines, and mathematically adjusted their findings at the end of the survey period to make up for voters they might have missed.

But several described these as stop-gap measures that have been only partly successful. Pollsters are under intense pressure to move quickly and hold down costs. They are uncomfortable with the kind of statistical adjustments used to compensate for missed or refused calls.

In particular, pollsters said they might be undercounting the growing number of younger voters who only have cellphones, as well as elderly voters who, they said, tend to be especially wary of any call that sounds like a solicitation. Several pollsters said the rise in the number of unlisted telephone numbers was more pronounced in minority and low-income neighborhoods.

"There is a lot of evidence that all of this is making our life more difficult and hurting our efforts," Mark A. Schulman, the president of the American Association of Public Opinion Research, said yesterday.

But, Mr. Schulman added, "I'm not ready to run up the white flag and concede defeat."

Matthew Dowd, a Republican pollster who advises the White

In particular, pollsters said they might be undercounting the growing number of younger voters who only have cellphones, as well as elderly voters who, they said, tend to be especially wary of any call that sounds like a solicitation.

House, said: "Right now, I'd still make the argument that polling is the best way to find things out. You haven't gotten to a point where you can't trust it, but you have gotten to a point you have to weigh it."

One prominent pollster said the number of telephone calls that were not completed—either because no one answers the telephone or because they answer and refuse to participate—had jumped in recent years, to about 30 percent from 10 percent. The number is even higher in New York and in South Florida.

"Response rates are falling," said Tom W. Smith of the National Opinion Research Center at the University of Chicago. "Either you spend a lot more time and money doing your survey or you end up being stuck with a much lower response rate than is traditionally acceptable."

Mr. Smith said that to complicate things for people in his profession, new screening machinery had been developed that can, in theory, identify calls that are being made by a mass dialer or can refuse calls from any unknown number.

Cellphones have posed another complication for pollsters. There is no directory of cellphone numbers, and an increasing number of people use cellphones as their home telephones. Mr. Schulman said federal regulations barred pollsters from calling people on their cellphones without permission, because the recipients of the calls are obliged to pay the cost.

Several pollsters said yesterday that they would prefer, if possible, not to conduct interviews with people on cellphones. These interviews typically take 20 minutes or so, and were intended to be done with people sitting at home rather than chatting on a cellphone from a car or restaurant.

"We haven't come to grips with the cellphone issue yet, I'll be honest with you about that," Mr. Schulman said. "Up to this point, the cellphone has generally been the second phone for the hard-wire phone in the household. In the future, we've got to figure out a strategy to deal with this."

Think About It

- In your experience, who do you think are the types of Americans who are now hardest to reach due to the development of cell phones and caller ID?
- Do you think young people like you are likely becoming harder to interview for surveys as a result of these technologies?

- One of the pollsters interviewed in this article claims that polling will eventually be done via the Internet instead of the phone. What do you see as the possible advantages and disadvantages of such a change?
- Does this article make you more skeptical about polls you read about in the newspaper?

Public opinion polls these days are mostly done over the telephone. Interviewers, most of whom are young people (and frequently college students), sit in front of computer terminals and read the questions that appear on the screen to randomly chosen individuals they have reached on the phone. They then enter the appropriate coded responses directly into the computer database. Such efficient procedures make it possible for analysts to get survey results very quickly.

The Role of Polls in American Democracy

Polls help political candidates detect public preferences. Supporters of polling insist that it is a tool for democracy. With it, they say, policymakers can keep in touch with changing opinions on the issues. No longer do politicians have to wait until the next election to see whether the public approves or disapproves of the government's course. If the poll results suddenly turn, then government officials can make corresponding midcourse corrections. Indeed, it was George Gallup's fondest hope that polling could contribute to the democratic process by providing a way for public desires to be heard at times other than elections.

Critics of polling, by contrast, say it makes politicians more concerned with following than leading. Polls might have told the constitutional convention delegates that the Constitution was unpopular or might have told President Thomas Jefferson that people did not want the Louisiana Purchase. Certainly they would have told William Seward not to buy Alaska, a transaction known widely at the time as "Seward's Folly." Polls may thus discourage bold leadership, like that of Winston Churchill, who once said,

> Nothing is more dangerous than to live in the temperamental atmosphere of a Gallup poll, always taking one's pulse and taking one's temperature. . . . There is only one duty, only one safe course, and that is to try to be right and not to fear to do or say what you believe.[16]

Recent research by Jacobs and Shapiro argues that the common perception of politicians pandering to the results of public opinion polls may be mistaken. Their examination of major policy debates in the 1990s finds that political leaders "track public opinion not to make policy but rather to determine how to craft their public presentations and win public support for the policies they and their supporters favor."[17] Staff members in both the White House and the Congress repeatedly remarked that their purpose in conducting polls was not to set policies, but rather to find the keywords and phrases with which to "sell" policies. Thus, rather than using polls to identify centrist approaches that will have the broadest popular appeal, Jacobs and Shapiro argue that elites use them to formulate strategies that enable them to avoid compromising on what they want to do.

Polls can also weaken democracy by distorting the election process. They are often accused of creating a *bandwagon effect*. The wagon carrying the band was the centerpiece of nineteenth-century political parades, and enthusiastic supporters would literally jump on it. Today, the term refers to voters who support a candidate merely because they see that others are doing so. Although only 2 percent of people in a recent CBS/*New York Times* poll said that poll results had influenced them, 26 percent said they thought others had been influenced (showing that Americans feel "It's the other person who's susceptible"). Beyond this, polls play to the media's interest in who's ahead in the race. The issues of recent presidential campaigns have sometimes been drowned out by a steady flood of poll results.

Probably the most widely criticized type of poll is the Election Day **exit poll**. For this type of poll, voting places are randomly selected around the country. Workers are then sent to these places and told to ask every tenth person how they voted. The results are accumulated toward the end of the day, enabling the television networks to project the outcomes of all but very close races before the polls even close. In the presidential elections of 1980, 1984, 1988, and 1996, the networks declared a national winner while millions on the West Coast still had hours to vote. Critics have charged that this practice discourages many people from voting and thereby affects the outcome of some state and local races.

In 2000, the exit polls received much of the blame for the media's inaccurate calls of the Florida result on election night. But contrary to common perception, the exit polls deserve only a portion of the blame for the networks' fiasco. Because the Florida exit poll showed a small advantage for Gore, the networks could not have called the election based on this information alone. Inaccurate reports and estimates of actual votes threw off the network prognostications most. The early call for Gore was apparently largely caused by underestimating the size of the absentee vote, which favored Bush. Then, near the end of the counting on election night, they estimated that there were only about 180,000 votes left to count when there were actually twice as many. Hence, they prematurely gave the state (and the presidency) to Bush, not realizing how much of a chance there was for Gore to close the gap. The chances of such a comedy of errors recurring is relatively small. Furthermore, the networks have made a number of changes in their procedures for predicting winners that resulted in slower but more reliable predictions in 2004.

Perhaps the most pervasive criticism of polling is that by altering the wording of a question, pollsters can usually get the results they want. Sometimes subtle changes in question wording can produce dramatic differences. For example, a month before the start of the 1991 Gulf War, the percentage of the public who thought we should go to war was 18 percentage points higher in the ABC/*Washington Post* poll than in the CBS/*New York Times* poll. The former poll asked whether the United States should go to war "at some point after January 15 or not," a relatively vague question; in contrast, the latter poll offered an alternative to war, asking whether the "U.S. should start military actions against Iraq, or should the U.S. wait longer to see if the trade embargo and other economic sanctions work."[18] It is therefore important to evaluate carefully how questions are posed when reading public opinion data.

Polling sounds scientific with its talk of random samples and sampling error; it is easy to take results for solid fact. But being an informed consumer of polls requires more than just a nuts-and-bolts knowledge of how they are conducted. You should think about whether the questions are fair and unbiased before making too much of the results. The good—or the harm—that polls do depends on how well the data are collected and how thoughtfully the data are interpreted.

What Polls Reveal About Americans' Political Information

Abraham Lincoln spoke stirringly of the inherent wisdom of the American people: "It is true that you may fool all of the people some of the time; and you can even fool some of the people all of the time; but you can't fool all of the people all the time." Obviously, Lincoln recognized the complexity of public opinion.

exit poll

Public opinion surveys used by major media pollsters to predict electoral winners with speed and precision.

War, Peace, and Public Opinion

Thomas Jefferson and Alexander Hamilton had very different views about the wisdom of common people. Jefferson trusted people's good sense and believed that education would enable them to take the tasks of citizenship ever more seriously. Toward that end, he founded the University of Virginia. Hamilton held a contrasting view. His infamous words "Your people, sir, are a great beast" do not reflect confidence in people's capacity for self-government.

If there had been polling data in the early days of the American republic, Hamilton would probably have delighted in throwing some of the results in Jefferson's face. If public opinion analysts agree about anything, it is that the level of public knowledge about politics is dismally low. As discussed in Chapter 1, this is particularly true for young people, but the overall levels of political knowledge are not particularly encouraging either. For example, in the 2004 National Annenberg Election Study conducted by the University of Pennsylvania, a national sample of Democrats were asked a set of questions about the Democratic contenders during the ten days prior to the New Hampshire primary. The results were as follows:

- 59 percent knew which candidate had been a general (Clark)
- 42 percent knew which candidate had been a decorated Vietnam veteran (Kerry)
- 33 percent knew which candidate would repeal all the Bush tax cuts (Dean)
- 25 percent knew which candidate had been a trial lawyer (Edwards)

If so many voters did not know these very basic facts about the candidates, then there is little doubt that most were also unaware of the detailed policy platforms they were running on.

No amount of Jeffersonian faith in the wisdom of the common people can erase the fact that Americans are not well informed about politics. Polls have regularly found that less than half the public can name their representative in the House, much less say how he or she generally votes. Asking most people to explain their opinion on whether trade policy toward China should be liberalized, the proposed "Star Wars" missile defense system, or whether the strategic oil reserve should be tapped when gasoline prices skyrocket often elicits blank looks. When trouble flares in a far-off country, polls regularly find that people have no idea where that country is. In fact, surveys show that citizens around the globe lack a basic awareness of the world around them (see "America in Perspective: Citizens Show Little Knowledge of Geography.")

As Lance Bennett points out, these findings provide "a source of almost bitter humor in light of what the polls tell us about public information on other subjects."[19] He notes that more people know their astrological sign (76 percent) than know the name of their representative in the House. Slogans from TV commercials are better recognized than famous political figures. When people were asked which vegetable President George Bush did not like in the late 1980s, a poll found that 75 percent could identify this as broccoli, but relatively few people knew his stand on a tax cut for capital gains.

How can Americans, who live in the most information-rich society in the world, be so ill-informed about politics? Some blame the schools. E. D. Hirsch, Jr. criticizes schools for a failure to teach "cultural literacy."[20] People, he says, often lack the basic contextual knowledge—for example, where Afghanistan is, what the Vietnam War was about, and so forth—necessary to understand and use the information they receive from the news media or from listening to political candidates. Indeed, it has been found that increased levels of education over the last four decades have scarcely raised public knowledge about politics.[21] Despite the apparent glut of information provided by the media, Americans do not remember much about what they are exposed to through the media. (Of course, there are many critics who say that the media fail to provide much meaningful information, a topic that will be discussed in Chapter 7.)

Why It Matters

Political Knowledge of the Electorate

The average American clearly has less political information than most analysts consider to be desirable. While this level of information is surely adequate to maintain our democracy, survey data plainly show that citizens with above average levels of political knowledge are more likely to vote and to have stable and consistent opinions on poicy issues. If political knowledge were to increase overall, it would in all likelihood be good for American democracy.

America in Perspective

Citizens Show Little Knowledge of Geography

In 2002, a major cross-national study sponsored by National Geographic interviewed representative samples of 18- to 24-year-olds to assess their knowledge of world geography. The results were discouraging, particularly with regard to American youth, who came in last in terms of placing countries accurately on the map, as shown in the test shown here. The average young person in the United States got less than half the questions right. Believe it or not, 11 percent of young Americans could not even find their own country on the map. Despite the American military campaign in Afghanistan after September 11, only 17 percent could correctly place this country on the map. Such lack of basic geographic knowledge is fairly common throughout the world. Here is the average score for each of the 10 countries in which the test was administered:

COUNTRY	AVERAGE % CORRECT
Sweden	79
Germany	77
Italy	75
France	71
Japan	62
Canada	56
United Kingdom	54
Mexico	49
United States	**46**

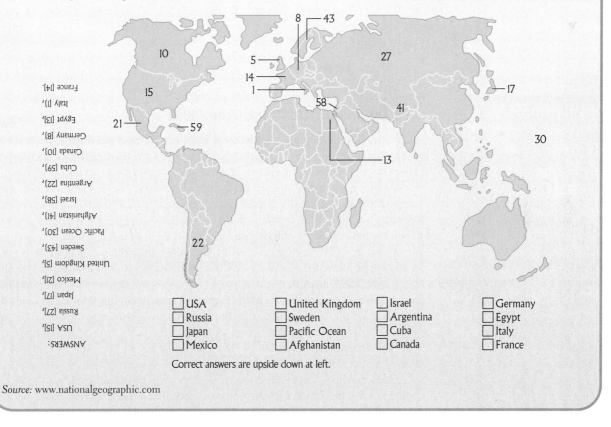

ANSWERS: USA [15], Russia [27], Japan [17], Mexico [21], United Kingdom [5], Sweden [43], Pacific Ocean [30], Afghanistan [41], Israel [58], Argentina [22], Cuba [59], Canada [10], Germany [8], Egypt [13], Italy [1], France [14].

☐ USA ☐ United Kingdom ☐ Israel ☐ Germany
☐ Russia ☐ Sweden ☐ Argentina ☐ Egypt
☐ Japan ☐ Pacific Ocean ☐ Cuba ☐ Italy
☐ Mexico ☐ Afghanistan ☐ Canada ☐ France

Correct answers are upside down at left.

Source: www.nationalgeographic.com

The "paradox of mass politics," says Russell Neuman, is that the American political system works as well as it does given the discomforting lack of public knowledge about politics.[22] Part of the reason for this phenomenon is that people may not know the ins and outs of policy questions or the actors on the political stage, but they know what basic values they want upheld.

Figure 6.4   The Decline of Trust in Government, 1958–2004

This graph shows how people have responded over time to the following question: How much of the time do you think you can trust the government in Washington to do what is right—just about always, most of the time, or only some of the time?

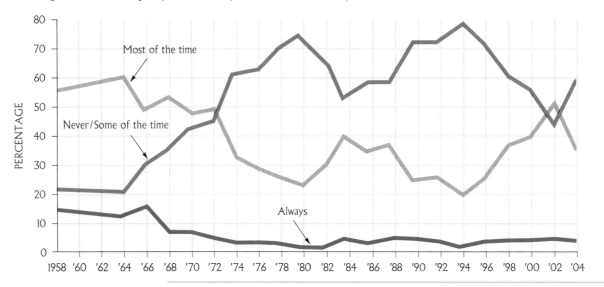

Source: Authors' analysis of 1958–2002 American National Election Study data; CBS/*New York Times* Poll, July 11–15, 2004.

The Decline of Trust in Government

Sadly, the American public has become increasingly dissatisfied with government over the last four decades, as you can see in Figure 6.4. In the late 1950s and early 1960s about three-quarters of Americans said that they trusted the government in Washington to do the right thing always or mostly. Following the 1964 election, however, researchers started to see a precipitous drop in public trust in government. First Vietnam and then Watergate shook the people's confidence in the federal government. The economic troubles of the Carter years and the Iran hostage crisis helped continue the slide; by 1980, only a quarter of the public thought the government could be trusted most of the time or always. During the Reagan years, public cynicism abated a bit, but by 1994, trust in government had plummeted again to another all-time low. Since 1994, trust in government has improved somewhat, but it seems unlikely that we will see a long-lasting return to the optimistic levels of trust in government of the early 1960s. For a brief time after September 11, media polls showed trust in government had risen to nearly this level, but by the summer of 2004 trust levels were back to where they were in 1998.

Some analysts have noted that a healthy dose of public cynicism helps to keep politicians on their toes. Others, however, note that a democracy is based on the consent of the governed and that a lack of public trust in the government is a reflection of their belief that the system is not serving them well. These more pessimistic analysts have frequently wondered whether such a cynical population would unite behind their government in a national emergency. Although the decrease in political cynicism after September 11 was not too great, the fact that it occurred at all indicates that cynicism will not stop Americans from rallying behind their government in times of national crisis. Widespread political cynicism about government apparently only applies to "normal" times; it has not eroded Americans' fundamental faith in our democracy.

What Americans Value: Political Ideologies

A coherent set of values and beliefs about public policy is a **political ideology**. Liberal ideology, for example, supports a wide scope for the central government, often involving policies that aim to promote equality. Conservative ideology, in contrast, supports a less active scope of government that gives freer reign to the private sector. Table 6.2 attempts to summarize some of the key differences between liberals and conservatives.

Who Are the Liberals and Conservatives?

Overall, more Americans consistently choose the ideological label of conservative over liberal. The 2000 National Annenberg Election Study found that of those who labeled themselves, 37 percent were conservatives, 40 percent were moderates, and just 23 percent were liberals. The predominance of conservative thinking in America is one of the most important reasons for the relatively restrained scope of government activities compared to most European nations.

Yet, there are some groups that are more liberal than others, and thus would generally like to see the government do more. Among people under the age of 30, there are just as many liberals as conservatives, as shown in "Young People and Politics: How Younger and Older Americans Compare on the Issues." The younger the individual, the less likely that person is to be a conservative. The fact that younger people are also less likely to vote means that conservatives are overrepresented at the polls.

political ideology

A coherent set of beliefs about politics, public policy, and public purpose. It helps give meaning to political events, personalities, and policies. See also **liberalism** and **conservatism**.

Visual Literacy

Who Are Liberals and
Conservatives?

Table 6.2   How To Tell a Liberal from a Conservative

Liberal and *conservative*—these labels are thrown around in American politics as though everyone knows what they mean. Here are some of the political beliefs likely to be preferred by liberals and conservatives. This table, to be sure, is oversimplified.

	LIBERALS	CONSERVATIVES
Foreign Policy		
Military spending	Believe we should spend less	Believe we should maintain peace through strength
Use of force	Less willing to commit troops to action, such as in the 2003 war with Iraq	More likely to support military intervention around the world
Social Policy		
Abortion	Support "freedom of choice"	Support "right to life"
Prayer in schools	Are opposed	Are supportive
Affirmative action	Favor	Oppose
Economic Policy		
Scope of government	View government as a regulator in the public interest	Favor free-market solutions
Taxes	Want to tax the rich more	Want to keep taxes low
Spending	Want to spend more on the poor	Want to keep spending low
Crime		
How to cut crime	Believe we should solve the problems that cause crime	Believe we should stop "coddling criminals"
Defendants' rights	Believe we should guard them carefully	Believe we should stop letting criminals hide behind laws

Young People and Politics

How Young and Old People Compare on the Issues

The following table compares young adults and senior citizens on a variety of issues. Because younger citizens are much less likely to vote than older people, the differences between the two groups give us some indication of how public opinion is not accurately reflected at the polls. As you can see, younger people are substantially more likely to call themselves liberal than senior citizens. Befitting their liberalism, they are more supportive of government policies to reduce income differences. And their spending priorities are more on the liberal side as well. They are more in favor of spending on education and environmental protection and less inclined than seniors to spend more on defense. Younger voters are also more supportive of gay rights.

However, younger people are not always more likely to take the liberal side of an issue. Younger people are more supportive of investing Social Security funds in the stock market and more in favor of schools vouchers to help parents send their children to private schools. Both of these reform proposals have been primarily championed by conservative politicians such as George W. Bush. The fact that young adults are the most likely to support them suggests that the nation's youth are most open to new ideas, be they liberal or conservative.

Questions for Discussion

- Only a few issues could be covered in this table due to space limitations. Are there other issues on which you think there are likely to be differences of opinion between young and old people?
- Do you think the differences shown above are important? If so, what difference might it make to the American political agenda if young people were to vote at the same rate as the elderly?

	18–29 YEARS OLD	65 AND OLDER
Very liberal	7	2
Liberal	25	14
Moderate	39	39
Conservative	24	38
Very conservative	5	7
Favor investing Social Security funds in the stock market	71	45
Oppose investing Social Security funds in the stock market	29	55
Favor school vouchers	44	30
Oppose school vouchers	56	70
Spending on education should be increased	81	53
Spending on education is about right	16	34
Spending on education should be reduced	3	13
Military spending should be increased	35	65
Military spending is about right	49	30
Military spending should be reduced	16	5
Favor gays in the military	64	53
Oppose gays in the military	36	47
Favor government policies to reduce income differences	61	42
Oppose government policies to reduce income differences	39	58
Spending to protect the environment should be increased	77	59
Spending to protect the environment is about right	18	28
Spending to protect the environment should be decreased	5	13

Source: 2000 National Annenberg Election Study.

In general, groups with political clout tend to be more conservative than groups whose members have often been shut out from the halls of political power. This is because excluded groups have often looked to the government to rectify the inequalities they have faced. For example, African Americans benefited from government activism in the form of the major civil rights bills of the 1960s to bring them into the mainstream of American life. Many African-American leaders currently place a high priority on retaining social welfare and affirmative action programs in order to assist their progress. It should come as little surprise then that African Americans are more liberal than the national average. Similarly, Hispanics also are less conservative than Whites, and if this pattern continues the influx of many more Hispanics into the electorate will move the country in a slightly liberal direction.

Women are not a minority group, making up about 54 percent of the population, but they have nevertheless been politically and economically disadvantaged. Compared to men, women are more likely to support spending on social services and to oppose the higher levels of military spending, which conservatives typically advocate. These issues concerning the priorities of government rather than the issue of abortion—on which men and women actually differ very little—lead women to be significantly less conservative than men. This ideological difference between men and women has led to the **gender gap,** which refers to the regular pattern by which women are more likely to support Democratic candidates. Bill Clinton carried the women's vote while Bob Dole was preferred among men in 1996, making Clinton the first president who can be said to be elected via the support of only one gender. In 2004, exit polls showed that women were about 7 percent more likely to support John Kerry than men.

The gender gap is a relatively new predictor of ideological positions, dating back only to 1980 when Ronald Reagan was first elected. A much more traditional source of division between liberals and conservatives has been financial status, or what is often known as social class. But in actuality, the relationship between family income and ideology is now relatively weak. As a result, social class has become much less predictive of political behavior than it used to be.[23]

The role of religion in influencing political ideology has also changed greatly in recent years. Catholics and Jews, as minority groups who struggled for equality, have long been more liberal than Protestants. Today, Jews remain by far the most liberal demographic group in the country.[24] However, the ideological gap between Catholics and Protestants is now smaller than the gender gap. Ideology is now determined more by religiosity—that is, the degree to which religion is important in one's life—than by religious denomination. What is known as the new Christian Right consists of Catholics and Protestants who consider themselves fundamentalists or "born again." The influx of new policy issues dealing with matters of morality and traditional family values has recently tied this aspect of religious beliefs to political ideology. Those who identify themselves as born-again Christians are currently the most conservative demographic group. On the other hand, people who say they have no religious affiliation (roughly one-tenth of the population) are more liberal than conservative.

Just as some people are very much guided by their religious beliefs whereas others are not, the same is true for political ideology. It would probably be a mistake to assume that when conservative candidates do better than they have in the past that this necessarily means people want more conservative policies, for not everyone thinks in ideological terms.

Do People Think in Ideological Terms?

The authors of the classic study *The American Voter* first examined how much people rely on ideology to guide their political thinking.[25] They divided the public into four groups, according to ideological sophistication. Their portrait of the American electorate was not flattering. Only 12 percent of the people showed evidence of thinking

Participation

Are You a Liberal or a Conservative?

gender gap

A term that refers to the regular pattern by which women are more likely to support Democratic candidates. Women tend to be significantly less conservative than men and are more likely to support spending on social services and to oppose higher levels of military spending.

in ideological terms and thus were classified as *ideologues*. These people could connect their opinions and beliefs with broad policy positions taken by parties or candidates. They might say, for example, that they liked the Democrats because they were more liberal or the Republicans because they favored a smaller government. Forty-two percent of Americans were classified as *group benefits* voters. These people thought of politics mainly in terms of the groups they liked or disliked; for example, "Republicans support small business owners like me" or "Democrats are the party of the working person." Twenty-four percent of the population were *nature of the times* voters. Their handle on politics was limited to whether the times seemed good or bad to them; they might vaguely link the party in power with the country's fortune or misfortune. Finally, 22 percent of the voters were devoid of any ideological or issue content in their political evaluations. They were called the *no issue content* group. Most of them simply voted routinely for a party or judged the candidates solely by their personalities. Overall, at least during the 1950s, Americans seemed to care little about the differences between liberal and conservative politics.

There has been much debate about whether this portrayal accurately characterizes the public today. Nie, Verba, and Petrocik took a look at the changing American voter, arguing that voters were more sophisticated in the 1970s than in the 1950s.[26] Others, though, have concluded that people only seemed more informed and ideological because the wording of the questions had changed.[27] If the exact same methods are used to update the analysis of *The American Voter* through more recent elections, one finds some increase in the proportion of ideologues, but not much. The last time these methods were employed was in 1988, and then just 18 percent were classified as ideologues, as compared to 12 percent in 1956. Given that George Bush continually labeled his 1988 opponent Michael Dukakis as "that liberal Governor from the most liberal state in the country," it is striking how few people actually evaluated the parties and candidates in ideological terms.

These findings do not mean that the vast majority of the population does not have a political ideology. Rather, for most people the terms *liberal* and *conservative* are just not as important as they are for the political elite such as politicians, activists, journalists, and the like. Relatively few people have ideologies that organize their political beliefs as clearly as shown in Table 6.2. Thus, the authors of *The American Voter* concluded that to speak of election results as indicating a movement of the public either left (to more liberal policies) or right (to more conservative policies) is not justified because most voters do not think in such terms. Furthermore, those who do are actually the least likely to shift from one election to the next. The relatively small percentage of voters who made up their minds in the last couple days of the Bush-Gore campaign in 2000 were far more concerned with integrity and competence than ideology.

How Americans Participate in Politics

In politics, as in many other aspects of life, the squeaky wheel gets the grease. The way citizens "squeak" in politics is to participate. Americans have many avenues of political participation open to them.

- Mrs. Jones of Iowa City goes to a neighbor's living room to attend her local precinct's presidential caucus.
- Demonstrators against abortion protest at the Supreme Court on the anniversary of the *Roe v. Wade* decision.
- Parents in Alabama file a lawsuit to oppose textbooks that, in their opinion, promote "secular humanism."
- Mr. Smith, a Social Security recipient, writes to his senator to express his concern about a possible cut in his cost-of-living benefits.
- Over 100 million people vote in a presidential election.

All these activities are types of political participation. **Political participation** encompasses the many activities in which citizens engage to influence the selection of political leaders or the policies they pursue.[28] Participation can be overt or subtle. The mass protests throughout Eastern Europe in the fall of 1989 represented an avalanche of political participation, yet quietly writing a letter to your congressperson also represents political participation. Political participation can be violent or peaceful, organized or individual, casual or consuming.

Generally, the United States has a culture that values political participation. Americans express very high levels of pride in their democracy: 79 percent say they are proud of how democracy works in the United States[29] Nevertheless, just 55 percent of adult Americans voted in the presidential election of 2004, and only 39 percent turned out for the 2002 midterm elections. At the local level, the situation is even worse, with elections for city council and school board often drawing less than 10 percent of the eligible voters. (For more on voter turnout and why it is so low, see Chapter 10.)

political participation

All the activities used by citizens to influence the selection of political leaders or the policies they pursue. The most common but not the only means of political participation in a **democracy** is voting. Other means include **protest** and **civil disobedience**.

Conventional Participation

Although the line is hard to draw, political scientists generally distinguish between two broad types of participation: conventional and unconventional. Conventional participation includes many widely accepted modes of influencing government—voting, trying to persuade others, ringing doorbells for a petition, running for office, and so on. In contrast, unconventional participation includes activities that are often dramatic, such as protesting, civil disobedience, and even violence.

For a few, politics is their lifeblood; they run for office, work regularly in politics, and live for the next election. The number of Americans for whom political activity is an important part of their everyday life is minuscule; they number at most in the tens of thousands. To these people, policy questions are as familiar as slogans on TV commercials are to the average citizen. They are the political elites—activists, party leaders, interest group leaders, judges, members of Congress, and other public officials. (Part 3 of this book will discuss the political elite in detail.)

Millions take part in political activities beyond simply voting. In two comprehensive studies of American political participation conducted by Sidney Verba and his colleagues, samples of Americans were asked in 1967 and 1987 about their role in various

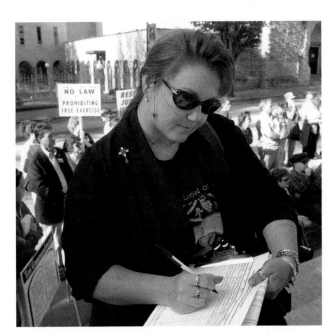

There are many ways of participating in politics beyond voting. One conventional form of participating is to sign a petition concerning a political issue. Here, a woman in Georgia is shown signing a petition in support of public displays of the Ten Commandments.

Making a Difference

Granny D and Her Walk for Campaign Finance Reform

At the age of 89 Doris Haddock resolved to do something unusual that would draw people's attention to the issue of campaign finance reform: a cross-country walk from California to Washington, D.C. Moving at a pace of 10 miles per day, Granny D—the nickname Mrs. Haddock assumed for publicity purposes—soon encountered desert heat and wind that would discourage most young and healthy people from continuing. But for over a year she continued on, until she finally made it all the way to Congress' front door. Along the way, she had publicized her cause through numerous media interviews and met with various members of Congress in their local offices. Tens of thousands of ordinary citizens had come out to see her, sign her petition, and sometimes walk along with her for a while. The National Association of Secretaries of State issued a resolution commending her "for showing that one person can make a difference."

kinds of political activities.[30] Included were voting, working in campaigns, contacting government officials, and working on local community issues. Voting was the only aspect of political participation that a majority of the population reported engaging in, but also the only political activity for which there is evidence of a decline in participation in recent years. Substantial increases in participation were found on the dimensions of giving money to candidates and contacting public officials, and small increases are evident for all the other activities. Thus, although the decline of voter turnout is a development Americans should rightly be concerned about (see Chapter 10), a broader look at political participation reveals some positive developments for participatory democracy.

Protest as Participation

From the Boston Tea Party to burning draft cards, to demonstrating against abortion, Americans have engaged in countless political protests. **Protest** is a form of political participation designed to achieve policy change through dramatic and unconventional tactics. The media's willingness to cover the unusual can make protests worthwhile, drawing attention to a point of view that many Americans might otherwise never encounter. For example, when an 89-year-old woman decided to try to walk across the country to draw attention to the need for campaign finance reform, she put this issue onto the front page of newspapers most everywhere she traveled (see "Making a Difference: Granny D and Her Walk for Campaign Finance Reform").

The right of political protest is constitutionally protected as an integral part of freedom of speech in the United States. Virtually every controversial governmental decision ends up generating some organized political protest sooner or later.

Nonviolent civil disobedience was one of the most effective techniques of the civil rights movement in the American South. Young African Americans sat at "Whites only" lunch counters to protest segregation. Photos such as this drew national attention to the injustice of racial discrimination.

Using much more flamboyant means, the AIDS activist group appropriately called "ACT-UP" interrupts political gatherings to draw attention to the need for AIDS research. In fact, protests today are often orchestrated to provide television cameras with vivid images. Demonstration coordinators steer participants to prearranged staging areas and provide facilities for press coverage.

Throughout American history, individuals and groups have sometimes used **civil disobedience** as a form of protest; that is, they have consciously broken a law that they thought was unjust. In the 1840s, Henry David Thoreau refused to pay his taxes as a protest against the Mexican War and went to jail; he stayed only overnight because his friend Ralph Waldo Emerson paid the taxes. Influenced by India's Mahatma Gandhi, Reverend Martin Luther King, Jr. won a Nobel Peace Prize for his civil disobedience against segregationist laws in the 1950s and 1960s. His "Letter from a Birmingham Jail" is a classic defense of civil disobedience.[31]

protest

A form of **political participation** designed to achieve policy change through dramatic and unconventional tactics.

civil disobedience

A form of **political participation** that reflects a conscious decision to break a law believed to be immoral and to suffer the consequences.

Perhaps the best known image of American political violence from the late 1960s to early 1970s period: A student lies dead on the Kent State campus, one of four killed when members of the Ohio National Guard opened fire on anti-Vietnam War demonstrators.

How You Can Make a Difference

Getting Involved

Whether it's campaign finance reform or any other issue you feel strongly about, there are ways *you* can make a difference. First, if you have not done so already, immerse yourself in the issues. Learn the ins and outs of existing laws pertaining to the issue you are concerned about. If the issue is campaign finance, learn about the role of political action committees (PACs), campaign finance laws, and soft money. Similarly, develop a basic understanding of such corrective legislation as the McCain-Feingold Act. For information on these topics, including lists of books, federal resources, interest groups, etc., go to *www.campaignfinance.homestead.com* or go to *www.commoncause.org* for an amazing amount of easily understood and well-organized information on campaign finance reform.

Another thing to do is to join an interest group that represents your posi-

tion on the issue. If you can't find one, start your own!

Find out where your congressperson and senators stand on the issue. Write, call, or e-mail their offices informing them of your position and asking them to support or introduce appropriate legislation. Keep up the writing campaign until your representative promises results.

If feasible, organize an event to garner media exposure for your views. An effective event can be anything from a classic protest march to something more original like a mock auction of congressional votes, a controversial art exhibit on special interests, or in the case of Granny D, a walk across the country. Be creative, but stay within the bounds of the law unless you are willing to pay the consequences.

Volunteer your time to support candidates who promise to legislate for the

issue you hold dear. If you live in a state that allows public initiatives, start or get involved with a group to place an initiative on the ballot.

On Election Day, send a clear signal by voting for those who support what you favor.

What you can do:
- Educate yourself on issues and current legislation.
- Join an interest group that represents your position or start one of your own.
- Contact your elected representatives and know where they stand on the issues.
- When possible, organize events to get media exposure for your issue and position.
- Support political campaigns of candidates who share your views.
- Vote!

Figure 6.5　Political Participation by Family Income

The following graph shows, by their income status, the percentage of the adult population who said they participated in various forms of political activity.

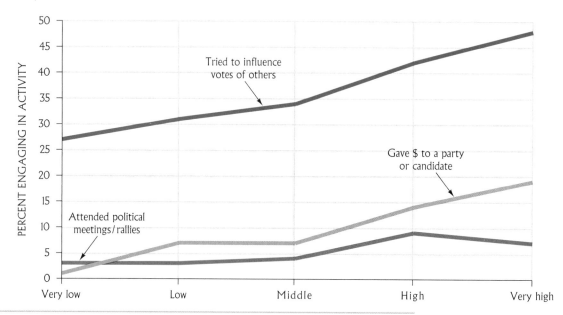

Source: Authors' analysis of 2000 National Election Study data.

Sometimes political participation can be violent. The history of violence in American politics is a long one—not surprising, perhaps, for a nation born in rebellion. The turbulent 1960s included many outbreaks of violence. African-American neighborhoods in American cities were torn by riots. College campuses were sometimes turned into battle zones as protestors against the Vietnam War fought police and National Guard units. At a number of campuses, demonstrations turned violent; students were killed at Kent State and Jackson State in 1970. Although supported by few people, violence has been a means of pressuring the government to change its policies throughout American history.

Class, Inequality, and Participation

The rates of political participation are unequal among Americans. Virtually every study of political participation has come to the conclusion that "citizens of higher social economic status participate more in politics. This generalization "holds true whether one uses level of education, income, or occupation as the measure of social status."[32] Figure 6.5 presents recent evidence on this score. Note that not only are people with higher incomes more likely to donate money to campaigns, but also to participate in other ways that do not require financial resources. Theorists who believe that America is ruled by a small, wealthy elite make much of this fact to support their view.

The participation differences between African Americans and Hispanics and the national average are no longer enormous, however. For African Americans, participation in 2000 was just 12 percentage points below the national average; for Hispanic citizens it was 11 percent. One reason for this relatively small participation gap is that minorities have a group consciousness that gives them an extra incentive to vote. In fact, when African Americans, Hispanics, and Whites of equal income and education are compared, the minorities participate more in politics.[33] In other words, a poor Hispanic or African American is more likely to participate than a poor White. In general, lower rates of political participation among these minority groups are linked with lower socioeconomic status.

People who believe in the promise of democracy should definitely be concerned with the inequalities of political participation in America. Those who participate are easy to listen to; nonparticipants are easy to ignore. Just as the makers of denture cream do not worry too much about people with healthy teeth, many politicians don't concern themselves much with the views of groups with low participation rates, such as the young and people with low incomes. Who gets what in politics therefore depends in part on who participates.

Understanding Public Opinion and Political Action

In 2004, many people in Iraq called for democracy in their country. Some said they wanted their political system to be like America's in the sense that ordinary people's opinions determine how the government is run. However, as this chapter has shown, there are many limits on the role public opinion plays in the American political system. The average person is not very well informed about political issues, including the crucial issue of the scope of government.

Public Attitudes Toward the Scope of Government

Central to the ideology of the Republican Party is the belief that the scope of American government has become too wide-ranging. According to Ronald Reagan, probably the most admired Republican in recent history, government was not the solution to society's

Why It Matters

Political Participation
Inequality in political participation is a problem in a representative democracy. Public policy debates and outcomes would probably be substantially different if people of all age and income groups participated equally. If young adults participated more, politicians would be more inclined to work on ways by which the government could help young people get the training necessary to get good jobs. And if the poor participated at higher levels, government programs to alleviate poverty would likely be higher on the political agenda than they are today.

problems—it was the problem. He called for the government to "get off the backs of the American people."

Reagan's rhetoric about an overly intrusive government was reminiscent of the 1964 presidential campaign rhetoric of Barry Goldwater, who lost to Lyndon Johnson in a landslide. Indeed, Reagan first made his mark in politics by giving a televised speech on behalf of the embattled Goldwater campaign. Although the rhetoric was much the same when Ronald Reagan was first elected president in 1980, public opinion about the scope of government had changed dramatically. In 1964, only 30 percent of the population thought the government was getting too powerful; by 1980, this figure had risen to 50 percent.

For much of the population, however, questions about the scope of government have consistently elicited no opinion at all. Indeed, when this question was last asked in the 2000 National Election Study, 42 percent of those interviewed said they had not thought about the question (among those under 25 years of age, this figure was 60 percent). The question of government power is a complex one, but as *Government in America* will continue to emphasize, it is one of the key controversies in American politics today. Once again, it seems that the public is not nearly so concerned with political issues as would be ideal in a democratic society.

Nor does public opinion on different aspects of the same issue exhibit much consistency. Thus, although more people today think the government is too active, a plurality has consistently called for more spending on such programs as education, health care, aid to big cities, protecting the environment, and fighting crime. Many political scientists have looked at these contradictory findings and concluded that Americans are ideological conservatives but operational liberals—meaning that they oppose the idea of big government in principle but favor it in practice. The fact that public opinion is often contradictory in this respect contributes to policy gridlock because it is hard for politicians to know which aspect of the public's attitudes to respond to.

Democracy, Public Opinion, and Political Action

Comparing Public Opinion

Remember, though, that American democracy is representative rather than direct. As *The American Voter* stated many years ago, "The public's explicit task is to decide not what government shall do but rather who shall decide what government shall do."[34] When individuals under communist rule protested for democracy, what they wanted most was the right to have a say in choosing their leaders. Americans can—and often do—take for granted the opportunity to replace their leaders at the next election. Protest is thus directed at making the government listen to specific demands, not overthrowing it. In this sense, it can be said that American citizens have become well socialized to democracy.

If the public's task in democracy is to choose who is to lead, we must still ask whether it can do so wisely. If people know little about where candidates stand on issues, how can they make rational choices? Most choose performance criteria over policy criteria. As Morris Fiorina has written, citizens typically have one hard bit of data to go on: "They know what life has been like during the incumbent's administration. They need not know the precise economic or foreign policies of the incumbent administration in order to see or feel the results of those policies."[35] Thus, even if they are only voting according to the nature of the times, their voices are clearly being heard—holding public officials accountable for their actions.

Summary

American society is amazingly varied. The ethnic makeup of America is changing to a minority majority. Americans are moving toward warmer parts of the country and growing older as a society. All these changes have policy consequences. One way of understanding the American people is through demography—the science of population changes. Demography, it is often said, is destiny.

Another way to understand the American people is through examination of public opinion in the United States. What Americans believe—and what they believe they know—is public opinion, the distribution of people's beliefs about politics and policy issues. Polling is one important way of studying public opinion; polls give us a fairly accurate gauge of public opinion on issues, products, and personalities. On the positive side for democracy, polls help keep political leaders in touch with the feelings of their constituents. On the negative side, polls may lead politicians to "play to the crowds" instead of providing leadership.

Polls have revealed again and again that the average American has a low level of political knowledge. Far more Americans know their astrological sign than know the names of their representatives in Congress. Ideological thinking is not widespread in the American public, nor are people necessarily consistent in their attitudes. Often they are conservative in principle but liberal in practice; that is, they are against big government but favor more spending on a wide variety of programs.

Acting on one's opinions is political participation. Although Americans live in a participatory culture, their actual level of participation is less than spectacular. In this country, participation is a class-biased activity; certain groups participate more than others. Those who suffer the most inequality sometimes resort to protest as a form of participation. Perhaps the best indicator of how well socialized Americans are to democracy is that protest typically is aimed at getting the attention of the government, not overthrowing it.

KEY TERMS

public opinion	reapportionment	exit poll
demography	political socialization	political ideology
census	sample	gender gap
melting pot	random sampling	political participation
minority majority	sampling error	protest
political culture	random-digit dialing	civil disobedience

INTERNET RESOURCES

www.census.gov
The census is the best source of information on America's demography. Go to the list of topics to find out the range of materials that are available.

www.gallup.com
The Gallup poll regularly posts reports about their political surveys at this site.

www.census.gov/statab/www/
The *Statistical Abstract of the United States* contains a wealth of demographic and political information and is available in Adobe Acrobat format off the Internet.

www.demographics.com/publications/ad/index.htm
American Demographics magazine publishes many interesting stories summarizing how America's population is currently changing.

GET CONNECTED

Public Opinion and SLOPs

Public opinion polls play an important role in American politics and government. Some observers even argue that policymakers keep an eye on polls when trying to develop policy, a practice that may be to the detriment of our system of government. Some polls are conducted scientifically and provide useful information about what Americans are thinking. There are other polls called self-selected opinion polls, or SLOPs, that may provide biased or misleading information. You may have seen SLOPs on an interest group's website or even on the local news. How are scientific polls conducted and how do they differ from SLOPs?

Search the Web

The Gallup Organization is one of the oldest public opinion polling firms in the country. Go to the "How Polls are Conducted" page at the Gallup website: *http://www.gallup.com/help/FAQs/poll1.asp*. Now review the National Council on Public Polls' "Statement about Internet Polls" *http://www.ncpp.org/internet.htm*. While the National Council on Public Polls' statement is about Internet polls, this type of public opinion poll could have the same shortcomings as the self-selected opinion poll you might see on television or find on an interest group's website.

Questions to Ask

- What are the important characteristics about Gallup's polling methods that allow people to have confidence in the findings revealed by the organization's polls?
- Why does the National Council on Public Polls think it is important to know if people were able to participate in the poll more than once?
- What are the shortcomings of any public opinion poll?

Why It Matters

The people are able to voice their opinions through public opinion polls, but polls may cause problems for our political system if they are not conducted correctly. It is important for the consumers of public opinion polls, including policymakers and voters, to have confidence in the information such polls present.

Get Involved

Find the results of an Internet poll at the CNN website (*http://www.cnn.com*), Fox News Channel's website (*http://www.foxnews.com*), or in your local media. Interest groups also run Internet polls. A list of interest groups and their web addresses can be found at *http://www.csuchico.edu/~kcfount/index.html*. Evaluate the poll using the National Council on Public Polls' "Statement about Internet Polls." Contact the person or group who published the poll and ask them to answer the questions on the statement if the poll doesn't provide the answers directly. Consult this issue brief from The Pew Research Center for the People and the Press *http://people-press.org/commentary/ display.php3?AnalysisID=20* to offer suggestions on how to improve the poll.

To see more Get Connected exercises for Chapter 6, go to www.ablongman.com/edwards.

FOR FURTHER READING

Asher, Herbert. *Polling and the Public: What Every Citizen Should Know*, 4th ed. Washington, D.C.: Congressional Quarterly Press, 1998. A highly readable introduction to the perils and possibilities of polling and surveys.

Campbell, Andrea Louise. *How Policies Make Citizens: Senior Political Activism and the American Welfare Sate*. Princeton, NJ: Princeton University Press, 2003. Senior citizens have bucked the trend of declining political participation in recent years; Campbell explains why.

Campbell, Angus, et al. *The American Voter*. New York: Wiley, 1960. The classic study of the American voter, based on data from the 1950s.

Conway, M. Margaret. *Political Participation*, 3rd ed. Washington, D.C.: Congressional Quarterly Press, 2000. A good review of the literature on political participation.

Delli Carpini, Michael X., and Scott Keeter. *What Americans Know About Politics and Why It Matters*. New Haven, CT: Yale University Press, 1996. The best study of the state of political knowledge in the electorate.

DeSipio, Louis. *Counting on the Latino Vote*. Charlottesville: University of Virginia Press, 1996. An examination of the current state of Latino public opinion, and how more Latinos could be politically mobilized in the future.

Jacobs, Lawrence R., and Robert Y. Shapiro. *Politicians Don't Pander*. Chicago: University of Chicago Press, 2000. Contrary to popular notions that politicians hold their fingers to the wind and try to follow the polls, Jacobs and Shapiro argue that politicians use polls to figure out how to best persuade the public to support their preferred policies.

Jennings, M. Kent, and Richard G. Niemi. *Generations and Politics: A Panel Study of Young Adults and Their Parents*. Princeton, NJ: Princeton University Press, 1981. A highly influential study of the class of 1965, their parents, and how both generations changed over the course of eight years.

Nie, Norman H., Jane Junn, and Kenneth Stehlik-Barry. *Education and Democratic Citizenship in America*. Chicago: University of Chicago Press, 1996. An in-depth investigation of the role of education in fostering political tolerance and participation.

Page, Benjamin I., and Robert Y. Shapiro. *The Rational Public: Fifty Years of Trends in Americans' Policy Preferences*. Chicago: University of Chicago Press, 1992. The authors argue that the public, as a whole, responds in a reasonable fashion to changing political circumstances and information.

Tate, Katherine. *From Protest to Politics: The New Black Voters in American Elections*, enlarged edition. Cambridge, MA: Harvard University Press, 1998. An excellent examination of public opinion and participation among the African-American community.

Verba, Sidney, and Norman H. Nie. *Participation in America*. New York: Harper & Row, 1972. A landmark study of American political participation.

Verba, Sidney, Kay Lehman Schlozman, and Henry E. Brady. *Voice and Equality: Civic Voluntarism in American Politics*. Cambridge, MA: Harvard University Press, 1995. A worthy update and extension to *Participation in America*.

The Mass Media and the Political Agenda

Chapter Outline

The Mass Media Today

The Development of Media Politics

Reporting the News

The New York Times Issues of the Times

The News and Public Opinion

The Media's Agenda-Setting Function

Understanding the Mass Media

Summary

■ In Washington's Smithsonian Museum, the television console used by President Lyndon Johnson in the mid-1960s can be seen on permanent display. Not wanting to miss anything on TV, Johnson asked for three screens to be installed in one console so he could monitor CBS, NBC, and ABC all at the same time. White House technicians rigged up a special remote control for the president, enabling him to switch the audio easily from one network to another. According to many observers, whenever he saw his picture appear, he immediately turned on the audio from that screen to hear what was being said about him.

As a piece of genuine Americana, LBJ's triple TV set symbolizes the tremendous importance television had assumed in U.S. politics by the mid-1960s. Interestingly, the same year that Lyndon Johnson finished his term as president, former Vice President Al Gore completed his senior thesis at Harvard on the impact of television on the conduct of the presidency. The essence of Gore's student thesis was that TV had an inherent bias toward individuals over institutions that over time would bring more attention to the president at the expense of the other branches of government. With a president's power increasingly stemming from his ability to dominate the airwaves, Gore's thesis argued that the ability to communicate well through the visual medium of television was becoming crucial to governing. Ironically for a politician who regularly joked that the difference between himself and his Secret Service agents was that "he's the stiff one," the young Gore speculated that future presidents would have to have personalities that play well to the TV cameras.

The rise of television has had a profound impact on the two central questions we emphasize in this text—*How should we govern?* and *What should government do?* Television has brought an immediacy to how we govern, removing the filter of time from events. Whatever the problem or event, it is happening now—live on the TV screen. People thus have more reason than ever to expect immediate governmental responses. However, the Founding Fathers

designed a very deliberative governing process, in which problems would be considered by multiple centers of political power and acted upon only after lengthy give and take. Given the difficulties of getting quick action through the American political system, it is no wonder the public has come to be more dissatisfied with our government in the television age.

In some cases, though, television has set the stage for leaders to take quick action affecting the scope of government. Lyndon Johnson was watching his triple screen TV set when NBC interrupted its airing of "Judgment at Nuremberg" to show film that had just become available of civil rights demonstrators being brutally attacked by police in Selma, Ala. Sensing the public outrage at this violence and injustice, Johnson soon proposed and pushed through the historic Voting Rights Act of 1965 (see Chapter 5). Today, any time a president takes strong action on some important policy problem, television sets the stage by focusing attention on the issue and putting it high on the policy agenda.

high-tech politics

A politics in which the behavior of citizens and policymakers and the political agenda itself are increasingly shaped by technology.

mass media

Television, radio, newspapers, magazines, the Internet, and other means of popular communication.

The American political system has entered a new period of **high-tech politics**—a politics in which the behavior of citizens and policymakers, as well as the political agenda itself, is increasingly shaped by technology. The **mass media** are a key part of this technology. Television, radio, newspapers, magazines, the Internet, and other means of popular communication are called *mass media* because they reach and profoundly influence not only the elites but also the masses. This chapter examines media politics, focusing on:

- The rise of modern media in America's advanced technological society.
- The making of the news and its presentation through the media.
- The biases in the news.
- The impact of the media on policymakers and the public.

This chapter also reintroduces the concept of the policy agenda, in which the media play an important role.

The Mass Media Today

Whether promoting a candidate, drawing attention to a social issue, or generating a government program, effectively communicating a message is critical to political success. The key is gaining control over the political agenda, which involves getting one's priorities presented at the top of the daily news. Politicians have learned that one way to guide the media's focus successfully is to limit what they can report on to carefully scripted events. A **media event** is staged primarily for the purpose of being covered. If the media were not there, the event would probably not happen or would have little significance. For example, on the eve of the 2004 New Hampshire primary, John Kerry went door-to-door in a middle-class neighborhood with TV crews in tow. The few dozen people he met could scarcely have made a difference, but Kerry was not really there to win votes by personal contact. Rather, the point was to get television coverage of him reaching out to ordinary people. Getting the right image on TV news for just 30 seconds can easily have a greater payoff than a whole day's worth of handshaking. Whereas once a candidate's G.O.T.V. program stood for "Get Out the Vote," today it is more likely to mean "Get on TV."

media events

Events purposely staged for the media that nonetheless look spontaneous. In keeping with politics as theater, media events can be staged by individuals, groups, and government officials, especially presidents.

In addition, a large part of today's so-called 30-second presidency is the slickly produced TV commercial. Approximately 60 percent of presidential campaign spending is now devoted to TV ads. In recent presidential elections, about two-thirds of the prominently aired ads were negative commercials.[1] Many people are worried that the tirade of accusations, innuendoes, and countercharges in political advertising is poisoning the American political process and possibly even contributing to declining turnout.[2] Other democracies typically allocate their parties free air time for longer ads that go into more depth than is possible than with the American-style 30-second ad (see "America in Perspective: How Campaign Advertising Compares Across Five Nations").

Image making does not stop with the campaign; it is also a critical element in day-to-day governing. Politicians' images in the press are seen as good indicators of their clout. Image is especially important for presidents, who in recent years have devoted much attention to maintaining a well-honed public image, as shown in the following internal White House memo written by President Nixon.

> When I think of the millions of dollars that go into one lousy 30-second television spot advertising a deodorant, it seems to me unbelievable that we don't do a better job in seeing that presidential appearances always have the very best professional advice whenever they are to be covered on TV. . . . The President should never be without the very best professional advice for making a television appearance.[3]

Few, if any, administrations devoted so much effort and energy to the president's media appearance as did Ronald Reagan's. It has often been said that Reagan played to the media as he had played to the cameras in Hollywood. According to Mark

America in Perspective

How Campaign Advertising Compares Across Five Nations

Campaign advertising in the United States differs greatly from that in other democracies. Most other countries have party-sponsored ads, provided by the state, with limits on both ad number and length. How do you think American elections might change if the government provided the parties with free air time like the British and French?

	UNITED STATES	BRITAIN	FRANCE	GERMANY	ISRAEL
Sponsorship	mostly candidate	party	party	party	party
Method of allocating ads	purchase	allocated by the state	allocated by the state	allocated by the state	allocated by the state
Limitations on number of ads	no	yes	yes	yes	yes
Duration of ads	unlimited, but typically only 30 seconds	2–3 minutes	up to 4 minutes	2-1/2 minutes	5 minutes

Source: Lynda Lee Kaid and Christina Holtz-Bacha, eds., *Political Advertising in Western Democracies: Parties and Candidates on Television* (Thousand Oaks, CA: Sage, 1995).

Hertsgaard, news management in the Reagan White House operated on the following seven principles: (1) plan ahead, (2) stay on the offensive, (3) control the flow of information, (4) limit reporters' access to the president, (5) talk about the issues you want to talk about, (6) speak in one voice, and (7) repeat the same message many times.[4]

To Ronald Reagan, the presidency was often a performance, and his aides helped to choreograph his public appearances. Perhaps there will never again be a president so concerned with public relations as Reagan, but for a president to ignore the power of image and the media would be perilous. In today's high-tech age, presidents can

The Reagan administration carefully—and masterfully—controlled the president's image as presented by the media. To avoid having Reagan give unrehearsed answers, for example, his advisers would place the media at a distance and rev a helicopter engine so the president could not hear reporters' questions.

Television enables many more people to see candidates for elected office than would ever be possible in person. In fact, people have become so accustomed to seeing politicians' faces when they speak that giant TV screens are now often used to enable those attending political events to see the speakers' facial expressions.

hardly lead the country if they cannot communicate effectively with it. President Clinton once reflected on the unexpected dimensions of his job on *Larry King Live*: "The thing that has surprised me most is how difficult it is . . . to really keep communicating what you're about to the American people. That to me has been the most frustrating thing." According to Bob Woodward, Clinton confided to a friend that "I did not realize the importance of communications and the overriding importance of what is on the evening television news. If I am not on, or there with a message, someone else is, with their message."[5]

The Development of Media Politics

There was virtually no daily press when the United States Constitution was written. The daily newspaper is largely a product of the mid-nineteenth century; radio and television have been around only since the first half of the twentieth century. As recently as the presidency of Herbert Hoover (1929–1933), reporters submitted their questions to the president in writing, and he responded in writing—if at all. As Hoover put it, "The President of the United States will not stand and be questioned like a chicken thief by men whose names he does not even know."[6]

Hoover's successor, Franklin D. Roosevelt (1933–1945), practically invented media politics. To Roosevelt, the media were a potential ally. Roosevelt promised reporters two **press conferences**—presidential meetings with reporters—a week, resulting in about 1,000 press conferences during his 12 years in the White House. FDR was

press conferences

Meetings of public officials with reporters.

also the first president to use radio, broadcasting a series of reassuring "fireside chats" to the Depression-ridden nation. Roosevelt's crafty use of radio helped him win four presidential elections. Theodore White tells the story of the time in 1944 when FDR found out that his opponent, Thomas E. Dewey, had purchased 15 minutes of air time on NBC immediately following FDR's address. Roosevelt spoke for 14 minutes and then left 1 minute silent. Thinking that the network had experienced technical difficulties, many listeners changed their dials before Dewey came on the air.[7]

Another of Roosevelt's talents was knowing how to feed the right story to the right reporter. He used presidential wrath to warn reporters off material he did not want covered, and he chastised news reports he deemed inaccurate. His wrath was rarely invoked, however, and the press revered him, never even reporting to the American public that the president was confined to a wheelchair. The idea that a political leader's health status might be public business was alien to journalists in FDR's day.

This relatively cozy relationship between politicians and the press lasted through the early 1960s. ABC's Sam Donaldson said that when he first came to Washington in 1961, "Many reporters saw themselves as an extension of the government, accepting, with very little skepticism, what government officials told them."[8] And coverage of a politician's personal life was generally off-limits. For example, as a young reporter R.W. Apple, Jr. of the *New York Times* once observed a beautiful woman being escorted to President Kennedy's suite. Thinking he had a major scoop, he rushed to tell his editor. But he was quickly told, "Apple, you're supposed to report on political and diplomatic policies, not girlfriends. No story."[9]

The events of the Vietnam War and the Watergate scandal, though, soured the press on government. Today's newspeople work in an environment of cynicism. To them, politicians rarely tell the whole story; the press sees ferreting out the truth as their job. No one has demonstrated this attitude better in recent years than Sam Donaldson. In his book, *Hold On, Mr. President!*, Donaldson wrote,

> *If you send me to cover a pie-baking contest on Mother's Day, I'm going to ask dear old Mom whether she used artificial sweetener in violation of the rules, and while she's at it, could I see the receipt for the apples to prove she didn't steal them. I maintain that if Mom has nothing to hide, no harm will have been done. But the questions should be asked.*[10]

When the Clinton-Lewinsky scandal broke, the entire press corps reacted in this fashion. So strong was the desire to find out what the president had to hide in his personal life that 75 percent of the questions asked during the daily White House press briefing concerned this scandal in the first week after the story broke.[11] The Middle East was in crisis, the United States was building up its forces against Iraq, and the president was preparing a State of the Union address. But on TV and radio talk shows programming could best be described as "All Monica, All the Time."

Many political scientists are critical of **investigative journalism**—the use of detective-like reporting methods to unearth scandals—which often pits reporters against political leaders. There is evidence that TV's fondness for investigative journalism has contributed to greater public cynicism and negativity about politics.[12]

In his analysis of media coverage of presidential campaigns since 1960, Thomas Patterson found that news coverage of presidential candidates has become increasingly less favorable. His tally of *Time* and *Newsweek* stories about the campaigns reveals that favorable references about Kennedy and Nixon outnumbered unfavorable ones by a 3-to-1 margin. In contrast, in 1992 there were three negative references regarding Clinton and Bush for every two favorable references. Patterson's careful analysis uncovers several aspects of the trend toward more negative media coverage of the candidates over the last three decades. First, he finds that the emphasis of campaign reporting has changed dramatically from "what" to "why." Patterson's content analysis of front-page *New York Times* stories revealed that in 1960 over 90 percent of news stories employed a descriptive framework, whereas by 1992 less than 20 percent did so. Second, the type of interpretative story that has become more prominent is hard-biting analysis of political maneuvering and the horse race.

investigative journalism

The use of in-depth reporting to unearth scandals, scams, and schemes, which at times puts reporters in adversarial relationships with political leaders.

When someone becomes an instant political celebrity it takes a police escort to get them through the hordes of cameras and reporters. Here, Monica Lewinsky leaves a federal courthouse amid much commotion after providing evidence for the special prosecutor's investigation into charges of wrongdoing by President Clinton.

Such reporting tends toward unfavorable impressions of the candidates because the unstated assumption behind much of today's coverage of the issues has shifted from policy statements to campaign controversies. Coverage of such issues as whether George W. Bush fulfilled his military obligations or John F. Kerry lied about his experiences in Vietnam are not likely to draw favorable references. Those who run campaigns naturally complain about such coverage. As Karl Rove, one of George W. Bush's top political advisers said after the 2000 election was over:

> "The general nature of the tone of the coverage was very much in keeping with what Patterson suggests, that it is process oriented, highly cynical, negative, dismissive of issue positions, focused on the internals of the campaign and not on the big messages and really serves to trivialize the whole contest."[13]

Whether or not such media coverage is ultimately in the public's best interest is much debated. The press maintains that the public is now able to get a complete, accurate, and unvarnished look at the candidates. Critics of the media charge that they overemphasize the controversial aspects of the campaign at the expense of an examination of the major issues.

Scholars distinguish between two kinds of media: the **print media,** which include newspapers and magazines, and the **broadcast media,** which include radio, television, and the Internet. Each has reshaped political communication at different points in American history. It is difficult to assess the likely impact of the Internet at this point, but there is at least some reason to believe that political communication is being reshaped once again.

print media

Newspapers and magazines, as compared with **broadcast media.**

broadcast media

Television and radio, as compared with **print media.**

Three Centuries of American Mass Media

The Print Media

The first American daily newspaper was printed in Philadelphia in 1783, but such papers did not proliferate until the technological advances of the mid-nineteenth century. The ratification of the First Amendment in 1791, guaranteeing freedom of speech, gave even the earliest American newspapers freedom to print whatever they saw fit. This has given the media a unique ability to display the government's dirty linen, a propensity that continues to distinguish the American press today.

At the turn of the century, newspaper magnates Joseph and William Randolph Hearst ushered in the era of "yellow journalism." This sensational style of reporting focused on violence, corruption, wars, and gossip, often with a less than scrupulous regard for the truth. On a visit to the United States at that time, young Winston Churchill said that "the essence of American journalism is vulgarity divested of

The White House press room is often the scene of much activity, with daily briefings on the president's activities each day the president is in residence. Contrary to the image that is often presented on television, reporters work in a cramped environment at the White House.

truth."[14] In the midst of the Spanish-American conflict over Cuba, Hearst once boasted of his power over public opinion by telling a news artist "You furnish the pictures and I'll furnish the war."

Among the press there is a pecking order. Almost from the beginning, the *New York Times* was a cut above most newspapers in its influence and impact; it is the nation's "newspaper of record" and can be found on line at *www.nytimes.com*. Its clearest rival in government circles is the *Washington Post* (*www.washingtonpost.com*), offering perhaps the best coverage inside Washington and a sprightlier alternative to the *Times*. Papers such as the *Chicago Tribune* (*www.chicagotribune.com*) and the *Los Angeles Times* (*www.latimes.com*), as well as those in Atlanta, Boston, and other big cities, are also major national institutions. For most newspapers in medium-sized and small towns, though, the main source of national and world news is the Associated Press wire service, whose stories are reprinted in small newspapers across the country. With 2,700 reporters, photographers, and editors scattered around every major location in the United States, the Associated Press has more news-gathering ability than any other news organization.

Ever since the rise of TV news, however, newspaper circulation rates have been declining, as you can see in Figure 7.1. Most political scientists who have studied the role of media in politics believe this is an unfortunate trend, as studies invariably find that regular newspaper readers are better informed and more likely to vote.[15] This should hardly be surprising given the greater degree of information available in a newspaper compared to TV. A major metropolitan newspaper averages roughly 100,000 words daily, whereas a typical broadcast of the nightly news on TV will amount to only about 3,600 words.[16] It remains to be seen whether the availability of most newspapers on the web will lead more people to look at newspapers in the future, or rather will prove to be a desperate gasp for a fading business.

Magazines, the other component of the print media, are also struggling in the Internet age, especially when it comes to the few that are heavily concerned with political events. The so-called newsweeklies—mainly *Time*, *Newsweek*, and *U.S. News and World Report*—rank well behind such popular favorites as the *Reader's Digest*, *TV Guide*, and *National Geographic*. Although *Time*'s circulation is a bit better than that of the *National Enquirer*, *Playboy* and *People* edge out *Newsweek* in sales competition. Serious magazines of political news and opinion tend to be read by the educated elite; magazines such as the *New Republic*, the *National Review*, and the *Atlantic Monthly*

Simulation

You Are a News Editor

Figure 7.1　The Decline of Newspaper Circulation

Following is the average number of newspapers sold daily per 1,000 Americans over the age of 18. Whereas one newspaper was sold for every two adults in 1960, by 2004 only one paper was sold for every four adults.

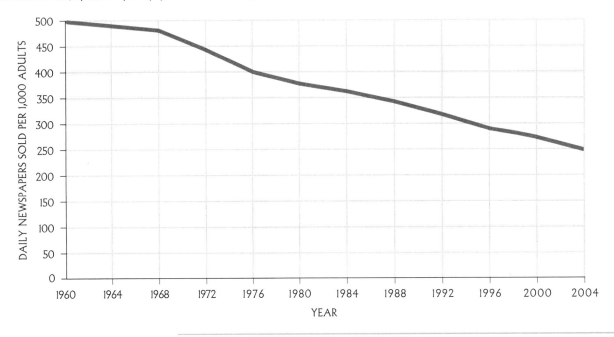

Source: Editor and Publisher; U.S. Census Bureau.

are outsold by American favorites such as *Hot Rod*, *Weightwatchers Magazine*, and *Organic Gardening*.

The Broadcast Media

Gradually, the broadcast media have displaced the print media as Americans' principal source of news and information. By the middle of the 1930s, radio ownership had become almost universal in America, and during World War II, radio went into the news business in earnest. The 1950s and early 1960s were the adolescent years for American television. During those years, the political career of Richard Nixon was made and unmade by television. In 1952, while running as Dwight Eisenhower's vice-presidential candidate, Nixon made a famous speech denying that he took gifts and payments under the table. He did admit accepting one gift—his dog, Checkers. Noting that his daughters loved the dog, Nixon said that regardless of his political future, they would keep it. His homey appeal brought a flood of sympathetic telegrams to the Republican National Committee, and party leaders had little choice but to leave him on the ticket.

In 1960, Nixon was again on television's center stage, this time in the first televised presidential debate against Senator John F. Kennedy. Nixon blamed his poor appearance in the first of the four debates for his narrow defeat in the election. Haggard from a week in the hospital and with his five o'clock shadow and perspiration clearly visible, Nixon looked awful compared to the crisp, clean, attractive Kennedy. The poll results from this debate illustrate the visual power of television in American politics; people listening on the radio gave the edge to Nixon, but those who saw the debate on television thought Kennedy won. Russell Baker, who covered the event for the *New York Times*, writes in his memoirs that "television replaced newspapers as the most important communications medium in American politics" that very night.[17]

Just as radio had taken the nation to the war in Europe and the Pacific during the 1940s, television took the nation to the war in Vietnam during the 1960s. TV exposed governmental naïveté (some said it was outright lying) about the progress of the war. Every night, in living color, Americans watched the horrors of war on television. President Johnson soon had two wars on his hands, one in faraway Vietnam and the other at home with antiwar protesters—both covered in detail by the media. In 1968, CBS anchor Walter Cronkite journeyed to Vietnam for a firsthand look at the state of the war. In an extraordinary TV special, Cronkite reported that the war was not being won, nor was it likely to be. Watching from the White House, Johnson sadly remarked that if he had lost Cronkite, he had lost the support of the American people.[18]

With the growth of cable TV, particularly the Cable News Network (CNN), television has recently entered a new era of bringing the news to people—and to political leaders—as it happens. Michael Bohn writes that CNN has become a valuable source of breaking information in the White House Situation Room.[19] President George W. Bush and his aides regularly watched CNN during the military campaign in Afghanistan; Osama Bin Laden's videotaped messages were regularly broadcast in part on CNN, enabling him to get his message out to a worldwide audience. A frequent response from U.S. officials to reporters' questions during the war against terrorism was something along the lines of "I don't know any more than what you saw on CNN."

Since 1963, surveys have consistently shown that more people rely on TV for the news than any other medium. Furthermore, by a regular 2-to-1 margin, people think television reports are more believable than newspaper stories.[20] (Consider the old sayings "Don't believe everything you read" and "I'll believe it when I see it.") Whereas people are predisposed to be skeptical about what they read in a newspaper, with television seeing is believing.

Government Regulation of the Broadcast Media

When broadcast media first appeared with the invention of radio, a number of problems that the government could help with (such as overlapping use of the same frequency) soon became apparent. In 1934, Congress created the Federal Communications Commission (FCC) to regulate the use of airwaves. Today, the FCC regulates communications via radio, television, telephone, cable, and satellite. The FCC is an independent regulatory body, but in practice it is subject to many political pressures. Congress uses its control over the purse strings of the agency to influence the commission, and presidential appointments to it are naturally made with political considerations in mind.

The FCC has regulated the airwaves in three important ways. First, to prevent near-monopolies of control over a broadcast market, it has instituted rules to limit the number of stations owned or controlled by one company. This once involved a variety of limitations but since 1996 has been simplified to simply state that no single owner can control more than 35 percent of the broadcast market. Second, the FCC conducts periodic examinations of the goals and performance of stations as part of its licensing authority. Congress long ago stipulated that in order to receive a broadcasting license a station must serve the public interest. The FCC has only on rare occasions withdrawn licenses for failing to do so, such as when a Chicago station lost its license for neglecting informational programs and for presenting obscene movies. Third, the FCC has issued a number of fair treatment rules concerning access to the airwaves for political candidates and officeholders. The equal time rule stipulates that if a station sells advertising time to one candidate it must be willing to sell equal time to other candidates for the same office. And the right-of-reply rule states if a person is attacked on a broadcast other than the news then that person has a right to reply via the same station. For many years, the fairness doctrine was in place, which required broadcasters to give time to opposing views if they broadcast a program slanted to one side of a controversial issue. But with the development of so many TV

Why It Matters

The Increasing Speed of News Dissemination
When Samuel Morse sent the first telegraph message from the U.S. Capitol building, he tapped out a question, "What hath God wrought?" The answer back was, "What is the news from Washington?" Ever since then, the transmission of news via electronic means has become faster and faster. As a result, over time there has been less and less time for deliberative action to provide for the future and the political agenda has come to focus more on the here and now.

Making a Difference

Matt Drudge

Matt Drudge was 30 years old when he broke his first story about Monica Lewinsky's relationship with President Clinton, which would become the biggest political scandal of the 1990s. He had neither verified the story nor done any extensive research on it. All he had to go on was the rumor that *Newsweek* had been working on this story. But for Drudge, a rumor was good enough to report on. When Drudge posted the Lewinsky story on his website (*www.drudgereport.com*), he knew his life would be changed forever, and for quite some time so would the nation's. Opinions on Matt Drudge and his reporting techniques vary widely. Because of his penchant for reporting rumors and gossip, the *New York Times* has called him "the nation's chief mischief maker." Others have dubbed him the first Internet superstar and praised how he has paved the way for communication power to be transferred from media giants to anyone with a modem. However one views him, it is clear that Matt Drudge has made a difference. Currently, his website draws over 2 billion hits a year.

---

narrowcasting

Media programming on cable TV or the Internet that is focused on one topic and aimed at a particular audience. Examples include MTV, ESPN, and C-SPAN.

Democracy and the Internet

channels via cable, this was seen as an unnecessary rule by the late 1980s, when it was abolished.

Narrowcasting: Cable TV and the Internet

The future of political communication seems destined to bring more and more choices regarding what we can see about our government. About two-thirds of the American public currently subscribes to cable television, thereby giving them access to dozens of channels. Sometime in the not-too-distant future it is expected that most cable systems will offer 500 channels. How will this explosion of TV channels impact political communication? Our best guess, based on developments with cable TV to date, is that information about politics will be presented in a way that appeals to a narrow and specific audience rather than to the public at large.

The first major networks—ABC, NBC, and CBS—adopted the term "broadcasting" in the names of their companies because their signal was being sent out to a broad audience. As long as these networks dominated the industry, each would have to deal with general topics that the public as a whole was concerned with, such as politics and government. But with the development of cable TV, market segmentation has taken hold. Sports buffs can watch ESPN all day, music buffs can tune to MTV or VH1, history buffs can glue their dial to the History Channel, and so forth. If you are interested in politics, you can channel surf between C-SPAN, C-SPAN2, CNN, MSNBC, Fox News Channel, and others. Rather than appealing to a general audience, channels such as ESPN, MTV, and C-SPAN focus on a narrow particular interest. Hence, their mission can be termed "**narrowcasting**," rather than traditional "broadcasting." This is even more true for websites, which require minimal start-up costs and hence can be successful with a very small and specific audience. An analysis of media usage patterns by age shows that young adults are the most likely to be using the Internet to learn about politics. (See "Young People and Politics: How the Under-30 Crowd Learns from Different Media Sources Compared to Older Americans").

As the number of channels and websites proliferates, it is clear that political junkies will find more political information readily available than ever before. Rumors once carefully verified by careful journalists are now immediately disseminated around the world electronically (see "Making a Difference: Matt Drudge"). But with so many readily available sources of information for so many specific interests, it will also be extremely easy for those who are not very interested in politics to completely avoid news and public affairs. And as Doris Graber writes, "While available food for political thought has grown, despite much overlap and redundancy, the appetite for it and the capacity to consume it remain limited."[21] Some scholars are worried that the result could well be a growing inequality of political information, with the politically interested becoming more knowledgeable while the rest of the public slips further into political apathy.

Private Control of the Media

One of the main reasons America has such a rich diversity of media sources is that journalism has long been big business in the United States, with control of virtually all media outlets being in private hands. Only a relatively small number of TV stations are publicly owned in America, and these PBS stations play a minimal role in the news business, attracting low ratings. In contrast, in many other countries major TV net-

Young People and Politics

How the Under-30 Crowd Learns from Different Media Sources Compared to Older Americans

In January of 2004, the Pew Research Center asked a representative sample whether they regularly learned about the presidential campaign from a variety of media sources. This table shows the results, broken down by age. Notice that young people are substantially more likely to learn from the Internet and comedy TV shows. In contrast, older people are more likely to learn from the traditional sources of newspapers and network TV news (i.e., NBC, CBS, and ABC). Because so many young people are bypassing these sources, newspapers and network news are both facing the likely prospect of declining audiences for some time to come.

Cable TV news—CNN, MSNBC, and the Fox News Channel—have seen their audiences expand in recent years, as Americans of all ages have come to rely on them fairly heavily. However, given how little time most people stay tuned to these channels one has to be skeptical that people are getting much more than basic headlines from these sources. In theory, the Internet offers all the details about public policy and government that anyone could want. Whether very many of those who learn about politics via the Internet take advantage of the opportunities offered there remains to be seen. Comedy shows, on the other hand, offer very limited chances for learning about politics. Young people seem to enjoy them, though, and are at least having a good time learning from them.

% SAYING THEY REGULARLY LEARN SOMETHING ABOUT THE PRESIDENTIAL CAMPAIGN FROM:	AGE 18–29	AGE 30–49	AGE 50–64	AGE 65+
Cable news networks	37	37	43	37
Nightly network news	23	32	44	49
Daily newspaper	23	27	37	45
Comedy TV shows	21	6	5	2
Internet	20	16	11	3
Late-night TV talk shows like Letterman and Leno	13	7	7	9

Source: January 2004 survey by The Pew Research Center for the People and the Press. http://people-press.org/reports/isplay.php3?ReportID=200.

Questions for Discussion

- How much do you think can really be learned about politics from the comedy shows that one out of five young people say they learn from?
- Why do you think young people are so much less likely to learn from the traditional major news sources—TV network news and newspapers?

works are owned by the government. In Canada the most prominent stations are part of the state-run Canadian Broadcasting Company, and most anywhere in Europe the major networks are government-owned. In these established democracies, government ownership is not supposed to inhibit journalists from criticizing the government because the journalists are assured autonomy. In underdeveloped countries like China, where democracy has yet to take root, it is a different story: Both television and newspapers are typically government enterprises and have to carefully avoid any criticism of their country's government. Private ownership of the media as well as the First Amendment right to free speech has long meant that American journalists have an unfettered capacity to criticize government leaders and policies.

Although the American media is free and independent when it comes to journalistic content, they are totally dependent on advertising revenues to keep their businesses going. Public ownership means that the media can serve the public interest without worrying about the size of their audience; private ownership means that

chains

Newspapers published by massive media conglomerates that account for over four-fifths of the nation's daily newspaper circulation. Often these chains control **broadcast media** as well.

getting the biggest audience is the primary—indeed, sometimes the only—objective. The major media in America are big business today and potentially the source of great profits. In recent years, the major television networks have been bought out by giant corporations. The Disney Corporation bought ABC, General Electric acquired NBC, Viacom (a conglomerate that owns many entertainment companies, including Blockbuster, Paramount Pictures, MTV, and Simon & Schuster) took over CBS, and CNN became part of Time Warner. Major metropolitan newspapers are mostly owned by **chains,** such as Gannett, Knight-Ridder, and Newhouse. Today's massive media conglomerates control newspapers with over 80 percent of the nation's daily circulation.[22] Thus, four out of five newspaper subscribers now read a newspaper owned not by a fearless local editor but by a corporation headquartered elsewhere. Often these chains control television and radio stations as well.

With corporate business managers increasingly calling the shots, American journalism has definitely been affected. For example, the major television networks once had bureaus all over the world and felt a responsibility to report on world affairs. Such foreign bureaus became an easy target for cost-cutting business executives, as they were expensive to operate and survey data showed that the public was not much interested in news from overseas. A study of network news broadcasts found that ABC, NBC, and CBS broadcast just 1,382 minutes of foreign news in 2000 compared to 4,032 minutes in 1989.[23] Consequently, by September 11, 2001, the American public was largely unfamiliar with overseas news and the TV networks had to scramble to establish an ability to cover it. As we shall see in the following section, striving for profits greatly shapes how the news is reported in America.

Reporting the News

As journalism students will quickly tell you, news is what is timely and different. It is a man biting a dog, not a dog biting a man. An oft-repeated speech on foreign policy or a well-worn statement on fighting drug abuse is less newsworthy than an odd episode. The public rarely hears about the routine ceremonies at state dinners, but when President George Bush threw up all over the Japanese prime minister in 1992, the world's media jumped on the story. Similarly, when Howard Dean screamed to a crowd of supporters after the 2004 Iowa caucuses, the major networks and cable news channels played the clip over 600 times in the following four days, virtually obliterating any serious discussion of the issues. In its search for the unusual, the news media can give its audience a peculiar view of events and policymakers.

Millions of new and different events happen every day; journalists must decide which of them are newsworthy. A classic look into how the news is produced can be found in Edward J. Epstein's *News from Nowhere,*[24] which summarizes his observations from a year of observing NBC's news department from inside the organization. Epstein found that in their pursuit of high ratings, news shows are tailored to a fairly low level of audience sophistication. To a large extent, TV networks define news as what is entertaining to the average viewer. A dull and complicated story would have to be of enormous importance to get on the air; in contrast, relatively trivial stories can make the cut if they are interesting enough. Leonard Downie, Jr. and Robert Kaiser argue that entertainment has increasingly pushed out information in the TV news business. In 2002, they wrote that the history of TV news can be summarized in a couple sentences:

> As audiences declined, network executives decreed that news had to become more profitable. So news divisions sharply reduced their costs, and tried to raise the entertainment value of their broadcasts.[25]

Regardless of the medium, it cannot be emphasized enough that news reporting is a business in America. The quest for profits shapes how journalists define what is

How You Can Make a Difference

The Internet and Political Action

Until very recently, the average citizen had little voice within the mass media beyond opinion pages in newspapers. The advent of the Internet, however, has changed this—as the story of Matt Drudge breaking the Monica Lewinsky story clearly demonstrates. With the modest exception of small low-frequency radio stations and low-cost alternative newspapers that reach relatively few people, before the Internet no media allowed ordinary people to do so immediately and powerfully affect public opinion and to challenge politicians and governments.

In fact, the meaning of grass-roots activism has changed as the world has become increasingly web savvy. In the comfort of a dorm room, today's college students can help topple foreign governments and pressure domestic government agencies into action. The governments in China, Malaysia, and Mexico have all been targets of Internet activists pressing for improved human rights. For example, the small and largely ineffectual Zapatista National

Liberation Army led by the ski-masked Subcommante Marcos has used the Internet to raise funds and convince thousands in Europe, North America, and Latin America to picket Mexican consulates in support of autonomy for the indigenous people of Chiapas. Jagdish Parikh of Human Rights Watch notes that "... what is making the difference is that ordinary people are now coming to this medium." This is especially true in the more technically advanced United States where the Internet and computers have become a necessity rather than a luxury. In the late 1990s, Internet postings and e-mails from civil liberties groups convinced the Federal Deposit Insurance Corporation to maintain strict privacy rules. According to *Business Week*, the FDIC got 205,000 e-mails opposing any loosening of their privacy policy compared to less than 100 in favor of a change.

Some observers note that many of the accepted rules of politics expressed in this textbook may become obsolete as the power of the Internet grows and

changes the political landscape. While other pundits caution that the impact of the Internet can be exaggerated especially outside the United States, Jagdish Parikh wisely considers, "How many people in China have Internet access? Not many. But then why is the government there rushing to make laws restricting access? It's because the Internet makes people realize that they should have the legal, codified right to information."

What you can do:
- *Clearly* define the issue that concerns you.
- Employ the necessary tools to make your online campaign effective.
- Visit *www.onenw.org/toolkit* for resources on making your campaign effective.

Source: Pete Engardio, Richard Dunham, Heidi Dawley, Irene Kunji, and Elisabeth Malkin, "Activists Without Borders," *Business Week* (October 4, 1999): 144–149.

newsworthy, where they get their information, and how they present it. Because some types of news stories attract more viewers or readers than others, certain biases are inherent in what the American public sees and reads.

Finding the News

Americans' popular image of correspondents or reporters somehow uncovering the news is accurate in some cases, yet most news stories come from well-established sources. Major news organizations assign their best reporters to particular **beats**—specific locations from which news often emanates, such as Congress. For example, during the 1991 Gulf War, more than 50 percent of the lead stories on TV newscasts came from the White House, Pentagon, and State Department beats.[26] Numerous studies of both the electronic and the print media show that journalists rely almost exclusively on such established sources to get their information.[27]

Those who make the news depend on the media to spread certain information and ideas to the general public. Sometimes they feed stories to reporters in the form of **trial balloons**: information leaked to see what the political reaction will be. For example, a few days prior to President Clinton's admission that he had an "inappropriate relationship" with Monica Lewinsky, top aides to the president leaked the story to Richard Berke of the *New York Times*. The timing of the leak was obvious; the story

beats

Specific locations from which news frequently emanates, such as Congress or the White House. Most top reporters work a particular beat, thereby becoming specialists in what goes on at that location.

trial balloons

An intentional **news leak** for the purpose of assessing the political reaction.

During the 2003 Iraqi War, a number of journalists were embedded with fighting units, meaning that they traveled along with them day after day and literally became part of the unit. Being right in with the action enabled an immediacy of reporting that was never possible before. One much-praised example of embedded reporting was that of NBC's David Bloom, who sent back stunningly clear pictures of what it was like to move through the desert with an infantry division. Sadly, Bloom was one of a number of journalists who died during the conflict with Iraq. He suffered a pulmonary embolism, a condition that may have been brought on by long hours confined to a very small space inside an armored tank.

appeared just before Clinton had to decide how to testify before Kenneth Starr's grand jury. When the public reacted that it was about time he admitted this relationship, it was probably easier for him to do so—at least politically.

Reporters and their official sources have a symbiotic relationship. Newsmakers rely on journalists to get their message out at the same time that reporters rely on public officials to keep them in the know. When reporters feel that their access to information is being impeded, complaints of censorship become widespread. During the 1991 Gulf War, reporters' freedom of movement and observation was severely restricted. After the fighting was over, 15 influential news organizations sent a letter to the secretary of defense complaining that the rules for reporting the war were designed more to control the news than to facilitate it.[28] In response to complaints about the lack of access for reporters in the first Gulf War, the Pentagon embedded about 500 reporters with coalition fighting forces during the 2003 Iraq War, thus enabling them to report on combat activity as it happened. The public response to this new form of war reporting was largely positive, as you can see in the polling data displayed in Table 7.1.

Although journalists are typically dependent on familiar sources, an enterprising reporter occasionally has an opportunity to live up to the image of the crusading truth seeker. Local reporters Carl Bernstein and Bob Woodward of the *Washington Post* uncovered important evidence in the Watergate case in the early 1970s. Ever since the Watergate scandal, news organizations have regularly sent reporters on beats to expose the uglier side of government corruption and inefficiency. Such reporting is highly valued among the media elite.

There are many cases of good investigative reporting making a difference in politics and government. For example, in 1997 the *New York Times* won a Pulitzer for their in-depth reports on how a proposed gold-mining operation threatened the environment of part of Yellowstone National Park. When President Clinton vacationed at nearby Jackson Hole, he decided to go up and see the mine because he had been reading about it in the *New York Times*. Soon afterward, the project was stopped and the government gave the owners of the property a financial settlement. In 1999, the *Chicago Tribune* documented the experiences of numerous Illinois men sentenced to death who had been convicted on questionable evidence or coerced into confessing. Soon after the series was published, the governor of Illinois suspended all executions in the state. And in 2000 a Houston TV station reported on Ford Explorers equipped with Firestone tires that were involved in a series of fatal traffic accidents. Its reports led to the recall of millions of tires and probably saved many lives.

Table 7.1 Embedded Reporting of the Iraq War: Opposing Opinions

About two weeks after the start of hostilities against Iraq the *Los Angeles Times* poll asked a representative sample of the U.S. population a carefully balanced question about the embedded reporting of the war. The question was:

Reporters have been assigned to U.S. military units in the region of Iraq and given unprecedented access to military action and personnel. Which of the following statements comes closer to your view: (1) "Greater media coverage of the military action and U.S. personnel in Iraq is good for the country because it gives the American people an uncensored view of events as they unfold" or (2) "Greater media coverage of the military action and U.S. personnel in Iraq is bad for the country because it provides too much information about military actions as they unfold?"

The results are presented here for the sample as a whole, as well as by gender.

	ALL	MEN	WOMEN
Embedded reporting good for the country	55%	58%	52%
Embedded reporting bad for the country	37%	34%	41%
Don't know	8%	8%	7%

Source: Los Angeles Times national poll conducted April 2–3, 2003.

Presenting the News

Once the news has been "found," it has to be neatly compressed into a 30-second news segment or fit in among the advertisements in a newspaper. If you had to pick a single word to describe news coverage by the print and broadcast media, it would be *superficial.* "The name of the game," says former White House Press Secretary Jody Powell, "is skimming off the cream, seizing on the most interesting, controversial, and unusual aspects of an issue."[29] Editors do not want to bore or confuse their audience. TV news, in particular, is little more than a headline service. According to CBS anchor Dan Rather, "You simply cannot be a well-informed citizen by just watching the news on television."[30]

Except for the little-watched, but highly regarded "NewsHour" on PBS and ABC's late-night "Nightline," analysis of news events rarely lasts more than a minute. Patterson's study of campaign coverage (see Chapter 9) found that only skimpy attention was given to the issues during a presidential campaign. Clearly, if coverage of political events during the height of an election campaign is thin, coverage of day-to-day policy questions is even thinner. Issues such as reforming the Medicare system, adjusting how the consumer price index is calculated, and deregulating the communications industry are highly complex and difficult to treat in a short news clip. A careful study of media coverage of President Clinton's comprehensive health care proposal early in his first term found that the media focused much more on strategy and who was winning the political game than on the specific policy issues involved.[31]

Strangely enough, as technology has enabled the media to pass along information with greater speed, news coverage has become less thorough.[32] Modern high-tech communications equipment has helped reporters do their job faster but not necessarily better, as you can read about in "Issues of the Times: Has Technology Really Improved the Quality of Political Reporting?" on pages 228–229. Newspapers once routinely reprinted the entire text of important political speeches; now the *New York Times* is virtually the only paper that does so—and even the *Times* has cut back sharply on this practice. In place of speeches, Americans now hear **sound bites** of 15 seconds or less on TV. As you can see in Figure 7.2, the average length of time that a presidential candidate has been given to talk uninterrupted on the TV news has declined precipitously since the late 1960s. Responding to criticism of sound-bite journalism, in 1992 CBS News briefly vowed that it would let a candidate speak for at least 30 seconds at a time. However, CBS found this to be unworkable and soon dropped the

sound bites

Short video clips of approximately 15 seconds; typically all that is shown from a politician's speech or activities on the nightly television news.

threshold to 20 seconds, noting that even this was flexible.[33] In 2000, the average sound bite of a candidate shown talking on the nightly news once again averaged less than 10 seconds.

Even successful politicians sometimes feel frustrated by sound-bite journalism. A year after his election to the presidency, Jimmy Carter told a reporter that

> ... it's a strange thing that you can go through your campaign for president, and you have a basic theme that you express in a 15- or 20-minute standard speech, ... but the traveling press—sometimes exceeding 100 people—will never report that speech to the public. The peripheral aspects become the headlines, but the basic essence of what you stand for and what you hope to accomplish is never reported.[34]

Rather than presenting their audience with the whole chicken, the media typically give just a McNugget. Why should politicians work to build a carefully crafted case for their point of view when a catchy line will do just as well? As former CBS anchor Walter Cronkite writes, "Naturally, nothing of any significance is going to be said in seven seconds, but this seems to work to the advantage of many politicians. They are not required to say anything of significance, and issues can be avoided rather than confronted."[35] Cronkite and others have proposed that in order to force candidates to go beyond sound bites they should be given blocks of free air time for a series of nights to discuss their opposing views (see "You Are the Policymaker: Should the Networks Have To Provide Free Air Time to Presidential Candidates?" on page 230).

Over the last decade, politicians have found it increasingly difficult to get their message covered on the major networks, as ratings pressures have led to a decrease in political coverage, leaving the field to the much-less watched channels like CNN and MSNBC. The three major networks *together* devoted an average of 12.6 minutes per night to the exceedingly close 2000 presidential election campaign; just half the 24.6 minutes they devoted to the 1992 campaign.[36] Indeed, in the presidential election of 2000 voters had to bypass the network television newscasts and watch the TV talk shows to hear candidates deliver their messages. George Bush was on-screen for a total of 13 minutes during his appearance on "Late Night With David Letterman" on October 19, which exceeded his entire speaking time on all three network news shows during that month. Similarly, Al Gore received more speaking time on his September 14 Letterman appearance than he did during the entire month of September on the network evening newscasts.[37]

During the Cold War, presidents could routinely obtain coverage for their speeches on the three major networks anytime they requested it. Now, with the networks able to shunt the coverage to CNN and other cable news outlets, it is easy for them to say "no" to even the president. In May of 2000, for example, Clinton was rebuffed when he asked for time on ABC, NBC, and CBS to address U.S.-China relations. "Are you crazy? It's sweeps month!" was one of the responses.[38]

Figure 7.2 The Incredible Shrinking Sound Bite

Following is the average length of time a presidential candidate was shown speaking uninterrupted on the evening network news from 1968 to 2000.

1968	1972	1976	1980	1984	1988	1992	1996	2000
43.1 seconds	25.2 seconds	18.2 seconds	12.2 seconds	9.9 seconds	8.9 seconds	8.4 seconds	8.2 seconds	7.0 seconds

Source: Daniel Hallin, "Sound Bite News: Television Coverage of Elections," *Journal of Communications,* Spring 1992; 1992–2000 data from studies by the Center for Media and Public Affairs.

BEFORE SOUND BITES:

FOURSCORE AND SEVEN YEARS AGO, OUR FOREFATHERS BROUGHT FORTH ON THIS CONTINENT A NEW NATION, CONCEIVED IN LIBERTY, AND DEDICATED TO THE PROPOSITION THAT ALL MEN ARE CREATED EQUAL...

AFTER SOUND BITES:

READ MY LIPS: NO SLAVES.

Until September 11, the Bush White House was finding it harder to get media attention than any administration in a long time. A study of the first 60 days of coverage of the presidencies of Bill Clinton and George W. Bush on ABC, NBC, CBS, PBS, the section fronts and opinion pages of the *Washington Post*, the *New York Times*, and *Newsweek* found that there were 41 percent fewer stories on Bush than on Clinton. *Newsweek* stories on the president had decreased by 59 percent over the eight years, while network coverage was down 43 percent and the *Post* and the *Times* had fallen off by 38 percent.[39] Although the prominence of the president increased after the September 11 terrorist attacks, there is no reason to think the trend toward less coverage of the White House has been permanently reversed.

Bias in the News

Many people believe that the news is biased in favor of one point of view. During the 1996 presidential campaign, Bob Dole often charged that the press was against him. "Annoy the Media—Elect Dole" became one of his favorite lines. The charge that the media have a liberal bias has become a familiar one in American politics, and there is some limited evidence to support it. A lengthy study by the *Los Angeles Times* in the mid-1980s found that reporters were twice as likely to call themselves liberal as the general public.[40] A 2002 survey of 1,149 journalists found that 37 percent identified themselves as Democrats, compared to just 19 percent who said they were Republicans.[41]

However, the vast majority of social science studies have found that reporting is not systematically biased toward a particular ideology or party.[42] Most stories are presented in a "point/counterpoint" format in which two opposing points of view (such as liberal versus conservative) are presented, and the audience is left to draw its own conclusions. Two factors explain why the news is typically characterized by such political neutrality. Most reporters strongly believe in journalistic objectivity, and those who practice it best are usually rewarded by their editors. In addition, media outlets have a direct financial stake in attracting viewers and subscribers and do not want to lose their audience by appearing biased—especially when multiple versions of the same story are readily available. It seems paradoxical to say that competition produces uniformity, but this often happens in the news business.

Why It Matters

Media as a Business
In his classic book *Understanding Media*, Marshall McLuhan coined the famous phrase, "The medium is the message." By this, McLuhan meant that the way we communicate information can be more influential than the information itself. In the United States, news is a commodity controlled by the media, not a public service. Therefore, the news media have far more incentive to make their reports interesting than informative about policy issues. The public would probably be exposed to more policy information were it not for this incentive system.

Issues of the Times

The Issue: Has Technology Really Improved the Quality of Political Reporting?

Good journalists have always been concerned about getting news to the public quickly. But recent developments in communications technology have made it perhaps too easy for journalists to send out information to their home offices. The constant pressure to feed stories back to the newsroom has left journalists with little time for contemplation or checking their stories for accuracy. On the positive side, more information can be conveyed than ever before. Yet, there is debate about whether the quality of political reporting has been improved as a result.

Read All About It

Making of the Digital Press Corps, 2004

By Katharine Q. Seelye
January 29, 2004

Howard Dean was taking questions from a crowd of New Hampshire voters the other day when a young man asked him, "Governor Dean, can I pray for you?"

Dr. Dean, the Democratic presidential candidate and former governor of Vermont, responded that he could use all the prayers he could get. Whereupon the young man immediately began a dialogue with the Almighty.

"Oh, I didn't know you meant right now!" Dr. Dean interjected, before telling him to go ahead.

As bizarre campaign moments go, this one was brief and not really all that bizarre. But Mike Roselli, a producer for CNN, thought it was worth alerting his bosses in case they needed fresh tape of Dr. Dean.

So Mr. Roselli quickly punched an e-mail message into his BlackBerry. He titled it "Pray For Me," concisely recounted the incident and concluded: "The prayer includes a plea to God asking him to cure Dean's cold.". . .

. . . Mr. Roselli, a campaign veteran, thought the prayer was more interesting than some of the material being beamed from CNN producers who were following other candidates ("Candidate X drinks a chocolate milkshake!") but conceded that he had sent it partly because he could. And he worried that someone else might.

"Four years ago, I wouldn't have called that in until the event was over," he said. "But there's more competition now, 24 hours a day."

Please see Press   **Page 229**

Press

Continued from Page 228

A deadline every minute, once the preserve of the wire services, is now the motto for most of the press corps, from print reporters with newspaper Web sites to still photographers, cable producers and bloggers. The news cycle has condensed into one endless loop, and with it has come a endless stream of technology to accommodate it, or fuel it, since it is hard to say which came first.

Campaign reporters, like war correspondents, are not necessarily gadget geeks. But the rapacious 24-hour news cycle has forced them onto the cutting edge to do their jobs better—or at least faster. The equipment is even altering the shape of the correspondent's day, which now includes scrolling in the morning through "The Note," an online political briefing from ABC News, and checking one another's Web sites at night, trying all the while to get a jump on everyone else.

The great leaps forward for print reporters in this campaign cycle are wireless laptops and digital tape recorders with software that allows them to download a candidate's speech immediately onto the laptops as an audio file. For television reporters, it is the ubiquitous hand-held minicam, which blurs the line between home video and politically revealing moments, like those captured by Alexandra Pelosi in "Journeys With George," her movie of George W. Bush shot with a hand-held camera during the 2000 campaign. . . .

The digital tape recorder that produces audio files has become essential for reporters trying to keep track of multiple speeches and bang out an article before flying off to another location.

> ## A deadline every minute, once the preserve of the wire services, is now the motto for most of the press corps.

With the audio software, up comes an image of a tape recorder on the computer screen. "It's so easy to play, rewind and play a quote over and over until you've got it," said Glen Johnson of *The Boston Globe,* who has been following Dr. Dean and Senator John Kerry of Massachusetts.

Mr. Johnson said his Sony digital recorder solved two problems. "It's got a much longer capacity than the standard reel-to-reel recorder, with up to five hours," he said. "And I can archive and organize all the speeches and permanently keep everything that's said on the trail without having to lug around a bunch of tapes and be out on the road without the tape I want."

He can also e-mail the audio files back to *The Globe,* which can put the sound bite on its Web site. . . .

Not every reporter, to be sure, is enamored of what technology has wrought. Jules Witcover, 76, a columnist for *The Baltimore Sun,* who covered his first campaign in 1960 by handing his copy to a Western Union boy, said he prefers to stick with the basics. . . .

[H]e does not like what the proliferation of gadgets has done to journalism, or to journalists. "Technology has impinged on reporting," he said. He said that candidates used to schmooze with reporters on the plane because they could pick whom they wanted to talk with and others would respect their privacy. Now, he said, if a candidate comes back, everybody gathers around. And with boom microphones and discreet recording gear and phones that can secretly take pictures and transmit them instantly, the candidate cannot relax.

"Rather than take a chance, they don't do it," Mr. Witcover said. "It has eroded the relationship that you could build up with a candidate."

Beyond that, he said, even a long bus ride at night is no fun anymore because most people are on their cellphones—and always on deadline.

Think About It

- What are the possible disadvantages of making it so easy for journalists to report on every little detail almost instantly? Do you think these disadvantages outweigh the advantages of greater access to information?

- Do you think editors should encourage some reporters to focus on sending back every detail whereas others are assigned to take their time and carefully analyze what they have seen and heard?

You Are the Policymaker

Should the Networks Have to Provide Free Air Time to Presidential Candidates?

In 1996, a group of prominent political and media figures proposed the idea of a series of free prime-time television appearances for presidential candidates to address the issues. The Coalition for Free Air Time called upon the networks to turn over 2 to 5 minutes a night to the candidates in the month before the presidential election. Furthermore, the coalition suggested that these segments should be "roadblocked"—shown simultaneously on all networks, PBS, and interested cable stations so that people watching prime-time entertainment would be sure to see the candidates. The coalition hoped this format would promote a nightly dialogue on the issues, with candidates making news with their replies to each other's previous segments. The only

requirement would be that the candidates look straight into the camera and talk. There would be no manipulation of images or unseen narrators—just candidates making their case directly to the biggest potential audience every night.

Most of the networks did eventually grant the candidates some free time in 1996, but the approach was a scattershot one. The segments varied from 1 to 2-1/2 minutes, and each network chose a different time to broadcast them. A survey done by the Annenberg School of Communication immediately after the election found that only 22 percent of registered voters even knew that the free-time effort existed. Virtually everyone involved was disappointed with the results. The results

from the 2000 election were similarly disheartening, as once again the networks adopted different approaches and the audiences tended to be relatively small.

Many observers believe that the experience of the recent presidential elections has demonstrated the necessity of adopting a common format and time for all networks; some even advocate using the government's regulatory powers to force the networks to adopt this approach. Others point to the poor ratings of the televised debates as an example of the ineffectiveness of roadblocking political dialogue when the public just isn't interested. You be the policymaker. Is this an experiment that the government should mandate in future presidential elections?

Participation

Are the Media Biased?

talking head

A shot of a person's face talking directly to the camera. Because this is visually unappealing, the major commercial networks rarely show a politician talking one-on-one for very long.

To conclude that the news contains little explicit partisan bias is not to argue that it does not distort reality in its coverage. Former CBS News reporter Bernard Goldberg spoke for the view of many observers when he wrote in his recent best-selling book entitled *Bias* that "real media bias comes not so much from what party they attack. Liberal bias is the result of how they see the world."[43] Goldberg argues on social issues like feminism, gay rights, and welfare that the nightly news clearly leans to the left, shaped by the cosmopolitan big-city environment in which network reporters live. He asks a telling question when he writes, "Do we really think that if the media elites worked out of Nebraska instead of New York; and if they were overwhelmingly social conservatives instead of liberals . . . do we really think that would make no difference?"[44]

Ideally, the news should mirror reality; in practice there are far too many possible stories for this to be the case. Journalists must choose which stories to cover and to what degree. The overriding bias is toward stories that will draw the largest audience. As Bernard Goldberg writes, "In the United States of Entertainment there is no greater sin than to bore the audience. A TV reporter could get it wrong from time to time. He could be snippy and snooty. But he could not be boring."[45] Surveys show that people are most fascinated by stories with conflict, violence, disaster, or scandal, as can be seen in Table 7.2. Good news is unexciting; bad news has the drama that brings in big audiences.

Television is particularly biased toward stories that generate good pictures. Seeing a **talking head** (a shot of a person's face talking directly to the camera) is boring; viewers will switch channels in search of more interesting visual stimulation. For example, during an unusually contentious and lengthy interview of George Bush by Dan Rather concerning the Iran-Contra scandal in the 1980s, CBS's ratings actually went down as people tired of watching two talking heads argue for an extended period of time.[46] A shot of ambassadors squaring off in a fistfight at the United Nations, on the other hand, will increase the ratings. Such a scene was shown three times in one day on CBS. Not once, though, was the cause of the fight discussed.[47] Network practices like these have led observers such as Lance Bennett to write that "the public is exposed to a world driven into chaos by seemingly arbitrary and mysterious forces."[48]

The News and Public Opinion

How does the threatening, hostile, and corrupt world often depicted by the news media shape what people believe about the American political system? This question is difficult to answer. Studying the effects of the news media on people's opinions and behaviors is a difficult task. One reason is that it is hard to separate the media from other influences. When presidents, legislators, and interest groups—as well as news organizations—are all discussing an issue, it is not easy to isolate the opinion changes that come from political leadership from those that come from the news. Moreover, the effect of one news story on public opinion may be trivial; the cumulative effect of dozens of news stories may be important.

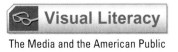

Visual Literacy

The Media and the American Public

For many years, students of the subject tended to doubt that the media had more than a marginal effect on public opinion. The "minimal effects hypothesis" stemmed from the fact that early scholars were looking for direct impacts—for example, whether the media affected how people voted.[49] When the focus turned to how the media affect *what Americans think about*, more positive results were uncovered. In a series of

Table 7.2   Stories Citizens Have Tuned in and Stories They Have Tuned out

Since 1986, the monthly survey of the Pew Research Center for the People and the Press has asked Americans how closely they have followed major news stories. As one would expect, stories involving disaster or human drama have drawn more attention than complicated issues of public policy. A representative selection of their findings is presented here. The percentage in each case is the proportion who reported following the story "very closely."

The explosion of the space shuttle *Challenger* in 1986	80%
Terrorist attacks on the World Trade Center and Pentagon	74%
San Francisco earthquake	73%
Los Angeles riots	70%
Rescue of baby Jessica McClure from a well	69%
School shootings at Columbine High School in Colorado	68%
Iraq's invasion of Kuwait in 1990	66%
Hurricane Andrew	66%
Sniper shootings near Washington, D.C.	65%
Start of hostilities against Iraq in 2003	57%
Supreme Court decision on flag burning	51%
Opening of the Berlin Wall	50%
Arrest of O. J. Simpson	48%
Nuclear accident at Chernobyl	46%
Capture of Saddam Hussein	44%
Controversy over whether Elian Gonzalez should have to return to Cuba	39%
2000 presidential election outcome	38%
Iran-Contra hearings	33%
Impeachment trial of President Clinton in the Senate	31%
Prescription drug benefit added to the Medicare program	25%
2004 Republican National Convention	22%
Release of President Bush's education plan in 2002	21%
Congressional debate about NAFTA	21%
Passage of the Communications Deregulation Bill	12%
Election of Ariel Sharon in Israel in 2001	9%
2003 Supreme Court decision upholding campaign finance reform	8%

Source: The Pew Research Center for the People and the Press.

Conservative Republicans often criticize the media for being biased against them. Studies have indeed shown that TV and newspaper reporters are more likely to be liberals than conservatives. However, there is little evidence that the personal views of reporters influence their coverage.

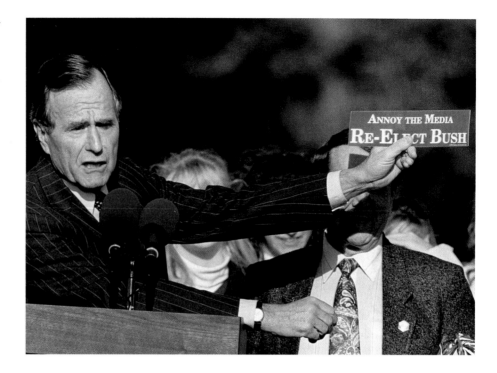

controlled laboratory experiments, Shanto Iyengar and Donald Kinder subtly manipulated the stories participants saw on the TV news.[50] They found that they could significantly affect the importance people attached to a given problem by splicing a few stories about it into the news over the course of a week. Iyengar and Kinder do not maintain that the networks can make something out of nothing or conceal problems that actually exist. But they do conclude that "what television news does, instead, is alter the priorities Americans attach to a circumscribed set of problems, all of which are plausible contenders for public concern."[51] Subsequent research by Miller and Krosnick has revealed that agenda-setting effects are particularly strong among politically knowledgeable citizens who trust the media. Thus, rather than the media manipulating the public, they argue that agenda-setting reflects a deliberate and thoughtful process on the part of sophisticated citizens who rely on what they consider to be a credible institutional source of information.[52]

This effect has far-reaching consequences. By increasing public attention to specific problems, the media influence the criteria by which the public evaluates political leaders. When unemployment goes up but inflation goes down, does public support for the president increase or decrease? The answer could depend in large part on which story the media emphasized. The fact that the media emphasized the country's slow economic growth in 1992, rather than the good news of low inflation and interest rates, was clearly detrimental to George Bush's failed reelection attempt the same year. Similarly, the emphasis on candidate character in 2000 as opposed to the excellent economic performance under the Clinton-Gore administration clearly helped the candidacy of George W. Bush.

The media can even have a dramatic effect on how the public evaluates specific events by emphasizing one particular news aspect over all others. When the press gave substantial coverage to President Ford's misstatement about Soviet domination of Eastern Europe, this coverage had an impact on the public. Polls showed that most people did not realize the president had made an error until the press told them so. Afterward, pro-Ford evaluations of the debate declined noticeably as voters' concerns for competence in foreign policymaking became salient.[53] Similarly, the media's focus on Al Gore's misstatements during the first presidential debate of 2000 had an impact on public opinion. In the days immediately following this debate the percentage who thought that Gore had beaten Bush declined markedly.[54]

Much remains unknown about the effects of the media and the news on American political behavior. Enough is known, however, to conclude that media is a key political institution. The media control much of the technology that in turn controls much of what Americans believe about politics and government. For this reason, it is important to look at the American policy agenda and the media's role in shaping it.

The Media's Agenda-Setting Function

Someone who asks you "What's your agenda?" wants to know something about your priorities. As discussed in Chapter 1, governments also have agendas. John Kingdon defines **policy agenda** as "the list of subjects or problems to which government officials, and people outside of government closely associated with those officials, are paying some serious attention at any given time."[55] Interest groups, political parties, individual politicians, public relations firms, bureaucratic agencies—and, of course, the president and Congress—are all pushing for their priorities to take precedence over others. Health care, education, unemployment, welfare reform—these and scores of other issues compete for attention from the government.

Political activists depend heavily on the media to get their ideas placed high on the governmental agenda. Political activists are often called **policy entrepreneurs**—people who invest their political "capital" in an issue (as an economic entrepreneur invests capital in an idea for making money). Kingdon says that policy entrepreneurs can "be in or out of government, in elected or appointed positions, in interest groups or research organizations."[56] Policy entrepreneurs' arsenal of weapons includes press releases, press conferences, and letter writing; convincing reporters and columnists to tell their side; trading on personal contacts; and, in cases of desperation, resorting to staging dramatic events.

The media are not always monopolized by political elites; the poor and downtrodden have access to them too. Civil rights groups in the 1960s relied heavily on the media to tell their stories of unjust treatment. Many believe that the introduction of television helped to accelerate the movement by showing Americans—in the North and South alike—just what the situation was.[57] Protest groups have learned that if they can stage an interesting event that attracts the media's attention, at least their point of view will be heard. Radical activist Saul Alinsky once dramatized the plight of one

policy agenda

The issues that attract the serious attention of public officials and other people actively involved in politics at the time.

policy entrepreneurs

People who invest their political "capital" in an issue. According to John Kingdon, a policy entrepreneur "could be in or out of government, in elected or appointed positions, in interest groups or research organizations."

neighborhood by having its residents collect rats and dump them on the mayor's front lawn. The story was one that local reporters could hardly resist. In 2002, graduate students at the University of California, Irvine camped out in tents in the campus park to protest the lack of investment in on-campus housing. The prime organizer, a teaching assistant for an introduction to American government course, issued press releases and made calls to news directors urging them to come down and take a look. Soon after several stations put the sorry scene on TV, the university administration gave in to the graduate students' demands.

Conveying a long-term, positive image via the media is more important than a few dramatic events. Policy entrepreneurs—individuals or groups, in or out of government—depend on good will and good images. Sometimes it helps to hire a public relations firm that specializes in getting a specific message across. Groups, individuals, and even countries have hired public relations firms to improve their image and their ability to peddle their issue positions.[58]

Understanding the Mass Media

The media act as key linkage institutions between the people and the policymakers, and have a profound impact on the political policy agenda. Bernard Cohen goes so far as to say "No major act of the American Congress, no foreign adventure, no act of diplomacy, no great social reform can succeed unless the press prepares the public mind."[59] If Cohen is right, then the growth of government in America would have been impossible without the need for it being established through the media.

The Media and the Scope of Government

The media's watchdog function helps to restrict politicians. Many observers say the press is biased against whoever holds office at the moment and that reporters want to expose officeholders. They argue that reporters hold disparaging views of most public officials and believe that they are self-serving, hypocritical, lacking in integrity, and preoccupied with reelection. Thus, it is not surprising that journalists see a need to debunk public officials and their policy proposals.

As every new proposal is met with much skepticism, regular constraints are placed on the scope of what government can do. The watchdog orientation of the press can be characterized as neither liberal nor conservative, but reformist. Reporters often see their job as crusading against foul play and unfairness in government and society. This focus on injustice in society inevitably encourages enlarging the scope of government. Once the media identify a problem in society—such as poverty, inadequate medical care for the elderly, or poor education for certain children—reporters usually begin to ask what the government is doing about it. Could it be acting more effectively to solve the problem? What do people in the White House and Congress, as well as state and local government, have to say about it? In this way, the media portray government as responsible for handling almost every major problem. Though skeptical of what politicians say and do, the media report on America's social problems in a manner that often also encourages government to take on more and more tasks.

Individualism and the Media

More than any other development in the last century, the rise of television broadcasting has reinforced and furthered individualism in the American political process. Candidates are now much more capable of running for office on their own by appealing to people directly through television. Individual voters can see the candidates "up close and personal" for themselves, and they have much less need for political parties or social groups to help them make their decisions.

When the TV networks projected Al Gore to be the winner in Florida early on Election Night 2000, most observers thought he was well on his way to being declared the president-elect. When it became clear that these projections were based on faulty data and that the race was too close to call, as shown in these newspaper headlines, the national media were incredibly embarrassed. Some members of Congress have suggested regulations to prevent the media from making such erroneous projections in the future, but First Amendment considerations probably make this impossible.

Television finds it easier to focus on individuals than on groups. As a result, parties have declined, and candidate personality is more important than ever. Congress is difficult to cover on television because there are 535 members, but there is only one president; thus, as Al Gore predicted in his senior thesis (see chapter opening) the presidency has increasingly received more exposure than the Congress. Doris Graber's study of nightly news broadcasts found that 60 percent of the coverage devoted to the three branches of government was devoted to the president as compared to 37 percent for the Congress. The Supreme Court, which does not allow TV cameras to cover its proceedings and whose members rarely give interviews, is almost invisible on TV newscasts, receiving only a mere 3 percent of the coverage.

Democracy and the Media

As Ronald Berkman and Laura Kitch remark, "Information is the fuel of democracy."[60] Widespread access to information could be the greatest boon to democracy since the secret ballot, yet most observers think it has fallen far short of this potential. Noting the vast increase in information available through the news media, Berkman and Kitch state that "If the sheer quantity of news produced greater competency in the citizenry, then we would have a society of political masters. Yet, just the opposite is happening."[61] The rise of the "information society" has not brought about the rise of the "informed society."

Whenever the media are criticized for being superficial, their defense is to say that this is what people want. Network executives remark that if people suddenly started to watch in-depth shows such as PBS's "NewsHour," then they would gladly imitate them. If the American people wanted serious coverage of the issues, networks would be happy to give it to them. Network executives claim they are in business to make a profit and that to do so, they must appeal to the maximum number of people. As Matthew Kerbel observes, "The people who bring you the evening news would like it to be informative *and* entertaining, but when these two values collide, the shared orientations of the television news world push the product inexorably toward the latter."[62] It is not their fault if the resulting news coverage is superficial, network executives argue; blame capitalism, or blame the people—most of whom like news to be more entertaining than educational. Thus, if people are not better informed in the high-tech

Comparing News Media

age, it is largely because they do not care to hear about complicated political issues. In this sense, one can say that the people really do rule through the media.

Summary

Plenty of evidence points to the power of the media in American politics. The media are ubiquitous. There is evidence that the news and its presentation are an important—perhaps the most important—shaper of public opinion on political issues. The media are an important ingredient in shaping the policy agenda, and political entrepreneurs carefully use the media for this purpose.

Gradually, the broadcast media have replaced the print media as the principal source of news. Recently, the development of cable TV channels and websites has led to narrowcasting—appealing to specific segments of the mass public rather than to the entire population. The media largely define "news" as people and events out of the ordinary. Because of economic pressures, the media are biased in favor of stories with high drama that will attract people's interest, instead of extended analyses of complex issues. With the media's superficial treatment of important policy issues, it should be no surprise that the incredible amount of information available to Americans today has not visibly increased their political awareness or participation.

KEY TERMS

high-tech politics	print media	trial balloons
mass media	broadcast media	sound bites
media event	narrowcasting	talking head
press conferences	chains	policy agenda
investigative journalism	beats	policy entrepreneurs

INTERNET RESOURCES

www.people-press.org
The Pew Center for the People and the Press regularly surveys people regarding their attitudes toward the media's coverage of politics, and measures which news events people follow most closely.

www.appcpenn.org
The Annenberg Public Policy Center conducts studies that analyze the content of TV coverage of politics, which they post at this site.

www.usnpl.com
Listings for newspapers all over the country, including web links where available.

www.cmpa.com
The Center for Media and Public Affairs posts their studies of the content of media coverage of politics at this site.

www.ammi.org/livingroomcandidate/
A great collection of classic and recent political commercials from 1952 through 2004.

GET CONNECTED

Campaign Advertising

Today's political campaigns rely heavily on campaign advertising to reach voters. Television stations also appear to rely on political campaigns to produce revenue for the station. The Alliance for Better Campaigns found that local television stations increased the prices of candidate ads in the two months before the 2002 elections. How much did candidates in your state spend on political advertising?

Search the Web

Go to the "In Your State" page at the Alliance for Better Campaigns' website at *http://freeairtime.org/docs/index.php?DocID=21*. Look at how much the TV stations you watch earned from political advertising. Compare that amount with the amounts in neighboring states.

Questions to Ask

- How much money did your local television stations earn from campaign advertising?
- How does this compare to the amount of money stations in neighboring states earned? What might explain the differences you find?
- The Alliance for Better Campaigns advocates providing free air time for candidates. You can read about this proposal on the organization's web page. Does it sound like a good idea to provide free air time to candidates?

Why It Matters

In order for voters to make informed decisions in a world with increasingly complicated issues, more detailed information is necessary. Often sound bites don't provide enough information or the right kind of information. The costs of television advertising sometimes cause candidates to end their campaigns and some candidates can't afford to advertise on television. If television is the primary way that most voters get political information, it is possible that some candidates' messages may not be heard.

Get Involved

Do you agree or disagree with the Alliance for Better Campaigns' goals? Send them an e-mail to let them know. The Alliance lists their state partner organizations on their web page. Contact these state organizations to find out what they are doing in your state.

To see more Get Connected exercises for Chapter 7, go to www.ablongman.com/edwards.

FOR FURTHER READING

Dautrich, Kenneth, and Thomas H. Hartley. *How the News Media Fail American Voters: Causes, Consequences and Remedies.* New York: Columbia University Press, 1999. A highly critical look at how the news media covered the 1996 presidential election.

Downie, Leonard, Jr., and Robert G. Kaiser. *The News About the News: American Journalism in Peril.* New York: Alfred A. Knopf, 2002. A good look at how the changing economics of the news profession is altering media values and practices.

Epstein, Edward J. *News from Nowhere: Television and the News.* New York: Randopm House, 1973. Although dated, this account still provides an excellent view of network news.

Frantzich, Stephen, and John Sullivan. *The C-SPAN Revolution.* Norman: University of Oklahoma Press, 1996. An account of the network for political junkies.

Goldberg, Bernard. *Bias: A CBS Insider Exposes How the Media Distort the News.* Washington, D.C.: Regnery, 2002. A bestselling account of the network news that argues there is a liberal bias on many issues, especially social policies.

Graber, Doris A. *Mass Media and American Politics*, 6th ed. Washington, D.C.: Congressional Quarterly Press, 2002. The standard textbook on the subject.

Hertsgaard, Mark. *On Bended Knee: The Press and the Reagan Presidency.* New York: Farrar, Straus & Giroux, 1988. An in-depth look at how the press treated Reagan, and vice versa.

Iyengar, Shanto, and Donald R. Kinder. *News that Matters.* Chicago: University of Chicago Press, 1987. Two political psychologists show how the media can affect the public agenda.

Jamieson, Kathleen Hall. *Eloquence in an Electronic Age.* New York: Oxford University Press, 1988. A noted communications scholar takes a look at how television has altered political discourse.

Kalb, Marvin. *One Scandalous Story: Clinton, Lewinsky, and Thirteen Days that Tarnished American Journalism.* New York: The Free Press, 2001. An indictment of how journalistic standards have been compromised in recent years, as illustrated by the media's coverage of the Lewinsky scandal.

Kingdon, John W. *Agendas, Alternatives, and Public Policy*, 2nd ed. New York: HarperCollins, 1995. The best overall study of the formation of policy agendas.

Patterson, Thomas E. *Out of Order.* New York: Knopf, 1993. A highly critical and well-documented examination of how the media covers election campaigns.

West, Darrell M. *Air Wars: Television Advertising in Election Campaigns, 1952–2000.* Washington, D.C.: Congressional Quarterly Press, 2001. An analysis of how TV campaign ads have evolved over the last four decades and what impact they have had on elections.

Political Parties

Chapter Outline

The Meaning of Party

The Party in the Electorate

The New York Times **Issues of the Times**

The Party Organizations: From the Grass Roots to Washington

The Party in Government: Promises and Policy

Party Eras in American History

Third Parties: Their Impact on American Politics

Understanding Political Parties

Summary

In the 2002 midterm elections the Democrats were expecting to gain seats in the House of Representatives, as the party opposing the incumbent president generally does in midterm elections. When they ended up losing seats instead, many analysts blamed the Democrats' poor performance in 2002 on their seeming failure to offer clear alternatives to the president's policies.

The story of the 2002 midterms differed greatly from that of 1994, when the Republicans took control of the House of Representatives after 40 years of Democratic control. In that year, 367 House Republican candidates stood on the steps of the U.S. Capitol in late September of 1994 to sign a document they entitled "Contract With America." This document outlined reforms the Republicans promised to pass on the first day of the new Congress, as well as ten bills they agreed would be brought to the floor for a vote within the first 100 days of the new Republican-controlled House of Representatives. The contract was the brainchild of Newt Gingrich and Richard Armey, both of whom were college professors before they were elected to Congress. Gingrich and Armey thought the Republicans needed a stronger message in 1994 than simply saying they opposed President Clinton's policies. The contract was an attempt to offer voters a positive program for reshaping American public policy and reforming how Congress works. Without actually knowing much about the individual candidates themselves, voters would know what to expect of the signers of the contract and would be able to hold them accountable for these promises in the future. In this sense, the contract endeavored to make politics user-friendly for the voters.

America's Founding Fathers were more concerned with their fear that political parties could be forums for corruption and national divisiveness than they were with the role that parties could play in making politics user friendly for ordinary voters. Thomas Jefferson spoke for many when he said, "If I could not go to heaven but with a party, I would not go there at all." In his farewell address, George Washington also warned of the dangers of parties.

Today, most observers would agree that political parties have contributed greatly to American democracy. In one of the most frequently—and rightly—quoted observations about American politics, E. E. Schattschneider said that "political parties created democracy . . . and democracy is unthinkable save in terms of the parties."[1] Political scientists and politicians alike believe that a strong party system is desirable.

The strength of the parties has an impact not only on how we are governed but also on what government does. The major historical developments in the expansion or contraction of the scope of government have generally been accomplished through the implementation of one party's platform. Currently, the Democrats and Republicans differ greatly on the issue of the scope of government. Which party controls the presidency and whether or not the same party also controls the Congress makes a big difference.

party competition

The battle of the parties for control of public offices. Ups and downs of the two major parties are one of the most important elements in American politics.

political party

According to Anthony Downs, a "team of men [and women] seeking to control the governing apparatus by gaining office in a duly constituted election."

The alternating of power and influence between the two major parties is one of the most important elements in American politics. **Party competition** is the battle between Democrats and Republicans for the control of public offices. Without this competition there would be no choice, and without choice there would be no democracy. Americans have had a choice between two major political parties since the early 1800s, and this two-party system remains intact more than two centuries later.

The Meaning of Party

Almost all definitions of political parties have one thing in common: Parties try to win elections. This is their core function and the key to their definition. By contrast, interest groups do not nominate candidates for office, though they may try to influence elections. For example, no one has ever been elected to Congress as the nominee of the National Rifle Association, though many nominees have received the NRA's endorsement. Thus, Anthony Downs defined a **political party** as a "team of men [and women] seeking to control the governing apparatus by gaining office in a duly constituted election."[2]

The word *team* is the slippery part of this definition. Party teams may not be so well disciplined and single-minded as teams fielded by top football coaches. Party teams often run every which way and are difficult to lead. Party leaders often disagree about policy, and between elections the party organizations seem to all but disappear. So who are the members of these teams? A widely adopted way of thinking about parties in political science is as "three-headed political giants." The three heads are (1) the party in the electorate, (2) the party as an organization, and (3) the party in government.[3]

The *party in the electorate* is by far the largest component of an American political party. Unlike many European political parties, American parties do not require dues or membership cards to distinguish members from nonmembers. Americans may register as Democrats, Republicans, Libertarians, or whatever, but registration is not legally binding and is easily changed. To be a member of a party, you need only claim to be a member. If you call yourself a Democrat, you are one—even if you never talk to a party official, never work in a campaign, and often vote for Republicans.

The *party as an organization* has a national office, a full-time staff, rules and bylaws, and budgets. In addition to a national office, each party maintains state and local headquarters. The party organization includes precinct leaders, county chairpersons, state chairpersons, state delegates to the national committee, and officials in the party's Washington office. These are the people who keep the party running between elections and make its rules. From the party's national chairperson to its local precinct captain, the party organization pursues electoral victory.

The *party in government* consists of elected officials who call themselves members of the party. Although presidents, members of Congress, governors, and lesser officeholders may share a common party label, they do not always agree on policy. Presidents and governors may have to wheedle and cajole their own party members into voting for their policies. In the United States, it is not uncommon to put personal principle—or ambition—above loyalty to the party's leaders. These leaders are the main spokespersons for the party, however. Their words and actions personify the party to millions of Americans. If the party is to translate its promises into policy, the job must be done by the party in government.

Political parties are everywhere in American politics—present in the electorate's mind, as an organization, and in government offices—and one of their major tasks is to link the people of the United States to their government and its policies.

Tasks of the Parties

The road from public opinion to public policy is long and winding. All 295 million Americans cannot raise their voices to the government and indicate their policy preferences in unison. In a large democracy, **linkage institutions** translate inputs from the public into outputs from the policymakers. Linkage institutions sift through all the issues, identify the most pressing concerns, and put these onto the governmental agenda. In other words, linkage institutions help ensure that public preferences are heard loud and clear. In the United States, there are four main linkage institutions: parties, elections, interest groups, and the media.

Kay Lawson writes that "parties are seen, both by the members and by others, as agencies for forging links between citizens and policymakers."[4] Here is a checklist of the tasks parties perform, or should perform, if they are to serve as effective linkage institutions:

Parties Pick Candidates.   Almost no one above the local level (and often not even there) gets elected to a public office without winning a party's endorsement.[5] A party's endorsement is called a *nomination.* Up until the early twentieth century, American parties chose their candidates with little or no input from the voters. Progressive reformers led the charge for primary elections, in which citizens would have the power to choose nominees for office. The innovation of primary elections spread rapidly, transferring the nominating function from the party organization to the party identifiers.

Parties Run Campaigns.   Through their national, state, and local organizations, parties coordinate political campaigns. However, television has made it easier for candidates to campaign on their own, without the help of the party organization. For example, Ross Perot received 18.9 percent of the presidential vote in 1992 and 8.5 percent in 1996 with hardly any organizational support at all.

Parties Give Cues to Voters.   Most voters have a **party image** of each party; that is, they know (or think they know) what the Republicans and Democrats stand for. Liberal, conservative, probusiness, prolabor—these are some of the elements of each party's image. Even in the present era of weakened parties, many voters still rely on a party to give them cues for voting.

Parties Articulate Policies.   Within the electorate and within the government, each political party advocates specific policy alternatives. For example, the Democratic Party has clearly supported abortion rights, and the Republican Party has repeatedly called for restrictions on abortion.

Parties Coordinate Policymaking.   In America's fragmented government, parties are essential for coordination among the branches of government. Virtually all major public officials are also members of a party. When they need support to get something done, the first place they look is to their fellow partisans.

The importance of these tasks makes it easy to see why most political scientists accept Schattschneider's famous assertion that modern democracy is unthinkable without competition between political parties.

Parties, Voters, and Policy: The Downs Model

The parties compete, at least in theory, as in a marketplace. A party is in the market for voters; its products are its candidates and policies. Anthony Downs has provided a working model of the relationship among citizens, parties, and policy, employing a

linkage institutions

The channels through which people's concerns become political issues on the government's policy agenda. In the United States, linkage institutions include elections, political parties, interest groups, and the media.

party image

The voter's perception of what the Republicans or Democrats stand for, such as **conservatism** or **liberalism**.

Why It Matters

Political Parties
Parties perform many important tasks in American politics. Among the most important are: generating symbols of identification and loyalty, mobilizing majorities in the electorate and in government, recruiting political leaders, implementing policies, and fostering stability in government. Hence, it has often been argued that the party system has to work well for the government to work well.

rational-choice theory

A popular theory in political science to explain the actions of voters as well as politicians. It assumes that individuals act in their own best interest, carefully weighing the costs and benefits of possible alternatives.

rational-choice perspective.[6] **Rational-choice theory** "seeks to explain political processes and outcomes as consequences of purposive behavior. Political actors are assumed to have goals and to pursue those goals sensibly and efficiently."[7] Downs argues that (1) voters want to maximize the chance that policies they favor will be adopted by government, and (2) parties want to win office. Thus, in order to win office, the wise party selects policies that are widely favored. Parties and candidates may do all sorts of things to win—kiss babies, call opponents ugly names, even lie and cheat—but in a democracy they will primarily use their accomplishments and policy positions to attract votes. If Party A figures out what the voters want more accurately than does Party B, then Party A should be more successful.

The long history of the American party system has shown that successful parties rarely stray far from the midpoint of public opinion. In the American electorate, a few voters are extremely liberal and a few are extremely conservative, but the majority are in the middle (see Figure 8.1). If Downs is right, then centrist parties will win, and extremist parties will be condemned to footnotes in the history books. Indeed, occasionally a party may misperceive voters' desires or take a risky stand on a principle—hoping to persuade voters during the campaign—but in order to survive in a system where the majority opinion is middle-of-the-road, parties must stay fairly near the center.

We frequently hear criticism that there is not much difference between the Democrats and the Republicans. Given the nature of the American political market, however, these two parties have little choice. We would not expect two competing department stores to locate at opposite ends of town when most people live on Main Street. Downs also notes, though, that from a rational-choice perspective, one should expect the parties to differentiate themselves at least somewhat. Just as Chrysler tries to offer something different from and better than General Motors in order to build buyer loyalty, so Democrats and Republicans have to forge different identities to build voter

Figure 8.1   The Downs Model: How Rational Parties Match Voters' Policy Preferences

In 2000, the National Election Study asked a sample of the American electorate to classify themselves on a 7-point scale from extremely liberal to extremely conservative. The graph shows how the people located themselves in terms of ideology and how they perceived the ideology of the parties.

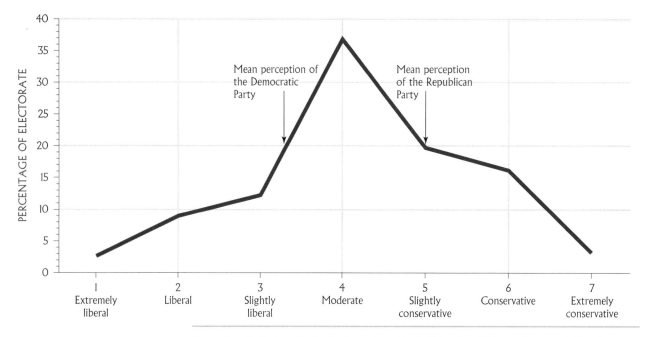

Source: From the National Election Studies conducted by the University of Michigan, Center for Political Studies, 2000.

loyalty. In recent years, the American National Election Study has found that two-thirds of the population believes that important differences exist between the parties. When asked what those differences are, respondents most frequently comment that the Republicans favor lower taxes and less domestic spending, whereas Democrats favor more government programs to help the working class and less-advantaged Americans.

Deciding on a Political Party

The Party in the Electorate

In most European nations, being a party member means formally joining a political party. You get a membership card to carry around, you pay dues, and you vote to pick your local party leaders. In America, being a party member takes far less work. There is no formal "membership" in the parties at all. If you believe you are a Democrat or a Republican, then you are a Democrat or a Republican. Thus the party in the electorate consists largely of symbolic images and ideas. For most people the party is a psychological label. They may never go to a party meeting, but they have images of the parties' stances on issues and of which groups the parties generally favor or oppose.

Party images help shape people's **party identification,** the self-proclaimed preference for one party or the other. Because many people routinely vote for the party they identify with (all else being equal), even a shift of a few percentage points in the distribution of party identification is important. Since 1952, the National Election Study surveys have asked a sample of citizens, "Generally speaking, do you usually think of yourself as a Republican, a Democrat, or an Independent?" Repeatedly asking this question permits political scientists to trace party identification over the past five decades (see Table 8.1). The clearest trend has been *the increasing percentage who decline to identify with either major party.* In 2000, 41 percent of the population called themselves Independents. As you can see in "Young People and Politics: The Parties Face an Independent Youth," survey data demonstrate that the younger one is the more likely he or she is to be a political independent.

Not only are there more Independents now, but those who still identify with a party are no longer so loyal in the voting booth. In recent years, **ticket-splitting**— voting with one party for one office and the other for other offices—has reached record proportions.[8] An examination of a random sample of over 8,000 actual 1994 ballots

party identification

A citizen's self-proclaimed preference for one party or the other.

ticket-splitting

Voting with one party for one office and with another party for other offices. It has become the norm in American voting behavior.

Table 8.1   Party Identification in the United States, 1952–2004[a]

YEAR	DEMOCRATS	INDEPENDENTS	REPUBLICANS
1952	48.6	23.3	28.1
1956	45.3	24.4	30.3
1960	46.4	23.4	30.2
1964	52.2	23.0	24.8
1968	46.0	29.5	24.5
1972	41.0	35.2	23.8
1976	40.2	36.8	23.0
1980	41.7	35.3	23.0
1984	37.7	34.8	27.6
1988	35.7	36.3	28.0
1992	35.8	38.7	25.5
1996	39.3	32.9	27.8
2000	34.8	41.0	24.2
2004	34.6	33.6	31.8

[a]In percentage of people; the small percentage who identify with a minor party or who cannot answer the question are excluded.
Source: American National Election Studies, 1952–2000; National Annenberg Election Study, 2004.

The major parties have different demographic bases of support. Of all social groups, African Americans tend to be the most solidly aligned with one party. Ever since the Civil Rights Act of 1964, they have voted overwhelmingly for Democratic candidates. In 2004, African-American voters cast 88 percent of their votes for John Kerry.

Young People and Politics

The Parties Face an Independent Youth

Younger people have always had a tendency to be more independent of the major political parties than older people. But this has rarely been so evident in survey data as it is now. As you can see from the 2002 survey data displayed here, 55 percent of people between the ages of 18 and 24 said they were political independents. In contrast, only about half as many of people over 65 called themselves independents. As one looks down the age groups in the table, it is clear that what varies by age is not the ratio of Democrats to Republicans, but rather the likelihood of someone being an independent. Data over time indicate that as people get older they become more likely to identify with one of the major parties. But whether this will be true for the current generation of youth remains to be seen.

Questions for Discussion
- Do you think that as the current generation of young people ages they will become more likely to identify with the major political parties?
- Because younger people are so likely to be independent, does this mean many young voters are particularly open to persuasion during campaigns? If so, why don't the Democrats and Republicans pay special attention to getting them on their side?
- In some states, such as New York and Florida, only voters who are registered with a party can participate in that party's primary. Given that younger people are less likely to identify with a party, does this mean that their influence in primary elections is diminished in such states?

AGE	DEMOCRAT	INDEPENDENT	REPUBLICAN
18–24	25	55	19
25–34	33	42	24
35–44	32	39	29
45–54	32	38	30
55–64	33	33	35
65+	41	28	31

Source: Authors' analysis of the 2002 General Social Survey.

from Los Angeles County compiled by Anthony Salvanto reveals that only 30 percent cast a complete and straight vote for all 11 partisan offices contested that year.[9] The result of voters failing to make an across-the-board choice between the parties has often been divided party government, at both the federal and state levels.

The Party Organizations: From the Grass Roots to Washington

An organizational chart is usually shaped like a pyramid, with those who give orders at the top and those who carry them out at the bottom. In drawing an organizational chart of an American political party, you could put the national committee and national convention of the party at the apex of the pyramid, the state party organizations in the middle, and the thousands of local party organizations at the bottom. Such a chart, however, would provide a misleading depiction of an American political party. The president of General Motors is at the top of GM in fact as well as on paper. By contrast, the chairperson of the Democratic or Republican national committee is on top on paper, but not in fact.

As organizations, American political parties are decentralized and fragmented. One can imagine a system in which the national office of a party resolves conflicts among its state and local branches, states the party's position on the issues, and then passes orders down through the hierarchy. One can even imagine a system in which the party leaders have the power to enforce their decisions by offering greater influence and resources to officeholders who follow the party line and by punishing those who do not. Many European parties work just that way, but in America the formal party organizations have little such power. Candidates in the United States can get elected on their own. They do not need the help of the party most of the time, and hence the party organization is relegated to a comparatively limited role.

Local Parties

The urban political party was once the main political party organization in America. From the late nineteenth century through the New Deal of the 1930s, scores of cities were dominated by **party machines.** A machine is a kind of party organization, very different from the typical fragmented and disorganized political party in America today. It can be defined as a party organization that depends on rewarding its members in some material fashion.

Patronage is one of the key inducements used by party machines. A patronage job is one that is awarded for political reasons rather than for merit or competence alone. In the late nineteenth century, political parties routinely sold some patronage jobs to the highest bidder. Party leaders made no secret of their corruption, openly selling government positions to raise money for the party. Some of this money was used to buy votes, but a good deal went to line the pockets of the politicians themselves. The most notable case was that of Boss Tweed of New York, whose ring reportedly made between $40 million and $200 million from tax receipts, payoffs, and kickbacks.

At one time, urban machines in Albany, Chicago, Philadelphia, Kansas City, and elsewhere depended heavily on ethnic group support. Some of the most fabled machine leaders were Irish politicians, including New York's George Washington Plunkett, Boston's James Michael Curley, and Chicago's Richard J. Daley. Daley's Chicago machine was the last survivor, steamrolling its opposition amid charges of racism and corruption. Even today there are remnants of the Chicago machine, particularly in White and ethnic neighborhoods. The survival of machine politics in Chicago can be traced to its ability to limit the scope of reform legislation. A large proportion of city jobs were classified as "temporary" even though they had been held by the same person for decades, and these positions were exempted from the merit system of hiring. At its

party machines

A type of political party organization that relies heavily on material inducements, such as patronage, to win votes and to govern.

patronage

One of the key inducements used by party machines. A patronage job, promotion, or contract is one that is given for political reasons rather than for merit or competence alone.

height, the Daley machine in Chicago dispensed 40,000 patronage jobs, the recipients of which were expected to deliver at least 10 votes each on Election Day and to kick back 5 percent of their salary in the form of a donation to the local Democratic Party.[10]

Urban party organizations are also no longer very active as a rule. Progressive reforms that placed jobs under the merit system rather than at the machine's discretion weakened the machines' power. Regulations concerning fair bidding on government contracts also took away much of their ability to reward the party faithful. As ethnic integration occurred in big cities, the group loyalties that the machines often relied on no longer seemed very relevant to many people.

Partly filling in the void created by the decline of the inner-city machines has been a revitalization of party organization at the county level—particularly in affluent suburbs. These county organizations distribute yard signs and campaign literature, get out the vote on Election Day, and help state and local candidates any way they can. Traditionally, local organizations relied on personal knowledge of individuals in the neighborhood who could be persuaded to support the party. Today, these organizations have access to computerized lists with all sorts of details about registered voters that they use to try to tailor their appeals to each individual. You can read more about this issue in "Issues of the Times: Should the Political Parties Be Gathering Data About You?" on pages 248–249.

The 50 State Party Systems

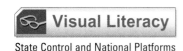

Visual Literacy

State Control and National Platforms

closed primaries

Elections to select party nominees in which only people who have registered in advance with the party can vote for that party's candidates, thus encouraging greater party loyalty.

open primaries

Elections to select party nominees in which voters can decide on Election Day whether they want to participate in the Democratic or Republican contests.

blanket primaries

Elections to select party nominees in which voters are presented with a list of candidates from all the parties. Voters can then select some Democrats and some Republicans if they like.

American national parties are a loose aggregation of state parties, which are themselves a fluid association of individuals, groups, and local organizations. There are 50 state party systems, and no two are exactly alike. In a few states, the parties are well organized, have sizable staffs, and spend a lot of money. Pennsylvania is one such state. In other states, however, parties are weak. California, says Kay Lawson, "has political parties so weak as to be almost nonexistent; it is the birthplace of campaigning by 'hired guns'; and it has been run by special interests for so long that Californians have forgotten what is special about that."[11]

The states are allowed wide discretion in the regulation of party activities, and how they choose to organize elections influences the strength of the parties profoundly. Some states give parties greater power than others to limit who can participate in their nomination contests. In **closed primaries** only people who have registered in advance with the party can vote in its primary, thus encouraging greater party loyalty. In contrast, **open primaries** allow voters to decide on Election Day whether they want to participate in the Democratic or Republican contests. And most antiparty of all are **blanket primaries,** which present voters with a list of candidates from all the parties and allow them to pick some Democrats and some Republicans if they like. (See "You Are the Policymaker: Was the Blanket Primary a Good Idea?")

When it comes to the general election, some states promote voting according to party by listing the candidates of each party down a single column, whereas others place the names in random order. About a third of the states currently have a provision on their ballots that enables a voter to cast a vote for all of one party's candidates with a single act. This option clearly encourages straight-ticket voting and makes the support of the party organization more important to candidates in these states.

Organizationally, state parties are on the upswing throughout the country. As recently as the early 1960s, half the state party organizations did not even maintain a permanent headquarters; when the state party elected a new chairperson, the party organization simply shifted its office to his or her hometown.[12] In contrast, almost all state parties today have a permanent physical headquarters, typically in the capital city or the largest city. State party budgets have also increased greatly, as parties have acquired professional staffs and high-tech equipment. As of 1999, the typical state party budget for an election year was more than eight times greater than it was 20 years earlier.[13]

You Are the Policymaker

Was the Blanket Primary a Good Idea?

In the 1996 California primary, voters were presented with an initiative to change the state's closed primary process to a blanket primary. Proponents of this initiative argued that a closed primary system favors the election of party hard-liners, contributes to legislative gridlock, and stacks the deck against moderate problem solvers. By opening up the primary process to allow voters to vote for any set of candidates they like regardless of partisanship, advocates of the blanket primary argued that politicians would be encouraged to focus on the median voter rather than a narrow group of partisans. They also noted that participation in primary elections would increase by allowing Independents a chance to take part, and by giving minority party voters in noncompetitive districts a real say in selecting their representatives.

Both the Democratic and Republican state parties of California came out strongly against this initiative. They argued that the blanket primary would be an invitation to political mischief, with political consultants and special interests manipulating the system to help the candidate they'd most like to face in November get the other party's nomination. A frequently used analogy

during the campaign was that allowing members of one party a large voice in choosing another party's nominee was like letting UCLA's football team choose USC's head coach. Rather than seeing this reform as giving voters more choice, opponents argued that it would diminish choice in the long run by muddling the differences between major parties.

In the end, the voters approved the blanket primary by a margin of 60 to 40. The exit polls showed that the initiative was supported by Democrats and Republicans alike. However, the party organizations immediately took the case to federal court, arguing that the blanket primary infringed on their constitutional rights of freedom of association by giving nonmembers a say in their activities. U.S. District Judge David Levy listened to a variety of testimony from political consultants, party leaders, and political scientists (including one of the coauthors of this book). In *Democratic Party et al. v. Jones* he ruled that although the blanket primary weakened the parties it was what the voters wanted and shouldn't be overruled by the courts. Subsequently, the Ninth Circuit Court of Appeals upheld the ruling. But the Supreme Court had

the final word in June of 2000, ruling that the blanket primary violated the parties' right to freedom of association. Writing for the majority, Justice Antonin Scalia stated that the blanket primary forces the parties "to adulterate their candidate-selection process—the basic function of a political party—by opening it up to persons wholly unaffiliated with the party."

Upon hearing of the Supreme Court decision, California's Democratic governor and Republican secretary of state both pledged to try to retain a blanket primary system by making primary elections nonpartisan, as currently practiced in Louisiana. In his opinion, Justice Scalia indicated that such a system is constitutional because party nominees are not chosen through such a process; indeed, sometimes this system leads to a general election between two members of the same party. It would be ironic if the parties' court victory led them to be excluded from the primary process in some states altogether.

You be the policymaker: Should the Supreme Court have outlawed California's blanket primary? Is the nonpartisan blanket primary an idea that should now be tried in a number of states?

In terms of headquarters and budgets, state parties are better organized than they used to be. Nevertheless, as John Bibby points out, they mostly serve to supplement the candidates' own personal campaign organizations; thus, state party organizations rarely manage campaigns. The job of the state party, writes Bibby, is merely "to provide technical services" within the context of a candidate-centered campaign.[14]

The National Party Organizations

The supreme power within each of the parties is its **national convention.** The convention meets every four years, and its main task is to write the party's platform and then nominate its candidates for president and vice president. (Chapter 9 will discuss conventions in detail.) Keeping the party operating between conventions is the job of the **national committee,** composed of representatives from the states and territories.

national convention

The meeting of party delegates every four years to choose a presidential ticket and write the party's platform.

national committee

One of the institutions that keeps the party operating between conventions. The national committee is composed of representatives from the states and territories.

Issues of the Times

The Issue: Should the Political Parties Be Gathering Data About You?

Until the advent of television, the heart of political party activity revolved around an army of activists going door-to-door to try to persuade and mobilize their friends and neighbors to support the party's candidates. A good party organization would consist of activists who really knew the people they were contacting and how to best approach them. Then, television allowed candidates to speak directly to the people, so personal contacts were no longer necessary. Today, as this article discusses, detailed computer databases have made it possible to communicate *individualized* messages to people once again. Whether or not this is a positive development for American party politics remains to be seen, as this article makes clear.

Read All About It

The Very, Very Personal Is the Political

By Jon Gertner
February 15, 2004

Suppose, for the sake of argument, that you are called into the boss's office and asked to help sell the citizens of the United States on one of two presidential candidates in the 2004 campaign. Hard work, but what makes it especially tough is that you've been directed to try something experimental, something

that's never been done before in a national election. Instead of creating a traditional political narrative for your candidate—one that highlights charisma or character, for instance, or one that hews to a message on taxes or Social Security—you've been told to focus on nothing but the people who might be persuaded to vote. Think about what they like, what they do, what they consume. Think about them one by one. Name

by name, address by address, phone by phone.

These are the customers you have to get to buy your Brand A over Brand B. So who are they? Where are they? Are they rich, with three kids and a jumbo mortgage? Do they own fly rods and drive minivans? Do they go to church or temple? And maybe most important,

Please see Political   Page 249

Political

Continued from Page 248

who among them has never voted, or rarely voted, or voted in ways that may deserve the special status of swing voter? To do the job right, of course, to really win this thing, you've got to find them, woo them and get them to the polls. Where to start?

These days, the first stop is a comprehensive database of U.S. voters. There are fewer than half a dozen of them. One, named Voter Vault, belongs to the Republican National Committee; another, named Datamart, belongs to the Democratic National Committee. Over the past few years, thanks to technological advances and an escalating arms race between the parties, Republicans and Democrats have gone to great lengths to make campaigning more like commercial marketing. Moreover, both parties have begun to sort through their troves of information in order to identify and then court individual voters. Variations on the new political sharpshooting have been tested successfully by the Republican and Democratic Parties in several recent statewide elections. . . .

Each party's databank has the name of every one of the 168 million or so registered voters in the country, cross-indexed with phone numbers, addresses, voting history, income range and so on—up to as many as several hundred points of data on each voter. The information has been acquired from state voter-registration rolls, census reports, consumer data-mining companies

and direct marketing vendors. The parties have also amassed detailed information about the political and social beliefs that you might have shared with canvassers who have phoned or knocked on the door over the past few years. . . .

Both national committees see their detailed breakdown of the American electorate as a high-tech variation of pretelevision techniques—from the 1930s, say, or

> **Among privacy advocates the new databases are almost uniformly viewed as a trespass into our zone of political privacy.**

even the 1950s—when politics was driven by the one-to-one contact of a precinct worker who might know how to deliver an individualized political message simply because he knew your family, your job, your ethnicity, your values. Within the Republican Party, the 72-Hour Task Force and Voter Vault are considered proof of its return to grassroots organizing, whereby the party will get to better understand, and keep track of, its supporters. . . .

[D]ata-mining technology offers three significant advantages. First, by locating likely voters with greater accuracy, it enables campaigns to spend their dollars more wisely and efficiently. Second, it

opens up innovative ways of discovering and turning out new voters. Third, it creates the option of creating a narrow or individualized message—delivered by a friend, through the mail, over the phone or on cable TV—so that parties can talk to potential supporters about exactly the things they care about most. . . .

Among privacy advocates the new databases are almost uniformly viewed as a trespass into our zone of political privacy. Oscar Gandy of the University of Pennsylvania has further noted that political targeting may effectively disenfranchise portions of the electorate that are less likely to vote, or less likely to be persuadable. Why reach out to someone a statistician or a computer program does not consider a viable target?

Meanwhile, other privacy advocates say they worry about the dangers of assembling an individualized message from voter data—a message to that 50-year-old Ford Explorer driver who likes gardening and cares about tort reform, for example. "The nightmare scenario is that the databases create puppet masters," Peter Swire, a privacy expert who worked at the Office of Management and Budget during the Clinton administration, told me. "In the nightmare, every voter will get a tailored message based on detailed information about the voter. . . . The candidate knows everything about the voter, but the media and the public know nothing about what the candidate really believes. . . .

Think About It

- After this article was printed the *New York Times* asked online: "Should the political parties be compiling data about you?" Seventy-nine percent of those who responded clicked "no." How would you respond?

- What about young people? Given the information laid out in this article concerning how these computerized lists are created, do you think young people are substantially less likely to be on them? If so, might this mean that the parties will soon be concentrating even more on older people if they rely on such technology?

Making a Difference

Maria Cino and the Republican Party

In 2004, Maria Cino served as the deputy chair of the Republican National Committee. Though unknown to the public at large before being appointed to this important position, she had toiled on behalf of Republican campaigns for 20 years, working in a variety of staff positions. Most notably she had managed the National Republican Congressional Committee's daily operations in 1994 when the GOP stunned the political world by winning the majority of seats for the House. And in 2000 she was national political director for the Bush campaign, a job that gave her responsibility for hiring and supervising a vast national field operation.

national chairperson

The national chairperson is responsible for the day-to-day activities of the party and is usually hand-picked by the presidential nominee.

coalition

A group of individuals with a common interest upon which every political party depends.

Typically, each state has a national committeeman and a national committeewoman as delegates to the party's national committee. The Democratic committee also includes assorted governors, members of Congress, and other party officials.

Day-to-day activities of the national party are the responsibility of the party's **national chairperson.** The national party chairperson hires the staff, raises the money, pays the bills, and attends to the daily duties of the party. When asked what their biggest organizational challenge was at a 1998 joint appearance, the chairs of the Democratic and Republican parties both promptly responded "money."[15]

The chairperson of the party that controls the White House is normally selected by the president (subject to routine ratification by the national committee). In the early 1970s, two of the people who served for a while as chair of the Republican Party at the request of President Nixon were Bob Dole and George Bush, both of whom used this position as a means of political advancement. These days the party chairs and deputy chairs are typically career staffers who have worked their way up through a series of behind-the-scenes jobs to the role of a visible spokesperson for the party. (See "Making a Difference: Maria Cino and the Republican Party").

The Party in Government: Promises and Policy

Which party controls which of America's many elected offices matters because each party and the elected officials who represent it generally try to turn campaign promises into action. As a result, the party that has control over the most government offices will have the most influence in determining who gets what, where, when, and how.

Voters are attracted to a party in government by its performance and policies. What a party has done in office, and what it promises to do greatly influences who will join its **coalition**—a set of individuals and groups supporting it. Sometimes voters suspect that political promises are made to be broken. To be sure, there are notable instances in which politicians have turned—sometimes 180 degrees—from their policy promises. Lyndon Johnson repeatedly promised in the 1964 presidential campaign that he would not "send American boys to do an Asian boy's job" and involve the United States in the Vietnam War, but he did. In the 1980 campaign, Ronald Reagan asserted that he would balance the budget by 1984, yet his administration quickly ran up the largest deficit in American history. Throughout the 1988 campaign George Bush proclaimed, "Read my lips—no new taxes," but he reluctantly changed course two years later when pressured on the issue by the Democratic majority in Congress. Bill Clinton promised a tax cut for the middle class during the 1992 campaign, but after he was elected he backed off, saying that first the deficit would have to be substantially reduced.

It is all too easy to forget how often parties and presidents do exactly what they say they will do. For every broken promise, many more are kept. Ronald Reagan promised to step up defense spending and cut back on social welfare expenditures, and his administration quickly delivered on these pledges. Bill Clinton promised to support bills providing for family leave, easing voting registration procedures, and tightening gun control that had been vetoed by his predecessor. He lobbied hard to get these measures through Congress again and proudly signed them into law once they arrived on his desk. George W. Bush promised a major tax cut for every taxpayer in America and he delivered just that in 2001. In sum, the impression that politicians and parties never produce policy out of promises is largely erroneous.

In fact, the parties have done a fairly good job over the years of translating their platform promises into public policy. Gerald Pomper has shown that party platforms are excellent predictors of a party's actual policy performance in office. He tabulated specific pledges in the major parties' platforms over a number of years, tabulating 3194 specific policy pronouncements. Pomper then looked to see whether the party that won the presidency actually fulfilled its promises. Nearly three-fourths of all promises resulted in policy actions. Others were tried but floundered for one reason or another. Only 10 percent were ignored altogether.[16]

If parties generally do what they say they will, then the party platforms adopted at the national conventions represent blueprints, however vague, for action. Consider what the two major parties promised the voters in 2004 (see Table 8.2). There is little doubt that the choice between Democratic and Republican policies in 2004 was a clear one on many important issues facing the country.

Party Eras in American History

While studying political parties, remember the following: *America is a two-party system and always has been.* Of course, there are many minor parties around—Libertarians, Socialists, Reform, Greens—but they rarely have a chance of winning a major office. In contrast, most democratic nations have more than two parties represented in their national legislature. Throughout American history, one party has been the dominant majority party for long periods of time. A majority of voters identify with the party in power; thus this party tends to win a majority of the elections. Political scientists call these periods **party eras.**

Punctuating each party era is a **critical election.**[17] A critical election is an electoral earthquake: Fissures appear in each party's coalition, which begins to fracture; new issues appear, dividing the electorate. Each party forms a new coalition—one that endures for years. A critical election period may require more than one election before change is apparent, but in the end, the party system will be transformed.

This process is called **party realignment**—a rare event in American political life that is akin to a political revolution. Realignments are typically associated with a major crisis or trauma in the nation's history. One of the major realignments, when the Republican Party emerged, was connected to the Civil War. Another was linked to the Great Depression of the 1930s, when the majority Republicans were displaced by

party eras

Historical periods in which a majority of voters cling to the party in power, which tends to win a majority of the elections.

critical election

An electoral "earthquake" where new issues emerge, new coalitions replace old ones, and the majority party is often displaced by the minority party. Critical election periods are sometimes marked by a national crisis and may require more than one election to bring about a new party era.

party realignment

The displacement of the majority party by the minority party, usually during a **critical election** period.

Table 8.2   Party Platforms, 2004

Although few people actually read party platforms, they are one of the best written sources for what the parties believe in. A brief summary of some of the contrasting positions in the Democratic and Republican platforms of 2004 illustrates major differences in beliefs between the two parties.

REPUBLICANS	DEMOCRATS
The War in Iraq The best intelligence available at the time indicated that Saddam Hussein was a threat. While the stockpiles of weapons of mass destruction we expected to find in Iraq have not yet materialized, we have confirmed that Saddam Hussein had the capability to reconstitute his weapons programs and the desire to do so. . . . President Bush had a choice to make: Trust a madman or defend America. He chose defending America.	**The War in Iraq** People of good will disagree about whether America should have gone to war in Iraq, but this much is clear: this administration badly exaggerated its case, particularly with respect to weapons of mass destruction and the connection between Saddam's government and Al Qaeda. This administration did not build a true international coalition. Ignoring the advice of military leaders, this administration did not send sufficient forces into Iraq to accomplish the mission.
Fighting Terrorism President Bush recognized that to overcome the dangers of our time, America would have to take a new approach in the world. That approach is marked by a determination to challenge new threats, not ignore them, or simply wait for future tragedy — and by a commitment to building a hopeful future in hopeless places, instead of allowing troubled regions to remain in despair and explode in violence.	**Fighting Terrorism** The Bush doctrine of unilateral preemption has driven away our allies and cost us the support of other nations. With John Kerry as Commander-in-Chief, we will never wait for a green light from abroad when our safety is at stake, but we must enlist those whose support we need for ultimate victory.
Abortion We say the unborn child has a fundamental individual right to life that cannot be infringed.	**Abortion** We stand proudly for a woman's right to choose, consistent with *Roe v. Wade*, and regardless of ability to pay.
Gay Marriage We strongly support President Bush's call for a constitutional Amendment that fully protects marriage, and we believe that neither federal nor state judges nor bureaucrats should force states to recognize other living arrangements as equivalent to marriage.	**Gay Marriage** In our country, marriage has been defined at the state level for 200 years, and we believe it should continue to be defined there. We repudiate President Bush's divisive effort to politicize our Constitution by pursuing a "Federal Marriage Amendment."
Health Care We must attack the root causes of high health care costs by: aiding small businesses in offering health care to their employees; empowering the self-employed through access to affordable coverage; putting patients and doctors in charge of medical decisions; and reducing junk lawsuits and limiting punitive damage awards that raise the cost of health care.	**Health Care** We believe that health care is a right and not a privilege. We will offer individuals and businesses tax credits to make quality, reliable health coverage more affordable. We will provide tax credits to Americans who are approaching retirement age and those who are between jobs so they can afford quality, reliable coverage. We will expand coverage for low income adults through existing federal-state health care programs.
Taxes We believe that good government is based on a system of limited taxes and spending. . . . Our party endorses the president's proposals to make tax-relief permanent, so that families and businesses can plan for the future with confidence.	**Taxes** We must restore our values to our tax code. We want a tax code that rewards work and creates wealth for more people, not a tax code that hoards wealth for those who already have it. We should set taxes for families making more than $200,000 a year at the same level as in the late 1990s.
Education The President and Republicans in Congress recognize that states and local communities are most directly responsible for the quality of education in their schools. That is why the No Child Left Behind Act stipulates that the states, not the federal government, develop an accountability plan that will work best for them.	**Education** Under Kerry and Edwards, we will offer high quality early learning opportunities, smaller classes, more after school activities, and more individualized attention for our students. . . . The federal government will meet its financial obligations for elementary and secondary education and for special education.

Source: Excerpts from party platforms as posted on the websites of each organization.

the Democrats. The following sections look more closely at the various party eras in American history.

1796–1824: The First Party System

In the *Federalist Papers*, James Madison warned strongly against the dangers of "factions," or parties. But Alexander Hamilton, one of the coauthors of the *Federalist Papers*, did as much as anyone to inaugurate our party system.[18] Hamilton was the nation's first secretary of the treasury, for which service his picture appears on today's $10 bill. To garner congressional support for his pet policies, particularly a national bank, he needed votes. From this politicking and coalition building came the rudiments of the Federalist Party, America's first political party. The Federalists were also America's shortest lived major party. After Federalist candidate John Adams was defeated in his reelection bid in 1800, the party quickly faded. The Federalists were poorly organized, and by 1820 they no longer bothered to offer up a candidate for president. In this early period of American history, most party leaders did not regard themselves as professional politicians. Those who lost often withdrew completely from the political arena. The ideas of a loyal opposition and rotation of power in government had not yet taken hold.[19] Each party wanted to destroy the other party, not just defeat it—and such was the fate of the Federalists.

The party that crushed the Federalists was led by Virginians, Jefferson, Madison, and Monroe, each of whom was elected president for two terms in succession. They were known as the Democratic-Republicans, or sometimes as the Jeffersonians. The Democratic-Republican Party derived its coalition from agrarian interests rather than from the growing number of capitalists who supported the Federalists. This made the party particularly popular in the largely rural South. As the Federalists disappeared, however, the old Jeffersonian coalition was torn apart by factionalism as it tried to be all things to all people.

1828–1856: Jackson and the Democrats Versus the Whigs

More than anyone else, General Andrew Jackson founded the modern American political party. In the election of 1828, he forged a new coalition that included Westerners as well as Southerners, new immigrants as well as settled Americans. Like most successful politicians of his day, Jackson was initially a Democratic-Republican, but soon after his ascension to the presidency his party became known as simply the Democratic Party, which continues to this day. The "Democratic" label was particularly appropriate for Jackson's supporters because their cause was to broaden political opportunity by eliminating many vestiges of elitism and mobilizing the masses.

Aaron Burr dealt a near-death blow to the Federalist Party when he killed its leader, Alexander Hamilton, in this 1804 duel. Burr, then vice president, challenged Hamilton to the duel after the former treasury secretary publicly called him a traitor.

Whereas Jackson was the charismatic leader, the Democrats' behind-the-scenes architect was Martin Van Buren, who succeeded Jackson as president. Van Buren's one term in office was relatively undistinguished, but his view of party competition left a lasting mark. He "sought to make Democrats see that their only hope for maintaining the purity of their own principles was to admit the existence of an opposing party."[20] A realist, Van Buren argued that a party could not aspire to pleasing all the people all the time. He argued that a governing party needed a loyal opposition to represent parts of society that it could not. This opposition was provided by the Whigs. The Whig Party included such notable statesmen as Henry Clay and Daniel Webster, but it was able to win the presidency only when it nominated aging but popular military heroes such as William Henry Harrison (1840) and Zachary Taylor (1848). The Whigs had two distinct wings—Northern industrialists and Southern planters—who were brought together more by the Democratic policies they opposed than by the issues on which they agreed.

1860–1928: The Two Republican Eras

In the 1850s, the issue of slavery dominated American politics and split both the Whigs and the Democrats. Slavery, said Senator Charles Sumner, an ardent abolitionist, "is the only subject within the field of national politics which excites any real interest."[21] Congress battled over the extension of slavery to the new states and territories. In *Dred Scott v. Sandford*, the Supreme Court of 1857 held that slaves could not be citizens and that former slaves could not be protected by the Constitution. This decision further sharpened the divisions in public opinion, making civil war increasingly likely.

The Republicans rose in the late 1850s as the antislavery party. Folding in the remnants of several minor parties, in 1860 the Republicans forged a coalition strong enough to elect Abraham Lincoln president and to ignite the Civil War. The "War Between the States" was one of those political earthquakes that realigned the parties. After the war, the Republican Party thrived for more than 60 years. The Democrats controlled the South, though, and the Republican label remained a dirty word in the old Confederacy.

A second Republican era was initiated with the watershed election of 1896, perhaps the most bitter battle in American electoral history. The Democrats nominated William Jennings Bryan, populist proponent of "free silver" (linking money with silver, which was more plentiful than gold, and thus devaluing money to help debtors). The Republican Party made clear its positions in favor of the gold standard, industrialization, the banks, high tariffs, and the industrial working classes, as well as its positions against the "radical" Western farmers and "silverites." "Bryan and his program were greeted by the country's conservatives with something akin to terror."[22] The *New York Tribune* howled that Bryan's Democrats were "in league with the Devil." On the other side, novelist Frank Baum lampooned the Republicans in his classic novel, *The Wizard of Oz*. Dorothy follows the yellow brick road (symbolizing the gold standard) to the Emerald City (representing Washington) only to find that the Wizard (whose figure resembles McKinley) is powerless. But by clicking on her *silver* slippers (the color was changed to ruby for technicolor effect in the movie), she finds that she can return home.

Political scientists call the 1896 election a realigning one because it shifted the party coalitions and entrenched the Republicans for another generation. (For more on the election of 1896, see Chapter 10.) For the next three decades the Republicans continued as the nation's majority party, until the stock market crashed in 1929. The ensuing Great Depression brought about another fissure in the crust of the American party system.

1932–1964: The New Deal Coalition

President Herbert Hoover's handling of the Depression turned out to be disastrous for the Republicans. He solemnly pronounced that economic depression could not be cured by legislative action. Americans, however, obviously disagreed, and voted for

Franklin D. Roosevelt, who promised the country a *New Deal.* In his first 100 days as president, Roosevelt prodded Congress into passing scores of anti-Depression measures. Party realignment began in earnest after the Roosevelt administration got the country moving again. First-time voters flocked to the polls, pumping new blood into the Democratic ranks and providing much of the margin for Roosevelt's four presidential victories. Immigrant groups in Boston and other cities had been initially attracted to the Democrats by the 1928 campaign of Al Smith, the first Catholic to be nominated by a major party for the presidency.[23] Roosevelt reinforced the partisanship of these groups, and the Democrats forged the **New Deal coalition.**

The basic elements of the New Deal coalition were:

- *Urban dwellers.* Big cities such as Chicago and Philadelphia were staunchly Republican before the New Deal realignment; afterward, they were Democratic bastions.
- *Labor unions.* FDR became the first president to support unions enthusiastically, and they returned the favor.
- *Catholics and Jews.* During and after the Roosevelt period, Catholics and Jews were strongly Democratic.
- *The poor.* Though the poor had low turnout rates, their votes went overwhelmingly to the party of Roosevelt and his successors.
- *Southerners.* Ever since pre-Civil War days, White Southerners had been Democratic loyalists. This alignment continued unabated during the New Deal. For example, Mississippi voted over 90 percent Democratic in each of FDR's four presidential election victories.
- *African Americans.* The Republicans freed the slaves, but under FDR the Democrats attracted the majority of African Americans.

As you can see in Figure 8.2, many of the same groups that supported FDR's New Deal continue to shape the party coalitions today.

The New Deal coalition made the Democratic Party the clear majority party for decades. Harry S Truman, who succeeded Roosevelt in 1945, promised a Fair Deal.

New Deal coalition

A coalition forged by the Democrats, who dominated American politics from the 1930s to the 1960s. Its basic elements were the urban working class, ethnic groups, Catholics and Jews, the poor, Southerners, African Americans, and intellectuals.

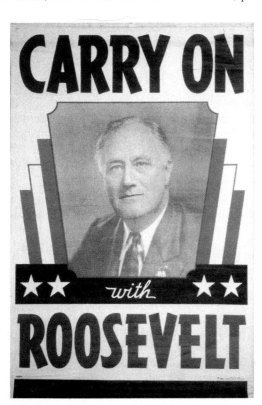

Franklin Roosevelt reshaped the Democratic Party, bringing together a diverse array of groups that had long been marginalized in American political life. Many of the key features of the Democratic Party today, such as support from labor unions, can be traced to the FDR era.

Figure 8.2   Party Coalitions Today

The two parties continue to draw support from very different social groups, many of which have existed since the New Deal era. This figure shows the percentage identifying as Democrats and Republicans for various groups in 2004.

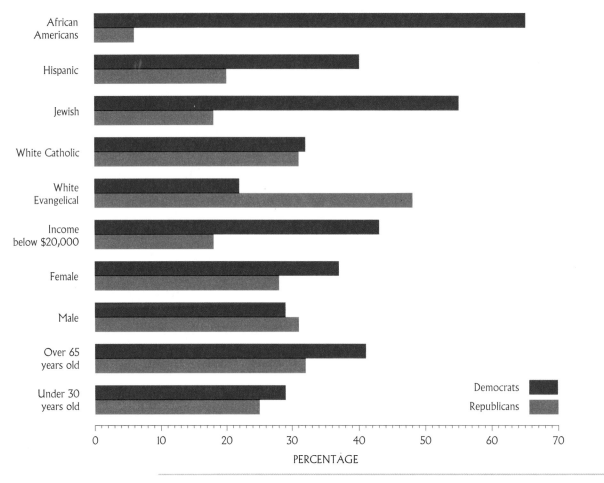

Source: Pew Research Center [http://people-press.org/commentary/display.php3?AnalysisID=95].

World War II hero and Republican Dwight D. Eisenhower broke the Democrats' grip on power by being elected president twice during the 1950s, but the Democrats regained the presidency in 1960 with the election of John F. Kennedy. His New Frontier was in the New Deal tradition, with platforms and policies designed to help labor, the working classes, and minorities. Lyndon B. Johnson, picked as Kennedy's vice president because he could help win Southern votes, became president upon Kennedy's assassination and was overwhelmingly elected to a term of his own in 1964. Johnson's Great Society programs included a major expansion of government programs to help the poor, the homeless, and minorities. His War on Poverty was reminiscent of Roosevelt's activism in dealing with the Depression. Johnson's Vietnam War policies, however, tore the Democratic Party apart in 1968, leaving the door to the presidency wide open for Republican candidate Richard M. Nixon.

1968–Present: The Era of Divided Party Government

Throughout most of American history, newly elected presidents have routinely swept a wave of their fellow partisans into office with them. For example, the Democrats gained 62 seats in the House when Woodrow Wilson was elected in 1912 and 97 when FDR was elected in 1932. The first time in the twentieth century that a newly elected president moved into the White House without having his party in control of both houses of Congress was when Nixon won the 1968 election. Nixon's election was not to be an exception, however, but rather the beginning of a common pattern—repeated in the presidential elections won by Ronald Reagan and George Bush. For a time, it seemed that the normal state of affairs in Washington was to have a Republican president and a Democratic Congress.

Bill Clinton's election in 1992 briefly restored united party government until the Republicans won both houses of Congress in the 1994 elections. After the 1994 elections, Republican leaders were optimistic that they were at last on the verge of a new Republican era in which they would control both the presidency and Congress simultaneously. On the other side, Democratic leaders were hopeful that voters would not like the actions of the new Republican Congress and would restore unified Democratic control of the government. In the end, the ambitions of both sides were frustrated as voters opted to continue divided party government in 1996. The election of George W. Bush in 2000 led to a very brief period of united Republican control of the White House in Congress. But four months after Bush took the inaugural oath, Senator James Jeffords of Vermont defected from the GOP, thereby giving the Democrats the majority in the upper chamber. The 2002 election restored GOP control of the Senate by a narrow margin. And in 2004, unified Republican government was ratified by the people when President George W. Bush was reelected with partisan majorities in both the House and the Senate.

With fewer voters attached to the two major parties, it may well be difficult for either one to gain a strong enough foothold to maintain simultaneous control of both sides of Pennsylvania Avenue for very long. All told, both houses of Congress and the presidency have been simultaneously controlled by the same party for just 10.3 of the 38 years from 1969 to 2006.[24] The discrepancy between the patterns of presidential and congressional voting during this era of divided party government is unprecedented in American history.

Divided party government is frequently seen not only at the federal level but at the state level as well. As Morris Fiorina shows, the percentage of states that have unified party control of the governorship and the state legislature has steadily declined for over four decades.[25] Whereas 85 percent of state governments had one party controlling both houses of the legislature and the governorship in 1946, by 2005 this was the case in only 40 percent of the states (see Figure 8.3). Divided government, once an occasional oddity in state capitols, is now commonplace.

The recent pattern of divided government has caused many political scientists to believe that the party system has dealigned rather than realigned. Whereas realignment involves people changing from one party to another, **party dealignment** means that people are gradually moving away from both parties. When your car is realigned, it is adjusted in one direction or another to improve its steering. Imagine if your mechanic were to remove the steering mechanism instead of adjusting it—your car would be useless and ineffective. This is what many scholars fear has been happening to the parties.

In the parties' heyday, it was said that people would vote for a yellow dog if their party nominated one. Now, more than 90 percent of all Americans insist that "I always vote for the person whom I think is best, regardless of what party they belong to."[26] Rather than reflecting negative attitudes toward the parties, the recent dealignment has been characterized by a growing **party neutrality**. For example, 25 percent of the 2000 National Election Study respondents answered as follows to a set of four open-ended questions about the parties:

Q. Is there anything in particular that you like about the Democratic Party?
A. No.
Q. Is there anything in particular that you don't like about the Democratic Party?
A. No.
Q. Is there anything in particular that you like about the Republican Party?
A. No.
Q. Is there anything in particular that you don't like about the Republican Party?
A. No.

Why It Matters

Divided Party Government
When one party controls the White House and the other party controls one or both houses of Congress, divided party government exists. Given that one party can check the other's agenda, it is virtually impossible for a party to say what it is going to do and then actually put these policies into effect. This situation is bad if you want clear lines of accountability on policy, but it is good if you prefer that the two parties be forced to work out compromises.

party dealignment

The gradual disengagement of people and politicians from the parties, as seen in part by shrinking party identification.

party neutrality

A term used to describe the fact that many Americans are indifferent toward to two major political parties.

Figure 8.3   Partisan Control of State Governments: 2005

This map shows which states as of 2005 were totally under Democratic or Republican control—that is, had one party controlling both Houses of the legislature as well as the governorship. Divided party control means that either one or both Houses of the legislature are controlled by a party different than the governor. Nebraska has a nonpartisan legislature and hence cannot be classified.

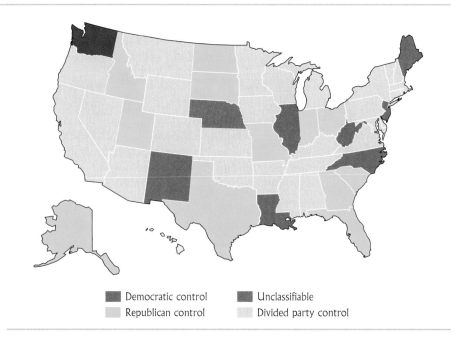

Democratic control   Unclassifiable

Republican control   Divided party control

When these questions were first asked in the 1950s, only about 10 percent of respondents answered in this neutral way, generally indicating that they were not following politics at all. Now, many of those who say nothing about the parties are quite aware of the candidates. Lacking any party anchoring, though, they are easily swayed one way or the other. As a result, they are often referred to as "the floating voters." More than any other group, these independent-minded voters will determine the ups and downs of party fortunes in the twenty-first century.

Third Parties: Their Impact on American Politics

third parties

Electoral contenders other than the two major parties. American third parties are not unusual, but they rarely win elections.

Third Parties in American History

The story of American party struggle is primarily the story of two major parties, but **third parties** are a regular feature of American politics and occasionally attract the public's attention. Third parties come in three basic varieties. First are parties that promote certain causes—either a controversial single issue (prohibition of alcoholic beverages, for example) or an extreme ideological position such as socialism or libertarianism. Second are splinter parties, which are offshoots of a major party. Teddy Roosevelt's Progressives in 1912, Strom Thurmond's States' Righters in 1948, and George Wallace's American Independents in 1968 all claimed they did not get a fair hearing from Republicans or Democrats and thus formed their own new parties. Finally, some third parties are merely an extension of a popular individual with presidential aspirations. Both John Anderson in 1980 and Ross Perot in 1992 and 1996 offered voters who were dissatisfied with the Democratic and Republican nominees another option.

Although third party candidates almost never win office in the United States, scholars believe they are often quite important.[27] They have brought new groups into the electorate and have served as "safety valves" for popular discontent. The Free Soilers of the 1850s were the first true antislavery party; the Progressives and the Populists put many social reforms on the political agenda. George Wallace told his supporters in 1968 they had the chance to "send a message" to Washington—a message of support for tougher law and order measures, which is still being felt to this day. Ross Perot used his saturation of the TV airwaves in 1992 to ensure that the issue of the federal deficit was not ignored in the campaign. In 1998, a former professional

One's party affiliation is an important part of one's political identity. Although clubs of college Republicans and college Democrats are common on campuses around the country, roughly half of college-age Americans do not have a party affiliation, preferring to call themselves Independents.

wrestler stunned the political world when he won the governorship of Minnesota as a third party candidate. And in 2000 Green Party candidate Ralph Nader forced more attention on environmental issues and ultimately cost Gore the presidency by drawing away a small percentage of liberal votes.

Despite the regular appearance of third parties, the two-party system is firmly entrenched in American politics. Would it make a difference if America had a multiparty system, as so many European countries have? The answer is clearly yes. The most obvious consequence of two-party governance is the moderation of political conflict. If America had many parties, each would have to make a special appeal in order to stand out from the crowd. It is not hard to imagine what a multiparty system might look like in the United States. Quite possibly, African-American groups would form their own party, pressing vigorously for racial equality. Environmentalists could constitute another party, vowing to clean up the rivers, oppose nuclear power, and save the wilderness. America

Ralph Nader challenged the two-party system in 2000 by running for president on the ticket of the Green Party. Exit polls show his voters preferred Gore over Bush by a margin of five to two. With the margin being as close as it was in 2000, it seems readily apparent that Nader's presence in the race influenced the outcome. In 2004, Nader's Independent candidacy garnered only 0.3 percent of the vote.

America in Perspective

Multiparty Systems in Other Countries

One of the major reasons why the United States has only two parties represented in government is structural. America has a **winner-take-all system,** in which whoever gets the most votes wins the election. There are no prizes awarded for second or third place. Suppose there are three parties; one receives 45 percent of the vote, another 40 percent, and the third 15 percent. Though it got less than a majority, the party that finished first is declared the winner. The others are out in the cold. In this way, the American system discourages small parties. Unless a party wins, there is no reward for the votes it gets. Thus, it makes more sense for a small party to form an alliance with one of the major parties than to struggle on its own with little hope. In this example, the second- and third-place parties might merge (if they can reach an agreement on policy) to challenge the governing party in the next election.

In a system that employs **proportional representation,** however, such a merger would not be necessary. Under this system, which is used in most European countries, legislative seats are allocated according to each party's percentage of the nationwide vote. If a party wins 15 percent of the vote, then it receives 15 percent of the seats. Even a small party can use its voice in Parliament to be a thorn in the side of the government, standing up strongly for its principles. Such has often been the role of the Greens in Germany, who are ardent environmentalists. After the 2002 German election they formed a **coalition government** along with Germany's Social Democratic Party. Together the coalition controls over half the seats. Coalition governments are common in Europe. Italy has regularly been ruled by a coalition since the end of World War II, for example.

Even with proportional representation, not every party gets represented in the legislature. To be awarded seats, a party must always achieve a certain percentage of votes, which varies from country to country. Israel has one of the lowest thresholds at 1.5 percent. This explains why there are always so many parties represented in the Israeli Knesset. The founders of Israel's system wanted to make sure that all points of view were represented, but sometimes this has turned into a nightmare, with small extremist parties holding the balance of power.

Parties have to develop their own unique identities to appeal to voters in a multiparty system. This requires strong stands on the issues, but after the election compromises must be made to form a coalition government. If an agreement cannot be reached on the major issues, the coalition is in trouble. Sometimes a new coalition can be formed; other times the result is the calling of a new election. In either case, it is clear that proportional representation systems are more fluid than the two-party system in the United States.

winner-take-all system

An electoral system in which legislative seats are awarded only to the candidates who come in first in their constituencies. In American presidential elections, the system in which the winner of the popular vote in a state receives all the electoral votes of that state.

proportional representation

An electoral system used throughout most of Europe that awards legislative seats to political parties in proportion to the number of votes won in an election.

coalition government

When two or more parties join together to form a majority in a national legislature. This form of government is quite common in the multiparty systems of Europe.

could have religious parties, union-based parties, farmers' parties, and all sorts of others. As in some European countries, there could be half a dozen or more parties represented in Congress (see "America in Perspective: Multiparty Systems in Other Countries").

The American two-party system contributes to political ambiguity. Why should parties risk taking a strong stand on a controversial policy if doing so will only antagonize many voters? Ambiguity is a safe strategy,[28] as extremist candidates Barry Goldwater in 1964 and George McGovern in 1972 found out the hard way. The two-party system thus throttles extreme or unconventional views.

Understanding Political Parties

Political parties are considered essential elements of democratic government. Indeed, one of the first steps taken toward democracy in formerly communist Eastern European countries was the formation of competing political parties to contest elections. After years of one-party totalitarian rule, Eastern Europeans were ecstatic to be able to adopt a multiparty system like those that had proved successful in the West. In contrast, the founding of the world's first party system in the United States was seen as a risky adventure in the then uncharted waters of democracy. Wary of having parties at all, the Founders designed a system that has greatly restrained their political role to this day. Whether American parties should continue to be so loosely organized is at the heart of today's debate about their role in American democracy.

Democracy and Responsible Party Government

Ideally, in a democracy candidates should say what they mean to do if elected and, once they are elected, should be able to do what they promised. Critics of the American party system lament that this is all too often not the case, and have called for a "more responsible two-party system."[29] Advocates of the **responsible party model** believe the parties should meet the following conditions:

1. Parties must present distinct, comprehensive programs for governing the nation.
2. Each party's candidates must be committed to its program and have the internal cohesion and discipline to carry out its program.
3. The majority party must implement its programs, and the minority party must state what it would do if it were in power.
4. The majority party must accept responsibility for the performance of the government.

A two-party system operating under these conditions would make it easier to convert party promises into governmental policy. A party's officeholders would have firm control of the government, so they would be collectively, rather than individually, responsible for their actions. Voters would therefore know whom to blame for what the government does and does not accomplish.

As this chapter has shown, American political parties fall far short of these conditions. They are too decentralized to take a single national position and then enforce it.

responsible party model

A view favored by some political scientists about how parties should work. According to the model, parties should offer clear choices to the voters, who can then use those choices as cues to their own preferences of candidates. Once in office, parties would carry out their campaign promises.

Comparing Political Parties

How You Can Make a Difference

Minor Political Parties

If you do not support either major political party, why not join one of the smaller political parties such as the Green Party, the Libertarian Party, or the Reform Party? Sometimes minor parties can win, such as when Jesse Ventura won the gubernatorial race in Minnesota in 1998. Minor parties suffer at the polls due to restrictive ballot access laws and lack of money. Many states will not let minor parties be on the ballot unless they demonstrate a lot of support in that state. Most states require a certain number of signatures of registered votes on petitions to allow a minor party on the ballot. You can help these parties get on the ballot in your state by carrying petitions and getting signatures. You can also help register new members of the party, distribute leaflets, write letters to the editors of newspapers, or in any other way your local party leaders need.

What you can do:

There are statewide organizations for most of the smaller political parties, and many local chapters as well. You can find the nearest one by checking the party's website.

- Green Party: *www.gp.org*. The Green Party is a progressive party that supports environmentalism, grassroots democracy, social justice, and peace/nonviolence. Ralph Nader was the Green Party candidate for the 2000 presidential election. Many believe his candidacy influenced the final outcome.
- Libertarian Party: *www.lp.org*. The Libertarian Party is both very liberal and very conservative. It favors absolute freedom in both the economic realm (free trade, nonintervention in foreign affairs, unrestricted free market, no government programs such as Social Security, welfare, interstate highways, or public schools) and in social/personal issues (no restrictions on abortions, drug use, prostitution, and so forth).
- Reform Party: *www.reformparty .org*. The Reform Party was started

by Ross Perot and his followers in the early 1990s and reflects concerns such as favoring a balanced federal budget, campaign finance reform, a new tax system, and trade that protects American workers.

- Communist Party USA: *www. cpusa.org*. This party is a Marxist-Leninist working-class party that believes capitalism has failed and is angry at the continuing injustices and suffering they say it brings. They work for a socialist economy that puts people before profits and for full equality of all races and both genders.
- Constitution Party: *www.constitu tionparty.com*. This conservative group wishes to return the U.S. government to its constitutional boundaries and limitations by restricting much current government activity.

Most candidates are self-selected, gaining their nomination by their own efforts rather than the party's. Virtually anyone can vote in party primaries; thus, parties do not have control over those who run under their labels. In 1991, for example, a former grand wizard of the Ku Klux Klan, David Duke, became the Republican nominee for governor of Louisiana despite denunciations from President Bush, who ultimately said he preferred the Democratic nominee. Had Duke won the election, the Republican Party would have been powerless to control his actions in office.

In America's loosely organized party system, there simply is no mechanism for a party to discipline officeholders and thereby ensure cohesion in policymaking. As David Mayhew writes, "Unlike most politicians elsewhere, American ones at both legislative and executive levels have managed to navigate the last two centuries of history without becoming minions of party leaders."[30] Thus, it is rare to find congressional votes in which over 90 percent of Democrats vote in opposition to over 90 percent of Republicans. Indeed, Mayhew's analysis of historic legislation from 1946 to 1990 failed to uncover a single case in which a major law was passed by such a clearly partisan vote.[31] The 1998 vote in the House to impeach President Clinton was unparalleled in recent times, with 98 percent of each party's members sticking to the party line.

Not everyone thinks that America's decentralized parties are a problem, however. Critics of the responsible party model argue that the complexity and diversity of American society are too great to be captured by such a simple model of party politics. Local differences need an outlet for expression, they say. One cannot expect Texas Democrats always to want to vote in line with New York Democrats. In the view of those opposed to the responsible party model, America's decentralized parties are appropriate for the type of limited government the Founders sought to create and most Americans wish to maintain.[32]

The Founding Fathers were very concerned that political parties would trample on the rights of individuals. They wanted to preserve individual freedom of action by various elected officials. With America's weak party system, this has certainly been the case. Individual members of Congress and other elected officials have great freedom to act as they see fit rather than toeing the party line.

American Political Parties and the Scope of Government

The lack of disciplined and cohesive European-style parties in America goes a long way to explain why the scope of governmental activity in the United States is not as broad as it is in other established democracies. The absence of a national health care system in America provides a perfect example. In Britain, the Labour Party had long proposed such a system, and after it won the 1945 election, all its members of Parliament voted to enact national health care into law. On the other side of the Atlantic, President Truman also proposed a national health care bill in the first presidential election after World War II. But even though he won the election and had majorities of his own party in both houses of Congress, his proposal never got very far. The weak party structure in the United States allowed many congressional Democrats to oppose Truman's health care proposal. Over four decades later, President Clinton again proposed a system of universal health care and had a Democratic-controlled Congress to work with. His experience in 1994 was much the same as Truman's: The Clinton health care bill never even came up for a vote in Congress because of the president's inability to get enough members of his own party to go along with him. Substantially increasing the scope of government in America is not something that can be accomplished through the disciplined actions of one party's members, as is the case in other democracies.

On the other hand, because no single party in the United States can ever be said to have firm control over the government, the hard choices necessary to cut back on existing government spending are rarely addressed. A disciplined and cohesive governing party would have the power to say no to various demands on the government.

America's decentralized political parties have little control over candidates, as shown by the Senate nomination of Oliver North, who figured prominently in the Iran-Contra scandal. North obtained the Republican nomination in Virginia despite being denounced by the state's senior Republican Senator, John Warner, as well as by former Presidents Reagan and Bush.

In contrast, America's loose party structure makes it possible for many individual politicians—Democrats and Republicans alike—to focus their efforts on getting more from the government for their own constituents.

Is the Party Over?

The key problem for American political parties is that they are no longer the main source of political information, attention, and affection. The party of today has rivals that appeal to voters and politicians alike, the biggest of which is the media. With the advent of television, voters no longer need the party to find out what the candidates are like and what they stand for. The interest group is another party rival. As Chapter 11 will discuss, the power of interest groups has grown enormously in recent years. Interest groups, not the parties, pioneered much of the technology of modern politics, including mass mailings and sophisticated fund-raising.

The parties have clearly been having a tough time lately, but there are indications that they are beginning to adapt to the high-tech age. Although the old city machines are largely extinct, state and national party organizations have become more visible and active than ever. More people are calling themselves Independents and splitting their tickets, but the majority still identify with a party, and this percentage seems to have stabilized.

For a time, some political scientists were concerned that parties were on the verge of disappearing from the political scene. A more realistic view is that parties will continue to play an important, but significantly diminished, role in American politics. Leon Epstein sees the situation as one in which the parties have become "frayed." He concludes that the parties will "survive and even moderately prosper in a society evidently unreceptive to strong parties and yet unready, and probably unable, to abandon parties altogether."[33]

Summary

Even though political parties are one of Americans' least beloved institutions, political scientists see them as a key linkage between policymakers and the people. Parties are pervasive in politics; for each party there is a *party in the electorate*, a *party organization*, and a *party in government*. Political parties affect policy through their platforms.

Despite much cynicism about party platforms, they are taken seriously when their candidates are elected.

America has a two-party system. This fact is of fundamental importance in understanding American politics. The ups and downs of the two parties constitute party competition. In the past, one party or the other has dominated the government for long periods of time. These periods were punctuated by critical elections, in which party coalitions underwent realignment. Since 1968, however, American government has experienced a unique period of party dealignment. Although parties are currently weaker at the mass level, they are somewhat stronger and richer in terms of national and state organization. Some would have them be far more centralized and cohesive, following the responsible party model. The loose structure of American parties allows politicians to avoid collective responsibility but also promotes individualism that many Americans value.

KEY TERMS

party competition	open primaries	party dealignment
political party	blanket primaries	party neutrality
linkage institutions	national convention	third parties
party image	national committee	winner-take-all system
rational-choice theory	national chairperson	proportional
party identification	coalition	representation
ticket-splitting	party eras	coalition government
party machines	critical election	responsible party model
patronage	party realignment	
closed primaries	New Deal coalition	

INTERNET RESOURCES

www.rnc.org
The official site of the Republican National Committee.

www.democrats.org
The Democratic Party online.

www.lp.org
Although Libertarians rarely get more than a few percent of the vote, they are consistently getting many of their candidates on the

ballot for many offices. You can learn more about their beliefs at this official site.

www.gp.org
The official website for the Green Party, which emphasizes environmental protection over corporate profits. The Greens nominated Ralph Nader in 2000 and David Cobb in 2004.

GET CONNECTED

Third Parties

Most people have heard of the Democratic and Republican Parties, but many people would be surprised to learn that there are many other parties besides these. The text notes that these other parties, called "minor parties" or "third parties," come in three basic varieties: those that promote certain causes, those that are offshoots of the major parties, and those organized around popular individuals. What do these third parties stand for? Should you identify with one of the third parties?

Search the Web

Go to the Party Matchmaking Service *http://www.3pc.net/matchmaker/* and take the quiz. Think about the questions carefully and try to answer honestly.

Questions to Ask

- According to the quiz, with which party do you have the highest compatibility? Do you already identify with this party?
- Were you surprised by the results? Why?

- Find out whether this party has had a candidate for federal office on the ballot in your state in recent elections. (You can try checking your state's Secretary of State or Election Board web pages, or even try a web search on Google.) If so, did the candidate win?

Why It Matters

Despite the fact that their candidates are rarely elected, third parties exist because of the diversity of ideas in America, and they play an important role in our system of government. Third parties propose policies that are often adopted by the two major parties and sometimes are enacted into law. Third parties also allow voters a "protest" vote when they don't like the Democratic or Republican candidate. In some parts of the country, third party candidates are the only opponents faced by Democratic or Republican candidates.

Get Involved

You can find the contact information and web page addresses of political parties at the Politics1.com website *http://www.politics1.com/parties.htm*. Research the party with which you are most compatible according to the quiz results. Are you interested in associating with this party? If so, find out how you can become an active member.

To see more Get Connected exercises for Chapter 8, go to www.ablongman.com/edwards.

FOR FURTHER READING

Black, Earl, and Merle Black. *The Rise of Southern Republicanism.* Cambridge, MA: Harvard University Press, 2002. An excellent examination of the transformation of party politics in the South.

Downs, Anthony. *An Economic Theory of Democracy.* New York: Harper & Row, 1957. An extremely influential theoretical work that applies rational-choice theory to party politics.

Epstein, Leon. *Political Parties in the American Mold.* Madison: University of Wisconsin Press, 1986. Epstein demonstrates the remarkable persistence of both parties during a century of profound social change.

Green, John C., and Daniel M. Shea. *The State of the Parties*, 4th ed. Lanham, MD: Rowman & Littlefield, 2003. A diverse set of articles on numerous aspects of party politics, with an emphasis on how well the party system is working.

Hershey, Marjorie Randon. *Party Politics in America*, 11th ed. New York: Longman, 2003. The standard textbook on political parties.

Maisel, L. Sandy, ed. *The Parties Respond: Changes in the American Parties and Campaigns*, 3rd ed. Boulder, CO: Westview Press, 1998. A good collection of readings on how parties have adapted to changes in the political system.

Mayhew, David R. *Electoral Realignments: A Critique of an American Genre.* New Haven, CN: Yale University Press, 2002. A critical look at the historical evidence concerning realignment theory.

Rosenstone, Steven, Roy Behr, and Edward Lazarus. *Third Parties in America*, 2nd ed. Princeton, NJ: Princeton University Press, 1996. An analytical study of why third parties appear, when they do, and what effect they have.

Sundquist, James L. *Dynamics of the Party System*, rev. ed. Washington, D.C.: Brookings Institution, 1983. One of the best books ever written on the major realignments in American history.

Tarrance, V. Lance Jr., and Walter DeVries with Donna L. Mosher. *Checked and Balanced: How Ticket-Splitters Are Shaping the New Balance of Power in American Politics.* Grand Rapids, MI: Eerdmans, 1998. A good basic presentation of trends in ticket-splitting, which also contains in-depth interviews that shed light on the meaning of such votes.

Wattenberg, Martin P. *The Decline of American Political Parties, 1952–1996.* Cambridge, MA: Harvard University Press, 1998. An account of the decline of parties in the electorate.

Nominations and Campaigns

Chapter Outline

The Nomination Game

The New York Times **Issues of the Times**

The Campaign Game

Money and Campaigning

The Impact of Campaigns

Understanding Nominations and Campaigns

Summary

■ Campaigning for any major office has become a massive undertaking in today's political world. Consider George W. Bush's grueling schedule for March 28–29, 2000, a relatively low-key period of the presidential campaign:

- The governor begins his day with an early morning flight from his home in Austin, Texas, to Dulles Airport in Northern Virginia.
- Upon landing in Virginia, Bush goes to a reception to raise money for his campaign. After lunch, he goes to the headquarters of Sallie Mae, a corporation that helps students finance educational expenses, to give a speech about his views on government and higher education.
- Governor Bush then boards his campaign plane again for a flight to Newark, N.J., where he participates in another fund-raiser and gives his standard campaign speech at dinner. After dinner, he goes to Manville, N.J., to address the Somerset County Republican Party convention. Finally, after 15 hours of traveling and campaigning, his day ends when he checks in at the Newark Hilton at 9:30 P.M.

- The next morning, Bush goes to the North Star Academy Charter school in Newark to give another speech on education. He then rides in a limousine to New York City to give a lunch speech on foreign affairs.
- After this quick stop in New York, Bush flies to Baltimore, Md., to meet with the local press, attend a youth rally, and deliver his standard campaign speech yet again at a dinner event. Finally, Bush takes his fourth flight in two days—this time to Eau Claire, Wis., where he arrives after 14 hours on the go.

It is often said that the presidency is the most difficult job in the world, but getting elected to the position may well be tougher. It is arguable that the long campaign for the presidency puts candidates under more continuous stress than they could ever face in the White House.

The current American style of long and arduous campaigns has evolved from the belief of reformers that the cure for the problems of democracy is more democracy. Whether this approach is helpful or harmful to democracy is a question that arouses much debate with respect to American political campaigns. Some scholars believe it is important that presidential candidates go through a long and

difficult trial by fire. Others, however, worry that the system makes it difficult for politicians with other responsibilities—such as incumbent governors and senior senators—to take a run at the White House.

The consequences for the scope of government are also debatable. Anthony King argues that American politicians do too little governing because they are always "running scared," in today's perpetual campaign.[1] From King's perspective, the campaign process does not allow politicians the luxury of trying out solutions to policy problems that might be initially unpopular but would work well in the long run. The scope of government thus stays pretty much as is, given that politicians are usually too concerned with the next election to risk fundamental change. Of course, many analysts would argue that having officeholders constantly worrying about public opinion is good for democracy and that changes in the scope of government shouldn't be undertaken without extensive public consultation.

As you read this chapter, consider whether today's nomination and campaign process provides *too much* opportunity for interaction between the public and candidates for office. Also, consider whether the entire process takes too much time and costs too much money—two very important topics of debate in American politics today.

With about half a million elected officials in this country, there is always someone somewhere running for office. This chapter will focus mainly on the campaign for the world's most powerful office: the presidency of the United States. On some topics that are broadly generalizable, such as money and campaigning, we will include examples from congressional races as well. Chapter 12 will specifically discuss the congressional election process.

Campaigns in American politics can be divided into two stages: first, nominations, and second, campaigns between the two nominees. The prize for a nomination campaign is garnering a party's nod as its candidate; the prize for an Election Campaign is winning an office. This chapter discusses what happens up to election day. Chapter 10 explores how people decide whether to vote and whom to vote for.

The Nomination Game

nomination

The official endorsement of a candidate for office by a **political party**. Generally, success in the nomination game requires momentum, money, and media attention.

A **nomination** is a party's official endorsement of a candidate for office. Anyone can play the nomination game, but few have any serious chance of victory. Generally, success in the nomination game requires money, media attention, and momentum. **Campaign strategy** is the way in which candidates attempt to manipulate each of these elements to achieve the nomination.

Deciding To Run

campaign strategy

The master game plan candidates lay out to guide their electoral campaign.

Believe it or not, not every politician wants to run for president. One reason why is that campaigns have become more physically and emotionally taxing than ever. As former Speaker of the House Thomas Foley once said, "I know of any number of people who I think would make good presidents, even great presidents, who are deterred from running by the torture candidates are obliged to put themselves through."[2] Running for president is an around-the-clock endurance test for over a year: sleep deprivation and strange hotel beds, countless plane rides, junk food eaten on the run, a lack of regular exercise and copious amounts of stress. As 1984 Democratic nominee Walter Mondale once said, "For four years, that's all I did. I mean, all I did. That's all you think about. That's all you talk about. . . . That's your leisure. That's your luxury. . . . I told someone, 'The question is not whether I can get elected. The question is whether I can be elected and not be nuts when I get there.'"[3]

In most advanced industrialized countries, campaigns last no more than two months according to either custom and/or law. In contrast, American campaigns seem endless; a presidential candidacy needs to be either announced or an open secret for at least a year before the election. In the winter of 2003, it was already clear to most observers that John Kerry, Howard Dean, John Edwards, Joe Lieberman, Dick Gephardt, and others were laying the groundwork for a shot at the Democratic presidential nomination for 2004.

The road to the convention is long and full of stumbling blocks. From the convention, held in the summer of election years, only one candidate emerges as each party's nominee.

Competing For Delegates

national party convention

The supreme power within each of the parties. The convention meets every four years to nominate the party's presidential and vice-presidential candidates and to write the party's platform.

In some ways, the nomination game is tougher than the general election game; it whittles a large number of players down to two. The goal of the nomination game is to win the majority of delegates' support at the **national party convention**—the supreme power within each of the parties, which functions to select presidential and vice presidential candidates and to write a party platform.

There are 50 different roads to the national convention, one through each state. From February through June of the election year, the individual state parties busily choose their delegates to the national convention via either caucuses or primaries. Candidates try to ensure that delegates committed to them are chosen.

The Caucus Road. Before primaries existed, all state parties selected their delegates to the national convention in a meeting of state party leaders called a **caucus.** Sometimes one or two party "bosses" ran the caucus show, such as Mayor Daley of Chicago or Governor Connally of Texas. Such state party leaders could control who went to the convention and how the state's delegates voted once they got there. They were the kingmakers of presidential politics who met in smoke-filled rooms at the convention to cut deals and form coalitions.

caucus

A meeting of all state party leaders for selecting delegates to the **national party convention.** Caucuses are usually organized as a pyramid.

Today's caucuses are different from those of the past. In the dozen states that still have them, caucuses are now open to all voters who are registered with the party. Caucuses are usually organized like a pyramid. Small, neighborhood, precinct-level caucuses are held initially—often meeting in a church, an American Legion hall, or even someone's home. At this level, delegates are chosen, on the basis of their preference for a certain candidate, to attend county caucuses and then congressional district caucuses, where delegates are again chosen to go to a higher level—a state convention. At the state convention, which usually occurs months after the precinct caucuses, delegates are finally chosen to go to the national convention.

Since 1972 the state of Iowa has held the nation's first caucuses. Because the Iowa caucuses are the first test of the candidates' vote-getting ability, they usually become a full-blown media extravaganza.[4] Well-known candidates like Dick Gephardt in 2004 and John Glenn in 1984 have seen their campaigns virtually fall apart as a result of poor showings in Iowa. Most important, some candidates have received tremendous boosts from unexpected strong showings in Iowa. An obscure former Georgia governor named Jimmy Carter took his first big presidential step by winning there in 1976. Four years later, George Bush also made his first big step into the national scene with an upset victory over Ronald Reagan in Iowa. In 2004, John Kerry's surprise victory in Iowa gave newfound life to a campaign that had been on the ropes. Because of the impact that Iowa's first-in-the-nation caucus can have, candidates spend more time during the nomination season than they do in the big states like California, Texas, and Florida. Howard Dean and John Edwards went to the trouble of visiting each of Iowa's 99 counties in their efforts to win Iowa in 2004.

The Primary Road. Today, most of the delegates to the Democratic and Republican national conventions are selected in **presidential primaries,** in which voters in a state go to the polls and vote for a candidate or delegates pledged to that candidate. The presidential primary was promoted around the turn of the century by reformers who wanted to take nominations out of the hands of the party bosses. The reformers wanted to let the people vote for the candidate of their choice and then bind the delegates to vote for that candidate at the national convention.

presidential primaries

Elections in which voters in a state vote for a candidate (or delegates pledged to him or her). Most delegates to the **national party conventions** are chosen this way.

The increase in the number of presidential primaries occurred after the Democratic Party's disastrous 1968 national convention led many to rethink the delegate selection procedures then in place. As the war in Southeast Asia raged, another war of sorts took place in the streets of Chicago during the Democratic convention. Demonstrators against the war battled Mayor Richard Daley's Chicago police in what an official report later called a "police riot." Beaten up in the streets and defeated in the convention hall, the antiwar faction won one concession from the party regulars: a special committee to review the party's structure and delegate selection procedures, which they felt had discriminated against them. Minorities, women, youth, and other groups that had been poorly represented in the party leadership also demanded a more open process of convention delegate selection. The result was a committee of inquiry, which was chaired first by Senator George McGovern and later by

Televised debates have become a regular part of presidential primaries. Here, candidates for the 2004 Democratic nomination are shown participating in a TV forum.

McGovern-Fraser Commission

A commission formed at the 1968 Democratic convention in response to demands for reform by minority groups and others who sought better representation.

Representative Donald Fraser, who took over when McGovern left the committee to run for president.

The **McGovern-Fraser Commission** had a mandate to try to make Democratic Party conventions more representative. As a result of their decisions, no longer could party leaders handpick the convention delegates virtually in secret. All delegate selection procedures were required to be open, so that party leaders had no more clout than college students or anyone else who wanted to participate. One of the unforeseen results of these new rules was that many states decided that the easiest way to comply was simply to hold primary elections to select convention delegates.[5] Because state laws instituting primaries typically apply to selection of both parties' selection of delegates, the Republican Party's nomination process was similarly transformed.

Few developments have changed American politics as much as the proliferation of presidential primaries. Presidential election watcher Theodore White calls the primaries the "classic example of the triumph of goodwill over common sense." Says White,

Riots at the 1968 Democratic national convention led to the creation of the McGovern-Fraser Commission, which established open procedures and affirmative action guidelines for delegate selection. These reforms have made party conventions more representative than they once were.

delegates, who were supposed to be free to vote by their own common sense and conscience, have become for the most part anonymous faces, collected as background for the television cameras, sacks of potatoes packaged in primaries, divorced from party roots, and from the officials who rule states and nation.[6]

Whereas once many of the delegates were experienced politicians who knew the candidates, today they are typically people who have worked on a candidate's campaign and who owe their position as a delegate strictly to that candidate's ability to pull in primary votes.

The Democratic Party became so concerned about the lack of a role for party leaders at their conventions that starting in 1984 they automatically set aside about 15 percent of their delegate slots for public officeholders and party officials. These politicians who are awarded convention seats on the basis of their position are known as **superdelegates.** The addition of these delegates to the Democratic national convention was designed to restore an element of "peer review" to the process, ensuring participation of the people most familiar with the candidates. However, to date the primaries have proved to be far more crucial than the superdelegates.

The primary season begins during the winter in New Hampshire. Like the Iowa caucuses, the importance of New Hampshire is not the number of delegates or how representative the state is, but rather that it is traditionally the first primary.[7] At this early stage, the campaign is not for delegates, but for images—candidates want the rest of the country to see them as front-runners. The frenzy of political activity in this small state is given lavish attention in the national press. During the week of the primary, half the portable satellite dishes in the country can be found in Manchester, N. H., and the networks move their anchors and top reporters to the scene to broadcast the nightly news. In recent years, over a fifth of TV coverage of the nomination races has been devoted to the New Hampshire primary.[8]

At one time, it was considered advantageous for a state to choose its delegates late in the primary season so that it could play a decisive role. However, in recent years states that have held late primaries, such as Pennsylvania and New Jersey, have found their primary results irrelevant given that one candidate had already sewn up the nomination by the time their primaries were held. With so much attention being paid to the early contests, more states have moved their primaries up in the calendar to capitalize on the media attention. This **frontloading** of the process resulted in 71 percent of pledged Democratic delegates being chosen within six weeks of the New Hampshire primary in 2004. For 2008, at least one big state—California—has decided to move its primary back to the end of the calendar, as you can read about in "Issues of the Times: Will the Presidential Candidates Pay Any Attention to California in 2008?"

State laws determine how the delegates are allocated, operating within the general guidelines set by the parties. Some are closed to only people who are registered with the party, whereas others are open. The Democrats require all states to use some form of proportional representation in which a candidate who gets 15 percent or more of a state's vote is awarded a roughly proportional share of the delegates. The Republicans practice what they preach, giving states a large degree of discretion. Some states like California allocate all Republican delegates to whoever wins the most votes, others like Texas award delegates according to who wins each congressional district, and yet others employ some form of proportional representation.

Week after week, the primaries serve as elimination contests, as the media continually monitor the count of delegates won. The politicians, the press, and the public all love a winner. Candidates who fail to score early wins get labeled as losers and typically drop out of the race. Usually they have little choice since losing quickly inhibits a candidate's ability to raise the money necessary to win in other states. As one veteran fundraiser put it, "People don't lose campaigns. They run out of money and can't get their planes in the air. That's the reality."[9]

In the 1980 delegate chase, a commonly used football term became established in the language of American politics. After George Bush scored a surprise victory over

superdelegates

National party leaders who automatically get a delegate slot at the Democratic **national party convention.**

frontloading

The recent tendency of states to hold primaries early in the calendar in order to capitalize on media attention.

Why It Matters

Early Delegate Contests
In baseball, no one would declare a team out of the pennant race after it lost the first two games of the season. But in the race for the presidential nomination, the results of the Iowa caucus and the New Hampshire primary frequently end the campaigns of many candidates after only a handful of national delegates have been selected. These contests are important not because of the number of delegates that are chosen, but rather that they are the first indicators of public support. If a candidate does not do well in these first two contests, money and media attention dry up quickly.

Issues of the Times

The New York Times   nytimes.com

The Issue: Will the Presidential Candidates Pay Any Attention to California in 2008?

In 2004, states that failed to schedule their primary early in the calendar were irrelevant to the nomination process. Most of these states were stuck with dates that were traditional for them. Given the frontloading of the process, states that want to be influential have in recent decades moved their primary dates earlier and earlier. But as we look ahead to 2008, our nation's largest state—California—has surprised many observers by deciding to move its primary date three months later than it was in 2004. This represents the first time in recent history that a major state had moved its presidential primary date backwards. Whether or not this is good or bad for California, as well as the nation as a whole, is likely to be debated for the next several years.

Read All About It

California Moves To Reschedule Its Primary from March to June

By Dean E. Murphy
August 30, 2004

SACRAMENTO—The state that helped push the presidential primary season into a fast-forward frenzy more than a decade ago is now abruptly shifting it into reverse.

A bill that would move the California presidential primary to June from March beginning in 2008 breezed through the State Legislature this week with bipartisan support.

The move would amount to unconditional surrender by the country's most delegate-rich state in the contest to influence the presidential nomination process.

"It defies logic," said Robert D. Loevy, a professor of political science at Colorado College and a scholar of presidential primaries. "You would think in a democracy with a presidency which is the top governing officer that state legislatures would be working hard to see

their citizens have as much influence as possible."

California held a June primary for a half-century before the Legislature voted in 1993 to move the primary to March, largely in response to the so-called Super Tuesday primaries scheduled by Southern states in the 1980s, which were draining the California vote of its influence.

Please see California   Page 273

California

Continued from Page 272

For many years, the June date made California a kingmaker in both parties, as presidential candidates methodically worked their way West in a primary system that involved far fewer contests than today. California was crucial to Barry Goldwater against Nelson Rockefeller in 1964. But the last time California played a pivotal role was in 1984, when Walter F. Mondale emerged from a tight battle with Gary Hart for the Democratic nomination.

California backers of the original June date say the three presidential elections with a March primary—in 1996, 2000 and this year—show that it failed in reviving California's fortunes. In all three of those elections, either the parties had settled on a nominee before the March primary here or candidates chose to focus their attention on other states that had also moved their primaries forward—and are much smaller and cheaper to campaign in.

Even with the move to March, California found itself behind some 20 other states in a primary sweepstakes that has states already jockeying for advantage in 2008. In New Hampshire, which has the country's first primary, state law requires that the primary be held at least one week before any other state's.

"It is a constant friction with other states where people want to keep moving their primaries to an earlier date," said Art Torres, chairman of the California Democratic Party, who supports moving the date back to June. "By the time you are done, we will have primaries at Halloween. You can never win at that level."

To make matters worse, the March elections in California have been a flop among voters: turnout this March was the lowest for any presidential primary in the state's history in percentage terms, making it difficult for candidates for offices on the same ballot to rouse interest in their races.

"People realize the March primary has been a disaster," said Susie Swatt, chief of staff for State Senator Ross Johnson, the Orange County Republican who wrote the bill.

In 2002, the Legislature considered another solution: separating the presidential primary from the state primary. That way the presidential vote could be held in March—or even earlier—and the primary for state and local offices could return to June. But the added cost of holding two primaries was considered too prohibitive, and the bill was vetoed by Gov. Gray Davis.

Dan Schnur, who has worked on four presidential campaigns, including that of Senator John McCain in 2000, said the March date remained a big inconvenience for local and state campaigns, partic-

ularly because it means candidates must decide whether to run much earlier. But Mr. Schnur said the biggest losers have been the voters.

"The voters' body clocks aren't ready for politics the day after the bowl games end," said Mr. Schnur, who favored the switch to March but now prefers June.

Kathy Sullivan, chairwoman of the Democratic Party in New Hampshire, said part of her longs for the old days when New Hampshire held its primary in March (when there was less snow) and California held its in June (when the vote still mattered). Ms. Sullivan said those days were probably gone forever, but she said the primary system has compensated in a way that keeps California relevant.

"People have come to recognize in this process, and I think you saw it with the Democrats in the early states this year, that we need to nominate a candidate who is going to be able to run an effective race nationwide," Ms. Sullivan said. "So people were not necessarily choosing who is best for New Hampshire or Iowa or Michigan or South Carolina."

Professor Loevy said that should not be good enough for the country's most populous state. He said California's mistake in 1993 was not moving its primary even earlier. He said a Halloween election was preferable to one in June with no meaning.

"Now they are going in exactly the wrong direction," he said.

Think About It

- After the California legislature passed this bill, the *New York Times* wrote an editorial praising California for trying to reverse the pattern of front-loading of presidential primaries. Do you agree with the position of the *New York Times* editorial board that this was a good move on California's part?

- Do you think other states will now move their primary dates back for 2008? Should they? Why or why not?

For a number of months, Howard Dean's formidable fundraising and high poll standing made him the frontrunner in the race for the 2004 Democratic presidential nomination. But when he repeatedly screamed during a concession speech after the first delegate contest in Iowa, his reputation took a drastic hit from which his campaign never recovered.

American Electoral Rules:
How Do They Influence Campaigns?

Ronald Reagan in Iowa, he proudly claimed to possess "the big mo"—momentum. Actually, Bush had only a little "mo" and quickly fell victim to a decisive Reagan victory in New Hampshire. But the term neatly describes what candidates for the nomination are after. Primaries and caucuses are more than an endurance contest, though they are certainly that; they are also proving grounds. Week after week, the challenge is to do better than expected. Learning from his father's experience, George W. Bush jokingly told the reporters on his 2000 campaign plane to: "Please stow your expectations securely in your overhead bins, as they may shift during the trip and can fall and hurt someone—especially me."[10]

To get "mo" going, candidates have to beat people they were not expected to beat, collect margins above predictions, and—above all else—never lose to people they were expected to trounce. Momentum is good to have, but it is no guarantee of victory because candidates with a strong base sometimes bounce back. Political scientist Larry Bartels found that "substantive political appeal may overwhelm the impact of momentum."[11] Indeed, after being soundly trounced by John McCain in New Hampshire in 2000, George W. Bush quickly bounced back to win the big states necessary to get the Republican nomination.

Evaluating the Primary and Caucus System.   The primaries and the caucuses are here to stay. That reality does not mean, however, that political scientists or commentators are particularly happy with the system. Criticisms of this marathon campaign are numerous; here are a few of the most important:

- *Disproportionate attention goes to the early caucuses and primaries.* Take a look at Figure 9.1, which shows how critics think America's media-dominated campaigns are distorted by early primaries and caucuses. Neither New Hampshire nor Iowa is particularly representative of the national electorate. Both are rural, both have only small minority populations, and neither is at the center of the political mainstream. Whereas Iowa is more liberal than the nation as a whole, New Hampshire is the reverse. Although Iowa and New Hampshire are not always "make or break"

Figure 9.1   The Inflated Importance of Iowa and New Hampshire

In 2004, the Wisconsin Advertising Project found that 48 percent of the money spent by candidates for the Democratic nomination on TV ads were run in either Iowa or New Hampshire, even though these two small states selected only about 2 percent of the convention delegates. The incredible degree to which the candidates and the media focus on these two small states has become a regular feature of the presidential nominating process. Here, you can see a map of the 50 states drawn to scale in terms of the media attention their primaries and caucuses received in 1996; note how blown out of proportion Iowa and New Hampshire are on the map.

Source: Center for Media and Public Affairs, as reported in Harold W. Stanley and Richard G. Niemi, *Vital Statistics on American Politics,* 6th ed. (Washington, D.C.: Congressional Quarterly Press), 1998, 172–174.

contests, they play a key—and a disproportionate—role in building momentum, generating money, and generating media attention.

- *Prominent politicians find it difficult to take time out from their duties to run.* Running for the presidency has become a full-time job. It is hard to balance the demands of serving in high public office with running a presidential campaign. Of the six Democratic candidates for the presidency in 2004 who were serving in Congress, the average voting participation rate in 2003 was a mere 52 percent— far below the average congressional attendance rate of about 90 percent.[12]
- *Money plays too big a role in the caucuses and primaries.* Momentum means money—getting more of it than your opponents do. Many people think that money plays too large a role in American presidential elections. (This topic will be discussed in detail shortly.) Candidates who drop out early in the process often lament that their inability to raise money left them without a chance to compete.
- *Participation in primaries and caucuses is low and unrepresentative.* Although about 50 percent of the population votes in the November presidential election, only about 20 percent casts ballots in presidential primaries. Participation in caucus states is much smaller because a person must usually devote several hours to attending a caucus. Except for Iowa, where the extraordinary media attention usually boosts the participation, only about 5 percent of registered voters typically show up for caucuses. Moreover, voters in primaries and caucuses are hardly representative of voters at large; they tend to be older and more affluent than the typical citizen.
- *The system gives too much power to the media.* Critics contend that the media have replaced the party bosses as the new kingmakers. Deciding who has momentum at any given moment, the press readily labels candidates as winners and losers. The fact that the press accepted Bill Clinton's interpretation of his second-place finish in New Hampshire as a great comeback may well have saved his campaign in 1992.

Is this the best way to pick a president? Critics think not and have come up with a number of reform proposals (see "You Are the Policymaker: National and Regional Presidential Primary Proposals").

You Are the Policymaker

National and Regional Presidential Primary Proposals

The idea of holding a **national primary** to select party nominees has been discussed virtually ever since state primaries were introduced. In 1913, President Woodrow Wilson proposed it in his first message to Congress. Since then over 250 proposals for a national presidential primary have been introduced in Congress. These proposals do not lack public support; opinion polls have consistently shown that a substantial majority of Democrats, Republicans, and Independents alike favor such reform.

According to its proponents, a national primary would bring directness and simplicity to the process for the voters as well as the candidates. The length of the campaign would be shortened, and no longer would votes in one state have more political impact than votes in another. The concentration of media coverage on this one event, say its advocates, would increase not only political interest in the nomination decision but also public understanding of the issues involved.

A national primary would not be so simple, respond the critics. Because Americans would not want a candidate nominated with 25 percent of the vote from among a field of six candidates, in most primaries a runoff election between the top two finishers in each party would have to be held. So much for making the campaign simpler,

national primary critics note. Each voter would have to vote three times for president—twice in the primaries and once in November.

Another common criticism of a national primary is that only well-established politicians would have a shot at breaking through in such a system. Big money and big attention from the national media would become more crucial than ever. Obscure candidates, such as Jimmy Carter or Bill Clinton, would never have a chance. Do Americans, however, really want politicians without an established reputation to become president?

Perhaps more feasible than a national primary is holding a series of **regional primaries** in which, say, states in the eastern time zone would vote one week, those in the central time zone the next, and so on. This would impose a more rational structure and cut down on candidate travel. A regional primary system would also put an end to the jockeying between states for an advantageous position in the primary season. After the 2000 campaign was over, the National Association of Secretaries of State—the organization of the leading election officials of the states—endorsed a plan to establish regional primaries.

The major problem with the regional primary proposal, however, is the

advantage gained by whichever region goes first. For example, if the Western states were the first to vote, any candidate from California would have a clear edge in building momentum. Although most of the proposed plans call for the order of the regions to be determined by lottery, this would not erase the fact that regional advantages would surely be created from year to year.

Another prominent proposal is to have states vote in four stages according to their population size, with the least populous states leading off and the big states like California and Texas voting last. Such a proposal received serious consideration from the Republican National Committee in 2000 and was about to be voted on at the convention until George W. Bush let it be known that he did not favor it. Bush expressed concern that the plan would be unworkable because candidates would be asked to campaign all over the country in each stage.

Put yourself in the role of policymaker. Do the advantages of the reform proposals outweigh the disadvantages? Would any of them represent an improvement over the current system? Keep in mind that there are almost always unintended consequences associated with reforms.

---

national primary

A proposal by critics of the **caucuses** and **presidential primaries**, which would replace these electoral methods with a nationwide **primary** held early in the election year.

Barring some major reform, states will continue to select delegates in primaries and caucuses who will attend the national conventions, where the nominees are formally chosen.

The Convention Send-off

At one time party conventions provided great drama. Great speeches were given, dark-horse candidates suddenly appeared, and numerous ballots were held as candidates jockeyed to win the nomination. It took the Democrats 46 ballots in 1912, 44 in 1920, and a record 103 in 1924 to nominate their presidential standard bearer. Multiballot conventions died out after 1952, however, with the advent of television.

Today, the drama has largely been drained from the conventions because the winner is a foregone conclusion. No longer can a powerful governor shift a whole block of votes at the last minute. Delegates selected in primaries and open caucuses have known preferences. The last time there was any doubt about who would win at the convention was in 1976, when Gerald Ford barely edged out Ronald Reagan for the Republican nomination.

Without such drama, the networks have substantially scaled back the number of hours of coverage in recent years, as you can see in Figure 9.2. Even with the condensed TV coverage, the Nielsen ratings have fallen to abysmal levels.[13] The biggest convention audience in 2000 occurred when 22 million viewers tuned in to watch Al Gore's speech to the Democratic convention, which was covered by all the major broadcast networks as well as the cable news channels. By contrast, the next week CBS alone got 58 million viewers for its final episode of "Survivor."

Although conventions are no longer very interesting, they are a significant rallying point for the parties. As George W. Bush said prior to the Republican convention in 2000, "The convention system provides a system of rewards for hardworking, grassroots people who end up being delegates. I view it as an opportunity for these people to go back home, energized to help me get elected."[14] Modern conventions are carefully scripted to present the party in its best light. Delegates are no longer there to argue for their causes but merely to support their candidate. The parties carefully orchestrate a massive send-off for the presidential and vice-presidential candidates. The party's leaders are there in force, as are many of its most important followers—people whose input will be critical during the general election campaign.

The conventions are also important in developing the party's policy positions and in promoting political representation. In the past, conventions were essentially an

regional primaries

A proposal by critics of the **caucuses** and **presidential primaries** to replace these electoral methods with a series of primaries held in each geographic region.

Figure 9.2   The Declining Coverage of Conventions on Network TV

Believe it or not, Democratic and Republican conventions once got far more coverage on the major networks (CBS, NBC, and ABC) than the Summer Olympics. As the number of presidential primaries has increased, however, nominations have come to be decided in these contests. Thus, by the time the conventions are held, there is little element of political suspense. Hence, the networks have drastically cut back on their coverage of these events, as you can see in the data displayed here.

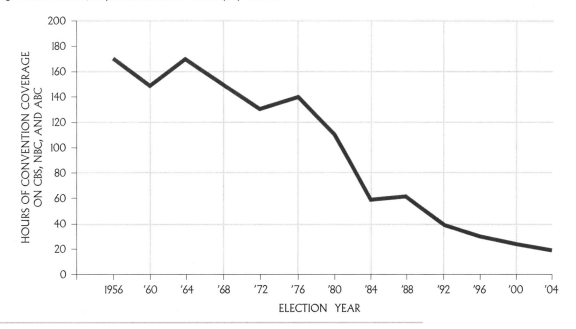

Source: For 1956–1984, calculated from data reported in Byron E. Schafer, *Bifurcated Politics: Evolution and Reform in the National Party Convention* (Cambridge, MA: Harvard University Press, 1988), 274; updated by the authors for 1988 through 2004.

assembly of party leaders, gathered together to bargain over the selection of the party's ticket. Almost all delegates were White, male, and over 40. Lately, party reformers, especially among the Democrats, have worked hard to make the conventions far more demographically representative. Meeting in an oversized, overstuffed convention hall in a major city, a national convention is a short-lived affair. The highlight of the first day is usually the keynote speech, in which a dynamic speaker recalls party heroes, condemns the opposition party, and touts the nominee apparent.

The second day centers on the **party platform**—the party's statement of its goals and policies for the next four years. The platform is drafted prior to the convention by a committee whose members are chosen in rough proportion to each candidate's strength. Any time over 20 percent of the delegates to the platform committee disagree with the majority, they can bring an alternative minority plank to the convention floor for debate. In former times, contests over the platform were key tests of candidates' strength before the actual nomination. When a peace plank failed to be adopted by the 1968 Democratic national convention it was clear that Vice President Hubert Humphrey would defeat antiwar candidate Eugene McCarthy. In contrast, recent contests over the platform have served mostly as a way for the minority factions in the party to make sure that their voices are heard. Since 1992, pro-choice Republicans have tried in vain every four years to force a vote on the solidly antiabortion plank in the GOP platform. Fearing the negative publicity the party would incur by showing open disagreement on this emotionally charged issue, pro-choice Republican leaders have dissuaded delegates from forcing such a confrontation.

The third day of the convention is devoted to formally nominating a candidate for president. One of each candidate's eminent supporters gives a speech extolling the candidate's virtues; a string of seconding speeches then follow. Toward the end of the evening, balloting begins as states announce their votes. After all the votes are counted, the long-anticipated nomination becomes official.

The vice-presidential nominee is chosen by roll call vote on the convention's final day, though custom dictates that delegates simply vote for whomever the presidential nominee recommends. The vice-presidential candidate then comes to the podium to

party platform

A political party's statement of its goals and policies for the next four years. The platform is drafted prior to the party convention by a committee whose members are chosen in rough proportion to each candidate's strength. It is the best formal statement of a party's beliefs.

In writing a party platform, disagreements between various factions of the party often become evident. In recent years, Ann Stone has led a movement of Republican women in favor of a pro-choice plank on abortion. Although Ann Stone's efforts have received a fair amount of media attention, she has been unsuccessful in getting the Republican convention to consider changing its pro-life platform.

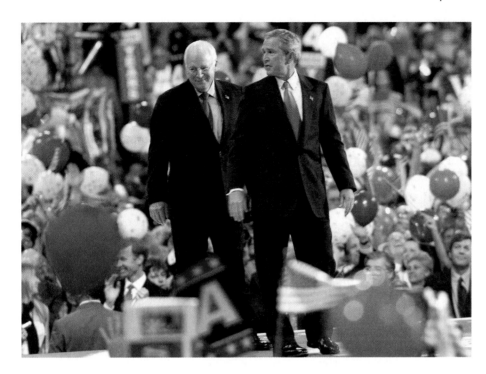

The first major decision that any new nominee for the presidency has to make is whom to recommend to the convention for vice president. In 2000, George W. Bush put Richard Cheney in charge of his search process to evaluate possible candidates for vice president. In working closely with Cheney, Bush ultimately decided that he would like Cheney to fill the role.

make a brief acceptance speech. This speech is followed by the grand finale—the presidential candidate's acceptance speech, in which the battle lines for the coming campaign are drawn. Afterward, all the party leaders come out to congratulate the party's ticket, raise their hands, and bid the delegates farewell.

The Campaign Game

Once nominated, candidates concentrate on campaigning for the general election. These days, the word *campaign* is part of the American political vocabulary, but it was not always so. The term was originally a military one: Generals mounted campaigns, using their scarce resources to achieve strategic objectives. Political campaigns proceed in a similar fashion, with candidates allocating their scarce resources of time, money, and energy to achieve their political objectives.

Campaigns involve more than organization and leadership. Artistry also enters the picture, for campaigns deal in images. The campaign is the canvas on which political strategists try to paint portraits of leadership, competence, caring, and other images Americans value in presidents. Campaigning today is an art and a science, heavily dependent—like much else in American politics—on technology.

The High-Tech Media Campaign

The new machines of politics have changed the way campaigns are run. During the first half of the twentieth century, candidates and their entourage piled onto a campaign train and tried to speak to as many people as time, energy, and money would allow. Voters journeyed from miles around to see a presidential whistle-stop tour go by and to hear a few words in person from the candidate. Today, television is the most prevalent means used by candidates to reach voters. Thomas Patterson stresses that "today's presidential campaign is essentially a mass media campaign. . . . It is no exaggeration to say that, for the majority of voters, the campaign has little reality apart

Technology has changed the way campaigns are run and the way candidates attempt to reach the people. Most serious candidates for a major office these days have their own official website. This provides an effective way to make their policy positions available for anyone interested. Here, you can see the front page of Representative Stephanie Herseth's website.

Television and Presidential Campaigns

direct mail

A high-tech method of raising money for a political cause or candidate. It involves sending information and requests for money to people whose names appear on lists of those who have supported similar views or candidates in the past.

from its media version."[15] Technology has made it possible for candidates to speak directly to the American people in the comfort of their living rooms, or in front of their computer monitors. At the grass-roots level, some candidates now distribute videotapes of themselves speaking rather than the old-fashioned political pamphlet. During the 2004 New Hampshire primary, Howard Dean's campaign passed out 75,000 videotape copies of Diane Sawyer's interview with Dean and his wife, in which they tried to soften his image.

The computer revolution has also now overtaken political campaigns. At the end of the first presidential debate in 1996, Bob Dole encouraged viewers to go to his website for more information on his issue stands. So many people immediately tried to check it out that the server soon crashed. Following his stunning win in the 2000 New Hampshire primary, John McCain's campaign received millions of dollars in donations through its website in just a few days. Howard Dean's recent record fund-raising for a Democrat was powered by small donations via the Internet; and once John Kerry sewed up the 2004 Democratic nomination, his campaign successfully copied the Dean campaign's methods for Internet fund-raising. There is little doubt that the Internet will play an increasingly important role in the campaigns of the twenty-first century.

One of the most important uses of computer technology in campaigns thus far has been the use of targeted mailings to prospective supporters. The technique of **direct mail** involves locating potential supporters by sending information and a request for money to huge lists of people who have supported candidates of similar views in the past. Conservative fund-raiser Richard Viguerie pioneered the mass-mailing list, including in his computerized list the names and addresses of hundreds of thousands of individuals who contributed to conservative causes. The accumulation of mailing lists enables candidates to pick almost any issue, be it helping the homeless, opposing abortion, aiding Israel, or anything else, and write to a list of people concerned about that issue. Direct mail induces millions of people each year to contribute over $1 billion to various candidates and political causes.[16] The high-tech campaign is no longer a luxury. Candidates *must* use the media and computer technology just to stay competitive.

The most important goal of any media campaign is simply to get attention. Media coverage is determined by two factors: (1) how candidates use their advertising budget and (2) the "free" attention they get as newsmakers. The first, obviously, is relatively easy to control; the second is more difficult but not impossible. Almost every logistical decision in a campaign—where to eat breakfast, whom to include on the rostrum, when to announce a major policy proposal—is calculated according to its intended media impact. In the first half of the twentieth century, the biggest item in a campaign budget might have been renting a railroad train. Today the major item is unquestionably television advertising. At least half the total budget for a presidential or U.S. Senate campaign will be used for television advertising.

Simulation

You Are a Media Consultant
to a Political Candidate

Many observers worry that we have entered a new era of politics in which the slick slogan and the image salesperson dominates—an era when Madison Avenue is more influential than Main Street. Most political scientists, however, are concluding that such fears are overblown. Research has shown that campaign advertising can be a source of information about issues as well as about images. Thomas Patterson and Robert McClure examined the information contained in TV advertising and found that viewers learned more about candidates' stands on the issues from watching their ads than from watching the nightly news. Most news coverage stresses where the candidates went, how big their crowds were, and other campaign details. Only rarely do the networks delve into where the candidates stand on the issues. In contrast, political ads typically address issues; a study of 230,000 candidate ads that ran in 1998 found that spots that emphasized policy outnumbered those that stressed personal image by a 6 to 1 ratio.[17] Most candidates apparently believe that their policy positions are a crucial part of their campaign, and they are willing to pay substantial sums to communicate them to voters.

Candidates have much less control over the other aspect of the media, news coverage. To be sure, most campaigns have press aides who feed "canned" news releases to reporters. Still, the media largely determine for themselves what is happening in a campaign. Campaign coverage seems to be a constant interplay between hard news about what candidates say and do and the human interest angle, which most journalists think sells newspapers or interests television viewers.

Apparently, news organizations believe that policy issues are of less interest to voters than the campaign itself. The result is that news coverage is disproportionately devoted to campaign strategies, speculation about what will happen next, poll results, and other aspects of the campaign game. Patterson tabulated the amount of media attention to the campaign itself and the amount of attention to such substantive issues as the economy in the 1976 presidential race. Examining several newspapers and news magazines as well as television network news, he found that attention to the "game" far exceeded attention to substance, and subsequent research through the 2000 election has found that this pattern continues to hold true.[18] Once a candidate has taken a policy position and it has been reported, it becomes old news. The latest poll showing Smith ahead of Jones is thus more newsworthy in the eyes of the media. Republican media consultant Roger Ailes calls this his "orchestra pit" theory of American politics: "If you have two guys on stage and one guy says, 'I have a solution to the Middle East problem,' and the other guy falls in the orchestra pit, who do you think is going to be on the evening news?"[19]

Organizing the Campaign

In every campaign, there is too much to do and too little time to do it. Every candidate must prepare for nightly banquets and endless handshaking. More important, to organize their campaigns effectively, candidates must do the following:

Simulation

You Are a Professional
Campaign Manager

- *Get a campaign manager.* Some candidates try to run their own campaign, but they usually end up regretting it. A professional campaign manager can keep the

Making a Difference

Mary Beth Cahill and the Kerry Campaign

Mary Beth Cahill is credited by many observers for turning around John Kerry's campaign for the 2004 Democratic nomination. When she took over the job of Kerry's campaign manager in November 2003, the campaign had developed a reputation for being disorganized, with no one clearly being in charge. On her first day she laid down the law that she would be in charge from now on and that anyone who had a problem with this should quit immediately. A few did, but most stayed on. Cahill's contribution from then on was not any brilliant innovative strategy, but rather simply keeping the campaign on track and staying on message. Doing so in any campaign is always easier said than done, and in steadily guiding the Kerry campaign for the Democratic nomination Mary Beth Cahill surely made a difference.

Simulation

You Are a Presidential
Campaign Consultant

candidate from getting bogged down in organizational details. This person also bears the day-to-day responsibility for keeping the campaign square on its message

and setting its tone (see "Making a Difference: Mary Beth Cahill and the Kerry Campaign").

- *Get a fund-raiser.* Money, as this chapter will soon discuss in detail, is an important key to election victory.
- *Get a campaign counsel.* With all the current federal regulation of campaign financing, legal assistance is essential to ensure compliance with the laws.
- *Hire media and campaign consultants.* Candidates have more important things to do with their time than plan ad campaigns, contract for buttons and bumper stickers, and buy TV time and newspaper space. Professionals can get them the most exposure for their money.
- *Assemble a campaign staff.* It is desirable to hire as many professionals as the campaign budget allows, but it is also important to get a coordinator of volunteers to ensure that envelopes are licked, doorbells rung, and other small but vital tasks addressed. Many campaign volunteers are typically young people, who are the most likely to have the energy for this sort of work. However, in recent years high school seniors have expressed less and less interest in participating in campaigns (see "Young People and Politics: Declining Interest in Working in Campaigns").
- *Plan the logistics.* A modern presidential campaign involves jetting around the country at an incredible pace.

Good advance people handle the complicated details of candidate scheduling and see to it that events are well publicized and well attended.

- *Get a research staff and policy advisers.* Candidates have little time to master the complex issues reporters will ask about. Policy advisers—often distinguished academics—feed them the information they need to keep up with events.
- *Hire a pollster.* Dozens of professional polling firms conduct opinion research to tell candidates how the voters view them and what is on the voters' minds.
- *Get a good press secretary.* Candidates running for major office have reporters dogging them every step of the way. The reporters need news, and a good press secretary can help them make their deadlines with stories that the campaign would like to see reported.
- *Establish a website.* A website is a relatively inexpensive way of getting a candidate's message out.

Most of these tasks cost money. Campaigns are not cheap, and the role of money in campaigns is a controversial one.

Money and Campaigning

There is no doubt that campaigns are expensive and, in America's high-tech political arena, growing more so. As the old saying goes, "Money is the mother's milk of politics." Candidates need money to build a campaign organization and to get their message out. Many people and groups who want certain things from the government are all too willing to give it; thus, there is the common perception that money buys votes and influence. The following sections examine the role of money in campaigns.

Young People and Politics

Declining Interest in Working in Campaigns

Walk into any campaign headquarters and chances are good that you'll find a lot of young people at work. Many of our nation's leaders got their political start working in a campaign when they were young. If you want to get involved in politics as a possible career, this is where you begin. The work is often tedious, the hours are long, and the financial rewards are usually minimal. Hence, full-time campaign work is not really suitable for someone with an active career or for a retired person. Campaign jobs have been and likely will continue to be filled primarily by young people.

Nevertheless, as you can see in this figure, there has been a decline in interest in working on campaigns among high school seniors over the last quarter-century. Whereas between 15 to 20 percent of those interviewed in the late 1970s and early 1980s said they planned to work on a campaign or had already done so, in recent years only about 10 percent have expressed an interest in campaign work.

Questions for Discussion

- At the same time that young people have been expressing less interest in working on political campaigns, they have been volunteering for community organizations at record rates. Might the decline in interest in campaign work simply be because today's young people are focusing on nonpolitical forms of community action?
- Do you think that one reason young people may not be very interested in working in campaigns may be that the issues discussed in recent campaigns aren't of much interest to them? If so, what sort of issues might stimulate more young people to sign up for campaign work?
- If more young people were to volunteer for work in campaigns, what difference might it make? Do you think the tenor of recent campaigns would have been changed if more young people had been involved?

PLAN TO WORK ON A CAMPAIGN
OR HAVE DONE SO

2002	11.3
2001	9.9
2000	11.1
1999	9.4
1998	10.2
1997	12.3
1996	12.1
1995	11.0
1994	11.7
1993	13.7
1992	10.7
1991	10.5
1990	10.7
1989	13.2
1988	13.4
1987	14.5
1986	13.9
1985	15.7
1984	15.0
1983	15.7
1982	14.7
1981	17.4
1980	15.8
1979	17.2
1978	18.6
1977	20.3
1976	17.8

Source: Authors' analysis of annual Monitoring the Future national surveys of high school seniors.

The Maze of Campaign Finance Reforms

As the costs of campaigning skyrocketed with the growth of television, and as the Watergate scandal exposed large, illegal campaign contributions, momentum developed for campaign finance reform in the early 1970s. Several public interest lobbies (see Chapter 11), notably Common Cause and the National Committee for an Effective Congress, led the drive. In 1974, Congress passed the **Federal Election**

How You Can Make a Difference

Volunteering for Political Campaigns

In order to change how government operates or to maintain a desired policy, you generally have to get involved. Personal involvement in politics and the political system is important.

One way to do this is to volunteer on a political campaign. You may wish to help out at a local level by helping a candidate in a race for school board, city council, or mayor. For most local elections you can call the candidate yourself and offer your services. You may wish to work on a race for the state legislature. If you are interested in assisting a candidate for a major office, call the candidate's campaign headquarters and ask to talk with the volunteer coordinator. The campaigns for top tier political offices such as state governor, U.S. senator, U.S. congressperson,

or president are generally huge operations that require the assistance of numerous volunteers. Candidates for these offices will usually have a big campaign organization somewhere in your state and maybe smaller campaign headquarters in regional cities. You can find these by calling the candidate's local party office and asking where the election headquarters is located and how to contact it. Then talk with the volunteer coordinator at headquarters.

All political campaigns need volunteers, and campaign work is fun. You will meet all sorts of people from all over your city, your state, or the nation and make lots of new friends. You will do things like go door-to-door distributing campaign literature, put up yard signs, stuff envelopes, and answer tele-

phones at campaign headquarters. You'll play an important role in helping elect someone who will work for your ideals. Many colleges and universities offer credit for campaign work. Ask at your school. You can be an intern on a campaign, do a useful bit for democracy, earn college credits, and maybe even get paid.

What you can do:
- Call your local political party office (Democratic, Republican, Green, etc).
- Contact a candidate you support and volunteer your services.
- Contact your school's political science department to see if you can receive internship credit for your work.

Federal Election Campaign Act

A law passed in 1974 for reforming campaign finances. The act created the **Federal Election Commission** (FEC), provided public financing for presidential primaries and general elections, limited presidential campaign spending, required disclosure, and attempted to limit contributions.

Federal Election Commission (FEC)

A six-member bipartisan agency created by the **Federal Election Campaign Act** of 1974. The FEC administers and enforces campaign finance laws.

Presidential Election Campaign Fund

Money from the $3 federal income tax check-off goes into this fund, which is then distributed to qualified candidates to subsidize their presidential campaigns.

Campaign Act. It had two main goals: tightening reporting requirements for contributions and limiting overall expenditures. The 1974 act and its subsequent amendments:

- *created the **Federal Election Commission** (FEC).* A bipartisan body, the six-member FEC administers the campaign finance laws and enforces compliance with their requirements.
- *created the **Presidential Election Campaign Fund.*** The Federal Election Commission is in charge of doling out money from this fund to qualified presidential candidates. Money for this fund is raised via a $3 voluntary check-off box on income tax returns, which currently only about 11 percent of taxpayers do (see Figure 9.3).
- *provided partial public financing for presidential primaries.* Presidential candidates who raise $5,000 on their own in at least 20 states can get individual contributions of up to $250 matched by the federal treasury. Money received at this stage of the campaign is commonly known as **matching funds.** If presidential candidates accept federal support, they agree to limit their campaign expenditures to an amount prescribed by federal law. For 2004, this amounted to approximately $45 million in the primaries. Because of this limit, President Bush, Senator Kerry, and Governor Dean all decided not to accept matching funds during the 2004 primaries.
- *provided full public financing for major party candidates in the general election.* For the general election, each major party nominee gets a fixed amount of money to cover all their campaign expenses. For 2004 this amounted to $75 million. Unlike in the primaries, the FEC pays all the costs of general election campaigns, thereby making the offer too good for anyone to turn down. Thus, although George W. Bush and John Kerry each decided not to accept federal support in the campaign

Figure 9.3   The Decline in Income Tax Check-off Participation for Federal Financing of Campaigns

This figure displays the percentage of income tax filers checking off the voluntary box to contribute to the federal financing of presidential campaigns. By checking this box, taxpayers do *not* add to their tax bill but simply specify that they would like $3 of their taxes to go to this fund. As you can see from the data displayed here, the percentage of taxpayers who have checked this box has declined substantially since this program was created in the mid-1970s. Because of a shortage of funds, all the candidates who were accepting matching funds received slightly less than half the money they were entitled to in February 2004. They either had to take bank loans, using the money owed to them by the Federal Election Commission as collateral, or wait until the funds became available.

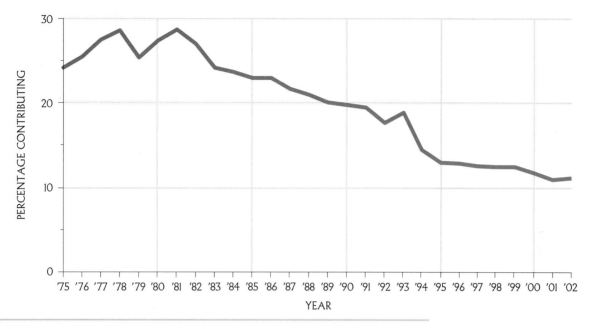

Source: Campaign Finance Institute.

for their party's nomination, they followed the practice of all previous major party nominees in taking federal money for the fall campaign.

- *required full disclosure.* Regardless of whether they accept any federal funding, all candidates for federal office must file periodic reports with the FEC, listing who contributed and how the money was spent. In the spirit of immediate disclosure, some 2004 presidential candidates regularly posted updated campaign contribution information on their websites.

- *limited contributions.* Scandalized to find out that some wealthy individuals had contributed $1 million to the 1972 Nixon campaign, Congress limited individual contributions to presidential and congressional candidates to $1,000. The McCain-Feingold Act increased this limit to $2,000 as of 2004, and provided for it to be indexed to rise along with inflation in the future.

Although the 1974 campaign reforms were generally welcomed by both parties, the constitutionality of the Federal Election Campaign Act was challenged in the 1976 case of *Buckley v. Valeo.* In this case the Supreme Court struck down, as a violation of free speech, the portion of the act that had limited the amount individuals could contribute to their own campaigns. This aspect of the Court ruling made it possible for Ross Perot to spend over $60 million of his own fortune on his independent presidential candidacy in 1992, and for John Kerry to loan his campaign over $7 million for the 2004 Democratic nomination contest.

Another loophole was opened in 1979 with an amendment to the original act that made it easier for political parties to raise money for voter registration drives and the distribution of campaign material at the grass-roots level or for generic party advertising. Money raised for such purposes is known as **soft money** and is not subject to

matching funds

Contributions of up to $250 are matched from the Presidential Election Campaign Fund to candidates for the presidential nomination who qualify and agree to meet various conditions, such as limiting their overall spending.

soft money

Political contributions earmarked for party-building expenses at the grass-roots level or for generic party advertising. Unlike money that goes to the campaign of a particular candidate, such party donations are not subject to contribution limits. For a time, such contributions were unlimited, until they were banned by the McCain-Feingold Act.

AT LAST, BIPARTISANSHIP...

MCCAIN-FEINGOLD LOOPHOLE LAB

3·22·02 THE PHILADELPHIA INQUIRER. UNIVERSAL PRESS SYNDICATE.

any contribution limits. In 2000, an unprecedented amount of money flowed into the coffers of the national parties through this loophole. Nearly half a billion dollars was raised by the two parties in 2000 via soft money contributions, with many of the contributions coming in increments of hundreds of thousands of dollars. AT&T alone gave over $3 million in soft money, as did the American Federation of State, County, and Municipal Employees.

Senators John McCain (R-AZ) and Russell Feingold (D-WI) crusaded for years to remove the taint of large soft money campaign contributions from the political system. Their efforts finally came to fruition in 2002 when their bill was passed by the Congress and signed into law by President George W. Bush. The McCain-Feingold Act: (1) banned soft money contributions; (2) increased the amount that individuals could give to candidates from $1000 to $2000 and indexed the latter amount to rise in the future along with inflation; and (3) barred groups from running "issue ads" within 60 days of a general election if they refer to a federal candidate and are not funded through a PAC (i.e., with funds regulated by the campaign finance system). These provisions were challenged in the Courts, and in the 2003 case of *McConnell v. Federal Election Commission* the Supreme Court ruled in favor of the new law by a 5-4 margin.

Overall, there is little doubt that campaign finance legislation since 1974 has made campaigns more open and honest. Small donors are encouraged, and the rich are restricted—at least in terms of the money they can give directly to a candidate. All contribution and expenditure records are now open for all to examine, and FEC auditors try to make sure that the regulations are enforced. As Frank Sorauf writes, the detailed FEC reports have "become a wonder of the democratic political world. Nowhere else do scholars and journalists find so much information about the funding of campaigns, and the openness of Americans about the flow of money stuns many other nationals accustomed to silence and secrecy about such traditionally private matters."[20]

The Proliferation of PACs

The campaign reforms of the 1970s also encouraged the spread of **political action committees,** generally known as PACs. Before the 1974 reforms, corporations were technically forbidden to donate money to political campaigns, but many wrote big

Political Action Committees (PACs)

Funding vehicles created by the 1974 campaign finance reforms. A corporation, union, or some other interest group can create a PAC and register it with the **Federal Election Commission (FEC)**, which will meticulously monitor the PAC's expenditures.

When President Clinton was in the White House, he regularly allowed big donors of soft money contributions to the Democratic Party to spend a night in the famous Lincoln bedroom (shown here). This practice was highly criticized and led to increased support for banning the practice of unlimited soft money contributions to the parties.

checks anyway. Unions could make indirect contributions, although limits were set on how they could aid candidates and political parties. The 1974 reforms created a new, more open way for interest groups such as business and labor to contribute to campaigns. Any interest group, large or small, can now get into the act by forming its own PAC to directly channel contributions of up to $5,000 per candidate in both the primary and the general election.

Buckley v. Valeo extended the right of free speech to PACs, and they can now spend unlimited amounts indirectly, that is, if such activities are not coordinated with the campaign. For example, in 1988 it was a PAC that aired the infamous "Willie Horton" ad accusing Democratic candidate Michael Dukakis of allowing criminals such as Horton out on parole, during which time they committed other crimes. Because the ad showed a sinister looking photo of the African-American Horton, many thought it was a veiled attempt to stimulate racist feelings. The Bush campaign responded to such criticism by saying there was nothing they could do about the ad because it was sponsored by a PAC who had not coordinated it with them.

As of 2004, the FEC reported that there were 3,868 PACs. In the 2002 congressional elections, PACs contributed over $258 million to House and Senate candidates. A PAC is formed when a business association, or some other interest group, decides to contribute to candidates whom it believes will be favorable toward its goals. The group registers as a PAC with the FEC and then puts money into the PAC coffers. The PAC can collect money from stockholders, members, and other interested parties. It then donates the money to candidates, often after careful research on their issue stands and past voting records. One very important ground rule prevails: All expenditures must be meticulously reported to the FEC. If PACs are corrupting democracy, as many believe, at least they are doing so openly.

Visual Literacy

PACs and the Money Trails

Candidates need PACs because high-tech campaigning is expensive. Tightly contested races for the House of Representatives can sometimes cost over $1 million; Senate races can easily cost $1 million for television alone. PACs play a major role in paying for expensive campaigns. Thus there emerges a symbiotic relationship between the PACs and the candidates: Candidates need money, which they insist can be used without compromising their integrity; PACs want access to officeholders, which they insist can be gained without buying votes. Most any lobbyist will tell their clients that politicians will listen to any important interest group but that with a sizable PAC donation they'll listen better.

There is an abundance of PACs willing to help out the candidates. There are big PACs, such as the Realtors Political Action Committee and the American Medical Association Political Action Committee. There are little ones, too, representing smaller

Why It Matters

Money and Elections
As the 2004 primaries approached, most pundits argued that any serious candidate for the presidency needed to raise $15 million by the end of 2003 in order to be classified as a serious contender. Raising money is one concrete indicator of support before the first votes are cast. In addition, money provides a campaign with the ability to hire sufficient staff and advertising time to get its message out. A campaign that is short on money can hardly get its message out.

Participation

The Debate over Campaign Finance Reform

industries or business associations: EggPAC, FishPAC, FurPAC, LardPAC, and—for the beer distributors, SixPAC.[21] Table 9.1 lists the business, labor, and ideological PACs that gave the most money to congressional candidates in 2000 and shows which party each favored.

Critics of the PAC system worry that all this money leads to PAC control over what the winners do once in office. Archibald Cox and Fred Wertheimer write that the role of PACs in campaign finance "is robbing our nation of its democratic ideals and giving us a government of leaders beholden to the monied interests who make their election possible."[22] On some issues, it seems clear that PAC money has made a difference. The Federal Trade Commission, for example, once passed a regulation requiring that car dealers list known mechanical defects on the window stickers of used cars. The National Association of Automobile Dealers quickly became one of the largest donors to congressional incumbents, contributing just over $1 million to candidates of both parties. Soon afterward, 216 representatives cosponsored a House resolution nullifying the FTC regulation. Of these House members, 186 had been aided by the auto dealers' PAC.[23]

It is questionable, however, whether such examples are the exception or the rule. Most PACs give money to candidates who agree with them in the first place. For instance, the antiabortion PACs will not waste their money supporting pro-choice candidates. Frank Sorauf's careful review of the subject concludes that "there simply are no data in the systematic studies that would support the popular assertions about the 'buying' of the Congress or about any other massive influence of money on the legislative process."[24]

The impact of PAC money on presidents is even more doubtful. Presidential campaigns, of course, are partly subsidized by the public and so are less dependent upon PACs. Moreover, presidents have well-articulated positions on most important issues. A small contribution from any one PAC is not likely to turn a presidential candidate's head.

Money matters in campaigns and sometimes also during legislative votes. Although the influence of PACs may be exaggerated, the high cost of running for office ensures their continuing major role in the campaign process.

Are Campaigns Too Expensive?

Every four years, Americans spend over $2 billion on national, state, and local elections. This seems like a tremendous amount of money. Yet American elections cost, per person, about as much as a DVD movie. Bradley Smith, who currently serves as commissioner on the Federal Election Commission, writes that the proportion of the nation's GDP spent on political activity is a mere .05 percent.[25]

What bothers politicians most about the rising costs of high-tech campaigning is that fund-raising takes up so much of their time. Many American officeholders feel that the need for continuous fund-raising distracts them from their jobs as legislators. They look with envy at how politicians in other countries can win major office without worrying about raising huge sums of money (see "America in Perspective: Arlene McCarthy's Election to the European Parliament").

Public financing of congressional campaigns would take care of this problem. Some lawmakers support some sort of public financing reform; however, it will be very difficult to get Congress to consent to equal financing for the people who will challenge them for their seats. Incumbents will not readily give up the advantage they have in raising money.

Perhaps the most basic complaint about money and politics is that there may be a direct link between dollars spent and votes received. Few have done more to dispel this charge than political scientist Gary Jacobson. His research has shown that "the more incumbents spend, the worse they do."[26] This fact is not as odd as it sounds. It simply

Table 9.1 The Big-Spending PACs

According to an analysis of Federal Election Commission data by the Center for Responsive Politics, here are the largest business, labor, and ideological/single-issue PAC contributors to congressional candidates for the 1999–2000 election cycle and the percentage that they gave to Republicans.

	AMOUNT CONTRIBUTED	PERCENTAGE GIVEN TO REPUBLICANS
Business		
Microsoft	$3,942,435	53
Goldman Sachs Group	3,546,432	32
AT&T	3,510,391	62
National Association of Realtors	3,298,100	58
Association of Trial Lawyers	2,951,500	12
United Parcel Service	2,919,584	74
Philip Morris	2,830,985	80
Labor		
American Federation of State/County/Municipal Employees	6,500,889	1
Service Employees International Union	4,724,664	4
Communication Workers of America	3,687,614	1
International Brotherhood of Electrical Workers	3,369,840	3
United Food and Commercial Workers Union	3,242,057	1
Ideological/Single-Issue		
National Rifle Association	2,884,127	92
Emily's List	1,979,829	0

Source: Center for Responsive Politics.

means that incumbents who face a tough opponent must raise more money to meet the challenge. When a challenger is not a serious threat, as they all too often are not, incumbents can afford to campaign cheaply.

More important than having "more" money is having "enough" money. Herbert Alexander calls this "the doctrine of sufficiency." As he writes, "Enough money must be spent to get a message across to compete effectively but outspending one's opponent is not always necessary—even an incumbent with a massive ratio of higher spending."[27] One case in point is that of the late Paul Wellstone, a previously obscure political science professor who beat an incumbent senator in 1990 despite being outspent by 5 to 1. Another example is the 1994 California Senate race, in which Dianne Feinstein prevailed even though she was outspent by Republican challenger Michael Huffington, who poured $28 million of his own money into the race.

The Impact of Campaigns

Almost all politicians presume that a good campaign is the key to victory. Many political scientists, however, question the importance of campaigns. Reviewing the evidence, Dan Nimmo concluded, "Political campaigns are less crucial in elections than most politicians believe."[28] For years, researchers studying campaigns have stressed that campaigns have three effects on voters: reinforcement, activation, and conversion. Campaigns can reinforce voters' preferences for candidates; they can activate voters, getting them to contribute money or ring doorbells as opposed to merely voting; and they can convert, changing voters' minds.

Over half a century of research on political campaigns leads to a single message: Campaigns mostly reinforce and activate; only rarely do they convert. The evidence on

America in Perspective

Arlene McCarthy's Election to the European Parliament

Arlene McCarthy is one of Europe's up-and-coming young politicians. She was first elected to represent England in the European Parliament at the age of 33, and since then she has twice been easily reelected. When asked if she could have won a similar election in the United States, she responds with a firm "No—I would never have been able to raise enough money."

A substantial bankroll, however, was not required for Ms. McCarthy to get her start in European politics. All told, she estimates that she spent about $1,600 to get the Labour Party's nomination in her district. Of this, roughly half was spent on new clothes, with the rest going for traveling costs, such as hotels, gasoline, and food. No one contributed any money to support her campaign for the nomination, and she never felt this was necessary. The party took charge of sending out information about her to the voters who would decide the nomination, and all candidates were forbidden from sending out anything else. Only 4500 dues-paying members of the party could participate in the nomination process, thus making it possible for Ms. McCarthy to speak personally with many of the activists who ultimately gave her a start in politics. Her major appeal was that she had gained much knowledge about how the European Parliament worked during her service as a staff member there, and that she could effectively represent the interests of people back home in England.

About 1800 voters returned their mail ballot, and Arlene McCarthy finished first among five candidates. The general election loomed only six weeks away when she became the Labour Party's nominee, but the party took charge of her campaign from this point on. The party provided her with about $40,000 in campaign funds, as well as staff and campaign literature. When Labour won a smashing victory across the country, Ms. McCarthy was swept into office, and had suddenly gone from being a young staff member to a member of the European Parliament.

The nomination and general election campaign of Arlene McCarthy illustrates several differences between European campaigns and those of the United States. Had she run a similar campaign in the United States she would have had to raise far more money, appeal to far more people to get her party's nomination, and run a much longer campaign. Which type of campaign do you think is best? Does the European-style campaign make it easier for young people and women to break into political office?

Source: Personal interview with Arlene McCarthy, December 12, 1998.

Comparative

Comparing Political Campaigns

---

selective perception

The phenomenon that people often pay the most attention to things they already agree with and interpret them according to their own predispositions.

the impact of campaigns points clearly to the conclusion that the best laid plans of campaign managers change very few votes. Given the billions of dollars spent on political campaigns, it may be surprising to find that they do not have a great effect. Several factors tend to weaken campaigns' impact on voters:

- Most people pay relatively little attention to campaigns in the first place. People have a remarkable capacity for **selective perception**—paying most attention to things they already agree with and interpreting events according to their own predispositions.
- Factors such as party identification—though less important than they used to be—still influence voting behavior regardless of what happens in the campaign.
- Incumbents start with a substantial advantage in terms of name recognition and an established track record.

Such findings do not mean, of course, that campaigns never change voters' minds or that converting a small percentage is unimportant. In tight races, a good campaign can make the difference between winning and losing.

All candidates for federal offices have to file detailed campaign finance reports with the Federal Election Commission quarterly. These reports must list every contribution and itemize every expense. Here, two of Howard Dean's staff members are shown wheeling in their campaign's lengthy financial report for the third quarter of 2003.

Understanding Nominations and Campaigns

Throughout the history of American politics, election campaigns have become longer and longer as the system has become increasingly open to public participation. Reformers in the nineteenth and twentieth centuries held that the solution to democratic problems was more democracy—or as John Lennon sang, "Power to the people." In principle, more democracy always sounds better than less, but it is not such a simple issue in practice.

Are Nominations and Campaigns Too Democratic?

If American campaigns are judged solely by how open they are, then certainly the American system must be viewed favorably. In other countries, the process of leadership nomination occurs within a relatively small circle of party elites. Thus, politicians must work their way up through an apprenticeship system. In contrast, America has an entrepreneurial system in which the people play a crucial role at every stage from nomination to election. In this way, party outsiders can get elected in a way virtually unknown outside the United States. By appealing directly to the people, a candidate can emerge from obscurity to win the White House. For example, former one-term Governor Jimmy Carter was scarcely known outside of his home state a year before his election to the presidency. After serving a dozen years as governor of Arkansas, Bill Clinton was only in a slightly better position than Carter in terms of name recognition when he announced his first campaign for the presidency in 1991. In this sense, the chance to win high office is open to almost any highly skilled politician with even a small electoral base.

There is a price to be paid for all this openness, however. The process of selecting American leaders is a long and convoluted one that has little downtime before it revs up all over again. George W. Bush had scarcely been reelected when potential candidates for 2008 started to schedule visits to Iowa and New Hampshire. Some analysts have even called the American electoral process "the permanent campaign."[29] Many wonder whether people would pay more attention to politics if it did not ask so much of them. Given so much democratic opportunity, many citizens are simply overwhelmed by the process and stay on the sidelines. Similarly, the burdens of the modern campaign can discourage good candidates from throwing their hats into the ring. One of the most worrisome burdens that candidates face is amassing a sufficient campaign treasury. The system may be open, but it requires a lot of fund-raising to be able to take one's case to the people.

Today's campaigns clearly promote individualism in American politics. The current system of running for office has been labeled by Wattenberg the "candidate-centered age."[30] It allows for politicians to decide on their own to run, to raise their own campaign funds, to build their own personal organizations, and to make promises about how they specifically will act in office. The American campaign game is one of individual candidates, by individual candidates, and for individual candidates.

Do Big Campaigns Lead to an Increased Scope of Government?

Today's big campaigns involve much more communication between candidates and voters than America's Founders ever could have imagined. In their view, the presidency was to be an office responsible for seeing to the public interest as a whole. They wished to avoid "a contest in which the candidates would have to pose as 'friends' of the people or make specific policy commitments."[31] Thus, the Founders would probably be horrified by the modern practice in which candidates make numerous promises during nomination and election campaigns.

States are the key battlegrounds of presidential campaigns, and candidates must tailor their appeals to the particular interests of each major state. When in Iowa, for instance, candidates typically promise to keep agricultural subsidies high and support the ethanol program; in New York, to help big cities with federal programs; in Texas, to help the oil and gas industry. To secure votes from each region of the country, candidates end up supporting a variety of local interests. Promises mount as the campaign goes on, and these promises usually add up to new government programs and money. The way modern campaigns are conducted is thus one of many reasons why politicians usually find it easier to promise, at least, that government will do more. Furthermore,

The American political system allows citizens a voice at almost every point of the election process, unlike many countries where a political elite controls the nomination process. Bill Clinton, for example, was little known outside the state of Arkansas at the beginning of the 1992 calendar year.

with their finger constantly to the wind assessing all the different political crosscurrents, it is hard for politicians to promise that the scope of government will be limited through specific cuts.

Summary

In this age of high-tech politics, campaigns have become more media oriented and far more expensive. There are really two campaigns of importance in presidential (and other) contests: the campaign for nomination and the campaign for election.

There are two ways by which delegates are selected to the national party conventions: state caucuses and primaries. The first caucus is traditionally held in Iowa, the first primary in New Hampshire. These two small, atypical American states have disproportionate power in determining who will be nominated and thus become president. This influence stems from the massive media attention devoted to these early contests and the momentum generated by winning them.

Money matters in political campaigns. As the costs of campaigning have increased, it has become more essential to amass large campaign war chests. Although federal campaign finance reform in the 1970s lessened the impact of big contributors, it also allowed the proliferation of PACs. Some observers believe that PACs have created a system of legal graft in campaigning; others say that the evidence for this view is relatively weak.

In general, politicians tend to overestimate the impact of campaigns; political scientists have found that campaigning serves primarily to reinforce citizens' views rather than to convert them. American election campaigns are easily the most open and democratic in the world—some say too open. They are also extraordinarily long, leading politicians to make many promises that contribute to big government.

KEY TERMS

nomination
campaign strategy
national party convention
caucus
presidential primaries
McGovern-Fraser
    Commission
superdelegates
frontloading

national primary
regional primaries
party platform
direct mail
Federal Election
    Campaign Act
Federal Election
    Commission (FEC)

Presidential Election
    Campaign Fund
matching funds
soft money
political action
    committees (PACs)
selective perception

INTERNET RESOURCES

www.fec.gov
The Federal Election Commission's reports on campaign spending can be found at this site.

www.fundrace.org
This site allows one to look up donations from particular individuals and to map contribution patterns for particular areas.

www.opensecrets.org
The Center for Responsive Politics posts a wealth of analysis about PAC contributions at its site.

www.campaignline.com
Campaigns and Elections magazine posts some of its articles here.

GET CONNECTED

The Delegate Selection Process and Presidential Nominations

Running for president is a very demanding job. It begins years before the election. An important part of the process for each candidate involves getting delegates pledged to him or her at the national party conventions. The nomination process involves a complex procedure that is neatly outlined on a web page called "The Green Papers."

Search the Web

Go to the Green Papers page on the nomination process for 2004 *http://www.thegreenpapers.com/P04/*. Find your state and examine the number of delegates that were selected for the Democratic and Republican national conventions in 2004. Also, look at neighboring states, and then find when your state selected the delegates.

Questions to Ask

- How many delegates did your state send to the Democratic and Republican national conventions in 2004? Were they selected through a primary or a caucus or some combination of methods?
- How does your state compare with neighboring states? How about states with more or less population than yours?
- Considering your state's vote for president in 2004, will your state have more or fewer delegates to the national conventions in 2008?

Why It Matters

Presidential candidates spend much time, energy, and money trying to accumulate delegates pledged to their candidacy who will attend the national convention. The media also focus on "delegate count" as an important measure to determine which candidate is leading the presidential race. It is important for you to understand how the delegate selection process works.

Get Involved

As we get closer to the 2008 presidential election, find out how you can become a delegate from your state to your party's national convention. The political parties are particularly interested in getting younger people involved.

To see more Get Connected exercises for Chapter 9, go to www.ablongman.com/edwards.

FOR FURTHER READING

Bartels, Larry M. *Presidential Primaries and the Dynamics of Public Choice.* Princeton, NJ: Princeton University Press, 1988. An excellent analysis of voters' decision-making process in the nominating season.

Bimber, Bruce, and Richard Davis. *Campaigning Online: The Internet in U.S. Elections.* New York: Oxford, 2003. An interesting study of how candidates use websites and how voters react to them.

Brown, Clifford W. Jr., Lynda W. Powell, and Clyde Wilcox. *Serious Money: Fundraising and Contributing in Presidential Nomination Campaigns.* New York: Cambridge University Press, 1995. A unique look into who contributes to presidential campaigns and why.

Farnsworth, Stephen J., and S. Robert Lichter, *The Nightly News Nightmare: Network Television's Coverage of U.S. Presidential Elections, 1988–2000.* Lanham, MD: Rowman & Littlefield, 2003. An interesting study of the content of TV news coverage of four recent presidential election campaigns.

Jamieson, Kathleen Hall, and Paul Waldman, eds. *Electing the President 2000: The Insiders' View.* Philadelphia: University of Pennsylvania Press, 2001. The campaign managers for all the 2000 presidential candidates gathered at the University of Pennsylvania to discuss their experiences in the primaries and the general election.

King, Anthony. *Running Scared.* New York: Free Press, 1997. King argues that American politicians campaign too much and govern too little.

Mayer, William G., ed. *The Making of the Presidential Candidates 2004*. Lanham, MD: Rowman and Littlefield, 2004. A good set of current readings on the presidential nomination process.

Orren, Gary R., and Nelson W. Polsby, eds. *Media and Momentum*. Chatham, NJ: Chatham House, 1987. The story of the exaggerated impact of New Hampshire on our presidential selection process.

Patterson, Thomas E. *Out of Order*. New York: Knopf, 1993. A good review of the role of the media in elections.

Smith, Bradley A. *Unfree Speech: The Folly of Campaign Finance Reform*. Princeton, NJ: Princeton University Press, 2001. A provocative book that argues that most regulations concerning donations to political campaigns should be eliminated.

Winebrenner, Hugh. *The Iowa Precinct Caucuses: The Making of a Media Event*, 2nd ed. Ames: Iowa State University Press, 1998. A highly critical view of the Iowa caucuses from one of the state's leading political analysts.

Elections and Voting Behavior

Chapter Outline

How American Elections Work

A Tale of Three Elections

Whether To Vote: A Citizen's First Choice

The New York Times **Issues of the Times**

How Americans Vote: Explaining Citizens' Decisions

The Last Battle: The Electoral College

Understanding Elections and Voting Behavior

Summary

■ One of the most memorable images of the 2000 presidential election was the regularly repeated scene of Florida election officials holding up a ballot to the light to try to determine whether a punch was present or not. When Joseph Harris, professor of political science at the University of California at Berkeley, invented the first punch-card voting system in the early 1960s it was hailed as a great technological innovation, enabling unprecedented speed in vote counting. But although also reputed to be more accurate than previous methods of voting, by 2000 the punch cards had become antiquated technology compared to modern scantron and touch-screen methods. Embarrassed election officials were quick to admit that they had long been aware of the problems with punch-card voting systems. Such systems theoretically worked fine, as long as people followed the directions—placing the cards in the machines properly, and punching the chads through the card completely. But as we saw in Florida in 2000, many

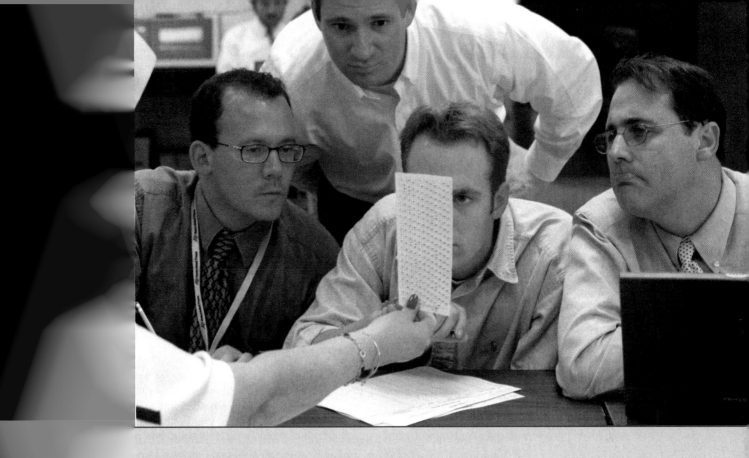

ollow the instructions. With the elec-
vn to just hundreds of votes, the ques-
ether election officials could
airly ascertain the intent of voters
d not been properly punched.
counted if one, two, or three of the
he chad had been perforated? How
imple was visible on the chad, indi-
oter had at least touched the stylus to
point? Election officials struggled to
could by holding them up to the
ning them carefully. Some applauded
valiant attempt to make sure every
d, whereas others criticized them for
the intent of the voter."
analyze elections have a seemingly
ring out the meaning of the vote
have been counted. But as Walter
of the most astute observers of
s, once remarked:

We call an election an expression of the popular will.
But is it? We go into a polling booth and mark a cross
on a piece of paper for one of two, or perhaps three or
four names. Have we expressed our thoughts on the
public policy of the United States? Presumably we have
a number of thoughts on this and that with many buts
and ifs and ors. Surely the cross on a piece of paper
does not express them.[1]

This chapter will discuss why it is difficult for
elections to be a faithful mechanism for expressing
the public's desires concerning what government
should do. The fact that only about half the eligible
electorate participates is one such factor. And those
who do go to the polls often have to choose from
candidates who obscure the issues. Even on an issue
as fundamental as the scope of government, it has
not always been crystal clear regarding what the candidates would do if they were elected. As you read
this chapter, the crucial question to consider is: Are
the people represented by elections in America?

297

Elections serve a critical function in American society. They *institutionalize* political activity, making it possible for most political participation to be channeled through the electoral process rather than bubbling up through demonstrations, riots, or revolutions. Elections provide *regular access to political power*, so that leaders can be replaced without being overthrown. This is possible because elections have **legitimacy** in the eyes of the American people; that is, they are almost universally accepted as a fair and free method of selecting political leaders. Furthermore, by choosing who is to lead the country, the people—if they make their choices carefully—can also guide the policy direction of the government.

This chapter will give you a perspective on how elections function in the American system, as well as how voters generally behave—both in terms of their decisions on whether to vote and how those who do vote make their choices. The focus here is primarily on presidential elections; Chapter 12 on the Congress will examine congressional elections in detail.

legitimacy

A characterization of elections by political scientists meaning that they are almost universally accepted as a fair and free method of selecting political leaders. When legitimacy is high, as in the United States, even the losers accept the results peacefully.

How American Elections Work

The United States has three general kinds of elections: primary elections in which voters select party nominees, general elections that are contested between the nominees of the parties, and elections on specific policy questions in which voters engage in making or ratifying legislation. Primary elections were covered in the previous chapter, and general elections will be the main topic of this chapter. But before turning to this subject, we briefly examine elections that decide policy questions because such contests are becoming increasingly important in many states.

At present, there is no constitutional provision for specific policy questions to be decided by a nationwide vote. It is certainly conceivable that this may come to pass sometime in the twenty-first century,[2] as a number of European democracies have recently started to put questions of great importance—such as joining the European Monetary Union—to a national vote. Procedures allowing the public to pass legislation directly have been in effect for quite some time in many American states. There are two methods for getting items on a state ballot. The first is via a **referendum**, whereby voters are given the chance to approve or disapprove some legislative act, bond issue, or constitutional amendment proposed by the legislature. The second method is through an **initiative petition,** which typically requires gaining signatures on a proposed law equal to 10 percent of the number of voters in the previous election.

Initiative petitions are often portrayed as lawmaking from the ground up, with the people taking charge of the political agenda. In this way, citizens can force a decision on an issue upon which state legislatures have failed to act. Twenty-four states, mostly in the West, currently enable voters to propose and decide legislation through the route of an initiative petition. The most famous example is California's Proposition 13, which in 1978 put a limit on the rise in property taxes in California. Eighteen years and 196 propositions later, California voters passed Proposition 209, a measure intended to end affirmative action programs in the state. In 2002, many initiatives were voted on around the country. A ballot measure was passed in Florida that would set maximum class sizes in all public schools (from 18 students per class in the earliest grades to 25 in high school). North Dakotans voted 2 to 1 against the "Youth Investment Initiative," which would pay as much as $10,000 to anyone who agreed to live in North Dakota for five years after finishing college. In California and Colorado voters rejected initiatives to establish Election Day registration in their states. And Oklahoma voters approved an initiative to outlaw cockfighting in the state.

Although such initiatives require the support of a majority of voters, Daniel Smith argues that they often stem from the actions of a dedicated political entrepreneur more than anything.[3] For example, in 1998 actor and director Rob Reiner spearheaded a California initiative to raise cigarette taxes to discourage teenage smoking and to pay

referendum

A state-level method of direct legislation that gives voters a chance to approve or disapprove proposed legislation or a proposed constitutional amendment.

initiative petition

A process permitted in some states whereby voters may put proposed changes in the state constitution to a vote if sufficient signatures are obtained on petitions calling for such a referendum.

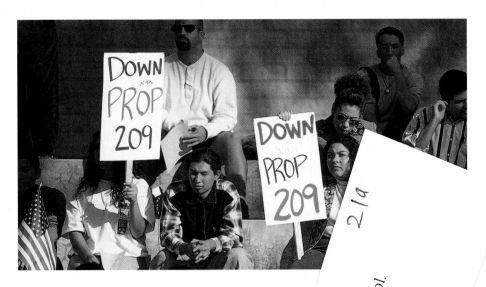

One recent referendum that has drawn national attention is California's vote on Proposition 209, which ended affirmative action programs in the state. Here, opponents make their point of view clear.

for additional educational programs for children. R only was the spokesman for the initiative in TV co but also paid for much of the cost of getting the initi ballot in the first place. Yet, Smith's examples of preneurs who successfully used the initiative pro public notoriety and personal wealth. These case ple who have spearheaded major initiative car strate how ordinary individuals can someti course of public policy, as you can see in "Ma Barbara Anderson and the Politics c Massachusetts."

A Tale of Three Electi

Times change, and so do elections. M high-tech affairs. A glance at three 1896, and 2004—should give you have changed over nearly two ce

1800: The First Elector

By current standards, the 18 tion at all. There were no ¡ no candidate speeches, incumbent President Jefferson were nomina in Congress—Fede Republicans for Jef back and let their and travel were to campaigning wa

At that tim for that matter sition's candi.

[handwritten note overlaid, tilted:] The decorations committee for Tolo is meeting on Tuesday the 23rd after school. Since the art club is interested in helping with Tolo decorations we ask that you please attend this meeting. Also please bring any ideas you have for decorations.

Isabella Lotz,
ASB Executive Board
Thanks,

... n elec- ...ntions, ...rs. Both ...Thomas ...esentatives ...emocratic- ...candidates sat ...omote their cause. Communication ...r message across themselves. Besides, ...f the presidential office. ...ttle concerned with dignity, or honesty ...did all they could to run down the oppo- ...nounced as a Bible-burning atheist, the

*[sidebar feature — partially obscured:]*

...**a Difference**

...**ara Anderson**
...**the Politics**
...**ax Relief in**
...**assachusetts**

...e state of Massachusetts has long been labeled as ...axachusetts" due to the high level of taxes in the ...ate. Though without previous experience in polit- ...ics, Barbara Anderson dedicated herself to doing something to change the system. Starting as a volunteer, she worked herself up to the position of executive director of a group called Citizens for Limited Taxation. This organization placed a proposition on the 1980 Massachusetts ballot to limit taxes on property to 2-1/2 percent per year of their cash value. Anderson helped put together a TV ad campaign featuring a now famous "Alka Seltzer spot," showing increases in taxation over the years in a series of bar graphs, and how Proposition 2-1/2 could turn reactions of "oooh" from high taxes into "ahhhs" of relief. On Election Day, Anderson's forces won a stunning 59 to 41 victory, which years later is still considered one of the most significant tax-cutting propositions enacted in any state.

father of mulatto children (much later shown to be probably true based on DNA tests), and a mad scientist. Adams, on the other hand, was said to be a monarchist "whose grand object was to destroy every man who differed from his opinions."[4]

The focus of the campaign was not on voters, but rather on the state legislatures, which had the responsibility for choosing members of the electoral college. When the dust settled, the Jeffersonians had won a slim victory in terms of electoral votes; however, they had also committed a troubling error. In the original constitutional system each elector cast two ballots, and the top vote getter was named president and the runner-up became vice president.[5] In 1796 Jefferson had become Adams' vice president by virtue of finishing second. Not wanting Adams to be his vice president, Jefferson made sure that all his electors also voted for his vice-presidential choice—Aaron Burr of New York. The problem was that when each and every one of them did so, Jefferson and Burr ended up tied for first. This meant that the Federalist-controlled House of Representatives would have to decide between the two Democratic-Republican candidates. Burr saw the chance to steal the presidency from Jefferson by cutting a deal with the Federalists, but his efforts failed. After 35 indecisive ballots in the House, the Federalists finally threw their support to Jefferson. On March 4, 1801, the transition from Adams to Jefferson marked the first peaceful transfer of power between parties via the electoral process in world history.

1896: A Bitter Fight over Economic Interests

Nearly a century later the election of 1896 was largely fought over economics. By then national nominating conventions had become well established, and Republicans, meeting in St. Louis for their convention, nominated former Congressman William McKinley. The Republicans' major issues were support for the gold standard and high tariffs. The gold standard linked money to this scarce precious metal so that debtors never got a break from inflation. Tariffs protected capitalists and their workers from foreign competition.

The Democrats met in Chicago's sticky July heat. They had an issue—unlimited coinage of silver—but no clear front-runner. The high point of the Chicago convention was a speech by 36-year-old William Jennings Bryan of Nebraska, who proclaimed the virtues of the silver rather than the gold standard. Bryan went on to win the nomination on the fifth ballot and to become the youngest nominee of a major party in American history.

William Jennings Bryan was the Democratic Party's standard bearer at the turn of the century. Eastern industrialists, fearing Bryan's powerful speeches and populist politics, used their financial clout to help William McKinley defeat "The Boy Orator of the Platte" (thus named after a river in his native Nebraska) in the 1896 and 1900 presidential elections.

The flamboyant Bryan broke with tradition and took to the stump in person. He gave 600 speeches as his campaign train traveled through 26 states, logging 18,000 miles. Debtors and silver miners were especially attracted to Bryan's pitch for cheap silver money. In contrast, the serene McKinley was advised to sit home in Ohio and run a front-porch campaign. He did, and managed to label the Democrats as the party of depression ("In God We Trust, With Bryan We Bust").

Bryan won the oratory, but McKinley won the election. Eastern manufacturers contributed a small fortune to the Republicans. Only White Southerners, Westerners in the silver-producing states, and rural debtors lined up behind the Democrats. The Republicans won overwhelmingly in the industrial Northeast and Midwest, and became firmly entrenched as the nation's majority party for the next several decades. McKinley triumphed by a margin of 271 to 176 in the electoral college. Nearly 80 percent of the eligible electorate voted in one of the highest turnouts ever.

2004: The Ratification of a Polarizing Presidency

In 2004, George W. Bush became the fourth Republican president since William McKinley to win a second term. Unlike twice-elected Republicans in the interim years—Dwight Eisenhower, Richard Nixon, and Ronald Reagan—George W. Bush was the first to repeat William McKinley's feat of winning two consecutive elections while leading the Republicans to majorities in both the Senate and the House of Representatives. The completeness of the Republican victory in 2004 led many pundits to talk of George W. Bush's presidency as ushering in a new era of Republican dominance reminiscent of the McKinley era. Whether or not this proves to be the case, only time will tell. But certainly the reelection of George W. Bush will go down in history books as one of the most important and hard-fought presidential elections ever.

The intensity of the battle over the presidency in 2004 was at least partially due to the controversial way Bush gained the presidency four years earlier. Election Night 2000 provided a wild night of entertainment, full of ups and downs for everyone. The networks first reported that Al Gore had won the crucial state of Florida, but within an hour they rescinded this call. Early in the morning, they at last called Florida for Bush and declared him the president-elect. But just as Gore was ready to give his concession

In 2000, a national firestorm erupted over problems with punch card voting machines in Palm Beach, Miami-Dade, and Broward counties in Florida. As a result of this controversy, Florida invested a good deal of effort and money in upgrading their voting equipment. Here, voters in Miami can be seen voting on new touch screen machines. To everyone's relief, the voting proceeded smoothly in 2004.

speech, the word broke that the networks were again rescinding their call, as the margin had narrowed to less than a thousand votes.

Because Bush's lead over Gore in the initial count was less than one-tenth of 1 percent, Florida law mandated an automatic recount. Few novelists would have dared imagine the scene of a nation watching transfixed as county-by-county recount figures came in from a state where 6 million people voted. Ultimately, with the margin between Bush and Gore down to 537 votes, the election hinged on whether or not the undervotes (ballots that showed no vote for president) would be examined by hand. The Gore campaign pointed out that in counties that used punch-card systems (such as Palm Beach, Miami-Dade, and Broward), that 1.5 percent of the ballots showed no presidential vote whereas only 0.3 percent of the ballots in counties that used scantrons were recorded as blank. The reason offered for this difference was that some people do not punch holes all the way through the card, thereby not fully removing the indentation — the now-famous "chad." The Gore campaign was hoping to find enough chads to turn the vote count in Gore's favor. Naturally, the Bush campaign realized this and opposed any manual recount. They argued that such a review of the ballots was inherently arbitrary, and subject to manipulation and differing standards.

And the Winner is . . .
Close Calls in
Presidential Elections

As with any legal dispute, this one ended up in the courts, which played a pivotal role in deciding the presidential election. The Florida Supreme Court ultimately ruled in favor of Gore's request, ordering counties to apply the standard of "the clear intention of the voter" in evaluating ballots. However, the U.S. Supreme Court in *Bush v. Gore* (2000) overruled the Florida Supreme Court and held that more precise and consistent standards for evaluating ballots would have to be applied in all counties. Most importantly, they ruled that there was not enough time to recount all the ballots in an orderly fashion by the time the electors were to vote. Thus, the U.S. Supreme Court ultimately determined that George W. Bush would emerge the winner.

Despite winning office by the narrowest of margins, Bush governed boldly, making numerous consequential decisions that reshaped American public policy. Many of his decisions further polarized his political allies from his political opponents. On the domestic side, his tax cuts were praised by his supporters as stimulating the economy, whereas Bush opponents frequently denounced them as a boon for millionaires that turned a budget surplus into a record budget deficit. The Bush doctrine of striking potential enemies first before they could use weapons of mass destruction was praised by supporters as keeping America safe from further strikes like those that occurred on September 11. But many opponents charged this was a reckless go-it-alone foreign policy that had alienated America from its traditional allies.

Into this maelstrom stepped John F. Kerry, a Democratic senator from Massachusetts since 1984. Kerry was used to being in the thick of battle, as both a decorated Vietnam War hero and subsequently as head of the controversial Vietnam Veterans Against the War. No sooner had Kerry wrapped up the Democratic nomination for president than George W. Bush's campaign launched a set of negative TV ads against him in order to try to define him in the public mind before he could define himself. Never before had a new nominee been attacked so early or so often. But Kerry soon raised ample resources to fight back, as his campaign raised far more money than any Democratic campaign had ever done before — $243 million, compared to $286 million for the Bush campaign. Some critics of the McCain-Feingold campaign finance reform bill worried that it would be hard to raise sufficient campaign funds once soft money was banned. But such fears were unfounded due to the high level of interest in the 2004 campaign.

The Kerry campaign sought to portray President Bush as a reckless leader who had rushed the country into an unnecessary war in Iraq. But it faced the problem of explaining how the senator had voted to authorize the president to use force in Iraq. When asked whether he would vote the same way again now that he knew that Iraq did not possess weapons of mass destruction, Kerry seemed to undercut his criticism of the war by saying that he would indeed. And Kerry put his foot in his mouth when he said that he initially voted for a supplemental appropriation of $87 million to fund further military operations in Iraq before he voted against it on final passage. Statements like these led the Bush campaign to charge that Kerry was a "flip-flopper" who could not be trusted to lead America in a dangerous time.

According to exit polls, strong leadership in the war on terrorism ended up being one of people's major reasons for voting for Bush. Many Bush voters also said that "moral values" was the most important issue to them. Bush's strength with evangelical white Christians was clearly instrumental in his victory, with 78 percent supporting his reelection. Voters whose top concern was taxes also favored Bush, who promised to stay the course with his tax-cutting agenda. On the other hand, Kerry won votes among those who were most concerned with the war in Iraq, the economy, health care, and education.

As shown in the Electoral College results displayed in Figure 10.1, there were sharp regional divisions in the vote in 2004. Bush ran strong in the South and Mountain West,

Figure 10.1   The Electoral College Results for 2000 and 2004

The two maps below show the number of votes each state had in the electoral college in 2000 and 2004, and which states were carried by the Democrats (green) and Republicans (rose).

2000

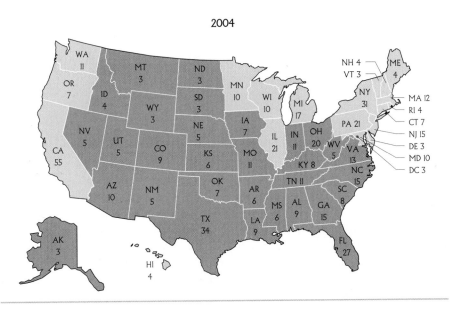

2004

whereas Kerry turned in a good showing in the Northeast and the Pacific Coast states. Like the 2000 election, the Electoral College winner hinged on just one big battleground state. This time it was Ohio, whose 20 electors gave Bush a victory of 286 to 252 in the Electoral College, but only by a narrow margin of about 135,000 votes out of 5.5 million votes cast. Unlike in 2000, when Bush lost the popular vote to Gore by about one-half of one percent, this time he won the popular vote by about three percent (51 percent to 48 percent).

In 2004, as in all election years, voters faced two key choices: whether to vote and, if they chose to do so, how to vote. The following sections will investigate how voters make these choices.

Whether To Vote: A Citizen's First Choice

suffrage

The legal right to vote, extended to African Americans by the **Fifteenth Amendment,** to women by the **Nineteenth Amendment,** and to people over the age of 18 by the **Twenty-sixth Amendment.**

Over two centuries of American electoral history include greatly expanded **suffrage** — the right to vote. In the election of 1800, only property-owning White males over the age of 21 were typically allowed to vote. Now virtually everyone over the age of 18 — male or female, White or non-White, rich or poor — has the right to vote. (For these developments, particularly as they affect women and minorities, see Chapter 5.) The two major exceptions concern noncitizens and convicted criminals. No state currently permits residents who are not citizens to vote. Some immigrant groups feel that this ought to at least be changed at the local level, as you can read about in "Issues of the Times: Should Noncitizen Permanent Residents Be Allowed To Vote in Local Elections?" State law varies widely when it comes to crime and voting: 46 states deny prisoners the right to vote, 32 states extend the ban to people on parole, and 10 states impose a lifetime ban on convicted felons.

Interestingly, as the right to vote has been extended, proportionately fewer of those eligible have chosen to exercise that right. In the past 100 years, the 80 percent turnout in the 1896 election was the high point of electoral participation. In 2004, only 55 percent of the adult population voted in the presidential election (see Figure 10.2).

Figure 10.2   The Decline of Turnout: 1892–2004

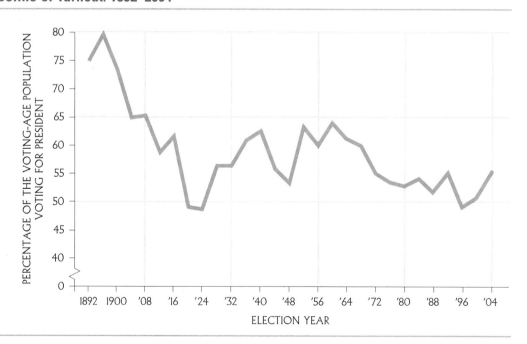

Sources: For data up to 1968, Historical Statistics of the United States (Washington, D.C.: Government Printing Office, 1975), part 2, 1071. For 1972–1988, *Statistical Abstract of the United States, 1990* (Washington, D.C.: Government Printing Office, 1990), 264. Subsequent years from census reports and authors' calculations.

Deciding Whether To Vote

Realistically, when over 100 million people vote in a presidential election, as they did in 2004, the chance of one vote affecting the outcome is very, very slight. Once in a while, of course, an election is decided by a small number of votes, as occurred in Florida in 2000. It is more likely, however, that you will be struck by lightning during your lifetime than participate in an election decided by a single vote.

Not only does your vote probably not make much difference to the outcome, but voting is somewhat costly. You have to spend some of your valuable time becoming informed, making up your mind, and getting to the polls. If you carefully calculate your time and energy, you might rationally decide that the costs of voting outweigh the benefits. Indeed, the most frequent response given by nonvoters in the 2000 Census Bureau survey on turnout was that they could not take time off from work or school that day.[6] Some scholars have therefore proposed that one of the easiest ways to increase American turnout levels would be to move election day to Saturday or make it a holiday.[7]

Economist Anthony Downs, in his model of democracy, tries to explain why a rational person would ever bother to vote. He argues that rational people vote if they believe that the policies of one party will bring more benefits than the policies of the other party.[8] Thus people who see policy differences between the parties are more likely to join the ranks of voters. If you are an environmentalist and you expect the Democrats to pass more environmental legislation than the Republicans, then you have an additional incentive to go to the polls. On the other hand, if you are truly indifferent—that is, if you see no difference whatsoever between the two parties—you may rationally decide to abstain.

Another reason why many people vote is that they have a high sense of **political efficacy**—the belief that ordinary people can influence the government. Efficacy is measured by asking people to agree or disagree with statements such as "I don't think public officials care much what people like me think." Those who lack strong feelings of efficacy are being quite rational in staying home on Election Day because they don't think they can make a difference. Yet even some of these people will vote anyway, simply to support democratic government. In this case, people are impelled to vote by a sense of civic duty. The benefit from doing one's **civic duty** is the long-term contribution made toward preserving democracy.

Participation

The Prepared Voter Kit

political efficacy

The belief that one's **political participation** really matters—that one's vote can actually make a difference.

civic duty

The belief that in order to support democratic government, a citizen should always vote.

Young people have one of the lowest rates of election turnout. Music stars like P. Diddy have tried to change this by actively participating in events that encourage young people to vote.

Issues of the Times

The Issue: Should Noncitizen Permanent Residents Be Allowed To Vote in Local Elections?

The U.S. Constitution is silent on whether or not people living in the United States who are not citizens may be permitted to vote. And Congress has not enacted any federal requirement stating that voters must be citizens. Currently, no U.S. state permits residents who are not citizens to vote. But as this article points out, this was not always the case prior to the 1920s. And today, with the great rise in immigration the United States has seen over the last two decades, many immigrants believe they shouldn't have to wait to attain citizenship in order to have a vote in local elections that determine how their local communities are run. In many communities where immigrants now make up a substantial portion of the population and pay a substantial proportion of the taxes, this is likely to be a hotly debated issue for some time to come.

Read All About It

Immigrants Raise Call for Right To Be Voters

By Rachel L. Swarns
August 9, 2004

WASHINGTON—For months, the would-be revolutionaries plotted strategy and lobbied local politicians here with the age-old plea, "No taxation without representation!" Last month, some of the unlikely insurgents—Ethiopian-born restaurateurs, travel agents and real estate developers in sober business suits—declared that victory finally seemed within reach.

Five City Council members announced their support for a bill that would allow thousands of immigrants to vote in local elections here, placing the nation's capital among a handful of cities across the country in the forefront of efforts to offer voting rights to noncitizens.

"It will happen," said Tamrat Medhin, a civic activist from Ethiopia who lives here. "Don't you believe that if people are working in the community and paying taxes, don't you agree that they deserve the opportunity to vote?"

Calling for "democracy for all," immigrants are increasingly press-

Please see Immigrants Page 307

Immigrants

Continued from Page 306

ing for the right to vote in municipal elections. In Washington, the proposed bill, introduced in July, would allow permanent residents to vote for the mayor and members of the school board and City Council.

Efforts to expand the franchise to noncitizens are also bubbling up in New York, Connecticut and elsewhere. Several cities, including Chicago, and towns like Takoma Park, Md., already allow noncitizens to vote in municipal or school elections.

The proposals have inspired fierce opposition from critics who say the laws would undermine the value of American citizenship and raise security concerns in the aftermath of the Sept. 11 terrorist attacks. Washington's mayor, Anthony Williams, has expressed his support for extending voting rights to permanent residents, but has yet to garner a majority of supporters on the 13-member City Council. In San Francisco, critics have questioned whether the law would violate the state's Constitution.

In this city, where Ethiopian restaurants and El Salvadoran travel agents dot many urban streets, advocates argue that permanent residents are paying taxes and fighting and dying for the United States as soldiers in Iraq while lacking a voice in local government. They describe the ban on immigrant voting as akin to the kind of taxation without representation that was a major cause of the American Revolution.

They also note that the United States has a long history of allowing noncitizens to vote. Twenty-two states and federal territories at various times allowed noncitizens to vote—even as blacks and women were barred from the ballot box—in the 1800s and 1900s.

Concerns about the radicalism of immigrants arriving from southern and Eastern Europe in the late 19th and early 20th centuries led states to restrict such voting rights. By 1928, voting at every level had been restricted to United States citi-

---

Calling for "democracy for all," immigrants are increasingly pressing for the right to vote in municipal elections.

---

zens. Today, some argue, those rights should be restored to noncitizens.

"They're paying taxes, they're working, they're contributing to our prosperity," said Jim Graham, the councilman who introduced the bill here. "And yet they're not able to exercise the franchise.

"This is part of our history. A lot of people don't know what the history of this nation is in terms of immigrant voting; they don't understand even that localities can determine this issue. It's a very healthy discussion."

Critics counter that the proposed laws would make citizenship irrelevant and pledges of allegiance to the United States meaningless. It is a touchy political issue, particularly in an election year when many politicians across party lines are lobbying for support from Hispanic voters, and many politicians have tried to sidestep it altogether.

Democrats have most often sponsored the initiatives, but some also oppose them. In Washington, where Congress has the right to override city laws, some Republicans said they would try to overturn the immigrant voting bill if it passed.

In San Francisco, some critics have also argued that the proposals raise security concerns. Louise Renne, a former city attorney in San Francisco and a longtime critic of the concept, recently raised the question of whether terrorists would soon be allowed access to the polls. "If noncitizens can vote," she asked reporters, "can Osama bin Laden vote in a school election?"

Advocates for noncitizen voting rights dismiss concerns about threats to national security, noting that several countries, including Belgium and Ireland, allow noncitizens to vote in local elections. New Zealand allows permanent residents to vote in local and national elections.

They argue that immigrants will still aspire to citizenship because it is the only way they can vote in federal elections. And having the right to vote, they argue, will help noncitizens feel more politically engaged and committed to this country.

"A lot of communities are not represented by representatives who reflect the diversity in their communities and are responsive to their needs," said Ron Hayduk, a professor of political science at the Borough of Manhattan Community College and an advocate for immigrant voting rights. "It raises basic fundamental questions about democracy."

Think About It

- Do you think that noncitizens should be allowed to vote in local elections? Why or why not?
- If noncitizens were allowed to vote, what difference do you think this might make? Would the politics of your local community be changed if they were allowed to vote? If so, how?

America in Perspective

Why Turnout in the United States Is So Low Compared to Other Countries

Despite living in a culture that encourages participation, Americans have a woefully low turnout rate compared to other democracies. Here are some figures on turnout rates among the voting-age population in the United States and other nations as shown in the table on the right.

There are several reasons given for Americans' abysmally low turnout rate. Probably the reason most often cited is the American requirement of voter registration. The governments of many, but not all, other democracies take the responsibility of seeing to it that all their eligible citizens are on the voting lists. In America, the responsibility for registration lies solely with the individual. If we were to be like the Scandinavian countries and have the government take care of registering every eligible citizen, no doubt our turnout rate would be higher.

A second difference between the United States and other countries is that the American government asks citizens to vote far more often. Whereas the typical European voter may be called upon to cast two or three ballots in a four-year period, many Americans are faced with a dozen or more separate elections in the space of four years. Furthermore, Americans are expected to vote for a much wider range of political offices.

With 1 elected official for every 442 citizens and elections held somewhere virtually every week, it is no wonder that it is so difficult to get Americans to the polls. It is probably no coincidence that the one European country that has a lower turnout rate—Switzerland—has also overwhelmed its citizens with voting opportunities, typically asking people to vote three times every year.

Finally, the stimulus to vote is low in the United States because the choices offered Americans are not as stark as in other countries. This is because the United States is quite unusual in that it has always lacked a major left-wing socialist party. When European voters go to the polls, they are deciding on whether their country will be run by parties with socialist goals or by conservative (and in some cases religious) parties. The consequences of their vote for redistribution of income and the scope of government are far greater than the ordinary American voter can imagine.

Source: Martin P. Wattenberg, *Where Have All the Voters Gone?* (Cambridge, MA: Harvard University Press, 2002), p. 15.

Note: Turnout rates for all countries are calculated based on the percentage of the voting-age population casting ballots.

Indonesia, 1997, parliamentary	92.8
Italy, 1996, parliamentary	87.4
Iceland, 1996, parliamentary	87.0
Israel, 1996, parliamentary and prime minister	84.7
Denmark, 1998, parliamentary	83.1
Belgium, 1999, parliamentary	82.6
Greece, 2000, parliamentary	82.0
Australia, 1998, parliamentary	81.9
Spain, 1996, parliamentary	80.6
Finland, 2000, presidential	79.4
Sweden, 1998, parliamentary	77.8
Brazil, 1998, presidential	77.2
Portugal, 1996, parliamentary	77.2
Norway, 1997, parliamentary	76.9
New Zealand, 1999, parliamentary	75.7
Germany, 1998, parliamentary	75.2
Austria, 1999, parliamentary	72.8
France, 1995, presidential	72.3
Netherlands, 1998, parliamentary	70.2
Russia, 1996, presidential	67.5
Ireland, 1997, parliamentary	66.7
Bangladesh, 1996, parliamentary	64.6
Japan, 2000, parliamentary	62.0
Mexico, 2000, presidential	60.0
India, 1999, parliamentary	59.7
United Kingdom, 2001, parliamentary	55.4
Canada, 2000, parliamentary	53.4
United States, 2000, presidential	51.2
Switzerland, 1999, parliamentary	34.9

Registering To Vote

voter registration

A system adopted by the states that requires voters to register well in advance of Election Day. A few states permit Election Day registration.

A century ago politicians used to say, "Vote early and often." Cases such as West Virginia's 159,000 votes being cast by 147,000 eligible voters in 1888 were not that unusual. Largely to prevent corruption associated with stuffing ballot boxes, states adopted **voter registration** laws around the turn of the century, which require individuals to first place their name on an electoral roll in order to be allowed to vote. Although these laws have made it more difficult to vote more than once, they have also discouraged some people from voting at all. Voter registration requirements in the United States are, in part, to blame for why Americans are significantly less likely to go to the polls than citizens of other democratic nations (see "America in Perspective: Why Turnout in the United States Is So Low Compared to Other Countries").

You Are the Policymaker

Registering and Voting by E-Mail?

Although modern technology is widely available, Americans have not harnessed much of it to improve democracy. Though many precincts now use computer touch screens to record votes, the high-tech age has not yet made much of an impact on the voting process. There is good reason to expect that this will change in the twenty-first century.

The development of the personal computer and the World Wide Web are likely to facilitate the process of voter registration. Already, one can go to the website of the Federal Election Commission *(http://www.fec.gov/votregis/vr.htm)* and download the "National Mail Voter Registration Form." Twenty-two states currently accept copies of this application printed from the computer image, signed by the applicant, and mailed in the old-fashioned way. As e-mail becomes ever more popular and "snail mail" fades into a method reserved for packages, the entire voter registration process may someday be conducted mostly through electronic

means. In an age where personal computers in the home are nearly as common as television sets are today, this technology would clearly make registering to vote more user-friendly.

If people can register by computer, the next step is voting by e-mail. A growing trend in the Pacific Coast states has been voting by mail. In 1998, Oregon voters approved a referendum to eliminate traditional polling places and conduct all future elections by mail. In California, approximately 25 percent of the votes cast currently come in via the post office. Again, as e-mail takes the place of regular mail, why not have people cast their votes through cyberspace?

Voting through the Internet would be less costly for the state, as well as easier for the average citizen—assuming that computer literacy reaches near-universal proportions sometime in the future. The major concerns, of course, would be ensuring that no one votes more than once and preserving the confidentiality of the vote. These security

concerns are currently being addressed by some of the world's top computer programmers, as commercial enterprises look toward using the Internet to conduct business. If the technology can be perfected to allow trillions of dollars of business to be conducted via the Internet, then it seems reasonable that similar problems can be overcome with regard to the voting process.

Whether these possible developments will improve democracy in America is debatable. Making voting more user-friendly should encourage turnout, but people will still have to be interested enough in the elections of the future to send in their e-mail ballots. If old-style polling places are relegated to the history books and everyone votes electronically in the convenience of their own homes, the sense of community on Election Day may be lost. This loss could lead to even lower turnout. You be the policymaker: Do the benefits of voting by e-mail outweigh the potential costs?

Registration procedures currently differ from state to state. In sparsely populated North Dakota there is no registration at all, and in Minnesota, Wisconsin, Wyoming, Idaho, New Hampshire, and Maine voters can register on Election Day. Advocates of this user-friendly procedure are quick to point out that these states all ranked near the top in voter turnout in 2004. For many years, some states—particularly in the South—had burdensome registration procedures, such as requiring people to make a trip to their county courthouse during normal business hours. As a result of the 1993 **Motor Voter Act,** this is no longer the case. The Motor Voter Act made voter registration easier by requiring states to allow eligible voters to register by simply checking a box on their driver's license application or renewal form. Nevertheless, its impact on turnout has thus far been disappointing, as you can see in Figure 10.2.

Future reform designed to increase turnout may well focus on conducting elections through e-mail (see "You are the Policymaker: Registering and Voting by E-Mail?").

Motor Voter Act

Passed in 1993, this act went into effect for the 1996 election. It requires states to permit people to register to vote at the same time they apply for their driver's license.

Who Votes?

When just over half the population votes, the necessity of studying nonvoters takes on added importance. Table 10.1 displays data regarding the turnout rates of various groups in the 2000 presidential election. This information reveals numerous demographic factors that are related to turnout:

Voter Turnout: Who Votes?

Table 10.1   Reported Turnout Rate in 2000

Social Groups	Percent
18–20	29
21–24	35
25–44	50
45–64	65
65 and over	68
No HS diploma	31
High school	49
Some college	60
College	72
White	56
African American	44
Hispanic citizens	45
Asian American	43
Men	53
Women	56
Married	61
Single	45
Union member	65
Not union member	53

Source: Authors' analysis of 2000 U.S. Census Bureau survey.

Why It Matters

Youth Turnout

Voter turnout rates in the United States have been declining for quite some time. The very low participation rate of young people has been one of the biggest reasons for this decline. Who votes matters not only because these individuals decide who wins elections, but also because politicians pay attention primarily to voters. The fact that so few young people vote means that politicians are not likely to pay too much attention to their opinions or to promote policies that will particularly help them.

- *Education.* People with higher than average educational levels have a higher rate of voting than people with less education. Among all factors affecting turnout, this one is the most important. Highly educated people are more capable of discerning the major differences between the candidates. In addition, their educational training comes in handy in clearing the bureaucratic hurdles imposed by registration requirements.

- *Age.* Older people are far more likely to vote than younger people. Younger citizens are less likely to be registered, but even just analyzing turnout patterns among registered voters yields wide differences by age. For example, Georgia's Secretary of State reported that of those on the registration rolls under 25 years of age only 22 percent voted in 2002 as compared to 68 percent among those over 65 years of age.[9]

- *Race.* African Americans and Hispanics are underrepresented among voters relative to their share of the population. This finding can largely be explained by their generally low levels of education. African Americans and Hispanics with high levels of education have a higher turnout rate than Whites with comparable educational achievement.

- *Gender.* In an earlier period many women were discouraged from voting, but today women actually participate in elections at a slightly higher rate than men.

- *Marital status.* People who are married are more likely to vote than those who are not. This pattern is true among all age categories and generally reflects the fact that married people are more tied into their community.

- *Union membership.* Unions have long been active in the political process and often devote considerable resources to encouraging their members to vote. People who live in a household with a union member do indeed have higher than average turnout levels.

These differences in turnout rates are cumulative. Possessing several of these traits (say, being elderly, well educated, and married) adds significantly to one's likelihood of voting. Conversely, being young, poorly educated, and single is likely to add up to a very low probability of voting. If you possess many of the demographic traits of nonvoters, then the interests of people like you are probably not drawing a great deal of attention from politicians—regardless of whether you personally vote or not. Politicians listen far more carefully to groups with high turnout rates, as they know their fate may well be in their hands. Who votes does matter.

How Americans Vote: Explaining Citizens' Decisions

A common explanation of how Americans vote—one favored by journalists and politicians—is that people vote because they agree more with the policy views of Candidate A than with those of Candidate B. Of course, the candidates have invested a lot of time and money to get those views implanted in the public mind. Because citizens vote for the candidate whose policy promises they favor, many journalists and politicians say that the election winner has a mandate from the people to carry out the promised policies. This idea is sometimes called the **mandate theory of elections.**

Politicians, of course, are attracted to the mandate theory. It lets them justify what they want to do by claiming public support for their policies. As President Clinton said

mandate theory of elections

The idea that the winning candidate has a mandate from the people to carry out his or her platforms and politics. Politicians like the theory better than political scientists do.

You mean, like, wow, we can actually get rid of, you know, incumbents with this whatchamacallit?"

Why It Matters

Mandate Theory of Elections
The mandate theory of elections asserts that voters send a policy message when they elect one candidate over another. Ideally, American democracy would work this way. The fact that it often does not indicates that leaders may be more claiming support from the people for their policies than is really justified.

How You Can Make a Difference
Voter Registration and Voting

The close presidential election of 2000 was notable not only for the postelection struggle in Florida but also for efforts to bring new voters to the polls—especially African-American citizens. The NAACP, through its National Voter Fund, spent over $10 million to register and bring people to the polls. Though the money is necessary in some efforts, the individual volunteers and staffers must always perform the hard work. This is where you can make a difference.

How can you improve voter turnout? Start by initiating a voter registration drive on campus and throughout your community. While the impetus to register is highest around presidential elections, organizing voters for local elections usually has a far greater impact on politics than in presidential elections. Working through existing political organizations (Democratic, Repub-lican, Green, Reform, League of

Women Voters) both on campus and in the community can help you overcome potential financial and administrative difficulties. You should remain nonpartisan in this effort and clearly post a sign that your voter registration service is available to all voters without reference to their political preferences. Do not campaign for a particular candidate or tell a person how they should vote while taking part in a registration campaign. You must also take care to educate newly registered voters in the correct voting procedure to avoid the problems faced by confused voters in Florida during the 2000 election.

Finally, you need to remind people to actually vote. Getting people registered is only half the battle. You may need to provide transportation if necessary or try to ensure convenient polling places on campus. You can also distribute straightforward, nonpartisan voting

guides (League of Women Voters) on candidates and their stances on issues. At some colleges, many of your friends may already be registered in their hometowns and do not want to switch their place of residence for a variety of reasons. This should not hinder your efforts. Instead, your turnout drive should also include an educational component that continually reminds students to request absentee ballots. Using all these strategies along with e-mail, bulletin boards, and campus newspapers, you can boost voter participation at little or no cost.

What you can do:
- Get educated on the issues and strategies involved in voter registration by visiting the NAACP's National Voter Fund at *www.naacpnvf.org* or Rock the Vote at *www.rockthevote.org*.

during the final presidential debate in 1992: "That's why I am trying to be so specific in this campaign—to have a mandate, if elected, so the Congress will know what the American people have voted for." Immediately after declaring victory in the 2004 presidential election, President Bush forcefully asserted that he had a mandate to enact his proposed policies over the next four years.

Political scientists, however, think little of the mandate theory of elections.[10] Whereas victorious politicians are eager to proclaim "the people have spoken," political scientists know that the people rarely vote a certain way for the same reasons. Instead, political scientists focus on three major elements of voters' decisions: (1) voters' party identification; (2) voters' evaluation of the candidates; and (3) the match between voters' policy positions and those of the candidates and parties—a factor termed "policy voting."

Party Identification

Party identifications are crucial for many voters because they provide a regular perspective through which voters can view the political world. "Presumably," say Niemi and Weisberg, "people choose to identify with a party with which they generally agree." As a result they need not concern themselves with every issue that comes along, but can generally rely on their party identification to guide them."[11] Parties tend to rely on groups that lean heavily in their favor to form their basic coalition. Even before an election campaign begins, Republicans usually assume they will not receive much support from African Americans, Jews, and Hispanic Americans. Democrats have an uphill struggle attracting groups that are staunchly Republican in their leanings, such as conservative evangelical Christians or upper-income voters. As you can see in Table 10.2, there have been substantial changes in how various groups have voted for president since 1960.

With the emergence of television and candidate-centered politics, the parties' hold on voters eroded substantially during the 1960s and 1970s, and then stabilized at a new and lower level.[12] In the 1950s, scholars singled out party affiliation as the best single predictor of a voter's decision. It was said that many Southern Democrats would vote for a yellow dog if their party nominated one. "My party—right or wrong" was the motto that typified strong party identifiers. Voting along party lines is less common, particularly in elections for the House of Representatives, where incumbency is now paramount (see Chapter 12). Many voters now feel that they no longer need the parties to guide their choices, given that modern technology makes it possible for them to evaluate and make their own decisions about the candidates. Thus, American voters have become increasingly individualistic. Voting choices have become largely a matter of individual choice, and many voters are up for grabs in each election (the so-called "floating voters"). Young people are particularly likely to be up for grabs and

Table 10.2   Changing Patterns in Voting Behavior: 1960 and 2004 Compared

The demographic correlates of presidential voting behavior have changed in a number of important ways since 1960. When Kennedy was elected in 1960 Protestants and Catholics voted very differently, as Kennedy's Catholicism was a major issue during the campaign. Although John Kerry was the first major party nominee since Kennedy to be of the Catholic faith, Catholics were only slightly more likely to support him than Protestants. Today, the major difference along religious lines involves how often one attends religious services, with those who attend regularly being substantially more likely to support Republican presidential candidates. The least likely group to support Republicans these days is African-Americans. As you can see in data below, Kerry clearly drew more support from African Americans than did Kennedy. Another advantage that Democrats now enjoy is with female voters, who preferred Kerry by 7 percent more than men. Interestingly, women were actually slightly less likely than men to have supported the handsome JFK in 1960. Finally, the rapidly expanding Hispanic population in the U.S. has reshaped the electoral scene with their tendency to support Democratic candidates. Hispanics numbered only about 1 percent of voters.

	KENNEDY	NIXON		KERRY	BUSH
Protestant	36	63		40	59
Catholic	83	17		47	52
Jewish	89	11		74	25
Regularly attend religious services	49	50		39	60
Often attend regligious services	36	64		49	50
Seldom attend religious services	55	44		54	45
Never attend religious services	51	49		62	36
White	48	52		41	58
African American	71	29		88	11
Hispanic	NA	NA		57	40
Male	52	48		44	55
Female	47	53		51	48
18–29	53	47		54	45
30–44	51	49		46	53
45–64	50	50		47	52
65+	39	61		47	52
No HS diploma	55	45		50	49
High school diploma	52	48		47	52
Some college	33	67		46	54
College degree	38	62		49	50

Source: 1960 National Election Study and 2004 National Voter Exit Poll.

Young People and Politics

How Young Voters Have Consistently Been More Supportive of Third Party Candidates

Over the last four decades there have been a number of important third party or independent candidates for the presidency. These candidates differed a great deal according to political ideology. George Wallace ran in 1968 as a conservative; Ross Perot offered the voters a centrist choice in the 1992 and 1996 elections; and John Anderson in 1980 and Ralph Nader in 2000 were liberals. Yet all of these candidates had one thing in common in terms of their supporters—they all drew a higher percentage of the votes of young adults than any other age group, as you can see in the national survey findings displayed here.

The reason young voters have been consistently more supportive of third party or independent candidates is that they are more likely to be political independents, without habitual ties to the Democrats or Republicans. As we saw in Chapter 8, young people are more likely to be political independents, and independents are more open to alternatives outside the two-party system. Thus, when a conservative third party candidate is on the ballot young conservatives are more likely to vote for him than older conservatives, and when a liberal third party candidate runs young liberals are more likely to support him than older liberals. Should a third party candidate ever win nation-

wide it is likely that young voters will be in forefront of his or her political supporters.

	George Wallace 1968	John Anderson 1980	Ross Perot 1992	Ross Perot 1996	Ralph Nader 2000
18–29	15	16	28	14	5
30–44	11	11	19	11	2
45–64	12	8	17	7	2
65+	8	3	12	5	2

Sources: 1968, 1980, 1992, and 1996 National Election Studies; 2000 National Voter Exit Poll.

Questions for Discussion
- Are young people sending a message to the two major parties by supporting alternative candidates?
- If America were like most European countries in using proportional representation in its elections, would young people be the supporters of new parties that might have a big impact?

open to the possibility of voting for candidates who are neither Democrats nor Republicans, as you can read about in "Young People and Politics: How Young Voters Have Consistently Been More Supportive of Third Party Candidates."

Candidate Evaluations: How Americans See the Candidates

All candidates try to present a favorable personal image. Using laboratory experiments, political psychologists Shawn Rosenberg and Patrick McCafferty showed that it is possible to manipulate a candidate's appearance in a way that affects voters' choices. Holding a candidate's policy views and party identification constant, they found that when good pictures are substituted for bad ones, a candidate's vote-getting ability is significantly increased. Although a laboratory setting may not be representative of the real world, Rosenberg and McCafferty conclude that "with appropriate pretesting and adequate control over a candidate's public appearance, a campaign consultant should be able to significantly manipulate the image projected to the voting public."[13]

To do so, a consultant would need to know what sort of candidate images voters are most attuned to. Research by Miller, Wattenberg, and Malanchuk shows that the three most important dimensions of candidate image are integrity, reliability, and competence.[14] In 2000, one of the key factors that helped George W. Bush was that he was rated fairly positively on integrity whereas Gore scored rather poorly on this dimension. In addition to honesty and integrity, a good candidate should also be seen as dependable and decisive—traits that Miller, Wattenberg, and Malanchuk label as "reliability." When George Bush broke his "no new taxes" pledge prior to the 1992 campaign, his image of reliability clearly suffered. The personal traits most often mentioned by voters, though, involve competence. Incumbent presidents typically score much higher on competence, as they have proven experience in dealing with national and international crises. This is one of the biggest reasons why it is so difficult to defeat a sitting president who is running for a second term.

Such evaluations of candidate personality are sometimes seen as superficial and irrational judgments. Miller and his colleagues disagree with this interpretation, arguing that voters rely on their assessments of candidates' personalities to predict how they would perform in office. If a candidate is too incompetent to carry out policy promises, or too dishonest for those promises to be trusted, it makes perfect sense for a voter to pay more attention to personality than policies. Interestingly, Miller and his colleagues find that college-educated voters are actually the most likely to view the candidates in terms of their personal attributes. They argue that better educated voters are able to make important issue-oriented inferences from these attributes (for example, that a candidate who is unreliable may not be the right person to be the commander in chief of the armed forces).

Policy Voting

Policy voting occurs when people base their choices in an election on their own issue preferences. True policy voting can only take place when four conditions are met. First, voters must have a clear view of their own policy positions. Second, voters must know where the candidates stand on policy issues. Third, they must see differences between the candidates on these issues. And finally, they must actually cast a vote for the candidate whose policy positions coincide with their own. Given these conditions, policy voting is not always easy—even for the educated voter. Abramson, Aldrich, and Rohde analyzed responses to nine questions about policy issues in the 2000 National

policy voting

Electoral choices that are made on the basis of the voters' policy preferences and on the basis of where the candidates stand on policy issues.

"It's a good speech—just a couple of points that need obfuscation."

Election Study. They found that 51 percent of the respondents met the first three informational criteria for policy voting on the average issue. About 68 percent of the time, when someone knew the candidates' stances and saw differences between them, they voted for the candidate closest to their own position.[15] Of course, we should never expect all votes to be consistent with policy views, as many people will prefer one candidate on some policies and another candidate on other policies.

One regular obstacle to policy voting is that candidates often decide that the best way to handle a controversial issue is to cloud their positions in rhetoric. For example, in 1968 both major party candidates—Nixon and Humphrey—were deliberately ambiguous about what they would do to end the Vietnam War. This made it extremely difficult for voters to cast their ballots according to how they felt about the war. The media may not be much help, either, as they typically focus more on the "horse race" aspects of the campaign than on the policy stands of the candidates, as discussed in Chapter 7. Voters thus often have to work fairly hard just to be well informed enough to potentially engage in policy voting.

In today's political world, it is somewhat easier for voters to vote according to policies than it was in the 1950s or 1960s. The key difference is that candidates are now regularly forced to take clear stands to appeal to their own party's primary voters. As late as 1968, it was still possible to win a nomination by dealing with the party bosses; today's candidates must appeal first to the issue-oriented activists in the primaries. Whatever the major issues are in the next presidential election, it is quite likely that the major contenders for the Democratic and Republican nominations will be taking stands on them in order to gain the support of these activists. Thus, what has changed is not the voters, but the electoral process that now provides much more incentive for candidates to draw clear policy distinctions between one another.

Party voting, candidate evaluation, and policy voting all play a role in elections. Their impact is not equal from one election to another, but they are the main factors affecting voter decisions. Once voters make their decisions in presidential elections, it is not just a simple matter of counting the ballots to see who has won the most support nationwide. Rather, the complicated process of determining electoral college votes begins.

The Last Battle: The Electoral College

electoral college

A unique American institution, created by the Constitution, providing for the selection of the president by electors chosen by the state parties. Although the electoral college vote usually reflects a popular majority, the winner-take-all rule gives clout to big states.

It is the members of the **electoral college,** not the people at large, who actually cast the determining votes for president and vice president of the United States. The electoral college is a unique American institution, created by the Constitution. The American Bar Association once called it, "archaic, undemocratic, complex, ambiguous, indirect, and dangerous."[16] Many, but certainly not all, political scientists oppose its continued use, as do most voters.

The Founders wanted the president to be selected by the nation's elite, not directly by the people. They created the electoral college for this purpose, and left the decision as to how the electors are chosen to each state. Since 1828, though, political practice has been for electors to vote for the candidate who won their state's popular vote. This is how the electoral college system works today:

- Each state, according to the Constitution, has as many electoral votes as it has U.S. senators and representatives.[17] The state parties select slates of electors, positions they use as a reward for faithful service to the party.
- Aside from Maine and Nebraska, each state has a winner-take-all system.[18] Electors vote as a bloc for the winner, whether the winner got 35 percent or 95 percent of the popular vote in their state.
- Electors meet in their states in December, following the November election, and then mail their votes to the vice president (who is also president of the Senate). The vote is counted when the new congressional session opens in January, and reported by the vice president. Thus, Dick Cheney had the duty of announcing the reelection of George W. Bush in January of 2005.

Participation

The Electoral College

Table 10.3 Presidential Vote in 2000 by State Representation in the Electoral College (in Percents)

States with less than seven electoral votes are overrepresented in the electoral college. Therefore, the fact that George W. Bush did especially well in these states in 2000, as shown in this table, helped him to win the presidency without winning the popular vote—the first time a candidate accomplished this feat since 1888.

	BUSH	GORE	NADER	OTHERS
Electoral votes < 7	52.5	42.3	3.7	1.5
7–18	48.9	47.6	2.5	1.0
> 18	45.7	50.7	2.7	0.9

Source: Calculated by the authors from official election returns.

- If no candidate receives an electoral college majority, then the election is thrown into the House of Representatives, which must choose from among the top three electoral vote winners. A significant aspect of the balloting in the House is that each state delegation has one vote, thus giving the 1 representative from Wyoming an equal say with the 53 representatives from California. Though the Founders envisioned that the House would often have to vote to choose the president, this has not occurred since 1828.

The electoral college is important to the presidential election for two reasons. First, it introduces a bias into the campaign and electoral process. Because each state gets two electors for its Senators regardless of population, the less populated states are overrepresented. One of the key reasons that George W. Bush won the electoral college vote in 2000 without winning the popular vote was that he did better in the small states, as shown in Table 10.3. Secondly, the winner-take-all rule means that candidates will necessarily focus on winning the states where the polls show that there appears to be a close contest. Thus, Bush and Kerry paid a great deal of attention to Ohio and Florida during the last month of the 2004 campaign but spent no time or money on states where the outcome seemed to be a foregone conclusion, such as New York and Texas.

Understanding Elections and Voting Behavior

Elections accomplish two tasks according to democratic theory. First, and most obviously, they *select the policymakers*. Second, elections are supposed to help *shape public policy*. Whether elections in fact make the government pay attention to what the people think is at the center of debate concerning how well democracy works in America. In the hypothetical world of rational choice theory and the Downs model (see Chapter 8), elections do in fact guide public policy; however, over a generation of social science research on this question has produced mixed findings. It is more accurate to describe the connection between elections and public policy as a two-way street: Elections, to some degree, affect public policy, and public policy decisions partly affect electoral outcomes.

Democracy and Elections

There will probably never be a definitive answer to the question of how much elections affect public policy—for it is a somewhat subjective matter. The broad contours of the answer, however, seem reasonably clear: *The greater the policy differences between the candidates, the more likely voters will be able to steer government policies by their choices.*

Of course, the candidates do not always help to clarify the issues. One result is that the policy stands are often shaped by what Benjamin Page once called "the art of ambiguity," in which "presidential candidates are skilled at appearing to say much while

The final chapter of any presidential campaign is the swearing in of the winner at noon on the following January 20. Here, Chief Justice Rehnquist administers the oath to George W. Bush as Laura Bush holds the Bible.

retrospective voting

A theory of voting in which voters essentially ask this simple question: "What have you done for me lately?

actually saying little."[19] Learning how to sidestep controversial questions and hedge answers is indeed part of becoming a professional politician, as you can observe at almost every presidential press conference.

When individual candidates do offer a plain choice to the voters (what 1964 Republican nominee Barry Goldwater once called "a choice, not an echo"), voters are better able to guide the government's policy direction. Ronald Reagan followed in Goldwater's footsteps in the 1980s by making clear his intention to cut the growth of domestic spending, reduce taxes, and build up American military capability. Once elected, he proceeded to do much of what he said he would—demonstrating that elections can sometimes dramatically affect public policy.

If elections affect policies, then policies can also affect elections. Most policies have consequences for the well-being of certain groups or the society as a whole. Those who feel better off as a result of certain policies are likely to support candidates who pledge to continue those policies, whereas those who feel worse off are inclined to support opposition candidates. This is known as the theory of **retrospective voting**,[20] in which voters essentially ask the simple question, "What have you done for me lately?" Incumbents who provide desired results are rewarded; those who fail to do so are not reelected.

Nothing makes incumbent politicians more nervous than the state of the economy. When the economy takes a downturn, the call to "throw the rascals out" usually sweeps the nation. In presidential elections, people unhappy with the state of the economy tend to blame the incumbent. Republican Herbert Hoover was in office when the stock market crash of 1929 sparked the Great Depression. Hoover and his fellow Republicans were crushed by Franklin Roosevelt in the 1932 elections. In 2004, Democrats were still hitting the Republicans with the memory of Hoover—calling George W. Bush a modern day Hoover whose administration had presided over more job losses than gains nationwide.

Clearly, elections affect policy, and public policy—especially the perception of economic policy impacts—can affect elections. Once in office, politicians use fiscal policy to keep the American economy running on an even keel. (How they try to do this is considered in Chapter 17.) If economic troubles mount, voters point their fingers at incumbent policymakers, and those fingers are more likely to pull the lever for the challengers on Election Day. In recent elections people who felt the national econ-

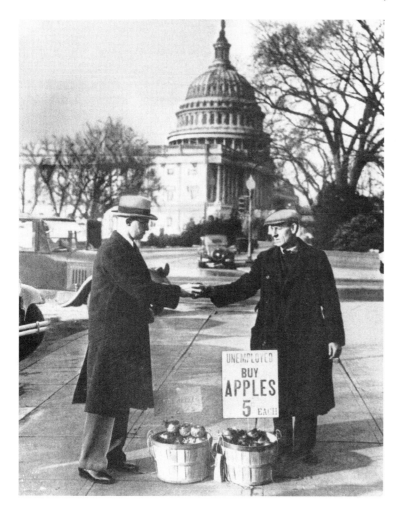

Economic conditions can have a profound effect on election outcomes. In 1932, voters expressed their despair over the Great Depression by electing Franklin Roosevelt in a landslide over Herbert Hoover. Here, an unemployed man sells "Hoover apples" in front of the capitol.

omy had improved voted strongly for the incumbent whereas those who thought the economy had gotten worse strongly favored the major challenger. As V. O. Key once wrote, "The only really effective weapon of popular control in a democratic regime is the capacity of the electorate to throw a party from power."[21]

Elections and the Scope of Government

While the threat of electoral punishment constrains policymakers, it also helps to increase generalized support for government and its powers. Voters know that the government can be replaced at the next election, so they are much more likely to feel that it will be responsive to their needs. Furthermore, when people have the power to dole out electoral reward and punishment, they are more likely to see government as their servant instead of their master. As Benjamin Ginsberg writes, "Democratic elections help to persuade citizens that expansion of the state's powers represents an increase in the state's capacity to serve them."[22]

Therefore, rather than wishing to be protected from the state, citizens in a democracy often seek to benefit from it. It is no coincidence that "individuals who believe they can influence the government's actions are also more likely to believe, in turn, that the government should have more power."[23] Voters like to feel that they are sending a message to the government to accomplish something. It should thus be no surprise that as democracy has spread government has come to do more and more, and its scope has grown.

Comparing Voting and Elections

Summary

This chapter has examined the final act in the electoral drama. Once the parties have made their nominations and the campaign has concluded, voters take center stage. Elections have changed dramatically since 1800 when Adams ran against Jefferson. By 1896, it was acceptable for candidates to campaign in person, and William Jennings Bryan did so with a vengeance. At that time suffrage—the right to vote—was still limited mostly to White males. Now the democratization of elections has made suffrage available to virtually all American citizens over the age of 18.

Voters make two basic decisions at election time. The first is whether to vote. Americans' right to vote is well established, but in order to do so citizens must go through the registration process. Although registration reform has been touted as the answer to America's low turnout problems, the Motor Voter Act of 1993 has yet to produce the benefit of greater voter participation that most people hoped for. Turnout in 2004 was still relatively low, identical to what it was in 1992. Second, those who choose to vote must decide for whom to cast their ballots. Over a generation of research on voting behavior has helped political scientists understand the dominant role played by three factors in voters' choices: party identification, candidate evaluations, and policy positions.

Elections are the centerpiece of democracy. Few questions are more important in understanding American government than this: Do elections matter? Under the right conditions, elections can influence public policy, and policy outcomes can influence elections. Elections also legitimize the power of the state, thereby making it easier to expand the scope of the government.

KEY TERMS

legitimacy	civic duty	policy voting
referendum	voter registration	electoral college
initiative petition	Motor Voter Act	retrospective voting
suffrage	mandate theory of	
political efficacy	elections	

INTERNET RESOURCES

www.umich.edu/~nes
The National Election Studies are a standard source of survey data about voting behavior. You can find information about these studies, as well as some of the results from them, at this site.

www.annenbergpublicpolicycenter.org/naes/
A good source of information on public views during the 2004 presidential campaign.

www.census.gov/population/www/socdemo/voting.html
The Census Bureau's studies of registration and turnout can be found at this address.

GET CONNECTED

The Help America Vote Act

On October 29, 2002, President Bush signed HR 3295, the Help America Vote Act (HAVA). This federal legislation created many new mandates for state and local government. The new law was enacted to improve voting system technology and election administration procedures. It was a result of the problems that occurred during the 2000 presidential election, especially the problems with outdated punch-card voting technology.

Search the Web

Go to the National Association of Secretaries of State webpage on HAVA *http://www.nass.org/electioninfo/HAVApage.htm* to find out how your state is implementing the federal law. Take a look at the League of Women Voters' page on HAVA *http://www.lwv.org/join/elections/hava_resources.html* and read about the group's suggestions for implementing HAVA and some of the issues related to electronic voting technology.

Questions to Ask

- What actions are election officials in your state taking to implement HAVA?
- What are some of the issues raised by election officials in your state in implementing HAVA?
- Are there any problems with electronic voting technology? What are those problems?

Why It Matters

Voting is an integral part of the American form of government. It is through voting that people can voice their concerns and choose people to represent them. If the voting technology does not adequately record votes, then voters will lose confidence in their ability to change government through their vote. We certainly do not want a repeat of the public problems that plagued voting in the 2000 presidential elections.

Get Involved

Find out what voting technology is used in your local area. Working with your local election officials, prepare a guidebook to help voters better understand that technology so they are less likely to be intimidated by the technology when they enter the polling place.

To see more Get Connected exercises for Chapter 10, go to www.ablongman.com/edwards.

FOR FURTHER READING

Abramson, Paul R., John H. Aldrich, and David W. Rohde. *Change and Continuity in the 2000 Elections.* Washington, D.C.: Congressional Quarterly Press, 2002. A good overview of voting behavior in the 2000 elections, which also focuses on recent historical trends.

Campbell, Angus, et al. *The American Voter.* New York: John Wiley, 1960. The classic study of the American electorate in the 1950s, which has shaped scholarly approaches to the subject ever since.

Kelley, Stanley G., Jr., *Interpreting Elections.* Princeton, NJ: Princeton University Press, 1983. Presents a theory of "the simple act of voting."

Nie, Norman H., Sidney Verba, and John R. Petrocik. *The Changing American Voter.* Cambridge, MA: Harvard University Press, 1976. Challenges some of the assumptions of Campbell et al.'s *The American Voter.*

Niemi, Richard G., and Herbert F. Weisberg, eds. *Controversies in Voting Behavior,* 4th ed. Washington, D.C.: Congressional Quarterly Press, 2001. An excellent set of readings on some of the most hotly debated facets of voting.

Polsby, Nelson W., and Aaron Wildavsky. *Presidential Elections,* 11th ed. Lanham, MD: Rowman and Littlefield, 2004. The classic text on the subject.

Pomper, Gerald M., et al. *The Election of 2000: Reports and Interpretations.* Chatham, NJ: Chatham House, 2001. A good collection of readings on a variety of aspects of the 2000 campaign.

Smith, Daniel A. *Tax Crusaders and the Politics of Direct Democracy.* New York: Routledge, 1998. A collection of interesting essays about activists who have made a difference through their advocacy of tax cut initiatives.

Wattenberg, Martin P. *Where Have All the Voters Gone?* Cambridge, MA: Harvard University Press, 2002. A review of the reasons for declining voter turnout, both in the United States and other advanced industrialized countries.

Wolfinger, Raymond E., and Steven J. Rosenstone. *Who Votes?* New Haven, CT: Yale University Press, 1980. A classic quantitative study of who turns out and why.

Interest Groups

11

Chapter Outline

The Role of Interest Groups

Theories of Interest Group Politics

What Makes an Interest Group Successful?

The Interest Group Explosion

How Groups Try To Shape Policy

The New York Times **Issues of the Times**

Types of Interest Groups

Understanding Interest Groups

Summary

■ Just before Christmas of 2002, a very unusual quarter-page advertisement appeared in the *New York Times* and other major papers around the country. It was placed by the public interest journal entitled *TomPaine.commonsense (www.tompaine.com)*. The bold headline read "Reward $10,000: For Information Leading to the Identification of the Eli Lilly Bandit." The story they told was one of corporate lobbyists using their influence to get a special provision written into law at the last minute with no one watching. As a public interest journal, *TomPaine.commonsense* strives to insure open and accountable government. They regularly seek to expose cases of corporations getting sweet deals from government policymakers. Eli Lilly & Company, a giant drug manufacturer, had gotten such a deal, and *TomPaine.commonsense* sought to at least publicize this fact, if not get to the bottom of how their lobbyists accomplished the feat.

The mystery is one worthy of Sherlock Holmes. In November 2002, Congress passed a 475-page bill creating the new Department of Homeland Security. Somehow or other, a little provision was slipped into this bill that seemingly had nothing to do with the topic of homeland security. This provision gave Eli Lilly & Company something it badly wanted—a shield from multimillion-dollar lawsuits. Lilly was facing numerous lawsuits from parents who claimed that their children's autism was linked to Thimerosal, a mercury-based preservative made by

Lilly that is a common ingredient in childhood vaccines. The provision diverted those suits from state courts to a federal vaccine court, where damages are capped at $250,000. How did such a measure end up in a bill dealing with homeland security? It was slipped in during the conference committee negotiations, which are held behind closed doors. But who slipped it in? That's what *TomPaine.commonsense* offered $10,000 to find out.

Strangely, in a city where knowledge is power and where people are usually eager to take credit for any political accomplishment, no one in Washington was willing to take credit for the passage of the measure helping Eli Lilly. The company's lobbyists claimed ignorance. Of course they had long wanted to get something like this passed, but they claimed they had never thought of getting it into the Homeland Security Act. And Office of Management and Budget Director Mitch Daniels, a former company executive at Eli Lilly, went to considerable lengths to deny any knowledge of the matter. As of this writing, the mystery still remains and the $10,000 reward money remains unclaimed.

The worst and oldest stereotype of a lobbyist is of someone who bribes a lawmaker to get a favorable policy decision. In contrast, whoever the "Eli Lilly Bandit" was, he or she used leverage with members of Congress that was probably obtained by open and legal means. The fact that Eli Lilly & Company had donated $1.6 million to the national parties and to federal candidates in the preceding two years likely had something to do with what happened. Note that such donations were perfectly legal and a matter of public record.

By making the American political system so openly democratic, the means have been created for an incredible array of interests to be heard loud and clear in Washington. Some critics believe the basic problem is that there are too many interest groups making demands on the government; others say the real problem is that the moneyed interests get a disproportionate share of access and influence. Those who are concerned the system is too democratic often argue that the result is the frustration of any proposals for changing the existing scope of government. For those most concerned with the domination of well-off interest groups, the scope of government that results is inevitably seen as helping the rich get richer. Nevertheless, there are scholars who believe the interest group system is working pretty much as the Founders intended. James Madison argued in *Federalist Paper No.10* that the sphere of influence must be extended in order to prevent any one group from having too much power. Whether we are far along in reaching this goal is a crucial question for you to consider when reading this chapter.

Our nation's capital has become a hub of interest group activity. On any given day, it is possible to observe pressure groups in action in many forums. In the morning, you could attend congressional hearings in which you are sure to see interest groups testifying for and against proposed legislation. At the Supreme Court, you might stop in to watch a public interest lawyer arguing for strict enforcement of environmental regulations. Take a break for lunch at a nice Washington restaurant, and you may see a lobbyist entertaining a member of Congress.

You could spend the afternoon in any department of the executive branch (such as commerce, labor, or the interior), where you might catch bureaucrats working out rules and regulations with friendly—or sometimes unfriendly—representatives of the interests they are charged with overseeing. You could stroll past the impressive headquarters of the National Rifle Association, the AFL-CIO, or the American Association of Retired Persons to get a sense of the size of some of the major lobbying organizations. To see some lobbying done on college students' behalf, you might drop by One Dupont Circle, where all the higher education groups have their offices. These groups lobby for student loans and scholarships, as well as for aid to educational institutions. At dinner time, if you are able to finagle an invitation to a Georgetown cocktail party, you may see lobbyists trying to get the ear of government officials—both elected and unelected.

All this lobbying activity poses an interesting paradox: Although turnout in elections has declined since 1960, participation in interest groups has mushroomed. As Kay Schlozman and John Tierney write, "Recent decades have witnessed an expansion of astonishing proportions in the involvement of private organizations in Washington politics."[1] This chapter will explore the factors behind the interest group explosion, how these groups enter the policymaking process, and what they get out of it.

The Role of Interest Groups

All Americans have some interests they want represented. Organizing to promote these interests is an essential part of democracy. The right to organize groups is protected by the Constitution, which guarantees people the right "peaceably to assemble, and to petition the Government for a redress of grievances." This important First Amendment right has been carefully defended by the Supreme Court. The freedom to organize is as fundamental to democratic government as freedom of speech and freedom of the press.

interest group

An organization of people with shared policy goals entering the policy process at several points to try to achieve those goals. Interest groups pursue their goals in many arenas.

The term *interest group* seems simple enough to define. Interest refers to a policy goal; a group is a combination of people. An **interest group,** therefore, is an organization of people with similar policy goals who enter the political process to try to achieve those aims. Whatever their goals—outlawing abortion or ensuring the right to one, regulating tax loopholes or creating new ones—interest groups pursue them in many arenas. Every branch of government is fair game; every level of government, local to federal, is a possible target. A policy battle lost in Congress may be turned around when it comes to bureaucratic implementation or to the judicial process.

This multiplicity of policy arenas helps distinguish interest groups from political parties. Parties fight their battles through the electoral process; they run candidates for public office. Interest groups may support candidates for office, but American interest groups do not run their own slate of candidates, as in some other countries (see "America in Perspective: Interest Groups as Parties in Other Democracies" on page 326). In other words, no serious candidate is ever listed on the ballot as a candidate of the National Rifle Association or Common Cause. It may be well known that a candidate is actively supported by a particular group, but that candidate faces the voters as a Democrat, a Republican, or a third-party candidate.

Another key difference between parties and interest groups is that interest groups are often policy specialists, whereas parties are policy generalists. Most interest groups have a handful of key policies to push: A farm group cares little about the status of

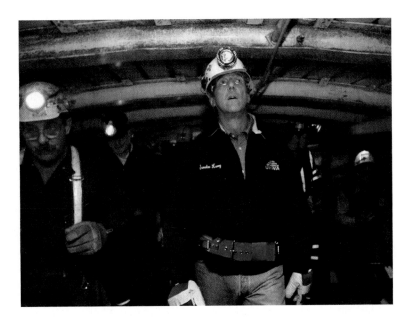

All candidates for public office seek to obtain the votes of various interest groups. Here, John Kerry tours a coal mine in order to learn about concerns of coal miners and to show that he cares about people like them.

urban transit; an environmental group has its hands full bringing polluters into court without worrying about the minimum wage. Unlike political parties, these groups do not face the constraints imposed by trying to appeal to everyone.

Theories of Interest Group Politics

Understanding the debate over whether honest lobbying—and interest groups in general—create problems for government in America requires an examination of three important theories, which were introduced in Chapter 1. **Pluralist theory** argues that interest group activity brings representation to all. According to pluralists, groups compete and counterbalance one another in the political marketplace. In contrast, **elite theory** argues that a few groups (primarily the wealthy) have most of the power. Finally, **hyperpluralist theory** asserts that too many groups are getting too much of what they want, resulting in government policy that is often contradictory and lacking in direction. The following sections will examine each of these three theories with respect to interest groups.

pluralist theory

A theory of government and politics emphasizing that politics is mainly a competition among groups, each one pressing for its own preferred policies.

elite theory

A theory of government and politics contending that societies are divided along class lines and that an upper-class elite will rule, regardless of the formal niceties of governmental organization.

hyperpluralist theory

A theory of government and politics contending that groups are so strong that government is weakened. Hyperpluralism is an extreme, exaggerated, or perverted form of **pluralism.**

"YOU'LL LIKE THEM ... THEIR SPECIAL INTEREST IS GIVING AWAY MORE MONEY THAN OTHER SPECIAL INTEREST GROUPS!"

America in Perspective

Interest Groups as Parties in Other Democracies

In many countries with multiparty systems, interest groups form their own political parties to push for their demands. With proportional representation systems (see Chapter 8), all it takes is between 1 and 5 percent of the vote, depending on the country, for a narrowly based party to win seats in the national legislature. Although special interest groups usually cannot win very many seats, their impact can be large if their votes are crucial in obtaining a majority in the Parliament.

In many of the Scandinavian countries, for example, farmers' parties have long been in existence. Typically, the farmers' party has received between 10 and 20 percent of the vote in nations such as Sweden and Finland. For a conservative, nonsocialist government to be formed, their support is often critical. Therefore, any conservative government in these countries will be quite responsive to agrarian interests. If you are troubled by the fact that American agricultural policy is heavily influenced by congressional representatives from farm states, imagine a situation where key officeholders owe their election exclusively to this single economic interest.

Many new interest groups in Europe have formed parties not on the basis of shared economic interests, such as labor or agriculture, but rather on the basis of shared values. In particular, Green parties have sprung up throughout Western Europe to represent the concerns of environmentalists. Imagine having two dozen members of the American Congress insist on discussing the environmental impact of every decision. These members might not often win, but they would certainly draw more attention to the issue of environmental protection. This is the situation in countries such as Germany where the Greens have won enough votes to enter the national legislature and are currently part of the governing coalition.

Pluralism and Group Theory

Pluralist theory rests its case on the many centers of power in the American political system. Pluralists consider the extensive organization of competing groups evidence that influence is widely dispersed among them. They believe that groups win some and lose some but that no group wins or loses all the time. Pluralist theorists offer a *group theory of politics*, which contains several essential arguments.[2]

- *Groups provide a key link between people and government.* All legitimate interests in the political system can get a hearing from government once they are organized.
- *Groups compete.* Labor, business, farmers, consumers, environmentalists, and other interests constantly make competing claims on the government.
- *No one group is likely to become too dominant.* When one group throws its weight around too much, its opponents are likely to intensify their organization and thus restore balance to the system. For every action, there is a reaction.
- *Groups usually play by the "rules of the game."* In the United States, group politics is a fair fight, with few groups lying, cheating, stealing, or engaging in violence to get their way.
- *Groups weak in one resource can use another.* Big business may have money on its side, but labor has numbers. All legitimate groups are able to affect public policy by one means or another.

Pluralists would never deny that some groups are stronger than others or that competing interests do not always get an equal hearing. Still, they can point to many cases in which a potential group organized itself and, once organized, affected policy decisions. African Americans, women, and consumers are all groups who were long ignored by government officials but who, once organized, redirected the course of public policy. In sum, pluralists argue that lobbying is open to all and is therefore not to be regarded as a problem.

Elites and the Denial of Pluralism

Whereas pluralists are impressed by the vast number of organized interests, elitists are impressed by how insignificant most of them are. Real power, elitists say, is held by relatively few people, key groups, and institutions. They maintain that the government is run by a few big interests looking out for themselves—a view that the majority of the public has usually agreed with in recent decades, as you can see in Figure 11.1.

Elitists critique pluralist theory by pointing to the concentration of power in a few hands. Where pluralists find dispersion of power, elitists find interlocking and concentrated power centers. About one-third of top institutional positions—corporate boards, foundation boards, university trusteeships, and so on—are occupied by people who hold more than one such position.[3] Elitists see the rise of mighty multinational corporations as further tightening the control of corporate elites. A prime example is America's giant oil companies. Robert Engler has tried to show that government has always bent over backward to maintain high profits for the oil industry.[4] When they come up against the power of these multinational corporations, consumer interests are readily pushed aside, according to elitists.

In sum, the elitist view of the interest group system makes the following assertions:

- The fact that there are numerous groups proves nothing because groups are extremely unequal in power.
- Awesome power is held by the largest corporations.
- The power of a few is fortified by an extensive system of interlocking directorates.
- Other groups may win many minor policy battles, but the corporate elites prevail when it comes to the big decisions.

Figure 11.1   Perceptions of the Dominance of Big Interests

Would you say the government is pretty much run by a few big interests looking out for themselves or that it is run for the benefit of all the people?

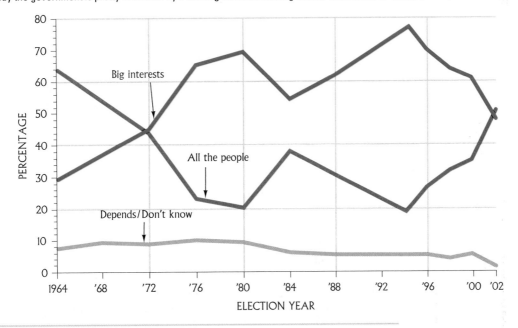

Source: Authors' analysis of 1964–2002 American National Election Study data.

Thus, even honest lobbying is a problem, say elite theorists, because it benefits few at the expense of many.

Hyperpluralism and Interest Group Liberalism

Hyperpluralists, also critical of pluralism, argue that the pluralist system is out of control. Theodore Lowi coined the phrase *interest group liberalism* to refer to the government's excessive deference to groups. Interest group liberalism holds that virtually all pressure group demands are legitimate and that the job of the government is to advance them all.[5]

In an effort to please and appease every interest, agencies proliferate, conflicting regulations expand, programs multiply, and of course, the budget skyrockets. If environmentalists want clean air, government imposes clean-air rules; if businesses complain that cleaning up pollution is expensive, government gives them a tax write-off for pollution control equipment. If the direct-mail industry wants cheap rates, government gives it to them; if people complain about junk mail, the postal service gives them a way to take their names off mailing lists. If cancer researchers convince the government to launch an antismoking campaign, tobacco sales may drop; if they do, government will subsidize tobacco farmers to ease their loss.[6]

Interest group liberalism is promoted by the network of **subgovernments** in the American political system that exercise a great deal of control over specific policy areas. These subgovernments, which are also known as iron triangles, are composed of key interest group leaders interested in policy X, the government agency in charge of administering policy X, and the members of congressional committees and subcommittees handling policy X.

All the elements composing subgovernments have the same goal: protecting their self-interest. The network of subgovernments in the agricultural policy area of tobacco is an excellent example. Tobacco interest groups include the Tobacco Institute, the Retail Tobacco Distributors of America, and the tobacco growers. Various agencies in the Department of Agriculture administer tobacco programs, and they depend on the tobacco industry's clout in Congress to help keep their agency budgets safe from cuts. Finally, most of the members of the House Tobacco Subcommittee are from tobacco-growing regions. All these elements want to protect the interests of tobacco farmers. Similar subgovernments of group-agency-committee ties exist in scores of other policy areas.

Hyperpluralists' major criticism of the interest group system is that relations between groups and the government have become too cozy. Hard choices about national policy are rarely made. Instead of making choices between X and Y, the government pretends there is no need to choose and instead tries to favor both policies. It is a perfect script for policy gridlock. In short, the hyperpluralist position on group politics is that:

- Groups have become too powerful in the political process as government tries to appease every conceivable interest.
- Interest group liberalism is aggravated by numerous subgovernments—comfortable relationships among a government agency, the interest group it deals with, and congressional subcommittees.
- Trying to please every group results in contradictory and confusing policy.

Ironically, the recent interest group explosion is seen by some scholars as weakening the power of subgovernments. As Morris Fiorina writes, "A world of active public interest groups, jealous business competitors, and packs of budding investigative reporters is less hospitable to subgovernment politics than a world lacking in them."[7] With so many more interest groups to satisfy, and with many of them competing against one another, a cozy relationship between groups and the government is plainly more difficult to sustain.

---

subgovernments

A network of groups within the American political system that exercise a great deal of control over specific policy areas. Also known as iron triangles, subgovernments are composed of interest group leaders interested in a particular policy, the government agency in charge of administering that policy, and the members of congressional committees and subcommittees handling that policy.

Why It Matters

Theories of Interest Group Politics

Suppose James Madison's descendants were studying American government in order to assess how well the system he devised controls the power of special interests. They would definitely draw different conclusions depending on whether they assessed the current system using pluralist, elitist, or hyperpluralist interpretations. A pluralist interpretation could be seen as evidence that Madison's system has worked as intended. An elitist interpretation would hold that the wealthy in particular hold too much power, whereas a hyperpluralist interpretation would indicate would indicate that too many groups have too much power.

What Makes an Interest Group Successful?

In recent years, *Fortune* magazine has issued a yearly list of the 25 most powerful interest groups in politics. Table 11.1 displays one of their lists and a quick look will probably reveal some surprises. Some of these powerful lobbying groups are relatively unknown.

Many factors affect the success of an interest group, as indicated by the diversity of groups in *Fortune's* "Power 25." Among these factors are the size of the group, its intensity, and its financial resources. While greater intensity and more financial resources work to a group's advantage, surprisingly, smaller groups are more likely to achieve their goals than larger groups.

The Surprising Ineffectiveness of Large Groups

In one of the most oft-quoted statements concerning interest groups, E.E. Schattschneider wrote that "pressure politics is essentially the politics of small groups. . . . Pressure tactics are not remarkably successful in mobilizing general interests."[8] There are perfectly good reasons why consumer groups are less effective than producer groups, patients are less effective than doctors, and energy conservationists are less effective than oil companies: Small groups have organizational advantages over large groups.

Table 11.1   The Power 25

Fortune magazine has long been famous for its lists of the richest companies and individuals in the country. Lately, editors have expanded their analysis to ranking the most powerful lobbying associations. Members of Congress, prominent congressional staffers, senior White House aides, and top-ranking officers of the largest lobbying groups in Washington were asked to assess, on a scale of 0 to 100, the political clout of 87 major trade associations, labor unions, and interest groups. Here is the list of the groups that finished in the top 25 in terms of political clout in 2001:

1. National Rifle Association
2. American Association of Retired Persons
3. National Federation of Independent Business
4. American Israel Public Affairs Committee
5. Association of Trial Lawyers of America
6. AFL-CIO
7. Chamber of Commerce
8. National Beer Wholesalers Association
9. National Association of Realtors
10. National Association of Manufacturers
11. National Association of Homebuilders
12. American Medical Association
13. American Hospital Association
14. National Education Association
15. American Farm Bureau Federation
16. Motion Picture Association of America
17. National Association of Broadcasters
18. National Right to Life Committee
19. Health Insurance Association of America
20. National Restaurant Association
21. National Governors' Association
22. Recording Industry
23. American Bankers Association
24. Pharmaceutical Research and Manufacturers of America
25. International Brotherhood of Teamsters

Source: Fortune magazine.

potential group

All the people who might be **interest group** members because they share some common interest. A potential group is almost always larger than an actual group.

actual group

That part of the **potential group** consisting of members who actually join.

collective good

Something of value (money, a tax write-off, prestige, clean air, and so on) that cannot be withheld from a group member.

free-rider problem

The problem faced by unions and other groups when people do not join because they can benefit from the group's activities without officially joining. The bigger the group, the more serious the problem.

Olson's law of large groups

Advanced by Mancur Olson, a principle stating that "the larger the group, the further it will fall short of providing an optimal amount of a collective good."

selective benefits

Goods (such as information publications, travel discounts, and group insurance rates) that a group can restrict to those who pay their annual dues.

To shed light on this point, it is important to distinguish between a potential and an actual group. A **potential group** is composed of all people who might be group members because they share some common interest.[9] In contrast, an **actual group** is composed of those in the potential group who choose to join. Groups vary enormously in the degree to which they enroll their potential membership. Consumer organizations are minuscule when compared with the total number of consumers, which is almost every American. Some organizations, however, do very well in organizing virtually all their potential members. The National Beer Wholesalers Association (ranked #8 in Table 11.1), the Tobacco Institute, and the Air Transport Association include a good portion of their potential members. Compared with consumers, these groups are tightly organized.

Economist Mancur Olson explains this phenomenon in *The Logic of Collective Action*.[10] Olson points out that all groups, unlike individuals, are in the business of providing collective goods. A **collective good** is something of value, such as clean air, that cannot be withheld from a potential group member. When the AFL-CIO wins a higher minimum wage, all low-paid workers benefit, regardless of whether they are members of the union. In other words, members of the potential group share in benefits that members of the actual group work to secure. If this is the case, an obvious and difficult problem results: Why should potential members work for something if they can get it free? Why join the group, pay dues, and work hard for a goal when a person can benefit from the group's activity without doing anything at all? A perfectly rational response is thus to sit back and let other people do the work. This is commonly known as the **free-rider problem.**

The bigger the group, the more serious the free-rider problem. That is the gist of **Olson's law of large groups:** "The larger the group, the further it will fall short of providing an optimal amount of a collective good."[11] Small groups thus have an organizational advantage over large ones. In a small group, members' shares of the collective good may be great enough that they will try to secure it. The old saying that "everyone can make a difference" is much more credible in the case of a relatively small group. In the largest groups, however, each member can expect to get only a tiny share of the policy gains. Weighing the costs of participation against the relatively small benefits, the temptation is always to "let somebody else do it." Therefore, as Olson argues, the larger the potential group, the less likely potential members are to contribute.

This distinct advantage of small groups helps explain why consumer groups have a hard time making ends meet. Such groups claim to seek "public interest" goals, but the gains they win are usually spread thin over millions of people. In contrast, the lobbying costs and benefits for business are concentrated. Suppose, for example, that consumer advocates take the airlines to court over charges of price fixing and force the airlines to return $10 million to consumers in the form of lower prices. This $10 million settlement is spread over 295 million Americans—about 4 cents per person (actually, the benefit is a little higher if one divides only by the number of people who use airlines). The $10 million airline loss is shared by 60 carriers at over $165,000 apiece. One can quickly see which side will be better organized in such a struggle.

In sum, Olson's law of large groups explains why interest groups with relatively few members are often so effective. The power of business in the American political system is thus due to more than just money, as proponents of elite theory would have us believe. Besides their financial strength, wealthy corporations also enjoy an inherent size advantage. Because there are a limited number of multinational corporations, these businesses have an easier time organizing themselves for political action than larger potential groups, such as consumers. Once well organized, large groups may be very effective, but it is much harder for them to get together in the first place.

The primary way for large potential groups to overcome Olson's law is to provide attractive benefits for only those who join the organization. **Selective benefits** are goods that a group can restrict to those who pay their yearly dues, such as information publications, travel discounts, and group insurance rates. The #2 rated group in *Fortune's* "Power 25"—the American Association of Retired Persons (AARP)—has built

Figure 11.2 The Benefits of Membership in the AARP

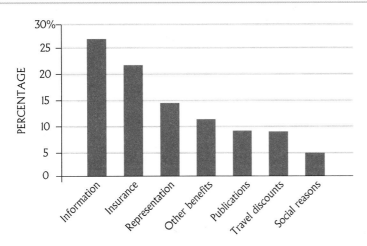

This chart illustrates the answers given by a sample of AARP members when they were asked why they had joined the organization.

Source: American Association for Retired Persons.

up a membership list of 35 million senior citizens by offering a variety of selective benefits (see Figure 11.2). Similarly, Consumers Union gains most of its members not because of its efforts on behalf of product safety but by offering the selective benefit of receiving *Consumer Reports*, a monthly magazine that rates the reliability, safety, and cost-effectiveness of products.

Intensity

Another way a large potential group may be mobilized is through an issue that people feel intensely about. Intensity is a psychological advantage that can be enjoyed by small and large groups alike. When a group shows that it cares deeply about an issue, politicians are more likely to listen; many votes may be won or lost on a single issue. The rise of single-issue groups (discussed in Chapter 1) has been one of the most dramatic political developments in recent years. Even college students have gotten into the act, forming groups to lobby against tuition increases in recent years, as you can read about in "Young People and Politics: The Virginia 21 Coalition."

A **single-issue group** can be defined as a group that has a narrow interest, dislikes compromise, and single-mindedly pursues its goal. Anti-Vietnam War activists may have formed the first modern single-issue group. Opponents of nuclear power plants, gun control (ranked #1 in "The Power 25"), and abortion are some of the many such groups that exist today. All these groups deal with issues that evoke the strong emotions characteristic of single-interest groups.

Perhaps the most emotional issue of recent times has been that of abortion. As befits the intensity of the issue, activities have not been limited to conventional means of political participation. Protesting—often in the form of blocking entrances to abortion clinics—has now become a common practice for antiabortion activists. Prochoice activists have organized as well, especially in the wake of the 1989 *Webster v. Reproductive Health Services* case, which allowed states greater freedom to restrict abortions. Both groups' positions are clear, not subject to compromise, and influence their vote. Regardless of which side candidates for political office are on, they will be taking heat on the abortion issue for years to come.

Financial Resources

One of the major indictments of the American interest group system is that it is biased toward the wealthy. When he was the majority leader in the Senate, Bob Dole once remarked that he had never been approached by a Poor People's PAC. There is no

single-issue groups

Groups that have a narrow interest, tend to dislike compromise, and often draw membership from people new to politics. These features distinguish them from traditional **interest groups.**

Young People and Politics

The Virginia 21 Coalition

As budget crunches have hit most states in recent years, many state legislatures have cut back on funding for higher education and approved sharp increases in tuition at public colleges and universities. In response, college students in some states have started to form interest groups to fight for more state subsidies for higher education and for limiting tuition increases. In Virginia, a group called the "21st Century Virginia Coalition," or simply "Virginia 21" for short, has recently had some success in getting the state's politicians to listen to the opinions of college students regarding funding for higher education.

Virginia 21 first entered the political scene with a campaign to garner support for a bond referendum on the 2002 Virginia ballot to provide over $900 million to state universities for capital improvements. The group raised over $17,000 to support the campaign, made roughly 20,000 telephone calls to round up votes for it, and aired a student-written and produced radio commercial on behalf of the referendum.

More recently, Virginia 21 has been active in pushing for a 1 cent increase in the state's sales tax that would be dedicated to increasing funds available for education. The organ-ization collected over 10,000 signatures for a petition entitled "Fund Virginia's Future" and presented them to the state legislature. But they grabbed more attention when they dropped off over 200,000 pennies at the office of the State Treasurer in support of the proposed 1 cent increase in the sales tax. The pennies weighed approximately three-quarters of a ton and the gesture was designed to show that college students care a ton about the funding of higher education. The local media could hardly ignore such a gripping visual image.

Virginia 21 may or may not prevail in getting the state legislature to substantially increase funds for higher education, but it does seem destined to at least make sure that the views of college students are heard by policymakers.

Source: http://www.virginia21.org/.

Questions for Discussion:
- Would you give money and/or volunteer for a group in your state like Virginia 21? Why or why not?
- Which of the strategies of interest group lobbying discussed in this chapter do you think would be most effective for a group like Virginia 21?

doubt that money talks in the American political system, and those who have it get heard. All groups listed in Table 11.1 spend over a million dollars a year on lobbying and campaign contributions. A big campaign contribution may ensure a phone call, a meeting, or even a favorable vote or action on a particular policy. When Lincoln Savings and Loan Chair Charles Keating was asked whether the $1.3 million he had funneled into the campaigns of five U.S. senators had anything to do with these senators later meeting with federal regulators on his behalf, he candidly responded, "I certainly hope so."

It is important to emphasize, however, that even on some of the most important issues, the big interests do not always win. An excellent example of this is the Tax Reform Act of 1986. In *Showdown at Gucci Gulch*, two reporters from the *Wall Street Journal* chronicle the improbable victory of sweeping tax reform.[12] In this case, a large group of well-organized, highly paid (and Gucci-clad) lobbyists were unable to preserve many of their most prized tax loopholes. One of the heroes of the book, former Senator Robert Packwood of Oregon, was Congress' top PAC recipient during the tax reform struggle; he had raked in $992,000 for his reelection campaign. As chair of the Senate Finance Committee, however, Packwood ultimately turned against the hordes of lobbyists trying to get his ear on behalf of various loopholes. The only way to deal with the tax loophole problem, he concluded, was to go virtually cold turkey by eliminating all but a very few. "There is special interest after special interest that is hit in this bill," Packwood gloated, pointing out that many of them contributed to his campaign. In the end, passage of the reform bill offered "encouraging proof that moneyed interests could not always buy their way to success in Congress."[13]

The Interest Group Explosion

The number of interest groups in the United States has been increasing rapidly over the last several decades. Although no one has ever compiled a *Who's Who* of interest groups, the closest thing is the annual *Encyclopedia of Associations*.[14] Between 1959 and 2001, the number of groups listed in the *Encyclopedia* skyrocketed from about 6,000 to 22,000.[15] As you can see in Figure 11.3, the increase in the number of groups

Figure 11.3   Associations by Type

The following two pie charts illustrate how the interest group world has become more diverse since the late 1950s.

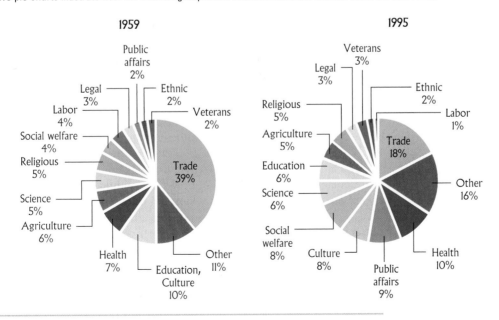

Source: Data from Frank R. Baumgartner and Beth L. Leech, *Basic Interests: The Importance of Groups in Politics and in Political Science* (Princeton, NJ: Princeton University Press, 1998), 109.

reflects a growing diversity in the interest group universe. Whereas trade groups clearly dominated the picture in 1959, this is no longer the case.

It seems that there is now an organized group for every conceivable interest. Jack Walker studied 564 groups listed in the *Washington Information Directory* and tried to trace their origins and expansion.[16] He found that 80 percent of the groups originated from occupational, industrial, or professional memberships. Interestingly, half the groups he studied were established after World War II. Walker also found a gravitation of groups to Washington, D.C. In 1960, only 66 percent of the groups in his study were headquartered in the nation's capital; today, over 90 percent are located there. Very few occupations or industries now go without an organized group to represent them in Washington. Even lobbyists themselves now have lobbies to represent their profession, such as the American League of Lobbyists.

There are many reasons for this explosion in the number of interest groups. Certainly one of the major factors has been the development of sophisticated technology. Andrew McFarland observes that

> *Technological innovations have made the coordination of constituents' activities and efforts of lobbyists much easier. Many lobbyists, for example, have available computerized lists of names and phone numbers of group members that can be easily arranged by congressional district or state. Address labels can be printed automatically or members can be called by WATS line from a group's headquarters.*[17]

Technology has also made it easier for groups back on Main Street to make their voices immediately heard in Washington. A well-organized interest group can deluge members of Congress with tens of thousands of faxes and e-mail messages in a matter of hours. Technology did not create interest group politics, but it has surely made the process much easier.

How Groups Try To Shape Policy

No interest group has enough staff, money, or time to do everything possible to achieve its policy goals. Interest groups must therefore choose from a variety of tactics. The four basic strategies are lobbying, electioneering, litigation, and appealing to the public.

Lobbying

lobbying

According to Lester Milbrath, a "communication, by someone other than a citizen acting on his own behalf, directed to a governmental decision maker with the hope of influencing his decision."

The term **lobbying** comes from the place where petitioners used to collar legislators. In the early years of politics in Washington, members of Congress had no offices and typically stayed in boarding houses or hotels while Congress was in session. A person could not call them up on the phone or make an appointment with their secretary; the only sure way of getting in touch with a member of Congress was to wait in the lobby where he was staying to catch him either coming in or going out. These people were dubbed *lobbyists* because they spent so much of their time waiting in lobbies.

Of course, merely loitering in a lobby does not make one a lobbyist; there must be a particular reason for such action. Lester Milbrath has offered a more precise definition of the practice. He writes that lobbying is a "communication, by someone other than a citizen acting on his or her own behalf, directed to a governmental decision maker with the hope of influencing his or her decision."[18] Lobbyists, in other words, are political persuaders who represent organized groups. They usually work in Washington, handling groups' legislative business. They are often former legislators themselves.

There are two basic types of lobbyists. Members of the first type are regular, paid employees of a corporation, union, or association. They may hold a title such as vice president for government relations, but everyone knows that their office is in Washington for a reason, even if the company headquarters is in Houston. Members of the second type are available for hire on a temporary basis. One group may be too small to afford a full-time lobbyist; another may have a unique, but temporary, need for access to Congress or the executive branch. Several thousand Washingtonians are available as "lobbyists for hire."

Although lobbyists are primarily out to influence members of Congress, it is important to remember that they can be of help to them as well. Ornstein and Elder list four important ways in which lobbyists can help a member of Congress.[19]

You Are a Lobbyist

- *They are an important source of information.* Members of Congress have to concern themselves with many policy areas; lobbyists can confine themselves to only one area and can thus provide specialized expertise. If information is power, then lobbyists can often be potent allies.
- *They can help politicians with political strategy for getting legislation through.* Lobbyists are politically savvy people, and they can be useful consultants. When Leon Panetta served as White House chief of staff, he regularly convened a small group of Washington lobbyists to discuss how the administration should present its proposals.[20]
- *They can help formulate campaign strategy and get the group's members behind a politician's reelection campaign.* Labor union leaders, for example, often provide help in how to appeal to typical working people, and they often provide volunteers to help out in campaigns as well.
- *They are a source of ideas and innovations.* Lobbyists cannot introduce bills, but they can peddle their ideas to politicians eager to attach their name to an idea that will bring them political credit.

Like anything else, lobbying can be done crudely or gracefully. Lobbyists can sometimes be heavy handed. They can threaten or cajole a legislator, implying that electoral defeat is a certain result of not "going along." They can even make it clear that money flows to the reelection coffers of those who cooperate. It is often difficult to tell the difference between lobbying as a shady business and lobbying as a strictly professional representation of legitimate interests. How much communication policymakers should have with lobbyists is a debatable question, as you can read about in "Issues of the Times: How Much Contact With Lobbyists is Too Much?"

Political scientists disagree about the effectiveness of lobbying. Much evidence suggests that lobbyists' power over policy is often exaggerated. A classic 1950s study of the influence of groups on foreign trade policy started with the hypothesis that when major business lobbies spoke, Congress listened—and acted accordingly.[21] Instead, the study found groups involved in trade policy to be ineffective, understaffed, and underfinanced. Usually the lobbyists were too disorganized to be effective. Members of Congress often had to pressure the interest groups to actively support legislation that would be in their own interest. Similarly, Milbrath concluded his own analysis of lobbying by arguing that "there is relatively little influence or power in lobbying per se."[22] Lobbyists are most effective as information sources, he claims, and are relatively ineffectual in winning over legislators.

Plenty of other evidence, however, suggests that sometimes lobbying can persuade legislators to support a certain policy.[23] The National Rifle Association, which for years kept major gun control policies off the congressional agenda, has long been one of Washington's most effective lobbying groups.[24] In a more specific example, intensive lobbying by the nation's most wealthy senior citizens—enraged by the tax burden imposed upon them by the Catastrophic Health Care Act—led Congress to repeal the act only a year after it was passed in the late 1980s.

Nailing down the specific effects of lobbying is difficult, partly because it is difficult to isolate its effects from other influences. Lobbying clearly works best on people already committed to the lobbyist's policy position. Thus, like campaigning, lobbying is directed primarily toward activating and reinforcing supporters. For example, antiabortion lobbyists would not think of approaching California's Barbara Boxer to

Issues of the Times

The Issue: How Much Contact With Lobbyists Is Too Much?

As Harold Lasswell said many years ago, "Politics is about who gets what, when, and how." Lobbyists are in business to get more of whatever there is to get from government for their clients. Politicians are often criticized for giving high-priced lobbyists too much of their time and to pandering to them in order to gain campaign contributions. When John Kerry was criticized for having too cozy relations with various lobbyists, he took the unprecedented step of releasing information about meetings he had with hundreds of lobbyists, as you can read about in the following article.

Read All About It

Kerry Releases a List of His Lobbyist Meetings

By Glen Justice
April 23, 2004

WASHINGTON—In the last 15 years, Senator John Kerry has met with more than 300 lobbyists and other advocates representing interests as diverse as organized labor and major corporations, according to a partial list released Thursday by his campaign.

The list, detailing meetings between 1989 and late last year that were often held over lunch, dinner or cocktails, identifies many participants who have contributed to his campaigns and, in some cases, become fund-raisers for his presidential run.

The Kerry organization produced the list after President Bush's campaign asserted that the senator had not been forthcoming in disclosing information like his military records. The release Thursday was intended as a contrast to the position of the Bush administration, which has not made public a similar list of meetings with lobbyists.

Those on the list have given a total of hundreds of thousands of dollars to Mr. Kerry's campaigns, according to PoliticalMoneyLine, a group that tracks campaign finance. A handful have gone further, each raising on their own at least $50,000, and often $100,000 or more, for his presidential race.

One example is Ivan Schlager, a partner in the communications practice at Skadden, Arps, Slate, Meagher & Flom, a firm that is home to at least two other six-figure Kerry fund-raisers as well.

The two men met in Mr. Kerry's Senate office in March 2002 to discuss broadband issues, according to the list. Mr. Schlager was representing companies like SBC Communications and AOL Time Warner on telecommunications policy at the time, lobbying disclosures show, though he no longer counts those two among his clients. And Mr. Kerry sat on the

Please see Meetings   Page 337

Meetings

Continued from Page 336

Senate Commerce Committee, which has jurisdiction over telecommunications.

Other fund-raisers on the list include John Merrigan, a lobbyist with Piper Rudnick who is now Mr. Kerry's finance chairman for the Middle Atlantic; Norman Brownstein, chairman of the law firm of Brownstein, Hyatt & Farber; and Jack Manning, chief executive of Boston Capital, who is a long-time friend.

Harold M. Ickes, the former Clinton aide, is also on the list. Mr. Ickes, who met with Mr. Kerry over dinner in May 2002, has since helped found the Media Fund, a group that has spent about $11 million on this year's races, much of it for television advertisements attacking Mr. Bush. Mr. Ickes said the meeting had been set up by a Kerry aide so that he and the senator, who were acquaintances, could get to know each other better. "He just wanted to get some ideas," Mr. Ickes said.

Campaign officials say the list is the best accounting that could be gathered from schedules and other materials. Though it necessarily omits many informal encounters — those by chance and otherwise — that are integral to lobbying, it goes far beyond what lawmakers or lobbyists are required to disclose. It offers dates, locations and in some cases the purpose of the meeting.

In issuing the list, the Kerry campaign challenged Mr. Bush to release the names of lobbyists who met with a task force that was created early in the administration to set energy policy. Vice President Dick Cheney headed the task force, and his refusal to disclose such a list is one issue in a bitter case still being litigated.

"George Bush and Dick Cheney have one of the most secretive governments in American history," said Chad Clanton, a Kerry spokesman.

The Bush campaign rejected the challenge as a "political ploy," and counterpunched. "Senator Kerry used to say he would show special interests the door," said Scott Stanzel, a spokesman. "It looks like he's showing them the revolving door."

Mr. Kerry's list is filled with recognizable names. Steve Ballmer, chief executive at Microsoft, met with Mr. Kerry. So did Thomas Hale Boggs Jr., who heads one of Washington's most powerful lobbying firms, Patton Boggs.

Mr. Kerry met with representatives of organized labor, trade associations of restaurateurs and bankers, environmental groups like the Sierra Club and the League of Conservation Voters, and companies as diverse as ValuJet Airlines, Raytheon and United States Tobacco.

Ed Yingling, executive director for government relations at the American Bankers Association, found himself on the list after just one meeting with Mr. Kerry, in 1989, a "courtesy call" in which, he says, he pressed no agenda. Such visits "help build our relationships," he said.

Also at that meeting was Christopher O'Neill, a lobbyist at O'Neill, Athy & Casey who is the son of the late Thomas P. O'Neill Jr., speaker of the House. Mr. O'Neill had at least four meetings with the senator on behalf of clients like Showtime and AT&T. "That's what we do," he said. "He always gave us a fair hearing."

Think About It

- Should all members of Congress, as well as major White House officials, be required to disclose their contacts with lobbyists, as Kerry did in this instance? Why or why not? Why do you think some members of Congress would oppose requiring such disclosures?

- Do you think contacts such as those disclosed by Kerry indicate that special interests have too much access to policymakers and too much power in the making of public policy? How much contact between lobbyists and politicians do you think there should be?

For years, the National Rifle Association has successfully lobbied against gun control measures, arguing that the Second Amendment to the Constitution guarantees all citizens the right to bear arms. Charlton Heston has long been a prominent member of the group, and served for a time as its president.

attempt to convert her to their position, because Boxer clearly supports the pro-choice movement. If Senator Boxer is lobbied by anyone on the abortion issue, it will be by the pro-choice faction, urging her not to compromise with the opposition.

Electioneering

electioneering

Direct group involvement in the electoral process. Groups can help fund campaigns, provide testimony, and get members to work for candidates, and some form **political action committees (PACs)**.

political action committees (PACs)

Political funding vehicles created by the 1974 campaign finance reforms. A corporation, union, or some other interest group can create a PAC and register it with the **Federal Election Commission (FEC)**, which will meticulously monitor the PAC's expenditures.

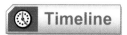

Interest Groups and
Campaign Finance

Because lobbying works best with those already on the same side, getting the right people into office and keeping them there is also a key strategy of interest groups. Many groups therefore get involved in **electioneering**—aiding candidates financially and getting group members out to support them. Pressure group involvement in campaigns is nothing new. In the election of 1896 (see Chapter 10) silver-mining interests poured millions into the losing presidential campaign of William Jennings Bryan, who advocated unlimited coinage of silver.

Political action committees (PACs) provide a means for groups to participate in electioneering. The number of PACs has exploded from 608 in 1974 to 3,868 in 2004, according to the Federal Election Commission. No major interest group seeking to exert influence on the political process these days can pass up the opportunity to funnel money honestly and openly into the campaign coffers of its supporters. For example, Major League Baseball's PAC gave $288,000 to congressional candidates and the major parties during the 2002 election cycle, mostly to members of congressional committees who were considering legislation that might impact the business of baseball. As economist Roger Noll of Stanford University remarked about the activity of baseball's PAC: "Any industry that has any kind of dependence on government is pretty much forced to do what they're doing," he said. "Unfortunately, this has become the cost of doing business."[25]

As campaign costs have risen, PACs have come along to help pay the bill. In recent years, nearly half the candidates running for reelection to the House of Representatives have received the majority of their campaign funds from PACs. Furthermore, their challengers did not enjoy this advantage. PACs gave a whopping $134 million to House incumbents during the 1999–2000 election cycle, compared to a mere $17 million to the challengers. Why does PAC money go so overwhelmingly to incumbents? The answer is that PAC contributions are basically investments for the future, and incumbents are the most likely to return the investment. When R. Kenneth

Godwin and Barry J. Seldon asked a sample of PAC directors to explain why their PACs gave money to certain candidates, the top five answers were that these candidates were (1) on committees that are important to their interests; (2) very supportive of issues important to them; (3) from a district or state where they had facilities; (4) helping them with executive and regulatory agencies; and (5) in leadership positions that enabled them to influence issues that affect the PAC.[26]

Only a handful of serious congressional candidates have resisted the lure of PAC money in recent years. One candidate described his experiences trying to get on the PAC bandwagon. When Democrat Steve Sovern ran for the House from Iowa's Second District, he made the now common pilgrimage to Washington to meet with potential contributors. "I found myself in line with candidates from all over," he reported. Each PAC had eager candidates fill out a multiple-choice questionnaire on issues important to the PAC. Candidates who shared the same concerns and views and who looked like winners got the money. Sovern later reported that "the process made me sick." After his defeat, he organized his own PAC called LASTPAC (for Let the American System Triumph), which urged candidates to shun PAC campaign contributions.[27] There have been serious calls to do away with PACs altogether, as discussed in "You Are the Policymaker: Should PACs Be Eliminated?"

Litigation

If interest groups fail in Congress or get only a vague piece of legislation, the next step is to go to court in the hope of getting specific rulings. Karen Orren has linked much of the success of environmental interest groups to their use of lawsuits. "Frustrated in Congress," she wrote, "they have made an end run to the courts, where they have skillfully exploited and magnified limited legislative gains."[28] Environmental legislation, such as the Clean Air Act, typically includes written provisions allowing ordinary citizens to sue for enforcement. As a result, every federal agency involved in environmental regulation now has hundreds of suits pending against it at any given time. These suits may not halt environmentally troublesome practices, but the constant threat of a lawsuit increases the likelihood that businesses will consider the environmental impact of what they do.

Perhaps the most famous interest group victories in court were by civil rights groups in the 1950s. While civil rights bills remained stalled in Congress, these groups won major victories in court cases concerning school desegregation, equal housing, and labor market equality. More recently, consumer groups have used suits against businesses and federal agencies as a means of enforcing consumer regulations. As long as law schools keep producing lawyers, groups will fight for their interests in court.

Why It Matters

PACs
The great increase in the number of PACs over the last quarter of a century has enabled far more groups to become involved in electioneering. If more participation is always desirable, then the increase of PACs has to be considered a positive development. But given that only groups that can successfully organize and raise substantial sums of money can take advantage of the PAC system, some obvious biases have been introduced to the electoral process due to the increased importance of PACs.

You Are the Policymaker

Should PACs Be Eliminated?

The effect of PAC campaign contributions on congressional votes has become a perennial issue in American politics. Critics of PACs are convinced that they are distorting the democratic process and corrupting our political system in favor of those who can raise the most money. Many politicians freely admit—once they are out of office—that it is a myth to think that the PACs don't want something in return. They may only want to be remembered on one or two crucial votes or with an occasional intervention with government agencies, but multiply this by the thousands of special interests that are organized today and the worst fears of the hyperpluralists could be realized—a government that constantly yields to every special interest.

Common Cause (*www.common-cause.org*) has made it their primary mission to expose what they see as the evils of the PAC system. They argue that the influence of corporate PACs on Capitol Hill has led to "corporate welfare" and costs taxpayers billions of dollars. For example, Common Cause

maintains that the timber industry prevailed against a Clinton administration proposal in 1997 to eliminate logging subsidies because of their $8 million in recent PAC contributions. Similarly, they argue that $5 million in PAC contributions from the broadcast industry led to a massive government giveaway of free digital TV licenses worth as much as $70 billion. And Common Cause and others have attributed the failure of Congress to further regulate tobacco and cigarette advertising to the more than $30 million of PAC contributions from tobacco companies over the past decade.

However, others argue that connection is not causation. They believe that most members of Congress are not affected by PAC contributions, which largely come from groups they already agree with anyway. Defenders of the PAC system also point out that the PAC system further increases participation in the political process. As opposed to individual donations, PACs—which represent groups of people—allow better representation of occupational

groups. The PAC system allows people with common professional interests, such as farmers, lawyers, dentists, and college professors, to express their support of candidates jointly through political contributions.

Similarly, corporation PACs represent the interests of many stockholders and employees with common political interests. If James Madison's notion that the key to controlling the power of interest groups is to expand their sphere of participation, then PACs certainly do this according to their defenders. Beyond this, the money for today's expensive media campaigns has to come from somewhere. Those who wish to maintain the PAC system typically point to the alternative of public financing of campaigns as impractical and unpopular given the low rate of participation on the voluntary income tax check-off box (see Chapter 9).

You be the policymaker: What would you do? Would you consider eliminating PACs? Or, as a middle course, would you favor further limits on the amount of money they can donate?

amicus curiae briefs

Legal briefs submitted by a "friend of the court" for the purpose of raising additional points of view and presenting information not contained in the briefs of the formal parties. These briefs attempt to influence a court's decision.

class action suits

Lawsuits permitting a small number of people to sue on behalf of all other people similarly situated.

One tactic that lawyers employ to make the views of interest groups heard by the judiciary is the filing of **amicus curiae** ("friend of the court") **briefs.** Amicus briefs consist of written arguments submitted to the courts in support of one side of a case. Through these written depositions, a group states its collective position as well as how its own welfare will be affected by the outcome of the case. Numerous groups may file amicus briefs in highly publicized and emotionally charged cases. For example, in the case of *Regents of the University of California v. Bakke* (see Chapter 5), which challenged affirmative action programs as reverse discrimination, over 100 different groups filed amicus briefs. A study of participation in amicus briefs by Caldeira and Wright found that the Supreme Court has been accessible to a wide array of organized interests, in terms of deciding both which cases to hear and how to rule.[29]

A more direct judicial strategy employed by interest groups is the filing of **class action lawsuits,** which enable a group of people in a similar situation to combine their common grievances into a single suit. For instance, flight attendants won a class action suit against the airline industry's regulation that all stewardesses be unmarried. As one lawyer who specializes in such cases states, "The class action is the greatest, most effective legal engine to remedy mass wrongs."[30]

Going Public

Groups are also interested in the opinions of the public. Because public opinion ultimately makes its way to policymakers, interest groups carefully cultivate their public image and use public opinion to their advantage when they can. As Ken Kollman finds, even the wealthiest and most powerful groups in America appeal to public opinion to help their cause. For example, when the government instituted a requirement for tax-withholding on savings accounts, the American Bankers Association appealed to their customers to protest this to their congressional representatives. After 22 million postcards flooded into Congress, lawmakers quickly reversed the policy.[31]

Interest groups market not only their stand on issues but also their reputations. Business interests want people to see them as "what made America great," not as wealthy Americans trying to ensure large profits. The Teamsters Union likes to be known as a united organization of hard-working men and women, not as an organization that has in the past been influenced by organized crime. Farmers promote the image of a sturdy family working to put bread on the table, not the huge agribusinesses that have largely replaced family farms. In this way, many groups try to create a reservoir of goodwill with the public.

Interest groups' appeals to the public for support have a long tradition in American politics. In 1908, AT&T launched a major magazine advertising campaign to convince people of the need for a telephone monopoly. Similarly, after President Truman proposed a system of national health insurance in 1948, the American Medical Association spent millions of dollars on ads attacking "socialized medicine." In 1994, the Health Insurance Association of America ran a $15 million nationally televised ad campaign criticizing President Clinton's health care package, which many analysts believe lessened public support for the reform bill. So many groups placed advertisements regarding the Clinton health care reform package and so much money was spent (over $100 million), that many observers compared this activity to a national electoral campaign.

Lately, more and more organizations have undertaken expensive public relations (PR) efforts. After September 11, the media was full of ads from various groups expressing their sympathy for the victims. Some other recent examples include Phillip Morris running ads countering the arguments of antitobacco legislation, Microsoft condemning its prosecution by the Justice Department for alleged monopolistic practices, and Ford and Bridgestone defending themselves against charges of negligence regarding defective tires. Mobil Oil has long run a visible corporate PR effort to influence the public with its regular editorial-style ads in the *New York Times* and other major publications. These ads typically address issues that affect the oil industry and big business in general. Once Mobil even ran an ad entitled "Why Do We Buy This Space?" It answered "that business needs voices in the media, the same way labor unions, consumers, and other groups in our society do."[32] No one knows just how effective these

Paid for by the Coalition to Scare Your Pants Off

Interest groups spent over $50 million appealing to public opinion during the debate over health care in 1994. In a counter-ad produced by the Democratic National Committee, the argument was made that opponents of the Clinton health care plan were using scare tactics. You can see the tag end of the ad in this photo.

image-molding efforts are, but many groups seem to believe firmly that advertising pays off.

Types of Interest Groups

Simulation

You Are the Leader
of Concerned Citizens
for World Justice

Whether they are lobbying, electioneering, litigating, or appealing to the public, interest groups are omnipresent in the American political system. As with other aspects of American politics and policymaking, political scientists loosely categorize interest groups into clusters. Among the most important clusters are those that deal with: (1) economic issues, (2) environmental concerns, (3) equality issues, and (4) the interests of all consumers. An examination of these four distinct types of interest groups will give you a good picture of much of the American interest group system.

Economic Interests

All economic interests are ultimately concerned with wages, prices, and profits. In the American economy, government does not determine these directly. Only on rare occasions has the government imposed wage and price controls. This has usually been during wartime, although the Nixon administration briefly used wage and price controls to combat inflation. More commonly, public policy in America has economic effects through regulations, tax advantages, subsidies and contracts, and international trade policy.

Business, labor, and farmers all fret over the impact of government regulations. Even a minor change in government regulatory policy can cost industries a great deal or bring increased profits. Tax policies also affect the livelihood of individuals and firms. How the tax code is written determines whether people and producers pay a lot or a little of their incomes to the government. Because government often provides subsidies to farmers, small businesses, railroads, minority businesses, and others, every economic group wants to get its share of direct aid and government contracts. In this era of economic global interdependence, all groups worry about import quotas, tariffs (fees imposed on imports), and the soundness of the American dollar. In short, business executives, factory workers, and farmers seek to influence government because regulations, taxes, subsidies, and international economic policy all affect their economic livelihoods. The following sections discuss some of the major organized interests and their impact on economic policy.

Participation

Farm Subsidies
and Domestic Policy

Labor.   Labor has more affiliated members than any other interest group except the American Association for Retired Persons. Fourteen million workers are members of unions belonging to the AFL-CIO—itself a union of unions. Several million others are members of non-AFL-CIO unions, such as the National Education Association, which represents schoolteachers.

Like labor unions everywhere, American unions press for policies to ensure better working conditions and higher wages. Recognizing that many workers would like to enjoy union benefits without actually joining a union and paying dues, unions have fought hard to establish the **union shop,** which requires new employees to join the union representing them. In contrast, business groups have supported **right-to-work laws,** which outlaw union membership as a condition of employment. They argue that such laws deny a basic freedom—namely, the right not to belong to a group. In 1947, the biggest blow ever to the American labor movement occurred when Congress passed the Taft-Hartley Act, permitting states to adopt right-to-work laws (known as "slave labor laws" within the AFL-CIO). Most of the states that have right-to-work laws are in the South, which traditionally has had the lowest percentage of unionized workers.

The American labor movement reached its peak in 1956, when 33 percent of the nonagricultural workforce belonged to a union; since then, the percentage has

union shop

A provision found in some collective bargaining agreements requiring all employees of a business to join the union within a short period, usually 30 days, and to remain members as a condition of employment.

right-to-work law

A state law forbidding requirements that workers must join a union to hold their jobs. State right-to-work laws were specifically permitted by the Taft-Hartley Act of 1947.

declined to about 16 percent. One factor behind this decline is that low wages in other countries have diminished the American job market in a number of key manufacturing areas. Steel, once made by American workers, is now made more cheaply in Korea and imported to the United States. The United Auto Workers has found its clout greatly reduced as Detroit has faced heavy competition from Japanese automakers. Some political scientists, however, believe labor's problems result from more than the decline of blue-collar industries. Paul Johnson argues that the biggest factor causing the decline in union membership is the problems unions have had in convincing today's workers that they will benefit from unionization. In particular, Johnson argues that this task has become more difficult in recent years because of employers' efforts to make nonunion jobs satisfying.[33]

Whatever the reason, it is clear that labor unions' ability to shape public policy has decreased. Labor is still a major Democratic constituency, and it surely preferred Bill Clinton to George W. Bush on many issues, such as raising the minimum wage. But the Clinton agenda and labor's agenda were hardly one and the same. Organized labor could not expect to be protected from policies that may have cost their members jobs when the Democrats were in office. In particular, labor found themselves battling in vain to stop trade agreements negotiated by Bill Clinton.

Business.   If the elite theorists are correct, however, and there is an American power elite, it certainly must be dominated by leaders of the biggest banks, insurance companies, and multinational corporations. Elitists' views may or may not be exaggerated, but business is certainly well organized for political action. Most large firms, such as AT&T and Ford, now have offices in Washington that monitor legislative activity. Schlozman and Tierney report that 70 percent of all interest group organizations that have a Washington presence represent business.[34] Furthermore, business PACs have increased more dramatically than any other category of PACs over the last several decades. Two umbrella organizations, the National Association of Manufacturers (NAM) and the Chamber of Commerce, include most corporations and businesses and speak for them when general business interests are at stake.

Different business interests compete on many specific issues, however. Microsoft and Netscape both have their lobbyists on Capitol Hill pressing their competing interests. Trucking and construction companies want more highways, but railroads do not. An increase in international trade will help some businesses expand their markets, but others may be hurt by foreign competition. Business interests are generally unified

Strikes are among labor unions' most powerful weapons. This strike by United Parcel Service workers attracted a great deal of public attention and affected people all over the country who were expecting packages. The workers got much of what they asked for.

when it comes to promoting greater profits, but are often fragmented when policy choices have to be made.

The hundreds of trade and product associations are far less visible than the NAM and the Chamber of Commerce, but they are at least as important in pursuing policy goals for their members. These associations fight regulations that would reduce their profits and seek preferential tax treatment as well as government subsidies and contracts. America's complex schedules of tariffs are monuments to the activities of the trade associations. Although they are the least visible of Washington lobbies, their successes are measured in amendments won, regulations rewritten, and exceptions made. It is not only American trade associations that are concerned with these policies, but foreign corporations and governments as well. The practice of foreign economic interests hiring influential former governmental officials to lobby on their behalf has recently led to a number of reform proposals.[35]

Environmental Interests

Among the newest political interest groups are the environmentalists. A handful, such as the Sierra Club and the Audubon Society, have been around since the nineteenth century, but many others trace their origins to the first Earth Day, April 22, 1970. On that day, ecology-minded people marched on Washington and other places to symbolize their support for environmental protection. Twenty years later, one estimate pegged the number of environmental groups at over 10,000 and their combined revenues at $2.9 billion—demonstrating "how widely and deeply green values had permeated the society."[36] Environmental groups continue to be formed all the time—for example, Earth 2000 was founded by an enterprising 12-year-old in order to provide an outlet for teenagers to participate in environmental protection (see "Making a Difference: Danny Seo").

Environmental groups have promoted pollution-control policies, wilderness protection, and population control. Perhaps more significant, however, is what they have opposed. Their hit list has included strip-mining, supersonic aircraft, the Alaskan oil pipeline, offshore oil drilling, and nuclear power plants. On these and other issues,

Earth Day was first held in 1970. Its mood was one of protest, as speakers demanded that the government take stronger action to protect the environment. Today, Earth Day is more of an occasion for people to conduct local clean-up efforts and to publicize things that everyone can do to protect the environment. Here, a University of Maine student displays some ideas at an Earth Day awareness ceremony.

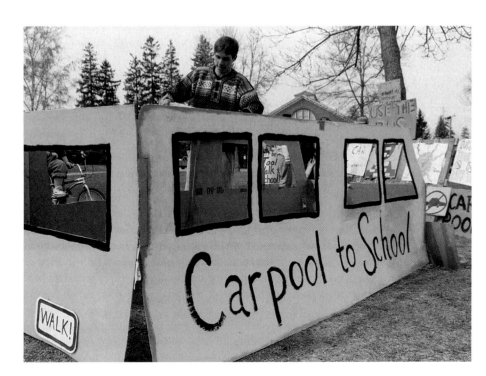

environmentalists have exerted a great deal of influence on Congress and state legislatures.

The concerns of environmentalists often come into direct conflict with energy goals. Environmentalists insist that, in the long run, energy supplies can be ensured without harming the environment or risking radiation exposure from nuclear power plants. On the issue of nuclear power plants, their arguments have had a profound impact on public policy. No new nuclear power plants have been approved since 1977, and many that had been in the works were canceled.[37] Short-term energy needs, however, have won out over environmental concerns in many other cases. Energy producers argue that environmentalists oppose nearly every new energy project. Given that there is no sign of a major drop in energy demands, they argue that some limited risks have to be taken. What is worse, they ask, an occasional oil spill off the shore of Alaska or long lines every day at the gas pumps? Thus, despite the opposition of environmentalists, Congress subsidized the massive trans-Alaskan pipeline, which a consortium of companies use to transport oil from Alaska's North Slope. Similarly, the strip-mining of coal continues despite constant objections from environmentalists. Group politics intensifies with the clash of two public interests such as environmental protection and an ensured supply of energy.

Making a Difference

Danny Seo

Danny Seo was born on Earth Day in 1977. On his twelfth birthday, he devoted his birthday party to forming an environmental group with his friends. Over the next few years this group promoted recycling, took on the cause of protecting 66 acres of forest and wetlands near their home from development, and successfully pressured the Pennsylvania legislature to pass a bill giving students the right to refuse to dissect animals. Now in his late-20s, Danny Seo is an internationally renowned environmental activist, author, and public speaker. He has his own website (*www.dannyseo.com*) and has published several books, including one called *Generation React*, which presents his ideas for political activism among young people. He has been named one of the "50 most beautiful people in the world" by *People* magazine, and "one of the most powerful twenty-somethings in America" by *Swing*.

Equality Interests

The Fourteenth Amendment guarantees equal protection under the law. American history, though, shows that this is easier said than done. Two sets of interest groups, representing minorities and women, have made equal rights their main policy goal. Chapter 5 reviewed the long history of the civil rights movement; this section is concerned with its policy goals and organizational base.

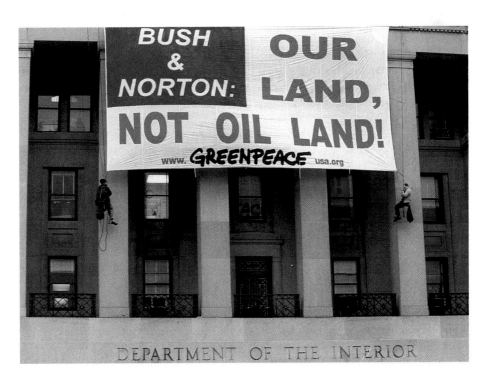

A few interest groups use unconventional methods to get attention for their views and demands. The environmental activist group Greenpeace is well known for coming up with activities the media can hardly ignore. Here, group members can be seen protesting the Bush administration's policies by placing a huge banner in front of the main entrance of the Department of the Interior early in the morning.

Equality at the polls, in housing, on the job, in education, and in all other facets of American life has long been the dominant goal of African-American groups. The oldest and largest of these groups is the National Association for the Advancement of Colored People (NAACP). It argued and won the monumental *Brown v. Board of Education* case in 1954, in which the Supreme Court held that segregated schools were unconstitutional. Although the NAACP has won many victories in principle, equality in practice has been much slower in coming. Today, civil rights groups continue to push for more effective affirmative action programs to ensure that minority groups are given educational and employment opportunities. In recent years, the NAACP's main vehicle has been the Fair Share program, which negotiates agreements with national and regional businesses to increase minority hiring and the use of minority contractors.[38] As an issue, affirmative action is not as emotionally charged as was desegregation, but it too has been controversial.

Although the work of civil rights interest groups in fighting segregation and discrimination is well known, Dona and Charles Hamilton argue that "much less is known about the 'social welfare agenda,'—the fight for social welfare policies to help the poor."[39] They argue that since the 1930s, civil rights groups have been concerned with larger and more universal economic problems in American society.

When the NAACP was just beginning, suffragists were in the streets and legislative lobbies were demanding women's right to vote. The Nineteenth Amendment, ratified in 1920, guaranteed women the vote, but other guarantees of equal protection remained absent from the Constitution. More recently, women's rights groups, such as the National Organization for Women (NOW), have lobbied for an end to gender discrimination. Their primary goal has been the passage of the Equal Rights Amendment (ERA), which states that "equality of rights under the law shall not be abridged on account of sex."

In the first month after the ERA was approved by Congress in 1972, it was overwhelmingly ratified by 15 states. Even Texas and Kansas, fairly conservative states, voted decisively for the ERA in the first year. The quiet consensual politics of the ERA ratification process soon came to a boisterous end, however, when Phyllis Schlafly, a conservative activist from Alton, Ill., began a highly visible STOP ERA movement. She and her followers argued the ERA would destroy the integrity of the family, require communal bathrooms, lead to women in combat, and eliminate legal protections that women already had. Their emotional appeal was just enough to stop the ERA 3 states short of the 38 necessary for ratification.

Though the ERA seems dead for the moment, NOW remains committed to enacting the protection that the amendment would have constitutionally guaranteed by advocating the enactment of many individual statutes. As is often the case with interest group politics, issues are rarely settled once and for all; rather, they shift to different policy arenas.

Consumers and Public Interest Lobbies

public interest lobbies

According to Jeffrey Berry, organizations that seek "a collective good, the achievement of which will not selectively and materially benefit the membership or activities of the organization."

Pluralist theory holds that for virtually every interest in society, there is an organized group. But what about the interests of all of us—the buying public? Today thousands of organized groups are championing various causes or ideas "in the public interest." These **public interest lobbies** are organizations that seek "a collective good, the achievement of which will not selectively and materially benefit the membership or activists of the organization."[40] If products are made safer by the lobbying of consumer protection groups, it is not the members of such groups alone that benefit. Rather, everyone should be better off, regardless of whether they joined in the lobbying.

If ever a lobbying effort was spurred by a single person, it was the consumer movement. At first, Ralph Nader took on American business almost single-handedly in the name of consumerism. He was propelled to national prominence by his book, *Unsafe at Any Speed*, which attacked General Motors' Corvair as a mechanically deficient and dangerous automobile. General Motors made the mistake of hiring a private detective to dig into Nader's background and follow him around, hoping that there might be some dirt they could uncover that would discredit him. Nader eventually learned about the investigation, sued General Motors for invasion of privacy, and won a hefty damage settlement in court. He used the proceeds to launch the first major consumer group in Washington.

Consumer groups have won many legislative victories. In 1973, Congress responded to consumer advocacy by creating the Consumer Product Safety Commission. Congress authorized it to regulate all consumer products and even gave it the power to ban particularly dangerous ones, bearing in mind that household products are responsible for 30,000 deaths annually. Among the products the commission has investigated are children's sleepwear (some of which contained a carcinogen), hot tubs, and lawn mowers.

Consumer groups are not the only ones that claim to be public interest groups. Groups speaking for those who cannot speak for themselves seek to protect children, animals, and the mentally ill; good-government groups such as Common Cause push for openness and fairness in government; and religious groups like the Christian Coalition crusade for the protection of ethical and moral standards in American society.

Understanding Interest Groups

The problem of interest groups in America today remains much the same as Madison defined it over 200 years ago. A free society must allow for the representation of all groups that seek to influence political decision-making. Yet groups are usually more concerned with their own self-interest than with the needs of society as a whole, and for democracy to work well, it is important that they not be allowed to assume a dominant position.

Interest Groups and Democracy

James Madison's solution to the problems posed by interest groups was to create a wide-open system in which many groups would be able to participate. In such an extended sphere of influence, according to Madison, groups with opposing interests would counterbalance one another. Pluralist theorists believe that a rough approximation of the public interest emerges from this competition.

With the tremendous growth of interest group politics in recent years, some observers say that Madison may at last have gotten his wish. For every group with an interest, there now seems to be a competing group to watch over it—not to mention

Like other public interest groups, the Children's Defense Fund works against Olson's law of large groups; that is, it is easier to organize a small group with clear economic goals than it is to organize a large group with broader goals.

How You Can Make a Difference

Interest Groups

Student activism for political causes has a long and proud history in the United States. You can be part of this—and help make a difference! Is there an issue or cause that is dear to you? Something about the country you would like to protect or to change? If so, get involved. There are groups representing just about every conceivable viewpoint. Find the one that matches your views. Join, go to meetings, and volunteer. Give your time and money to a group that fights for what you believe in. Know your legislators (local, state, and national) and how to contact them. Learn how legislation is made and how it can be blocked or overturned. If conventional political tactics don't produce the result you want, consider adopting unconventional tactics to attract media attention.

What else you can do:
One way to find interest groups that reflect your own views is through the Internet. Just about all interest groups have their own websites. You can also use the resources and directories listed here to local specific interest groups:

- Political science resources: links to political parties, interest groups, and other political groups around the world *www.psr.keele.ac.uk /parties.*
- Activist groups director: *www.good money.com/directory_active. htm.*

- Environmental action groups: *www.mamagaia.com/ecogroups a–1.htm* and *www.mamagia.com /ecogroupsm-z.htm.*
- Links to activist groups on affirmative action, civil liberties, free speech, disability rights, and ethnic and minority rights: *www.ncec .org/links/issues.htm.*
- Index of activist groups: *www.politicalindex.com/sect 10.htm.*
- Youth activist groups: *www. politicalusa.com /youth1.htm.*
- Other activist groups: *www.crash. ihug.co.nz/~bwmm/groups.htm.*

public interest lobbies to watch over them all. Robert Salisbury argues that "the growth in the number, variety, and sophistication of interest groups represented in Washington" has transformed policymaking such that it "is not dominated so often by a relatively small number of powerful interest groups as it may once have been."[41] Paradoxically, Salisbury concludes that the increase in lobbying activity has resulted in less clout overall for interest groups—and better democracy.

Elite theorists clearly disagree with this conclusion and point to the proliferation of business PACs as evidence of more interest group corruption in American politics than ever. A democratic process requires a free and open exchange of ideas in which candidates and voters should be able to hear one another out, but PACs—the source of so much money in elections—distort the process. Elite theorists particularly note that wealthier interests are greatly advantaged by the PAC system. It is true that there are nearly four thousand PACs, but the relatively few big-spending ones dominate the fund-raising game. In 2002, just 6 percent of all the registered PACs accounted for over 60 percent of PAC contributions to House candidates.[42]

PACs can sometimes link money to politics at the highest levels. The old party machines may have bought votes in the voting booth; the new PACs are accused of buying votes in legislatures. Technology, especially television, makes American elections expensive; candidates need money to pay for high-tech campaigns, and PACs are able to supply that money. In return, they ask only to be remembered when their interests are clearly at stake.

Hyperpluralist theorists maintain that whenever a major interest group objects strongly to proposed legislation, policymakers will bend over backward to try to accommodate it. With the formation of so many groups in recent years, and with so many of them having influence in Washington, hyperpluralists argue that it has been increasingly difficult to accomplish major policy change in Washington. Thus hyperpluralist theory offers a powerful explanation for the policy gridlock evident in American politics today.

Interest Groups and the Scope of Government

Though individualistic, Americans are also very associational. As Alexis de Tocqueville wrote in the 1830s, "Americans of all ages, all conditions, and all dispositions constantly form associations."[43] This is not at all contradictory. By joining a number of political associations, Americans are able to politicize a variety of aspects of their own individualism. The multiplicity of the American interest group structure and the openness of American politics to inputs from interest groups allow individuals many channels for political participation and thus facilitate representation of individual interests.

Comparing Interest Groups

Though individualism is most often treated in this book as being responsible for the relatively small scope of American government, when it works its way through interest group politics, the result is just the opposite. Individual interest groups fight to sustain government programs that are important to them, thereby making it hard for politicians ever to reduce the scope of government. Both President Carter and President Reagan remarked at the end of their time in office that their attempts to cut waste in federal spending had been frustrated by interest groups. In his farewell address, Carter "suggested that the reason he had so much difficulty in dealing with Congress was the fragmentation of power and decision making that was exploited by interest groups."[44] Similarly, Reagan remarked a month before leaving office that "special interest groups, bolstered by campaign contributions, pressure lawmakers into creating and defending spending programs."[45] Above all, most special interest groups strive to maintain established programs that benefit them.

However, one can also argue that the growth in the scope of government in recent decades accounts for a good portion of the proliferation of interest groups. The more areas in which the federal government has become involved, the more interest groups have developed to attempt to influence policy. As William Lunch notes, "a great part of the increase was occasioned by the new government responsibility for civil rights, environmental protection, and greater public health and safety."[46] For example, once the government got actively involved in protecting the environment, many groups sprung up to lobby for strong standards and enforcement. Given the tremendous effects of environmental regulations on many industries, it should come as no surprise that these industries also organized to ensure that their interests were taken into account. As Salisbury writes, many groups have "come to Washington out of need and dependence rather than because they have influence."[47] He argues that interest groups spend much of their time merely monitoring policy developments in order to alert their membership and develop reactive strategies.

Summary

This chapter discusses the vast array of interest groups in American politics—all vying for policies they prefer. Pluralists see groups as the most important way people can have their policy preferences represented in government. Hyperpluralists, though, fear that too many groups are getting too much of what they want, skillfully working the many subgovernments in the American system. Elitist theorists believe that a few wealthy individuals and multinational corporations exert control over the major decisions regarding distribution of goods and services.

A number of factors influence a group's success in achieving its policy goals. Most surprising is that small groups have an organizational advantage over large groups. Large groups often fall victim to the free-rider problem, which is explained by Olson's law of large groups. Both large and small groups can benefit from the intensity of their members' beliefs. Money always helps lubricate the wheels of power, though it is hardly a surefire guarantee of success.

Interest groups use four basic strategies to maximize their effectiveness. Lobbying is one well-known group strategy. Although the evidence on its influence is mixed, it is clear that lobbyists are most effective with those legislators already sympathetic to their side. Thus electioneering becomes critical because it helps put supportive people in office. Often today, groups operate in the judicial as well as the legislative process, using litigation in the courts when lobbying fails or is not enough. Many also find it important to project a good image, employing public relations techniques to present themselves in the most favorable light.

This chapter also examined some of the major kinds of interest groups, particularly those concerned with economic, environmental, and equality policy. Public interest lobbies claim to be different from other interest groups, representing, they say, an important aspect of the public interest. Recently there has been a rapid growth of single-interest groups, which focus narrowly on one issue and are not inclined to compromise.

The issue of controlling interest groups remains as crucial to democracy today as it was in Madison's time. Some scholars believe that the growth of interest groups has worked to divide political influence just as Madison hoped it would. Other scholars point to the PAC system as the new way in which special interests corrupt American democracy.

KEY TERMS

interest group	free-rider problem	political action
pluralist theory	Olson's law of large	committees (PACs)
elite theory	groups	*amicus curiae* briefs
hyperpluralist theory	selective benefits	class action lawsuits
subgovernments	single-issue group	union shop
potential group	lobbying	right-to-work laws
actual group	electioneering	public interest lobbies
collective good		

INTERNET RESOURCES

www.aarp.org
The official site of the American Association of Retired Persons.

www.aflcio.org
The nation's largest labor association, the AFL-CIO, posts material at this site.

www.nea.org
The site of the National Education Association.

www.greenpeaceusa.org
The place to go to learn more about the activities of this environmental protection group.

www.commoncause.org
The official site of Common Cause, one of the nation's oldest and largest public affairs interest groups.

www.freespeech.org
A site for an interest group that represents young people, particularly on Social Security issues.

GET CONNECTED

Interest Groups and PACs

Many interest groups try to influence government by getting the right people into office and helping them stay there. This process is called electioneering, aiding candidates financially and getting members of the interest group out to vote for them. In order to contribute to campaigns, interest groups create political action committees, or PACs. The costs of campaigns have risen over the past few decades and PACs have stepped in to help with the costs. PACs typically give to incumbent candidates, especially those who serve on committees important to the group. From what interests do the U.S. senators from your state receive campaign contributions?

Search the Web

Go to the United States Senate website *http://www.senate.gov* and find the senators from your state. Also find the committees on which they serve. Develop a hypothesis about the groups that might contribute to the senators based on their committee membership. Then go to the website of the Center for Responsive Politics *http://www.opensecrets.org*. Look at the most recent filings for the senators. You also may want to look at the records for the senators' opponents, if they had opponents in their most recent election.

Questions To Ask

- Which interest groups contributed the most to each senator?
- Was your hypothesis supported? Did the senators receive support from groups with an interest in the senators' committees?
- Did different interest groups contribute to each of the senators? Does it appear that political party makes a difference? How about seniority or leadership position in the Senate?
- Have you heard of any of the interest groups that contributed to your senators?

Why It Matters

As the size of government has grown, so has the number of interest groups. These groups participate in politics in part by contributing money to political campaigns. Some people complain that the amount of money is hurting politics and government in the United States. You should try to learn about the interest groups that contribute to the elected public officials who represent you. It is possible that one or more of the groups advocate a position similar to your feelings on an issue.

Get Involved

Find our more about the groups that contribute to your senators by sending one or more of them an e-mail request for information. You can find a useful list of interest groups at this website: *http://www.csuchico.edu/~kcfount/*. You may want to consider joining an interest group as well.

To see more Get Connected exercises for Chapter 11, go to www.ablongman.com/edwards.

FOR FURTHER READING

Baumgartner, Frank R., and Beth L. Leech. *Basic Interests: The Importance of Groups in Politics and in Political Science*. Princeton, NJ: Princeton University Press, 1998. An excellent review and analysis of the academic literature on interest groups.

Berry, Jeffrey M. *The Interest Group Society*, 3rd ed. New York: Longman, 1997. One of the best contemporary textbooks on interest groups.

Berry, Jeffrey M. *The New Liberalism: The Rising Power of Citizen Groups*. Washington, D.C.: Brookings, 1999. Berry argues that citizen groups have been strikingly successful in influencing the policy agenda in recent decades.

Birnbaum, Jeffrey H., and Alan S. Murray. *Showdown at Gucci Gulch: Lawmakers, Lobbyists, and the Unlikely Triumph of Tax Reform*. New York: Vintage, 1987. A fascinating account of how the 1986 tax reform bill passed over the objections of the Gucci-clad lobbyists.

Cigler, Allan J., and Burdett A. Loomis, eds. *Interest Group Politics*, 6th ed. Washington, D.C.: Congressional Quarterly Press, 2002. An excellent collection of original articles on the modern interest group system.

CQ Press Editors, *Public Interest Group Profiles, 2004–5*. Washington, D.C.: Congressional Quarterly Press, 2004. A comprehensive reference book about interest groups that provides information about internship and employment opportunities with many groups.

Dye, Thomas R. *Who's Running America?*, 7th ed. Englewood Cliffs, NJ: Prentice-Hall, 2002. A good summary of the elitist view of interest groups.

Herrnson, Paul S., Ronald G. Shaiko, and Clyde Wilcox, eds. *The Interest Group Connection*. Chatham, NJ: Chatham House, 1998. A collection of essays on interest groups with the added bonus of commentaries from major lobbyists themselves.

Kollman, Ken. *Outside Lobbying: Public Opinion and Interest Group Strategies*. Princeton, NJ: Princeton University Press, 1998. An insightful study of how many interest groups use public opinion in the lobbying process.

Lowi, Theodore J. *The End of Liberalism*, 2nd ed. New York: Norton, 1979. A critique of the role of subgovernments and the excessive deference to interest groups in the American political system.

Olson, Mancur. *The Logic of Collective Action*. Cambridge, MA: Harvard University Press, 1965. Develops an economic theory of groups, showing how the cards are stacked against larger groups.

Rauch, Jonathan. *Demosclerosis: The Silent Killer of American Government*. New York: Random House, 1994. A good treatment of hyperpluralism in American politics.

Rozell, Mark J., and Clyde Wilcox. *Interest Groups in American Campaigns*. Washington, D.C.: Congressional Quarterly Press, 1999. A good review of how interest groups are playing an increasingly important role in electioneering.

12

Congress

Chapter Outline

The Representatives and Senators

Congressional Elections

How Congress Is Organized To Make Policy

The Congressional Process

The New York Times Issues of the Times

Understanding Congress

Summary

■ David Boren of Oklahoma decided to quit. He was a senior U.S. senator in good health and could look forward to years of prominence in making public policy. Yet he chose to leave office midterm to become president of the University of Oklahoma. The same year, a record number of Boren's colleagues decided to voluntarily retire from the Senate. They had had enough.

To many Americans, being a U.S. senator may seem rather glamorous. What citizens do not see is the 14-hour days spent dashing from one meeting to the next, the continuous travel between Washington and constituencies, the lack of time for reflection or exchange of ideas, the constant fund-raising, the partisan rancor that permeates Congress, and—perhaps most important of all—the feeling that Congress is making little headway in solving the country's problems.

It is ironic that such frustrations exist in an organization whose members put so much blood, sweat, and tears into joining. Yet it *is* difficult to get anything done. The movement of legislation through the congressional labyrinth has never been more

wer is fragmented within Congress,
f Congress are often fiercely inde-
r Senate Majority Leader Howard
that moving the Senate is like "trying
oodle."
re is the president. Often the major-
and the chief executive are of differ-
ties. Even if a bill passes Congress, it
t the other end of Pennsylvania
agreement between the two
ven lead to a shutdown of the gov-
pened during the battle over the

enators and representatives ask them-
he point of serving? The public
regard, the pundits criticize us con-
e get little done. Isn't it better to be
g else?"
nt with Congress among its own
ironic. The framers of the
ceived of the legislature as the cen-
ing in America. The great disputes
cy were to be resolved there, not in
e or the Supreme Court. Although
of Congress has ebbed and flowed

over the course of American history, in recent years
Congress has been the true center of power in
Washington.

Congress is not only our central policymaking
branch, but is also our principal *representative*
branch. As such, it lies at the heart of American
democracy. How does Congress combine its roles of
representing constituents *and* making effective public policy? Not very well, according to many critics.
Some argue that Congress is too responsive to constituents and, especially, to organized interests and is
thus unable to make difficult choices regarding public policy. Conversely, others argue that Congress is
too insulated from ordinary citizens. Many critics
even support efforts to force members of Congress to
retire after serving just a few terms.

Other critics focus on Congress as the source of
government expansion. If Congress is responsive to a
multitude of interests and those interests want government policies to aid them in some way, the logi-
cal result is an increase in the size of the public
sector. In addition, do the benefits of servicing constituents provide an incentive for members of
Congress to tolerate—even to expand—an already
big government?

353

Congress' tasks become more difficult each year. On any day a representative or senator can be required to make a sensible judgment about nuclear missiles, nuclear waste dumps, abortion, trade competition with Japan, income tax rates, the soaring costs of Social Security and Medicare, and countless other issues. President Clinton's 1993 health care reform proposal was 1,342 pages long and weighed 6 pounds. Just finding time to think about these issues—much less debate them—has become increasingly difficult.

Despite the many demands of the job, there is no shortage of men and women running for congressional office. The following sections will introduce you to these people.

The Representatives and Senators

Being a member of Congress is a difficult and unusual job. A person must be willing to spend considerable time, trouble, and money to obtain a crowded office on Capitol Hill. To nineteenth-century humorist Artemus Ward, such a quest was inexplicable: "It's easy to see why a man goes to the poorhouse or the penitentiary. It's because he can't help it. But why he should voluntarily go live in Washington is beyond my comprehension."

The Job

Hard work is perhaps the most prominent characteristic of a congressperson's job. Representatives and senators deeply resent common beliefs that they are overpaid, underworked, corrupt, and ineffective. Members have even commissioned their own time and motion studies of their efficiency to demonstrate that they do work hard (see Table 12.1). For example, the typical representative is a member of about six committees and subcommittees; a senator is a member of about ten. Members are often scheduled to be in two places at the same time.

There are attractions to the job, however. First and foremost is power. Members of Congress make key decisions about important matters of public policy. In addition, the salary and the perks that go with the job help make it tolerable. Members of Congress receive the following:

- A salary of $158,100 in 2004, about four times the income of the typical American family, but well below that of hundreds of corporate presidents who earn several times as much
- Generous retirement benefits
- Office space in Washington and in their constituencies
- A substantial congressional staff who serve individual members, committees, and party leaders
- Handsome travel allowances to see their constituents each year, plus opportunities to travel at low fares or even free to foreign nations on congressional inquiries (what critics call "junkets")
- Franking privileges—the free use of the mail system to communicate with constituents, and machines that duplicate a member's signature in real ink
- Plenty of small privileges, such as free flowers from the National Botanical Gardens, research services from the Library of Congress, and access to exercise rooms and pools

Despite the salaries, the perquisites, and the thousands of staff members, Congress is relatively inexpensive. Per citizen, it costs Americans about the same amount to run the nation's legislature for a year as to buy a hamburger, fries, and cola at a fast food franchise.

Table 12.1   A Day in the Life of a Member of Congress

TYPICAL SCHEDULE IN WASHINGTON		TYPICAL SCHEDULE IN CONSTITUENCY	
8:00 A.M.	Budget Study Group:—Chair Leon Panetta, Budget Committee	7:30 A.M.	Business group breakfast: 20 leaders of the business community
8:45 A.M.	Mainstream Forum meeting	8:45 A.M.	Hoover Elementary School: 6th grade class assembly
9:15 A.M.	Meeting with Consulting Engineers Council from constituency about various issues of concern	9:45 A.M.	National Agriculture Day: speech
		10:45 A.M.	Supplemental Food Shelf: pass foodstuffs to needy families
9:45 A.M.	Meet with Soybean Association representatives regarding agriculture appropriations projects	12:00 NOON	Community college: student/faculty lunch, speech and Q & A
10:15 A.M.	WCHL radio interview (by phone)	1:00 P.M.	Sunset Terrace Elementary School: assembly 4th, 5th, 6th grades, remarks/Q & A
10:30 A.M.	Tape weekly radio show—budget		
11:00 A.M.	Meet with former student, now an author, about intellectual property issue	(Travel Time: 1:45 P.M.–2:45 P.M.)	
1:00 P.M.	Agriculture Subcommittee Hearing— Budget Overview and General Agriculture Outlook	2:45 P.M.	Plainview Day Care Facility: discuss changes in federal law with owner
2:30 P.M.	Meeting with Chair Bill Ford and Southern Democrats regarding HR5, Striker Replacement Bill, possible amendments	4:00 P.M.	Town Hall meeting: American Legion
		(Travel Time: 5:00 P.M.–5:45 P.M.)	
3:15 P.M.	Meet with Close-up students from district on steps of Capitol for photo and discussions	5:45 P.M.	PTA meeting: speech on education issues before Congress (also citizen involvement with national associations)
3:45 P.M.	Meet with professor regarding energy research programs	6:30 P.M.	Annual Dinner: St. John's Lutheran Church Development Activity Center
4:30 P.M.	Meet with constituent of Kurdish background regarding situation in Iraq	7:15 P.M.	Association for Children for Enforcement of Support meeting: discuss problems of enforcing child support payments
5:30–7:00 P.M.	Reception—Sponsored by National Association of Home Builders, honoring new president Mark Tipton from constituency	(Travel Time 8:00 P.M.–8:30 P.M.)	
		8:30 P.M.	Students Against Drunk Driving (SADD) meeting: speech on drinking age, drunk driving, uniform federal penalties
6:00–8:00 P.M.	Reception—Honoring retiring Rep. Bill Gray	9:30 P.M.	State university class: discuss business issues before Congress
6:00–8:00 P.M.	Reception—Sponsored by Firefighters Association		
6:00–8:00 P.M.	Reception—Sponsored by American Financial Services Association		

Sources: Adapted by permission from Craig Schultz, ed., *Setting Course: A Congressional Management Guide.* Copyright © 1994 Congressional Management Foundation, Washington, D.C. and from David E. Price, *The Congressional Experience: A View from the Hill.* Copyright © 1999 Westview Press, a division of HarperCollins Publishers. Reprinted by permission of Westview Press, a member of Perseus Books, L.L.C.

The Members

There are 535 members of Congress. An even hundred, two from each state, are members of the Senate. The other 435 are members of the House of Representatives. The Constitution specifies only that members of the House must be at least 25 years old and American citizens for seven years; senators must be at least 30 and American citizens for nine years. In addition, all members of Congress must be residents of the states from which they are elected.

Members of Congress are not typical or average Americans, however, as the figures in Table 12.2 reveal. Elite theorists are quick to point out that members come largely from occupations with high status and usually have substantial incomes. Although calling the Senate a "millionaires' club" is an exaggeration, the proportion of millionaires and near-millionaires is much higher in Congress than in an average crowd of 535 people. Business and law are the dominant prior occupations; other elite occupations such as academia are also well represented.

Law especially attracts persons interested in politics and provides the flexibility (and often the financial support of a law firm) to wage election campaigns. In addition, many government positions in which aspiring members of Congress can make their marks, such as district attorney, are reserved for lawyers.

Less than 10 percent of the House are African American (compared with about 12 percent of the total population), and most (but not all) of these representatives have been elected from overwhelmingly African-American constituencies. No state is predominantly African American, and there is one African American in the Senate. There are 25 Hispanics in the House and two in the Senate. Asian and Native Americans are also underrepresented. In terms of numbers, however, women are the most underrepresented group; more than half the population is female, but only 14 senators and 64 voting representatives are female (the representative from Washington, D.C. does not vote).

How important are the personal characteristics of members of Congress? Can a group of predominantly White, upper-middle-class, middle-aged Protestant males adequately represent a much more diverse population? Would a group of more typical citi-

Table 12.2   A Portrait of the 109th Congress: Some Statistics

CHARACTERISTIC	HOUSE (435 TOTAL)	SENATE (100 TOTAL)
Party		
Democrat	202	44
Republican	232	55
Independent	1	1
Gender		
Men	371	86
Women	64	14
Race		
Asian	4	1
African American	38	1
Hispanic	25	2
White and other	368	96
Religion		
Protestant	268	63
Roman Catholic	128	24
Jewish	26	11
Other and unspecified	10	2
Prior Occupation*		
Law	160	58
Business	162	30
Education	86	12
Public service/politics	163	32
Agriculture	28	5
Journalism	10	7
Real estate	38	3
Medicine	15	4
Other	61	6

*Some members specify more than one occupation.
Source: Congressional Quarterly.

Despite their gains in recent congressional elections, women are the most underrepresented demographic group in Congress. Here a group of female representatives advocates legislation that would require federal employees' health insurance plans to cover the cost of prescription contraceptives.

zens be more effective in making major policy decisions? Because power in Congress is highly decentralized, the backgrounds of representatives and senators can be important if they influence how issues are prioritized and how officials vote on these issues. There is evidence that African-American members are more active than White members in serving African-American constituents,[1] and they appear to increase African-American constituents' contact with and knowledge about Congress.[2] Similarly, on the average, women legislators seem to be more active than men in pursuing the interests of women.[3]

Obviously, members of Congress cannot claim *descriptive* representation—that is, representing constituents by mirroring their personal, politically relevant characteristics. They may, however, engage in *substantive* representation—representing the interests of groups.[4] For example, members of Congress with a background of wealth and privilege, such as Senator Edward Kennedy, can be champions for the interests of the poor. Moreover, most members of Congress have lived in the constituencies they represent for many years, and share the beliefs and attitudes of at least a large proportion of their constituents. If they do not share such perspectives, they may find it difficult to keep their seats come election time. At the same time, females and African Americans who are in Congress are achieving important positions on committees, increasing the chances of making descriptive representation effective.[5]

Congressional Elections

Congressional elections are demanding, expensive,[6] and, as you will see, generally foregone conclusions—yet the role of politician is the most universal one in Congress. Men and women may run for Congress to forge new policy initiatives, but they also run because they are politicians, they enjoy politics, and they consider a position in Congress near the top of their chosen profession. Even if they dislike politics, without reelection they will not be around long enough to shape policy.

Members of Congress who do not share their constituents' economic and social backgrounds can nonetheless represent their concerns. Senator Edward Kennedy, for example, born into one of America's wealthiest families, has championed the poor and underprivileged throughout his career. Here, Kennedy speaks to workers concerned over proposed cuts in their pay and benefits.

Who Wins Elections?

Everyone in Congress is a politician, and politicians continually have their eyes on the next election. The players in the congressional election game are the incumbents and the challengers.

Incumbents are individuals who already hold office. Sometime during each term, the incumbent must decide whether to run again or to retire voluntarily. Most decide to run for reelection. They enter their party's primary, almost always emerge victorious, and typically win in the November general election, too. Indeed, the most important fact about congressional elections is this: *Incumbents usually win.*

Thus, the key to ensuring an opponent's defeat is not having more money than the opponent, although that helps. It is not being more photogenic, although that helps, too. The best thing a candidate can have going for him or her is simply to be the incumbent (see Figure 12.1). Even in a year of great political upheaval such as 1994, in which the Republicans gained 8 seats in the Senate and 53 seats in the House, 92 percent of incumbent senators and 89 percent of incumbent representatives won their bids for reelection.

Not only do more than 90 percent of the incumbents seeking reelection win, but most of them win with more than 60 percent of the vote. Perhaps most astonishing is the fact that even when challengers' positions on the issues are closer to the voters' positions, incumbents still tend to win.[7]

The picture for the Senate is a little different. Even though senators still have a good chance of beating back a challenge, the odds of reelection are often not as handsome as for House incumbents; senators typically win by narrower margins.

One reason for the greater competition in the Senate is that an entire state is almost always more diverse than a congressional district and thus provides a larger base for opposition to an incumbent. At the same time, senators have less personal contact with their constituencies, which on average are nearly 10 times larger than those of members of the House of Representatives. Senators also receive more coverage in the media than representatives do and are more likely to be held accountable on controversial issues. Moreover, senators tend to draw more visible challengers, such as governors or members of the House, whom voters already know and who have substantial financial backing—a factor that lessens the advantages of incumbency. Many of these

incumbents

Those already holding office. In congressional elections, incumbents usually win.

Figure 12.1 The Incumbency Factor in Congressional Elections

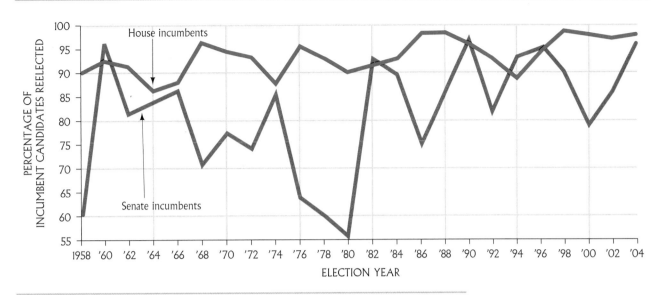

Source: Norman J. Ornstein, Thomas E. Mann, and Michael J. Malbin, *Vital Statistics on Congress, 1997–1998* (Washington, D.C.: Congressional Quarterly Press, 1998). Data for 1998–2004 compiled by the authors. Figures reflect incumbents running in both primary and general elections.

challengers know that the Senate is a stepping stone to national prominence and sometimes even the presidency.

Despite their success at reelection, incumbents often feel quite vulnerable. As Thomas Mann put it, members of Congress perceive themselves as "unsafe at any margin."[8] Thus, they have been raising and spending more campaign funds, sending more mail to their constituents, visiting their states and districts more often, and staffing more local offices than ever before.[9] They realize that with the decline of partisan loyalty in the electorate, they bear more of the burden of obtaining votes.

The Advantages of Incumbency

There are several possible explanations for the success of incumbents. One is that voters know how their elected representatives vote on important policy issues and agree with their stands, sending them back to Washington to keep up the good work. This, however, is usually not the case. In fact, voters are rather oblivious to how their senators and representatives actually vote. One study found that only about one-fifth of Americans can make an accurate guess about how their representatives have voted on any issue in Congress.[10] As one expert put it, "Mass public knowledge of congressional candidates declines precipitously once we move beyond simple recognition, generalized feelings, and incumbent job ratings."[11]

Another possibility is that voter assessments of presidential candidates influence their voting for Congress. Most stories of presidential "coattails" (when voters support congressional candidates because of their support for the president), however, seem to be just stories.[12] Bill Clinton received a *smaller* percentage of the vote than did almost every winning Democrat in Congress in both 1992 and 1996. The same was true for George W. Bush and Republicans in 2000. He had little in the way of coattails.

Journalists often claim that voters are motivated primarily by their pocketbooks. Yet members of Congress do not gain or lose many votes as a result of the ups and downs of the economy.[13]

What accounts for the success of congressional incumbents? Members of Congress engage in three primary activities that increase the probability of their reelection:

Visual Literacy

Why Is it So Hard to Defeat
an Incumbent?

advertising, credit claiming, and position-taking.[14] In addition, the lack of strong opponents further ensures their success.

Advertising.   For members of Congress, advertising means much more than placing ads in the newspapers and on television. Most congressional advertising takes place between elections in the form of contact with constituents. The goal is *visibility.*

Members of Congress work hard to get themselves known in their constituencies, and they usually succeed. Not surprisingly, members concentrate on staying visible. Trips home are frequent. In a typical week, members spend some time in their home districts,[15] even though their districts may be hundreds of miles from Washington. Similarly, members use the franking privilege to mail newsletters to every household in their constituency.

Credit Claiming.   Congresspersons also engage in credit claiming, which involves enhancing their standing with constituents through service to individuals and the district. One member told Richard Fenno about the image he tried to cultivate in his constituency:

> [I have] a very high recognition factor. And of all the things said about me, none of them said, "He's a conservative or a liberal," or "He votes this way on such and such an issue." None of that at all. There were two things said. One, "He works hard." Two, "He works for us." Nothing more than that. So we made it our theme, "O'Connor gets things done"; and we emphasized the dams, the highways, the buildings, the casework.[16]

Morris Fiorina has emphasized this close link between service and success.[17] Members of Congress, he says, *can* go to the voters and stress their policymaking record and their stands on new policy issues on the agenda. The problem with facing the voters on one's record—past, present, and future—is that policy positions make enemies as well as friends. A member of Congress' vote for reducing government spending may win some friends, but it will make enemies of voters who happen to link that vote with service cutbacks. Besides, a congressperson can almost never show that he or she alone was responsible for a major policy. Being only 1 of 435 members of the House or 1 of 100 senators, a person can hardly promise to end inflation, cut taxes, or achieve equal rights for women single-handedly.

One thing, though, always wins friends and almost never makes enemies: *servicing the constituency.* There are two ways in which members of Congress can do so: through casework and through the pork barrel. **Casework** is helping constituents as individuals—cutting through some bureaucratic red tape to give people what they think they have a right to get. The **pork barrel** is the mighty list of federal projects, grants, and contracts available to cities, businesses, colleges, and institutions.

Do you have trouble getting your check from the Social Security Administration on time? Call your congressperson; he or she can cut red tape. Does your town have trouble getting federal bureaucrats to respond to its request for federal construction money? Call your congressperson. Representatives and senators can single-handedly take credit for each of these favors. Fiorina puts it like this:

> Even committee chairmen have a difficult time claiming credit for a piece of major legislation, let alone a rank-and-file congressman. Ah, but casework, and the pork barrel. In dealing with the bureaucracy, the congressman is not merely 1 vote in 435. Rather he is a nonpartisan power, someone whose phone calls snap an office to attention. He is not kept on hold. The constituent who receives aid believes that his congressman and his congressman alone got results. Similarly, congressmen find it easy to claim credit for federal projects awarded in their districts. The congressman may have instigated the project in the first place, issued regular progress reports, and ultimately announced the award through his office. Maybe he can't claim credit for the 1965 Voting Rights Act, but he can take credit for Littletown's spanking new sewage treatment plant.[18]

Getting things done for the folks back home often gets an incumbent the chance to serve them again.

casework

Activities of members of Congress that help constituents as individuals; cutting through bureaucratic red tape to get people what they think they have a right to get.

pork barrel

The mighty list of federal projects, grants, and contracts available to cities, businesses, colleges, and institutions available in a congressional district.

Representative Silvio Conte used a pig nose and ears to protest pork barrel spending—until he wanted multimillion-dollar federal grants for his Massachusetts district. Because credit claiming is so important to reelection, members of Congress rarely pass up the opportunity to increase federal spending in their state or district.

As a result of the advantages of incumbency in advertising and credit claiming, incumbents, especially in the House, are usually much better known and have a more favorable public image than do their opponents.[19] Shrewd use of the resources available to incumbents may give them an advantage, but by themselves, casework and pork barrel do not determine congressional elections.[20]

Position-Taking.   Members of Congress must also engage in position-taking on issues when they vote and when they respond to constituents' questions. In establishing their public images, members of Congress emphasize their personal qualities as experienced, hard-working, trustworthy representatives who have served their constituencies—an image often devoid of partisan or programmatic content. Nevertheless, all members must take policy stands, and the positions they take may affect the outcome of an election, especially if the issues are on matters salient to voters and the candidates' stands differ from those of a majority of their constituents. This is especially true in elections for the Senate, in which issues are likely to play a greater role than in House elections.

Weak Opponents.   Another advantage for incumbents is that they are likely to face weak opponents. Confronted with the advantages of incumbency, potentially effective opponents are often unlikely to risk challenging members of the House.[21] Those individuals who do run are usually not well known or well qualified and lack experience and organizational and financial backing.[22] The lack of adequate campaign funds is a special burden because challengers need money to compensate for the "free" recognition incumbents receive from their advertising and credit claiming.[23]

Campaign Spending.   It costs a great deal of money to elect a Congress. In the 2001–2002 election cycle, congressional candidates spent nearly a *billion* dollars to win the election. Challengers have to raise large sums if they hope to defeat an incumbent, and the more they spend, the more votes they receive. Money buys them name recognition and a chance to be heard. Incumbents, by contrast, already have high levels of recognition among their constituents and benefit less (but still benefit) from campaign spending; what matters most is how much their opponents spend. (In contests for open seats, the candidate who spends the most usually wins.) In the end, however, challengers are usually substantially outspent by incumbents.[24] In the House races in 2002, the typical incumbent outspent the typical challenger by a rating of 12 to 1.[25]

Where do campaign funds come from? And, more important, what do they buy? Although most of the money spent in congressional elections comes from individuals, about 30 percent of the funds raised by candidates for Congress comes from political action committees (PACs) (see Chapters 9 and 11). Critics of PACs offer plenty of complaints about the present system of campaign finance. Why, they ask, is money spent to pay the campaign costs of a candidate who is already heavily favored to win? Even more interesting is that PACs often make contributions *after* the election.

There is a continuous debate in America today on whether PACs "buy" votes in Congress (see "You Are the Policymaker: Should We Do Away With PACs?" in Chapter 11). Although this question remains unresolved, everyone agrees that at the very least, PACs seek *access* to policymakers. Thus they give most of their money to incumbents, who are likely to win anyway. When they support someone who loses, they quickly make amends and contribute to the winner. PACs want to keep the lines of communication open and create a receptive atmosphere in which to be heard. Because each PAC is limited to an expenditure of $5,000 per candidate (most give less), a single PAC can at most account for only a small percentage of a winner's total spending. If one PAC does not contribute to a candidate, there are always other PACs from which to seek funds.

Aside from the question of whether money buys influence, what does it buy the candidates who spend it? In 2000, Jon Corzine of New Jersey spent more than $60 million to win a Senate seat. However, Rick Lazio spent more than $40 million to win a Senate seat in New York—and lost. In 1994, Californian Michael Huffington spent nearly $30 million—most of it his own money—about twice the expenditures of his rival, Senator Dianne Feinstein, and still lost. Oliver North spent about $20 million in the much smaller state of Virginia, and he lost as well. Obviously, prolific spending in a campaign is no guarantee of success.

The Role of Party Identification

At the base of every electoral coalition are the members of the candidate's party in the constituency. Although party loyalty at the voting booth is not as strong as it was a generation ago, it is still a good predictor of voting behavior. In the 2002 congressional elections, for example, nearly 90 percent of voters who identified with a party voted for the House candidates of their party. Most members of Congress represent constituencies in which their party is in the majority.

Defeating Incumbents

In light of the advantages of incumbents, it is reasonable to ask why anyone challenges them at all. One of the main reasons is simply that challengers are often naïve about their chances of winning. Because few have money for expensive polls, they rely on friends and local party leaders, who often tell them what they want to hear. Sometimes they do get some unexpected help; incumbents almost have to beat themselves, and some do.

An incumbent tarnished by scandal or corruption becomes instantly vulnerable. Clearly, voters do take out their anger at the polls. For example, representatives who bounced large numbers of checks at the House bank were much more likely to lose their seats in the 1992 elections than their more fiscally responsible colleagues.[26] In a close election, negative publicity can turn victory into defeat.[27]

Incumbents may also be redistricted out of their familiar turfs. After each federal census, Congress reapportions its membership. States that have gained significantly in population will be given more House seats; states that have lost substantial population will lose one or more of their seats. The state legislatures must then redraw their states' district lines; one incumbent may be moved into another's district, where the two must battle for one seat. A state party majority is more likely to move two of the opposition party's representatives into a single district than two of its own.

"WE'RE ASKING VOTERS WHY THEY'VE SHOWN SO LITTLE INTEREST IN THIS YEAR'S CONGRESSIONAL RACES..."

"WELL, THANKS TO GERRY-MANDERING LEGISLATURES, MOST DISTRICTS ARE TOTALLY DOMINATED BY ONE PARTY!"

"SO, MOST OF US HAVE A CHOICE BETWEEN AN ENTRENCHED INCUMBENT AND A SACRIFICIAL LAMB!"

"AND WHERE THERE ARE REAL RACES, THERE'S NO SERIOUS DEBATE, JUST MARKET-TESTED SOUND BITES AND UNFAIR ATTACK ADS!"

"PLUS, YOU LOCAL TV GUYS DON'T COVER POLITICS, YOU JUST DO FIRES, CAR CHASES AND LAME MAN-IN-THE-STREET INTERVIEWS!"

"UH, YEAH, WELL... I GUESS IT REMAINS A MYSTERY WHY VOTERS DON'T SEEM TO CARE."

Finally, major political tidal waves occasionally roll across the country, leaving defeated incumbents in their wake. One such wave occurred in 1994, when the public mood turned especially sour and voters took out their frustration on Democratic incumbents, defeating 34 in the House and 2 in the Senate.

Open Seats

When an incumbent is not running for reelection and the seat is open, there is greater likelihood of competition. If the party balance in a constituency is such that either party has a chance of winning, each side may offer a strong candidate—each with enough money to establish name recognition among the voters. Most of the turnover in the membership of Congress results from vacated seats.

Stability and Change

Because incumbents usually win reelection, there is some stability in the membership of Congress. This provides the opportunity for representatives and senators to gain some expertise in dealing with complex questions of public policy. At the same time, it also may insulate them from the winds of political change. Safe seats make it more difficult for citizens to "send a message to Washington" with their votes. Particularly in the House, it takes a large shift in votes to affect the outcomes of most elections. To increase turnover in the membership of Congress, some reformers have proposed *term limitations* for representatives and senators[28] (see "You Are the Policymaker: Should We Impose Term Limits on Members of Congress?").

How Congress Is Organized To Make Policy

Of all the senators' and representatives' roles, making policy is the toughest. Congress is a collection of generalists trying to make policy on specialized topics. Members are short on time and expertise. As amateurs in almost every subject, they are surrounded

You Are the Policymaker

Should We Impose Term Limits on Members of Congress?

In the late 1980s many reformers were concerned that the incumbency advantage enjoyed by legislators created, in effect, lifetime tenure, which served as a roadblock to change and encouraged ethics abuses. To increase turnover among legislators, these reformers proposed term limitations, generally restricting representatives to 6 or 12 consecutive years in office.

The movement to limit the terms of legislators spread rapidly across the country. Within a few years, 23 states enacted term limitations for members of their state legislatures. The House Republicans made terms limits for Congress part of their Contract With America in the 1994 election. Yet changing the terms of members of Congress requires changing the Constitution, which is difficult

to do, and many members of Congress have fought term limitations fiercely.

Opponents of term limitations object to the loss of experienced legislators and of the American people's ability to vote for whomever they please. In addition, they add, there is plenty of new blood in the legislature: At the beginning of the 105th Congress (1997), more than half the members of House and 40 percent of the senators had no more than four years of experience in their chambers. Moreover, recent research indicates that the movement of party fortunes in the House follows the movement of citizen preferences for public policy.*

Proponents of term limits suffered two setbacks in 1995 when Congress failed to pass a constitutional amendment on term limitations (it also failed

in 1997), and when the Supreme Court, in *U.S. Term Limits, Inc. et al. v. Thornton et al.*, decided that state-imposed term limits on members of Congress were unconstitutional. In the meantime, most people seem comfortable with their own representatives and senators and appear content to reelect them again and again.

Nevertheless, many Americans support a constitutional amendment to impose term limitations on members of Congress. You be the policymaker: What would *you* do?

*Suzanna De Boef and James A. Stimson, "The Dynamic Structure of Congressional Elections," *Journal of Politics* 57 (August 1995): 630–648.

by people who know (or claim to know) more than they do—lobbyists, agency administrators, even their own staffs. Even if they had time to study all the issues thoroughly, making wise national policy would be difficult. If economists disagree about policies to fight unemployment, how are legislators to know which policies may work better than others?

When ringing bells announce a roll-call vote, representatives or senators rush into the chamber from their offices or from a hearing—often unsure of what is being voted on. Frequently, "uncertain of their position, members of Congress will seek out one or two people who serve on the committee which considered and reported the bill, in whose judgment they have confidence."29

The Founders gave Congress' organization just a hint of specialization when they split it into the House and the Senate. The complexity of today's issues, however, requires much more specialization. Congress tries to cope with policymaking demands through its elaborate committee system.

American Bicameralism

bicameral legislature

A legislature divided into two houses. The U.S. Congress and every American state legislature except Nebraska's are bicameral.

A **bicameral legislature** is a legislature divided into two houses. The U.S. Congress is bicameral, as is every American state legislature except Nebraska's, which has one house (unicameral). As we learned in Chapter 2, the Connecticut Compromise at the Constitutional Convention created a bicameral Congress. Each state is guaranteed 2 senators, and its number of representatives is determined by the population of the state (California has 53 representatives; Alaska, Delaware, Montana, North Dakota,

Table 12.3 House Versus Senate: Some Key Differences

CHARACTERISTIC	HOUSE OF REPRESENTATIVES	SENATE
Constitutional powers	Must initiate all revenue bills; must pass all articles of impeachment	Must give "advice and consent" to many presidential nominations; must approve treaties; tries impeached officials
Membership	435 members	100 members
Term of office	2 years	6 years
Constituencies	Smaller	Larger
Centralization of power	More centralized; stronger leadership	Less centralized; weaker leadership
Political prestige	Less prestige	More prestige
Role in policymaking	More influential on budget; more specialized	More influential on foreign affairs; less specialized
Turnover	Small	Moderate
Role of seniority	More important in determining power	Less important in determining power
Procedures	Limited debate; limits on floor amendments allowed	Unlimited debate

South Dakota, Vermont, and Wyoming have just 1 each). By creating a bicameral Congress, the Constitution set up yet another check and balance. No bill can be passed unless both House and Senate agree on it; each body can thus veto the policies of the other. Some of the basic differences between the two houses are shown in Table 12.3.

The House. More than four times larger than the Senate, the House is also more institutionalized—that is, more centralized, more hierarchical, and less anarchic.[30] Party loyalty to leadership and party-line voting are more common in the House than in the Senate. Partly because there are more members, leaders in the House do more leading than do leaders in the Senate. First-term House members are more likely to be seen and not heard, and they have less power than senior representatives.[31]

Both the House and the Senate set their own agendas. Both use committees, which we will examine shortly, to winnow down the thousands of bills introduced. One institution unique to the House, however, plays a key role in agenda setting: the **House Rules Committee.** This committee reviews most bills coming from a House committee before they go to the full House. Performing a traffic cop function, the Rules Committee gives each bill a "rule," which schedules the bill on the calendar, allots time for debate, and sometimes even specifies what kind of amendments may be offered. Today, the committee often brings controversial legislation to the floor under a closed rule that prohibits amendments and thus the opportunities for the minority to propose changes. The Rules Committee is generally responsive to the House leadership, in part because the Speaker of the House now appoints the committee's members.

The Senate. The Constitution's framers thought the Senate would protect elite interests to counteract the tendencies of the House to protect the masses. They gave the House power to initiate all revenue bills and to impeach officials; they gave the Senate the responsibility to ratify all treaties, to confirm important presidential nominations (including nominations to the Supreme Court), and to try impeached officials. History shows that when the same party controls each chamber, the Senate is just as

House Rules Committee

An institution unique to the House of Representatives that reviews all bills (except revenue, budget, and appropriations bills) coming from a House committee before they go to the full House.

liberal as, and perhaps more liberal than, the House.[32] The real differences between the bodies lie in the Senate's organization and decentralized power.

Smaller than the House, the Senate is also less disciplined and less centralized. Today's senators are more nearly equal in power than representatives are. They are also more nearly equal in power than senators have been in the past. Even incoming senators sometimes get top committee assignments; they may even become chairs of key subcommittees.

Committees and the party leadership are important in determining the Senate's legislative agenda, just as they are in the House. Party leaders do for Senate scheduling what the Rules Committee does in the House.

filibuster

A strategy unique to the Senate whereby opponents of a piece of legislation try to talk it to death, based on the tradition of unlimited debate. Today, 60 members present and voting can halt a filibuster.

One activity unique to the Senate is the **filibuster.** This is a tactic by which opponents of a bill use their right to unlimited debate as a way to prevent the Senate from ever voting on a bill. Unlike their fellow legislators in the House, once senators have the floor in a debate, tradition holds that they can talk as long as they wish. Strom Thurmond of South Carolina once held forth for a full 24 hours. Working together, then, like-minded senators can practically debate forever, tying up the legislative agenda until the proponents of a bill finally give up their battle. In essence, they literally talk the bill to death.

The power of the filibuster is not absolute, however. Sixty members present and voting can halt a filibuster by voting for *cloture* on debate, but many senators are reluctant to vote for cloture for fear of setting a precedent to be used against them when *they* want to filibuster.

At its core the filibuster raises profound questions about American democracy because it is used by a minority, sometimes a minority of one, to defeat a majority. Southern senators once used filibusters to prevent civil rights legislation.[33] More recently, the opponents of all types of legislation have used them. Indeed, during Bill Clinton's presidency, filibusters became the weapon of first resort for even the most trivial matters. Each senator knows that he or she has at least six opportunities to filibuster a single bill and that these opportunities can be used one after another. In addition, the tactical uses of a filibuster have expanded. A senator might threaten to filibuster an unrelated measure in order to gain concessions on a bill he or she opposes.

If the minority is blocking the majority, why doesn't the majority change the rules to prevent filibuster? The answer is twofold. First, changing the rules requires 67 votes. It is always difficult to obtain the agreement of two-thirds of the Senate on a controversial matter. Second, every senator knows that he or she might be in the minority on an issue at some time. A filibuster gives senators who are in the minority a powerful weapon for defending their (or their constituents') interests.

In the meantime, Americans complain about gridlock in Congress. Nevertheless, senators have decided that they are more concerned with allowing senators to block legislation they oppose than with expediting the passage of legislation a majority favors.

Congressional Leadership

Leading 100 senators or 435 representatives in Congress—each jealous of his or her own power and responsible to no higher power than the constituency—is no easy task. "Few members of the House, fewer still in the Senate," Robert Peabody once wrote, "consider themselves followers."[34] Chapter 8 discussed the party in government. Much of the leadership in Congress is really party leadership. There are a few formal posts whose occupants are chosen by nonparty procedures, but those who have the real power in the congressional hierarchy are those whose party put them there.

Speaker of the House

An office mandated by the Constitution. The Speaker is chosen in practice by the majority party, has both formal and informal powers, and is second in line to succeed to the presidency should that office become vacant.

The House.   Chief among leadership positions in the House of Representatives is the **Speaker of the House.** This is the only legislative office mandated by the Constitution.

In practice, the majority party selects the Speaker. Before each Congress begins, the majority party presents its candidate for Speaker, who—because this person attracts the unanimous support of the majority party—turns out to be a shoo-in. Typically, the Speaker is a senior member of the party. J. Dennis Hastert of Illinois, who has served in Congress since 1987, was elected Speaker in 1999. The Speaker is also two heartbeats away from the presidency, being second in line (after the vice president) to succeed a president who resigns, dies in office, or is convicted after impeachment.

Years ago, the Speaker was king of the congressional mountain. Autocrats such as "Uncle Joe Cannon" and "Czar Reed" ran the House like a fiefdom. A great revolt in 1910 whittled down the Speaker's powers and gave some of them to committees, but six decades later, members of the House restored some of the Speaker's powers. Today the Speaker

- presides over the House when it is in session
- plays a major role in making committee assignments, which are coveted by all members to ensure their electoral advantage
- appoints or plays a key role in appointing the party's legislative leaders and the party leadership staff
- exercises substantial control over which bills get assigned to which committees

In addition to these formal powers, the Speaker has a great deal of informal clout inside and outside Congress. When the Speaker's party differs from the president's party, as it frequently does, the Speaker is often a national spokesperson for the party. The bank of microphones in front of the Speaker of the House is a commonplace feature of the evening news. A good Speaker also knows the members well—including their past improprieties, the ambitions they harbor, and the pressures they feel.

Leadership in the House, however, is not a one-person show. The Speaker's principal partisan ally is the **majority leader**—a job that has been the main stepping stone to the Speaker's role. The majority leader is responsible for scheduling bills in the House. More important, the majority leader is responsible for rounding up votes on behalf of the party's position on legislation. Working with the majority leader are the party's **whips,** who carry the word to party troops, counting votes before they are cast and leaning on waverers whose votes are crucial to a bill. Party whips also report the views and complaints of the party rank and file back to the leadership. The current majority leader is Tom DeLay of Texas.

The minority party is also organized, poised to take over the Speakership and other key posts if it should win a majority in the House. The Republicans had been the minority party in the House for 40 years before 1995, although they had a president to look to for leadership for much of that period. Now the Democrats are experiencing minority status, led by the **minority leader,** Nancy Pelosi of California.

The Senate.   The Constitution makes the vice president of the United States the president of the Senate; this is the vice president's only constitutionally defined job. But even the mighty Lyndon Johnson, who had been the Senate majority leader before becoming vice president, found himself an outsider when he returned as the Senate's president. Vice presidents usually slight their senatorial chores, leaving power in the Senate to party leaders. Senators typically return the favor, ignoring vice presidents except in the rare case when their vote can break a tie.

Thus the Senate majority leader (currently, Tennessee Senator Bill Frist)—aided by the majority whips—is a party's workhorse, corralling votes, scheduling the floor action, and influencing committee assignments. The majority leader's counterpart in the opposition, the minority leader (currently Harry Reid of Nevada), has similar responsibilities. Power is widely dispersed in the contemporary Senate; it no longer lies in the hands of a few key members of Congress who are insulated from the public. Therefore party leaders must appeal broadly for support, often speaking to the country directly or indirectly over television.

Timeline

The Power of the Speaker of the House.

majority leader

The principal partisan ally of the Speaker of the House or the party's manager in the Senate. The majority leader is responsible for scheduling bills, influencing committee assignments, and rounding up votes in behalf of the party's legislative positions.

whips

Party leaders who work with the **majority leader** or **minority leader** to count votes beforehand and lean on waverers whose votes are crucial to a bill favored by the party.

minority leader

The principal leader of the minority party in the House of Representatives or in the Senate.

Dennis Hastert of Illinois was elected Speaker of the House in 1999. Minority Leader Nancy Pelosi leads the Democrats in the House. Bill Frist of Tennessee is the Senate Majority Leader, which makes him the most powerful member of that body. Nevertheless, in the decentralized power structure in the upper chamber, even he must work for support.

Congressional Leadership in Perspective. Despite their stature and power, congressional leaders are not in strong positions to move their troops. Both houses of Congress are highly decentralized and rarely show an inclination for major changes in the way they operate. Leaders are elected by their party members and must remain responsive to them. Except in the most egregious cases (which rarely arise), leaders cannot punish those who do not support the party's stand, and no one expects members to vote against their constituents' interests. Senator Robert Dole nicely summed up the leader's situation when he once dubbed himself the "Majority Pleader."

Nevertheless, party leadership, at least in the House, has been more effective in recent years. As the party contingents have become more homogeneous, there has been more policy agreement within the parties and thus more party unity in voting on the floor. Increased agreement has made it easier for the Speaker to exercise his prerogatives regarding the assignment of bills and members to committees, the rules by which legislation is brought to the floor, and the use of an expanded whip system—all developments that have enabled the parties to advance an agenda that reflects party preferences.[35] Following the Republican takeover of Congress in 1995, Speaker Newt Gingrich began centralizing power and exercising vigorous legislative leadership.

The Committees and Subcommittees

Will Rogers, the famous Oklahoman humorist, once remarked that "outside of traffic, there is nothing that has held this country back as much as committees." Members of the Senate and the House would apparently disagree. Most of the real work of Congress goes on in committees, and committees dominate congressional policymaking in all its stages.

Committees regularly hold hearings to investigate problems and possible wrongdoing and to oversee the executive branch. Most of all, *they control the congressional agenda and guide legislation* from its introduction to its send-off to the president for his signature. Committees can be grouped into four types, the first of which is by far the most important.

standing committees

Separate subject-matter committees in each house of Congress that handle **bills** in different policy areas.

joint committees

Congressional committees on a few subject-matter areas with membership drawn from both houses.

1. **Standing committees** are formed to handle bills in different policy areas (see Table 12.4). Each house of Congress has its own standing committees; members do not belong to a committee in the other house. In the 109th Congress, the typical representative served on two committees and four subcommittees; senators averaged three committees and seven subcommittees each. Subcommittees are smaller units of a committee created out of the committee membership.

2. **Joint committees** exist in a few policy areas, such as the economy and taxation; their membership is drawn from both the Senate and the House.

Table 12.4   Standing Committees in the Senate and in the House

SENATE COMMITTEES	HOUSE COMMITTEES
Agriculture, Nutrition, and Forestry	Agriculture
Appropriations	Appropriations
Armed Services	Armed Services
Banking, Housing, and Urban Affairs	Financial Services
Budget	Budget
Commerce, Science, and Transportation	Energy and Commerce
Energy and Natural Resources	Education and the Workforce
Environment and Public Works	Government Reform
Finance	House Administration
Foreign Relations	International Relations
Governmental Affairs	Judiciary
Health, Education, Labor, and Pensions	Resources
Judiciary	Rules
Rules and Administration	Science
Small Business	Small Business
Veterans' Affairs	Standards of Official Conduct
	Transportation and Infrastructure
	Veterans' Affairs
	Ways and Means

Why It Matters

Weak Parties
Parties organize Congress, but historically they have been relatively weak. If parties are strong, they can enforce strict party loyalty and thus are better able to keep their promises to voters. At the same time, strict party loyalty makes it more difficult for members of Congress to break from the party line to represent their constituents' special needs and interests.

3. **Conference committees** are formed when the Senate and the House pass a particular bill in different forms. Appointed by the party leadership, a conference committee consists of members of each house chosen to iron out Senate and House differences and to report back a compromise bill.
4. **Select committees** are appointed for a specific purpose. The Senate select committee that investigated Watergate is a well-known example.

The Committees at Work: Legislation and Oversight. With more than 11,000 bills submitted by members every two years, some winnowing is essential. Every bill goes to a committee, which has virtually the power of life and death over it. The whole House or Senate usually considers only bills that obtain a favorable committee report.

New bills sent to a committee typically go directly to a subcommittee, which can hold hearings on the bill. Sizable committee and subcommittee staffs conduct research, line up witnesses for hearings, and write and rewrite bills. Committees and their subcommittees report on proposed legislation; these reports are typically bound in beige or green covers and are available from the Government Printing Office. A committee's most important output, however, is the "marked up" (rewritten) bill itself, submitted to the full House or Senate for debate and voting.

The work of committees does not stop when the bill leaves the committee room. Members of the committee usually serve as "floor managers" of the bill, helping party leaders hustle votes for it. They are also the "cue givers" to whom other members turn for advice. When the Senate and House pass different versions of the same bill, some committee members serve on the conference committee.

The committees and subcommittees do not leave the scene even after legislation is passed. They stay busy in **legislative oversight,** the process of monitoring the bureaucracy and its administration of policy. Oversight is handled mainly through hearings. When an agency wants a bigger budget, the use of its present budget is reviewed. Even if no budgetary issues are involved, members of committees constantly monitor how a law is being implemented. Agency heads and even cabinet secretaries testify, bringing graphs, charts, and data on the progress they have made and the problems they face. Committee staffs and committee members grill agency heads about particular problems. For example, a member may ask a Small Business Administration

conference committees

Congressional committees formed when the Senate and the House pass a particular **bill** in different forms. Party leadership appoints members from each house to iron out the differences and bring back a single bill.

select committees

Congressional committees appointed for a specific purpose, such as the Watergate investigation.

legislative oversight

Congress' monitoring of the bureaucracy and its administration of policy, performed mainly through hearings.

Most of Congress' work takes place—and most of its members' power is wielded—in the standing committees and their numerous subcommittees. Here, a Senate committee investigates the electrical power shortage in California in 2002.

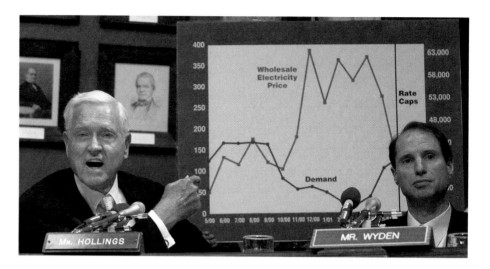

official why constituents who are applying for loans get the runaround. On another committee, officials charged with listing endangered species might defend the gray wolf against a member of Congress whose sheep-ranching constituents are not fond of wolves.

Oversight, one of the checks Congress can exercise on the executive branch, gives Congress the power to pressure agencies and, in extreme cases, cut their budgets in order to secure compliance with congressional wishes and even congressional whims.[36] Oversight also provides an opportunity to refine existing policies or respond to new problems.

Occasionally, congressional oversight rivets the nation's attention. In 1973 the Senate established the Select Committee on Presidential Campaign Activities to investigate the misdeeds and duplicity of the 1972 presidential campaign, otherwise known as the Watergate scandal. This action was followed the next year by the House Judiciary Committee's hearings on the impeachment of President Nixon for his conduct in attempting to cover up the scandal. Shortly after the Judiciary Committee recommended three articles of impeachment, the president resigned.

More recently, a special joint committee was established in 1987 to investigate what became known as the Iran-Contra affair, a term that refers to the secret sale of arms to Iran (for which President Reagan hoped to obtain the release of American hostages held in the Middle East) and the diversion of some of the funds from these sales to the Contras fighting the Sandinista government in Nicaragua (in the face of congressional prohibition of such aid). Many people thought the hearings, especially the testimony of Lieutenant Colonel Oliver North, made for great spy novel entertainment but did little to illuminate the issues involved in the matter.

Congress keeps tabs on more routine activities of the executive branch through its committee staff members. These members have specialized expertise in the fields and agencies that their committees oversee and maintain an extensive network of formal and informal contacts with the bureaucracy. By reading the voluminous reports that Congress requires of the executive and by receiving information from numerous sources—agencies, complaining citizens, members of Congress and their personal staff, state and local officials, interest groups, and professional organizations—staff members can keep track of the implementation of public policy.[37]

Nevertheless, members of Congress have many competing responsibilities, and there are few political payoffs for carefully watching a government agency to see whether it is implementing policy properly. It is difficult to go to voters and say, "Vote for me. I oversaw the routine handling of road building." Because of this lack of incentives, problems may be overlooked until it is too late to do much about them. A major scandal involving the Department of Housing and Urban Development's administration of housing programs during the Reagan presidency was not uncovered until 1989, after Reagan had left office. Similarly, taxpayers could have saved well over $100 billion if Congress had insisted that the agencies regulating the savings and loan industry enforce their regulations more rigorously.

Nevertheless, Congress *did* substantially increase its oversight activities in the 1970s and 1980s. As the size and complexity of the national government grew in the 1960s, and after numerous charges that the executive branch had become too powerful (especially in response to the widespread belief that Presidents Johnson and Nixon had abused their power), Congress responded with more oversight. The tight budgets of recent years have provided additional incentives for oversight, as members of Congress have sought to protect programs they favor from budget cuts and to get more value for the tax dollars spent on them. As the publicity value of receiving credit for controlling governmental spending has increased, so has the number of representatives and senators interested in oversight.[38]

Getting on a Committee. One of the first worries for an incoming member of Congress (after paying off campaign debts) is getting on the right committee. Although it is not always easy to figure out what the right committee is, it is fairly easy to recognize some wrong committees. The Iowa newcomer does not want to get stuck on the Financial Services Committee; the Brooklyn freshman would like to avoid Agriculture. Members seek committees that will help them achieve three goals: reelection, influence in Congress, and the opportunity to make policy in areas they think are important.[39]

Just after their election, new members write to the party's congressional leaders and members of their state delegation, indicating their committee preferences. Every committee includes members from both parties, but a majority of each committee's members, as well as its chair, come from the majority party. Each party in each house has a slightly different way of picking its committee members. Party leaders almost always play a key role.

Those who have supported the leadership are favored in the committee selection process, but generally the parties try to grant members' requests for committee assignments whenever possible. They want their members to please their constituents (being on the right committee should help them represent their constituency more effectively and reinforce their ability to engage in credit claiming) and to develop expertise in an area of policy. The parties also try to apportion the influence that comes with committee membership among the state delegations, in order to accord representation to diverse components of the party.[40]

Getting Ahead on the Committee: Chairs and the Seniority System. If committees are the most important influencers of the congressional agenda, **committee chairs** are the most important influencers of the committee agenda. Committee chairs play dominant roles in scheduling hearings, hiring staff, appointing subcommittees, and managing committee bills when they are brought before the full house.

Until the 1970s, there was a simple way of picking committee chairs: the **seniority system.** If committee members had served on their committee longest and their party controlled the chamber, they got to be chairs—regardless of their party loyalty, mental state, or competence.

Woodrow Wilson, a political scientist before he became a politician, once said that the government of the United States was really government by the chairs of the standing committees of Congress. The chairs were so powerful for most of the twentieth century that they could bully members or bottle up legislation at any time—and with almost certain knowledge that they would be chairs for the rest of their electoral

committee chairs

The most important influencers of the congressional agenda. They play dominant roles in scheduling hearings, hiring staff, appointing subcommittees, and managing committee bills when they are brought before the full house.

seniority system

A simple rule for picking **committee chairs,** in effect until the 1970s. The member who had served on the committee the longest and whose party controlled Congress became chair, regardless of party loyalty, mental state, or competence.

Why It Matters

The Committee System
The committee system in Congress is highly decentralized. As a result, it is open to the appeals of a wide range of "special" interests, especially those represented by highly paid lobbyists. If Congress were more *centralized* and only those interests cleared by the elected leadership received a hearing, special interests might be constrained. However, there is also a danger that only the interests reflecting the views of the leadership would be heard.

caucus (congressional)

A group of members of Congress sharing some interest or characteristic. Most are composed of members from both parties and from both houses.

life. Richard Fenno, a veteran congressional observer, once remarked that the "performance of Congress as an institution is very largely the performance of its committees" but that the committee system is the "epitome of fragmentation and decentralization."[41] The more that power is dispersed, the more difficult it is to make coherent policy.

In the 1970s, younger members of Congress revolted. Both parties in both branches permitted members to vote on committee chairs; in 1975, the House Democrats dumped four chairs with 154 years of seniority among them. The Democrats also increased the independence of subcommittees, which limited the chairs' power and widened the distribution of authority, visibility, and resources in both chambers.[42]

Today seniority remains the *general rule* for selecting chairs, but there are plenty of exceptions. House Republicans skipped over several senior representatives when they named committee chairs in 1995 and have continued to do so in subsequent Congresses. Partially in response to the problems of decentralized power in the House, the Republicans passed other prominent committee reforms when they took control in 1995. Committee chairs were allowed to choose the chairs of subcommittees on their committees and to hire all the committee and subcommittee staff. Some subcommittees were simply eliminated. These changes centralized more power in the committee chairs.

At the same time, both committee and subcommittee chairs were limited to three consecutive two-year terms as chair (Senate Republicans also adopted this rule), and committee chairs lost the power to cast proxy votes for those committee members not in attendance. The Speaker also put the committees on short leashes, giving them instructions regarding the legislation they were to report and a timetable for reporting it. In a few instances, the leadership bypassed committees by setting up separate task forces to prepare legislation.

By 1997, however, the leadership backed off. Weakened by his low ratings in the polls, Speaker Newt Gingrich gave committee chairs greater leeway to set their committee's agenda and promised to allow legislation to be first fashioned by committees. The fact remains, however, that committee chairs are not as powerful as they were before the reform era, and the party leadership in the House has much more control over legislation.

Caucuses: The Informal Organization of Congress

Although the formal organization of Congress consists of its party leadership and its committee structures, the informal organization of the House and Senate is also important. The informal networks of trust and mutual interest can spring from numerous sources. Friendship, ideology, and geography are long-standing sources of informal organization.

Lately, these traditional informal groupings have been dominated by a growing number of caucuses. In this context, a **caucus** is a group of members of Congress who share some interest or characteristic. In the 109th Congress, there are about 300 of these caucuses, most of them containing members from both parties, and some containing members from both the House and the Senate. The goal of all caucuses is to promote the interests around which they are formed. Within Congress they press for committees to hold hearings, they push particular legislation, and they pull together votes on bills they favor. They are somewhat like interest groups, but with a difference: Their members are members of Congress, not petitioners to Congress on the outside looking in. Thus caucuses—interest groups within Congress—are nicely situated to pack more punch than interest groups outside Congress.[43]

Some, such as the Black Caucus, the Congresswomen's Caucus, and the Hispanic Caucus, are based on the characteristics of their members. Others, such as the Sunbelt Caucus and the Northeast-Midwest Congressional Coalition, are based on regional

The proliferation of congressional caucuses gives members of Congress an informal yet powerful means of shaping the policy agenda. Composed of legislative insiders who share similar concerns, the caucuses—such as the Black Caucus pictured here—exert a much greater influence on policy-making than most citizen-based interest groups can.

groupings. Still others, such as the Moderate/Conservative Democrats, are ideological groupings. And still others, such as the Steel, Travel and Tourism, Coal, and Mushroom caucuses, are based on some economic interest that is important to a set of constituencies (yes, there really is a Mushroom Caucus; it is composed of members interested in protecting the interests of mushroom growers).

This explosion of informal groups in Congress has made the representation of interests in Congress a more direct process. The caucuses proceed on the assumption that no one is a more effective lobbyist than a senator or representative. The proliferation of informal caucuses has also tended to decentralize power in Congress. In an effort to limit their importance, the new Republican majority in the House prohibited members from using appropriations for their office allowances to fund caucuses.

Congressional Staff

As we discussed earlier, members of Congress are overwhelmed with responsibilities. It is virtually impossible to master the details of the hundreds of bills on which they must make decisions each year or to prepare their own legislation. They need help to meet their obligations, so they turn to their staff.[44]

Personal Staff. Most staff members work in the personal offices of individual members. The average representative has 17 assistants and the average senator has 40. In total, about 11,200 individuals serve on the personal staffs of members of Congress. (Another 400 serve the congressional leaders.) In the summer, about 4,000 interns also work in members' offices on Capitol Hill (see "Young People and Politics: Are Opportunities To Intern Biased in Favor of the Wealthy?").

Most of these staffers spend their time providing services to constituents, the casework we discussed earlier regarding congressional elections. They answer mail, communicate the member's views to voters, and help constituents solve problems. Nearly one-half of these House staffers and nearly one-third of the Senate personal staff work in members' offices in their constituencies, not in Washington. This makes it easier for people to make contact with the staff. Other personal staff help members of Congress with legislative functions, including drafting legislation, meeting with lobbyists and administrators, negotiating agreements on behalf of their

Young People and Politics

Are Opportunities to Intern Biased in Favor of the Wealthy?

Many college students spend their summers working to pay for their studies during the rest of the year. Others, in contrast, serve as interns. Many of the interns have parents who support them financially during the summer. According to some experts, the focus on internships as a tool for professional success has never been greater, and about 80 percent of graduating college seniors have done a paid or unpaid internship. To some, an internship is an essential stepping stone to career success.

Because Washington internships are in high demand, in most cases they do not pay or pay very little. The White House does not pay the interns who work there during the summer; in most cases the Supreme Court does not pay its undergraduate interns; and a vast majority of congressional offices do not pay the 4,000 summer interns who work on Capitol Hill, though a few, mostly on the Senate side, provide a limited stipend. To make matters worse, Washington is an expensive place to live, widening the gap between the haves and have-nots in the opportunities to gain experience as an intern. In some cases, universities or other programs provide some financial help, but most interns are left on their own.

As internships rise in importance as critical milestones along the path to success, some people question whether they are creating a class system that discriminates against students from less affluent families who must turn down unpaid internships to earn money for college expenses. To the extent that Washington internships serve as a pipeline for people to become policymakers in the nation's capital, critics fear that over time internships, like the rising costs of college tuition, will squeeze voices from the working class and even the middle class out of high-level policy debates.

Source: Jennifer Lee, "Crucial Unpaid Internships Increasingly Separate the Haves from the Have-Nots," the *New York Times,* August 10, 2004.

Questions for Discussion
- Is the internship system in Washington likely to bias policymaking in the future?
- Should Congress appropriate funds so internships are more available to students from less wealthy backgrounds?

bosses, writing questions to ask witnesses at committee hearings, summarizing bills, and briefing legislators. Senators, who must cover a wider range of committee assignments than members of the House, are especially dependent on staff. Indeed, members of both houses are now more likely to deal with each other through staff intermediaries than through personal interactions.

Committee Staff.   The committees of the House and Senate employ another 2,100 staff members. These staff members organize hearings, research legislative options, draft committee reports on bills, write legislation, and, as we have seen, keep tabs on the activities of the executive branch. Committee staff members often possess high levels of expertise and can become very influential in policymaking (see "Making a Difference: Tony Battista"). As a result, lobbyists spend a lot of time cultivating these staffers both to obtain information about likely legislative actions and to plant ideas for legislation.

Staff Agencies.   Finally, Congress has three important staff agencies that aid it in its work. The first is the *Congressional Research Service (CRS),* administered by the Library of Congress. The CRS employs nearly 750 researchers, many with advanced degrees and highly developed expertise. Each year it responds to more than 250,000

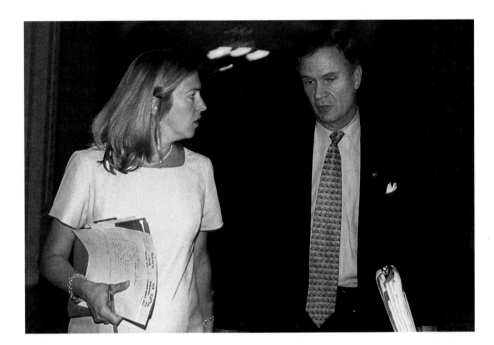

Members of Congress depend heavily on their staffs for everything from information and advice to scheduling and negotiating with other members of Congress. Here former Senator John Breaux of Louisiana consults with a member of his staff.

congressional requests for information and provides members with nonpartisan studies. CRS also tracks the progress of major bills, prepares summaries of bills, and makes this information available electronically.

The *Government Accountability Office (GAO)*, with more than 3,200 employees, helps Congress perform its oversight functions by reviewing the activities of the executive branch to see if it is following the congressional intent of laws and by investigating the efficiency and effectiveness of policy implementation. The GAO also sets government standards for accounting, provides legal opinions, and settles claims against the government.

The *Congressional Budget Office (CBO)* (discussed in more detail in Chapter 14) employs about 230 people. Its principal focus is on analyzing the president's budget and making economic projections about the performance of the economy, the costs of proposed policies, and the economic effects of taxing and spending alternatives.

Committees, caucuses, and individual legislators follow bills from their introduction to their approval. The next sections will discuss this process, which is often termed "labyrinthine" to reflect the fact that getting a bill through Congress is very much like navigating a difficult, intricate maze.

Making a Difference

Tony Battista

Tony Battista was a legendary staffer for the House Armed Services Committee. A weapons expert and a tireless foe of duplication and inefficiency, Battista grilled generals mercilessly and often succeeded against highly paid lobbyists for defense contractors. Technical expertise, intelligence, thorough homework, fearlessness, and tenacity were at the core of his success. Members from both sides of the aisle trusted him to provide a bipartisan assessment of weapons systems. In the process, he saved taxpayers millions of dollars in defense expenditures.

The Congressional Process

Congress' agenda is, of course, a crowded one—about 11,000 bills are introduced in each Congress. A **bill** is a proposed law, drafted in precise, legal language. Anyone—even you or I—can draft a bill. The White House and interest groups are common sources of polished bills. However, only members of the House or the Senate can formally submit a bill for consideration. The traditional route for a bill as it works its way through the legislative labyrinth is depicted in Figure 12.2. Most bills are quietly killed off early in the process. Some are introduced mostly as a favor to a group or a

bill

A proposed law, drafted in precise, legal language. Anyone can draft a bill, but only a member of the House of Representatives or the Senate can formally submit a bill for consideration.

constituent; others are private bills, granting citizenship to a constituent or paying a settlement to a person whose car was demolished by a postal service truck. Still other bills may alter the course of the nation.

Congress is typically a reactive and cumbersome decision-making body. Rules are piled upon rules, and procedures upon procedures.[45] Moreover, reforms in the 1970s decentralized the internal distribution of power in Congress, making legislating more difficult. The polarized political climate of the 1980s also exacerbated the problems of legislating. Party leaders sought ways to cope with these problems, and what Barbara Sinclair has termed *unorthodox lawmaking* has become common in the congressional process, especially for the most significant legislation.[46]

You Are a Member
of Congress

In both chambers party leaders involve themselves in the legislative process on major legislation earlier and more deeply, using special procedures to aid the passage of legislation. Bills are often referred to several committees at the same time, bringing more interests to bear on an issue but complicating the process of passing legislation. Since committee leaders cannot always negotiate compromises *among* committees, party leaders have accepted this responsibility, often negotiating compromises and making adjustments to bills after a committee or committees report legislation. On the other hand, committees may be bypassed altogether when party leaders form special task forces for high-priority legislation.

In the House, special rules from the Rules Committee have become powerful tools for controlling floor consideration of bills and sometimes for shaping the outcomes of votes. Often party leaders from each chamber negotiate among themselves instead of creating conference committees. Sometimes, special "summits" between the legislative and executive branches are employed to obtain agreement on the passage of legislation. Party leaders also use *omnibus* legislation that addresses numerous and perhaps unrelated subjects, issues, and programs to create winning coalitions.

These new procedures are generally under the control of party leaders in the House, but in the Senate, leaders have less leverage and *individual* senators have retained great opportunities for influence (such as using the filibuster). As a result, it is often more difficult to pass legislation in the Senate.

There are, of course, countless influences on this legislative process. Presidents, parties, constituents, interest groups, the congressional and committee leadership structure—these and other influences offer members cues for their decision making.

Presidents and Congress: Partners and Protagonists

Political scientists sometimes call the president the *chief legislator*, a phrase that might have appalled the Constitution writers, with their insistence on separation of powers. Presidents do, however, help create the congressional agenda. They are also their own best lobbyists.

Presidents have their own legislative agenda, based in part on their party's platform and their electoral coalition. Their task is to persuade Congress that their agenda should also be Congress' agenda. Lyndon Johnson once claimed (with perhaps a touch of overstatement), "If an issue is not included on the presidential agenda, it is almost impossible—short of crisis—to get the Congress to focus on it."[47]

Presidents have many resources with which to influence Congress. (The next chapter will examine presidential leadership.) They may try to influence members directly—calling up wavering members and telling them that the country's future hinges on their votes, for example—but they do not do this often. If presidents were to pick just one key bill and spend 10 minutes on the telephone with each of the 535 members of Congress, they would spend 89 hours chatting with them. Instead, presidents wisely leave most White House lobbying to the congressional liaison office and work mainly through regular meetings with the party's leaders in the House and Senate.

Figure 12.2   How a Bill Becomes a Law

Many bills travel full circle, coming first from the White House as part of the presidential agenda, then returning to the president at the end of the process. In the interim, there are two parallel processes in the Senate and House, starting with committee action. If a committee gives a bill a favorable report, the whole chamber considers it. When it is passed in different versions by the two chambers, a conference committee drafts a single compromise bill.

CONGRESS

Bill introduction

HOUSE	SENATE
Bill introduction	**Bill introduction**
Bill is introduced by a member and assigned to a committee, which usually refers it to a subcommittee.	Bill is introduced by a member and assigned to a committee, which usually refers it to a subcommittee.

Committee action

Subcommittee	**Subcommittee**
Subcommittee performs studies, holds hearings, and makes revisions. If approved, the bill goes to the full committee.	Subcommittee performs studies, holds hearings, and makes revisions. If approved, the bill goes to the full committee.
Committee	**Committee**
Full committee may amend or rewrite the bill, before deciding whether to send it to the House floor, to recommend its approval, or to kill it. If approved, the bill is reported to the full House and placed on the calendar.	Full committee may amend or rewrite the bill, before deciding whether to send it to the Senate floor, to recommend its approval, or to kill it. If approved, the bill is reported to the full Senate and placed on the calendar.
Rules Committee	**Leadership**
Rules Committee issues a rule governing debate on the House floor and sends the bill to the full House.	Senate leaders of both parties schedule Senate debate on the bill.

Floor action

Full House	**Full Senate**
Bill is debated by full House, amendments are offered, and a vote is taken. If the bill passes in a different version from that passed in the Senate, it is sent to a conference committee.	Bill is debated by full Senate, amendments are offered, and a vote is taken. If the bill passes in a different version from that passed in the House, it is sent to a conference committee.

Conference action

Conference Committee
Conference committee composed of members of both House and Senate meet to iron out differences between the bills. The compromise bill is returned to both the House and Senate for a vote.

Full House	**Full Senate**
Full House votes on conference committee version. If it passes, the bill is sent to the president.	Full Senate votes on conference committee version. If it passes, the bill is sent to the president.

Presidential decision

President signs or vetoes the bill. Congress may override a veto by a two-thirds vote in both the House and Senate.

Law

It seems a wonder that presidents, even with all their power and prestige, can push and wheedle anything through the labyrinthine congressional process. The president must usually win at least ten times to hope for final passage:

1. in one House subcommittee
2. in the full House committee
3. in the House Rules Committee to move to the floor
4. on the House floor
5. in one Senate subcommittee
6. in the full Senate committee
7. on the Senate floor
8. in the House-Senate conference committee to work out the differences between the two bills
9. back to the House floor for final passage
10. back to the Senate floor for final passage

As one scholar put it, presidential leadership of Congress is *at the margins.*[48] In general, successful presidential leadership of Congress has not been the result of the dominant chief executive of political folklore who reshapes the contours of the political landscape to pave the way for change. Rather than creating the conditions for important shifts in public policy, the effective American leader is the less heroic *facilitator* who works at the margins of coalition building to recognize and exploit opportunities presented by a favorable configuration of political forces. Of course, presidents can exercise their veto to *stop* legislation they oppose.

Presidents are only one of many claimants for the attention of Congress, especially on domestic policy. As we will show in the next chapter, popular presidents and presidents with a large majority of their party in each house of Congress have a good chance of getting their way. Yet, presidents often lose. Ronald Reagan was considered a strong chief executive, and budgeting was one of his principal tools for affecting public policy. Yet the budgets he proposed to Congress were typically pronounced DOA, dead on arrival. Members of Congress truly compose an independent branch.

Party, Constituency, and Ideology

Presidents come and go; the parties linger on. Presidents do not determine a congressional member's electoral fortunes; constituents do. Where presidents are less influential, on domestic policies especially, party, personal ideology, and constituency are more important.

Party Influence.   On some issues, members of the parties stick together like a marching band. They are most cohesive when Congress is electing its official leaders. A vote for Speaker of the House is a straight party-line vote, with every Democrat on one side and every Republican on the other. On other issues, however, the party coalition may come unglued. In the past, votes on civil rights policies, for example, revealed deep divisions within each party.

Differences between the parties are sharpest on questions of social welfare and economic policy.[49] When voting on labor issues, Democrats traditionally cling together, leaning toward the side of the unions, whereas Republicans almost always vote with business. On social welfare issues—poverty, unemployment aid, help to the cities— Democrats are more generous than Republicans are. This split between the parties should not be too surprising if you recall the party coalitions described in Chapter 8. Once in office, party members favor their electoral coalitions. Because the constituencies of House members are now more solidly Republican or Democrat, the differences between party members in the House have increased (see "Issues of the Times: Polarized Politics in Congress").

Party leaders in Congress help "whip" their members into line. Their power to do so is limited, of course. They cannot drum a recalcitrant member out of the party. Leaders have plenty of influence, however, including making committee assignments, boosting a member's pet projects, and the subtle but significant influence of providing critical information to a member.

The congressional parties can also impact who sits in Congress. The congressional campaign committees have energized both parties, helping to recruit candidates, running seminars in campaign skills, and conducting polls. They are also a source of funding, as are PACs headed by members of the party leadership.

Constituency Versus Ideology. Members of Congress are representatives; their constituents expect them to represent their interests in Washington. In 1714, Anthony Henry, a member of the British Parliament, received a letter from some of his constituents asking him to vote against an excise tax. He is reputed to have replied in part:

> Gentlemen: I have received your letter about the excise, and I am surprised at your insolence in writing to me at all...may God's curse light upon you all, and may it make your homes as open and as free to the excise officers as your wives and daughters have always been to me while I have represented your rascally constituency.[50]

Needless to say, notions of representation have changed since Henry's time.

Sometimes representation requires a balancing act. If some representatives favor more defense spending but suspect that their constituents do not, what are they to do? The English politician and philosopher Edmund Burke favored the concept of legislators as *trustees*, using their best judgment to make policy in the interests of the people. Others prefer the concept of representatives as *instructed delegates*, mirroring the preferences of their constituents. Actually, members of Congress are *politicos*, adopting both trustee and instructed delegate roles as they strive to be both representatives and policymakers.[51]

The best way constituents can influence congressional voting is also simple: Elect a representative or senator who agrees with their views. John Sullivan and Robert O'Connor discovered that congressional candidates tend to take policy positions different from their opponent's. Moreover, the winners generally vote on roll calls as they said they would during their campaigns.[52] If voters use their good sense to elect candidates who share their policy positions, then constituents *can* influence congressional policy.

Simulation

You Are an Informed Voter

If voters miss their chance and elect someone out of step with their thinking, it may be difficult to influence that person's votes. It is difficult even for well-intentioned legislators to know what people want. Some legislators pay careful attention to their mail, but the mail is a notoriously unreliable indicator of people's thinking; individuals with extreme opinions on an issue are more likely to write than those with moderate views. Some members send questionnaires to constituents, but the answers they receive are unreliable because few people respond. Some try public opinion polling, but it is expensive if professionally done and unreliable if not.

Defeating an incumbent is no easy task. Even legislators whose votes conflict with the views of their constituents tend to be reelected. Most citizens have trouble recalling the names of their congressional representatives (one study found that only 28 percent of the public could name their representatives in the House),[53] let alone keeping up with their representatives' voting records. According to one expert, "Probably less than a third of all constituents can recognize who their representatives are and what policy positions they have generally taken—and even that third tends not to evaluate incumbents on the basis of policy."[54] A National Election Study found that only 11 percent of the people even claimed to remember how their congressperson voted on a particular issue.

On some controversial issues, however, legislators ignore constituent opinion at great peril. For years, Southern members of Congress would not have dared to vote for a civil rights law. Lately, representatives and senators have been concerned about the many new single-issue groups. Such groups care little about a member's overall record;

Issues of the Times

The Issue: Polarized Politics in Congress

One of the most interesting and important developments in Congress over the past generation has been the increased homogeneity of the two parties, especially in the House of Representatives, and their increased polarization. By this we mean that differences among the elected representatives *within* party have diminished while differences between the average members of each party have increased.

Thus, although most people in the United States are in the center of the political spectrum, the people's elected representatives are not. The polarization of Congress has made passing legislation more challenging because the further apart the parties, the more difficult it is to reach a compromise. In addition, most members of the House represent safe seats, so it is difficult to dislodge them in order to change public policies.

Read All About It

In the House at Least, Moderation Is No Virtue

BY ROBIN TONER
November 17, 2002

It seemed, to many Republicans, too good to be true: Representative Nancy Pelosi, an archetypal San Francisco Democrat, assumed the leadership of the House Democrats last week. Republicans cheerfully revived all the old stereotypes of the loony left—the latte-drinking, culturally alien, soft-on-national-defense limousine liberals.

In all the chortling, a few political realities got lost. Yes, Ms. Pelosi is a liberal's liberal, with a rating from Americans for Democratic Action of 100 percent and a district that gave just 15 percent of its presidential vote to George W. Bush. But she is no more of a liberal than Representative Tom DeLay, the new majority leader of the Republicans, is a conservative, with his zero ratings from the A.D.A. and the League of Conservation Voters. The two representatives represent the heart of

their parties' caucuses in the House with far more ideological purity than either party would like to admit.

"It's perfectly symmetrical," said Charles Cook, an independent expert on Congressional elections. "I don't know that San Francisco is any further from the ideological 50-yard line than Sugar Land, Tex., is," he added, referring to the hometown of Mr. DeLay.

Please see House   Page 381

House

Continued from Page 380

In fact, the ascension of Ms. Pelosi and Mr. DeLay reflects a long-running trend in Congress, particularly in the House. While presidential candidates race to the center, Congressional candidates often head the other way.

Congressional Republicans have grown more consistently conservative, and Congressional Democrats more consistently liberal, over the past 30 years, scholars said. Not surprisingly, their leaders come from that base, said Ross K. Baker, an expert on Congress at Rutgers University. "She's drawn fire for being some outlier, but she's not," he added of Ms. Pelosi.

The ideological polarization on Capitol Hill was most apparent in 1994, when Newt Gingrich took control of the House and claimed a mandate for revolutionary change. His party lost seats in the next two elections, in part because Democrats were able to campaign against him as a conservative extremist.

Since then, leaders of both parties have grown far more savvy about the image they project. Republican leaders were carefully pledging to reach across the aisle and build bipartisan coalitions last week, while Ms. Pelosi was arguing, with a centrist's smile, "It's not about left and right." As she noted at one point, "I'm a liberal Democrat, but I'm a conservative Catholic—put that into the mix."

But the fact remains that the Congressional wings of both parties have grown further apart, particularly as the South has realigned to the Republicans over the last three decades, thinning the ranks of conservative Southern Democrats on Capitol Hill. Party unity scores, a measure of how often members vote

---

In fact, the ascension of Ms. Pelosi and Mr. DeLay reflects a long-running trend in Congress, particularly in the House. While presidential candidates race to the center, Congressional candidates often head the other way.

---

with the majority of their party, were substantially higher in recent years than they were 30 years ago, according to an analysis by Congressional Quarterly. The philosophical divisions between the two parties are acutely apparent when the debate turns to issues like the role of government and health care.

The reasons for the great divide in the House are partly structural. While presidential candidates are forced to focus on swing voters in big states, House members are often elected from politically safe districts where their chief concern may be a challenge in the primary—not the general election. . . .

But the ultimate counterweight to the Congressional parties may be the president or, in the case of the Democrats, the nominee. . . . In a similar situation in 1996, President Clinton famously "triangulated," and found a third way by maneuvering between two polarized parties.

As for the Democrats, even those who praised Ms. Pelosi said her days as the main voice and image of the party will be numbered. "Nancy Pelosi is going to be like most other minority leaders in the end," said Peter Hart, a Democratic pollster. "They can help shape and direct the message of the party, but they are not the message of the party—that will be created by the nominee."

Al From, the leader of the Democratic Leadership Council, which is devoted to pushing the party to the center, argued that the party's presidential candidate is who really matters. "Bob Michel didn't define the Republican Party," alluding to the Republican House leader in the early 1980s. "Ronald Reagan did. Gephardt and Foley didn't define the Democratic Party in 1992. Bill Clinton did."

Think About It

- Would you rather see the congressional parties reflect clear ideological differences or be composed of pragmatists who are willing to bargain to pass legislation?
- Do you prefer districts to be safe for members of the House, or would you prefer to redraw district lines to make seats more competitive?

- How do you feel about congressional parties projecting images more moderate than they actually are?
- Is the president able to counter the ideological polarization of the congressional parties to forge compromises?

to them, a vote on one issue—gun control, abortion, the ERA—is all that counts. Ready to pounce on one wrong vote and pour money into an opponent's campaign, these new forces in constituency politics make every legislator nervous. When issues are visible and salient to voters and easy for them to understand, their representatives are likely to be quite responsive to constituency opinion.[55]

Nevertheless, many issues are complex, obscure, and not salient to voters. On such issues legislators can safely ignore constituency opinion. On a typical issue, the prime determinant of a congressional member's vote is personal ideology. On issues where ideological divisions are sharp and constituency preferences and knowledge are likely to be weak, such as defense and foreign policy, ideology is virtually the only determinant of voting.[56] As ideological divisions weaken and constituency preferences strengthen, members are more likely to deviate from their own position and adopt those of their constituencies.[57] Thus, when they have differences of opinion with their constituencies, members of Congress consider constituency preferences but are not controlled by them.[58]

Lobbyists and Interest Groups

The nation's capital is crawling with lawyers, lobbyists, registered foreign agents, public relations consultants, and others—more than 14,000 individuals representing nearly 12,000 organizations at last count—all seeking to influence Congress.[59] Several dozen groups are concerned with the single issue of protecting Alaska's environment; the bigger the issue, the more lobbyists are involved in it. Any group interested in influencing national policymaking—and that includes almost everyone—either hires Washington lobbyists or sends its own. Washington lobbyists can be a formidable group.

Lobbyists spend nearly $2 billion on lobbying Congress—plus millions more in campaign contributions and attempts to try to persuade members' constituents to send messages to Washington.[60] Such spending gives lobbyists a bad name, no doubt often deserved. But lobbyists have a job to do—namely, to represent the interests of their organizations. Lobbyists, some of them former members of Congress, can provide legislators with crucial information and often with assurances of financial aid in the next campaign. They often coordinate their efforts at influencing members with party leaders who share their views. Grass-roots lobbying—such as computerized mailings to encourage citizens to pressure their representatives on an issue—is a common activity. Interest groups also distribute scorecards of how members of Congress voted on issues important to the groups, threatening members with electoral retaliation if they do not support the groups' stands.

The easiest way to frustrate lobbyists is to ignore them. Lobbyists usually make little headway with their opponents anyway: The lobbyist for General Motors arguing against automobile pollution controls would not have much influence with a legislator concerned about air pollution. Members of Congress can also make life uncomfortable for lobbyists. They can embarrass them, expose heavy-handed tactics, and spread the word among an organization's members that it is being poorly represented in Washington.

Congress can also regulate lobbyists. In 1995, it passed a law requiring anyone hired to lobby members of Congress, congressional staff members, White House officials, and federal agencies to report what issues they were seeking to influence, how much they were spending on the effort, and the identities of their clients. This law was designed to close loopholes in a 1946 law that allowed most lobbyists to avoid registering and had permitted those who did to disclose only limited information about their activities. Congress also placed severe restrictions on the gifts, meals, and expense-paid travel that public officials may accept from lobbyists. In theory, these reporting

Lobbyists have never been held in high esteem by the public, and they have come under especially harsh criticism in recent years. Nevertheless, lobbyists play an important role in the legislative process.

requirements and restrictions not only prevent shady deals between lobbyists and members of Congress but also curb the influence of special interests.

There are many forces that affect senators and representatives as they decide how to vote on a bill. After his exhaustive study of influences on congressional decision-making, John Kingdon concluded that none was important enough to suggest that congresspeople vote as they do because of one influence.[61] The process is as complex for individual legislators as it is for those who want to influence their votes.

Understanding Congress

Congress is a complex institution. Its members want to make sound national policy, but they also want to return to Washington after the next election. How do these sometimes conflicting desires affect American democracy and the scope of American government?

Congress and Democracy

In a large nation, the success of democratic government depends on the quality of representation. Americans could hardly hold a national referendum on every policy issue on the government agenda; instead, they delegate decision-making power to representatives. If Congress is a successful democratic institution, it must be a successful representative institution.

Certainly, some aspects of Congress make it very *un*representative. Its members are an American elite (see "America in Perspective: The Russian Duma: A Reformer's Paradise"). Its leadership is chosen by its own members, not by any vote of the American people. Voters have little direct influence over the individuals who chair key committees or lead congressional parties. Voters in just a single constituency control the fate of committee chairs and party leaders. Voters in the other 434 House districts and the other 49 states have no real say, for example, about who chairs a committee

How You Can Make a Difference

Gun Control

Besides abortion, perhaps no other issue under consideration by Congress evokes more emotion and public attention than gun control. On both sides of this issue, advocate organizations constantly press members of Congress to either pass or defeat legislation favorable to their position. Like abortion, the gun control debate involves not only matters of life and death but also constitutional concerns and interpretations. This issue remains contentious not only because of strong emotions of those involved but also because of convincing arguments and impressive organizations on both sides of the debate.

Organizations in favor of gun control tend to emphasize grass-roots organization and local visibility. Although most gun control organizations agree upon the key issues, a smorgasbord of organizations allow individuals favorable to gun control legislation to find a group with agreeable tactics and positions. The Educational Fund to End Handgun Violence (*www.endhandgunviolence.org*) provides a good entry point to antigun organizations on the Internet including the Children's Defense Fund, Coalition To Stop Gun Violence, Handgun Control, Inc., Mothers Against Violence in America, and many others.

Opponents of gun control rally to the NRA (*www.nra.org*). With a single dominant organization, gun supporters can mount a more organized, better funded, more centralized campaign. This advantage is clear in the NRA's influence on Capitol Hill on issues of gun control. On the downside, a single organization makes it easier for opponents to target the entire issue by identifying it with one organization. Another drawback of such a strong, nearly monolithic organization is that it cannot easily accommodate diverse opinions about the issue.

If you examine the websites of these organizations, you'll find that nearly all ask for money to support their causes. Being a college student and most likely short on cash, you would likely make a far greater impact by writing your congressional representatives a personal, handwritten letter. Even better, you could organize a letter-writing campaign on campus in your dorm or fraternity/sorority, at church, or in your neighborhood. Be sure to insist on handwritten letters because they convey a personal interest that massproduced form letters, e-mails, and petitions cannot hope to duplicate. Tell your fellow letter writers to be short,

include a name, address, and phone number, and if possible, to incorporate a memorable personal story. You can also make a personal phone call to your legislators by dialing the congressional switchboard at 202-224-3121. Though you'll only get to talk to a legislative aide, these assistants are influential in bringing information and legislation to the attention of their bosses. Involvement in high profile marches, protests, and rallies also can influence how members of Congress, especially in swing districts, eventually vote on gun control issues.

These inexpensive, low-tech approaches are effective precisely because they demonstrate to members of Congress a high level of concern among their constituents.

What else you can do:
- Become better educated about the arguments on both sides of the gun control debate by visiting the websites for the Educational Fund to End Handgun Violence and the NRA. You'll be a much stronger advocate for either side if you are well-versed on the various issues involved in the debate.

Gun Rights and Gun Control

considering new forms of energy, a committee considering defense buildups, or a committee making economic policy.

Nevertheless, the evidence in this chapter demonstrates that Congress *does* try to listen to the American people. Whom voters elect makes a difference in how congressional votes turn out; which party is in power affects policies. Linkage institutions actually link voters to policymakers. Perhaps Congress could do a better job at representation than it does, but there are many obstacles to improved representation. Legislators find it hard to know what constituents want. Groups may keep important issues off the legislative agenda. Members may spend so much time servicing their constituencies that they have little time left to represent those constituencies in the policymaking process.

Members of Congress are responsive to the people, if the people make clear what they want. For example, in response to popular demands, Congress established a program in 1988 to shield the elderly against the catastrophic costs associated with acute

America in Perspective

The Russian Duma: A Reformer's Paradise

The next time you grow exasperated at Congress, just remember the Russian Duma, the 450-member lower house of Parliament. In the anything-goes world of the Duma, there are no rules of sexual conduct, no sensitivities about political correctness, and no ethics investigations. Sergie Semyonov was recently the deputy chair of the committee on women, families, and youth. His expertise in the area seems to be a result of living with three women. He proposed a bill to legalize polygamy, arguing that he had "the money and energy to keep all my women fully satisfied."

But Mr. Semyonov appears positively chivalrous compared to the ultranationalist Vladimir V. Zhirinovsky.

Mr. Zhirinovsky got into a fistfight on the floor of the Duma and punched another deputy—a woman—in the face. He later claimed he was fending off her sexual advances!

Parliamentary immunity attracts candidates who face criminal charges and want to escape prosecution by becoming legislators. They should feel right at home. There are no financial scandals in the Duma because no one even tries to hide their conflicts of interest. Graft and corruption are blatant, and there is no way to trace illicit money, no oversight committees, no paper trail for prosecutors to follow, and no watchdog press to hold lawmakers accountable.

Such ethical improprieties seem to have replaced the work ethic as a norm of behavior. Often the deputies simply do not show up at all, even for key votes. In several instances, all the leaders were absent, leaving Communist Party leader Anatoly Lukyanov, who supported the 1991 coup against Mikhail Gorbachev, in charge. There is one saving grace for the Russian people, however. The newest Russian constitution has stripped the Duma of most of its power.

Source: Alesandra Stanley, "Russia's Gross National Legislature," in the *New York Times*, January 19, 1997, D3.

illness. In 1989, in response to complaints from the elderly about higher Medicare premiums, Congress abolished most of what it had created the previous year.

Representativeness Versus Effectiveness.   The central legislative dilemma for Congress is combining the faithful representation of constituents with making effective public policy. Supporters see Congress as a forum in which many interests compete for a spot on the policy agenda and over the form of a particular policy—which is just as the Founders intended it to be.

Critics charge that Congress is responsive to so many interests that policy is as uncoordinated, fragmented, and decentralized as Congress itself. Interest groups grow on committees and subcommittees like barnacles on a boat. After a while, these groups develop intimacy and influence with "their" committee. Committee decisions usually carry over to the roll-call vote. Thus the committee system links congressional policymaking to a multiplicity of interests, rather than to a majority's preferences.

In addition, some observers believe Congress is too representative—so much so that it is incapable of taking decisive action to deal with difficult problems. The agricultural committees busily tend to the interests of tobacco farmers, while committees on health and welfare spend millions for lung cancer research. One committee wrestles with domestic unemployment while another makes tax policy that encourages businesses to open new plants out of the country. One reason why government spends too much, critics say, is that Congress is protecting the interests of too many people. As long as each interest tries to preserve the status quo, bold reforms cannot be enacted.

On the other hand, defenders of Congress point out that, thanks to its being decentralized, there is no oligarchy in control to prevent the legislature from taking comprehensive action. In fact, Congress has enacted the huge tax cuts of 1981 and 2001, the comprehensive (and complicated) tax reform of 1986, and various bills structuring the budgetary process designed to balance the budget.[62]

Comparing Legislatures

Cable television's live coverage of Congress has further democratized the legislative process by letting Americans see their representatives at work. Here, the U.S. House of Representatives is shown discussing security at U.S. embassies.

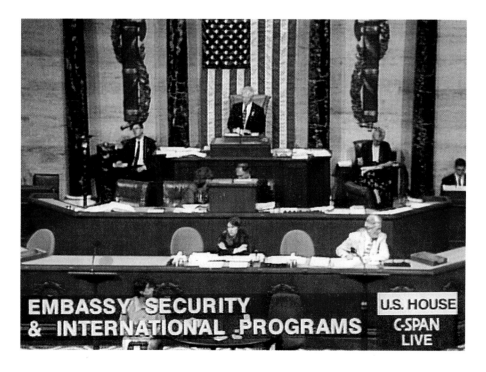

There is no simple solution to Congress' dilemma. It tries to be both a representative and an objective policymaking institution. As long as this is true, it is unlikely that Congress will please all its critics.

Congress and the Scope of Government

If Congress is responsive to a multitude of interests and those interests desire government policies to aid them in some way, does the nature of Congress predispose it to continually increasing the scope of the public sector? Do the benefits of servicing constituents provide an incentive for members of Congress to tolerate, even to expand, an already big government? The more policies there are, the more potential ways members can help their constituencies. The more bureaucracies there are, the more red tape members can help cut. Big government helps members of Congress get reelected and even gives them good reason to support making it bigger.

Members of Congress vigorously protect the interests of their constituents. At the same time, there are many members who agree with Ronald Reagan that government is not the answer to problems but rather *is* the problem. These individuals make careers out of fighting against government programs (although these same senators and representatives typically support programs aimed at aiding *their* constituents).

Americans have contradictory preferences regarding public policy. As we have noted in previous chapters, they want to balance the budget and pay low taxes, but they also support most government programs. Congress does not impose programs on a reluctant public; instead, it responds to the public's demands for them.

Summary

According to the Constitution, members of Congress are the government's policymakers, but legislative policymaker is only one of the roles of members of Congress. They are also politicians, and politicians always keep one eye on the next election. Success in congressional elections may be determined as much by constituency service—casework and the pork barrel—as by policymaking. Senators and representatives have become so skilled at constituency service that incumbents have a big edge over challengers, making it more difficult to bring about major changes in the makeup, and thus the policies, of Congress.

The structure of Congress is so complex that it seems remarkable that legislation gets passed at all. Its bicameral division means that bills have two sets of committee hurdles to clear. Because power is often decentralized, especially in the Senate, the job of leading Congress is more difficult than ever.

Presidents try hard to influence Congress, and parties and elections can also shape legislators' choices. The impact of these factors clearly differs from one policy area to another. Party impacts are clearest on issues for which the party's coalitions are clearest, especially social welfare and economic issues. Constituencies influence policy mostly by the initial choice of a representative. Members of Congress do pay attention to voters, particularly on visible issues, but most issues do not interest voters. On these less visible issues other factors, such as lobbyists and members' individual ideologies, influence policy decisions.

Congress clearly has some undemocratic and unrepresentative features. Its members are hardly average Americans. Even so, members pay attention to popular preferences, when they can figure out what they are. People inside and outside the institution, however, think that Congress is ineffective. Its objective policymaking decisions and representative functions sometimes conflict, yet from time to time Congress does show that it can deal with major issues in a comprehensive fashion. Many members of Congress have incentives to increase the scope of the federal government, but the people who put those representatives in office provide these incentives.

KEY TERMS

incumbents	majority leader	legislative oversight
casework	whips	committee chairs
pork barrel	minority leader	seniority system
bicameral legislature	standing committees	caucus
House Rules Committee	joint committees	bill
filibuster	conference committees	
Speaker of the House	select committees	

INTERNET RESOURCES

www.house.gov/
The official House website contains information on the organization, operations, schedule, and activities of the House and its committees. The site also contains links to the offices of members and committees and enables you to contact your representative directly.

www.senate.gov/
The official Senate website contains information and links similar to those for the House.

Thomas.loc.gov/
Information on the activities of Congress, the status and text of legislation, the *Congressional Record*, committee reports, and historical documents.

www.rollcall.com/
Roll Call, the online version of the Capitol Hill newspaper.

www.fec.gov/
Federal Election Commission data on campaign expenditures.

www.opensecrets.org
The Center for Responsive Politics website with data on the role of money in politics.

www.c-span.org
Video coverage of Congress in action.

GET CONNECTED

The Organization of Congress

Both the Senate and the House are organized into committees, where much of the real work on the Congress takes place. As the text notes, senators and representatives seek membership on committees that have something to do with their home state or district. They seek membership on the right committees because good work on the right committees will help them get reelected, make good policy, and gain influence in Congress. See whether you can pick the committees on which your local representative serves.

First, make a list of the important characteristics of your district, such as whether it is urban or rural, whether it has a lot of farming or industry, whether it has a large international airport or sits next to the ocean, or whether there is a lot of military in the district or not. Your list should have five or six items on it. Next, go the House of Representatives and look at the jurisdictional duties of each standing House committee. Based upon your list, pick the committees on which you think your representative might serve. Once you've done that, go to your representative's website to see how accurate you are.

Search the Web

Go to *http://www.house.gov/rules/comm_jurisdiction.htm* to review the jurisdiction of the standing committees. Go to *http://www.house.gov/* to find your representative's website to check the accuracy of your picks.

Questions To Ask

- Does your representative appear to be on the kinds of committees that will allow him or her to best represent your district?
- If you could place your representative on another committee, one that might be more important to the district, which would it be? Why?
- Not all committees are focused on district-level interests. Some deal with broader issues such as foreign affairs, national defense, and tax policy. Is your representative on a committee on which he or she can influence policies critical to the nation?

Why It Matters

One job of congressional representatives is to represent the issues and concerns of their constituents. Because the committees are where most work gets done in Congress, it is important for representatives to be on a committee that will allow them to best represent their districts. Constituents also have broader interests, however, and the committees on which their representatives serve are an opportunity to influence important policies.

Get Involved

Send your representative an e-mail asking why he or she serves on certain committees. Ask why they serve on a committee that does not seem to fit the district and not on a committee that seems important for the district. Ask also whether the representative has any plans to change committee assignments in the future.

To see more Get Connected exercises for Chapter 12, go to www.ablongman.com/edwards.

FOR FURTHER READING

Aberbach, Joel D. *Keeping a Watchful Eye: The Politics of Congressional Oversight.* Washington, D.C.: Brookings Institution, 1990. A thorough study of congressional oversight of the executive branch.

Bernstein, Robert A. *Elections, Representation, and Congressional Voting Behavior.* Englewood Cliffs, NJ: Prentice-Hall, 1989. Examines the issue of constituency control over members of Congress.

Binder, Sarah A. *Stalemate.* Washington, D.C.: Brookings Institution, 2003. Discusses the causes and consequences of legislative gridlock.

Deering, Christopher J., and Steven S. Smith. *Committees in Congress,* 3rd ed. Washington, D.C.: Congressional Quarterly Press, 1997. A thorough overview of the complex committee structure in the House and Senate.

Dodd, Lawrence C., and Bruce I. Oppenheimer. *Congress Reconsidered,* 8th ed. Washington, D.C.: Congressional Quarterly, 2005. Excellent essays covering many aspects of Congress.

Fenno, Richard F., Jr. *Home Style.* Boston: Little, Brown, 1978. How members of Congress mend fences and stay in political touch with the folks back home.

Fiorina, Morris P. *Congress: Keystone of the Washington Establishment,* 2nd ed. New Haven, CT: Yale University Press, 1989. Argues that members of Congress are self-serving in representing their constituents, ensuring their reelection but harming the national interest.

Jacobson, Gary C. *The Politics of Congressional Elections*, 6th ed. New York: Addison-Wesley Longman, 2004. An excellent review of congressional elections.

Kingdon, John W. *Congressmen's Voting Decisions*, 3rd ed. Ann Arbor: University of Michigan Press, 1989. A thorough and insightful study of congressional voting decisions.

Lee, Frances E., and Bruce I. Oppenheimer. *Sizing Up the Senate: The Unequal Consequences of Equal Representation.* Chicago: University of Chicago Press, 1999. How representation in the Senate affects how people are represented, the distribution of government benefits, and the nature of election campaigns.

Mayhew, David R. *Congress: The Electoral Connection* 2nd ed. New Haven, CT: Yale University Press, 2005. An analysis of Congress based on the premise that the principal motivation of congressional behavior is reelection.

Sinclair, Barbara. *Unorthodox Lawmaking*, 2nd ed. Washington, D.C.: Congressional Quarterly Press, 2000. Explains how Congress tries to cope with decentralization and polarization.

The Presidency

Chapter Outline

The Presidents

Presidential Powers

Running the Government: The Chief Executive

Presidential Leadership of Congress: The Politics of Shared Powers

The President and National Security Policy

Power from the People: The Public Presidency

The President and the Press

The New York Times **Issues of the Times**

Understanding the American Presidency

Summary

■ As George W. Bush stood before a joint session of Congress in early 2005, he could reflect on his first term in office. It had certainly been eventful. Elected without even a plurality of the vote and after a protracted battle in the courts, he had to create a new administration under the difficult circumstances of a substantially shortened transition period. Once in office, he had led the successful fight on his highest priority—a major tax cut. Soon, however, his approval ratings dropped and the Senate switched to control by the Democratic opposition. Shortly afterward, terrorists launched a devastating attack on the United States, and the focus of his administration abruptly changed to a war on terrorism. His approval ratings rocketed to the highest on record and his party won majorities in Congress in the midterm elections. Nevertheless, Congress was often resistant to his proposals and members of both Congress and the press raised disturbing questions about the bureaucracy's performance regarding homeland security. Even more frustrating were the difficulties he faced in pacifying and democratizing Iraq.

Powerful, strong, leader of the Free World, commander in chief—these are common images of the

American president. The president epitomizes American government. The only place in the world where television networks assign a permanent camera crew is the White House. The presidency is power—at least according to popular myth.

In this presidency-as-powerhouse myth, presidents are the government's command center. Problems are brought to their desk, they decide on the right courses of action, they issue orders, and an army of aides and bureaucrats carry out their commands.

As George W. Bush and all other presidents soon discover, nothing could be further from the truth. The main reason why presidents have trouble getting things done is that other policymakers with whom they deal have their own agendas, their own interests, and their own sources of power. Presidents operate in an environment filled with checks and balances and competing centers of power. As one presidential aide put it, "Every time you turn around people resist you."[1] Congress is beholden not to the president but to the individual constituencies of its members. Cabinet members often push their departmental interests and their constituencies (the Department of Agriculture has farmers as its constituency, for example). Rarely can presidents rely on unwavering support from their party, the public, or even their own appointees.

As the pivotal leader in American politics, the president is the subject of unending political analysis and speculation. A perennial question focuses on presidential power. World history is replete with examples of leaders who have exceeded the prescribed boundaries of their power. Can the presidency become too powerful and thus pose a threat to democracy? Or is the Madisonian system strong enough to check any such tendencies? On the other hand, is the president *strong enough* to stand up to the diverse interests in the United States? Does the president have enough power to govern on behalf of the majority?

A second fundamental question regarding democratic leaders is the nature of their relationship with the public and its consequences for public policy. The president and vice president are the only officials elected by the entire nation. In their efforts to obtain public support from the broad spectrum of interests in the public, are presidents natural advocates of an expansion of government? Do they promise more than they should in order to please the voters? As they face the frustrations of governing, do presidents seek to centralize authority in the federal government, where they have greater influence, while reducing that of the states? Does the chief executive seek more power through increasing the role of government?

Since not everyone bends easily to even the most persuasive president, the president must be a *leader.* As Richard Neustadt has argued, presidential power is the power to *persuade,* not to command.[2] To accomplish policy goals, the president must get other people—important people—to do things they otherwise would not do. To be effective, the president must have highly developed *political skills* to mobilize influence, manage conflict, negotiate, and fashion compromises. Presidential leadership has varied over the years, depending in large part on the individual who holds our nation's highest office.

The Presidents

The presidency is an institution composed of the roles presidents must play, the powers at their disposal, and the large bureaucracy at their command. It is also a highly personal office. The personality of the individual serving as president makes a difference.

Great Expectations

When a new president takes the oath of office, he faces many daunting tasks. Perhaps the most difficult is living up to the expectations of the American people. Americans expect the chief executive to ensure peace, prosperity, and security.[3] As President Carter remarked, "The President is held to be responsible for the state of the economy and for the inconveniences, or disappointments, or the concerns of the American people."[4] Americans want a good life, and they look to the president to provide it.

Americans are of two minds about the presidency. On the one hand, they want to believe in a powerful president, one who can do good. They look back longingly on the great presidents of the first American century—Washington, Jefferson, Lincoln—and some in the second century as well, especially Franklin D. Roosevelt and John F. Kennedy.

On the other hand, Americans dislike a concentration of power. Although presidential responsibilities have increased substantially in the past few decades, there has been no corresponding increase in presidential authority or administrative resources to meet these new expectations. Americans are basically individualistic and skeptical of authority. According to Samuel Huntington, "The distinctive aspect of the American Creed is its antigovernment character. Opposition to power, and suspicion of government as the most dangerous embodiment of power, are the central themes of American political thought."[5] The American political culture's tenets of limited government, liberty, individualism, equality, and democracy generate a distrust of strong leadership, authority, and the public sector in general.

Because Americans' expectations of the presidency are so high, who serves as president is especially important. Just who are the people who have occupied the Oval Office?

Who They Are

When Warren G. Harding, one of the least illustrious American presidents, was in office, attorney Clarence Darrow remarked, "When I was a boy, I was told that anybody could become president. Now I'm beginning to believe it." The Constitution simply states that the president must be a natural-born citizen at least 35 years old and must have resided in the United States for at least 14 years. In fact, all American presidents have been White, male, and (except for John Kennedy) Protestant. In other ways, however, the recent collection of presidents suggests considerable variety. Since World War II, the White House has been home to a Missouri haberdasher, a war hero, a Boston-Irish politician, a small-town Texas boy who grew up to become the biggest wheeler-dealer in the Senate, a California lawyer described by his enemies as "Tricky Dick" and by his friends as a misunderstood master of national leadership, a former Rose Bowl player who had spent his entire political career in the House of

Representatives, a former governor who had been a Georgia peanut wholesaler, an actor who was also a former governor of California, a CIA chief and ambassador who was the son of a U.S. senator, an ambitious governor from a small state, and a former managing director of a major league baseball team who won his first election only six years before becoming president (see Table 13.1).

So far, no woman or minority group member has served as president. This situation is likely to change, however, as social prejudices diminish and as more women and minorities are elected to positions that serve as stepping stones to the presidency.

All manner of men have occupied the Oval Office. Thomas Jefferson was a scientist and scholar who assembled dinosaur bones when presidential business was slack. Woodrow Wilson, the only political scientist ever to become president, combined a Presbyterian moral fervor and righteousness with a professor's intimidating style of leadership and speech making. His successor, Warren G. Harding, became president because Republican leaders thought he looked like one. Poker was his pastime. Out of his element in the job, Harding is almost everyone's choice as the worst American president. His speech making, said opponent William G. McAdoo, sounded "like an army of pompous phrases marching across the landscape in search of an idea." Harding's friends stole the government blind, prompting his brief assessment of the presidency: "God, what a job!"

How They Got There

No one is born to be the future president of the United States solely because of royal lineage like the future kings or queens of England. Regardless of their background or character, all presidents must come to the job through one of two basic routes.

Elections: The Normal Road to the White House.   Most presidents take a familiar journey to 1600 Pennsylvania Avenue: They run for president through the electoral process, which is described in Chapters 9 and 10. Once in office, presidents are guaranteed a four-year term by the Constitution, but the **Twenty-second Amendment,** passed in 1951, limits them to two terms.

Only 12 of the 42 presidents before George W. Bush have actually served two or more full terms in the White House: Washington, Jefferson, Madison, Monroe,

Twenty-second Amendment

Passed in 1951, the amendment that limits presidents to two terms of office.

'Okay, bring in the new guy . . .'

Table 13.1   Recent Presidents

PRESIDENT	TERM	PARTY	BACKGROUND	SIGNIFICANT EVENTS
Harry S Truman	1945–1953	Democrat	• U.S. senator from Missouri • chosen as FDR's running mate in 1944 • became president when FDR died	• made decision to drop atomic bombs on Japan to end World War II • presided over postwar recovery • laid foundation for Cold War policy • relatively unpopular during term
Dwight D. Eisenhower	1953–1961	Republican	• commander of Allied forces in Europe in World War II • never voted until he ran for president	• presided over relatively tranquil 1950s • conservative domestic policies • cool crisis management • enjoyed strong public approval
John F. Kennedy	1961–1963	Democrat	• U.S. senator from Massachusetts • from very wealthy family • war hero	• known for personal style • presided over Cuban missile crisis • ushered in era of liberal domestic policies • assassinated in 1963
Lyndon B. Johnson	1963–1969	Democrat	• Senate majority leader • chosen as Kennedy's running mate; succeeded him after the assassination	• skilled legislative leader with a coarse public image • launched the Great Society • won passage of major civil rights laws • escalated the Vietnam War • war policies proved unpopular; did not seek reelection
Richard M. Nixon	1969–1974	Republican	• U.S. senator from California • served two terms as Eisenhower's vice president • lost presidential election of 1960 to John F. Kennedy	• presided over period of *domestic policy* innovation • *reopened* relations with China • ended Vietnam War • resigned as result of Watergate scandal

Jackson, Grant, Cleveland (whose terms were not consecutive), Wilson, Franklin Roosevelt, Eisenhower, Reagan, and Clinton. A few decided against a second term ("Silent Cal" Coolidge said simply, "I do not choose to run"). Five other presidents (Polk, Pierce, Buchanan, Hayes, and Lyndon Johnson) also threw in the towel at the end of one full term. Seven others (both the Adamses, Van Buren, Taft, Hoover, Carter, and George Bush) thought they had earned a second term, but the voters disagreed.

Succession and Impeachment.   For more than 10 percent of American history, the presidency has actually been occupied by an individual who was not elected to the office. About one in five presidents got the job because they were vice president when the incumbent president either died or (in Nixon's case) resigned (see Table 13.2). In the twentieth century, almost one-third (5 of 18) of those who occupied the office were "accidental presidents." The most accidental of all was Gerald Ford, who did not run for either the vice presidency or the presidency before taking office. Ford was nominated vice president by President Nixon when Vice President Spiro Agnew resigned; Ford then assumed the presidency when Nixon himself resigned.

Table 13.1   Recent Presidents (*continued*)

PRESIDENT	TERM	PARTY	BACKGROUND	SIGNIFICANT EVENTS
Gerald R. Ford	1974–1977	Republican	• House minority leader • only person ever nominated as vice president under Twenty-fifth Amendment	• pardoned Richard Nixon • helped heal the nation's wounds • lost election in 1976 to Jimmy Carter
Jimmy Carter	1977–1981	Democrat	• governor of Georgia • peanut farmer	• viewed as honest, but politically unskilled • managed Iranian hostage crisis • lost bid for reelection 1980 • brokered peace between Egypt and Israel
Ronald W. Reagan	1981–1989	Republican	• governor of California • well-known actor	• won a substantial tax cut • led fight for a large increase in defense spending • hurt by Iran/Contra scandal • known as the Great Communicator
George Bush	1989–1993	Republican	• U.S. representative from Texas • director of CIA • ambassador to UN • served two terms as Reagan's vice president	• led international coalition to victory in Gulf War • presided over end of Cold War • popular until economy stagnated • lost reelection bid in 1992
William J. Clinton	1993–2001	Democrat	• governor of Arkansas • Rhodes Scholar	• moved Democrats to center • presided over balanced budget • benefited from strong economy • tenure marred by Monica Lewinsky scandal • impeached but not convicted
George W. Bush	2001–	Republican	• governor of Texas • son of President George Bush • elected without plurality of the vote	• launched war on terrorism • won large tax cut • established Department of Homeland Security • began war with Iraq

Table 13.2   Incomplete Presidential Terms

PRESIDENT	TERM	SUCCEEDED BY
William Henry Harrison	March 4, 1841–April 4, 1841	John Tyler
Zachary Taylor	March 4, 1849–July 9, 1850	Millard Fillmore
Abraham Lincoln	March 4, 1865–April 15, 1865[a]	Andrew Johnson
James A. Garfield	March 4, 1881–September 19, 1881	Chester A. Arthur
William McKinley	March 4, 1901–September 14, 1901[a]	Theodore Roosevelt
Warren G. Harding	March 4, 1921–August 2, 1923	Calvin Coolidge
Franklin D. Roosevelt	January 20, 1945–April 12, 1945[b]	Harry S Truman
John F. Kennedy	January 20, 1961–November 22, 1963	Lyndon B. Johnson
Richard M. Nixon	January 20, 1973–August 9, 1974[a]	Gerald R. Ford

[a]Second term.
[b]Fourth term.

impeachment

The political equivalent of an indictment in criminal law, prescribed by the Constitution. The House of Representatives may impeach the president by a majority vote for "Treason, Bribery, or other high Crimes and Misdemeanors."

Watergate

The events and scandal surrounding a break-in at the Democratic National Committee headquarters in 1972 and the subsequent cover-up of White House involvement, leading to the eventual resignation of President Nixon under the threat of **impeachment.**

Twenty-fifth Amendment

Passed in 1951, this amendment permits the vice president to become acting president if both the vice president and the president's cabinet determine that the president is disabled. The amendment also outlines how a recuperated president can reclaim the job.

Removing a discredited president before the end of a term is not easy. The Constitution prescribes the process through **impeachment,** which is roughly the political equivalent of an indictment in criminal law. The House of Representatives may, by majority vote, impeach the president for "Treason, Bribery, or other high Crimes and Misdemeanors." Once the House votes for impeachment, the case goes to the Senate, which tries the accused president, with the chief justice of the Supreme Court presiding. By a two-thirds vote, the Senate may convict and remove the president from office.

Only two presidents have been impeached. The House impeached Andrew Johnson, Lincoln's successor, in 1868 on charges stemming from his disagreement with radical Republicans. He narrowly escaped conviction. Richard Nixon came as close to impeachment as anyone since. By July 31, 1974, the House Judiciary Committee voted to recommend his impeachment to the full House as a result of the **Watergate** scandal. Nixon escaped a certain vote for impeachment by resigning. In 1998, the House voted two articles of impeachment against President Clinton on party-line votes. The public clearly opposed the idea, however, and the Senate voted to acquit the president on both counts in 1999 (see "You Are the Policymaker: Should President Clinton Have Been Convicted?").

Constitutional amendments cover one other important problem concerning the presidential term: presidential disability and succession. Several times a president has become disabled, incapable of carrying out the job for weeks or even months at a time. After Woodrow Wilson suffered a stroke, his wife, Edith Wilson, became virtual acting president. The **Twenty-fifth Amendment** (1967) clarifies some of the Constitution's vagueness about disability. The amendment permits the vice president to become acting president if the vice president and the president's cabinet determine that the president is disabled or if the president declares his own disability, and it outlines how a recuperated president can reclaim the Oval Office. Other laws specify the order of presidential succession—from the vice president, to the Speaker of the House, to the president *pro tempore* of the Senate and down through the cabinet members in the order their departments were created.

The Twenty-fifth Amendment also created a means for selecting a new vice president when the office becomes vacant (a more frequent occurrence). The president nominates a new vice president, who assumes the office when both houses of Congress approve the nomination.

Richard Nixon was the only American president ever to resign his office. Nixon decided to resign rather than face impeachment for his role in the Watergate scandal, a series of illegal wiretaps, break-ins, and cover-ups.

You Are the Policymaker

Should President Clinton Have Been Convicted?

Monica Lewinsky became a household name in January 1998. By the end of the year, the most intimate details of her two-year affair with President Bill Clinton were known to almost everyone in the country. The nation had to do more than live through a new soap opera of sex and politics, however. The question became whether the president should be removed from office.

In September, Independent Counsel Kenneth Starr issued a report to Congress accusing President Clinton of 11 counts of possible impeachable offenses, including perjury, obstruction of justice, witness tampering, and abuse of power. The president's detractors used the report as a basis for charging that he had broken the law, failed in his primary constitutional duty to take care that the laws be faithfully executed, betrayed the public's trust, and dishonored the nation's highest office. As a result, they argued the president should be removed from office through the process of impeachment. They also argued that other public officials would be removed from office for having an affair with a young intern. Why, they asked, should the president be held to lower standards?

The White House fought back. First, the president apologized to the nation—sort of. Then he engaged in a round of expressions of remorse before a variety of audiences. At the same time, the White House accused Starr of engaging in an intrusive investigation motivated by a political vendetta against the president. The White House argued

that the president made a mistake in his private behavior, apologized for it, and should continue to do the job he was elected to do. Impeachment, the president's defenders said, was grossly disproportionate to the president's offense.

The Constitution provides only the most general guidelines as to the grounds for impeachment. Article II, Section 4, says "The President, Vice President and all civil Officers of the United States, shall be removed from Office on Impeachment for, and Conviction of, Treason, Bribery, or other high Crimes and Misdemeanors."

There is agreement on at least four points regarding impeachable offenses.
1. Impeachable behavior does not have to be a crime. If the president refused to work or chose to invade a country solely to increase his public support, his actions could be grounds for impeachment, even though they would not violate the law.
2. The offense should be grave for it to be impeachable. A poker game in the White House, even though it may violate the law, would not constitute an impeachable offense.
3. A matter of policy disagreement is not grounds for impeachment. The only president who had been impeached before Clinton was Andrew Johnson, who was tried in 1868. He survived by one vote. The real issue was disagreement between the president and Congress over the policy of Reconstruction following the Civil War. Johnson's impeachment and trial are widely viewed as an abuse of impeachment power.

4. Impeachment is an inherently political process and the grounds for impeachment are ultimately whatever Congress decides they are because the Constitution assigns these calibrations to members' political judgment.

Beyond these points of agreement, we enter speculative territory. In 1974, the House Judiciary Committee passed three articles of impeachment against President Richard Nixon, but the president resigned before the House took up the charges. The three articles charged that Nixon had (1) obstructed justice, (2) abused his power, and (3) failed to comply with congressional subpoenas. The Democrats overwhelmingly supported all three articles, and the Republicans generally opposed them.

In 1998 and 1999, the tables were turned, as the Republicans supported a lower threshold for an impeachable offense while the Democrats argued for a higher one. In December 1998, the House voted two articles of impeachment against President Clinton on nearly straight party-line votes. The articles charged him with lying to a grand jury and obstructing justice.

Most Americans felt that the president had behaved improperly, but they also felt he was doing a good job as president. Most opposed impeaching Clinton. Opinion among officeholders and journalists was more negative toward the president, however. After a Senate trial, senators voted to acquit the president. If you were a member of the Senate, would *you* have voted to convict the president?

Presidential Powers

The contemporary presidency hardly resembles the one the Constitution framers designed in 1787. The executive office they conceived had more limited authority, fewer responsibilities, and much less organizational structure than today's presidency. The

Comparing Chief Executives

America in Perspective

President or Prime Minister?

The Founders selected a presidential system of government for the United States. Most democracies in developed countries, however, have chosen a parliamentary system. In such a system the chief executive, the prime minister, is selected by the legislature, not the voters. The prime minister is a member of the legislature, elected from one district as a member of parliament. The majority party, or the largest bloc of votes in the legislature if there is no majority party, votes its party leader to be prime minister. The prime minister may remain in power for a long time—as long as his or her party or coalition has a majority of the seats and supports the leader.

Presidents and prime ministers govern quite differently. Prime ministers never face divided government, for example. Since they represent the majority party or coalition, they can almost always depend on winning on votes. In addition, party discipline is better in parliamentary systems than in the United States. Parties know that if the prime minister should lose on an important vote, the government might have to call elections under circumstances unfavorable to the majority. As a result, members of parliament almost always support their leaders.

Prime ministers generally differ in background from presidents as well. They must be party leaders, as we have seen, and they are usually very effective communicators with skills honed in the rough and tumble of parliamentary debate. In addition, they have had substantial experience dealing with national issues, unlike American governors who may move directly into the presidency. Cabinet members, who are usually senior members of parliament, have similar advantages.

So why does the United States maintain a presidential system? The Founders were concerned about the concentration of power, such as that found in the prime minister. Instead, they wanted to separate power so that the different branches could check each other. More concerned with the abuse of power than its effective use, they chose a presidential system—the first world had ever known.

Why It Matters

Standards of Impeachment
It is not easy to impeach a president; the threshold for an impeachable offense is a high one. This standard makes it very difficult to remove a president Congress feels is performing poorly *between* elections. A lower threshold for impeachment would have the potential to turn the United States into a parliamentary system in which the chief executive could be changed at any time.

Founders feared both anarchy and monarchy. They wanted an independent executive but disagreed about both the form the office should take and the powers it should exercise. In the end, they created an executive unlike any the world had ever seen[6] (see "America in Perspective: President or Prime Minister?").

Constitutional Powers

The Constitution says remarkably little about presidential power. The discussion of the presidency begins with these general words: "The executive power shall be vested in a president of the United States of America." It goes on to list just a few powers (see Table 13.3). The framers' invention fit nicely within the Madisonian system of shared power and checks and balances. There is little that presidents can do on their own, and they share executive, legislative, and judicial power with the other branches of government.

Institutional balance was essential to the convention delegates, who had in mind the abuses of past executives (including both the king and colonial governors) combined with the excesses of state legislatures (discussed in Chapter 2). The problem was how to preserve the balance without jeopardizing the independence of the separate branches or impeding the lawful exercise of their authority. The framers resolved this problem by checking those powers they believed to be most dangerous, the ones that historically had been subject to the greatest abuse (for example, they gave Congress the power to declare war and the Senate the power to approve treaties and presidential appointments), while protecting the general spheres of authority from encroachment (the executive, for instance, was given a qualified veto).

Provisions for reelection and a short term of office also encouraged presidential responsibility. For those executives who flagrantly abused their authority, impeachment was the ultimate recourse.

Table 13.3 Constitutional Powers of the President

National Security Powers
Serve as commander in chief of the armed forces
Make treaties with other nations, subject to the agreement of two-thirds of the Senate
Nominate ambassadors, with the agreement of a majority of the Senate
Receive ambassadors of other nations, thereby conferring diplomatic recognition on other
   governments

Legislative Powers
Present information on the state of the union to Congress
Recommend legislation to Congress
Convene both houses of Congress on extraordinary occasions
Adjourn Congress if the House and Senate cannot agree on adjournment
Veto legislation (Congress may overrule with two-thirds vote of each house)

Administrative Powers
"Take care that the laws be faithfully executed"
Nominate officials as provided for by Congress and with the agreement of a majority of the
   Senate
Request written opinions of administrative officials
Fill administrative vacancies during congressional recesses

Judicial Powers
Grant reprieves and pardons for federal offenses (except impeachment)
Nominate federal judges, who are confirmed by a majority of the Senate

The Expansion of Power

Today there is more to presidential power than the Constitution alone suggests, and that power is derived from many sources. The role of the president has changed as America has increased in prominence on the world stage; technology has also reshaped the presidency. George Washington's ragtag militias (mostly disbanded by the time the first commander in chief took command) were much different from the mighty nuclear arsenal that today's president commands.

Simulation

Presidential Leadership:
Which Hat Do You Wear?

Presidents themselves have taken the initiative to develop new roles for the office. In fact, many presidents have enlarged the power of the presidency by expanding the president's responsibilities and political resources. Thomas Jefferson was the first leader of a mass political party. Andrew Jackson presented himself as the direct representative of the people. Abraham Lincoln mobilized the country for war. Theodore Roosevelt mobilized the public behind his policies. He and Woodrow Wilson set precedents for presidents to serve as world leaders; Wilson and Franklin D. Roosevelt developed the role of the president as manager of the economy.

Perspectives on Presidential Power

During the 1950s and 1960s it was fashionable for political scientists, historians, and commentators to favor a powerful presidency. Historians rated presidents from strong to weak—and there was no question that "strong" meant good and "weak" meant bad. Political scientists waxed eloquent about the presidency as the epitome of democratic governments.[7]

By the 1970s, many felt differently. The Vietnam War was unpopular. Lyndon Johnson and the war made people reassess the role of presidential power, and Richard Nixon and the Watergate scandal heightened public distrust. Presidential duplicity was revealed in the *Pentagon Papers*, a series of secret documents slipped to the press by Daniel Ellsberg. Nixon's "enemies list" and his avowed goal to "screw our enemies" by illegally auditing their taxes, tapping their phones, and using "surreptitious entry" (a euphemism for burglary) asserted that presidents considered themselves above the law. Nixon's lawyers argued solemnly to the Supreme Court and Congress that the presidency has "inherent powers" permitting presidents to order acts that otherwise would be illegal. Nixon protected himself with an umbrella defense of executive privilege, claiming that he did not need to provide evidence to Congress or the courts.

Early defenders of a strong presidency made sharp turnabouts in their position. In his book *The Imperial Presidency*, historian Arthur Schlesinger, an aide of John Kennedy's, argued that the presidency had become too powerful for the nation's own good.[8] (Critics pointed out that Schlesinger did not seem to feel that way when he worked in the White House.) Whereas an older generation of scholars had written glowing accounts of the presidency, a newer generation wrote about "The Swelling of the Presidency" and "Making the Presidency Safe for Democracy."[9]

The Nixon era was followed by the presidencies of Gerald Ford and Jimmy Carter, whom many critics saw as weak leaders and failures. Ford himself spoke out in 1980, claiming that Carter's weakness had created an "imperiled" presidency. In the 1980s, Ronald Reagan experienced short periods of great influence and longer periods of frustration as the American political system settled back into its characteristic mode of stalemate and incremental policymaking. The Iran-Contra affair kept concern about a tyrannical presidency alive, while, in most instances, Reagan's inability to sway Congress evoked a desire on the part of some (mostly conservatives) for a stronger presidency. Reagan's immediate successors, George Bush, Bill Clinton, and George W. Bush, often found it difficult to get things done.

The following sections will explore the relationship between the president's responsibilities and resources by examining how contemporary presidents try to lead the nation.

Running the Government: The Chief Executive

Although the president is often called the "chief executive," it is easy to forget that one of the president's most important roles is presiding over the administration of government. This role does not receive the same publicity as other functions do, such as appealing to the public for support of policy initiatives, dealing with Congress, or negotiating with foreign powers, but it is of great importance nevertheless.

The Constitution exhorts the president to "take care that the laws be faithfully executed." In the early days of the republic, this clerical-sounding function was fairly easy. Today, the sprawling federal bureaucracy spends more than $2 trillion a year and numbers about 4.2 million civilian and military employees. Running such a large organization would be a full-time job for even the most talented of executives, yet it is only one of the president's many jobs.

One of the resources for controlling this bureaucracy is the presidential power to appoint top-level administrators. New presidents have about 500 high-level positions available for appointment—cabinet and subcabinet jobs, agency heads, and other noncivil service posts—plus 2,500 lesser jobs. Since passage of the Budgeting and Accounting Act of 1921, presidents have had one other important executive tool: the power to recommend agency budgets to Congress.

The vastness of the executive branch, the complexity of public policy, and the desire to accomplish their policy goals have led presidents in recent years to pay even closer attention to appointing officials who will be responsive to the president's policies. Presidents have also taken more interest in the regulations issued by agencies. This trend toward centralizing decision-making in the White House pleases those who think the bureaucracy should be more responsive to elected officials. On the other hand, it dismays those who believe that increased presidential involvement in policymaking will undermine the "neutral competence" of professional bureaucrats by encouraging them to follow the president's policy preferences rather than the intent of laws as passed by Congress.

Chapter 15 on the bureaucracy explores the president's role as chief executive further. This chapter will focus on how presidents go about organizing and using the parts of the executive branch most under their control—the vice president, the cabinet, the Executive Office of the President, and the White House staff.

The Vice President

Neither politicians nor political scientists have paid much attention to the vice presidency. Once the choice of a party's "second team" was an afterthought; now it is often an effort to placate some important symbolic constituency. Southerner Jimmy Carter selected a well-known liberal, Walter Mondale, as his running mate, and Ronald Reagan chose his chief rival, George Bush, in part to please Republican moderates.[10]

Vice presidents have rarely enjoyed the job. John Nance Garner of Texas, one of Franklin Roosevelt's vice presidents, declared that the job was "not worth a pitcher of warm spit." Some have performed so poorly that they were deemed an embarrassment to the president. After Woodrow Wilson's debilitating stroke, almost everyone agreed that Vice President Thomas Marshall—a man who shirked all responsibility, including cabinet meetings—would be a disaster as acting president. Spiro Agnew, Richard Nixon's first vice president, had to resign and was convicted of evading taxes (on bribes he had accepted).

Once in office, vice presidents find that their main job is waiting. Constitutionally, they are assigned the minor tasks of presiding over the Senate and voting in case of a tie among the senators. As George Bush put it when he was vice president, "the buck doesn't stop here." Recent presidents, though, have taken their vice presidents more seriously, involving them in policy discussions and important diplomacy.[11]

Jimmy Carter and Ronald Reagan, both Washington outsiders, chose vice presidents who had substantial Washington experience: Walter Mondale and George Bush. To become intimates of the president, both had to be completely loyal, losing their political independence in the process. Vice President Bush, for example, was accused of knowing more about the Iran-Contra affair than he admitted, but he steadfastly refused to reveal his discussions with President Reagan on the matter.

When his turn came to choose a vice president, Bush selected Senator Dan Quayle of Indiana, considered by many a political lightweight. Albert Gore, Bill Clinton's vice president, was a Washington insider and played a prominent role in the administration. He met regularly with the president, represented him in discussions with the leaders of numerous countries, and chaired a prominent effort to "reinvent" government. George W. Bush chose Richard Cheney, who had extensive experience in high-level positions in the national government, as his vice president and assigned him a central role in his administration. Cheney has advised the president on a wide range of issues and chaired task forces dealing with major policy issues.

The Cabinet

Although the Constitution does not mention the group of presidential advisers known as the **cabinet**, every president has had one. The cabinet is too large and too diverse, and its members are too concerned with representing the interests of their departments for it to serve as a collective board of directors, however. The major decisions remain in the president's hands. Legend has it that Abraham Lincoln asked his cabinet to vote on an issue, and the result was unanimity in opposition to his view. He announced the decision as "seven nays and one aye, the ayes have it."

George Washington's cabinet was small, consisting of just three secretaries (state, treasury, and war) and the attorney general. Presidents since Washington have

cabinet

A group of ppresidential advisors not mentioned in the Constitution, although every president has had one. Today the cabinet is composed of 14 secretaries and the attorney general.

Members of the president's cabinet are important for both the power they exercise and the status they symbolize. President George W. Bush formed a cabinet that was representative of America's demographic diversity. Pictured here is President Bush with Secretary of Education Rod Paige, an African American, who served in Bush's first term.

increased the size of the cabinet by requesting that new executive departments be established. These requests must be approved by Congress, which creates the departments. Today 14 secretaries and the attorney general head executive departments and constitute the cabinet (see Table 13.4). In addition, presidents may designate other officials (the ambassador to the United Nations is a common choice) as cabinet members.[12]

Even in making his highest level appointments, the president is subject to the constitutional system of checks and balances. President George Bush met resistance when he nominated John Tower, a former senator, to be secretary of defense. After a bitter

Table 13.4 The Cabinet Departments

DEPARTMENT	YEAR CREATED	FUNCTION
State	1789	Makes foreign policy, including treaty negotiations
Treasury	1789	Serves as the government's banker
Defense	1947	Formed by the consolidation of the former Departments of the Army and the Navy
Justice	1870	Serves as the government's attorney; headed by the attorney general
Interior	1849	Manages the nation's natural resources, including wildlife and public lands
Agriculture	1862	Administers farm and food stamp programs and aids farmers
Commerce	1903	Aids businesses and conducts the U.S. census
Labor	1913	Formed through separation from the Department of Commerce; runs programs and aids labor in various ways
Health and Human Services	1953	Originally created as the Department of Health, Education, and Welfare, it lost its education function in 1979 and Social Security in 1995
Housing and Urban Development	1966	Responsible for housing and urban programs
Transportation	1966	Responsible for mass transportation and highway programs
Energy	1977	Responsible for energy policy and research, including atomic energy
Education	1979	Responsible for the federal government's education programs
Veterans Affairs	1988	Responsible for programs aiding veterans
Homeland Security	2002	Responsible for protecting against terrorism and responding to natural disasters

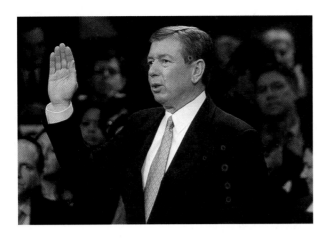

The president must sometimes fight for his nominees, even to his cabinet. President George W. Bush met resistance to his nomination of John Ashcroft, shown here being sworn in during his Senate confirmation hearing as attorney general. Ultimately, Ashcroft was confirmed and served during the president's first term.

debate (which focused on the nominee's use of alcohol and relations with women), the Senate handed the president a serious defeat by rejecting Tower. President Clinton's first nominee to serve as attorney general, Zoe Baird, withdrew from consideration after she came under fire from senators of both parties for hiring an illegal alien as her babysitter and for failing to pay Social Security taxes for her employee.

The Executive Office

Next to the White House sits an ornate building called the EEOB, or Eisenhower Executive Office Building. It houses a collection of offices and organizations loosely grouped into the Executive Office of the President.[13] Some of these offices (such as the Council of Economic Advisors) are created by legislation, and some are organized essentially by the president. The Executive Office started small in 1939 when President Roosevelt established it, but has grown with the rest of government. In the Executive Office are housed three major policymaking bodies—the National Security Council, the Council of Economic Advisors, and Office of Management and Budget—along with several other units that serve the president (see Figure 13.1).

The **National Security Council (NSC)** is the committee that links the president's key foreign and military policy advisors. Its formal members include the president, vice president, and secretaries of state and defense, but its informal membership is broader. The president's special assistant for national security affairs plays a major role in the NSC. The occupant of this post has responsibility for running the council's staff; together they provide the president with information and policy recommendations on national security, aid the president in national security crisis management, coordinate agency and departmental activities bearing on national security, and monitor the implementation of national security policy.

The **Council of Economic Advisors (CEA)** has three members, each appointed by the president, who advise him on economic policy. They prepare the annual *Economic Report of the President*, which includes data and analysis on the current state and future trends of the economy, and help the president make policy on inflation, unemployment, and other economic matters.

The **Office of Management and Budget (OMB)** grew out of the Bureau of the Budget (BOB) created in 1921. The OMB is composed of a handful of political appointees and more than 600 career officials, many of whom are highly skilled professionals. Its major responsibility is to prepare the president's budget (discussed in Chapter 14). President Nixon revamped the BOB in 1970 in an attempt to make it a managerial as well as a budgetary agency, changing its name in the process to stress its managerial functions.

Because each presidential appointee and department have their own agenda, presidents need a clearinghouse—the OMB. Presidents use the OMB to review legislative

National Security Council (NSC)

An office created in 1947 to coordinate the president's foreign and military policy advisors. Its formal members are the president, vice president, **secretary of state,** and **secretary of defense,** and it is managed by the president's national security assistant.

Council of Economic Advisors (CEA)

A three-member body appointed by the president to advise the president on economic policy.

Office of Management and Budget (OMB)

An office that grew out of the Bureau of the Budget, created in 1921, consisting of a handful of political appointees and hundreds of skilled professionals. The OMB performs both managerial and budgetary functions. See also **Congressional Budget Office.**

Figure 13.1   Executive Office of the President

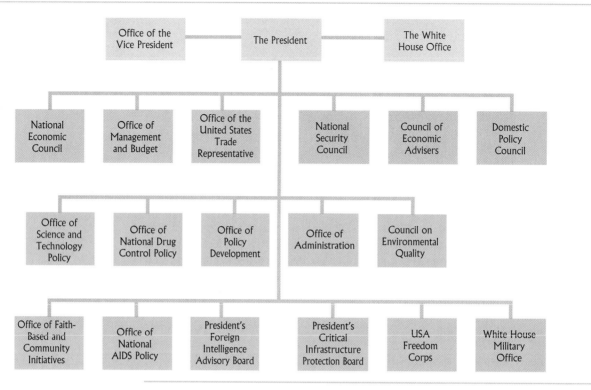

Source: Office of the Federal Register, *The United States Government Manual, 2003/2004* (Washington, D.C.: U.S. Government Printing Office, 2004), 87–102; *http://www.whitehouse.gov/government/eop.html.*

proposals from the cabinet and other executive agencies so that they can determine whether they want an agency to propose these initiatives to Congress. The OMB assesses the proposals' budgetary implications and advises presidents on the proposals' consistency with their overall program. The OMB also plays an important role in reviewing regulations proposed by departments and agencies.

Though presidents find that the Executive Office is smaller and more manageable than the cabinet departments, it is still filled with people performing jobs required by law and whose primary allegiance is to their office, rather than to the president. There is, however, one part of the presidential system that presidents can truly call their own: the White House staff.

The White House Staff

Before Franklin D. Roosevelt, the president's personal staff resources were minimal. Only one messenger and one secretary served Thomas Jefferson. One hundred years later the president's staff had grown only to 13, including clerks and secretaries. Woodrow Wilson was in the habit of typing his own letters. As recently as the 1920s, the entire budget for the White House staff was no more than $80,000 per year.

The White House staff consists of the key aides the president sees daily: the chief of staff, congressional liaison people, a press secretary, a national security assistant, and a few other administrative and political assistants. Today, there are about 600 people at work on the White House staff—many of whom the president rarely sees—who provide the chief executive with a wide variety of services ranging from making advance travel preparations to answering the avalanche of letters received each year (see Figure 13.2).

The top aides in the White House hierarchy are people who are completely loyal to the president, and the president turns to them for advice on the most serious or mun-

Figure 13.2 Principal Offices in the White House

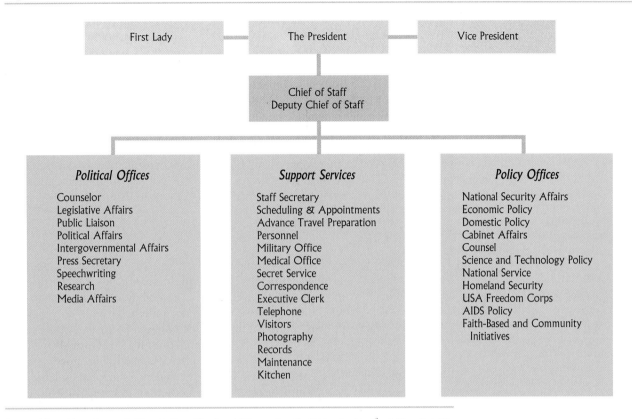

Source: Adapted from George C. Edwards III and Stephen J. Wayne, *Presidential Leadership,* 6th ed. (New York: St. Martin's Press, 2003), Figure 6-2.

dane matters of governance. Good staff people are self-effacing, working only for the boss and shunning the limelight. The 1939 report of the Brownlow Committee, which served as the basis for the development of the modern White House staff, argued that presidential assistants should have a "passion for anonymity." So important are their roles, though, that the names of top White House aides quickly become well known. Woodrow Wilson's Colonel Edward M. House, Franklin D. Roosevelt's Harry Hopkins, Richard Nixon's Henry Kissinger, and George Bush's John Sununu, for example, did much to shape domestic and global policy.

Presidents rely heavily on their staffs for information, policy options, and analysis. Different presidents have different relationships with their staffs. They all organize the White House to serve their own political and policy needs and their own decision-making style. Most presidents end up choosing some form of *hierarchical* organization with a chief of staff at the top, whose job it is to see that everyone else is doing his or her job and that the president's time and interests are protected. A few presidents, such as John F. Kennedy, have employed a *wheel-and-spokes* system of White House management in which many aides have equal status and are balanced against one another in the process of decision-making.[14] Whatever the system, White House aides are central in the policymaking process—fashioning options, negotiating agreements, writing presidential statements, controlling paperwork, molding legislative details, and generally giving the president their opinions on most matters.

No presidential management styles contrasted more sharply than those of Presidents Carter and Reagan. Carter was a detail man, pouring endlessly over memoranda and facts. President Reagan was the consummate delegator. George Bush's operating style fell between the extremes of his two immediate predecessors. He consulted widely both within and outside of government, and he insisted on letting others' views reach him unfiltered by his staff. He was considerably more accessible than Reagan and devoted more energy to decision-making. At the same time, he liked to delegate responsibility to his subordinates and took little initiative in domestic policy.

President Clinton, like Carter, immersed himself in the details of policy. He ran an open White House, dealing directly with a large number of aides and reading countless policy memoranda. His emphasis on deliberation and his fluid staffing system generated criticism that his White House was "indecisive" and "chaotic." George W. Bush is more likely to delegate and his White House has been a more orderly one.

Despite presidents' reliance on their staffs, it is the president who sets the tone for the White House. Although it is common to blame presidential advisors for mistakes made in the White House, it is the president's responsibility to demand that staff members analyze a full range of options and their probable consequences before they offer the president their advice. If the chief executive does not demand quality staff work, then the work is less likely to be done, and disaster or embarrassment may follow.

The First Lady

The First Lady has no official government position, yet she is often at the center of national attention. The media chronicles every word she speaks and every hairstyle she adopts. Although many people think of First Ladies as well-dressed homemakers presiding over White House dinners, there is much more to the job.

Abigail Adams (an early feminist) and Dolley Madison counseled and lobbied their husbands. Edith Galt Wilson was the most powerful First Lady, virtually running the government when her husband, Woodrow, suffered a paralyzing stroke in 1919. Eleanor Roosevelt wrote a nationally syndicated newspaper column and tirelessly traveled and advocated New Deal policies. She became her crippled husband's eyes and ears around the country and urged him to adopt liberal social welfare policies. Lady Bird Johnson chose to focus on one issue, beautification, and most of her successors followed this single-issue pattern. Rosalyn Carter chose mental health, Nancy Reagan selected drugs, and Barbara Bush advocated literacy. Laura Bush, a former librarian, has also chosen to focus on increasing literacy.

In what was perhaps a natural evolution in a society where women have moved into positions formerly held only by males, Hillary Rodham Clinton attained the most

Although the First Lady has no official government position, she is often at the center of national attention. In recent years, First Ladies have taken active roles in promoting policies ranging from highway beautification and mental health to literacy and health care. Here First Lady Laura Bush reads to Washington-area students.

responsible and visible leadership position ever held by a First Lady. She was an influential advisor to the president, playing an active role in the selection of nominees for cabinet and judicial posts, for example. Most publicly, she headed the planning for the president's massive health care reform plan in 1993 and became, along with her husband, its primary advocate.

Although many have hailed her as a model for our times, successfully combining career and family, others have criticized her as a political liability. The health plan failed to pass Congress and was seen by many observers as a leading cause of the Democrats' crushing defeat in the 1994 congressional elections. As a result, she retreated to a more traditional role, focusing on representing the United States abroad and on advocating policies to help children and women in developing countries. In 2000, however, she was elected to the U.S. Senate.

Presidents not only have responsibility for running the executive branch, they must also deal intensively with the legislative branch. These dealings are the topic of the following section.

Presidential Leadership of Congress: The Politics of Shared Powers

Near the top of any presidential job description would be "working with Congress." The American system of separation of powers is actually one of *shared* powers, so if presidents are to succeed in leaving their stamp on public policy, much of their time in office must be devoted to leading the legislature to support presidential initiatives.

Chief Legislator

Nowhere does the Constitution use the phrase *chief legislator*; it is strictly a phrase invented to emphasize the executive's importance in the legislative process. The Constitution does require that the president give a State of the Union address to Congress and instructs the president to bring other matters to Congress' attention "from time to time." In fact, as noted in Chapter 12, the president plays a major role in shaping the congressional agenda.

The Constitution also gives the president power to **veto** congressional legislation. Once Congress passes a bill, the president may (1) sign it, making it law; (2) veto it, sending it back to Congress with the reasons for rejecting it; or (3) let it become law after 10 working days by not doing anything. Congress can pass a vetoed law, however, if two-thirds of each house vote to override the president. At one point in the lawmaking process the president has the last word, however: If Congress adjourns within 10 days after submitting a bill, the president can simply let it die by neither signing nor vetoing it. This process is called a **pocket veto.** Table 13.5 shows how frequently recent presidents have used the veto.

The presidential veto is usually effective; only about 4 percent of all vetoed bills have been overridden by Congress since the nation's founding. Thus, even the threat of a presidential veto can be an effective tool for persuading Congress to give more weight to the president's views. On the other hand, the veto is a blunt instrument. Presidents must accept or reject bills in their entirety; they cannot veto only the parts they do not like (most governors have a *line-item veto* that allows them to veto particular portions of a bill). As a result, the White House often must accept provisions of a bill it opposes in order to obtain provisions that it desires. For example, in 1987, Congress passed the entire discretionary budget of the federal government in one bill (called an "omnibus" bill). President Reagan had to accept the whole package or lose appropriations for the entire government.

veto

The constitutional power of the president to send a bill back to Congress with reasons for rejecting it. A two-thirds vote in each house can override a veto.

pocket veto

A veto taking place when Congress adjourns within 10 days of submitting a bill to the president, who simply lets it die by neither signing nor vetoing it.

Table 13.5   Presidential Vetoes

PRESIDENT	REGULAR VETOES	VETOES OVERRIDDEN	PERCENTAGE OF VETOES OVERRIDDEN	POCKET VETOES	TOTAL VETOES
Eisenhower	73	2	3	108	181
Kennedy	12	0	0	9	21
Johnson	16	0	0	14	30
Nixon	26	7	27	17	43
Ford	48	12	25	18	66
Carter	13	2	15	18	31
Reagan	39	9	23	39	78
G. Bush	29	1	3	15	44
Clinton	37	2	5	1	38
G. W. Bush*	0	0	0	0	0

*Through 2004.

Why It Matters

The President's Veto
Unlike most governors, the president does not have the power to veto parts of a bill. As a result, he cannot choose to delete what he views as wasteful items from the budget. At the same time, the lack of a line-item veto helps to maintain the delicate balance of separate institutions sharing powers.

In 1996, Congress passed a law granting the president authority to propose rescinding funds in appropriations bills and tax provisions that apply to only a few people. Once the president signed tax or spending bills, he had five days to propose rescissions; such provisions could become law only if Congress passed them as separate bills—which would then be subject to a presidential veto. The 1996 law was immediately challenged in the courts as being an unconstitutional grant of power to the president. In 1998 the Supreme Court agreed in *Clinton v. City of New York*, and voided the law.

The presidential veto is an inherently negative resource. It is most useful for preventing legislation. Much of the time, however, presidents are more interested in passing their own legislation. To do so, they must marshal their political resources to obtain positive support for their programs. Presidents' three most useful resources are their party leadership, public support, and their own legislative skills.

Party Leadership

No matter what other resources presidents may have at their disposal, they remain highly dependent on their party to move their legislative programs. Representatives and senators of the president's party usually form the nucleus of coalitions supporting presidential proposals and provide considerably more support than do members of the opposition party. Thus, party leadership in Congress is every president's principal task when countering the natural tendency toward conflict between the executive and legislative branches that is inherent in the government's system of checks and balances.[15]

The Bonds of Party.   For most senators and representatives, being in the same political party as the president creates a psychological bond. Personal loyalties or emotional commitments to their party and their party leader, a desire to avoid embarrassing "their" administration and thus hurting their chances for reelection, and a basic distrust of the opposition party are inclinations that produce support for the White House. Members of the same party also agree on many matters of public policy, and they are often supported by similar electoral coalitions, reinforcing the pull of party ties.

If presidents could rely on their party members to vote for whatever the White House sent up to Capitol Hill, presidential leadership of Congress would be rather easy. All presidents would have to do is make sure members of their party showed up to vote. If their party had the majority, presidents would always win. If their party was in the minority, presidents would only have to concentrate on converting a few members of the other party.

Presidents depend heavily on their parties' leaders in Congress to pass their initiatives. They also must frequently seek support from the opposition party. Here President George W. Bush meets with (from left to right) House Majority Leader Tom DeLay, House Minority Leader Nancy Pelosi, House Speaker Dennis Hastert, Senate Majority Leader Bill Frist, and former Senate Minority Leader Tom Daschle.

Slippage in Party Support.   Things are not so simple, however. Despite the pull of party ties, all presidents experience substantial slippage in the support of their party in Congress. Presidents can count on their own party members for support no more than two-thirds of the time, even on key votes. Presidents are thus forced to be active in party leadership and to devote their efforts to conversion as much as to mobilization of members of their party.

The primary obstacle to party unity is the lack of consensus on policies among party members, especially in the Democratic Party. Jimmy Carter, a Democrat, remarked, "I learned the hard way that there was no party loyalty or discipline when a complicated or controversial issue was at stake—none."[16]

This diversity of views often reflects the diversity of constituencies represented by party members. For many years the frequent defection of Southern Democrats from Democratic presidents (such defectors were called "boll weevils") was one of the most prominent features of American politics. When constituency opinion and the president's proposals conflict, members of Congress are more likely to vote with their constituents, whom they rely on for reelection. If the president is not popular with their constituencies, congressional party members may avoid identifying too closely with the White House.

Leading the Party.   The president has some assets as party leader, including congressional party leaders, services and amenities for party members, and campaign aid. Each asset is of limited utility, however.

The president's relationship with party leaders in Congress is a delicate one. Although the leaders are predisposed to support presidential policies and typically work closely with the White House, they are free to oppose the president or lend only symbolic support; some party leaders may be ineffective themselves. Moreover, party leaders, especially in the Senate, are not in strong positions to reward or discipline members of Congress on the basis of presidential support.

To create goodwill with congressional party members, the White House provides them with many amenities, ranging from photographs with the president to rides on Air Force One. Although this arrangement is to the president's advantage and may earn the benefit of the doubt on some policy initiatives, party members consider it their right to receive benefits from the White House and as a result are unlikely to be especially responsive to the president.

Just as the president can offer a carrot, so too can the president wield a stick in the form of withholding favors, although this is rarely done. Despite the resources available to the president, if party members wish to oppose the White House, there is little the president can do to stop them. The parties are highly decentralized, as we saw in Chapter 8. National party leaders do not control those aspects of politics that are of vital concern to members of Congress—nominations and elections. Members of Congress are largely self-recruited, gain their party's nomination by their own efforts and not the party's, and provide most of the money and organizational support needed for their elections. Presidents can do little to influence the results of these activities.

One way for the president to improve the chances of obtaining support in Congress is to increase the number of fellow party members in the legislature. The phenomenon of **presidential coattails** occurs when voters cast their ballots for congressional candidates of the president's party because those candidates support the president. Most recent studies show a diminishing connection between presidential and congressional voting, however, and few races are determined by presidential coattails.[17] The change in party balance that usually emerges when the electoral dust has settled is strikingly small. In the 14 presidential elections between 1952 and 2004, the party of the winning presidential candidate gained an average of 7 seats (out of 435) per election in the House. In the Senate the opposition party actually gained seats in seven of the elections (1956, 1960, 1972, 1984, 1988, 1996, and 2000), and there was no change in 1976 and 1992. The net gain for the president's party in the Senate averaged less than one seat per election (see Table 13.6).

What about midterm elections—those held between presidential elections? Can the president depend on increasing the number of fellow party members in Congress then? Actually, the picture is even bleaker than during presidential elections. As you can see in Table 13.7, the president's party typically *loses* seats in these elections. In 1986, the Republicans lost 8 seats in the Senate, depriving President Reagan of a majority. In 1994, the Democrats lost 8 Senate seats and 52 House seats, losing control of both houses in the process.[18] Recently there have been exceptions, however. In 1998, the Democrats gained 5 seats in the House, and in 2002, Republicans made small gains in both houses.

presidential coattails

These occur when voters cast their ballots for congressional candidates of the president's party because they support the president. Recent studies show that few races are won this way.

Table 13.6　Congressional Gains or Losses for the President's Party in Presidential Election Years

Presidents cannot rely on their coattails to carry their party's legislators into office to help pass White House legislative programs. The president's party typically gains few, if any, seats when the president wins election. For instance, the Republicans lost seats in both houses when President George W. Bush was elected in 2000.

YEAR	PRESIDENT	HOUSE	SENATE
1952	Eisenhower (R)	+22	+1
1956	Eisenhower (R)	−2	−1
1960	Kennedy (D)	−22	−2
1964	Johnson (D)	+37	+1
1968	Nixon (R)	+5	+6
1972	Nixon (R)	+12	−2
1976	Carter (D)	+1	0
1980	Reagan (R)	+34	+12
1984	Reagan (R)	+14	−2
1988	G. Bush (R)	−3	−1
1992	Clinton (D)	−10	0
1996	Clinton (D)	+9	−2
2000	G. W. Bush (R)	−2	−4
2004	G. W. Bush (R)	+4	+4
	Average	+7	+.7

Table 13.7　Congressional Gains or Losses for the President's Party in Midterm Election Years

For decades the president's party typically *lost* seats in midterm elections. Thus, presidents could not be certain of helping to elect members of their party once in office. The elections of 1998 and 2002 deviated from this pattern, and the president's party gained a few seats.

YEAR	PRESIDENT	HOUSE	SENATE
1954	Eisenhower (R)	−18	−1
1958	Eisenhower (R)	−47	−13
1962	Kennedy (D)	−4	+3
1966	Johnson (D)	−47	−4
1970	Nixon (R)	−12	+2
1974	Ford (R)	−47	−5
1978	Carter (D)	−15	−3
1982	Reagan (R)	−26	0
1986	Reagan (R)	−5	−8
1990	G. Bush (R)	−9	−1
1994	Clinton (D)	−52	−8
1998	Clinton (D)	+5	0
2002	G. W. Bush (R)	+6	+2
	Average	−21	−3

To add to these party leadership burdens, the president's party often lacks a majority in one or both houses of Congress. Since 1953 there have been 28 years in which Republican presidents faced a Democratic House of Representatives and 20 years in which they encountered a Democratic Senate. President Clinton faced both a House and a Senate with Republican majorities from 1995 through 2000. George W. Bush faced a Democratic Senate from May 2001 through December 2002.

As a result of election returns and the lack of dependable party support, the president usually has to solicit help from the opposition party. This is often a futile endeavor, however, since the opposition is generally not fertile ground for seeking support. Nevertheless, even a few votes may be enough to give the president the required majority.

Public Support

One of the president's most important resources for leading Congress is public support. Presidents who enjoy the backing of the public have an easier time influencing Congress. Said one top aide to Ronald Reagan, "Everything here is built on the idea that the president's success depends on grassroots support."[19] Presidents with low approval ratings in the polls find it difficult to influence Congress. As one of President Carter's aides put it, "No president whose popularity is as low as this president's has much clout on the Hill."[20] Members of Congress and others in Washington closely watch two indicators of public support for the president: approval in the polls and mandates in presidential elections.

Public Approval. Members of Congress anticipate the public's reactions to their support for or opposition to presidents and their policies. They may choose to be close to or independent of the White House—depending on the president's standing with the public—to increase their chances for reelection. Representatives and senators may also use the president's standing in the polls as an indicator of presidential ability to mobilize public opinion against presidential opponents.

Public approval also makes other leadership resources more efficacious. If the president is high in the public's esteem, the president's party is more likely to be responsive, the public is more easily moved, and legislative skills become more effective. Thus public approval is the political resource that has the most potential to turn a stalemate between the president and Congress into a situation supportive of the president's legislative proposals.

Public approval operates mostly in the background and sets the limits of what Congress will do for or to the president. Widespread support gives the president leeway and weakens resistance to presidential policies. It provides a cover for members of Congress to cast votes to which their constituents might otherwise object. They can defend their votes as support for the president rather than support for a certain policy alone.

Lack of public support strengthens the resolve of the president's opponents and narrows the range in which presidential policies receive the benefit of the doubt. In addition, low ratings in the polls may create incentives to attack the president, further eroding an already weakened position. For example, after the arms sales to Iran and the diversion of funds to the Contras made the headlines in late 1986, it became more acceptable in Congress and in the press to raise questions about Ronald Reagan's capacities as president. Disillusionment is a difficult force for the White House to combat.

The impact of public approval or disapproval on the support the president receives in Congress is important, but it occurs at the margins of the effort to build coalitions behind proposed policies. No matter how low presidential standing dips, the president still receives support from a substantial number of senators and representatives. Similarly, no matter how high approval levels climb, a significant portion of Congress will still oppose certain presidential policies. Members of Congress are unlikely to vote against the clear interests of their constituencies or the firm tenets of their ideology out of deference to a widely supported chief executive, as George W. Bush learned following the terrorist attacks on September 11, 2001. Public approval gives the president leverage, not command.[21]

In addition, presidents cannot depend on having the approval of the public, and it is not a resource over which they have much control, as we will see later. Once again, it is clear that presidents' leadership resources do not allow them to dominate Congress.

Mandates.   The results of presidential elections are another indicator of public opinion regarding presidents. An electoral mandate—the perception that the voters strongly support the president's character and policies—can be a powerful symbol in American politics. It accords added legitimacy and credibility to the newly elected president's proposals. Moreover, concerns for both representation and political survival encourage members of Congress to support new presidents if they feel the people have spoken.

More important, mandates change the premises of decisions. Following Roosevelt's decisive win in the 1932 election, the essential question became *how* government should act to fight the Depression rather than *whether* it should act. Similarly, following Johnson's overwhelming win in the 1964 election, the dominant question in Congress was not whether to pass new social programs but how many social programs to pass and how much to increase spending. In 1981, the tables were turned; Ronald Reagan's victory placed a stigma on big government and exalted the unregulated marketplace and large defense efforts. Reagan had won a major victory even before the first congressional vote.

Although presidential elections can structure choices for Congress, merely winning an election does not provide presidents with a mandate. Every election produces a winner, but mandates are much less common. Even large electoral victories, such as Richard Nixon's in 1972 and Ronald Reagan's in 1984, carry no guarantee that Congress will interpret the results as mandates from the people to support the president's programs. Perceptions of a mandate are weak if the winning candidate did not stress his policy plans in the campaign or if the voters also elected majorities in Congress from the other party (of course, the winner may *claim* a mandate anyway).[22]

Legislative Skills

Presidential legislative skills come in a variety of forms, including bargaining, making personal appeals, consulting with Congress, setting priorities, exploiting "honeymoon" periods, and structuring congressional votes. Of these skills, bargaining receives perhaps the most attention from commentators on the presidency, and by examining it, one can learn much about the role that a president's legislative skills play in leading Congress.

Bargains occur in numerous forms. Reagan's budget director David Stockman recalled that "the last 10 or 20 percent of the votes needed for a majority of both houses on the 1981 tax cut had to be bought, period." The concessions for members of Congress included special breaks for oil-lease holders, real estate tax shelters, and generous loopholes that virtually eliminated the corporate income tax. "The hogs were really feeding," declared Stockman. "The greed level, the level of opportunities, just got out of control."[23]

Nevertheless, bargaining, in the form of trading support on two or more policies or providing specific benefits for representatives and senators, occurs less often and plays a less critical role in the creation of presidential coalitions in Congress than one might think. For obvious reasons, the White House does not want to encourage the type of bargaining Stockman describes, and there is a scarcity of resources with which to bargain, especially in an era where balancing the budget is a prominent goal for policy-makers (discussed in Chapter 14).

Moreover, the president does not have to bargain with every member of Congress to receive support. On controversial issues on which bargaining may be useful, the president usually starts with a sizable core of party supporters and may add to this group those of the opposition party who provide support on ideological or policy grounds. Others may support the president because of relevant constituency interests or strong public approval. The president needs to bargain only if this coalition does not provide a majority (or two-thirds on treaties and one-third on veto overrides).

Presidents may improve their chances of success in Congress by making certain strategic moves. It is wise, for example, for a new president to be ready to send legislation to the Hill early during the first year in office in order to exploit the "honeymoon" atmosphere that typically characterizes this period. Obviously, this is a one-shot opportunity.

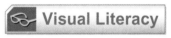

Visual Literacy

Presidential Success in
Polls and Congress

An important aspect of presidential legislative strategy can be establishing priorities among legislative proposals. The goal of this effort is to set Congress' agenda. If presidents are unable to focus the attention of Congress on their priority programs, these programs may become lost in the complex and overloaded legislative process. Setting priorities is also important because presidents and their staffs can lobby effectively for only a few bills at a time. Moreover, each president's political capital is inevitably limited, and it is sensible to focus on a limited range of personally important issues; otherwise, this precious resource might be wasted.

In 1981 Ronald Reagan followed both of these strategies, moving fast and setting priorities. He had great success—obtaining passage of a large tax cut, a substantial increase in defense expenditures, and sizable decreases in the rate of spending for domestic policies. George Bush, in contrast, did not enter the White House geared for legislative action and did little to articulate his priorities. With a large budget deficit, few legislative goals, and the opposition in the majority in both the House and Senate, he did not feel it necessary or useful to focus his energies on Congress. From the outset Bush seemed destined to make his mark on foreign policy, where the president has more latitude to maneuver.

Within a month after taking office, President Clinton presented Congress with an ambitious agenda, including tax increases and both spending cuts and increases. He proposed a major health care reform bill and the North American Free Trade Agreement later in the year. The president lacked the political capital to pass much of his agenda, however, and some of the most important proposals fell prey to Republican opposition. By failing to focus on his priorities, Clinton spent his political capital on

Presidents influence the legislative agenda more than any other political figure. One of Ronald Reagan's chief legislative skills was the ability to communicate his policy priorities effectively to Congress and the public. No matter what a president's skills are, however, the "chief legislator," as the president is often called, can rarely exercise complete control over the agenda.

matters of less importance. Although he engaged in an endless campaign of public appearances and congressional meetings to build support for his legislation, in the end he met with substantial disappointment and was rebuffed by the voters in the 1994 midterm elections as the Republicans captured both houses of Congress. In his early months in office, George W. Bush followed Reagan's example of moving rapidly and focusing on his priority legislation.

The president is the nation's key agenda builder; what the administration wants strongly influences the parameters of Washington debate.[24] John Kingdon's careful study of the Washington agenda found that "no other single actor in the political system has quite the capability of the president to set agendas."[25] There are limits to what the president can do, however.

By his second year in office, Ronald Reagan's honeymoon with Congress was over, and he had lost control of the legislative agenda. Although the White House can put off dealing with many national issues at the beginning of a new president's term in order to focus on its highest priority legislation, it cannot do so indefinitely. Eventually it must make decisions about a wide range of matters. Soon the legislative agenda is full and more policies are in the pipeline, as the administration attempts to satisfy its constituents and responds to unanticipated or simply overlooked problems. Moreover, Congress is quite capable of setting its own agenda, providing competition for the president's proposals.

In general, presidential legislative skills must compete—as presidential public support does—with other, more stable factors that affect voting in Congress: party, ideology, personal views and commitments on specific policies, constituency interests, and so on. By the time a president tries to exercise influence on a vote, most members of Congress have made up their minds on the basis of these other factors.

After accounting for the status of the president's party in Congress and standing with the public, systematic studies have found that presidents known for their legislative skills (such as Lyndon Johnson) are no more successful in winning votes, even close ones, or obtaining congressional support than those considered less adept at dealing with Congress (such as Jimmy Carter).[26] The president's legislative skills are not at the core of presidential leadership of Congress. Even skilled presidents cannot reshape the contours of the political landscape and *create* opportunities for change. They can, however, recognize favorable configurations of political forces—such as existed in 1933, 1965, and 1981—and effectively exploit them to embark on major shifts in public policy.

Presents find the role of legislative leader a challenging one. Often they must compromise with opponents in Congress, as President Bill Clinton did in 1996 when he signed the welfare reform bill.

Perhaps the most important role of presidents—and their heaviest burden—is their responsibility for national security. Dealing with Congress is only one of the many challenges presidents face in the realm of defense and foreign policy.

The President and National Security Policy

Constitutionally, the president has the leading role in American defense and foreign policy (often termed *national security* policy). Such matters, ranging from foreign trade to war and peace, occupy much of the president's time. There are several dimensions to the president's national security responsibilities, including negotiating with other nations, commanding the armed forces, waging war, managing crises, and obtaining the necessary support in Congress.

Chief Diplomat

The Constitution allocates certain powers in the realm of national security exclusively to the executive. The president alone extends diplomatic recognition to foreign governments—as Jimmy Carter did on December 14, 1978, when he announced the exchange of ambassadors with the People's Republic of China and the downgrading of the U.S. Embassy in Taiwan. The president can also terminate relations with other nations, as Carter did with Iran after Americans were taken hostage in Tehran.

The president also has the sole power to negotiate treaties with other nations, although the Constitution requires the Senate to approve them by a two-thirds vote. Sometimes presidents win and sometimes they lose when presenting a treaty to the Senate. After extensive lobbying, Jimmy Carter persuaded the Senate to approve a treaty returning the Panama Canal to Panama (over objections such as those of one senator who declared, "We stole it fair and square"). Carter was not so lucky when he presented the SALT II treaty on arms control; it never even made it to a vote on the Senate floor. At other times senators add "reservations" to the treaties they ratify, altering the treaty in the process.[27]

In addition to treaties, presidents also negotiate *executive agreements* with the heads of foreign governments. However, executive agreements do not require Senate ratification (although they are supposed to be reported to Congress and may require implementing legislation passed by majorities of each house). Most executive agreements are routine and deal with noncontroversial subjects such as food deliveries or customs enforcement, but some, such as the Vietnam peace agreement and the SALT I agreement limiting offensive nuclear weapons, implement important and controversial policies.

Occasionally presidential diplomacy involves more than negotiating on behalf of the United States. Theodore Roosevelt won the Nobel Peace Prize for his role in settling the war between Japan and Russia. One of Jimmy Carter's greatest achievements was forging a peace treaty between Egypt and Israel. For 13 days he mediated negotiations between the leaders of both countries at his presidential retreat, Camp David.

As the leader of the Western world, the president must try to lead America's allies on matters of both economics and defense. This is not an easy task, given the natural independence of sovereign nations; the reduced status of the United States as an economic power relative to other countries, such as Japan and Germany; and the many competing influences on policymaking in other nations. As in domestic policymaking, the president must rely principally on persuasion to lead.

Commander in Chief

Because the Constitution's framers wanted civilian control of the military, they made the president the commander in chief of the armed forces. President George Washington actually led troops to crush the Whiskey Rebellion in 1794. Today, presidents do not take the task quite so literally, but their military decisions have changed the course of history. Bill Clinton joined the ranks of presidents exerting their prerogatives as commander in chief when he sent American troops to occupy Haiti, keep the peace in Bosnia, restore order in Somalia, prevent an invasion of Kuwait, and bomb Yugoslavia, Iraq, Afghanistan, and the Sudan. George W. Bush ordered an attack on the Taliban government in Afghanistan—and on terrorists everywhere.

When the Constitution was written, the United States did not have—nor did anyone expect it to have—a large standing or permanent army. Today the president is commander in chief of about 1.5 million uniformed men and women. In his farewell

Presidents usually conduct diplomatic relations through envoys, but occasionally they engage in personal diplomacy. Here, President Carter celebrates a peace agreement he brokered between Israeli Prime Minister Menachem Begin and Egyptian President Anwar Sadat.

In 1950, President Harry Truman fulfilled his role as commander in chief by pinning a distinguished service medal on the shirt of General Douglas MacArthur, who was commanding American troops in Korea. The following year, Truman exercised his powers by dismissing MacArthur for disobeying orders—an unpopular decision given MacArthur's fame as a World War II hero.

address, George Washington warned against permanent alliances, but today America has commitments to defend nations across the globe. Even more important, the president commands a vast nuclear arsenal. Never more than a few steps from the president is "the football," a briefcase with the codes needed to unleash nuclear war. The Constitution, of course, states that only Congress has the power to declare war, but it is unreasonable to believe that Congress can convene, debate, and vote on a declaration of war in the case of a nuclear attack. The House and Senate chambers would be gone—*literally* gone—before the conclusion of a debate.

War Powers

Perhaps no issue of executive-legislative relations generates more controversy than the continuing dispute over war powers. Though charged by the Constitution with declaring war and voting on the military budget, Congress long ago accepted that presidents make short-term military commitments of troops or naval vessels. In recent decades, however, presidents have paid even less attention to constitutional details; for example, Congress never declared war during the conflicts in either Korea or Vietnam.

In 1973 Congress passed the **War Powers Resolution** (over President Nixon's veto). As a reaction to disillusionment about American fighting in Vietnam and Cambodia, the law was intended to give Congress a greater voice in the introduction of American troops into hostilities. It required presidents to consult with Congress, whenever possible, before using military force, and it mandated the withdrawal of forces after 60 days unless Congress declared war or granted an extension. Congress could at any time pass a concurrent resolution (which could not be vetoed) ending American participation in hostilities.

The War Powers Resolution cannot be regarded as a success for Congress, however. All presidents serving since 1973 have deemed the law an unconstitutional infringement on their powers, and there is reason to believe the Supreme Court would consider the law's use of the **legislative veto** (the ability of Congress to pass a resolution to override a presidential decision) to be a violation of the doctrine of separation of

War Powers Resolution

A law passed in 1973 in reaction to American fighting in Vietnam and Cambodia that requires presidents to consult with Congress whenever possible prior to using military force and to withdraw forces after 60 days unless Congress declares war or grants an extension. Presidents view the resolution as unconstitutional.

legislative veto

The ability of Congress to override a presidential decision. Although the **War Powers Resolution** asserts this authority, there is reason to believe that, if challenged, the Supreme Court would find the legislative veto in violation of the doctrine of separation of powers.

Why It Matters

War Powers
The question as to the president's war powers has never been fully resolved. Some feel we would be less likely to go to war if the president could only send troops into combat after a congressional resolution authorizing the use of force. Others see such a requirement as unduly hampering the president's ability to conduct an effective foreign policy.

crisis

A sudden, unpredictable, and potentially dangerous event requiring the president to play the role of crisis manager.

powers. Presidents have largely ignored the law and sent troops into hostilities, sometimes with heavy loss of life, without effectual consulting with Congress. The legislature has found it difficult to challenge the president, especially when American troops were endangered, and the courts have been reluctant to hear a congressional challenge on what would be construed as a political, rather than a legal, issue.[28]

Following numerous precedents, George Bush took an expansive view of his powers as commander in chief. On his own authority, he ordered the invasion of Panama in 1989 and moved half a million troops to Saudi Arabia to liberate Kuwait after its invasion by Iraq in 1990. Matters came to a head in January 1991. President Bush had given President Saddam Hussein of Iraq until January 15 to pull out of Kuwait. At that point, President Bush threatened to move the Iraqis out by force. Debate raged over the president's power to act unilaterally to engage in war. A constitutional crisis was averted when Congress passed (on a divided vote) a resolution on January 12 authorizing the president to use force against Iraq.

In a sweeping assertion of presidential authority, Bill Clinton moved toward military intervention in Haiti in 1994 and essentially dared Congress to try to stop him. Congress did nothing but complain to block military action, even though a majority of members of both parties clearly opposed an invasion. In the end, an invasion (as opposed to a more peaceful "intervention") was avoided, but Congress was unlikely to have cut off funds for such an operation had it occurred. In 1999, the president authorized the United States to take the leading role in a sustained air attack against Serbia, but Congress could not agree on a resolution supporting the use of force.

George W. Bush faced little opposition to responding to the terrorist attacks of September 11, 2001. Congress immediately passed a resolution authorizing the use of force against the perpetrators of the attacks. The next year, Congress passed a resolution authorizing the president to use force against Iraq.

Questions continue to be raised about the relevance of America's 200-year-old constitutional mechanisms for engaging in war. Some observers worry that the rapid response capabilities afforded the president by modern technology allow him to bypass congressional opposition, thus undermining the separation of powers. Others stress the importance of the commander in chief having the flexibility to meet America's global responsibilities and combat international terrorism without the hindrance of congressional checks and balances. All agree that the change in the nature of warfare brought about by nuclear weapons inevitably delegates to the president the ultimate decision to use such weapons.

Crisis Manager

The president's roles as chief diplomat and commander in chief are related to another presidential responsibility: crisis management. A **crisis** is a sudden, unpredictable, and potentially dangerous event. Most crises occur in the realm of foreign policy. They often involve hot tempers and high risks; quick judgments must be made on the basis of sketchy information. Be it American hostages held in Iran or the discovery of Soviet missiles in Cuba, a crisis challenges the president to make difficult decisions. Crises are rarely the president's doing, but handled incorrectly, they can be the president's undoing. On the other hand, handling a crisis well can remake a president's image, as George W. Bush found following the terrorist attacks of September 11, 2001.

Early in American history there were fewer immediate crises. By the time officials were aware of a problem, it often had resolved itself. Communications could take weeks or even months to reach Washington. Similarly, officials' decisions often took weeks or months to reach those who were to implement them. The most famous land battle of the War of 1812, the Battle of New Orleans, was fought *after* the United States had signed a peace treaty with Great Britain. Word of the treaty did not reach the battlefield; thus, General Andrew Jackson won a victory for the United States that contributed nothing toward ending the war, although it did help put him in the White House as the seventh president.

Crisis management may be the most difficult of the president's many roles. By definition, crises are sudden, unpredictable, and dangerous. Here President George W. Bush stands with firefighters and rescue workers at of the World Trade Center site three days after the terrorist attacks on September 11, 2001.

With modern communications, the president can instantly monitor events almost anywhere. Moreover, because situations develop more rapidly today, there is a premium on rapid action, secrecy, constant management, consistent judgment, and expert advice. Congress usually moves slowly (one might say deliberately), and it is large (making it difficult to keep secrets), decentralized (requiring continual compromising), and composed of generalists. As a result, the president—who can come to quick and consistent decisions, confine information to a small group, carefully oversee developments, and call upon experts in the executive branch—has become more prominent in handling crises.

Working With Congress

As America moves through its third century under the Constitution, presidents might wish the framers had been less concerned with checks and balances in the area of national security. In recent years, Congress has challenged presidents on all fronts, including foreign aid; arms sales; the development, procurement, and deployment of weapons systems; the negotiation and interpretation of treaties; the selection of diplomats; and the continuation of nuclear testing.

Congress has a central constitutional role in making national security policy, although this role is often misunderstood. The allocation of responsibilities for such matters is based on the Founders' apprehensions about the concentration of power and the subsequent potential for its abuse. They divided the powers of supply and command, for example, in order to thwart adventurism in national security affairs. Congress can thus refuse to provide the necessary authorizations and appropriations for presidential actions, whereas the chief executive can refuse to act (for example, by not sending troops into battle at the behest of the legislature).

Despite the constitutional role of Congress, the president is the driving force behind national security policy, providing energy and direction. Congress is well organized to deliberate openly on the discrete components of policy, but it is not well designed to take the lead on national security matters. Its role has typically been overseeing the executive rather than initiating policy. Congress frequently originates proposals for domestic policy, but it is less involved in national security policy.[29]

The president has a more prominent role in foreign affairs as the country's sole representative in dealing with other nations and as commander in chief of the armed forces (functions that effectively preclude a wide range of congressional diplomatic and military initiatives). In addition, the nature of national security issues may make the failure to integrate the elements of policy more costly than in domestic policy. Thus, members of Congress typically prefer to encourage, criticize, or support the president rather than to initiate their own national security policy. If leadership occurs, it is usually centered in the White House.

Commentators on the presidency often refer to the "two presidencies"—one for domestic policy and the other for national security policy.[30] By this phrase they mean that the president has more success in leading Congress on matters of national security than on matters of domestic policy. The typical member of Congress, however, supports the president on roll-call votes about national security only slightly more than half the time. There is a significant gap between what the president requests and what members of Congress are willing to give. Certainly the legislature does not accord the president automatic support on national security policy.[31]

Nevertheless, presidents do end up obtaining much, often most, of what they request from Congress on national security issues. Some of the support they receive is the result of agreement on policy, but presidential leadership also plays an important role. That role is not one in which presidents simply bend the legislature to their will, however; rather, they lead by persuasion.

Presidents need resources to persuade others to support their policies. One important presidential asset can be the support of the American people. The following sections will take a closer look at how the White House tries to increase and use public support.

Power from the People: The Public Presidency

"Public sentiment is everything. With public sentiment nothing can fail; without it nothing can succeed." These words, spoken by Abraham Lincoln, pose what is perhaps the greatest challenge to any president—to obtain and maintain the public's support. Because presidents are rarely in a position to command others to comply with their wishes, they must rely on persuasion. Public support is perhaps the greatest source of influence a president has, for it is difficult for other power holders in a democracy to deny the legitimate demands of a president who has popular backing.

Going Public

Presidents are not passive followers of public opinion. The White House is a virtual whirlwind of public relations activity.[32] John Kennedy, the first "television president," held considerably more public appearances than did his predecessors. Kennedy's successors, with the notable exception of Richard Nixon, have been even more active in making public appearances. Indeed, they have averaged more than one appearance every weekday of the year. Bill Clinton and George W. Bush invested enormous time and energy in attempting to sell their programs to the public.

Often the president's appearances are staged purely to get the public's attention. When George Bush introduced his clean-air bill in 1989, he traveled to Wyoming to use the eye-catching Grand Tetons as a backdrop. He announced his support for a constitutional amendment to prohibit flag burning in front of the Iwo Jima Memorial in Arlington National Cemetery. In cases such as these, the president could have simply made an announcement, but the need for public support drives the White House to employ public relations techniques similar to those used to publicize commercial products.

In many democracies, different people occupy the jobs of head of state and head of government. For example, the queen is head of state in England, but she holds little power in government and politics. In America, these roles are fused. As head of state, the president is America's ceremonial leader and symbol of government. Trivial but time-consuming activities—tossing out the first baseball of the season, lighting the White House Christmas tree, meeting an extraordinary Boy or Girl Scout—are part of the ceremonial function of the presidency. Meeting foreign heads of state, receiving ambassadors' credentials, and making global goodwill tours represent the international side of this role. Presidents rarely shirk these duties, even when they are not inherently

Presidents often use commercial public relations techniques to win support for their policy initiatives. President George Bush, for example, used the spectacular backdrop of the Grand Tetons to gain public approval for renewal and strengthening of the Clean Air Act.

important. Ceremonial activities give them an important symbolic aura and a great deal of favorable press coverage, contributing to their efforts to build public support.

Presidential Approval

Much of the energy the White House devotes to public relations is aimed at increasing the president's public approval. The White House believes that the higher the president stands in the polls, the easier it is to persuade others to support presidential initiatives. Because of the connection between public support and presidential influence, the president's standing in the polls is monitored closely by the press, members of Congress, and others in the Washington political community. For years, the Gallup Poll has asked Americans: "Do you approve or disapprove of the way John Kennedy, George W. Bush, etc. is handling his job as president?" You can see the results in Figure 13.3.

Presidents frequently do not have widespread public support, often failing to win even majority approval. Figure 13.4 shows the average approval levels of recent presidents. Presidents Nixon, Ford, and Carter did not receive approval from 50 percent of the public on the average. Ronald Reagan had only a 52 percent approval level. For three years, George Bush enjoyed much higher levels of approval on the average than his

Participation

Rate the Presidents

Figure 13.3   Average Yearly Presidential Approval

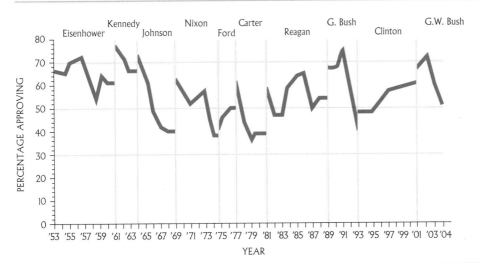

For years the Gallup Poll has asked Americans, "Do you approve or disapprove of the way _____ is handling his job as president?" Here you can track the percentage approving of presidential performance from Eisenhower to George W. Bush. Notice that most presidents seem to be most popular when they first enter office; later on, their popularity often erodes. Bill Clinton was an exception.

Source: George C. Edwards III, *Presidential Approval* (Baltimore, MD: Johns Hopkins University Press, 1990); updated by the authors.

predecessors did. In his fourth year, however, his ratings dropped below the 40 percent mark. President Clinton struggled to rise above the 50 percent mark in his first term, and George W. Bush was at 51 percent before the September 11, 2001 terrorist attacks.

Presidential approval is the product of many factors.[33] At the base of presidential evaluations is the predisposition of many people to support the president. Political party identification provides the basic underpinning of approval or disapproval and mediates the impact of other factors. On average, those who identify with the president's party give approval more than 40 percentage points higher than do those who identify with the opposition party. Moreover, partisans are not inclined to approve presidents of the other party. Predispositions provide the foundations of presidential approval and furnish it with a basic stability.

Presidents also usually benefit from a "honeymoon" with the American people after taking office. Some observers believe that "honeymoons" are fleeting phenomena in which the public affords new occupants of the White House only a short grace period before they begin their inevitable descent in the polls. You can see in Figure 13.3 that declines do take place, but they are neither inevitable nor swift. Throughout his two terms in office, Ronald Reagan experienced considerable volatility in his relations with the public, but his record certainly does not indicate that the loss of public support is inexorable or that support cannot be revived and maintained. George Bush obtained more public support in his third year in office than in his first two years, and Bill Clinton enjoyed more approval in his second term in office than in his first.

Changes in approval levels appear to reflect the public's evaluation of how the president is handling policy areas such as the economy, war, and foreign affairs. Different policies are salient to the public at different times. For example, if communism is collapsing, then foreign policy is likely to dominate the news and to be on the minds of Americans. If the economy turns sour, then people are going to be concerned about unemployment.

Contrary to conventional wisdom, citizens seem to focus on the president's efforts and stands on issues rather than on personality ("popularity") or simply how presidential policies affect them (the "pocketbook"). Job-related personal characteristics of the president, such as integrity and leadership skills, also play an important role in influencing presidential approval.

Sometimes public approval of the president takes sudden jumps. One popular explanation for these surges of support is "rally events," which John Mueller defined as events that are related to international relations, directly involve the United States and particularly the president, and are specific, dramatic, and sharply focused.[34] A classic

Figure 13.4   Average Presidential Approval for Entire Terms in Office

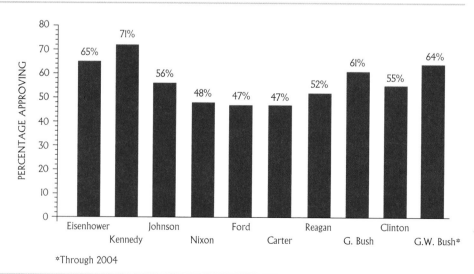

Source: George C. Edwards III, *Presidential Approval* (Baltimore, MD: Johns Hopkins University Press, 1990); updated by the authors.

*Through 2004

example is the 18-percentage-point rise in President George Bush's approval ratings immediately after the fighting began in the Gulf War in 1991. George W. Bush's approval shot up 39 percentage points in September 2001. Such occurrences are unusual and isolated events, however; they usually have little enduring impact on a president's public approval. President Bush, for example, dropped precipitously in the polls and lost his bid for reelection in 1992.

The criteria on which the public evaluates presidents—such as the way they are handling the economy, where they stand on complex issues, and whether they are "strong" leaders—are open to many interpretations. The modern White House makes extraordinary efforts to control the context in which presidents appear in public and the way they are portrayed by the press, to try to influence how the public views them. The fact that presidents are frequently low in the polls anyway is persuasive testimony to the limits of presidential leadership of the public. As one student of the public presidency put it, "The supply of popular support rests on opinion dynamics over which the president may exert little direct control."[35]

Policy Support

Commentators on the presidency often refer to it as a "bully pulpit," implying that presidents can persuade or even mobilize the public to support their policies if they are skilled communicators. Certainly presidents frequently do attempt to obtain public support for their policies with television or radio appearances and speeches to large groups.[36] All presidents since Truman have had media advice from experts on lighting, makeup, stage settings, camera angles, clothing, pacing of delivery, and other facets of making speeches.

Despite this aid and despite the experience that politicians have in speaking, presidential speeches designed to lead public opinion have typically been rather unimpressive. In the modern era only Franklin D. Roosevelt, John Kennedy, Ronald Reagan, and Bill Clinton could be considered especially effective speakers. The rest were not, and they appeared unimpressive under the glare of hot lights and the unflattering gaze of television cameras. Partly because of his limitations as a public speaker, President George Bush waited until he had been in office for over seven months before making his first nationally televised address in 1989.

Moreover, the public is not always receptive to the president's message. Chapter 6 showed that Americans are not especially interested in politics and government; thus, it is not easy to get their attention (see "Young People and Politics: The Generation Gap in Watching the President"). Citizens also have predispositions about public policy

John Kennedy was the first president to use public appearances regularly to seek popular backing for his policies. Despite his popularity and skills as a communicator, Kennedy was often frustrated in his attempts to win widespread support for his administration's "New Frontier" policies.

Young People and Politics

The Generation Gap in Watching the President

If the president is to persuade the public to support him and his policies, he must have the public's attention. He has been getting less of it, however. When President Nixon went on TV to give a speech or hold a press conference in the 1970s, many viewers had little other choice but to watch him if they had their TV on at that time. Today, when regular programming is preempted on the major networks for a presidential address, most people now can turn to either the many alternatives offered via cable TV or to a videotape or DVD if they are not interested in seeing what the president has to say. As a result, presidential speeches have been viewed by a smaller percentage of the American public in recent decades. The president cannot rely on a captive audience for a speech.

As described in Chapter 7, a whole generation has now grown up in the "narrowcasting" age, in which a number of cable stations that cater to particular audiences with a specific interest (such as ESPN, MTV, and C-SPAN) are available, as opposed to traditional "broadcasting." The Reagan years coincided with the rise of narrowcasting. Scholars have found that people over 65 years of age were about twice as likely to view the typical Reagan speech than those under 35. In addition, older people who tuned in were also much more attentive to President Reagan. When senior citizens said they watched a speech, two out of every three said they watched the whole thing. In contrast, less than out one out of every three young viewers said they watched a typical speech in its entirety. Channel surfing, as facilitated by the widespread diffusion of TV and cable remote controls during the 1980s, apparently caught on much

faster with young adults—who used them to switch away from President Reagan's speeches.

The pattern of young people being less attentive to presidential messages has persisted, even for the high profile address President Bush delivered to Congress nine days after the September 11, 2001, terrorist attacks. Older citizens were about 20 percent more likely to tune in to hear from the president than were young adults. One might expect that young people would be especially attentive to speeches regarding the onset of a war that their cohort would be asked to fight. Yet, this was not the case. Young people were about 25 percent less likely to have tuned in to Bush's 2003 State of the Union speech, delivered shortly before the war with Iraq.

In sum, the audience for presidential speeches is now one that is unrepresentative of the general adult public in terms of age. When presidents address the nation in the narrowcasting age, they are actually likely to reach a much larger percentage of older than younger citizens. In some sense, then, presidents are in a less powerful position than in earlier decades. They have lost the ability to communicate directly with the American public anytime they see fit, making it more difficult to obtain the public's support.

Questions for Discussion
- Will the relative inattention to the president by today's young people persist as they age?
- Do you think presidents can govern effectively if they cannot connect to the people?

(however ill-informed) that act as screens for presidential messages. In the absence of national crises, most people are unreceptive to political appeals.[37]

The public may misperceive or ignore even the most basic facts regarding presidential policy. For example, at the end of October 1994, 59 percent of the public thought the economy was still in recession (although it was growing so fast that the Federal Reserve Board was taking strong action to cool it off), only 34 percent knew the deficit had decreased since Clinton became president (it had decreased substantially), and 65 percent thought taxes on the middle class had increased during that period (income taxes had been raised for less than 2 percent of the public).[38] Partly as a consequence of these misconceptions, Clinton was frustrated repeatedly in his efforts to obtain public support for his policy initiatives.[39]

Ronald Reagan, sometimes called the "Great Communicator," was certainly interested in policy change and went to unprecedented lengths to influence public opinion on behalf of such policies as deregulation, decreases in spending on domestic policy, and increases in the defense budget. Bill Clinton was also an extraordinarily able communicator, and he traveled widely and spoke out constantly on behalf of his policies such as those dealing with the economy, health care reform, and free trade. Nevertheless, both presidents were typically unable to obtain the public's support for their initiatives and generally saw public opinion moving against them.[40]

Mobilizing the Public

Sometimes merely changing public opinion is not sufficient, and the president wants the public to communicate its views directly to Congress. Mobilization of the public may be the ultimate weapon in the president's arsenal of resources with which to influence Congress. When the people speak, especially when they speak clearly, Congress listens.

Mobilizing the public involves overcoming formidable barriers and accepting substantial risks. It entails the double burden of obtaining both opinion support and political action from a generally inattentive and apathetic public. If the president tries to mobilize the public and fails, the lack of response speaks clearly to members of Congress.

Perhaps the most notable recent example of the president's mobilization of public opinion to pressure Congress is Ronald Reagan's effort to obtain passage of his tax-cut bill in 1981. Shortly before the crucial vote in the House, the president made a televised plea for support of his tax-cut proposals and asked the people to let their representatives in Congress know how they felt. Evidently Reagan's plea worked; thousands of phone calls, letters, and telegrams poured into congressional offices. On the morning of the vote, Speaker Tip O'Neill declared, "We are experiencing a telephone blitz like this nation has never seen. It's had a devastating effect."[41] The president easily carried the day.

The Reagan administration's effort to mobilize the public on behalf of the 1981 tax cut is significant not only because of the success of presidential leadership but also because it appears to be an anomaly. In the remainder of Reagan's tenure, the president went repeatedly to the people regarding a wide range of policies, including the budget, aid to the Contras in Nicaragua, and defense expenditures. Despite high levels of approval for much of that time, Reagan was never again able to arouse many in his audience to communicate their support of his policies to Congress. Substantial tax cuts hold more appeal to the public than most other issues.

The President and the Press

Despite all their efforts to lead public opinion, presidents do not directly reach the American people on a day-to-day basis. The mass media provide people with most of what they know about chief executives and their policies. The media also interpret and analyze presidential activities, even the president's direct appeals to the public. The press is thus the principal intermediary between the president and the public, and relations with the press are an important aspect of the president's efforts to lead public opinion.

No matter who is in the White House or who reports on presidential activities, presidents and the press tend to be in conflict. George Washington complained that the "calumnies" against his administration were "outrages of common decency." Thomas Jefferson once declared that "nothing in a newspaper is to be believed." Presidents are inherently policy advocates. They want to control the amount and timing of information about their administration, whereas the press wants all the information that exists without delay. As long as their goals are different, presidents and the media are likely to be adversaries.

Because of the importance of the press to the president, the White House monitors the media closely. Some presidents have installed special televisions so they can watch the news on all the networks at once; Lyndon Johnson even had news tickers from AP, UPI, and Reuters in the Oval Office. The White House also goes to great lengths to encourage the media to project a positive image of the president's activities and policies. About one-third of the high-level White House staff members are directly involved in media relations and policy of one type or another, and most staff members are involved at some time in trying to influence the media's portrayal of the president.

The person who most often deals directly with the press is the president's *press secretary*, who serves as a conduit of information from the White House to the press. Press secretaries conduct daily press briefings, giving prepared announcements and answering questions. They and their staff also arrange private interviews with White House officials (often done on a background basis, in which the reporter may not attribute remarks to the person being interviewed), photo opportunities, and travel arrangements for reporters when the president leaves Washington.

The best known direct interaction between the president and the press is the formal presidential press conference. Since the presidency of George Bush, however, prime time, televised press conferences have become rare events. Bill Clinton took office with an antagonistic attitude toward the national media and planned to bypass it rather than use it as part of his political strategy. After a rocky start in his press relations, the president made himself somewhat more accessible to the national press. Like Clinton, George W. Bush has relied more on travel around the country to gain television time to spread his message than on formal press conferences.

Despite their visibility, press conferences are not very useful means of eliciting information. Presidents and their staffs can anticipate most of the questions that will be asked and prepare answers to them ahead of time, reducing the spontaneity of the sessions. Moreover, the large size and public nature of press conferences reduce the candor with which the president responds to questions.

Most of the news coverage of the White House comes under the heading "body watch." In other words, reporters focus on the most visible layer of the president's personal and official activities and provide the public with step-by-step accounts. They are interested in what presidents are going to do, how their actions will affect others, how they view policies and individuals, and how they present themselves, rather than in the substance of policies or the fundamental processes operating in the executive branch. Former ABC White House correspondent Sam Donaldson tells of covering a meeting of Western leaders on the island of Guadeloupe. It was a slow news day, so Donaldson did a story on the roasting of the pig the leaders would be eating that night, including "an exclusive look at the oven in which the pig would be roasted."[42] Because there are daily

The press secretary is the primary channel through which the White House communicates with the media. Here, President George W. Bush's press secretary, Scott McClellan, responds to reporters' questions.

deadlines to meet and television reporters must squeeze their stories into sound bites measured in seconds, not minutes, there is little time for reflection, analysis, or comprehensive coverage.

Bias is the most politically charged issue in relations between the president and the press. A large number of studies have concluded that the news media, including the television networks and major newspapers, are not biased *systematically* toward a particular person, party, or ideology, as measured in the amount or favorability of coverage.[43]

To conclude that the news contains little explicitly partisan or ideological bias is not to argue that the news does not distort reality in its coverage of the president. As the following excerpt from Jimmy Carter's diary regarding a visit to a U.S. Army base in Panama in 1978 illustrates, "objective" reporting can be misleading.

> I told the Army troops that I was in the Navy for 11 years, and they booed. I told them that we depended on the Army to keep the Canal open, and they cheered. Later, the news reports said that there were boos and cheers during my speech.[44]

Making a Difference

Helen Thomas

Journalist Helen Thomas is in her 80s and has been covering the White House since the Kennedy administration. She often arrives at 5:30 A.M., where her office is a tiny cubicle the size of a phone booth. The dean of the White House press, she, more than anyone else, sets the tone for White House coverage and ensures that Americans know as much as possible about the presidency. With a legendary nose for news that can anticipate a story days before it breaks, there is no more tenacious questioner in the press corps.

We learned in Chapter 7 that the news is fundamentally superficial, oversimplified, and often overblown, all of which provides the public with a distorted view of, among other things, presidential activities, statements, policies, and options. We have also seen that the press prefers to frame the news in themes, which both simplifies complex issues and events and provides continuity of persons, institutions, and issues. Once these themes are established, the press tends to maintain them in subsequent stories. Of necessity, themes emphasize some information at the expense of other data, often determining what information is most relevant to news coverage and the context in which it is presented.

Once a stereotype of President Ford as a "bumbler" was established, every stumble was magnified as the press emphasized behavior that fit the mold. He was repeatedly forced to defend his intelligence, and many of his acts and statements were reported as efforts to "act" presidential. Once Ford was typecast, his image was repeatedly reinforced and was very difficult to overcome.[45]

News coverage of the presidency often tends to emphasize the negative (even if the negative stories are presented in a seemingly neutral manner),[46] a trend that has increased over the past 20 years.[47] In the 1980 election campaign, the press portrayed President Carter as mean and Ronald Reagan as imprecise rather than Carter as precise and Reagan as pleasant. The emphasis, in other words, was on the candidates' negative qualities. George Bush received extraordinarily negative press coverage during the 1992 election campaign, and the television networks' portrayal of the economy, for which Bush was blamed, got worse as the economy actually improved to a robust rate of growth![48]

President Clinton received mostly negative coverage during his tenure in office, with a ratio of negative to positive comments on network television of about 2 to 1.[49] When the story broke regarding his affair with Monica Lewinsky, the press engaged in a feeding frenzy, providing an extraordinary amount of information on both the affair and the president's attempts to cover it up. Little of this coverage was favorable to the president.

White House reporters are always looking to expose conflicts of interest and other shady behavior of public officials. In addition, many of their inquiries revolve around the question "Is the president up to the job?" Reporters who are confined in the White House all day may attempt to make up for their lack of investigative reporting with sarcastic and accusatory questioning. Moreover, the desire to keep the public interested and the need for continuous coverage may create in the press a subconscious bias against the presidency that leads to negative stories.

Issues of the Times

The Issue: Who Controls White House News?

A vibrant democracy requires an informed public. The media provide people with most of what they know about chief executives and their policies. The media also interpret and analyze presidential activities. Dealing with the press is an important aspect of every presidency.

Despite their need for each other, the relationship between the White House and the press is often adversarial. The president wishes to control the amount and timing of information about his administration, whereas the press wants all the information that exists without delay. The president's press secretary, who conducts daily press briefings, must manage this difficult relationship. The following article discusses the efforts of George W. Bush's first press secretary, Ari Fleischer, to manage the White House press.

Read All About It

White House Keeps a Grip on Its News

BY JIM RUTENBERG
October 14, 2002

When he stands before the blue curtain of the White House press briefing area, Ari Fleischer, President Bush's press secretary, often seems downright chummy with re-porters as they quiz him about the news of the day.

But in the privacy of his well-ordered office, he is not always so complimentary.

"There can be a tendency," he said in an interview, "of reporters kind of peacocking in front of each other to show each other and their editors, 'I'm the one, I can ask the same question a different way for the 18th time

to get the press secretary to say something different.'"

And the same goes for reporters, who often put on a cordial face during Mr. Fleischer's briefings but, privately, are often fuming.

"If the National Hurricane Center were as stingy with its information, there would be thousands dead," John Roberts, the senior CBS News White House correspondent, deadpanned in his West Wing broadcast booth the other day.

Mr. Roberts may have been joking, but the sentiment was real. "Ari has the uncanny ability to suck information out of a room," he added.

Tensions have escalated far beyond the inevitable grousing

between press secretaries and journalists, who said they could not remember a White House that was more grudging or less forthcoming in informing the press. Complaints from the White House press corps ranged from the paucity of presidential press conferences to fewer briefings from administration policy experts to instances where they believe they have been frozen out by White House officials when they ask questions considered out of bounds.

The White House in turn says these complaints are the result of its strict adherence to its own message,

Please see Grip   Page 429

Grip

Continued from Page 428

and a break from the tradition of gossip-mongering in the press.

Certainly, there have been strains between reporters and the press secretary in previous White Houses, and every administration has tried to prevent leaks and control spin.

But complaints about White House secrecy have reached new levels. White House reporters say they have been given very limited information about the cost, the length, and the risk of any military action in Iraq. They also contend that after Sept. 11, many more policy and governmental decisions are considered off limits for questions because of national security.

"We have a gap between information the public wants to know and information the White House has provided," said Bob Deans, the Cox Newspapers White House correspondent and the president of the White House Correspondents' Association.

"In this administration, the controls on information are tighter than in any other one I have covered," said Bill Plante, a CBS News White House correspondent, who has reported on the presidency since 1980.

Reporters also protest that they get little opportunity to directly quiz the president. Invitations to peek in on meetings between the president and foreign leaders, they say, do not come as often as they did in the past.

White House officials are proud of the discipline that reporters grouse about, and say they have such a relatively low leak factor because the president does not tolerate them, and officials have no interest in them. Still, Mr. Fleischer contends that reporters get as much information as needs to be available at the appropriate time, and have ample opportunity to ask questions at various presidential photo opportunities, pool events and appearances with foreign leaders, which the White House puts at over 100.

"The press has plenty of access," Mr. Fleischer said. "I don't think it's a matter of withholding information— we withhold gossip."

With talk of war increasing, the White House press briefing room has become more confrontational. There, a fierce joust plays out day after day, as members of the White House press

---

Tensions have escalated far beyond the inevitable grousing between press secretaries and journalists, who said they could not remember a White House that was more grudging or less forthcoming in informing the press.

---

corps devise ways to draw Mr. Fleischer out in greater detail on the administration's case against Saddam Hussein—and Mr. Fleischer refuses to venture beyond his message of the day, often carried live on cable news.

For many reporters and producers, the briefings have become an exercise in frustration, a White House-produced television program in which they say they feel like unamused straight men, there to set up policy punchlines for Mr. Fleischer.

"I think Ari goes into the briefing with a message that he intends to deliver," said Campbell Brown, an NBC News White House correspondent, "and what questions are asked is almost irrelevant."

Mr. Fleischer often does seem to stick to practiced catch phrases. Early this month, as the administration worked hard for stiffer United Nations weapons inspections terms, Mr. Fleischer warned six times that Mr. Hussein would play "cat-and-mouse games." During the same briefing, he repeated six times that the president would not accept a congressional war resolution that "ties his hands."

Mr. Fleischer said it was his policy to share new information only when the administration is ready to do so. "Why do they have to have everything spoon-fed ahead of time?" he asked.

Certain bits of information, he said, are withheld for good reason when the president is weighing action in Iraq on one front and considering homeland defense on the other. He said, for instance, that it was not in the administration's interests to divulge how far it was willing to compromise in negotiating over the congressional war resolution.

Mr. Fleischer expressed exasperation at what he considered to be a silly—and ultimately futile—exercise by reporters to prod him to say something controversial.

"Reporters who are polite, who gather their information with honey instead of vinegar, are going to get farther," he said. "I think the days of the shouting, the screaming, cynical approach have really ended."

As far as Mr. Fleischer is concerned, the press will never be satisfied. "I think there is a difference between the press's demand for information and the public's demand for information," he said. "Sometimes I think the press won't be satisfied until there's Oval Cam, and people can watch the president 24 hours a day in the Oval Office."

Think About It

- Do you think you are able to learn everything you need to know to evaluate the president and his policies?
- Should the relationship between the president and the press be adversarial, or should the press limit itself to transmitting what the White House wishes to say?
- Should the press be able to directly question the president more often?

On the other hand, the president has certain advantages in dealing with the press. He is typically portrayed with an aura of dignity and treated with deference.[50] According to Sam Donaldson, who was generally considered an aggressive White House reporter, "For every truly tough question I've put to officials, I've asked a dozen that were about as tough as Grandma's apple dumplings."[51] Thus, when he left after serving as President Reagan's press secretary for six years, Larry Speakes told reporters they had given the Reagan administration "a fair shake."[52]

Remember that the White House can largely control the environment in which the president meets the press—even going so far as to have the Marine helicopters revved as Ronald Reagan approached them so that he could not hear reporters' questions and give unrehearsed responses. (See "Issues of the Times: Who Controls White House News?")

Understanding the American Presidency

Because the presidency is the single most important office in American politics, there has always been concern about whether the president is a threat to democracy. The importance of the president has raised similar concerns for the scope of government in America.

The Presidency and Democracy

From the time the Constitution was written, there has been a fear that the presidency would degenerate into a monarchy or a dictatorship. Even America's greatest presidents have heightened these fears at times. Despite George Washington's well-deserved reputation for peacefully relinquishing power, he also had certain regal tendencies that fanned the suspicions of the Jeffersonians. Abraham Lincoln, for all his humility, exercised extraordinary powers at the outbreak of the Civil War. Since that time, political commentators have alternated between extolling and fearing a strong presidency.

Concerns over presidential power are generally closely related to policy views. Those who oppose the president's policies are the most likely to be concerned about *too much* presidential power. As you have seen, however, aside from acting outside the law and the Constitution, there is little prospect that the presidency will be a threat to democracy. The Madisonian system of checks and balances remains intact.

This system is especially evident in an era characterized by divided government—government in which the president is of one party and a majority in each house of Congress is of the other party. Some observers are concerned that there is too much checking and balancing and too little capacity to act on pressing national challenges. More potentially important legislation fails to pass under divided government than when one party controls both the presidency and Congress.[53] However, major policy change *is* possible under a divided government. One author found that major change is just as likely to occur when the parties share control as when one party holds both the presidency and a majority in each house of Congress.[54]

The Presidency and the Scope of Government

Some of the most noteworthy presidents in the twentieth century (including Theodore Roosevelt, Woodrow Wilson, and Franklin Roosevelt) have successfully advocated substantial increases in the role of the national government. Supporting an increased role for government is not inherent in the presidency, however; leadership can move in many directions.

All seven presidents since Lyndon Johnson have championed constraints on government and limits on spending, especially in domestic policy. It is often said that the American people are ideologically conservative and operationally liberal. For most of the past generation, it has been their will to choose presidents who reflected their ide-

How You Can Make a Difference

The Fast Track to the White House

Since the scandal involving President Clinton and Monica Lewinsky, presidential interns have become the butt of late night comedians' jokes. However, this bad publicity should not discourage you from investigating one of the best experiences available to college students who are eager to get a taste of politics at the top. This prestigious and highly competitive program allows you to actively participate in the federal government's policy decisions from inside the White House.

The White House Internship Program allows select college students to work within over 30 different offices under the control of the Executive Office of the President. Interns work in the more familiar offices of the chief of staff, communications, and press secretary's office as well as the lesser-known offices of the counsel of the president, executive clerk's office, and National Economic Council. Most of these internships are not located within the West Wing (where the president works) but at other buildings, especially the Eisenhower Executive Office Building, within the White House complex. In fact, fewer than a third of the over 500 interns at any one time ever secure

valid passes granting them access to the West Wing. Because the purpose of this program is primarily educational, interns learn skills and information that prove extremely valuable after graduation, whether one pursues a career in public office or the private sector. The work, though, is grinding and seldom glamorous. Long hours and hard work can gain an intern the reputation as a "trooper," a long sought-after title. Intense competition between interns for recognition is normal. Many interns hope to translate their internship into a paid position within the White House or another government agency after graduation.

How you do become a White House intern? There are two routes. First, according to Mike McCurry, former White House spokesman, it helps to have connections. "Many of [the interns] are sons and daughters of supporters," he said. Most college students, however, will compete purely on merit with the other applicants. To learn more, go to the White House homepage (*www.whitehouse.gov/government/wh-intern.html*) to download an application. Along with the application, you must submit a résumé, a personal statement, a writing sample, two letters of recom-

mendation, and a transcript. Although one is only required to be 18 years or older, most interns are either juniors or seniors in college. Among the criteria considered in the selection process are community service, academic achievement, extracurricular activity, and writing skills. Also, be aware that you must pass a background investigation to be admitted to the White House complex. Remember, in a few years, those late night comedy skits will be ancient history, but the opportunity to serve as a White House intern will remain with you (and your résumé) for a lifetime!

What you can do:

- Log onto *www.whitehouse.gov/government/wh-intern.html* for further information.
- Volunteer for a political campaign office in order to gain valuable experience.
- Ask your parents or friends if they know anybody in government. You never know!

Source: Duncan Moon, "Washington Interns: Lots of Gofer Work, Little Glamour," *Christian Science Monitor* 90 (January 29, 1998), 44:12.

ology and a Congress that represented their appetite for public service. It has been the president more often than Congress who has said "no" to government growth.

Summary

Americans expect a lot from presidents—perhaps too much. The myth of the president as a powerhouse clouds Americans' image of presidential reality. Presidents mainly have the power to persuade, not to impose their will.

Presidents do not work alone. Gone are the days when the presidency meant the president plus a few aides and advisors. The cabinet, the Executive Office of the President, and the White House staff all assist today's presidents. These services come at a price, however, and presidents must organize their subordinates effectively for decision-making and policy execution.

Although presidential leadership of Congress is central to all administrations, it often proves frustrating. Presidents rely on their party, the public, and their own legislative skills to persuade Congress to support their policies, but most of the time their efforts are at the margins of coalition building. Rarely are presidents in a position to create—through their own leadership—opportunities for major changes in public policy. They may, however, use their skills to exploit favorable political conditions to bring about policy change.

Some of the president's most important responsibilities fall in the area of national security. As chief diplomat and commander in chief of the armed forces, the president is the country's crisis manager. Still, disputes with Congress over war powers and presidential discretion in foreign affairs demonstrate that even in regard to national security, the president operates within the Madisonian system of checks and balances.

Because presidents are dependent on others to accomplish their goals, their greatest challenge is to obtain support. Public opinion can be an important resource for presidential persuasion, and the White House works hard to influence the public. Public approval of presidents and their policies is often elusive, however; the public does not reliably respond to presidential leadership. The press is the principal intermediary between the president and the public, and relations with the press present yet another challenge to the White House's efforts to lead public opinion.

KEY TERMS

Twenty-second Amendment	National Security Council (NSC)	veto
impeachment	Council of Economic	pocket veto
Watergate	Advisors (CEA)	presidential coattails
Twenty-fifth Amendment	Office of Management	War Powers Resolution
cabinet	and Budget (OMB)	legislative veto
		crisis

INTERNET RESOURCES

www.whitehouse.gov/
Links to presidential speeches, documents, schedules, radio addresses, federal statistics, and White House press releases and briefings.

www.whitehouse.gov/government/eop.html
Information about the Executive Office of the President.

www.ibiblio.org/lia/president/
Links to presidents and presidential libraries.

http://www.ipl.org/div/potus
Background on presidents and their administrations.

www.lib.umich.edu/govdocs/fedprs.html
Wide range of documents regarding the president's activities.

http://www.presidency.ucsb.edu/
Presidential papers, documents, and data.

www.archives.gov/digital_classroom/lessons/watergate_and_ constitution/chronology.html
Contains background and details of the Watergate scandal.

GET CONNECTED

Approving of the President

The White House invests a great deal of time and energy in its public relations efforts designed to increase the president's public approval. A president who is popular with the people may find it easier to enact his initiatives. Throughout a president's term in office, approval ratings rise and fall in reaction to current events in the United States and abroad as well as in response to actions taken by the president. Different polling agencies use different questions to gauge presidential approval, but most follow the pattern set by the Gallup Poll: "Do you approve of the way [name of president] is handling his job as president?"

Search the Web

Go to the Polling Report's Politics & Policy page *http://www.pollingreport.com/POLPOL.htm* and click on "White House" to access the president's job approval ratings. Compare the ratings of the president to the historical information on presidential approval ratings presented in the textbook.

Questions To Ask

- When were the president's job approval ratings the highest? The lowest? Are the ratings trending up or down for the president?
- How similar are the ratings of different polling organizations?
- What were the major reasons for changes in the president's approval?

Why It Matters

Presidents believe that public approval is the political resource that has the most potential to turn a stalemate between the president and Congress into a supportive situation for the president's legislative proposals. The White House also believes that lack of public support strengthens the resolve of the president's opponents and narrows the range in which presidential policies receive the benefit of the doubt.

Get Involved

Keep track of how presidential approval is reported in your local newspaper and on the national television networks. Also watch to see whether Congress is more responsive and press coverage is more positive when the president ranks high in the polls.

To see more Get Connected exercises for Chapter 13, go to www.ablongman.com/edwards.

FOR FURTHER READING

Burke, John P. *The Institutional Presidency*, 2nd ed. Baltimore: Johns Hopkins University Press, 2000. Examines White House organization and presidential advising.

Burke, John P., and Fred I. Greenstein. *How Presidents Test Reality*. New York: Russell Sage Foundation, 1989. Excellent work on presidential decision-making.

Cooper, Phillip J. *By Order of the President*. Lawrence: University Press of Kansas, 2002. The use and abuse of executive direct action.

Edwards, George C., III. *At the Margins: Presidential Leadership of Congress*. New Haven, CT: Yale University Press, 1989. Examines the presidents' efforts to lead Congress and explains their limitations.

Edwards, George C., III. *On Deaf Ears: The Limits of the Bully Pulpit*. New Haven, CT: Yale University Press, 2003. The effect of the president's efforts to change public opinion in the White House's pursuit of popular support.

Fisher, Louis. *Constitutional Conflicts Between Congress and the President*, 4th ed. rev. Lawrence: University Press of Kansas, 1997. Presents the constitutional dimensions of the separation of powers.

Greenstein, Fred. *The Presidential Difference*. New York: Free Press, 2000. Leadership styles of modern presidents.

Hart, John. *The Presidential Branch*, 2nd ed. Chatham, NJ: Chatham House, 1995. Discusses the Executive Office of the President and the White House staff.

Jacobs, Lawrence R., and Robert Y. Shapiro. *Politicians Don't Pander*. Chicago: University of Chicago Press, 2000. The relationship between leaders and public opinion.

Neustadt, Richard E. *Presidential Power and the Modern Presidents*. New York: Free Press, 1990. The most influential book on the American presidency; argues that presidential power is the power to persuade.

Pfiffner, James P. *The Strategic Presidency*, 2nd ed. Lawrence: University Press of Kansas, 1996. Organizing the presidency.

The Congress, the President, and the Budget: The Politics of Taxing and Spending

14

Chapter Outline

Sources of Federal Revenue

The New York Times **Issues of the Times**

Federal Expenditures

The Budgetary Process

Understanding Budgeting

Summary

In 1776 the cry of "no taxation without representation" was enough to spark a revolution. Today issues of taxes and budgetary measures continue to dominate national public policy: How much should we spend for homeland security, health care for the elderly, subsidized student loans, or cleaning up the environment? And how should we pay for these programs?

In the presidential election of 2004, George W. Bush argued that we should make temporary tax cuts permanent while John Kerry proposed increasing taxes on the wealthiest Americans. Kerry was also more supportive of investing in new or expanded programs.

Politicians who attempt to make tough decisions about the budget risk incurring voters' wrath. In 1985, Republican senators took the lead with a reform that was designed to balance the budget. In the 1986 congressional elections, Republicans lost control of the

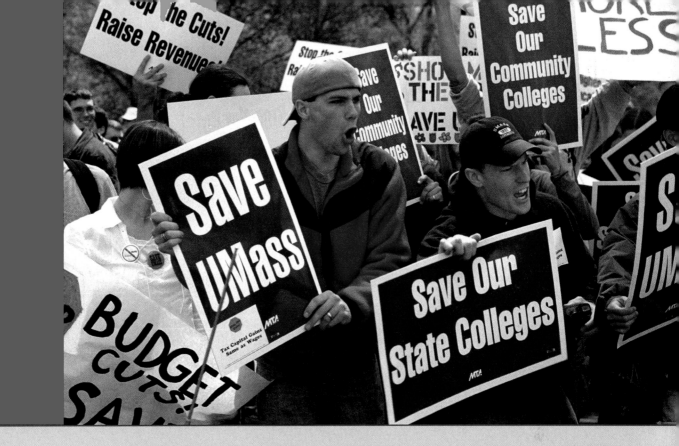

Senate. In 1990, President George Bush bit the bullet and reversed his pledge not to raise taxes. He agreed to a budget deal with the congressional Democrats that succeeded in reducing the deficit and limiting spending. In 1992, he lost his bid for reelection.

In 1993, President Clinton followed Bush's precedent and reversed his promise to lower taxes with a program of higher taxes and spending constraints. In the 1994 elections, Republicans won majorities in both houses of Congress for the first time since 1952. They pledged to cut taxes, balance the budget, and reduce expenditures for important social welfare programs. A two-year political battle ensued between congressional Republicans and President Clinton, who vigorously opposed the scope of their proposals. In the end, little changed, and each side vowed to take its case to the American people in the 1996 elections.

The public—which typically seeks a balanced budget, little or no cut in government programs, and tax relief—split its decision. The Democrats won the presidency, but Republicans won both houses of Congress—the only time that had *ever* happened. In the 1998 elections, little changed. George W. Bush advocated a large tax cut as the centerpiece of his campaign in the 2000 presidential election and won

following what was perhaps the closest election in American history. Congress was also narrowly divided. It is not surprising that the battle of the budget remains at the center of American politics.

Two questions are central to public policy: *Who bears the burdens of paying for government? Who receives the benefits?* Some observers are concerned that democracy poses a danger to budgeting. Do politicians seek to "buy" votes by spending public funds on things voters will like—and will remember on Election Day? Or is spending the result of demands made on government services by the many segments of American society? In addition, does the public choose to "soak the rich" with taxes that redistribute income?

Budgets are central to our theme of the scope of government. Indeed, for many programs, budgeting *is* policy. The amount of money spent on a program determines how many people are served, how well they are served, or how much of something (weapons, vaccines, and so on) the government can purchase. The bigger the budget, the bigger the government. But is the growth of the government's budget inevitable? Or are the battles over the allocation of scarce public resources actually a *constraint* on government?

The Constitution allocates various tasks to both the president and Congress, but it generally leaves to each branch the decision of whether to exercise its power to perform a certain task. There is an exception, however. Every year the president and Congress must appropriate funds. If they fail to do so, the government will come to a standstill. The army will be idled, Social Security offices will close, and food stamps will not be distributed to the poor.

Everyone has a basic understanding of budgeting. Public budgets are superficially like personal budgets. Aaron Wildavsky has remarked that a budget is a document that "contains words and figures that propose expenditures for certain objects and purposes." There is more to public budgets than bookkeeping, however, because such a **budget** is a policy document allocating burdens (taxes) and benefits (expenditures). Thus, "budgeting is concerned with translating financial resources into human purposes. A budget therefore may also be characterized as a series of goals with price tags attached."[1]

Over the past 30 years, the national government has run up large annual budget deficits. A budget **deficit** occurs when **expenditures** exceed **revenues** in a fiscal year. In other words, the national government spends more money than it receives in taxes. As a result, the total national debt rose sharply during the 1980s, increasing from less than $1 trillion to more than $8 trillion by the year 2005. About 9 percent of all current budget expenditures go to paying just the *interest* on this debt.

The president and Congress have often been caught in a budgetary squeeze: Americans want them to balance the budget, maintain or increase the level of government spending on most policies, and keep taxes low. As a result, the president and Congress are preoccupied with budgeting, trying to cope with these contradictory demands.

In this chapter you will learn how the president and Congress produce a budget, making decisions on both taxes and expenditures. In short, you will look at how government manages its money—which is, of course, really *your* money.

Sources of Federal Revenue

"Taxes," said the late Supreme Court Justice Oliver Wendell Holmes, Jr., "are what we pay for civilization." Despite his assertion that "I like to pay taxes," most taxpayers throughout history do not agree. The art of taxation, said Jean-Baptiste Colbert, Louis XIV's finance minister, is in "so plucking the goose as to procure the largest quantity of feathers with the least possible amount of hissing."[2] In Figure 14.1, you can see where the federal government has been getting its feathers. Only a small share comes from excise taxes (a tax levied upon the manufacture, transportation, sale, or consumption of a good—for example, those on gasoline) and other sources; the three major sources of federal revenues are the personal and corporate income tax, social insurance taxes, and borrowing.

Income Tax

Millions of bleary-eyed American taxpayers struggle to the post office before midnight every April 15th to mail their income tax forms. Individuals are required to pay the government a portion of the money they earn; this portion is an **income tax.** Although the government briefly adopted an income tax during the Civil War, the first peacetime income tax was enacted in 1894. Even though the tax was only 2 percent of income earned beyond the then magnificent sum of $4,000, a lawyer opposing it called the tax the first step of a "communist march." The Supreme Court wasted little time in declaring the tax unconstitutional in *Pollock v. Farmer's Loan and Trust Co.* (1895).

In 1913, the **Sixteenth Amendment** was added to the Constitution, explicitly permitting Congress to levy an income tax. Congress was already receiving income tax revenue before the amendment was ratified, however, and the *Internal Revenue Service*

---

budget

A policy document allocating burdens (taxes) and benefits (expenditures).

deficit

An excess of federal **expenditures** over federal **revenues.**

expenditures

Federal spending of **revenues.** Major areas of such spending are social services and the military.

revenues

The financial resources of **the federal government.** The individual income tax and Social Security tax are two major sources of revenue.

income tax

Shares of individual wages and corporate revenues collected by the government. The **Sixteenth Amendment** explicitly authorized Congress to levy a tax on income. See also **Internal Revenue Service.**

Sixteenth Amendment

The constitutional amendment adopted in 1913 that explicitly permitted Congress to levy an **income tax.**

Figure 14.1   Federal Revenues

Forty-three percent of federal revenues come from individual income taxes. Another 40 percent comes from social insurance taxes.

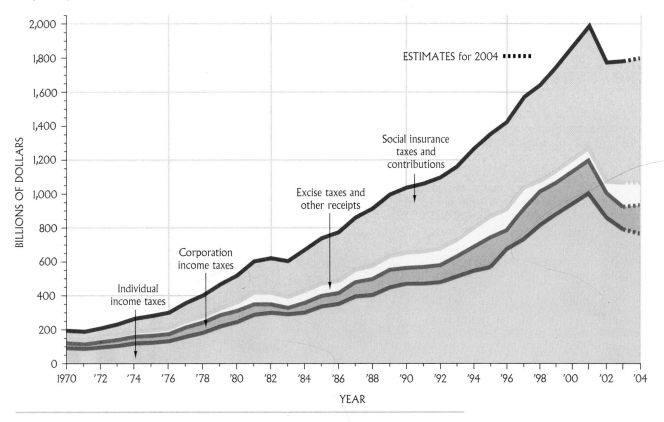

Source: Budget of the United States Government, Fiscal Year 2005: Historical Tables (Washington, D.C.: U.S. Government Printing Office, 2004), Table 2.1.

was established to collect it. Today the IRS receives more than 130 million individual tax returns each year. People or computers scrutinize each return. In addition, the IRS audits in greater detail more than 750,000 returns, investigates thousands of suspected criminal violations of the tax laws, and annually prosecutes and secures the conviction of thousands of errant taxpayers or nonpayers.[3] Never a popular agency, in recent years the IRS has received substantial criticism for abusing taxpayers with its aggressive efforts to enforce the tax code. In 1998 Congress passed a law designed to rein in the IRS and make it a more consumer-oriented agency.

Corporations, like individuals, pay income taxes. Although corporate taxes once yielded more revenues than individual income taxes, this is no longer true. Today corporate taxes yield about 9 cents of every federal revenue dollar, compared with 43 cents from individual income taxes.

The income tax is generally *progressive*, meaning that those with more taxable income not only pay more taxes but also pay higher *rates* of tax on that income. As a result, the 10 percent of taxpayers with the highest incomes pay about two-thirds of all the income taxes in the country while those in the bottom 50 percent of taxable income pay less than 4 percent of all income taxes.[4] Some people feel that a progressive tax is the fairest type of taxation because those who have the most pay higher rates. Others see things differently and propose a "flat" tax, with everyone taxed at the same rate. Still others suggest that we abandon the income tax altogether and rely on a national sales tax, much like the sales taxes in most states. As you can see, it is easy to criticize the income tax but difficult to obtain agreement on a replacement (see "Issues of the Times: Who Should Bear the Burden of Taxes?").

Issues of the Times

The Issue: Who Should Bear the Burden of Taxes?

Individuals in the United States are subject to two main types of taxes: income taxes and social insurance taxes (often called "payroll"). People with higher incomes pay a higher rate of taxes on their income, and many Americans pay no income taxes at all. Americans paid payroll taxes, which support Social Security and Medicare, on the first $87,900 of income in 2004, and everyone pays the same rate (although higher income people pay a small tax for Medicare on all their income).

A perennial source of conflict in politics is the question of how high taxes should be and who should pay them. President George W. Bush made income tax reduction a priority in his first term. Republicans argued that it was quite appropriate to reduce the taxes on wealthier taxpayers because they pay most of the income taxes. Democrats responded that the president's income tax cuts increased the deficit and allocated most of the benefits to the

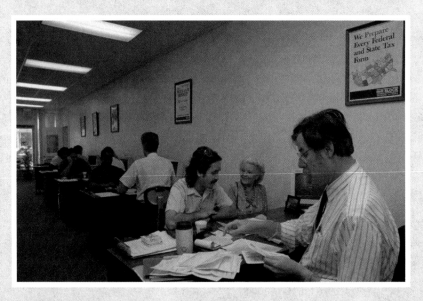

wealthy, who ought to bear the burden of income taxation. Moreover, they say, the less well-off Americans still bear the burden

of social insurance taxes. In his second term, President Bush is considering changing the basic structure of federal taxes.

Read All About It

Proposals Would Shift Burden From Wealthy to Middle Class

By Edmund L. Andrews
October 6, 2004

Almost all experts agree that the current tax code is hideously complicated and often unfair. But they also say that accomplishing any fundamental change will be hideously difficult. . .

Republican and Democratic tax experts caution that making the tax code simpler would almost certainly set off a fierce political battle over the issue of fairness, because most options under discussion would shift a substantial share of the tax burden from high-income families to middle-income earners. . . .

Supporters of a consumption tax, which can take many different forms, say it could be far simpler than today's system and would greatly increase incentives for people to save and to invest.

Please see Burden   Page 439

Burden

Continued from Page 438

The options range from a flat tax on wages to some sort of national sales tax to an income tax that excludes almost all earnings from investment and business profits. Best of all, from the viewpoint of many economists, would be a pure consumption tax, which requires people to pay taxes only on the amount of money they spend each year.

To Republicans, "most of the tax reform ideas revolve around the idea of taxing consumption," said Representative Paul Ryan, Republican of Wisconsin and a staunch proponent of a major tax overhaul. "It can be a flat tax or a sales tax or anything in between, but all of those are consumption taxes."

The political obstacles, however, are enormous. An internal report by the Treasury Department in 2002, which analyzed five approaches to tax reform, concluded that either a flat income tax or a flat consumption tax would benefit higher income families at the expense of others.

"Any reform is likely to have vocal losers and largely silent winners," said the report, which was recently made public by Ron Suskind, author of a book on Paul H. O'Neill, Mr. Bush's first Treasury secretary. "In other countries, adoption of a consumption tax has led to election losses for the incumbent party." . . .

Republican tax experts acknowledge that tax reform would ignite a bitter battle over fairness.

"Contrary to popular belief, the existing tax system is very progressive," said Kenneth Kies, a tax lobbyist and former staff director of the Joint Committee on Taxation. "The rich basically pay the income tax. It's very hard to take any of the reform options out there and do them without having a progressivity problem."

> ## Republican tax experts acknowledge that tax reform would ignite a bitter battle over fairness.

Supporters of a consumption tax or a flat income tax say such a system could still place a heavier tax burden on high-income people. A system that imposed a national sales tax or a European-style value-added tax, for example, could provide rebates to lower income people and include an extra tax for people with high incomes.

But most experts say it would be hard to design a consumption tax that did not shift some of the tax burden away from high-income taxpayers, because most taxable investment income goes to a very small slice of people at the very top of the income spectrum. Wealthy people typically spend a smaller share of their earnings than those with less income.

Leonard E. Burman, a senior analyst at the Urban Institute, estimated that half of all stock dividends in 2000 went to the top 3.8 percent of households, those with incomes higher than $200,000 a year. Wealthy people also devote a much smaller share of their incomes to consumption—about a third for families with incomes above $200,000, compared with about 93 percent for families with incomes between $20,000 and $30,000.

"You cannot do reform without spending a huge amount of money and identifying a huge number of losers," Mr. Burman said. "It's almost impossible to design a consumption tax that doesn't shift some of the tax burden from high-income tax payers." . . .

Tax reform could easily clash with Mr. Bush's call for an ownership society. Even as he called for a simpler system at the Republican convention, he proposed new tax breaks for businesses that build single-family homes and implied that he would preserve the deduction for home mortgage interest.

"You can't separate the ownership society and tax reform," said C. Eugene Steuerle, a senior fellow at the Urban Institute who coordinated the Treasury Department's last big effort at overhauling the income tax, under President Reagan in 1986. "We now have $150 billion in housing subsidies, most of that in the tax system." . . .

Think About It

- Who should bear the burden of taxes? Should the rich pay not only more taxes but also a higher rate of taxation?
- Is it appropriate for a small percentage of Americans to receive most of the benefits from a policy?

- Is it healthy for American society that a small percentage of the people pay most of the income tax?
- Should average people pay for their own Social Security and Medicare benefits, or should wealthier citizens subsidize them?

Why It Matters

The Progressive Income Tax
The principal source of revenue for the federal government is the income tax, which is progressive in that those with higher incomes typically pay a higher rate of taxes. What if everyone paid the same rate? Most people would probably find it unfair to pay taxes at the same rate as a millionaire. If a uniform tax rate were set at a level that everyone could afford to pay, it would have to be set very low. In this case there may not be sufficient revenues to fund critical government programs.

---

federal debt

All the money borrowed by the federal government over the years and still outstanding. Today the federal debt is more than $8 trillion.

Social Insurance Taxes

Both employers and employees pay Social Security taxes. Money is deducted from employees' paychecks and matched by their employers. Unlike other taxes, these payments do not go into the government's general money fund but are earmarked for a specific purpose: the Social Security Trust Fund that pays benefits to the elderly, the disabled, the widowed, and the unemployed.

Social Security taxes have grown faster than any other source of federal revenue, and they will continue to grow as the population ages. In 1957, these taxes made up a mere 12 percent of federal revenues; today they account for nearly 40 percent. In 2004, employees and employers each paid a Social Security tax equal to 6.2 percent of the first $87,900 of earnings, and for Medicare they paid another 1.45 percent on all earnings.

Borrowing

Like families and firms, the federal government may borrow money to make ends meet. When families and firms need money, they go to their neighborhood bank, savings and loan association, or moneylender. When the federal government wants to borrow money, the Treasury Department sells bonds, guaranteeing to pay interest to the bondholder. Citizens, corporations, mutual funds, and other financial institutions can all purchase these bonds; there is always a lively market for government bonds. In addition, the federal government has "intragovernmental" debt on its books. This debt is what the Treasury owes various Social Security and other trust funds because the government has been using for its general purposes payroll taxes and other taxes designated to fund specific programs.

Most government borrowing is not for its capital needs (such as a house or a factory) but for its day-to-day expenses. Most families wisely do not borrow money for their food and clothing, yet the government has largely borrowed money for its farm subsidies, its military pensions, and its aid to states and cities.

Today the **federal debt**—all the money borrowed over the years that is still outstanding—exceeds $8 *trillion* (see Figure 14.2). Nine percent of all federal expenditures go to paying interest on this debt rather than paying for current policies. Yesterday's consumption of public policies is at the expense of tomorrow's taxpayers because borrowing money shifts the burden of repayment to future taxpayers who will have to service the debt and pay the principal. Every dollar that the government borrows today will cost taxpayers many more dollars in interest over the next 30 years. These dollars cannot be spent on health care, education, or lower taxes. Paying the interest on the debt is not optional.

Many economists and policymakers are concerned about the national debt.[5] Government borrowing may crowd out private borrowers, both individuals and businesses, from the loan marketplace. For instance, your local bank may know that you are a low-risk borrower, but it thinks the federal government is an even lower risk. Over the past 70 years a substantial percentage of all the net private savings in the country have gone to the federal government. Most economists believe that under some conditions this competition to borrow money increases interest rates and makes it more difficult for businesses to invest in capital expenditures (such as new plants and equipment) that produce economic growth. Higher interest rates also raise the costs to individuals of financing homes or credit card purchases.

Large deficits also make the American government dependent on foreign investors, including other governments, to fund its debt—not a favorable position for a superpower. Foreign investors currently hold about one-fifth of the national debt.

Others say such fears are overblown and that the national debt has relatively little to do with the overall health of the U.S. economy. Our national debt, they argue, is a smaller percentage of our economy and of the total amount of money available for borrowing than in past years. For decades a defining principle of the Republican

Figure 14.2   Total National Debt

The national debt climbed steadily throughout the 1980s, leveled off in the 1990s, and rose again in this decade.

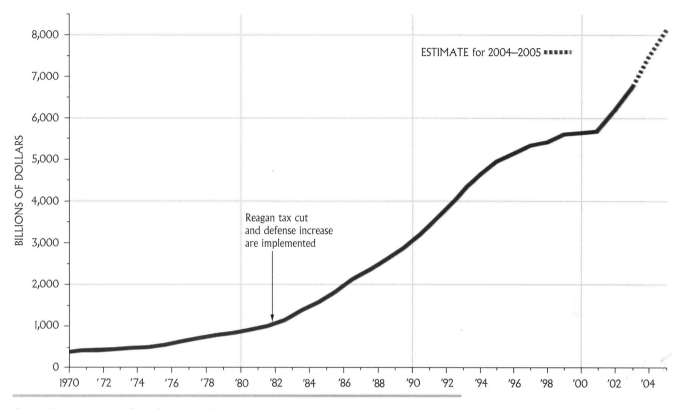

Source: Budget of the United States Government, Fiscal Year 2005: Historical Tables (Washington, D.C.: U.S. Government Printing Office, 2004), Table 7.1.

Party was to curtail federal spending to reduce the federal deficit. In recent years, however, this philosophy has changed and Republicans now support cutting taxes (and thus decreasing revenues), hopefully to stimulate the economy so that it produces more tax revenue in the long run. George W. Bush's tax-cut proposals were based on this principle. Democrats see the issue differently, arguing that the tax cuts never replace the lost revenue and leave the country with an ever-increasing debt to service in the future.

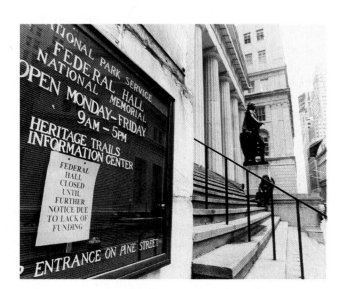

Because budgetary policy is so important, decision makers may be reluctant to compromise. In 1995–1996, the inability of the president and Congress to reach agreement led to the shutdown of the federal government.

Why It Matters

Deficit Spending

The federal government can run a deficit and borrow money to pay its current expenses. States and cities can only borrow (by issuing bonds) for long-term capital expenses such as roads and schools. If the Constitution required a balanced budget, the federal government could not borrow money to provide increased services during an economic downturn; nor could it cut taxes to stimulate the economy in such a situation.

Sometimes politicians complain that because families and businesses and even state and local governments balance their budgets, the federal government ought to be able to do the same. Such statements reflect a fundamental misunderstanding of budgeting, however. Most families do *not* balance their budgets. They use credit cards to give themselves instant loans, and they go to the bank to borrow money to purchase automobiles, boats, and, most important, homes. The mortgages on their homes are debts they owe for most of their lives.

Unlike state and local governments and private businesses, the federal government does not have a *capital budget*, a budget for expenditures on items that will serve for the long term, such as equipment, roads, and buildings. Thus, for example, when airlines purchase new airplanes or when school districts build new schools, they do not pay for them out of current income. Instead, they borrow money, often through issuing bonds. These debts do not count against the operating budget. When the federal government purchases new jets for the air force or new buildings for medical research, however, these purchases are counted as current expenditures and run up the deficit.

Despite its borrowing habits, most of the government's income still comes from taxes. Few government policies provoke more heated discussion than taxation.

Taxes and Public Policy

No government policy affects as many Americans as tax policy. In addition to raising revenues to finance its services, the government can use taxes to make citizens' incomes more nearly or less nearly equal, to encourage or discourage growth in the economy, and to promote specific interests. Whereas Chapters 17 and 18 discuss how taxes affect economic and equality issues, the following sections focus on how tax policies can promote the interests of particular groups or encourage specific activities.

Tax Loopholes.   No discussion of taxes goes very far before the subject of tax loopholes comes up. Difficult to define, a *tax loophole* is presumably a tax break or tax benefit. The IRS Code, which specifies what income is subject to taxation, contains many legal exemptions, deductions, and special cases. Of course, some taxpayers benefit more from these loopholes than others. Jimmy Carter, campaigning for the presidency, called the American tax system a "national disgrace" because of its special treatment of favored taxpayers. Businesspeople, he complained, could deduct costly "three-martini lunches" as business expenses, whereas ordinary workers, carrying coffee in a Thermos and a sandwich to work, could not write off their lunch expenses.

In 1975, Texas computer magnate and 1992 and 1996 presidential candidate H. Ross Perot hired a former Internal Revenue Service commissioner to lobby for a change in the tax code. The proposed change would have saved Perot $15 million in taxes. The amendment passed through the House Ways and Means Committee (billionaire Perot was reported to be a generous contributor to the campaign chests of several members) but was killed on the House floor when the press reported that only Perot would benefit from the proposed provision.[6]

Tax loopholes may offend Americans' sense of fair play, but they cost the treasury relatively little because they apply to only a few people. Loopholes are actually only one type of tax expenditure.

tax expenditures

Revenue losses that result from special exemptions, exclusions, or deductions on federal tax law.

Tax Expenditures.   What does cost the federal budget a substantial sum is the system of **tax expenditures,** defined by the 1974 Budget Act as "revenue losses attributable to provisions of the federal tax laws which allow a special exemption, exclusion, or deduction." These expenditures represent the difference between what the government actually collects in taxes and what it would have collected without special exemptions. Thus tax expenditures amount to subsidies for different activities. For example,

- The government *could* send checks for billions of dollars to charities. Instead, it permits some taxpayers to deduct their contributions to charities from their income. Thus the government encourages charitable contributions.
- The government *could* give cash to families with the desire and financial means to buy a home. Instead, it permits homeowners to deduct from their income the billions of dollars they collectively pay each year in mortgage interest.
- The government *could* write a check to all businesses that invest in new plants and equipment. Instead, it allows such businesses to deduct these expenses from their taxes at a more rapid rate than they deduct other expenses. In effect, the owners of these businesses, including stockholders, get a subsidy that is unavailable to owners of other businesses.

Tax expenditures are among the most obscure aspects of a generally obscure budgetary process, partly because they receive no regular review by Congress—a great advantage for those who benefit from a tax expenditure. Few ordinary citizens seem to realize their scope; you can see the magnitude of tax expenditures in Table 14.1.

On the whole, tax expenditures benefit middle- and upper-income taxpayers and corporations. Poorer people, who tend not to own homes, can take little advantage of provisions that permit homeowners to deduct mortgage interest payments. Likewise, poorer people in general can take less advantage of a deduction for charitable expenses. Students, however, are an exception to this generalization (see "Young People and Politics: Education and the Federal Tax Code").

Table 14.1   Tax Expenditures: The Money Government Does Not Collect

Tax expenditures are essentially monies that government could collect but does not because they are exempted from taxation. The Office of Management and Budget estimated that the total tax expenditures in 2005 would be nearly $750 billion—an amount equal to more than 40 percent of the total federal receipts. Individuals receive most of the tax expenditures, and corporations get the rest. Here are some of the largest tax expenditures and their cost to the treasury:

TAX EXPENDITURE	MAIN BENEFICIARY	COST
Exclusion of company-paid benefits	Families	$122 billion
Exclusion of company contributions to pension funds	Families	$121 billion
Deduction of mortgage interest on owner-occupied houses	Families	$77 billion
Deductions for state and local taxes	Families	$66 billion
Capital gains	Families	$50 billion
Deductions for charitable contributions	Families and corporations	$37 billion
Child credit	Families	$30 billion
Exclusion of Social Security benefits	Families	$27 billion
Exclusion for interest earned on state and local government bonds	Families	$26 billion
Exclusion of interest on life insurance savings	Families	$22 billion
Deferral of capital gains on home sales	Families	$21 billion
Exclusion of Individual Retirement Account contributions and earnings	Families	$20 billion

Government could lower overall tax rates by taxing things it does not currently tax, such as Social Security benefits, pension fund contributions, charitable contributions, and the like. You can easily figure out, though, that these are not popular items to tax, and doing so would evoke strong opposition from powerful interest groups.

Source: Budget of the United States Government, Fiscal Year 2005: Analytical Perspectives (Washington, D.C.: U.S. Government Printing Office, 2004), Table 18.3.

Young People and Politics

Education and the Federal Tax Code

If you think that the federal income tax is something that does not affect you much as a student, you are wrong. If you are footing the costs of higher education for yourself or your family, education tax credits can help offset these costs. On the other hand, if you think the rules for obtaining a tax credit are simple, you are also wrong.

First, there is the Hope Credit, which applies only for the first two years of post-secondary education, such as college or vocational school. It can be worth up to $1,500 per eligible student, per year. It does not apply to graduate and professional-level programs. You are allowed 100 percent of the first $1,000 of qualified tuition and related fees paid during the tax year, plus 50 percent of the next $1,000. To receive the credit, you must be enrolled at least half-time.

The Lifetime Learning Credit applies to undergraduate, graduate, and professional degree courses, including instruction to acquire or improve your job skills. If you qualify, your credit equals 20 percent of the first $10,000 of post-secondary tuition and fees you pay during the year for all eligible students, for a maximum credit of $2,000 per tax return.

The Hope Credit and the Lifetime Learning Credit are education credits you can subtract in full from your federal income tax, not just deduct from your taxable income.

Naturally, there are restrictions on claiming these credits. To qualify for either credit, you must pay post-secondary tuition and fees for yourself, your spouse, or your dependent. The credit may be claimed by the parent or the student, but not by both. However, if the student was claimed as a dependent, the student cannot claim the credit. Moreover, you cannot claim both the Hope and Lifetime Learning Credits for the same student (such as yourself) in the same year. Parents with children or attending school themselves can claim more than one Hope credit but only one Lifetime Learning Credit.

These credits are not for everyone. They are phased out for Modified Adjusted Gross Income (AGI) above $41,000 ($83,000 for married filing jointly) and eliminated completely for Modified AGI of $51,000 or more ($103,000 for married filing jointly). If a taxpayer is married, the credit may be claimed only on a joint return. In addition, the Hope Credit is not allowed for a student convicted of a felony drug offense.

A taxpayer may also take a deduction for up to $4,000 of higher education expenses, but only when opting not to use the education credits. A different deduction lets taxpayers recoup some of the cost of student loan interests. It and other deductions and credits also begin to diminish as taxpayers earn more.

Welcome to the federal tax code. As you can see, Congress has chosen to give students benefits in the tax code, but it has also been concerned that people do not abuse these benefits. Thus, even students have to face the intricacies of the federal tax code and work out the myriad tax credits and deductions that help defray the costs of a college education. In the end, however, it is worth the effort.

Questions for Discussion
- Why doesn't Congress simply appropriate money for students and send them a check instead of relying on the tax code?
- What are the obstacles to simplifying the tax code?

To some, tax expenditures such as business-related deductions, tuition tax credits, and capital gains tax rates are loopholes. To others, they are public policy choices that support a social activity worth subsidizing. Either way, they amount to the same thing: revenues that the government loses because certain items are exempted from normal taxation or are taxed at lower rates. The Office of Management and Budget (OMB) estimates that the total tax expenditures equal more than 40 percent of the federal government's total receipts.

Tax Reduction. The annual rite of spring—the preparation of individual tax returns—is invariably accompanied by calls for tax reform and, frequently, tax reduction. Early in his administration, President Reagan proposed a massive tax-cut bill. Standing in the way of tax cuts is never popular, and in July 1981, Congress passed Reagan's tax-cutting proposal. Over a three-year period, the federal tax bills of Americans were reduced 25 percent, corporate income taxes were also reduced, new tax incentives were provided for personal savings and corporate investment, and taxes were *indexed* to the cost of living. Indexing taxes meant that beginning in 1985, government no longer received a larger share of income when inflation pushed incomes into higher brackets while the tax rates stayed the same. (This point is important because people with high incomes also pay a higher *percentage* of their incomes in taxes.)

Families with high incomes saved many thousands of dollars on taxes, but those at the lower end of the income ladder saw little change in their tax burden because social insurance and excise taxes (which fall disproportionately on these people) rose during the same period. Many blamed the massive deficits of the 1980s and 1990s at least partially on the 1981 tax cuts, as government continued to spend but at the same time reduced its revenues.

To deal with these deficits, in 1993 President Clinton persuaded Congress to raise the income tax rate on those in the top 2 percent of income and the top corporate income tax rate. Congress also increased a small energy tax that would be paid by all but those with low incomes.

When budget surpluses materialized (briefly) in the late 1990s, cutting taxes was once again a popular rallying cry for some politicians, including George W. Bush. In 2001, Congress enacted a tax cut that gradually lowered tax rates over the next ten years, and in 2003 it reduced the tax rates on capital gains and dividends. When deficits reappeared, critics charged that the president was fiscally irresponsible. The appropriate level of taxation remains one of the most vexing problems in American politics (see "America in Perspective: How Much Is Too Much?").

Simulation

You Are Trying to Get a Tax Cut

America in Perspective

How Much Is Too Much?

No one likes to pay taxes, and it is common for Americans—and citizens all over the world—to complain that taxes are too high. The figures in the accompanying graph show that the national, state, and local governments in the United States tax a smaller percentage of the resources of the country than do those in almost all other democracies with developed economies. The Scandinavian countries of Sweden, Finland, and Denmark take about half the wealth of the country in taxes each year.

Comparatively, citizens in the United States have a rather light tax burden. Naturally, tax levels are related to the level of public services that governments provide. If you compare this graph with "America in Perspective: How Big Is Too Big?" you will see that the big taxers are also the big spenders.

Source: Organization for Economic Cooperation and Development, 2004.

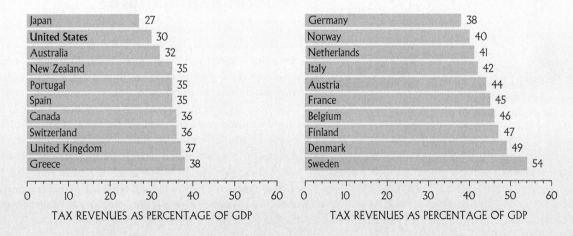

TOTAL GOVERNMENT TAX REVENUES AS A PERCENTAGE OF THE GROSS DOMESTIC PRODUCT

Country	Tax revenue (% of GDP)
Japan	27
United States	30
Australia	32
New Zealand	35
Portugal	35
Spain	35
Canada	36
Switzerland	36
United Kingdom	37
Greece	38
Germany	38
Norway	40
Netherlands	41
Italy	42
Austria	44
France	45
Belgium	46
Finland	47
Denmark	49
Sweden	54

TAX REVENUES AS PERCENTAGE OF GDP

President Reagan signs the Tax Reform Act of 1986, passed with the backing of congressional leaders and administration officials. The legislation—the most wide-ranging reform of federal tax policy since the Sixteenth Amendment legalized income taxes in 1913—was implemented despite protests from numerous interest groups that did not want to lose their tax deductions.

Tax Reform.   Gripes about taxes in America are at least as old as the Boston Tea Party. When President Reagan first revealed his massive tax simplification plan in 1985 — with its proposals to eliminate many tax deductions and tax expenditures—it was met with howls of protest. The insurance industry, for example, launched a $6 million advertising campaign to save the tax deductions for fringe benefits (much of which are in the form of life and health insurance) that employers set aside for employees. A pitched battle raged between tax reformers and interest groups determined to hold on to their tax benefits.

For once, however, a tax reform plan was not derailed. Democrats, including the powerful House Ways and Means Committee chair, Dan Rostenkowski, were enthusiastic about tax reform. They also did not want the Republicans to get all the credit for it. In fact, the president actually had more problems obtaining the support of those in his own party and had to make an unusual trip to Capitol Hill to plead with House Republicans to support the tax bill after its initial defeat when it came to the floor.

The Senate posed an even bigger problem because the bill was loaded with special tax treatments for a wide variety of groups. While the president was on a trip abroad, the Finance Committee met behind closed doors and emerged with a bill similar in spirit to the bill supported by the president and the House. The *Tax Reform Act of 1986* was one of the most sweeping alterations in federal tax policy history. It eliminated or reduced the value of many tax deductions, removed several million low-income individuals from the tax rolls, and greatly reduced the number of tax brackets (categories of income that are taxed at different rates).

Making a Difference

Robert McIntyre

Robert McIntyre is the director of Citizens for Tax Justice, a nonpartisan research and advocacy group that fights against the armies of special interest lobbyists for corporations and the wealthy. His report on "The Top Ten Corporate Freeloaders" became an instant media sensation and was a key turning point in the debate over tax reform that led to the Tax Reform Act of 1986. He frequently testifies before Congress, appears on television, and writes articles for major newspapers and magazines, raising important questions about tax policies and keeping public officials and private corporations on their toes.

Federal Expenditures

In 1932, when President Franklin D. Roosevelt took office in the midst of the Great Depression, the federal government was spending just over $3 billion a year. Today, that sum would get the federal government through less than a day. Program costs once measured in the millions are now measured in billions. Comparisons over time are a little misleading, of course, because they do not account for changes in the value of the dollar. You can see in Figure 14.3 how the federal budget has grown in actual dollars (not controlling for changes in the value of the dollar).

Figure 14.3 makes two interesting points. First, the policies and programs on which the government spends money change over time. Second, expenditures keep rising. The following sections explore three important questions: Why are government

Figure 14.3   Federal Expenditures

The biggest category of federal expenditures is payments to individuals. National defense accounts for about one-fifth of the budget.

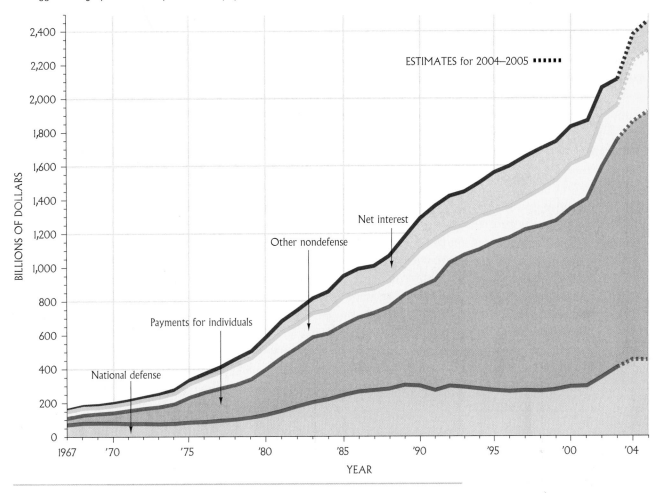

Source: Budget of the United States Government, Fiscal Year 2005: Historical Tables (Washington, D.C.: U.S. Government Printing Office, 2004), Table 6.1.

budgets so big? Where does the money go? Why is it difficult to control federal expenditures?

Big Governments, Big Budgets

One answer to the question of why budgets are so large is simple: Big budgets are necessary to pay for big governments. Among the most important changes of the twentieth century is the rise of large governments.[7] Actually, as you can see in "America in Perspective: How Big Is Too Big?" among Western nations, America has one of the *smallest* public sectors relative to the size of the economy, which is measured as the gross domestic product (GDP). Nevertheless, it is difficult to characterize the national government, with a budget of more than $2 trillion per year, as anything but large — some critics would say enormous.

As with other Western nations, the growth of government in the United States has been dramatic. Political scientist E. E. Schattschneider described the small beginnings of American government:

> President Washington made his budget on a single sheet of paper. Jefferson ran his Department of Foreign Affairs with a staff of six writing clerks. . . . As late as 1822 the

America in Perspective

How Big Is Too Big?

When one hears about trillion-dollar federal budgets and budget deficits that may run $500 billion in a single year, it's easy to think of "big government." The figures in the accompanying graph, however, show that the national, state, and local governments in the United States actually spend a smaller percentage of their country's resources than those in most other democracies with developed economies. Compared with these countries, the United States has a rather modest public sector.

Source: Organization for Economic Cooperation and Development, 2004.

TOTAL GOVERNMENT EXPENDITURES AS A PERCENTAGE OF THE GROSS DOMESTIC PRODUCT

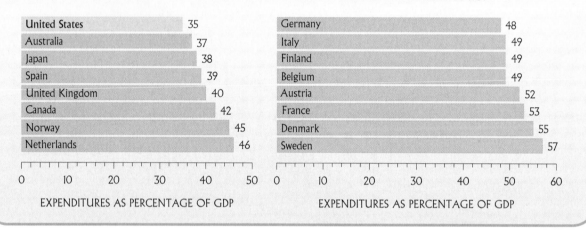

Country	%
United States	35
Australia	37
Japan	38
Spain	39
United Kingdom	40
Canada	42
Norway	45
Netherlands	46
Germany	48
Italy	49
Finland	49
Belgium	49
Austria	52
France	53
Denmark	55
Sweden	57

EXPENDITURES AS PERCENTAGE OF GDP

government spent $1,000 for the improvement of rivers and harbors and President Monroe vetoed a $9,000 appropriation for the repair of the Cumberland Road.[8]

This relatively tiny government was, said Schattschneider, the "grain of mustard seed" from which today's huge government has grown. American governments—national, state, and local—spend an amount equal to one-third of the gross domestic product. The national government's expenditures alone equal about 20 percent of the GDP.

Of course, no one knows for sure exactly why government has grown so rapidly in all the Western democracies. William Berry and David Lowery launched a major investigation into the question, but their findings were mixed. Overall, however, they found that the public sector expands principally in response to the public's preferences and changes in economic and social conditions that affect the public's level of demand for government activity.[9] This is why the rise of big government has been strongly resistant to reversal: Citizens like government services. Even Ronald Reagan, a strong leader with an antigovernment orientation, succeeded only in slowing the growth of government, not in actually trimming its size. When he left office, the federal government employed more people and spent more money than when he was inaugurated.

Two conditions associated with government growth in America are the rise of the national security state and the rise of the social service state.

The Rise and Decline of the National Security State

A generation ago, the most expensive part of the federal budget was not its social services but its military budget. Until World War II, the United States customarily disbanded a large part of its military forces at the end of a war. After World War II, however, the "Cold War" with the Soviet Union resulted in a permanent military establishment and expensive military technology. Fueling the military machine greatly increased the cost of government. It was President Eisenhower—not some liberal anti-military activist—who coined the phrase *military industrial complex* to characterize the close relationship between the military hierarchy and the defense industry that supplies its hardware needs.

In the 1950s and early 1960s, spending for past and present wars amounted to more than half the federal budget. The Department of Defense received the majority of federal dollars. Liberals complained that government was shortchanging the poor while lining the pockets of defense contractors. Things soon changed, however. Over 15 years, from the mid-1960s to the early 1980s, defense expenditures crept downward in real dollars while social welfare expenditures more than doubled.

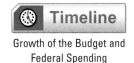

Timeline

Growth of the Budget and Federal Spending

Although President Reagan proposed eliminating scores of domestic programs in his annual budget requests, he also urged Congress to increase the defense budget substantially. Throughout his entire second term, Congress balked, however, and in the 1990s defense expenditures decreased in response to the lessening tensions in Europe (discussed in Chapter 20). Defense expenditures increased again following the terrorist attacks of September 11, 2001. Nevertheless, the budget of the Department of Defense, once the driving force in the expansion of the federal budget, now constitutes only about one-fifth of all federal expenditures (see Figure 14.4).

Payrolls and pensions for the more than 7 million persons who work for the Pentagon, serve in the reserves, or receive military retirement pay, veterans pensions, or disability compensation constitute a large component of the defense budget. So do the research, development, and *procurement* (purchasing) of military hardware. The costs of procurement are high, even though total military expenditures have declined as a percentage of American GDP since the end of World War II. The cost of advanced technology makes any weapon, fighter plane, or component more expensive than its predecessors. Moreover, cost overruns are common. The American fleet of Stealth Bombers will cost several times the original estimate—over a *billion* dollars each.

Figure 14.4   Trends in National Defense Spending

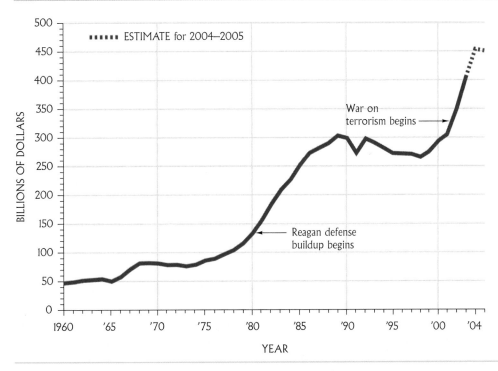

Defense expenditures increased rapidly during the Reagan administration, but they declined with the end of the Cold War. They increased again after the September 11, 2001, terrorist attacks.

Source: Budget of the United States Government, Fiscal Year 2005: Historical Tables (Washington, D.C.: U.S. Government Printing Office, 2004), Table 3.1.

The U.S. Air Force unveiled its new Stealth Bomber in 1989. The plane's unusual shape allows it to fly undetected by enemy radar, but such technology costs money—over $1 billion per plane. These huge expenditures contributed to substantial increases in the defense budget in the 1980s.

The Rise of the Social Service State

The biggest slice of the budget pie, once reserved for defense, now belongs to *income security* expenditures, a bundle of policies extending direct and indirect aid to the elderly, the poor, and the needy. In 1935, during the Great Depression and the administration of President Franklin D. Roosevelt, Congress passed the **Social Security Act.** The act was intended to provide a minimal level of sustenance to older Americans, saving them from poverty.

In January 1940, the treasurer of the United States sent the nation's first Social Security check to Ida Fuller of Brattleboro, Vt., in the amount of $22.54. An early entrant into the fledgling Social Security program, Fuller had contributed less than the amount of her first check to the system. By the time she died in December 1974 at the age of 100, she had collected $22,888.92 from the Social Security Administration. These days, about 45 million Americans receive payments from the Social Security system each month. The typical retired worker received $922 a month in 2004.

In the 1950s, disability insurance became a part of the Social Security program; thus, workers who had not retired but who were disabled could also collect benefits. In 1965, **Medicare,** which provides both hospital and physician coverage to the elderly, was added to the system. Although most Social Security checks go to retired workers, many also go to the disabled, to Medicare patients, and to widows and widowers of workers. Congress added an expensive prescription drug benefit to Medicare in 2003.

Social Security is less an insurance program than a kind of intergenerational contract. Essentially, money is taken from the working members of the population and spent on the retired members. Today, however, demographic and economic realities threaten to dilute this intergenerational relationship. In 1940, the entire Social Security system was financed with a 3 percent tax on payrolls; by 1990, the tax exceeded 15 percent. In 1945, 50 workers paid taxes to support each Social Security beneficiary. In 1990, about three workers supported each beneficiary. By the year 2025, when people born in the late 1950s will be getting their Social Security checks, only two workers will be supporting each beneficiary.

Not surprisingly, by the early 1980s the Social Security program faced a problem. As Paul Light candidly described it: "It was going broke fast."[10] And that was only the short-term problem. The aging population has added more people to the Social Security rolls annually; once there, people tend to stay on the rolls because life expectancies are

Social Security Act

A 1935 law passed during the Great Depression that was intended to provide a minimal level of sustenance to older Americans and thus save them from poverty.

Medicare

A program added to the Social Security system in 1965 that provides hospitalization insurance for the elderly and permits older Americans to purchase inexpensive coverage for doctor fees and other health expenses.

increasing. Congress responded by increasing social insurance taxes so that more was coming into the Social Security Trust Fund than was being spent. The goal was to create a surplus to help finance payments when the baby boomers retire.

In 1999, President Clinton proposed allocating much of the new budget surplus to Social Security and investing some of it in the stock market. Everyone agreed that saving Social Security was a high priority, but not everyone agreed with the president's solutions. As a result, no major changes occurred. George W. Bush faced similar resistance to his proposals for investing part of individuals' tax payments in the stock market. Nevertheless, the fiscal clock keeps ticking and by 2018 Social Security's costs will begin to exceed its income from tax collections.

Social Security is the largest social policy of the federal government (Social Security and Medicare account for about one-third of the federal budget). However, other social service expenditures have paralleled the upward growth of income security. In health, education, job training, and many other areas, the rise of the social service state has also contributed to America's growing budget. No brief list can do justice to the range of government social programs, which provide funds for the elderly, businesses run by minority entrepreneurs, consumer education, drug rehabilitation, environmental education, food subsidies for the poor, guaranteed loans to college students, housing allowances for the poor, inspections of hospitals, and so on. Liberals often favor these programs to assist individuals and groups in society; conservatives see them as a drain on the federal treasury. In any event, they cost money—a lot of it (see Figure 14.5).

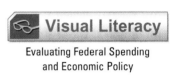

Visual Literacy

Evaluating Federal Spending and Economic Policy

Figure 14.5   Trends in Social Service Spending

Social Service spending has increased rapidly since the 1960s.

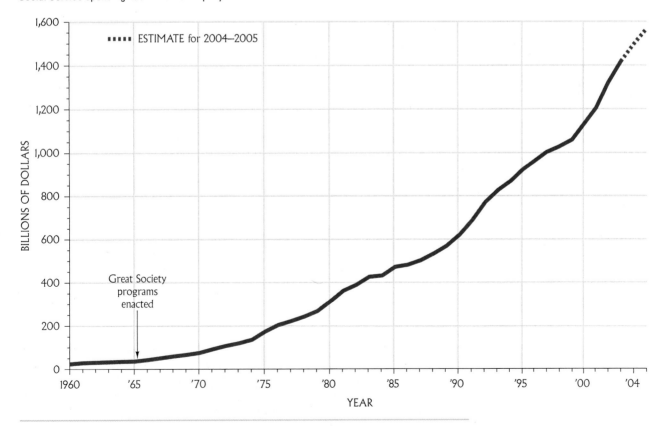

Source: Budget of the United States Government, Fiscal Year 2005: Historical Tables (Washington, D.C.: U.S. Government Printing Office, 2004), Table 3.1

Lyndon Johnson's "Great Society" initiatives in the mid-1960s greatly expanded America's social services network, adding Medicare and Medicaid to the Social Security system and creating many new programs designed to aid the poor. Here, LBJ campaigns during the 1964 presidential election.

The rise of the social service state and the national security state are linked with much of American governmental growth since the end of World War II. Although American social services expanded less than similar services in Western European nations, for most of the postwar period American military expenditures expanded more rapidly. Together, these factors help explain why the budget is the center of attention in American government today. Why is it so difficult to bring this increasing federal budget under control?

Incrementalism

incrementalism

The belief that the best predictor of this year's **budget** is last year's budget, plus a little bit more (an increment). According to Aaron Wildavsky, "Most of the budget is a product of previous decisions."

Sometimes political scientists use the term *incrementalism* to describe the spending and appropriations process. **Incrementalism** means simply that the best predictor of this year's budget is last year's budget plus a little bit more (an increment). According to Wildavsky and Caiden, "The largest determining factor of the size and content of this year's budget is last year's. Most of each budget is a product of previous decisions."[11] Incremental budgeting has several features:

- Very little attention is focused on the budgetary base—the amounts agencies have had over the previous years.
- Usually, agencies can safely assume they will get at least the budget they had the previous year.
- Most of the debate and most of the attention of the budgetary process are focused on the proposed increment.
- The budget for any given agency tends to grow by a little bit every year.

This picture of the federal budget is one of constant growth. Expenditures mandated by an existing law or obligation (such as Social Security) are particularly likely to follow a neat pattern of increase.[12] There are exceptions, however. Paul Schulman observed that budgets for the National Aeronautics and Space Administration (NASA) were hardly incremental; they initially rose as fast as a NASA rocket but later plummeted to a fraction of their former size.[13] Incrementalism may be a general tendency of the budget, but it does not fully describe all budgetary politics.

Because so much of the budgetary process looks incremental, there is a never-ending call for budgetary reform. The idea is always to make it easier to compare programs so that the "most deserving" ones can be supported and the "wasteful" ones cut. Nevertheless, the budgetary process, like all aspects of government, is affected by groups with interests in taxes and expenditures. These interests make it difficult to pare the budget. In addition, the budget is too big to review from scratch each year, even for the most systematic and conscientious members of Congress. The federal budget is a massive document, detailing annual outlays larger than the entire economies of individual countries except those of the United States, Japan, and Russia. Although efforts to check incrementalism have failed, so have attempts to reduce more rapidly rising expenses. Much of the federal budget has become "uncontrollable."

"Uncontrollable" Expenditures

At first glance, it is hard to see how one could call the federal budget uncontrollable. After all, Congress has the constitutional authority to budget—to add or subtract money from an agency. Indeed, Presidents Reagan, Bush, and Clinton proposed and Congress adopted some proposals to cut the growth of government spending. How, then, can one speak of an uncontrollable budget?

Consider for a moment what we might call the "allowance theory" of the budget. Using this theory, a government budget works like an allowance. Mom and Dad hand over to Mary Jean and Tommy a monthly allowance, say $10 each, with the stern admonition, "Make that last to the end of the month because that's all we're giving you until then." In the allowance model of the budget, Congress plays this parental role; the agencies play the roles of Mary Jean and Tommy. Congress thus allocates a lump sum—say, $5.2 billion—and instructs agencies to meet their payrolls and other expenses throughout the fiscal year. When most Americans think of the government's budget, they envision the budget as a kind of allowance to the agencies.

About two-thirds of the government's budget, however, does not work this way at all. **Uncontrollable expenditures** result from policies that make some group automatically eligible for some benefit or by previous obligations of the government, such as pensions and interest on the national debt. The government does not decide each year, for example, whether it will pay the interest on the federal debt, or that it will chop the pensions earned by former military personnel in half.

Many expenditures are uncontrollable because Congress has in effect obligated itself to pay X level of benefits to Y number of recipients. Congress writes the eligibility rules; the number of people eligible and their level of guaranteed benefits determine how much Congress must spend. Such policies are called **entitlements,** and they range from agricultural subsidies to veterans' aid. Each year, Congress' bill is a straightforward function of the X level of benefits times the Y beneficiaries. The biggest uncontrollable expenditure of all is the Social Security system, including Medicare, which costs about $800 billion per year. The Social Security Administration does not merely provide benefits on a first-come, first-served basis until the money runs out. Instead, eligible individuals automatically receive Social Security payments. Of course, Congress can, if it desires, cut the benefits or tighten eligibility restrictions. Doing so, however, would provoke a monumental outcry from millions of elderly voters.

The Budgetary Process

Budgets are produced through a long and complex process that starts and ends with the president and has the Congress squarely in the middle. Because budgets are so important to almost all other policies, the budgetary process is the center of political battles in Washington and involves nearly everyone in government. The distribution of the government's budget is the outcome of a very complex budgetary process. Nestled inside the tax and expenditures figures are thousands of policy choices, each prompting plenty of politics.

uncontrollable expenditures

Expenditures that are determined not by a fixed amount of money appropriated by Congress but by how many eligible beneficiaries there are for a program or by previous obligations of the government.

entitlements

Policies for which Congress has obligated itself to pay X level of benefits to Y number of recipients. Social Security benefits are an example.

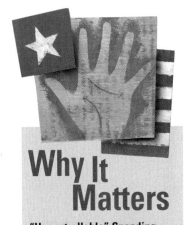

Why It Matters

"Uncontrollable" Spending
Much of the federal budget is "uncontrollable" in the sense that it does not come up for reauthorization on a regular basis. If entitlement programs were subject to annual authorizations as most other programs are, they would probably have less secure funding. We might spend less money on them and more on other services. This flexibility might please some people, especially those not receiving entitlement benefits, but those receiving Social Security and Medicare payments, for example, prefer more reliable funding.

Budgetary Politics

Public budgets are the supreme example of Harold Lasswell's definition of politics as "who gets what, when, and how." Budget battles are fought over contending interests, ideologies, programs, and agencies.

Stakes and Strategies.   Every political actor has a stake in the budget. Mayors want to keep federal grants-in-aid flowing in; defense contractors like a big defense budget; scientists push for a large budget for the National Science Foundation. Agencies within the government also work to protect their interests. Individual members of Congress act as policy entrepreneurs for new ideas and support constituent benefits, both of which cost money. Presidents try to use budgets to manage the economy and leave their imprint on Congress' policy agenda.

Think of budgetary politics as resembling a game in which players choose among strategies.[14] Agencies pushing their budgetary needs to the president and Congress, for instance, try to link the benefits of their program to a senator's or representative's electoral needs.[15] Almost invariably, agencies pad their requests a bit, hoping that the almost inevitable cuts will be bearable. President John Adams justified this now common budgetary gambit by saying to his cabinet, "If some superfluity not be given Congress to lop off, they will cut into the very flesh of the public necessities." Interest groups try to identify their favorite programs with the national interest. Mayors tell Congress not how much they like to receive federal aid but how crucial cities are to national survival. Farmers stress not that they like federal aid but that feeding a hungry nation and world is the main task of American agriculture. In the game of budgetary politics, there are plenty of players, all with their own strategies.

The Players.   Deciding how to carve up one-fifth of the GDP is a process likely to attract plenty of interest—from those formally required to participate in the budgeting process as well as those whose stakes are too big to ignore it. Here are the main actors in the budgetary process:

- *The interest groups.* No lobbyist worth his or her pay would ignore the budget. Lobbying for a group's needs takes place in the agencies, with presidents (if the lobbyist has access to them), and before congressional committees. A smart agency head will be sure to involve interest groups in defending the agency's budget request.
- *The agencies.* Convinced of the importance of their mission, the heads of agencies almost always push for higher budget requests. They send their requests to the Office of Management and Budget and later get a chance to present themselves before congressional committees as well.[16]
- *The Office of Management and Budget (OMB).* The OMB is responsible to the president, its boss, but no president has the time to understand and make decisions about the billions of dollars in the budget—parceled out to hundreds of agencies, some of which the chief executive knows little or nothing about. The director and staff of the OMB have considerable independence from the president, which makes them major actors in the annual budget process.
- *The president.* The president makes the final decisions on what to propose to Congress. In early February, the president unveils the proposed budget; the president then spends many a day trying to ensure that Congress will stick close to the recommendations.
- *The Tax Committees in Congress.* The government cannot spend money it does not have. The **House Ways and Means Committee** and the **Senate Finance Committee** write the tax codes, subject to the approval of Congress as a whole.
- *The Budget Committees and the Congressional Budget Office (CBO).* The CBO—which is the congressional equivalent of the OMB—and its parent committees,

---

House Ways and Means Committee

The House of Representatives committee that, along with the **Senate Finance Committee**, writes the tax codes, subject to the approval of Congress as a whole.

Senate Finance Committee

The Senate committee that, along with the **House Ways and Means Committee**, writes the tax codes, subject to the approval of Congress as a whole.

the Senate and House Budget Committees, set the parameters of the congressional budget process through examining revenues and expenditures in the aggregate and proposing resolutions to bind Congress within certain limits.

- *The subject-matter committees.* Committees of Congress, ranging from Agriculture to Veterans' Affairs, write new laws, which require new expenditures. Committee members may use hearings either to publicize the accomplishments of their pet agencies, thus supporting larger budgets for them, or to question agency heads about waste or overspending.
- *The Appropriations Committees and their subcommittees.* The Appropriations Committee in each house decides who gets what. These committees take new or old policies coming from the subject-matter committees and decide how much to spend. Appropriations subcommittees hold hearings on specific agency requests.
- *The Congress as a whole.* The Constitution requires that Congress as a whole approve taxes and appropriations, and senators and representatives alike have a strong interest in delivering federal dollars to their constituents. A dam here, a military base there, and a job-training program somewhere else—these are items that members look for in the budget.
- *The Government Accountability Office (GAO).* Congress' role does not end when it has passed the budget. The GAO works as Congress' eyes and ears, auditing, monitoring, and evaluating what agencies are doing with their budgets.

Budgeting involves a cast of thousands. However, their roles are carefully scripted and their time on stage is limited because budget making is both repetitive (the same things must be done each year) and sequential (actions must occur in the proper order and more or less on time). The budget cycle begins in the executive branch a full 19 months before the fiscal year begins.

The President's Budget

Until 1921, the various agencies of the executive branch sent their budget requests to the secretary of the treasury, who in turn forwarded them to the Congress. Presidents played a limited role in proposing the budget; sometimes they played no role at all. Agencies basically peddled their own budget requests to Congress. In 1921 Congress, concerned about retiring the debt the country had accumulated during World War I, passed the Budget and Accounting Act, which required presidents to propose an executive budget to Congress, and created the Bureau of the Budget to help them. In the 1970s, President Nixon reorganized the Bureau of the Budget and gave it a new name, the Office of Management and Budget (OMB). The OMB, whose director is a presidential appointee requiring Senate approval, now supervises preparation of the federal budget and advises the president on budgetary matters.

It takes a long time to prepare a presidential budget.[17] By law, the president must submit a budget by the first Monday in February. The process begins almost a year before (see Table 14.2), when the OMB communicates with each agency, sounding out its requests and tentatively issuing guidelines. By the summer, the president has decided on overall policies and priorities and has established general targets for the budget. These are then communicated to the agencies.

The budget makers now get down to details. During the fall, the agencies submit formal, detailed estimates for their budgets, zealously pushing their needs to the OMB. Budget analysts at the OMB pare, investigate, weigh, and meet on agency requests. Typically, the agency heads ask for hefty increases; sometimes they threaten to go directly to the president if their priorities are not met by the OMB. As the Washington winter sets in, the budget document is readied for final presidential approval. There is usually some last-minute juggling—agencies may be asked to change their estimates to conform with the president's decisions, or cabinet members may make a last-ditch effort to bypass the OMB and convince the president to increase their funds. With only

Table 14.2   The President's Budget: An Approximate Schedule

Spring Budget policy developed	The OMB presents the president with an analysis of the economic situation, and they discuss the budgetary outlook and policies. The OMB then gives guidelines to the agencies, which in turn review current programs and submit to the OMB their projections of budgetary needs for the coming year. The OMB reviews these projections and prepares recommendations to the president on final policy, programs, and budget levels. The president establishes guidelines and targets.
Summer Agency estimates submitted	The OMB conveys the president's decisions to the agencies and advises and assists them in preparing their budgets.
Fall Estimates reviewed	The agencies submit to the OMB formal budget estimates for the coming fiscal year, along with projections for future years. The OMB holds hearings, reviews its assessment of the economy, and prepares budget recommendations for the president. The president reviews these recommendations and decides on the agencies' budgets and overall budgetary policy. The OMB advises the agencies of these decisions.
Winter President's budget determined and submitted	The agencies revise their estimates to conform with the president's submitted decisions. The OMB once again reviews the economy and then drafts the president's budget message and prepares the budget document. The president revises and approves the budget message and transmits the budget document to Congress.

days—or hours—left before the submission deadline, the budget document is rushed to the printers. Then the president sends it to Capitol Hill. The next steps are up to Congress.

Congress and the Budget

According to the Constitution, Congress must authorize all federal appropriations. Thus, Congress always holds one extremely powerful trump card in national policymaking: the power of the purse.[18] Congress decides how to spend more than $2 trillion each year.

Reforming the Process.   For years Congress budgeted in a piecemeal fashion. A subcommittee of the House and Senate Appropriations Committees handled each agency request; then all these appropriations were added to produce a total budget. People never quite knew what the budget's bottom line would be until all the individual bills were totaled up. What Congress spent had little to do with any overall judgment of how much it should spend.

Congressional Budget and Impoundment Control Act of 1974

An act designed to reform the congressional budgetary process. Its supporters hoped that it would also make Congress less dependent on the president's budget and better able to set and meet its own budgetary goals.

The **Congressional Budget and Impoundment Control Act of 1974** was designed to reform the congressional budgetary process. Its supporters hoped that it would also make Congress less dependent on the president's budget and more able to set and meet its own budgetary goals. The act established:

- A *fixed budget calendar.* Each step in the budgetary process has an established completion date. In the past, Congress sometimes failed to appropriate money to agencies until after the fiscal year was over, leaving agencies drifting for months with no firm budget. Now there is a timetable mandated by law, which has been amended several times (see Table 14.3).
- A *budget committee in each house.* These two committees are supposed to recommend target figures to Congress for the total budget size by April 1 of each year. By April 15, Congress is to agree on the *total* size of the budget, which guides the Appropriations Committee to juggling figures for individual agencies.

Table 14.3   The Congressional Budget Process: Targets and Timetables

DATE	ACTION TO BE COMPLETED
First Monday in February	Congress receives the president's budget.
February 15	The CBO submits a budget report to the House and Senate Budget Committees, including an analysis of the president's budget.
February 25	Other committees submit reports on outlays and revenues to Budget Committees in each house.
April 1	Budget Committees report concurrent resolution on the budget, which sets a total for budget outlays, an estimate of expenditures for major budget categories, and the recommended level of revenues. This resolution acts as an agenda for the remainder of the budgetary process.
April 15	Congress completes action on concurrent resolution on the budget.
May 15	Annual appropriations bills may be considered in the House.
June 10	House Appropriations Committee reports last annual appropriations bill.
June 15	Congress completes action on reconciliation legislation, bringing budget totals into conformity with established ceilings.
June 30	House completes action on annual appropriation bills.
October 1	The new fiscal year begins.

Source: From Howard E. Shuman, *Politics and the Budget*, 3rd ed. (Englewood Cliffs, NJ: Prentice-Hall, 1992), 67.

- *A Congressional Budget Office.* The **Congressional Budget Office (CBO)** advises Congress on the probable consequences of its budget decisions, forecasts revenues, and is a counterweight to the president's OMB.

One purpose of the new budgeting system was to force Congress to consider the budget (both projected expenditures and projected revenues) as a whole, rather than in bits and pieces as it had done before. An important part of the process of establishing a budget is to set limits on expenditures on the basis of revenue projections—a step that is supposed to be done through a **budget resolution.** Thus, in April of each year, both houses are expected to agree on a budget resolution—thereby binding Congress to a total expenditure level that should form the bottom line of all federal spending for all programs. Only then is Congress supposed to begin acting on the individual appropriations.

In terms of a family budget, Family A might decide to budget by adding up all its needs and wants and calling that its budget. Such a strategy almost guarantees overspending the family income. Family B, though, might begin by looking first at its revenue and then trying to bring its total expenditures into line with its revenue before dealing with its individual expenditure decisions. With its 1974 reforms, Congress was trying to force itself to behave more like Family B than Family A.

Like the president's budget proposal, the congressional budget resolution often requests that certain changes be made in law, primarily to achieve savings incorporated into the spending totals and thus meet the budget resolution. These changes are legislated in two separate ways.

First is budget **reconciliation,** a process by which program authorizations are revised to achieve required savings; it frequently also includes tax or other revenue

Congressional Budget Office (CBO)

Advises Congress on the probable consequences of its decisions, forecasts revenues, and is a counterweight to the president's OMB.

budget resolution

A resolution binding Congress to a total expenditure level, supposedly the bottom line of all federal spending for all programs.

reconciliation

A congressional process through which program authorizations are revised to achieve required savings. It usually also includes tax or other revenue adjustments.

adjustments. Usually reconciliation comes near the end of the budgetary process. However, in an attempt to strike while his political standing was high and to overcome the opposition of special interests and the parochialism and power of congressional committees, President Reagan in 1981 successfully proposed using an extremely complex reconciliation bill to reduce the budget by approximately $40 billion. Reagan thought that he could obtain substantial cuts only if he lumped them all together in one bill in which everyone lost something. The preparation of the bill was so hurried that few members of Congress could give it serious consideration.

The second way that laws are changed to meet the budget resolution (or to create or change programs for other reasons) involves more narrowly drawn legislation. An **authorization bill** is an act of Congress that establishes a discretionary government program or an entitlement, or that continues or changes such programs. Authorizations specify program goals and, for discretionary programs, set the maximum amount that they may spend. For entitlement programs, an authorization sets or changes eligibility standards and benefits that must be provided by the program. Authorizations may be for one year, or they may run for a specified or indefinite number of years.

An additional measure, termed an **appropriations bill,** must be passed to fund programs established by authorization bills. Appropriations bills usually fund programs for one year and cannot exceed the amount of money authorized for a program; in fact, they may appropriate *less* than was authorized.

authorization bill

An act of Congress that establishes, continues, or changes a discretionary government program or an entitlement. It specifies program goals and maximum expenditures for discretionary programs.

appropriations bill

An act of Congress that actually funds programs within limits established by authorization bills. Appropriations usually cover one year.

The Success of the 1974 Reforms.   Have these reforms worked? If *worked* means that Congress has brought its spending into line with its revenues, then the reforms have been almost a total failure. Congressional budgets were in the red every year between the 1974 amendments and 1998. In fact, the red ink grew from a puddle to an ocean (see Figure 14.6). Presidents made matters worse, submitting budget proposals that contained large deficits.

In addition, Congress has often failed to meet its own budgetary timetable. There has been too much conflict over the budget for the system to work according to design. Moreover, in many instances Congress has not been able to reach agreement and pass appropriations bills at all and has instead resorted to **continuing resolutions**—laws that allow agencies to spend at the previous year's level. Sometimes, as in 1986 and 1987, appropriations bills have been lumped together in one enormous and complex bill (rather than in the 13 separate appropriations bills that are supposed to pass), precluding adequate review by individual members of Congress and forcing the president either to accept unwanted provisions or to veto the funding for the entire government. These omnibus bills in 1986 and 1987 also became magnets for unrelated and controversial pieces of legislation that could not pass on their own.

continuing resolutions

When Congress cannot reach agreement and pass appropriations bills, these resolutions allow agencies to spend at the level of the previous year.

On the other hand, the 1974 reforms have helped Congress view the entire budget early in the process; now Congress can at least see the forest as well as the trees. The problem is not so much the procedure as disagreement over how scarce resources should be spent—or whether they should be spent at all.

More Reforms.   By 1985 Congress was desperate. President Reagan refused to consider tax increases to pay for federal spending and continued to submit budgets that contained huge deficits. In response to growing frustration at its inability to reduce annual budget deficits substantially, Congress enacted the Balanced Budget and Emergency Deficit Control Act, better known as Gramm-Rudman-Hollings after its cosponsors, Senators Phil Gramm (R) of Texas, Warren Rudman (R) of New Hampshire, and Ernest Hollings (D) of South Carolina.

This legislation, as it was amended in 1987, mandated maximum allowable deficit levels for each year until 1993, when the budget was supposed to be in balance. If Congress failed to meet the deficit goals, automatic across-the-board spending cuts, called *sequestrations*, were to be ordered by the president (a number of programs, including Social Security and interest on the national debt, were exempt from this process).

Figure 14.6   Annual Federal Deficits

Yearly deficits mushroomed during the Reagan administration (1981–1988), despite the president's oft-repeated commitment to a balanced budget. The deficit disappeared during the Clinton administration, and the nation began running a surplus in fiscal year 1998. By 2002, however, the United States was back in the red.

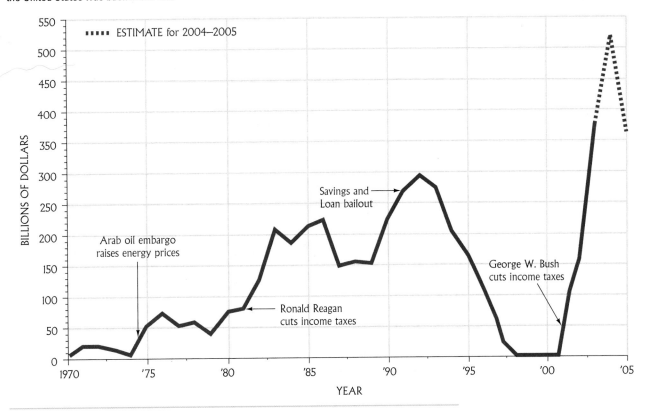

Source: Budget of the United States Government, Fiscal Year 2005: Historical Tables (Washington, D.C.: U.S. Government Printing Office, 2004), Table 1.1.

Gramm-Rudman-Hollings was clearly an indelicate, unthinking approach to budgeting; no one liked the arbitrary nature of the automatic budget cuts, half of which were to come from defense and half from domestic programs. Even Senator Rudman described it as "a bad idea whose time has come." In the absence of consensus on spending priorities, Congress believed it had no other way to force itself to reduce the deficit. Success was elusive, however, as you can see in Figure 14.6.

Near the end of 1990, Congress abandoned Gramm-Rudman-Hollings and approved a major change in budgeting policy. It decided to shift its focus from controlling the size of the deficit to controlling increases in spending. Discretionary spending was divided into three categories: domestic, defense, and international. Any new spending in any of these categories had to be offset by decreases elsewhere within the category. Violations of these strictures would lead to across-the-board sequestration within the affected category. Spending for entitlement programs such as Medicare was placed on a "pay-as-you-go" basis, requiring that any expansion be paid for by a corresponding entitlement cut or revenue increase. Similarly, any tax cut was to be paid for by a compensating tax increase or entitlement cut.

President Clinton presented his first budget to Congress in 1993. After the dust cleared following a highly partisan legislative battle, the president and Congress had made a significant decrease in the deficit. There was a single cap for all discretionary spending (rather than one for each of the three components), imposing a hard freeze on appropriations, yet there was little prospect of balancing the budget in the foreseeable future.

You Are the Policymaker
Balancing the Budget

You have seen that the national government is running large budget deficits and that the national debt continues to grow. Here is the situation you would face as a budget decision maker: According to the OMB, in fiscal year 2005 the national government will have revenues (including Social Security taxes) of about $2,036 billion. Mandatory expenditures for domestic policy (entitlements such as Social Security and other prior obligations) total about $1,371 billion. Nondiscretionary payments on the national debt

will cost another $178 billion. National defense will cost an additional $451 billion. That leaves you with just $36 billion to spend and still balance the budget. The president's proposals for discretionary domestic policy programs will take $466 billion, however. If you spend this amount you will run a deficit of $430 billion—and you will not even have had a chance to fund any significant new programs.

What would you do? Would you drastically reduce defense expenditures? Or would you leave them alone and close

down substantial portions of the rest of the government, such as programs for space and science, transportation and public works, economic subsidies and development, education and social services, health research and services, or law enforcement and other core functions of government—programs that also have broad public support? Perhaps you would show great political courage and seek a tax increase to pay for these programs.

What would *you* do?

The results of the 1994 congressional elections once again altered the budgetary game. In 1995, the new Republican majorities in each house, determined to balance the budget within seven years, argued for substantial cuts in the rate of growth of popular entitlement programs such as Medicaid and for the outright elimination of many other programs. Most Democrats strongly opposed these proposals. The president agreed with the goal of balancing the budget—but on his terms—and took his case to the voters in 1996. The outcome, as we have seen, was divided government.

In 1997, the president and Congress agreed to a budget that was to be in balance—by 2002. Each political party claimed victory, but the path to a balanced budget was eased by the booming economy, which produced more tax revenues than either side had anticipated. Indeed, the economy was so strong that the government began running surpluses. However, decreased tax revenues resulting from the economic downturn in 2000–2001 and the income tax cut of 2001 sent the budget into deficit again. In the meantime, the budget deficit continues as a source of conflict (see "You Are the Policymaker: Balancing the Budget").

Understanding Budgeting

Citizens and politicians alike fret about whether government is too big. In 1988 President Bush was elected by claiming that government had too many hands in Americans' pockets. He promised not to raise taxes to pay for more government spending. Of course, not everyone agrees that the national government is too large—even Bush backtracked on his "no new taxes" pledge by 1990 and was defeated by the more activist Bill Clinton in 1992. There is agreement on the centrality of budgeting to modern government and politics, however.

Democracy and Budgeting

Almost all democracies have seen a substantial growth in government in the twentieth century. One explanation for this growth is that politicians spend money to "buy" votes. They do not buy votes in the sense that a corrupt political machine pays voters to vote

Long a goal of many elected officials, balancing the budget was aided by the booming economy that produced far more tax revenues than anticipated and the budget agreements of the 1990s that constrained spending. Here President Clinton shows how the deficit fell during his tenure.

for its candidates; rather, policymakers spend public money on things voters will like—and will remember on Election Day. As you saw in Chapter 12, members of Congress have incentives to make government grow; they use both constituency services and pork barrel policies to deliver benefits to the folks back home, and government grows as a result.

Economists Allan Meltzer and Scott Richard have argued that government grows in a democracy because of the equality of suffrage. They maintain that in the private sector people's incomes are unequal, whereas in the political arena power is much more equally distributed. Each voter has one vote. Parties must appeal to a majority of the voters. Hence, claim Meltzer and Richard, poorer voters will always use their votes to support public policies that redistribute benefits from the rich to the poor. Even if such voters cannot win in the marketplace, they can use the electoral process to their

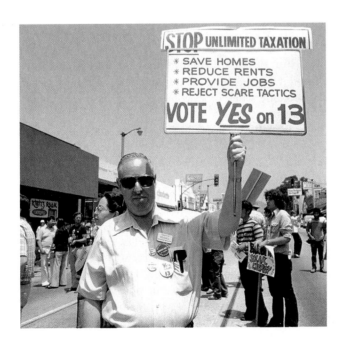

Public opinion is a key element in the budgeting process. Occasionally, the public has a direct role in budget making, as when the citizens of California voted on Proposition 13, a referendum proposing strict limits to local property taxes. Despite protests against the proposed legislation—many citizens argued that tax limits would restrict many government services—the proposition was passed.

How You Can Make a Difference

The Federal Government and Student Loans

Since 1965, the Federal Family Education Program (FFEL) has provided federally guaranteed student loans worth nearly $200 billion. Under this system, private banks issue the loans and profit from them while the federal government subsidizes the interest rate and guarantees the loans. The Clinton administration, however, advocated that the federal government provide direct funding to the students and bypass private banks. If the pilot program were adopted on a permanent basis, the government's partnership with the private banking sector would likely end.

Is direct lending better than the traditional public/private venture used for 35 years? According to the proponents of direct lending, college students would likely pay lower interest rates on their student loans under a direct plan. Likewise, critics of the traditional system point out that even the Congressional Budget Office notes that because these loans have been subsidized and guaran-

teed by the federal government, private banks take on less risk and reap hefty profits from student loan programs. In short, many college and student interest groups claim that the only reason to continue the present system is to guarantee larger profits to private banks.

The Alliance To Save Student Aid is a coalition of 50 educational organizations. By calling them at 1-800-574-4243, you can get information about the current status of government funding for student loans. Give them your zip code, and the Alliance will directly connect you to your congressional representative's office to voice your educated opinion.

Many citizens, especially libertarians and fiscal conservatives, strongly oppose expansion of the direct lending program. The Heritage Foundation (*www.heritage.org*) argues that the direct lending plan costs the government more money in administrative costs but also adds to the national debt.

In fact, a similar program in the 1970s failed because of poor management and soaring default rates due to poor loan collection. In short, the argument against direct lending remains both ideological (in favor of limited government) and practical (direct lending did not work the last time around).

However you view this debate, do not let your short tenure as a college student keep you from participating. Although nothing may get done while you are still an undergraduate student, your involvement in this debate may impact your graduate education funding.

What you can do:

- Call 1-800-574-4243 to contact the Alliance to Save Student Aid.
- Review a more detailed list of student aid lobbying and advocacy groups and their websites, from both sides of the spectrum. See *www.finaid.org/ questions/ advocacy*.

advantage.[19] Many politicians willingly cooperate with the desire of the working-class voters to expand their benefits because voters return the favor at election time. Not surprisingly, the most rapidly growing areas of expenditures are Social Security, Medicaid, Medicare, and social welfare programs, which benefit the poor more than the rich.

Many believe that elites, particularly corporate elites, oppose big government. However, Lockheed, United Airlines, and Chrysler Corporation appealed to the government for large bailouts when times got rough. Corporations support a big government that offers them contracts, subsidies, and other benefits. A $150 billion procurement and research and development budget at the Department of Defense benefits defense contractors, their workers, and their shareholders.

Low-income and wealthy voters alike have voted for parties and politicians who promised them benefits. When the air is foul, Americans expect government to help clean it up. When Americans get old, they expect a Social Security check. In a democracy, what people want affects what government does. Citizens are not helpless victims of big government and its big taxes; they are at least coconspirators.

Government also grows by responding to groups and their demands. The parade of PACs is one example of groups asking government for assistance. From agricultural lobbies supporting loans to zoologists pressing for aid from the National Science Foundation, groups seek to expand their favorite part of the budget. They are aided by committees and government agencies that work to fund projects favored by supportive groups (see the discussion on iron triangles in Chapter 15).

You have also seen, however, that some politicians compete for votes by promising not to spend money. After all, Ronald Reagan did not win election to the presidency twice by promising to raise taxes and provide more services, nor did the Republicans who took control of Congress in 1995. No country has a more open political system than the United States, but as the *America in Perspective* features in this chapter demonstrate, Americans have chosen to tax less and spend less on public services than almost all other democracies with developed economies. The size of government budgets varies widely among democratic nations. Democracy may encourage government spending, but it does not compel it.

One of the most common criticisms of government is its failure to balance the budget. Public officials are often criticized for lacking the will to deal with the problem, yet it is not lack of resolve that prevents a solution to enormous budget deficits. Instead, it is a lack of consensus on policy. Americans want to spend but not pay taxes and, being a democracy, this is exactly what the government does. The inevitable result is red ink.

The Budget and the Scope of Government

Issues regarding the scope of government have pervaded this chapter. The reason is obvious—in many ways, the budget *is* the scope of government. The bigger the budget, the bigger the government.

The budgetary process can also limit government. One could accurately characterize policymaking in the American government since 1980 as the "politics of scarcity"—scarcity of funds, that is. Thus, the budget can be a force for reining in the government as well as for expanding its role.[20] President Clinton came into office hoping to make new investments in education, worker training, and the country's physical infrastructure, such as roads and bridges. He soon found, however, that there was no money to fund new programs.

The president was reduced to speaking loudly and carrying a small budgetary stick in other policy areas as well. Because there was not enough money in the budget to pay for health care reform, he had to accept a reduced benefits package and advocate the politically difficult option of forcing employers to pay for their employees' health insurance. Welfare reform faced a similar obstacle. America's large budget deficits have been as much a constraint on government as they have been evidence of a burgeoning public sector.

Summary

When the federal government's budget consumes one-fifth of America's gross domestic product, it demands close attention. The government's biggest revenue source remains the income tax, but the Social Security tax is becoming increasingly important. Lately, much of the government's budget has been financed through borrowing. Annual deficits exceeding $100 billion—and sometimes $400 billion—boosted the federal debt to more than $8 trillion by 2005.

In all Western democracies, government budgets grew during the twentieth century. In the United States, government spending also experienced significant change. Defense spending dominated the 1950s; social services spending dominated the 1990s. President Reagan, for one, wanted to reverse this trend by increasing military expenditures and cutting domestic ones. Nonetheless, much of the American budget consists of "uncontrollable" expenditures that are extremely difficult to pare. Many of these expenditures are associated with Social Security payments and with grants-in-aid.

Budget making is complex, with many actors playing many roles. The president sets the budgetary agenda, whereas Congress and its committees approve the budget itself.

Some critics believe that democracy turns politics into a bidding war for votes, increasing the size of the budget in the process. In the United States, however, many candidates campaign on *not* spending money or increasing taxes. Although larger budgets mean larger government, the budget, at least in times of substantial deficits such as those the United States experienced in the previous decade, can also serve as a constraint on further government growth.

KEY TERMS

budget
deficit
expenditures
revenues
income tax
Sixteenth Amendment
federal debt
tax expenditures
Social Security Act
Medicare
incrementalism

uncontrollable
   expenditures
entitlements
House Ways and Means
   Committee
Senate Finance
   Committee
Congressional Budget and
   Impoundment Control
   Act of 1974

Congressional Budget
   Office (CBO)
budget resolution
reconciliation
authorization bill
appropriations bill
continuing resolutions

INTERNET RESOURCES

www.access.gpo.gov/eop/
The *Economic Report of the President* and the budget for the federal government.

www.irs.ustreas.gov
The Internal Revenue Service homepage, containing a wealth of information about taxes.

www.whitehouse.gov/omb
The Office of Management and Budget homepage.

www.cbo.gov/
Congressional Budget Office homepage, containing budgetary analyses and data.

www.taxpolicycenter.org
A joint venture of the Urban Institute and the Brookings Institution containing many studies of budgets and taxes.

www.taxfoundation.org/
The Tax Foundation site with a wealth of tax information.

www.concordcoalition.org/
The nonpartisan Concord Coalition provides studies of budgetary issues.

GET CONNECTED

The Budgetary Process

The process of making the federal budget is long and cumbersome. Although the Constitution gives the legislative branch the responsibility to tax and spend, the president is heavily invested in the budget process. Indeed, Congress requires the president to recommend what the federal budget should be. Its thinking was that since the executive branch was responsible for spending most of the money Congress allocated, it only made sense to ask the president to recommend a budget each year. Recommending a budget is not an easy job. Economists say that running a large deficit is bad for the economy, and so is running a large surplus. Usually, the government should spend about what it collects in taxes each year. Try putting together a budget on your own. Go to the National Budget Simulation and create a budget that reflects your values.

Search the Web

Go to the National Budget Simulation (Short Version) *http://www.budgetsim.org/nbs/shortbudget02.html* and create your budget. Once you have made your choices, see how well you did.

Questions To Ask
- Did your budget balance, or did you have a large surplus or deficit?
- How did you make your decisions on what to change in making your budget?
- Do you think your decisions expressed conservative, liberal, or centrist values?

Why It Matters
The federal budget is more than $2 *trillion* (that is $2,000,000,000,000), and it is supposed to reflect the values of the nation. Because presidents recommend the annual budget to Congress, their values have a large influence on the budget.

Get Involved
How do you feel about the current federal budget? Do you think the president is recommending the right kind of budget or not? What would you change?

To see more Get Connected exercises for Chapter 14, go to www.ablongman.com/edwards.

FOR FURTHER READING

Bennett, Linda L. M., and Stephen Earl Bennett. *Living With Leviathan.* Lawrence: University Press of Kansas, 1990. Examines Americans' coming to terms with big government and their expectations of government largesse.

Berry, William D., and David Lowery. *Understanding United States Government Growth.* New York: Praeger, 1987. An empirical analysis of the causes of the growth of government in the period since World War II.

King, Ronald F. *Money, Taxes, and Politics.* New Haven, CT: Yale University Press, 1993. Explains why democratically elected officials approve tax policies that make rich people richer.

Light, Paul. *Artful Work: The Politics of Social Security Reform.* New York: Random House, 1985. A case study of the perennial crisis of Social Security and what has been done about it.

Rubin, Irene S. *Balancing the Federal Budget.* New York: Chatham House, 2003. Explains how the budget was balanced in the late 1990s.

Schick, Allen. *The Federal Budget,* rev. ed. Washington, D.C.: Brookings Institution, 2000. A useful "hands-on" view of federal budgeting.

Schuman, Howard E. *Politics and the Budget,* 3rd ed. Englewood Cliffs, NJ: Prentice-Hall, 1992. An excellent primer on the entire budgetary process.

Wildavsky, Aaron, and Naomi Caiden. *The New Politics of the Budgetary Process,* 4th ed. New York: Longman, 2001. The standard work on the budgetary process.

15

The Federal Bureaucracy

Chapter Outline

The Bureaucrats

The New York Times **Issues of the Times**

How Bureaucracies Are Organized

Bureaucracies as Implementors

Bureaucracies as Regulators

Understanding Bureaucracies

Summary

■ Americans do not want to worry about the safety of the food we eat. Indeed, food safety is something we take for granted. But who assures this safety? Bureaucrats. It is their job to keep our food safe from contamination. Although we rarely think about food inspections, they represent one of the most important regulatory functions of government. The fact that we rarely think about food safety is testimony to the success of bureaucrats in carrying out their tasks.[1]

Policing the food supply is not a straightforward task, however. It involves a complex web of federal agencies with overlapping jurisdictions. Twelve agencies and 35 statutes regulate food safety. Eggs in the shell fall under the purview of the Food and Drug Administration (FDA), but once cracked and processed, they come under the jurisdiction of the U.S. Department of Agriculture (USDA). The USDA is responsible for regulating meat and poultry, while the FDA handles most other food products, including seafood and produce. Cheese pizzas are the FDA's responsibility, but if they have pepperoni on top, Agriculture inspectors step in. Other parts of the government also play a prominent role in enforcing food safety laws. For example, the Environmental Protection Agency oversees pesticides applied to crops, and the Centers for Disease Control and Prevention track food-related illnesses.

Is this complex system the result of bureaucratic maneuvering? No, the system was created by Congress layer on top of layer, with little regard to

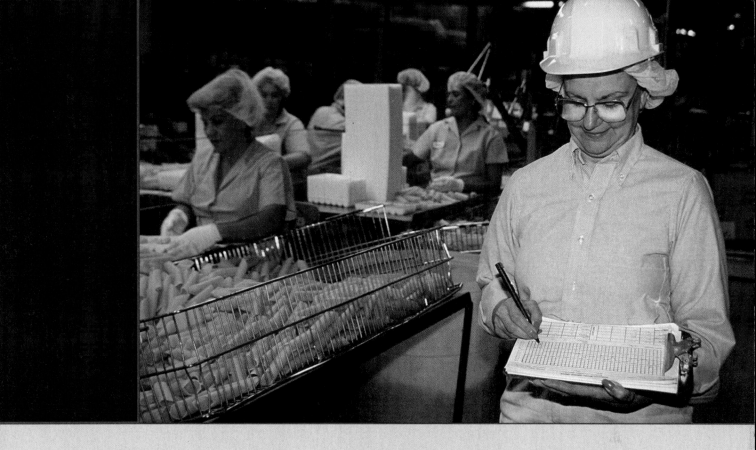

how it should work as a whole. Critics argue that the system is outdated and it would be better to create a single food safety agency that could target inspections, streamline safety programs, and use resources more efficiently. Such proposals have generated little enthusiasm in Congress, however, where committees are sensitive about losing jurisdiction over agencies. For example, in the House the Commerce Committee has oversight over the FDA while the Agriculture Committee has responsibility for the USDA. Growers and manufacturers fear a single agency would impose onerous new regulations, product recalls, and fines, and could be used by empire-building bureaucrats to expand their budget and regulatory authority. So little change occurs.

Bureaucrats face other challenges in insuring safe food. The FDA has only about 430 inspectors to keep tabs on more than 53,000 establishments that produce, process, or store food other than meat and poultry. The agency carries out about 5,000 inspections per year, so the average company is subject to an FDA inspection just once every 10 years.

Bureaucrats are central to our lives. They provide essential public services. They possess crucial information and expertise that make them partners with the president and Congress in decision-making about public policy. Who knows more than bureaucrats about Social Security recipients or the military capabilities of China? Bureaucrats are also central to poli-

tics. They do much more than simply follow orders. Because of their expertise, bureaucrats inevitably have discretion in carrying out policy decisions, which is why congressional committees and interest groups take so much interest in what they do.

Bureaucratic power extends to every corner of American economic and social life, yet bureaucracies are scarcely hinted at in the Constitution. Each bureaucratic agency is created by Congress, which sets its budget and writes the policies it administers. Most agencies are responsible to the president, whose constitutional responsibility to "take care that the laws shall be faithfully executed" sheds only a dim light on the problems of managing so large a government. How to manage and control bureaucracies is a central problem of democratic government.

Reining in the power of bureaucracies is also a common theme in debates over the scope of government in America. Some political commentators see the bureaucracy as the prime example of a federal government growing out of control. They view the bureaucracy as acquisitive, constantly seeking to expand its size, budgets, and authority while being entwined in red tape and spewing forth senseless regulations. Others see the bureaucracy as laboring valiantly against great odds to fulfill the missions elected officials have assigned it. Where does the truth lie? The answer is less obvious than you may think. Clearly, bureaucracies require closer examination.

467

bureaucracy

According to Max Weber, a hierarchical authority structure that uses task specialization, operates on the merit principle, and behaves with impersonality. Bureaucracies govern modern states.

The classic conception of bureaucracy was advanced by the German sociologist Max Weber, who stressed that the bureaucracy was a "rational" way for a modern society to conduct its business.[2] According to Weber, a **bureaucracy** depends on certain elements: It has a *hierarchical authority structure*, in which power flows from the top down and responsibility flows from the bottom up; it uses *task specialization* so that experts instead of amateurs perform technical jobs; and it develops extensive *rules*, which may seem extreme at times, but which allow similar cases to be handled similarly instead of capriciously. Bureaucracies operate on the *merit principle*, in which entrance and promotion are awarded on the basis of demonstrated abilities rather than on "who you know." Bureaucracies behave with *impersonality* so that all their clients are treated impartially. Weber's classic prototype of the bureaucratic organization depicts the bureaucracy as a well-organized machine with plenty of working, but hierarchical, parts.

The Bureaucrats

Bureaucrats are typically much less visible than the president or members of Congress. As a result, Americans usually know little about them. This section will examine some myths about bureaucrats and explain who they are and how they got their jobs.

Some Bureaucratic Myths and Realities

Bureaucrat baiting is a popular American pastime. George Wallace, former Alabama governor and frequent presidential hopeful, warmed up his crowds with a line about "pointy-headed Washington bureaucrats who can't even park their bicycles straight." Even successful presidential candidates climbed aboard the antibureaucracy bandwagon. Jimmy Carter complained about America's "complicated and confused and overlapping and wasteful" bureaucracies; Gerald Ford complained about the "dead weight" of bureaucracies; and Ronald Reagan insisted that bureaucrats "overregulated" the American economy, causing a decline in productivity.

Any object of such unpopularity will spawn plenty of myths. The following are some of the most prevalent myths about bureaucracy:

- *Americans dislike bureaucrats.* Despite the rhetoric about bureaucracies, Americans are generally satisfied with bureaucrats and the treatment they get from them. Americans may dislike bureaucracies, but they like individual bureaucrats. Surveys have found that two-thirds or more of those who have had encounters with a bureaucrat evaluate these encounters positively. In most instances, bureaucrats are described as helpful, efficient, fair, courteous, and working to serve their clients' interests.[3]

- *Bureaucracies are growing bigger each year.* This myth is half true and half false. The number of government employees has been expanding, but not the number of *federal* employees. Almost all the growth in the number of public employees has occurred in state and local governments. The 18.7 million state and local public employees far outnumber the 4.2 million civilian and military federal government employees (see Figure 15.1). As a percentage of America's total workforce, *federal* government employment has been shrinking, not growing; it now accounts for about 3 percent of all civilian jobs. Of course, many state and local employees work on programs that are federally funded, and the federal government hires many private contractors to provide goods and services ranging from hot meals to weapons systems.[4]

- *Most federal bureaucrats work in Washington, D.C.* Only about 12 percent of federal civilian employees work in the Washington, D.C. metropolitan area. California leads the nation in federal employees, with 248,000. Texas has 162,000, New York 134,000. About 91,000 federal employees work in foreign countries and American territories.[5] You can see where federal bureaucrats work by looking in your local phone book under "U.S. Government." You will probably find listings

Figure 15.1   Growth in Civilian Government Employees

The number of government employees has grown since 1965. The real growth, however, has been in the state and local sector, with its millions of teachers, police officers, and other service deliverers. Many state and local employees and programs, though, are supported by federal grants-in-aid. (Note that the figures for federal employment do not include military personnel.)

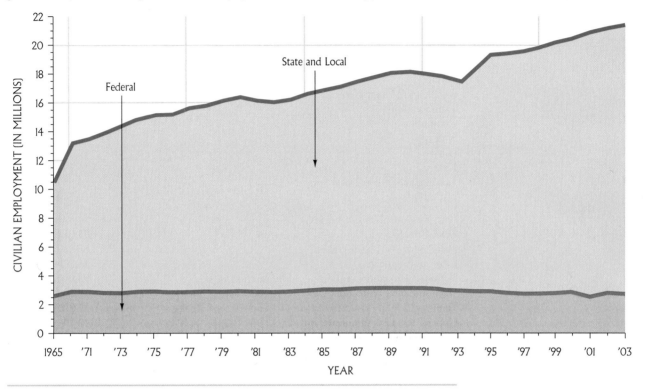

Source: Budget of the United States Government, Fiscal Year 2005: Historical Tables (Washington, D.C.: U.S. Government Printing Office, 2004), Table 17–5.

for the local offices of the Postal Service, the Social Security Administration, the FBI, the Department of Agriculture's county agents, recruiters for the armed services, air traffic controllers, the Internal Revenue Service, and many others.

- *Bureaucracies are ineffective, inefficient, and always mired in red tape.* No words describing bureaucratic behavior are better known than "red tape."[6] Bureaucracy, however, is simply a way of organizing people to perform work. General Motors, a college or university, the U.S. Army, the Department of Health and Human Services, and the Roman Catholic Church are all bureaucracies. Bureaucracies are a little like referees: When they work well, no one gives them much credit, but when they work poorly, everyone calls them unfair, incompetent, or inefficient. Bureaucracies may be inefficient at times, but no one has found a substitute for them; and no one has yet demonstrated that government bureaucracies are more or less inefficient, ineffective, or mired in red tape than private bureaucracies.[7]

Anyone who looks with disdain on American bureaucracies should contemplate life without them. Despite all the complaining about bureaucracies, the vast majority of tasks carried out by governments at all levels are noncontroversial. Bureaucrats deliver mail, test milk, clean streets, issue Social Security and student loan checks, run national parks, and perform other routine governmental tasks in a perfectly acceptable manner. Most of the people who work for cities, states, and the national government are typical Americans, the type who are likely to be your neighbors.

Most federal civilian employees work for just a few of the agencies (see Table 15.1). The Department of Defense (DOD) employs about one-fourth of federal *civilian* workers in addition to the 1.5 million men and women in uniform. Altogether,

Table 15.1   Federal Civilian Employment

EXECUTIVE DEPARTMENTS	NUMBER OF EMPLOYEES[a]
Defense (military functions)	647,800
Veterans Affairs	218,300
Homeland Security	144,000
Treasury	115,900
Justice	112,600
Agriculture	101,700
Interior	71,400
Health and Human Services	61,600
Transportation	58,500
Commerce	36,100
State	30,300
Labor	17,300
Energy	16,100
Housing and Urban Development	10,600
Education	4,500
Larger Non-Cabinet Agencies	
U.S. Postal Service	773,958
Social Security Administration	65,000
Corps of Engineers	24,800
National Aeronautics and Space Administration	18,900
Environmental Protection Agency	17,600
Tennessee Valley Authority	13,200
General Services Administration	12,500

[a]Figures are for 2004.
Source: *Budget of the United States Government, Fiscal Year 2005: Analytical Perspectives* (Washington, D.C.: U.S. Government Printing Office, 2004), Tables 23.1, 23.3.

the DOD makes up more than half the federal bureaucracy. The postal service accounts for an additional 30 percent of the federal civilian employees, and the Department of Veterans Affairs, clearly related to national defense, has more than 218,000 employees. All other functions of government, including homeland security, are handled by the remaining 25 percent of federal employees.

Who They Are and How They Got There

Who Wants to Be a Bureaucrat?

Because there are 2.7 million civilian bureaucrats (more than 21 million if we include state and local public employees), it is hard to imagine a statistically typical bureaucrat. Bureaucrats are male and female, all races and religions, well paid and not so well paid. Like other institutions, the federal government has been under pressure to expand its hiring of women and minorities. Congress has ordered federal agencies to make special efforts to recruit and promote previously disadvantaged groups, but women and non-Whites still cluster at the lower ranks. As a whole, however, the permanent bureaucracy is more broadly representative of the American people than are legislators, judges, or presidential appointees in the executive branch[8] (see Figure 15.2).

The diversity of bureaucratic jobs mirrors the diversity of private-sector jobs, including occupations literally ranging from A to Z. Accountants, bakers, census analysts, defense procurement specialists, electricians, foreign service officers, guards in federal prisons, home economists, Indian Affairs agents, judges, kitchen workers, lawyers, missile technologists, narcotics agents, ophthalmologists, postal carriers, quarantine specialists, radiologists, stenographers, truck drivers, underwater demolition experts, virologists, wardens, X-ray technicians, youth counselors, and zoologists all work for the government (see Table 15.2).

Figure 15.2   Characteristics of Federal Civilian Employees[a]

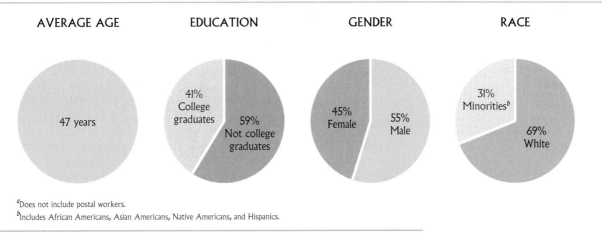

[a]Does not include postal workers.
[b]Includes African Americans, Asian Americans, Native Americans, and Hispanics.

Source: Data from United States Office of Personnel Management, *The Factbook, 2003* (Washington, D.C.: U.S. Government Printing Office, 2004), 10–13.

Civil Service: From Patronage to Protection.   Until roughly a hundred years ago, a person got a job with the government through the patronage system. **Patronage** is a hiring and promotion system based on political reasons rather than on merit or competence. Working in a congressional campaign, making large donations, and having the right connections helped people secure jobs with the government. Nineteenth-century presidents staffed the government with their friends and allies, following the view of Andrew Jackson that "to the victors belong the spoils." Scores of office seekers would swarm the White House after Inauguration Day. It is said that during a bout

patronage

One of the key inducements used by political machines. A patronage job, promotion, or contract is one that is given for political reasons rather than for merit or competence alone. Compare **civil service** and the **merit principle.**

Table 15.2   Full-Time Civilian White-Collar Employees of the Federal Government

SELECTED OCCUPATIONAL CATEGORIES	NUMBER OF EMPLOYEES
General administrative, clerical, and office services	363,953
Medical, dental, and public health	139,132
Engineering and architecture	123,183
Accounting and budget	115,369
Investigation	93,897
Business and industry	87,292
Legal and kindred	86,377
Social science, psychology, and welfare	67,496
Biological sciences	58,779
Transportation	45,864
Personnel management and industrial relations	40,673
Physical sciences	33,470
Education	32,632
Supply	31,272
Information and the arts	18,197
Mathematics and statistics	13,624
Equipment, facilities, and services	12,164
Quality assurance, inspection, and grading	10,028
Library and archives	8,045
Copyright, patent, and trademark	3,864
Veterinary medical science	2,088

Source: U.S. Office of Personnel Management, *Occupations of Federal White-Collar and Blue-Collar Workers, Federal Civilian Workforce Statistics, as of September 30, 1999* (Washington, D.C.: U.S. Government Printing Office, 2000), Table W-2.

Pendleton Civil Service Act

Passed in 1883, an Act that created a federal **civil service** so that hiring and promotion would be based on merit rather than **patronage.**

civil service

A system of hiring and promotion based on the **merit principle** and the desire to create a nonpartisan government service.

merit principle

The idea that hiring should be based on entrance exams and promotion ratings to produce administration by people with talent and skill.

Hatch Act

A federal law prohibiting government employees from active participation in partisan politics.

Office of Personnel Management (OPM)

The office in charge of hiring for most agencies of the federal government, using elaborate rules in the process.

GS (General Schedule) rating

A schedule for federal employees, ranging from GS 1 to GS 18, by which salaries can be keyed to rating and experience.

Senior Executive Service (SES)

An elite cadre of about 9,000 federal government managers, established by the Civil Service Reform Act of 1978, who are mostly career officials but include some political appointees who do not require Senate confirmation.

with malaria, Lincoln told an aide to "send in the office seekers" because he finally had something to give them.

A disappointed office seeker named Charles Guiteau helped end this "spoils system" of federal appointments in 1881. Frustrated because President James A. Garfield would not give him a job, Guiteau shot and killed Garfield. The so-called Prince of Patronage himself, Vice President Chester A. Arthur, then became president. Arthur, who had been collector of the customs for New York—a patronage-rich post—surprised his critics by encouraging passage of the **Pendleton Civil Service Act** (1883), which created the federal Civil Service. Today, most federal agencies are covered by some sort of civil service system.

All **civil service** systems are designed to hire and promote members of the bureaucracy on the basis of merit and to create a nonpartisan government service. The **merit principle**—using entrance exams and promotion ratings to reward qualified individuals—is intended to produce an administration of people with talent and skill. Creating a nonpartisan civil service means insulating government workers from the risk of being fired when a new party comes to power. At the same time, the **Hatch Act,** originally passed in 1939 and amended most recently in 1993, prohibits civil service employees from actively participating in partisan politics while on duty. While off duty they may engage in political activities, but they cannot run for partisan elective offices or solicit contributions from the public. Employees with sensitive positions, such as those in the national security area, may not engage in political activities even while off duty.

The **Office of Personnel Management (OPM)** is in charge of hiring for most federal agencies. Its director is appointed by the president and confirmed by the Senate. The OPM has elaborate rules about hiring, promotion, working conditions, and firing. To get a civil service job, usually candidates must first take a test. If they pass, their names are sent to agencies when jobs requiring their particular skills become available. For each position open, the OPM will send three names to the agency. Except under unusual circumstances, the agency must hire one of these three individuals. (This process is called the "rule of three.") Each job is assigned a **GS (General Schedule) rating** ranging from GS 1 to GS 18. Salaries are keyed to rating and experience. You can see how many people are employed in each rating and their average salaries in Table 15.3.

At the very top of the civil service system (GS 16–18) are about 9,000 members of the **Senior Executive Service (SES),** the "cream of the crop" of the federal employees.

Table 15.3   GS Employment and Salaries

GENERAL SCHEDULE GRADE	NUMBER OF EMPLOYEES	AVERAGE SALARY
1	397	$16,636
2	1,657	19,229
3	11,666	21,850
4	51,485	25,158
5	109,238	29,038
6	83,511	32,964
7	127,840	36,463
8	48,958	41,235
9	127,840	44,022
10	15,221	49,863
11	169,945	53,485
12	205,120	64,299
13	168,881	77,004
14	76,866	91,724
15	39,579	110,065

Source: U.S. Office of Personnel Management, *Pay Structure of the Federal Civil Service as of March 31, 2002* (Washington, D.C.: U.S. Government Printing Office, 2003), Table 4.

These executives earn high salaries and may be moved from one agency to another as leadership needs change.

Once hired, and after a probationary period, civil servants are protected—overprotected, critics claim—by the civil service system. Ensuring a nonpartisan civil service requires that workers have protection from dismissals that are politically motivated. Protecting all workers against political firings may also protect a few from dismissal for good cause. Firing incompetents is hard work. In a recent year, the government managed to fire only 500 employees for poor performance, a tiny fraction of civilian federal workers. According to Civil Service regulations, the right of appeal must be exhausted before one's paycheck stops. Appeals can consume weeks, months, or even years. More than one agency has decided to tolerate incompetents, assigning them trivial or no duties, rather than invest its resources in the nearly hopeless task of discharging them. Firing incompetent female, minority, or older workers may be even more difficult than dislodging incompetent young or middle-aged White males. These groups not only have the usual Civil Service protections but also can resort to antidiscrimination statutes to appeal their dismissals. After a protracted battle, President George W. Bush limited job protection for employees in the Department of Homeland Security (see "Issues of the Times: Managing the Federal Bureaucracy").

The Other Route to Federal Jobs: Recruiting from the Plum Book

As an incoming administration celebrates its victory and prepares to take control of the government, Congress publishes the *plum book*, which lists top federal jobs (that is, "plums") available for direct presidential appointment, often with Senate confirmation. There are about 400 of these top policymaking posts (mostly cabinet secretaries, undersecretaries, assistant secretaries, and bureau chiefs) and about 2,500 lesser positions.

All incoming presidents launch a nationwide talent search for qualified personnel. Presidents seek individuals who combine executive talent, political skills, and sympathy for policy positions similar to those of the administration. Often, the president tries to include men and women, Whites and non-Whites, people from different regions, and party members who represent different interests (although few recent presidents have appointed as high a percentage of middle-aged White males as did Ronald Reagan). Some positions, especially ambassadorships, go to large campaign contributors. A few of these appointees will be civil servants, temporarily elevated to a "political" status; most, though, will be political appointees, "in-and-outers" who stay for a while and then leave.[9]

Why It Matters

The Merit System
People obtain positions in the federal bureaucracy through a merit system and are protected against losing their jobs because of their political views. If the president could appoint a substantial percentage of bureaucrats, it is likely that they would be more responsive to the president but also likely that they would be less qualified to serve the public interest than today's bureaucrats.

Doonesbury

BY GARRY TRUDEAU

LOT #1 IS 166 SQ. MILES OF CARIBBEAN BEACHFRONT...

HAUNTINGLY BEAUTIFUL, IT FEATURES BALMY WEATHER, AMIABLE LOCALS AND A VIBRANT CULTURE...

LADIES AND GENTLEMEN, AS YOU KNOW, THE PROCEEDS FROM TONIGHT'S AUCTION BENEFIT A VERY WORTHY CAUSE, SO I'D LIKE TO SEE SOME SPIRITED BIDDING ON THIS LOT! LET'S BEGIN, SHALL WE?

WHAT AM I BID FOR THE POST OF AMBASSADOR TO BARBADOS?

$100,000!

$150,000!

Issues of the Times

The Issue: Managing the Federal Bureaucracy

One of the most important, but often overlooked, jobs of the president is to manage the 2.7 million civilians and 1.5 million uniformed military who comprise the federal bureaucracy. The chief executive wants the bureaucracy to provide services as efficiently as possible and to be responsive to his leadership. Recently, President George W. Bush has tried his hand at increasing the efficiency and responsiveness of government.

The civil service system provides job security for civil servants and protects them from dismissals that are politically motivated. These benefits are necessary to recruit able people to government service, which often pays less than the private sector. At the same time, it is difficult to dismiss incompe-

tent people or transfer competent bureaucrats to other jobs. The president is also torn between having a bureaucracy large enough to

accomplish the tasks assigned to it and limiting the size—and the cost—of government.

Read All About It

The Incredible Shrinking Government, Bush Style

BY Richard W. Stevenson
December 8, 2002

Unlike Ronald Reagan, who insisted government is the problem not the solution, President Bush has never cast himself as an anti-Washington crusader. Indeed, national security concerns have forced him to put aside any ideological qualms he has about big government to support a striking expansion of federal powers and bureaucracy.

Yet over the past several months, Mr. Bush has picked a fight with the federal work force in a way that has revived concern among labor unions—and hope among conservatives—that he is

intent on being a hard-nosed, confrontational chief operating officer for Washington Inc. even as he rallies the government and the nation behind him in his role as commander in chief.

His impetus may be more managerial than ideological. But if Mr. Bush prevails, he could end up doing more to overhaul the Civil Service and to advance the conservative small-government agenda than any of his predecessors, Mr. Reagan included. After a long battle in Congress, Mr. Bush won the right to hire, fire and move the 170,000 workers who will staff the new Department of Homeland Security with more ease than

Democrats and public employee unions wanted to give him.

He also laid out a plan to transfer as many as 850,000 government jobs—nearly half the federal civilian work force—to private companies as a way to save money and improve performance. Saying the country could not afford to grant a bigger raise in wartime, he set next year's pay increase for 1.8 million federal employees below the level sought by Congress, and then set off a storm by acknowledging that the administration had quietly re-established a

Please see Bush   **Page 475**

Bush

Continued from Page 474

bonus pool this year for more than 2,000 political appointees.

Ever since he was governor of Texas, Mr. Bush has been a master at blurring ideological lines while hewing by and large to conservative principles. To administration officials, there is no dissonance in his presiding over one of the largest expansions of government in decades while simultaneously seeking to rein in the bureaucracy.

"The president sees the federal government as an agent of positive change on behalf of a compassionate conservative agenda," said Ari Fleischer, the White House spokesman. "He thinks the government can do things well, and it's important that the government do them efficiently as it does them well."

But he has heads swiveling, or shaking, among experts on governance across the political spectrum. To conservatives who have watched with dismayed resignation as the demands of fighting terrorism have trumped their goal of reducing the size of the federal government, Mr. Bush's actions in the last few months were welcome, if minimal, reassurance.

"These are half measures," said Ronald D. Utt, a senior fellow at the Heritage Foundation, a conservative research group, "but it's about as far as he can go politically." Some experts on the bureaucracy, Democrats among them, say Mr. Bush is right to push for more management flexibility within the civil service, which is under increasing pressure to attract better educated workers and redefine jobs for changing needs. But they also wonder whether management reform by a

Republican president is cover for slashing domestic programs.

Labor leaders and analysts said Mr. Bush seems intent on a showdown with government-employee unions, the biggest source of growth in union membership in recent decades and a major supporter of Democrats.

"Not since the Patco strike in 1981 has any administration con-

---

If Mr. Bush prevails, he could end up doing more to overhaul the Civil Service and to advance the conservative small-government agenda than any of his predecessors, Mr. Reagan included.

---

fronted federal labor unions as aggressively," said Joseph A. McCartin, a labor historian at Georgetown University, referring to President Reagan's decision to replace striking air traffic controllers. "It's clearly an exercise in trying to diminish the power of federal employee unions, and by doing so it has tremendous implications for the labor movement in general."

Elements of the administration's policy, especially the push to privatize many jobs, from mowing lawns to running laboratories, could also have broad implications for the economy.

Government employment has long been a stepping stone into the middle class for workers, especially blacks and women, who benefited

greatly from efforts by the public sector to reduce discrimination in hiring.

Even today, black and female workers remain more reliant on government jobs than white workers. Robert I. Lerman, director of the labor and social policy center at the Urban Institute, a research group, said that among black men, federal, state and local government jobs currently account for 15 percent of employment, versus 11 percent for white males.

Critics of privatizing federal employment say it can lead to job losses, salary and benefit cuts and less job security, a trend that would expand if state and local governments follow Washington's lead. Even people who say privatization of government work can lead to savings for taxpayers and better government services warn against permitting the practice to reduce opportunities for women and minority groups.

Clearly sensitive to the perception that he is hostile to workers and their unions, Mr. Bush invited leaders of government employee unions to the White House for the signing of the bill creating the Department of Homeland Security. He has also taken pains in recent weeks to praise federal employees, especially for their role in keeping the nation safe from terrorists.

But the administration's critics accused Mr. Bush of saying one thing and doing another.

"Republican businessmen will tell you you can't expect to achieve widespread organizational change without the participation of the workers, and the unions if they are unionized," said Elaine Kamarck, who ran the Clinton administration's "reinventing government" program.

Think About It

- Is the federal bureaucracy large enough to accomplish the tasks the president and Congress have assigned it?
- How important is the goal of preserving government jobs for women and minorities?

- Do you think the private sector can provide better and lower-cost services than the public sector?
- How important are job protections for attracting people to work for government?

Once in office, these administrative policymakers constitute what Hugh Heclo has called a "government of strangers." Their most important trait is their transience. The average assistant secretary or undersecretary lasts about 22 months.[10] Few top officials stay long enough to know their own subordinates well, much less people in other agencies. Administrative routines, budget cycles, and legal complexities are often new to them. To these new political executives, the possibilities of power may seem endless. Nevertheless, although plum book appointees may have the outward signs of power, many of them find it challenging to exercise real control over much of what their subordinates do and have difficulty leaving their mark on policy. They soon learn that they are dependent on senior civil servants who know more, have been there longer, and will outlast them.

How Bureaucracies Are Organized

A complete organizational chart of the American federal government would be big enough to occupy a large wall. You could pore over this chart, trace the lines of responsibility and authority, and see how government is organized—at least on paper. A very simplified organizational chart of the executive branch appears in Figure 15.3. A much easier way to look at how the federal executive branch is organized is to group agencies into four basic types: cabinet departments, regulatory agencies, government corporations, and independent executive agencies.

The Cabinet Departments

Each of the 15 cabinet departments is headed by a secretary (except the Department of Justice, which is headed by the attorney general), chosen by the president, and approved by the Senate. Undersecretaries, deputy undersecretaries, and assistant secretaries report to the secretary. Each department manages specific policy areas (see the list in Table 13.4, page 402), and each has its own budget and its own staff.

Each department has a unique mission and is organized somewhat differently. The Department of the Interior, charged with overseeing the nation's natural resources and administering policies that affect Native Americans, is a well-established and traditional department (see Figure 15.4). The real work of a department is done in the bureaus, which divide the work into more specialized areas (a bureau is sometimes called a *service, office, administration,* or other name).

Until the 1970s, the largest cabinet department was the Department of Defense. From then until 1995, the Department of Health and Human Services (HHS) was the largest federal department in dollars spent (although the Department of Defense still had more employees). The Social Security Administration split from HHS and became an independent agency in 1995, spending one-third of the federal budget on the massive programs of Social Security and Medicare.

Sometimes status as a cabinet department can be controversial. For several years, Republicans have been trying to disband the Departments of Education, Energy, and Commerce, arguing that they waste tax dollars and implement policies that should be terminated.

independent regulatory agency

A government agency responsible for some sector of the economy, making and enforcing rules to protect the public interest. It also judges disputes over these rules.

The Regulatory Agencies

Each **independent regulatory agency** has responsibility for some sector of the economy, making and enforcing rules designed to protect the public interest. The independent regulatory agencies also judge disputes over these rules.[11] They are also sometimes called the alphabet soup of American government because most such agencies are known in Washington by their initials. For example:

Figure 15.3   Organization of the Executive Branch

The President
Executive Office of the President

Department of State — Department of the Treasury — Department of Defense — Department of Justice

Department of the Interior — Department of Agriculture — Department of Commerce — Department of Labor — Department of Transportation

Department of Housing and Urban Development — Department of Health and Human Services — Department of Energy — Department of Education — Department of Veterans Affairs — Department of Homeland Security

INDEPENDENT ESTABLISHMENTS AND GOVERNMENT CORPORATIONS

African Development Foundation
Central Intelligence Agency
Commodity Futures Trading Commission
Consumer Product Safety Commission
Corporation for National and
   Community Service
Defense Nuclear Facilities Safety Board
Environmental Protection Agency
Equal Employment Opportunity
   Commission
Export-Import Bank of the United States
Farm Credit Administration
Federal Communications Commission
Federal Deposit Insurance Corporation
Federal Election Commission
Federal Emergency Management Agency
Federal Housing Finance Board
Federal Labor Relations Authority
Federal Maritime Commission
Federal Mediation and Conciliation Service
Federal Mine Safety and Health Review
   Commission

Federal Reserve System
Federal Retirement Thrift Investment Board
Federal Trade Commission
General Services Administration
Inter-American Foundation
Merit Systems Protection Board
National Aeronautics and Space
   Administration
National Archives and Records
   Administration
National Capital Planning Commission
National Credit Union Administration
National Foundation on the Arts and
   Humanities
National Labor Relations Board
National Mediation Board
National Railroad Passenger Corporation
   (Amtrak)
National Science Foundation
National Transportation Safety Board
Nuclear Regulatory Commission
Occupational Safety and Health Review
   Commission

Office of Government Ethics
Office of Personnel Management
Office of Special Counsel
Overseas Private Investment
   Corporation
Peace Corps
Pension Benefit Guaranty Corporation
Postal Rate Commission
Railroad Retirement Board
Securities and Exchange Commission
Selective Service System
Small Business Administration
Social Security Administration
Tennessee Valley Authority
Trade and Development Agency
U.S. Agency for International
   Development
U.S. Commission on Civil Rights
U.S. International Trade Commission
U.S. Postal Service

Source: Office of the Federal Register, *United States Government Manual 2003–2004* (Washington, D.C.: U.S. Government Printing Office, 2004), 22.

- *FRB (the Federal Reserve Board)*, charged with governing banks and, even more important, regulating the supply of money and thus interest rates
- *NLRB (the National Labor Relations Board)*, created to regulate labor-management relations

Figure 15.4   Organization of the Department of the Interior

Source: Office of the Federal Register, *United States Government Manual 2003–2004* (Washington, D.C.: U.S. Government Printing Office, 2004), 252.

- *FCC (the Federal Communications Commission)*, charged with licensing radio and TV stations and regulating their programming in the public interest, as well as with regulating interstate long-distance telephone rates, cable television, and the Internet
- *FTC (the Federal Trade Commission)*, responsible for regulating business practices and controlling monopolistic behavior, and now involved in policing the accuracy of advertising
- *SEC (the Securities and Exchange Commission)*, created to police the stock market

Each of these independent regulatory agencies is governed by a small commission, usually with 5 to 10 members appointed by the president and confirmed by the Senate for fixed terms. Unlike cabinet officers and members of the president's staff, regulatory commission members cannot be fired easily by the president. The Supreme Court made this ruling after President Franklin Roosevelt fired a man named Humphrey from the Federal Trade Commission. Humphrey took the matter to court but died shortly afterward. The angry executors of his estate sued for back pay, and the Court held that presidents could not fire members of regulatory agencies without just cause (*Humphrey's Executor v. United States*, 1935). "Just cause" has never been defined clearly, and no member of a regulatory commission has been fired since.

Interest groups consider the rule making by independent regulatory agencies (and, of course, their membership) very important. The FCC can deny a multimillion-dollar TV station a license renewal—a power that certainly sparks the interest of the National Association of Broadcasters. The FTC regulates business practices—a power that prompts both business and consumers to pay careful attention to its activities and membership.

Interest groups are so concerned with these regulatory bodies that some critics point to the "capture" of the regulators by the regulatees.[12] It is common for members of commissions to be recruited from the ranks of the regulated. Sometimes, too, members of commissions or staffs of these agencies move on to jobs in the very industries they were regulating. Some lawyers among them use contacts and information gleaned at the agency when they represent clients before their former employers at the agency. A later section of this chapter will discuss the bureaucracy's relationship with interest groups.

The Government Corporations

The federal government also has a handful of **government corporations.** These are not exactly like private corporations in which you can buy stock and collect dividends, but they *are* like private corporations—and different from other parts of the government—in two ways. First, they provide a service that *could be* handled by the private sector. Second, they typically charge for their services, though often at rates cheaper than those the consumer would pay to a private-sector producer.

The granddaddy of the government corporations is the Tennessee Valley Authority (TVA). Established in 1933 as part of the New Deal, it has controlled floods, improved navigation, protected the soil against erosion, and provided inexpensive electricity to millions of Americans in Tennessee, Kentucky, Alabama, and neighboring states. Through Comsat—a modern-day government corporation that sells time-sharing on

government corporation

A government organization that, like business corporations, provides a service that could be provided by the private sector and typically charges for its services. The U.S. Postal Service is an example. Compare **independent regulatory agency** and **independent executive agency.**

The Environmental Protection Agency is the federal government's largest independent regulatory agency, overseeing the administration of all environmental legislation. Here, EPA workers clean up hazardous waste.

NASA satellites—you can rent time on a space satellite for radio communications. The post office, one of the original cabinet departments (first headed by Benjamin Franklin), has become the government's largest corporation: the U.S. Postal Service.

Occasionally the government has taken over a "sick industry" and turned it into a government corporation. Amtrak, the railroad passenger service, is one example. Congress grumbles about Amtrak's multibillion-dollar subsidy (although some critics point out that billions of dollars in federal highway funds also constitute something of a subsidy for the auto industry), but members of Congress have only reluctantly agreed to let Amtrak shed its most unprofitable runs.

The Independent Executive Agencies

The **independent executive agencies** are essentially all the rest of the government—not cabinet departments, not regulatory commissions, and not government corporations. Their administrators typically are appointed by the president and serve at his will. These scores of bureaus are listed in the current issue of the *United States Government Manual*. A few of the biggest independent executive agencies (in size of budget) are:

- *General Services Administration (GSA)*, the government's landlord, which handles buildings, supplies, and purchasing
- *National Science Foundation (NSF)*, the agency supporting scientific research
- *National Aeronautics and Space Administration (NASA)*, the agency that takes Americans to the moon and points beyond

Bureaucracies as Implementors

Today, bureaucracies are essentially *implementors* of policy. They take congressional, presidential, and sometimes even judicial pronouncements and develop procedures and rules for implementing policy goals. They also manage the routines of government, from delivering mail to collecting taxes to training troops.

What Implementation Means

Public policies are rarely self-executing. One of the few policies that administers itself is the president's decision to "recognize" a foreign government. It is entirely the chief executive's prerogative to do so, and once it is done, diplomatic relations with the country are thereby established.

Most policies, however, are not self-executing. Congress typically announces the goals of a policy in broad terms, sets up an administrative apparatus, and leaves the bureaucracy the task of working out the details of the program. In other words, the bureaucracy is left to implement the program. **Policy implementation** is the stage of policymaking between the establishment of a policy (such as the passage of a legislative act, the issuing of an executive order, the handing down of a judicial decision, or the promulgation of a regulatory rule) and the results of the policy for individuals.[13] To paraphrase loosely a famous line about war from German General Karl von Clausewitz: "Implementation is the continuation of policymaking by other means."[14] At a minimum, implementation includes three elements:

1. Creation of a new agency or assignment of a new responsibility to an old agency
2. Translation of policy goals into operational rules and development of guidelines for the program
3. Coordination of resources and personnel to achieve the intended goals[15]

---

independent executive agency

The government not accounted for by **cabinet** departments, **independent regulatory agencies**, and **government corporations**. Its administrators are typically appointed by the president and serve at the president's pleasure. NASA is an example.

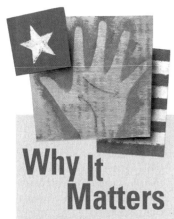

Why It Matters

Independent Regulatory Agencies

Independent regulatory agencies, such as the Federal Reserve Board, are designed to be somewhat insulated from the influence of politics. Their independence makes them less responsive to the president and Congress than other agencies. It also provides the potential—but not the certainty—of taking a long-range view and acting in the public interest.

---

policy implementation

The stage of policymaking between the establishment of a policy and the consequences of the policy for the people whom it affects. Implementation involves translating the goals and objectives of a policy into an operating, ongoing program. See also **judicial implementation**.

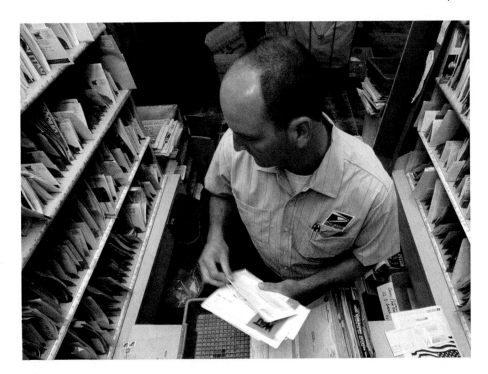

In an effort to make the agency financially independent as well as more responsive to consumers, in 1970, Congress transformed the Post Office Department into the U.S. Postal Service, the government's largest corporation. The agency has improved its fiscal performance (partly as a result of increased postal rates), although it is now subject to direct competition from private businesses that offer parcel and overnight mail services.

Why the Best-Laid Plans Sometimes Flunk the Implementation Test

The Scottish poet Robert Burns once wrote: "The best laid schemes o'mice and men/Gang aft a-gley [often go awry]." So, too, with the best intended public policies. Policies that people expect to work often fail. In 1996, Congress overwhelmingly passed a bill to guarantee health insurance to millions of Americans when they change or lose their jobs or lose coverage. Yet the law has been ineffective because insurance companies often charge these individuals premiums far higher than standard rates.[16] High expectations followed by dashed hopes are the frequent fate of well-intended public policies.

Program Design.   Implementation can break down for several reasons. One is faulty program design. "It is impossible," said Eugene Bardach, "to implement well a policy or program that is defective in its basic theoretical conception." Consider, he suggested, the following hypothetical example:

> If Congress were to establish an agency charged with squaring the circle with compass and straight edge—a task mathematicians have long ago shown is impossible—we could envision an agency coming into being, hiring a vast number of consultants, commissioning studies, reporting that progress was being made, while at the same time urging in their appropriations request for the coming year that the Congress augment the agency's budget.[17]

And the circle would remain round.[18]

Lack of Clarity.   Congress is fond of stating a broad policy goal in legislation and then leaving implementation up to the bureaucracies. Members of Congress can thus escape messy details, and place blame for the implementation decisions elsewhere (see "Young People and Politics: Drug Offenses and Financial Aid").

Such was the case with the controversial Title IX of the Education Act of 1972,[19] which said: "No person in the United States shall, on the basis of sex, be excluded from participation in, be denied the benefits of, or be subjected to discrimination under any

Young People and Politics

Drug Offenses and Financial Aid

In 1998, Congress wrote a provision into the law governing financial aid for college students that prohibits students who have been convicted of drug offenses from receiving grants and loans from the federal government. It does not matter whether the conviction was relatively minor or whether the conviction happened years ago—if a student has ever been convicted of a drug offense as an adult, he or she can be denied financial aid from one year to life, depending on the number of offenses and severity of conviction. Not surprisingly, the law has been a matter of contention.

The law itself might seem a bit severe, but there is more. Someone convicted of armed robbery, rape, or even murder would not be in the same predicament. Once out of prison, such a person is entitled to government grants and loans with no questions asked. But under the law, tens of thousands of would-be college students have been denied financial aid because of drug offenses, even though the crimes may have been committed long ago and the sentences already served.

Members of Congress have accused the Clinton and Bush administrations of distorting the law's intent. They argue that the Department of Education, which administers financial aid programs, should not be strict in its interpretation of the law. The department responds that Congress wrote a vague law—one that refers to "a student who has been convicted," and that it is faithfully imple-

menting the letter of the law. In effect, the department is arguing that it has no discretion in the matter and cannot act on its own to make financial aid policy more just.

It might seem easy for Congress to simply change the law. No such luck. A bill to repeal the law is a long way from having enough support to come to a floor vote, much less to pass. The George W. Bush administration suggested ending the prohibition on aid for those who violated drug laws before entering college. However, it wants to continue the aid ban for those who commit such crimes while enrolled in college. Its goal, the administration said, is to discourage students from using drugs. The problem, as others see it, is that such a rule would still impose stiffer penalties for drug use than for any other crime. It would also have the effect of barring some first-time, minor offenders from getting financial aid while restoring it for more serious drug lawbreakers.

Anticipating implementation problems is difficult. Putting together coalitions within Congress is also difficult. One consequence of these difficulties is that laws are often vague—and often have unintended consequences as well.

Questions for Discussion
- How much discretion should a bureaucratic unit have to correct injustices in laws?
- Why is it so difficult for Congress to anticipate problems implementing laws?

education program or activity receiving federal financial assistance." Because almost every college and university receives some federal financial assistance, almost all were thereby forbidden to discriminate on the basis of gender. Interest groups supporting women's athletics convinced Congress to include a provision about college athletics as well. Thus Section 844 reads,

> The Secretary of [Health, Education, and Welfare (HEW) then, today of Education] shall prepare and publish . . . proposed regulations implementing the provisions of Title IX relating to prohibition of sex discrimination in Federally assisted education programs which shall include with respect to intercollegiate athletic activities reasonable provisions considering the nature of the particular sports.

Just what does this section mean? Proponents of women's athletics thought it meant that discrimination against women's sports was also prohibited. Some, with good reason, looked forward to seeing women's sports on an equal footing with men's. One member of the House-Senate Conference Committee proposed language specifically exempting "revenue-producing athletics" (meaning men's football and basketball) from the prohibition. The committee rejected this suggestion, but to colleges and universities with big-time athletic programs, and to some alumni, the vague

Bureaucracies are often asked to implement unclear laws. When Congress decided to prohibit gender discrimination in college athletics, for example, it left bureaucrats the task of creating guidelines that would end discrimination while addressing the diverse needs of different sports. It took years—and several lawsuits—to establish the law's meaning.

Section 844 called for equality in golf and swimming, not men's football and basketball programs, which could continue to have the lion's share of athletic budgets.

Joseph Califano, President Carter's secretary of HEW, was the man in the middle on this tricky problem. His staff developed a "policy interpretation" of the legislation, which he announced in December 1978. HEW's interpretation of the 100 or so words of Section 844 of Title IX numbered 30 pages. The interpretation recognized that football was "unique" among college sports. If football was unique, then the interpretation implied (but did not directly say) that male-dominated football programs could continue to outspend women's athletic programs.

Supporters of equal budgets for male and female athletics were outraged. Charlotte West of the Association for Intercollegiate Athletics for Women called HEW's interpretation "a multitude of imprecise and confusing explanations, exceptions, and caveats." Even the football-oriented National Collegiate Athletic Association was wary of the interpretation. One of its lawyers allowed, "They are trying to be fair. The question is how successful they are." A 100-word section in a congressional statute, which prompted a 30-page interpretation by the bureaucracy, in turn prompted scores of court cases. The courts have had to rule on such matters as whether Title IX requires that exactly equivalent dollar amounts be spent on women's and men's athletics. Litigation continues to this day.

The complex case of implementing Title IX for intercollegiate athletics contains an important lesson: Policy problems that Congress cannot resolve are not likely to be easily resolved by bureaucracies.

Bureaucrats receive not only unclear orders but also contradictory ones. James Q. Wilson points out that the Immigration and Naturalization Service was supposed to keep out illegal immigrants but let in necessary agricultural workers; to carefully screen foreigners seeking to enter the country but facilitate the entry of foreign tourists; and to find and expel illegal aliens but not break up families, impose hardships, violate civil rights, or deprive employers of low-paid workers. "No organization can accomplish all of these goals well, especially when advocates of each have the power to mount newspaper and congressional investigations of the agency's 'failures'."[20] Similarly, the National Park Service is ordered to preserve the environmental quality of national parks; it is also obliged to keep them accessible to tourists at the same time. The Forest Service is supposed to help timber companies exploit the lumber potential in the national forests *and* preserve the natural environment.

Lack of Resources.   As noted earlier, bureaucracies are often perceived as bloated. The important issue, however, is not the size of the bureaucracy in the abstract but whether it is the appropriate size to do the job it has been assigned to do. As big as a bureaucracy may seem in the aggregate, it frequently lacks the staff—along with the necessary training, funding, supplies, and equipment—to carry out the tasks it has been assigned. Recently, for example, the news has been filled with complaints such as:

You Are the President
of MEDICORP

- A shortage of staff at the Federal Drug Administration has been responsible for delays in the testing of new drugs to combat AIDS.
- Because of lack of funding, the popular Head Start program serves fewer than half the children who are theoretically eligible to participate.
- The Immigration and Naturalization Service (INS) lacked the personnel to track aliens who overstayed their visas or who engaged in suspicious activities such as taking flight training that did not include take-offs and landings. The INS also lacked the resources even to identify, much less deport, more than 10 percent of the 200,000 convicted criminal aliens in the United States. It even lacked the personnel to open letters containing checks for application fees.
- In their inspections of facilities handling and storing hazardous wastes, inadequately trained inspectors for the Environmental Protection Agency overlooked more than half the serious violations.
- The FBI lacks computers at its headquarters that allow it to search its own databases for multiple terms such as "aviation" and "schools."
- The lack of financing to maintain national parks may lead to permanent deterioration of such treasured American vacation spots as Yosemite and Yellowstone.
- The Federal Aviation Agency lacks the proper personnel and equipment to direct the nation's air traffic safely.
- The computer system used by the Environmental Protection Agency to track and control water pollution is obsolete, full of faulty data, and does not take into account thousands of significant pollution sources.
- The Internal Revenue Service lacks the appropriate computer systems to integrate the dozens of databases that contain the information necessary to collect the nearly $2 trillion in taxes that finance the federal government.
- There is a shortage of epidemiologists who are trained to recognize and investigate the outbreak of infectious disease.

Why It Matters

Bureaucratic Resources
A case can be made that some bureaucracies are too small. By substantially increasing the resources available to those who implement policies, it is possible that the quality of government services would improve.

Agencies may also lack the *authority* necessary to meet their responsibilities. For example, many observers believe that the Food and Drug Administration (FDA) lacks adequate powers to protect the public from dangerous drugs such as the sleeping pill Halcion and the sedative Versed. The FDA does no testing of its own and must rely entirely on the test results submitted by manufacturers. Yet it lacks the subpoena power to obtain documents when it suspects that drug companies are withholding data about adverse drug reactions or misrepresenting test results. It often lacks access to potentially damaging company documents that have been involved in private product-liability cases. Similarly, the Department of Agriculture lacks authority to close meat processing plants—even ones with serious violations of food safety standards.

standard operating procedures

Better known as SOPs, these procedures are used by bureaucrats to bring uniformity to complex organizations. Uniformity improves fairness and makes personnel interchangeable. See also **administrative discretion.**

Administrative Routine.   For most bureaucrats, administration is a routine matter most of the time. They follow **standard operating procedures,** better known as SOPs, to help them make numerous everyday decisions. Standard rules save time. If a Social Security caseworker had to invent a new rule for every potential client and then have it cleared at higher levels, few clients would be served. Thus detailed manuals are written to cover as many particular situations as officials can anticipate. The regulations elaborating the Internal Revenue Code compose an IRS agent's bible. Similarly, a customs agent has binders filled with rules and regulations about what can and cannot be brought into the United States duty-free.

SOPs also bring uniformity to complex organizations. Justice is better served when rules are applied uniformly, as in the implementation of welfare policies that distribute benefits to the needy or in the levying of fines for underpayment of taxes. Uniformity also makes personnel interchangeable. Soldiers, for example, can be transferred to any spot in the world and still find out how to do their job by referring to the appropriate manual.

Routines are essential to bureaucracy. Yet they sometimes become frustrating to citizens, who term them "red tape" when they do not seem appropriate to a situation. SOPs then become obstacles to action. In an October 1983 terrorist attack on their barracks outside Beirut, Lebanon, 241 Marines were killed while they slept. A presidential commission appointed to examine the causes of the tragedy concluded that, among other factors contributing to the disaster, the Marines in the peacekeeping force were "not trained, organized, staffed, or supported to deal effectively with the terrorist threat."[21] In other words, they had not altered their SOPs regarding security, which is basic to any military unit, to meet the unique challenges of a terrorist attack.

Sometimes an agency simply fails to establish routines that are necessary to complete its tasks. For example, in late 1997, the General Accounting Office found that the Federal Aviation Agency (FAA) failed to determine whether the violations its inspectors uncovered at aircraft repair stations were ever corrected. The FAA did not keep the proper paperwork for adequate follow-up activities.

Problems with SOPs are nothing new. They certainly frustrated Franklin D. Roosevelt:

> The Treasury is so . . . ingrained in its practices that I find it impossible to get the action and results I want. . . . But the Treasury is not to be compared with the State Department. You should go through the experience of trying to get any changes in the thinking, policy, and action of the career diplomats. . . . But both put together are nothing as compared to the Na-a-vy. . . . To change anything in the Na-a-a-vy is like punching a feather bed. You punch it with your right and you punch it with your left until you are finally exhausted, and then you find the damn bed just as it was before you started punching.[22]

Sometimes routines seem impenetrable to the average citizen, who must understand them in order to make use of the service bureaucracies offer. The Clinton administration made an effort to simplify government regulations. You can see an example of one success in "Making a Difference: Harry Carey and Sara Pratt."

Making a Difference

Harry Carey and Sara Pratt

Harry Carey and Sara Pratt worked in the Office for Fair Housing Enforcement. They won the "No Gobbledygook Award" in 1998 for putting into plain language a regulation on how to file a housing discrimination complaint, Originally the language read:

(a) Except as provided in paragraph (b) of this section, a complaint is filed when it is received by HUD, or dual filed with HUD through a substantially equivalent State or local agency, in a form that reasonably meets the standards of Sec. 103.30.
(b) The Assistant Secretary may determine that a complaint is filed for the purposes of the one-year period for the filing of complaints, upon the submission of written information (including information provided by telephone and reduced to writing by an employee of HUD) identifying the parties and describing generally the alleged discriminatory housing practice.
(c) Where a complaint alleges a discriminatory housing practice that is continuing, as manifested in a number of incidents of such conduct, the complaint will be timely if filed within one year of the last alleged occurrence of that practice.

Carey and Pratt changed the language to:

Is there a time limit on when I can file?
Yes. You must notify us within one year that you are a victim of discrimination. If you indicate there is more than one act of discrimination, or that it is continuing, we must receive your information within one year of the last incident.

Administrators' Dispositions. Paradoxically, bureaucrats operate not only within the confines of routines, but often with considerable discretion to behave independently. **Administrative discretion** is the authority of administrative actors to select among various responses to a given problem.[23] Discretion is greatest when rules do not fit a particular case, and this is often the case—even in agencies with elaborate rules and regulations.

administrative discretion

The authority of administrative actors to select among various responses to a given problem. Discretion is greatest when routines, or **standard operating procedures,** do not fit a case.

Although the income tax code is massive and detailed, the IRS wields vast discretion because of the complexity of the U.S. economy and the multitude of tax situations it produces. Here are a few examples:[24]

- Congress and the IRS code say that medical expenses above a certain percentage of income are deductible, but how about the expenses of a vasectomy? (The IRS said yes.)
- A girl who had been ordered to take strenuous exercise under the supervision of a doctor was enrolled by her father in $8,436 worth of ballet lessons. Was it deductible? (The IRS said no.)
- Congress and the IRS code say that business expenses are deductible, but can an airline flight attendant deduct the cost of uniforms? (The IRS said yes.)
- Are taxi expenses incurred in visiting your stockbroker a deductible expense? (The IRS said yes.)

street-level bureaucrats

A phrase coined by Michael Lipsky, referring to those bureaucrats who are in constant contact with the public and have considerable **administrative discretion.**

Some administrators exercise more discretion than others. Michael Lipsky coined the phrase **street-level bureaucrats** to refer to those bureaucrats who are in constant contact with the public (often a hostile one) and have considerable discretion; they include police officers, welfare workers, and lower-court judges.[25] No amount of rules, not even the thousands of pages of IRS rules, will eliminate the need for bureaucratic discretion on some policies. The highway patrol officer who stops you can choose to issue you a warning or a ticket.

Because bureaucrats will inevitably exercise discretion, it is important to understand how they use it. Ultimately, how they use discretion depends on their dispositions about the policies and rules they administer. Although bureaucrats may be indifferent to the implementation of many policies, other policies may conflict with their views or their personal or organizational interests. When people are asked to execute orders with which they do not agree, slippage is likely to occur between policy decisions and performance. A great deal of mischief may occur as well.

On one occasion, President Nixon ordered Secretary of Defense Melvin Laird to bomb a Palestine Liberation Organization hideaway, a move Laird opposed. According to the secretary, "We had bad weather for forty-eight hours. The Secretary of Defense can always find a reason not to do something."[26] The president's order was stalled for days and eventually rescinded.

Controlling the exercise of discretion is a difficult task. It is not easy to fire bureaucrats in the civil service, and removing appointed officials may be politically embarrassing to the president, especially if those officials have strong support in Congress and among interest groups. In the private sector, leaders of organizations provide incentives such as pay raises to encourage employees to perform their tasks in a certain way. In the public sector, however, special bonuses are rare, and pay raises tend to be small and across the board. Moreover, there is not necessarily room at the top for qualified bureaucrats. Unlike a typical private business, a government agency cannot expand just because it is performing a service effectively and efficiently.

In the absence of positive and negative incentives, the government relies heavily on rules to limit the discretion of implementors. As former Vice President Al Gore put it in a report issued by the National Performance Review,

Because we don't want politicians' families, friends, and supporters placed in "no-show" jobs, we have more than 100,000 pages of personnel rules and regulations defining in exquisite detail how to hire, promote, or fire federal employees. Because we don't want employees or private companies profiteering from federal contracts, we create procurement processes that require endless signatures and long months to buy almost anything. Because we don't want agencies using tax dollars for any unapproved purpose, we dictate precisely how much they can spend on everything from telephones to travel.[27]

Often these rules end up creating new obstacles to effective and efficient governing, however. As U.S. forces were streaming toward the Persian Gulf in the fall of 1990 to liberate Kuwait from Iraq, the air force placed an emergency order for 6,000 Motorola

Bureaucrats typically apply thousands of pages of rules in the performance of routine tasks, but many bureaucrats—especially street-level bureaucrats—must use administrative discretion as well. These border patrol officers, shown arresting illegal immigrants on the U.S.-Mexican border, must decide whom they will search carefully and whom they will let pass with a quick check.

commercial radio receivers. But Motorola refused to do business with the air force because of a government requirement that the company set up separate accounting and cost-control systems to fill the order. The only way the U.S. Air Force could acquire the much-needed receivers was for Japan to buy them and donate them to the United States!

Fragmentation. Sometimes responsibility for a policy is dispersed among several units within the bureaucracy. The federal government has more than 150 training and employment programs spread across 15 departments, agencies, and commissions. In the field of welfare, 10 different departments and agencies administer more than 100 federal human services programs. The Department of Health and Human Services has responsibility for basic welfare grants to families, the Department of Housing and Urban Development provides housing assistance, the Department of Agriculture runs the food stamp program, and the Department of Labor administers training programs and provides assistance in obtaining employment.

This diffusion of responsibility makes the coordination of policies both time consuming and difficult. For years, efforts to control the flow of illicit drugs into the country have been hindered by lack of cooperation among the Drug Enforcement Administration in the Department of Justice, the Customs Service in the Treasury Department, the State Department, and other relevant agencies. Similarly, the failure of the FBI and the CIA to share information hindered recognition of a possible terrorist attack in 2001.

The resources and authority necessary for the president to attack a problem comprehensively are often distributed among many bureaucratic units. President George W. Bush's creation of the Office of Homeland Security in 2001 dramatically illustrates the challenge of diffusion of responsibility. The president ordered the office to coordinate the implementation of a comprehensive national strategy to protect the United States from terrorist threats or attacks. This involved directing the counterterrorism efforts of 46 federal agencies, encompassing much of the federal government. Of course, each of these agencies also reported to other officials for other purposes.

One piece of the puzzle of homeland security is securing our borders. Table 15.4 lists the agencies with responsibilities for border control in 2002. As you can see, at least 33 departments and agencies had responsibility for protecting America's borders, focusing on threats ranging from illegal immigrants and chemical toxins to missiles

Table 15.4   Departments and Agencies with Responsibility for Border Security in 2002

Department of Agriculture
Animal and Plant Health Inspection Service

Central Intelligence Agency

Department of Commerce
Critical Infrastructure Assurance Office
National Oceanic and Atmospheric Administration

Department of Defense
Defense Intelligence Agency
Inspector General
National Guard
National Reconnaissance Office
National Security Agency
North American Aerospace Defense Command

Department of Energy
Office of Science and Technology Policy

Environmental Protection Agency
Office of International Activities

Department of Justice
Bureau of Alcohol, Tobacco, and Firearms
Drug Enforcement Administration
Federal Bureau of Investigation

Immigration and Naturalization Service
Marshals Service
Office of Special Investigations

Department of State
Bureau of Consular Affairs
Bureau of Intelligence and Research
Bureau of Population, Refugees, and Migration
Bureau for International Narcotics and Law Enforcement
    Agencies
Passport Office

Postal Service

Department of Treasury
Customs Service
Financial Crimes Enforcement Network
Internal Revenue Service
Office of the Inspector General
Secret Service

Department of Transportation
Coast Guard
Federal Aviation Agency
Federal Motor Carrier Administration
Maritime Administration

and electronic sabotage. It is difficult to coordinate so many different agencies, especially when they lack a history of trust and cooperation. Moreover, there are often physical obstacles to cooperation, such as the largely incompatible computer systems of the Immigration and Naturalization Service and the Coast Guard. Once the borders have been breached and an attack has occurred, many other offices get involved in homeland security, including hundreds of state and local agencies.

If fragmentation is a problem, why not reorganize the government? The answer lies in hyperpluralism and the decentralization of power. Congressional committees recognize that they would lose jurisdiction over agencies if these agencies were merged with others. Interest groups (such as the nuclear power industry) do not want to give up the close relationships they have developed with "their" agencies. Agencies themselves do not want to be submerged within a broader bureaucratic unit. All these forces fight reorganization, and they usually win.[28] President Clinton's proposal to merge the Drug Enforcement Administration and the Customs Service met with immediate opposition from the agencies and their congressional allies. Pursuing the merger became too costly for the president, who had to focus on higher-priority issues.

Nevertheless, under the right conditions, reorganization is possible. In 2001, congressional Democrats proposed a new Department of Homeland Security. In the summer of 2002, President George W. Bush concluded that the only way to overcome the fragmentation of agencies involved in providing homeland security was to create a new department, one that combined many of the agencies listed in Table 15.4. Congress created the new department at the end of 2002, the largest reorganization of the federal government in half a century.

A Case Study: The Voting Rights Act of 1965

Even when a policy is controversial, implementation can be effective if goals are clear and there are adequate means to achieve them. In 1965, Congress, responding to generations of discrimination against prospective African-American voters in the South,

How You Can Make a Difference

NASA

"Romantic" and "exciting" are adjectives rarely used to describe the federal bureaucracy in the United States. Unless that agency happens to be NASA—the National Aeronautics and Space Administration, that is. Since its creation in 1958, few other branches of the national government have captured people's imagination like NASA. The National Air and Space Museum in Washington, D.C. remains one of the most popular museums in the world. From the TV show "I Dream of Jeannie" to the movie "Armageddon," NASA has become a featured staple in American popular culture. However, in an era of budget cutting and a leaner federal government, NASA's future remains uncertain. And, given the crash of the space shuttle *Columbia*, NASA is under close scrutiny.

As Brian Chase, executive director of the National Space Society says, "Students are critical in shaping our future in space. The next generation of explorers is in school right now, so it's important that the sense of wonder and curiosity that helps drive our need to explore be nurtured and encouraged. And while space explorers today are scientists, engineers, and pilots, future explorers will come from every walk of life and every profession. Permanent space settlements will need not only technical skills but also lawyers, business managers, poets, artists, chefs, and

historians, to name just a few." It's only through action and support from average citizens like you that the dreams of NASA's space exploration can thrive.

One way to advance the cause of space exploration is to join one of the many advocacy groups for space exploration. To encourage political action, the National Space Society (*www.nss.org*) highlights key legislation pertaining to NASA that is moving through Congress and needs public lobbying. Calls, e-mails, and handwritten letters to your representatives are crucial in sustaining the U.S. space program. The Planetary Society (*www.planetary.org*), founded in 1980 by Carl Sagan and others, is another organization that seeks to encourage human exploration of space and further the search for extraterrestrial life. Through their volunteer network, the Planetary Society sponsors lectures and activities to stir up public interest in the space program. Joining one of these organizations is perhaps the single biggest step you can take to return NASA to its position of prominence and funding.

Beyond writing letters and contacting government officials regarding budget support for NASA, you can also help build public support for space exploration—starting with your neighborhood and campus. With chapters at universities and colleges around the world, Students for the Exploration and

Development of Space (*www.seds.org*) is a great place to start. SEDS works to build public awareness of space exploration by conducting programs at area elementary and secondary schools. This organization believes that the enthusiasm of young people is the necessary prerequisite to jump-start human exploration of space again.

Of course, there are those who believe that NASA is spending money that could be better spent on more practical things—that's a possibility you could consider as well. Whether you want to cut spending or increase spending—going through Congress is the way to go. Public support is the one sure way of getting Congress to increase spending—so join in. If you want to go to the moon someday on a vacation when you retire—then start working on it now!

What you can do:
- Visit the websites for the National Space Society, the Planetary Society, or Students for the Exploration of Space. Join and help out.
- Complete an internship with NASA or an aerospace contractor.
- Write your congressional representative today.
- Get involved in public awareness and education in favor of space exploration.

passed the Voting Rights Act. The act singled out six states in the Deep South in which the number of registered African-American voters was minuscule. Congress ordered the Justice Department to send federal registrars to each county in those states to register qualified voters. Congress outlawed literacy tests and other tests previously used to discriminate against African-American registrants. The government promised stiff penalties for those who interfered with the work of federal registrars.

Congress charged the attorney general with implementing the Voting Rights Act. He acted quickly and dispatched hundreds of registrars—some protected by U.S. marshals—to Southern counties. Within seven-and-a-half months after the act's passage, more than 300,000 new African-American voters were on the rolls. The proportion of the Southern African-American population registered to vote increased from 43 percent in 1964 to 66 percent in 1970, partly (though not entirely) because of the Voting Rights Act.[29]

The Voting Rights Act of 1965 was successfully implemented because its goal was clear: to register African Americans to vote in Southern counties where their voting rights had been denied for years. This federal registrar, like hundreds of others working for the Department of Justice, helped bring the vote to some 300,000 African Americans in less than a year.

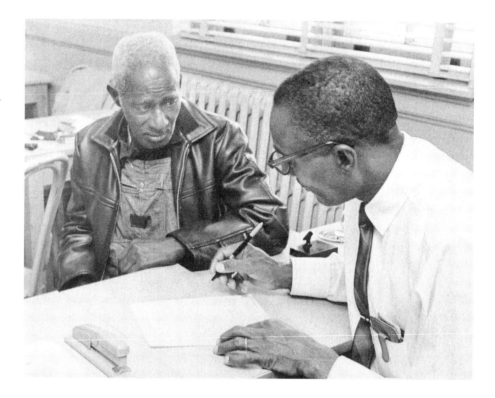

The Voting Rights Act was a successful case of implementation by any standard, but not because it was popular with everyone. Southern representatives and senators were outraged by it, and a filibuster delayed its passage in the Senate. It was successful because its goal was clear (to register large numbers of African-American voters), its implementation was straightforward (sending out people to register them), and the authority of the implementors was clear (they had the support of the attorney general and even U.S. marshals) and concentrated in the Justice Department, which was disposed to implementing the law vigorously.

Bureaucracies as Regulators

regulation

The use of governmental authority to control or change some practice in the private sector. Regulations pervade the daily lives of people and institutions.

Government **regulation** is the use of governmental authority to control or change some practice in the private sector. Regulations by government pervade Americans' everyday lives and the lives of businesses, universities, hospitals, and other institutions. Federal regulations now fill more than 200 volumes. Regulation is the most controversial role of the bureaucracies, yet Congress gives bureaucrats broad mandates to regulate activities as diverse as interest rates, the location of nuclear power plants, and food additives.

Regulation in the Economy and in Everyday Life

The notion that the American economy is largely a "free enterprise" system, unfettered by government intervention, is about as up to date as a Model T Ford. You can begin to understand the sweeping scope of governmental regulation by examining how the automobile industry is regulated.

- The Securities and Exchange Commission regulates buying and selling stock in an automobile corporation.
- Relations between the workers and managers of the company come under the scrutiny of the National Labor Relations Board.
- Affirmative action in hiring workers is mandated and administered by the Department of Labor and the Equal Employment Opportunity Commission because automakers are major government contractors.

Most government regulation is clearly in the public interest. For example, the U.S. Department of Agriculture is charged with regulating the quality of meat products, a task it was given after novelist Upton Sinclair exposed the meat-packaging industry's unsanitary conditions at the turn of the century.

- The Environmental Protection Agency, the National Highway Traffic Safety Administration, and the Department of Transportation require pollution-control, energy-saving, and safety devices.
- Unfair advertising and deceptive consumer practices in marketing cars come under the watchful eye of the Federal Trade Commission.

A Full Day of Regulation.   Everyday life itself is the subject of bureaucratic regulation. Almost all bureaucratic agencies—not merely the ones called independent regulatory agencies—are in the regulatory business. Consider a typical factory worker (we'll name him John Smith) who works in the city of Chicago and lives with his wife, Joan Smith, and their three young children in suburban Mount Prospect, Ill. Both at work and at home, federal regulations affect John's life. At 5:30 A.M. he is awakened by his clock radio, which is set to a country music station licensed to operate by the Federal Communications Commission. For breakfast he has cereal, which has passed inspection by the Food and Drug Administration, as has the lunch Joan packs for him. The processed meat in his sandwich is packed under the supervision of the Food Safety and Quality Service of the U.S. Department of Agriculture.

John takes the train to work and buys a quick cup of coffee before the journey. The FDA has warned that the caffeine in his coffee has caused birth defects in laboratory animals, and there is discussion in Washington about regulating it. After paying his fare (regulated by the state government), he hops aboard and shortly arrives at work, a small firm that makes equipment for the food industry.

At home, Joan Smith is preparing breakfast for the children. The price of the milk she serves is affected by the dairy price supports regulated by the Agricultural Stabilization and Conservation Service. As the children play, she evaluates the toys they use, wanting to avoid any that could be dangerous. A Washington agency, the Consumer Product Safety Commission, also takes note of children's toys, regulating their manufacture and sale. The Consumer Product Safety Commission also regulates the lawn mower, the appliances, the microwave oven, and numerous other items around the Smith house.

Setting out for the grocery store and the bank, Joan encounters even more government regulations. The car has seat belts mandated by the National Highway Traffic Safety Administration, and the Department of Transportation certifies its gas mileage. The car's pollution-control devices are now in need of service because they do not meet the requirements of the Environmental Protection Agency. The bank where Joan deposits money and writes a check is among the most heavily regulated institutions she encounters in her daily life. Her passbook savings rate is regulated by the Depository Institutions Deregulation Committee, and her account is insured by the Federal Deposit Insurance Commission.

Meanwhile, John Smith is at work assembling food-processing machinery. He and the other workers are members of the International Association of Machinists. Their negotiations with the firm are held under rules laid down by the National Labor Relations Board. Not long ago, the firm was visited by inspectors from the Occupational Safety and Health Administration (OSHA), a federal agency charged with ensuring worker safety. OSHA inspectors noted several violations and forwarded a letter recommending safety changes to the head of the firm.

Back at home, John has a beer before dinner. It was made in a brewery carefully supervised by the Bureau of Alcohol, Tobacco, and Firearms, and federal and state taxes were collected when it was sold. After dinner (almost all the food served has been transported by the regulated trucking industry), the children are sent to bed. An hour or so of television, broadcast on regulated airwaves, is followed by bedtime. A switch will turn off the electric lights, whose rates are regulated by the Illinois Commerce Commission and the Federal Energy Regulatory Commission.[30]

Regulation: How It Grew, How It Works

Timeline

The Evolution of the
Federal Bureaucracy

From the beginnings of the American republic until 1887, the federal government made almost no regulatory policies; the little regulation produced was handled by state and local authorities. Even the minimal regulatory powers of state and local governments were much disputed. In 1877, the Supreme Court upheld the right of government to regulate the business operations of a firm. The case, *Munn v. Illinois*, involved the right of the state of Illinois to regulate the charges and services of a Chicago warehouse. During this time, farmers were seething about alleged overcharging by railroads, grain elevator companies, and other business firms. In 1887—a decade after *Munn*—Congress created the first regulatory agency, the Interstate Commerce Commission (ICC), and charged it with regulating the railroads, their prices, and their services to farmers; the ICC thus set the precedent for regulatory policymaking.

As regulators, bureaucratic agencies typically operate with a large grant of power from Congress, which may detail goals to be achieved but may also permit the agencies to sketch out the regulatory means. In 1935, for example, Congress created the National Labor Relations Board to control "unfair labor practices," but the NLRB had to play a major role in defining "fair" and "unfair." Most agencies charged with regulation must first develop a set of rules, often called *guidelines*. The appropriate agency may specify how much food coloring it will permit in a hot dog, how many contaminants it will allow an industry to dump into a stream, how much radiation from a nuclear reactor is too much, and so forth. Guidelines are developed in consultation with, and sometimes with the agreement of, the people or industries being regulated.

Next, the agency must apply and enforce its rules and guidelines, either in court or through its own administrative procedures. Sometimes it waits for complaints to come to it, as the Equal Employment Opportunity Commission does; sometimes it sends inspectors into the field, as the Occupational Safety and Health Administration does; and sometimes it requires application for a permit or license to demonstrate performance consistent with congressional goals and agency rules, as the Federal Communications Commission does. Often government agencies take violators to court, hoping to secure a judgment and fine against an offender (see "You Are the Policymaker:

command-and-control policy

According to Charles Schultze, the existing system of **regulation** whereby government tells business how to reach certain goals, checks that these commands are followed, and punishes offenders. Compare **incentive system.**

You Are the Policymaker

How Should We Regulate?

Almost every regulatory policy was created to achieve some desirable social goal. When more than 6,000 people are killed annually in industrial accidents, who would disagree with the goal of a safer workplace? Who would dissent from greater highway safety, when more than 40,000 die each year in automobile accidents? Who would disagree with policies to promote equality in hiring, when the history of opportunities for women and minorities is one of discrimination? Who would disagree with policies to reduce industrial pollution, when pollution threatens health and lives? However, there may be more than one way to achieve these—and many other—desirable social goals.

Charles L. Schultze, former chair of President Carter's Council of Economic Advisors, is—like Murray L. Weidenbaum, who held the same position under President Reagan—a critic of the current state of federal regulation. Schultze reviewed the regulatory activities of the Environmental Protection Agency (EPA) and the Occupational Safety and Health Administration (OSHA). Neither agency's policies, he concluded, had worked very well. He

described the existing system as **command-and-control policy:** The government tells business how to reach certain goals, checks that these commands are followed, and punishes offenders.

Schultze advocates an **incentive system.** He argues that instead of telling construction businesses how their ladders must be constructed, measuring the ladders, and charging a small fine for violators, it would be more efficient and effective to levy a high tax on firms with excessive worker injuries. Instead of trying to develop standards for 62,000 pollution sources, as the EPA now does, it would be easier and more effective to levy a high tax on those who cause pollution. The government could even provide incentives in the form of rewards for such socially valuable behavior as developing technology to reduce pollution. Incentives, Schultze argues, use market-like strategies to regulate industry. They are, he claims, more effective and efficient than command-and-control regulation.

Not everyone is as keen on the use of incentives as Schultze. Defenders of the command-and-control system of

regulation compare the present system to preventive medicine—it is designed to minimize pollution or workplace accidents before they become too severe. Defenders of the system argue, too, that penalties for excessive pollution or excessive workplace accidents would be imposed only after substantial damage had been done. They also add that if taxes on pollution or unsafe work environments were merely externalized (that is, passed along to the consumer as higher prices), they would not be much of a deterrent. Moreover, it would take a large bureaucracy to monitor carefully the level of pollution discharged, and it would require a complex calculation to determine the level of tax necessary to encourage businesses not to pollute.

The issue of the manner of regulation is a complex one. What would *you* do?

Sources: Charles L. Schultze, *The Public Use of the Private Interest* (Washington, D.C.: Brookings Institution, 1977); and Steven Kelman, *What Price Incentives? Economists and the Environment* (Boston: Auburn House, 1981).

How Should We Regulate?"). Whatever strategy Congress permits a regulating agency to use, all regulation contains these elements: (1) *a grant of power and set of directions from Congress,* (2) *a set of rules and guidelines* by the regulatory agency itself, and (3) *some means of enforcing compliance* with congressional goals and agency regulations.

Government regulation of the American economy and society has, of course, grown in recent decades. The budgets of regulatory agencies, their level of employment, and the number of rules they issue are all increasing—and did so even during the conservative Reagan administration. As we have seen, few niches in American society are *not* affected by regulation. Not surprisingly, this situation has led to charges that government is overdoing it.

Toward Deregulation

Deregulation—the lifting of government restrictions on business, industry, and professional activities—is currently a fashionable term.[31] The idea behind deregulation is that the number and complexity of regulatory policies have made regulation too complicated

You Are a Federal Administrator

incentive system

According to Charles Schultze, a more effective and efficient policy than **command-and-control**; in the incentive system, market-like strategies are used to manage public policy.

deregulation

The lifting of restrictions on business, industry, and professional activities for which government rules had been established and that bureaucracies had been created to administer.

and burdensome. To critics, the problem with regulation is that it raises prices, distorts market forces, and—worst of all—does not work. They claim that the regulatory system:

- *Raises prices.* If the producer is faced with expensive regulations, the cost will inevitably be passed on to the consumer in the form of higher prices.
- *Hurts America's competitive position abroad.* Other nations may have fewer regulations on pollution, worker safety, and other business practices than the United States. Thus American products may cost more in the international marketplace, undermining sales in other countries.
- *Does not always work well.* Tales of failed regulatory policies are numerous. Regulations may be difficult or cumbersome to enforce. Critics charge that regulations sometimes do not achieve the results that Congress intended and maintain that they simply create massive regulatory bureaucracies.

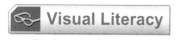

The Changing Face of the
Federal Bureaucracy

President Reagan's conservative political philosophy was opposed to much government regulation, but even before the Reagan administration, sentiment favoring deregulation was building in the Washington community. Even liberals sometimes joined the antiregulation chorus; for example, Senator Edward Kennedy of Massachusetts pushed for airline deregulation. The airline industry also pressed for deregulation and in 1978 the Civil Aeronautics Board (CAB) began to deregulate airline prices and airline routes. In 1984, the CAB formally disbanded; it even brought in a military bugler to play taps at its last meeting.

Not everyone, however, believes that deregulation is in the nation's best interest.[32] For example, critics point to severe environmental damage resulting from lax enforcement of environmental protection standards during the Reagan administration. Similarly, many observers attribute at least a substantial portion of the blame for the enormously expensive bailout of the savings and loan industry to deregulation in the 1980s. Many people now argue for more regulation of savings and loan institutions. Californians found that deregulation led to severe power shortages in 2001.

In addition, many regulations have proved beneficial to Americans. As a result of government regulations, we breathe cleaner air,[33] we have lower levels of lead in our blood, miners are safer at work,[34] seacoasts have been preserved,[35] and children are more likely to survive infancy.[36]

Understanding Bureaucracies

As both implementors and regulators, bureaucracies are making public policy, not just administering someone else's decisions. The fact that bureaucrats, who are not elected, compose most of the government raises fundamental issues about who controls governing and what the bureaucracy's role should be.

Bureaucracy and Democracy

Bureaucracies constitute one of America's two unelected policymaking institutions (courts are the other). In democratic theory, popular control of government depends on elections, but we could not possibly elect the 4.2 million federal civilian and military employees, or even the few thousand top men and women, though they spend more than $2 trillion of the American GDP. Furthermore, the fact that voters do not elect civil servants does not mean that bureaucracies cannot respond to and represent the public's interests. When we compare the backgrounds of bureaucrats with those of members of Congress or presidents, we find that bureaucrats are more representative than elected officials. Much depends on whether bureaucracies are effectively controlled by the policymakers citizens do elect—the president and Congress.[37]

Presidents Try To Control the Bureaucracy. Chapter 13 looked at some of the frustrations presidents endure in trying to control the government they are elected to

America in Perspective

Influencing Independent Agencies

We often think of the president as head of the executive branch, but there are agencies, such as the Federal Reserve Board, that are very powerful and are generally free from the chief executive's direction. This often leaves presidents frustrated, as when they wish the Federal Reserve Board to lower interest rates to stimulate the economy. There are even more autonomous agencies in Latin America, however—agencies removed from the direct control of the president and the legislature.

Why would Latin American governments create agencies they cannot control? The primary reason is to protect a new agency providing a new service from changes in policy made by future decision makers. Those who create an agency fear that its policies will be undone by a new administration or legislature, so they make it autonomous.

These agencies often have their own sources of revenue and thus can increase their budgets without going through the public and controversial process of government budget debates. They are also freer from legislative oversight and formal presidential controls than are regular agencies, and conflict over their programs is less visible. Expenditures for autonomous agencies also allow the government to engage in creative financing because when these agencies contract debt, it does not count against the central government's debt (which is substantial in Latin America).

Autonomy is decidedly a mixed blessing, however. Creative financing is not necessarily good for a nation, nor is the difficulty policymakers have in consolidating bureaucracies and increasing their efficiency. The lack of traditional means of influence also makes it difficult to alter the priorities of agencies, such as shifting the emphasis from building roads to building apartments.

Sources: Michelle M. Taylor, "When Are Juridically Autonomous Agencies Responsive to Elected Officials? A Simulation Based on the Costa Rican Case," *Journal of Politics* 57 (November 1995): 1,070–1,092; and Bruce M. Wilson, Juan Carlos Rodríguez Cordero, and Roger Handberg, "The Best Laid Schemes . . . Gang Aft A-gley: Judicial Reform in Latin America—Evidence from Costa Rica," *Journal of Latin American Studies* 36 (August 2004).

run. Presidents try hard—not always with success—to impose their policy preferences on agencies (see "America in Perspective: Influencing Independent Agencies"). Following are some presidential methods of exercising control over bureaucracies:

- *Appoint the right people to head the agency.* Normally, presidents control the appointments of agency heads and subheads. Putting their people in charge is one good way for presidents to influence agency policy,[38] yet even this has its problems. President Reagan's efforts to whittle the powers of the Environmental Protection Agency led to his appointment of controversial Anne Gorsuch to head the agency. Gorsuch had previously supported policies contrary to the goals of the EPA. When Gorsuch attempted to implement her policies, legal squabbles with Congress and political controversy ensued, ultimately leading to her resignation. To patch up the damage Gorsuch had done to his reputation, Reagan named a moderate and seasoned administrator, William Ruckelshaus, to run the agency. Ironically, Ruckelshaus demanded, and got, more freedom from the White House than Gorsuch had sought.
- *Issue orders.* Presidents can issue **executive orders** to agencies. These orders carry the force of law and are used to implement statutes, treaties, and provisions of the Constitution.[39] Sometimes presidential aides simply pass the word that "the President was wondering if . . ." These messages usually suffice, although agency heads are reluctant to run afoul of Congress or the press on the basis of a broad presidential hint. The president's rhetoric in speeches outside the bureaucracy may also influence the priorities of bureaucrats.[40]
- *Tinker with an agency's budget.* The Office of Management and Budget is the president's own final authority on any agency's budget. The OMB's threats to cut here or add there will usually get an agency's attention. Each agency, however, has its constituents within and outside of Congress, and Congress, not the president, does the appropriating.

Comparing Bureaucracies

executive orders

Regulations originating from the executive branch. Executive orders are one method presidents can use to control the bureaucracy.

The Executive Order Over Time

- *Reorganize an agency.* Although President Reagan promised, proposed, and pressured to abolish the Department of Energy and the Department of Education, he never succeeded—largely because each department was in the hands of an entrenched bureaucracy backed by elements in Congress and strong constituent groups. Reorganizing an agency is hard to do if it is a large and strong agency; reorganizing a small and weak agency is often not worth the trouble.

Congress Tries To Control the Bureaucracy.   Congress exhibits a paradoxical relationship with the bureaucracies. On the one hand (as we have seen), members of Congress may find a big bureaucracy congenial.[41] Big government provides services to constituents, who may show their appreciation at the polls. Moreover, when Congress lacks the answers to policy problems, it hopes the bureaucracies will find them. Unable itself, for example, to resolve the touchy issue of equality in intercollegiate athletics, Congress passed the ball to the Department of Health, Education, and Welfare. Unable to decide how to make workplaces safer, Congress produced the Occupational Safety and Health Administration (OSHA). As you saw in Chapter 12, Congress is increasingly the problem-identifying branch of government, setting the bureaucratic agenda but letting the agencies decide how to implement the goals it sets.

On the other hand, Congress has found it hard to control the government it helped create. There are several measures Congress can take to oversee the bureaucracy:

- *Influence the appointment of agency heads.* Even when senatorial approval of a presidential appointment is not required, members of Congress are not shy in offering their opinions about who should and should not be running the agencies. When congressional approval is required, members are doubly influential. Committee hearings on proposed appointments are almost guaranteed to produce lively debates if some members find the nominee's probable orientations objectionable.
- *Tinker with an agency's budget.* With the congressional power of the purse comes a mighty weapon for controlling bureaucratic behavior. At the same time, Congress knows that agencies perform services that its constituents demand. Too much budget cutting may make an agency more responsive—at the price of losing an interest group's support for a reelection campaign.
- *Hold hearings.* Committees and subcommittees can hold periodic hearings as part of their oversight job. Flagrant agency abuses of congressional intent can be paraded in front of the press, but responsibility for oversight typically goes to the

Former FBI Director J. Edgar Hoover is an example of a powerful bureaucrat who worked outside the law. Hoover took over the new agency in 1924 and, after consolidating his power following World War II, began collecting information on presidents, members of Congress, and later, liberal groups and civil rights leaders. Partly because they were afraid of what he might have in his files, elected officials were unwilling to control Hoover, who did not relinquish power until his death in 1972.

very committee that created a program; the committee thus has some stake in showing the agency in a favorable light.

- *Rewrite the legislation or make it more detailed.* Every statute is filled with instructions to its administrators. To limit bureaucratic discretion and make its instructions clearer, Congress can write new or more detailed legislation. Still, even voluminous detail (as in the case of the IRS) can never eliminate discretion.

Through these and other devices, Congress tries to keep bureaucracies under its control. Never entirely successful, Congress faces a constant battle to limit and channel the vast powers that it delegated to the bureaucracy in the first place.

Sometimes these efforts are detrimental to bureaucratic performance. The explosion of legislative subcommittees has greatly increased Congress' oversight activities. Numerous subcommittees may review the actions of a single agency. A half-dozen or more subcommittees may review the activities of the Department of Energy, the Department of Agriculture, or the Department of Commerce. Different committees may send different signals to the same agency. One may press for stricter enforcement, another for more exemptions. As the oversight process has become more vigorous, it has also become more fragmented, thus limiting the effectiveness of the bureaucracies.

Iron Triangles and Issue Networks. Agencies' strong ties to interest groups on the one hand and to congressional committees and subcommittees on the other further complicate efforts to control the bureaucracy. Chapter 11 illustrated that bureaucracies often enjoy cozy relationships with interest groups and with committees or subcommittees of Congress. When agencies, groups, and committees all depend on one another and are in close, frequent contact, they form what are sometimes called **iron triangles** or *subgovernments*. These triads have advantages on all sides (see Figure 15.5).

iron triangles

A mutually dependent relationship between bureaucratic agencies, interest groups, and congressional committees or subcommittees. Iron triangles dominate some areas of domestic policymaking.

There are plenty of examples of subgovernments at work. A subcommittee on aging, senior citizens' interest groups, and the Social Security Administration are likely to agree on the need for more Social Security benefits. Richard Rettig has recounted how an alliance slowly jelled around the issue of fighting cancer. It rested on three pillars: cancer researchers, agencies within the National Institutes of Health, and members of congressional health subcommittees.[42]

When these iron triangles shape policies for senior citizens, cancer, tobacco, or any other interest, each policy is made independently of the others, sometimes even in contradiction to other policies. For example, for years the government has supported tobacco farmers in one way or another while encouraging people not to smoke. Moreover, the iron triangles' decisions tend to bind larger institutions, such as Congress and the White House. Congress often defers to the decisions of committees and subcommittees, especially on less visible issues. The White House may be too busy wrestling with global concerns to fret over agricultural issues or cancer. Emboldened by this lack of involvement, subgovernments flourish and add a strong decentralizing and fragmenting element to the policymaking process.

Hugh Heclo points out that the system of subgovernments is now overlaid with an amorphous system of *issue networks*. There is more widespread participation in bureaucratic policymaking, and many of the participants have technical policy expertise and are drawn to issues because of intellectual or emotional commitments rather than material interests. Those concerned with environmental protection, for example, have challenged formerly closed subgovernments on numerous fronts (see Chapter 19). This opening of the policymaking process complicates the calculations and decreases the predictability of those involved in the stable and relatively narrow relationships of subgovernments.[43]

Although subgovernments are often able to dominate policymaking for decades, they are not indestructible.[44] For example, the subgovernment pictured in Figure 15.5 long dominated smoking and tobacco policy, focusing on crop subsidies to tobacco farmers. But increasingly, these policies have come under fire from health authorities, who were not involved in tobacco policymaking in earlier years. Similarly, pesticide

Figure 15.5   Iron Triangles: One Example

Iron triangles—composed of bureaucratic agencies, interest groups, and congressional committees or subcommittees—have dominated some areas of domestic policymaking by combining internal consensus with a virtual monopoly on information in their area. The tobacco triangle is one example; there are dozens more. Iron triangles are characterized by mutual dependency, in which each element provides key services, information, or policy for the others. The arrows indicate some of these mutually helpful relationships. In recent years, a number of well-established iron triangles, including the tobacco triangle, have been broken up.

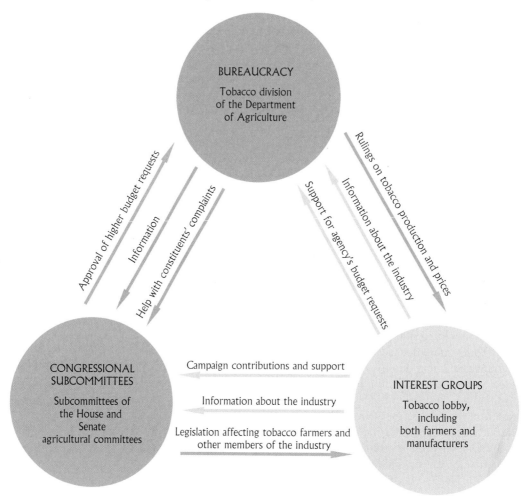

policy, once dominated by chemical companies and agricultural interests, is no longer considered separately from environmental and health concerns.

An especially vivid example of the death of an iron triangle is the case of nuclear power.[45] During the 1940s and 1950s, Americans were convinced that the technology that had ended World War II could also serve peaceful purposes. Nuclear scientists spoke enthusiastically about harnessing the atom to achieve all sorts of goals, eventually making electricity so inexpensive that it would be "too cheap to meter." Optimism in progress through science was the rule, and the federal government encouraged the development of nuclear power through a powerful iron triangle.

A special congressional joint committee, the Joint Committee on Atomic Energy, was established and given complete control over questions of nuclear power in Congress. A new executive agency, the Atomic Energy Commission (AEC), was created, and together with the private companies that built the nuclear power plants and the electrical utilities that wanted to operate them, they formed a powerful subgovernment. America built more nuclear power plants than any other country in the world, and American technology was exported overseas to dozens of nations.

Nuclear power today—after the accidents at Three Mile Island and Chernobyl and the various cost overruns associated with the industry—bears almost no resemblance to that of the early 1960s when the iron triangle was at its peak. What happened? The experts lost control. When questions arose concerning the safety of the plants and when opponents were able to get local officials to question the policies publicly, the issue grew into a major political debate of the late 1960s, associated with the growth of environmentalism. Two of the most powerful legs of the iron triangle were destroyed. The Joint Committee on Atomic Energy was disbanded; a variety of congressional committees now claim some jurisdiction over nuclear power questions. Similarly, the AEC was replaced by two new agencies: the Nuclear Regulatory Commission and the Department of Energy.

The nuclear power industry has been devastated: No new nuclear power plants have been built in the United States since 1978, and almost all those under construction at that time have been abandoned at huge financial loss. In sum, the wave of environmental concern that developed in the late 1960s swept away one of the most powerful iron triangles in recent American history.

Bureaucracy and the Scope of Government

To many, the huge American bureaucracy is the prime example of the federal government growing out of control. As this chapter discussed earlier, some observers view the bureaucracy as acquisitive, constantly seeking to expand its size, budgets, and authority. Much of the political rhetoric against big government also adopts this line of argument, along with complaints about red tape, senseless regulations, and the like. It is easy to take pot shots at a faceless bureaucracy that usually cannot respond.

One should keep in mind, however, that the federal bureaucracy has not grown over the past two generations, as Figure 15.1 illustrates. If one considers the fact that the population of the country has grown significantly over this period, then the federal bureaucracy has actually *shrunk* in size relative to the population it serves.

Originally, the federal bureaucracy had the modest role of promoting the economy, defending the country, managing foreign affairs, providing justice, and delivering the mail. Its role gradually expanded to include providing services to farmers, businesses, and workers. The discussion of federalism in Chapter 3 showed that as the economy and the society of the United States changed, additional demands were made on government. Government—and the bureaucracy—are now expected to play an active role in dealing with social and economic problems. A good case can be made that the bureaucracy is actually too *small* for many of the tasks currently assigned to it—tasks ranging from the control of illicit drugs to protection of the environment.

In addition, it is important to remember that when the president and Congress have chosen to deregulate certain areas of the economy or cut taxes, the bureaucracy could not and did not prevent them from doing so. The question of what and how much the federal government should do—and thus how big the bureaucracy should be—is answered primarily at the polls and in Congress, the White House, and the courts—not by faceless bureaucrats.

Summary

Americans rarely congratulate someone for being a good bureaucrat. Unsung, taunted by cartoonists, and maligned by columnists, bureaucrats are the scapegoats of American politics. Americans may call presidents great and reelect members of Congress, but almost no one praises bureaucrats. Those who compose the bureaucracy, however, perform most of the vital services provided by the federal government.

Bureaucrats shape policy as administrators, as implementors, and as regulators. In this chapter we examined who bureaucrats are, how they got their positions, and what they do. Today, most bureaucrats working for the federal government get their jobs through the civil service system, although a few at the very top are appointed by the president.

In general, there are four types of bureaucracies: the cabinet departments, the regulatory agencies, the government corporations, and the independent executive agencies.

As policymakers, bureaucrats play three key roles. First, they are policy implementors, translating legislative policy goals into programs. Policy implementation does not always work well, and when it does not, bureaucrats usually take the blame, whether they deserve it or not. Second, bureaucrats administer public policy. Much of administration involves a prescribed routine, but nearly all bureaucrats still have some discretion. Third, bureaucrats are regulators. Congress increasingly delegates large amounts of power to bureaucratic agencies and expects them to develop rules and regulations. Scarcely a nook or cranny of American society or the American economy escapes the long reach of bureaucratic regulation.

Although bureaucrats are not elected, bureaucracies are not necessarily undemocratic. Bureaucracies must be controlled by elected decision makers, but presidential or congressional control over bureaucracies is difficult. Bureaus have strong support from interest groups—a factor that contributes to pluralism because interest groups try to forge common links with bureaucracies and congressional committees. These subgovernments tend to decentralize policymaking, thereby contributing to hyperpluralism.

Although there are many critics of the increasing size of government, the federal bureaucracy has not grown over the past two generations. Instead, it has shrunk, even as the country has grown and the public has made additional demands on government.

KEY TERMS

bureaucracy	Senior Executive Service	regulation
patronage	independent regulatory	deregulation
Pendleton Civil Service	agency	command-and-control
Act	government corporations	policy
civil service	independent executive	incentive system
merit principle	agency	executive orders
Hatch Act	policy implementation	iron triangles
Office of Personnel	standard operating	
Management (OPM)	procedures	
GS (General Schedule)	administrative discretion	
rating	street-level bureaucrats	

INTERNET RESOURCES

www.gpoaccess.gov/gmanual/index.html
U.S. Government Manual that provides information on the organization of the U.S. government.

www.gpoaccess.gov/fr/index.html
The Federal Register, which provides information on U.S. laws and regulations.

www.whitehouse.gov/government/cabinet.html
Information on federal cabinet departments.

www.whitehouse.gov/government/independent-agencies.html
Information on federal independent agencies and commissions.

www.opm.gov/feddata/
Federal employment statistics.

www.opm.gov
Office of Personnel Management website with information on federal jobs and personnel issues.

www.govexec.com/
The website for *Government Executive* magazine.

GET CONNECTED

How Bureaucracies Are Organized

On January 24, 2003, President George W. Bush signed legislation that created a new department and the largest federal bureaucracy since 1947. The new department, called the Department of Homeland Security, was proposed first by Congress in the aftermath of the September 11, 2001, terrorist attacks. The department's mission is to better coordinate the nation's homeland defenses. Do you know how this new bureaucracy is organized? Could you contact the Department of Homeland Security if you needed to? Let us look at this department's web page to learn more about the agency.

Search the Web

Go to *http://www.dhs.gov/dhspublic/faq.jsp* and review the information on that page. Then review *America at Risk: A Homeland Security Report Card* published by the Progressive Policy Institute at *http://www.ppionline.org/documents/HomeSecRptCrd_0703.pdf*.

Questions To Ask

- How many agencies have been combined to create the new Department of Homeland Security?
- What are some of the challenges the Progressive Policy Institute identifies for the new Department of Homeland Security?

Why It Matters

The Department of Homeland Security is the most dramatic change in the federal bureaucracy in half a century. It is likely that, as with most other agencies, citizens will come into contact with the new agency often, especially as they travel.

Get Involved

Do you have a question about the Department of Homeland Security? If so, go to *http://www.dhs.gov/dhspublic/contactus* and send your question. Discuss the response you get with your class. You also may follow issues related to homeland security by visiting the web page of the United States House of Representatives Select Committee on Homeland Security *http://hsc.house.gov/*.

To see more Get Connected exercises for Chapter 15, go to www.ablongman.com/edwards.

FOR FURTHER READING

Aberbach, Joel D., and Bert A. Rockman. *In the Web of Politics.* Washington, D.C.: Brookings Institution, 2000. Examines federal executives and the degree to which they are representative of the country and responsive to elected officials.

Arnold, Peri E. *Making the Managerial Presidency*, 2nd ed. Princeton, NJ: Princeton University Press, 1996. A careful examination of efforts to reorganize the federal bureaucracy.

Derthick, Martha, and Paul J. Quirk. *The Politics of Deregulation.* Washington, D.C.: Brookings Institution, 1985. Explains why advocates of deregulation prevailed over the special interests that benefited from regulation.

Edwards, George C., III. *Implementing Public Policy.* Washington, D.C.: Congressional Quarterly Press, 1980. A good review of the issues involved in implementation.

Goodsell, Charles T. *The Case for Bureaucracy*, 4th ed. Washington, D.C.: Congressional Quarterly, 2004. A strong case on behalf of the effectiveness of bureaucracy.

Gormley, William T., Jr. *Taming the Bureaucracy.* Princeton, NJ: Princeton University Press, 1989. Examines remedies for controlling bureaucracies.

Gormley, William T., Jr., and Steven J. Balla. *Bureaucracy and Democracy: Accountability and Performance.* Washington, D.C.: Congressional Quarterly, 2003. Discusses the accountability of unelected bureaucrats in a democracy.

Heclo, Hugh M. *Government of Strangers: Executive Politics in Washington.* Washington, D.C.: Brookings Institution, 1977. A study of the top executives of the federal government, who constitute (says the author) a "government of strangers."

Kerwin, Cornelius M. *Rulemaking: How Government Agencies Write Law and Make Policy*, 3rd ed.. Washington, D.C.: Congressional Quarterly Press, 2003. Explains how agencies write regulations to implement laws.

Osborne, David, and Ted Gaebler. *Reinventing Government.* Reading, MA: Addison-Wesley, 1992. Simplistic but important view of making government more entrepreneurial and responsive to citizens.

Savas, E. S. *Privatization: The Key to Better Government.* Chatham, NJ: Chatham House, 1987. A conservative economist's argument that many public services performed by bureaucracies would be better handled by the private sector.

Wilson, James Q. *Bureaucracy.* New York: Basic Books, 1989. Presents a "bottom-up" approach to understanding how bureaucrats, managers, and executives decide what to do.

The Federal Courts

16

Chapter Outline

The Nature of the Judicial System

The Structure of the Federal Judicial System

The Politics of Judicial Selection

The Backgrounds of Judges and Justices

The Courts as Policymakers

The Courts and the Policy Agenda

Understanding the Courts

The New York Times Issues of the Times

Summary

■ Say that you are involved in a lawsuit regarding the application of an affirmative action policy in your college or university. A trial is held in a federal district court. After the trial, a verdict is rendered and you lose. Not content to accept this decision, you appeal to the court of appeals. Once again, you lose. Now you have only two options left: accept the decision or appeal to the U.S. Supreme Court. You decide to appeal, and of the thousands of petitions for hearings presented to the Court each year, yours is one of a few dozen the Court selects.

On the day of the oral argument (there are no trials in the Supreme Court), you walk up the steep steps of the Supreme Court building, the impressive "Marble Palace" with the motto "Equal Justice Under Law" engraved over its imposing columns. The Court's surroundings and procedures suggest the nineteenth century. The justices, clothed in black robes, take their seats at the bench in front of a red velvet curtain. Behind the bench there are still spittoons, one for each justice. (Today, the spittoons are used as wastebaskets.)

Your case, like most of the cases the Court selects for oral arguments, is scheduled for about an hour. Lawyers arguing before the Court often wear formal clothing. They find a goose quill pen on their desk, purchased by the Court from a Virginia supplier. (Lawyers may take the pen with them as a memento of their day in court.) As is the norm, each side is allotted 30 minutes to present its case. The justices may, and do, interrupt the lawyers with questions. When the time is up, a discreet red light goes on at your lawyer's lectern, and he immediately stops talking.

That is the end of the hearing, but not the end of the process. You have asked the Court to overrule a policy established by your state legislature. As the Court considers doing so, it recognizes that its decision will become precedent for all such policies across the nation. Months will go by, as the justices deliberate and negotiate an opinion, before the Court announces its decision. If you win, it will take many more months for your university, aided by lower courts, to interpret the decision and implement it.

The scope of the Supreme Court's power is great, extending even to overruling the decisions of elected officials. Despite the trappings of tradition and majesty, however, the Court does not reach its decisions in a political vacuum. Instead, it works in a context of political influences and considerations, a circumstance that raises important questions about the role of the judiciary in the U.S. political system.

The federal courts pose a special challenge to American democracy. Although it is common for state judges to be elected in one fashion or another, federal judges are *appointed* to their positions—for

life. The framers of the Constitution purposefully insulated federal judges from the influence of public opinion. How can we reconcile powerful courts populated by unelected judges with American democracy? Do they pose a threat to majority rule? Or do the federal courts actually function to protect the rights of minorities and thus maintain the type of open system necessary for democracy to flourish?

The power of the federal courts also raises the issue of the appropriate scope of judicial power in our society. Federal courts are frequently in the thick of policymaking on issues ranging from affirmative action and abortion to physician-assisted suicide and the financing of public schools. Numerous critics argue that judges should not be actively involved in determining public policy. Instead, the critics say, judges should focus on settlement of routine disputes and leave the determination of policy to elected officials. On the other hand, advocates of a more aggressive role for the courts emphasize that judicial decisions have often met pressing needs—especially needs of those who are politically or economically weak—left unmet by the normal processes of policymaking. For example, we have already seen the leading role that the federal courts played in ending legally supported racial segregation in the United States. To determine the appropriate role of the courts in our democracy, we must first understand the nature of our judicial system.

However impressive the Supreme Court may be, only the tiniest fraction of American judicial policy is made there. To be sure, the Court decides a handful of key issues each year. Some will shape people's lives, perhaps even decide issues of life and death. In addition to the Supreme Court, there are 12 federal courts of appeal, a Court of Appeals for the Federal Circuit, 91 federal district courts, and thousands of state and local courts (the latter will be discussed in Chapter 21). Most of America's legal business is transacted in these less august courts. This chapter will focus on federal courts and the judges who serve on them—the men and women in black robes who are important policymakers in the American political system.

The Nature of the Judicial System

The judicial system in the United States is, at least in principle, an adversarial one in which the courts provide an arena for two parties to bring their conflict before an impartial arbiter (a judge). The system is based on the theory that justice will emerge out of the struggle between two contending points of view. The task of the judge is to apply the law to the case, determining which party is legally correct. In reality, most cases never go to trial because they are settled by agreements reached out of court.

There are two basic kinds of cases: criminal law cases and civil law cases. In a *criminal law* case, the government charges an individual who violated specific laws, such as those prohibiting robbery. The offense may be harmful to an individual or to society as a whole, but in either case it warrants punishment, such as imprisonment or a fine. In a *civil law* case, there is no charge of criminality—no charge that a law has been violated. Such a case involves a dispute between two parties (one of whom may be the government itself) and defines relationships between them. Civil law cases range from divorce proceedings to mergers of multinational companies. Civil law consists of both statutes (laws passed by legislatures) and common law (the accumulation of judicial decisions).

Just as it is important not to confuse criminal and civil law, it is important not to confuse state and federal courts. The vast majority of all criminal and civil cases involve state law and are tried in state courts. Criminal cases such as burglary and civil cases such as divorce normally begin and end in the state, not the federal, courts.

Participants in the Judicial System

The serenity and majesty of the U.S. Supreme Court are a far cry from the grimy urban courts where strings of defendants are bused from the local jails for their day—often only a few minutes—in court. Yet every case has certain components in common, including litigants, attorneys, and judges. Sometimes organized groups are also directly involved. Judges are the policymakers of the American judicial system, and we examine them extensively in later sections of this chapter. Here we will discuss the other regular participants in the judicial process.

Litigants. Federal judges are restricted by the Constitution to deciding "cases" or "controversies"—that is, actual disputes rather than hypothetical ones. Judges do not issue advisory opinions on what they think (in the abstract) may be the meaning or constitutionality of a law. The judiciary is essentially passive, dependent on others to take the initiative.

Thus two parties must bring a case to the court before it may be heard. Every case is a dispute between a *plaintiff* and a *defendant* in which the former brings some charge against the latter. Sometimes the plaintiff is the government, which may bring a charge against an individual or a corporation. The government may charge the defendant with the brutal murder of Jones or charge the XYZ Corporation with illegal trade practices. All cases are identified with the name of the plaintiff first and the defendant second, for example, *State v. Smith* or *Anderson v. Baker*. In many (but not all) cases, a *jury*, a group of citizens (usually 12), is responsible for determining the outcome of a lawsuit.

Litigants end up in court for a variety of reasons. Some are reluctant participants—the defendant in a criminal case, for example. Others are eager for their day in court. For some, the courts can be a potent weapon in the search for a preferred policy. For example, in the 1960s, atheist Madalyn Murray O'Hair was an enthusiastic litigant, always ready to take the government to court for promoting religion.

Not everyone can challenge a law, however. Plaintiffs must have what is called **standing to sue**; that is, they must have serious interest in a case, which is typically determined by whether they have sustained or are in immediate danger of sustaining a direct and substantial injury from another party or an action of government. Except in cases pertaining to governmental support for religion, merely being a taxpayer and being opposed to a law do not provide the standing necessary to challenge that law in court. Nevertheless, Congress and the Supreme Court have liberalized the rules for standing, making it somewhat easier for citizens to challenge governmental and corporate actions in court.

In recent years, the concept of standing to sue has been broadened. **Class action suits** permit a small number of people to sue on behalf of all other people in similar circumstances. These suits may be useful in cases as varied as civil rights, in which a few persons seek an end to discriminatory practices on behalf of all who might be discriminated against, and environmental protection, in which a few persons may sue a polluting industry on behalf of all who are affected by the air or water the industry pollutes. Following an explosion of such cases, in 1973 the Supreme Court began making it more difficult to file class action suits.

Conflicts must not only arise from actual cases between litigants with standing in court, but they must also be **justiciable disputes**—issues that are capable of being settled by legal methods. One would not go to court to determine whether Congress should fund the Strategic Defense Initiative (SDI), for the matter could not be resolved through legal methods or knowledge.

Groups. Because they recognize the courts' ability to shape policy, interest groups often seek out litigants whose cases seem particularly strong. Few groups have been more successful in finding good cases and good litigants than the National Association for the Advancement of Colored People, which selected the school board of Topeka, Kans., and a young schoolgirl named Linda Brown as the litigants in *Brown v. Board of Education* (1954). NAACP legal counsel Thurgood Marshall (see "Making a

standing to sue

The requirement that **plaintiffs** have a serious interest in a **case,** which depends on whether they have sustained or are likely to sustain a direct and substantial injury from a party or an action of government.

class action suits

Lawsuits permitting a small number of people to sue on behalf of all other people similarly situated.

justiciable disputes

A requirement that to be heard a case must be capable of being settled as a matter of law rather than on other grounds as is commonly the case in legislative bodies.

Sometimes people find themselves involved in extraordinary court decisions. Linda Brown was a plaintiff in *Brown v. Board of Education,* a key civil rights case in which the Supreme Court overturned its earlier *Plessy v. Ferguson* ruling that legalized segregation.

Difference: Thurgood Marshall") believed that Topeka represented a stronger case than other school districts in the United States in the effort to end the policy of "separate but equal"—meaning racially segregated—public education because the city provided segregated facilities that were otherwise genuinely equal. The courts could not resolve the case simply by insisting that expenditures for schools for White and African-American children be equalized.

The American Civil Liberties Union is another interest group that is always seeking cases and litigants to support in its defense of civil liberties. One ACLU attorney, stressing that principle took priority over a particular client, even admitted that the ACLU's clients are often "pretty scurvy little creatures. . . . It's the principle that we're going to be able to use these people for that's important."[1] (For an example, review the case in Chapter 4 of the Nazis who tried to march in Skokie, Ill.)

At other times groups do not directly argue the case for litigants, but support them instead with *amicus curiae* ("friend of the court") briefs that attempt to influence the Court's decision, raise additional points of view, and present information not contained in the briefs of the attorneys for the official parties to the case. In controversial cases, there may be many such briefs submitted to the Court; 102 were presented in the University of Michigan case on affirmative action in 2003.

Attorneys. Lawyers are indispensable actors in the judicial system. Law is one of the nation's fastest growing professions. The United States counted about 100,000 lawyers in 1960 but has nearly 800,000 today. Lawyers busily translate policies into legal language and then enforce or challenge them.

amicus curiae **briefs**

Legal briefs submitted by a "friend of the court" for the purpose of raising additional points of view and presenting information not contained in the briefs of the formal parties. These briefs attempt to influence a court's decision.

Once lawyers were primarily available to the rich. Today, public interest law firms can sometimes handle legal problems of the poor and middle classes. The federally funded Legal Services Corporation employs lawyers to serve the legal needs of the poor, although the Reagan administration made drastic cuts in legal aid. State and local governments provide public defenders for poor people accused of crimes. Some employers and unions now provide legal insurance, which works like medical insurance. Members with legal needs—for a divorce, a consumer complaint, or whatever—can secure legal aid through prepaid plans. As a result, more people than ever before can take their problems to the courts. Equality of access, of course, does not mean equality of representation. The wealthy can afford high-powered attorneys who can invest many hours in their cases and arrange for testimony by expert witnesses. The poor are often served by overworked attorneys with few resources to devote to an individual case.

The audience for the judicial drama is a large and attentive one that includes interest groups, the press (a close observer of the judicial process, especially of its more sensational aspects), and the public, who often have very strong opinions about how the process works. All these participants—plaintiffs, defendants, lawyers, interest groups, and others—play a role in the judicial drama, even though many of their activities take place outside the courtroom. How these participants arrive in the courtroom and which court they go to reflect the structure of the court system.

Making a Difference

Thurgood Marshall

Thurgood Marshall led a civil rights revolution in the twentieth century that forever changed the landscape of American society. As director and legal counsel of the NAACP's Legal Defense and Education Fund, Marshall coordinated the organization's effort to end racial segregation. He won an astonishing 29 of 32 cases he argued before the Supreme Court, including the landmark *Brown v. Board of Education* case. He later served on the Court for 23 years, where he was a vigorous advocate for protections under law for African Americans, women, children, prisoners, and the homeless.

You Are a Young Lawyer

The Structure of the Federal Judicial System

The Constitution is vague about the structure of the federal court system. Aside from specifying that there will be a Supreme Court, the Constitution left it to Congress' discretion to establish lower federal courts of general jurisdiction. In the Judiciary Act of

Figure 16.1　Organization of the Federal Court System

1789, Congress created these *constitutional courts*, and although the system has been altered over the years, America has never been without them. The current organization of the federal court system is displayed in Figure 16.1.

Congress has also established *legislative courts* for specialized purposes. These courts include the Court of Military Appeals, the Court of Claims, the Court of International Trade, and the Tax Court. These legislative courts are staffed by judges who have fixed terms of office and who lack the protections against removal or salary reductions that judges on constitutional courts enjoy. The following sections, however, will focus on the courts of general jurisdiction.

First, we must understand another difference among courts. Courts with **original jurisdiction** are those in which a case is heard first, usually in a trial. These are the courts that determine the facts about a case, whether it is a criminal charge or a civil suit. More than 90 percent of court cases begin and end in the court of original jurisdiction.

Lawyers can sometimes appeal an adverse decision to a higher court for another decision. Courts with **appellate jurisdiction** hear cases brought to them on appeal from a lower court. Appellate courts do not review the factual record, only the legal issues involved. At the state level, the appellate process normally ends with the state's highest court of appeal, which is usually called the state supreme court. Appeals from a state high court can be taken only to the U.S. Supreme Court.

District Courts

The entry point for most litigation in the federal courts is one of the 91 **district courts,** at least one of which is located in each state, in addition to one in Washington, D.C. and one in Puerto Rico (there are also three somewhat different territorial courts for Guam, the Virgin Islands, and the Northern Mariana Islands). The district courts are courts of original jurisdiction; they hear no appeals. They are the only federal courts in which trials are held and in which juries may be impaneled. The 680 district court judges usually preside over cases alone, but certain rare cases require that three judges constitute the court. Each district court has between 2 and 28 judges, depending on the amount of judicial work within its territory.

The jurisdiction of the district courts extends to

- Federal crimes
- Civil suits under federal law
- Civil suits between citizens of different states where the amount in question exceeds $75,000

original jurisdiction

The jurisdiction of courts that hear a case first, usually in a trial. These are the courts that determine the facts about a case.

appellate jurisdiction

The jurisdiction of courts that hear cases brought to them on appeal from lower courts. These courts do not review the factual record, only the legal issues involved.

district courts

The 91 federal courts of original jurisdiction. They are the only federal courts in which trials are held and in which juries may be impaneled.

- Supervision of bankruptcy proceedings
- Review of the actions of some federal administrative agencies
- Admiralty and maritime law cases
- Supervision of the naturalization of aliens

It is important to remember that about 98 percent of all the criminal cases in the United States are heard in state and local court systems, not in the federal courts. Moreover, only a small percentage of the persons convicted of federal crimes in the federal district courts actually have a trial. Most enter guilty pleas as part of a bargain to receive lighter punishment.

Most civil suits in the United States are also handled in state and local courts. The vast majority of civil cases that commence in the federal courts are settled out of court. Only about 2 percent of the more than 250,000 civil cases resolved each year are decided by trials.

Diversity of citizenship cases involve civil suits between citizens of different states (such as a citizen of California suing a citizen of Texas) or suits in which one of the parties is a citizen of a foreign nation and the matter in question exceeds $75,000. Congress established this jurisdiction to protect against the possible bias of a state court in favor of a citizen from that state. In these cases, federal judges are to apply the appropriate state laws.

An elaborate supporting cast assists district judges. In addition to clerks, bailiffs, law clerks, stenographers, court reporters, and probation officers, U.S. marshals are assigned to each district to protect the judicial process and to serve the writs that the judges issue. Federal magistrates, appointed to eight-year terms, issue warrants for arrest, determine whether to hold arrested persons for action by a grand jury, and set bail. They also hear motions subject to review by their district judge and, with the consent of both parties in civil cases and of defendants in petty criminal cases, preside over some trials. As the workload for district judges increases (there were more than 315,000 cases in 2003),[2] magistrates are becoming essential components of the federal judicial system.

Another important player at the district court level is the U.S. attorney. Each of the 91 regular districts has a U.S. attorney who is nominated by the president and confirmed by the Senate and who serves at the discretion of the president (U.S. attorneys do not have lifetime appointments). These attorneys and their staffs prosecute violations of federal law and represent the U.S. government in civil cases.

Most of the cases handled in the district courts are routine, and few result in policy innovations. Usually district court judges do not even publish their decisions. Although most federal litigation ends at this level, a large percentage of these cases that district court judges actually decide (as opposed to those settled out of court or by guilty pleas in criminal matters) are appealed by the losers. A distinguishing feature of the American legal system is the relative ease of appeals. U.S. law gives everyone a right to an appeal to a higher court. The loser in a case only has to request an appeal to be granted one. Of course, the loser must pay a substantial legal bill to exercise this right.

Courts of Appeal

courts of appeal

Appellate courts empowered to review all final decisions of district courts, except in rare cases. In addition, they also hear appeals to orders of many federal regulatory agencies. Compare **district courts.**

The U.S. **courts of appeal** are courts empowered to review all final decisions of district courts, except in rare instances in which the law provides for direct review by the Supreme Court (injunctive orders of special three-judge district courts and certain decisions holding acts of Congress unconstitutional). Courts of appeal also have authority to review and enforce orders of many federal regulatory agencies, such as the Securities and Exchange Commission and the National Labor Relations Board. About 75 percent of the more than 60,000 cases heard in the courts of appeal each year come from the district courts.

Figure 16.2   The Federal Judicial Circuits

Not shown are Puerto Rico (First Circuit), Virgin Islands (Third Circuit), and Guam and the Northern Mariana Islands (Ninth Circuit).

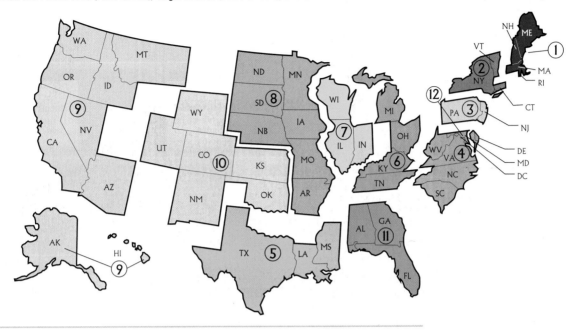

The United States is divided into 12 judicial circuits, including one for the District of Columbia (see Figure 16.2). Each circuit serves at least two states and has between 6 and 28 permanent circuit judgeships (179 in all), depending on the amount of judicial work in the circuit. Each court of appeal normally hears cases in panels consisting of three judges, but each may sit *en banc* (with all judges present) in particularly important cases. Decisions in either arrangement are made by majority vote of the participating judges.

There is also a special appeals court called the U.S. Court of Appeals for the Federal Circuit. Composed of 12 judges, it was established by Congress in 1982 to hear appeals in specialized cases, such as those regarding patents, claims against the United States, and international trade.

The courts of appeal focus on correcting errors of procedure and law that occurred in the original proceedings of legal cases, such as when a district court judge gave improper instructions to a jury or misinterpreted the rights provided under a law. These courts are appellate courts and hold no trials and hear no testimony. Their decisions set precedent for all the courts and agencies within their jurisdictions.

The Supreme Court

Sitting at the pinnacle of the American judicial system is the U.S. **Supreme Court.** The Court does much more for the American political system than decide individual cases. Among its most important functions are resolving conflicts among the states and maintaining national supremacy in the law. The Supreme Court also plays an important role in ensuring uniformity in the interpretation of national laws. For example, in 1984 Congress created a federal sentencing commission to write guidelines aimed at reducing the wide disparities in punishment for similar crimes tried in federal courts. By 1989, more than 150 federal district judges had declared the law unconstitutional, and another 115 had ruled it valid. Only the Supreme Court could resolve this inconsistency in the administration of justice, which it did when it upheld the law.

Supreme Court

The pinnacle of the American judicial system. The Court ensures uniformity in interpreting national laws, resolves conflicts among states, and maintains national supremacy in law. It has both **original jurisdiction** and **appellate jurisdiction,** but unlike other federal courts, it controls its own agenda.

Figure 16.3   The Organization and Jurisdiction of the Courts

UNITED STATES SUPREME COURT

Original jurisdiction of the Supreme Court	Appellate jurisdiction of the Supreme Court (federal route)	Appellate jurisdiction of the Supreme Court (state route)
Cases involving foreign diplomats Cases involving a state: • Between the United States and a state • Between two or more states • Between one state and citizens of another state • Between a state and a foreign country	U.S. Courts of Appeal Court of Appeals for the Federal Circuit Legislative Courts	State Courts of Last Resort

There are nine justices on the Supreme Court: eight associates and one chief justice (only members of the Supreme Court are called justices; all others are called judges). The Constitution does not require this number, however, and there have been as few as six justices and as many as ten. The size of the Supreme Court was altered many times between 1801 and 1869. In 1866, Congress reduced the size of the Court from ten to seven members so that President Andrew Johnson could not nominate new justices to fill two vacancies. When Ulysses S. Grant took office, Congress increased the number of justices to nine because it was confident that he would nominate members to its liking. Since then, the number of justices has remained stable.

All nine justices sit together to hear cases and make decisions. But they must first decide which cases to hear. A familiar battle cry for losers in litigation in lower courts is "I'll appeal this all the way to the Supreme Court!" In reality, this is unlikely to happen. Unlike other federal courts, the Supreme Court decides which cases it will hear.

You can see in Figure 16.3 that the Court does have an original jurisdiction, yet very few cases arise under it, as Table 16.1 illustrates. Almost all the business of the Court comes from the appellate process, and cases may be appealed from both federal and state courts. In the latter instance, however, a "substantial federal question" must be involved. In deference to the states, the Supreme Court hears cases from state courts only if they involve federal law, and then only after the petitioner has exhausted all the potential remedies in the state court system. Cases from state courts cannot be appealed to any other federal court.

The Court will not try to settle matters of state law or determine guilt or innocence in state criminal proceedings. To obtain a hearing in the Supreme Court, a defendant convicted in a state court might demonstrate, for example, that the trial was not fair as required by the Bill of Rights, which was extended to cover state court proceedings by

Table 16.1   Sources of Full Opinions in the Supreme Court

TYPE OF CASE	NUMBER OF CASES
Original jurisdiction	1
Civil actions from lower federal courts	46
Federal criminal and *habeas corpus* cases	24
Civil actions from state courts	0
State criminal cases	9
TOTAL	80

Source: "The Supreme Court, 2003 Term: The Statistics," *Harvard Law Review* 118 (November 2004): 507–509.

the due process clause of the Fourteenth Amendment. The majority of cases heard by the Supreme Court come from the lower federal courts.

The central participants in the judicial system are, of course, the judges. Once on the bench, they must draw on their backgrounds and beliefs to guide their decision-making. Some, for example, will be more supportive of abortion or of prayer in the public schools than others. Because presidents and others involved in the appointment process know perfectly well that judges are not neutral automatons who methodically and literally interpret the law, they work diligently to place candidates sympathetic to presidential policies on the bench. Who are the men and women who serve as federal judges and justices, and how did they obtain their positions?

The Politics of Judicial Selection

Appointing a federal judge or a Supreme Court justice is a president's chance to leave an enduring mark on the American legal system. Guaranteed by the Constitution the right to serve "during good behavior," federal judges and justices enjoy, for all practical purposes, lifetime positions. They may be removed only by conviction of impeachment, which has occurred a mere seven times in two centuries under the Constitution. No Supreme Court justice has ever been removed from office, although one, Samuel Chase, was tried but not convicted by the Senate in 1805. Nor can members of the federal judiciary have their salaries reduced, a stipulation that further insulates them from political pressures.

Although the president nominates persons to fill judicial slots, the Senate must confirm each nomination by majority vote. Because the judiciary is a coequal branch, the upper house of the legislature sees no reason to be especially deferential to the executive's recommendations. Because of the Senate's role, the president's discretion is actually less important than it appears.

The Lower Courts

The customary manner in which the Senate handles state-level federal judicial nominations is through **senatorial courtesy.** Under this unwritten tradition (which began under George Washington in 1789), nominations for lower-court positions are not confirmed when opposed by a senator of the president's party from the state in which the nominee is to serve. In the case of judges for courts of appeal, nominees are not confirmed if opposed by a senator of the president's party from the state of the nominee's residence.

To invoke the right of senatorial courtesy, the relevant senator usually simply states a general reason for opposition. Other senators then honor their colleague's views and oppose the nomination, regardless of their personal evaluations of the candidate's merits.

Because of the strength of this informal practice, presidents usually check carefully with the relevant senator or senators ahead of time to avoid making a nomination

senatorial courtesy

An unwritten tradition whereby nominations for state-level federal judicial posts are not confirmed if they are opposed by a senator of the president's party from the state in which the nominee will serve. The tradition also applies to courts of appeal when there is opposition from the nominee's state senator.

Why It Matters

Senatorial Courtesy
Because of the practice of senatorial courtesy, senators actually end up nominating persons to be district court judges. If the Senate abolished this practice, it would allow the president greater freedom in making nominations and give the White House more opportunity to put its stamp on the judiciary.

that will fail to be confirmed. In many instances, this is tantamount to giving the power of nomination to these senators. Typically, when there is a vacancy for a federal district judgeship, the one or two senators from the state where the judge will serve suggest one or more names to the attorney general and the president. If neither senator is of the president's party, then the party's state congresspersons or other state party leaders may make suggestions. Other interested senators may also try to influence a selection.[3]

Once several names have been submitted to the president, the Department of Justice and the Federal Bureau of Investigation conduct competency and background checks on these persons, and the president usually selects a nominee from those who survive the screening process. It is difficult for the president to reject the recommendation of the party's senator in favor of someone else if the person recommended clears the hurdles of professional standing and integrity. Thus the Constitution is often turned on its head, and the Senate ends up making nominations, which the president then approves.

Others have input in judicial selection as well. The Department of Justice may ask sitting judges, usually federal judges, to evaluate prospective nominees. Sitting judges may also initiate recommendations to advance or retard someone's chances of being nominated. In addition, candidates for the nomination are often active on their own behalf. They have to alert the relevant parties that they desire the position and may orchestrate a campaign of support. As one appellate judge observed, "People don't just get judgeships without seeking them."[4]

The president usually has more influence in the selection of judges to the federal courts of appeal than to federal district courts. The decisions of appellate courts are generally more significant than those of lower courts, so the president naturally takes a greater interest in appointing people to these courts. At the same time, individual senators are in a weaker position to determine who the nominee will be because the jurisdiction of an appeals court encompasses several states. Although custom and pragmatic politics require that these judgeships be apportioned among the states in a circuit, the president has some discretion in doing this and therefore has a greater role in recruiting appellate judges than in recruiting district court judges. Even here, however, senators of the president's party from the state in which the candidate resides may be able to veto a nomination.

The increasing polarization of partisan politics in recent years has affected courts of appeals nominations. The time for confirmation has increased dramatically,[5] which has decreased the chances of confirmation. Senators of the opposition party have filibustered or otherwise derailed the confirmations of a number of high-profile nominations of Presidents Clinton and George W. Bush. In response, Bush appointed some judges to the courts of appeals as recess appointments. Such appointments are unusual and good only for the remainder of a congressional term. They are also likely to anger opposition senators.

Simulation

You Are Appointing a Supreme Court Justice

The Supreme Court

The president is vitally interested in the Supreme Court because of the importance of its work and will generally be intimately involved in recruiting potential justices. Nominations to the Court may be a president's most important legacy to the nation.

A president cannot have much impact on the Court unless there are vacancies to fill. Although on the average there has been an opening on the Supreme Court every two years, there is a substantial variance around this mean.[6] Franklin D. Roosevelt had to wait five years before he could nominate a justice; in the meantime, he was faced with a Court that found much of his New Deal legislation unconstitutional. More recently, Jimmy Carter was never able to nominate a justice. Between 1972 and 1984, there were only two vacancies on the Court. Nevertheless, Richard Nixon was able to nominate four justices in his first three years in office, and Ronald Reagan had the opportunity to add three new members.

When the chief justice's position is vacant, the president may nominate either someone already on the Court or someone from outside to fill the position. Usually presidents choose the latter course to widen their range of options, but if they decide to elevate a sitting associate justice—as President Reagan did with William Rehnquist in 1986—the nominee must go through a new confirmation hearing by the Senate Judiciary Committee.

The president operates under fewer constraints in nominating persons to serve on the Supreme Court than in naming persons to be judges in the lower courts. Although many of the same actors are present in the case of Supreme Court nominations, their influence is typically quite different. The president usually relies on the attorney general and the Department of Justice to identify and screen candidates for the Court. Sitting justices often try to influence the nominations of their future colleagues, but presidents feel little obligation to follow their advice.

Why It Matters

Judicial Elections
The public directly elects most state and local judges. All federal judges and justices are nominated by the president and confirmed by the Senate for lifetime tenures. If we elected federal judges, their decisions on highly visible issues might be more responsive to the public—but less responsive to the Constitution.

Senators also play a lesser role in the recruitment of Supreme Court justices than in the selection of lower-court judges. No senator can claim that the jurisdiction of the Court falls within the realm of his or her special expertise, interest, or sphere of influence. Thus presidents typically consult with senators from the state of residence of a nominee after they have decided whom to select. At this point, senators are unlikely to oppose a nomination because they like having their state receive the honor and are well aware that the president can simply select someone from another state.

Candidates for nomination usually keep a low profile. Little can be accomplished through aggressive politicking, and because of the Court's standing, actively pursuing the position might offend those who play important roles in selecting nominees. The American Bar Association's Standing Committee on the federal judiciary has played a varied but typically modest role at the Supreme Court level. Presidents have not generally been willing to allow the committee to prescreen candidates before their nominations are announced. George W. Bush chose not to seek its advice at all.

Through 2004, there have been 148 nominations to the Supreme Court, and 108 persons have served on the Court. Four people were nominated and confirmed twice, eight declined appointment or died before beginning service on the Court, and 28 failed to secure Senate confirmation. Presidents have failed 20 percent of the time to appoint the nominees of their choice to the Court—a percentage much higher than for any other federal position.

Although home-state senators do not play prominent roles in the selection process for the Court, the Senate as a whole does. Through its Judiciary Committee, it may probe a nominee's judicial philosophy in great detail.

For most of the twentieth century, Supreme Court nominations were routine affairs. Only one nominee failed to win confirmation in the first two-thirds of the century (see Table 16.2). But the 1960s were tumultuous times and bred ideological conflict. Although John F. Kennedy had no trouble with his two nominations to the Court—Byron White and Arthur Goldberg—his successor, Lyndon Johnson, was not so fortunate. Johnson had to withdraw his nomination of Abe Fortas (already serving on the Court) to serve as chief justice in the face of strong opposition; therefore, the Senate never voted on Homer Thornberry, Johnson's nominee to replace Fortas as an associate justice. Richard Nixon, the next president, had two nominees rejected in a row after bruising battles in the Senate.

The most recent failed nominations occurred in 1987. President Reagan nominated Robert H. Bork to fill the vacancy created by the resignation of Justice Lewis Powell. Bork testified before the Senate Judiciary Committee for 23 hours. A wide range of interest groups entered the fray, mostly in opposition to the nominee, whose views they claimed were extremist. In the end, following a bitter floor debate, the Senate rejected the president's nomination by a vote of 42 to 58.

Six days after the Senate vote on Bork, the president nominated Judge Douglas H. Ginsburg to the high court. Just nine days later, however, Ginsburg withdrew his nomination after disclosures that he had used marijuana while a law professor at Harvard.

Table 16.2   Twentieth-Century Senate Rejections of Supreme Court Nominees

NOMINEE	YEAR	PRESIDENT
John J. Parker	1930	Hoover
Abe Fortas[a]	1968	Johnson
Homer Thornberry[b]	1968	Johnson
Clement F. Haynesworth, Jr.	1969	Nixon
G. Harrold Carswell	1970	Nixon
Robert H. Bork	1987	Reagan
Douglas H. Ginsburg[a]	1987	Reagan

[a]Nomination withdrawn. Fortas was serving on the Court as an associate justice and was nominated to be chief justice.
[b]The Senate took no action on Thornberry's nomination.

In June 1991, at the end of the Supreme Court's term, Associate Justice Thurgood Marshall announced his retirement from the Court. Shortly thereafter, President Bush announced his nomination of another African American, federal appeals judge Clarence Thomas, to replace Marshall on the Court. Thomas was a conservative, so this decision was consistent with the Bush administration's emphasis on placing conservative judges on the federal bench.

The president claimed that he was not employing quotas when he chose another African American to replace the only African American ever to sit on the Supreme Court. Not everyone believed him, but liberals were placed in a dilemma. On the one hand, they favored a minority group member serving on the nation's highest court. On the other hand, Thomas was unlikely to vote the same way as Thurgood Marshall had voted. Instead, Thomas presented the prospect of strengthening the conservative trend in the Court's decisions. In the end, this ambivalence inhibited spirited opposition to Thomas, who was circumspect about his judicial philosophy in his appearances before the Senate Judiciary Committee. The committee sent his nomination to the Senate floor on a split vote.

Just as the Senate was about to vote on the nomination, however, charges of sexual harassment leveled against Thomas by University of Oklahoma law professor Anita Hill were made public. Hearings were reopened on the charges in response to criticism that the Senate was sexist for not seriously considering them in the first place. For several days, citizens sat transfixed before their television sets as Professor Hill calmly

In 1991, after two weeks of riveting hearings in which Clarence Thomas was charged with sexual harassment, the Senate narrowly confirmed his nomination to the Supreme Court. Historically, about one-fifth of those nominated to the Court have failed to obtain confirmation.

and graphically described her recollections of Thomas's behavior. Thomas then emphatically denied any such behavior and charged the Senate with racism for raising the issue. Ultimately, public opinion polls showed that most people believed Thomas, and he was confirmed in a 52–48 vote—the closest vote on a Supreme Court nomination in more than a century.

The Senate's treatment of President Clinton's two nominees harks back to the Kennedy era. Neither Ruth Bader Ginsburg nor Stephen Breyer caused much controversy. It is unlikely that the days of deference to the president have returned, however.

Nominations are most likely to run into trouble under certain conditions. Presidents whose parties are in the minority in the Senate or who make a nomination at the end of their terms face a greatly increased probability of substantial opposition.[7] Presidents whose views are more distant from the norm in the Senate or who are appointing a person who might alter the balance on the Court are also likely to face additional opposition. Equally important, opponents of a nomination usually must be able to question a nominee's competence or ethics in order to defeat a nomination. Opposition based on a nominee's ideology is generally not considered a valid reason to vote against confirmation. For example, liberals disagreed strongly with the views of William Rehnquist, but he was easily confirmed as chief justice. Questions of the legal competence and ethics of nominees must usually be raised by their opponents in order to attract moderate senators to their side and to make ideological protests seem less partisan.

The Backgrounds of Judges and Justices

The Constitution sets no special requirements for judges or justices, but most observers conclude that the federal judiciary is composed of a distinguished group of men and women. Competence and ethical behavior are important to presidents for reasons beyond merely obtaining Senate confirmation of their judicial nominees. Skilled and honorable judges and justices reflect well on the president and are likely to do so for many years. Moreover, these individuals are more effective representatives of the president's views. Although the criteria of competence and character screen out some possible candidates, there is still a wide field from which to choose. Other characteristics then play prominent roles.

The judges serving on the federal district and circuit courts are not a representative sample of the American people (see Table 16.3). They are all lawyers (although this is not a constitutional requirement), and they are overwhelmingly White males. Jimmy Carter appointed 40 women, 37 African Americans, and 16 Hispanics to the federal bench, more than all previous presidents combined. Ronald Reagan did not continue this trend, although he was the first to appoint a woman to the Supreme Court. His administration placed a higher priority on screening candidates on the basis of ideology than on screening them in terms of ascriptive characteristics. From 1989 to 1992 George Bush continued to place conservatives on the bench, but he was much more likely to appoint women and minorities than was Reagan. Bill Clinton nominated Democrats, who are more liberal than the nominees of Reagan and Bush, and a large percentage of them were women and minorities. George W. Bush's nominees have been similar to those of his father.

Federal judges have typically held office as a judge or prosecutor, and often they have been involved in partisan politics. This involvement is generally what brings them to the attention of senators and the Department of Justice when they seek nominees for judgeships. As former U.S. Attorney General and Circuit Court Judge Griffin Bell once remarked, "For me, becoming a federal judge wasn't very difficult. I managed John F. Kennedy's presidential campaign in Georgia. Two of my oldest and closest friends were senators from Georgia. And I was campaign manager and special unpaid counsel for the governor."[8]

Table 16.3 Backgrounds of Recent Federal District and Appeals Court Judges

Characteristic	Appeals Court					District Court				
	G.W. BUSH[a]	CLINTON	BUSH	REAGAN	CARTER	G.W. BUSH[a]	CLINTON	BUSH	REAGAN	CARTER
Total number of nominees	16	61	37	78	56	83	305	148	290	202
Occupation (%)										
Politics/government	6	7	11	6	5	8	12	11	13	4
Judiciary	50	53	60	55	47	48	48	42	37	45
Large law firm	6	18	16	14	11	24	15	26	18	14
Moderate-size firm	13	13	11	9	16	10	13	15	19	19
Solo or small firm	6	2	—	1	5	5	8	5	10	14
Professor of law	13	8	3	13	14	2	2	1	2	3
Other	6	—	—	1	2	2	1	1	1	1
Experience (%)										
Judicial	69	59	62	60	54	53	52	47	46	54
Prosecutorial	25	38	30	28	30	51	41	39	44	38
Neither one	25	30	32	35	39	23	29	28	29	31
Party (%)										
Democrat	13	85	5	—	82	7	88	6	5	91
Republican	81	7	89	96	7	83	6	89	92	5
Independent	—	8	8	3	11	—	6	5	3	5
Past party activism (%)	75	54	70	67	73	57	50	64	60	61
Ethnicity or race (%)										
White	81	74	89	97	79	86	75	89	92	79
African American	19	13	5	1	16	7	17	7	2	14
Hispanic	—	12	5	1	4	7	6	4	5	7
Asian	—	2	—	—	2	—	1	—	1	1
Gender (%)										
Male	81	67	81	95	80	80	72	80	92	86
Female	19	33	19	5	20	21	28	20	8	14
Average age	51	51	49	50	52	50	50	48	49	50

[a] As of January 1, 2003.
Source: From Sheldon Goldman, Gerard Gryski, Gary Zuk, and Sara Schiavoni, "W. Bush Remaking the Judiciary," in *Judicature* 86 (No. 6, 2003), 304, 308.

Most members of the federal judiciary have backgrounds atypical of most Americans. Sandra Day O'Connor, nominated in 1981, is the first woman to sit on the Supreme Court.

Like their colleagues on the lower federal courts, Supreme Court justices share characteristics that qualify them as an elite group. All have been lawyers, and all but four (Thurgood Marshall, nominated in 1967; Sandra Day O'Connor, nominated in 1981; Clarence Thomas, nominated in 1991; and Ruth Bader Ginsburg, nominated in 1993) have been White males. Most have been in their fifties and sixties when they took office, from the upper-middle or upper class, and Protestants.[9]

Race and gender have become more salient criteria in recent years. In the 1980 presidential campaign, Ronald Reagan promised to appoint a woman to the first vacancy on the Court if he were elected. In 1991, President George Bush chose to replace the first African-American justice, Thurgood Marshall, with another African American, Clarence Thomas. Women and minorities may serve on all federal courts more frequently in the future because of increased opportunity for legal education and decreased prejudice against their judicial activity, as well as because of their increasing political clout.

Geography was once a prominent criterion for selection to the Court, but it is no longer very important. Presidents do like to spread the slots around, however, as when Richard Nixon decided that he wanted to nominate a Southerner. At various

Table 16.4   Supreme Court Justices, 2005

NAME	YEAR OF BIRTH	PREVIOUS POSITION	NOMINATING PRESIDENT	YEAR OF APPOINTMENT
William H. Rehnquist[a]	1924	Assistant U.S. Attorney General	Nixon	1971
John Paul Stevens	1920	U.S. Court of Appeals	Ford	1975
Sandra Day O'Connor	1930	State Court of Appeals	Reagan	1981
Antonin Scalia	1936	U.S. Court of Appeals	Reagan	1986
Anthony M. Kennedy	1936	U.S. Court of Appeals	Reagan	1988
David H. Souter	1939	U.S. Court of Appeals	Bush	1990
Clarence Thomas	1948	U.S. Court of Appeals	Bush	1991
Ruth Bader Ginsburg	1933	U.S. Court of Appeals	Clinton	1993
Stephen G. Breyer	1938	U.S. Court of Appeals	Clinton	1994

[a]William Rehnquist was promoted from associate justice to chief justice by President Reagan in 1986.

The U.S. Supreme Court: Front row, left to right: Antonin Scalia, John Paul Stevens, William Rehnquist, Sandra Day O'Connor, and Anthony Kennedy. Second row, left to right: Ruth Bader Ginsburg, David Souter, Clarence Thomas, and Stephen Breyer.

times there have been what some have termed a "Jewish seat" and a "Catholic seat" on the Court, but these guidelines are not binding on the president. For example, after a half-century of having a Jewish justice, the Court did not have one from 1969 to 1993.

Typically, justices have held high administrative or judicial positions before moving to the Supreme Court (see Table 16.4). Most have had some experience as a judge, often at the appellate level, and many have worked for the Department of Justice. Some have held elective office, and a few have had no government service but have been distinguished attorneys. The fact that many justices, including some of the most distinguished ones, have not had previous judicial experience may seem surprising, but the unique work of the Court renders this background much less important than it might be for other appellate courts.

Partisanship is another important influence on the selection of judges and justices. Only 13 of 108 members of the Supreme Court have been nominated by presidents of a different party. Moreover, many of the 13 exceptions were actually close to the president in ideology, as was the case in Richard Nixon's appointment of Lewis Powell. Herbert Hoover's nomination of Benjamin Cardozo seems to be one of the few cases in which partisanship was completely dominated by merit as a criterion for selection. Usually more than 90 percent of presidents' judicial nominations are of members of their own parties.

The role of partisanship is really not surprising. Most of a president's acquaintances are made through the party, and there is usually a certain congruity between party and political views. Most judges and justices have at one time been active partisans—an experience that gave them visibility and helped them obtain the positions from which they moved to the courts.

Judgeships are also considered very prestigious patronage plums. Indeed, the decisions of Congress to create new judgeships, and thus new positions for party members, are closely related to whether the majority party in Congress is the same as the party of the president. Members of the majority party in the legislature want to avoid providing an opposition party president with new positions to fill with their opponents.

Ideology is as important as partisanship in the selection of judges and justices. Presidents want to appoint people who share their views to the federal bench. In effect, all presidents try to "pack" the courts. They want more than "justice"; they want policies with which they agree. Presidential aides survey candidates' decisions (if they have served on a lower court),[10] speeches, political stands, writings, and other expressions of opinion. They also glean information from people who know the candidates well. Although it is considered improper to question judicial candidates about upcoming court cases, it is appropriate to discuss broader questions of political and judicial philosophy. The Reagan administration was especially concerned about such matters and had each potential nominee fill out a lengthy questionnaire and be interviewed by a special committee in the Department of Justice. Like its predecessor, the George Bush administration was attentive to appointing conservative judges. Bill Clinton was less concerned with the ideology of his nominees, at least partly to avoid costly confirmation fights. Instead, he focused on identifying persons with strong legal credentials, especially women and minorities. George W. Bush reverted to the Reagan policy of naming clear conservatives to the federal courts.

Members of the federal bench also play the game of politics, of course, and may try to time their retirements so that a president with compatible views will choose their successor. This is one reason why justices remain on the Supreme Court for so long, even when they are clearly infirm. William Howard Taft, a rigid conservative, even feared that a successor would be named by Herbert Hoover, a more moderate conservative.[11]

Presidents are typically pleased with the performance of their nominees to the Supreme Court and through them have slowed or reversed trends in the Court's decisions. Franklin D. Roosevelt's nominees substantially liberalized the Court, whereas Richard Nixon's turned it in a conservative direction.

Nevertheless, it is not always easy to predict the policy inclinations of candidates, and presidents have been disappointed in their nominees about one-fourth of the time. President Eisenhower, for example, was displeased with the liberal decisions of both Earl Warren and William Brennan. Once, when asked whether he had made any mistakes as president, he replied, "Yes, two, and they are both sitting on the Supreme Court."[12] Richard Nixon was certainly disappointed when Warren Burger, whom he had nominated as chief justice, wrote the Court's decision calling for immediate desegregation of the nation's schools shortly after his confirmation. This turn of events did little for the president's "Southern strategy." Burger also wrote the Court's opinion in *United States v. Nixon*, which forced the president to release the Watergate tapes. Nixon's resignation soon followed.

Presidents influence policy through the values of their judicial nominees, but this impact is limited by numerous legal and "extra-legal" factors beyond the chief executive's control. As Harry Truman put it, "Packing the Supreme Court can't be done . . . I've tried it and it won't work. . . . Whenever you put a man on the Supreme Court, he ceases to be your friend. I'm sure of that."[13]

There is no doubt that various women's, racial, ethnic, and religious groups desire to have their members appointed to the federal bench. At the very least, judgeships have symbolic importance for them.[14] Presidents face many of the same pressures for representativeness in selecting judges that they experience when they name their cabinet.

What is less clear is what policy differences result when presidents nominate persons with different backgrounds to the bench. The number of female and minority group judges is too few and their service too recent to serve as a sound basis for generalizations about their decisions. Many members of each party have been appointed, of course, and it appears that Republican judges in general are somewhat more conservative than Democratic judges. Former prosecutors serving on the Supreme Court have tended to be less sympathetic toward defendants' rights than other justices. It seems that background does make some difference,[15] yet for reasons that we will examine in the following sections, on many issues, party affiliation and other characteristics bring no more predictability to the courts than they do to Congress.

The Courts as Policymakers

"Judicial decision making," a former Supreme Court law clerk wrote in the *Harvard Law Review*, "involves, at bottom, a choice between competing values by fallible, pragmatic, and at times nonrational men and women in a highly complex process in a very human setting."[16] This is an apt description of policymaking in the Supreme Court and in other courts, too. The next sections will look at how courts make policy, paying particular attention to the role of the U.S. Supreme Court. Although it is not the only court involved in policymaking and policy interpretation, its decisions have the widest implications for policy.

Accepting Cases

Visual Literacy

Case Overload

Deciding what to decide about is the first step in all policymaking. Courts of original jurisdiction cannot very easily refuse to consider a case; appeals courts, including the U.S. Supreme Court, have much more control over their agendas. The approximately 7,500 cases submitted annually to the U.S. Supreme Court must be read, culled, and sifted. Figure 16.4 shows the stages of this process. At least once each week, the nine justices meet in conference. With them in the conference room sit some 25 carts, each wheeled in from the office of one of the nine justices, and each filled with petitions, briefs, memoranda, and every item the justices are likely to need during their discussions. These meetings operate under the strictest secrecy; only the justices themselves attend.

Simulation

You Are a Clerk to Supreme Court Justice Judith Gray

At these weekly conferences two important matters are hammered out. First is an agenda: The justices consider the chief justice's "discuss list" and decide which cases they want to discuss. Because few of the justices can take the time to read materials on every case submitted to the Court, most rely heavily on their law clerks (each justice has up to four to assist them in considering cases and writing opinions) to screen each case. If four justices agree to grant review of a case (the "rule of four"), it can be scheduled for oral argument or decided on the basis of the written record already on file with the Court.

The most common way for the Court to put a case on its docket is by issuing to a lower federal or state court a *writ of certiorari*, a formal document that calls up a case. Until 1988, some cases—principally those in which federal laws had been found unconstitutional, in which federal courts had concluded that state laws violated the federal Constitution, or in which state laws had been upheld in state courts despite claims that they violated federal law or the Constitution—were technically supposed to be heard by the Court "on appeal." In reality, however, the Court always exercised broad discretion over hearing these and other cases.

Cases that involve major issues—especially civil liberties, conflict between different lower courts on the interpretation of federal law (as when a circuit court of appeals in Texas prohibits the use of affirmative action criteria in college admissions and a court of appeals in Michigan approves them), or disagreement between a majority of the Supreme Court and lower-court decisions—are likely to be selected by the Court.[17]

Figure 16.4 Obtaining Space on the Supreme Court's Docket

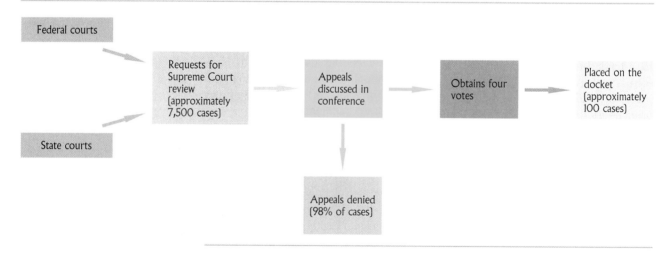

Because getting into the Supreme Court is half the battle, it is important to remember this chapter's earlier discussion of standing to sue (litigants must have serious interest in a case, having sustained or being in immediate danger of sustaining a direct and substantial injury from another party or an action of government)—a criterion the Court often uses to decide whether to hear a case. In addition, the Court has used other means to avoid deciding cases that are too politically "hot" to handle or that divide the Court too sharply,[18] as we will discuss later in this chapter.

Another important influence on the Supreme Court is the **solicitor general.** As a presidential appointee and the third-ranking official in the Department of Justice, the solicitor general is in charge of the appellate court litigation of the federal government. The solicitor general and a staff of about two dozen experienced attorneys have four key functions: (1) to decide whether to appeal cases the government has lost in the lower courts, (2) to review and modify the briefs presented in government appeals, (3) to represent the government before the Supreme Court, and (4) to submit a brief on behalf of a litigant in a case in which the government is not directly involved.[19] Unlike attorneys for private parties, the solicitors general are careful to seek Court review only of important cases. By avoiding frivolous appeals and displaying a high degree of competence, they typically earn the confidence of the Court, which in turn grants review of a large percentage of the cases they submit.[20]

Ultimately, the Supreme Court decides very few cases. In recent years, the Court has made fewer than 100 formal written decisions per year in which their opinions could serve as precedent and thus as the basis of guidance for lower courts. In a few dozen additional cases, the Court reaches a *per curiam decision*—that is, a decision without explanation. Such decisions resolve the immediate case but have no value as precedent because the Court does not offer reasoning that would guide lower courts in future decisions.[21]

solicitor general

A presidential appointee and the third-ranking office in the Department of Justice. The solicitor general is in charge of the appellate court litigation of the federal government.

Making Decisions

The second task of the justices' weekly conferences is to discuss cases actually accepted and argued before the Court. Beginning the first Monday in October and lasting until June, the Court hears oral arguments in two-week cycles: two weeks of courtroom arguments followed by two weeks of reflecting on cases and writing opinions about them. Figure 16.5 shows the stages in this process.

Before the justices enter the courtroom to hear the lawyers for each side present their arguments, they have received elaborately prepared written briefs from each party involved. They have also probably received several *amicus curiae* briefs from parties (often groups) who are interested in the outcome of the case but who are not formal litigants.

Amicus curiae briefs have another important role: The government, under the direction of the solicitor general, may submit them in cases in which it has an interest. For instance, a case between two parties may involve the question of the constitutionality of a federal law. The federal government naturally wants to have its voice heard on such matters, even if it is not formally a party to the case. These briefs are also a means to urge the Court to change established doctrine. For example, the Reagan administration frequently submitted *amicus curiae* briefs to the Court to try to change the law dealing with defendants' rights.

Figure 16.5   The Supreme Court's Decision-Making Process

In most instances, the attorneys for each side have only a half-hour to address the Court. During this time they summarize their briefs, emphasizing their most compelling points. The justices may listen attentively, interrupt with penetrating or helpful questions, request information, talk to one another, read (presumably briefs), or simply gaze at the ceiling. After 25 minutes, a white light comes on at the lectern from which the lawyer is speaking, and five minutes later a red light signals the end of that lawyer's presentation, even if he or she is in midsentence. Oral argument is over.[22]

Back in the conference room, the chief justice, who presides over the Court, raises a particular case and invites discussion, turning first to the senior associate justice. Discussion can range from perfunctory to profound and from courteous to caustic. If the votes are not clear from the individual discussions, the chief justice may ask each justice to vote. Once a tentative vote has been reached, it is necessary to write an **opinion**, a statement of the legal reasoning behind the decision.

Opinion writing is no mere formality. In fact, the content of an opinion may be as important as the decision itself. Broad and bold opinions have far-reaching implications for future cases; narrowly drawn opinions may have little impact beyond the case being decided. Tradition in the Supreme Court requires that the chief justice, if in the majority, write the opinion or assign it to another justice in the majority. The chief justice often writes the opinion in landmark cases, as Earl Warren did in *Brown v. Board of Education* and Warren Burger did in *United States v. Nixon*. If the chief justice is part of the minority, the senior associate justice in the majority assigns the opinion. Drafts are then circulated among the majority, suggestions are made, and negotiations are conducted among the justices.[23] Votes can be gained or lost by the content of the opinion. An opinion that proves unacceptable to a clear majority is reworked and redrafted.

Justices are free to write their own opinions, to join in other opinions, or to associate themselves with part of one opinion and part of another. *Dissenting opinions* are those written by justices opposed to all or part of the majority's decision. *Concurring opinions* are those written not only to support a majority decision but also to stress a different constitutional or legal basis for the judgment. When the opinions are written and the final vote is taken, the decision is announced. At least six justices must participate in a case, and decisions are made by majority vote. If there is a tie (because of a vacancy on the Court or because a justice chooses not to participate), the decision of the lower court from which the case came is sustained. Five votes in agreement on the reasoning underlying an opinion are necessary for the logic to serve as precedent for judges of lower courts.

The vast majority of cases that reach the courts are settled on the principle of *stare decisis* ("let the decision stand"), meaning that an earlier decision should hold for the case being considered. All courts rely heavily on **precedent**—the way similar cases

opinion

A statement of legal reasoning behind a judicial decision. The content of an opinion may be as important as the decision itself.

stare decisis

A Latin phrase meaning "let the decision stand." Most cases reaching appellate courts are settled on this principle.

precedents

How similar cases have been decided in the past.

The content of a Supreme Court opinion may be as important as the decision itself, and justices may spend months negotiating a majority opinion. Here, William H. Rehnquist, chief justice of the Supreme Court, prepares a written opinion.

were handled in the past—as a guide to current decisions. Lower courts, of course, are expected to follow the precedents of higher courts in their decision-making. If the Supreme Court, for example, rules in favor of the right to abortion under certain conditions, it has established a precedent that lower courts are expected to follow. Lower courts have much less discretion than the Supreme Court.

The Supreme Court is in a position to overrule its own precedents, and it has done so more than 200 times.[24] One of the most famous of such instances occurred with *Brown v. Board of Education* (1954) (see Chapter 5), in which the court overruled *Plessy v. Ferguson* (1896) and found that segregation in the public schools violated the Constitution.

What happens when precedents are unclear? This is especially a problem for the Supreme Court, which is more likely than other courts to handle cases at the forefront of the law. Precedent is typically less firmly established on these matters. Moreover, the justices are often asked to apply to concrete situations the vague phrases of the Constitution ("due process of law," "equal protection," "unreasonable searches and seizures") or vague statutes passed by Congress. This ambiguity provides leeway for the justices to disagree (only about one-third of the cases in which full opinions are handed down are decided unanimously) and for their values to influence their judgment.

As a result, it is often easy to identify consistent patterns in the decisions of justices. For example, if there is division on the Court (indicating that precedent is not clear) and you can identify a conservative side to the issue at hand, it is likely that Chief Justice William Rehnquist will be on that side. Ruth Bader Ginsburg may very well be voting on the other side of the issue. Liberalism and conservatism have several dimensions, including freedom, equality, and economic regulation. The point is that policy preferences do matter in judicial decision-making, especially on the nation's highest court[25] (see "You Are the Policymaker: The Debate over Original Intentions").

Once a decision is announced, copies of it are conveyed to the press as the decision is formally announced in open court. Media coverage of the Court remains primitive—short and shallow. Doris Graber reports that "much reporting on the courts—even at the Supreme Court level—is imprecise and sometimes even wrong."[26] More important to the legal community, the decisions are bound weekly and made available to every law library and lawyer in the United States. There is, of

"Call it 'legislating from the bench,' if you will, but on this occasion I should like to repeal the First Amendment."

You Are the Policymaker

The Debate over Original Intentions

The most contentious issue involving the courts is the role of judicial discretion. According to Christopher Wolfe: "The Constitution itself nowhere specifies a particular set of rules by which it is to be interpreted. Where does one go, then, in order to discover the proper way to interpret the Constitution?"

Some have argued for a jurisprudence of **original intent** (sometimes referred to as *strict constructionism*). This view holds that judges and justices should attempt to determine the intent of the framers of the Constitution regarding a particular matter and decide cases in line with that intent. Such a view is popular with conservatives.

Advocates of strict constructionism view it as a means of constraining the exercise of judicial discretion, which they see as the foundation of the liberal decisions of the past four decades, especially on matters of civil liberties, civil rights, and defendants' rights (discussed in Chapters 4 and 5).

They also see following original intent as the only basis of interpretation consistent with democracy. Judges, they argue, should not dress up constitutional interpretations with *their* views on "contemporary needs," "today's conditions," or "what is right." It is the job of legislators, not judges, to make such judgments.

Other jurists, such as former Justice William Brennan, disagree. They maintain that what appears to be deference to the intentions of the framers is simply a cover for making conservative decisions. Opponents of original intent assert that the Constitution is subject to multiple meanings by thoughtful people in different ages. Judges will differ in time and place about what they think the

Constitution means. Thus, basing decisions on original intent is not likely to have much effect on judicial discretion.

In addition, Brennan and his supporters contend that the Constitution is not like a paint-by-numbers kit. Trying to reconstruct or guess the framers' intentions is very difficult. Recent key cases before the Supreme Court have concerned issues such as school busing, abortions, the Internet, and wire tapping, that the framers could not have imagined; there were no public schools or buses, no contraceptives or modern abortion techniques, and certainly no computers or electronic surveillance equipment or telephones in 1787.

The Founders embraced general principles, not specific solutions when they wrote the Constitution. They frequently lacked discrete, discoverable intent. Moreover, there is often no record of their intentions, nor is it clear whose intentions should count—those of the writers of the Constitution, those of the more than 1,600 members who attended the ratifying conventions, or those of the voters who sent them there. This problem grows more complex when you consider the amendments to the Constitution, which involve thousands of additional "framers."

Historian Jack N. Rakove points out that there is little historical evidence that the framers believed their intentions should guide later interpretations of the Constitution. In fact, there is some evidence for believing that Madison—the key delegate—left the Constitutional Convention bitterly disappointed with the results. What if Madison had one set of intentions but—like anyone working in a committee—got a different set of results?

The lines are drawn. On one side is the argument that any deviation from following the original intentions of the Constitution's framers is a deviation from principle, leaving unelected judges to impose their views on the American people. If judges do not follow original intentions, then on what do they base their decisions?

On the other side are those who believe that it is often impossible to discern the views of the framers, and that there is no good reason to be constrained by the views of the eighteenth century, which reflect a more limited conception of constitutional rights. In order to cope with current needs, they argue, it is necessary to adapt the principles in the Constitution to the demands of each era.

The choice here is at the very heart of the judicial process. If you were a justice sitting on the Supreme Court and were asked to interpret the meaning of the Constitution, what would *you* do?

Sources: Christopher Wolfe, *The Rise of Modern Judicial Review* (New York: Basic Books, 1986); Raoul Berger, *Government by Judiciary: The Transformation of the Fourteenth Amendment* (Cambridge, MA: Harvard University Press, 1977); Traciel V. Reid, "A Critique of Interpretivism and Its Claimed Influence upon Judicial Decision Making," *American Politics Quarterly* 16 (July 1988): 329–356; Jack N. Rakove, ed., *Interpreting the Constitution* (Boston: Northeastern University Press, 1990); and Arthur S. Miller, "In Defense of Judicial Activism," in Stephen C. Halpern and Charles M. Lamb, eds., *Supreme Court Activism and Restraint* (Lexington, MA: D.C. Heath, 1982).

course, an air of finality to the public announcement of a decision. In fact, however, even Supreme Court decisions are not self-implementing; they are actually "remands" to lower courts, instructing them to act in accordance with the Court's decisions.

Virgil Hawkins' unsuccessful struggle to attend the all-White University of Florida Law School illustrates how judicial implementation can affect the impact of court decisions. The Supreme Court ordered the school to admit Hawkins in 1956, but the school and state refused to implement the ruling, and continued to appeal the case. Two years later a Florida district court again denied admission to Hawkins, although it did order the school's desegregation.

Implementing Court Decisions

Reacting bitterly to one of Chief Justice Marshall's decisions, President Andrew Jackson is said to have grumbled: "John Marshall has made his decision; now let him enforce it." Court decisions carry legal, even moral, authority, but courts must rely on other units of government to enforce their decisions. **Judicial implementation** refers to how and whether court decisions are translated into actual policy, thereby affecting the behavior of others.

You should think of any judicial decision as the end of one process—the litigation process—and the beginning of another process—the process of judicial implementation. Sometimes delay and stalling follow even decisive court decisions. There is, for example, the story of the tortured efforts of a young African American named Virgil Hawkins to get himself admitted to the University of Florida Law School. Hawkins's efforts began in 1949, when he first applied for admission, and ended unsuccessfully in 1958, after a decade of court decisions. Despite a 1956 order from the U.S. Supreme Court to admit Hawkins, continued legal skirmishing produced a 1958 decision by a U.S. district court in Florida ordering the admission of non-Whites but upholding the denial of admission to Hawkins himself. Other courts and other institutions of government can be roadblocks in the way of judicial implementation.

Charles Johnson and Bradley Canon suggest that implementation of court decisions involves several elements.[27] First, there is an *interpreting population*, heavily composed of lawyers and judges. They must correctly understand and reflect the intent of the original decision in their subsequent actions. Usually lower-court judges do follow the Supreme Court, but sometimes they circumvent higher-court decisions to satisfy their own policy interests.[28]

Second, there is an *implementing population*. Suppose the Supreme Court held (as it did) that prayers organized by school officials in the public schools are unconstitutional. The implementing population (school boards and school administrators) must then actually abandon prayers. Police departments, hospitals, corporations, government agencies—all may be part of the implementing population. With so many implementors, many of whom may disagree with a decision, there is plenty of room for "slippage" between what the Supreme Court decides and what actually occurs. Judicial decisions are more likely to be implemented smoothly if implementation is concentrated in the hands of a few highly visible officials, such as the president or state legislators.

Third, every decision involves a *consumer population*. The potential "consumers" of an abortion decision are those who want abortions (and those who oppose them);

original intent

A view that the Constitution should be interpreted according to the original intent of the framers. Many **conservatives** support this view.

judicial implementation

How and whether court decisions are translated into actual policy, thereby affecting the behavior of others. The courts rely on other units of government to enforce their decisions.

Why It Matters

The Lack of a Judicial Bureaucracy
The federal courts lack a bureaucracy to implement their decisions. In fact, some of the Supreme Court's most controversial decisions, such as those dealing with school integration and school prayers, have been implemented only with great difficulty. If the courts had a bureaucracy to enforce their decisions, justice might be better served, but such a bureaucracy would have to be enormous to monitor, for example, every school and police station.

the consumers of the *Miranda* decision (see Chapter 4) are criminal defendants and their attorneys. The consumer population must be aware of its newfound rights and stand up for them.

Congress and presidents can also help or hinder judicial implementation. The Supreme Court held in 1954 that segregated schools were "inherently unconstitutional" and the next year ordered public schools desegregated "with all deliberate speed." President Eisenhower refused to state clearly that Americans should comply with this famous decision in *Brown v. Board of Education*, which may have encouraged local school boards to resist the decision. Congress was not much help either; only a decade later, in the wake of the civil rights movement discussed in Chapter 5, did it pass legislation denying federal aid to segregated schools. Different presidents have different commitments to a particular judicial policy. After years of court and presidential decisions supporting busing to end racial segregation, in December 1984 the Reagan administration went before the Supreme Court and argued *against* school busing in a case in Norfolk, Va.

The fate and effect of a Supreme Court decision are complex and unpredictable. The implementation of any court decision involves many actors besides the justices, and the justices have no way of ensuring that their decisions and policies will be implemented. Courts have made major changes in public policies, however, not because their decisions are automatically implemented, but because the courts both reflect and help to determine the national policy agenda.[29]

The Courts and the Policy Agenda

Even though American courts and judges work largely alone and in isolation from daily contact with other political institutions, they play a key role in shaping the policy agenda. Ultimately, their decisions affect us all (see "Young People and Politics: The Supreme Court Is Closer than You Think"). Like all policymakers, the courts are choice-takers. Confronted with controversial policies, they make controversial decisions that leave some people winners and others losers. The courts have made policy about slavery and segregation, corporate power and capital punishment, and dozens of other controversial matters.

A Historical Review

Until the Civil War, the dominant questions before the Court concerned the strength and legitimacy of the federal government and slavery. These issues of nation building were resolved in favor of the supremacy of the national government. From the Civil War until 1937, questions of the relationship between the federal government and the economy predominated. During this period, the Court restricted the power of the federal government to regulate the economy. From 1938 to the present, the paramount issues before the Court have concerned personal liberty and social and political equality. In this era, the Court has enlarged the scope of personal freedom and civil rights and has removed many of the constitutional restraints on the regulation of the economy.

Few justices played a more important role in making the Court a significant national agenda setter than John Marshall, chief justice from 1801 to 1835. His successors have continued not only to respond to the political agenda but also to shape discussion and debate about it.

The Chief Justice of the United States

John Marshall and the Growth of Judicial Review.   Scarcely was the government housed in its new capital when Federalists and Democratic-Republicans clashed over the courts. In the election of 1800, Democratic-Republican Thomas Jefferson had beaten Federalist John Adams. Determined to leave at least the judiciary in trusted hands, Adams tried to fill it with Federalists. He is alleged to have stayed

Young People and Politics

The Supreme Court Is Closer than You Think

The Supreme Court of the United States may seem remote and not especially relevant to a college student. Yet a surprising number of its most important decisions have been brought by young adults seeking protection for their civil rights and liberties. For example, we saw in Chapter 5 that in *Rostker v. Goldberg* (1981) several young men filed a suit claiming that the Military Selective Service Act's requirement that only males register for the draft was unconstitutional. Although the Court held that the requirement was constitutional, draft registration was suspended temporarily during the suit.

Students were the center of *Board of Regents of University of Wisconsin System v. Southworth* (2000), in which the Court upheld that the University of Wisconsin's requirement of a fee to fund speakers on campus—even if the speakers advocated views that offended some students. The right of the police to search newspaper files was fought over the actions of a campus newspaper in *Zurcher v. Stanford Daily* (1978). In 1992, the Supreme Court ruled that legislatures and universities may not single out racial, religious, or sexual insults or threats for prosecution as "hate speech" or "bias crimes" (*R.A.V. v. St. Paul*). From Gregory Johnson's burning an American flag at the 1984 Republican National Convention to protest nuclear arms buildup (which the Court protected in *Texas v. Johnson*,

1989) to burning a draft card (which the Court did not protect in *United States v. O'Brien*, 1968), young adults have also been pioneers in the area of symbolic speech.

Issues of religious freedom have also prominently featured college students. In *Widmar v. Vincent* (1981), the Court decided that public universities that permit student groups to use their facilities must allow student religious groups on campus to use the facilities for religious worship. In 1995, the Court held that the University of Virginia was constitutionally required to subsidize a student religious magazine on the same basis as other student publications (*Rosenberger v. University of Virginia*). However, in 2004 the Court held that the state of Washington was within its rights when it excluded students pursuing a devotional theology degree from its general scholarship program (*Locke v. Davey*).

Thus, the Supreme Court has a long history of dealing with issues of importance to young adults. Often it is young adults themselves who initiate the cases—and who take them all the way to the nation's highest court.

Questions for Discussion
- Why do you think cases involving young people tend to involve civil liberties issues?
- What other issues of particular importance to young people should the Supreme Court decide?

---

at his desk until 9 P.M. signing commissions on his last night in the White House (March 3, 1801).

In the midst of this flurry, Adams appointed William Marbury to the minor post of justice of the peace in the District of Columbia. In the rush of last-minute business, however, Secretary of State John Marshall failed to deliver commissions to Marbury and 16 others. He left the commissions to be delivered by the incoming secretary of state, James Madison.

Madison and Jefferson were furious at Adams' actions and refused to deliver the commissions. Marbury and three others in the same situation sued Madison, asking the Supreme Court to order Madison to give them their commissions. They took their case directly to the Supreme Court under the Judiciary Act of 1789, which gave the Court original jurisdiction in such matters.

The new chief justice was none other than Adams's former secretary of state and arch-Federalist John Marshall, himself one of the "midnight appointments" (he took his seat on the Court barely three weeks before Adams's term ended). Marshall and his Federalist colleagues were in a tight spot. Threats of impeachment came from Jeffersonians fearful that the Court would vote for Marbury. Moreover, if the Court ordered Madison to deliver the commissions, he was likely to ignore the order, putting

John Marshall, chief justice from 1801 to 1835, established the Supreme Court's power of judicial review in the 1803 case *Marbury v. Madison*. In their ruling on the case, Marshall and his associates declared that the Court has the power to determine the constitutionality of congressional actions.

Marbury v. Madison

The 1803 case in which Chief Justice John Marshall and his associates first asserted the right of the **Supreme Court** to determine the meaning of the **U.S. Constitution.** The decision established the Court's power of **judicial review** over acts of Congress, in this case the Judiciary Act of 1789.

judicial review

The power of the courts to determine whether acts of Congress, and by implication the executive, are in accord with the **U.S. Constitution.** Judicial review was established by John Marshall and his associates in *Marbury v. Madison.* See also **judicial interpretation.**

the nation's highest court at risk over a minor issue. Marshall had no means of compelling Madison to act.

The Court could also deny Marbury's claim. Taking that option, however, would concede the issue to the Jeffersonians and give the appearance of retreat in the face of opposition, thereby reducing the power of the Court.

Marshall devised a shrewd solution to the case of ***Marbury v. Madison.*** In February 1803, he delivered the unanimous opinion of the Court. First, Marshall and his colleagues argued that Madison was wrong to withhold Marbury's commission. The Court also found, however, that the Judiciary Act of 1789, under which Marbury had brought suit, contradicted the plain words of the Constitution about the Court's original jurisdiction. Thus Marshall dismissed Marbury's claim, saying that the Court, according to the Constitution, had no power to require that the commission be delivered.

Conceding a small battle over Marbury's commission (he did not get it), Marshall won a much larger war, asserting for the courts the power to determine what is and what is not constitutional. As Marshall wrote, "An act of the legislature repugnant to the Constitution is void," and "it is emphatically the province and duty of the judicial department to say what the law is." The chief justice established the power of **judicial review,** the power of the courts to hold acts of Congress, and by implication the executive, in violation of the Constitution.

Marbury v. Madison was part of a skirmish between the Federalists on the Court and the Democratic-Republican-controlled Congress. Partly, for example, to rein in the Supreme Court, the Jeffersonian Congress in 1801 abolished the lower federal appeals courts and made the Supreme Court judges return to the unpleasant task of "riding circuit" — serving as lower-court judges around the country. This was an act of studied harassment of the Court by its enemies.

After *Marbury*, angry members of Congress, together with other Jeffersonians, claimed that Marshall was a "usurper of power," setting himself above Congress and the president. This view, however, was unfair. State courts, before and after the Constitution, had declared acts of their legislatures unconstitutional. In the *Federalist Papers*, Alexander Hamilton had expressly assumed the power of the federal courts to review legislation, and the federal courts had actually done so. *Marbury* was not even the first case to strike down an act of Congress; a lower federal court had done so in 1792, and the Supreme Court itself had approved a law after a constitutional review in 1796. Marshall was neither inventing nor imagining his right to review laws for their constitutionality.

The case also illustrates that the courts must be politically astute in exercising their power over the other branches. By in effect reducing its *own* power—the authority to hear cases such as Marbury's under its original jurisdiction—the Court was able to assert the right of judicial review in a fashion that the other branches could not easily rebuke.

More than any other power of the courts, judicial review has embroiled them in policy controversy. Before the Civil War the Supreme Court, headed by Chief Justice Roger Taney, held the Missouri Compromise unconstitutional because it restricted slavery in the territories. The decision was one of many steps along the road to the Civil War. After the Civil War, the Court was again active, this time using judicial review to strike down dozens of state and federal laws curbing the growing might of business corporations.

The "Nine Old Men."   Never was the Court so controversial as during the New Deal. At President Roosevelt's urging, Congress passed dozens of laws designed to end the Depression. However, conservatives—most nominated by Republican presidents—who viewed federal intervention in the economy as unconstitutional and tantamount to socialism dominated the Court.

The Supreme Court began to dismantle New Deal policies one by one. The National Industrial Recovery Act was one of a string of anti-Depression measures. Although it was never particularly popular, the Court sealed its doom in *Schechter Poultry Corporation v. United States* (1935), declaring the Act unconstitutional because it regulated purely local business that did not affect interstate commerce.

Incensed, Roosevelt in 1937 proposed what critics called a "court-packing plan." Noting that the average age of the Court was over 70, Roosevelt railed against those "nine old men." Because Congress can determine the number of justices, he proposed that Congress expand the size of the Court, a move that would have allowed him to appoint additional justices sympathetic to the New Deal. Congress objected and never passed the plan. Indeed, it became irrelevant when two justices, Chief Justice Charles Evans Hughes and Associate Justice Owen Roberts, began switching their votes in favor of New Deal legislation. (One wit called it the "switch in time that saved nine.") Shortly thereafter Associate Justice William Van Devanter retired, and Roosevelt got to make the first of his many appointments to the Court.

The Warren Court.   Few eras of the Supreme Court have been as active in shaping public policy as that of the Warren Court (1953–1969), presided over by Chief Justice Earl Warren. Scarcely had President Eisenhower appointed Warren when the Court faced the issue of school segregation. In 1954, it held that laws requiring segregation of the public schools were unconstitutional. Later it expanded the rights of criminal defendants, extending the right to counsel and protections against unreasonable search and seizure and self-incrimination (see Chapter 4). It ordered states to reapportion both their legislatures and their congressional districts according to the principle of one person, one vote, and it prohibited organized prayer in public schools. So active was the Warren Court that right-wing groups, fearing that it was remaking the country, posted billboards all over the United States urging Congress to "Impeach Earl Warren."[30]

The Burger Court. Warren's retirement in 1969 gave President Richard Nixon his hoped-for opportunity to appoint a "strict constructionist" —that is, one who interprets the Constitution narrowly—as chief justice. He chose Minnesotan Warren E. Burger, then a conservative judge on the District of Columbia Court of Appeals. As Nixon hoped, the Burger Court turned out to be more conservative than the liberal Warren Court. It narrowed defendants' rights, though it did not overturn the fundamental contours of the *Miranda* decision. The conservative Burger Court, however, also wrote the abortion decision in *Roe v. Wade*, required school busing in certain cases to eliminate historic segregation, and upheld affirmative action programs in the *Weber* case (see Chapter 5). One of the most notable decisions of the Burger Court weighed against Burger's appointer, Richard Nixon. At the height of the Watergate scandal (see Chapter 13), the Supreme Court was called upon to decide whether Nixon had to turn his White House tapes over to the courts. It unanimously ordered him to do so in **United States v. Nixon** (1974), thus hastening the president's resignation.

United States v. Nixon

The 1974 case in which the Supreme Court unanimously held that the doctrine of executive privilege was implicit in the Constitution but could not be extended to protect documents relevant to criminal prosecutions.

The Rehnquist Court. By the late 1990s, the conservative nominees of Republican presidents, led by Chief Justice William Rehnquist, composed a clear Supreme Court majority. Like the Burger Court, it has been both conservative and like both the Warren and Burger Courts, it has been neither deferential to Congress nor reluctant to enter the political fray. The Court's decision in *Bush v. Gore* (2000) that decided the 2000 presidential election certainly represents a high point of judicial activism.

However one evaluates the Court's current direction, in most cases the Rehnquist Court has not created a revolution in constitutional law. Instead, as discussed in Chapters 4 and 5, it has limited rather than reversed rights established by liberal decisions such as those regarding defendants' rights and abortion. Although its protection of the First Amendment rights of free speech and free press remains robust, the Court no longer sees itself as the special protector of individual liberties and civil rights for minorities (affirmative action laws are at risk). In the area of federalism, however, the Court has blazed new paths in constraining the federal government's power over the states.

The Supreme Court frequently makes controversial decisions regarding important matters of politics and public policy. Critics often argue that unelected judges are making policy decisions that should be made by elected officials. Here demonstrators protest the Supreme Court's decisions regarding counting the ballots in the 2000 presidential election.

Understanding the Courts

Powerful courts are unusual; few nations have them. The power of American judges raises questions about the compatibility of unelected courts with a democracy and about the appropriate role for the judiciary in policymaking.

The Courts and Democracy

Announcing his retirement in 1981, Justice Potter Stewart made a few remarks to the handful of reporters present. Embedded in his brief statement was this observation: "It seems to me that there's nothing more antithetical to the idea of what a good judge should be than to think it has something to do with representative democracy." He meant that judges should not be subject to the whims of popular majorities. In a nation that insists so strongly that it is democratic, where do the courts fit in?

In some ways, the courts are not a very democratic institution. Federal judges are not elected and are almost impossible to remove. Indeed, their social backgrounds probably make the courts the most elite-dominated policymaking institution. If democracy requires that key policymakers always be elected or be continually responsible to those who are, then the courts diverge sharply from the requirements of democratic government.

As you saw in Chapter 2, the Constitution's framers wanted it that way. Chief Justice Rehnquist, a judicial conservative, put the case as follows: "A mere change in public opinion since the adoption of the Constitution, unaccompanied by a constitutional amendment, should not change the meaning of the Constitution. A merely temporary majoritarian groundswell should not abrogate some individual liberty protected by the Constitution."[31]

The courts are not entirely independent of popular preferences, however. Turn-of-the-century Chicago humorist Finley Peter Dunne had his Irish saloonkeeper character "Mr. Dooley" quip that "th' Supreme Court follows th' iliction returns." Many years later, political scientists have found that the Court usually reflects popular majorities.[32] Even when the Court seems out of step with other policymakers, it eventually swings around to join the policy consensus,[33] as it did in the New Deal. A study of the period from 1937 to 1980 found that the Court was clearly out of line with public opinion only on the issue of prayers in public schools.[34]

Despite the fact that the Supreme Court sits in a "marble palace," it is not as insulated from the normal forms of politics as one might think. The two sides in the abortion debate flooded the Court with mail, targeted it with advertisements and protests, and bombarded it with 78 *amicus curiae* briefs in the *Webster v. Reproductive Health Services* (1989) case. Members of the Supreme Court are unlikely to cave in to interest group pressures, but they are aware of the public's concern about issues, and this awareness becomes part of their consciousness as they decide cases. Political scientists have found that the Court is more likely to hear cases for which interest groups have filed *amicus curiae* briefs.[35]

Courts can also promote pluralism. When groups go to court, they use litigation to achieve their policy objectives.[36] Both civil rights groups and environmentalists, for example, have blazed a path to show how interest groups can effectively use the courts to achieve their policy goals. Thurgood Marshall, the legal wizard of the NAACP's litigation strategy, not only won most of his cases but also won for himself a seat on the Supreme Court. Almost every major policy decision these days ends up in court. Chances are good that some judge can be found who will rule in an interest group's favor. On the other hand, agencies and businesses commonly find themselves ordered by different courts to do opposite things. The habit of always turning to the courts as a last resort can add to policy delay, deadlock, and inconsistency (see "America in Perspective: Courts and Culture").

How You Can Make a Difference

Teen Court

Unknown to most college students, a branch of many state and local court systems known as "teen court" needs smart and ambitious volunteers. A teenage defendant (between the ages of 10 and 17) who has already pleaded guilty to a misdemeanor (curfew violation, smoking, trespassing, littering, larceny, disorderly conduct, etc.) can request to bypass the traditional juvenile court and enter the teen court system. Though teen courts vary from city to city and state to state, this basic system remains fairly consistent. The bailiff, defense attorneys, prosecutors, and members of the jury are literally the defendant's peers—they are all teenagers. Usually a local judge, lawyer, or other court official serves as the teen court judge. Since guilt has already been decided, the teen court focuses on sentencing the defendant. After the prosecuting and defense "attorneys" present their cases, the jury members are usually allowed to question the defendant to gather enough information to make a fair ruling. Jurors are usually presented with a menu of sen-

tencing options including community service, monetary restitution, a written essay, and/or a written apology to the victim. After deliberation, the jury announces its binding decision to the defendant and his or her parent(s). This is not a game but a serious procedure requiring training, maturity, and hard work.

These courts desperately need volunteers to help organize and train teenagers to correctly function within the court system, said Peggy Jones, a former undergraduate student who helped develop the teen court system in northern Kentucky. Peggy took a primary role in recruiting and training high school students to participate in the program. This program put her in touch with lawyers, judges, and the court system for the first time. Her curiosity about law school soon blossomed into a firm determination to succeed. By working alongside the president of the Kentucky Bar Association, local judges, and lawyers, Peggy not only gained invaluable preparation for law school but also

contacts and references that helped her law school application stand out from countless others.

If teen courts interest you, contact your local, county, or state judicial system to see if a teen court is already in place. If not, you can follow Peggy's example by helping to develop one with the assistance and permission of local lawyers and judges. The American Probation and Parole Association with the National Youth Court Center conduct several training seminars per year for those interested in developing a teen court system. You can also download an implementation guide that shows how to organize teen court, recruit volunteers, and develop a program model at *www.youthcourt.net/peerjustice*.

What you can do:
- Contact your local judicial system to see if a teen court already exists.
- Develop a teen court by calling a local attorney or judge.
- Attend training seminars.
- Visit *www.youthcourt.net*.

What Courts Should Do: The Scope of Judicial Power

The courts, Alexander Hamilton wrote in *The Federalist Papers*, "will be least in capacity to annoy or injure" the people and their liberties.[37] Throughout American history, critics of judicial power have disagreed. They see the courts as too powerful for their own—or the nation's—good. Yesterday's critics focused on John Marshall's "usurpations" of power, on the proslavery decision in *Dred Scott*, or on the efforts of the "nine old men" to kill off Franklin D. Roosevelt's New Deal legislation. Today's critics are never short of arguments to show that courts go too far in making policy.

Courts make policy on both large and small issues. In the last few decades, courts have made policies on major issues involving school busing, abortion, affirmative action, nuclear power, legislative redistricting, bilingual education, prison conditions, counting votes in the 2000 presidential election, and many other key issues.[38]

There are strong disagreements about the appropriateness of allowing the courts to have a policymaking role. Many scholars and judges favor a policy of **judicial restraint,** in which judges adhere closely to precedent and play minimal policymaking roles, leaving policy decisions strictly to the legislatures. These observers stress that the federal courts, composed of unelected judges, are the least democratic branch of government and question the qualifications of judges for making policy decisions and

judicial restraint

A judicial philosophy in which judges play minimal policymaking roles, leaving that duty strictly to the legislatures.

America in Perspective

Courts and Culture

The Japanese and Americans have many things in common. Both live in nations that are modern industrial giants with developed economies and complex societies. However, the role of the law and the judiciary in the daily life of the people of Japan is quite different from that in the United States.

The role of the courts in Japan is influenced by the prevailing attitude toward law and the court system. The Japanese typically find adversary proceedings distasteful and will resort to going to court only when all the preferred traditional forms of informal mediation and negotiation have failed. Most people prefer to settle disputes through a compromise agreement arrived at with the mediation of friends, relatives, or influential persons, rather than engage in litigation in courts.

The Japanese have traditionally preferred amicable and harmonious social relations, relations that would be jeopardized by clear-cut court decisions based on the assertion of individuals'

legal rights and on the assignment of moral fault. They prefer to deemphasize conflict and the existence of disputes and to seek compromise solutions. The Japanese are also less likely to desire others to apply the universalistic standards that characterize the law. Instead, they favor participating in the settlement of disputes, applying their personal criteria for reconciling differences.

This attitude toward litigation is reflected in the small number of practicing lawyers in Japan. There are far fewer lawyers per capita in Japan than in the United States (about one-twentieth as many), and only about one-fourth as many civil suits per capita come to court in Japan as in the United States.

All is not well in the land of the rising sun, however. Some of the functions performed by American lawyers are handled in Japan by legal specialists and by graduates of law faculties who have knowledge of the law but who are not professionally trained as lawyers. Moreover, the increased tempo of life

in modern Japan has brought greater use of courts and legal procedures, especially in commercial matters.

There is also more involved here than just the cultural preferences of potential litigants. The Japanese government has deliberately restricted access to the courts through a formidable system of procedural barriers. In addition, the number of courts and lawyers is purposely kept small to encourage Japanese citizens to resolve their differences in other forums.

Sources: Bradley M. Richardson and Scott C. Flanagan, *Politics in Japan* (Boston: Little, Brown, 1984), 59–60; Marc Galanter, "Reading the Landscape of Disputes: What We Know and Don't Know (and Think We Know) About Our Allegedly Contentious and Litigious Society," *UCLA Law Review* 31 (October 1983): 51–59; and Louis D. Hayes, *Introduction to Japanese Politics* (New York: Paragon House, 1992), 66–68.

Comparing Judiciaries

Interest groups often use the judicial system to pursue their policy goals, forcing the courts to rule on important social issues. Some Hispanic parents, for example, have successfully sued local school districts to compel them to offer bilingual education.

judicial activism

A judicial philosophy in which judges make bold policy decisions, even charting new constitutional ground. Advocates of this approach emphasize that the courts can correct pressing needs, especially those unmet by the majoritarian political process.

political questions

A doctrine developed by the federal courts and used as a means to avoid deciding some cases, principally those involving conflicts between the president and Congress.

balancing interests. Advocates of judicial restraint believe that decisions such as those on abortion and prayer in public schools go well beyond the "referee" role they say is appropriate for courts in a democracy.

On the other side are proponents of **judicial activism,** in which judges make bolder policy decisions, even charting new constitutional ground with a particular decision. Advocates of judicial activism emphasize that the courts may alleviate pressing needs—especially needs of those who are politically or economically weak—left unmet by the majoritarian political process. (For current views about interpreting the law, see "Issues of the Times: How Should the Courts Interpret the Law?")

It is important not to confuse judicial activism or restraint with liberalism or conservatism. In Table 16.5, you can see the varying levels of the Supreme Court's use of judicial review to void laws passed by Congress in different eras. In the early years of the New Deal, judicial activists were conservatives. During the tenure of Earl Warren as chief justice (1953–1969), activists made liberal decisions. The Courts under Chief Justices Warren Burger (1969–1986) and William Rehnquist (1986–), composed of mostly conservative nominees of Republican presidents, marked the most active use of judicial review in the nation's history.

The problem remains of reconciling the American democratic heritage with an active policymaking role for the judiciary. The federal courts have developed a doctrine of **political questions** as a means to avoid deciding some cases, principally those that involve conflicts between the president and Congress. The courts have shown no willingness, for example, to settle disputes regarding the War Powers Resolution (see Chapter 13).

Similarly, judges typically attempt, whenever possible, to avoid deciding a case on the basis of the Constitution, preferring less contentious "technical" grounds. They also employ issues of jurisdiction, mootness (whether a case presents a real controversy in which a judicial decision can have a practical effect), standing, ripeness (whether the issues of a case are clear enough and evolved enough to serve as the basis of a decision), and other conditions to avoid adjudication of some politically charged cases. The Supreme Court refused to decide, for example, whether it was legal to carry out the war in Vietnam without an explicit declaration of war from Congress.

As you saw in the discussion of *Marbury v. Madison*, from the earliest days of the republic, federal judges have been politically astute in their efforts to maintain the legitimacy of the judiciary and to conserve their resources. (Remember that judges are typically recruited from political backgrounds.) They have tried not to take on too many politically controversial issues at one time. They have also been much more likely to find state and local laws unconstitutional (about 1,100) than federal laws (fewer than 200, as shown in Table 16.5).

Another factor that increases the acceptability of activist courts is the ability to overturn their decisions. First, the president and the Senate determine who sits on the federal bench. Second, Congress, with or without the president's urging, can begin the process of amending the Constitution to overcome a constitutional decision of the Supreme Court. Although this process does not occur rapidly, it is a safety valve. The Eleventh Amendment in 1795 reversed the decision in *Chisolm v. Georgia*, which permitted an individual to sue a state in federal court; the Fourteenth Amendment in 1868 reversed the decision in *Scott v. Sandford*, which held African Americans not to be citizens of the United States; the Sixteenth Amendment in 1913 reversed the decision in *Pollock v. Farmer's Loan and Trust Co.*, which prohibited a federal income tax; and the Twenty-sixth Amendment in 1971 reversed part of *Oregon v. Mitchell*, which voided a congressional act according 18- to 20-year-olds the right to vote in state elections.

Even more drastic options are available as well. Just before leaving office in 1801, the Federalists created a tier of circuit courts and populated them with Federalist judges; the Jeffersonian Democrats took over the reins of power and promptly abolished the entire level of courts. In 1869, the Radical Republicans in Congress altered the appellate jurisdiction of the Supreme Court to prevent it from hearing a case (*Ex*

Table 16.5   Supreme Court Rulings in Which Federal Statutes Have Been Found Unconstitutional[a]

PERIOD	STATUTES VOIDED
1798–1864	2
1864–1910	33 (34)[b]
1910–1930	24
1930–1936	14
1936–1953	3
1953–1969	25
1969–1986	35
1986–present	35
TOTAL	171

[a]In whole or in part.
[b]An 1883 decision in the *Civil Rights Cases* consolidated five different cases into one opinion declaring one act of Congress void. In 1895, *Pollock v. Farmers Loan and Trust Co.* was heard twice, with the same result both times.
Source: From *The Judicial Process: An Introductory Analysis of the Courts of the United States, England, and France,* 7th ed., by Henry J. Abraham. Copyright 1993 by Henry J. Abraham. Used by permission of Oxford University Press, Inc. Updated by the authors.

parte McCardle) that concerned the Reconstruction Acts. This kind of alteration has never recurred, although Congress did threaten to employ the method in the 1950s regarding some matters of civil liberties.

Finally, if the issue is one of **statutory construction,** in which a court interprets an act of Congress, then the legislature routinely passes legislation that clarifies existing laws and, in effect, overturns the courts.[39] In 1984, for example, the Supreme Court ruled in *Grove City College v. Bell* that when an institution receives federal aid, only the program or activity that actually gets the aid, not the entire institution, is covered by four federal civil rights laws. In 1988 Congress passed a law specifying that the entire institution is affected. The description of the judiciary as the "ultimate arbiter of the Constitution" is hyperbolic; all the branches of government help define and shape the Constitution.

statutory construction

The judicial interpretation of an act of Congress. In some cases where statutory construction is an issue, Congress passes new legislation to clarify existing laws.

Summary

The American judicial system is complex. Sitting at the pinnacle of the judicial system is the Supreme Court, but its importance is often exaggerated. Most judicial policymaking and enforcement of laws take place in the state courts and the lower federal courts.

Throughout American political history, courts have shaped public policy with regard to the economy, liberty, equality, and, most recently, ecology. In the economic arena, until the time of Franklin D. Roosevelt, courts traditionally favored corporations, especially when government tried to regulate them. Since the New Deal, however, the courts have been more tolerant of government regulation of business, shifting much of their policymaking attention to issues of liberty and equality. From *Dred Scott* to *Plessy* to *Brown,* the Supreme Court has moved from a role of reinforcing discriminatory policy toward racial minorities to a role of shaping new policies for protecting civil rights. Most recently, environmental groups have used the courts to achieve their policy goals.

A critical view of the courts claims that they are too powerful for the nation's own good and are rather ineffective policymakers besides. Throughout American history, however, judges have been important agenda setters in the political system. Many of the most important political questions make their way into the courts at one time or

Issues of the Times

The Issue: How Should the Courts Interpret the Law?

Judges must interpret both the Constitution and statutes. But *how* should they do so? The Constitution provides little help in answering this basic question. One source of conflict is the debate over interpreting the original intentions of the Constitution's framers (discussed in the *You Are the Policymaker* feature in this chapter). A related issue is the debate between those who favor interpreting the Constitution based on the exact text or language of the Constitution or a law, and those who argue that judges should also be influenced by the purpose of a law and the effects of a decision on that purpose.

Those who support textual interpretation want clear rules of interpretation and insist it is irresponsible to leave the law in a state of indeterminacy, changing from one year to the next. Moreover, they want to constrain the discretion of judges in interpreting the law. Those favoring an important role for context, on the other hand, argue that often there

is not a clear meaning to the text of the Constitution or a statute, and ignoring the context and purpose of either leads to judicial decisions that are inconsistent

with the real intent of the framers or law's drafters and do not provide for the potential of new legal understanding of laws and the Constitution.

Read All About It

Judicial Intent: The Competing Visions of the Role of the Court

By Linda Greenhouse
July 7, 2002

Labels that once comfortably described the range of views on the Supreme Court don't work so well these days. "Liberal" versus "conservative" means less than it did back when old-fashioned liberals sat on the court. And the new judicial "activism" on the right has stripped much usefulness from a handy insult once flung exclusively at liberal judges.

Yet with the court deeply divided, there remains a need to identfy and analyze its current dichotomies. In fact, two justices, Antonin Scalia and Stephen G. Breyer, spent much of the term just ended engaged in a debate about how the court should approach its work. It is in terms of that debate, and in the competing visions of the judicial role emerging from it, that one of the most interesting and potentially important fault lines on the

current Supreme Court can be understood.

It is a debate over text versus context. For Justice Scalia, who focuses on text, language is supreme, and the court's job is to derive and apply rules from the words chosen by the Constitution's framers or a statute's drafters. For Justice Breyer, who looks to context, language is only a starting point to

Please see Intent   Page 537

Intent

Continued from Page 536

an inquiry in which a law's purpose and a decision's likely consequence are the more important elements.

This debate is taking place not only in the court's opinions but, significantly, in the two justices' outside writing and speaking. Not since the Roosevelt era, when Justice Hugo L. Black (text) and Justice Felix Frankfurter (context) battled over the meaning of the Bill of Rights, has the court had two justices willing to engage each other—and the public—in a debate over basic principles.

Justice Scalia's vision is the more familiar, pungently expressed in 16 years of Supreme Court opinions and through much speaking and writing off the bench; his 1995 Tanner Lectures at Princeton became a book, "A Matter of Interpretation." He is a seeker of bright lines and boundaries, a transmitter of rules, whether derived from the framers' original understanding or from the unannotated text of federal statutes.

For Justice Scalia, constitutional principles are fixed, not evolving—"The Constitution that I interpret and apply is not living, but dead," he declared at a conference earlier this year—and Congress needs to be held to the words it wrote, not to interpretations written by committee aides or judges. "Our first responsibility is not to make sense of the law—our first responsibility is to follow the text of the law," he said from the bench. In his view, the Supreme Court's job is to give lower court judges not factors to weigh, but rules to apply.

For much of Justice Breyer's eight years on the court, his premises were not equally clear, though it was obvious that context, for him,

counted far more than rules. His tone was often diffident, his doubts openly acknowledged.

It was during the past term that Justice Breyer presented an integrated theory of the role he sees for the court in society and for himself as a justice. Delivering New York University Law School's James Madison Lecture last October, he said three principles should guide the court's decision-making.

> Not since the Roosevelt era, when Justice Hugo L. Black (text) and Justice Felix Frankfurter (context) battled over the meaning of the Bill of Rights, has the court had two justices willing to engage each other—and the public—in a debate over basic principles.

First was the purpose (as opposed to text) of the constitutional provision or law under review. Second was the likely consequence of a decision, which he contrasted to "a more 'legalistic' approach that places too much weight upon language, history, tradition and precedent alone." Without mentioning Justice Scalia by name, he said the "literalist" approach leads to a result "no less subjective but which is far less transparent than a decision that directly addresses consequences in constitutional terms."

Third, Justice Breyer said, the court should bear in mind the Constitution's overall objective, that of fostering "participatory democratic self-government." The court should be wary, he said, about preempting a "national conversation" in which new legal understanding "bubbles up from below."

Justice Breyer's lecture did more than clarify his own approach. It meant that Justice Scalia was no longer the solitary voice framing the debate on the role of the court. In an influential *Harvard Law Review* article 10 years ago, Kathleen M. Sullivan described "The Justices of Rules and Standards." Justice Scalia was the quintessential and selfdefined justice of rules. Justice Breyer was not on the court then, but Professor Sullivan, now dean of Stanford Law School, agreed last week that he is the quintessential justice of standards, an approach she defined as "evolutionary, pragmatic, always asking what makes sense, what would serve the purpose of the law."

Neither approach carries an ideological guarantee. Justice Black's rules (text) led him to the liberal side of the spectrum, while Justice Frankfurter's use of standards (context) had a conservative tilt. In recent cases, Justice Scalia's rules led him to write—over a dissent by Chief Justice William H. Rehnquist—that for the police to aim a thermal imaging device at a home was a search for which the framers would have required a warrant, while Justice Breyer's satisfaction that a school district's broad drug-testing policy was the product of an authentically democratic community debate led him to align with the four more conservative justices to uphold the policy.

Think About It

- How should judges interpret the Constitution and statutes?
- If judges follow the contextual approach, are they freer to make law rather than just interpret it?

- If judges follow the textual approach, will they be able to determine the intent of the Constitution's framers, who wrote the document 220 years ago?

another. The judiciary is an alternative point of access for those seeking to obtain public policy decisions to their liking, especially those who are not in the majority.

Once in court, litigants face judges whose discretion in decision-making is typically limited by precedent. Nevertheless, on questions that raise novel issues (as do many of the most important questions that reach the Supreme Court), the law is less firmly established. Here there is more leeway and judges become more purely political players, balancing different interests and linked to the rest of the political system by their own policy preferences and the politics of their selection.

The unelected and powerful federal courts raise important issues of democracy and the scope of judicial power. Yet court decisions are typically consistent with public opinion and judges and justices have often used their power to promote democracy. Reconciling the American democratic heritage with an active policymaking role for the judiciary remains a matter of debate. The courts have been sensitive to the issue of their power and often avoid the most controversial issues, at least for a time. It has also been easier for opponents of court decisions to accept judicial power because it is possible to overturn judicial decisions.

KEY TERMS

standing to sue	Supreme Court	*Marbury v. Madison*
class action suits	senatorial courtesy	judicial review
justiciable disputes	solicitor general	*United States v. Nixon*
amicus curiae briefs	opinion	judicial restraint
original jurisdiction	*stare decisis*	judicial activism
appellate jurisdiction	precedents	political questions
district courts	original intent	statutory construction
courts of appeal	judicial implementation	

INTERNET RESOURCES

www.supremecourtus.gov/
Official site of the U.S. Supreme Court with information about its operations.

supct.law.cornell.edu/supct/
Decisions of the Supreme Court, background, schedule, and rules of the Court; also includes backgrounds of the justices serving on the Court.

www.oyez.org/oyez/frontpage
Website that allows you to hear oral arguments before the Supreme Court. Also provides information on the Supreme Court and its docket.

www.courttv.com/trials/
Information on recent trials.

www.uscourts.gov/
Explains the organization, operation, and administration of federal courts.

www.usdoj.gov/olp/judicialnominations.htm
Information on current judicial nominations.

GET CONNECTED

The Background of Judges and Justices

As the text notes, the Constitution sets no requirements for judges and historically judges have not represented the cultural diversity of America. For instance, federal judges have been more male and more White than the rest of the population. Advocates of race and gender equality have in recent years increased their call for greater race and gender diversity on the federal bench. Let us look at the current list of judicial nominations and compare their background characteristics with the background characteristics detailed in Table 16.3 of the text.

Search the Web

Go to *http://www.usdoj.gov/olp/nominations.htm* and click on the name of the judge to view his or her biography. Do this for all the nominees.

Questions To Ask

- How does the current list of nominees compare with the characteristics outlined in Table 16.3?
- In general is President George W. Bush nominating judges who will greatly alter the general characteristics of the judiciary or not? If so, how?

Why It Matters

We want the most qualified judges to sit on the bench, and most people also want the judiciary to reflect American cultural diversity. Judges from different backgrounds, such as women and racial and ethnic minorities, may be more sensitive to the implications of issues especially relevant to their experiences.

Get Involved

Find out more about the nominees from your federal district court or federal court of appeals circuit. Contact one or both of your U.S. Senators *http://www.senate.gov/* to tell him or her your opinions of the nominee.

To see more Get Connected exercises for Chapter 16, go to www.ablongman.com/edwards.

FOR FURTHER READING

Abraham, Henry J. *Justices, Presidents, and Senators: A History of the U.S. Supreme Court Appointments from Washington to Clinton.* Lanham, MD: Rowman and Littlefield, 1999. A readable history of the relationships between presidents and the justices they appointed.

Baum, Lawrence. *The Supreme Court,* 8th ed. Washington, D.C.: Congressional Quarterly Press, 2004. An excellent work on the operations and impact of the Court.

Carp, Robert A., Ronald Stidham, and Kenneth L. Manning. *Judicial Process in America,* 6th ed. Washington, D.C.: Congressional Quarterly Press, 2004. An overview of federal and state courts.

Ely, John Hart. *Democracy and Distrust.* Cambridge, MA: Harvard University Press, 1980. An appraisal of judicial review and an effort to create a balanced justification for the role of the courts in policymaking.

Epstein, Lee, and Jack Knight. *The Choices Justices Make.* Washington, D.C.: Congressional Quarterly Press, 1997. A strategic account of Supreme Court decision-making.

Epstein, Lee, and Joseph F. Kobylka. *The Supreme Court and Legal Change.* Chapel Hill: University of North Carolina Press, 1992. Examines how interest groups propelled issues regarding abortion and the death penalty to the Supreme Court, and how the way they framed their legal arguments affected outcomes on these issues.

Gates, John B., and Charles A. Johnson, eds. *The American Courts: A Critical Assessment.* Washington, D.C.: Congressional Quarterly Press, 1991. Useful essays covering many aspects of judicial politics.

Goldman, Sheldon. *Picking Federal Judges.* New Haven, CT: Yale University Press, 1997. The definitive work on backgrounds and the politics of recruiting lower-court judges.

Jacob, Herbert. *Law and Politics in the United States,* 2nd ed. Boston: HarperCollins, 1995. An introduction to the American legal system with an emphasis on linkages to the political arena.

Johnson, Charles A., and Bradley C. Canon. *Judicial Policies: Implementation and Impact,* 2nd ed. Washington, D.C.: Congressional Quarterly Press, 1999. One of the best overviews of judicial policy implementation.

O'Brien, David M. *Storm Center,* 6th ed. New York: Norton, 2002. An overview of the Supreme Court's role in American politics.

Rowland, C. K., and Robert A. Carp. *Politics and Judgment in Federal District Courts.* Lawrence: University Press of Kansas, 1996. An important work on the operations of the federal district courts.

Segal, Jeffrey A., and Harold J. Spaeth. *The Supreme Court and the Attitudinal Model.* Cambridge, MA: Cambridge University Press, 1993. Examines how the attitudes and values of justices affect their decisions.

Economic Policymaking

Chapter Outline

Government, Politics, and the Economy

Policies for Controlling the Economy

The New York Times **Issues of the Times**

Why It Is Hard To Control the Economy

Politics, Policy, and the International Economy

Arenas of Economic Policymaking

Understanding Economic Policymaking

Summary

■ After the president delivers his State of the Union address to Congress in January, he usually hits the road to sell his policy agenda. President Bush did just that after his January 20, 2004, State of the Union address. Air Force One took him to Ohio, Arizona, and New Mexico—three "battleground states" whose electoral votes he wanted in November. (No Republican had ever won the White House without Ohio.) He had some jobs proposals in the State of the Union address, which he had bundled as a "Jobs for the Twenty-first Century" plan. At Owens Community College near Toledo on January 21, the president told Ohioans that "Nationwide, this economy is strong." Even so, he acknowledged, "In Ohio, there are still troubled times. The manufacturing sector here is sluggish at best." In neighboring Michigan, on January 16, just before the President's tour, Sweden's Electrolux, the world's largest home appliance maker, announced that it was closing its plant in Greenville, population 8,000. The Electrolux refrigerator factory there employed 2,700 people and had been in town since 1877. Electrolux's press release said it was going to spend $150 million to build a new factory in Mexico. Michigan had even offered Electrolux a 20-year tax-free deal to stay.[1]

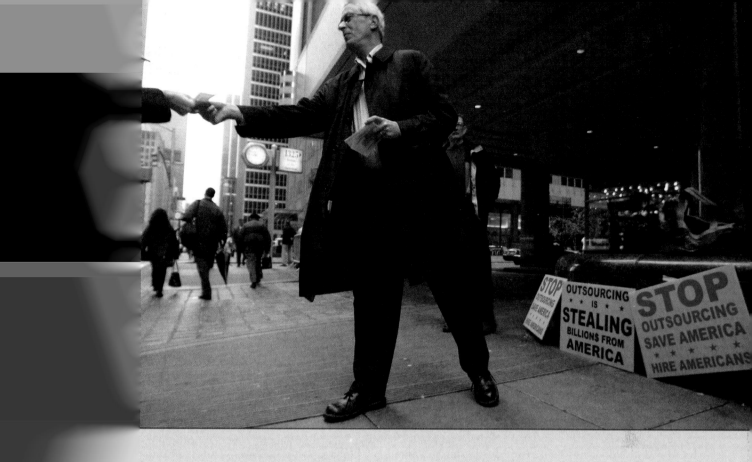

ame day the president was in Ohio, at
Times Square Hotel in New York
ce opened on "Offshore Outsourcing:
ney Work for Your Corporation."
rcing (sometimes called offshoring) is
or moving operations and jobs to
, which is what Electrolux was doing.
onstrators stood outside the hotel in
weather. A protest sign on an easel
g Creates Jobless Americans, State
Higher Taxes." One Pennsylvania
r protested with a "Will Code for
le, one attendee reported "I have yet
urcing conference with this many
f the speakers were a little sensitive.
om the offshoring consulting firm
Co., barred the press from his session
ring Unpatriotic?"
sh was still on his barnstorming trip
g conference in New York was in its
n the University of Maryland's
rnational Policy Attitudes released its
cans' attitudes toward foreign trade
conomy. Its survey found that many
eeply suspicious that foreign trade,
g that comes with it, is responsible

for much of the unemployment in the United States.
Twice as many Americans said they knew someone
who had lost their job because of "globalization and
the growth of foreign trade" than said they knew
someone who got a job from a globalizing economy
(39 percent to 17 percent).[2] All through the 2004
campaign, Democrats were pounding George Bush
on 1.6 million jobs lost during his presidency.

Virtually every economist in the world pushes the
virtues of free trade. Three recent presidents also
pushed globalization and free trade (on free trade
agreements, see Chapter 20). The first President
Bush negotiated the North American Free Trade
Agreement; President Clinton strong-armed his own
party to get an agreement creating the World Trade
Organization; President George W. Bush reiterated
in the 2004 State of the Union address that his
administration was "promoting free and fair trade to
open up markets for American manufacturers and
farmers." Voters, however, were not as sure about the
virtues as economists and presidents.

The United States is imbedded as never before in
the world economy. In this chapter, we will examine
why the economy is so important to politics and vice
versa.

If George Washington was the father of the country and James Madison the father of the Constitution, then Alexander Hamilton was the father of the American economy. Bright, arrogant, and with a good head for numbers, Hamilton was the first U.S. secretary of the Treasury. We may remember Thomas Jefferson better because he became president, but his economic ideas favoring farmers and small towns quickly became outmoded.

The word "capitalism" wasn't even introduced until the middle of the nineteenth century, but Hamilton's economic system laid the basis for it. **Capitalism** is an economic system in which individuals and corporations own the principal means of production, through which they seek to reap profits. The American economic system was never one of pure capitalism by this definition. Hamilton's economic system created a **mixed economy,** in which the government, while not commanding the economy, is deeply involved in economic decisions. Written in an agrarian era, the Constitution still gave large powers over the economy to the new national government. It was Hamilton's job to put them into operation.

Far-sighted as he was, though, even Hamilton would not recognize today's interplay between government and the economy, the topic of our chapter. Today we live in a global economy with all its problems and opportunities. Corporations have been getting bigger and bigger. **Multinational corporations**—businesses with vast holdings in many countries such as Disney, Coca-Cola, and Microsoft—dominate the world's economy. From your neighborhood Wal-Mart—China's biggest customer—to presidential candidates on the campaign trail arguing about jobs, issues about government and the economy are vital. People expect government to keep the economy moving. Rightly or wrongly, voters often punish politicians when the economy turns sour. Politics and economics are powerful forces, intertwined like the strands of a double helix.

capitalism

An economic system in which individuals and corporations, not the government, own the principal means of production and seek profits.

mixed economy

An economic system in which the government is deeply involved in economic decisions through its role as regulator, consumer, subsidizer, taxer, employer, and borrower.

multinational corporations

Businesses with vast holdings in many countries, many of which have annual budgets exceeding that of many foreign governments.

Government, Politics, and the Economy

The American economy is made up of the millions or billions of decisions made by corporations, workers, producers, consumers, regulators, and even policymakers. There is an entire academic discipline (called "economics") devoted to understanding it. In one chapter, we could not possibly give you more than a hint about how our economy works. But that is not our goal. We are interested in understanding two things: how government and its policies affect the economy, and how economics affect policymakers and politicians.

To do this, we are going to begin with an institution almost all Americans are familiar with: Wal-Mart. A look at Wal-Mart will illustrate two key points. First, the government's long arm of regulation (which we first met in Chapter 15) affects Wal-Mart, as it does the hundreds of thousands of other U.S. companies. Second, Wal-Mart epitomizes the imbedding of the U.S. economy in the global economy, a trend that will continue to have an enormous impact on the domestic economy and the politics of economic policy. We will take up the topics of business and economic policy and the impact of globalization again later in this chapter.

Economic Policy at Work: An Illustration

It is the store that has saved millions billions. Headquartered in tiny Bentonville, Ark., Wal-Mart, the world's largest company, generated $273 billion in 2003 and ranked first on *Fortune Magazine's* 500 biggest corporations list.[3] That made it about as big as the economy of Saudi Arabia and more than half the size of Australia's. It generated as much revenue as California—the world's sixth largest economy—collected in taxes. It made Sam Walton's widow and children five of the ten richest people in the world, *each* with assets of $20 billion.[4] Wal-Mart, known for its low prices, is also famous for shaving fractions of pennies from every supplier and every worker. That is why Wal-Mart is partly responsible for the low rate of inflation in the United States. One consulting firm estimated that Wal-Mart was alone responsible for 12 percent of all productivity growth in the United States during the 1990s.[5] Next, we will consider how government economic policy affects such a key player in our economy.

Government Regulation and Business Practices. Government regulation affects the way Wal-Mart, like most U.S. companies, does business. The main government regulatory agency responsible for the regulation of business practices is the **Securities and Exchange Commission (SEC)**, a federal agency created in 1934 to regulate stock fraud. The SEC regulates stock transactions and the stock market. Wal-Mart is a publicly traded company, listed on the New York Stock Exchange (its "ticker symbol" is WMT), and so its stock trading is regulated by the SEC. Wal-Mart's officers cannot, for example, enrich themselves by buying and selling Wal-Mart stock on the basis of insider knowledge. Buyers of Wal-Mart stock are entitled to accurate knowledge from the company. The SEC requires that companies hire an auditor and publish an annual review. Crooked accounting led to the demise of one of the nation's hottest and biggest companies, Enron, in 2001. Martha Stewart (her product lines are sold by Wal-Mart's bankrupt rival K-Mart) was convicted of lying about insider information on a stock trade.

Government also affects a company's labor practices. About 1.4 million people work for Wal-Mart—about 1 out of every 100 workers in the United States. Workers there and almost everywhere else are entitled to collect a **minimum wage,** now $5.15 per hour. Its workers have a right to join a **labor union,** a workers' organization for bargaining with an employer. Wal-Mart remains fiercely nonunion, however. In the United States, union membership and political power have been declining, partly because of the rise of companies like Wal-Mart, and the decline of the manufacturing sector. First guaranteed by law in 1935, labor unions engage in **collective bargaining** about wages and working conditions with their employers under rules controlled by the National Labor Relations Board. When Wal-Mart was ready to expand its grocery operations to Southern California, existing grocery chains with unionized workers insisted that workers accept reduced benefits. Only that way, the stores said, could they compete with the coming Wal-Mart onslaught. The chains won a bitter strike, and union workers accepted cuts in wages and health benefits.

Federal law also regulates working conditions and hiring practices. Worker safety is governed by the rules of the Occupational Health and Safety Administration. Like other employers, Wal-Mart is supposed to abide by hiring and employment regulations and laws. U.S. companies cannot employ illegal aliens. In October 2003, federal immigration officers raided 67 Wal-Marts and arrested 250 illegal aliens working on cleaning crews.[6] Wal-Mart, like other companies, cannot discriminate in its hiring, firing,

Securities and Exchange Commission (SEC)

The federal agency created during the New Deal that regulates stock fraud.

minimum wage

The legal minimum hourly wage for large employers.

labor union

An organization of workers intended to engage in collective bargaining.

collective bargaining

Negotiations between representatives of labor unions and management to determine pay and acceptable working conditions.

With more than 3,000 stores in the United States, and more than 1,000 abroad, Arkansas-based retail giant Wal-Mart is a major force in the global economy. Known for its deeply discounted prices, Wal-Mart has also been criticized for its labor practices.

You Are the Judge

Is It OK for a Company To Discriminate Against Younger Workers?

Companies face a lot of federal regulations about their workers. For example, companies are required to provide a safe working environment and they are obligated to follow laws against discrimination. Of course, a company cannot legally say "we are not going to hire you because you are a woman" or "we do not hire people from your racial group." There is also a federal law against age discrimination. The Age Discrimination in Employment Act of 1967 (ADEA) prohibits discrimination because of an individual's age. Specifically, the law says a company cannot discriminate against workers over 40. A company could not, for example, conclude that a worker over 40 was too expensive and could be fired so two cheaper entry-level workers could be hired.

Like many companies, General Dynamics Land Systems Inc. faced rising costs for workers' health plans. As many companies have done, they decided to continue to offer, under a renegotiated union contract, benefits to workers over 50, but not to younger workers. Instead, younger workers would have to provide their own health benefits. Some of General Dynamics' workers who were 40 but not yet 50 sued, claiming that they were discriminated against because of their age. The law against age discrimination should, they claimed, protect them against discrimination because of their age.

You Be the Judge: Does the ADEA permit a company to provide benefits to older workers but deny the same benefits to younger ones?

Answer: In the *General Dynamics Land Systems Inc. v. Cline* case in 2004, the Supreme Court ruled that Congress intended for the ADEA to protect older workers from age discrimination, not younger ones. The Court could not have been clearer. In its opening paragraph, it said, "The Age Discrimination in Employment Act forbids discriminatory preference for the young over the old. The question in this case is whether it also prohibits favoring the old over the young. We hold that it does not." Younger workers will find it next to impossible to sue when they think a company favors older workers.

and promotion. It cannot refuse to hire or promote someone because of the person's sex or race. Federal law also protects older workers from job discrimination. (Does federal law, though, protect younger workers from age discrimination? See "You Are the Judge: Is It OK for a Company To Discriminate Against Younger Workers?")

Wal-Mart and the World Economy. No institution better epitomizes America's imbedding in the world economy than Wal-Mart. Perhaps ironically in retrospect, Wal-Mart founder Sam Walton's autobiography was subtitled "Made in America," the slogan Wal-Mart first used way back in the 1980s. At one point, much of its merchandise was even tagged with a "Made in America" label. Today, the slogan is long gone. Opening one new store a day, Wal-Mart is typical of the globalization of the entire economy. Over the last generation, the proportion of the U.S. Gross Domestic Product accounted for by international trade has tripled, to about 30 percent. The elimination of trade barriers among nations has probably added about $2000 to the annual income of the average U.S. family in the form of cheaper products.[7] The Waltons and the other Wal-Mart stockholders take full advantage of what economists call "comparative advantage." Its $12 billion in imports from China constituted one-tenth of all of China's exports to the United States. The U.S. supplier who cannot provide the retailer with goods cheaply enough can always be replaced with a company elsewhere. So can the Chinese supplier. A company that sells 26 percent of the toothpaste (and about that share of almost every other consumer product) in the United States has real clout. *Business Week* believes that Wal-Mart's "hard line on costs has forced many factories to move overseas."[8]

As we saw in the chapter opener and will discuss again later in this chapter, when U.S. factories move overseas, jobs do as well. Offshore outsourcing is a key concern of the new global economy. The dean of Yale's management school speculates that amid all the debate about globalization in the 2004 election campaign, "Global capitalism could have a new face, Wal-Mart. That would be bad news."[9]

Wal-Mart is more than a microcosm of the American economy. In many ways, it symbolizes the new U.S. economy.[10] Sam Walton may have had as much influence on the American economy as Henry Ford's invention of the assembly line. It is a major player in the globalization of the U.S. economy. Still, as we saw in this illustration, there are lots of government rules and regulations that affect Wal-Mart and other American businesses and consumers. When it comes to the economy, politics and policies matter. Indeed, the economy was one of the major issues in the 2004 presidential election, as it is in nearly every election. Let us see why.

"It's the Economy, Stupid": Voters, Politicians, and Economic Policy

It was the most famous sign ever to adorn a campaign headquarters: "It's the economy, stupid." Arkansas Governor William Jefferson Clinton, once the longest of long shots in the 1992 presidential race, was running against an incumbent president, George H. W. Bush ("Bush 41," his son's advisers sometimes called him because he was the forty-first president), whose Gulf War against Iraq had shot his presidential approval into the stratosphere. The economy, though, was weak when the Democrats nominated Bill Clinton in 1992. Clinton hammered home a constant message: The economy under George H. W. Bush was ailing and Bush didn't understand. Political folklore has it that in the "war room" of the Clinton campaign headquarters in Little Rock, a sign was hung with big letters: "It's the economy, stupid." Presumably this would constantly focus the attention of the campaign staff on the Clinton attack theme.[11] Campaign manager James Carville "drilled [it] into our heads, and every speech, every event, every attack" had to be "on message."[12]

"Bush 41's" son, George W., became president after the bitter 2000 election. As the economy waned in the early years of the younger President Bush's term, White House aides constantly looked over their shoulders at the fate of "41." They knew that voters pay attention to what President Harry S Truman called "the most sensitive part of their anatomies," their pocketbooks. We saw earlier in *Government in America* that economic conditions affect both voting behavior (see Chapter 10) and presidential approval (see Chapter 13). Voters, the parties, and politicians are riveted on economic issues, especially at election time.

Hundreds, if not thousands, of studies by political scientists have reaffirmed the wisdom of Harry S Truman's observations about voters and their pocketbooks. Summarizing a generation of research, two political scientists put it plainly: "There is little doubt that economic conditions profoundly affect voters' electoral decisions."[13] Economic conditions are the best single predictor of voters' evaluation of how the president is doing his job.[14] Voters may (as we will see) exaggerate the importance of politicians in shaping the economy, but the more sophisticated the voter, the more likely she or he is to engage in "pocketbook voting."[15]

The connection between economic conditions and voting is real, but complex. Mary Voter may lose her job, but she does not quickly jump to the conclusion that the current president deserves to be thrown out. Voters in general engage is what political scientists call "sociotropic" voting, assessing the overall rate of employment and unemployment more than their individual circumstances.[16]

Like voters, the parties are economic animals. The two parties have different economic centers of gravity. Traditionally in American politics, Democrats stress the importance of employment. Republicans are worried about inflation. This reflects their constituencies. Democrats appeal to working-class voters, to poorer people, to union members, and to minority groups. Republicans appeal to the "investor class," professionals and business people who can save and invest, and worry that inflation will erode their savings. Presidential and congressional elections usually see "Republicans

Why It Matters

Employment Discrimination
Employers have a lot of discretion about whom they hire and fire. Federal law, though, prohibits many kinds of job discrimination in hiring, firing and promoting. Employers cannot use race or gender as a qualification for job decisions. Age, though, is a different matter. Federal law prohibits discrimination in hiring, firing or promotion if you are over 40, but not if you are younger. Under the law, an employer could legally say to you "I am not hiring you because you are too young," if you are under the age of 40.

focusing on the ills of inflation and Democrats on the ills of unemployment."[17] Let us look at the twin economic—and political—quagmires of unemployment and inflation. Too much unemployment and inflation can increase unemployment among politicians.

The 2004 presidential election was one more election where economics mattered. People whose main issue concern was the economy or jobs voted 4-1 for Democrat John Kerry. (Exactly the same percent of people whose main concern was "moral values" split for President Bush.) People who thought their family was doing better economically went 4-1 for the incumbent; people who thought they were faring less well went 4-1 for Kerry. Presidents seemed to be glued to the performance of the economy during their term. Voters, though, probably overestimate the impact any president has on their economic fortunes. As we will see in the rest of this chapter, government has a lot to do with the economy. It may not have much to do, though, with whether you have a job or not.

Two Major Worries: Unemployment and Inflation

unemployment rate

As measured by the Bureau of Labor Statistics (BLS), the proportion of the labor force actively seeking work but unable to find jobs.

The **unemployment rate** is the percentage of Americans seeking work who are unable to find it. Measuring how many and what types of workers are unemployed is one of the major jobs of the Bureau of Labor Statistics (BLS) in the Department of Labor. To carry out this task, the BLS conducts a huge statistical survey of the population every month. It then announces changes in the "unemployment rate." We have to increase the number of U.S. jobs by about 125,000 every month just to keep up with new entrants (graduates, for example) into the labor force. Of course, the unemployment rate varies from time to time and group to group. Young adults actually face more serious unemployment problems than other sectors of the population. (See "Young People and Politics: Unemployment and Young Workers.") Most people are out of work for only a short time (which is why the connection between the poverty rate and the unemployment rate is weak). Even so, the official unemployment rate underestimates unemployment because it leaves out "discouraged workers," who have given up their job search altogether. Figure 17.1 shows what has happened to unemployment rates in

Figure 17.1   Unemployment: Joblessness in America, 1960–2003

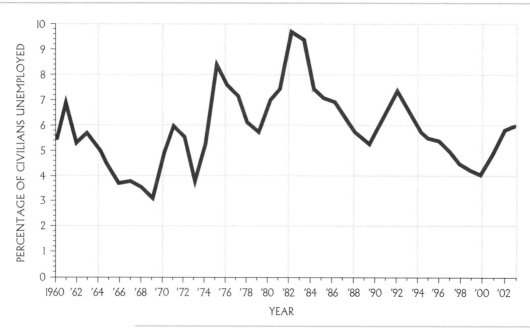

Source: Economic Report of the President, 2004 (Washington, D.C.: U.S. Government Printing Office, 2004).

Young People and Politics

Unemployment and Young Workers

The unemployment rate is one of the nation's most important economic indicators, and a political issue, too. To measure the rate of unemployment, the Bureau of Labor Statistics (BLS) in the Department of Labor surveys about 60,000 individuals every month. From this, the Bureau produces the familiar "unemployment rate," a number watched carefully by the White House and policymakers. The higher the unemployment rate, the higher their level of worry.

Every year the BLS counts the employment rates for young Americans, ages 16 to 24. Young Americans have very high unemployment rates compared to middle-aged and older Americans. Few things plunge a person into unemployment more certainly and more quickly than dropping out of high school. More than 400,000 young men and women drop out of high school each year. For October 2003, the unemployment rate of recent high school dropouts was a staggering 30.8 percent.

Even recent high school graduates, though, face higher-than-average unemployment. Here are the percentages of unemployment for 2003's high school graduates:

Men	21.0%
Women	17.1
White	13.6
African Americans	50.9
Hispanic	16.9

Half of all African-American recent high school graduates face unemployment. Overall, recent high school graduates are still about four times more likely to be unemployed than the rest of the work force.

Most high school graduates (about 64 percent) go to college. Although college does not come cheap, it pays off economically in the long run. People with college degrees have as much as a million dollar income advantage over their working lifetimes.

High unemployment rates among the young adult population compete with many other economic issues on the agenda. Partly because young adults are such poor participators in elections, their unemployment rates never seem to rank very high as a campaign issue. If voter turnout were to improve dramatically among young Americans, however, it is likely that their concerns would capture the attention of more politicians and policymakers.

Questions for Discussion

- Which, if any, government policies have an effect on the high youth unemployment rate in the United States?
- What accounts for the variations in jobless rates among ethnic and racial groups?

Source: For the unemployment statistics among young adults, see the Bureau of Labor Statistics press release entitled "College Enrollment and Work Activity of 2003 High School Graduates," April 27, 2004.

---

recent decades. When the unemployment rate increases, public opinion pushes policymakers to "do more" to "expand employment."[18] (See "Issues of the Times: Should the Government Help Create Jobs?" on pages 550–551.) Doing something about U.S. companies outsourcing U.S. jobs was a key theme of the 2004 campaigns.

The problem of **inflation**—the rise in prices for consumer goods—is the other half of policymakers' regular economic concern. For decades the government has also kept tabs on inflation via the **consumer price index (CPI),** which measures the change in the cost of buying a fixed basket of goods and services. Each month, the BLS's data-gatherers fan out over the country looking at the prices of some 80,000 items from eggs to doctor visits. Even so, the CPI is an imperfect index at best (most taxes are excluded, for example). The BLS itself says that "the CPI is frequently called a cost of living index, but it differs in important ways from a complete cost of living measure."[19] Figure 17.2 shows changes in the CPI since 1960. Huge spikes in energy costs, among other things, contributed to soaring inflation in the 1970s. In recent years, inflation has been barely noticeable, thanks in part to the enormous effect Wal-Mart has on the economy, directly and (by forcing competitors to hold down prices) indirectly. Tame today, soaring inflation rates contributed to the defeat of one recent incumbent president, Jimmy Carter, in 1980.

inflation

The rise in prices for consumer goods.

consumer price index (CPI)

The key measure of inflation that relates the rise in prices over time.

Figure 17.2   Inflation: Increases in the Cost of Living, 1960–2003

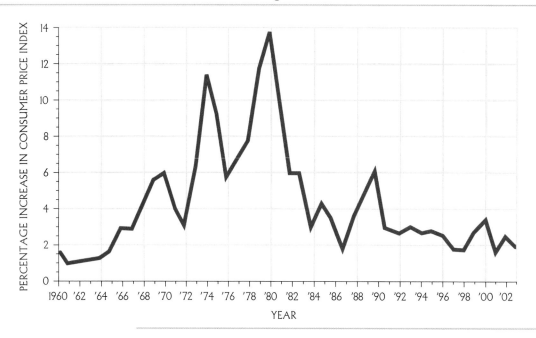

Source: Economic Report of the President, 2004 (Washington, D.C.: U.S. Government Printing Office, 2004).

Policies for Controlling the Economy

The time when government could ignore economic problems, confidently asserting that the private marketplace could handle them, has long passed, if it ever really existed. Especially since the Great Depression and the New Deal, government has been actively involved in steering the economy. When the stock market crash of 1929 sent unemployment soaring, President Herbert Hoover clung to **laissez-faire**—the principle that government should not meddle with the economy. In the next presidential election, Hoover was handed a crushing defeat by Franklin D. Roosevelt, whose New Deal programs experimented with dozens of new federal policies to put the economy back on track. Since the New Deal, policymakers have regularly sought to control the economy. The American political economy offers two important tools to guide the economy: monetary policy and fiscal policy.

Monetary Policy and "The Fed"

The most important tool government has to manage the economy is its control over the money supply. Government's main economic policy is **monetary policy**, that is, manipulation of the supply of money and credit in private hands. An economic theory called **monetarism** holds that the supply of money is the key to the nation's economic health. Monetarists believe that having too much cash and credit in circulation generates inflation. Essentially, they advise holding the growth in money supply to the rise in the gross domestic product, the total value of all the goods and services a nation produces. Politicians worry constantly about the money supply because it affects the rate of interest their constituents have to pay for home loans, new cars, starting up new businesses, and so on.

The main agency for making monetary policy is "the Fed," whose formal title is the Board of Governors of the **Federal Reserve System.** Created by Congress in 1913 to regulate the lending practices of banks and thus the money supply, the Federal Reserve System is intended to be formally beyond the control of the president and Congress. Its seven-member Board of Governors—appointed by the president and con-

laissez-faire

The principle that government should not meddle in the economy.

monetary policy

Based on **monetarism**, monetary policy is the manipulation of the supply of money in private hands by which the government can control the economy.

monetarism

An economic theory holding that the supply of money is the key to a nation's economic health. Monetarists believe that too much cash and credit in circulation produces inflation.

Federal Reserve System

The main instrument for making **monetary policy** in the United States. It was created by Congress in 1913 to regulate the lending practices of banks and thus the money supply.

Federal Reserve Chair Alan Greenspan before the Joint Economic Committee on Capitol Hill. Greenspan made fighting inflation the Federal Reserve's top priority, based on the theory that when inflation is controlled, investors will put their money into enterprises that will produce goods and services, people will be employed, and pensions will be secure.

firmed by the Senate—is expected to do its job without regard to partisan politics. Accordingly, members of the Fed's Board of Governors are given 14-year terms designed to insulate them from political pressures.

Here is how "the Fed" works to affect the supply of money and credit: Its Federal Open Market Committee, the policymaking body, meets eight times a year in Washington. Studying carefully a vast amount of economic data, the FOMC sets the "federal funds rate," the interest rate banks can charge each other for overnight loans. The Fed itself purchases or sells government bonds from banks. By buying or selling bonds from banks, the Fed determines whether banks have more or less money to lend out. The more money banks have to lend, the cheaper borrowing is; if banks have less to loan, loans become more expensive and interest rates rise.

Thus, the amount of money available, interest rates, inflation, and the availability of jobs are all affected either directly or indirectly by the complicated financial dealings of the Fed. The Fed can profoundly influence the state of the economy; no wonder it attracts the attention of politicians. With so much riding on its decisions, presidents quite naturally try to persuade the Fed to pursue policies in line with presidential plans for the country. Long-time Fed Chair Alan Greenspan did indeed lead the Fed to hold the line on interest rates, thus adding more evidence to the general finding that the Fed is responsive to the White House, though not usually to the extent of trying to influence election outcomes.[20] The chair of the Federal Reserve Board probably has more power over the U.S. economy than any other person, presidents included.

Fiscal Policy of Presidents and Parties

Presidents don't have as much power over the economy as we think they do, but on matters of economic policy, the president *is* his party. While "the Fed" is almost entirely responsible for monetary policy, presidents and Congress are responsible for **fiscal policy,** the impact of the federal budget—taxing, spending, and borrowing—on the economy. According to the Constitution, Congress got most of the economic powers (coining money, regulating trade, and so on). As the federal budget grew, its impact on the economy skyrocketed. We saw in Chapter 13, though, that the president has now gained the informal title of "chief economist." Presidents or their parties have to run on their economic record. When the economy sags, they need to change the subject. To the Republicans in 2004, "national security" trumped "job losses"; to the Democrats, it was the other way around.

Why It Matters

Interest Rates
Interest rates are the amount you pay to borrow money for a house or a car, for example. Banks or finance companies charge you these rates, but how high they are—and what you pay—are strongly influenced by decision of the Fed. Even a great credit rating cannot get you a low interest rate if the Federal Reserve Board is keeping the money supply tight.

fiscal policy

The policy that describes the impact of the federal budget—taxes, spending, and borrowing—on the economy. Fiscal policy is almost entirely determined by Congress and the president, who are the budget makers.

Issues of the Times

The Issue: Should the Government Help Create Jobs?

Jobs are at the core of the economy—and of the everyday life of Americans. If people do not have jobs, they cannot spend money, and if people do not spend money, the economy sags. Closer to home, jobs determine the lifestyles of Americans, and whether they have access to health care, vacations, or college educations for their children.

Over the last few years, the economy has not created jobs at the same rate as it has during economic recoveries in the past. Even the large tax cuts of the George W. Bush years have yet to lead to a steady expansion in employment. Indeed, employment fell during the president's first term. In the past, it was common for political leaders to call for government action to create jobs. Today, there is less demand for the government to act.

Nevertheless, many people are concerned about unemployment and under-

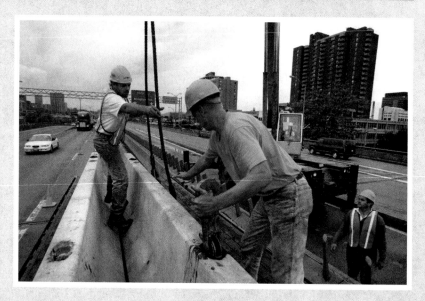

employment. Because jobs are so central to the economy and the lives of Americans, the issue of government action is still with us.

Read All About It

Maybe It's Time For Another New Deal

By Louis Uchitelle
April 11, 2004

Can the private sector generate enough jobs to return the United States to full employment? Or must government play a much greater supporting role in job creation?

That question, once hotly debated, is barely mentioned today. It should be. For 30 years, the assumption has been that the private sector

would generate full employment on its own. It has not, except for a five-year stretch in the late 1990's. Now the situation has become worse. Despite robust economic growth, the private sector is generating fewer jobs than ever in a recovery.

Never mind that private employers added 277,000 jobs in March. It was the biggest one-month gain in the two and a half years since the last recession. It was also some-

what of a mirage. Most of the 277,000 jobs were canceled out by a decline in total hours worked and total weekly pay.

"The normal rule of thumb by which a certain increase in the gross domestic product would produce a concomitant increase in jobs does not appear to apply," Representative

Please see Jo5

Jobs

Barney Frank, a Massachusetts Democrat, declared in a speech before the House last month.

The situation cries out for government job creation, Mr. Frank said in an interview last week. But public pressure is lacking. "People have so attacked government," he said, "that now when there is a need for it to help create jobs, they cannot recognize a positive role for government."

Such views are rare today. They are often dismissed as heresy. Among politicians they show up, when they show up at all, in the liberal wing of the Democratic Party. Mr. Frank is a member of that dwindling wing. John Kerry, the presidential candidate, is not. He is a centrist, in the Clinton mode. He counts on the private sector to generate full employment, with government playing a peripheral role, mainly in tax incentives that encourage companies to create more jobs.

After World War II, millions of Americans took for granted a robust government role in job creation. The Depression had amply demonstrated the private sector's failure and, with military spending winding down, there was widespread concern that corporate America could not generate enough jobs. The New Deal reflected that concern, and early drafts of the Employment Act of 1946 included clauses mandating government job creation through public spending—in effect, supplementing insufficient demand for private-sector workers.

The Employment Act, as finally enacted, fell well short of making government the employer of last resort. But, as the economy boomed, who really noticed? The combination of private-sector hiring and huge government spending for the Korean War, the Vietnam War, the space program and the Interstate System of highways, among other things, created, de facto, a private-public partnership that generated nearly full

Can the private sector generate enough jobs to return the United States to full employment? Or must government play a much greater supporting role in job creation?

employment. That generally means an unemployment rate below 5 percent and enough upward pressure on wages to prevent the income inequality that is now so glaring.

When the postwar boom finally faded in the 1970's, some in Con-gress tried once again to make government the employer of last resort. That language was written into early drafts of the Humphrey-Hawkins Act of 1978. The attempt failed, even backfired. The final act gave equal billing to fighting inflation and to full employment. Soon the Federal Reserve was trading higher unemployment for less inflation. And,

simultaneously, government was gaining a reputation as an obstacle to job creation.

Free markets work best when government stays in the background, encouraging the private sector through various supportive measures. President Bill Clinton made that claim and took credit for the full employment that finally reappeared in the late 1990's. President Bush has staked out roughly the same ground, although the job creation he promises as a result of his tax cuts has not occurred. It will, Mr. Kerry says, if we cancel the most egregious Bush tax cuts and substitute incentives that encourage corporate hiring.

The public wonders. Years of layoffs, wage stagnation, outsourcing and now offshore contracting have made people skeptical. Mr. Frank plays to that skepticism. So do a few others, the most important being Senator Edward M. Kennedy, a Democratic leader who in recent speeches appears to be trying to push his party back toward New Deal policies. The government job creation in his proposals would be coupled with much-needed public spending.

School and highway construction are examples. "Every billion dollars invested in highway construction produces 47,500 jobs," the senator said in a speech. He added: "We must create new and meaningful jobs for all Americans. And we must do this by recognizing once again that government—an enlightened government—has an extraordinary responsibility to assist in this task."

Think About It

- What responsibility does the government have in creating jobs?
- If government creates jobs, what kind will they be?
- Would it be better for government to spend money that could be used directly to hire people, such as construction jobs, or is it better to stimulate the economy (and hopefully job growth) through incentives for private investment?

How You Can Make a Difference
Fair Lending Practices

In the not too distant past, discrimination against religious and racial minorities in the financial and banking sector was common and obvious. The policy of redlining, for example, refers to the practice of loan officers who used to deny loans to applicants living in the boundaries of segregated or integrated neighborhoods that were marked by a red line on their office map. In the wake of the civil rights movement, things changed with the passage of federal laws such as the Home Ownership and Equity Protection Act (HOEPA), the Community Reinvestment Act (CRA), and the Home Mortgage Disclosure Act (HMDA), which gave the Federal Reserve Board authority to stop such unfair lending practices.

Though blatant, old-style redlining may have been eradicated, many activist groups are looking for volunteers to help continue the fight against economic injustice in America. Instead of being rejected purely on the basis of color, these activists maintain that many Americans, particularly ethnic minorities in the inner cities, remain ignored or "unbanked" by reputable financial institutions and become victims of predatory lending practices. Nearly all advances in curbing these financial abuses were achieved in conjunction with such community activist organizations. For over 30 years, the Association of Community Organizations for Reform Now (ACORN) has conducted training sessions for rallying local communities to action and for providing technical and financial assistance. The Woodstock Institute in Chicago (www.woodstockinst.org), for example, recently initiated a unique, permanent dialogue between community groups and federal bank regulators (including those from the Federal Reserve Board and Federal Deposit Insurance Corporation) to improve financial service to inner cities across the Midwest. The National Community Reinvestment Coalition (www.ncrc.org), a coalition of 640 community and regional organizations across the country, helps to coordinate activity among the various organizations. Recently, the NCRC issued a nationwide call to action when the Federal Reserve revised HOEPA.

What can you do by contacting these groups? If you have accounting and financial skills, you can volunteer your services in a nearby area. Even if you can't balance your own checkbook, you can still write letters to congressmen and Federal Reserve officials on behalf of pending legislation and action that would aid the movement, such as the proposed revisions of HOEPA highlighted by the NCRC. For the more ambitious, several organizations, most particularly ACORN, stage regional and national protest rallies to convince the public, governments, and financial institutions to change their attitudes and policies.

What you can do:

- Write letters to your congressional representatives and Federal Reserve officials.
- Join a protest rally.
- Volunteer your financial and accounting skills.

Both parties have their presidential icons as economic leaders. If the parties could give out Nobel Prizes for economic leadership, Democrats would honor Franklin D. Roosevelt (1933–1945). The Republicans lionize Ronald Reagan (1981–1989).

Roosevelt, himself a wealthy New Yorker, inherited the Great Depression and created the New Deal. FDR was architect of the Social Security system and federal aid to the poor, and also created dozens of regulatory agencies to manage the economy. Conrad Black, his most recent biographer, says that when he left office, "Capitalism was no longer a destructive force" and that the United States "enjoyed unexampled prosperity—more than twice as great as when he entered office."[21] Roosevelt was president during the rise of Keynesian economics, named after its founder, English economist John Maynard Keynes. **Keynesian economic theory** emphasized that government could be a positive force in weathering economic ups and downs. Governments should spend more in bad times, and contract some in the good times.

More than three decades later, Republicans had a president who crystallized their economic philosophy. For years before he became president, Ronald Reagan gave what his aides called "The Speech." It contained, said Sidney Milkis, "a single, abstract idea, universal in application: the idea that centrally administered government tended to weaken a free people's character."[22] From his inaugural platform in 1981, he argued

Keynesian economic theory

The theory emphasizing that government spending and deficits can help the economy weather its normal ups and downs. Proponents of this theory advocate using the power of government to stimulate the economy when it is lagging.

President George W. Bush takes part in a panel discussion with economics experts and business people at a December 2004 White House Conference on the Economy intended to boost President Bush's economic policy proposals for his second term.

that "Government is not the solution to our problem; government is the problem." He was the anti-New Deal president. Yet, Reagan spoke warmly of Roosevelt. The *New York Times* even called him "Franklin Delano Reagan" after his first nomination.[23] Republicans had their icon.

Ronald Reagan brought the nation, and especially the Republican Party, a new economic philosophy. Reagan proposed a radically different theory based on the premise that the key task for government economic policy is to stimulate the supply of goods, not their demand.[24] This theory has been labeled **supply-side economics.** In economists' language, Keynes focused on the demand side of the economy, while supply-siders focused on the supply side. To supply-siders, big government soaked up too much of the gross domestic product. By taxing too heavily, spending too freely, and regulating too tightly, government actually curtailed economic growth. To supply-siders, "By lowering tax rates, you could increase the motivation to work longer, increase savings and investments, and produce more."[25] Economist Arthur Laffer proposed (legend says he did so on the back of a cocktail napkin) a curve suggesting that the more government taxed, the less people worked, and thus the smaller the government's tax revenues. In its most extreme form, this theory held that by taking a smaller percentage of people's income, the government would actually get more total revenue as production increased. Cutting taxes was Job One for the supply-siders. Both Presidents Reagan and George W. Bush were so committed to supply- side economics that they were willing to risk massive budget deficits in its name.

Supply-side economics is far from the mainstream of the discipline of economics, but it seems to be etched into the Republican DNA. President Reagan used it to justify huge tax cuts to Congress. The second President Bush used supply-side logic to justify his $1.3 trillion, 10-year tax cuts of 2001. His second chair of the Council of Economic Advisers, Gregory Mankiw, had once called it "fad economics" proposed by "charlatans" in his best selling macroeconomics text. Mankiw soon came on board, though, once he became President Bush's top economist.

The president is required by law to send to Congress an annual *Economic Report*, which is prepared by his Council of Economic Advisers. The president signs it, sends it to Congress, and sends out press releases about it. The report makes predictions about jobs, inflation rates, and other economic indicators for the coming year. President Bush caught some flak in 2004 when his economic adviser, Gregory Mankiw, penned a report that predicted a huge increase in jobs and, even worse, appeared to endorse "outsourcing" of jobs to other countries. "Offshoring," he said, "in only the latest manifestation of the gains from trade."

supply-side economics

An economic theory advocated by President Reagan holding that too much income goes to taxes so too little money is available for purchasing, and the solution is to cut taxes and return purchasing power to consumers.

Why It Is Hard To Control the Economy

Managing the economy is a lot harder than many politicians seem to believe. It is harder than most voters think, too. Government can do about as much to control the economy as the average parent can do to control the average teenager. Economist Robert Samuelson doubted that presidents have much impact on the economy. "If presidents could create jobs," he says, "the unemployment rate would rarely exceed 3.5 percent."[26] Even so, some political scientists have tried hard to show that politicians manipulate the economy for short-run advantage to win elections. This was sometimes called a "political business cycle."[27] Presidents, so this argument goes, stimulate the economy just before elections, putting more money (even more government benefits) in voters' hands weeks or months before an election. Presidential power over the economy is—under the best of circumstances—more limited than that.[28] Politicians and presidents may wish they had the kind of power to swing elections. They rarely do—even though voters may blame them for economic woes. Presumably President Bush wished more than anyone that more than 1.6 million jobs had not disappeared during his presidency (even the most partisan Democrats did not think he deliberately set out to cause more unemployment).

Government makes economic policy very slowly. Most policies must be decided upon a year or more before they will have their full impact on the economy. The president's budget, for example, is prepared many months in advance of its enactment into law. The budgetary process, as we saw in Chapter 14, is dominated by "uncontrollable expenditures." These expenditures are mandated by law. In addition, benefits such as Social Security are now indexed. They go up automatically as the cost of living increases. Even conservative Republican presidents see federal expenditures rise on their watch. Given that law already mandates so much spending, it is difficult to make substantial cuts. Keynesianism is thus largely irrelevant in the twenty-first century.

Government in America is big; it is important. Big and important as it is, though, the billions of economic choices made by consumers and businesses are far more important. The American capitalist system itself imposes the biggest restraint on controlling the economy. Because the private sector is much larger than the public sector, it dominates the economy. Big as the federal government it, it still spends less than 20 percent of our gross domestic product. Consumers and businesses still make the vast majority of our economic decisions. This is even truer for the international economy.

Politics, Policy, and the International Economy

If it is difficult for policymakers to control the U.S. economy, it is even more difficult for them to control an increasingly global one.[29] Today's economy is worldwide. A street scene in the Middle East may be played out for television cameras in front of a multinational corporate logo. The U.S. economy depends on international trade for its survival. In the world as a whole, nearly a quarter of world GDP is based on exports. Foreign-owned assets in the United States quadrupled in the 1990s to $8 trillion.[30] "American" cars have U.S. brands on them, but may be made almost entirely abroad; "foreign" cars have a Japanese, German, or Korean brand, but may be mostly made here. The distinction between U.S. and other economies has become transparent. "Globalization" has become an issue dividing international institutions and governments on the one hand, and protesters on the other. What U.S. policymakers do about the economy can never again be decided in a vacuum. (We will return to these issues again in Chapter 20.)

Most emerging economies want to follow an economic policy of **protectionism,** letting their own fragile economies grow while keeping out products from other countries. Ours was no exception. Alexander Hamilton was our first secretary of the Treasury and our first protectionist. In the very first Congress he supported a set of tariffs— essentially a tax—on foreign products imported into the new United States. For most

protectionism

Economic policy of shielding an economy from imports.

of the nineteenth century, the tariff was the major source of federal revenues. For two centuries, economists have been virtually united against tariffs and protectionism. Politicians, though, are another matter. Seeing constituents lose jobs because the products they make will be undersold by another country's products is painful. One country's tariff, though, is likely to provoke retaliation from another country and so on and on. The Smoot-Hawley tariff, a 20 percent hike in U.S. tariffs in 1930, was one of the major causes of the Great Depression.

After World War II, the world's governments moved slowly but steadily toward free trade and the reductions of tariffs. Two political scientists called this "the growing willingness of national governments to open up their national economy to global market forces."[31] This was harder for Democrats, who depended on labor union votes—worried about job losses to other countries—than for Republicans, whose business supporters wanted new markets. Presidents Bush, Clinton, and Bush pressed Congress hard for more free trade and fewer tariffs. Democratic President Clinton had to overcome the resistance of unions and many Democrats in Congress to pass the World Trade Agreement Treaty, creating an international **World Trade Organization (WTO)**. The WTO would become the international organization promoting free trade and punishing protectionist restrictions.

World Trade Organization (WTO)

International organization that regulates international trade.

Unions feared that free trade would essentially promote "a race to the bottom," where massive international corporations would "constantly ransack the globe searching for low costs and high returns."[32] A specter was haunting first the manufacturing worker and later the software engineer: Their jobs were going somewhere else. And, sure enough, that is just the issue that cropped up as the Democrats' "jobs, jobs, jobs" campaign theme in 2004. The virtues of free trade are hard to explain to someone who has just lost his job and sees a similar one crop up in another country. (The Electrolux press release we described in our introduction to this chapter dramatized the problem.)

Nothing in the great offshoring debate generated more passion than stories of U.S. workers being required to train their own foreign replacements before they were fired. (See "Making a Difference: Mike Emmons.") Congress passed an immigration law permitting companies to bring their foreign employees to the United States for training and then to pay them at their foreign salary rate. This L-1B visa program infuriated U.S. unions and workers.

An oft-quoted report by the consulting firm Forrester Research estimated more than 3 millions U.S. jobs would move offshore by 2015. "Not so fast," said most economists. Even if those estimates were accurate, counting jobs lost to foreign trade is only half the story. Jobs are gained from foreign trade, too. Catherine Mann, an economist with the Institute for International Economics, predicts a new surge of technology employment in the United States because of the explosion of international trade.[33] This is a political science book, though, and not an economics book. Horror stories about the evils of offshoring carry more weight with voters than even the best weighty economics studies. International trade almost certainly creates long-term gain. It may also create short-term pain. Rightly or wrongly, politics is often about the short run.

Making a Difference

Mike Emmons

Mike Emmons was laid off from his computer programming job by Siemens, the giant German electronics firm. In April 2002, Siemens told Emmons and his entire information technology (IT) department that it would be outsourcing IT services to an Indian firm, and in July, Indian computer programmers arrived in Emmons' office for training. Emmons was going to be paid a $13,000 severance fee for training his own replacements. They were there under a program called an L-1B visa, which permits a company to bring overseas employees to the United States and train them—paying them their old wages, not U.S. salaries—to learn new skills. Emmons rebelled after he finished the work, launching a campaign against L-1B visas and offshore outsourcing. His campaign brought attention to the issue and helped reduce the number of these visas.

Arenas of Economic Policymaking

Economic interests far outnumber any other kind of interest group (see Chapter 11). Liberal or conservative, most interest groups seek benefits, protection from unemployment, tax breaks, or safeguards against some other economic evil (as they see it). Business, consumers, and labor are three of the major actors in, and objects of, government economic policy. In our Wal-Mart illustration, we looked at some issues relevant to the business and labor arenas. Here, we will look at a few more and will also consider consumers and economic policy.

Business and Public Policy

President Calvin Coolidge's saying "The business of America is business" rings particularly true when Republican administrations are in office, but some would argue that it applies almost all the time. One of the reasons why Washington, D.C. is so hospitable to business interests is that industry lobbyists in Washington are well organized and well funded (see Chapter 11). Nobody lobbies like business lobbies. Domestic and foreign corporations and their trade associations "account for the preponderance of politically active groups within the United States."[34] On some issues, business sings in a well-tuned chorus, all together. Almost every business wants its Washington representatives to work to keep taxes on business low and regulation sparse. Much business lobbying, though, pits one business interest against another. Cable TV and the broadcast networks, for example, compete for regulatory advantage. And railroads are not interested in government subsidies for the airlines or truckers.

Corporate Corruption and Concentration.   The corporation has long stood at the center of the American economy. In the 1990s, the corporations and their CEOs were the modern symbols of American success. As the century turned, they seemed to be the symbol of American excess. A go-go time for the stock market turned into a plummeting earnings loss for millions of American investors and retirees. Though there were many culprits in this downturn, corporate corruption also played a part. A string of corporate leaders from Enron, Tyco, Healthsouth, and other companies were charged with fraud and many went to prison. Corporate corruption did not come cheap. Washington's Brookings Institution estimated in 2002 that the first-year fallout of corporate accounting scandals would cost the economy around $35 billion—about what the country was spending on homeland security.[35]

Since the early 1980s, a new form of entrepreneurship has flourished—merger mania. Conglomerates buying up and buying out other companies have spent billions. There are now only two U.S. major credit card companies (Visa and MasterCard); only four publishers publish the vast majority of all school textbooks (two of them owned by European megapublishers—one a publisher of this book); there are only six cell phone companies; oil companies have bought one another out, leaving only a half-dozen major ones. Not all these mergers have been happy ones. The massive publisher and media conglomerate, Time-Warner, was gobbled up by AOL, and shareholders have rued it ever since.

At the turn of the twentieth century, powerful corporate titans took control of entire industries. After they eliminated competitors, they could charge customers essentially whatever they wanted. John D. Rockefeller's control of oil refining and processing was the most famous example. This was the era of the trusts, as monopolies were then called. Government regulation of business is at least as old as the first antitrust act, the Sherman Act of 1890. The purpose of **antitrust policy** is to ensure competition and prevent monopoly (control of a market by one company). Antitrust legislation permits the Justice Department to sue in federal court to break up companies that control too much of the market. The Clinton administration filed a major antitrust lawsuit against Microsoft, which produces the operating system for about 90 percent of the world's computers. Microsoft lost, but hardly blinked.

antitrust policy

A policy designed to ensure competition and prevent monopoly, which is the control of a market by one company.

Regulating and Benefiting Business.   In our Wal-Mart illustration, we examined the role of the Security and Exchange Commission in regulating stock trade. Not surprisingly, the corporate scandals of the early twenty-first century led to a new wave of calls for business regulation. Congress passed a law in 2002 that provided tougher criminal penalties for stock fraud. It created an Accounting Oversight Board within the SEC to regulate accounting industry practices.

Though business owners and managers, especially in small business, often complain about regulation, they should also remember some of the benefits they get from government. One of the oldest protections government gives to business is found in the Constitution: protection for inventions and creative works in the form of patents and copyrights. The Department of Commerce collects data on products and markets through the Census Bureau, helps businesses export their wares, and protects inventions through the Patent Office. The Small Business Administration is the government's counselor, adviser, and loan maker to small businesses. Several agencies fund research that is valued by businesses involved with natural resources, transportation, electronics and computers, and health. In fact, the federal government is the principal source of research and development funding in the United States.

Businesses organized for lobbying have been around for years; consumer groups, by contrast, are a relatively new arrival on the economic policy stage.

Consumer Policy: The Rise of the Consumer Lobby

Years ago the governing economic principle of consumerism was "let the buyer beware." With a few exceptions, public policy ignored consumers and their interests. The first major consumer protection policy in the United States was the Food and Drug Act of 1906, which prohibited the interstate transportation of dangerous or impure foods and drugs. Today, the **Food and Drug Administration (FDA)** has broad regulatory powers over the manufacturing, contents, marketing, and labeling of food and drugs. It is the FDA's responsibility to ascertain the safety and effectiveness of new drugs before approving them for marketing in the United States.

Food and Drug Administration (FDA)

The federal agency formed in 1913 and assigned the task of approving all food products and drugs sold in the United States. All drugs, with the exception of tobacco, must have FDA authorization.

Consumerism was a sleeping political giant until the 1960s, when self-proclaimed consumer activists such as Ralph Nader awakened it. Uncovering clear cases of unsafe products and false advertising, these activists argued that it was the government's responsibility to be a watchdog on behalf of the consumer. As they garnered broad public support, the 1960s and 1970s saw a flood of consumer protection legislation. Created in 1972 by the Product Safety Act, the Consumer Product Safety Commission (CPSC) has broad powers to ban hazardous products from the market. Today the CPSC regulates the safety of items ranging from toys to lawn mowers.

The Federal Trade Commission (FTC), traditionally responsible for regulating trade practices, also jumped into the business of consumer protection in the 1960s and 1970s, becoming a defender of consumer interests in truth in advertising. It has made new rules about product labeling, exaggerated product claims, and the use of celebrities in advertising. Congress has also made the FTC the administrator of the new Consumer Credit Protection Act. This act stipulates that whenever you borrow money, even if only by using a credit card, you must receive a form stating the exact amount of interest you must pay. The FTC enforces truth in lending through such forms and other means.

Labor and Government

Throughout most of the nineteenth century and well into the twentieth, the federal government allied with business elites to squelch labor unions. The courts interpreted the antitrust laws as applying to unions as well as businesses. Until the Clayton Antitrust Act of 1914 exempted unions from antitrust laws, the mighty arm of the federal government was busier busting unions than trusts.

The major turnabout in government policy toward labor took place during the New Deal. In 1935 Congress passed the **National Labor Relations Act,** often called the Wagner Act after its sponsor, Senator Robert Wagner of New York. The Wagner Act guaranteed workers the right of collective bargaining—the right to have labor union

National Labor Relations Act

A 1935 law, also known as the Wagner Act, that guarantees workers the right of **collective bargaining**, sets down rules to protect unions and organizers, and created the National Labor Relations Board to regulate labor-management relations.

Unionization began in the late 1800s not only because of low wages, but because of working conditions for men, women, and children we would call inhumane. Coal mining was then—and it is now—one of the most dangerous jobs in the country. Union power and membership grew for nearly a hundred years, but began to decline in the 1970s.

representatives negotiate with management to determine working conditions. It also established rules to protect unions and organizers. For example, under the Wagner Act, an employer cannot fire or discriminate against a worker who advocates unionizing.

After World War II, a series of strikes and a new Republican majority in Congress tilted federal policy somewhat back in the direction of management. The Taft-Hartley Act of 1947 continued to guarantee unions the right of collective bargaining, but it prohibited various unfair practices by unions as well. The act also gave the president power to halt major strikes by seeking a court injunction for an 80-day "cooling off" period. Most important, section 14B of the law permitted states to adopt what union opponents call right-to-work laws. Such laws forbid labor contracts from requiring workers to join unions to hold their jobs.

Unions have had some notable successes over the years, which have become staples of the American economy. First, partly as the result of successful union lobbying, the government provides unemployment compensation—paid for by workers and employers—to cushion the blows of unemployment. Second, since the New Deal, the government has guaranteed a minimum wage, setting a floor on the hourly wages earned by employees. No issue of economic policy more sharply divides the parties than minimum wage. Democrats argue for its increase, appealing in part to their core constituents. Republicans argue that increasing it would lead employers to lay off or not hire low-paid workers.

As we discussed earlier in the chapter, lately labor unions have fallen on hard times. Membership has dropped and political power has been declining. Union members themselves no longer vote solidly Democratic as they once did, but instead split their votes about evenly. Unions find it hard to unionize high-tech workers or at-home workers (the "telecommuters"), and many companies discourage organizing efforts. The rise of companies such as Wal-Mart, which relies almost exclusively on nonunionized, relatively low-paid labor, also makes it difficult for unionized workers to compete or to bargain with their employers for benefits or pay increases.

Understanding Economic Policymaking

One of the major battles of the twentieth century was the conflict between market-based economic systems and centrally planned ones. The market won. In the Communist system envisioned by Karl Marx, all the means of production would be owned by the state—in which each citizen would be an equal shareholder. The Communist system in the Soviet Union collapsed in the 1980s. Ever since, Russia has been trying to patch together a market economy and a democratic political system. China's Communist system retains much of its harsh political reality, even as it strug-

America in Perspective

China, Trade, and the Internet

China is the world's fasting growing economy, roaring along at the astounding growth rate of 10 percent a year. China is also one of America's biggest trading partners. If Wal-Mart were a separate nation, it would rank as China's fifth-largest trading partner, ahead of Germany and Britain. With 1.3 billion people, China has the world's largest population as well. Can more trade and more economic openness ever lead to political change in China?

Over the centuries, Chinese governments have been among the world's most totalitarian. Human rights groups annually document the jailing of union and religious leaders and political dissidents. China's critics claim that its government-owned factories rely on slave labor to keep low labor costs even lower. Congress only reluctantly gave China free trade sta-

tus with the United States, and China's human rights abuses were the reason for the delay.

What all the human rights censuring could not accomplish, however, the Internet might. It is difficult to manage a huge economy without the fast, free exchange of information on the Internet. By 2006, China will surpass the United States as the world's most connected nation. The Internet is hard even for China to censor. An event called The BMW Incident would never have been discussed in a newspaper, but it traveled fast over the Internet in China. In the city of Harbin, a rich Chinese woman ran over a peasant woman with her BMW and received only a suspended sentence. People all over China heard about it over the Internet.

The Chinese government has been getting tougher on Internet-related

"offenses." Amnesty International reported a crackdown on "cyber-dissidents" with the arrest of 40 offenders, a pinprick in a nation of 150 million Internet users. Today, a nation cannot really run a modern, trade-driven economy without high-speed communications. China is no exception. But just as the United States has discovered that it is hard to control pornography on the Internet, China is discovering that it is hard to control free speech on the Internet.

Source: The information about Wal-Mart comes from Peter S. Goodman and Philip P. Pan, "Chinese Workers Pay for Wal-Mart's Low Prices," *Washington Post*, February 8, 2004, p. A1. On China and the Internet, see the stories in *Business Week*, March 15, 2004. The Amnesty International Report on China is dated October 1, 2003.

gles to mix a market economy with a tightly controlled political system. (See "America in Perspective: China, Trade, and the Internet" on China's explosion of the Internet and the wedge it may provide for more political freedom.)

Comparing Economic Policy

Democracy and Economic Policymaking

Democratic control means that public policy follows at least in a general way the preference of voters. What voters expect of politicians, though, is not always what politicians can deliver. In the economic arena, voters often expect more of politicians than they can realistically control—at least in a mixed economy. It is even harder in an international economy, where economic decisions are made by corporations and others not easily influenced by U.S. public policy. For the last two generations, U.S. policymakers have followed the near-universal advice of economists ("the theory of comparative advantage") and created international trade agreements. President Clinton had to browbeat his own Democratic Party—traditionally skittish about free trade—to support free trade agreements. Still, it is hard for a party or candidate to tell a voter who lost her job that more free trade is good for her. Sometimes, economic theory and democratic theory may even be at cross purposes.

The conflicts about jobs in the 2004 election remind us of another dilemma of democracy: Sometimes economics requires some bitter pills. Sometimes there is short-run pain but long-term gain. If virtually every economist and every recent president of both parties is correct, freer trade is good for the American economy. If voters voted directly on policies, many, perhaps most, would support walls around America to keep our jobs at home. It is a challenge to politicians to carry on serious discussions about economic changes without playing demagogue. Short-run interests and long-run interests may not coincide. Because they have so much at stake, economic policy brings out special interests. In particular, groups that may be adversely affected by an economic policy have many avenues through which they can work to block it. More interest groups are involved in economic issues than any other arena. Groups go to government for special benefits, protections, tax breaks, or regulations. Therefore, one of the consequences of democracy for economic policymaking is that it is difficult to make decisions that hurt particular groups or that involve short-term pain for long-term gain.

Economic Policymaking and the Scope of Government

Liberals and conservatives fundamentally disagree about the scope of government involvement in the economy. Liberals think the economy, especially business, needs a lot of regulating; conservatives don't think so. In general, liberals look to the writings of economists such as John Maynard Keynes, whose works offer justification for an expanded role of government in stimulating the economy during times of recession. Today, government is a major regulator of the economy. Government policy toward the market is central to conflict between the parties today. Republicans favor a light touch, Democrats a heavier hand. Republicans have become the "supply-side party," which makes tax cuts their favored solution to almost every economic problem. The parties' different positions on the economy and the scope of government are deeply rooted in their constituencies. Whereas liberals focus on the imperfections of the market and what government can do about them, conservatives focus on the imperfections of government.

Summary

In the United States, the political and economic sectors are closely intermingled. Our tour of Wal-Mart showed the role of regulation and the growth of the international economy. Voters expect a lot from politicians, probably more than they can deliver on the economy. Voters want unemployment kept low and inflation in check. Although politicians have strong feelings about the economy and pay close attention to it, only scattered evidence indicates that they can successfully manipulate the economic situation at election time, even though voters think they can work wonders with economic policy. The two parties do have different economic policies, particularly with respect to unemployment and inflation; Democrats try to curb unemployment more than Republicans, though they risk inflation in so doing, and Republicans are generally more concerned with controlling inflation. Two major instruments are available to government for managing the economy: monetary policy and fiscal policy. Republicans have become the party of supply-side economics, believing that tax cuts will lead to economic growth and jobs. Democrats disagree. That is why jobs were such a hot issue in the 2004 presidential election.

KEY TERMS

capitalism
mixed economy
multinational corporation
Securities and Exchange
    Commission
minimum wage
labor unions
collective bargaining
unemployment rate
inflation

consumer price index
    (CPI)
laissez-faire
monetary policy
monetarism
Federal Reserve System
fiscal policy
Keynesian economic
    theory
supply-side economics

protectionism
World Trade
    Organization (WTO)
antitrust policy
Food and Drug
    Administration (FDA)
National Labor
    Relations Act

INTERNET RESOURCES

www.whitehouse.gov/cea
Reports of the President's Council of Economic Advisers, such as the annual Economic Report of the President.

www.federalreserve.gov
Information about the activities of the Federal Reserve Board.

www.cbpp.org
The Council on Budget and Policy Priorities presents information and research on economics and the budget from a liberal perspective.

www.cato.org
The Cato Institute is a conservative organization with plenty of papers and data on the economy.

GET CONNECTED

Do Something About the Economy!

Congratulations! You have been elected to Congress. As you prepare to head to Washington for orientation and to complete all the tasks that face a new member of the House of Representatives, you remember that you promised to do something about the economy. In fact, exit polls show that a majority of the people who voted for you wanted you to do something about the economy.

Search the Web

Go to Public Agenda's issues page on the economy *http://www.publicagenda.com/issues/debate.cfm?issue_type=economy* and read the detailed perspectives and the section on how the perspectives differ. As a member of Congress, think about which perspective would help your constituents back in the district, as well as the entire United States. It is possible that one perspective might not fit your constituency and you may need to combine ideas presented in each of the perspectives. You also may find that none of the perspectives fits your district terribly well. What potential solutions can you recommend? Remember that it will be difficult to satisfy all the people all the time.

Questions To Ask

- How would you defend your choice of strategies against other members of Congress who may support another strategy?
- What characteristics of your district (the type of industries, the age of the people, etc.) did you consider in evaluating the perspectives?
- If you did not think any of the perspectives would work to help your district, what was missing from the perspectives?

Why It Matters

Economic policy is important to most Americans, even when they do not think about it or even understand how economic policy is made. High levels of inflation make goods and services less affordable to many Americans. Too much government regulation may also increase the prices of goods and services. High levels of unemployment also negatively impact Americans' "pursuit of happiness."

Get Involved

Talk with your parents or older relatives or friends about life in the United States during some of the recessions of recent decades, especially the 1970s, late 1980s, and early 1990s. Did the recession affect their lives in any way?

To see more Get Connected exercises for Chapter 17, go to www.ablongman.com/edwards.

FOR FURTHER READING

Barber, Benjamin. *Jihad vs. McWorld.* 1996. A very readable account of globalization and its consequences.

Gilder, George. *Wealth and Poverty.* New York: Basic Books, 1981. A supply-sider's bible.

Gosling, James J. *Politics and the American Economy, 2000.* New York: Longman, 2002. A brief introduction to the politics of economic policy.

Greider, William. *Secrets of the Temple: How the Federal Reserve Runs the Country.* New York: Simon & Schuster, 1987. A book that demystifies the Fed.

Henwood, Doug. *After the New Economy.* New York: New Press, 2003. A look at the twenty-first-century economy, sometimes even humorously.

Sloan, John. *The Reagan Effect.* Lawrence: University Press of Kansas, 1999. The enduring effect of Ronald Reagan's supply-side economics on the economy and political system.

Yergin, Daniel, and Joseph Stanislaw. *The Commanding Heights: The Battle for the World Economy.* New York: Touchstone, 2002. A good exposition of the new global economy.

18

Social Welfare Policymaking

Chapter Outline

What Is Social Welfare and Why Is It So Controversial?

Income, Poverty, and Public Policy

Helping the Poor? Social Policy and Poverty

Living on Borrowed Time: Social Security

The New York Times **Issues of the Times**

Social Welfare Policy Elsewhere

Understanding Social Welfare Policy

Summary

■ Social policy—the topic of this chapter—is about many things. For one thing, it is about money. Our social policies represent far and away the most expensive things government funds in the United States. But social policy is also about families. Everyone knows what a family is. Or do they? What is the definition of the word "family" in America today? Is there just one definition?

Some people connect the word "family" only or mainly with marriage, or with married couples with children. "Married with children" was once the norm, and not just the name of a TV show. In fact, today only about 5 percent of all Americans live in the very traditional family in which dad works and mom stays home with the kids. Only 50 percent of all adults are married and 40 percent of all mothers today have never been married. Singles will outnumber marrieds by the next census in 2010.

Yet even as the traditional family has waned, it crowds its way onto center stage of the political agenda. Politicians sometimes peddle "family values." The Republican convention that nominated President George Bush in 1988 made "family values" its theme. Later, his son President George W. Bush wanted to push marriage and spend federal funds to do so. And Americans were sharply divided about the wisdom of permitting same-sex couples to marry. People in traditional families are more likely to vote Republican; singles lean more toward Democrats.

Traditionally, families have also been among our most important economic institutions. Long before there were government programs, families had the economic responsibility for people too young or too old to work. Debates about social policy are often debates about social responsibility for dependent populations. With the rapid growth of an aged population—80–90 year old Americans are the fastest growing age group—few families would be able to pick up financial support for their elderly relatives today. That is one reason why Social Security—a major topic of this chapter—has become the most expensive public policy in the history of the world.

Government gives lots of advantages to families—tax deductions for children, the right to share Social Security and pension benefits, and breaks on estate taxes. Even the private sector favors families. Thousands of companies, big and small, subsidize benefits for children and for spouses (to the growing annoyance of singles).

Even so, despite all the benefits that families enjoy, a lot of them still feel strapped. There were about 1.5 million individual and family bankruptcies filed in 2003. Elizabeth Warren and her daughter Amelia Warren Tyagi think they understand part of the family economic plight. Warren teaches bankruptcy courses at Harvard Law School; Tyagi is a financial consultant. In *The Two Income Trap*, they argue that more and more families these days rely on two breadwinners in large part to support schooling for their children (buying a house in the best school district even if they can barely afford it). Two incomes were once a luxury; now they have become a necessity. When a crunch comes, though, and one worker loses a job or gets ill, there is no slack in the family budget; bankruptcies are often the only alternative.[1] And these are the middle classes. David Shipler surveyed the 35 million Americans called *The Working Poor*—contrary to popular impression, most of the poor work—who are even closer to the economic margins.[2]

Social welfare policies involve the vast range of public policies that support individuals and families. The parties differ sharply on the desirable size and scope of such policies. In this chapter, we will see what the debate is about.

Americans believe strongly that people should take personal responsibility for themselves. Many are suspicious of government programs in general. Congress hammered out a major reform of public welfare in 1996 to "end welfare as we know it," in President Clinton's words. The new law was called the *Personal Responsibility and Work Opportunity Reconciliation Act* (PRWORA). While skeptical of a government "handout," Americans also believe in a "hand up." Even the late President Reagan, one of the most conservative of recent presidents, favored a "safety net" of social programs, partly to signal his sympathy with poor people. President George W. Bush had a slogan about "compassionate conservatism." Even in these days of terrorism and costly wars, federal spending on social programs (about $1.4 trillion) dwarfs federal spending on the Iraq war (about $150 billion) and homeland security (about $40 billion).

Debates about social policy are debates about social responsibility. Americans believe the people are—or should be—masters of their own fate. Social policies are often called "social insurance," however, because they are intended to "insure" people against life's crises and catastrophes—serious sickness, disability, the ravages of aging, or job loss.[3] You (or you and your employer) have paid into a benefit program designed to ease the burden of aging or job loss. Social Security and unemployment compensation are social insurance programs. More than people in any other country, though, Americans believe that they are only inches away from the promise of riches. People in 44 countries were asked if they agreed that "success in life is pretty much determined by forces outside our control." Almost two-thirds of Americans—far more than in any other country—disagreed. Just after President Reagan's death, the *New York Times* looked at why Americans shared the late president's sunny optimism. Those beliefs that hard work, and good luck, are the most important ingredients in success help account for Americans' suspicions about social policy.[4]

What Is Social Policy and Why Is It So Controversial?

social welfare policies

Policies that provide benefits to individuals, either through entitlements or means testing.

Social welfare policies broadly refer to the hundreds of programs through which government provides support and assistance to specific groups of people. The Social Security check for the retired grandmother, the food stamp coupon for the poor fam-

People who receive food stamps and use them for buying groceries, as shown here, must pass a means test in order to receive this government benefit.

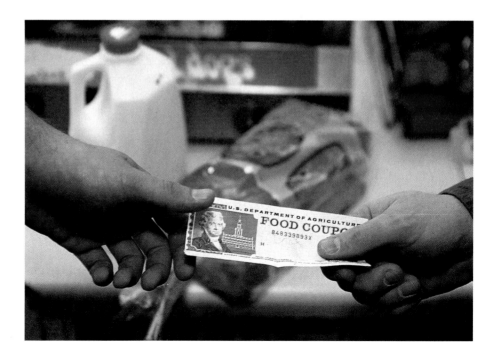

ily, the school buildings and programs, and the Medicare reimbursement for a hip replacement are but a few examples.

No public policy stimulates more argument and causes more confusion than social welfare. Here is one major confusion: Many Americans equate social welfare exclusively with government moneys given to the poor. Yet the government gives far more money to the nonpoor than to people below the poverty line. Political scientist Martin Gilens says that while "the welfare state is often associated with aid to the poor," in fact about five-sixths of all money for social programs goes to universally available benefit programs (Social Security and Medicare being the biggest examples) available to middle class and well-off Americans; only 17 percent of social spending goes to the poor.[5] Few Americans have the slightest qualms about assisting older Americans with government programs (even though most retirees will get back in benefits many times what they put in). Handing out money to the poor may be another matter. As two political scientists put it, Americans may be humanitarians, but they are not egalitarians.[6]

Social welfare policies consist of two kinds of programs. First are the **entitlement programs** (see Chapter 14). An entitlement is any benefit provided by law and regardless of need. Entitlement programs are sometimes called "social insurance" programs because people typically pay into them and later get money back. The two biggest entitlement programs are Social Security and Medicare. You don't have to be poor to get an entitlement, nor does being rich disqualify you. Most "entitlement" programs are really social insurance—programs you (or you and your employer) contributed to in the first place.

Means-tested programs, on the other hand, provide benefits selectively only to people with specific needs. To be eligible for means-tested programs, people have to prove that they qualify for them. Entitlement programs are rarely controversial in America. They are often overwhelmingly popular (perhaps because everyone is *entitled* to them). Means-tested programs, though, generate powerful political controversy. Much of that conflict has to do with how people see the poor and the causes of poverty. People who see the poor as mostly shiftless and irresponsible are hostile to what they see as "government handouts" to the poor. If people see poverty as largely beyond people's control, they are much more sympathetic to governmental assistance. Thus Americans have often distinguished between the "deserving poor" and the "undeserving poor." The deserving poor are victims of things they are not responsible for: the loss of the breadwinner, disabilities, or poor economic opportunities. The undeserving poor have presumably created their own problems and do not warrant government's help. With respect to helping the poor, "Throughout the twentieth century, U.S. welfare policy was caught between two competing values: the desire to help those who could not help themselves, and the concern that charity would create dependency."[7]

Let's look, therefore, at who's rich, who's poor, who's in between—and what public policy has to do with income.

Income, Poverty, and Public Policy

Americans are a rich people. Only a handful of nations have higher per capita incomes than the United States, but most other countries have—by our standards— staggering costs of living, and staggering tax rates, too. When we factor in purchasing power, only tiny Luxembourg ranks ahead of the United States. The Census Bureau reported that in 2003 the median American household income was $43,300—that is, half of American households made more, and half less than this amount. However, no industrialized country has wider extremes of income than the United States. Andrew Hacker reports that "among the world's modernized countries, the United States has the most glaring income gaps."[8] Income is important to politics, just as it is important to people. McCarty, Poole, and Rosenthal argue that American politics is becoming more polarized and the main "conflict is basically over income redistribution."[9]

entitlement programs

Government benefits that certain qualified individuals are entitled to by law, regardless of need.

means-tested programs

Government programs available only to individuals below a poverty line.

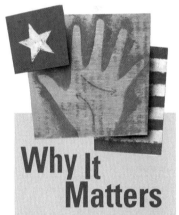

Why It Matters

Views of the Poor
Our views of the poor are likely to affect our views about the best policies for government. Americans have often distinguished between the "deserving" and the "undeserving" poor. The desering poor are poor because of circumstances beyond their control. The undeserving poor are depicted as lazy, unwilling to work, and living off welfare benefits. These "pictures of the poor" shape our views of public policy toward the poor. Portrayals of the poor as "welfare queens" added fuel to the movement for welfare reform in 1996.

Table 18.1   Who Gets What? Income Shares of American Households

The following table demonstrates how much of the nation's income is received by people within each quintile (or fifth) of the population. In other words, the 3.5 percent in 2002 means that people whose income placed them in the lowest 20 percent received just 3.5 percent of the nation's income in that year while the highest fifth got 49.7 percent. The rich are getting richer and the poor poorer. What accounts for the growing divide between rich and poor? Why would it be growing wider even though the 1990s were a time of surging economic growth?

INCOME QUINTILE	1960	1970	1980	1990	2002
Lowest fifth	4.9	5.5	5.1	4.6	3.5
Second fifth	11.8	12.0	11.6	10.8	8.8
Third fifth	17.6	17.4	17.5	16.6	14.8
Fourth fifth	23.6	23.5	24.3	23.8	23.3
Highest fifth	42.0	41.6	41.6	44.3	49.7

Source: U.S. Census Bureau, "Income in the United States," Table A-3, 2003.

Liberals and conservatives divide about many things, but "who gets what" is a major battleground.

Who's Getting What?

The novelist F. Scott Fitzgerald once wrote to his friend Ernest Hemingway, "The rich are different from you and me." "Yes," replied Hemingway, "they have more money." In fact, the distribution of income across segments of the American population is quite uneven. The concept of **income distribution** describes the share of national income earned by various groups in the United States. You can see in Table 18.1 how income distribution has changed in recent decades. During the 1960s and 1970s, the distribution of income was rather constant. The 1980s and 1990s, however, proved the old adage true: The rich get richer and the poor get poorer.[10]

Although the words *income* and *wealth* might seem similar, they are not the same thing. **Income** is the amount of money collected between any two points in time; **wealth** is the value of one's assets, including stocks, bonds, bank accounts, cars, houses, and so forth. Studies of wealth show even more inequality than those of income: one-third of America's wealth is held by the wealthiest 1 percent of the population; about one-third is held by the next 9 percent; and about one-third is held by the other 90 percent. For most people in the lower half of the wealth distribution, the value of their house constitutes 60 percent of their wealth.[11] *Forbes* Magazine fancies itself the chronicler of the very rich, and publishes an annual list of the 400 richest people in the world. In 2004, Bill Gates, Microsoft's founder, still held his edge, with a wealth of $46.6 billion, followed closely by Omaha investor Warren Buffett with $42.9 billion. Five Wal-Mart heirs, though, constituted half the top ten, with a combined wealth of $100 billion, more than Gates and Buffett put together.[12] Harry Potter author J. K. Rowling made *Forbes'* latest list with $2.7 billion, making her the 128th richest person in the world.

There are a couple of hundred billionaires, but a couple of million millionaires. Broker Merrill Lynch compiles an annual "World Wealth Report." It reported in 2004 that there were 2.22 million millionaires in the United States, down, though, nearly 2 percent from the previous year. These are people whose net wealth is at least $1 million, excluding real estate. The good news for them: While the stock market as a whole dropped 22 percent in the previous year, they suffered only a 2.1 percent reduction in their combined $7.4 trillion wealth.[13] Americans see CEOs of large corporations making millions, of course, but we pay our celebrities well, too. The average New York Yankee makes $4.6 million.

---

income distribution

The "shares" of the national income earned by various groups.

income

The amount of funds collected between any two points in time.

wealth

The value of assets owned.

The United States is a wealthy nation but one that also has tremendous inequality in wealth. In many parts of the country, affluent suburban neighborhoods can be found less than 10 miles away from poverty-stricken areas.

Who's Poor in America?

At the other end of the income scale are the poor. In one sense, poverty is relative. Compared with most people in India or Haiti or Nigeria, poor Americans seem almost prosperous. But it would be scant comfort to poor Americans for politicians to tell them how well off they are in comparison to people in other countries, or, for that matter, to their own ancestors (in 1900 the average income was only $246 a year).

To count the poor, the U.S. Bureau of the Census has established the **poverty line,** which takes into account what a family must spend to maintain an "austere" standard of living. This official statistic was designed by Mollie Orshansky during the 1960s (see "Making a Difference: Mollie Orshansky and the Origins of the Poverty Threshold").

poverty line

A method used to count the number of poor people, it considers what a family must spend for an "austere" standard of living.

Making a Difference

Mollie Orshansky and the Origins of the Poverty Threshold

How should we measure "poverty"? Rarely in the history of public policy has a single measure been so profoundly influenced by a single person. Mollie Orshansky, a statistician at the Social Security Administration, invented one of the most influential measures of all time, the "poverty rate."

Orshansky's measure was based on a Department of Agriculture 1955 study (the latest then available) showing that poor families spent about a third of their income for food. She took the cost of this diet, adjusted for family size, and suggested this as a very rough estimate of the "poverty threshold." Orshansky's measure, taking on a life of its own, became the metric by which Americans think of poverty, and it is still the basis for allocating billions of dollars of federal aid—and how we think of poverty itself.

For 2003, the Census Bureau defined a family of three as falling below the poverty level if it had an annual income below $14,824. Officially, 35.9 million Americans, about 12.5 percent of the population, are poor.

The official poverty counts tend to *underestimate* the seriousness of poverty in America because it is a snapshot and not a moving picture. A count of the poor for one year can conceal millions who drop into and out of poverty. Divorce, the loss of a breadwinner, job setbacks, and the addition of a new mouth to feed can precipitate the fall below the poverty line. Rank and Hirschl looked at the overall incomes of Americans during their working lifetimes. An impressive 50.4 percent of all working Americans experienced at least a year of poverty during their lifetimes.[14]

Journalist Barbara Ehrenreich chronicled the life of millions of these "near poor" in America.[15] She took a string of low-wage jobs—working at lower-end retail stores and doing janitorial work, for example—and pieced together a meager living. Even during her short stint as a near-poor person, she was lucky: She never got sick, or had to work below the minimum wage, and had no children to feed, house, and clothe. She also had a real life to go back to. Contrary to popular impression, most of the poor work. They often have low-wage jobs, however, which still leave them poor, and often without health insurance.[16]

Who's officially poor? Although the poor are a varied group, poverty is more common among some groups—African Americans, Hispanics, unmarried women, and inner-city residents—than among others. Race and ethnicity are major factors. Figure 18.1 reports the characteristics of persons in America living below the poverty line by race and ethnicity over three decades. African Americans and Hispanic Americans have a little better than a 1 in 5 chance of being in poverty. The group the Census Bureau calls "White Nonhispanic" has a less than 10 percent chance.

Estimates vary, but most experts believe that around 1 million Americans—like this man across the street from the White House—are homeless. Cuts to government programs that funded low-income housing and unemployment benefits, in addition to the deinstitutionalization of the mentally ill, forced thousands of people out into the streets during the 1980s.

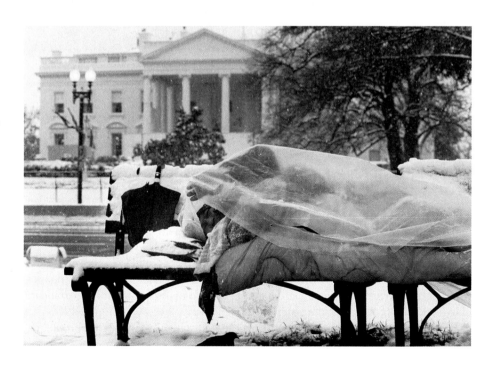

Figure 18.1   Poverty Rates by Race and Hispanic Origin: 1959 to 2003

Ever since the federal government started measuring the poverty rate (about 1960), poverty rates for some groups have been consistently higher than for others. Black and Hispanic groups consistently have had higher rates of poverty. In this graph, you can trace the changes in the poverty rates of groups over the last few decades.

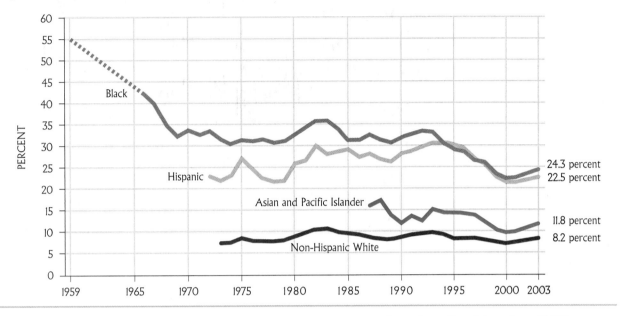

Source: U.S. Census Bureau, Current Population Survey, 1960–2003 Annual Demographic Supplements, Census Bureau, Press Release, August 26, 2004.

Note: The data points represent the midpoints of the respective years. The latest recession began in March 2001. Data for Blacks are not available from 1960 to 1965. Data for the other race and Hispanic origin groups are shown from the first year available. Hispanics may be of any race.

We began our discussion of social policy by focusing on the family. Families have a lot to do with poverty. Once poverty claimed the elderly as its main victims. Now it mostly claims women and children. When Social Security was created in 1935, poverty was largely—not entirely—a problem for older Americans. For decades, the constant expansion of the Social Security system and the increase in its benefits have significantly reduced poverty among the elderly. Today, however, unmarried women and their children now greatly outnumber the elderly among the ranks of the poor. Poverty scholar Harrell Rodgers entitled his study of contemporary poverty *Poor Women, Poor Children.*[17] Because of the high incidence of poverty among unmarried mothers and their children, experts on poverty often describe the problem today as the **feminization of poverty.** Female-headed families run almost a 30 percent chance of poverty, while families with two parents around have less than a 6 percent poverty rate. Having children out of wedlock, Rodgers says, is the "superhighway to poverty."[18] The unwed mother collecting welfare checks is among the most negative of all images of the poor. "Despite two decades of heated ideological controversy," Christopher Jencks says, "we don't know how much a father's absence (or a stepfather's presence) affects a child's social or emotional development. We do know, however, that not having a man in the house has serious economic consequences."[19]

feminization of poverty

The increasing concentration of poverty among women, especially unmarried women and their children.

What Part Does Government Play?

When government spends a third of our Gross Domestic Product, it is bound to have an effect on income. Actually, politicians almost never directly debate about income distribution in America. Income distribution is hiding way off the political agenda. No party platform is likely to proclaim "If elected, we will make the rich richer and the poor poorer." Nor will one claim, "When we are elected, we will take from the rich in order to end poverty." There are two important ways in which government does

Poverty in America is concentrated among a few groups. More than one-third of single parent, female-headed families, for example, live below the poverty line.

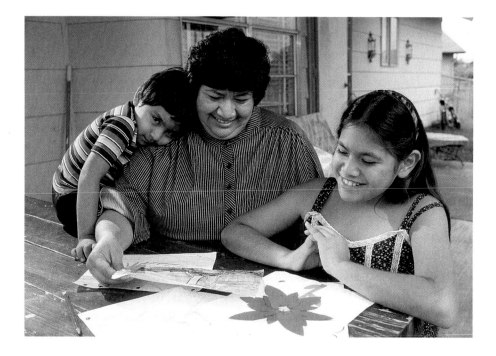

indeed affect people's incomes. One is through its taxes; the other is through its expenditures.

Taxation.   "Nothing," said Benjamin Franklin, "is certain in life but death and taxes." Taxes at least became a little lower in Summer 2001, when Congress passed President Bush's number one policy proposal, a 10-year, $1.35 trillion (that's trillion with a "t") federal income tax cut. Tax cuts are a mantra of the modern Republican Party.

There are three general types of taxes, and each can affect citizens' incomes in a different way. A **progressive tax** takes a bigger bite from the incomes of the rich than from those of the poor; an example is charging millionaires 50 percent of their income and the poor 5 percent of theirs. Second, a **proportional tax** takes the same percentage from everyone, rich and poor alike. And finally, a **regressive tax** takes a higher percentage from those at lower income levels than from the well-to-do.

A tax is rarely advocated or defended because it is regressive, but some taxes do take a bigger bite from the poor than they do the rich. Chief among these is the sales tax from which many states derive more than half their revenues. A sales tax looks proportional—6 percent of every purchase, for example, is taxed. However, since poor families spend more of their income on the necessities subject to the tax—food, clothing, and school supplies, for example—they wind up paying a higher percent of their incomes in taxes than do the rich.

In general, and even after the Bush tax cuts, federal taxes are progressive (you only have to look at the rates on your tax forms to see this). The rich send a bigger proportion of their incomes to Washington than the poor. How government helps well-off people—in contrast to poorer people—is through tax expenditures (see Chapter 14). The federal government spends about $18 billion in food stamps for the poor. By contrast, it permits individuals to deduct about $68 billion for employer-sponsored pension plans; another $67 billion is written off as interest on home mortgage interest. Few of the working poor—the folks Barbara Ehrenreich worked with, for example—can take advantage of employer pension plans or home ownership tax breaks, for example. Overall, of the $800 billion in tax breaks, people making less than $50,000 got only 15 percent of them.[20]

In fact, if you are poor enough, you can get money back from the government in lieu of paying income tax. Through the **Earned Income Tax Credit (EITC)**, the working poor receive a check from Washington instead of sending one. The EITC is a spe-

progressive tax

A tax by which the government takes a greater share of the **income** of the rich than of the poor—for example, when a rich family pays 50 percent of its income in taxes and a poor family pays 5 percent.

proportional tax

A tax by which the government takes the same share of income from everyone, rich and poor alike—for example, when a rich family and a poor family both pay 20 percent.

regressive tax

A tax in which the burden falls relatively more heavily upon low-income groups than upon wealthy taxpayers. The opposite of a **progressive tax**, in which tax rates increase as income increases.

Earned Income Tax Credit (EITC)

A "negative income tax" that provides income to very poor individuals in lieu of charging them federal income taxes.

cial tax benefit for working people who earn low incomes. In 2003, workers who were raising one child in their home and had family incomes of less than $29,666 could get an EITC of up to $2,312. The Brookings Institution estimates that the EITC puts as much as $20 billion a year into the hands of poor and near-poor families.[21]

Government Expenditures. The second way government can affect personal income is through the expenditure side of the ledger. Each year millions of government checks are mailed from federal computers to Social Security beneficiaries, retired government employees, veterans, and others. The government also provides "in-kind" benefits, something with cash value that is not cash itself, such as food stamps, for example. About 19 million people got food stamps in 2002 (down from a high of 28.9 million in 1994). A low-interest loan for a college education is another in-kind benefit. The federal Children's Health Insurance Program—CHIPs—subsidizes health care insurance for poor families with children. Together these benefits are called **transfer payments;** they transfer money from the federal treasury to individuals.

Table 18.2 summarizes the major government social welfare programs that affect our incomes. Social Security and Medicare are the two major entitlement programs. They are also the most costly social welfare programs. Unemployment payments also count as entitlement programs. Companies and their employees pay into these social insurance programs to provide income in case of job loss. The other programs are means-tested and are available only to the poor or the very poor.

transfer payments

Benefits given by the government directly to individuals. Transfer payments may be either cash transfers, such as Social Security payments and retirement payments to former government employees, or in-kind transfers, such as food stamps and low-interest loans for college education.

Table 18.2   The Major Social Welfare Programs

PROGRAM	DESCRIPTION	BENEFICIARIES	FUNDING
The Entitlement Programs—"Social Insurance":			
Social Security	monthly payments; entitlement program	retired or disabled people and surviving members of their families	payroll tax on employees and employers
Medicare (Part A)	partial payment of cost of hospital care; entitlement	retired and disabled people	payroll taxes on employees and employers
Medicare (Part B)	voluntary program of medical insurance (pays physicians); entitlement	persons 65 or over and disabled Social Security beneficiaries	beneficiaries pay premiums
Unemployment Insurance (UI)	weekly payments; benefits vary by state; entitlement	workers who have been laid off and cannot find work	taxes on employers; states determine benefits
The Means-Tested Programs:			
Medicaid	medical and hospital aid; means-tested	the very poor	federal grants to state health programs
Food stamps	coupons that can be used to buy food	people whose income falls below a certain level	general federal revenues
Temporary Assistance for Needy Families (TANF)	payment	families with children, either one-parent families or, in some states, two-parent families where the breadwinner is unemployed	paid partly by states and partly by the federal government
Supplementary Security Income (SSI)	cash payments	elderly, blind, or disabled people whose income is below a certain amount	general federal revenues
Children's Health Insurance Program (CHIPs)	subsidies for insurance	poor families with children	federal and state revenues

Helping the Poor? Social Policy and Poverty

"Welfare" as We Knew It

For centuries, societies considered family welfare a private concern. Children were to be nurtured by their parents and, in turn, later nurture them in their old age. When children cast off their parents or when parents let their children go hungry, significant social pressure was often enough to make people accept their proper family responsibilities. Governments took little responsibility for feeding and clothing the poor or anyone else. The life of the poor in America and elsewhere was grim almost beyond our imagining. In England, governments passed Poor Laws intended, historians argue, to make the life of the poor so miserable that people would do almost anything to avoid the specter, disgrace, and agony of poverty.[22] It was scarcely better in the United States.

The **Social Security Act of 1935**—the same one that created our vast entitlement program for the aged—also created a national program to assist the poor, or some of the poor. The program brought together scattered, uneven state programs under a single federal umbrella. It was first called "aid to dependent children," then in 1959 "AFDC," Aid to Families with Dependent Children. The federal government established some uniform standards for the states and subsidized their efforts to help children in families with no breadwinner. However, states were free to give generous or skimpy benefits, and payments ranged widely. For the first quarter century of the program, enrollments remained small. In 1960 only 1.7 percent of all U.S. families received welfare, and those typically for short periods of time. The Civil Rights Movement of the 1960s and the succession of Lyndon Johnson to the presidency in 1963 combined to boost federal and state support for AFDC and other means-tested programs. Johnson declared a national "War on Poverty" in 1964, adding food stamps and other programs to the arsenal of poverty-fighting policies. These programs—collectively called "welfare"—came to bitterly divide Republicans from Democrats and conservatives from liberals.

If Lyndon Johnson had declared war on poverty, the late President Ronald Reagan declared war on antipoverty programs. In 1981, he persuaded Congress to cut welfare benefits, lower the number of Americans on welfare rolls, and cut benefits for many beneficiaries. Conservatives during Reagan's time—and many liberals agreed—convinced many policymakers that welfare was a failure. Conservative economist Charles Murray has offered an influential and provocative argument that the social welfare programs of the Great Society and later administrations not only failed to curb the advance of poverty, but actually made the situation worse.[23] The problem, Murray maintained, was that these public policies discouraged the poor from solving their problems. He contended that the programs made it profitable to be poor, and discouraged people from pursuing means by which they could rise out of poverty. For example, Murray pointed out that poor couples could obtain more benefits if they weren't married; thus most would not marry, a decision that leads to further disintegration of the family. Not all poverty scholars agreed. They mattered little, though, as press and politics came to shape America's condemnation of welfare. No public policy had a worse public perception than welfare. "Deadbeat dads" who ran out on their families, leaving them on welfare, and images of "welfare queens" who collected money they didn't deserve, coexisted as media and popular images of a broken system.

No one could be clearer or blunter about why Americans hate welfare than political scientist Martin Gilens.[24] He found that Americans tend to see welfare recipients (wrongly) as overwhelmingly African American. Whites' welfare attitudes were strongly influenced by whether they viewed African Americans as lazy or not.[25] Negative views of African-American welfare mothers were more politically potent and generated greater opposition to welfare than comparative views of White welfare mothers. The media was a major culprit here. Gilens counted magazine and newspaper stories about poor people over several decades. About a third of all welfare recipients have been

---

Social Security Act of 1935

Created both the Social Security Program and a national assistance program for poor children, usually called AFDC.

Timeline

The Evolution of Social Welfare Policy

African American, but the media portrayed approximately three-quarters of poor people as African American.[26] Attitudes toward welfare became "race coded." It was not far to jump to the conclusion that lots of the "undeserving poor" were on welfare. The stage for a major welfare reform was set with the 1992 presidential election. Bill Clinton, a centrist Democratic president, and the new Republican congressional majority after 1994 were gunning for the welfare system.

Ending Welfare as We Knew It: The Welfare Reforms of 1996

Bill Clinton was determined to be a "centrist" president, fearing the "tax and spend" label Republicans so eagerly applied to liberal Democrats. In the 1992 presidential election campaign, Bill Clinton promised to "end welfare as we know it," by providing two years of support—training, child care, and health care—in exchange for an agreement to return to work. The congressional Republican Party was even more enthusiastic about welfare reform than the new president. In 1995 Newt Gingrich, the new Republican Speaker of the House, launched new war on poverty programs. In August 1996 the president and the congressional Republicans completed a welfare reform bill that received almost unanimous backing among congressional Republicans but that was opposed by half of congressional Democrats. The law bore the lofty name of the **Personal Responsibility and Work Opportunity Reconciliation Act (PRWORA).** The major provisions of this bill were: (1) each state would receive a *fixed* amount of money to run its own welfare programs, (2) people on welfare would have to find work within two years or lose all their benefits, and (3) a lifetime maximum of five years on welfare was set.

Symbolically, the welfare reform policies also changed the name of "welfare as we knew it." The cash payments to poor families once called Aid to Families with Dependent Children (AFDC) now became known as **Temporary Assistance for Needy Families (TANF)**, today's name for the means-tested aid for the poorest of the poor. TANF benefits today are small and declining. The average recipient family collects about $363 monthly in TANF benefits.

In one sense, welfare reform certainly "worked." It got millions off welfare. From the Act's signing in 1996 until September 2002, the number of welfare recipients declined from 12.2 million to 5 million. The welfare reform law stipulated that adults must be working in no fewer than 25 percent of the families on welfare, or else states would be subject to financial penalties at the start of 1999. Most states met this target, with the nationwide data showing that 33 percent of adults on welfare rolls were engaged in some sort of work activity by the end of 2000. Welfare "leavers" sometimes do get work, but their wages are low (about $10,400 per year) and constitute their family's main source of support.[27] Welfare reform got millions off welfare and many into the job market.

President George W. Bush pushed for one other welfare reform: encouraging people to marry. The welfare reform legislation permitted states to use some of their money for programs to promote marriage, and President Bush, and several states, pushed marriage as one solution to the perpetual problem of poverty. (See "You Are the Policymaker: Should the Government Promote Marriage?")

Did we win, lose, or draw what President Johnson called a "war on poverty"? For those looking for the "right" answer, the evidence is clearly mixed. Scholars disagree on how beneficial the programs were and are. One of the soundest assessments comes from economist Rebecca Blank who warns about the fight on poverty: "Don't declare success too quickly." Very likely no one single strategy—the war on poverty, income subsidies, the Earned Income Tax Credit, welfare reform—can claim the credit for improving poverty. It is hard to beat a strong economy to help the poor.[28] The proportion of the poor—measured, remember, by the cost of Mollie Orshansky's "emergency" food budget—has declined a little since we first started measuring poverty. But

Participation

Making a Difference:
Welfare Reform

Personal Responsibility and Work Opportunity Reconciliation Act (PRWORA)

The official name of the welfare reform law of 1996.

Temporary Assistance for Needy Families (TANF)

Once called "Aid to Families With Dependent Children," the new name for public assistance to needy families.

Why It Matters

Ending Welfare
President Clinton said that the United States should "end welfare are we know it" and that is what Congress intended with the PRWORA of 1996. In fact, the PRWORA has reduced both TANF recipients and their benefits. Welfare reform, though, took hold as the economy was moving into a recession. This made it hard for them to find jobs.

You Are the Policymaker

Should the Government Promote Marriage?

Fifty years ago, only 4 percent of all babies were born to unmarried women; today about 33 percent are. Marriage rates are on the decline in the United States, partly because people are simply getting married later than they used to. But in the face of such changes, "family values" is a familiar refrain of politicians. The federal government even passed what is called the "Defense of Marriage Act," although it was sponsored by a twice-divorced member of Congress (it was designed to prevent gay marriages by permitting states not to recognize other states' marriages). Social scientists are nearly unanimous in showing that marriage is associated with ("associated with" is not the same thing as "caused by") substantial benefits for the partners as well as the children. Children from two parent homes have fewer behavior problems, do better in school, and are less likely to be poor. A survey of high school seniors reports that 82 percent of girls and 73 percent of boys think it is "extremely important" to have a good marriage.

But should the government promote marriage? Oklahoma—which, despite its reputation as the "buckle of the Bible Belt," has one of the nation's highest divorce rates—uses some of its Temporary Assistance for Needy Families (TANF) funds to support workshops on marriage. A third of Oklahoma adults are divorced, compared to a fifth of all Americans. West Virginia actually gives its TANF recipients a $100 a month bonus for being married. As a part of the renewal of the welfare reform legislation in 2004, President Bush proposed spending $1.5 billion to promote marriage. Realistically, in a $2.4 trillion budget, the amount was miniscule. Still, the President argued, we should be willing to spend this for a series of demonstration projects around the country to see what worked to get and keep people married. His critics thought this was little more than a campaign initiative to please religious conservatives. Theodoro Ooms worried that "the conflict mostly isn't about research, however, but about values." She feared that it might stigmatize single parents, "many of whom do a terrific job under difficult circumstances."

One of the purposes of government is to support public goals. Liberals and conservatives alike favor government policies to reduce pollution, encourage savings, and even support home ownership. The federal government lets people deduct about $70 billion from their income tax bill for the interest on their mortgage payments. The justification: Home ownership is a valued public goal. What is so different about marriage? Couldn't government spend a bit to see if marriage can be improved? Or should government stay neutral about marriage? Or does the issue carry so much political baggage—gay marriage, for example—that marriage policy is too controversial to consider?

Sources: For information about marriage attitudes, including the survey reported here and other data, see the 2003 *State of Our Unions* report from the Rutgers University, National Marriage Project, available at their website. See also Linda Waite and Maggie Gallagher, *The Case for Marriage: Why Married People Are Happier, Healthier and Better Off Financially* (New York: Doubleday, 2000). The Ooms quotation is from her article "Marriage Plus," *American Prospect*, April 2002. On the Oklahoma experiment, see Kim Cobb, "Oklahoma Embraces Pro-Marriage Experiment," *Houston Chronicle*, February 22, 2004, p. A12.

the rich get a larger share of the nation's income, and the poor a smaller one since we declared war on poverty. And the kinds of people who were poor then are still the poorest now—except for older Americans, to whom we now turn.

Living on Borrowed Time: Social Security

If you work, you should be getting those official-looking letters about your Social Security benefits. Beginning in 1998, the federal government launched the largest mass mailing in history. The commissioner of Social Security wrote to every single American who pays Social Security taxes. The letter is entitled "Your Social Security Statement." The massive computers of the Social Security Administration in Baltimore, Md., churned out millions of individualized letters reporting what each individual had paid year by year. The letters also reported estimated benefits. Based on what you had paid in so far, you could expect to receive—if you kept working until the retirement age—so many dollars per month.

About 75 million "Baby Boomers" will start retiring in about 2010. Chances are, they will live longer and healthier lives than any generation before—and run up even bigger costs for the Social Security system and its health care cousin, Medicare. (We discuss Medicare in the next chapter.) There are some—President George Bush is among them—who think Social Security needs some reform. It is a time bomb, most experts think, ticking away, moving inexorably toward the day when the costs will exceed the income. But what, exactly, is Social Security? Here, we examine its history—and its future.

The New Deal, the Elderly, and the Growth of Social Security

Social Security, the most expensive public policy in the United States, began modestly enough as a "pay-as-you-go" plan during Franklin Roosevelt's New Deal. Its official name is OASDI, for Old Age, Survivors and Disability Insurance. Social Security was designed in part to get older Americans out of the workforce during the Great Depression of the 1930s. At first it was "a deal that couldn't be beat."[29] The idea was that money in payroll taxes would have to come into the Treasury before money could go out to the beneficiaries. President Roosevelt wanted a plan so fiscally solid that "no damn politician can ever scrap my social security program." Over the years, Americans have tended to believe that their Social Security payments were just getting out what was paid in. But that wasn't true even for the very first Social Security recipient, a woman named Ida May Fuller from Brattleboro, Vt. Her total contributions were a mere $22.54, but her lifetime benefits were $22,888.92 because she lived to old age. But Ida May Fuller's deal is no longer available. Take a young woman beginning a career today at the age of 22. There will be only about two workers for every one recipient by the time she retires (in contrast to about 25 to 1 when the program began).

No event has shaped American social welfare policy more than the Great Depression. Franklin Roosevelt's administration initiated hundreds of New Deal programs in its efforts to help citizens like these jobless men. Government spending on social welfare has continued to grow, even during the Bush administration.

Visual Literacy

Where the Money Goes . . .

Social Security Trust Fund

The "bank account" into which Social Security contributions are "deposited" and used to pay out eligible recipients.

Social Security grew over the years, in large part because it worked. More than 90 percent of people polled, year after year, support Social Security. No one gets rich off Social Security. The mean monthly check is about $800. Still, for the cost of a tiny administrative fee to run it, Social Security got the elderly off the bottom of the poverty ladder. In 1965, Congress tacked onto Social Security a new program, Medicare, to assist the elderly with medical costs (see Chapter 19). By the turn of the twenty-first century, Social Security and Medicare had become the most expensive public policies in the history of the world. In a decade, they will consume more than half the federal budget.

Here is how Social Security works: Government taxes workers and their employers a percent of the employee's income up to a maximum. Both employee and employer contributions are paid into the **Social Security Trust Fund.** If you work, you are contributing 6.2 percent of your wages (up to $90,000) and your employer matches it. (If you are making $90,000, you and Bill Gates are paying the same dollar amount into Social Security.) Your contributions, as well as those of more than a hundred million other workers, go into this huge government "bank account." The Trust Fund, of course, is not a literal bank account. As long as there is more money paid in than going out, the Trust Fund stays in the black. Though the sums are huge, the math is not all that complicated. Today's average Social Security payment is equal to about 36 percent of the average worker's wages. Currently, there are about 3.4 workers per recipient. Thus, the cost to each worker is about 10.5 percent of a worker's earnings (36/3.4=10.5). Current Social Security payroll taxes are 12.4 percent. Thus, for the moment, more money is going into the Trust Fund than is being paid out. By law, the Trust Fund can do only one thing with these moneys: invest them in U.S. treasury bonds. It cannot buy McDonald's stock or Wal-Mart stock or Joe's Hot New Internet stock.

Essential to this arithmetic is the ratio of workers to beneficiaries. The more retirees, relative to workers, the thinner the Social Security blanket stretches. If instead of 3.4 workers per beneficiaries, there are only 2, then the math changes. The cost to each worker rises from 10.5 percent of earnings to 18 percent of earnings (36/2 = 18)— and Social Security turns from black to red ink.[30] That will soon happen.

The Future of Social Security

The Social Security program may be living on borrowed time. Americans are aging. When Social Security was first established, the life expectancy of the average American was lower than the 65 years pegged for the worker to collect benefits. Thus, the "average" American would not even live long enough to collect his or her benefits. Things changed when birth rates began to soar after World War II (the "Baby Boomers") and better medicine kept us alive longer. Of the generation reaching age 65 in 2000, 69 percent of males lived to be 65; those who did will live another 16.2 years. Women have even longer life expectancies.

The Social Security dilemma is this: The number of Social Security contributors (the workers) is growing slowly, while the number of Social Security recipients (the retired) is growing rapidly. As the number of retirees grows, and their average benefit is constantly increased to cover the cost of living (called a Cost of Living Allowance), Social Security expenditures are going to increase. The more retirements and the more benefits, the higher the costs. At some point—about 2038 unless something changes— payouts will exceed income.[31] The Trust Fund's accumulated trillions will be gone. If this happens, Congress would have to use regular appropriations to pay out benefits to claimants as they retired. If taxes were not raised, a dollar, which would have gone to the military or homeland security or the national parks, would have to be diverted to the retirees. No solution is a politically pleasant one. Cutting benefits to retirees is no more popular than raising taxes on working contributors. Hard choices lie ahead. Many young Americans suspect that Social Security is not going to be around for them anyway. (See "Young People and Politics: Social Security and UFOs.")

Labor union members rally against the plan supported by President George W. Bush to privatize Social Security. Bush made Social Security reform a key issue of his second term.

Politicians tread gingerly on the terrain of Social Security, fearing a backlash from elderly Americans. George W. Bush and the Republicans proposed diverting a small portion (the suggested figure was 2 percent—that is a bit less than a third of your contribution of 6.2 percent) of Social Security contributions to private retirement funds. Each individual could, presumably, reduce his or her contribution to the Social Security system and instead put the money into a private account, a stock, a bond, or another investment. Chile, Great Britain, Australia, Poland, and Brazil have done just that. Democrats feared what Franklin Roosevelt warned about, that some "damn politicians" were about to scrap the nearly sacred Social Security program.

President Bush—long before the events of September 11—appointed a Commission to Strengthen Social Security. The commission was filled with advocates for the "privatization" of Social Security. The late New York Democratic Senator Daniel Patrick Moynihan, one of the few Democrats to favor privatization, and Richard Parsons, AOL-Time Warner's CEO and one of the most prominent African-American business leaders, cochaired the Commission. Most presidential commissions release their report in the glare of television cameras, often in a showy presentation in the White House. The Moynihan-Parsons commission released its final report on December 21, 2001, while most Americans were Christmas shopping. Its warnings were dire (the warnings of almost every commission to study Social Security are dire).[32] It pushed the idea of limited privatization of Social Security. Workers could put a portion (say a third) of their contributions into the stock or bond market. The problem, the Democrats emphasized, was that permitting people to divert money from the system, even for good reason, would merely hasten its bankruptcy. The report couldn't have come at a worse time for advocates of privatization. Stocks were swooning before the commission reported, and slumped further thereafter. One critic called the whole idea of privatizing Social Security the "Trillion Dollar Hustle," a plan only Wall Street could love.[33] The stock slump of the early twenty-first century eroded public and political support of the whole idea.[34] (See "Issues of the Times: Should We Privatize Social Security?" on pages 580–581.)

At his first post-election news conference in 2004, President George W. Bush announced that he would make reforming Social Security his top domestic policy priority. It would be hard, he said—if it were easy, it would have been done already. For

Young People and Politics

Social Security and UFOs

The story that more young adults believe in UFOs than in the future of Social Security has been repeated so often that it has almost become an urban legend—one of those off-beat, oft-told stories that just might be true. President Clinton told an audience at the University of Illinois that "there are polls that say that young people in their twenties think it's more likely that they will see UFOs than that they will ever collect Social Security." The story has been repeated by countless politicians, on ABC's 20/20, CNN's Capital Gang and elsewhere. How did such an odd "factoid" come into popular lore?

A group called Third Millennium that favors Social Security reform commissioned two surveys in 1994, one of Americans 65 and older and one of young adults. They hired pollster Frank Luntz to conduct the surveys. Luntz asked the young adults if they thought Social Security would exist by the time they retired, and only 28 percent said "yes." At the very end of the questionnaire, he asked an out-of-the-blue question: "And one final question, and I ask you to take this seriously—Do you think UFOs exist?" Some 46 percent said yes. That was the basis for the claim that young people believe more in UFOs than in Social Security. (Or, in President Clinton's further embellishment, that "they will see UFOs.")

There was a little more to the survey than that. Interestingly, young people were more likely than seniors themselves (48 percent to 35 percent) to think that older people were getting "less than their fair share of government benefits." But the quirky finding about UFOs became a part of national lore. Anyone with a complaint about Social Security could trot out the isolated numbers and make something out of them.

Indeed, the "factoid" made so much news that, a few years later, the Employee Benefit Research Institute surveyed people ages 18–34, and asked this question: "Which do you have greater confidence in, receiving Social Security benefits after retirement or that alien life from outer space exists?" It found that 63 percent have greater confidence in getting their Social Security and 33 percent thought alien life was more likely.

Americans, even young Americans, remain pretty committed to Social Security. Fay Lomax Cook and Lawrence R. Jacobs examined public opinion about Social Security over the last two decades and found that 90 percent of the population consistently believed that we spend either "too little" or "the right amount" as a nation for Social Security. About half of all Americans were either somewhat confident or very confident about the future of Social Security, and older Americans continue to vote more heavily than younger ones.

Questions for Discussion

- In 2004, both candidates promised to protect Social Security benefits for older Americans. What could—or should—we do about younger Americans?
- How much do you plan to rely on Social Security?

Sources: The Third Millennium poll is available at their website http://www.third.mil.org/. The Employee Benefit Research Institute Report is "Public Attitudes on Social Security," EBRI News, 19 (March 1998), p. 1. The Lomax-Jacobs report is in the National Academy of Social Insurance, "American Attitudes Toward Social Security: Popular Claims Meet Hard Data," March 2001, pp. 1–8.

years, Bush had advocated permitting workers to take a portion—about a sixth, perhaps—of their Social Security payments and divert them to private stock and bond accounts. Presumably, Tom or Mary Worker could decide how to invest their self-directed portion of their Social Security payments. They could collect their gains—or perhaps face their losses—when they were eligible to collect Social Security.

The problem with the idea was universally acknowledged. If people are putting less into the common Social Security pool, perhaps a few trillion dollars less, the Social Security System would run out of money even faster. (If you are saving $100 a month toward a new computer, but start taking $10 a month out of it, your fund for the new computer is going to leak.) How to cover that gap (indeed, whether to cover the gap at all) would become the central issue of Social Security reform.

Social Welfare Policy Elsewhere

The future of social welfare policies is just as complex (if somewhat less controversial) in other democratic countries. Most industrial nations not only provide social policy benefits but also are usually more generous with them than the U.S. government. The scope of social benefits in health, child care, parental leave, unemployment compensation, and benefits to the elderly are far greater in European nations than in ours. Europeans often think of their countries as "welfare states," with all the generous benefits—and staggering taxes by U.S. standards—that this implies.[35] European old age programs are in even bigger trouble than ours are, though, partly because their labor forces are not being replenished by immigration.

Other national governments and their citizens often take quite a different approach to the problems of poverty and social welfare. Americans tend to see poverty and social welfare needs as individual rather than governmental concerns, whereas European nations tend to support greater governmental responsibility for these problems. Also, Europeans often have a more positive attitude toward government, whereas Americans are more likely to distrust government action in areas such as social welfare policy.

Comparing Social
Welfare Policy

Most Americans would be amazed at the range of social benefits in the average European country. French parents, for example, are guaranteed the right to put their toddlers in *crèches* (day care centers), regardless of whether the parents are rich or poor, at work or at home. French unemployment benefits are generous by American standards (and French unemployment rates are two to three times higher than ours). In many European countries, treatments at health spas come with free or low-cost government health care policies. The United States has very limited policies about family leave for a new baby (essentially that your employer cannot fire you if you take a little time off at your own expense). Europeans have generous policies. (See "America in Perspective: Family Policies Here and in Western Europe.")

Europeans pay a high price for generous benefits. Taxes in Western European nations far exceed those in the United States (see Chapter 14). There, taxes approach (or even exceed) 50 percent of income. Every problem the United States faces in funding Social Security is even bigger in Europe. As in the United States, there has been a backlash against the welfare state in Europe. Parties of the Left, advocating generous public benefits, once ruled nearly every European country. Today, conservative parties—like the Republicans in the United States—often win by bashing the welfare state.

Understanding Social Welfare Policy

Social welfare policies are going to be controversial in a capitalist, democratic political system. Very few issues divide liberals and conservatives more sharply. Americans struggle to balance individual merit and the rewards of initiative with the reality of systemic inequalities and the need to provide support to many. Citizens disagree on how much government can or should do to even out the competition and protect those who are less able or too old to compete.

Social Welfare Policy and the Scope of Government

Nothing more clearly accounts for the growth of government in America than social welfare spending. Americans tend to overestimate how much government spends on the poor. They probably underestimate how much support for the elderly costs, thinking that Social Security is merely "getting back what I paid in." Ever since the New Deal and the invention of Social Security, the growth of government has been driven by the growth of social welfare policies. Conservatives complain about the "welfare state."

Issues of the Times

The Issues: Should We Privatize Social Security?

Social Security—the program in which workers and employees pay into an old-age pension fund—is the country's most expensive public policy. It also may be the most important policy as well, because tens of millions of Americans rely heavily upon it for income after they retire.

Unfortunately, the taxes paid by employees and employers do not sit in the treasury but have been spent for other purposes. In return, the Social Security system receives an IOU from the federal government. In addition, more people are retiring and living longer and there are fewer workers paying into the system for each retiree than in the past. The result is a looming budget crunch.

We could raise Social Security taxes, but this option, for obvious reasons, is not very popular. Another idea is for workers to take some of the money they now pay to Social Security and invest it in private retirement accounts.

Advocates argue that this practice would allow pension funds to grow more rapidly and thus reduce the need to raise taxes. Opponents worry that private accounts are risky and could leave many elderly people without adequate income if the stock market sours.

Read All About It

AARP Opposes Bush Plan to Replace Social Security With Private Accounts

By Robert Pear
November 12, 2004

Gearing up for battle over the future of Social Security, AARP, the influential lobby for older Americans, said Thursday that it opposed President Bush's plan to divert some payroll taxes into private retirement accounts. But it supports new incentives for private accounts that supplement Social Security.

Working closely with Congress and the White House, AARP helped shape legislation adding drug benefits to Medicare last year. Social Security is an even bigger issue, politically and financially, and lawmakers said Congress was unlikely to make major changes in Social Security over the organization's objections.

Marie F. Smith, president of the organization, said, "AARP adamantly opposes replacing any part of Social Security with individual accounts." But Ms. Smith added that the group supported incentives for people to establish personal retirement accounts in addition to Social Security.

John C. Rother, the organization's policy director, said, "We favor private accounts when they

Please see Accounts   Page 581

Accounts

Continued from Page 580

are in addition to Social Security, but not as a substitute."

The fight over Social Security, pitting Mr. Bush's vision of an "ownership society" against the Democrats' determination to preserve a cornerstone of the New Deal, is reflected in a battle over the proper terminology.

The White House dislikes the word "privatization," which it sees as a misleading and imprecise way to describe Mr. Bush's ideas for Social Security. Democrats insist that the term is accurate.

E-mail messages circulated within AARP in recent weeks indicated that the group would avoid the word whenever possible.

One message, by an editor of an AARP magazine, says, "There is a new forbidden word at AARP: Social Security privatization."

Another e-mail message, by a manager of its Web site, says, "The term 'privatization' is stricken from our vocabulary forever."

David M. Certner, the organization's director of federal affairs, said "privatization" had no fixed meaning or definition. To some people, he said, it means "getting rid of the entire program"—a goal not favored by the White House.

Martis J. Davis, a spokesman for the organization, said it was sensitive to the views of younger workers and retirees.

"Younger people think private accounts make sense," Mr. Davis said. "Polls by some organizations suggest that young people believe in flying saucers more than in Social Security. We have a problem with that. We don't want to end up being perceived as dinosaurs, and we don't want to be labeled as greedy geezers, because we are not."

In interviews this week, three Republican members of Congress—Representative E. Clay Shaw Jr. of Florida and Senators Lindsey Graham of South Carolina and John E. Sununu of New Hampshire—said Mr. Bush would make a major effort next year to overhaul Social Security.

AARP adamantly opposes replacing any part of Social Security with individual accounts.

"The election results have given new life to proposals for Social Security reform," Mr. Graham said.

Mr. Sununu said, "The president is very committed to an approach based on personal accounts."

House Democrats have begun to devise a strategy to oppose private accounts.

"Privatizing Social Security will divert trillions of dollars from the trust funds and force significant benefit cuts," said Representative Robert T. Matsui, Democrat of California.

In general, Social Security payroll taxes are credited to the Social Security trust funds, and revenues not needed to pay benefits in the current year are invested in government securities. White House officials and many Republicans in Congress say workers could get higher rates of return if some of their retirement savings were invested in private stocks and bonds rather than in government securities.

Mr. Shaw, who is chairman of the House Ways and Means subcommittee on Social Security, said private accounts were "the only way we can take care of our kids in the future, when we'll have more retirees and fewer workers."

White House officials said it was unfair to portray the president as supporting privatization.

"I do not favor 'privatization' of Social Security," Mr. Bush wrote last month in the AARP Bulletin. "Those workers who do not want a personal account would continue to receive their benefits from the federally administered Social Security system. Even those who choose a personal account would continue to draw traditional Social Security benefits."

Mr. Bush said his proposal would give workers ownership and control of their accounts, allowing them to pass wealth to their heirs. But AARP says retirees would bear a substantial investment risk and would have to accept lower guaranteed benefits under the president's plan.

The Cato Institute, a libertarian research center, established a Project on Social Security Privatization in 1995, but in 2002 it was renamed the Project on Social Security Choice.

"Republicans in Congress do not like the word 'privatization' because it does not poll well," said Michael Tanner, director of the project. "The word polls more poorly than the actual concept, in part because people do not understand what it means."

Think About It

- Do you think we should create private accounts for younger people within the Social Security system?
- If we create private accounts and the stock market crashes, what should government's response be to those who have lost a substantial portion of their life savings?
- Why do Democrats and Republicans disagree about private accounts? Do their differences reflect more basic ideologies?
- Can the United States afford to have *both* traditional Social Security benefits and private accounts?

America in Perspective

Family Policies Here and in Western Europe

American politicians often talk about their commitment to "family values." This fuzzy phrase can mean many different things to many different people (perhaps that's why they say it). But Americans and Western Europeans have sharply different views about family policy. Every European country provides for generous (by U.S. standards) child care, usually at state expense. Parents can take *paid* leaves from their jobs to spend time with young children.

In the United States it took a major political struggle to permit *unpaid* leave for parents to tend to children or other family needs. One of the first laws passed under the Clinton administration was the Family and Medical Leave Act. This law requires employers with 50 or more employees to provide workers with up to 12 weeks of unpaid leave for the birth or adoption of a child or for the illness of a close family member. To qualify, a person must have worked for the employer for at least a year and worked at least 1,250 hours during that

year. However, an employer can deny unpaid leave to a worker who is among the company's top 10 percent in salary and whose leave would result in "substantial and grievous economic injury" to the business. President Clinton hailed the Family and Medical Leave Act as a landmark piece of legislation, whereas the majority of Republicans denounced it as yet another example of intrusive government.

This is what you could expect in some European countries if you wanted to take parental leave:

- **Belgium:** Three months of full-time leave or six months of part-time leave until the child is four. Payment of $482 a month during the leave.
- **Italy:** Ten months leave any time until the child is eight. The leave is extended by one month if the father takes at least three months. Pay is equivalent to 30 percent of earnings during the leave.

- **France:** Full-time leave until the child is three. For two or more children, the payment is $439 a month.
- **Norway:** Fifty-six weeks of full-time leave at 80 percent of earnings or 42 weeks of leave at full earnings.
- **Germany:** Full-time leave until the child is three. Payment of $292 a month until the child is two.

In the United States, about two of every three mothers with small children work. Even with larger employers, the best you can do in the United States is get a short stint of unpaid leave. Child care policies here are thin in comparison to child care policies in Western European countries.

Source: The information on other countries' programs is reported in *USA Today*, July 12, 2000, p. 12A. On child care as a policy issue in the United States, see William T. Gormley, *Everybody's Children* (Washington, D.C.: Brookings, 1995).

Even if ours is small relative to those of other nations, the American social welfare system grows generation by generation. American attitudes toward the growth of social welfare often depend upon their assessment of what Schneider and Ingram call "target groups."[36] Groups viewed favorably—the elderly who have worked hard or the "deserving poor"—are one thing. The "undeserving poor" are another. Part of the debate about the scope of social welfare policies is a debate about how deserving various groups are and how big they are. We have cut back on aid to the poor, but there is no sign that the elderly will go quietly if political candidates propose cutting back on Social Security.

Democracy and Social Welfare

There is an extensive social welfare system in every major democracy. Ours, in fact, is the least extensive of all. As with other policies, competing demands have to be resolved by government decision makers, but decision makers do not act in a vacuum. They are aligned with and pay allegiance to various groups in society. These groups include members of their legislative constituencies, members of their electoral coalitions, and members of their political party. Many of these groups provide the financial assistance that the decision makers need to seek and retain political office.

In the social welfare policy arena, the competing groups are often quite unequal in terms of political resources. For example, the elderly are relatively well organized and

How You Can Make a Difference

Social Security Reform

Look at your last paycheck. Notice that line titled FICA with the comparatively large amount of money underneath it? That's your contribution to the Social Security Administration. Considering the increasingly larger percentage of people's income diverted to this federal program, the future of Social Security should be of vital interest to today's younger college students. Everyone agrees that the Social Security Administration requires reform in order to remain solvent when today's youth reach retirement age. There is little agreement, however, on exactly what kind of reform is needed.

One increasingly visible proposal advocated by Republicans as well as some Democrats is the partial privatization of Social Security funds. By privatization, this plan's advocates call for a small portion of the program's funds to be invested in private enterprise and the stock market. The Cato Institute, a venerable libertarian think tank, clearly states its opposition to the current trend and looks for more creative solutions. Their proposal at *www.socialsecurity.org*, similar to George W. Bush's campaign in 2004, looks beyond establishing mere solvency of the Social Security program and toward privatization. Individuals should be given a choice of investments while still keeping current beneficiaries' checks flowing.

Others, including most Democrats and progressive liberals, find this privatization too risky. The New Century Alliance for Social Security is an advocacy organization comprised of a broad coalition of labor groups (NEA and AFL-CIO), liberal academics, civil rights organizations, feminists, and environmentalists. Associated with this coalition, the Campaign for America's Future (*www.ourfuture.org*) distributes a handbook for antiprivatization advocates and a "Sign the Pledge" campaign to uncover which candidates oppose privatization of Social Security and Medicare. Also, the 2030 Center (*www.2030.org*), is a public policy organization for young people/college students. One of their key areas of focus aims is preserving Social Security for their generation. Rather than put forward any radical plans of their own, most of these progressive groups advocate spending budget surpluses on financing the Social Security system in order to maintain current benefits without changes that could hurt lower-income and disabled Americans.

The future of this debate is undecided. You can enter this still-fluid debate by joining one of these organizations, writing letters, and attending town hall meetings.

What you can do:
- Explore the issue for yourself. Find out if you're in favor of privatization or if you have another plan to rescue the program.
- Check out the different perspectives on the issue at *www.socialsecurity.org*, *www.ourfuture.org*, and *www.2030.org*.
- Write letters and get your friends involved in this debate. Their vote and interest probably matter more than anything else!

often have the resources needed to wield significant influence in support of programs they desire. As a result, they are usually successful in protecting and expanding their programs. For the poor, however, influencing political decisions is more difficult. They vote less frequently and lack strong, focused organizations and money. In this unequal battle, cutting welfare benefits is easier than tampering with the Social Security system.

Summary

Our social welfare policies have taken two distinct paths. First are the entitlement policies, dominated by Social Security and Medicare. In the United States, we spend more money on federal entitlements than on any other single thing the government does. Rich or poor, Americans are entitled to Social Security benefits by law. The other road includes the means-tested programs, government's expenditures for poorer Americans.

You have seen in this chapter that government action and inaction can play a major role in affecting the social welfare status of many poor and elderly Americans. Entitlement programs such as Social Security and Medicare have significantly improved the lot of the elderly, but these very costly programs threaten to grow ever larger and more expensive. Programs aimed more specifically at the poor cost less (and perhaps have accomplished less), but they seem likely to remain objects of political controversy for many years to come.

As the century turned, social welfare policies were under fire more than any period since the New Deal. A Democratic president and a Republican Congress had already reformed welfare. Social Security seemed ripe for reassessment. Like most domestic policy issues, terrorism shoved it further down the policy agenda. Neither poverty, nor the Social Security crunch, though, are going away soon.

KEY TERMS

social welfare policies
entitlement programs
means-tested programs
income distribution
income
wealth
poverty line
feminization of poverty

progressive tax
proportional tax
regressive tax
Earned Income Tax
    Credit
transfer payments
Social Security Act of
    1935

Personal Responsibility
    and Work Opportunity
    Reconciliation Act
Temporary Assistance for
    Needy Families
Social Security Trust
    Fund

INTERNET RESOURCES

www.aecf.org
The Annie E. Casey Foundation produces a wealth of information about America's children, including its *Kid's Count* databook.

www.csss.gov
Report of the President's Commission to Strengthen Social Security.

www.marriage/rutgers.edu
Rutgers' University publishes an annual "State of Our Unions" report on marriages and families.

www.ssa.gov
The official site of the Social Security Administration, where you can learn about the history of the program and find out how to calculate your own benefits.

www.tanf.gov
Annual reports on the effects of the 1996 welfare reforms.

GET CONNECTED

Insuring Children

Children tend to be the group of Americans least likely to have health insurance coverage. A provision in the Balanced Budget Act of 1997 established the State Children's Health Insurance Program (SCHIP). This program allowed each state to offer health insurance for children, up to age 19, who are not already insured. SCHIP is a state-administered program and each state sets its own guidelines regarding eligibility and services. Let us look a little closer at the State Children's Health Insurance Program.

Search the Web

Go to the United States Department of Health and Human Services page on the State Children's Health Insurance Program *http://www.cms.hhs.gov/schip/consumers_default.asp*. Find the link to your state's program. The department also built a website "Insure Kids Now!" that provides more direct links to information about each state's insurance plan. Visit it at *http://www.insurekidsnow.gov/* and find the link to the website created by your state. Look around your state's website. Access some of the pages for states near your state. Also look at the page for a state that is far from your state.

Questions To Ask

- Who determines who is eligible to participate in the Children's Health Insurance Program?
- Who is eligible to participate in the program in your state? How does this compare with the eligibility in surrounding states? How about a state far away from your state?

- Can you see a relationship between who is eligible and the political culture in the states you looked at? For some help identifying the states' political cultures, you may want to consult *http://academic.regis.edu/jriley/421elazar.html/*.

Why It Matters

The State Children's Health Insurance Program was created because many families cannot afford adequate health insurance coverage. Sick children who are uninsured are often taken to hospital emergency rooms, where the care tends to be more expensive than that received from a family doctor. Usually the American taxpayer pays for the emergency room visit through the Medicaid program because the family can't afford to pay for it.

Get Involved

One of the challenges that has faced the State Children's Health Insurance Program is getting eligible children enrolled in the program. Find out if your state has experienced this problem and think about how to create an outreach plan to reach those children. You can research your state's program by searching the index of the newspaper in your state's capital or your local newspaper. This website *http://www.urban.org/urlprint.cfm?ID=7233* discusses some of the reasons why more children have not enrolled in the insurance program. Look over the items linked on *http://www.financeprojectinfo.org/win/HC_CHIPmisc.asp* for more information on the challenges facing the program.

To see more Get Connected exercises for Chapter 18, go to www.ablongman.com/edwards.

FOR FURTHER READING

Blank, Rebecca. *It Takes a Nation: A New Agenda for Fighting Poverty.* Princeton, NJ: Princeton University Press, 1998. One of the nation's most distinguished economists examines poverty.

Ehrenreich, Barbara. *Nickel and Dimed: On (Not) Getting By in America.* New York: Owl Books, 2001. A well-educated—with a Ph.D. in biology—journalist experiences the difficulties of getting by in America while working a string of low-wage jobs.

Gilens, Martin. *Why Americans Hate Welfare: Race, Media, and the Politics of Antipoverty Policy.* Chicago: University of Chicago Press, 2000. Gilens argues that public opposition to welfare is fed by a combination of racial and media stereotyping about the true nature of America's poor.

Kotlikoff, Lawrence J., and Scott Burns. *The Coming Generational Storm.* Cambridge, MA: M.I.T. Press, 2004. The authors argue we are rapidly shifting resources to older Americans with awful consequences.

Murray, Charles. *Losing Ground: American Social Policy, 1950–1980.* New York: Basic Books, 1984. A classic conservative argument that social policies have not worked and have actually made things worse.

Page, Benjamin I., and James R. Simmons. *What Government Can Do: Dealing With Poverty and Inequality.* Chicago: University of Chicago Press, 2000. A liberal analysis of and agenda for antipoverty policy.

Rodgers, Harrell, Jr. *American Poverty in a New Era of Reform.* New York: M.E. Sharpe, 2000. Discusses what has happened to poverty since the welfare reforms.

Schieber, Sylvester J., and John B. Shoven. *The Real Deal: The History and Future of Social Security.* New Haven, CT: Yale University Press, 2000. An excellent analysis of the past, present, and future of Social Security.

Shipler, David K. *The Working Poor: Invisible in America.* New York: Knopf, 2004. How people who work still risk poverty.

Skocpol, Theda. *Social Policy in the United States.* Princeton, NJ: Princeton University Press, 1995. Skocpol takes a historical approach to social welfare programs.

Weil, Alan, and Kenneth Finegold, eds. *Welfare Reform: The Next Act.* Washington, D.C.: Urban Institute Press, 2002. What happened after welfare reform and what should be done.

Policymaking for Health Care and the Environment

Chapter Outline

Health Care Policy

The New York Times **Issues of the Times**

Environmental Policy

Energy Policy

Groups, Energy, and the Environment

Understanding Health Care and Environmental Policy

Summary

■ Carl Moore had made and lost a fortune in Oklahoma. Once rich enough to afford two private jets, an oil bust in the 1980s forced him into bankruptcy. His wife Corey, whom he divorced in 2002, had breast cancer and the costs of her drugs were staggering. His son, Joe-Max, had become a professional soccer player and was doing well financially. In 2002, with Joe-Max's backing, Moore opened a drugstore in Tulsa called Rx Depot, and quickly expanded his business to 22 more stores across the country. All were small operations with only one or two people on duty. They were not full-service pharmacies, however. Carl and Joe-Max had one simple business model: importing prescription drugs from Canada. Drugs in Canada often cost half the U.S. price. Canada has a national medical care system and the Canadian government negotiates wholesale prices with giant U.S. pharmaceutical companies and then resells them to Canadian pharmacies. It is, however, a violation of U.S. law to commercially reimport these drugs into the United States. Several million Americans either cross the border to visit Canadian pharmacies or they order Canadian pills on the Internet every year. Mr. Moore was going to be their middleman.[1]

The Food and Drug Administration is the federal agency responsible for the safety of medicines and drugs. Its agents planned a sting operation for the Rx Depot. In May 2003, an agent in Maryland downloaded an Rx Depot form and filled out an order for the antidepressant Serzone. Another agent took it to the Oklahoma City office of Rx Depot on May 10. Rx Depot got the prescription filled in Winnepeg, Canada. The FDA took Carl Moore to court. On November 6, the federal district court for the Northern District of Oklahoma shut the company down.[2]

Across the country, the Mayor of Springfield, Mass., Michael Albino, had a buy-Canada program of his own. Prescription drug costs for his employees had doubled to $18 million in eight years and he estimated that buying prescriptions for them north of the border could cut that cost in half. Springfield became the first U.S. city to import drugs from Canada. Illinois Governor Rod Blagojevich, worried over his state's $340 million drug bill, asked the FDA whether Illinois could import Canadian drugs. A commission he appointed had concluded that pharmacy practices in Canada met or exceeded U.S. standards. The FDA, however, told him no.

Actually, Congress passed a law during the Clinton administration permitting the importation of Canadian low-priced drugs, but only if the secretary of Health and Human Services certified them as safe. Neither Clinton's nor Bush's HHS secretaries would budge, though, and reimporting Canadian drugs remained illegal. The Medicare drug benefit law, in fact, even made it illegal for the federal government to negotiate with drug companies to get better prices. Dr. Mark McClelland, the FDA commissioner, thought other countries should raise their prices to help support U.S. drug companies' research. It might cost, he said, a hundred million dollars, which the FDA didn't have, to insure the safety of imported drugs. An odd political alliance in Congress pressed for Canadian drug importation. Conservative Indiana Republican Dan Burton and the only Independent member of the House, Vermont's self-proclaimed Socialist Bernie Sanders, were for once on the same side.

This chapter is about two major public policy issues—health care and the environment—that have two things in common. First, unlike many other policies, they both involve life and death decisions. Medical care in the United States is incredibly expensive, involving hundreds of thousands of life and death choices every day. Environmental issues are also critical. Pollution is not merely unsightly or unpleasant; it is also a serious health risk. Second, both health policy and environmental decisions involve sophisticated technologies that are expensive and sometimes controversial. Many of these issues— human cloning and stem cell research, for example— involve moral debates as well.

587

Health Care Policy

America's health policy paradox is this: As a nation we spend a far larger share of our national income on health than any other industrialized country and yet we are far from having the healthiest population. There are few things more important to people than their health. It is often said that Americans enjoy the best health care in the world, and some do. Americans, compared to people in other countries, pay a lot for their health care. Yet it is not clear whether they always get their money's worth. Unlike other countries, we do not have a government-run health care system. Nor do we have a completely private one. Like American politics itself, the system is vast, complex, and controversial.

The Health of Americans

Although Americans are generally healthy (which is to be expected given the country's wealth), health care statistics show that they still lag behind other countries in some key health care categories (see "America in Perspective: We Pay a Lot for Health Care, but What Do We Get for the Investment?").

The average American has a life expectancy of 77 years—a high number, but one surpassed by citizens of most other developed nations. Despite advances in medical technology the average American does not live as long as the average Canadian. Using a measure of healthy longevity, the World Health Organization ranked the United States twenty-fourth among the world's nations.[3] The second common indicator of a healthy population is its infant mortality rate, the chances that a baby will live beyond

America in Perspective

We Pay a Lot for Health Care, but What Do We Get for the Investment?

The World Health Organization (WHO) compiles a list of health indicators for countries around the world. Just a few years ago, WHO tabulated what countries spend on their health and measured various health outcomes, mainly how long their citizens live and how healthy children are. We spend a large percent of our Gross Domestic Product on health care—more than almost any other nation, at nearly 14 percent. On two major indicators of a healthy population—our longevity and the percent of infants and young children who die—our expenditures do not buy better health care. This is the American health care paradox.

COUNTRY	PER CAPITA SPENDING IN U.S. DOLLARS	PERCENT OF GDP SPENT ON HEALTH	LIFE EXPECTANCY IN YEARS	DEATHS OF CHILDREN UNDER 5 (PER 1,000)
United States	$4,887	13.9%	77.3	9
Canada	2,163	9.5	79.8	6
France	2,109	9.6	79.7	5
Germany	2,412	10.8	78.7	5
Italy	1,584	8.4	79.7	5
Japan	2,627	8.0	81.9	4
United Kingdom	1,835	7.6	78.2	7

Source: World Health Organization, *World Health Report 2003*, Annex Table 1.

its crucial first year. The chances in the United States of a baby dying in the first year of life are more than 50 percent higher than those of a baby born in Japan. Indeed, the United States ranks only eighteenth among the world's nations in infant mortality. The health care system in the United States may be part of the explanation.

The Cost of Health Care

American health care does not come cheap. The United States spends a higher proportion of its income on health care than any other country. Americans now spend about $1.5 *trillion* on health care. Health expenditures are one of the largest single components of America's economy, accounting for *one-seventh* (14 percent) of the GDP. Canada, France, and Germany provide universal health care coverage for their citizens but spend only 8 to 11 percent of their GDPs on health care, and Britain and Japan spend only 8 percent for universal coverage. In America, not only are costs high, they are increasing faster than any other good or service we purchase. Health care costs in America are skyrocketing. In constant 2002 dollars we spent $1,313 per person on health care in 1970; by 2002, we were spending $5,449.[4] In 1970, we spent a mere 7 percent of our Gross Domestic Product on health care. Today, we spend almost 14 percent of our GDP on health services.

Why are health care expenditures in the United States so high? For one thing, American medicine is high-tech medicine. New technologies, drugs, and procedures often add to the cost of health care by addressing previously untreatable conditions or by providing better, but more expensive, care. Much of the money Americans pay for health care goes to services like organ transplants, kidney dialysis, and other treatments not widely available outside the United States. Americans believe that more care is better care, yet there is little evidence that high costs and more care translate into healthier patients.[5] No one can even imagine the costs of widespread availability of the sort of technologies available from stem cell research and other high-tech medicine.

Because insurance companies and government programs pay for most health care expenses, most patients have no reason to ask for cheaper care—they do not directly face the full financial consequences of their care. Health care providers, such as physicians, are also insulated from competing with each other to offer less expensive care. In fact, with the rise in medical malpractice suits, doctors may be ordering extra tests, however expensive they may be, to ensure that they cannot be sued—an approach sometimes called "defensive medicine." Such practices drive up the costs of medical care for everyone. Because insurance companies pay the bills, patients do not protest. However, increased costs associated with medical care are making insurance rates skyrocket—about 12 percent a year recently—and one way or another, through taxes, insurance, or out of our own pockets, the consumer-taxpayer pays for it all. The level of care varies widely from one group to another in part because money drives the system.

Uneven Coverage, Uneven Care

Americans gain access to health care in a variety of ways. The most common means of access is through private plans. The traditional form of such a plan is a health insurance policy, in which a policyholder pays an annual premium and then is entitled to have the insurance company pay a certain amount of the cost of health care for the year. Today, many people and their employers contract with a **Health Maintenance Organization (HMO)** that directly provides all or most of a person's health care for a yearly fee. The government-subsidized Medicare program covers older Americans, and many of those living below the poverty line are covered by another government program, Medicaid (discussed in the next section). Some people must pay all health care expenses out of their own pocket. They, of course, are hit the hardest.

health maintenance organization (HMO)

Organization contracted by individuals or insurance companies to provide health care for a yearly fee. Such network health plans limit the choice of doctors and treatments. About 60 percent of Americans are enrolled in HMOs or similar programs.

Access to health care is one of the greatest challenges to health care policy. The quality of health care varies substantially among Americans; so does the health of different groups in society.

Health Insurance.   Most Americans have health insurance of some kind (an individual policy or membership in an HMO), but more than 43.0 million people are without health insurance coverage.[6] The *Wall Street Journal*—no friend of government programs—reported the story of a Ms. Amandeep Kaur, whose deteriorating eye stretched her resources far beyond what she made from her newsstand. Ms. Kaur pays far more than most for her eyedrops because she is uninsured; people who are insured get cheaper medicines. In the long run, she will need to have her eye removed at a cost of $12,000. Her best hope at the moment: Save enough to get back to her native India, where surgery is cheaper.[7] The most common reason for lacking health insurance is being poor. But the most common reason for losing health insurance is not being poor, but losing or changing a job.

Unlike in other countries, health insurance in America is usually tied to a person's employment. The reason we get health insurance from our jobs is a historical quirk. During World War II, wage controls forbade employers from increasing worker wages. Employers decided to attract good new people by offering to pay their health insurance instead.[8] Today, about 60 percent of Americans get health insurance from their jobs.

Age is one of the biggest predictors of being uninsured. Most of the uninsured are under 65 because nearly everyone 65 and older participates in Medicare, a government-subsidized program. Young adults are the least insured Americans. Children and older people are far more likely to have health insurance than young people. Lacking health insurance, though, matters a lot more than many young Americans think it does. Young Americans think—rightly—that diseases are far more common among older people. What hits them hardest is the most expensive single point in the health care system: the emergency room. (See "Young People and Politics: Health Insurance, Emergency Rooms, and Young Americans.")

Access to health insurance in the United States is also closely tied to race and income. A majority of the uninsured are non-Whites. Thirty-two percent of the poor lack health insurance, despite the existence of government-subsidized programs such as Medicaid and Medicare. The higher a family's income, the more likely that its members are insured.[9] Long-term studies show that people without health insurance face a 25 percent higher risk of dying than those with insurance.[10]

Discrepancies in access to health care are reflected in the health of different groups. The story is a familiar one: Minority groups get worse care. Minority Americans have higher rates of most diseases, shorter life spans, and face much higher infant mortality rates.

Young People and Politics

Health Insurance, Emergency Rooms, and Young Americans

In the United States, more than 40 million Americans do not have health insurance for some part of a year and about 20 million lack it all year. Young adults, some people say, see themselves as more or less invincible to illness or death and pay little attention to the unpleasant prospects of getting seriously ill or dying. And, in fact, the uninsured are disproportionately young Americans between the ages of 18 and 35. In contrast, less than 10 percent of children are uninsured, and virtually all Americans over 65 are insured through Medicare.

Young people are certainly right about their fairly low chances of needing medical care for serious illnesses. Chances of getting heart disease or cancer increase with age. Young adults' medical problems mostly come from injuries and accidents—particularly traffic accidents—that require expensive emergency care that is difficult to afford without health insurance coverage.

Indeed, the statistics show that except for the very old (those over 75), young adults are the biggest users of emergency rooms. About 45 out of every 100 young adults aged 15 to 24 visit an emergency room annually, far more than kids under 15 (37 per 100) or even people 65 to 74 (36 per 100). Young people are even more likely than people over 75 to go to an emergency room for an injury. Apparently, those summer jobs can also be hazardous to your health. *Newsweek* reports that 70,000 young people are injured on the job and go to the emergency room each year. Teens are twice as likely as adults to be hurt on the job.

Because of charges of "patient dumping," where some emergency rooms were accused of denying service to desperate patients, Congress passed a 1986 law called EMTALA (Emergency Medical Treatment and Labor Act). EMTALA makes it illegal for emergency rooms to turn away people. The emergency room is therefore the only place in the American health care system that is required by law to treat you. Still, one of the first questions you are likely to be asked on the stretcher is "what is your insurance situation?" Young adults actually have a harder time answering that question than any other age group, and they can find themselves with big medical debts at the same time they are trying to establish a good credit history and start a family. Emergency rooms provide great care, but are the most expensive single component of the health care system.

Questions for Discussion

- Should young Americans—or all Americans—be required to purchase health insurance, just as they are required to purchase collision insurance on their cars?
- Should emergency rooms be required by law to treat everyone who comes in?

Source: The data come from two reports by the Communicable Disease Center: "Early Release of Selected Estimates Based on Data from the January-June 2003 National Health Interview Study," December 12, 2003, and "National Hospital Ambulatory Medical Care Summary: 2001 Emergency Department Survey," *Advance Data*, June 4, 2003. See also *Newsweek*, May 31, 2004, p. 61.

Managed Care.   One of the biggest constraints on obtaining health insurance has been its cost. In recent years, private market forces have transformed the country's health care system dramatically. Insurers choose HMOs or restricted physician lists for the provision of care, negotiate with physician groups and hospitals on fees and costs, and try to monitor most aspects of care to control unnecessary use. At least three-fourths of all doctors have signed contracts, covering at least some of their patients, to cut their fees and accept oversight of their medical decisions. Enrollment in managed care plans grew slowly in the 1970s, but more than tripled in the 1980s and doubled again in the 1990s. Today these plans cover about 60 percent of all Americans, representing about 85 percent of workers who receive health insurance.

Managed care grew on the strength of its claims to provide better service at a lower cost. Traditional insurance gave doctors incentives to provide additional, and perhaps unnecessary, services and no incentive to provide preventive medicine. Doctors treated patients with little concern about cost, and insurance companies paid the bills with few questions asked.

ELDON FLAGLER WAS AWARDED the NOBEL PRIZE FOR MEDICINE TODAY FOR DISCOVERING HOW TO GET HIS HMO TO PAY FOR an OVERNIGHT HOSPITAL STAY FOLLOWING QUADRUPLE BYPASS SURGERY.

By Borgman for *The Cincinnati Enquirer*

patients' bill of rights

A controversial proposal before Congress that would give patients certain rights against medical providers, particularly HMOs, including the right to sue them.

Partly because of their cost containment efforts, HMOs have become the medical care system everyone loves to hate. Employer-sponsored benefits plans are governed by a complex federal law limiting lawsuits against them. Consumer groups have pressed Congress for a **patients' bill of rights,** which would give patients rights against HMO decisions to deny care. President Clinton first proposed a patients' bill of rights, which included a right to see the doctor of one's choice, obtain access to reasonable emergency care without prior authorization from a plan, secure the right to appeal a plan's refusal to provide medical treatments, attain easier access to out-of-network doctors, receive more information on their plan's regulations, and acquire the right to sue a plan for malpractice. Democrats have preferred including a right to sue HMOs for bad decisions; Republicans, always at odds with trial lawyers (2004 Democratic Vice Presidential candidate John Edwards was a trial lawyer), want suits limited in scope. A few states (Texas, for example, when George W. Bush was governor) passed laws permitting people to sue their HMOs. The cases went to court. But the U. S. Supreme Court held in *Aetna Health Care v. Davila* (2004) that federal law generally prohibits suing one's HMO. Few issues about health care more sharply divide Democrats and Republicans than the right to sue.

The Role of Government in Health Care

Medical care in the United States differs from that in most other democracies in one important way: the role the government plays. The United States has the most thoroughly privatized medical care system in the developed world. National, state, and local governments pay for 46 percent of the country's total health bill, whereas the median for all industrialized countries is about 77 percent. The government also subsidizes employer-provided health insurance with tax breaks worth about $77 billion per year, the benefits of which go disproportionately to affluent, highly paid workers.

Forty-six percent amounts to much more than most Americans realize. Many hospitals are connected to public universities, and much medical research is financed through the National Institutes of Health (NIH), for example. Further, the federal government pays for much of the nation's medical bills through the Medicare program for the elderly, the Medicaid program for the poor, and health care for veterans. More than 20,000 physicians work for the federal government, and nearly all the rest receive

Figure 19.1 The Nation's Health Care Dollar: Who Pays?

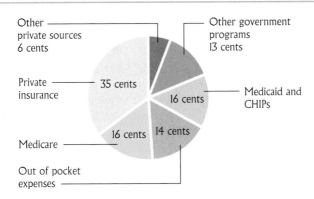

The United States has a mixed system of paying for health care. Private individuals still pay for the bulk of medical costs (out of their own pockets and through their insurance), but governments pay for about 45 cents of every medical care dollar.

Source: Department of Health and Human Services, Centers for Medicare and Medicaid Services, *Annual Report,* 2002.

payments from it. The government thus plays an important health care role in America, though less so than in other countries.

Who pays for the rest of Americans' health care? Private insurance companies cover one-third, and Americans pay nearly one-fifth of their health care costs out of their own pockets (see Figure 19.01). Americans often think insurance companies pay most health care costs, but in fact the government is more heavily involved than the private insurance industry.

More than 50 years ago Harry S Truman was the first president to call for **national health insurance,** a compulsory insurance program to finance all Americans' medical care. The idea was strongly opposed by the American Medical Association, the largest physicians' interest group, which called this program socialized medicine because it would be run by the government. Although every other industrial nation in the world has adopted some form of national health insurance, the United States remains the exception. Today, about 62 percent of Americans would prefer a universal, governmentally funded medical care system.[11] Even the American Medical Association has done an about face on the issue. Divided by conflicts about markets and government, though, the United States has tried mostly incremental reform.

In 1965 Congress sought to rectify the special health care problems of elderly Americans by adopting **Medicare.** Medicare is part of the Social Security system and covers 40 million people. Part A of Medicare provides hospitalization insurance and short-term nursing care; Part B, which is voluntary, permits older Americans to purchase inexpensive coverage for doctor fees and other nonhospital medical expenses. Because the number of elderly Americans grows rapidly—and because the cost of medical care is growing just as fast (Medicare cost about $250 billion in 2002)—the funding of health care for the elderly is one of the country's most pressing public policy issues.

Like Social Security, Medicare costs are outrunning contributions to the Medicare Trust Fund. While Social Security is likely to last until about 2038, the safe horizon for Medicare is much shorter. By 2008, expenditures will outrun revenues. It is the most rapidly increasing component of the federal budget. Today it is about 12 percent of the federal budget. Without reform, it will soar to nearly 30 percent by 2030.[12] The cost squeeze, though, is here today. More and more hospitals, physicians, and insurance companies have abandoned Medicare patients because Medicare payments do not cover their costs. To save itself money, Medicare constantly cuts back on the fees it will pay doctors and hospitals. One result: Fewer and fewer doctors treat Medicare patients. If Medicare will pay $1,200 for a $1,400 procedure, the physician loses money. "I have Medicare" is no guarantee that a doctor will treat you at the rate Medicare will reimburse.

Medicare's biggest gap has been coverage of prescription drugs. When it was created in 1965, drugs were a minor matter in medical care and little thought was given to

national health insurance

A compulsory insurance program for all Americans that would have the government finance citizens' medical care. First proposed by President Harry S Truman, the plan was soundly opposed by the American Medical Association.

Medicare

A program added to the Social Security system in 1965 that provides hospitalization insurance for the elderly and permits older Americans to purchase inexpensive coverage for doctor fees and other medical expenses.

including drugs in the Medicare package. Drugs—"wonder drugs" we sometimes call them—have increased in price faster than any other component of the costly medical care system. Medicare beneficiaries spent an average of $1,051 out of their own pockets on drugs in 2002. Seniors near the Canadian border can trek across the border to (illegally) purchase cheaper drugs.

Republicans and Democrats have been as bitterly divided on prescription drug coverage for Medicare recipients as on a patients' bill of rights. Democrats want government to subsidize drugs. Republicans want to encourage private plans to do it. Finally, in 2003, the Republican-run Congress passed the Medicare Prescription Drug Improvement and Modernization Act. Medicare beneficiaries would be able to get a price reduction on their drugs. Congress and the White House squabbled about the cost, but all agreed it would be high—probably $530 billion over its first decade. Seniors would pay an annual premium of at least $420. Some seniors found the law confusing; others feared that increases in drug costs would eat up the potential savings before the program was off the ground. Congress, though, forbade Medicare from negotiating with drug companies—as Canada does—to get wholesale prices for seniors. (See "Issues of the Times: Should the Government Negotiate Drug Prices?")

Skyrocketing Medicare bills would soar even higher under a new Medicare policy announced in July 2004, defining obesity as a disease. Obesity has about the same health effect as 20 years of aging, a more serious result than smoking or problem drinking.[13] The Centers for Disease Control and Prevention estimates that obesity will overtake smoking as the nation's leading cause of preventable deaths by 2005.[14] Treating it, though, is not going to be cheap.

Not to be confused with Medicare is **Medicaid,** a program designed to provide health care for the poor that serves about 42.7 million people. Like other public assistance programs, Medicaid is funded by both the states and the national government (in 2002 the government spent $267 billion on Medicaid). Unlike Medicare, which goes to elderly Americans regardless of their income, Medicaid is a means-tested program. Medicaid is for the poorest of the poor (only 42 percent of people below the poverty line even qualify). Like Medicare, the future of Medicaid is tenuous as costs soar. Insurers and providers who cannot afford Medicare patients cannot afford Medicaid patients either. Government also subsidizes insurance for poor children through a program called "CHIPS" (which stands for state Children's Health Insurance Programs).

Government in America plays an important role in health care, even if it is less involved than in other countries. One way to explain our mixed system—and mixed results—is to look at politics and policymaking for health care.

Policymaking for Health Care

The Politics of Health Care.   In countries with national health care systems (or national health insurance), government policymakers have focused more on ensuring equality of care and on containing costs, especially administrative costs. In the United States, equality of care and cost containment have taken a back seat to technological advance.

One reason for uneven government and private health care policies involves the representation of interests. Powerful lobbying organizations representing hospitals, doctors, and the elderly want Medicare to pay for the latest techniques. Politicians hardly feel comfortable denying these lifesaving measures to those who may have voted them into office. On the other hand, many groups are unrepresented in government. Their health needs may not be met simply because no well-organized groups are insisting that the government meet them.

The elderly are now one of the most powerful voting and lobbying forces in American politics. Health care policy that favors the elderly is one of the results of this interest group activity. The American Association of Retired Persons (AARP) has grown from about 150,000 members in 1959 to more than 35 million today, making it the largest voluntary association in the world. This single group now can claim to repre-

---

Medicaid

A public assistance program designed to provide health care for poor Americans. Medicaid is funded by both the states and the national government.

Why It Matters

National Health Insurance
The United States is the only Western, industrialized nation without a national health insurance system. Health care systems in other countries try to maintain a level of adequate care for everyone, even if it means squeezing high-cost drug expenditures and high-tech medicine. If we had a national health insurance system, we would probably have a higher level of care for the uninsured, but people who could afford it might have to pay more for care beyond the ordinary. Which do you favor? Why?

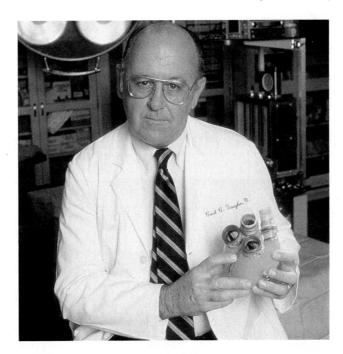

Health care policymaking involves difficult ethical issues. For example, should limited federal funds be spent on the expensive, unproven, but potentially lifesaving artificial heart technology shown here? Or should public money be devoted to less dramatic medical procedures that could help many more Americans?

sent one American in eight and its numbers may swell as the baby boomer generation reaches retirement. It claims to speak with authority on all questions associated with the elderly. Elderly Americans dependent on Social Security and Medicare are vigorous participators in American elections.[15]

One group that is increasingly active in health care policymaking is business. Conflict between the government (which pays many medical bills) and private employers (who pay much of the insurance premiums for their employees) is increasing. Each side wants the other to assume more of the health care burden. As private insurance rates increase, employers complain that they are paying inflated premiums for their workers to cover the costs of those who cannot pay or whose insurance provides only partial reimbursement for medical care. Employers then may attempt to reduce their burden by cutting out benefits that are covered by government programs.

Insurance companies are also major players in health care policymaking. They have been making it more difficult for doctors and hospitals to pass along the costs of others' unpaid bills to them, causing a cost crunch for some institutions, including inner-city hospitals and trauma centers that serve the poor. In addition, the health insurance industry has a huge stake in the outcome of the debate on national health insurance. A program funded and run by the national government would leave insurance companies without a function (or a profit). All these political fractures came together to defeat President Bill Clinton's major health care reform plan.

The Clinton Health Care Reform Plan.   President Clinton made health care reform the centerpiece of his first administration. His 5-pound, 1,342-page Health Security Act proposal was an effort to deal with the two great problems of health care policy: costs and access. The difficulties the president faced with this proposal reveal much about the challenge of reforming health care in America.[16]

Clinton's main concern was guaranteeing health care coverage for all Americans. His plan would particularly have benefited people without any health insurance, but it would also have extended coverage for millions of others with inadequate health insurance.

Paying for the plan would have necessitated either broad-based taxes, which were politically unpalatable, or a requirement that employers provide health insurance for their employees or pay a premium into a public fund (which would also cover Medicaid and Medicare recipients). The president chose the employer insurance option, but the

Issues of the Times

The Issue: Should the Government Negotiate Drug Prices?

Prescription drugs compose an increasingly large percentage of the nation's health costs. They are especially important for the nation's 41 million elderly and disabled people covered by Medicare. In 2003, Congress passed a law that will provide coverage of some of the cost of prescription drugs for Medicare patients starting in 2006.

Everyone agrees that it is important not to waste taxpayers' dollars. However, there is much less agreement on how to run the new program most efficiently. The American Medical Association argues that the federal government should use its buying power to negotiate lower prices from drug manufacturers. Those who wrote the law, however, banned the government from doing exactly that, arguing that private companies would do a better job in negotiating prices and that public officials should not be involved in setting the prices of drugs.

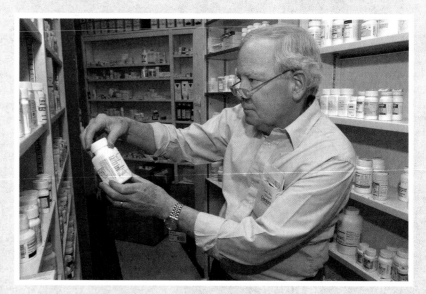

Of course, no one knows how well private companies will do in their negotiations and what ramifications the results will have for both the cost of this very important policy and the drugs that are available to patients.

Read All About It

A.M.A. Says Government Should Negotiate on Drugs

BY ROBERT PEAR
October 17, 2004

The American Medical Association says the government should negotiate directly with drug manufacturers to secure lower prices on prescription medicines for the nation's elderly.

Under the new Medicare law, signed by President Bush last December, 41 million elderly and disabled people will have access to drug benefits in 2006. Medicare will rely on private health plans to deliver the benefits. The law says the government "may not interfere" in negotiations with drug companies.

Authors of the law included that provision out of fear that government involvement could overwhelm the free market, leading to federal regulation of drug prices—"price-fixing" by federal bureaucrats, in the words of Senator Charles E. Grassley, Republican of Iowa.

Please see Drugs **Page 597**

Drugs

Continued from Page 596

The American Medical Association lobbied last year for the Medicare law, which makes hundreds of changes in the giant health insurance program.

The association now says Congress should pass legislation giving the secretary of health and human services authority to negotiate contracts with manufacturers of drugs that will be covered by Medicare.

The association, often viewed as a conservative voice for organized medicine, is influential on Capitol Hill. It strongly supports Republican efforts to limit damages that can be awarded in medical malpractice lawsuits.

But it is Democrats who have taken the lead in trying to repeal the ban on federal negotiations with drug manufacturers under Medicare.

Senator John Kerry, the Democratic nominee, said Medicare should be allowed to save money through "bulk purchasing" of drugs. But, Mr. Kerry said, "rather than help seniors have less expensive drugs, the president made it illegal, illegal, for Medicare to actually go out and bargain for lower prices." As a result, he said, drug companies will receive a "windfall profit."

Within hours after Mr. Bush signed the Medicare law last year, the Democratic leaders of the House and the Senate, Representative

Nancy Pelosi of California and Senator Tom Daschle of South Dakota, introduced bills to give federal officials the "authority to negotiate prices with manufacturers" of drugs covered by Medicare.

Dr. Andrew F. Calman of San Francisco, an ophthalmologist who pushed for the new policy adopted by the medical association, said: "I don't think it's a Democratic or a Republican issue. We have the sup-

---

Government should negotiate directly with drug manufacturers to secure lower prices on prescription medicines for the nation's elderly

---

port of doctors from different points on the political spectrum. We're very concerned about patients' access to affordable drugs. I have some glaucoma patients who need to take three or four different types of eye drops to avoid going blind, and each medication may cost $50 to $100 a month."

Ms. Pelosi said: "I'm pleased to have the A.M.A.'s support for negotiating lower prices and look forward to working with them on this issue. Their support will be a significant help."

Under the new law, competing private plans will buy drugs for

Medicare beneficiaries. The Bush administration and the Congressional Budget Office contend that these plans will be able to obtain large discounts from drug manufacturers, saving just as much money as the government could in such negotiations.

The secretary of health and human services "would not be able to negotiate prices that further reduce federal spending to a significant degree," said Douglas J. Holtz-Eakin, director of the budget office.

In asserting that Medicare officials should be able to negotiate with drug companies, the medical association said that other federal agencies, like the Department of Veterans Affairs and the Defense Department, had "negotiated favorable rates on prescription drugs on behalf of their beneficiaries, resulting in very substantial cost savings."

Moreover, it said, "others delivering medical services under federal health care programs, including physicians, have long been under government-imposed limits on their fees."

Doctors and hospitals often complain about federal regulation of the payments they receive under Medicare, and some suggest that it would be an anomaly if drugs were completely exempt from such restraints. Some doctors worry that rapid growth in Medicare spending on prescription drugs could create new pressure to hold down payments to doctors and other health care providers in the program.

Think About It

- Do you think the federal government should negotiate with drug companies to obtain lower prices for prescription drugs for those covered by Medicare?
- Would private companies do a better job of negotiating lower drug prices?

- Would government negotiations lead to "price fixing" for prescription drugs?
- If "price fixing" did occur, what would be the consequences for the development of new drugs?

Many Americans lack access to health care. President Clinton, appearing here at a rally in Minneapolis, made improved health care a centerpiece of his administration.

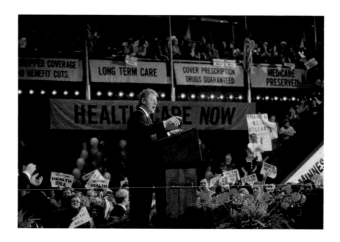

small business community was adamantly opposed to bearing the cost of providing health insurance. The president also proposed raising taxes on cigarettes, which angered the tobacco industry, and imposing a small tax on other large companies.

To contain health care costs, the administration would have required states to set up large consumer groups called "health alliances" to collect premiums, bargain with health plans, and handle payments. Most companies would have had to buy coverage through an alliance. The proposal would also have limited the annual increase in the price of health insurance premiums and capped government spending for Medicare (threatening the elderly) and Medicaid.

Because the White House reform plan for health care was bureaucratic and complicated, it was easy for opponents to label it a government takeover of the health care system. Interest groups of all shapes and sizes organized against it. An aggressive advertising campaign mounted by the health insurance industry characterized the president's plan as being expensive and experimental, as providing lower-quality and rationed care, and as killing jobs. The health insurance industry's famous "Harry and Louise" ads—Harry and Louise mull over the Clinton plan around their kitchen table and conclude, "There's got to be a better way"—were one of the most effective policy-oriented campaigns in history. After a long and tortuous battle, the plan died in Congress.

The Health Policy Issues Ahead.   The massive effort by President Clinton failed, but health care issues remain high on the policy agenda. While Americans are fairly satisfied with their own health care, a careful analysis of public opinion surveys show that people think the nation's health care system needs a great deal of reform.[17] Most of these concerns focus on the very issues we have examined here: cost and access.

Nothing suggests Americans' medical care is likely to get any cheaper in the decades ahead. The biomedical revolution promises cures around the corner. Just a month before the September 11 disasters, President Bush was wrestling with one of the major health care issues of his presidency—stem cell research. He made a televised speech from his Texas ranch on August 9, 2001, about the thorny scientific and political issue of fetal stem cells. Stem cells are "master cells" that can grow into virtually any sort of cell in the human body. Using stem cells, many scientists and research advocates are nearly certain that a range of human diseases could be ameliorated, prevented, or even cured. Prominent among them were Parkinson's disease and spinal cord injuries. Congressional hearings on stem cell research brought out celebrities with various diseases that might be cured by stem cell research (for example, Michael J. Fox for Parkinson's and the late Christopher Reeve for spinal cord injuries).

"In recent weeks," Bush said in his stem cell address, "we learned that scientists have created human life in test tubes solely for the purpose of experimenting on them. I strongly oppose human cloning, as do most Americans." He proposed permitting federal funds to be used for 60 existing lines of stem cells, but banning the creation of new ones. Scientists doubted that 60 cell lines existed.

The stem cell argument was not only political, but religious and linguistic, too. No one was proposing using federal moneys—or even private moneys—to create new human beings. Proponents of stem cell research—Senator Arlen Specter, the moderate Republican from Pennsylvania was one—objected to the very name "cloning," or its milder version, "therapeutic cloning." Stem cell research, he argued, is not cloning at all because it is not meant to produce a baby. Nancy Reagan, wife of former president Ronald Reagan, became an advocate for stem cell research. It might, she believed, provide a cure for Alzheimer's disease, which took her husband's life. Reagan's son also spoke in favor of stem cell research at the 2004 Democratic convention.

The stem cell research argument nationally was mired in "right to life" issues, but California voted in 2004 to create a $3 billion state fund to support stem cell research. This would dwarf the $25 million the federal government allots annually for stem cell research. California universities geared up to hire new researchers from other states and nations.

How You Can Make a Difference

Health Care

Have you thought about health care lately? Many traditional-age college students don't. You're young, invincible, healthy, and maybe still on your parents' insurance plan. Most college students don't find health insurance debates particularly relevant. Health insurance issues and prescription drug coverage is something senior citizens discuss, right? If you've been fortunate enough so far to avoid being confronted with this issue, start preparing for life after college when you'll no longer be on your parents' insurance. Even if you'll never face a problem with health insurance (a dicey bet), what about the plight of those who are uninsured?

First, you need to discern the different policy alternatives to solving the health care crisis. A particularly useful website, *www.publicagenda.com*, has a section on health care that sketches the three main approaches and lists the key players and organizations in this debate. Investigate all these approaches carefully. Some advocate the necessity for employing free market mechanisms and controlling costs. Others advocate universal health care for all. Still other

activists emphasize the need for quality in health care. Chances are you will find that each approach has strengths and weaknesses.

The advocates of universal health care tend to produce the most vocal grassroots activists in this debate. Even if you disagree with their conclusions, you should examine their tactics and strategies in getting grassroots support for your position. Different groups from health care professionals to faith-based organizations to disabled citizens have all voiced their opinion on this issue.

While primarily targeted at medical students in favor of universal health care, the AMSA—the American Medical Student Association (*www.amsa.org*)—provides an extraordinarily useful model for undergraduate student activists. Their website details various activities designed to heighten awareness of this issue on campus. For example, you could hold a candlelight vigil on campus for the uninsured by using their well-designed how-to guide. This guide walks you through the various steps necessary for your event to be a success—and how to not spend a fortune! For

example, where to buy candles, how to get a speaker, how to garner publicity, etc. Or you can learn how to organize a lobbying effort on behalf of key health care legislation. With an updated list of key congressional legislation and a congressional scorecard on how your congressional representatives have voted on particular issues, this site is useful to activists of all opinions.

What you can do:

- Learn about the issue by examining the section on health care issues at *www.publicagenda.com*.
- Investigate key websites from various activists to learn different approaches and tactics. Examine the AMSA (*www.amsa.org*), Universal Health Care Action Network (*www.uhcan.org*), and find a list of other organizations at *www.politics1.com* in the health care sections of "Ideologies and Issues."
- Hold a candlelight vigil and plan a Lobby Day on behalf of key legislation that you support.

In two decades, the United States has moved from a time when a "test tube baby" seemed an oddity to a time when cloning people may be as easy as cloning mice.[18] Cost containment, access to medical care, and the moral issues of medical care are all parts of the American health care policy debate.

Believing that medical care is close to a right, Americans have been reluctant to face up to the "rationing" of medical care. Medical care may not be a constitutional right, but Americans treat it as if it were. We do not like to admit that "rationing" of medical care goes on all the time in our system.[19] Much rationing is informal; physicians and families quietly agree not to provide further care to a loved one. Some of it is formal. Medical boards have elaborate rules for allocating donated organs. When we ration openly and publicly, though, conflict erupts. Oregon took the lead on the issue of rationing health care, trying to set priorities for medical treatments under the Medicaid program, which is funded by both the state and the national government. In 1991, the state came up with a list of 709 treatments/conditions. The Oregon legislature agreed to fund 587 of these from its tight Medicaid budget. As a result, Oregon does not pay for some costly treatments that might save or merely prolong people's lives, but by doing so it can use its resources to provide medical care to a larger pool of people. Though Oregon's plan was controversial at first, evidence shows that it works well and that patient satisfaction is higher after the plan than it was before.[20] Most Americans continue to believe, though, that they and their loved ones are entitled to all the medical care they—or someone else—can pay for.

There is little doubt that government will continue to struggle with regulating the costs of health care and helping those who fall through the cracks of the American health care system. Our part-public, part-private system remains complex, confusing, uneven, and expensive.

Environmental Policy

Making a Difference

Robert Bullard

Sociologists rarely make much difference in politics. Robert Bullard, though, is one who did. In 1979, his wife, Linda McKeever Bullard, was going to file suit against a major waste hauler called Southwestern Waste Management in Houston. The suit claimed that the company, now called BFI, was creating toxic landfills mostly in minority neighborhoods. Bullard gathered some data for his wife's lawsuit and wrote a paper called "Solid Waste Sites and the Houston Black Community." It was published four years later in a small sociological journal called *Sociological Inquiry*. Bullard turned it into a book called *Dumping on Dixie* (1993). The Bullard and Bullard lawsuit represented the first suit against a corporation claiming "environmental racism" under federal civil rights law. Robert's small-scale study in Houston provided evidentiary groundwork for hundreds of lawsuits about environmental justice. Now he runs the Environmental Justice Resource Center at Clark Atlanta University.

Environmentalists have been telling us for years that our air, water, and land need protection. A generation of environmental policies—started mostly by President Nixon in the 1970s—has targeted dirty air and water. One "skeptical environmentalist," as he calls himself, though, thinks the world's environmental plight is greatly exaggerated. Danish political scientist Bjorn Lomborg piled on 2,730 footnotes in a 515-page book to argue that environmentalists overlook plenty of improvements in the world's resource supply and environment.[21] Scientists and environmentalists reacted with fury. *Scientific American* headlined a string of rebuttals "Science Defends Itself Against the Skeptical Environmentalist."[22] (One critic gleefully noted Lomborg's own admission that "I am not myself an expert as regards environmental problems.")

One might think that such a cherished national treasure as the natural environment would be above politics. Everyone likes clear water and clean air. Everyone wants plenty of cheap, clean-burning energy with none of the byproducts of pollution.

As in other areas, however, politics infuses itself into the debate over the environment. Minority neighborhoods have complained for years that they are the victims of higher environmental dangers than suburban, White areas. An "environmental justice movement" has used court challenges and citizen action to make environmental quality into a civil rights issue. (See "Making a Difference: Robert Bullard.")

Attempts to control air quality or limit water pollution often affect political choices through their impact on business, economic growth, and jobs. And although Americans may be generally in favor of "doing something" about the environment, specific proposals to limit suburban growth, encourage carpooling, and limit access to national parks have met with strong resistance. Many Americans think it a stretch to put cans and bottles in a separate container for the garbage truck's recycling. Few are willing to pay more for oil to conserve gasoline; SUVs seem like America's chariots. Yet 60 cents of every dollar put into the gas tank goes to other countries, some of whom are none too friendly. And by 2004 Americans were spending well over $2 a gallon—in some states more than $3 a gallon—to fuel that car.

Politics puts oil and energy on the nation's front burner. Our oil is running low. Oil refining capacity is almost at its peak. Surging economic growth in China increases demand elsewhere. As we went to war with Iraq, Americans learned more about where their oil comes from. Less and less of it comes from our own wells. Two decades ago, President Carter vowed to make the United States energy independent. Yet we are more dependent on foreign oil than when he made the pledge. These days, we debate ferociously over measures that, at best, would extend U.S. oil production by a few years. Soon after taking office, President Bush pushed for further opportunities for oil companies to drill in Alaska's tundra. The Democratic Senate defeated it, preferring a pristine Arctic to oil drilling.

Environmental Policies in America

Until the early 1960s, environmental protection was not a prominent element of federal policy. What policy existed then focused largely on conservation and the national parks. It was President Richard Nixon who pressed for most of the nation's first environmental legislation. Spearheading government efforts is the **Environmental Protection Agency (EPA),** now the nation's largest federal regulatory agency. The EPA has a wide-ranging mission; it is charged with administering policies dealing with land, air, and water quality.

Environmental Impacts. The centerpiece of federal environmental policy is the **National Environmental Policy Act (NEPA),** passed in 1969. This law required both government and private agencies to complete **environmental impact statements (EIS).** Every time an agency proposes to undertake a policy that is potentially disruptive to the natural environment, it must file an EIS with the Environmental Protection Agency, detailing possible effects of the policy. Big dams and small post offices, major port construction and minor road widening—proposals for all these projects must include an EIS.

Clean Air. Another landmark piece of legislation affecting the environment is the **Clean Air Act of 1970,** which charges the Department of Transportation (DOT) with the responsibility of reducing automobile emissions. You have probably met the Clean Air Act if you have bought a new car or even looked at one. Cars today use far cleaner fuels (and less of it) than before the Clean Air Act. For years after the act's passage, fierce battles raged between the automakers and the DOT about how stringent the requirements had to be. Automakers claimed it was impossible to meet DOT standards; the DOT claimed that automakers were deliberately dragging their feet in hopes Congress would delay or weaken the requirements. In fact, Congress did weaken them, again and again. Still, the smaller size of American cars, the use of unleaded gasoline, and the lower gas consumption of new cars are all due in large part to DOT regulations. In 1990 Congress passed a reauthorization of the Clean Air Act, which significantly increased the controls on cars, oil refineries, chemical plants, and coal-fired utility plants. This bill was the strongest step forward in the fight to clean the air since the bill's original passage 20 years earlier.

The Clean Air Act Amendments of 1990 also marked one of the most radical innovations in pollution control policy. Congress permitted utility companies to use emissions trading, essentially the right to buy and trade rights to pollute on the open market (there is even a market for these emissions credits on the Chicago Board of Trade). A

Environmental Protection Agency (EPA)

An agency of the federal government created in 1970 and charged with administering all the government's environmental legislation. It also administers policies dealing with toxic wastes. The EPA is the largest federal independent regulatory agency.

National Environmental Policy Act (NEPA)

The law passed in 1969 that is the centerpiece of federal environmental policy in the United States. The NEPA established the requirements for **environmental impact statements.**

environmental impact statement (EIS)

A report required by the National Environmental Policy Act that specifies the likely environmental impact of a proposed action. NEPA requires that whenever any agency proposes to undertake a policy that impacts the environment, the agency must file a statement with the EPA.

Clean Air Act of 1970

The law that charged the Department of Transportation with the responsibility to reduce automobile emissions.

These damaged trees in Tennessee show the devastating effects of acid rain, which is formed when tall smokestacks at coal-burning plants belch pollution high into the atmosphere. Much of the acid rain caused by American industries actually falls in Canada; officials there estimate that more than 2,000 lakes have "died" as a result of acid rain.

Simulation

You Are an
Environmental Activist

Water Pollution Control Act of 1972

A law intended to clean up the nation's rivers and lakes. It requires municipal, industrial, and other polluters to use pollution control technology and secure permits from the **Environmental Protection Agency** for discharging waste products into waters.

utility generating cleaner fuel could "bank" its savings and sell them to other utilities around the country. Some environmentalists were horrified at these "licenses to pollute," but evidence shows the trading program has helped reduce pollution rates.[23]

Overall, we have cleaner air today than before this string of air pollution policies. President Bush's Council of Economic Advisers borrowed EPA data in 2004 to summarize our cleaner air.[24] Taking the levels of various pollutants in 1970 as 100, lead has been cut to nearly zero, both carbon monoxide and sulfur dioxide by nearly two-thirds, and particulates by three-quarters.

Clean Water.   Congress acted to control pollution of the nation's lakes and rivers with the **Water Pollution Control Act of 1972.** This law was enacted in reaction to the tremendous pollution of Northeastern rivers and the Great Lakes. Since its passage, water quality has improved dramatically. In 1972 only one-third of U.S. lakes and rivers were safe for fishing and drinking. Today, the fraction has doubled to two-thirds. Similarly, the number of waterfowl in U.S. waters has increased substantially. But federal laws only regulate "point sources"—places where pollutants can be dumped in the water, such as a paper mill along a river. What is hard to regulate is the most important cause of water pollution, "runoff" from streets, roads, fertilized lawns, and service stations.

Wilderness Preservation.   In addition to protecting air and water, environmental policy literally aims to keep some parts of the environment intact. One component of the environment that has received special attention is wilderness—those areas that are largely untouched by human activities. Ever since the founding of the National Park system in 1916, the United States has been a world leader in wilderness preservation. Perhaps the most consistently successful environmental campaigns in the postwar era have been those aimed at preserving such wild lands.[25] There are now 378 national parks and 155 national forests. Still, only about 4 percent of the United States is now designated as wilderness, and half of that is in Alaska. The strains of overuse have forced our national parks to consider restricting the public's access to preserve them for future generations. In addition, wilderness areas—with the biological, recreational, and symbolic values they embody—come under increasing pressure from those, such as logging and mining interests, who stress the economic benefits lost by keeping them intact. President Bush and environmentalists were constantly at odds over logging on federal lands. President Clinton had put 60 million acres of federal land beyond the reach of logging. In July 2004, President Bush proposed to let the state governors decide whether there should be roads built—for loggers and others—on federal lands.

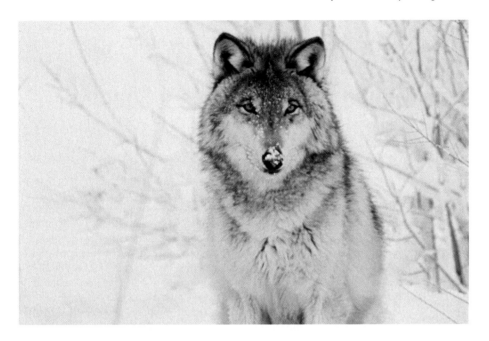

The gray wolf is an endangered species. In 1995–1996, the U.S. Fish and Wildlife Service reintroduced 31 gray wolves into Yellowstone National Park in an effort to reestablish its presence. They number 120 adults today. Environmentalists hail this effort as a great victory, but ranchers and farmers around Yellowstone complain that wolf packs will endanger their livestock.

Endangered Species.   National policy protects wildlife in other, more direct ways as well. One policy—saving endangered species—is among the most controversial. The **Endangered Species Act of 1973** created an endangered species protection program in the U.S. Fish and Wildlife Service. More important, the law required the government to actively protect each of the hundreds of species listed as endangered—regardless of the economic effect on the surrounding towns or region. Later, during the Reagan administration, the act was amended to allow exceptions in cases of overriding national or regional interest. These have been hard to come by, though. There has been plenty of controversy about the implementation of the Endangered Species Act. Bringing back the wolves in Yellowstone has a certain appeal to many Americans, but not to neighboring ranchers. In an expanding population, species and people come into conflict. You can think about the policy issues of saving species in "You Are the Policymaker: How Much Should We Do To Save a Species? The Florida Manatee."

Endangered Species Act of 1973

This law requires the federal government to protect actively each of the hundreds of species listed as endangered—regardless of the economic effect on the surrounding towns or region.

Toxic Wastes.   In 1980, Congress reacted to increased pressure to deal with toxic waste by establishing a **Superfund,** funded by taxing chemical products. The law established that those who polluted the land were responsible for paying to clean it up. A controversial retroactive liability provision holds companies liable even for legal dumping prior to 1980. The law also contains strict provisions for liability, under which the government can hold a single party liable for cleaning up an entire site that received waste from many sources.

Superfund

A fund created by Congress in 1980 to clean up hazardous waste sites. Money for the fund comes from taxing chemical products.

The Comprehensive Environmental Response, Compensation, and Liability Act (the formal name of the Superfund law) has virtually eliminated haphazard dumping of toxic waste, but it has been less successful in cleaning up existing waste. Instead, the law has led to endless rounds of litigation. Large companies facing multimillion-dollar clean-up bills have tried to recover some of their costs by suing small businesses that had contributed to the hazardous waste. They have also been embroiled in protracted court fights with their insurers over whether policies written in the early 1980s cover Superfund-related costs.[26]

Another serious environmental challenge is the disposal of nuclear waste, such as that from nuclear reactors and the production of nuclear weapons. It is necessary to protect not only ourselves but also the people of a distant future from radioactive materials. These wastes must be isolated for 10,000 years. At this point, 30,000 metric tons of highly radioactive nuclear waste are sitting in temporary sites around the country, most of them near nuclear power plants. Congress has studied, debated, and fretted for years over where to store the nation's nuclear waste. In the 1980s, Congress envisioned

You Are the Policymaker

How Much Should We Do to Save a Species? The Florida Manatee

The manatee (*Trichechus manatus latirostris*) is a walrus-like fresh-water animal weighing in at about 1,000 pounds. Plump and squinty-eyed, the Florida manatee is one of the charter members of the Department of Interior's Endangered Species list, first put there in 1967. Being on the Endangered Species list requires that both the federal and state governments enact policies to protect the habitat of the species. Few species have caused such a political conflict as the manatee. One of the major killers of manatees are the propellers on the thousands of boats in Florida's lakes and rivers. Biologists even use scar patterns from the propellers to identify individual manatees. In 2002, more than 95,000 Florida drivers paid an extra $20 for a "Save the Manatee" slogan on their license plates. Singer Jimmy Buffet has been a leader in the campaign to save the manatee, even writing a song ("Growing Older but Not Up") comparing himself to a prop-scarred manatee. Florida first passed a manatee protection law in 1893, making it illegal to kill manatees.

Enshrining an animal or plant as "endangered" puts policy into action.

Then politics enters. When the Fisheries and Wildlife Bureau of the Department of Interior lists a species as endangered, it has to design a recovery program. There are even fines and imprisonments for people who kill or injure an endangered species. (Only one person was ever prosecuted, though, and he paid a $750 fine and served a six-month prison term for having a butchered manatee on his boat.) In Florida, nearly one-quarter of the state's canals, rivers, and lakes were designated as manatee protection areas. Any construction project had to come to a halt if a manatee appeared within 100 feet, and could only resume if the animal left—as the regulation put it—"of its own volition." Boating was curtailed. Fishing was limited. Canal locks were refitted at a substantial cost.

When the Fish and Wildlife Service proposed reducing the manatee protection areas, environmentalists sued. In December 2002, 3,000 people swarmed into the Fort Myers Convention Center for a hearing on the proposed reduction in the protected habitat. One T-shirt read "Stop the Manatee Insanity." The Coastal Conservation Association of

Florida, a profishing group, produced data to show that the manatee population was increasing, and that regulations should be reduced and the habitat restrictions eased. One state legislator there compared environmentalists to watermelons ("green on the outside and red on the inside"). Environmentalists doubted the data.

If the purpose of the Endangered Species Act was to improve the chances of a species surviving, the Coastal Conservation group said, hadn't the Act served its purpose? Did the State really need to put a quarter of its waterways off limits to protect the manatee?

Often, the Endangered Species Act collides with other interests—economic growth, protecting property rights, and recreational activities. You be the policymaker. Do we want to save every single species (there may be 100 million of them)? When have we done enough to save a species?

Sources: On the Fort Myers meeting and the debate about the manatee, see Craig Pittman, "Fury over a Gentle Giant," *Smithsonian Magazine*, (February 2004), pp. 55–59.

that spent nuclear fuel would be consolidated and permanently buried. The search was on for the country's least sought-after public project. Early on, the "winner" appeared to be Nevada, a site about an hour from Las Vegas called Yucca Flats. Nevada's state government and congressional delegation battled the Yucca Flats site for more than a decade, but in July 2002 President Bush finally signed off on Congress' decision: Yucca Flats would be the nation's home for its nuclear wastes. Those 30,000 tons of nuclear waste would be making their way to Nevada by truck and rail (and these trips, some feared, would be inviting targets for terrorists).

Energy Policy

Energy Sources and Energy Politics

Modern American society depends on the availability of abundant energy. Americans are used to getting their energy cheaply and easily. Producing the amounts of energy necessary to retain our standard of living and accustomed patterns of life while at the same time preserving the environment has become increasingly difficult. Energy

Figure 19.2 Sources of America's Energy

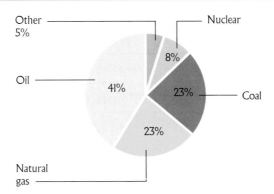

Despite the technological advances of society, America still relies on traditional sources for its energy: coal, oil, and natural gas. Coal generates a majority of our electricity; oil fuels our cars, trucks, and planes. Only 5 percent of our energy comes from renewable sources, mainly hydroelectricity and geothermal power.

Note: "Other" consists mostly of hydroelectricity, wood, and wind.

Source: Monthly Energy Review, May 2002, p. 6.

issues continually present thorny problems for policymakers to resolve, and government is constantly involved in battles concerning what forms of energy the country should be producing, and from what sources.

Once Americans used wood, animals, water, and people power for energy. Today 87 percent of the nation's energy comes from coal, oil, and natural gas (see Figure 19.2). Americans search continually for new and more efficient sources of energy, both to increase supplies and to reduce pollution. Much of the research on new energy sources and efficiencies comes from the government in Washington.

Coal is America's most abundant fuel. An estimated 90 percent of the country's energy resources are in coal deposits—enough to last hundreds of years. Although coal may be the nation's most plentiful fuel, unfortunately it is also the dirtiest. It contributes to global warming (discussed later in this chapter) and smog, and it is responsible for the "black lung" health hazard to coal miners and for the once soot-blackened cities of the Northeast. In addition, acid rain is traced to the burning of coal to produce electricity. Coal may be abundant, but most Americans do not want to rely on it exclusively for their energy needs. Coal accounts for only 23 percent of the energy Americans use.

Oil, which accounts for over 40 percent of the energy Americans use, is one of nature's nonrenewable resources. Some resources, such as the wind and solar energy, are renewable; that is, using them once does not reduce the amount left to be used in the future. These things are constantly renewed by nature. Oil, coal, and other common sources of energy, however, are not renewable. Natural gas and petroleum are somewhat cleaner than coal (though they too contribute to global warming), but petroleum imports inevitably lead to oil dependency.

To a large degree, America runs on oil. It powers our cars and trucks, makes our plastics, and—to some degree—fuels our politics. In 1940 Lyndon Johnson, then a young member of Congress, got Texas oil producers to pour unheard of sums into Franklin Roosevelt's reelection campaign.[27] Johnson's meteoric political career was greased by the oil industry. A company called Brown and Root footed the bills for much of Lyndon Johnson's rise to power. George W. Bush was the third president from Texas (his father was the second) with close ties to the oil industry. The remnants of Brown and Root are a core part of Halliburton, which Dick Cheney headed before he became George Bush's vice president.

Nature did not distribute oil evenly around the world, nor did it bless the biggest users with the most.[28] Compared to its usage, the United States is short of oil. Oil is counted and measured in barrels—whether it is being transported on a massive tanker or refined in Texas or Louisiana. Table 19.1 shows who has the oil in the world and who consumes it. The United States has about 2 percent of the world's oil, but uses more than a quarter of it. (Even Mexico has more oil reserves than the United States; Russia has twice as much.) Most of the oil—as most Americans know today—is in the Middle East. Nations of the Organization of Petroleum Exporting Countries (OPEC) have

Table 19.1   Where Is the Oil? Who Consumes It?

Oil is measured in barrels. The world's reserves of oil are mostly located in OPEC countries (including Iran, Iraq, Kuwait, Qatar, Saudi Arabia, the United Arab Emirates, Algeria, Libya, Nigeria, Indonesia, and Venezuela). The United States, with only 4 percent of the world's population, consumes more than a quarter of the world's annual oil production.

	Reserves		Consumption	
	BILLION BARRELS	RESERVE SHARE	MILLION BARRELS PER DAY	SHARE
United States	22	2%	19.6	26%
OPEC	814.5	79%	5.7	7%
Rest of world	191.6	19%	50.7	67%

Source: Office of Transportation Technologies, Department of Energy, June 11, 2002.

Why It Matters

Greenhouse Gases
Most scientists believe global warming will have dire consequences for the entire world. Because of its advanced economic system, the United States produces a larger quantity of greenhouse gases per person than any other nation. At the same time, no other nation can force the United States to reduce its emissions. Do you have any responsibility to help reduce greenhouse gases, or is that a problem for the next generation? What are our responsibilities to other peoples? How much cost, if any, should you and other Americans bear to benefit the rest of the world—and future generations?

nearly 80 percent of the world's reserves. The two nations with the largest oil reserves are Saudi Arabia and Iraq. Oil, of course, magnified the importance of Saddam Hussein, and contributed to the Gulf War during the first Bush administration. Seizing neighboring Kuwait, with its huge reserves, put Saddam Hussein within striking distance of Saudi Arabia's even bigger ones. If fear of terrorism was the text for "regime change" (in President Bush's oft-quoted phrase) in Iraq, oil was a strong subtext.

The most controversial energy source is nuclear power. During the 1940s and 1950s, Americans were convinced the technology that had ended World War II could be made to serve peaceful purposes. Nuclear scientists spoke enthusiastically about harnessing the atom to produce electricity that would be "too cheap to meter." These claims, however, were met with increasing skepticism in the light of huge cost overruns and the accidents at Three Mile Island in Pennsylvania and Chernobyl in the former Soviet Union. The wave of environmental concern that developed in the late 1960s devastated the nuclear power industry, and no new nuclear power plants have been built in the United States since 1978. Compared to oil and coal, its contribution to America's energy is tiny.

The Global Warming Debate Heats Up

One of the most intractable and potentially most serious issues relating to energy and the environment is global warming. When fossil fuels (coal, oil, and natural gas—the remnants of ancient plants and animals) are burned, they produce carbon dioxide. It, along with smaller quantities of methane and other gases, collects in the atmosphere, wrapping the Earth in an added layer of insulation and heating the climate. The "greenhouse effect" occurs when energy from the Sun is trapped under the atmosphere and warms the Earth as a result, much as in a greenhouse.[29]

Many scientists have found that the Earth is warming at a rapid rate and will be between 2 and 6 degrees warmer by the year 2100. This may not seem like a major change, but the world is now only 5–9 degrees warmer than during the depths of the last ice age, 20,000 years ago. Scientists predict that if the warming trend is not reversed, seas will rise (gobbling up shorelines and displacing millions of people), severe droughts, rainstorms, heat waves, and floods will become more common, and broad shifts in climatic and agricultural zones will occur, bringing famine, disease, and pestilence to some areas. Even that eternal optimist about the conditions of the environment, Danish political scientist Bjorn Lomborg, believes "Global warming is important. Its total costs could be about $5 trillion."[30]

In 1992, industrialized countries met in Rio de Janeiro and voluntarily agreed to cut greenhouse gas emissions to 1990 levels by the year 2000. The century turned, though, with no country coming close to meeting that goal.

At the end of 1997, 150 nations met in Kyoto, Japan, and agreed in principle to require 38 industrial nations to reduce their emissions of greenhouse gases below 1990 levels by about 2010. The European Union would reduce emissions by 8 percent, the United States by 7 percent, and Japan by 6 percent. The less developed nations argue that rich countries got rich by burning coal and oil and still produce most of the emissions today. (The United States alone, with only 4 percent of the world's population, produces more than 20 percent of the gases that cause global warming.) Thus, the less developed nations say developed nations should bear most of the burden in reducing global warming. Besides, less developed nations insist they are the ones who would be hurt worst by climate changes, and they are hard-pressed enough as it is.

The global warming problem has proved to be a hot political issue. A 2004 movie (*The Day After Tomorrow*) even imagined the world in the grip of a global warming disaster. Opponents of the Kyoto treaty in the United States—President Bush is one—fear that cutting greenhouse gases will cost a staggering sum. They also argue that it is unfair that the developed nations should bear the burden of cutting greenhouse emissions. After all, they say, less developed nations produce more emissions per dollar of gross domestic product than developed countries do. President Clinton never submitted the Kyoto treaty to the Senate. President Bush simply renounced it in 2001. When his own Department of Energy produced a "U.S. Climate Action Report" to the United Nations in 2002, tracing the U.S. contribution to global warming, President Bush merely grumbled "I've read the bureaucracy's report" and paid it no heed. Senators John McCain and Joseph Lieberman, though, proposed a Climate Stewardship Act that would require large companies to reduce their emissions to 1990 levels by 2020. A strong majority of Americans (about 8 in 10) supported that idea, even if it would increase their own energy costs.[31]

Groups, Energy, and the Environment

Nobody is against cleaning up the environment. The issue becomes a political question only because environmental concerns often conflict with equally legitimate concerns about foreign trade, economic growth, and jobs. Those who generate pollution do so in their efforts to make cars, to produce electricity, and to provide food and the consumer products Americans take for granted. On federally owned land, including national parks and forests, there has long been a policy of multiple use whereby mining, lumbering, and grazing leases are awarded to private companies or ranchers at a very low cost. Often the industries supported by these arrangements are important sources of jobs to otherwise depressed areas, and they may also lessen the country's dependence on foreign sources of oil and minerals.

Massive battles pitting lumbering interests against national and local environmental groups have raged in Alaska, where exports of lumber products to Japan provide jobs but decimate large parts of the Tongass National Forest. Similarly, harvesting old-growth timber on public lands has caused great concern in Oregon and Washington. In the Northwest and Alaska, environmentalists have complained that some of the few remaining large tracts of virgin forest, with trees hundreds of years old, are being felled by logging companies operating under generous lease agreements with the U.S. government, which owns the lands. Oil exploration on public lands and off shore in coastal waters also brings the goals of environmental protection and economic growth into conflict. Energy companies and environmentalists have battled over Alaska's reserves.

The 1960s and 1970s saw an explosion in the size and number of environmental interest groups.[32] Bosso and Guber report three environmental groups (the National Wildlife Federation, the Nature Conservancy, and the World Wildlife Fund) with more than a million members. The Sierra Club, Greenpeace, the National Audubon Society, the Natural Resources Defense Council, and others count a half million members each. Everyone loves the environment, but not everyone loves environmentalists. In an age where terrorism trumps every other policy issue, and where Republicans control Congress and the presidency, there is an "uncertain road ahead" for environmental groups.[33]

In March 1989, the *Exxon Valdez* ran aground off the southern coast of Alaska, spilling 11 million gallons of crude oil. Despite a $2 billion clean-up effort, the oil killed thousands of fish and animals and ruined miles of shoreline. No other single oil spill has drawn so much public attention to the environmental dangers of America's reliance on oil as an energy source.

Why It Matters

"NIMBY"

Most Americans say "NIMBY"—not in my backyard—when government proposes locating unwanted waste dumps, toxic disposal sites, and other unhealthy land uses near their homes. Would you always oppose the placement of environmental hazards in your neighborhood? Should government give every neighborhood a veto over having to house wastes? If every community, even sparsely populated areas, had a veto, where would society dispose of its hazardous materials?

No group proudly announces it is opposed to a clean environment. But there are many groups that oppose self-proclaimed environmentalists ("tree huggers," some sneer). They argue that the effects of environmental regulations on employment, economic growth, and international competitiveness must be part of the policymaking equation. Others, especially ranchers, miners, farmers, and loggers, demand inexpensive access to public land and the right to use their own property as they wish or else be compensated by government for being prohibited from doing so. In the West, groups that oppose the environmentalists often call themselves "wise use" advocates. Western proponents of mining interests formed People for the West. Republicans get a large share of their certain electoral votes from Western states. Ranching, grazing, logging, and mining interests loom large in this coalition. George W. Bush was generous in his appointments of "wise use" Westerners to key environmental posts. (Environmentalists thought this was leaving the fox to watch the henhouse.)

Widening opposition to potentially hazardous industrial facilities (such as toxic or nuclear waste dumps) has further complicated environmental policymaking in recent years. Local groups have often successfully organized resistance to planned development, rallying behind the cry "Not in My Backyard." The so-called NIMBY phenomenon highlights another difficult dilemma in environmental policy: How can government equitably distribute the costs associated with society's seemingly endless demand for new technologies, some of which turn out to be environmentally threatening? If, for example, we are to use nuclear power to keep our lights on, the waste it produces must go in someone's backyard. Government's answer: Nevada's.

For all these reasons, government policies designed to clean up the environment are sure to be controversial, expensive, and debated for years to come.

Understanding Health Care and Environmental Policy

The complex issues involved in making policy for health care and the environment pose many special problems in a democracy. These issues are difficult to understand when discussed in experts' terms, but most Americans do not want to leave them to "experts" to decide. This section discusses how democracies handle such issues and then considers the impact of these issues on the scope of government.

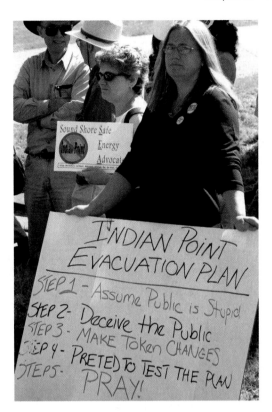

Citizen action is a powerful force even on highly technical issues such as nuclear power. Here, protesters oppose the Indian Point nuclear power plant in Buchanan, N.Y.

Democracy, Health Care, and Environmental Policy

Very few Americans actually understand how a nuclear power plant operates. Few know how much about a stem cell. Does such ignorance mean citizens should not be allowed to participate in the public policy debates concerning complex technologies? High-tech issues, more than any others, strain the limits of public participation in a democracy. Further, the issues associated with high technology are often so complex that many different levels of government—local, state, and national—become heavily involved. Whether it be the new ethical issues raised by machines and devices that can keep patients alive indefinitely—respirators, artificial kidneys, and the like—or whether it be the threats to public safety inherent in an accident at a nuclear power plant, governments are constantly called on to make decisions that involve tremendously complex technologies. Maintaining the right balance between public participation and technological competence is not an easy task.

High-technology issues make it especially difficult to include the public in a reasoned political debate. Many issues about health, energy, and environment are ethical issues, too. Debates about stem cell research or reproductive cloning are moral issues, and not merely technological ones. Often groups of specialists are the only ones who seem qualified to make decisions (and these specialists may have "special interest" in the issues on which they pass expert judgment). Still, in the United States, dramatic change has occurred. Environmental groups that once focused only on dramatic statements or loud protests now have their own staffs of scientists. Because knowledge is important in a highly complex debate, they have procured the resources to develop that knowledge. No longer are major public issues such as environmental pollution debated in the absence of well-informed groups looking out for the public interest.

Policymaking for technological issues seems to rely heavily on group representation. Individual citizens are unlikely to have the information or the resources to participate meaningfully because of the complexity of the debates. Interest groups—associations of professionals and citizens—play an active role in making the complicated decisions that will affect all Americans for generations.

The Scope of Government and Health Care and Environmental Policy

Americans do not hesitate to call for government to play a greater role in high-technology issues, and the scope of the federal government has grown in response to these demands. Medicare for the elderly, Medicaid for the poor, and tax subsidies for employer-provided health insurance are large, expensive public policies. Adding prescription drug coverage for the elderly will be a huge increase in the cost of governmentally supported medicine.

The most important single policy difference between the United States and all other industrialized governments is in health care. We have a mixed, mostly private system; other industrialized democracies have a nearly entirely public one. Creating a national health system would be the biggest domestic policy change since the New Deal. With the parties sharply divided on the scope of government, incremental, rather than fundamental, change may be all the American political system can produce.

Similarly, in the past three decades, concerns for environmental protection have placed additional demands on the federal government. Volumes of regulations and billions of dollars spent on environmental protection have enlarged the scope of government's environmental policy. Republicans think many of these demands are too onerous on private businesses; Democrats think regulation keeps the environment clean.

Summary

Americans live in an age driven by technology. Like so much in human history, technology brings its blessings and its curses. In particular, technology meets public policy in health care and the environment.

Health care already makes up one-seventh of America's GDP, and with increased technology, its costs will almost certainly continue to rise. These advances have improved health care, but tremendous problems also plague health care in America, including inadequate insurance coverage (or no coverage at all) for many people and ever-increasing costs for even routine medical attention. The paradox of health policy in the United States is that it spends more of its national income on health than other nations and is far from the healthiest.

Americans are also increasingly concerned with the environment. Environmental issues will continue to cause the government to become involved in many aspects of daily life, and they often pit citizens' groups against important economic interests. The government has become very active in ensuring the quality of America's air, land, and water and in protecting wildlife. We are dependent on energy, but the most common sources of energy, coal and oil, cause many environmental and health problems. Only a few decades ago, President Carter announced a national policy of energy independence. Today, though, 60 percent of our oil comes from other nations. Two-thirds of the world's oil supply is in the Middle East, fueling foreign policy issues.

In both of these public policy areas government is and will continue to be at the center of public debate. Furthermore, governmental activities can be expected to grow, rather than to decrease, in each of these areas. Finally, citizen participation has profoundly influenced government decisions. Voting and organizing interest group campaigns will continue to be important means of influencing health care and the environment.

KEY TERMS

health maintenance organization (HMO)	Environmental Protection Agency (EPA)	Clean Air Act of 1970
patients' bill of rights	National Environmental Policy Act (NEPA)	Water Pollution Control Act of 1972
national health insurance	environmental impact	Endangered Species Act of 1973
Medicare	statement (EIS)	
Medicaid		Superfund

INTERNET RESOURCES

www.census.gov/hhes/www/hlthins.html
Census Bureau data on health insurance coverage.

www.epa.gov
Official site for the Environmental Protection Agency, which provides information on policies and current environmental issues.

www.sierraclub.org/
Website for the Sierra Club, one of the most active environmental protection organizations.

www.epa.gov/superfund/sites/index.htm
Locate toxic waste sites in your state or city.

GET CONNECTED

Health Care Policy

America spends a large amount on health care yet has a population that is not any healthier than other industrial nations. In addition, about 45 million Americans don't have health insurance. The reason for this seeming paradox is that health care in America is market oriented, meaning it is a profit-making industry. Some argue that health care should not be open to market forces. One group, Physicians for a National Health Care Program (PNHC) advocates a single-payer system. Let us explore their idea.

Search the Web

Go to *http://www.pnhp.org/* and read about their single-payer plan.

Questions To Ask

- What is a single-payer plan?
- Who would pay the bill in a single-payer plan?
- Why do these physicians support a single-payer plan? Are there reasons to support the idea?
- Who would be the big winners and big losers if this plan were adopted?

Why It Matters

Health care is important for obvious reasons. The nation's health care system is under severe strain because costs continue to rise and at the same time around 15 percent of the population is not covered by any health insurance.

Get Involved

What kind of plan would you support? Talk to your parents about the cost of your family's health care. What kind of plan would they support? Talk with your doctor about the costs of health care. Would he or she support a single-payer plan?

To see more Get Connected exercises for Chapter 19, go to www.ablongman.com/edwards.

FOR FURTHER READING

Bonnickson, Andrea. *Crafting a Cloning Policy: From Dolly to Stem Cells.* Washington, D.C.: Georgetown University Press, 2002. The politics and policy issues of cloning.

Casamayou, Maureen Hogan. *The Politics of Breast Cancer.* Washington, D.C.: Georgetown University Press, 2001. How women's groups and others organized to elevate breast cancer research on the policy agenda.

Gore, Albert. *Earth in the Balance: Ecology and the Human Spirit.* Boston: Houghton Mifflin, 1992. The former vice president presents a manifesto for protecting the environment.

Henig, Robin Marantz. *Pandora's Baby.* Boston: Houghton Mifflin, 2004. Reproductive issues from in vitro fertilization to cloning.

Lomborg, Bjorn. *The Skeptical Environmentalist: Measuring the Real State of the World.* New York: Cambridge University Press, 2001. Controversial book arguing that the world is a lot better off than environmentalists think.

Skocpol, Theda. *Boomerang: Health Care Reform and the Turn Against Government.* New York: Norton, 1996. Why Clinton's health care reforms boomeranged.

Tobin, Richard. *The Expendable Future: U.S. Politics and the Protection of Biological Diversity.* Durham, NC: Duke University Press, 1990. The promise and problems of trying to protect endangered species.

Vig, Norman J., and Michael E. Kraft, eds. *Environmental Policy,* 5th ed. Washington, D.C.: Congressional Quarterly Press, 2003. Useful articles on a range of environmental policy issues.

20

National Security Policymaking

Chapter Outline

American Foreign Policy: Instruments, Actors, and Policymakers

The New York Times **Issues of the Times**

American Foreign Policy: An Overview

The Politics of Defense Policy

The New Global Agenda

Understanding National Security Policymaking

Summary

■ On September 11, 2001, America trembled. Terrorist attacks on the World Trade Center in New York and the Pentagon in Washington killed thousands and exposed the nation's vulnerability to unconventional attacks.

Less than 12 years after the fall of the Berlin Wall, the United States could no longer take comfort in its status as the world's only superpower. Suddenly the world seemed a more threatening place, with dangers lurking around every corner.

Communism was no longer the principal threat to the security of the United States, and our foreign policy goals suddenly changed to ending terrorism. Many important questions remained unsettled, however. What should be the role of the world's only remaining superpower? What should we do with our huge defense establishment?

The need to answer the question of the appropriate role of the national government in national security policy is more important and perhaps more difficult than ever. America's status in the world makes leadership unavoidable. Should we go it alone, or should we work closely with our allies on issues ranging from fighting terrorism and stopping nuclear proliferation to protecting the environment and encouraging trade? How should we deal with our former adversaries? Should we aid their transition to democracy?

At the same time, a number of critical areas of the world, such as the Middle East and the India-Pakistan border, exhibited a frightening tendency to conflict. Should the United States get involved in trying to end conflicts resulting from ethnic, religious, and regional differences? Does the United States have a choice about involvement when the conflict could affect its ability to fight terrorism or prevent the use of nuclear weapons?

And just how should we decide about national security policy? Should the American people delegate discretion in this area to officials who seem more at home with complex and even exotic issues of defense and foreign policy? Or should they and their representatives fully participate in the democratic policymaking process, just as they do in domestic policy? Can the public or its representatives in Congress or in interest groups have much influence on the elites who often deal in secrecy with national security policy?

The end of the Cold War has not lessened the importance of national security policy. New and complex challenges have emerged to replace the conflict with Communism. Some of these challenges, such as the fight against terrorism, are traceable to a malevolent enemy who can be contained or defeated—but many others are not.

American Foreign Policy: Instruments, Actors, and Policymakers

foreign policy

A policy that involves choice-taking, like domestic policy, but additionally involves choices about relations with the rest of the world. The president is the chief initiator of foreign policy in the United States.

Foreign policy, like domestic policy, involves making choices—but the choices involved are about relations with the rest of the world. Because the president is the main force behind foreign policy, every morning the White House receives a highly confidential intelligence briefing that might cover monetary transactions in Tokyo, last night's events in some trouble spot on the globe, or Fidel Castro's health. The briefing is part of the massive informational arsenal the president uses to manage American foreign policy.

Instruments of Foreign Policy

The instruments of foreign policy are, however, different from those of domestic policy. Foreign policies depend ultimately on three types of tools: military, economic, and diplomatic.

Military.   Among the oldest instruments of foreign policy are war and the threat of war. German General Karl von Clausewitz once called war a "continuation of politics by other means." As we learned in Chapter 13, the United States has been involved in only a few full-scale wars. It has often employed force to influence actions in other countries, however. Most of this influence has been close to home, in Central America and the Caribbean, as you can see in Figure 20.1.

In recent years, the United States has continued to use force in limited ways around the world: to topple Saddam Hussein's regime in Iraq and the Taliban regime in Afghanistan, to oppose ethnic cleansing in the Kosovo province of Yugoslavia, to prevent the toppling of the democratic government of the Philippines, to assist a UN peacekeeping mission in Somalia, to rescue stranded foreigners and protect our embassy in Liberia, to launch missile attacks on Baghdad in retaliation for an effort to assassinate former President Bush and for the failure to provide United Nations weapons inspectors access to suspected weapons sites. The United States also employed military forces to aid the democratic transfer of power in Haiti and for humanitarian relief operations in Yugoslavia, Iraq, Somalia, Bangladesh, Russia, and Bosnia.

Economic.   Today, economic instruments are becoming weapons almost as potent as those of war. The control of oil can be as important as the control of guns. Trade regulations, tariff policies, and monetary policies are other economic instruments of foreign policy. A number of studies have called attention to the importance of a country's economic vitality to its long-term national security.[1]

Diplomacy.   Diplomacy is the quietest instrument of influence. It is the process by which nations carry on relationships with each other. It often evokes images of ambassadors at chic cocktail parties, but the diplomatic game is played for high stakes. Sometimes national leaders meet in summit talks. More often, less prominent negotiators work out treaties covering all kinds of national contracts, from economic relations to aid for stranded tourists.

Figure 20.1   U.S. Military Interventions in Central America and the Caribbean Since 1900

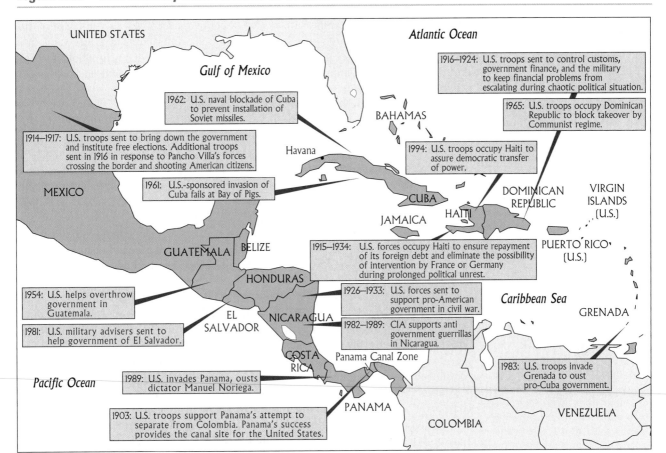

Actors on the World Stage

If all the world's a stage, then there are more actors on it than ever before. More than 125 nations have emerged since 1945—nearly two dozen in the 1990s alone. Once foreign relations were almost exclusively transactions among nations in which military, economic, or diplomatic methods were used to achieve foreign policy goals. Nations remain the main actors in international politics, but today's world stage is more crowded.

International Organizations.   Most of the challenges in international relations, ranging from peacekeeping and controlling weapons of mass destruction to protecting the environment and maintaining stable trade and financial networks, require the cooperation of many nations. It is not surprising that international organizations play an increasingly important role on the world stage.

The best known international organization is the **United Nations (UN)**. Housed in a magnificent skyscraper in New York City, the UN was created in 1945. Its members agree to renounce war and respect certain human and economic freedoms. The UN General Assembly is composed of 191 member nations. Each nation has one vote. Although not legally binding, General Assembly resolutions can achieve a measure of collective legitimization when a broad international consensus is formed on some matter concerning relations among states.

It is the *Security Council*, however, that is the seat of real power in the UN. Five of its 15 members (the United States, Great Britain, China, France, and Russia) are permanent members; the others are chosen from session to session by

United Nations (UN)

Created in 1945, an organization whose members agree to renounce war and to respect certain human and economic freedoms. The seat of real power in the UN is the Security Council.

the General Assembly. Each permanent member has a veto over Security Council decisions, including any decisions that would commit the UN to a military peace-keeping operation. The Secretariat is the executive arm of the UN and directs the administration of UN programs. Composed of 8,900 international civil servants, it is headed by the secretary general. In addition to its peacekeeping function, the UN runs a number of programs focused on economic development and on health, education, and welfare.

Since 1948 there have been 57 United Nations peacekeeping operations, 43 of which were created by the Security Council between 1988 and 2004. In 1990, the UN Security Council backed resolutions authorizing an embargo on the shipment of goods to or from Iraq in an attempt to force its withdrawal from Kuwait. Later, it authorized the use of force to compel Iraq to withdraw. In 1992, the UN assisted famine relief in Somalia. More recently, it supported the return of the democratically elected president of Haiti and has been active in trying to end the civil war in Bosnia-Herzegovina. In 2004 there were 14 UN missions under-way in the Democratic Republic of the Congo, Sierra Leone, Western Sahara, East Timor, India/Pakistan, Ethiopia and Eritrea, the Golan Heights, Ivory Coast, Liberia, Lebanon, Cyprus, Georgia, Kosovo, and the Middle East generally. However, the UN did not support the U.S.-led war in Iraq.

The United States often plays the critical role in implementing UN policies. Although President Clinton envisioned an expanded role for UN peacekeeping operations at the beginning of his term, he later concluded that the UN is often not capable of making and keeping peace, particularly when hostilities among parties still exist. He also backtracked on his willingness to place American troops under foreign commanders—always a controversial policy.

George W. Bush sought but did not receive UN sanction for the war with Iraq and has been skeptical of the organization's ability to enforce its own resolutions. Nevertheless, many countries feel the legitimacy of the UN is crucial for their participation in peacekeeping or other operations requiring the use of force.

The UN is only one of many international organizations. The International Monetary Fund, for example, helps regulate the chaotic world of international finance; the World Bank finances development projects in new nations; the World Trade Organization (WTO) attempts to regulate international trade; and the Universal Postal Union helps get the mail from one country to another.

Regional Organizations. *Regional organizations* have proliferated in the post-World War II era. These are organizations of several nations bound by a treaty, often for military reasons. The **North Atlantic Treaty Organization (NATO)** was created in 1949. Its members—the United States, Canada, most Western European nations, and Turkey—agreed to combine military forces and to treat a war against one as a war against all. During the Cold War, more than a million NATO troops (including about 325,000 Americans) were spread from West Germany to Portugal as a deterrent to foreign aggression. To counter the NATO alliance, the Soviet Union and its Eastern European allies formed the *Warsaw Pact*. The Warsaw Pact has since been dissolved, however, and the role of NATO has changed dramatically as the Cold War has thawed. In 1999, Poland, Hungary, and the Czech Republic, former members of the Warsaw Pact, became members of NATO. In 2002, seven additional Eastern European countries, including Slovakia, Slovenia, Bulgaria, Romania, Latvia, Estonia, and Lithuania, were invited to join the alliance.

Regional organizations can be economic as well as military. The **European Union (EU)** is a transnational government composed of most European nations. The EU coordinates monetary, trade, immigration, and labor policies so that its members have become one economic unit, just as the 50 United States are an economic unit. Other economic federations exist in Latin America and Africa, although none is as unified as the EU. Most EU nations have adopted a common currency, the Euro.

North Atlantic Treaty Organization (NATO)

Created in 1949, an organization whose members include the United States, Canada, most Western European nations, and Turkey, all of whom agreed to combine military forces and to treat a war against one as a war against all.

European Union (EU)

An alliance of the major Western European nations that coordinates monetary, trade, immigration, and labor policies, making its members one economic unit. An example of regional organization.

Multinational Corporations. Chapter 17 discussed the potent *multinational corporations*, or MNCs. Today, a large portion of the world's industrial output comes from these corporations, and they account for more than one-tenth of the global economy and one-third of world exports.[2] Sometimes more powerful (and often much wealthier) than the governments under which they operate, MNCs have voiced strong opinions about governments, taxes, and business regulations. They have even linked forces with agencies such as the Central Intelligence Agency (CIA) to overturn governments they disliked. In the 1970s, for example, several of these corporations worked with the CIA to "destabilize" the democratically elected Marxist government in Chile; Chile's military overthrew the government in 1973. Even when they are not so heavy handed, MNCs are forces to be reckoned with in nearly all nations.

Nongovernmental Organizations (NGOs). *Groups* are also actors on the global stage. Churches and labor unions have long had international interests and activities. Today, environmental and wildlife groups such as Greenpeace have also proliferated. Ecological interests are active in international as well as in national politics. Groups interested in protecting human rights, such as Amnesty International, have also grown (see "Making a Difference: Jody Williams").

Not all groups, however, are committed to saving whales, oceans, or even people. Some are committed to the overthrow of particular governments and operate as terrorists around the world. Airplane hijackings, and assassinations, bombings, and similar terrorist attacks have made the world a more unsettled place. Conflicts within a nation or region thus spill over into world politics.

Individuals. Finally, *individuals* are international actors. The recent explosion of tourism sends Americans everywhere and brings to America legions of tourists from Japan, Europe, and the less-developed world. Tourism creates its own costs and benefits and thus always affects the international economic system. Tourism may enhance friendship and understanding among nations. However, more tourists traveling out of the country than arriving in the country can create problems with a country's balance of payments (discussed later in this chapter). In addition to tourists, growing numbers of students are going to and coming from other nations; they are carriers of ideas and ideologies. So are immigrants and refugees, who also place new demands on public services.

Just as there are more actors on the global stage than in the past, there are also more American decision makers involved in foreign policy problems.

Making a Difference

Jody Williams

Landmines are a daily threat in dozens of countries and have caused hundreds of thousands of deaths and injuries in the past few decades. Mines also render large tracts of agricultural land unusable, wreaking environmental and economic devastation. Jody Williams, a former schoolteacher and director of humanitarian relief efforts in Central America, decided to do something about the landmine threat. She became the founding coordinator of the International Campaign to Ban Landmines (ICBL), which led the fight for change. By 1999, 133 countries had signed a treaty that bans the use, production, stockpiling, and transfer of antipersonnel mines. In 1997, the Nobel Peace Prize was awarded to the ICBL and its coordinator, Jody Williams.

The Policymakers

There are many policymakers involved with national security policy, but any discussion of foreign policymaking must begin with the president.

The President. The president, as you know from Chapter 13, is the main force behind foreign policy. As chief diplomat, the president negotiates treaties; as commander in chief of the armed forces, the president deploys American troops abroad. The president also appoints U.S. ambassadors and the heads of executive departments (with the consent of the Senate), and he has the sole power to accord official recognition to other countries and receive (or refuse to receive) their representatives.

Some presidential foreign policy is made through the formal mechanisms of treaties or executive agreements. Both are written accords in which the parties agree to specific actions. Since the end of World War II, presidents have negotiated thousands of executive agreements but only about 800 treaties. They both have legal standing, but only treaties must be ratified by two-thirds of the Senate. Presidents usually find it more convenient to use executive agreements. Most executive agreements deal with routine and noncontroversial matters, but they have also been used for matters of significance such as ending the Vietnam War and arms control agreements.

The president combines constitutional prerogatives with greater access to information than other policymakers and can act with speed and secrecy if necessary. The White House is also advantaged by the president's role as a leader of Congress and the public and by his ability to commit the nation to a course of action. Presidents do not act alone in foreign policy, however. They are aided (and sometimes thwarted) by a huge national security bureaucracy. In addition, they must contend with the views and desires of Congress, which also wields considerable clout in the foreign policy arena—sometimes doing so in opposition to a president.

secretary of state

The head of the Department of State and traditionally a key adviser to the president on **foreign policy.**

The Diplomats.   The State Department is the foreign policy arm of the U.S. government. As the department's chief, the **secretary of state** (Thomas Jefferson was the first) has traditionally been the key adviser to the president on foreign policy matters. In over 300 overseas posts from Albania to Zimbabwe, the State Department staffs U.S. embassies and consulates, representing the interests of Americans. Once a dignified and genteel profession, diplomacy is becoming an increasingly dangerous job. The November 1979 seizure of the American embassy in Tehran and the 1998 bombing of the American embassy in Nairobi, Kenya, are extreme examples of the hostilities diplomats can face.

The more than 30,000 people working in the State Department are organized into functional areas (such as economic and business affairs and human rights and humanitarian affairs) and area specialties (a section on Middle Eastern affairs, one on European affairs, and so on), each nation being handled by a "country desk." The political appointees who occupy the top positions in the department and the highly select members of the Foreign Service who compose most of the department are heavily involved in formulating and executing American foreign policy.

Many recent presidents have found the State Department too bureaucratic and intransigent. Even its colloquial name "Foggy Bottom," taken from the part of Washington where it is located, conjures up less than an image of cooperation. Some recent presidents have bypassed institutional arrangements for foreign policy decision-making and have instead established more personal systems for receiving policy advice. Presidents Nixon and Carter, for example, relied more heavily on their special assistants for national security affairs (Henry Kissinger and Zbigniew Brzezinski, respectively) than on their secretaries of state. Foreign policy was thus centered in the White House and was often disconnected from what was occurring in the State Department. Critics, however, charged that this situation led to split-level government and chronic discontinuity in foreign policy.[3] President Reagan, by contrast, relied less on his assistants for national security affairs (six different men filled the job in eight years) and more on Secretary of State George Schultz, who was a powerful player. George Bush continued this pattern, appointing his closest friend, James Baker, as secretary of state. President Clinton also relied heavily on his secretaries of state, Warren Christopher and Madeleine Albright. George W. Bush named Colin Powell, one of the most admired people in America, as secretary of state. Powell was the president's leading foreign policy adviser, but national security assistant Condoleezza Rice also played a prominent role. She replaced Powell as secretary of state in Bush's second term.

The National Security Establishment.   Foreign policy and military policy are closely linked. Thus the Department of Defense is a key foreign policy actor. Often called "the Pentagon" after the five-sided building in which it is located, the Defense

The secretary of state is typically the president's chief foreign policy adviser, presiding over a global bureaucracy of diplomats. Here, Colin Powell, who served in George W. Bush's first term, meets with South Korean President Kim Young-san.

Department was created after World War II. The U.S. Army, Navy, and Air Force were collected into one giant department, although they have never been thoroughly integrated and continue to plan and operate largely independently of one another. Reforms, made law under the Goldwater-Nichols Defense Reorganization Act of 1986, have increased interservice cooperation and centralization of the military hierarchy. The **secretary of defense** manages a budget larger than the entire budget of most nations and is the president's main civilian adviser on national defense matters.

The commanding officers of each of the services, along with a chairperson and vice chairperson, constitute the **Joint Chiefs of Staff.** American military leaders are sometimes portrayed as aggressive hawks in policymaking, presumably eager to crush some small nation with a show of American force. Richard Betts carefully examined the Joint Chiefs' advice to the president in many crises and found them to be no more likely than civilian advisers to push an aggressive military policy. (The most hawkish advice, incidentally, came from the admirals. The most dovish advice came from the army generals and the marine corps.)[4] On several occasions during the Reagan administration, the president's uniformed advisers cautioned against aggressive actions—including the use of military force—favored by the State Department. The military was similarly conservative regarding the use of force against Iraq in 1991[5] and intervention in the civil wars in Eastern Europe. Steeped in the mythology of generals like George Patton and Curtis LeMay, many Americans would be surprised at the cautious attitudes of America's top military leaders today.

American foreign and military policies are supposed to be coordinated. The *National Security Council (NSC)* was formed in 1947 for this purpose. The NSC is composed of the president, the vice president, the secretary of defense, and the secretary of state. The NSC staff is managed by the president's national security assistant—a position that first gained public prominence with the flamboyant, globe-trotting Henry Kissinger during President Nixon's first term.

Despite the coordinating role assigned to the NSC, conflict within the foreign policy establishment remains common. The NSC staff has sometimes competed with, rather than integrated, policy advice from cabinet departments—particularly State and Defense. It has also become involved in covert operations. A scandal erupted in November 1986 when NSC staff were found to be involved in a secret operation to sell battlefield missiles to Iran in return for Iranian help in gaining the release of hostages held by Iranian-backed terrorists in Lebanon. Some of the money from the sale was

secretary of defense

The head of the Department of Defense and the president's key adviser on military policy; a key **foreign policy** actor.

Joint Chiefs of Staff

The commanding officers of the armed services who advise the president on military policy.

Issues of the Times

The Issue: Managing Crises

A crisis is a sudden, unpredictable, and potentially dangerous event. Most crises focus on some aspect of national security policy. The stakes in a crisis are high, typically involving life and death. Someone must manage a crisis, and the job usually falls to the president, who can come to quick and consistent decisions, confine information to a small group, carefully oversee developments, and call upon experts in the executive branch.

What makes crisis management especially difficult is that crises do not necessarily occur serially. Instead, there is often more than one crisis occurring at a time. Multiple crises raise profound questions for governing. How well can a president focus on several critical matters at the same time? What is the personal toll on a president who manages multiple crises? Equally important, what happens to domestic policy issues when crises dominate the president's time, the media and the public's attention, and perhaps the budget as well?

Read All About It

Crises, Crises Everywhere. What Is a President to Do?

By Todd S. Purdum
February 9, 2003

If, as F. Scott Fitzgerald wrote, "the test of a first-rate intelligence is the ability to hold two opposed ideas in mind at the same time and still retain the ability to function," the test of a successful presidency may be the ability to multitask in crises. In fact, it's more or less the definition of the job.

Sure, President Bush had a full week: a space disaster and a wrenching memorial service, a $2.23 trillion budget proposal to Congress, a

North Korean threat of "total war," a dramatic showdown at the United Nations over Iraqi defiance of weapons inspections, a stepped-up orange-level terrorism alert based on ominous intelligence rumblings.

But the current confluence of challenging events is hardly new. Harry S. Truman faced almost non-stop crises from the moment he took office after Franklin D. Roosevelt's death in 1945. Roosevelt himself managed the Depression, then a global war, not to mention paralysis.

In 1957, Dwight D. Eisenhower was in the middle of a crisis over

desegregation of Central High School in Little Rock, Ark., when the Soviet Union launched Sputnik, a silver satellite the size of a beachball, setting off a panic about preparedness in the cold war. By his own account, Richard M. Nixon managed "Six Crises" before he ever reached the White House, then created a doozy of his own in Watergate. Bill Clinton complained that it was his bad luck to be president in placid times of plenty, when greatness cannot easily emerge, then

Please see Crises   **Page 621**

Crises

Continued from Page 620

managed to become the second president in history to be impeached.

"This is what a president is—a crisis manager," said the historian Robert Dallek, who wrote a two-volume biography of Johnson and has just finished another on Kennedy. "Of course, what suffers in all of this is any domestic agenda a president has. A standard reality is that war kills reform. The Spanish-American war killed populism, World War I killed Progressivism, World War II killed the New Deal, Korea killed the Fair Deal, Vietnam the Great Society."

Mr. Bush is not the first president to govern in a 24-hour news cycle, but the endless drumbeat no doubt worsens the sense of perpetual crisis. The media, and sometimes the politicians themselves, have a tendency to inflate every event, from a school shooting to a sniper on the loose to the prospect of nuclear war, into a round-the-clock happening.

Daniel Schorr, the veteran broadcast journalist, acknowledged on NPR last week that Washington has a hard time managing multiple problems and tends to be a "one-thing-at-a-time type of town." Attention spans are short, politicians rise and fall, issues come and go.

To all appearances, Mr. Bush often seems the calmest one in the storm. For months, he has remained steadily determined to disarm Saddam Hussein, first in the face of warnings that doing so without a Middle East peace risked Arab rage, and now despite worries that North Korea is the more volatile threat.

Ronald Reagan survived an assassination attempt after just weeks in office, then went on to face recession, survive the Iran-contra scandal and help end the cold war. Lyndon B. Johnson fared less well waging the Vietnam War while trying to build a Great Society, and was ultimately consumed by wrenching public division.

Harry C. McPherson Jr., who was Johnson's special counsel, said

> Mr. Bush is not the first president to govern in a 24-hour news cycle, but the endless drumbeat no doubt worsens the sense of perpetual crisis. The media, and sometimes the politicians themselves, have a tendency to inflate every event, from a school shooting to a sniper on the loose to the prospect of nuclear war, into a round-the-clock happening.

he marked the toll of White House crises in the annual albums of photographs that the Johnsons gave the senior staff at Christmas. "I got there in '65, and by '67 I looked pale and overtaxed and Johnson looked very gray."

There are costs and casualties for failing to keep up with events. The first President Bush soared to stratospheric approval ratings after the Persian Gulf war, but was seen as out of touch with a faltering economy and unemployed Americans. Jimmy Carter micromanaged the White House tennis courts but could not manage to confront a national malaise and the failure to rescue American hostages in Iran.

Sometimes the price is more personal. Everyone remembers Truman's acid letter to Paul Hume, The *Washington Post* music critic who panned the singing of his daughter, Margaret. Less well remembered is the week that led up to Truman's outburst.

On Nov. 28, 1950, Truman received word that the Chinese had plunged into the Korean War, with a quarter-million troops in a furious assault. Two days later, Truman set off a worldwide firestorm by suggesting at a news conference that the United States was prepared to use the atomic bomb in Korea. The man responsible for trying to calm that crisis was the president's press secretary, Charlie Ross, who was also his longtime friend.

On Tuesday, Dec. 5, Ross dropped dead of a heart attack, hours before Miss Truman's concert at Constitution Hall. The president kept the news from her until afterward. The next morning, when the president read Hume's assessment that Miss Truman "is flat a good deal of the time," he reached for paper and pen.

"Some day I hope to meet you," Truman wrote. "When that happens you'll need a new nose, a lot of beefsteak for black eyes, and perhaps a supporter below!"

Think About It

- How well do you think presidents have handled multiple crises?
- Are there changes the president could make in the way the White House works that would make it easier to handle crises?
- Would it be possible for the president to share the burden of managing crises?
- Is it necessary that crises abroad undermine attempts for reform at home?

funneled secretly to anti-Communist rebels (called *Contras*) fighting the Nicaraguan government, despite a congressional ban on such aid.

The scandal, termed the Iran-Contra affair, resulted in the resignation of the president's assistant for national security affairs, Vice Admiral John Poindexter, and the sacking of a number of lower-level NSC officials, including Lieutenant Colonel Oliver North. North went from obscurity to national prominence overnight as he described his involvement in the affair before a televised congressional inquiry in 1987. Both Poindexter and North were subsequently convicted of felony charges related to the diversion of funds and misleading Congress, but their convictions were overturned because their testimony before Congress, given under conditions of immunity, was judged to have been used against them in court.

No discussion of the institutional structures of foreign policy would be complete without mention of the **Central Intelligence Agency (CIA)**. "The Company," as the CIA is known to insiders, was created after World War II to coordinate American information- and data-gathering intelligence activities abroad and to collect, analyze, and evaluate its own intelligence. Technically, its budget and staff are secret; estimates put them at $5 billion and more than 20,000 people.

Central Intelligence Agency (CIA)

An agency created after World War II to coordinate American intelligence activities abroad. It became involved in intrigue, conspiracy, and meddling as well.

The CIA plays a vital role in providing information and analysis necessary for effective development and implementation of national security policy. Most of its activities are uncontroversial because the bulk of the material it collects and analyzes comes from readily available sources such as government reports and newspapers. However, the CIA also collects information by espionage. Most people accept the necessity of this form of information collection when it is directed against foreign adversaries. However, in the 1970s it was discovered that at times the agency had also engaged in wiretaps, interception of mail, and the infiltration of interest groups—in the United States. These actions violated the CIA's charter, and revelations of spying on Americans who disagreed with the foreign policy of the administration badly damaged the agency's morale and external political support.

The CIA also has a long history of involvement in other nations' internal affairs. After the end of World War II, when Eastern European nations had fallen under Moscow's shadow and Western European nations were teetering, the CIA provided aid to anti-Communist parties in Italy and West Germany. It was no less busy in the developing countries where, for example, it nurtured coups in Iran in 1953 and in

The national security establishment is large and the National Security Council is designed to integrate options and information for the president. Here President Bush talks to national security assistant Condoleezza Rice, who headed the NSC staff in the president's first term.

Guatemala in 1954. The CIA has also trained and supported armies—the most notable, of course, in Vietnam.

In the 1980s, a major controversy surrounded the CIA's activity in Central America, particularly in Nicaragua, where the Marxist government developed close ties with the Soviet Union and Cuba and embarked on a massive military buildup. Determined to undermine the regime, the Reagan administration aggressively supported armed rebels (Contras). Congressional inquiries into the Iran-Contra affair suggested that the CIA, under Director William Casey, was quietly involved in covert operations to assist the Contra rebels.[6]

Reconciling covert activities with the principles of open democratic government remains a challenge for public officials. With the end of the Cold War, there was less pressure for covert activities and a climate more conducive to conventional intelligence gathering. Currently, Congress requires the CIA to inform relevant congressional committees promptly of current and anticipated covert operations. In the meantime, there is substantial debate on the role of the CIA in the post-Cold War era.

The failure to predict the terrorist attack on September 11, 2001, increased the intensity of this debate, with many leaders calling for an increase in covert capabilities. Perhaps more disconcerting was the CIA's conclusion that Iraq possessed weapons of mass destruction. Destroying these weapons became the principal justification for the war, and their absence was a major embarrassment for the Agency and the Bush administration.

There are numerous other components of America's intelligence community. For example, the National Reconnaissance Office uses imagery satellites to monitor missile sites and other military activities around the world, and the National Security Agency is on the cutting edge of electronic eavesdropping capabilities.

After World War II, these military and foreign policy institutions grew steadily. As the American role on the world stage grew, so did the importance of these institutions as foreign policy instruments.

Congress.   The U.S. Congress shares with the president constitutional authority over foreign and defense policy (see Chapters 12 and 13). Congress has sole authority, for example, to declare war, raise and organize the armed forces, and appropriate funds for national security activities. The Senate determines whether treaties will be ratified and ambassadorial and cabinet nominations confirmed. The "power of the purse" (see Chapter 14) and responsibilities for oversight of the executive branch give Congress considerable clout, and each year senators and representatives carefully examine defense budget authorizations.[7]

Congress' important constitutional role in foreign and defense policy is sometimes misunderstood. It is a common mistake among some journalists, executive officials, and even members of Congress to believe that the Constitution vests foreign policy decisions solely in the president. Sometimes this erroneous view leads to perverse results, such as the Iran-Contra affair that dominated the news in late 1986 and much of 1987. Officials at high levels in the executive branch "sought to protect the president's 'exclusive' prerogative by lying to Congress, to allies, to the public, and to one another." Louis Fisher suggests that such actions undermined the "mutual trust and close coordination by the two branches that are essential attributes in building a foreign policy that ensures continuity and stability."[8]

American Foreign Policy: An Overview

Throughout most of its history, the United States followed a foreign policy course called **isolationism.** This policy, articulated by George Washington in his farewell address, directed the country to stay out of other nations' conflicts, particularly European wars. The famous *Monroe Doctrine*, enunciated by President James

isolationism

A **foreign policy** course followed throughout most of our nation's history, whereby the United States has tried to stay out of other nations' conflicts, particularly European wars. Isolationism was reaffirmed by the Monroe Doctrine.

From Stand-alone to
Superpower:
The Evolution of Foreign
and Military Policy

Monroe, reaffirmed America's inattention to Europe's problems but warned European nations to stay out of Latin America. The United States—believing that its own political backyard included Central and South America—did not hesitate to send marines, gunboats, or both to intervene in South American and Caribbean affairs. When European nations were at war, however, Americans relished their distance from the conflicts. So it was until World War I (1914–1918).

In the wake of World War I, President Woodrow Wilson urged the United States to join the League of Nations, a forerunner to the United Nations. The U.S. Senate refused to ratify the League of Nations treaty, indicating that the country was neither ready to abandon the long-standing American habit of isolationism nor was the Senate ready to turn over its war-making authority to an international body. It was World War II, which forced the United States into a global conflict, that dealt a deathblow to American isolationism. A charter for the United Nations was signed at a conference in San Francisco in 1945. The United States was an original signatory and soon donated land to house the United Nations permanently in New York City.

The Cold War

At the end of World War II, Germany and Japan were vanquished and much of Europe was strewn with rubble. The United States was unquestionably the dominant world power, both economically and militarily. It not only had helped to bring the war to an end but also had inaugurated a new era in warfare by dropping the first atomic bombs on Japan in August 1945. Because only the United States possessed nuclear weapons, Americans looked forward to an era of peace secured by their nuclear umbrella.

After World War II, the United States forged strong alliances with the nations of Western Europe. To help them rebuild their economies, the United States poured billions of dollars into war-ravaged European nations through a program known as the Marshall Plan—named after its architect, Secretary of State George C. Marshall. A military alliance was also forged; the creation of NATO in 1949 affirmed the mutual military interests of the United States and Western Europe, and NATO remains a cornerstone of American foreign and defense policy.

Containment Abroad and Anti-Communism at Home.   Although many Americans expected cooperative relations with their wartime ally, the Soviet Union, they soon abandoned these hopes. There is still much dispute about how the Cold War between the United States and the Soviet Union started.[9] Even before World War II ended, some American policymakers feared that their Soviet allies were intent on spreading Communism not only to their neighbors but everywhere. All of Eastern Europe fell under Soviet domination as World War II ended. In 1946, Winston Churchill warned that the Russians had sealed off Eastern Europe with an "iron curtain."

Communist support of a revolt in Greece in 1946 compounded fears of Soviet aggression. Writing in *Foreign Affairs* in 1947, foreign policy strategist George F. Kennan proposed a policy of "containment."[10] His **containment doctrine** called for the United States to isolate the Soviet Union—to "contain" its advances and resist its encroachments—by peaceful means if possible, but with force if necessary. When economic problems forced Great Britain to decrease its support of Greece, the United States stepped in with the Truman Doctrine of helping other nations oppose Communism. The Soviet Union responded with the Berlin Blockade of 1948–1949, in which it closed off land access to West Berlin (which was surrounded by Communist East Germany). The United States and its allies broke the blockade by airlifting food, fuel, and other necessities to the people of the beleaguered city.

The fall of China to Mao Zedong's Communist-led forces in 1949 seemed to confirm American fears that Communism was a cancer spreading over the "free world." In the same year, the Soviet Union exploded its first atomic bomb. The invasion of pro-

containment doctrine

A **foreign policy** strategy advocated by George Kennan that called for the United States to isolate the Soviet Union, "contain" its advances, and resist its encroachments by peaceful means if possible, but by force if necessary.

American South Korea by Communist North Korea in 1950 further fueled American fears of Soviet imperialism. President Truman said bluntly, "We've got to stop the Russians now" and sent American troops to Korea under United Nations auspices. The Korean War was a chance to put containment into practice. Involving China as well as North Korea, the war dragged on until July 27, 1953.

The 1950s were the height of the **Cold War**; though hostilities never quite erupted into armed battle between them, the United States and the Soviet Union were often on the brink of war. John Foster Dulles, secretary of state under Eisenhower, proclaimed a policy often referred to as "brinkmanship," in which the United States was to be prepared to use nuclear weapons in order to *deter* the Soviet Union and Communist China from taking aggressive actions.

Fear of Communism affected domestic as well as foreign policy. Most Americans believed that international Communism was conspiratorial, insidious, and bent on world domination and infiltrating American government and cultural institutions. Senator Joseph McCarthy exploited this atmosphere and with flimsy evidence accused scores of prominent Americans and State Department officials of being Communists. **McCarthyism** flowered during the Korean War. Domestic policy in general was deeply affected by the Cold War and by anti-Communist fears. A burgeoning defense budget during the Korean War and later in the 1950s was another result of the Cold War.

The Swelling of the Pentagon. The Cold War ensured that military needs and massive national security expenditures would remain fixtures in the American economy. As early as 1947, aircraft manufacturers noted that the decline of military procurement after World War II would injure the industry; to avert dislocation, they launched a campaign to sell planes to the U.S. Air Force.[11] Thus were forged some of the first links between policymakers' perceptions of the Soviet threat and corporations' awareness of potential profits from military hardware. Generals and admirals believed that they needed weapons systems, and private industry was happy to supply them for a profit. Defense expenditures grew to be the largest component of the federal budget in the 1950s, consuming $13 of every $100 of the gross domestic product (GDP) by 1954. Large parts of this defense budget were spent on weapons supplied by giant companies such as Westinghouse, RCA, Western Electric, and General Motors.

The interests shared by the armed services and defense contractors produced what some call a *military-industrial complex*. The phrase was coined not by a left-wing critic of the military but by President Dwight D. Eisenhower, a former general. Elite theorists especially pointed to this tight alliance between business and government.

In 1963, President John F. Kennedy looked over the Berlin Wall, which the Soviet Union had built to separate Communist East Berlin from the western sectors of the city. The wall stood as the most palpable symbol of the Cold War for almost 30 years until it was torn down in 1989.

Cold War

War by other than military means usually emphasizing ideological conflict, such as that between the United States and the Soviet Union from the end of World War II until the 1990s.

McCarthyism

The fear, prevalent in the 1950s, that international Communism was conspiratorial, insidious, bent on world domination, and infiltrating American government and cultural institutions. It was named after Senator Joseph McCarthy and flourished after the Korean War.

Simulation
You Are President
John F. Kennedy

arms race

A tense relationship beginning in the 1950s between the Soviet Union and the United States whereby one side's weaponry became the other side's goad to procure more weaponry, and so on.

Economist Seymour Melman wrote about *pentagon capitalism*, linking the military's drive to expand with the profit motives of private industry.[12] As the defense budget grew, so did the profits of aircraft producers and other defense contractors.

By the 1950s, the Soviet Union and the United States were engaged in an **arms race.** One side's weaponry goaded the other side to procure yet more weaponry, as one missile led to another. By the mid-1960s, the result of the arms race was a point of *mutual assured destruction (MAD)*, in which each side could annihilate the other, even after absorbing a surprise attack. Later sections of this chapter will examine efforts to control the arms race.

The Vietnam War.   Even though it reached its peak during the 1960s, American involvement in Vietnam began much earlier. The Korean War and the 1949 victory of Communist forces in China fixed the U.S. government's attention on Asian Communism. In 1950, while the Korean War raged and just after the fall of Chiang Kai-shek in China, President Truman decided to aid France's effort to retain its colonial possessions in Southeast Asia.[13]

Aided by the new Communist government in China, the Vietnamese Communists finally defeated the French in a battle at Dien Bien Phu in 1954. The morning after the battle, peace talks among the participants and other major powers began in Geneva, Switzerland.

Though a party to the resultant agreements, the United States never accepted the Geneva agreement, which stipulated that national elections be held in Vietnam in 1956. Instead, it began supporting one non-Communist leader after another in South Vietnam, each seemingly more committed than the last to defeating Communist forces in the north.

Vietnam first became an election-year issue in 1964. President Lyndon B. Johnson, who had succeeded John F. Kennedy, was seeking his first full term and promised that he would not "send American boys . . . to do what Asian boys ought to be doing" to defend the pro-American regime in South Vietnam. His Republican opponent, Barry Goldwater, advocated tough action in Vietnam; he promised to send American troops if necessary and even defoliate the jungles with chemicals so that the Communist guerrillas would have no place to hide.

There was a standing joke among Johnson's opponents after his victory in 1964: "They told me that if I voted for Goldwater, we'd have half a million American troops in Vietnam in four years. I did, and we do." Unable to contain the forces of the Communist guerillas and the North Vietnamese army with American military advisers, Johnson sent in American troops—more than 500,000 at the peak of the undeclared war. He dropped more bombs on Communist North Vietnam than the United States had dropped on Germany in all of World War II. American troops and massive firepower failed to contain the North Vietnamese, however. At home, widespread protests against the war contributed to Johnson's decisions not to run for reelection in 1968 and to begin peace negotiations.

The new Nixon administration prosecuted the war vigorously, in Cambodia as well as in Vietnam, but also negotiated with the Vietnamese Communists. A peace treaty was signed in 1973, but no one expected it to hold. South Vietnam's capital, Saigon, finally fell to the North Vietnamese army in 1975. South and North Vietnam were reunited into a single nation, and Saigon was renamed Ho Chi Minh City, in honor of the late leader of Communist North Vietnam.

Looking back on the Vietnam War, few Americans think it was worthwhile. It divided the nation and made citizens painfully aware of the government's ability to lie to them—and (perhaps worse) to itself. It reminded Americans that even a "great power" cannot prevail in a protracted military conflict against a determined enemy unless there is a clear objective and unless the national will is sufficiently committed to expend vast resources on the task.

The Vietnam War Memorial is one of Washington, D.C.'s most moving sights. Often called "The Wall," the memorial lists the names of more than 58,000 Americans killed during the Vietnam War.

The Era of Détente

Even while the Vietnam War was being waged, Richard Nixon—a veteran fighter of the Cold War—supported a new policy that came to be called *détente*. The term was popularized by Nixon's national security adviser and later secretary of state, Henry Kissinger.

Détente represented a slow transformation from conflict thinking to cooperative thinking in foreign policy strategy. It sought a relaxation of tensions between the superpowers, coupled with firm guarantees of mutual security. The policy assumed that the United States and the Soviet Union had no long-range, irrevocable sources of conflict; that both had an interest in peace and world stability; and that a nuclear war was—and should be—unthinkable. Thus foreign policy battles between the United States and the Soviet Union were to be waged with diplomatic, economic, and propaganda weapons; the threat of force was downplayed.

One major initiative emerging from détente was the *Strategic Arms Limitation Talks (SALT)*. These talks represented a mutual effort by the United States and the Soviet Union to limit the growth of their nuclear capabilities, with each power maintaining sufficient nuclear weapons to deter a surprise attack by the other. The first SALT accord was signed by Nixon in 1972 and was followed by negotiations for a second agreement, SALT II. After six years of laborious negotiations, the agreement was finally signed and sent to the Senate by President Carter in 1979. The Soviet invasion of Afghanistan that year caused Carter to withdraw the treaty from Senate consideration, however, even though both he and Ronald Reagan insisted that they would remain committed to the agreement's limitations on nuclear weaponry.

The United States applied the philosophy of détente to the People's Republic of China as well as to the Soviet Union. After the fall of the pro-American government in 1949, the United States refused to extend diplomatic recognition to the world's most populous nation, recognizing instead the government in exile on the nearby island of Taiwan. As a senator in the early 1950s, Richard Nixon had been an implacable foe of "Red China," even suggesting that the Democratic administration had traitorously "lost" China. Nevertheless, two decades later it was this same Richard Nixon who, as president, first visited the People's Republic and sent an American mission there. President Jimmy Carter extended formal diplomatic recognition to China in

détente

A slow transformation from conflict thinking to cooperative thinking in **foreign policy** strategy and policymaking. It sought a relaxation of tensions between the superpowers, coupled with firm guarantees of mutual security.

January 1979. Since then, cultural and economic ties between the United States and China have increased greatly.

Not everyone favored détente, however. Even Carter called for a substantial increase in defense spending after the Soviet Union invaded Afghanistan in 1979. Few people saw more threats from the Soviet Union than did Ronald Reagan, who called it the "Evil Empire." He viewed the Soviet invasion of Afghanistan as typical Russian aggression that, if unchecked, could only grow more common. He hailed anti-Communist governments everywhere and pledged to increase American defense spending.

The Reagan Rearmament

From the mid-1950s to 1981 (with the exception of the Vietnam War), the defense budget had generally been declining as a percentage of both the total federal budget and the GDP. In 1955, during the Eisenhower administration, the government was spending 61 percent of its budget for defense purposes, or about 10 percent of the GDP (the total value of all the goods and services produced annually by the United States). By the time President Reagan took office in 1981, less than 25 percent of the federal budget and 5.2 percent of the GDP were devoted to defense expenditures. These figures reflected a substantial cut indeed, although the decrease came about more because levels of social spending had increased than because military spending had declined. Still, Republican Richard Nixon used to boast that he was the first president in recent history who committed more of the national budget to social services than to military expenditures.

During his campaign for the presidency, Reagan argued that "We cannot negotiate arms control agreements that will slow down the Soviet military buildup as long as we let the Soviets move ahead of us in every category of armaments." According to Reagan, America faced a "window of vulnerability" because the Soviet Union was galloping ahead of the United States in military spending.

As president, Reagan was determined to reverse the trend of diminishing defense spending and proposed the largest peacetime defense spending increase in American history: a five-year defense buildup costing $1.5 trillion. The early days of the Reagan administration were the most critical in this defense buildup. The news came down to the Pentagon rank and file quickly: President Carter's last budget had proposed a large increase in defense spending, and the Reagan administration would add $32 billion on top of that. Defense officials were ordered to find places to spend more money.[14] These heady days for the Pentagon lasted only through the first term of Reagan's presidency, however. In his second term, concern over huge budget deficits brought defense spending to a standstill. After taking inflation into account, Congress appropriated no increase in defense spending at all from 1985 to 1988.

In 1983 President Reagan added another element to his defense policy—a new plan for defense against missiles. He called it the **Strategic Defense Initiative (SDI)**; critics quickly renamed it "Star Wars." Reagan's plans for SDI proposed creating a global umbrella in space, wherein computers would scan the skies and use various high-tech devices to destroy invading missiles. The administration proposed a research program that would have cost tens of billions of dollars over the next decade.

In the face of an onslaught of criticism regarding the feasibility of SDI, its proponents reduced their expectations about the size and capabilities of any defensive shield that could be erected over the next generation. Talk of a smaller system—capable of protecting against an accidental launch of a few missiles or against a threat by some third-world country with nuclear weapons—replaced the dream of an impenetrable umbrella over the United States capable of defeating a massive Soviet nuclear strike.

Strategic Defense Initiative (SDI)

Renamed "Star Wars" by critics, a plan for defense against the Soviet Union unveiled by President Reagan in 1983. SDI would create a global umbrella in space, using computers to scan the skies and high-tech devices to destroy invading missiles.

The Final Thaw in the Cold War

On May 12, 1989, in a commencement address at Texas A&M University, President Bush announced a new era in American foreign policy. He termed this era one "beyond containment"; the United States' goal would be more than containing Soviet expansion. Bush declared that it was time to seek the integration of the Soviet Union into the community of nations.

The Cold War ended as few had anticipated—spontaneously. Suddenly, the elusive objective of 40 years of post-World War II U.S. foreign policy—freedom and self-determination for Eastern Europeans and Soviet peoples and the reduction of the military threat from the East—occurred. Forces of change sparked by Soviet leader Mikhail Gorbachev led to a staggering wave of upheaval that shattered Communist regimes and the postwar barriers between Eastern and Western Europe. The Berlin Wall, the most prominent symbol of oppression in Eastern Europe, came tumbling down on November 9, 1989, and East and West Germany formed a unified, democratic republic. The former Soviet Union split into 15 separate nations, and non-Communist governments formed in most of them. Poland, Czechoslovakia (splitting into the Czech Republic and Slovakia), and Hungary established democratic governments, and reformers overthrew the old-line Communist leaders in Bulgaria and Romania.

Events were unfolding so fast and in so many places at once that no one was quite sure how to deal with them. President Bush declared, "Every morning I receive an intelligence briefing, and I receive the best information available to any world leader today. And yet, the morning news is often overtaken by the news that very same evening."[15]

In 1989, reform seemed on the verge of occurring in China as well as in Eastern Europe. That spring in Tiananmen Square, the central meeting place in Beijing, thousands of students held protests on behalf of democratization. Unable to tolerate challenges to their rule any longer, the aging Chinese leaders forcibly—and brutally—evacuated the square, crushing some protestors under armored tanks. It is still not clear how many students were killed and how many others arrested, but the reform movement in China received a serious setback. This suppression of efforts to develop democracy sent a chill through what had been a warming relationship between the United States and the People's Republic of China (see "You Are the Policymaker: Defending Human Rights").

Beginning in 1989, Communism in the Soviet Union and in Eastern Europe suddenly began to crumble. The end of the Cold War between East and West reduced the threat of nuclear war between the superpowers, but it also left a host of difficult new national security issues in its wake. Here, workers dismantle the head from a huge granite statue of Lenin in Berlin in 1991.

You Are the Policymaker
Defending Human Rights

Americans sat riveted to their television screens for several weeks in May and June of 1989 as they watched Chinese students and workers in Beijing's Tiananmen Square protest on behalf of greater democracy. This was heady stuff for the world's most populous country, apparently emerging from two generations of totalitarian rule.

For a time it looked as though China's rulers would accommodate demands for reform. On the night of June 3, however, the army violently crushed the democracy movement, killing hundreds—perhaps thousands—of protestors and beginning a wave of executions, arrests, and repression.

Westerners were shocked at the bloodshed and widely condemned the Chinese government. Regardless, in July and December 1989, President Bush sent national security adviser Brent Scowcroft and Deputy Secretary of State Lawrence Eagleburger to meet secretly with Chinese leaders. Later, Bush also lifted some economic sanctions against China. The president claimed he was not normalizing relations with China, but many political leaders criticized him for moral capitulation to the hard-line Communist leaders.

The president asked, "How else should nuclear powers deal with each other?" and pointed out that the United States maintains relations with many countries that have even more egregious records of human rights violations than China. In addition, Bush argued that keeping the lines of communication open would increase his ability to encourage the Chinese leaders to moderate their repression.

His critics responded, "How can you deal with immoral leaders who slaughter their own people for nonviolently advocating rights that Americans cherish? Is there no place for morality in international relations?"

President Clinton faced a similar dilemma. In his 1999 State of the Union message, he told the American people that stability in China could "no longer be bought at the expense of liberty." But then he added, "It's important not to isolate China. The more we bring China into the world, the more the world will bring change and freedom to China."

Both President Bush and President Clinton were also mindful of the potentially vast market that China provided for U.S. goods and services and the role of the contribution that capitalism might make to political freedom. Their critics argued that we should not sell out our principles for a greater market share.

If you were the president, what would *you* do?

Reform continued elsewhere, however. On June 17, 1992, Boris Yeltsin addressed a joint session of the U.S. Congress. When the burly, silver-haired president of the new Russian republic entered the House chamber, members of Congress greeted him with chants of "Bo-ris, Bo-ris" and hailed him with numerous standing ovations.

Yeltsin proclaimed to thunderous applause,

The idol of communism, which spread everywhere social strife, animosity and unparalleled brutality, which instilled fear in humanity, has collapsed . . . I am here to assure you that we will not let it rise again in our land.

The Cold War that had been waged for two generations had ended, and the West, led by the United States, had won.

The War on Terrorism

Perhaps the most troublesome issue in the national security area is the spread of terrorism—the use of violence to demoralize and frighten a country's population or government. Terrorism takes many forms, including the bombing of buildings (such as the attacks on New York and Washington on September 11, 2001, on the American embassy in Kenya in 1998, and on the World Trade Center in New York in 1993) and ships (such as the *USS Cole* in Yemen in 2000), the assassinations of political leaders (as when Iraq attempted to kill former president George Bush in 1993), and the kidnappings of diplomats and civilians (as when Iranians took Americans hostage in 1979).

It is difficult to defend against terrorism, especially in an open society. Terrorists have the advantage of stealth and surprise. Improved security measures and better intelligence gathering can help. So, perhaps, can punishing governments and organizations that engage in terrorist activities. In 1986, the United States launched an air attack on Libya in response to Libyan-supported acts of terrorism; in 1993, the United States struck at Iraq's intelligence center in response to a foiled plot to assassinate former president George Bush; and in 1998, the United States launched an attack in Afghanistan on Osama bin Laden, the leader of a terrorist organization.

Terrorism takes many forms, including the bombing of buildings and ships. Shown here are terrorist attacks on the World Trade Center in New York in 2001, the American embassy in Kenya in 1998, and the *USS Cole* in Yemen in 2000.

Following the September 11, 2001, attacks on New York and Washington, the United States declared war on terrorism. President George W. Bush made the war the highest priority of his administration, and the United States launched an attack on the Taliban regime that had been harboring terrorists in Afghanistan. The Taliban fell in short order, although many suspected terrorist members of Osama bin Laden's Al Qaeda network escaped. In the meantime, the president declared that Iran, Iraq, and North Korea formed an "axis of evil" and began laying plans to remove Iraqi President Saddam Hussein from power. In 2003, a U.S.-led coalition toppled Hussein.

Despite its risks and uncertainties, the Cold War was characterized by a stable and predictable set of relations among the great powers. Now international relations have entered an era of improvisation as nations struggle to develop creative responses to changes in the global balance of power and the new challenges that have emerged.

The threat posed by terrorist groups and the hostile states supporting them has forced America to reconsider basic tenets of its national security policy. President George W. Bush believes that the strategies and institutions that kept the peace during the Cold War are not suited to a twenty-first-century campaign against terrorism. He has concluded that multilateral alliances like NATO and bilateral partnerships like that with South Korea have proven ineffective in dealing with terrorism. Thus, the United States is moving away from a system of formal, structured alliances and into more fluid system of ad hoc alignments of nations in which the mission determines the alliance.

The Bush administration developed a new strategic doctrine that moves away from the Cold War pillars of containment and deterrence toward a policy that supports preemptive strikes against terrorists and hostile states with chemical, biological, or nuclear weapons. Thus, the president wishes to add preemption and "defensive intervention" as formal options.

The national security strategy doctrine issued by the Bush administration in September 2002 is the most dramatic and far-reaching change in national security policy in a half-century.[16] It substitutes preemption of potential threats for deterrence and containment of aggression by hostile nations or groups that appear determined to use weapons of mass destruction against the United States. The strategic doctrine also explicitly advocates U.S. preeminence in military capabilities and, if necessary, unilateral action in national security policy, contrary to decades of emphasis on grounding defense policy in alliances.[17]

The U.S. invasion of Iraq in 2003 followed directly from these premises. It was a policy designed to preempt future strikes against the United States and its allies. The absence of support from core members of NATO and the potential damage to our most enduring alliances did not deter the president. Nor did the lack of support from the United Nations.

Toppling dictators carries with it new problems, however. In the 2000 presidential campaign, George W. Bush spoke of "humility" in foreign affairs and warned against "nation-building" and overextending America's military. The threat of terrorism, leading to the invasions of both Afghanistan and Iraq, caused the president to rethink these views, and the administration began talking about meeting America's "unparalleled responsibilities." One of those responsibilities has been to rebuild and democratize Iraq. As both U.S. expenditures on the process and American casualties mounted in the period since the end of the war with Iraq, the public's support for the effort declined substantially and the president experienced a corresponding drop in his approval ratings.

Some see the war on terrorism as responding to a tactic (terrorism) rather than to the forces that generate it. Critics also fear that the arrogation of a unilateral right to define threats and use force is squandering America's moral authority and diminishing our global credibility. They argue that the Unites States cannot defend itself without the help of others and thus American national security is inextricably tied to international security.[18]

Almost everyone agrees that today's complicated international environment portends an overhaul of the American national security infrastructure. Armed forces and alliances, defense industries, and budgets built up since World War II are being reassessed in light of both the Cold War thaw and the war on terrorism.

The Politics of Defense Policy

The politics of national defense involves high stakes—the nation's security, for example. Domestic political concerns, budgetary limitations, and ideology all influence decisions on the structure of defense policy and negotiations with allies and adversaries. All public policies include budgets, people, and equipment. In the realm of national defense, these elements are especially critical because of the size of the budget and the bureaucracy, as well as the destructive potential of modern weapons.

At the core of defense policy is a judgment about what the United States will defend. The central assumption of current American defense policy is that the United States requires forces and equipment sufficient to win decisively a single major conflict, defend American territory against new threats, and conduct a number of holding actions elsewhere around the world. A large military infrastructure is necessary to meet these goals.

Defense Spending

Defense spending now makes up about one-fifth of the federal budget. Although this is a much smaller percentage than in earlier years (see Figure 20.2), vast sums of money and fundamental questions of public policy are still involved (see Chapter 14). Some scholars have argued that America faces a trade-off between defense spending and social spending. A nation, they claim, must choose between guns and butter, and more guns mean less butter. Evidence supporting the existence of such a trade-off is mixed, however. In general, defense and domestic policy expenditures appear to be independent of each other.[19] Ronald Reagan's efforts to increase military budgets while cutting back on domestic policy expenditures seem to have stemmed more from his own ideology than from any inevitable choice between the two.

Defense spending is a thorny political issue, entangled with ideological disputes. Conservatives advocate increases in defense spending, pointing out that many nations and terrorist organizations retain potent military capability, and insist that America maintain its readiness at a high level. They refer to the Gulf War and the Iraq War to prove that wars on a significant scale are still possible. In addition, they attribute the collapse of Communism in Eastern and Central Europe to Western toughness and the massive increase in defense spending that occurred in the early 1980s. When the Soviet Union saw that it could not outspend the United States, they argue, it finally decided not to continue to allocate so much of its scarce resources to defense and to loosen its grip on Eastern Europe.

Liberals have supported increased defense spending for the war on terrorism. More generally, however, they are skeptical of defense spending, maintaining that the Pentagon wastes money and that the United States buys too many guns and too little butter. The most crucial aspect of national defense, they argue, is a strong economy, which is based on investments in "human capital" such as health and education. Liberals insist that the erosion of the Communist Party's authority was well under way when Gorbachev rose to power. This erosion accelerated as *glasnost* (the Russian term for the new openness of society) made the party's failures a matter of public ridicule as democratization freed new forces to challenge the existing order.

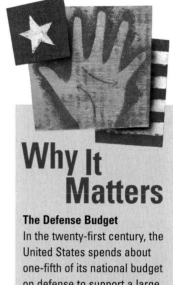

Why It Matters

The Defense Budget
In the twenty-first century, the United States spends about one-fifth of its national budget on defense to support a large defense establishment. This expenditure contributes to large annual budget deficits, but some argue that we should spend even more to protect the country against terrorism.

Figure 20.2   Trends in Defense Spending

John F. Kennedy took office in 1961 at the height of the Cold War. National defense was the dominant public policy for the U.S. government; it accounted for half of all the money ("outlays") the government spent that year. Things have changed dramatically since then, however. Although defense spending continued to increase until the 1990s, spending on other policies increased even more. As a result, defense spending is now only about one-fifth of the budget. Still, at nearly $500 billion per year, it remains a significant sum, one over which battles continue to be fought in Congress.

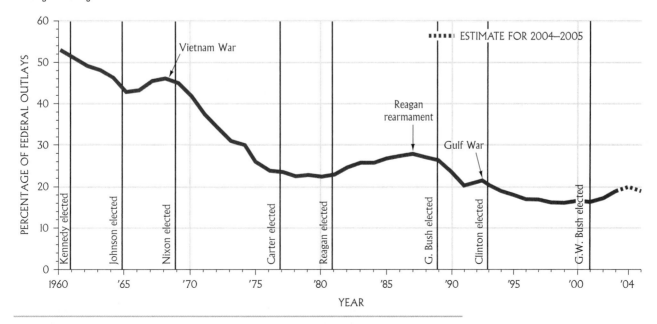

Source: Budget of the United States Government, Fiscal Year 2005: Historical Tables (Washington, D.C.: U.S. Government Printing Office, 2004), Table 3.1.

They contend that Gorbachev and his fellow reformers were responding primarily to internal, not external, pressures. Inadequacies and defects at the core of the Soviet economy—the inertia, wastefulness, and corruption inherent in the system—were the driving forces that brought change to the Soviet Union, not American defense spending.

In addition, scholars such as Paul Kennedy and David Calleo envision a new world order different from the bipolar dominance of the United States and the Soviet Union.[20] Kennedy warns of the historical dangers of "imperial overstretch," suggesting that great empires in a stage of relative economic decline vis-à-vis emerging powers accelerate their decline by clinging to vast military commitments.

Evaluating Defense Spending

Whatever its cause, the lessening of East-West tensions gave momentum to significant reductions in defense spending in the 1990s, what some called the *peace dividend*. Changing spending patterns was not easy, however. For example, military hardware developed during the early 1980s has proven to be increasingly expensive to purchase and maintain. And when the assembly lines at weapons plants close down, submarine designers, welders, and others lose their jobs. These programs become political footballs as candidates compete over promises to keep weapons systems such as the *Seawolf* submarine or the *Osprey* helicopter in production. Ideology plays a crucial role in the basic decisions members of Congress make regarding defense spending, but once these decisions are made, liberal as well as conservative representatives and senators fight hard to help constituencies win and keep defense contracts.[21]

The trend of reductions in defense spending was reversed abruptly in 2001 following the September 11 terrorist attacks. Whatever the proper level of spending, there is no question that the United States spends more on defense than the next 15 or 20 biggest spenders combined! It has overwhelming nuclear superiority, the world's dominant air force, the only truly blue-water navy (which also has impressive air power), and a unique capability to project power around the globe. No other country in modern history has come close to this level of military predominance, and the gap between the United States and other nations is increasing with more defense spending to support the war on terrorism. Moreover, the military advantages are even greater when one considers the quality as well as the quantity of U.S. defense capabilities. America has exploited the military applications of advanced communications and information technology and has developed the ability to coordinate and process information about the battlefield and to destroy targets from afar with extraordinary precision.

Personnel

The structure of America's defense has been based on a large standing military force and a battery of strategic nuclear weapons. The United States has about 1.4 million men and women on active duty and about 860,000 in the national guard and reserves (see Table 20.1). There are more than 250,000 active-duty troops deployed abroad, mostly in Europe, Japan, and South Korea,[22] and there were about 135,000 troops in Iraq in 2004. This is a very costly enterprise and one that frequently evokes calls to bring the troops home. Many observers believe that America's allies, especially prosperous nations such as Japan and Germany, should bear a greater share of common defense costs.

Cuts in defense spending led to reduced numbers of active-duty personnel in the armed services. As a result, the military now relies much more heavily on national guard and reserve units to maintain national security (the "Total Force" concept). The president mobilized national guard units and sent them into active duty in Bosnia, and national guard and reserve units have served in the war on terrorism, many for extended periods in Iraq.

Table 20.1   Size of the Armed Forces

BRANCH	PERSONNEL[a]
Army	482,400
Navy	365,900
Air Force	359,700
Marines	175,000
Subtotal	**1,383,000**
Reserves	860,900
Total	**2,243,900**

[a]2005 estimates
Sources: Office of Management and Budget, *Budget of the United States Government, Fiscal Year 2005: Appendix* (Washington, D.C.: U.S. Government Printing Office, 2004), 247.

Weapons

To deter an aggressor's attack, the United States has relied on a triad of nuclear weapons: ground-based intercontinental ballistic missiles (ICBMs), submarine-launched ballistic missiles (SLBMs), and strategic bombers. Both the United States and Russia have thousands of large nuclear warheads. These weapons, like troops, are costly (each Stealth bomber costs over a *billion* dollars), and they pose obvious dangers to human survival. The total cost of building nuclear weapons has been $5.5 *trillion* dollars![23]

The rapid drive toward democracy in Eastern Europe combined with Moscow's economic stagnation and the Pentagon's budgetary squeeze, pushed arms reduction inexorably onto the two superpowers' discussion agenda. Substantial progress has been made to end the arms race and what was known as "the balance of terror."

During the May 1988 Moscow summit meeting, President Reagan and Mikhail Gorbachev exchanged ratified copies of a new treaty eliminating *intermediate-range nuclear forces (INF)*. Reagan, who had built his reputation on fervid anti-Communism and had denounced earlier arms control efforts (such as Jimmy Carter's SALT II agreement), became the first American president to sign a treaty to reduce current levels of nuclear weapons. Under the terms of the INF treaty, more than 2,500 nuclear weapons with ranges between 300 and 3,400 miles were to be destroyed.

Superpower relations continued to improve at a dizzying pace, accelerated by the dissolution of the Soviet Union. On November 19, 1990, the leaders of 22 countries signed a treaty reducing conventional armed forces in Europe. The treaty slashed

President Reagan and Soviet President Mikhail Gorbachev begin their 1988 summit meeting in Moscow. The two presidents later signed a treaty eliminating intermediate-range nuclear missiles from Europe. The INF treaty marked the first time an American president had agreed to reduce current levels of nuclear weapons.

forces in Europe by 40 percent—the Soviet Union was called on to remove the most troops. A related change occurred in 1991 as the Warsaw Pact, the military alliance tying Eastern Europe to the Soviet Union, was dissolved.

On July 31, 1991, shortly before Soviet hard-liners attempted a coup to remove President Gorbachev and other reformers from power, he and President Bush signed the *Strategic Arms Reduction Treaty (START)*—after nine years of negotiations. The treaty had the distinction of being the first accord mandating the elimination of strategic nuclear weaponry. (The INF treaty banned a whole class of shorter-flying nuclear arms.)

The significance of these changes was soon overshadowed by other events, however, as the democratization of Eastern Europe, the restructuring of the Soviet Union, and the deterioration of the Soviet economy substantially diminished both Russia's inclination and potential to threaten the interests of the United States and its allies. President Bush broke ground with his decision in Fall 1991 to dismantle unilaterally some U.S. nuclear weapons, enticing President Gorbachev to follow suit shortly afterward.

In January 1993, Presidents Bush and Yeltsin signed an agreement (START II) to cut the U.S. and Russian (including those of Ukraine, Belarus, and Kazakhstan) nuclear arsenals to a total of no more than 6,500 weapons by the year 2003—less than one-third of the 20,000 long-range nuclear weapons the two possessed at the time. Large, accurate ICBMs with multiple warheads (MIRVs) were banned altogether. In 2002, President George W. Bush and Russian President Vladimir Putin signed a treaty to limit strategic nuclear weapons to no more than 2,200 for each country by 2012. At the same time, President George W. Bush has stepped up efforts to build a national missile defense. To pursue this system, in December 2001 the president withdrew the United States from the Anti-Ballistic Missile Treaty that it signed with the Soviet Union in 1972.

Nuclear weapons are the most destructive in America's arsenal, but they are by no means the only weapons. Jet fighters, aircraft carriers, and even tanks are extraordinarily complex and equally costly. The perception that space-age technology helped win the Gulf War in "100 hours" and topple the Taliban regime in Afghanistan with few American casualties, in addition to the fact that producing expensive weapons provides jobs for American workers, means that high-tech weapons systems will continue to play an important role in America's defense posture.

Reforming Defense Policy

Directly related to rethinking national security policy is reforming the nation's military. Reevaluating weapons systems and potentially skipping a generation to produce more technologically advanced systems is part of the effort. So is changing the force structure to make the armed forces lighter, faster, and more flexible. More effectively coupling intelligence with an increasingly agile military and a greater use of Special Forces are also significant breaks from the past. New approaches to military conflict inevitably follow from such transformations.

Although progress has been made on reducing tensions between East and West, other international matters clamor for attention. Even the mightiest nation can be mired in intractable issues.

The New Global Agenda

The global agenda is changing rapidly. As military competition with Communist powers has diminished, economic competition with the world has increased. Public opinion polls find that in the post-Cold War era, Americans are more likely to perceive threats to their security from the economic competition of allies than from military rivalry with old adversaries.[24] The gap between domestic and foreign policy is increasingly obscure. Dealing with allies such as Japan and Germany on trade and finance is as crucial as negotiating arms reductions with Russia. Maintaining access to petroleum in the Middle East is more crucial than ever, and determining policy regarding the global environment has taken on new prominence.

Regardless of the standards one uses for measurement, the United States is the world's mightiest military power. Its very strength seems to belie an essential weakness, however. Events on the world stage often appear to counter the American script. In the long and controversial Vietnam War, 500,000 American troops were not enough. U.S. economic vulnerability has increased. Our military might did not protect us from the deadly terrorist attacks on September 11, 2001. Oil supply lines depend on a precarious Middle Eastern peace and on the safe passage of huge tankers through a sliver of water called the Strait of Hormuz. We sometimes appear to be losing the highly publicized war on drugs to an international network of wealthy drug lords called *narcotraficantes*. Perhaps most important of all, our economy is increasingly dependent on international trade, placing us at the mercy of interest rates in Germany and restrictive markets in Japan and China.

There is an interesting paradox to American power: Although the United States is militarily and economically supreme, it is becoming increasingly dependent on other peoples to defeat terrorism, protect the environment, control weapons of mass destruction, regulate trade, and deal with other problems that cross national boundaries.[25] Even the effective use of U.S. military power requires military bases, ports, air fields, fuel supplies, and overflight rights that only its allies can provide.

There is much discussion in governing circles about whether America's military dominance will blind it to the need to cooperate with other nations. The George W. Bush administration has been assertive in acting unilaterally and defending U.S. interests rather than collective international interests. Many critics (including many of America's allies) complain that the United States undermines its ability to obtain the support of other countries when it fails to consult them, refuses to participate in the International Criminal Court, and rejects treaties to eliminate greenhouse gases, restrict antiballistic missile systems, prohibit land mines, and ban biological weapons testing.

The Decreasing Role of Military Power

Harvard political scientist Stanley Hoffman likened the United States' plight to that of Jonathan Swift's fictional character, Gulliver, the traveler seized and bound by the tiny Lilliputians.[26] For Americans, as for Gulliver, merely being big and powerful is no guarantee of dominance. Time after time and place after place, so it seems, the American Gulliver is frustrated by the Lilliputians.

One explanation for America's tribulations is that the nation's strong suit—military might—is no longer the primary instrument of foreign policy. Robert Keohane and Joseph Nye, in describing the diminishing role of military force in contemporary international politics, say that among the developed nations, "the perceived margin of safety has widened: fears of attack in general have declined, and fears of attacks by one another are virtually nonexistent."[27]

Today military power is losing much of its utility in resolving many international issues. "Force," argue Keohane and Nye, "is often not an appropriate way of achieving other goals (such as economic and ecological welfare) that are becoming more important" in world affairs.[28] Economic conflicts do not readily yield to nuclear weapons. America cannot persuade Arab nations to sell it cheap oil by bombing them, nor can it prop up the textile industry's position in world trade by resorting to military might. The United States is long on firepower at the very time when firepower is decreasing in its utility as an instrument of foreign policy.

According to Nye, it is "soft power"—the ability of a country to persuade others to do what it wants without force or coercion—that is often crucial to national security. American culture, ideals, and values have been important in helping Washington attract partners and supporters and countries require both hard and soft power to shape

Why It Matters

The Only Superpower
The United States is the world's only superpower. This puts us in a strong position to defend ourselves against other nations. However, it also means that America comes under more pressure from other nations to police the world's hot spots for peace-keeping and other humanitarian purposes. Being a superpower also does not protect us against attacks by non-state actors like terrorists.

Participation

Economic Sanctions and Cuba

long-term attitudes and preferences around the globe. Thus, security hinges as much on winning heats and minds as it does on winning wars.[29]

Conflict among large powers, the threat of nuclear war, and the possibility of conventional war have certainly not disappeared, but grafted onto them are new issues. Former Secretary of State Henry Kissinger described the new era eloquently:

> The traditional agenda of international affairs—the balance among major powers, the security of nations—no longer defines our perils or our possibilities. Now we are entering a new era. Old international patterns are crumbling; old slogans are uninstructive. The world has become interdependent in economics, in communications, in human aspirations.[30]

Despite these changes, military power remains an important element in U.S. foreign policy. The end of the Cold War emboldened local dictators and reignited age-old ethnic rivalries that had been held in check by the Soviet Union. The result: The number of regional crises likely to pose a threat to peace has grown exponentially in the post-Cold War era. Thus, although the end of the Cold War gives the United States unprecedented freedom to act, its status as the only superpower has meant that Washington is the first place people look for help when trouble erupts, even in Europe's backyard as in the case of the territory of the former Yugoslavia. One of the nation's most difficult foreign policy problems is in deciding when to send U.S. troops to police the world's hot spots.

Economic Sanctions.   An ancient tool of diplomacy, sanctions are nonmilitary penalties imposed on a foreign government in an attempt to modify its behavior. The penalties can vary broadly—a cutoff of U.S. aid, a ban on military sales, restrictions on imports, a denial of aircraft landing rights, a total trade embargo. The implied power behind sanctions is U.S. economic muscle and access to U.S. markets.

Economic sanctions are often a first resort in times of crises, as they are less risky than sending in troops. Sanctions are often the outgrowth of pressure from well-organized domestic political groups with ethnic, cultural, environmental, human rights, or religious grievances against a foreign regime. These groups and government officials want to curb unfair trade practices, end human rights abuses and drug trafficking, promote environmental initiatives, and stop terrorism.

There are examples of economic sanctions that accomplished the goals of their sponsors, such as the sanctions levied against South Africa in the mid-1980s that contributed to the demise of apartheid. Most experts, however, view these tools as having limited effect. The trade embargo the United Nations placed on Iraq after its 1990 invasion of Kuwait succeeded in isolating Iraq, diplomatically and economically, and prevented it from rebuilding its military to its former strength. Yet Saddam Hussein retained a firm grip on power until 2003.

Successful sanctions most often have broad international support, which is rare. Unilateral sanctions are doomed to failure. The sanctions leak and the real losers are U.S. companies that are forced to abandon lucrative markets. They are quickly replaced by their competitors around the globe. When President Carter imposed a grain embargo on the Soviet Union in 1980 in retaliation for the Soviet invasion of Afghanistan, only U.S. farmers were hurt. The Soviet Union simply bought grain elsewhere.

In addition, critics argue that sanctions are counterproductive because they can provoke a nationalist backlash. The decades-old sanctions against Cuba have not ousted Marxist dictator Fidel Castro, and the perennial threats of sanctions against China typically result in a hardening of China's attitude regarding human rights and other matters.

Nuclear Proliferation

The spread of technology has enabled the creation of nuclear weapons and the missiles to deliver them, encouraging U.S. officials to adopt a more assertive posture in attempting to deny these weapons of mass destruction to rogue states. American policymakers have sought to halt the spread of nuclear weapons since the signing of the Nuclear Non-Proliferation Treaty in 1968. The primary means of accomplishing this goal has been to encourage nations to agree that they would not acquire, or at least test, nuclear weapons. As you can see in Figure 20.3, only seven countries have declared that they have nuclear weapons capacities: the United States, Russia, Britain, France, China, India, and Pakistan. Israel is widely suspected of having nuclear weapons. South Africa and three countries that used to be part of the Soviet Union, Belarus, Kazakhstan, and Ukraine, have given up nuclear weapons. Algeria, Argentina, Brazil, Libya, South Korea, Sweden, and Taiwan have ended their nuclear weapons programs. The United States actively supported the UN weapons inspections of Iraq, which faced continuous harassment and obstruction from Saddam Hussein until he was driven from power. After it invaded Iraq in 2003, it found only a modest effort to develop nuclear weapons remained.

Currently, policymakers are most concerned about countries that are actively seeking nuclear weapons capabilities, principally North Korea and Iran. These nations, frequently branded as "outlaw" states, pose serious threats to their neighbors, and perhaps to the United States as well. The United States provided aid to North Korea in return for a promise to end its nuclear weapons program, but in 2002 North Korea declared its intention to continue the program and likely possesses a few nuclear

Simulation

You Are the President:
Policy Toward Iran

Figure 20.3 The Spread of Nuclear Weapons

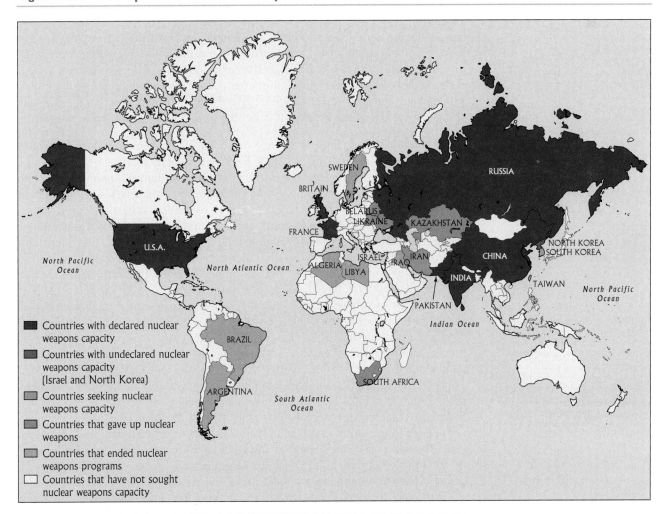

Source: *Congressional Quarterly Weekly Report,* May 23, 1998, 1,366. Updated by authors.

weapons now. Our efforts regarding Iran have been less effective yet, as we lack diplomatic relations with that nation.

Other nations have serious security concerns when faced with hostile neighbors possessing nuclear weapons. When India resumed testing of nuclear weapons in 1998, neighboring Pakistan quickly tested its first nuclear weapons. Their possession of nuclear weapons is a matter of special concern because of their history of conflict over Kashmir. Ending the proliferation of nuclear weapons will require resolving diplomatic tensions involving undeclared and nonnuclear states. In the meantime, the United States will focus on discouraging the deployment of nuclear weapons that have been developed.

The International Economy

Once upon a time, nations took pains to isolate themselves from the world. They erected high barriers to fend off foreign products and amassed large armies to defend their borders against intruders. Times have changed. One key word describes today's international economy: **interdependency,** a mutual reliance in which actions reverberate and affect other people's economic lifelines. The health of the American economy depends increasingly on the prosperity of its trading partners and on the smooth flow of trade and finance across borders (see "Young People and Politics: Embracing Globalization").

The *International Monetary Fund (IMF)* is a cooperative international organization of 185 countries intended to stabilize the exchange of currencies and the world economy. From 1997 to 1998, the decline of currencies in a number of Asian countries, including South Korea, Thailand, Indonesia, and the Philippines, threatened to force these nations to default on their debts—and throw the international economy into turmoil in the process. To stabilize these currencies, the IMF, to which the United States is by far the largest contributor, arranged for loans and credits of more than $100 billion. The IMF's intervention seems to have been successful, but the necessity of making the loans dramatically illustrates the world's economic interdependence.

International Trade.   Since the end of World War II, trade among nations has grown rapidly. U.S. exports and imports have increased twentyfold since 1970 alone (see Figure 20.4). Among the largest U.S. exporters are grain farmers, producers of computer hardware and software, aircraft manufacturers, moviemakers, heavy construction companies, and purveyors of accounting and consulting services. Foreign tourist spending bolsters the U.S. travel, hotel, and recreation industries. American colleges and universities derive a significant portion of their revenue from educating foreign students. The globalization of finances has been even more dramatic than the growth of trade. Worldwide computer and communications networks link financial markets in all parts of the globe instantaneously, making it easier to move capital across national boundaries but also increasing the probability that a steep decline in the Japanese stock market will send prices plummeting on Wall Street.

Coping with foreign economic issues is becoming just as difficult, and increasingly just as important, as coping with domestic ones. In a simpler time, the main instrument of international economic policy was the **tariff,** a special tax added to the cost of imported goods. Tariffs are intended to raise the price of imported goods and thereby protect American businesses and workers from foreign competition. Tariff making, though, is a game everyone can play. High U.S. tariffs encourage other nations to respond with high tariffs on American products. The high tariffs that the government enacted early in the Great Depression (and that some say aggravated this economic crisis) were the last of their kind. Since that time, the world economy has moved from a period of high tariffs and protectionism to one of lower tariffs and freer trade.

However, nontariff barriers such as quotas, subsidies, and quality specifications for imported products are common means of limiting imports. In recent years, the United States has placed quotas on the amount of steel that could be imported and negotiated

interdependency

Mutual dependency, in which the actions of nations reverberate and affect one another's economic lifelines.

tariff

A special tax added to imported goods to raise the price, thereby protecting American businesses and workers from foreign competition.

Young People and Politics

Embracing Globalization

The protests that regularly occur during economic summit meetings of the leaders of the world's most economically developed countries might lead you to conclude that young adults are in the forefront of opposition to globalization. Actually, the facts are quite different, according to the Pew *Global Attitudes Project*'s surveys.

In every country globalization has produced some political tensions. However, strong majorities in all regions believe that increased global interconnectedness is a good thing, and globalization is more popular among the young adults of the world. Everywhere but Latin America, young people are more likely than their elders to see advantages in increased global trade and communication, and they are more likely to support "globalization."

The hesitation among some older citizens to embrace the movement toward globalization may be due in part to national pride. People in all countries and of all ages are proud of their cultures. Yet it is only in the West (North America and Western Europe) where that pride is markedly stronger among the older generations. Younger people tend to be less wedded to their cultural identities. In the United States, 68 percent of those aged 65 and older agree with the statement "our people are not perfect, but our culture is superior," while only 49 percent of those aged 18 to 29 agree. The generation gap in Western Europe is similar. The difference between generations is particularly apparent in France, where only one-fifth of those under age 30 support the notion of cultural superiority, while more than half of those aged 65 and older say French culture is superior.

Despite the general attraction of globalization, solid majorities everywhere think their way of life needs to be protected against foreign influence. In most parts of the world, that desire cuts across all age groups. However, in the United States and Western Europe, older people are much more worried than the young about defending their country's way

of life. In the United States, 71 percent of people aged 65 and older want to shield their way of life from foreign influence, while just 55 percent of those ages 18 to 29 agree. This generation gap is even greater in France, Germany, and Britain, where older people are twice as likely as young people to be worried about erosion of their way of life.

Skepticism about foreign influence is evident in widespread, intense antipathy toward immigration. Majorities in nearly every country surveyed support tougher restrictions on people entering their countries. Immigrants are particularly unpopular across Europe, especially among the older generation, where half of those surveyed *completely agree* with the need for additional immigration controls. The anti-immigrant generation gap is widest in France, where 53 percent of those aged 65 and older *completely agree* that immigration should be restricted. Only 24 percent of younger French men and women shared such strong views. Anti-immigrant sentiment also runs high in the United States, especially among older Americans. Fifty percent of those aged 65 and older strongly support new controls on entry of people into the country. Only 40 percent young people share that intensity of sentiment.

There are many reasons why young adults may be more supportive of globalization than their elders. Better educated, more widely traveled, and more accustomed to the Internet, young adults seem to be less parochial, have less fear of change, and have more appreciation for the benefits of other cultures. Partially as a result of these attitudes, we should expect the trend toward globalization to accelerate over the coming decades.

Questions for Discussion
- Do young people you know fear foreign competition?
- Do you agree that education and experience are the best explanations for the greater support of globalization among young people?

---

voluntary limits on the importation of Japanese automobiles. Such policies do save American jobs involved in producing steel and automobiles, but they also raise the price of steel and automobiles that Americans buy, raising the costs of producing yet other products – and costing jobs in the process. American and European subsidies for agricultural products have been an obstacle to negotiating tariff reductions.

Recently, substantial progress has been made in lowering barriers to trade. In 1992, President Bush signed the *North American Free Trade Agreement (NAFTA)* with Canada and Mexico, which would eventually eliminate most tariffs among North American countries. In 1993, after a heated battle, President Clinton obtained congressional passage of the legislation implementing the agreement.

Comparing Foreign and Security Policy

Figure 20.4   Exports and Imports

Since 1975, the United States has imported more than it has exported, resulting in a mounting trade deficit.

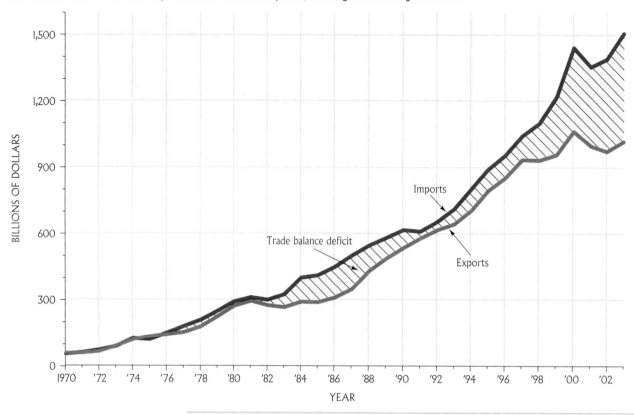

Source: U.S. Bureau of the Census, December 2003.

President Clinton submitted an even more important agreement to Congress in 1994. The *General Agreement on Tariffs and Trade (GATT)* is the mechanism by which most of the world's nations negotiate widespread trade agreements. In 1994, 117 nations agreed to (1) reduce tariffs 38 percent for developed countries; (2) eliminate certain nontariff barriers and subsidies; (3) broaden GATT principles to areas such as trade in services, investment, and intellectual property rights; and (4) apply more effective disciplines to agricultural trade. The GATT also included a charter to create a World Trade Organization (WTO) that would act as the arbiter of international trade disputes. In its last action, the 103rd Congress passed the legislation necessary to implement this agreement.

A persistent issue for the president is opening up foreign markets for U.S. goods and services. The White House is especially eager to open lucrative Japanese markets in areas such as automobiles, auto parts, telecommunications, insurance, and medical equipment. The United States lacks the influence to *demand* that these markets be opened, however. If we refuse to trade with another nation, that nation will deny *our* exports access to its markets, and U.S. consumers will lose access to its products. In addition, millions of Americans now work in foreign-owned companies in the United States, such as Japanese automobile assembly plants. Although foreign investments and the creation of jobs are good for the United States, a by-product is that Americans have a stake in averting a trade crisis with investing nations. Those benefiting from Japanese investments, for example, may flock to Tokyo's side on some important issues.

Balance of Trade.   Foreign products are not free. When Americans purchase foreign products, they send dollars out of the country. When an oil tanker arrives in

International trade is a controversial subject. Opponents believe that it undermines U.S. laws that protect the environment and workers' rights, costs some employees their jobs, and encourages the exploitation of foreign workers. Proponents argue that everyone benefits from increased trade. Here Seattle police face protesters during a World Trade Organization meeting in 1999.

Houston, dollars travel to Saudi Arabia. If other nations do not buy as many American products as Americans do of theirs, then the United States is paying out more than it is taking in. If the United States puts military bases in Germany, the money that soldiers spend for a night on the town goes into German pockets. When American tourists spend their dollars abroad, they too carry American dollars away. All these instances combine to upset the **balance of trade**: the ratio of what a country pays for imports to what it earns from exports. When a country imports more than it exports, it has a balance-of-trade *deficit*. Year after recent year, the American balance of trade has been preceded by a minus sign, and the deficit for the balance of trade was more than $489 billion in 2003.[31]

The excess of imports over exports decreases the dollar's buying power against other currencies, making Americans pay more for goods that they buy from other nations. This decline in the value of the dollar, however, also makes American products cheaper abroad, thereby increasing our exports. Since the late 1980s, the United States has experienced an export boom, exceeding $1 trillion in 2003.[32] Exports account for more than 10 percent of the GDP.

A poor balance of trade also exacerbates unemployment. Currently, 5 percent of all civilian employment in the United States is related to manufacturing exports. A substantial amount of white-collar employment—in the area of financial services, for example, is also directly tied to exports. The trade imbalance has caused not only dollars but also jobs to flow abroad. Because labor is cheaper in Mexico, Taiwan, Malaysia, and South Korea, products made there can be priced lower than American-made products. Sometimes American firms have shut down their domestic operations and relocated in countries where labor costs are lower. The AFL-CIO claims that hundreds of thousands of American jobs have been lost to foreign competition. Under a special act guaranteeing compensation to American workers who lose their jobs to foreign competition, the Department of Labor has aided thousands of workers. The Labor Department, however, would be the first to note that short-term aid is no substitute for a long-term job.

Even so, a cheaper dollar also makes the cost of American labor more competitive. In response to this and to criticism about the balance of trade, more foreign-owned companies are building factories in the United States—just as American companies have plants around the globe. Thus, many Hondas are made in the United States, and parts for some cars manufactured by General Motors are made abroad. The web of interdependency has become so tangled that it is increasingly difficult to define "imports."

balance of trade

The ratio of what is paid for imports to what is earned from exports. When more is imported than exported, there is a balance-of-trade deficit.

Why It Matters

Economic Interdependence
The world economy is increasingly interdependent. In fact, Americans have more investments abroad than citizens of any other nation. Investments and markets in other countries provide economic opportunities for Americans, but they also make Americans more dependent on the strength of economies over which they lack control and provide increased competition for American products and American workers.

In addition, the stability of the U.S. economy and the low value of the dollar have made the United States attractive to foreign investors, who buy everything from major motion picture studios to the Rockefeller Center. Although advantages accrue to the United States when investors pour money into the country, some fear that both profits and control will move outside our borders.

Organization of Petroleum Exporting Countries (OPEC)

An economic organization consisting primarily of Arab nations that controls the price of oil and the amount of oil its members produce and sell to other nations.

Energy.   In 1973, the **Organization of Petroleum Exporting Countries (OPEC)** responded to American support of Israel in the short war against Egypt by embargoing oil shipments to the United States and Western European nations. The fuel shortages and long lines at gas stations that resulted from the 1973 oil embargo convincingly illustrated the growing interdependency of world politics.

More than half the world's recoverable reserves of oil lie in the Middle East; Saudi Arabia alone controls much of this resource. States such as Texas, Oklahoma, Louisiana, and Alaska produce considerable amounts of oil within the United States, but not enough to meet the country's needs. America imports more than 60 percent of its annual consumption of oil from other countries, particularly from the Middle East. The United States is not as dependent on foreign sources of oil as many European countries, like France or Italy, which have virtually no oil of their own, or like Japan, which also imports all its oil. On the other hand, America's dependence on foreign oil is growing every year.

America's decision to respond to Iraq's invasion of Kuwait in 1990 was based in large part by this dependence. Kuwait, although a small country, produces about 10 percent of the world's oil; its neighbor, Saudi Arabia, possesses about a quarter of the world's proven oil reserves. Following a UN embargo and ultimatum to Iraq to pull out of Kuwait, the United States and its allies poured forces into Saudi Arabia (more than a half million soldiers from the United States alone). The allied forces quickly defeated the Iraqis and liberated Kuwait.

Circumstances may again restrict the availability of oil, however, and the United States is vulnerable because of its dependence on imported oil. Yet the Middle East— and America's sources of foreign oil—remain unstable.

Foreign Aid.   Presidents of each party have pressed for aid to nations in the developing world. Aside from simple humanitarian concern for those who are suffering, presidents have wanted to stabilize nations that were friendly to the United States or that possessed supplies of vital raw materials. Sometimes aid has been given in the form of grants, but often it has taken the form of credits and loan guarantees to purchase American goods, loans at favorable interest rates, and forgiveness of previous loans. At other times, the United States has awarded preferential trade agreements for the sale of foreign goods in the United States.

A substantial percentage of foreign aid is in the form of military assistance and is targeted to a few countries the United States considers to be of vital strategic significance: Israel, Egypt, Turkey, and Greece have received the bulk of such assistance in recent years. Foreign aid programs have also assisted with agricultural modernization, irrigation, and population control. Food for Peace programs have subsidized the sale of American agricultural products to poor countries (and simultaneously given an economic boost to American farmers). Peace Corps volunteers have fanned out over the globe to provide medical care and other services in less developed nations.

Nevertheless, foreign aid has never been very popular with Americans. Lacking a constituency, the president's foreign aid requests are typically cut by Congress, which currently appropriates about 1 percent of the federal budget to economic and humanitarian foreign aid. Moreover, many people believe that the provision of economic aid to other nations serves only to further enrich the few without helping the many within a poor nation. Although the United States donates more total aid (both for economic development and military assistance) than any other country, it devotes a smaller share of its GDP to foreign economic development than any other developed nation (see

America in Perspective

Ranking Largess

The United States is the largest donor of foreign aid, but it ranks lower than other industrialized nations in the percentage of its gross domestic product (GDP) it spends on economic development aid for needy nations. American private giving is substantial, however.

COUNTRY	TOTAL ECONOMIC AID (IN MILLIONS $)	PERCENTAGE OF GDP
Denmark	1,634	1.03
Netherlands	3,172	.82
Norway	1,346	.80
Sweden	1,666	.77
Belgium	867	.37
Switzerland	908	.34
France	4,198	.32
Finland	389	.32
United Kingdom	4,579	.32
Germany	4,990	.27
New Zealand	112	.25
Australia	873	.25
Austria	533	.29
Japan	9,847	.23
Canada	1,533	.22
Italy	1,627	.15
United States	**11,429**	**.11**

Source: Organization for Economic Cooperation and Development, *OECD in Figures, 2003 Edition*, Paris, 2004, pp. 64–65.

"America in Perspective: Ranking Largess"). It is important to note, however, that the United States provides a great deal more aid through grants from private voluntary organizations, foundations, religious organizations, corporations, universities, and individuals.[33]

Understanding National Security Policymaking

National security policy is perhaps the most exotic arena of public policy, dealing with issues and nations that are often far from America's shores. Nevertheless, the themes that have guided your understanding of American politics throughout *Government in America*—democracy and the scope of government—can also shed light on the topic of international relations.

National Security Policymaking and Democracy

To some commentators, democracy has little to do with America's international relations. Because domestic issues are closer to their daily lives and easier to understand, Americans are usually more interested in domestic policy than in foreign policy. This preference would seem to give public officials more discretion in making national

How You Can Make a Difference

Getting Involved in the Foreign Policy Process

Concerned about U.S. national security and its foreign policy positions in the wake of September 11? Do not fall into the trap of believing that your opinion is insignificant compared to highly paid news anchors and well-financed lobbyists. Average citizens, believe it or not, can have a large impact on governmental actions—especially during wartime and periods of unrest. Popular support of government actions can invigorate and strengthen national resolve (the home front during World War II) or it can force change (Vietnam War). Don't underestimate your influence and potential as college students in this realm! Remember—four freshmen at North Carolina A&T State University in Greensboro, N.C., started the "sit-in" movement that transformed the civil rights movement!

At the start of the twenty-first century, due to the terrorist attacks on September 11, foreign policy has become relevant to Americans to a degree unheard of since the end of the Vietnam War. Average American citizens are forming opinions about American foreign policy because it now seems to matter in their daily lives.

However, before going out and just doing "something"—whether acting on your instincts or being influenced by a charismatic professor—you should try to come to your own conclusions regarding the war on terror. Learn about the wide range of approaches and ideas regarding the war on terrorism after September 11. Do not just read works you agree with. If you are a conservative, read through some arguments put forth by thoughtful liberals at the Brookings Institution or the insightful libertarians at the Cato Institute. Look for differences among the spectrum of "liberal" approaches or "libertarian" perspectives. If you consider yourself a liberal, then read—with an open mind—some intelligent conservative theories at sites like the Heritage Foundation or the National Review.

Once you have come to some conclusions regarding terrorism and national security, do not blindly follow what past activists have done. It is not the 1960s—it is the twenty-first century—and tactics and strategies that may have worked against the war in Vietnam and segregation do not necessarily work today. This is a different time and a different struggle. Don't adopt antiwar positions just because your professors were antiwar during the 1960s and 1970s. Neither should you

be blindly patriotic because your grandparents fought against Adolf Hitler. Think for yourself and develop your own strategies and tactics. After all, the Greensboro college students definitely broke new ground in the area of civil rights protests!

What you can do:
- Read and research. Start by examining some of the organizations mentioned: *www.cato.org*, *www.heritage.org*, and *www.brook.edu*.
- Contact your legislative representatives with your ideas.
- Lobby for new legislation by supporting like-minded institutions.
- Start or join a forum on your campus—brainstorm with others to develop new approaches and tactics. See *www.sitins.com* to read about how the Greensboro Four carved a new approach.
- Question existing clubs and political groups on campus regarding their stance.
- Help in humanitarian efforts during spring break and Christmas vacation.

security policy. In addition, some say, those with the discretion are elites in the State Department and unelected military officers in the Pentagon.

There is little evidence, however, that policies at odds with the wishes of the American people can be sustained; civilian control of the military is unquestionable. When the American people hold strong opinions regarding international relations—as when they first supported and later opposed the war in Vietnam—policymakers are usually responsive. Citizens in democracies do not choose to fight citizens in other democracies, and studies have found that well-established democracies rarely go to war against one another.[34]

In addition, the system of separation of powers plays a crucial role in foreign as well as domestic policy. The president takes the lead on national security matters, but you saw in Chapter 12 that Congress has a central role in matters of international relations. Whether treaties are ratified, defense budgets appropriated, weapons systems authorized, or foreign aid awarded is ultimately at the discretion of the Congress—the government's most representative policymaking body. Specific issues such as the proper funding for the Strategic Defense Initiative rarely determine congressional elections, but public demands for and objections to policies are likely to be heard in Washington.

When it comes to the increasingly important arena of American international economic policy, pluralism is pervasive. Agencies and members of Congress, as well as their constituents, all pursue their own policy goals. For example, the Treasury Department and the Federal Reserve Board worry about the negative balance of trade, and the Department of Defense spends billions in other countries to maintain American troops abroad. The Departments of Agriculture and Commerce and their constituents—farmers and businesspeople—want to peddle American products abroad and generally favor freer trade. The Department of Labor and the unions worry that the nation may export not only products but also jobs to other countries where labor costs are low. Jewish citizens closely monitor U.S. policy toward Israel, whereas Greek Americans seek to limit military aid to Turkey, Greece's ancient rival. Even foreign governments hire lobbying firms and join in the political fray. As a result, a wide range of interests are represented in the making of foreign policy.

National Security Policymaking and the Scope of Government

America's global connections as a superpower have many implications for how active the national government is in the realm of foreign policy and national defense. Treaty obligations to defend allies around the world, the nation's economic interests in an interdependent global economy, and pressing new questions on the global agenda—ranging from illicit drugs to environmental protection—demand government action.

By any standard, the scope of government in these areas is large. The national defense consumes about one-fifth of the federal government's budget and requires about 2.2 million civilian and military employees for the Department of Defense. Even though the United States has improved relations with Eastern and Central Europe, it will remain a superpower and continue to have political, economic, and other interests to defend around the world. As long as these interests remain, the scope of American government in foreign and defense policy will be substantial.

Summary

The world—its politics and its economics—intrudes on Americans more each year. This chapter examined America's global connections and the contours of its foreign policy.

The Cold War began shortly after World War II, when the containment doctrine became the basis of American foreign policy. The Cold War led to actual wars in Korea and Vietnam when the United States tried to contain Communist advances. With containment came a massive military buildup, resulting in what some people called the *military-industrial complex*. Gradually, containment has been balanced by détente and then friendship with many of our former adversaries. This trend has accelerated with the democratization of Central and Eastern Europe and the dissolution of the Soviet Union. Nevertheless, the United States maintains an enormous defense capability, which was put to use again in the war on terrorism.

Although the United States has great military power, many of the issues facing the world today are not military issues. Nuclear proliferation and terrorism present new challenges to national security, challenges not easily met by advanced weaponry. Interconnected issues of equality, energy, and the environment have also become important. The international economic system pulls the United States deeper and deeper into the world's problems as global interdependency and its own vulnerability become more apparent.

KEY TERMS

foreign policy
United Nations (UN)
North Atlantic Treaty
    Organization (NATO)
European Union (EU)
secretary of state
secretary of defense
Joint Chiefs of Staff

Central Intelligence
    Agency (CIA)
isolationism
containment doctrine
Cold War
McCarthyism
arms race
détente

Strategic Defense
    Initiative (SDI)
interdependency
tariff
balance of trade
Organization of Petroleum
    Exporting Countries
    (OPEC)

INTERNET RESOURCES

www.state.gov/
Information about the Department of State and current foreign policy issues.

www.defenselink.mil/
Information about the Department of Defense and current issues in national security policy.

www.cia.gov/cia/publications/factbook/
The *CIA World Factbook.*

www.oecd.org/home/
The Organization for Economic Cooperation and Development (OECD) provides a wealth of economic information on the world's nations.

www.nato.int/
Contains background and activities of NATO.

www.un.org/
Background on the United Nations and its varied programs.

www.cfr.org
The Council on Foreign Relations is the most influential private organization in the area of foreign policy. Its website includes a wide range of information on foreign policy.

www.whitehouse.gov/nsc/
Information about the members and functions of the National Security Council.

GET CONNECTED

The Department of State

Congratulations! The president of the United States has just nominated you to be the secretary of state. You have been given advance notice that several members of the Senate Foreign Relations Committee will ask you about the "Palestinian Question" during your confirmation. Although you are aware that the relationship between Arabs and Israel has been a key element of United States foreign policy for decades, you want to provide the committee with some new thinking on possible answers to the Palestinian Question. One place you look for ideas is American public opinion.

Search the Web

Go to the "America's Global Role: Quick Takes" page at the Public Agenda website *http://www.publicagenda.org/ issues/angles.cfm?issue_type=americas_global_role.* There are several graphs under the heading "Middle East" that show American public opinion about the role the United States should play in the conflict between the Palestinians and Israel. Take a look at all three graphs.

Questions To Ask

- Who do most Americans believe should take the first step in trying to end the bombings and other violence in the region?
- What should the United States do to try to help the two sides find a peaceful resolution to the decades-long conflict?
- Where should the Palestinian-Israeli conflict be on the United States' foreign policy agenda?

Why It Matters

Israelis and Palestinians have been engaged in varying levels of conflict since Israel became an independent nation in 1948. The conflict has led to large numbers of Palestinian refugees, some of whom become terrorists. Achieving peace in the Middle East has been a foreign policy goal of the United States for decades, partly out of its longstanding support for a Jewish homeland and partly out of concern for the impact of violence in the Middle East on the supply of energy in the United States.

Get Involved

Learn a little more about the U.S. role in seeking answers to the Palestinian Question. What are the current administration's goals? How do your members of Congress feel about the potential for ending conflict between the Palestinians and the Israelis?

To see more Get Connected exercises for Chapter 20, go to www.ablongman.com/edwards.

FOR FURTHER READING

Brzezinski, Zbigniew. *The Choice: Global Domination or Global Leadership*. New York: Basic Books, 2004. An important critique of the Bush administration's national security strategy.

Daalder, Ivo H., and James M. Lindsay, *America Unbound: The Bush Revolution in Foreign Policy*. Washington, D.C.: Brookings Institution, 2003. A balanced analysis of the Bush administration's foreign policy.

Huntington, Samuel P. *The Clash of Civilizations and the Remaking of World Order*. New York: Simon & Schuster, 1996. Argues that civilizational identities built on religious empires of the past will be the source of international turmoil in the next century.

Kagan, Donald. *On the Origins of War and the Preservation of Peace*. New York: Doubleday, 1995. Provides insights gleaned from studying the origins of great wars.

Lindsay, James M. *Congress and the Politics of U.S. Foreign Policy*. Baltimore: Johns Hopkins University Press, 1994. A useful discussion of the role of Congress in setting U.S. foreign policy.

Mead, Walter Russell. *Power, Terror, Peace, and War*. New York: Alfred A. Knopf, 2004. Analyzes America's grand strategy in national security.

Nye, Joseph S., Jr. *The Paradox of American Power: Why the World's Only Superpower Can't Go It Alone*. New York: Oxford University Press, 2002. Although the U.S. is militarily and economically supreme, it is increasingly dependent on other nations to accomplish its goals.

Nye, Joseph S., Jr. *Soft Power: The Means To Success in World Politics*. Cambridge, MA: Harvard University Press, 2004. Argues that national security hinges as much on winning hearts and minds as it does on winning wars.

Woodward, Bob. *Plan of Attack*. New York: Simon and Schuster, 2004. The inside story of decision-making regarding the war with Iraq.

Yergin, Daniel. *Shattered Peace: The Origins of the Cold War and the National Security State*. Boston: Houghton Mifflin, 1977. An excellent political history of the early years of the Cold War and containment.

The New Face of State and Local Government

21

Chapter Outline

State Constitutions

State Elections

Governors and the Executive Branch

State Legislatures

State Court Systems

Direct Democracy

State and Local Government Relations

Local Governments

State and Local Finance Policy

The New York Times Issues of the Times

Understanding State and Local Governments

Summary

■ Following the terrorist attacks of September 11, 2001, the national government passed a variety of new laws that created new categories of crime for terrorist acts and increased the power and authority of federal law enforcement and intelligence agencies. At the same time, state governments adopted similar laws and took steps to consolidate bureaucratic agencies charged with law enforcement and emergency response. For example, by November 2002, 13 states had adopted laws that provided for the death penalty in cases of murder committed in the furtherance of a terrorist act. New Jersey even adopted a law that carries penalties for recruiting members of a terrorist organization.

Traditionally state and local governments have been responsible for most criminal justice policy and maintaining the civil order for situations contained within state borders. However, the national government response to September 11 reflects a pattern of growing federal involvement in criminal justice policy. And the states have likewise been reluctant to forfeit their policymaking role or their

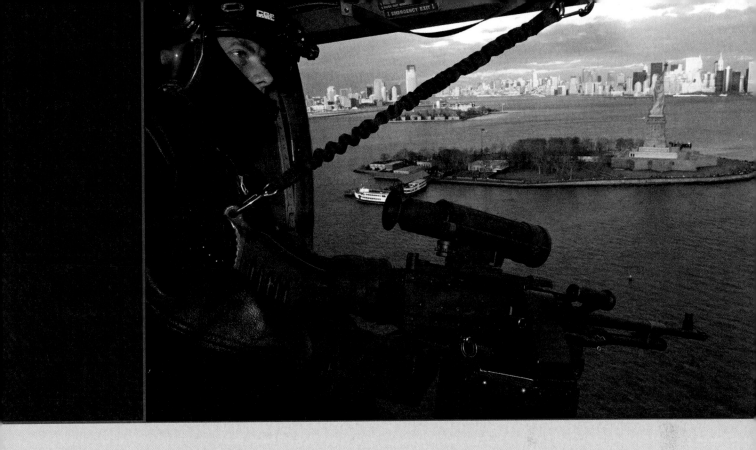

role in prosecuting criminals. This competition has led some to suggest that states should maintain their traditional dominant role in criminal justice policy, but in issues involving national security and defense, state and local governments should defer to the national government, or confusion will abound.[1] Such an example occurred in 2002 as Maryland and Virginia argued with the national government over who would be the first to prosecute the accused in the Washington, D.C.-area sniper case, with Virginia arguing it should go first and make use of its new antiterrorism law that carried the death penalty.

The debate over government jurisdiction in criminal justice policy is important for several reasons. First, maintaining the civil order is a fundamental role for any government. Without civil order, commerce cannot occur and democratic practices, such as elections, cannot take place. Second, the ultimate power of the government comes from its ability to take away the rights and liberties of

individuals. Our fear of this power has led us to place limits on the government and to traditionally keep this power close at hand—with state and local governments.

Does increasing federal involvement in criminal justice policy, from drug crimes to carjacking to terrorism, threaten our liberties more than traditional state and local government involvement in this area? On the other hand, are state governments threatening the security of our homeland by adopting their own policies and refusing to participate in federal intelligence-sharing programs? If the states defer to the national government, do we lose the accountability over our elected officials as opposed to the accountability we currently have over local and state officials? Clearly there are no simple answers, but the questions reflect the tensions within our federalist system between levels of government and the difficulty of establishing policy jurisdictions.

subnational governments

Another way of referring to state and local governments. Through a process of reform, modernization, and changing intergovernmental relations since the 1960s, subnational governments have assumed new responsibilities and importance.

State and local governments, or **subnational governments,** touch our lives every day. They pick up our garbage, educate us, keep us safe from criminals, protect our critical infrastructure systems, such as the water supply, and perform a myriad of other vital services. Odds are that you are attending a state or city university right now. You will drive home on locally maintained streets (and may perhaps be issued a speeding ticket from a local official). Subnational governments regulate a wide range of business activities, from generating electric power to cutting hair. The state government is also the single largest employer in every state; in aggregate, local governments employ even more people than do the states. So, as a consumer of government services, as a regulated businessperson, and/or as an employee, subnational governments are intimately involved in our lives.

Not long ago, however, some political observers predicted that state governments would cease to exist in the near future.[2] The states seemed to some like archaic accidents of history rather than meaningful political entities. For example, how could one possibly equate Wyoming, with less than a half million people and less than 5 people per square mile, to California with 34 million people and 217 people per square mile? What do Hawaii and Alaska have in common with Rhode Island and Louisiana as political entities? Some critics in the 1950s and 1960s thought, "not much." Further, a generation ago, state governments were ridiculed as being "horse and buggy" institutions in an era of space travel.[3] Their institutions were weak, outdated, resource-poor, and were simply not up to the task of running a modern state. The states were also seen by social liberals as obstacles to addressing the grievances of racial and ethnic minorities and urban dwellers—witness Governor George Wallace's stand against the racial integration of Alabama schools (Chapter 3). The federal government was seen as the modern engine of progressive policymaking, and the states were encouraged to step aside or get replaced.

But as Mark Twain said about his mistaken obituary, these reports of the death of the states were greatly exaggerated. Through a process of reform, modernization, and changing intergovernmental relations since the 1960s, subnational governments have become more vital to our democratic system than ever. They have assumed new and costly responsibilities in areas such as welfare, health, economic development, and criminal justice. States and localities have also gained importance as federal policymakers have confronted budgetary limits and policymakers have recognized the virtues of grass-roots democracy—of giving decision-making power to governments closer to the people.

In this chapter, we discuss subnational government with an eye toward two important characteristics: *revitalization* and *diversity.* Since the early 1960s, the states have become revitalized in their institutions, their personnel, and their role in the federal system.[4] State legislatures, governors' offices, courts, and even bureaucracies have undergone dramatic changes that have allowed them to move forward as strong and active players in the U.S. policymaking process. The people involved in governing the states and localities are more representative of their constituents than was previously the case, and they tend to be better educated, more professionalized, and have greater policy expertise. With the weight of the philosophical argument about where policymaking power should lie in the federal system swinging strongly toward the states for the past 35 years (Chapter 3), the federal government has provided the states and localities with increasing control over many policy areas.

The second characteristic important to understanding subnational government in the United States is diversity. As anyone who has ever traveled outside their hometown knows, government, policy, and political behavior differ from place to place. For example, in California citizens can propose and pass laws through the ballot box; in Delaware they can't. On the freeways of New Jersey, you may legally drive no faster than 65 mph at most, whereas until recently in Montana, the only limit was your own judgment and the power of your car's engine. In South Dakota, almost twice the proportion of eligible voters cast votes as in Louisiana. To understand this diversity among the states is to

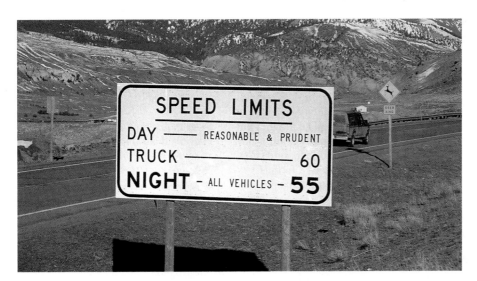

The long, straight, and empty freeways of Montana allowed policymakers there to set a speed limit that would be unthinkable on the crowded highways of New Jersey.

understand the politics and history of the United States better. This also raises the important questions of why these differences exist and what effects these differences have.

State Constitutions

Each state is governed by a separate and unique constitution that spells out the basic rules of that state's political game. Every state elects a governor as its chief executive officer, and most states have a legislature with two chambers like the Congress (except for Nebraska, which only has a senate). However, the states endow their governors with different powers and organize and elect their legislatures differently. Each state's constitution was written under unique historical conditions and with a unique set of philosophical principles in mind. Each is unique in its length and provisions. Some are modern documents; others were written over 100 years ago. The differences among these documents also reflect the diversity—social, economic, geographic, historic, and political—of the states.[5]

State constitutions are subordinate to the U.S. Constitution and the laws of the United States, but they take precedence over state law. State constitutions share many features in common with the U.S. Constitution. Both provide for separation of powers; the creation of executive, judicial, and legislative branches; means of taxation and finance; and all include a bill of rights. Figure 21.1 shows how the Texas state constitution arranges the state's governmental structure.

The key difference between the federal and state constitutions is that the state documents often provide far more detail about specific policies. The Oklahoma constitution, for example, requires that "stock feeding" be taught in public schools, and the South Dakota constitution authorizes a twine and cordage plant at its state penitentiary.[6] This level of specificity leads to constitutions that are long and sometimes confusing. Whereas the U.S. Constitution is a brief document of 8,700 words, state constitutions can be as long as Alabama's 220,000-word tome. In contrast, a few states try to stick to the point as closely as the federal constitution does—Vermont's constitution, adopted in 1793, is a model of brevity with only 6,880 words.

Why do some states try to embed specific policy into what is supposed to be a document detailing fundamental principles and government organization? It has long been argued that powerful interest groups have encouraged lengthy constitutions in order to protect their interests. It is far more difficult to amend a state constitution than to change a law, so activists try to include policy statements in the constitution in order to guard against their future repeal. In Southern states, where most constitutions were rewritten after the Civil War, state constitutions tend to be

Visual Literacy

Explaining Differences
in State Laws

Participation

Explore Your State Constitution

Figure 21.1   Government Under the Texas State Constitution

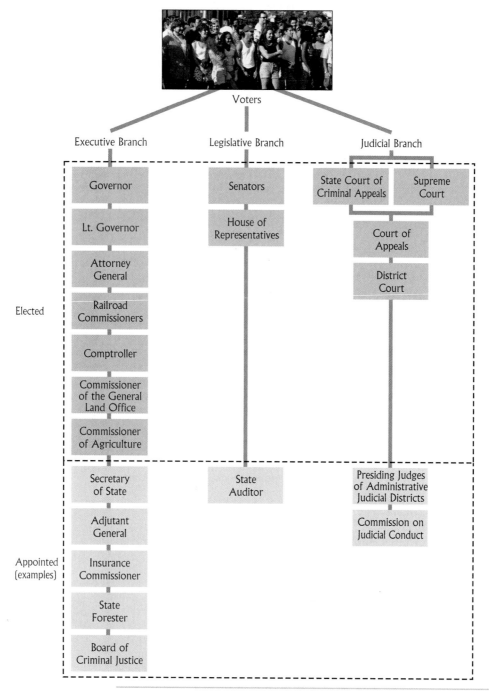

Source: Council of State Governments, 2004.

longer and more particularistic. Even so, some argue that longer constitutions help limit government interference with Americans' valued individualism.[7]

Amending State Constitutions

Periodically, a state considers changes to the rules of its political game. Most avoid the politically difficult process of writing an entirely new constitution. Massachusetts, for example, is governed by a constitution written in 1780. Mississippi, Nebraska, New

York, and Utah are among 29 states that have nineteenth-century constitutions. Although a few states have attempted to write entirely new constitutions since World War II (the most recent successful attempt being Georgia in 1983), most states have adapted their governing documents to the late twentieth century by the "cut and paste" method of constitutional amendment.

The most common way that state constitutions are amended is through a two-step process by which the legislature "proposes" an amendment (usually by passing a resolution to this effect by a vote of two-thirds of the legislature, and in 12 states doing so in two consecutive sessions) and a majority vote in the next general election "ratifies" it. Although this process is difficult, it is used every election year, typically for taxation and public debt issues. Indeed, California has amended its constitution 493 times since 1879. And across all states between 1898 and 1998, 827 direct (from voters) and indirect initiatives (through legislature) for constitutional amendments were proposed, and voters approved 343 (42 percent) measures.[8] State constitutions can also be amended through a constitutional convention. Although rare, Massachusetts used a convention in an attempt to address same-sex marriage in 2004.

State Elections

Most top-level state policymakers are elected to office. To an even greater extent than federal officials, state officials must achieve office through the ballot box and respond to the voters' preferences if they wish to remain there. At the federal level, voters can only elect one member of the executive branch (the president) while they can elect no one in the judicial branch. However, at the state level, voters usually have far more power to determine who governs them. For example, in California voters select eight statewide executive officers (including the governor, treasurer, and even the insurance commissioner), as well as many judges down to the trial court level.[9] Further, in many states voters are authorized to make law directly through the ballot box by using the direct democracy mechanisms we will discuss shortly.

Historically, state elections have been decided by the general political mood of the country or state, with those running for office having little ability to influence their own electoral fortunes. Voters cared little and knew less about state legislative or even gubernatorial races. But as the states have become more important and as their institutions have become more effective and respected in the past generation, average voters and political activists are more attentive to state elections. As a result, state officials look more like their constituents, in terms of partisanship, ideology, and demographics.

Gubernatorial Elections

Gubernatorial races have increasingly become focused on individual candidates rather than party affiliations. Political scientists call this the "presidentialization" of gubernatorial elections, since they have come to resemble the personality-focused mega-events that make up modern campaigns for the White House. This has occurred because of the increasing importance of television and money to gubernatorial campaigns, and the decoupling of gubernatorial races from presidential races and state political party organizations.[10]

Historically, most governors were elected during presidential years, either because their term of office was only two years, or because their four-year term coincided with that of the presidential term. But since the 1960s, most states have adopted a four-year gubernatorial term and shifted that term so that elections are held during nonpresidential election years. Today, only 11 states hold their gubernatorial elections at the same time as presidential elections.[11]

The change means that the gubernatorial race is the "top of the ticket" in most states, which makes it more likely that voters will pay attention. Races are therefore more likely to be decided on what voters think about the candidates than on any coattail effect from the presidential race. This means that candidates for governor can no longer expect to garner much help from a popular presidential candidate for their party, nor can they assume any candidate's campaign suffers from an unpopular presidential candidate topping the ticket. Political scientists refer to the pattern of running on your own as a "candidate-centered campaign"[12]

In order to run on their own, gubernatorial candidates have taken to television advertising in a big way, just as presidential candidates have, and largely for the same reasons. There are simply too many people in a state for a candidate to meet them all face-to-face. Gubernatorial candidates hire nationally known advertising agencies to develop slick ad campaigns. These campaigns are not cheap. The use of television is one of the main reasons why the costs of gubernatorial campaigns have skyrocketed. For elections between 1977 and 1980, the total cost of gubernatorial elections was $422.7 million (adjusted for 1997 dollars). That cost increased by 45 percent, to $611.8 million, for elections between 1994 and 1997. Although the largest states have some of the most expensive elections, if we adjust for the cost per general election vote, we find that the 2000 election cost the most in New Hampshire at $10.03 per vote, and the least in a relatively larger state like Washington at $2.78 per vote. However, collectively the elections in California and Texas have cost the most, with California at $114 million and Texas at $66 million in the 2002 election, and the four 2003 gubernatorial elections and California gubernatorial recall election cost nearly $104.5 million.[13]

Most of this money has to be raised by the candidates themselves. At one time, state political party organizations had a strong hand in funding these campaigns and in selecting the party nominees for the general election. Those days are long gone in most states. With the advent of the direct primary for nominating party candidates, a person who wants to become governor must organize and fund a major campaign in the primary. And by the time a candidate wins the primary, he or she has built a solid campaign organization and has little need for the party's help in the general election.

One result for the personalization of gubernatorial elections has been that parties have a harder time predicting their success. Because voters now become familiar with gubernatorial candidates during campaigns, they more frequently vote based on their attitude toward the candidates rather than resorting to party loyalty. This can lead to ticket splitting and divided government, as citizens vote for less well-known state legislative candidates strictly based on their party affiliation.[14] We see the results of this when states whose voters are predominantly of one party elect governors of the other party. For example, in 2002, Virginia voters elected Democrat Mark R. Warner to the governorship, even though registered Republican voters outnumber registered Democrats and Republicans maintained majorities in the state legislature, even after the 2003 elections. At the extreme, this has led to four Independent governors being elected in recent years. Two of these—Lowell Weicker of Connecticut and Walter Hickel of Alaska—were politicians formerly associated with a major party who challenged their parties' candidates in the general election due to intraparty squabbles. But the two governors serving in 2002—Angus King of Maine (Independent) and Jesse Ventura of Minnesota (Reform Party)—were truly independent of the Democratic and Republican Parties and owed their election completely to the efforts of their personal campaign organizations. However, both of these governors left office in 2003, leaving no Independents in governorships.

State Legislative Elections

Of all state- and federal-level officials, state legislators face the smallest constituencies, ranging from less than 3,000 people in a New Hampshire House of Representatives district to almost 800,000 people in a California Senate district, but with an average size of about 140,000 for state senate districts and 50,000 for state house districts.[15] By comparison, governors and members of the U.S. House of Representatives need to respond to considerably more constituents.

Throughout much of the twentieth century, state legislatures were horribly malapportioned, giving greater representation to rural areas than their population warranted. One hundred years ago, most state legislators represented rural areas because that was where people lived. However, by the early 1960s the population had become overwhelmingly urban. Since the legislative district boundaries had rarely changed, state legislatures continued to be dominated by rural politicians. The main reason for the underrepresentation of urban areas was that districts were often constructed on the basis of the boundaries of some local government, such as a county, regardless of how many people lived there. This meant that in many states, rural counties with a few thousand residents and urban counties with hundreds of thousands of residents all had the same representation in the state legislature.

In 1962, after decades of avoiding the issue, the U.S. Supreme Court ruled that the districts of the lower chamber of state legislatures must be based on the number of people living in them. This landmark decision in *Baker v. Carr* established the principle of "one person, one vote" in drawing up state house districts. Two years later, the Court ruled in *Reynolds v. Sims* that state senates must also be apportioned in this fashion.

These cases dramatically changed the face of state legislatures. Gone was the rural dominance of these chambers. New representatives arrived from the central cities and suburbs. Urban and metropolitan area problems became the focus of state legislatures.

Periodic redrawing of legislative districts is required as population shifts. This is now done following every decennial census, further changing the composition of state legislatures. The late twentieth-century migration of citizens to the suburbs has resulted in new voting power for suburban metropolitan interests and a decline in the power of central cities in state capitals.

Ironically, although state legislators have smaller districts than any other state or federal elected officials, they are the least well known by voters. This is largely due to the historic lack of media coverage given to state legislatures and the lack of campaign resources of candidates for the office. The result is that races for state legislature, at least in general elections, have been decided on the basis of forces beyond candidates' control—party identification of district voters, and the parties' candidates in the race for governor and president.[16]

But with the recent shifting of more policy responsibilities to the states and increases in state legislative salaries (discussed shortly) making the office both more important and attractive, campaigns for the state legislature have started to become more candidate centered, although not nearly to the extent that gubernatorial campaigns have. This "congressionalization" of state legislative races is encouraged by increased resources (mainly staff and time) for incumbent legislators to retain their seats, and increases in the activities of PACs at the state level willing to fund expensive campaigns.[17] Campaign costs skyrocketed for state legislative campaigns from the 1970s to 1990s, and continue to be high today, with candidates in large states such as California and Illinois finding it necessary to raise at least $100,000 and highly competitive races might cost over $2 million. Although it is still possible to run a less closely contested campaign in a less populous state for only several thousand dollars, this is no longer the norm.[18]

Because of the need to raise and spend more money on these campaigns, incumbent legislators appear to be more advantaged than they used to be. Incumbents can use the resources and prestige of office both to enhance their visibility with their constituents and to attract campaign contributions from PACs and others interested in garnering favor in the legislature. State legislative leaders also help incumbents through their own PACs and party funds in order to enhance their personal influence as leaders and the prospects of their party retaining or regaining control of their chamber.[19]

Partisan Competition, Legislative Turnover, and Term Limits.   The 2003–2004 elections continued the 20-year trend in state legislatures of increasing party competition, closer partisan splits, and changing party control (see Table 21.1). Although

Table 21.1 The Balance of Power, 2005

STATE BY STATE

THE BALANCE OF POWER

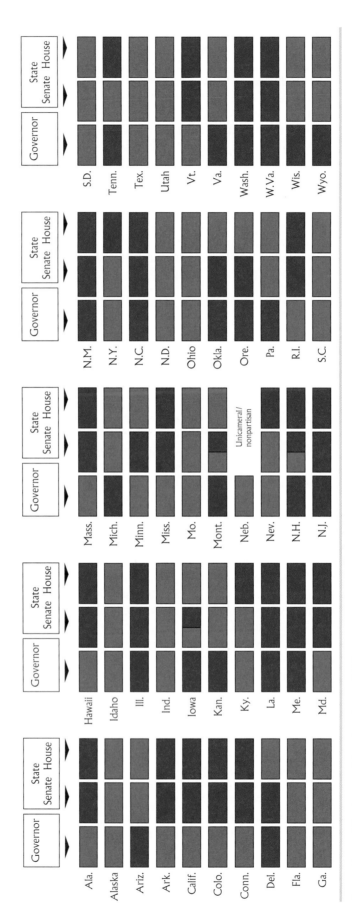

Source: National Conference of State Legislatures, 2004.

much of this change has occurred as a result of Republican gains in the South (for example, the South Carolina statehouse now has a majority of Republicans, as do both chambers of the Florida state legislature), even Northern states have been experiencing increasingly close legislative party divisions. Democrats hold 49.5 percent of all seats in state legislatures, continuing a steady downward trend since the Watergate scandals buoyed the party's fortunes in the mid-1970s.[20]

Although some state legislative chambers have very lopsided partisan splits (for example, in the Idaho state senate Republicans hold 80 percent of the seats and in the Massachusetts state senate Democrats hold 85 percent), some legislatures are closely divided. In nine legislative chambers, there are three or fewer seats separating the parties. The Montana senate is an extreme case, with exactly 25 Republicans and 25 Democrats. And finally, following the 2004 elections, 12 chambers changed majority party control or are now split. This change is consistent with a 16-year trend that indicates a remarkable period of increasing party competition in the state legislatures.

Divided government exists when a single party does not control both chambers of the state legislature and the governor's office. With divided government, it is usually much more difficult for coherent policy action to take place because the parties that control the different components of state government have conflicting policy and electoral goals. Increased switching of party control and party competition has inevitably led to more divided control of state government than in the past, when party affiliation of voters within states was more stable and electorates more homogeneous.[21] After the 2004 elections, 29 states had divided government. In contrast, in 1946 only seven states had divided government.

Increased party competition, divided government, and majority party switching in state legislatures has tended to increase legislative partisanship and polarize legislative deliberations, thereby making compromise harder to come by. Further, this sort of swinging from party to party can lead to a lack of policy continuity in a state. On the other hand, high levels of party competition tend to make elected officials more attentive and responsive to voters.[22]

Aside from partisan change there is the question of turnover in state legislatures. Turnover levels—the rate that state legislators are replaced from election to election—give us an understanding both of how much experience and expertise state legislators have relative to other political actors in the states and how closely they are "connected" to their constituencies and the normal life of a state citizen.

Recent history has shown that in any 10-year period, about 72 percent of state senate and 84 percent of state house legislative seats are turned over.[23] Thus, significant change in the people holding state legislative office is the norm. But annual turnover in most states has been on the decline over the past 40 years. During the 1990s, Delaware and Oklahoma had the lowest average annual percent turnover in their Senates (10 percent). Kansas and Louisiana had the highest annual turnover rates, both in their upper chambers, in the 1990s at 43 and 41 percent respectively.[24] Across all states the current average annual turnover rate in any election year is about 25 percent in lower chambers and 23 percent in upper chambers.[25]

In recent years voters in many states have attempted to increase turnover rates by legally restricting the number of terms a member may serve. Increasingly, voters appear to support the argument that professional, career-oriented legislators become so entrenched and difficult to unseat that they lose touch with their constituents and instead pander to special interests. Since 1990, 21 states have adopted term limits for state legislators, almost exclusively through direct democracy mechanisms (discussed shortly). However, four states have seen their term limits overturned in court, or in the case of Idaho and Utah, by the state legislature, leaving only 15 term limit laws intact.[26] The number of terms permitted varies from state to state. For example, California limits its assembly (their lower house) members to six years and its senators to eight years in office.[27] In the 2002 elections, term limited states had turnover rates in lower chambers that were 13 percentage points higher than non-term limited states and almost 9 percentage points higher in upper chambers.[28]

The Changing Face of State Elected Officials

In November 1996, Washington state voters chose Gary Locke, the son of Chinese immigrants, as their governor. Locke became the first Asian American ever to be elected governor of one of the 48 contiguous states. Seven years before, Virginia voters made Douglas Wilder the first elected African-American governor. Although these two governors are exceptions to the rule that governors are White, married men who are often lawyers, state voters are increasingly electing a wider variety of people to state offices.

Women have made strong inroads into the governors' offices (see Figure 21.2). Before 1974, only a few women had ever been governors, and those were elected because they were married to a former governor who could not run again. But in 1974, Ella Grasso was elected to the governor's office of Connecticut in her own right. Dixie Lee Ray followed her in 1976 in Washington. Since 1925, 26 women have served as governors in states as varied as Delaware, Oregon, Kansas, and Kentucky, representing both the Democratic and Republican Parties. At least two prominent female governors—Ann Richards of Texas and Christine Whitman of New Jersey— have been mentioned as potential presidential candidates. In 2002, 36 states were holding gubernatorial elections and in 14 of these states women were running for the office. In 2004 there were eight female state governors serving in the United States. Being female or a person of color is no longer an insurmountable hurdle to being elected to a state's highest office.

State legislatures too have been looking more and more like the diverse population of the United States.[29] In 2004, 22.5 percent of all state legislators were women, a tremendous increase over 1969, when only about 4 percent of state legislators were women.[30] Women are also taking more leadership roles in state legislatures. In 2003 there were 41 women in legislative leadership positions, serving in positions such as

Figure 21.2   Female Representation in State Government

Percentage of females in the state legislature in 2004.

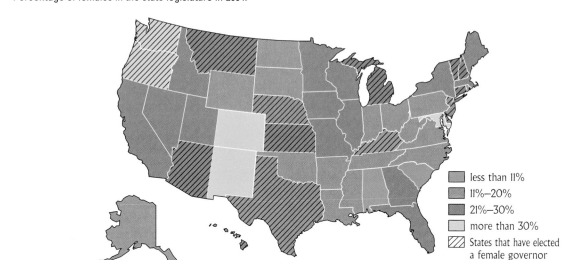

Legend:
- less than 11%
- 11%–20%
- 21%–30%
- more than 30%
- States that have elected a female governor since 1975

Source: Center for American Women and Politics, "Women in Elected Office 2004: Fact Sheet Summaries," *http://www.cawp.rutgers.edu/Facts/Officeholders/cawpfs.html,* June 14, 2004.

In 1998, women were elected to all five statewide executive offices in Arizona—governor, secretary of state, treasurer, superintendent of public instruction, and attorney general. The so-called "Fab Five" were sworn into office by another powerful Arizona female—U.S. Supreme Court Justice Sandra Day O'Connor.

senate or house majority leader. However, state legislatures do vary widely in the percentage of female legislators, from almost 37 percent in Washington to only 9 percent in South Carolina during the 2004 legislative session.

In 2003, there were 595 state legislators of African-American descent—8.1 percent, a figure that has also been mostly increasing for 30 years. Asians and Hispanics have also been increasing in their state legislative representation, primarily in Florida and the Western states. Indeed, almost 3 percent of state legislators were Hispanic in 2003.[31]

The less-than-representative percentage of women and ethnic minorities in state elected positions (although at a historic high) shows the slowness with which progress is made in this area, due at least in part to informal qualifications for higher-level offices that can include experience at lower level offices. Women and minorities are making the inroads today in the state and local offices that may well lead to them being elected more frequently to federal positions in the future. For example, the sharp jump in the representation of women in the U.S. Senate and statewide elective office in the 1990s was encouraged by increases in women being elected to state legislative positions in the 1970s and 1980s.

Governors and the Executive Branch

During his first several months as governor of California in 2003 and 2004, Arnold Schwarzenegger traveled to Israel, Japan, and China to promote investment in California industries, such as biotechnology, and to promote trade between those countries and his state. Schwarzenegger also appeared in television

Making a Difference

Rep. Tammy Baldwin (D-WI)

At an early age, Wisconsin-born Tammy Baldwin believed that she could impact people's lives through public service. In high school, she served on the student council and helped to solve problems between students and school neighbors.

After college, Baldwin served as an intern for Wisconsin Governor Tony Earl. In 1986, Baldwin was elected to serve on the Dane County Board of Supervisors for multiple terms and in 1992 she was elected to the Wisconsin State Assembly (District 78). In the state legislature she pursued health, civil rights, and women's issues.

In 1998 Tammy Baldwin made history as the first openly lesbian person elected to Congress, but she also became the first woman elected to Congress from Wisconsin.

Rep. Baldwin was reelected in 2000, 2002, and 2004, and continues her commitment to helping improve people's lives, work that she began at the local and state levels of government.

commercials aired oversees that promoted California. Such actions are becoming increasingly common for governors who are interested in creating more economic growth, even though they have no legal capacity to sign formal trade agreements with foreign nations. Governor Kathleen Sebelius of Kansas and former governor of Minnesota, Jesse Ventura, made similar trips to foreign countries, including Cuba.

The actions of these governors highlight the modern role of the governor. Not only is the governor the chief executive officer of a state, with the responsibility to execute the laws passed by the legislature, but he or she is also the best known state public official, to whom the public looks for leadership, assurance, conflict resolution, and policy initiatives. If administering public policy is the governor's main constitutional responsibility, then promoting his or her vision of what public policy ought to be is the modern governor's primary responsibility to the public.

The Job of Governor

Like presidents, governors are expected to wear many hats—sometimes fulfilling constitutionally assigned duties, sometimes performing political tasks. But the powers of governors are not always commensurate with citizens' expectations. State constitutions often hamstring a governor, dividing executive power among many different administrative actors and agencies. But a generation of modernization and reform has resulted in enhanced powers for governors by reducing the number of independently elected officials and independent boards and commissions in the state executive branch, as well as by enhancing governors' other formal powers.[32] These reforms have established clearer lines of authority and enhanced the governor's appointment, reorganization, and budgetary powers. Most states have also raised their governors' salaries and increased the number of years a governor can serve. Nevertheless, the limited formal powers of governors make it very difficult for them to fulfill their responsibilities to the state without resorting to more "informal powers," such as the use of the media and a public relations staff.

How powerful are the nation's governors? Political scientist Thad Beyle has devoted considerable attention to this subject. On the basis of an analysis of gubernatorial powers outlined in state constitutions and statutes, and in the strength of their party in their states' legislatures, he has rated each of the states' governor's institutional powers. Figure 21.3 displays this rating, based on the governor's ability to stay in office, make major appointments, prepare the state budget, veto legislation, and direct political parties. Seven states' governors—those in Hawaii, Maryland, New Jersey, New York, Ohio, Pennsylvania, and Utah—have very strong powers. Another 18 governors enjoy strong executive powers. Ten states accord their governors moderate powers. The remaining 15 states, including states as diverse as Massachusetts, California, and Nevada, give only weak powers to their governors.[33]

Two of a governor's most important formal powers for controlling state government are the veto and the executive budget. The governor's veto is similar to that of the president—a governor can refuse to sign a bill passed by the state legislature, blocking it from becoming law. But in most states, the governor's veto power is far more potent than the president's. First, gubernatorial vetoes have been very difficult for state legislatures to override historically, and this remains true today.[34] Although state legislatures have become more aggressive in overriding vetoes in recent years, still less than 10 percent of gubernatorial vetoes are overridden.

line-item veto

The power possessed by 42 state governors to veto only certain parts of a bill while allowing the rest of it to pass into law.

Further, 42 state governors have the **line-item veto,** which allows them to veto only certain parts of a bill while allowing the rest of the bill to pass into law. This keeps the legislature from being able to hold a bill hostage, forcing the governor to sign a popular bill even though it contains a provision that the governor thinks is unwise. This is especially useful on appropriations bills, allowing the governor to trim pork barrel spending as he or she sees fit. In Wisconsin, the governor is even allowed to veto individual words and letters from a bill, sometimes changing its basic meaning. In

Figure 21.3   Institutional Powers of the Governors

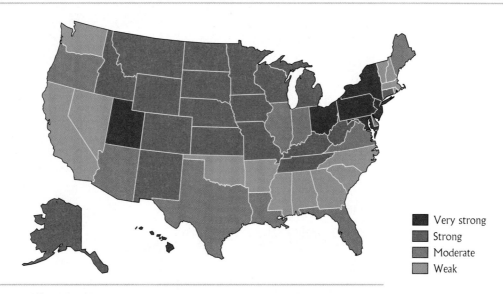

Very strong
Strong
Moderate
Weak

Source: Adapted from Thad Beyle, "The Governors," in Virginia Gray and Russell L. Hanson, eds., 8th ed., *Politics in the American States* (Washington, D.C.: Congressional Quarterly Press, 2004), 212–213.

1987, newly elected Governor Tommy Thompson used this power over 350 times on the budget passed by the Democratic state legislature.[35] With this power, a governor with a sizable minority in the legislature to support him or her can force or cajole the legislature into passing much of his or her agenda.

The governor also has the power to initiate the state budget process in almost all states. This allows the governor to set the agenda for what is by far the most important bill(s) of the state legislative session. The budget details how state tax dollars are going to be spent—it is where state public policy "puts up or shuts up." Although the legislature may amend and must pass the governor's proposal as it does any other bill, the limited staff and session time of most state legislatures, especially compared to that available to the governor, makes the massive budget sent by the governor difficult to change substantially. Further, since the governor has the ability to veto—and sometimes item veto—the budget passed by the legislature, he or she also has the last word in the process. This provides a governor the ability to gain help for his or her policy goals from both state legislators and bureaucrats interested in furthering their own policy goals through state spending.

To enhance their influence, governors supplement their formal institutional powers with more "personal powers."[36] A governor's real power depends on the way he or she uses character, leadership style, and persuasive abilities in conjunction with the formal prerogatives of the office. Building public support is an increasingly important part of the policymaking process. This is true as a means for influencing legislative decision making in all states, but also applies to influencing citizen behavior directly in states with direct democracy mechanisms. For example, in 2004 California Governor Schwarzenegger expended most of his informal powers on generating public support for ballot propositions concerning government finances rather than trying to influence legislators.

Not surprisingly, public relations and media experts have become a key part of many governors' staffs. Although press coverage of state politics is intermittent at best, focusing on only the most salient controversies and such predictable events as the governor's State of the State address, a savvy governor can create media events and opportunities that enhance his or her popularity and political clout. Whether it is Governor Arnold Schwarzenegger visiting the prime minister of Israel, or New York

To lead a state government successfully today, a governor must serve a variety of roles, including symbolic leader of the state during times of crisis. Here, Oregon Governor Theodore R. Kulongoski mourns with the wife of a U.S. solider who was killed in Afghanistan.

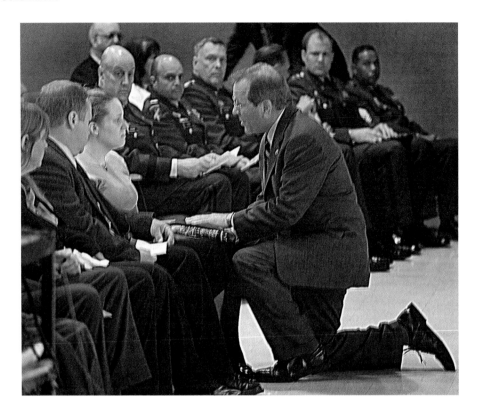

Governor George Pataki visiting Ground Zero of the World Trade Center, the media image of a caring, active, busy governor can be parlayed into political clout with the legislature and executive agencies. Likewise, governors are subjected to media frenzies over failures in the bureaucracies they oversee. For example, as Florida Governor Jeb Bush pursued what seemed to be an easy reelection in 2002, the media and Democrats attacked Bush over the unexplained disappearance of a 4-year-old girl in the state's foster care system and the system's reputation for being the worst in the country.

After languishing for most of the twentieth century as a political backwater office where political hacks, business leaders, and others went to cap off their careers before retiring to the country club, today's governors are politically savvy, active, and have strong policy agendas.[37] Modern governors are more likely to be bright, experienced, and capable of managing the diverse problems of a state. In addition to being better educated than their predecessors, recent governors have often had previous experience as a statewide elected official or held a federal position.

Today's governors increasingly have the tools and skills to control state government and guide the state in the policy directions they think are best. Demonstrating the esteem in which the modern governorship is held is the fact that in the last quarter of the twentieth century, the U.S. president has been a former governor in all but five years. In each presidential race in this period, at least one of the major party nominees was a sitting or former governor.

Other Executive Officers

lieutenant governor

Often the second-highest executive official in state government, who is elected with the governor as a ticket in some states and is elected separately in others. She or he may have legislative and executive branch responsibilities.

Unlike the U.S. president, most governors must work with an array of independently elected executive branch officials in conducting the affairs of state government. At various times, these officials may assist or oppose the governor. State voters choose a **lieutenant governor** in 43 states. The governor and lieutenant governor are elected as a team in 24 states. In states where the governor and lieutenant governor are chosen independently, it is possible for the two top state executives to be political rivals or even members of different political parties. This can result in some real battles between

As the state's legal counsel, the attorney general watches out for the state's legal interests. New York Attorney General Eliot Spitzer has fought against corporate corruption and greed, even going so far as to sue the former director of the famed New York Stock Exchange.

them. For example, in 1990 when then-Governor (and Democrat) Michael Dukakis of Massachusetts left the state on an international trade mission, Republican Lieutenant Governor Evelyn Murphy initiated major cuts in public employment in an attempt to jump-start her floundering campaign for governor.[38] Perhaps in anticipation of such antics, when Republican Steve Windom became lieutenant governor of Alabama, the Democrat-dominated state legislature and Democratic governor promptly stripped the office of almost all its powers.[39] Most lieutenant governors have few formal duties aside from presiding over the state senate and being in the succession path for governor.

Other major executive positions elected in some states include:

- Attorney General—the state's legal counsel and prosecutor (elected in 43 states)
- Treasurer—the manager of the state's bank accounts (elected in 38 states)
- Secretary of State—in charge of elections and record-keeping (elected in 36 states)
- Auditor—financial comptroller for the state (elected in 25 states)

Other officials elected in fewer states include education secretary and commissioners for land, labor, mines, agriculture, and utilities, among others.[40]

So many independent executives, commissions, and boards work within state governments that many politicians and scholars have called for major state government reorganization to allow governors more control and to increase efficiency generally. Every state has undertaken some kind of reorganization of the executive branch in the last 30 years. However, research shows that the expected benefits of reorganized state governments are not always achieved. Such reorganization only sometimes increases accountability and seldom results in cost saving and efficiency—benefits often promised by its proponents.[41] Although state residents may value smaller governments, they enjoy having electoral control over the leaders of state executive branches.

State Legislatures

State legislatures are often easy targets for criticism. Their work is not well understood and the institution does not typically receive the public attention that the governor's office or federal institutions do. Further, up until a generation ago, state legislatures and legislators had a history of poor performance that still haunts them. At that time, they were "malapportioned, unrepresentative, dominated by their governors and/or special interests, and unable and unwilling to deal with the pressing issues of the day."[42]

But between 1965 and 1985, many state legislatures underwent a metamorphosis into more full-time, professional bodies—several like state-level congresses. According to political scientist Alan Rosenthal, "They increased the time they spent on their tasks; they established or increased their professional staffs; and they streamlined their procedures, enlarged their facilities, invigorated their processes, attended to their ethics, disclosed their finances, and reduced their conflicts of interest."[43] As a result, state legislatures are far more active, informed, representative, and democratic today than they were 40 years ago.

You Are a State Legislator

State legislatures serve the same basic function in the states as Congress does in the federal government, and they do it with the same basic mechanisms. State legislatures make almost all the basic laws of the state by approving identical bills in each of their two-chambered bodies (except in Nebraska's unicameral legislature). They appropriate the money that is needed for state government to function. They oversee the activities of the executive branch through confirming gubernatorial appointments, controlling the budgets of the agencies, and investigating complaints and concerns of citizens and the press. State legislators themselves attend closely to the needs of their constituents, whether through voting on bills in line with their constituents' interests or chasing down problems a citizen has with a bureaucratic agency.

Members of the state legislature are at the front line of interaction between citizens and government. Because most state legislatures meet for only a limited number of months each year, and because state capitals are typically closer to their districts than Washington, D.C., is to the districts of most congresspersons, state legislators usually live among the people they represent. They are closely involved with their constituents not only at election time, but also throughout the year. They coach basketball and run restaurants; they teach school and preach at local churches; they are local attorneys and bankers. In short, the state legislature in almost all states comes closest to the sort of citizen-directed government envisioned by Thomas Jefferson over 200 years ago.

The reforms of the past generation designed to improve the efficiency and effectiveness of state legislatures are collectively called *legislative professionalism.*[44] That is, these are reforms designed "to enhance the capacity of the legislature to perform its role in the policymaking process with an expertise, seriousness, and effort comparable to that of other actors in the process."[45] Changes have been primarily in three areas. First, legislative sessions have been lengthened to give legislators more time to deal with the increasingly complex problems of the states. Before 1965, most state legislatures only met for several weeks each year, and many would only meet every other year. In 2004, 43 state legislatures had annual sessions, usually meeting for between three and five months, with a few (such as in Michigan, Massachusetts, and Wisconsin) meeting year-round.

The second legislative professionalism reform was to increase legislators' salaries so they could devote more of their time to considering the states' business, and less to their "regular" job. The idea was also that if service in the state legislature paid a living wage, legislators would have fewer conflicts of interest and a wider variety of people would be willing to serve. For instance, the only people who could afford to serve in the West Virginia state legislature in 1960 for a salary of $1,500 were those with either an outside source of income or who were independently wealthy. In 2004, the roughly $67,000 an Illinois state representative earned could allow him or her to focus full-time on legislative duties.

The third major professionalism reform was the increase in the staff available to help legislators in their duties. Even since 1979 (after many of the big professionalism changes had already occurred), permanent state legislative staff has increased over 60 percent.[46] By increasing their session length, salary, and staff, state legislatures have dramatically increased their ability to have an impact on the state policymaking process.

Not all the effects of this drive toward legislative professionalism are seen as good, and not all states have professionalized their legislatures to the same level. Some argue that professionalism leads to an overemphasis on reelection by state legislators, inflated campaign costs, and lack of leadership in the law-making process.[47] Legislative professionalism threatens the existence of the "citizen legislature," in which people leave their job for a couple of months each year to serve the state and inject some "common sense" into government. The recent spate of state term limits laws indicates the esteem in which many Americans hold this sort of nonprofessional state legislature. There is also some evidence that increased professionalism does not enhance even some of the aspects of the process that proponents argued it would, such as increasing membership diversity in state legislatures.[48]

It is also important to note that not all state legislatures are in any sense full-time, professional bodies. Members of the New Hampshire House of Representatives earn $200 for a two-year term, which consists of only one 30-day period of service in each year. These are clearly not professional legislators. On the other hand, across the border in Massachusetts, state legislators earn over $50,000 and meet virtually the entire year. Figure 21.4 shows roughly which states have professionalized legislatures, which still have citizen legislatures, and which have legislatures that are hybrids, having some characteristics of both. Those states that have developed professional legislatures tend to be those with large and heterogeneous populations that both need and can afford them, although there is a regional effect that may have to do with political preferences for a professional government.[49] Although this selective process makes it difficult to assess the independent effects of legislative professionalism, there is some evidence that more professionalism leads to more liberal welfare policy and perhaps more divided government in the states.[50]

We may now be seeing the beginning of a "deprofessionalizing" trend in some states, as some hearken back to the Jeffersonian ideal of the citizen legislature. Term

Figure 21.4   Legislative Professionalism

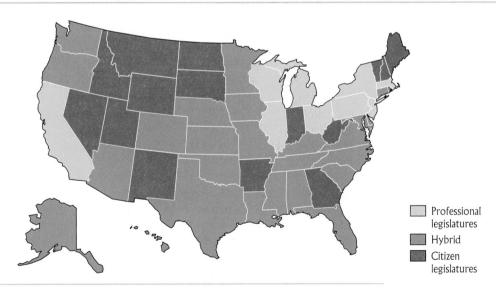

Legend:
- Professional legislatures
- Hybrid
- Citizen legislatures

Source: Adapted from Keith E. Hamm and Gary F. Moncrief, "Legislative Politics in the States," in Virginia Gray and Russell L. Hanson, eds., 8th ed., Politics in the American States (Washington, D.C.: Congressional Quarterly Press, 2004), 158.

limits laws are the most obvious manifestation of this, but recent laws in California limiting legislative staffing and in Colorado limiting the powers of the legislative leadership may also signal that the legislative professionalism movement is cyclical.[51]

State Court Systems

The organization of the states' courts reflects two major influences: (1) the model of organization set by the federal courts, and (2) the judicial preferences of each state's citizens as manifested in state constitutions and statutes. State courts are far more involved in administering justice than is the federal judiciary. Indeed, 98 percent of all litigation in the United States is settled in state courts. Recent data show that state courts have 85 times the number of criminal cases and 27 times more civil cases than federal courts with only 14 times as many judges.[52] In addition, state court workloads have been increasing in both criminal and civil cases, forcing states to experiment with alternatives to trial courts like mediation, arbitration, and plea bargaining, among others. The volume of cases heard by state courts is significant, but courts are also policy-making bodies. Particularly when the highest court in the state rules on a case, judges are doing more than just interpreting the law; they are often making policy in the same fashion as the U.S. Supreme Court.[53]

Since World War II, many state court systems have undergone reforms designed to modernize and rationalize their procedures and structure, much like the reforms undergone in the states' governors' offices and legislatures. These include reforms both of organizational structure and judicial selection.

State Court Organization

State court systems often developed as a hodgepodge of individual courts set up at odd times and for odd reasons at the subnational level. Many states have low-level courts, such as justices of the peace or magistrate courts, whose presiding officials may not even be lawyers. Many states developed a variety of specialized courts to deal with specific judicial matters involving traffic, family, or taxes. These systems, which included courts that were completely independent of any higher authority, often led to confusion, duplication of effort, and unfair treatment of cases and people.

In the past generation, efforts have been made to consolidate and coordinate many state courts systems so that they parallel the federal system, discussed in Chapter 16. First, specialized courts have been consolidated and subsumed into trial courts with more general jurisdiction. These courts are usually established for county-sized areas and are the setting for most trials. They are known by a variety of labels—district courts, circuit courts, superior courts, and (in the case of New York) supreme courts. Judges assigned to these trial courts often work in only one county and specialize in criminal, juvenile, or civil litigation. A single judge presides over each case, and citizens may be called upon to serve as jurors and members of grand jury panels.

Many states have also moved toward coordinating their court systems through their court of last resort, usually called the state supreme court. Under a coordinated system, the state supreme court serves not only as the court of final appeal for all cases in the state court system, but it also has the responsibility for administering and regulating the justice system in the state. This usually involves appointing a chief court administrator to handle the day-to-day budgeting, operations, and organization of all the courts in the state, and establishing boards to oversee and deal with complaints against lawyers and judges in the states.

A major innovation adopted by most states in the past 30 years is an *intermediate court of appeal.* Like federal appeals courts, states organize these courts on a regional

Figure 21.5   Prototypical Modern State Court System

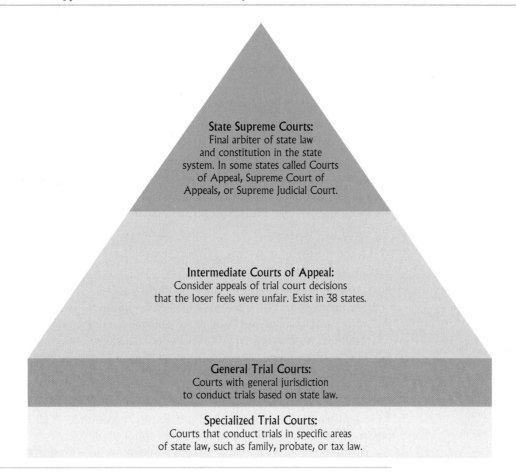

State Supreme Courts:
Final arbiter of state law and constitution in the state system. In some states called Courts of Appeal, Supreme Court of Appeals, or Supreme Judicial Court.

Intermediate Courts of Appeal:
Consider appeals of trial court decisions that the loser feels were unfair. Exist in 38 states.

General Trial Courts:
Courts with general jurisdiction to conduct trials based on state law.

Specialized Trial Courts:
Courts that conduct trials in specific areas of state law, such as family, probate, or tax law.

basis and with judges working together in panels of three or more, with a majority deciding each case. No witnesses are called before appellate courts, and juries are not used. Instead, judges read briefs and hear arguments prepared by lawyers that address whether the law was appropriately applied at the trial court level and whether due process of law was followed. The job of judges at this level is not to determine the facts of a case but to interpret the laws and the state or national constitution as they apply to the case.

The organizational purpose of an intermediate court of appeal is to reduce the pressure on the state supreme court of the many "routine" appeals of trial court decisions. These are appeals that have few implications for state policy or procedure; they are appeals that primarily impact only the case at hand. An intermediate appeals court frees up the state supreme court to consider only those cases with statewide policy importance. Twelve states, all with small populations, do not have intermediate courts of appeal,[54] so the appellate work in these states falls solely to the supreme court, reducing its ability to concentrate on making policy through judicial interpretation.

Selecting Judges

In contrast to federal judges, all of whom are appointed by the president for life, judges rise to the bench in the states in a variety of ways (see Table 21.2). These judicial selection mechanisms are each relics of values that were manifested in a series of reform movements over the past 200 years.

Table 21.2 State Judicial Selection Mechanisms

APPOINTMENT	ELECTION	MERIT PLAN
By Governor: DE, ME, MD, MA, NH, NM NJ, NY, RI, VT	Partisan: AL, AR, IL, IN, MS, NY, NC, PA, TN, TX, WV	AK, AZ, CA, CO, FL, IN, IA, KS, MD, MO, NE, OK, SD, TN, UT, WY
By Legislature: CT, HI, RI, SC, VA	Nonpartisan: AZ, CA, FL, GA, ID, KS, KY, LA, MI, MN, MT, NV, NM, ND, OH, OK, OR, SD, WA	

Note: States may appear more than once, since some states select different types of judges through different mechanisms. Minor local judges, such as justices of the peace, are not considered in this table.
Source: The Council of State Governments, *The Book of the States, 2003 Edition,* (Washington, D.C.: The Council of State Governments, 2004), 235.

Merit Plan

Method for selecting state judges in which governors appoint persons based on the recommendations of a committee. After serving a short term, the judge then often faces a retention election.

At the founding of the country, almost all state judges were appointed, as in the federal system, either by the governor or the state legislature, and 13 states still use this method of judicial selection for some or all their judges. With the Jacksonian democratic impulse of the early to mid-nineteenth century, states began to select their judges by partisan ballot, just as other state officials were selected. Currently, 11 states select some or all their judges this way. In the Progressive Era (1890–1920), reformers argued that to be administered fairly, justice should be nonpartisan because a judge elected on a party platform might be more biased in his or her decisions. Persuaded by this argument, many states changed their judicial selection mechanism to that of nonpartisan election, where candidates ran against one another but without a party label. Nineteen states still use nonpartisan elections to select some or all their judges. But electing judges remains both common and controversial.[55]

The most recent wave of judicial selection reforms since World War II has been 17 states adopting a hybrid system of appointment and election known as the **Merit Plan.** In this system, the governor appoints the state's judges from a list of persons recommended by the state bar or a committee of jurists and other officials. Each appointed judge then serves a short "trial run" term, usually one year, in which citizens may assess the judge's performance. After this, an election is held in which voters are asked whether the judge should be retained in office—they simply vote yes or no, not for one candidate or another. If voters approve retention by a majority vote (Illinois requires 60 percent), then the judge continues in office for a lengthy term (usually 6 to 12 years), after which another retention election is held if the judge wishes to continue serving. Few judges lose in this type of retention election, which raises the question of whether the Merit Plan's democratic component truly enhances responsiveness to citizens. Indeed, recent research suggests there is little difference between the various selection plans and election outcomes as well as the political responsiveness of judges.[56]

direct democracy

Government controlled directly by citizens. In some U.S. states, procedures such as the initiative, the referendum, and the recall give voters a direct impact on policymaking and the political process by means of the voting booth and can therefore be considered forms of direct democracy.

Direct Democracy

A method of policymaking that is unique in the United States to subnational governments is **direct democracy.** Three procedures—the initiative, the referendum, and the recall—provide voters with ways they can directly impact policymaking and the political process through the voting booth. One or more of these procedures is available in all but one state (Alabama); the referendum for ratifying constitutional amendments is especially common. The more proactive of these are less widely available—the initiative (24 states) and recall (17 states) (see Table 21.3). These procedures were devel-

Table 21.3   Direct Democracy Mechanisms

INITIATIVE[a]	LEGISLATIVE REFERENDUM[b]	RECALL
AK, AZ, AR, CA, CO, FL, ID, IL, ME, MA, MI, MS, MO, MT, NE, NV, ND, OH, OK, OR, SD, UT, WA, WY	AZ, AR, CA, DE, ID, IL, KY, ME, MD, MA, MI, MO, MT, NE, NV, NM, ND, OH, OK, OR, SD, UT, WA	AK, AZ, CA, GA, ID, KS, LA, MI, MN, MT, NV, NM, ND, OR, SD, WA, WI

[a]These states have at least one of the several forms of initiative.
[b]All states except Alabama allow or require a referendum for state constitutional amendments. The states listed in this column also allow referenda on the passage of legislative issues that are not constitutional amendments.
Source: The Council of State Governments, *The Book of the States, 2003 Edition*, (Washington, D.C.: The Council of State Governments, 2004), 281–287.

oped in the Progressive Era largely in the Western and Midwestern states as a way to bring more power to the people, by cutting out the middle persons in the policymaking system—political parties, politicians, and interest groups.

The **initiative** is the purest form of direct democracy. Although its details vary from state to state, the basic procedure is as follows. First, a citizen decides that he or she wants to see a law passed. The specific language of that proposal is then registered with a state official (typically the secretary of state), and permission to circulate a petition is given. The advocates of the proposal then try to get a specified number of eligible voters (typically 5–10 percent of those voting in the previous election) to sign a petition saying they would like to see the proposal on the ballot. When the appropriate number of signatures has been verified, the proposal is placed on the next general election ballot for an approve/disapprove vote. If a majority of voters approve it, the proposal becomes law. Between 1904 and 2003 at least 2,021 initiatives have been placed on state ballots and only 41 percent have passed. But both the number and passage rate of initiatives has increased in the past 15 years.[57]

The initiative allows for the adoption of policy that might otherwise be ignored or opposed by policymakers in the state legislature and governor's offices. The best example of this is the state legislative term limits movement of the 1990s. Since this policy would directly and negatively affect some state legislators, it is easy to see why such a policy would be difficult to pass through the state legislature. Of the 21 states that have passed such limits, only Louisiana does not have the initiative. Perhaps just as telling, of the 24 states that have the initiative in some form, only 4 (Alaska, Illinois, Mississippi, and North Dakota) have not passed term limits. Other sorts of ideas become state law through this process that might not otherwise do so, for good or ill. These include everything from a series of property tax limitations in many states in the 1970s and 1980s to recent initiatives allowing marijuana to be used for medical purposes in California and seven other states. Some research even suggests that legislatures in states with the initiative may pass laws more in line with citizen preferences when the threat of citizen action through the initiative is present,[58] but other research disputes this finding.[59]

Perhaps not surprisingly there is considerable debate over the wisdom of making state law through citizen-initiated proposals. Constitutional amendments and legislation passed through initiative are often poorly drafted and may contain ambiguous or contradictory provisions. As a result, initiatives often create new problems, leading to lawsuits and court interpretation, and often, action by the legislature.

It is also unclear to what extent the initiative process empowers citizens or merely gives new tools to well-financed interest groups. In larger states, special interests can pay professional firms to gather the required number of signatures. Monied interests also have the advantage in mounting expensive television advertising campaigns. These ads can present voters with a biased or incomplete set of facts on an issue they would otherwise know little about. For example, in the 1998 California initiative

initiative

A process permitted in some states whereby voters may place proposed changes to state law on the ballot if sufficient signatures are obtained on petitions calling for such a vote.

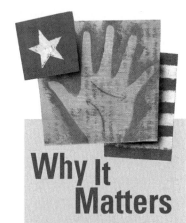

Why It Matters

Direct Democracy
Direct democracy has a special appeal to Americans, who believe in government by the people. But what if all laws passed by a state legislature had to be approved by the voters? We might adopt many policies that infringe on the rights of numerical minorities. We would also have to vote more often and spend more time voting. Extensive voting demands might decrease citizen participation and lead to ill-informed policy choices. At the same time, citizens would likely view government actions as more legitimate.

Timeline

The Initiative and Referendum

referendum

A state-level method of direct legislation that gives voters a chance to approve or disapprove legislation or a constitutional amendment proposed by the state legislature.

recall

A procedure that allows voters to call a special election for a specific official in an attempt to throw him or her out of office before the end of term. Recalls are only permitted in 17 states, seldom used because of their cost and disruptiveness, and rarely successful.

During the 2004 primary and general elections, 13 states passed constitutional amendments banning same-sex marriage via the referendum process. Here, State Rep. Nan Orrock (D-Atlanta) addresses an October 27, 2004 rally against the Georgia referendum (Amendment 1), which passed a week later by 76 to 24 percent.

campaign to legalize Indian tribal casinos, the gambling industry spent more than $71 million on *both sides* of the issue, with advertisements that were often confusing to citizens.[60] In initiative and referendum campaigns, complex public policy questions too often are reduced to simplistic sloganeering. As Ann O' M. Bowman and Richard C. Kearney argue,

Seldom are issues so simple that a yes-or-no ballot question can adequately reflect appropriate options and alternatives. A legislative setting, in contrast, fosters the negotiation and compromise that produce workable solutions. Legislatures are deliberative bodies, not instant problem solvers.[61]

A hybrid of legislative and direct democratic policymaking is the **referendum.** Unlike the initiative, which is proposed by a citizen or group, the referendum begins life as a legislative resolution. Typically, the state legislature deliberates on and passes the proposal in both chambers in identical form, as required for any bill to become law, but then instead of sending the bill to the governor for his or her approval, the proposal is presented to the voters in a general election. If a majority of voters approve it, it becomes law; otherwise, it does not. In all states (except Alabama), this procedure is required for amendments to the state constitution, and in many subnational governments referenda are required for bond issues (government debt), tax changes, and other fiscal matters.

The **recall** is different than the initiative or referendum because it is about elected officials rather than public policy. In essence, the recall allows voters to call a special election for a specific official in an attempt to throw him or her out of office before the end of his or her term. The process involves gathering signatures on a petition of voters in the jurisdiction of the official being recalled, much like an initiative. Once enough signatures are gathered, a special election is held, usually within three months, in which the official being recalled runs against any forthcoming challenger(s), if he or she desires to do so.

Needless to say, this is a drastic action and it is infrequently undertaken successfully. It is disruptive of the routine political process and very costly for the jurisdiction having to hold the special election. Because of this, only 17 states allow for the recall, and these states make it difficult to undertake, with the required number of signatures being much higher than that required to place an initiative on the ballot. Historically, those who have been recalled have been accused of a serious breach of propriety, morals, or ethics, and often are local officials or judges serving long terms. For example, in 1982 a district judge in Madison, Wis., made the highly publicized and inflammatory statement that he thought a very young victim in a sexual assault case appeared promiscuous; the judge was recalled and removed from office.[62] However, in recent

How You Can Make a Difference

Direct Democracy

If you live in a state with direct democracy mechanism such as initiative, recall, and referendum (see Table 21.3), you can get directly involved in shaping and passing legislation you support. Most people limit their participation to voting for or against a referendum or initiative, but you can do more by becoming a part of an initiative and referendum movement.

You can join the campaign staff for an initiative, or if you are very ambitious, you can start your own ballot initiative. Using the information found in the Initiative and Referendum Institute (*www.iandrinstitute.org*), you can discover the key steps to developing a ballot petition in your state. In Michigan, for example, after you decide on legislation you want enacted, you get the format of your initiative approved by the

state (though that step isn't required). Next, you must gather a sufficient number of valid signatures supporting the petition within 180 days in order to have it placed on the next statewide ballot. In 2004, a petition proposing a constitutional amendment in Michigan required 317,757 signatures.

The issues appearing on ballot initiatives are sometimes controversial ones that state legislatures want to avoid out of fear of casting a vote that would offend potential supporters. In recent years, hot topics have ranged from affirmative action, government benefits to illegal aliens, legalization of marijuana, vouchers and school choice, gun control, health care reform, bilingual education, same-sex marriage, and physician-assisted suicide. For a more detailed list of the issues in your state, check out the

Initiative and Referendum Institute, Ballot Watch (*www.ballotwatch.org*) and Ballot.org.

No matter what issues interest you, becoming active in an initiative or a referendum ballot election can be one of the surest ways to directly change government and your surrounding world.

What you can do:
- Consider what issues/concerns in your region have not been addressed.
- Go to Ballot Watch (*www.ballotwatch.org*) and *Ballot.org* to see what issues are already under consideration.
- Start a petition drive—go to *www.iandrinstitute.org* to discover how to start one in your state.

years, some state and local officials have been recalled for more policy-oriented reasons, such as for supporting tax increases in Michigan, a stadium sales tax in Wisconsin, and gun control in California. Most dramatically, California Governor Gray Davis was recalled in 2003 after voters came to believe that he had failed to solve the state's energy and fiscal crisis. California voters elected action-movie star Arnold Schwarzenegger. This was the first successful recall of a governor since North Dakota voters recalled Governor Lynn Frazier in 1921.

State and Local Government Relations

In Chapter 3, you read about the concept of federalism, and how the nation's Founders tried to strike a balance between the powers of the central government and those of the states. This state-federal *intergovernmental relationship* has evolved in the past 200 years through statutes passed by Congress, constitutional amendments and their interpretation by the U.S. Supreme Court, civil war, and tradition. The relationship between the states and the federal government is both contentious and one of the defining characteristics of government in the United States.

The intergovernmental relationship between the states and their inferior governments—local governments—is no less important in defining how our government works. But this relationship is far less ambiguous and involves no balance and little interpretation.

The basic relationship is that local governments are totally subservient to the state government. According to **Dillon's Rule** (after Iowa Judge John Dillon, who expressed this idea in an 1868 court decision) local governments have only those powers that are

Dillon's Rule

The idea that local governments have only those powers that are explicitly given them by the states. This means that local governments have very little discretion over what policies they pursue or how they pursue them. It was named for Iowa Judge John Dillon, who expressed this idea in an 1868 court decision.

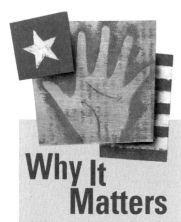

Why It Matters

State Boundaries
State boundaries typically result from historical accidents rather than efforts to define regions that have similar interests and needs. For example, the people of the Florida panhandle probably have more in common with those of southern Alabama and Georgia than those of south Florida. But what if the states were reconstructed so as to make them more homogenous and therefore more different from one another? How do you think this would affect state policy? For example, would state policies also be more dissimilar? Would citizens be happier with the policies in their state?

local charter

An organizational statement and grant of authority from the state to a local government, much like a state or federal constitution. States sometimes allow municipalities to write their own charters and to change them without permission of the state legislature, within limits. See also **home rule.**

home rule

The practice by which municipalities are permitted by the states to write their own charters and change them without permission of the state legislature, within limits. Today this practice is widely used to organize and modernize municipal government. See also **local charter.**

explicitly given to them by the states. Dillon argued definitively that local governments were "creatures of the state," and that the state legislature gave local governments the "breath of life without which they cannot exist."[63] This means that local governments have very little discretion over which policies they pursue or how they pursue them. In fact, the states have been known to take away policymaking and administrative power from local governments completely, as when the state of Missouri recently took over a school district that state officials felt was being run improperly. An extreme case of state usurpation of local power took place in 1997 when the Massachusetts state legislature actually *abolished* Middlesex County due to mismanagement and corruption![64]

The basis of this shocking imbalance of power is the U.S. Constitution. Although the Constitution discusses at length the role of the states and the relationship between the states and the central government, local governments are never explicitly mentioned. The establishment and supervision of local government has been interpreted to be one of the "reserve powers" for the states, under the Tenth Amendment of the Bill of Rights. The idea is that states have certain responsibilities and policy goals they must fulfill, but sometimes the best way to do this is through local units of government they establish. For example, the states have the responsibility to educate children, but all states (except Hawaii) have opted to establish regional school districts to do this for the states.

Although local governments have no constitutional sovereignty, local government officials are certainly not powerless in their efforts to control their own destiny. But the power of local government arises from informal political clout rather than formal powers. First, many people feel more strongly connected to their local governments than to the state. After all, it is the local government officials they see most frequently—the police officer responding to an emergency call, the teacher in the school caring for their child, the city council member helping to get the potholes filled in the street. State officials understand the sympathy (and political clout) these officials have among citizens, so they do not try to rile them without good reason. Further, local government officials of all stripes form interest groups to lobby state officials. In all states, organizations of local officials, such as the Wisconsin League of Municipalities or the Texas Association of Counties, are among the most powerful interest groups in the state capitol.[65]

Many cities have also managed to get state legislatures to grant them a degree of autonomy through a **local charter.** A charter is an organizational statement and grant of authority from the state to a local government, much like a state or federal constitution. States sometimes allow cities to write their own charters and to change them without permission from the state legislature, within limits. Today, this practice of **home rule** is widely used to organize and modernize city government.

Local Governments

The U.S. Bureau of the Census counts not only people but also governments. Its latest count revealed an astonishing 87,525 American local governments (see Table 21.4). In addition to being a citizen of the United States and of a state, the average citizen also resides within the jurisdiction of perhaps 10 to 20 local governments. The state of Illinois holds the current record for the largest number of local governments: 6,904 at the latest count. The six-county Chicago metropolitan area alone has more than 1,200 governments!

The sheer number of governments in the United States is, however, as much a burden as a boon to democracy. Citizens are governed by a complex maze of local governments—some with broad powers, others performing very specialized services. This plethora of local governments creates voter overload and ignorance, thereby defeating the democratic purpose of citizen control.

Table 21.4   Local Governments in the United States

TYPE OF GOVERNMENT	1962	2002	% CHANGE 1962–2002
All local governments	91,186	87,525	–4.1%
General-purpose governments:			
County	3,043	3,043	0.0%
Municipal	18,000	19,429	+7.4%
Township	17,142	16,504	–3.8%
Single-purpose governments:			
School district	34,678	13,506	–61.1%
Special district	18,323	35,052	+47.7%

Source: U.S. Bureau of the Census, *2002 Census of Governments, Volume 1, Number 1, Government Organization* (Washington, D.C.: U.S. Government Printing Office, 2002), 3.

Young People and Politics

Public Service Through Elective Office

Many young Americans are concerned about particular issues and government policy, and some are inspired to mobilize other young adults to register to vote, attend city council meetings, and sign petitions. However, even though issues such as public spending on education, economic development, and the drinking age have a direct impact on youth, few young people are motivated enough about these issues to run for public office. And because of age restrictions, most federal and statewide offices are closed to young adults. However, in most states there are no age requirements for state and local legislative positions, and some young adults successfully run for these offices.

In Kansas, 20-year-old Tanner Fortney ran for the Spring Hill city council in 2001 after becoming interested in public policy through his high school debate team and, later, through an internship with Congressman Dennis Moore (D-KS) and through his political science classes at the University of Kansas. Fortney survived the primary election for the city council, but lost the general election by 75 votes. After the election Fortney did not wallow in defeat. Instead he gained an appointment to the Spring Hill planning commission and immersed himself in the details of zoning and infrastructure.

Fortney's vigor impressed the town's mayor, and when a city council member resigned in October 2001, Mayor Mark Squire appointed Fortney to the council. The appointment made Fortney the Council's youngest member ever. Fortney focused his attention on development and economic growth issues, trying to make sure the town balanced residential and commercial development. Fortney's hard work, zeal, and fresh perspective helped to revitalize city government in the sleepy suburb of 3,000 near Kansas City. Voters appreciated Fortney's efforts and reelected him in April 2003 for a four-year term.

Fortney says that he will likely continue in public service, perhaps running for the county commission. In the meantime he will serve on the council, complete law school, and perhaps dream of serving in the state legislature. Fortney's example clearly demonstrates that young people can become involved and make a difference.

Questions for Discussion
- What are the minimum age limits for running for local and state offices in your state? Do you think they are too low or too high?
- Would you ever consider running for local or state office? Why or why not? Would a specific policy change encourage you to run? Explain.
- If you did run for office at a young age, what steps would you take to encourage more young people to become involved in politics?

Types of Local Government

Local governments can be classified into five types based on their legal purpose and the scope of their responsibilities: counties, townships, municipalities, school districts, and special districts.

Counties. The largest geographic unit of government at the local level is the *county* government, although they are called "parishes" in Louisiana and "boroughs" in Alaska. Texas has the most counties with 254, while Delaware and Hawaii have only 3. Los Angeles County serves the most people—over 9.5 million residents, whereas Loving County, Texas, serves only 67 residents.

The 3,034 county governments are administrative arms of state government. Typically, counties are responsible for keeping records of births, deaths, and marriages; establishing a system of justice and law enforcement; maintaining roads and bridges; collecting taxes; conducting voter registration and elections; and providing for public welfare and education. Rural residents more often rely on county governments for services because they have fewer local governments to turn to than city dwellers.

County governments usually consist of an elected *county commission*, the legislative body that makes policy, and a collection of "row officers," including sheriffs, prosecutors, county clerks, and assessors, who run county services. Some urban counties, such as Milwaukee County, St. Louis County, and Wayne (Detroit) County, now elect a county executive (like a mayor or governor). In some counties, such as Dade (Miami) County and Sacramento County, the county commission appoints a county administrator to take responsibility for the administration of county policies.

Townships. *Township* governments are found in only 20 states, including Maine, Michigan, New Hampshire, New York, Vermont, and Wisconsin. Most of the 16,504 township governments have limited powers and primarily just assist with county services in rural areas; however, some, such as those in New England, function much like city governments. Voters typically elect a township board, a supervisor, and perhaps a very small number of other executives. Township officers oversee public highways and local law enforcement, keep records of vital statistics and tax collections, and administer elections. However, most lack the power to pass local ordinances since they serve as administrative extensions of state and county governments.

Municipalities. Cities are more formally referred to as municipal governments or *municipalities*, and they supply most local programs and services for 19,429 communities in the United States. Municipalities typically provide police and fire protection, street maintenance, solid waste collection, water and sewer works, park and recreation services, and public planning. Some larger cities also run public hospitals and health programs, administer public welfare services, operate public transit and utilities, manage housing and urban development programs, and even run universities. Citizen satisfaction with the delivery of such services varies greatly.

Originally, many municipalities in the United States were run with a special form of direct democracy—the **town meeting.** Under this system, all voting-age adults in a community gathered once a year to make public policy such as passing new local laws, approving a town budget, and electing a small number of local residents to serve as town officials. But as cities became too large for the town meeting style of governance, three modern forms of municipal government developed.

Mayor-Council Government. In a typical mayor-council government (Figure 21.6), local residents elect a mayor and a city council. In "strong mayor" cities, such as New York City, the city council makes public policy, and the mayor and city bureaucrats who report to the mayor are responsible for policy implementation. Strong mayors may

---

town meeting

A special form of direct democracy under which all voting-age adults in a community gather once a year to make public policy. Now only used in a few villages in upper New England.

Figure 21.6   Mayor-Council Government

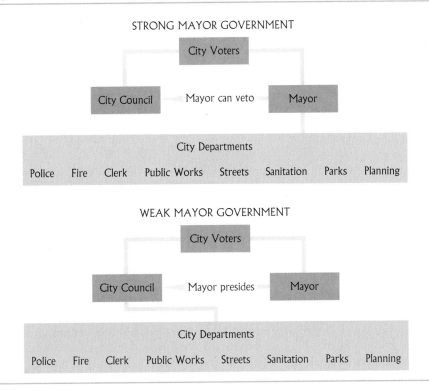

also veto actions of the city council. In "weak mayor" cities, most power is vested in the city council, which directs the activities of the city bureaucracy. The mayor serves as the presiding officer for city council meetings and as the ceremonial head of city government. Most mayor-council cities have this weak mayor form of governance because most of the numerous small cities of 10,000 or fewer residents use this system. San Diego is one major city that uses the weak mayor form of government.

Council-Manager Government. In this form of municipal government, voters elect a city council, and sometimes a mayor who often acts as both presiding officer and voting member of the council (see Figure 21.7). The council is responsible for setting policy for the city. The implementation and administration of the council's actions are placed in the hands of an appointed **city manager,** who is expected to carry out policy with the aid of city bureaucracy. More than one-third of cities use this form of government, including such major cities as Dallas, Kansas City, and Phoenix.

Commission Government. In commission government, voters elect a panel of city commissioners, each of whom serves as both legislator and executive. These officials make public policy just as city council members do in the other two forms of government. However, each member is also elected as a commissioner of a functional area of city government (for example, public safety), and bureaucrats report to a single commissioner. Among the few cities that still use a commission government are Vicksburg, Miss., and St. Petersburg, Fla.[66]

Most city council members and many mayors are elected in nonpartisan elections. Traditionally, city council members represented a district or ward of the city—a practice that permitted ward-based machine party bosses to control elections and to try to create public policies that were good for individual wards, rather than for the city as a whole. Reformers advocated at-large city elections, with all members of the city council

city manager

An official appointed by the city council who is responsible for implementing and administering the council's actions. More than one-third of U.S. cities use the council-manager form of government.

Figure 21.7   Council-Manager Government

chosen by voters throughout the city. These at-large representatives could not create public policies to benefit only their own neighborhoods because they would have to answer to all the city's voters. A majority of cities use at-large elections today.

A consequence of at-large elections is that they make it more difficult for minority group members to be elected to the city council. This is because African-American and other ethnic minorities in U.S. cities have tended to live in more or less homogeneous neighborhoods. Therefore, although they may be a minority of the entire city's population (and so fail to generate a majority in at-large elections), they may be a majority in smaller sections of the city, and so could elect candidates to pursue their interests in district-based electoral systems. Cities that employ district elections may have a greater degree of representational equity for African Americans and Hispanics on city councils than cities that use at-large elections.[67]

School Districts.   The nation's 13,506 *school districts* are responsible for educating children. Although some cities, counties, townships, and one state (Hawaii) operate dependent public school systems (a total of 1,508), school districts are run as independent local governments. Consolidation of small, often rural, districts into larger ones is the major reason for a 61 percent drop in the number of school districts during the past 40 years.

In an independent school district, voters within a geographically defined area are responsible for their own public education system, including electing a board of education, selecting administrators and teachers, building and operating schools, designing and running education programs, and raising the revenues to meet a locally adopted school budget. Because the states are ultimately responsible for public education, state governments adopt general standards for education, mandate certain school programs, and provide a system of state financial assistance to public schools. But within the guidelines of state policy and the parameters of state funding, locally elected school boards and their appointed administrators deliver education services to the nation's children.

School districts have become the focus for many emotionally charged issues at the local level. Prayer in public schools, sex education, equity in school funding, charter schools, and lingering racial discrimination are just a few of the more explosive issues surrounding schools in the 2000s. For example, although the Supreme Court declared that states have a responsibility to eliminate discrimination in education in such important decisions as *Brown v. Board of Education* (1954) and *Swann v. Charlotte-Mecklenberg County Schools* (1971) (see Chapter 5), inequities in the public school systems persist, with racial minorities still encountering poorly funded public education in many instances. In fact, political scientists have discovered an extensive pattern of second-generation discrimination—a shortage of minority teachers "which leads to negative outcome for minority students."[68]

This inequity is coupled with a financial crisis in many public school systems. States have widely divergent school aid policies—some states are good providers to their neediest local schools, whereas others leave the financing responsibility largely to local districts. Local revenue sources are disproportionately based on the local property tax—a policy choice that results in wealthier districts having an abundance of resources, while poorer districts have inadequate revenues for their schoolchildren.[69] Schools around the country continue to struggle with providing quality education with limited resources.

Special Districts. The fastest growing form of local government in the United States is the *special district*. The last official U.S. Census Bureau count showed 35,052 of these independent, limited-purpose governments. Generally, special districts provide only a single service, such as flood control, waste disposal, fire protection, public libraries, or public parks. There is no standard model of special district government organization—the types of organizational arrangements are almost as plentiful as the number of districts. Some districts have elected policymaking boards; a governor or mayor appoints others. Special districts are highly flexible units of local government because their boundary lines can be drawn across the usual municipal, county, and township borders. By providing services on a larger scale, they help localities realize certain economies and efficiencies.

However, important questions about democracy are inherent in the growth of special districts. Special districts are, to a great extent, invisible governments; the local press rarely covers their operations, and there is little direct public participation in their decision-making. Most citizens do not even know who serves on these district boards or when the boards meet. As a result, the public has great difficulty holding special districts accountable.

Fragmentation, Cooperation, and Competition

Each governing body in a fragmented metropolis tends to look at problems from its own narrow perspective. As a result, local bodies fail to cooperate with one another and plan effectively for the region's future needs. For example, the development of an effective mass transit system is often hindered when not all communities are willing to share in financing a new metropolitan bus network or light rail system; or a narrowly focused special district devoted to maintaining the region's road network may not be willing to divert its funds to help finance new rail construction.

Traditionally, regional cooperation on specific policy areas has been undertaken through the use of special districts. For example, local water and sewer needs transcend municipality borders. To address this issue, special sewer and water districts have been set up in most metropolitan areas to coordinate the delivery of this service.

But there are limits to the number of special districts that can be established efficiently and the level of coordination these districts can achieve. What can be done to coordinate a variety of public services in a metropolitan area? A few areas have developed super-locals, institutional arrangements that act almost as general purpose governments for an entire region. Seattle, Miami, and Minneapolis-St. Paul each have a metropolitan council that serves such a function. For example, the Minneapolis-St. Paul Metropolitan Council operates the region's bus service, provides sewer and water services, operates a regional housing and development authority, and funds and plans regional parks and trails, all activities that cut across traditional local governments physical and policy area boundaries.

Participation

The Courts and School Vouchers

Why It Matters

Local Services
The multitude of local governments with independent authority can make the delivery of public services in a metropolitan area inefficient, contentious, and just plain confusing. If all government services in a metropolitan area were taken over by a single government entity, such as the county, then these services might be provided more effectively and at a lower cost. And inequities in services between wealthy neighborhoods and poor neighborhoods might be resolved. However, such consolidation would allow fewer access points to government, perhaps making it less democratic.

America in Perspective

Urban Planning in the European Union and the United States

The nations of the European Union play a much stronger role in guiding urban development than does the United States. Europe's strong planning has helped to preserve cities, control the pace of development, protect agricultural land and the environment, and minimize urban sprawl to a degree that is hardly imaginable in the United States. Typically, these urban planning actions are initiated by regional agencies that get their authority from the central government.

In Great Britain, planners prevented the overgrowth of London by encircling the city with a "green belt"—a designated area in which the countryside would be preserved and no new development permitted. The growth of the region's population was absorbed in planned "new towns" that were built some distance from the central city. The result was a mixture of city and countryside in a metropolitan area and the avoidance of American-style urban sprawl.

Faced with the prospect of excessive growth in Paris, France's national agency for development steered new industries into the suburbs and more distant cities. Still the lure of Paris proved attractive. In response, central government and regional planners built

two new towns of high-rise office buildings, convention centers, and hotels in different spots just outside the city's borders. These towns became the main office centers of the metropolitan Paris area. High-rise residential new towns were built in a ring around Paris to absorb the area's rapidly growing population. These new commercial and residential centers were connected to the old city by a new commuter rail system.

The Netherlands has also relied on strong government planning and controls over land use to prevent the country's limited supply of land from being eaten up by rapid urbanization. Dutch planners saved valuable agricultural land and recreational space in a "green heart" in the midst of the metropolitan Amsterdam-The Hague-Rotterdam Randstad ("Ring City") area, one of the most densely populated areas in the world. Riding a train through the area today, you can easily see exactly where the city ends and the land designated for agricultural purposes begins. The planning boundaries are extremely clear and well guarded.

European planners now confront new problems. With the globalization of their economies, cities in Europe find that they are increasingly competing with one another for new business.

As a result, spatial planning considerations are sometimes sacrificed in order to give a corporation a site it desires. Citizens' demands for individual homes of their own have also led to pressures for continued suburban development, sometimes compromising the integrity of regional land-use plans. Rush-hour traffic jams have become increasingly commonplace in major European metropolises.

Despite these new problems, European nations have been able to ward off the ills of uncontrolled growth. In the United States, by contrast, the private sector and the free market—not government—play the dominant role in deciding where growth will occur. Compared to Europe, regional planning in the United States is essentially toothless.

Sources: Peter Hall, *Urban and Regional Planning*, 4th ed., Independence, KY: Routledge, 2002; H. V. Savitch, *Post-Industrial Cities: Politics and Planning in New York, Paris, and London*, Princeton, NJ: Princeton University Press, 1988; and Hans Thor Andersen and Ronald Van Kempen, *Governing European Cities: Social Fragmentation, Social Exclusion and Urban Governance*, London: Ashgate Publishing Co., 2000.

But examples of institutionalized regional coordination are the exception rather than the rule. For the most part, the prospects for promoting regional cooperation to correct the inequalities and coordination problems that result from metropolitan fragmentation have been dim. Generally speaking, the United States lacks the strong tradition of regional planning evident in Europe (see "America in Perspective: Urban Planning in the European Union and the United States"). In large part, this reflects the strong localism inherent in American democracy. Americans prefer living in small, autonomous communities.

In the United States, there is a tradition (or perhaps a myth) of people being able to "vote with their feet," that is, of people moving to the place where the government's policies best reflect their values.[70] This exacerbates the problem of regional coordination because local governments in different parts of the same metropolitan area will sometimes offer very different services to their citizens. This often manifests itself as a conflict between city dwellers and suburbanites.

Mass transit is one of the most visible services provided by local government, but the multiplicity of local governments in metropolitan areas makes coordination of service difficult.

A good (if disturbing) example of this is seen in the conflict over the racial integration of the Milwaukee public schools. When its schools were ordered to desegregate in the 1970s and 1980s, many White families moved out of the school district into neighboring suburban districts. In a classic case of "White flight," White student enrollment in the Milwaukee Public Schools dropped rapidly. In response, the federal court that issued the original desegregation order then expanded its order to include other school districts within Milwaukee County, thus attempting to force a regional coordination for educational policy by judicial fiat and with the backing of the federal government. But again, many White families voted with their feet and left the county entirely, making the attempt at coordination a failure.

Other typical conflicts between the preferences and needs of suburbanites and city dwellers involve taxes, roads, and central city services. Many people move to the suburbs because property taxes are lower and land is cheaper. The denser population of an urban area causes a higher need for most local government services, and therefore a higher tax burden. Regional coordination often looks to suburbanites as a way to get them to subsidize the taxes of the urban dwellers they left behind. Because suburbanites live more spread out and often far away from their jobs, they need plenty of good roads and highways on which to commute. Meanwhile, urban dwellers would rather that more transportation money be spent on mass transit, which is economical for dense populations. Urban dwellers also complain that suburbanites drive into the central city each workday, using city services like roads, police, water, and so forth, and then take themselves and their tax dollars back to the suburbs at night. These examples offer the barest outline of the differences in preferences and viewpoints of people in different areas of a metropolis. It is easy to understand why coordination and cooperation are hard to come by.

Local governments are also engaged in serious competition for economic development. That is, they try to expand their tax base through commercial and residential development. Some analysts believe that cities are quite limited in their ability to control economic change within their borders, but local officials often believe that development policies are a community's lifeblood.[71] A business owner can simply threaten to leave a community or locate facilities in another town if he or she is unhappy with local policies. Thus, business owners and corporate officials have great leverage to extract concessions from local officials because no local government wants to face the loss of jobs or tax base. As a result, cities compete with one another for desirable business facilities

You Are the Director of Economic Development for the City of Baltimore, Maryland

You Are a Restaurant Owner

council of governments (COG)

Councils in many areas of the country where officials from various localities meet to discuss mutual problems and plan joint, cooperative action.

by offering tax reductions, promises of subsidized infrastructure development, and other services demanded by business.

However, local governments can cooperate with one another when they find it in their mutual interest to do so. Central cities and suburbs are often willing, for instance, to share the costs of a new sewage disposal facility. They may also cooperate in ventures to attract a major new employer to the area, or to keep one, as in the case of the massive efforts by local governments in the Chicago metropolitan area to construct a new baseball stadium to keep the White Sox from leaving town in the late 1980s. Sometimes two or more governments may cooperate informally to share equipment and services. In many areas of the country, a **council of governments** (frequently referred to as a COG) exists wherein officials from various localities meet to discuss mutual problems and plan joint, cooperative action. These COGs are often formally very weak, being underfunded, poorly staffed, and lacking in any real legislative or taxing power.

State and Local Finance Policy

When a state or local government approves its budget for the next year, the basic policy objectives of the government have also been approved. These objectives are contained in the taxing and spending plans that make up the budget. Lofty speeches can be made and bills passed into law, but without some significant and specific budgetary commitment, a policy will usually have little impact on citizens' lives. Taxpayers increasingly demand more accountability and efficiency from their subnational governments, forcing officials to squeeze services and programs out of limited revenue dollars. Figure 21.8 shows how state governments get their money and how they spend it.

State government revenues are derived from a variety of sources. States receive the largest share of revenue, 42.8 percent, from taxes. States' major sources of tax revenue are sales taxes, income taxes, and motor vehicle and fuel taxes. The second-largest source of state revenue is intergovernmental revenue (21.7 percent)—almost all as grants from the federal government. The third major revenue source is state insurance programs (21.2 percent). Charges and fees for services such as state hospitals, college courses, and state parks have become an increasingly important source of revenue for states in the past 20 years (13.5 percent, along with miscellaneous revenue).

Changes in their constitutions over the past 40 years have given states wider access to income and sales taxes and other sources of revenue. Today, 45 states levy a general

Figure 21.8   State Government Revenues and Expenditures

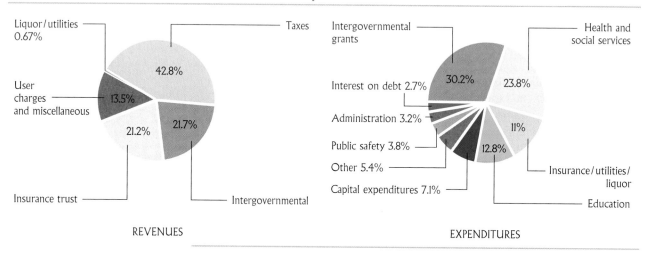

Source: U.S. Bureau of the Census, *Statistical Abstract of the United States, 2002* (Washington, D.C.: U.S. Government Printing Office, 2003).

sales tax; Alaska, Delaware, Montana, New Hampshire, and Oregon are the only hold-outs. Only seven states—Alaska, Florida, Nevada, South Dakota, Texas, Washington, and Wyoming—do not have a personal income tax, and New Hampshire and Tennessee have only a limited form of income tax. The modernization of state revenue structures gives the states new money to finance the public programs demanded by citizens.

How do states spend their money? Most of the states' money—about 50 percent—goes to operate state programs (in public safety, education, health and social services, etc.), construct state buildings, and provide direct assistance to individuals. Another 30 percent is allocated as aid to local governments. Since so much of the money that states spend is given to local governments (and since so much of the local governments' revenue comes from the states), the states have even more leverage over the locals than is given to them by Dillon's Rule.

Local government finances can be confusing because of the fragmentation of local governments and the varied ways in which states support and constrain their local authorities. This situation is primarily due to the different ways in which states and their local governments have sorted out the assignment of policy responsibilities among local governments. Figure 21.9 offers a snapshot of local government finances—combining county, city, township, school, and special district budgets—across the United States. Local governments receive their revenues from three main sources: taxes, user charges, and intergovernmental aid. Intergovernmental aid (primarily from the states) and "own source" taxes are now about equal in their contribution to local government revenue, again showing the great dependence of local governments on their states. Local taxes are mainly property taxes, but sales and income taxes also contribute to the revenue of some local governments. Charges on the users of certain services, such as libraries and recreation facilities, provide another 21 percent of local government revenue. They receive 8 percent of their revenue from the operation of municipally owned utilities and liquor sales.

Local governments allocate their monies to a range of services, but the main areas are public education (38 percent), health and social services (13 percent), and public safety (9 percent). These are services that citizens need on a regular basis, and expect local governments to provide.

The difference between state and local expenditures reflects the distribution of public services between these levels of government that has developed over the course of the history of the United States. Local government is expected to provide two of the

Figure 21.9   Local Government Revenues and Expenditures

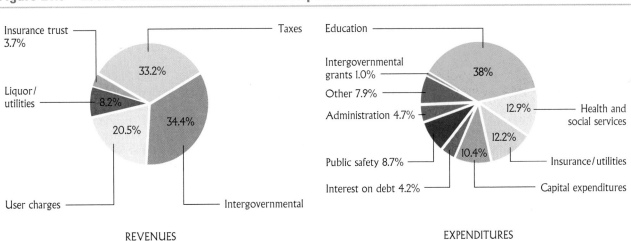

REVENUES   EXPENDITURES

Source: U.S. Bureau of the Census, Statistical Abstract of the United States, 2002 (Washington, D.C.: U.S. Government Printing Office, 2003).

Issues
of the Times

The Issue: Paying for Homeland Security in the States

All governments face difficult decisions regarding how to ensure public safety and maintain civil order. At the same time, subnational governments hope to generate a strong local economy by attracting business, tourism, and special activities, such as sporting events and conventions. The threat of terrorism, and the requirement that subnational governments pay part of the cost for homeland security, places a huge financial burden on local and state government, especially when those governments host high-profile events.

How are state and local officials balancing the need to attract dollars with the need to protect their citizens?

Read All About It

Fears of Attack at Conventions Drive New Plans

By David Johnston
July 5, 2004

The federal authorities, concerned about a terror attack during this summer's national political conventions, have begun a new effort to identify potential extremists inside the United States, including conducting interviews in communities where terrorists might seek refuge, government officials said.

The fears about an incident during the conventions or later in the year have also led state and local officials to impose extraordinary security precautions. Persistent if indistinct intelligence reports, based on electronic intercepts and live sources, indicate that Al Qaeda is determined to strike in the United States some time this year, the officials said in interviews last week.

Almost half the budgets in each convention city will be spent on security, local officials said. The Democratic National Convention will be held in Boston and the Republican National Convention will be held in New York at Madison Square Garden.

New York is regarded as a higher risk than Boston by counterterrorism officials because President Bush is a Republican and because of consistent intelligence. "Al Qaeda has unambiguous plans to hit the homeland again," James L. Pavitt, the C.I.A.'s outgoing head of clandestine operations, said in a speech in New York last week, "and New York City, I am certain, remains a prime target."

Convention planners expanded their security requirements, at the urging of federal officials, after the March 11 commuter train attacks in Madrid that killed 191 people.

In New York, Gov. George E. Pataki, a Republican, has called on a 10-state consortium of law enforcement agencies, from Maine to Delaware, to share intelligence about warning signs of terrorist planning.

"We think we know the targets that might have great economic impact or cause large loss of life," said James K. Kallstrom, a senior terrorism adviser to Mr. Pataki. "But we know terrorists might not be in proximity to those targets, so we have put a series of tripwires in place throughout New England."

Please see Fears   Page 685

Fears

Continued from Page 684

In New York, the cost of security is expected to exceed $75 million, of the total convention cost of about $166 million, as concerns have broadened to include not only the week of the convention, but also the weeks before and after it.

The Police Department will increase uniformed and plainclothes patrols in many parts of the city, focusing on landmarks, tourist sites, sites related to the convention, bridges and tunnels, airports and simply places where people gather. Much of the focus will be on the subway system.

For Boston, the security bill is now estimated to reach $50 million, twice the original estimate and more than half the roughly $95 million overall convention cost.

The Secret Service has ordered some 40 miles of roads closed around the Fleet Center, where the Democrats will meet, including Interstate 93, a section of which runs above ground just 40 feet from the arena. The shutdown of major roads near the convention site is the central and most controversial part of a complex security plan. The plan involves multiple police agencies and includes random checks of handbags and packages on buses and subways by police and bomb-sniffing dogs, as well as closed security zones.

New York is considered to be a more likely target, but security planners in Boston said that area had many potential targets of its own, including a complex infrastructure, prestigious universities and, perhaps most of all, symbolic sites.

"This is the seat of liberty," said Carlo A. Boccia, the city's director of homeland security, gesturing from the window of his City Hall office toward Faneuil Hall and the

---

> ## "Al Qaeda has unambiguous plans to hit the homeland again, and New York City, I am certain, remains a prime target."

Old State House. "You attack that, it's the very heart of America."

The Boston Police Department estimated that the security measures ordered by the Secret Service added about $9.5 million in police, firefighter and medical worker overtime for a total of $32.5 million, the largest portion of the security cost.

The traffic ban has outraged commuters as well as business owners who fear the city will be nearly deserted except for the 36,000 visitors expected for the convention. State employees have been encouraged to take the days of the convention off, and many businesses have told their employees to do the same.

Mayor Thomas M. Menino bristles at criticism. "This convention will be good for Boston," Mayor Menino said in an interview. He added, "Since 9/11, our whole world has changed drastically. The Secret Service is really dictating the conditions. It's remarkable how many public safety agencies have been working together."

As in Boston, security concerns in New York will focus on a fairly broad time frame. Raymond W. Kelly, the city police commissioner, said the heightened measures would be in place weeks before Aug. 30, when the Republican National Convention opens, and will continue after the event ends Sept. 2.

The Madrid bombing has also led to stepped-up security plans in New York. About 10,000 officers will be deployed, up from 6,500, to provide security at Madison Square Garden, city hotels, bridges and tunnels, demonstration areas, landmarks and other sites, according to a previously undisclosed May 10 memorandum prepared by the city's Washington lobbying office in an effort to obtain more federal money for security.

Securing the city's transportation system is a complex task. About seven million people a day ride the subway system. The Long Island Rail Road carries about 270,000 riders each day on 730 trains, while the Metro-North Railroad carries about 250,000 people daily.

In addition to increased subway patrols, the memorandum said, the department's efforts include deploying officers to Pennsylvania Station, beneath Madison Square Garden. . . .

Think About It

- What is the budget situation in your state? How likely is it that the demands of homeland security will take funds away from other areas, such as higher education? Will budget shortfalls lead to increases in your tuition for the school you attend now? How would you and students at your school respond to tuition increases?

- If your state faces a gubernatorial election, how significant a role will terrorism and homeland security play in the campaign and how citizens vote? Will new taxes be needed? Do voters in state elections always oppose new taxes? Do voters always punish officials who raise taxes?

- How much money should the federal government provide to the state and local governments to pay for homeland security?

- Should states establish their own departments of homeland security and consolidate bureaucracies as the federal government has? What are the benefits and drawbacks of such a move? Does your city need a special position or office of homeland security?

most important and broadly used services of all government in the United States—education and public safety (police and fire protection). State governments, on the other hand, are mainly in charge of making sure that the poorest of the state's citizens have their basic physical needs met. Further, the state is charged with gathering the state's resources and distributing them where they are most needed, via intergovernmental grants. While local governments are busy providing direct citizen service, the state governments can take a broader view to enhance equity in public service.

Understanding State and Local Governments

A full understanding of the complexity of subnational government cannot be gleaned from a single textbook chapter, but you should remember a few important points about these 87,909 governments.

Democracy at the Subnational Level

The very existence of so many governments to handle complex as well as ordinary—but needed—services, testifies to the health of our democracy. States have been willing to decentralize their governing arrangements to permit the creation of local governments to address citizens' policy demands. Today, local voters choose their own representatives to serve on county commissions, city councils, school boards, and some special district boards. As small legislatures elected from among the community's residents, these governing bodies are usually the policymaking institutions closest and most open to all citizens. In many ways, local governments encourage individual participation in government and promote the value of individualism at the local level.

The states also operate in an open policymaking environment. Many of the most important of state officials are elected to office, far more than in the federal government. Direct primaries permit voters to select nominees for state offices. The recall even allows voters to oust an official from office before his or her term is over in about one-third of the states. The initiative and the referendum permit voters in many states to make policy or amend their state constitutions directly. In most states, voters have a far more direct role in selecting judges than is the case in the federal court system. And by the 1990s, subnational elections were putting officials into office who are far more representative of the U.S. population demographically than is the case in the federal government today or subnational governments in previous years.

Even so, subnational politics may not be as democratic as this initial assessment would seem to indicate. Politics at the state level is poorly covered by the media and, as a result, is relatively invisible to the public. Voters can hardly hold elected officials accountable if they know little about what is going on in the state capital. Even at the local level, there is little press coverage of anything other than the results of city council meetings or a mayor's actions—and that doesn't even happen regularly in smaller communities or in suburbs that lack their own daily newspaper.

Comparing State and
Local Governments

When, as is often the case, only 30 to 35 percent of voters participate in statewide elections and fewer than 20 percent turn out for local elections, there are real concerns about the health of our grass-roots governments. In one effort to boost citizen participation, states have begun experimenting with vote-by-mail elections. Instead of having to show up on a specific day to cast a ballot, citizens in Oregon were able to mail in their ballots in 1996, and in 1998 Oregon voters passed an initiative making vote-by-mail the only way to vote for every election. Further, in a small number of cities, including Birmingham, Dayton, Portland, and St. Paul, vigorous programs of neighborhood democracy have been developed where citizen participation in public affairs goes far beyond voting. In these cities, neighborhood boards are given control over meaningful policy decisions and program resources, and their actions are not merely

You Are the Policymaker

Should Your State Take a Chance on Gambling?

No one likes taxes, but government services have to be paid for somehow. In the 1980s and 1990s many states tried to earn money for state programs "painlessly" through legalized gambling. Thirty years ago, only Nevada allowed most forms of gambling; in some states children couldn't even enter a sweepstakes on the back of a cereal box. Today, many states not only allow a variety of types of gambling, they even sponsor and earn money from such activities. Various states run lotteries and allow casino and riverboat gambling, horse and dog racing, slot machines, video lottery, bingo, and other forms of what proponents call "gaming."

Suppose you are a state legislator faced with the question of legalizing gambling in your state in order to earn extra revenue without raising taxes. To what extent are you willing to accept the negative aspects of gambling in order to gain its monetary rewards?

States earn money from gambling in two main ways. First, states may run a gambling operation outright. State lotteries are the best example. States skim off as much as 50 percent of the receipts from lottery tickets, offering most of the rest as prize money. Second, states may earn money from gambling by taxing bets and winnings heavily, as is commonly done with casino and racetrack gambling.

This sort of revenue is a very attractive alternative to direct taxation as a way to help states fund public services. First, it is seen as a voluntary source of revenue, rather than mandatory taxation. Some characterize it as a tax on stupidity. Second, some forms of gambling are argued to encourage economic development in a local area, thereby being a positive good aside from a source of revenue. The prosperity that some Native American tribes have gained through opening casinos (allowed by the federal government since 1988) is evidence in favor of this position. Third, there are those who view gambling as a harmless recreational activity that the state has no business banning anyway—why not make a little money on it?

Even though dozens of states have legalized and earned money from a wide variety of forms of gambling in the past 20 years, not all states have done so and not all people are convinced that it is good public policy. One argument against legalized gambling is that it is a regressive form of taxation because the people who gamble the highest proportions of their incomes are those who are relatively poor. There has been increasing concern about compulsive gambling, a psychological disorder akin to alcoholism that drives people to gamble incessantly. Like alcoholism, compulsive gambling can lead to financial ruin and the destruction of families. There are also those who argue that gambling is simply immoral, and that legalizing and especially encouraging it (as in state lottery TV commercials) leads people to pursue false hope and a destructive lifestyle. Finally, there is some debate as to just how much money a state can actually earn from gambling, now that it has become so commonplace in the United States.

As a state legislator, you must weigh the benefits of "painless" gambling revenue against the arguments of those who oppose it. Should your state legalize gambling? If so, what form should it adopt? Should it run a lottery? Should it allow casinos, and tax them? What difference does it make if neighboring states do or do not have legalized gambling? What would *you* do?

advisory. These cities also reward municipal officials who listen to the views of these neighborhood bodies. The experience in these and other cities shows that citizens will devote the considerable time necessary to participate in public affairs if they are convinced that participation is meaningful and that city officials are not just manipulating them.[72]

Competition between subnational governments for economic development also raises significant questions about democracy. As a result of this competition, state and local governments have subsidized business growth and economic development, often at the cost of slighting redistribution services and human resource needs. Business interests have substantial leverage in state and city affairs as a result of their ability to threaten to leave or locate facilities in another jurisdiction. The increasing importance of money in subnational elections has only added to the influence that special interests exert in state and local affairs.

The workings of democracy are often difficult to see in the judicial branch of government. Because most citizens do not attend trials and only lawyers and judges are directly involved in the appeals process, the proceedings of the judiciary are seldom visible to the public until a significant case or decision is announced. This judicial process is not subject to quite the same scrutiny as the legislative and executive functions of state governments. Even though most state and local judges and justices must face the voters to gain or retain their positions, the lack of information that voters have about the judicial process makes the level of true democracy in this process suspect. Citizens will have to take more interest in the crucial role of courts in our democracy in order for courts to assume the same political importance in states as the other branches of government.

The Scope of Subnational Government

Growth in subnational government employment has proceeded at a pace exceeding that of the federal government for most of this century, as we learned in Chapter 15. Most of this growth has been driven by citizen demand for more government services. Although most American voters want their elected representatives to control the size of government, voters also want government to provide them with more and better programs.

Has the reform and professionalization of subnational government in the past generation made any difference for taxpayers? In most cases, it has not resulted in smaller government. By its very nature, legislative professionalism costs tax dollars and leads to a legislature that is more permanent and continuous. School district consolidation has occurred, reducing the overall number of districts by 61 percent in the past 30 years. This declining number of school districts comes at a time of growing demand for more special district governments, which have increased by over 48 percent in three decades.

Most state governments have experimented with *sunset legislation*, which involves periodically reviewing agencies to control the growth of government and eliminate unneeded programs. States have also empowered their legislatures to review executive branch regulations and rules to ensure that citizens or businesses are not overregulated by government. These practices help limit the scope of governments.

But as citizen demand in the late twentieth century has led to growth and development in the areas of technology, communications, and public health and safety, subnational governments have had to grow, not diminish. More police, more health care providers, more computer technicians, and more social-welfare caseworkers have been needed to meet the expanding range of services and problems that confront people daily. Although some local governments are barely able to fulfill their basic responsibilities for public safety and maintenance of the local infrastructure, other cities and counties have become much more competent at managing local affairs. Indeed, recent research suggests that local governments often lead their states and the nation in devising innovative ways to deliver public services.[73]

In sum, with the greater responsibilities thrust upon them by the federal government and the demands of their citizens, subnational governments have responded by enhancing their capacity to provide services to their citizens. In the past 40 years, the enhanced capacity of democratically elected officials in the states, especially state legislators and governors, and the greater use of direct democracy mechanisms has led to stronger and more effective subnational governments that are also more extensive and expensive.

Summary

Our nation's 50 states and its tens of thousands of local governments are responsible for most public policies with which we are most familiar: education, fire protection, police protection, highway maintenance, public welfare, public health, and trash collection. The states are a diverse group, but each has a government that makes, enforces, and interprets laws for its citizens. The structure for state governments is specified in state constitutions—some very long, others quite short. Citizens may modify these state constitutions when necessary to keep pace with changing demands of government.

State legislatures include elected representatives who make laws, appropriate money, oversee the executive branch, perform casework, and help manage conflict across the state. Legislators are increasingly diverse demographically, but most tend to be from a somewhat higher socioeconomic position than the majority of the people they represent. Significant turnover takes place in state legislatures, and voters in some states have ensured that this will continue by enacting term limits for their public officials.

The governors of our states are elected to administer public policy and to attend to citizen needs. Once in office, a governor directs a complex set of state government institutions and programs, conducts state affairs with other governors and the president, initiates much of the legislation state legislatures will adopt, and helps manage conflict. Governors must often work with a number of other elected executive officials to produce public policy.

The state court systems are similar in organization to federal courts. Most states have trial courts, intermediate courts of appeal, and a court of last resort; all have jurisdiction over both civil and criminal cases. Judges may attain office through appointment, election, or a hybrid of both known as the Merit Plan. The actions of state judges, especially those serving on the court of last resort, can affect policy significantly.

Local governments in the United States—counties, municipalities, townships, school districts, and special districts—were established by the states to decide on and administer policy in limited geographic and policy areas. Most cities are run by city councils with either a mayor or a city manager directing the day-to-day affairs of city bureaucracies. Counties and townships help states perform many local functions, such as record-keeping and the administration of justice. School districts run public schools, and special districts provide limited services for multiple communities. The existence of nearly 88,000 local governments indicates that democracy truly thrives at the local level in the United States.

KEY TERMS

subnational governments	initiative	home rule
line-item veto	referendum	town meeting
lieutenant governor	recall	city manager
Merit Plan	Dillon's Rule	council of governments
direct democracy	local charter	

INTERNET RESOURCES

www.ezgov.com/portal/index.jsp/
Website of the Citizen Information Center with easy links to your state and local government as well as information on state and local politics.

www.statesnews.org/
Website of the Council of State Governments, with information on states and state public policies.

www.ncsl.org/
Website of the National Conference of State Legislatures, with information on state legislatures, elections, and members.

www.ncsc.dni.us/
Website of the National Center for State Courts with information on state courts.

www.nga.org/
Website of the National Governors' Association, with links to websites for each state.

www.usmayors.org/
U.S. Conference of Mayors website.

www.census.gov/
Website of the U.S. Census Bureau, with links to sites with data on states and local areas.

www.stateline.org/
Website of the Pew Center on the State, with lots of general and state-specific policy information.

GET CONNECTED

State Legislatures

After reading this chapter, it should be clear to you that state and local government officials regularly make decisions that affect you. And although many citizens can name officials in the federal government, such as the president, most of us do not know the names of our representatives in the state legislature. Indeed, in most states each citizen has two representatives in the state legislature, one in a lower chamber (usually called the Assembly or House), and one in the upper chamber (usually called the Senate). Let us take a closer look at the legislature in your state.

Search the Web

To find your state legislator or to track bills before your state legislature, go to your state's official government website or locate your state legislative homepage through *http://www.ncsl.org/* (click on legislatures), a website established by the National Council of State Legislatures for this purpose. Once you locate your state legislative homepage, select the directory for the lower or upper chamber and enter your address or zip code. All of the state websites differ, but on most sites you can locate biographical information about your representative, voting records, and his or her committee assignments and sponsored legislation. On most sites you can also track the progress of bills through the legislature by searching under key words, legislative sponsor, or bill number. Often you can find the text of legislative debate on a given bill through the chamber's official journal or calendar. If one issue interests you, state legislative websites will allow you to track similar bills in several states during the year.

Questions To Ask

- If your state's website is fairly complete, you should be able to develop an opinion about your legislator's voting record. What is your assessment of this record in terms of voting attendance and vote choices?
- In your view, is your legislator representing the views of citizens in your district?
- Does your legislator sponsor legislation or cast votes in a manner that supports your positions on issues?
- Does legislation sponsored by your legislator tend to pass or fail in a vote of the chamber?
- How do your legislator's committee assignments enhance the interests of your district?
- In comparing similar legislation across states, did the outcomes differ (did the legislation pass in one state and fail in another)?

Why It Matters

In a representative democracy, we elect representatives to serve in official positions and to speak for our interests. Each state has a legislature with representatives elected from districts. The expectation is that legislators will serve the constituents of their districts in the legislature. Many constituents may not be concerned about every issue facing the legislature, but each legislator is still expected to discern the district's interests and behave accordingly in the legislature. If a constituent has a specific problem that can be addressed by government, such as a concern about the safety of a nearby prison facility, he or she should have the attention of the state legislator on the issue.

Get Involved

Many constituents contact their legislators over the phone or by mail. As a citizen, you should tell your legislator about the issues you think are important by calling, e-mailing, or mailing your ideas.

To see more Get Connected exercises for Chapter 21, go to www.ablongman.com/edwards.

FOR FURTHER READING

Beyle, Thad L. *Governors and Hard Times.* Washington, D.C.: Congressional Quarterly Press, 1992. A timely monograph on the modern governor by one of the country's leading experts.

The Council of State Governments. *The Book of the States,* (annual). Lexington, KY: Council of State Governments. An overview of annual developments in state government.

Gray, Virginia, and Russell L. Hanson, eds. *Politics in the American States: A Comparative Analysis,* 8th ed. Washington, D.C.: Congressional Quarterly Press, 2004. A superb collection of essays that review the empirical literature on state politics.

Hedge, David M. *Governance and the Changing American States: Transforming American Politics.* Washington, D.C.: Congressional Quarterly Press, 1998. An in-depth and balanced assessment of the literature on the resurgence of state government institutions.

Hovey, Hal A., and Kendra A. Hovey. *CQ's State Fact Finder: Rankings Across America* (annual). Washington, D.C.: Congressional Quarterly Press. A data book with hundreds of state-by-state comparisons on economic, demographic, political, and policy variables.

International City/County Management Association. *The Municipal Year Book*. Washington, D.C.: ICMA, annual. Excellent current affairs updates on local governments and informative directories on civic affairs and public officials.

Nelson, Albert J. *Emerging Influentials in State Legislatures: Women, Blacks, and Hispanics*. New York: Praeger Publishers, 1991. Explores the power of minority and women legislators by focusing on their representation, turnover, and influence within party leadership and as chairs of committees.

Rosenthal, Alan. *The Decline of Representative Democracy: Process, Participation, and Power in State Legislatures*, Washington, D.C.: Congressional Quarterly Press, 1998. A detailed examination and evaluation of the state legislatures at the end of the millennium by the leading analyst of those bodies.

Weber, Ronald E., and Paul Brace, eds. *American State and Local Politics: Directions for the 21st Century*. Chatham, NJ: Chatham House, 1999. A collection of essays by top scholars focusing on recent reforms and their implications.

Welch, Susan, and Timothy Bledsoe. *Urban Reform and Its Consequences: A Study in Representation*. Chicago: University of Chicago Press, 1988. An important review and analysis of urban government today.

Appendix

The Declaration of Independence*

In Congress, July 4, 1776

The Unanimous Declaration of the Thirteen United States of America

When in the Course of human events it becomes necessary for one people to dissolve the political bands which have connected them with another, and to assume among the powers of the earth, the separate and equal station to which the Laws of Nature and of Nature's God entitle them, a decent respect to the opinions of mankind requires that they should declare the causes which impel them to the separation.

We hold these truths to be self-evident, that all men are created equal, that they are endowed by their Creator with certain unalienable Rights, that among these are Life, Liberty and the pursuit of Happiness.—That to secure these rights, Governments are instituted among Men, deriving their just powers from the consent of the governed,—That whenever any Form of Government becomes destructive of these ends, it is the Right of the People to alter or to abolish it, and to institute new Government, laying its foundation on such principles and organizing its powers in such form, as to them shall seem most likely to effect their Safety and Happiness. Prudence, indeed, will dictate that Governments long established should not be changed for light and transient causes; and accordingly all experience hath shewn that mankind are more disposed to suffer, while evils are sufferable, than to right themselves by abolishing the forms to which they are accustomed. But when a long train of abuses and usurpations, pursuing invariably the same Object evinces a design to reduce them under absolute Despotism, it is their right, it is their duty, to throw off such Government, and to provide new Guards for their future security.

Such has been the patient sufferance of these Colonies; and such is now the necessity which constrains them to alter their former Systems of Government. The history of the present King of Great Britain is a history of repeated injuries and usurpations, all having in direct object the establishment of an absolute Tyranny over these States. To prove this, let Facts be submitted to a candid world.

He has refused his Assent to Laws, the most wholesome and necessary for the public good.

He has forbidden his Governors to pass Laws of immediate and pressing importance, unless suspended in their operation till his Assent should be obtained; and when so suspended, he has utterly neglected to attend to them.

He has refused to pass other Laws for the accommodation of large districts of people, unless those people would relinquish the right of Representation in the Legislature, a right inestimable to them and formidable to tyrants only.

He has called together legislative bodies at places unusual, uncomfortable, and distant from the depository of their Public Records, for the sole purpose of fatiguing them into compliance with his measures.

He has dissolved Representative Houses repeatedly, for opposing with manly firmness his invasions on the rights of the people.

He has refused for a long time, after such dissolutions, to cause others to be elected; whereby the Legislative Powers, incapable of Annihilation, have returned to the People at large for their exercise; the State remaining in the mean time exposed to all the dangers of invasion from without, and convulsions within.

He has endeavored to prevent the population of these States; for that purpose obstructing the Laws for Naturalization of Foreigners; refusing to pass others to encourage their migration hither, and raising the conditions of new Appropriations of Lands.

He has obstructed the Administration of Justice, by refusing his Assent to Laws for establishing Judiciary powers.

He has made Judges dependent on his Will alone, for the tenure of their offices, and the amount and payment of their salaries.

He has erected a multitude of New Offices, and sent hither swarms of Officers to harass our people, and eat out their substance.

He has kept among us, in times of peace, Standing Armies without the Consent of our legislatures.

He has affected to render the Military independent of and superior to the Civil power.

He has combined with others to subject us to a jurisdiction foreign to our constitution, and unacknowledged by our laws; giving his Assent to their Acts of pretended Legislation:

For quartering large bodies of armed troops among us:

For protecting them, by a mock Trial, from punishment for any Murders which they should commit on the Inhabitants of these States:

For cutting off our Trade with all parts of the world:

For imposing Taxes on us without our Consent:

For depriving us in many cases, of the benefits of Trial by Jury:

For transporting us beyond Seas to be tried for pretended offences:

For abolishing the free System of English Laws in a neighboring Province, establishing therein an Arbitrary government, and enlarging its Boundaries so as to render it at once an example and fit instrument for introducing the same absolute rule into these Colonies:

For taking away our Charters, abolishing our most valuable Laws, and altering fundamentally the Forms of our Governments:

For suspending our own Legislatures, and declaring themselves invested with power to legislate for us in all cases whatsoever.

He has abdicated Government here, by declaring us out of his Protection and waging War against us.

He has plundered our seas, ravaged our Coasts, burnt our towns, and destroyed the lives of our people.

---

*This text retains the spelling, capitalization, and punctuation of the original.

He is at this time transporting large Armies of foreign Mercenaries to compleat the works of death, desolation and tyranny, already begun with circumstances of Cruelty & perfidy scarcely paralleled in the most barbarous ages, and totally unworthy the Head of a civilized nation.

He has constrained our fellow Citizens taken Captive on the high Seas to bear Arms against their Country, to become the executioners of their friends and Brethren, or to fall themselves by their Hands.

He has excited domestic insurrections amongst us, and has endeavored to bring on the inhabitants of our frontiers, the merciless Indian Savages, whose known rule of warfare, is an undistinguished destruction of all ages, sexes and conditions.

In every stage of these Oppressions We have Petitioned for Redress in the most humble terms: Our repeated Petitions have been answered only by repeated injury. A Prince, whose character is thus marked by every act which may define a Tyrant, is unfit to be the ruler of a free people.

Nor have We been wanting in attention to our British brethren. We have warned them from time to time of attempts by their legislature to extend an unwarrantable jurisdiction over us. We have reminded them of the circumstances of our emigration and settlement here. We have appealed to their native justice and magnanimity, and we have conjured them by the ties of our common kindred to disavow these usurpations, which would inevitably interrupt our connections and correspondence. They too have been deaf to the voice of justice and consanguinity. We must, therefore, acquiesce in the necessity, which denounces our Separation, and hold them, as we hold the rest of mankind, Enemies in War, in Peace Friends.

We, therefore, the Representatives of the United States of America, in General Congress, Assembled, appealing to the Supreme Judge of the world for the rectitude of our intentions, do, in the Name, and by Authority of the good People of these Colonies, solemnly publish and declare, That these United Colonies are, and of Right ought to be Free and Independent States; that they are Absolved from all Allegiance to the British Crown, and that all political connection between them and the State of Great Britain, is and ought to be totally dissolved; and that as Free and Independent States, they have full Power to levy War, conclude Peace, contract Alliances, establish Commerce, and to do all other Acts and Things which Independent States may of right do. And for the support of this Declaration, with a firm reliance on the protection of divine Providence, we mutually pledge to each other our Lives, our Fortunes and our sacred Honor.

John Hancock

NEW HAMPSHIRE
Josiah Bartlett,
Wm. Whipple,
Matthew Thornton.

MASSACHUSETTS BAY
Saml. Adams,
John Adams,
Robt. Treat Paine,
Elbridge Gerry.

RHODE ISLAND
Step. Hopkins,
William Ellery.

CONNECTICUT
Roger Sherman,
Samuel Huntington,
Wm. Williams,
Oliver Wolcott.

NEW YORK
Wm. Floyd,
Phil. Livingston,
Frans. Lewis,
Lewis Morris.

NEW JERSEY
Richd. Stockton,
Jno. Witherspoon,
Fras. Hopkinson,
John Hart,
Abra. Clark.

PENNSYLVANIA
Robt. Morris,
Benjamin Rush,
Benjamin Franklin,
John Morton,
Geo. Clymer,
Jas. Smith,
Geo. Taylor,
James Wilson,
Geo. Ross.

DELAWARE
Caesar Rodney,
Geo. Read,
Tho. M'kean.

MARYLAND
Samuel Chase,
Wm. Paca,
Thos. Stone,
Charles Caroll of
Carrollton.

VIRGINIA
George Wythe,
Richard Henry Lee,
Th. Jefferson,
Benjamin Harrison,
Thos. Nelson, jr.,
Francis Lightfoot Lee,
Carter Braxton.

NORTH CAROLINA
Wm. Hooper,
Joseph Hewes,
John Penn.

SOUTH CAROLINA
Edward Rutledge,
Thos. Heyward, Junr.,
Thomas Lynch, jnr.,
Arthur Middleton.

GEORGIA
Button Gwinnett,
Lyman Hall,
Geo. Walton.

The Federalist No. 10

James Madison

November 22, 1787

To the People of the State of New York.

Among the numerous advantages promised by a well constructed Union, none deserves to be more accurately developed than its tendency to break and control the violence of faction. The friend of popular governments, never finds himself so much alarmed for their character and fate, as when he contemplates their propensity to this dangerous vice. He will not fail therefore to set a due value on any plan which, without violating the principles to which he is attached, provides a proper cure for it. The instability, injustice and confusion introduced into the public councils, have in truth been the mortal diseases under which popular governments have every where perished; as they continue to be the favorite and fruitful topics from which the adversaries to liberty derive their most specious declamations. The valuable improvements made by the American Constitutions on the popular models, both ancient and modern, cannot certainly be too much admired; but it would be an unwarrantable partiality, to contend that they have as effectually obviated the danger on this side as was wished and expected. Complaints are every where heard from our most considerate and virtuous citizens, equally the friends of public and private faith, and of public and personal liberty; that our governments are too unstable; that the public good is disregarded in the conflicts of rival parties; and that measures are too often decided, not according to the rules of justice, and the rights of the minor party; but by the superior force of an interested and over-bearing majority. However anxiously we may wish that these complaints had no foundation, the evidence of known facts will not permit us to deny that they are in some degree true. It will be found indeed, on a candid review of our situation, that some of the distresses under which we labor, have been erroneously charged on the operation of our governments; but it will be found, at the same time, that other causes will not alone account for many of our heaviest misfortunes; and particularly, for that prevailing and increasing distrust of public engagements, and alarm for private rights, which are echoed from one end of the continent to the other. These must be chiefly, if not wholly, effects of the unsteadiness and injustice, with which a factious spirit has tainted our public administrations.

By a faction I understand a number of citizens, whether amounting to a majority or minority of the whole, who are united and actuated by some common impulse of passion, or of interest, adverse to the rights of other citizens, or to the permanent and aggregate interests of the community.

There are two methods of curing the mischiefs of faction: the one, by removing its causes; the other, by controlling its effects.

There are again two methods of removing the causes of faction: the one by destroying the liberty which is essential to its existence; the other, by giving to every citizen the same opinions, the same passions, and the same interests.

It could never be more truly said than of the first remedy, that it is worse than the disease. Liberty is to faction, what air is to fire, an aliment without which it instantly expires. But it could not be a less folly to abolish liberty, which is essential to political life, because it nourishes faction, than it would be to wish the annihilation of air, which is essential to animal life, because it imparts to fire its destructive agency.

The second expedient is as impracticable, as the first would be unwise. As long as the reason of man continues fallible, and he is at liberty to exercise it, different opinions will be formed. As long as the connection subsists between his reason and his self-love, his opinions and his passions will have a reciprocal influence on each other; and the former will be objects to which the latter will attach themselves. The diversity in the faculties of men from which the rights of property originate, is not less an insuperable obstacle to a uniformity of interests. The protection of these faculties is the first object of Government. From the protection of different and unequal faculties of acquiring property, the possession of different degrees and kinds of property immediately results: and from the influence of these on the sentiments and views of the respective proprietors, ensues a division of the society into different interests and parties.

The latent causes of faction are thus sown in the nature of man; and we see them every where brought into different degrees of activity, according to the different circumstances of civil society. A zeal for different opinions concerning religion, concerning Government and many other points, as well of speculation as of practice; an attachment to different leaders ambitiously contending for pre-eminence and power; or to persons of other descriptions whose fortunes have been interesting to the human passions, have in turn divided mankind into parties, inflamed them with mutual animosity, and rendered them much more disposed to vex and oppress each other, than to co-operate for their common good. So strong is this propensity of mankind to fall into mutual animosities, that where no substantial occasion presents itself, the most frivolous and fanciful distinctions have been sufficient to kindle their unfriendly passions, and excite their most violent conflicts. But the most common and durable source of factions, has been the various and unequal distribution of property. Those who hold, and those who are without property, have ever formed distinct interests in society. Those who are creditors, and those who are debtors, fall under a like discrimination. A landed interest, a manufacturing interest, a mercantile interest, a monied interest, with many lesser interests, grow up of necessity in civilized nations, and divide them into different classes, actuated by different sentiments and views. The regulation of these various and interfering interests forms the principal task of modern Legislation, and involves the spirit of party and faction in the necessary and ordinary operations of Government.

No man is allowed to be a judge in his own cause; because his interest would certainly bias his judgment, and, not improbably, corrupt his integrity. With equal, nay with greater reason, a body of men, are unfit to be both judges and parties, at the same time; yet, what are many of the most important acts of legislation, but so many judicial determinations, not indeed concerning the rights of single persons, but concerning the rights of large bodies of citizens, and what are the different classes of legislators, but advocates and parties to the causes which they determine? Is a law proposed concerning private debts? It is a question to which the creditors are parties on one side, and the debtors on the other. Justice ought to hold the balance between them. Yet the parties are and must be themselves the judges; and the most numerous party, or, in other words, the most powerful faction must be expected to prevail. Shall domestic manufactures be encouraged, and in what degree, by restrictions on foreign manufactures? are questions which would be differently decided by the landed and the manufacturing classes; and probably by neither, with a sole regard to justice and the public good. The apportionment of taxes on the various descriptions of property, is an act which seems to require the most exact impartiality; yet, there is perhaps no legislative act in which greater opportunity and temptation are given to a predominant party, to trample on the rules of justice. Every shilling with which they over-burden the inferior number, is a shilling saved to their own pockets.

It is in vain to say, that enlightened statesmen will be able to adjust these clashing interests, and render them all subservient to the public good. Enlightened statesmen will not always be at the helm: Nor, in many cases, can such an adjustment be made at all, without taking into view indirect and remote considerations, which will rarely prevail over the immediate interest which one party may find in disregarding the rights of another, or the good of the whole.

The inference to which we are brought, is, that the causes of faction cannot be removed; and that relief is only to be sought in the means of controlling its effects.

If a faction consists of less than a majority, relief is supplied by the republican principle, which enables the majority to defeat its sinister views by regular vote: It may clog the administration, it may convulse the society; but it will be unable to execute and mask its violence under the forms of the Constitution. When a majority is included in a faction, the form of popular government on the other hand enables it to sacrifice to its ruling passion or interest, both the public good and the rights of other citizens. To secure the public good, and private rights, against the danger of such a faction, and at the same time to preserve the spirit and the form of popular government, is then the great object to which our enquiries are directed: Let me add that it is the great desideratum, by which alone this form of government can be rescued from the opprobrium under which it has so long labored, and be recommended to the esteem and adoption of mankind.

By what means is this object attainable? Evidently by one of two only. Either the existence of the same passion or interest in a majority at the same time, must be prevented; or the majority, having such co-existent passion or interest, must be rendered, by their number and local situation, unable to concert and carry into effect schemes of oppression. If the impulse and the opportunity be suffered to coincide, we well know that neither moral nor religious motives can be relied on as an adequate control. They are not found to be such on the injustice and violence of individuals, and lose their efficacy in proportion to the number combined together; that is, in proportion as their efficacy becomes needful.

From this view of the subject, it may be concluded, that a pure Democracy, by which I mean, a Society, consisting of a small number of citizens, who assemble and administer the Government in person, can admit of no cure for the mischiefs of faction. A common passion or interest will, in almost every case, be felt by a majority of the whole; a communication and concert results from the form of Government itself; and there is nothing to check the inducements to sacrifice the weaker party, or an obnoxious individual. Hence it is, that such Democracies have ever been spectacles of turbulence and contention; have ever been found incompatible with personal security, or the rights of property; and have in general been as short in their lives, as they have been violent in their deaths. Theoretic politicians, who have patronized this species of Government, have erroneously supposed, that by reducing mankind to a perfect equality in their political rights, they would, at the same time, be perfectly equalized and assimilated in their possessions, their opinions, and their passions.

A republic, by which I mean a government in which the scheme of representation takes place, opens a different prospect, and promises the cure for which we are seeking. Let us examine the points in which it varies from pure democracy, and we shall comprehend both the nature of the cure and the efficacy which it must derive from the union.

The two great points of difference, between a democracy and a republic, are, first, the delegation of the government, in the latter, to a small number of citizens, elected by the rest; secondly, the greater number of citizens, and greater sphere of country, over which the latter may be extended.

The effect of the first difference is, on the one hand, to refine and enlarge the public views, by passing them through the medium of a chosen body of citizens, whose wisdom may best discern the true interest of their country, and whose patriotism and love of justice, will be least likely to sacrifice it to temporary or partial considerations. Under such a regulation, it may well happen, that the public voice, pronounced by the representatives of the people, will be more consonant to the public good, than if pronounced by the people themselves, convened for the purpose. On the other hand the effect may be inverted. Men of factious tempers, of local prejudices, or of sinister designs, may by intrigue, by corruption, or by other means, first obtain the suffrages, and then betray the interest of the people. The question resulting is, whether small or extensive republics are most favorable to the election of proper guardians of the public weal, and it is clearly decided in favor of the latter by two obvious considerations.

In the first place, it is to be remarked that, however small the republic may be, the representatives must be raised to a certain number, in order to guard against the cabals of a few; and that however large it may be, they must be limited to a certain number, in order to guard against the confusion of a multitude. Hence, the number of representatives in the two cases not being in proportion to that of the constituents, and being proportionally greatest in the small republic, it follows, that if the proportion of fit characters be not less in the large than in the small republic, the former will present a greater option, and consequently a greater probability of a fit choice.

In the next place, as each Representative will be chosen by a greater number of citizens in the large than in the small Republic, it will be more difficult for unworthy candidates to practise with success the vicious arts, by which elections are too often carried; and the suffrages of the people being more free, will be more likely to center on men who possess the most attractive merit, and the most diffusive and established characters.

It must be confessed, that in this, as in most other cases, there is a mean, on both sides of which inconveniences will be found to lie. By enlarging too much the number of electors, you render the representative too little acquainted with all their local circumstances and lesser interests; as by reducing it too much, you render him unduly attached to these, and too little fit to comprehend and pursue great and national objects. The Federal Constitution forms a happy combination in this respect; the great and aggregate interests being referred to the national, the local and particular, to the state legislatures.

The other point of difference is, the greater number of citizens and extent of territory which may be brought within the compass of Republican, than of Democratic Government; and it is this circumstance principally which renders factious combinations less to be dreaded in the former, than in the latter. The smaller the society, the fewer probably will be the distinct parties and interests composing it; the fewer the distinct parties and interests, the more frequently will a majority be found of the same party; and the smaller the number of individuals composing a majority, and the smaller the compass within which they are placed, the more easily will they concert and execute their plans of oppression. Extend the sphere, and you take in a greater variety of parties and interests; you make it less probable that a majority of the whole will have a common motive to invade the rights of other citizens; or if such a common motive exists, it will be more difficult for all who feel it to discover their own strength, and to act in unison with each other. Besides other impediments, it may be remarked, that where there is a consciousness of unjust or dishonorable purposes, communication is always checked by distrust, in proportion to the number whose concurrence is necessary.

Hence it clearly appears, that the same advantage, which a Republic has over a Democracy, in controlling the effects of faction, is enjoyed by a large over a small Republic—is enjoyed by the Union over the States composing it. Does this advantage consist in the substitution of Representatives, whose enlightened views and virtuous sentiments render them superior to local prejudices, and to schemes of injustice? It will not be denied, that the Representation of the Union will be most likely to possess these requisite endowments. Does it consist in the greater security afforded by a greater variety of parties, against the event of any one party being able to outnumber and oppress the rest? In an equal degree does the increased variety of parties, comprised within the Union, increase this security? Does it, in fine, consist in the greater obstacles opposed to the concert and accomplishment of the secret wishes of an unjust and interested majority? Here, again, the extent of the Union gives it the most palpable advantage.

The influence of factious leaders may kindle a flame within their particular States, but will be unable to spread a general conflagration through the other States: a religious sect may degenerate into a political faction in a part of the Confederacy but the variety of sects dispersed over the entire face of it, must secure the national Councils against any danger from that source: a rage for paper money, for an abolition of debts, for an equal division of property, or for any other improper or wicked project, will be less apt to pervade the whole body of the Union, than a particular member of it; in the same proportion as such a malady is more likely to taint a particular county or district, than an entire State.

In the extent and proper structure of the Union, therefore, we behold a Republican remedy for the diseases most incident to Republican Government. And according to the degree of pleasure and pride, we feel in being Republicans, ought to be our zeal in cherishing the spirit, and supporting the character of Federalists.

PUBLIUS

The Federalist No. 51

James Madison

February 6, 1788

To the People of the State of New York.

To what expedient then shall we finally resort for maintaining in practice the necessary partition of power among the several departments, as laid down in the constitution? The only answer that can be given is, that as all these exterior provisions are found to be inadequate, the defect must be supplied, by so contriving the interior structure of the government, as that its several constituent parts may, by their mutual relations, be the means of keeping each other in their proper places. Without presuming to undertake a full development of this important idea, I will hazard a few general observations, which may perhaps place it in a clearer light, and enable us to form a more correct judgment of the principles and structure of the government planned by the convention.

In order to lay a due foundation for that separate and distinct exercise of the different powers of government, which to a certain extent, is admitted on all hands to be essential to the preservation of liberty, it is evident that each department should have a will of its own; and consequently should be so constituted, that the members of each should have as little agency as possible in the appointment of the members of the others. Were this principle rigorously adhered to, it would require that all the appointments for the supreme executive, legislative, and judiciary magistracies, should be drawn from the same fountain of authority, the people, through channels, having no communication whatever with one another. Perhaps such a plan of constructing the several departments would be less difficult in practice than it may in contemplation appear. Some difficulties however, and some additional expense, would attend the execution of it. Some deviations therefore from the principle must be admitted. In the constitution of the judiciary department in particular, it might be inexpedient to insist rigorously on the principle; first, because peculiar qualifications being essential in the members, the primary consideration ought to be to select that mode of choice, which best secures these qualifications; secondly, because the permanent tenure by which the appointments are held in that department, must soon destroy all sense of dependence on the authority conferring them.

It is equally evident that the members of each department should be as little dependent as possible on those of the others, for the emoluments annexed to their offices. Were the executive magistrate, or the judges, not independent of the legislature in this particular, their independence in every other would be merely nominal.

But the great security against a gradual concentration of the several powers in the same department, consists in giving to those who administer each department, the necessary constitutional means, and personal motives, to resist encroachments of the others. The provision for defense must in this, as in all other cases, be made commensurate to the danger of attack. Ambition must be made to counteract ambition. The interest of the man must be connected with the constitutional right of the place. It may be a reflection on human nature, that such devices should be necessary to control the abuses of government. But what is government itself but the greatest of all reflections on human nature? If men were angels, no government would be necessary. If angels were to govern men, neither external nor internal controls on government would be necessary. In framing a government which is to be administered by men over men, the great difficulty lies in this: You must first enable the government to control the governed; and in the next place, oblige it to control itself. A dependence on the people is no doubt the primary control on the government; but experience has taught mankind the necessity of auxiliary precautions.

This policy of supplying by opposite and rival interests, the defect of better motives, might be traced through the whole system of human affairs, private as well as public. We see it particularly displayed in all the subordinate distributions of power;

where the constant aim is to divide and arrange the several offices in such a manner as that each may be a check on the other; that the private interest of every individual, may be a sentinel over the public rights. These inventions of prudence cannot be less requisite in the distribution of the supreme powers of the state.

But it is not possible to give to each department an equal power of self defense. In republican government the legislative authority, necessarily, predominates. The remedy for this inconveniency is, to divide the legislature into different branches; and to render them by different modes of election, and different principles of action, as little connected with each other, as the nature of their common functions, and their common dependence on the society, will admit. It may even be necessary to guard against dangerous encroachments by still further precautions. As the weight of the legislative authority requires that it should be thus divided, the weakness of the executive may require, on the other hand, that it should be fortified. An absolute negative, on the legislature, appears at first view to be the natural defense with which the executive magistrate should be armed. But perhaps it would be neither altogether safe, nor alone sufficient. On ordinary occasions, it might not be exerted with the requisite firmness; and on extraordinary occasions, it might be perfidiously abused. May not this defect of an absolute negative be supplied, by some qualified connection between this weaker department, and the weaker branch of the stronger department, by which the latter may be led to support the constitutional rights of the former, without being too much detached from the rights of its own department?

If the principles on which these observations are founded be just, as I persuade myself they are, and they be applied as a criterion, to the several state constitutions, and to the federal constitution, it will be found, that if the latter does not perfectly correspond with them, the former are infinitely less able to bear such a test.

There are moreover two considerations particularly applicable to the federal system of America, which place that system in a very interesting point of view.

First. In a single republic, all the power surrendered by the people, is submitted to the administration of a single government; and usurpations are guarded against by a division of the government into distinct and separate departments. In the compound republic of America, the power surrendered by the people, is first divided between two distinct governments, and then the portion allotted to each, subdivided among distinct and separate departments. Hence a double security arises to the rights of the people. The different governments will control each other; at the same time that each will be controlled by itself.

Second. It is of great importance in a republic, not only to guard the society against the oppression of its rulers; but to guard one part of the society against the injustice of the other part. Different interests necessarily exist in different classes of citizens. If a majority be united by a common interest, the rights of the minority will be insecure. There are but two methods of providing against this evil: The one by creating a will in the community independent of the majority, that is, of the society itself, the other by comprehending in the society so many separate descriptions of citizens, as will render an unjust combination of a majority of the whole, very improbable, if not impracticable. The first method prevails in all governments possessing an hereditary or self appointed authority. This at best is but a precarious security;

because a power independent of the society may as well espouse the unjust views of the major, as the rightful interests, of the minor party, and may possibly be turned against both parties. The second method will be exemplified in the federal republic of the United States. While all authority in it will be derived from and dependent on the society, the society itself will be broken into so many parts, interests and classes of citizens, that the rights of individuals or of the minority, will be in little danger from interested combinations of the majority. In a free government, the security for civil rights must be the same as for religious rights. It consists in the one case in the multiplicity of interests, and in the other, in the multiplicity of sects. The degree of security in both cases will depend on the number of interests and sects; and this may be presumed to depend on the extent of country and number of people comprehended under the same government. This view of the subject must particularly recommend a proper federal system to all the sincere and considerate friends of republican government: Since it shows that in exact proportion as the territory of the union may be formed into more circumscribed confederacies or states, oppressive combinations of a majority will be facilitated, the best security under the republican form, for the rights of every class of citizens, will be diminished; and consequently, the stability and independence of some member of the government, the only other security, must be proportionally increased. Justice is the end of government. It is the end of civil society. It ever has been, and ever will be pursued, until it be obtained, or until liberty be lost in the pursuit. In a society under the forms of which the stronger faction can readily unite and oppress the weaker, anarchy may as truly be said to reign, as in a state of nature where the weaker individual is not secured against the violence of the stronger: And as in the latter state even the stronger individuals are prompted by the uncertainty of their condition, to submit to a government which may protect the weak as well as themselves: So in the former state, will the more powerful factions or parties be gradually induced by a like motive, to wish for a government which will protect all parties, the weaker as well as the more powerful. It can be little doubted, that if the state of Rhode Island was separated from the confederacy, and left to itself, the insecurity of rights under the popular form of government within such narrow limits, would be displayed by such reiterated oppressions of factious majorities, that some power altogether independent of the people would soon be called for by the voice of the very factions whose misrule had proved the necessity of it. In the extended republic of the United States, and among the great variety of interests, parties and sects which it embraces, a coalition of a majority of the whole society could seldom take place on any other principles than those of justice and the general good; and there being thus less danger to a minor from the will of the major party, there must be less pretext also, to provide for the security of the former, by introducing into the government a will not dependent on the latter; or in other words, a will independent of the society itself. It is no less certain than it is important, notwithstanding the contrary opinions which have been entertained, that the larger the society, provided it lie within a practicable sphere, the more duly capable it will be of self government. And happily for the *republican cause*, the practicable sphere may be carried to a very great extent, by a judicious modification and mixture of the *federal principle.*

PUBLIUS

The Constitution of the United States of America*

(Preamble)

We the People of the United States, in Order to form a more perfect Union, establish Justice, insure domestic Tranquility, provide for the common defence, promote the general Welfare, and secure the Blessings of Liberty to ourselves and our Posterity, do ordain and establish this Constitution for the United States of America.

Article I.

(The Legislature)

Section 1.   All legislative Powers herein granted shall be vested in a Congress of the United States, which shall consist of a Senate and House of Representatives.

Section 2.   The House of Representatives shall be composed of Members chosen every second Year by the People of the several States, and the Electors in each State shall have the Qualifications requisite for Electors of the most numerous Branch of the State Legislature.

No person shall be a Representative who shall not have attained to the Age of twenty five Years, and been seven Years a Citizen of the United States, and who shall not, when elected, be an Inhabitant of that State in which he shall be chosen.

Representatives and direct [Taxes][1] shall be apportioned among the several States which may be included within this Union, according to their respective Numbers [which shall be determined by adding to the whole Number of free Persons, including those bound to Service for a Term of Years, and excluding Indians not taxed, three fifths of all other Persons].[2] The actual Enumeration shall be made within three Years after the first Meeting of the Congress of the United States, and within every subsequent Term of ten Years, in such Manner as they shall by Law direct. The Number of Representatives shall not exceed one for every thirty Thousand, but each State shall have at Least one Representative; and until such enumeration shall be made, the State of New Hampshire shall be entitled to chuse three, Massachusetts eight, Rhode-Island and Providence Plantations one, Connecticut five, New-York six, New Jersey four, Pennsylvania eight, Delaware one, Maryland six, Virginia ten, North Carolina five, South Carolina five, and Georgia three.

When vacancies happen in the Representation from any State, the Executive Authority thereof shall issue Writs of Election to fill such Vacancies.

The House of Representatives shall chuse their speaker and other Officers; and shall have the sole Power of Impeachment.

Section 3.   The Senate of the United States shall be composed of two Senators from each State [chosen by the Legislature thereof],[3] for six Years; and each Senator shall have one Vote.

Immediately after they shall be assembled in Consequence of the first Election, they shall be divided as equally as may be into three Classes. The Seats of the Senators of the first Class shall be vacated at the Expiration of the second year, of the second Class at the Expiration of the fourth Year, and of the third Class at the Expiration of the sixth Year, so that one third may be chosen every second Year [and if Vacancies happen by Resignation, or otherwise, during the Recess of the Legislature of any State, the Executive thereof may make temporary Appointments until the next Meeting of the Legislature, which shall then fill such Vacancies].[4]

No Person shall be a Senator who shall not have attained to the Age of thirty Years, and been nine Years a Citizen of the United States, and who shall not, when elected, be an Inhabitant of that State for which he shall be chosen.

The Vice President of the United States shall be President of the Senate, but shall have no Vote, unless they be equally divided.

The Senate shall chuse their other Officers, and also a President pro tempore, in the Absence of the Vice President, or when he shall exercise the Office of President of the United States.

The Senate shall have the sole Power to try all Impeachments. When sitting for that Purpose, they shall be on Oath or Affirmation. When the President of the United States is tried, the Chief Justice shall preside: And no Person shall be convicted without the Concurrence of two thirds of the Members present.

Judgment in Cases of Impeachment shall not extend further than to removal from Office, and disqualification to hold and enjoy any Office of honor, Trust or Profit under the United States; but the Party convicted shall nevertheless be liable and subject to Indictment, Trial, Judgment and Punishment, according to Law.

Section 4.   The Times, Places and Manner of holding Elections for Senators and Representatives, shall be prescribed in each State by the Legislature thereof; but the Congress may at any time by Law make or alter such Regulations, except as to the Places of chusing Senators.

[The Congress shall assemble at least once in every Year, and such Meeting shall be on the first Monday in December, unless they shall by Law appoint a different Day.][5]

---

*This text retains the spelling, capitalization, and punctuation of the original. Brackets indicate passages that have been altered by amendments.
[1]See Amendment XVI.
[2]See Amendment XIV.
[3]See Amendment XVII.
[4]See Amendment XVII.
[5]See Amendment XX.

Section 5. Each House shall be the Judge of the Elections, Returns and Qualifications of its own Members, and a Majority of each shall constitute a Quorum to do Business; but a smaller Number may adjourn from day to day, and may be authorized to compel the Attendance of absent Members, in such Manner, and under such Penalties as each House may provide.

Each House may determine the Rules of its Proceedings, punish its Members for disorderly Behaviour, and, with the Concurrence of two thirds, expel a Member.

Each House shall keep a Journal of its Proceedings, and from time to time publish the same, excepting such Parts as may in their judgment require Secrecy; and the Yeas and Nays of the Members of either House on any question shall, at the Desire of one fifth of those present, be entered on the Journal.

Neither House, during the Session of Congress, shall, without the Consent of the other, adjourn for more than three days, nor to any other Place than that in which the two Houses shall be sitting.

Section 6. The Senators and Representatives shall receive a Compensation for their Services, to be ascertained by Law, and paid out of the Treasury of the United States. They shall in all Cases, except Treason, Felony and Breach of the Peace, be privileged from Arrest during their Attendance at the Session of their respective Houses, and in going to and returning from the same; and for any Speech or Debate in either House, they shall not be questioned in any other Place.

No Senator or Representative shall, during the Time for which he was elected, be appointed to any civil Office under the Authority of the United States, which shall have been created, or the Emoluments whereof shall have been encreased during such time; and no Person holding any Office under the United States, shall be a Member of either House during his Continuance in Office.

Section 7. All Bills for raising Revenue shall originate in the House of Representatives; but the Senate may propose or concur with Amendments as on other Bills.

Every Bill which shall have passed the House of Representatives and the Senate, shall, before it becomes a Law, be presented to the President of the United States; If he approves he shall sign it, but if not he shall return it, with his Objections to that House in which it shall have originated, who shall enter the Objections at large on their Journal, and proceed to reconsider it. If after such Reconsideration two thirds of that House shall agree to pass the Bill, it shall be sent, together with the Objections, to the other House, by which it shall likewise be reconsidered, and if approved by two thirds of that House, it shall become a Law. But in all such Cases the Votes of both Houses shall be determined by yeas and Nays, and the Names of the Persons voting for and against the Bill shall be entered on the Journal of each House respectively. If any Bill shall not be returned by the President within ten Days (Sundays excepted) after it shall have been presented to him, the Same shall be a Law, in like Manner as if he had signed it, unless the Congress by their Adjournment prevent its Return, in which Case it shall not be a Law.

Every Order, Resolution, or Vote to which the Concurrence of the Senate and House of Representatives may be necessary (except on a question of Adjournment) shall be presented to the President of the United States; and before the Same shall take Effect, shall be approved by him, or being disapproved by him, shall be repassed by two thirds of the Senate and House of Representatives, according to the Rules and Limitations prescribed in the Case of a Bill.

Section 8. The Congress shall have Power To lay and collect Taxes, Duties, Imposts and Excises, to pay the Debts and provide for the common Defence and general Welfare of the United States; but all Duties, Imposts and Excises shall be uniform throughout the United States;

To borrow Money on the credit of the United States;

To regulate Commerce with foreign Nations, and among the several States, and with the Indian Tribes;

To establish a uniform Rule of Naturalization, and uniform Laws on the subject of Bankruptcies throughout the United States;

To coin Money, regulate the Value thereof, and of foreign Coin, and fix the Standard of Weights and Measures;

To provide for the Punishment of counterfeiting the Securities and current Coin of the United States;

To establish Post Offices and post Roads;

To promote the Progress of Science and useful Arts, by securing for limited Times to Authors and Inventors the exclusive Right to their respective Writings and Discoveries;

To constitute Tribunals inferior to the supreme Court;

To define and punish Piracies and Felonies committed on the high Seas, and Offences against the Law of Nations;

To declare War, grant Letters of Marque and Reprisal, and make Rules concerning Captures on Land and Water;

To raise and support Armies, but no Appropriation of Money to that Use shall be for a longer Term than two Years;

To provide and maintain a Navy;

To make Rules for the Government and Regulation of the land and naval Forces;

To provide for calling forth the Militia to execute the Laws of the Union, suppress Insurrections and repel Invasions;

To provide for organizing, arming, and disciplining, the Militia, and for governing such Part of them as may be employed in the Service of the United States, reserving to the States respectively, the Appointment of the Officers, and the Authority of training the Militia according to the discipline prescribed by Congress;

To exercise exclusive Legislation in all Cases whatsoever, over such District (not exceeding ten Miles square) as may, by Cession of particular States, and the Acceptance of Congress, become the Seat of the Government of the United States, and to exercise like Authority over all Places purchased by the Consent of the Legislature of the State in which the Same shall be, for the Erection of Forts, Magazines, Arsenals, dock-Yards, and other needful Buildings;—And

To make all Laws which shall be necessary and proper for carrying into Execution the foregoing Powers, and all other Powers vested by this Constitution in the Government of the United States, or in any Department or Officer thereof.

Section 9.   The Migration or Importation of such Persons as any of the States now existing shall think proper to admit, shall not be prohibited by the Congress prior to the Year one thousand eight hundred and eight, but a Tax or duty may be imposed on such Importation, not exceeding ten dollars for each Person.

The Privilege of the Writ of Habeas Corpus shall not be suspended, unless when in Cases of Rebellion or Invasion the public Safety may require it.

No Bill of Attainder or ex post facto Law shall be passed.

[No Capitation, or other direct, Tax shall be laid, unless in Proportion to the Census or Enumeration herein before directed to be taken.][6]

No Tax or Duty shall be laid on Articles exported from any State.

No Preference shall be given by any Regulation of Commerce or Revenue to the Ports of one State over those of another; nor shall Vessels bound to, or from, one State, be obliged to enter, clear, or pay Duties in another.

No Money shall be drawn from the Treasury, but in Consequence of Appropriations made by Law; and a regular Statement and Account of the Receipts and Expenditures of all public Money shall be published from time to time.

No Title of Nobility shall be granted by the United States: And no Person holding any Office of Profit or Trust under them, shall, without the Consent of the Congress, accept of any present, Emolument, Office, or Title, of any kind whatever, from any King, Prince, or foreign State.

Section 10.   No State shall enter into any Treaty, Alliance, or Confederation; grant Letters of Marque and Reprisal; coin Money; emit Bills of Credit; make any Thing but gold and silver Coin a Tender in Payment of Debts; pass any Bill of Attainder, ex post facto Law, or Law impairing the Obligation of Contracts, or grant any Title of Nobility.

No State shall, without the Consent of the Congress, lay any Imposts or Duties on Imports or Exports, except what may be absolutely necessary for executing its inspection Laws: and the net Produce of all Duties and Imposts, laid by any State on Imports or Exports, shall be for the Use of the Treasury of the United States; and all such Laws shall be subject to the Revision and Controul of the Congress.

No State shall, without the Consent of Congress, lay any Duty of Tonnage, keep Troops, or Ships of War in time of Peace, enter into any Agreement or Compact with another State, or with a foreign Power, or engage in War, unless actually invaded, or in such imminent Danger as will not admit of delay.

Article II.
(The Executive)

Section 1.   The executive Power shall be vested in a President of the United States of America. He shall hold his Office during the Term of four Years, and, together with the Vice President, chosen for the same Term, be elected, as follows.

Each State shall appoint, in such Manner as the Legislature thereof may direct, a Number of Electors, equal to the whole Number of Senators and Representatives to which the State may be entitled in the Congress; but no Senator or Representative, or Person holding an Office of Trust or Profit under the United States, shall be appointed an Elector.

[The Electors shall meet in their respective States, and vote by Ballot for two Persons, of whom one at least shall not be an Inhabitant of the same State with themselves. And they shall make a List of all the Persons voted for, and of the Number of Votes for each; which List they shall sign and certify, and transmit sealed to the Seat of the Government of the United States, directed to the President of the Senate. The President of the Senate shall, in the Presence of the Senate and House of Representatives, open all the Certificates, and the Votes shall then be counted. The Person having the greatest Number of Votes shall be the President, if such Number be a Majority of the whole Number of Electors appointed; and if there be more than one who have such Majority, and have an equal Number of Votes, then the House of Representatives shall immediately chuse by Ballot one of them for President; and if no Person have a Majority, then from the five highest on the List the said House shall in like Manner chuse the President. But in chusing the President, the Votes shall be taken by States, the Representation from each State having one Vote; A quorum for this Purpose shall consist of a Member or Members from two thirds of the States, and a Majority of all the States shall be necessary to a Choice. In every Case, after the Choice of the President, the Person having the greatest Number of Votes of the Electors shall be the Vice President. But if there should remain two or more who have equal Votes, the Senate shall chuse from them by Ballot the Vice President.][7]

The Congress may determine the Time of chusing the Electors, and the Day on which they shall give their Votes; which Day shall be the same throughout the United States.

No Person except a natural born Citizen, or a Citizen of the United States, at the time of the Adoption of this Constitution, shall be eligible to the Office of President; neither shall any Person be eligible to that Office who shall not have attained to the Age of thirty five Years, and been fourteen Years a Resident within the United States.

[In Case of the Removal of the President from Office, or of his Death, Resignation, or Inability to discharge the Powers and Duties of the said Office, the Same shall devolve on the Vice President, and the Congress may by Law provide for the Case

---

[6]See Amendment XVI.

[7]See Amendment XII.

of Removal, Death, Resignation or Inability, both of the President and Vice President, declaring what Officer shall then act as President, and such Officer shall act accordingly, until the Disability be removed, or a President shall be elected.][8]

The President shall, at stated Times, receive for his Services, a Compensation, which shall neither be encreased nor diminished during the Period for which he shall have been elected, and he shall not receive within that Period any other Emolument from the United States, or any of them.

Before he enter on the Execution of his Office, he shall take the following Oath or Affirmation:—"I do solemnly swear (or affirm) that I will faithfully execute the Office of President of the United States, and will to the best of my Ability, preserve, protect and defend the Constitution of the United States."

Section 2.   The President shall be Commander in Chief of the Army and Navy of the United States, and of the Militia of the several States, when called into the actual Service of the United States; he may require the Opinion, in writing, of the principal Officer in each of the executive Departments, upon any Subject relating to the Duties of their respective Offices, and he shall have Power to grant Reprieves and Pardons for Offences against the United States, except in Cases of Impeachment.

He shall have Power, by and with the Advice and Consent of the Senate, to make Treaties, provided two thirds of the Senators present concur; and he shall nominate, and by and with the Advice and Consent of the Senate, shall appoint Ambassadors, other public Ministers and Consuls, Judges of the supreme Court, and all other Officers of the United States, whose Appointments are not herein otherwise provided for, and which shall be established by Law: but the Congress may by Law vest the Appointment of such inferior Officers, as they think proper, in the President alone, in the Courts of Law, or in the Heads of Departments.

The President shall have Power to fill up all Vacancies that may happen during the Recess of the Senate, by granting Commissions which shall expire at the end of their next Session.

Section 3.   He shall from time to time give to the Congress Information of the State of the Union, and recommend to their Consideration such Measures as he shall judge necessary and expedient; he may, on extraordinary Occasions, convene both Houses, or either of them, and in Case of Disagreement between them, with Respect to the Time of Adjournment, he may adjourn them to such Time as he shall think proper; he shall receive Ambassadors and other public Ministers; he shall take Care that the Laws be faithfully executed, and shall Commission all the Officers of the United States.

Section 4.   The President, Vice President and all civil Officers of the United States, shall be removed from Office on Impeachment for, and Conviction of, Treason, Bribery, or other high Crimes and Misdemeanors.

---

[8]See Amendment XXV.

Article III.

(The Judiciary)

Section 1.   The judicial Power of the United States, shall be vested in one supreme Court, and in such inferior Courts as the Congress may from time to time ordain and establish. The Judges, both of the supreme and inferior Courts, shall hold their Offices during good Behaviour, and shall, at stated Times, receive for their Services, a Compensation, which shall not be diminished during their Continuance in Office.

Section 2.   The judicial Power shall extend to all Cases, in Law and Equity, arising under this Constitution, the Laws of the United States, and Treaties made, or which shall be made, under their Authority;—to all Cases affecting Ambassadors, other public Ministers and Consuls;—to all Cases of admiralty and maritime Jurisdiction;—to Controversies to which the United States shall be a Party;—to Controversies between two or more States; [—between a State and Citizens of another State;—][9] between Citizens of different States,—between Citizens of the same State claiming Lands under Grants of different States, [and between a State, or the Citizens thereof, and foreign States, Citizens or Subjects.][10]

In all Cases affecting Ambassadors, other public Ministers and Consuls, and those in which a State shall be Party, the supreme Court shall have original Jurisdiction. In all the other Cases before mentioned, the supreme Court shall have appellate Jurisdiction, both as to Law and Fact, with such Exceptions, and under such Regulations as the Congress shall make.

The Trial of all Crimes, except in Cases of Impeachment, shall be by Jury; and such Trial shall be held in the State where the said Crimes shall have been committed; but when not committed within any State, the Trial shall be at such Place or Places as the Congress may by Law have directed.

Section 3.   Treason against the United States, shall consist only in levying War against them, or in adhering to their Enemies, giving them Aid and Comfort. No Person shall be convicted of Treason unless on the Testimony of two Witnesses to the same overt Act, or on Confession in open Court.

The Congress shall have Power to declare the Punishment of Treason, but no Attainder of Treason shall work Corruption of Blood, or Forfeiture except during the Life of the Person attainted.

Article IV.

(Interstate Relations)

Section 1.   Full Faith and Credit shall be given in each State to the public Acts, Records, and judicial Proceedings of every other State. And the Congress may by general Laws prescribe the Manner in which such Acts, Records and Proceedings shall be proved, and the Effect thereof.

---

[9]See Amendment XI.
[10]See Amendment XI.

Section 2.   The Citizens of each State shall be entitled to all Privileges and Immunities of Citizens in the several States.

A Person charged in any State with Treason, Felony, or other Crime, who shall flee from Justice, and be found in another State, shall on Demand of the executive Authority of the State from which he fled, be delivered up, to be removed to the State having Jurisdiction of the Crime.

[No Person held to Service or Labour in one State under the Laws thereof, escaping into another, shall, in Consequence of any Law or Regulation therein, be discharged from such Service or Labour, but shall be delivered up on Claim of the Party to whom such Service or Labour may be due.][11]

Section 3.   New States may be admitted by the Congress into this Union; but no new State shall be formed or erected within the Jurisdiction of any other State; nor any State be formed by the Junction of two or more States, or Parts of States, without the Consent of the Legislatures of the States concerned as well as of the Congress.

The Congress shall have Power to dispose of and make all needful Rules and Regulations respecting the Territory or other Property belonging to the United States; and nothing in this Constitution shall be so construed as to Prejudice any Claims of the United States, or of any particular State.

Section 4.   The United States shall guarantee to every State in this Union a Republican Form of Government, and shall protect each of them against Invasion, and on Application of the Legislature, or of the Executive (when the Legislature cannot be convened) against domestic Violence.

Article V.

(Amending the Constitution)

The Congress, whenever two thirds of both Houses shall deem it necessary, shall propose Amendments to this Constitution, or, on the Application of the Legislatures of two thirds of the several States, shall call a Convention for proposing Amendments, which, in either Case, shall be valid to all Intents and Purposes, as Part of this Constitution, when ratified by the Legislatures of three fourths of the several States, or by Conventions in three fourths thereof, as the one or the other Mode of Ratification may be pro-

posed by the Congress; Provided that no Amendment which may be made prior to the Year One thousand eight hundred and eight shall in any Manner affect the first and fourth Clauses in the Ninth Section of the first Article; and that no State, without its Consent, shall be deprived of its equal Suffrage in the Senate.

Article VI.

(Debts, Supremacy, Oaths)

All Debts contracted and Engagements entered into, before the Adoption of this Constitution, shall be as valid against the United States under this Constitution, as under the Confederation.

This Constitution, and the laws of the United States which shall be made in Pursuance thereof; and all Treaties made, or which shall be made, under the Authority of the United States, shall be the supreme Law of the Land; and the Judges in every State shall be bound thereby, any Thing in the Constitution or Laws of any State to the Contrary notwithstanding.

The Senators and Representatives before mentioned, and the Members of the several State Legislatures, and all executive and judicial Officers, both of the United States and of the several States, shall be bound by Oath or Affirmation, to support this Constitution; but no religious Test shall ever be required as a Qualification to any Office or public Trust under the United States.

Article VII.

(Ratifying the Constitution)

The Ratification of the Conventions of nine States, shall be sufficient for the Establishment of this Constitution between the States so ratifying the Same.

Done in Convention by the Unanimous Consent of the States present the Seventeenth Day of September in the Year of our Lord one thousand seven hundred and Eighty seven and of the Independence of the United States of America the Twelfth. IN WITNESS whereof we have hereunto subscribed our Names.

Go. WASHINGTON
Presid't. and deputy from Virginia

Attest	CONNECTICUT	PENNSYLVANIA	MARYLAND	SOUTH CAROLINA
William Jackson	Wm. Saml. Johnson	B. Franklin	James McHenry	J. Rutledge
Secretary	Roger Sherman	Thomas Mifflin	Dan of St. Thos. Jenifer	Charles Cotesworth
		Robt. Morris	Danl. Carroll	Pinckney
DELAWARE	NEW YORK	Geo. Clymer		Charles Pinckney
Geo. Read	Alexander Hamilton	Thos. FitzSimons	VIRGINIA	Pierce Butler
Gunning Bedford jun		Jared Ingersoll	John Blair	
John Dickinson	NEW JERSEY	James Wilson	James Madison Jr.	GEORGIA
Richard Basset	Wh. Livingston	Gouv. Morris		William Few
Jaco. Broom	David Brearley		NORTH CAROLINA	Abr. Baldwin
	Wm. Paterson	NEW HAMPSHIRE	Wm. Blount	
MASSACHUSETTS	Jona. Dayton	John Langdon	Richd. Dobbs Spaight	
Nathaniel Gorbam		Nicholas Gilman	Hu. Williamson	
Rufus King				

---

[11]See Amendment XIII.

Articles in addition to, and amendment of the Constitution of the United States of America, proposed by Congress and ratified by the Legislatures of the several states, pursuant to the Fifth Article of the original Constitution.

(The first ten amendments were passed by Congress on September 25, 1789, and were ratified on December 15, 1791.)

Amendment I—Religion, Speech, Assembly, Petition

Congress shall make no law respecting an establishment of religion, or prohibiting the free exercise thereof; or abridging the freedom of speech, or of the press; or the right of the people peaceably to assemble, and to petition the Government for a redress of grievances.

Amendment II—Right to Bear Arms

A well regulated Militia, being necessary to the security of a free State, the right of the people to keep and bear Arms, shall not be infringed.

Amendment III—Quartering of Soldiers

No Soldier shall, in time of peace be quartered in any house, without the consent of the Owner, nor in time of war, but in a manner to be prescribed by law.

Amendment IV—Searches and Seizures

The right of the people to be secure in their persons, houses, papers, and effects, against unreasonable searches and seizures, shall not be violated, and no warrants shall issue, but upon probable cause, supported by Oath or affirmation, and particularly describing the place to be searched, and the persons or things to be seized.

Amendment V—Grand Juries, Double Jeopardy, Self-incrimination, Due Process, Eminent Domain

No person shall be held to answer for a capital, or otherwise infamous crime, unless on a presentment or indictment of a Grand Jury, except in cases arising in the land or naval forces, or in the Militia, when in actual service in time of War or public danger; nor shall any person be subject for the same offence to be twice put in jeopardy of life or limb; nor shall be compelled in any criminal case to be a witness against himself, nor be deprived of life, liberty, or property, without due process of law; nor shall private property be taken for public use, without just compensation.

Amendment VI—Criminal Court Procedures

In all criminal prosecutions, the accused shall enjoy the right to a speedy and public trial, by an impartial jury of the State and district wherein the crime shall have been committed, which district shall have been previously ascertained by law, and to be informed of the nature and cause of the accusation; to be con-fronted with the witnesses against him; to have compulsory process for obtaining witnesses in his favor, and to have the assistance of counsel for his defence.

Amendment VII—Trial by Jury in Common-law Cases

In Suits at common law, where the value in controversy shall exceed twenty dollars, the right of trial by jury shall be preserved, and no fact tried by a jury, shall be otherwise re-examined in any Court of the United States, than according to the rules of the common law.

Amendment VIII—Bails, Fines, and Punishment

Excessive bail shall not be required, nor excessive fines imposed, nor cruel and unusual punishments inflicted.

Amendment IX—Rights Retained by the People

The enumeration in the Constitution, of certain rights, shall not be construed to deny or disparage others retained by the people.

Amendment X—Rights Reserved to the States

The powers not delegated to the United States by the Constitution, nor prohibited by it to the States, are reserved to the States respectively, or to the people.

Amendment XI—Suits Against the States (Ratified February 7, 1795)

The Judicial power of the United States shall not be construed to extend to any suit in law or equity, commenced or prosecuted against one of the United States by Citizens of another State, or by Citizens or Subjects of any Foreign State.

Amendment XII—Election of the President and Vice-President (Ratified June 15, 1804)

The Electors shall meet in their respective states, and vote by ballot for President and Vice-President, one of whom, at least, shall not be an inhabitant of the same state with themselves; they shall name in their ballots the person voted for as President, and in distinct ballots the person voted for as Vice-President, and they shall make distinct lists of all persons voted for as President, and of all persons voted for as Vice-President, and of the number of votes for each, which lists they shall sign and certify, and transmit sealed to the seat of the government of the United States, directed to the President of the Senate;—The President of the Senate shall, in the presence of the Senate and House of Representatives, open all the certificates and the votes shall then be counted;—The person having the greatest number of votes for President, shall be the President, if such number be a majority of the whole number of Electors appointed; and if no person have such majority, then from the persons having the highest numbers not exceeding three on the list of those voted for as President, the House of Representatives shall choose immediately, by ballot, the President. But in choosing the President, the votes shall be taken by states, the representation from each state having one vote; a quorum for this purpose shall consist of a member or members from two-thirds of the states, and a majority of all the states shall be necessary to a Choice. [And if the House of Representatives shall not choose a President whenever the right of choice shall devolve upon them, before the fourth day of March next following, then the Vice-President shall act as President, as in the case of the death or other constitutional disability of the President.]^{12}—The person having the greatest number of votes as Vice-President, shall be the Vice-President, if such number be a majority of the whole number of Electors appointed, and if no person have a majority, then from the two highest numbers on the list, the Senate shall choose the Vice-President; a quorum for the purpose shall consist of two-thirds of the whole number of Senators, and a majority of the whole number shall be necessary to a choice. But no person constitutionally ineligible to the office of President shall be eligible to that of Vice-President of the United States.

Amendment XIII—Slavery (Ratified on December 6, 1865)

Section 1. Neither slavery nor involuntary servitude, except as a punishment for crime whereof the party shall have been duly convicted, shall exist within the United States, or any place subject to their jurisdiction.

Section 2. Congress shall have power to enforce this article by appropriate legislation.

Amendment XIV—Citizenship, Due Process, and Equal Protection of the Laws (Ratified on July 9, 1868)

Section 1. All persons born or naturalized in the United States, and subject to the jurisdiction thereof, are citizens of the United States and of the State wherein they reside. No State shall make or enforce any law which shall abridge the privileges or immunities of citizens of the United States; nor shall any State deprive any person of life, liberty, or property, without due process of law; nor deny to any person within its jurisdiction the equal protection of the laws.

Section 2. Representatives shall be apportioned among the several States according to their respective numbers, counting the whole number of persons in each State, excluding Indians not taxed. But when the right to vote at any election for the choice of electors for President and Vice President of the United States, Representatives in Congress, the Executive and Judicial officers of a State, or the members of the Legislature thereof, is denied to any of the male inhabitants of such State, being twenty-one years of age, and citizens of the United States, or in

any way abridged, except for participation in rebellion, or other crime, the basis of representation therein shall be reduced in the proportion which the number of such male citizens shall bear to the whole number of male citizens twenty-one years of age in such State.

Section 3. No person shall be a Senator or Representative in Congress, or elector of President and Vice President, or hold any office, civil or military, under the United States, or under any State, who, having previously taken an oath, as a member of Congress, or as an officer of the United States, or as a member of any State legislature, or as an executive or judicial officer of any State, to support the Constitution of the United States, shall have engaged in insurrection or rebellion against the same, or given aid or comfort to the enemies thereof. But Congress may by a vote of two-thirds of each House, remove such disability.

Section 4. The validity of the public debt of the United States, authorized by law, including debts incurred for payment of pensions and bounties for services in suppressing insurrection or rebellion, shall not be questioned. But neither the United States nor any State shall assume or pay any debt or obligation incurred in aid of insurrection or rebellion against the United States, or any claim for the loss or emancipation of any slave, but all such debts, obligations and claims shall be held illegal and void.

Section 5. The Congress shall have power to enforce, by appropriate legislation, the provisions of this article.

Amendment XV—The Right To Vote (Ratified on February 3, 1870)

Section 1. The right of citizens of the United States to vote shall not be denied or abridged by the United States or by any State on account of race, color, or previous condition of servitude.

Section 2. The Congress shall have power to enforce this article by appropriate legislation.

Amendment XVI—Income Taxes (Ratified on February 3, 1913)

The Congress shall have power to lay and collect taxes on incomes, from whatever source derived, without apportionment among the several States, and without regard to any census or enumeration.

Amendment XVII—Election of Senators (Ratified on April 8, 1913)

The Senate of the United States shall be composed of two Senators from each State, elected by the people thereof, for six years; and each Senator shall have one vote. The electors in each State shall have the qualifications requisite for electors of the most numerous branch of the State legislatures.

When vacancies happen in the representation of any State in the Senate, the executive authority of such State shall issue writs of

---

^{12}Amendment XX.

election to fill such vacancies: *Provided,* That the legislature of any State may empower the executive thereof to make temporary appointments until the people fill the vacancies by election as the legislature may direct.

This amendment shall not be so construed as to affect the election or term of any Senator chosen before it becomes valid as part of the Constitution.

Amendment XVIII—Prohibition (Ratified on January 16, 1919)

Section 1.　After one year from the ratification of this article the manufacture, sale, or transportation of intoxicating liquors within, the importation thereof into, or the exportation thereof from the United States and all territory subject to the jurisdiction thereof for beverage purposes is hereby prohibited.

Section 2.　The Congress and the several States shall have concurrent power to enforce this article by appropriate legislation.

Section 3.　This article shall be inoperative unless it shall have been ratified as an amendment to the Constitution by the legislatures of the several States, as provided in the Constitution, within seven years from the date of the submission hereof to the States by the Congress.[13]

Amendment XIX—Women's Right To Vote (Ratified on August 18, 1920)

The right of citizens of the United States to vote shall not be denied or abridged by the United States or by any State on account of sex.

Congress shall have power to enforce this article by appropriate legislation.

Amendment XX—Terms of Office, Convening of Congress, and Succession (Ratified February 6, 1933)

Section 1.　The terms of the President and Vice President shall end at noon on the 20th day of January, and the terms of Senators and Representatives at noon on the 3d day of January, of the years in which such terms would have ended if this article had not been ratified; and the terms of their successors shall then begin.

Section 2.　The Congress shall assemble at least once in every year, and such meeting shall begin at noon on the 3d day of January, unless they shall by law appoint a different day.

Section 3.　If, at the time fixed for the beginning of the term of the President, the President elect shall have died, the Vice President elect shall become President. If a President shall not have been chosen before the time fixed for the beginning of his term, or if the President elect shall have failed to qualify, then

the Vice President elect shall act as President until a President shall have qualified; and the Congress may by law provide for the case wherein neither a President elect nor a Vice President elect shall have qualified, declaring who shall then act as President, or the manner in which one who is to act shall be selected, and such person shall act accordingly until a President or Vice President shall have qualified.

Section 4.　The Congress may by law provide for the case of the death of any of the persons from whom the House of Representatives may choose a President whenever the rights of choice shall have devolved upon them, and for the case of the death of any of the persons from whom the Senate may choose a Vice President whenever the right of choice shall have devolved upon them.

Section 5.　Sections 1 and 2 shall take effect on the 15th day of October following the ratification of this article.

Section 6.　This article shall be inoperative unless it shall have been ratified as an amendment to the Constitution by the legislatures of three-fourths of the several States within seven years from the date of its submission.

Amendment XXI—Repeal of Prohibition (Ratified on December 5, 1933)

Section 1.　The eighteenth article of amendment to the Constitution of the United States is hereby repealed.

Section 2.　The transportation or importation into any State, Territory, or possession of the United States for delivery or use therein of intoxicating liquors, in violation of the laws thereof, is hereby prohibited.

Section 3.　This article shall be inoperative unless it shall have been ratified as an amendment to the Constitution by conventions in the several States, as provided in the Constitution, within seven years from the date of the submission hereof to the States by the Congress.

Amendment XXII—Number of Presidential Terms (Ratified on February 27, 1951)

No person shall be elected to the office of the President more than twice, and no person who has held the office of President, or acted as President, for more than two years of a term to which some other person was elected President shall be elected to the office of the President more than once. But this Article shall not apply to any person holding the office of President when this Article was proposed by the Congress, and shall not prevent any person who may be holding the office of President, or acting as President, during the term within which this Article becomes operative from holding the office of President or acting as President during the remainder of such term.

---

[13]Amendment XXI.

Amendment XXIII—Presidential Electors for the District of Columbia (Ratified on March 29, 1961)

Section 1.   The District constituting the seat of Government of the United States shall appoint in such manner as the Congress may direct:

A number of electors of President and Vice President equal to the whole number of Senators and Representatives in Congress to which the District would be entitled if it were a State, but in no event more than the least populous State; they shall be in addition to those appointed by the States, but they shall be considered, for the purposes of the election of President and Vice President, to be electors appointed by a State; and they shall meet in the District and perform such duties as provided by the twelfth article of amendment.

Section 2.   The Congress shall have power to enforce this article by appropriate legislation.

Amendment XXIV—Poll Tax (Ratified on January 23, 1964)

Section 1.   The right of citizens of the United States to vote in any primary or other election for President or Vice President, for electors for President or Vice President, or for Senator or Representative in Congress, shall not be denied or abridged by the United States or any State by reason of failure to pay any poll tax or other tax.

Section 2.   The Congress shall have power to enforce this article by appropriate legislation.

Amendment XXV—Presidential Disability and Vice Presidential Vacancies (Ratified on February 10, 1967)

Section 1.   In case of the removal of the President from office or of his death or resignation, the Vice President shall become President.

Section 2.   Whenever there is a vacancy in the office of the Vice President, the President shall nominate a Vice President who shall take office upon confirmation by a majority vote of both Houses of Congress.

Section 3.   Whenever the President transmits to the President pro tempore of the Senate and the Speaker of the House of Representatives his written declaration that he is unable to dis-

charge the powers and duties of his office, and until he transmits to them a written declaration to the contrary, such powers and duties shall be discharged by the Vice President as Acting President.

Section 4.   Whenever the Vice President and a majority of either the principal officers of the executive departments or of such other body as Congress may by law provide, transmit to the President pro tempore of the Senate and the Speaker of the House of Representatives their written declaration that the President is unable to discharge the powers and duties of his office, the Vice President shall immediately assume the powers and duties of the office as Acting President.

Thereafter, when the President transmits to the President pro tempore of the Senate and the Speaker of the House of Representatives his written declaration that no inability exists, he shall resume the powers and duties of his office unless the Vice President and a majority of either the principal officers of the executive department or of such other body as Congress may by law provide, transmit within four days to the President pro tempore of the Senate and the Speaker of the House of Representatives their written declaration that the President is unable to discharge the powers and duties of his office. Thereupon Congress shall decide the issue, assembling within forty-eight hours for that purpose if not in session. If the Congress, within twenty-one days after receipt of the latter written declaration, or, if Congress is not in session, within twenty-one days after Congress is required to assemble, determines by two-thirds vote of both Houses that the President is unable to discharge the powers and duties of his office, the Vice President shall continue to discharge the same as Acting President; otherwise, the President shall resume the powers and duties of his office.

Amendment XXVI—Eighteen-year-old Vote (Ratified on July 1, 1971)

Section 1.   The right of citizens of the United States, who are eighteen years of age or older, to vote shall not be denied or abridged by the United States or by any State on account of age.

Section 2.   The Congress shall have power to enforce this article by appropriate legislation.

Amendment XXVII—Congressional Salaries (Ratified on May 18, 1992)

Section 1.   No law varying the compensation for the services of the Senators and Representatives, shall take effect, until an election of Representatives shall have intervened.

Presidents of the United States

YEAR	PRESIDENTIAL CANDIDATES	POLITICAL PARTY	ELECTORAL VOTE	PERCENTAGE OF POPULAR VOTE
1789	**George Washington**	—	69	—
	John Adams		34	
	Others		35	
1792	**George Washington**	—	132	—
	John Adams		77	
	Others		55	
1796	**John Adams**	Federalist	71	—
	Thomas Jefferson	Democratic-Republican	68	
	Thomas Pinckney	Federalist	59	
	Aaron Burr	Democratic-Republican	30	
	Others		48	
1800	**Thomas Jefferson**	Democratic-Republican	73	—
	Aaron Burr	Democratic-Republican	73	
	John Adams	Federalist	65	
	C. C. Pinckney	Federalist	64	
	John Jay	Federalist	1	
1804	**Thomas Jefferson**	Democratic-Republican	162	—
	C. C. Pinckney	Federalist	14	
1808	**James Madison**	Democratic-Republican	122	—
	C. C. Pinckney	Federalist	47	
	George Clinton	Independent-Republican	6	
1812	**James Madison**	Democratic-Republican	128	—
	De Witt Clinton	Federalist	89	
1816	**James Monroe**	Democratic-Republican	183	—
	Rufus King	Federalist	34	
1820	**James Monroe**	Democratic-Republican	231	—
	John Q. Adams	Independent-Republican	1	
1824	**John Q. Adams**	Democratic-Republican	84	30.5
	Andrew Jackson	Democratic-Republican	99	
	Henry Clay	Democratic-Republican	37	
	W. H. Crawford	Democratic-Republican	41	
1828	**Andrew Jackson**	Democratic	178	56.0
	John Q. Adams	National Republican	83	
1832	**Andrew Jackson**	Democratic	219	55.0
	Henry Clay	National Republican	49	
	William Wirt	Anti-Masonic	7	
	John Floyd	Independent Democrat	11	
1836	**Martin Van Buren**	Democratic	170	50.9
	William H. Harrison	Whig	73	
	Hugh L. White	Whig	26	
	Daniel Webster	Whig	14	
1840	**William H. Harrison***	Whig	234	53.0
	Martin Van Buren	Democratic	60	
	(John Tyler, 1841)			
1844	**James K. Polk**	Democratic	170	49.6
	Henry Clay	Whig	105	
1848	**Zachary Taylor***	Whig	163	47.4
	Lewis Cass	Democratic	127	
	(Millard Fillmore, 1850)			

Note: Presidents are shown in boldface.
*Died in office, succeeding vice president shown in parentheses.

YEAR	PRESIDENTIAL CANDIDATES	POLITICAL PARTY	ELECTORAL VOTE	PERCENTAGE OF POPULAR VOTE
1852	**Franklin Pierce**	Democratic	254	50.8
	Winfield Scott	Whig	42	
1856	**James Buchanan**	Democratic	174	45.3
	John C. Fremont	Republican	114	
	Millard Fillmore	American	8	
1860	**Abraham Lincoln**	Republican	180	39.8
	J. C. Breckinridge	Democratic	72	
	Stephen A. Douglas	Democratic	12	
	John Bell	Constitutional Union	39	
1864	**Abraham Lincoln***	Republican	212	55.0
	George B. McClellan	Democratic	21	
	(Andrew Johnson, 1865)			
1868	**Ulysses S. Grant**	Republican	214	52.7
	Horatio Seymour	Democratic	80	
1872	**Ulysses S. Grant**	Republican	286	55.6
	Horace Greeley	Democratic	**	
1876	**Rutherford B. Hayes**	Republican	185	47.9
	Samuel J. Tilden	Democratic	184	
1880	**James A. Garfield***	Republican	214	48.3
	Winfield S. Hancock	Democratic	155	
	(Chester A. Arthur, 1881)			
1884	**Grover Cleveland**	Democratic	219	48.5
	James G. Blaine	Republican	182	
1888	**Benjamin Harrison**	Republican	233	47.8
	Grover Cleveland	Democratic	168	
1892	**Grover Cleveland**	Democratic	277	46.0
	Benjamin Harrison	Republican	145	
	James B. Weaver	People's	22	
1896	**William McKinley**	Republican	271	51.0
	William J. Bryan	Democratic	176	
1900	**William McKinley***	Republican	292	51.7
	William J. Bryan	Democratic	155	
	(Theodore Roosevelt, 1901)			
1904	**Theodore Roosevelt**	Republican	336	56.4
	Alton B. Parker	Democratic	140	
1908	**William H. Taft**	Republican	321	51.6
	William J. Bryan	Democratic	162	
1912	**Woodrow Wilson**	Democratic	435	41.8
	Theodore Roosevelt	Progressive	88	
	William H. Taft	Republican	8	
1916	**Woodrow Wilson**	Democratic	277	49.2
	Charles E. Hughes	Republican	254	
1920	**Warren G. Harding***	Republican	404	60.3
	James M. Cox	Democratic	127	
	(Calvin Coolidge, 1923)			
1924	**Calvin Coolidge**	Republican	382	54.1
	John W. Davis	Democratic	136	
	Robert M. LaFollette	Progressive	13	

**Horace Greeley died between the popular vote and the meeting of the presidential electors.

YEAR	PRESIDENTIAL CANDIDATES	POLITICAL PARTY	ELECTORAL VOTE	PERCENTAGE OF POPULAR VOTE
1928	**Herbert C. Hoover**	Republican	444	58.2
	Alfred E. Smith	Democratic	87	
1932	**Franklin D. Roosevelt**	Democratic	472	57.4
	Herbert C. Hoover	Republican	59	
1936	**Franklin D. Roosevelt**	Democratic	523	60.8
	Alfred M. Landon	Republican	8	
1940	**Franklin D. Roosevelt**	Democratic	449	54.7
	Wendell L. Willkie	Republican	82	
1944	**Franklin D. Roosevelt***	Democratic	432	53.4
	Thomas E. Dewey	Republican	99	
	(Harry S Truman, 1945)			
1948	**Harry S Truman**	Democratic	303	49.5
	Thomas E. Dewey	Republican	189	
	J. Strom Thurmond	States' Rights	39	
1952	**Dwight D. Eisenhower**	Republican	442	55.1
	Adlai E. Stevenson	Democratic	89	
1956	Dwight D. Eisenhower	Republican	457	57.4
	Adlai E. Stevenson	Democratic	73	
1960	**John F. Kennedy***	Democratic	303	49.7
	Richard M. Nixon	Republican	219	
	(Lyndon B. Johnson, 1963)			
1964	**Lyndon B. Johnson**	Democratic	486	61.0
	Barry M. Goldwater	Republican	52	
1968	**Richard M. Nixon**	Republican	301	43.4
	Hubert H. Humphrey	Democratic	191	
	George C. Wallace	American Independent	46	
1972	**Richard M. Nixon†**	Republican	520	60.7
	George S. McGovern	Democratic	17	
	(Gerald R. Ford, 1974)‡			
1976	**Jimmy Carter**	Democratic	297	50.1
	Gerald R. Ford	Republican	240	
1980	**Ronald Reagan**	Republican	489	50.7
	Jimmy Carter	Democratic	49	
	John B. Anderson	Independent	—	
1984	**Ronald Reagan**	Republican	525	58.8
	Walter Mondale	Democratic	13	
1988	**George Bush**	Republican	426	53.4
	Michael Dukakis	Democratic	112	
1992	**Bill Clinton**	Democratic	370	43.0
	George Bush	Republican	168	
	H. Ross Perot	Independent	—	
1996	**Bill Clinton**	Democratic	379	49.2
	Robert Dole	Republican	159	
	H. Ross Perot	Reform	—	
2000	**George W. Bush**	Republican	271	47.8
	Al Gore	Democratic	266	
	Ralph Nader	Green		
	Patrick J. Buchanan	Reform		
2004	**George W. Bush**	Republican	286	50.8
	John Kerry	Democratic	252	
	Ralph Nader	Independent	—	

†Resigned
‡Appointed vice president

Party Control of the Presidency, Senate, and House of Representatives in the Twentieth Century

			Senate			House		
CONGRESS	YEARS	PRESIDENT	D	R	OTHER*	D	R	OTHER*
57th	1901–03	McKinley T. Roosevelt	29	56	3	153	198	5
58th	1903–05	T. Roosevelt	32	58	—	178	207	—
59th	1905–07	T. Roosevelt	32	58	—	136	250	—
60th	1907–09	T. Roosevelt	29	61	—	164	222	—
61st	1909–11	Taft	32	59	—	172	219	—
62d	1911–13	Taft	42	49	—	228‡	162	1
63d	1913–15	Wilson	51	44	1	290	127	18
64th	1915–17	Wilson	56	39	1	230	193	8
65th	1917–19	Wilson	53	42	1	200	216	9
66th	1919–21	Wilson	48	48‡	1	191	237‡	7
67th	1921–23	Harding	37	59	—	132	300	1
68th	1923–25	Coolidge	43	51	2	207	225	3
69th	1925–27	Coolidge	40	54	1	183	247	5
70th	1927–29	Coolidge	47	48	1	195	237	3
71st	1929–31	Hoover	39	56	1	163	267	1
72d	1931–33	Hoover	47	48	1	216‡	218	1
73d	1933–35	F. Roosevelt	59	36	1	313	117	5
74th	1935–37	F. Roosevelt	69	25	2	322	103	10
75th	1937–39	F. Roosevelt	75	17	4	333	89	13
76th	1939–41	F. Roosevelt	69	23	4	262	169	4
77th	1941–43	F. Roosevelt	66	28	2	267	162	6
78th	1943–45	F. Roosevelt	57	38	1	222	209	4
79th	1945–47	Truman	57	38	1	243	190	2
80th	1947–49	Truman	45	51‡	—	188	246‡	1
81st	1949–51	Truman	54	42	—	263	171	1
82d	1951–53	Truman	48	47	1	234	199	2
83d	1953–55	Eisenhower	47	48	1	213	221	1
84th	1955–57	Eisenhower	48‡	47	1	232‡	203	—
85th	1957–59	Eisenhower	49‡	47	—	234‡	201	—
86th†	1959–61	Eisenhower	64‡	34	—	283‡	154	—
87th	1961–63	Kennedy	64	36	—	263	174	—
88th	1963–65	Kennedy Johnson	67	33	—	258	176	—
89th	1965–67	Johnson	68	32	—	295	140	—
90th	1967–69	Johnson	64	36	—	248	187	—
91st	1969–71	Nixon	58‡	42	—	243‡	192	—
92d	1971–73	Nixon	55‡	45	—	255‡	180	—
93d	1973–75	Nixon Ford	57‡	43	—	243‡	192	—
94th	1975–77	Ford	61‡	38	—	291‡	144	—
95th	1977–79	Carter	62	38	—	292	143	—
96th	1979–81	Carter	59	41	—	277	158	—
97th	1981–83	Reagan	47	53	—	243‡	192	—
98th	1983–85	Reagan	46	54	—	269‡	166	—
99th	1985–87	Reagan	47	53	—	253‡	182	—
100th	1987–89	Reagan	55‡	45	—	258‡	177	—
101st	1989–91	Bush	55‡	45	—	260‡	175	—
102d	1991–93	Bush	56‡	44	—	267‡	167	1
103d	1993–95	Clinton	57	43	—	258	176	1
104th	1995–97	Clinton	46	54	—	202	232	1
105th	1997–99	Clinton	45	55	—	206	228‡	1
106th	1999–01	Clinton	45	55	—	211	223	1
107th	2001–03	Bush	50	49	1	212	221	2
108th	2003–05	Bush	48	51	1	205	229	1
109th	2005–07	Bush	44	55	1	202	232	1

*Excludes vacancies at beginning of each session. Party balance immediately following election.

†The 437 members of the House in the 86th and 87th Congresses are attributable to the at-large representative given to both Alaska (January 3, 1959) and Hawaii (August 21, 1959) prior to redistricting in 1962.

‡Chamber controlled by party other than that of the president.

D=Democrat   R=Republican

Supreme Court Justices Serving in the Twentieth Century

NAME	NOMINATED BY	SERVICE
John M. Harlan	Hayes	1877–1911
Horace Gray	Arthur	1882–1902
Melville W. Fuller*	Cleveland	1888–1910
David J. Brewer	Harrison	1890–1910
Henry B. Brown	Harrison	1890–1906
George Shiras, Jr.	Harrison	1892–1903
Edward D. White	Cleveland	1894–1910
Rufus W. Peckham	Cleveland	1895–1909
Joseph McKenna	McKinley	1898–1925
Oliver W. Holmes	T. Roosevelt	1902–1932
William R. Day	T. Roosevelt	1903–1922
William H. Moody	T. Roosevelt	1906–1910
Horace H. Lurton	Taft	1910–1914
Edward D. White	Taft	1910–1921
Charles E. Hughes	Taft	1910–1916
Willis Van Devanter	Taft	1911–1937
Joseph R. Lamar	Taft	1911–1916
Mahlon Pitney	Taft	1912–1922
James C. McReynolds	Wilson	1914–1941
Louis D. Brandeis	Wilson	1916–1939
John H. Clarke	Wilson	1916–1922
William H. Taft	Harding	1921–1930
George Sutherland	Harding	1922–1938
Pierce Butler	Harding	1922–1939
Edward T. Sanford	Harding	1923–1930
Harlan F. Stone	Coolidge	1925–1941
Charles E. Hughes	Hoover	1930–1941
Owen J. Roberts	Hoover	1930–1945
Benjamin N. Cardozo	Hoover	1932–1938
Hugo L. Black	F. Roosevelt	1937–1971
Stanley F. Reed	F. Roosevelt	1938–1957
Felix Frankfurter	F. Roosevelt	1939–1962
William O. Douglas	F. Roosevelt	1939–1975
Frank Murphy	F. Roosevelt	1940–1949
Harlan F. Stone	F. Roosevelt	1941–1946
James F. Byrnes	F. Roosevelt	1941–1942
Robert H. Jackson	F. Roosevelt	1941–1954
Wiley B. Rutledge	F. Roosevelt	1943–1949
Harold H. Burton	Truman	1945–1958
Fred M. Vinson	Truman	1946–1953
Tom C. Clark	Truman	1949–1967
Sherman Minton	Truman	1949–1956
Earl Warren	Eisenhower	1953–1969
John M. Harlan	Eisenhower	1955–1971
William J. Brennan, Jr.	Eisenhower	1956–1990
Charles E. Whittaker	Eisenhower	1957–1962

NAME	NOMINATED BY	SERVICE
Potter Stewart	Eisenhower	1958–1981
Byron R. White	Kennedy	1962–1993
Arthur J. Goldberg	Kennedy	1962–1965
Abe Fortas	Johnson	1965–1969
Thurgood Marshall	Johnson	1967–1991
Warren E. Burger	Nixon	1969–1986
Harry A. Blackmun	Nixon	1970–1994
Lewis F. Powell, Jr.	Nixon	1971–1987
William H. Rehnquist	Nixon	1971–1986
John Paul Stevens	Ford	1975–
Sandra Day O'Connor	Reagan	1981–
William H. Rehnquist	Reagan	1986–
Antonin Scalia	Reagan	1986–
Anthony M. Kennedy	Reagan	1988–
David H. Souter	Bush	1990–
Clarence Thomas	Bush	1991–
Ruth Bader Ginsburg	Clinton	1993–
Stephen G. Breyer	Clinton	1994–

*Boldface type indicates service as chief justice.

Glossary

A

activation. One of three key consequences of electoral campaigns for voters, in which the voter is activated to contribute money or ring doorbells instead of just voting. See also **reinforcement** and **conversion.**

actual group. That part of the **potential group** consisting of members who actually join. See also **interest group.**

Adarand Constructors v. Pena. A 1995 Supreme Court decision holding that federal programs that classify people by race, even for an ostensibly benign purpose such as expanding opportunities for minorities, should be presumed to be unconstitutional. Such programs must be subject to the most searching judicial inquiry and can survive only if they are "narrowly tailored" to accomplish a "compelling governmental interest."

administrative discretion. The authority of administrative actors to select among various responses to a given problem. Discretion is greatest when routines, or **standard operating procedures,** do not fit a case.

advertising. According to David Mayhew, one of three primary activities undertaken by members of Congress to increase the probability of their reelection. Advertising involves contacts between members and their constituents between elections. See also **credit claiming** and **position taking.**

affirmative action. A policy designed to give special attention to or compensatory treatment for members of some previously disadvantaged group.

agenda. See **policy agenda.**

agents of socialization. Families, schools, television, peer groups, and other influences that contribute to **political socialization** by shaping formal and especially informal learning about politics.

Americans with Disabilities Act of 1990. A law passed in 1990 that requires employers and public facilities to make "reasonable accommodations" for people with disabilities and prohibits discrimination against these individuals in employment.

amicus curiae briefs. Legal briefs submitted by a "friend of the court" for the purpose of raising additional points of view and presenting information not contained in the briefs of the formal parties. These briefs attempt to influence a court's decision.

Anti-Federalists. Opponents of the American Constitution at the time when the states were contemplating its adoption. They argued that the Constitution was a class-based document, that it would erode fundamental liberties, and that it would weaken the power of the states. See also **Federalists** and **U.S. Constitution.**

antitrust policy. A policy designed to ensure competition and prevent monopoly, which is the control of a market by one company.

appellate jurisdiction. The jurisdiction of courts that hear cases brought to them on appeal from lower courts. These courts do not review the factual record, only the legal issues involved. Compare **original jurisdiction.**

appropriations bill. An act of Congress that actually funds programs within limits established by **authorization bills.** Appropriations usually cover one year.

arms race. A tense relationship beginning in the 1950s between the Soviet Union and the United States whereby one side's weaponry became the other side's goad to procure more weaponry, and so on.

Articles of Confederation. The first constitution of the United States, adopted by Congress in 1777 and enacted in 1781. The Articles established a national legislature, the Continental Congress, but most authority rested with the state legislatures.

authorization bill. An act of Congress that establishes, continues, or changes a discretionary government program or an entitlement. It specifies program goals and maximum expenditures for discretionary programs. Compare **appropriations bill.**

B

balance of trade. The ratio of what is paid for imports to what is earned from exports. When more is imported than exported, there is a balance-of-trade deficit.

balanced budget amendment. A proposed amendment to the Constitution that would instruct Congress to hold a national convention to propose to the states a requirement that peacetime federal budgets be balanced. The amendment has been passed in varied forms by the legislatures of nearly two-thirds of the states.

Barron v. Baltimore. The 1833 Supreme Court decision holding that the **Bill of Rights** restrained only the national government, not the states and cities. Almost a century later, the Court first ruled in **Gitlow v. New York** that state governments must respect some **First Amendment rights.**

beats. Specific locations from which news frequently emanates, such as Congress or the White House. Most top reporters work a particular beat, thereby becoming specialists in what goes on at that location.

bicameral legislature. A legislature divided into two houses. The U.S. Congress and every American state legislature except Nebraska's are bicameral.

bill. A proposed law, drafted in precise, legal language. Anyone can draft a bill, but only a member of the House of Representatives or the Senate can formally submit a bill for consideration.

Bill of Rights. The first ten amendments to the **U.S. Constitution,** drafted in response to some of the **Anti-Federalist** concerns. These amendments define such basic liberties as freedom of religion, speech, and press and offer protections against arbitrary searches by the police and being held without talking to a lawyer.

blanket primaries. Elections to select party nominees in which voters are presented with a list of candidates from all the parties. Voters can then select some Democrats and some Republicans if they like. See also **primaries.**

714

block grants. Federal grants given more or less automatically to states or communities to support broad programs in areas such as community development and social services. Compare **categorical grants.**

broadcast media. Television and radio, as compared with **print media.**

Brown v. Board of Education. The 1954 Supreme Court decision holding that school segregation in Topeka, Kans., was inherently unconstitutional because it violated the **Fourteenth Amendment's** guarantee of **equal protection.** This case marked the end of legal segregation in the United States. See also ***Plessy v. Ferguson.***

budget. A policy document allocating burdens (taxes) and benefits (expenditures). See also **balanced budget amendment.**

budget resolution. A resolution binding Congress to a total expenditure level, supposedly the bottom line of all federal spending for all programs.

bureaucracy. According to Max Weber, a hierarchical authority structure that uses task specialization, operates on the merit principle, and behaves with impersonality. Bureaucracies govern modern states.

C

cabinet. A group of presidential advisers not mentioned in the Constitution, although every president has had one. Today the cabinet is composed of 14 secretaries and the attorney general.

campaign strategy. The master game plan candidates lay out to guide their electoral campaign.

capitalism. An economic system in which individuals and corporations, not the government, own the principal means of production and seek profits. Pure capitalism means the strict noninterference of the government in business affairs. Compare **mixed economy.**

casework. Activities of members of Congress that help constituents as individuals; cutting through bureaucratic red tape to get people what they think they have a right to get. See also **pork barrel.**

categorical grants. Federal grants that can be used only for specific purposes, or "categories," of state and local spending. They come with strings attached, such as nondiscrimination provisions. Compare **block grants.**

caucus (congressional). A group of members of Congress sharing some interest or characteristic. Most are composed of members from both parties and from both houses.

caucus (state party). A meeting of all state party leaders for selecting delegates to the **national party convention.** Caucuses are usually organized as a pyramid.

censorship. Governmental regulation of media content.

census. A valuable tool for understanding demographic changes. The Constitution requires that the government conduct an "actual enumeration" of the population every ten years. See also **demography.**

Central Intelligence Agency (CIA). An agency created after World War II to coordinate American intelligence activities abroad. It became involved in intrigue, conspiracy, and meddling as well.

chains. See **newspaper chains.**

checks and balances. An important part of the Madisonian model designed to limit government's power by requiring that power be balanced among the different governmental institutions. These institutions continually check one another's activities. This system reflects Madison's goal of setting power against power. See also **separation of powers.**

city manager. An offical appointed by the city council who is responsible for implementing and administrating the council's actions. More than one-third of U.S. cities use the council-manager form of government.

civic duty. The belief that in order to support democratic government, a citizen should always vote.

civil disobedience. A form of **political participation** that reflects a conscious decision to break a law believed to be immoral and to suffer the consequences. See also **protest.**

civil law. The body of law involving cases without a charge of criminality. It concerns disputes between two parties and consists of both statutes and **common law.** Compare **criminal law.**

civil liberties. The legal constitutional protections against government. Although our civil liberties are formally set down in the **Bill of Rights,** the courts, police, and legislatures define their meaning.

civil rights. Policies designed to protect people against arbitrary or discriminitory treatment by government officials or individuals.

Civil Rights Act of 1964. The law that made racial discrimination against any group in hotels, motels, and restaurants illegal and forbade many forms of job discrimination. See also **civil rights movement** and **civil rights policies.**

civil rights movement. A movement that began in the 1950s and organized both African Americans and Whites to end the policies of segregation. It sought to establish equal opportunities in the political and economic sectors and to end policies that erected barriers between people because of race.

civil rights policies. Policies that extend government protection to particular disadvantaged groups. Compare **social welfare policies.**

civil service. A system of hiring and promotion based on the **merit principle** and the desire to create a nonpartisan government service. Compare **patronage.**

class action suits. Lawsuits permitting a small number of people to sue on behalf of all other people similarly situated.

Clean Air Act of 1970. The law that charged the Department of Transportation (DOT) with the responsibility of reducing automobile emissions.

Clean Water Act of 1972. A law intended to clean up the nation's rivers and lakes. It requires municipal, industrial, and other polluters to secure permits from the **Environmental Protection Agency** for discharging waste products into waters. According to the law, polluters are supposed to use "the best practicable [pollution] control technology."

closed primaries. Elections to select party nominees in which only people who have registered in advance with the party can vote for that party's candidates, thus encouraging greater party loyalty. See also **primaries.**

coalition. A group of individuals with a common interest upon which every political party depends. See also **New Deal Coalition.**

coalition government. When two or more parties join together to form a majority in a national legislature. This form of government is quite common in the multiparty systems of Europe.

coattails. See **presidential coattails.**

Cold War. War by other than military means usually emphasizing ideological conflict, such as that between the United States and the Soviet Union from the end of World War II until the 1990s.

collective bargaining. Negotiations between representatives of labor unions and management to determine acceptable working conditions.

collective good. Something of value (money, a tax write-off, prestige, clean air, and so on) that cannot be withheld from a group member.

command-and-control policy. According to Charles Schultze, the existing system of **regulation** whereby government tells business how to reach certain goals, checks that these commands are followed, and punishes offenders. Compare **incentive system.**

commercial speech. Communication in the form of advertising. It can be restricted more than many other types of speech but has been receiving increased protection from the Supreme Court.

commission government. A form of municipal government in which voters elect individuals to serve as city commissioners who will have legislative responsibilities to approve city policies and executive responsibilities to direct a functional area of city government, such as public safety or public works. See also **mayor-council government** and **council-manager government.**

committee chairs. The most important influencers of the congressional agenda. They play dominant roles in scheduling hearings, hiring staff, appointing subcommittees, and managing committee bills when they are brought before the full house.

committees (congressional). See **conference committees, joint committees, select committees,** and **standing committees.**

common law. The accumulation of judicial decisions applied in **civil law** disputes.

comparable worth. The issue raised when women are paid less than men for working at jobs requiring comparable skill.

conference committees. Congressional committees formed when the Senate and the House pass a particular **bill** in different forms. Party leadership appoints members from each house to iron out the differences and bring back a single bill. See also **standing committees, joint committees,** and **select committees.**

Congressional Budget and Impoundment Control Act of 1974. An act designed to reform the congressional budgetary process. Its supporters hoped that it would also make Congress less dependent on the president's budget and better able to set and meet its own budgetary goals.

Congressional Budget Office (CBO). A counterweight to the president's **Office of Management and Budget (OMB).** The CBO advises Congress on the probable consequences of budget decisions and forecasts revenues.

Connecticut Compromise. The compromise reached at the Constitutional Convention that established two houses of Congress: the House of Representatives, in which **representation** is based on a state's share of the U.S. population, and the Senate, in which each state has two representatives. Compare **New Jersey Plan** and **Virginia Plan.**

consensus. Agreement. Consensus is reflected by an opinion distribution in which a large majority see eye to eye.

consent of the governed. According to John Locke, the required basis for government. **The Declaration of Independence** reflects Locke's view that governments derive their authority from the consent of the governed.

conservatives. Those who advocate **conservatism.** Compare **liberals.**

constitution. A nation's basic law. It creates political institutions, assigns or divides powers in government, and often provides certain guarantees to citizens. Constitutions can be either written or unwritten. See also **U.S. Constitution.**

constitutional convention. A method of amending a state constitution in which voters may approve the calling of a convention of state citizens to propose amendments to the state constitution; the proposals are submitted to state voters for approval. See also **initiative** and **legislative proposal.**

constitutional courts. Lower federal courts of original jurisdiction created by Congress by the Judiciary Act of 1789. Compare **legislative courts.**

consumer price index (CPI). The key measure of **inflation** that relates the rise in prices over time.

containment doctrine. A **foreign policy** strategy advocated by George Kennan that called for the United States to isolate the Soviet Union, "contain" its advances, and resist its encroachments by peaceful means if possible, but by force if necessary.

continuing resolutions. When Congress cannot reach agreement and pass appropriations bills, these resolutions allow agencies to spend at the level of the previous year.

convention. See **national party convention.**

conversion. One of three key consequences of electoral campaigns for voters, in which the voter's mind is actually changed. See also **reinforcement** and **activation.**

cooperative federalism. A system of government in which powers and policy assignments are shared between states and the national government. They may also share costs, administration, and even blame for programs that work poorly. Compare **dual federalism.**

council-manager government. A common form of government used by municipalities in which voters elect a city council (and possibly an independent mayor) to make public policy for the city. The city council, in turn, appoints a professional city manager to serve as chief executive of the city and to administer public policy. See also **mayor-council government** and **commission government.**

Council of Economic Advisers (CEA). A three-member body appointed by the president to advise the president on economic policy.

council of governments (COG). Councils in many areas of the country where officials from various localities meet to discuss mutual problems and plan joint, cooperative action.

county. A political subdivision of state government that has a set of government officers to administer some local services—often on behalf of the state. Called a *parish* in Louisiana and a *borough* in Alaska. See also **county government.**

county government. A unit of local government that serves as the administrative arm of state government at the local level. It has many social service and record-keeping responsibilities. See also **county.**

court of last resort. The final appeals court in a state, often known as the state "supreme court."

courts. See **constitutional courts, legislative courts, district courts,** and **courts of appeal.**

courts of appeal. Appellate courts empowered to review all final decisions of district courts, except in rare cases. In addition, they also hear appeals to orders of many federal regulatory agencies. Compare **district courts.**

Craig v. Boren. In this 1976 Supreme Court decision, the Court determined that gender classification cases would have a "heightened" or "middle level" of scrutiny. In other words, the courts were to show less deference to gender classifications than to more routine classifications, but more deference than to racial classifications.

credit claiming. According to David Mayhew, one of three primary activities undertaken by members of Congress to increase the probability of their reelection. It involves personal and district service. See also **advertising** and **position taking.**

criminal law. The body of law involving a case in which an individual is charged with violating a specific law. The offense may be harmful to an individual or society and in either case warrants punishment, such as imprisonment or a fine. Compare **civil law.**

crisis. A sudden, unpredictable, and potentially dangerous event requiring the president to play the role of crisis manager.

critical election. An electoral "earthquake" whereby new issues emerge, new coalitions replace old ones, and the majority party is often displaced by the minority party. Critical election periods are sometimes marked by a national crisis and may require more than one election to bring about a new **party era.** See also **party realignment.**

cruel and unusual punishment. Court sentences prohibited by the **Eighth Amendment.** Although the Supreme Court has ruled that mandatory death sentences for certain offenses are unconstitutional, it has not held that the death penalty itself constitutes cruel and unusual punishment. See also **Furman v. Georgia, Gregg v. Georgia,** and **McClesky v. Kemp.**

culture of poverty. Negative attitudes and values toward work, family, and success that condemn the poor to low levels of accomplishment. The view that there is a culture of poverty is most commonly held by **conservatives.**

D

Dartmouth College v. Woodward. The 1819 case in which the Supreme Court held that Dartmouth's charter, as well as the charter of any corporation, is a legal contract that cannot be tampered with by a government.

dealignment. See **party dealignment.**

debate. See **presidential debate.**

debt. See **federal debt.**

Declaration of Independence. The document approved by representatives of the American colonies in 1776 that stated their grievances against the British monarch and declared their independence.

deficit. An excess of federal **expenditures** over federal **revenues.** See also **budget.**

delegate. See **instructed delegate.**

democracy. A system of selecting policymakers and of organizing government so that policy represents and responds to the public's preferences.

democratic theory. See **traditional democratic theory.**

demography. The science of population changes. See also **census.**

Dennis v. United States. A 1951 Supreme Court decision that permitted the government to jail several American Communist Party leaders under the Smith Act, a law forbidding advocacy of the violent overthrow of the U.S. government.

deregulation. The lifting of restrictions on business, industry, and professional activities for which government rules had been established and that bureaucracies had been created to administer.

détente. A slow transformation from conflict thinking to cooperative thinking in **foreign policy** strategy and policymaking. It sought a relaxation of tensions between the superpowers, coupled with firm guarantees of mutual security.

Dillon's Rule. The idea that local governments have only those powers that are explicitly given them by the states. This means that local governments have very little discretion over what policies they pursue or how they pursue them. It was named for Iowa Judge John Dillon, who expressed this idea in an 1868 court decision.

direct democracy. Procedures such as the initiative, the referendum, and the recall, by which voters can have a direct impact on policymaking and the political process by means of the voting booth.

direct mail. A high-tech method of raising money for a political cause or candidate. It involves sending information and requests for money to people whose names appear on lists of those who have supported similar views or candidates in the past.

direct primaries. **Primaries** used to select party nominees for congressional and state offices.

district courts. The 91 federal courts of original jurisdiction. They are the only federal courts in which no trials are held and in which juries may be empaneled. Compare **courts of appeal.**

dual federalism. A system of government in which both the states and the national government remain supreme within their own spheres, each responsible for some policies. Compare **cooperative federalism.**

due process clause. Part of the **Fourteenth Amendment** guaranteeing that persons cannot be deprived of life, liberty, or property by the United States or state governments without due process of law. See also **Gitlow v. New York.**

E

earned income tax credit (EITC). A "negative income tax" that provides income to very poor individuals in lieu of charging them federal tax.

efficacy. See **political efficacy.**

Eighth Amendment. The constitutional amendment that forbids **cruel and unusual punishment,** although it does not define this phrase. Through the **Fourteenth Amendment,** this **Bill of Rights** provision applies to the states.

elastic clause. The final paragraph of Article I, Section 8, of the Constitution, which authorizes Congress to pass all laws "necessary and proper" to carry out the enumerated powers. See also **implied powers.**

electioneering. Direct group involvement in the electoral process. Groups can help fund campaigns, provide testimony, and get members to work for candidates, and some form **political action committees (PACs).**

electoral college. A unique American institution created by the Constitution that provides for the selection of the president by electors chosen by the state parties. Although the electoral college vote usually reflects a popular majority, the winner-take-all rule gives clout to big states.

electoral mandate. A concept based on the idea that "the people have spoken." It is a powerful symbol in American electoral politics, according legitimacy and credibility to a newly elected president's proposals. See also **mandate theory of politics.**

elite. The upper class in a society that utilizes wealth for political power. According to the **elite and class theory** of government and politics, elites control policies because they control key institutions.

elite theory. A theory of government and politics contending that societies are divided along class lines and that an upper-class elite will rule, regardless of the formal niceties of governmental organization. Compare **hyperpluralism, pluralist theory,** and **traditional democratic theory.**

Endangered Species Act of 1973. This law requires the federal government to protect actively each of the hundreds of species listed as endangered—regardless of the economic effect on the surrounding towns or region.

Engel v. Vitale. The 1962 Supreme Court decision holding that state officials violated the **First Amendment** when they wrote a prayer to be recited by New York's schoolchildren. Compare *School District of Abington Township, Pennsylvania v. Schempp.*

entitlement programs. Policies for which expenditures are uncontrollable because Congress has in effect obligated itself to pay X level of benefits to Y number of recipients. Each year, Congress' bill is a straightforward function of the X level of benefits times the Y number of beneficiaries. Social Security benefits are an example.

entrepreneur. See **political entrepreneur.**

enumerated powers. Powers of the federal government that are specifically addressed in the Constitution; for Congress, these powers are listed in Article I, Section 8, and include the power to coin money, regulate its value, and impose taxes. Compare **implied powers.**

environmental impact statement (EIS). A report filed with the **Environmental Protection Agency (EPA)** that specifies what environmental effects a proposed policy would have. The **National Environmental Policy Act** requires that whenever any agency proposes to undertake a policy that is potentially disruptive of the environment, the agency must file a statement with the EPA.

Environmental Protection Agency (EPA). An agency of the federal government created in 1970 and charged with administering all the government's environmental legislation. It also administers policies dealing with toxic wastes. The EPA is the largest federal **independent regulatory agency.**

equal opportunity. A policy statement about equality holding that the rules of the game should be the same for everyone. Most of our **civil rights** policies over the past three decades have presumed that equality of opportunity is a public policy goal. Compare **equal results.**

equal protection of the laws. Part of the **Fourteenth Amendment** emphasizing that the laws must provide equivalent "protection" to all people. As one member of Congress said during debate on the amendment, it should provide "equal protection of life, liberty, and property" to all a state's citizens.

equal results. A policy statement about equality holding that government has a duty to help break down barriers to **equal opportunity. Affirmative action** is an example of a policy justified as promoting equal results rather than merely equal opportunities.

Equal Rights Amendment (ERA). A constitutional amendment originally introduced in 1923 and passed by Congress in 1972 and sent to the state legislatures for ratification, stating that "equality of rights under the law shall not be denied or abridged by the United States or by any state on account of sex." Despite substantial public support and an extended deadline, the amendment failed to acquire the necessary support from three-fourths of the state legislatures.

establishment clause. Part of the **First Amendment** stating that "Congress shall make no law respecting an establishment of religion."

European Union (EU). An alliance of the major Western European nations that coordinates monetary, trade, immigration, and labor policies, making its members one economic unit. An example of a regional organization.

exclusionary rule. The rule that evidence, no matter how incriminating, cannot be introduced into a trial if it was not constitutionally obtained. The rule prohibits use of evidence obtained through **unreasonable search and seizure.**

executive agency. See **independent executive agency.**

executive orders. Regulations originating from the executive branch. Executive orders are one method presidents can use to control the bureaucracy; more often, though, presidents pass along their wishes through their aides.

exit poll. Public opinion surveys used by major media pollsters to predict electoral winners with speed and precision.

expenditures. Federal spending of **revenues.** Major areas of such spending are social services and the military.

extradition. A legal process whereby an alleged criminal offender is surrendered by the officials of one state to officials of the state in which the crime is alleged to have been committed.

F

facilitator. According to George Edwards, the effective leader who works at the margin of coalition building to recognize and exploit opportunities presented by a favorable configuration of political forces.

factions. Interest groups arising from the unequal distribution of property or wealth that James Madison attacked in *Federalist*

Paper No. 10. Today's parties or interest groups are what Madison had in mind when he warned of the instability in government caused by factions.

federal debt. All the money borrowed by the federal government over the years and still outstanding. Today the federal debt is more than $8 trillion.

Federal Election Campaign Act. A law passed in 1974 for reforming campaign finances. The act created the **Federal Election Commission (FEC),** provided public financing for presidential primaries and general elections, limited presidential campaign spending, required disclosure, and attempted to limit contributions.

Federal Election Commission (FEC). A six-member bipartisan agency created by the **Federal Election Campaign Act** of 1974. The FEC administers the campaign finance laws and enforces compliance with their requirements.

Federal Regulation of Lobbying Act. Passed in 1946, an act requiring congressional lobbyists to register and state their policy goals. According to the Supreme Court, the law applies only to groups whose "principal" purpose is **lobbying.**

Federal Reserve System. The main instrument for making **monetary policy** in the United States. It was created by Congress in 1913 to regulate the lending practices of banks and thus the money supply. The seven members of its Board of Governors are appointed to 14-year terms by the president with the consent of the Senate.

Federal Trade Commission (FTC). The **independent regulatory agency** traditionally responsible for regulating false and misleading trade practices. The FTC has recently become active in defending consumer interests through its truth-in-advertising rule and the Consumer Credit Protection Act.

federalism. A way of organizing a nation so that two levels of government have formal authority over the same land and people. It is a system of shared power between units of government. Compare **unitary government.**

Federalist Papers. A collection of 85 articles written by Alexander Hamilton, John Jay, and James Madison under the name "Publius" to defend the Constitution in detail. Collectively, these papers are second only to the **U.S. Constitution** in characterizing the framers' intents.

Federalists. Supporters of the **U.S. Constitution** at the time the states were contemplating its adoption. See also **Anti-Federalists** and **Federalist Papers.**

feminization of poverty. The increasing concentration of poverty among women, especially unmarried women and their children.

Fifteenth Amendment. The constitutional amendment adopted in 1870 to extend **suffrage** to African Americans.

Fifth Amendment. The constitutional amendment designed to protect the rights of persons accused of crimes, including protection against double jeopardy, **self-incrimination,** and punishment without due process of law.

filibuster. A strategy unique to the Senate whereby opponents of a piece of legislation try to talk it to death, based on the tradition of unlimited debate. Today, 60 members present and voting can halt a filibuster.

First Amendment. The constitutional amendment that establishes the four great liberties: freedom of the press, of speech, of religion, and of assembly.

fiscal federalism. The pattern of spending, taxing, and providing grants in the federal system; it is the cornerstone of the national government's relations with state and local governments. See also **federalism.**

fiscal policy. The policy that describes the impact of the federal budget—taxes, spending, and borrowing—on the economy. Unlike **monetary policy,** which is mostly controlled by the **Federal Reserve System,** fiscal policy is almost entirely determined by Congress and the president, who are the budget makers. See also **Keynesian economic theory.**

Food and Drug Administration (FDA). The federal agency formed in 1913 and assigned the task of approving all food products and drugs sold in the United States. All drugs, with the exception of tobacco, must have FDA authorization.

foreign policy. A policy that involves choice taking, like domestic policy, but additionally involves choices about relations with the rest of the world. The president is the chief initiator of foreign policy in the United States.

formula grants. Federal **categorical grants** distributed according to a formula specified in legislation or in administrative regulations.

Fourteenth Amendment. The constitutional amendment adopted after the Civil War that states, "No State shall make or enforce any law which shall abridge the privileges or immunities of citizens of the United States; nor shall any state deprive any person of life, liberty, or property, without due process of law; nor deny to any person within its jurisdiction the **equal protection of the laws.**" See also **due process clause.**

fragmentation. A situation in which responsibility for a policy area is dispersed among several units within the bureaucracy, making the coordination of policies both time consuming and difficult.

free exercise clause. A **First Amendment** provision that prohibits government from interfering with the practice of religion.

free-rider problem. The problem faced by unions and other groups when people do not join because they can benefit from the group's activities without officially joining. The bigger the group, the more serious the free-rider problem. See also **interest group.**

frontloading. The recent tendency of states to hold primaries early in the calendar in order to capitalize on media attention. At one time, it was considered advantageous for a state to choose its delegates late in the primary season so that it could play a decisive role. However, in recent years, votes cast in states that have held late primaries have been irrelevant given that one candidate had already sewn up the nomination early on.

full faith and credit clause. A clause in Article IV, Section 1, of the Constitution requiring each state to recognize the official documents and civil judgments rendered by the courts of other states.

G

gender gap. A term that refers to the regular pattern by which women are more likely to support Democratic candidates. Women tend to be significantly less conservative than men and are more likely to support spending on social services and to oppose higher levels of military spending.

General Schedule rating. See **GS (General Schedule) rating.**

Gibbons v. Ogden. A landmark case decided in 1824 in which the Supreme Court interpreted very broadly the clause in Article I, Section 8, of the Constitution giving Congress the power to regulate interstate commerce, encompassing virtually every form of commercial activity. The commerce clause has been the constitutional basis for much of Congress' regulation of the economy.

Gideon v. Wainwright. The 1963 Supreme Court decision holding that anyone accused of a felony where imprisonment may be imposed, however poor he or she might be, has a right to a lawyer. See also **Sixth Amendment.**

Gitlow v. New York. The 1925 Supreme Court decision holding that freedoms of press and speech are "fundamental personal rights and liberties protected by the **due process clause** of the **Fourteenth Amendment** from impairment by the states" as well as the federal government. Compare *Barron v. Baltimore.*

government. The institutions and processes through which **public policies** are made for a society.

governmental corporation. A government organization that, like business corporations, provides a service that could be provided by the private sector and typically charges for its services. The U.S. Postal Service is an example. Compare **independent regulatory agency** and **independent executive agency.**

governor. The elected chief executive of state government who directs the administration of state government and the implementation of public policy in the state.

Gramm-Rudman-Hollings. Named for its sponsors and also known as the Balanced Budget and Emergency Deficit Act, legislation mandating maximum allowable deficit levels each year until 1991, when the budget was to be balanced. In 1987, the balanced budget year was shifted to 1993, but the Act was abandoned in 1991.

grandfather clause. One of the methods used by Southern states to deny African Americans the right to vote. In order to exempt illiterate Whites from taking a literacy test before voting, the clause exempted people whose grandfathers were eligible to vote in 1860, thereby disenfranchising the grandchildren of slaves. The grandfather clause was declared unconstitutional by the Supreme Court in 1913. See also **poll taxes** and **White primary.**

grants. See **categorical grants** and **block grants.**

Gregg v. Georgia. The 1976 Supreme Court decision that upheld the constitutionality of the death penalty, stating that "It is an extreme sanction, suitable to the most extreme of crimes." The court did not, therefore, believe that the death sentence constitutes **cruel and unusual punishment.**

gross domestic product. The sum total of the value of all the goods and services produced in a nation.

GS (General Schedule) rating. A schedule for federal employees, ranging from GS 1 to GS 18, by which salaries can be keyed to rating and experience. See **civil service.**

H

Hatch Act. A federal law prohibiting government employees from active participation in partisan politics.

health maintenance organizations (HMOs). Organizations contracted by individuals or insurance companies to provide health care for a yearly fee. Such network health plans limit the choice of doctors and treatments. About 60 percent of Americans are enrolled in HMOs or similar programs.

high-tech politics. A politics in which the behavior of citizens and policymakers and the political agenda itself are increasingly shaped by technology.

home rule. The practice by which municipalities are permitted by the states to write their own charters and change them without permission of the state legislature, within limits. Today this practice is widely used to organize and modernize municipal government. See also **local charter.**

House Rules Committee. An institution unique to the House of Representatives that reviews all bills (except revenue, budget, and appropriations bills) coming from a House committee before they go to the full House.

House Ways and Means Committee. The House of Representatives committee that, along with the **Senate Finance Committee,** writes the tax codes, subject to the approval of Congress as a whole.

hyperpluralism. A theory of government and politics contending that groups are so strong that government is weakened. Hyperpluralism is an extreme, exaggerated, or perverted form of **pluralism.** Compare **elite and class theory, pluralist theory,** and **traditional democratic theory.**

I

ideology. See **political ideology.**

impacts. See **policy impacts.**

impeachment. The political equivalent of an indictment in criminal law, prescribed by the Constitution. The House of Representatives may impeach the president by a majority vote for "Treason, Bribery, or other high Crimes and Misdemeanors."

implementation. The stage of policymaking between the establishment of a policy and the consequences of the policy for the people whom it affects. Implementation involves translating the goals and objectives of a policy into an operating, ongoing program. See also **judicial implementation.**

implied powers. Powers of the federal government that go beyond those enumerated in the Constitution. The Constitution states that Congress has the power to "make all laws necessary and proper for carrying into execution" the powers enumerated in Article I. Many federal policies are justified on the basis of implied powers. See also *McCulloch v. Maryland,* **elastic clause,** and **enumerated powers.**

incentive system. According to Charles Shultze, a more effective and efficient policy than **command-and-control;** in the incentive system, market-like strategies are used to manage public policy.

income. The amount of funds collected between any two points in time. Compare **wealth.**

income distribution. The "shares" of the national income earned by various groups.

income tax. Shares of individual wages and corporate revenues collected by the government. The first income tax was declared unconstitutional by the Supreme Court in 1895, but the **Sixteenth Amendment** explicitly authorized Congress to levy a tax on income. See also **Internal Revenue Service.**

incorporation doctrine. The legal concept under which the **Supreme Court** has nationalized the **Bill of Rights** by making most of its provisions applicable to the states through the **Fourteenth Amendment.**

incrementalism. The belief that the best predictor of this year's **budget** is last year's budget, plus a little bit more (an increment). According to Aaron Wildavsky, "Most of the budget is a product of previous decisions."

incumbents. Those already holding office. In congressional elections, incumbents usually win.

independent executive agency. The government not accounted for by **cabinet** departments, **independent regulatory agencies,** and **government corporations.** Its administrators are typically appointed by the president and serve at the president's pleasure. NASA is an example.

independent regulatory agency. A government agency responsible for some sector of the economy, making and enforcing rules supposedly to protect the public interest. It also judges disputes over these rules. Compare **government corporation** and **independent executive agency.**

individualism. The belief that individuals should be left on their own by the government. One of the primary reasons for the comparatively small scope of American government is the prominence of this belief in American political thought and practice.

industrial policy. An economic policy that advocates the federal government's support of key strategic industries, such as the making of computer chips, and protection of these industries from foreign competition by tariffs and other measures.

INF Treaty. The elimination of intermediate range nuclear forces (INF) through an agreement signed by President Reagan and Mikhail Gorbachev during the May 1988 Moscow summit. It was the first treaty to reduce current levels of nuclear weapons.

inflation. The rise in prices for consumer goods. Inflation hurts some but actually benefits others. Groups such as those who live on fixed incomes are particularly hard hit, while people whose salary increases are tied to the **consumer price index** but whose loan rates are fixed may enjoy increased buying power.

initiative. A process permitted in some states whereby voters may put proposed changes in the state constitution to a vote if sufficient signatures are obtained on petitions calling for such a referendum. See also **legislative proposal** and **constitutional convention.**

instructed delegate. A legislator who mirrors the preferences of his or her constituents. Compare **trustee.**

interdependency. Mutual dependency, in which the actions of nations reverberate and affect one another's economic lifelines.

interest group. An organization of people with shared policy goals entering the policy process at several points to try to achieve those goals. Interest groups pursue their goals in many arenas.

intergenerational equity. The issue of the distribution of government benefits and burdens among the generations and over time. Affected groups include children, the working and middle classes, and the elderly, all of whom are beneficiaries of public policies.

intergovernmental relations. The workings of the federal system—the entire set of interactions among national, state, and local governments.

Internal Revenue Service. The office established to collect federal **income taxes,** investigate violations of the tax laws, and prosecute tax criminals.

investigative journalism. The use of in-depth reporting to unearth scandals, scams, and schemes, which at times puts reporters in adversarial relationships with political leaders.

iron triangles. Entities composed of bureaucratic agencies, interest groups, and congressional committees or subcommittees, which have dominated some areas of domestic policymaking. Iron triangles are characterized by mutual dependency, in which each element provides key services, information, or policy for the others.

isolationism. A **foreign policy** course followed throughout most of our nation's history, whereby the United States has tried to stay out of other nations' conflicts, particularly European wars. Isolationism was reaffirmed by the Monroe Doctrine.

issue. See **political issue.**

item veto. The power possessed by 42 state governors to veto only certain parts of a bill while allowing the rest of it to pass into law.

J

Joint Chiefs of Staff. The commanding officers of the armed services who advise the president on military policy.

joint committees. Congressional committees on a few subject-matter areas with membership drawn from both houses. See also **standing committees, conference committees,** and **select committees.**

judicial activism. A judicial philosophy in which judges make bold policy decisions, even charting new constitutional ground. Advocates of this approach emphasize that the courts can correct pressing needs, especially those unmet by the majoritarian political process.

judicial implementation. How and whether court decisions are translated into actual policy, affecting the behavior of others. The courts rely on other units of government to enforce their decisions.

judicial interpretation. A major informal way in which the Constitution is changed by the courts as they balance citizens' rights against those of the government. See also **judicial review.**

judicial restraint. A judicial philosophy in which judges play minimal policymaking roles, leaving that strictly to the legislatures. Compare **judicial activism.**

judicial review. The power of the courts to determine whether acts of Congress, and by implication the executive, are in accord with the **U.S. Constitution.** Judicial review was established by John Marshall and his associates in **Marbury v. Madison.** See also **judicial interpretation.**

jurisdiction. See **original jurisdiction** and **appellate jurisdiction.**

justiciable disputes. A constraint on the courts, requiring that a case must be capable of being settled by legal methods.

K

Keynesian economic theory. The theory emphasizing that government spending and deficits can help the economy weather its normal ups and downs. Proponents of this theory advocate using the power of government to stimulate the economy when it is lagging. See also **fiscal policy.**

Korematsu v. United States. A 1944 Supreme Court decision that upheld as constitutional the internment of more than 100,000 Americans of Japanese descent in encampments during World War II.

L

labor union. An organization of workers intended to engage in **collective bargaining.**

laissez-faire. The principle that government should not meddle in the economy. See also **capitalism.**

leak. See **news leak.**

legislative courts. Courts established by Congress for specialized purposes, such as the Court of Military Appeals. Judges who serve on these courts have fixed terms and lack the protections of **constitutional court** judges.

legislative oversight. Congress' monitoring of the bureaucracy and its administration of policy, performed mainly through hearings.

legislative proposal. A method of state constitutional revision in which the state legislature offers a proposed change to state voters for approval (or may be used to describe a bill proposed by a legislator). See also **constitutional convention** and **initiative.**

legislative turnover. The rate at which incumbent state legislators leave office by choice or by defeat during a bid for reelection.

legislative veto. The ability of Congress to override a presidential decision. Although the **War Powers Resolution** asserts this authority, there is reason to believe that, if challenged, the Supreme Court would find the legislative veto in violation of the doctrine of separation of powers.

legislators. The elected representatives of state citizens who serve in the state legislature and make public policy.

legitimacy. A characterization of elections by political scientists meaning that they are almost universally accepted as a fair and free method of selecting political leaders. When legitimacy is high, as in the United States, even the losers accept the results peacefully.

Lemon v. Kurtzman. The 1971 Supreme Court decision that established that aid to church-related schools must (1) have a secular legislative purpose (2) have a primary effect that neither advances nor inhibits religion and (3) not foster excessive government entanglement with religion.

libel. The publication of false or malicious statements that damage someone's reputation.

liberalism. A **political ideology** whose advocates prefer a government active in dealing with human needs, support individual rights and liberties, and give higher priority to social needs than to military needs.

lieutenant governor. Often the second-highest executive official in state government, who is elected with the governor as a ticket in some states and is elected separately in others. May have legislative and executive branch responsibilities.

limited government. The idea that certain things are out of bounds for government because of the **natural rights** of citizens.

Limited government was central to John Locke's philosophy in the seventeenth century, and it contrasted sharply with the prevailing view of the divine rights of monarchs.

line-item veto. The power possessed by 42 state governors to veto only certain parts of a bill while allowing the rest of it to pass into law.

linkage institutions. The channels or access points through which issues and people's policy preferences get on the government's **policy agenda.** In the United States, elections, **political parties, interest groups,** and the **mass media** are the three main linkage institutions.

litigants. The **plaintiff** and the **defendant** in a **case.**

lobbying. According to Lester Milbrath, a "communication, by someone other than a citizen acting on his own behalf, directed to a governmental decisionmaker with the hope of influencing his decision."

local charter. An organizational statement and grant of authority from the state to a local government, much like a state or federal constitution. States sometimes allow municipalities to write their own charters and to change them without permission of the state legislature, within limits. See also **home rule.**

M

majority leader. The principal partisan ally of the Speaker of the House or the party's wheel horse in the Senate. The majority leader is responsible for scheduling bills, influencing committee assignments, and rounding up votes in behalf of the party's legislative positions.

majority rule. A fundamental principle of **traditional democratic theory.** In a democracy, choosing among alternatives requires that the majority's desire be respected. See also **minority rights.**

mandate. See **electoral mandate** and **mandate theory of elections.**

mandate theory of elections. The idea that the winning candidate has a mandate from the people to carry out his or her platforms and politics. Politicians like the theory better than political scientists do.

Mapp v. Ohio. The 1961 Supreme Court decision ruling that the Fourth Amendment's protection against **unreasonable searches and seizures** must be extended to the states as well as the federal government. See also **exclusionary rule.**

Marbury v. Madison. The 1803 case in which Chief Justice John Marshall and his associates first asserted the right of the **Supreme Court** to determine the meaning of the **U.S. Constitution.** The decision established the Court's power of **judicial review** over acts of Congress, in this case the Judiciary Act of 1789.

mass media. Television, radio, newspapers, magazines, and other means of popular communication. They are a key part of **high-tech politics.** See also **broadcast media** and **print media.**

matching funds. Contributions of up to $250 are matched from the Presidential Election Campaign Fund to candidates for the presidential nomination who qualify and agree to meet various conditions, such as limiting their overall spending.

mayor-council government. One of three common forms of municipal government in which voters elect both a mayor and a city council. In the weak mayor form, the city council is more powerful; in the strong mayor form, the mayor is the chief executive of city government. See also **council-manager government.**

McCarthyism. The fear, prevalent in the 1950s, that international communism was conspiratorial, insidious, bent on world domination, and infiltrating American government and cultural institutions. It was named after Senator Joseph McCarthy and flourished after the Korean War.

McCleskey v. Kemp. The 1987 Supreme Court decision that upheld the constitutionality of the death penalty against charges that it violated the **Fourteenth Amendment** because minority defendants were more likely to receive the death penalty than White defendants.

McCulloch v. Maryland. An 1819 Supreme Court decision that established the supremacy of the national government over state governments. In deciding this case, Chief Justice John Marshall and his colleagues held that Congress had certain **implied powers** in addition to the **enumerated powers** found in the Constitution.

McGovern-Fraser Commission. A commission formed at the 1968 Democratic convention in response to demands for reform by minority groups and others who sought better representation.

means-tested programs. Government programs available only to individuals below a poverty line.

media events. Events purposely staged for the media that nonetheless look spontaneous. In keeping with politics as theater, media events can be staged by individuals, groups, and government officials, especially presidents.

Medicaid. A public assistance program designed to provide health care for poor Americans. Medicaid is funded by both the states and the national government. Compare **Medicare.**

Medicare. A program added to the Social Security system in 1965 that provides hospitalization insurance for the elderly and permits older Americans to purchase inexpensive coverage for doctor fees and other expenses. Compare **Medicaid.**

melting pot. The mixing of cultures, ideas, and peoples that has changed the American nation. The United States, with its history of immigration, has often been called a melting pot.

merit plan. A hybrid system of appointment and election used to select judges in 17 states. In this system the governor appoints the state's judges from a list of recommended persons; an appointed judge then serves a short "trial run" term, after which a retention election is held. If voters approve retention by a majority vote, then the judge continues in office for a lengthy term.

merit principle. The idea that hiring should be based on entrance exams and promotion ratings to produce administration by people with talent and skill. See also **civil service** and compare **patronage.**

Miami Herald Publishing Company v. Tornillo. A 1974 case in which the Supreme Court held that a state could not force a newspaper to print replies from candidates it had criticized, illustrating the limited power of government to restrict the **print media.** See ***Red Lion Broadcasting Company v. FCC.***

Miller v. California. A 1973 Supreme Court decision that avoided defining obscenity by holding that community standards be used to determine whether material is obscene in terms of appealing to a "prurient interest."

minimum wage. The legal minimum hourly wage for large employers, currently $5.15 per hour.

minority leader. The principal leader of the minority party in the House of Representatives or in the Senate.

minority majority. The emergence of a non-Caucasian majority, as compared with a White, generally Anglo-Saxon majority. It is predicted that, by about 2060, Hispanic Americans, African Americans, and Asian Americans together will outnumber White Americans.

minority rights. A principle of **traditional democratic theory** that guarantees rights to those who do not belong to majorities and allows that they might join majorities through persuasion and reasoned argument. See also **majority rule.**

Miranda v. Arizona. The 1966 Supreme Court decision that sets guidelines for police questioning of accused persons to protect them against **self-incrimination** and to protect their right to counsel.

mixed economy. An economic system in which the government is deeply involved in economic decisions through its role as regulator, consumer, subsidizer, taxer, employer, and borrower. The United States can be considered a mixed economy. Compare **capitalism.**

monetarism. An economic theory holding that the supply of money is the key to a nation's economic health. Monetarists believe that too much cash and credit in circulation produces inflation. See also **monetary policy.**

monetary policy. Based on **monetarism,** monetary policy is the manipulation of the supply of money in private hands by which the government can control the economy. See also the **Federal Reserve System,** and compare **fiscal policy.**

Motor Voter Act. Passed in 1993, this Act went into effect for the 1996 election. It requires states to permit people to register to vote at the same time they apply for driver's licenses.

multinational corporations. Large businesses with vast holdings in many countries. Many of these companies are larger than most governments.

municipalities. Another name for *cities,* also known by the legal term *municipal corporations*; denotes a government created by charter granted from the state government or by home rule charter approved by local voters.

N

NAACP v. Alabama. The Supreme Court protected the right to assemble peaceably in this 1958 case when it decided the NAACP did not have to reveal its membership list and thus subject its members to harassment.

narrowcasting. As opposed to the traditional "broadcasting," the appeal to a narrow, particular audience by channels such as ESPN, MTV, and C-SPAN, which focus on a narrow particular interest.

national chairperson. One of the institutions that keeps the party operating between conventions. The national chairperson is responsible for the day-to-day activities of the party and is usually selected by the presidential nominee. See also **national committee.**

national committee. One of the institutions that keeps the party operating between conventions. The national committee is composed of representatives from the states and territories. See also **national chairperson.**

national convention. The meeting of party delegates every four years to choose a presidential ticket and write the party's platform.

National Environmental Policy Act (NEPA). The law passed in 1969 that is the centerpiece of federal environmental policy in the United States. The NEPA established the requirements for **environmental impact statements.**

national health insurance. A compulsory insurance program for all Americans that would have the government finance citizens' medical care. First proposed by President Harry S Truman, the plan has been soundly opposed by the American Medical Association.

National Labor Relations Act. A 1935 law, also known as the Wagner Act, that guarantees workers the right of **collective bargaining,** sets down rules to protect unions and organizers, and created the National Labor Relations Board to regulate labor management relations.

national party convention. The supreme power within each of the parties. The convention meets every four years to nominate the party's presidential and vice-presidential candidates and to write the party's platform.

national primary. A proposal by critics of the **caucuses** and **presidential primaries** systems who would replace these electoral methods with a nationwide **primary** held early in the election year.

National Security Council. An office created in 1947 to coordinate the president's foreign and military policy advisers. Its formal members are the president, vice president, **secretary of state,** and **secretary of defense,** and it is managed by the president's national security assistant.

NATO. See **North Atlantic Treaty Organization.**

natural rights. Rights inherent in human beings, not dependent on governments, which include life, liberty, and property. The concept of natural rights was central to English philosopher John Locke's theories about government, and was widely accepted among America's Founding Fathers. Thomas Jefferson echoed Locke's language in drafting the Declaration of Independence.

Near v. Minnesota. The 1931 Supreme Court decision holding that the **First Amendment** protects newspapers from **prior restraint.**

necessary and proper clause. See **elastic clause.**

New Deal Coalition. A **coalition** forged by the Democrats, who dominated American politics from the 1930s to the 1960s. Its basic elements were the urban working class, ethnic groups, Catholics and Jews, the poor, Southerners, African Americans, and intellectuals.

New Jersey Plan. The proposal at the Constitutional Convention that called for equal **representation** of each state in Congress regardless of the state's population. Compare **Virginia Plan** and **Connecticut Compromise.**

New York Times v. Sullivan. Decided in 1964, this case established the guidelines for determining whether public officials and public figures could win damage suits for libel. To do so, said the Court, such individuals must prove that the defamatory statements made about them were made with "actual malice" and reckless disregard for the truth.

news leak. A carefully placed bit of inside information given to a friendly reporter. Leaks can benefit both the leaker and the leakee.

newspaper chains. Newspapers published by massive media conglomerates that account for almost three-quarters of the nation's daily circulation. Often these chains control **broadcast media** as well.

Nineteenth Amendment. The constitutional amendment adopted in 1920 that guarantees women the right to vote. See also **suffrage.**

nomination. The official endorsement of a candidate for office by a **political party.** Generally, success in the nomination game requires momentum, money, and media attention.

nonrenewable resources. Minerals and other resources that nature does not replace when they are consumed. Many commonly used energy resources, such as oil and coal, are nonrenewable.

North Atlantic Treaty Organization (NATO). Created in 1949, an organization whose members include the United States, Canada, most Western European nations, and Turkey, all of whom agreed to combine military forces and to treat a war against one as a war against all. Compare **Warsaw Pact.**

O

Office of Management and Budget (OMB). An office that grew out of the Bureau of the Budget, created in 1921, consisting of a handful of political appointees and hundreds of skilled professionals. The OMB performs both managerial and budgetary functions, and although the president is its boss, the director and staff have considerable independence in the budgetary process. See also **Congressional Budget Office.**

Office of Personnel Management (OPM). The office in charge of hiring for most agencies of the federal government, using elaborate rules in the process.

Olson's law of large groups. Advanced by Mancur Olson, a principle stating that "the larger the group, the further it will fall short of providing an optimal amount of a collective good." See also **interest group.**

OPEC. See **Organization of Petroleum Exporting Countries.**

open primaries. Elections to select party nominees in which voters can decide on Election Day whether they want to participate in the Democratic or Republican contests. See also **primaries.**

opinion. A statement of legal reasoning behind a judicial decision. The content of an opinion may be as important as the decision itself.

Organization of Petroleum Exporting Countries (OPEC). An economic organization, consisting primarily of Arab nations, that controls the price of oil and the amount of oil its members produce and sell to other nations. The Arab members of OPEC caused the oil boycott in the winter of 1973–1974.

original intent. A view that the Constitution should be interpreted according to the original intent of the framers. Many **conservatives** support this view.

original jurisdiction. The jurisdiction of courts that hear a case first, usually in a trial. These are the courts that determine the facts about a case. Compare **appellate jurisdiction.**

oversight. The process of monitoring the bureaucracy and its administration of policy, mainly through congressional hearings.

P

PACs. See **political action committees (PACs).**

parliamentary governments. Governments, like the one in Great Britain, that typically select the political leader from membership in the parliament (the legislature).

participation. See **political participation.**

party. See **political party.**

party competition. The battle of the parties for control of public offices. Ups and downs of the two major parties are one of the most important elements in American politics.

party dealignment. The gradual disengagement of people and politicians from the parties, as seen in part by shrinking **party identification.**

party eras. Historical periods in which a majority of voters cling to the party in power, which tends to win a majority of the elections. See also **critical election** and **party realignment.**

party identification. A citizen's self-proclaimed preference for one party or the other.

party image. The voter's perception of what the Republicans or Democrats stand for, such as **conservatism** or **liberalism.**

party machines. A type of political party organization that relies heavily on material inducements, such as patronage, to win votes and to govern.

party neutrality. A term used to describe the fact that many Americans are indifferent toward the two major political parties. See also **party dealignment.**

party platform. A political party's statement of its goals and policies for the next four years. The platform is drafted prior to the party convention by a committee whose members are chosen in rough proportion to each candidate's strength. It is the best formal statement of what a party believes in.

party realignment. The displacement of the majority party by the minority party, usually during a **critical election period.** See also **party eras.**

patients' bill of rights. A controversial proposal before Congress that would give patients certain rights against medical providers, particularly HMOs, including the right to sue.

patronage. One of the key inducements used by political machines. A patronage job, promotion, or contract is one that is given for political reasons rather than for merit or competence alone. Compare **civil service** and the **merit principle.**

Pendleton Civil Service Act. Passed in 1883, an Act that created a federal **civil service** so that hiring and promotion would be based on merit rather than **patronage.**

per curiam decision. A court decision without explanation—in other words, without an **opinion.**

Personal Responsibility and Work Opportunity Reconciliation Act (PRWORA). The official name of the welfare reform law of 1996.

Planned Parenthood v. Casey. A 1992 case in which the Supreme Court loosened its standard for evaluating restrictions on abortion from one of "strict scrutiny" of any restraints on a "fundamental right" to one of "undue burden" that permits considerably more regulation.

plea bargaining. A bargain struck between the defendant's lawyer and the prosecutor to the effect that the defendant will plead guilty to a lesser crime (or fewer crimes) in exchange for the state's promise not to prosecute the defendant for a more serious (or additional) crime.

Plessy v. Ferguson. An 1896 Supreme Court decision that provided a constitutional justification for segregation by ruling that a Louisiana law requiring "equal but separate accommodations for the white and colored races" was not unconstitutional.

pluralist theory. A theory of government and politics emphasizing that politics is mainly a competition among groups, each one pressing for its own preferred policies. Compare **elite and class theory, hyperpluralism,** and **traditional democratic theory.**

pocket veto. A veto taking place when Congress adjourns within ten days of having submitted a **bill** to the president, who simply lets it die by neither signing nor vetoing it. See also **veto.**

policy. See **public policy.**

policy agenda. The issues that attract the serious attention of public officials and other people actually involved in politics at any given point in time.

policy differences. The perception of a clear choice between the parties. Those who see such choices are more likely to vote.

policy entrepreneurs. People who invest their political "capital" in an issue. According to John Kingdon, a policy entrepreneur "could be in or out of government, in elected or appointed positions, in interest groups or research organizations."

policy gridlock. A condition that occurs when no coalition is strong enough to form a majority and establish policy. The result is that nothing may get done.

policy impacts. The effects a policy has on people and problems. Impacts are analyzed to see how well a policy has met its goal and at what cost.

policy implementation. See **implementation.**

policymaking institutions. The branches of government charged with taking action on political issues. The U.S. Constitution established three policymaking institutions—the Congress, the presidency, and the courts. Today, the power of the bureaucracy is so great that most political scientists consider it a fourth policymaking institution.

policymaking system. The process by which political problems are communicated by the voters and acted upon by government policymakers. The policymaking system begins with people's needs and expectations for governmental action. When people confront government officials with problems that they want solved, they are trying to influence the government's policy agenda.

policy voting. Electoral choices that are made on the basis of the voters' policy preferences and on the basis of where the candidates stand on policy issues.

political action committees (PACs). Funding vehicles created by the 1974 campaign finance reforms. A corporation, union, or some other interest group can create a PAC and register it with the **Federal Election Commission (FEC),** which will meticulously monitor the PAC's expenditures.

political culture. An overall set of values widely shared within a society.

political efficacy. The belief that one's **political participation** really matters—that one's vote can actually make a difference.

political ideology. A coherent set of beliefs about politics, public policy, and public purpose. It helps give meaning to political events, personalities, and policies. See also **liberalism** and **conservatism.**

political issue. An issue that arises when people disagree about a problem and a public policy choice.

political participation. All the activities used by citizens to influence the selection of political leaders or the policies they pursue. The most common, but not the only, means of political participation in a **democracy** is voting. Other means include **protest** and **civil disobedience.**

political party. According to Anthony Downs, a "team of men [and women] seeking to control the governing apparatus by gaining office in a duly constituted election."

political questions. A doctrine developed by the federal courts and used as a means to avoid deciding some cases, principally those involving conflicts between the president and Congress.

political socialization. According to Richard Dawson, "the process through which an individual acquires his [or her] particular political orientations—his [or her] knowledge, feelings, and evaluations regarding his [or her] political world." See also **agents of socialization.**

political system. A set of institutions and activities that link together people, politics, and policy.

politics. The process by which we select our governmental leaders and what policies these leaders pursue. Politics produces authoritative decisions about public issues.

poll taxes. Small taxes, levied on the right to vote, that often fell due at a time of year when poor African-American sharecroppers had the least cash on hand. This method was used by most Southern states to exclude African Americans from voting registers. Poll taxes were declared void by the **Twenty-fourth Amendment** in 1964. See also **grandfather clause** and **White primary.**

polls. See **exit polls.**

pork barrel. The mighty list of federal projects, grants, and contracts available to cities, businesses, colleges, and institutions available in a congressional district.

position taking. According to David Mayhew, one of three primary activities undertaken by members of Congress to increase the probability of their reelection. It involves taking a stand on issues and responding to constituents about these positions. See also **advertising** and **credit taking.**

potential group. All the people who might be **interest group** members because they share some common interest. A potential group is almost always larger than an actual group.

poverty line. A method used to count the number of poor people, it considers what a family would need to spend for an "austere" standard of living.

power. The capacity to get people to do something they would not otherwise do. The quest for power is a strong motivation to political activity.

precedent. How similar cases have been decided in the past.

presidential approval. An evaluation of the president based on many factors, but especially on the predisposition of many people to support the president. One measure is provided by the Gallup Poll.

presidential coattails. The situation occurring when voters cast their ballots for congressional candidates of the president's party because they support the president. Recent studies show that few races are won this way.

presidential debate. A debate between presidential candidates. The first televised debate was between Richard Nixon and John Kennedy during the 1960 campaign.

Presidential Election Campaign Fund. Money from the $3 federal income tax check-off goes into this fund, which is then distributed to qualified candidates to subsidize their presidential campaigns.

presidential primaries. Elections in which voters in a state vote for a candidate (or delegates pledged to him or her). Most delegates to the **national party conventions** are chosen this way.

press conferences. Meetings of public officials with reporters.

press secretary. The person on the White House staff who most often deals directly with the press, serving as a conduit of information. Press secretaries conduct daily press briefings.

primaries. Elections that select candidates. In addition to **presidential primaries,** there are **direct primaries** for selecting party nominees for congressional and state offices and proposals for **regional primaries.**

print media. Newspapers and magazines, as compared with **broadcast media.**

prior restraint. A government's preventing material from being published. This is a common method of limiting the press in some nations, but it is usually unconstitutional in the United States, according to the **First Amendment** and as confirmed in the 1931 Supreme Court case of *Near v. Minnesota.*

privacy. See **right to privacy.**

privileges and immunities clause. A clause in Article IV, Section 2, of the Constitution according citizens of each state most of the privileges of citizens of other states.

probable cause. The situation occurring when the police have reason to believe that a person should be arrested. In making the arrest, police are allowed legally to search for and seize incriminating evidence. Compare **unreasonable searches and seizures.**

progressive tax. A tax by which the government takes a greater share of the **income** of the rich than of the poor—for example, when a rich family pays 50 percent of its income in taxes and a poor family pays 5 percent. Compare **regressive tax** and **proportional tax.**

project grants. Federal grants given for specific purposes and awarded on the basis of the merits of applications. A type of the **categorical grants** available to states and localities.

proportional representation. An electoral system used throughout most of Europe that awards legislative seats to political parties in proportion to the number of votes won in an election. Compare with **winner-take-all system.**

proportional tax. A tax by which the government takes the same share of income from everyone, rich and poor alike—for example, when a rich family pays 20 percent and a poor family pays 20 percent. Compare **progressive tax** and **regressive tax.**

protectionism. Economic policy of shielding an economy from imports.

protest. A form of **political participation** designed to achieve policy change through dramatic and unconventional tactics. See also **civil disobedience.**

public goods. Goods, such as clean air and clean water, that everyone must share.

public interest. The idea that there are some interests superior to the private interest of groups and individuals, interests we all have in common. See also **public interest lobbies.**

public interest lobbies. According to Jeffrey Berry, organizations that seek "a collective good, the achievement of which will not selectively and materially benefit the membership or activities of the organization." See also **lobbying** and **public interest.**

public opinion. The distribution of the population's beliefs about politics and policy issues.

public policy. A choice that **government** makes in response to a political issue. A policy is a course of action taken with regard to some problem.

R

random digit dialing. A technique used by pollsters to place telephone calls randomly to both listed and unlisted numbers when conducting a survey. See also **random sampling.**

random sampling. The key technique employed by sophisticated survey researchers, which operates on the principle that everyone should have an equal probability of being selected for the sample. See also **sample.**

rational-choice theory. A popular theory in political science to explain the actions of voters as well as politicians. It assumes that individuals act in their own best interest, carefully weighing the costs and benefits of possible alternatives.

realignment. See **party realignment.**

reapportionment. The process of reallocating seats in the House of Representatives every ten years on the basis of the results of the census.

recall. A procedure that allows voters to call a special election for a specific official in an attempt to throw him or her out of office before the end of his or her term. Recalls are only permitted in 17 states, are seldom used because of their cost and disruptiveness, and are rarely successful.

reconciliation. A congressional process through which program authorizations are revised to achieve required savings. It usually also includes tax or other revenue adjustments.

Red Lion Broadcasting Company v. FCC. A 1969 case in which the Supreme Court upheld restrictions on radio and television broadcasting, such as giving adequate coverage to public issues and covering opposing views. These restrictions on the **broadcast media** are much tighter than those on the **print media** because there are only a limited number of broadcasting frequencies available. See ***Miami Herald Publishing Company v. Tornillo.***

Reed v. Reed. The landmark case in 1971 in which the Supreme Court for the first time upheld a claim of gender discrimination.

referendum. A state-level method of direct legislation that gives voters a chance to approve or disapprove legislation or a constitutional amendment proposed by the state legislature.

Regents of the University of California v. Bakke. A 1978 Supreme Court decision holding that a state university could not admit less qualified individuals solely because of their race. The Court did not, however, rule that such **affirmative action** policies and the use of race as a criterion for admission were unconstitutional, only that they had to be formulated differently.

regional primaries. A proposal by critics of the **caucuses** and **presidential primaries** to replace these electoral methods with a series of primaries held in each geographic region.

registration. See **voter registration.**

regressive tax. A tax in which the burden falls relatively more heavily upon low-income groups than upon wealthy taxpayers. The opposite of a **progressive tax,** in which tax rates increase as income increases.

regulation. The use of governmental authority to control or change some practice in the private sector. Regulations pervade the daily lives of people and institutions.

regulatory agency. See **independent regulatory agency.**

reinforcement. One of three key consequences of electoral campaigns for voters, in which the voter's candidate preference is reinforced. See also **activation** and **conversion.**

relative deprivation. A perception by a group that it is doing less well than is appropriate in relation to a reference group. The desire of a group to correct what it views as the unfair distribution of resources, such as income or government benefits, is a frequent motivator for political activism.

representation. A basic principle of **traditional democratic theory** that describes the relationship between the few leaders and the many followers.

republic. A form of government that derives its power, directly or indirectly, from the people. Those chosen to govern are accountable to those whom they govern. In contrast to a direct democracy, in which people themselves make laws, in a republic the people select representatives who make the laws.

responsible party model. A view favored by some political scientists about how parties should work. According to the model, parties should offer clear choices to the voters, who can then use those choices as cues to their own preferences of candidates. Once in office, parties would carry out their campaign promises.

retrospective voting. A theory of voting in which voters essentially ask this simple question: "What have you done for me lately?"

revenues. The financial resources of the federal government. The individual income tax and Social Security tax are two major sources of revenue. Compare **expenditures.**

right to privacy. The right to a private personal life free from the intrusion of government. The right to privacy is implicitly protected by the **Bill of Rights.** See also **Privacy Act.**

right-to-work law. A state law forbidding requirements that workers must join a union to hold their jobs. State right-to-work laws were specifically permitted by the Taft-Hartley Act of 1947.

Roe v. Wade. The 1973 Supreme Court decision holding that a state ban on all abortions was unconstitutional. The decision forbade state control over abortions during the first trimester of pregnancy, permitted states to limit abortions to protect the mother's health in the second trimester, and permitted states to protect the fetus during the third trimester.

Roth v. United States. A 1957 Supreme Court decision ruling that "obscenity is not within the area of constitutionally protected speech or press."

S

sample. A relatively small proportion of people who are chosen in a survey so as to be representative of the whole.

sampling error. The level of confidence in the findings of a public opinion poll. The more people interviewed, the more confident one can be of the results.

Schenck v. United States. A 1919 decision upholding the conviction of a socialist who had urged young men to resist the draft during World War I. Justice Holmes declared that government can limit speech if the speech provokes a "clear and present danger" of substantive evils.

School District of Abington Township, Pennsylvania v. Schempp. A 1963 Supreme Court decision holding that a Pennsylvania law requiring Bible reading in schools violated the **establishment clause** of the **First Amendment.** Compare ***Engel v. Vitale.***

school districts. Units of local government that are normally independent of any other local government and are primarily responsible for operating public schools.

Scott v. Sandford. The 1857 Supreme Court decision ruling that a slave who had escaped to a free state enjoyed no rights as a citizen and that Congress had no authority to ban slavery in the territories.

search warrant. A written authorization from a court specifying the area to be searched and what the police are searching for.

secretary of defense. The head of the Department of Defense and the president's key adviser on military policy; a key **foreign policy** actor.

secretary of state. The head of the Department of State and traditionally a key adviser to the president on **foreign policy.**

Securities and Exchange Commission (SEC). The federal agency created during the New Deal that regulates stock fraud.

select committees. Congressional committees appointed for a specific purpose, such as the Watergate investigation. See also **joint committees, standing committees,** and **conference committees.**

selective benefits. Goods (such as information publications, travel discounts, and group insurance rates) that a group can restrict to those who pay their yearly dues.

selective perception. The phenomenon that people often pay the most attention to things they already agree with and interpret them according to their own predispositions.

self-incrimination. The situation occurring when an individual accused of a crime is compelled to be a witness against himself or herself in court. The **Fifth Amendment** forbids self-incrimination. See also ***Miranda v. Arizona.***

Senate Finance Committee. The Senate committee that, along with the **House Ways and Means Committee,** writes the tax codes, subject to the approval of Congress as a whole.

senatorial courtesy. An unwritten tradition whereby nominations for state-level federal judicial posts are not confirmed if they are opposed by the senator from the state in which the nominee will serve. The tradition also applies to courts of appeal when there is opposition from the nominee's state senator, if the senator belongs to the president's party.

Senior Executive Service (SES). An elite cadre of about 11,000 federal government managers, established by the Civil Service Reform Act of 1978, who are mostly career officials but include some political appointees who do not require Senate confirmation.

seniority system. A simple rule for picking **committee chairs,** in effect until the 1970s. The member who had served on the committee the longest and whose party controlled Congress became chair, regardless of party loyalty, mental state, or competence.

separation of powers. An important part of the **Madisonian model** that requires each of the three branches of government—executive, legislative, and judicial—to be relatively independent of the others so that one cannot control the others. Power is shared among these three institutions. See also **checks and balances.**

Shays' Rebellion. A series of attacks on courthouses by a small band of farmers led by revolutionary war Captain Daniel Shays to block foreclosure proceedings.

single-issue groups. Groups that have a narrow interest, tend to dislike compromise, and often draw membership from people new to politics. These features distinguish them from traditional **interest groups.**

Sixteenth Amendment. The constitutional amendment adopted in 1913 that explicitly permitted Congress to levy an **income tax.**

Sixth Amendment. The constitutional amendment designed to protect individuals accused of crimes. It includes the right to counsel, the right to confront witnesses, and the right to a speedy and public trial.

social policies. Policies that manipulate opportunities through public choice. They include policies related to income and policies related to opportunity.

Social Security Act. A 1935 law passed during the Great Depression that was intended to provide a minimal level of sustenance to older Americans and thus save them from poverty.

social welfare policies. Policies that provide benefits to individuals, particularly to those in need. Compare **civil rights policies.**

socialized medicine. A system in which the full cost of medical care is borne by the national government. Great Britain and the former Soviet Union are examples of countries that have socialized medicine. Compare **Medicaid** and **Medicare.**

soft money. Political contributions earmarked for party-building expenses at the grass-roots level (or for generic party advertising). Unlike money that goes to the campaign of a particular candidate, such party donations are not subject to contribution limits.

solicitor general. A presidential appointee and the third-ranking office in the Department of Justice. The solicitor general is in charge of the appellate court litigation of the federal government.

sound bites. Short video clips of approximately 15 seconds, which are typically all that is shown from a politician's speech or activities on television news.

Speaker of the House. An office mandated by the Constitution. The Speaker is chosen in practice by the majority party, has both formal and informal powers, and is second in line to succeed to the presidency should that office become vacant.

special districts. Limited-purpose local governments called *districts* or *public authorities* that are created to run a specific type of service, such as water distribution, airports, public transportation, libraries, and natural resource areas.

standard operating procedures. Better known as SOPs, these procedures are used by bureaucrats to bring uniformity to complex organizations. Uniformity improves fairness and makes personnel interchangeable. See also **administrative discretion.**

standing committees. Separate subject-matter committees in each house of Congress that handle **bills** in different policy areas. See also **joint committees, conference committees,** and **select committees.**

standing to sue. The requirement that **plaintiffs** have a serious interest in a **case,** which depends on whether they have sustained or are likely to sustain a direct and substantial injury from a party or an action of government.

stare decisis. A Latin phrase meaning "let the decision stand." Most cases reaching appellate courts are settled on this principle.

statutory construction. The judicial interpretation of an act of Congress. In some cases where statutory construction is an issue, Congress passes new legislation to clarify existing laws.

Strategic Defense Initiative (SDI). Renamed "Star Wars" by critics, a plan for defense against the Soviet Union unveiled by President Reagan in 1983. SDI would create a global umbrella in space, using computers to scan the skies and high-tech devices to destroy invading missiles.

street-level bureaucrats. A phrase coined by Michael Lipsky, referring to those bureaucrats who are in constant contact with the public and have considerable **administrative discretion.**

subgovernments. A network of groups within the American political system which exercise a great deal of control over specific policy areas. Also known as iron triangles, subgovernments are composed of interest group leaders interested in a particular policy, the government agency in charge of administering that policy, and the members of congressional committees and subcommittees handling that policy.

subnational governments. Another way of referring to state and local governments. Through a process of reform, modernization, and changing intergovernmental relations since the 1960s, subnational governments have assumed new responsibilities and importance.

suffrage. The legal right to vote, extended to African Americans by the **Fifteenth Amendment,** to women by the **Nineteenth Amendment,** and to people over the age of 18 by the **Twenty-sixth Amendment.**

Super Tuesday. Created by a dozen or so Southern states when they held their **presidential primaries** in early March 1988. These states hoped to promote a regional advantage as well as a more conservative candidate.

superdelegates. National party leaders who automatically get a delegate slot at the Democratic **national party convention.**

Superfund. A fund created by Congress in the late 1970s and renewed in the 1980s to clean up hazardous waste sites. Money for the fund comes from taxing chemical products.

supply-side economics. An economic theory, advocated by President Reagan, holding that too much income goes to taxes and too little money is available for purchasing and that the solution is to cut taxes and return purchasing power to consumers.

supremacy clause. Article VI of the Constitution, which makes the Constitution, national laws, and treaties supreme over state laws when the national government is acting within its constitutional limits.

Supreme Court. The pinnacle of the American judicial system. The Court ensures uniformity in interpreting national laws, resolves conflicts among states, and maintains national supremacy in law. It has both **original jurisdiction** and **appellate jurisdiction,** but unlike other federal courts, it controls its own agenda.

symbolic speech. Nonverbal communication, such as burning a flag or wearing an armband. The Supreme Court has accorded some symbolic speech protection under the **First Amendment.** See ***Texas v. Johnson.***

T

Taft-Hartley Act. A 1947 law giving the president power to halt major strikes by seeking a court injunction and permitting states to forbid requirements in labor contracts forcing workers to join a union. See also **right-to-work law.**

talking head. A shot of a person's face talking directly to the camera. Because this is visually unappealing, the major commercial networks rarely show a politician talking one-on-one for very long. See also **sound bites.**

tariff. A special tax added to imported goods to raise the price, thereby protecting American businesses and workers from foreign competition.

tax. See **proportional tax, progressive tax,** and **regressive tax.**

tax expenditures. Defined by the 1974 Budget Act as "revenue losses attributable to provisions of the federal tax laws which allow a special exemption, exclusion, or deduction." Tax expenditures represent the difference between what the government actually collects in taxes and what it would have collected without special exemptions.

tax incidence. The proportion of its income a particular group pays in taxes.

Temporary Assistance for Needy Families (TANF). Once called "Aid to Families with Dependent Children," the new name for public assistance to needy families.

Tenth Amendment. The constitutional amendment stating that "The powers not delegated to the United States by the Constitution, nor prohibited by it to the states, are reserved to the states respectively, or to the people."

term limits. Laws to restrict legislators from serving more than a fixed number of years or terms in office.

Texas v. Johnson. A 1989 case in which the Supreme Court struck down a law banning the burning of the American flag on the grounds that such action was **symbolic speech** protected by the **First Amendment.**

third parties. Electoral contenders other than the two major parties. American third parties are not unusual, but they rarely win elections.

Thirteenth Amendment. The constitutional amendment passed after the Civil War that forbade slavery and involuntary servitude.

ticket-splitting. Voting with one party for one office and with another party for other offices. It has become the norm in American voting behavior.

town meeting. A special form of direct democracy under which all voting-age adults in a community gather once a year to make public policy. Now only used in a few villages in upper New England, originally many municipalities in the United States were run by town meeting. The growth of most cities has made them too large for this style of governance.

township. A political subdivision of local government that is found in 20 states and often serves to provide local government services in rural areas. It is a particularly strong form of local government—comparable to a municipality—in the Northeast.

traditional democratic theory. A theory about how a democratic government makes its decisions. According to Robert Dahl, its cornerstones are equality in voting, effective participation, enlightened understanding, final control over the agenda, and inclusion.

transfer payments. Benefits given by the government directly to individuals. Transfer payments may be either cash transfers, such as Social Security payments and retirement payments to former government employees, or in-kind transfers, such as food stamps and low-interest loans for college education.

transnational corporations. Businesses with vast holdings in many countries—such as Microsoft, Coca-Cola, and McDonald's—many of which have annual budgets exceeding that of many foreign governments.

trial balloons. An intentional **news leak** for the purpose of assessing the political reaction.

trial courts. The lowest tier in the trial court system, in which the facts of a case are considered. These courts hear both civil and criminal matters.

trustee. A legislator who uses his or her best judgment to make policy in the interests of the people. This concept was favored by Edmund Burke. Compare **instructed delegate.**

Twenty-fifth Amendment. Passed in 1967, this amendment permits the vice president to become acting president if both the vice president and the president's cabinet determine that the president is disabled. The amendment also outlines how a recuperated president can reclaim the job.

Twenty-fourth Amendment. The constitutional amendment passed in 1964 that declared **poll taxes** void.

Twenty-second Amendment. Passed in 1951, the amendment that limits presidents to two terms of office.

U

uncontrollable expenditures. Expenditures that are determined not by a fixed amount of money appropriated by Congress but by how many eligible beneficiaries there are for some particular program or by previous obligations of the government. Three-fourths of the federal **budget** is uncontrollable. Congress can change uncontrollable expenditures only by changing a law or existing benefit levels.

unemployment rate. As measured by the Bureau of Labor Statistics (BLS), the proportion of the labor force actively seeking work but unable to find jobs.

unfunded mandates. When the federal government requires state and local action but does not provide the funds to pay for the action.

union shop. A provision found in some collective bargaining agreements requiring all employees of a business to join the union within a short period, usually 30 days, and to remain members as a condition of employment.

unitary government. A way of organizing a nation so that all power resides in the central government. Most national governments today, including those of Great Britain and Japan, are unitary governments. Compare **federalism.**

United Nations (UN). Created in 1945, an organization whose members agree to renounce war and to respect certain human and economic freedoms. The seat of real power in the UN is the Security Council.

United States v. Nixon. The 1974 case in which the Supreme Court unanimously held that the doctrine of executive privilege was implicit in the Constitution but could not be extended to protect documents relevant to criminal prosecutions.

unreasonable searches and seizures. Obtaining evidence in a haphazard or random manner, a practice prohibited by the Fourth Amendment. Both **probable cause** and a **search warrant** are required for a legal and proper search for and seizure of incriminating evidence.

unwritten constitution. The body of tradition, practice, and procedure that is as important as the written constitution. Changes in the unwritten **constitution** can change the spirit of the Constitution. **Political parties** and **national party conventions** are a part of the unwritten constitution in the United States.

urban underclass. The poorest of the poor in America. These are the Americans whose economic opportunities are severely limited in almost every way. They constitute a large percentage of the Americans afflicted by homelessness, crime, drugs, alcoholism, unwanted pregnancies, and other endemic social problems.

U.S. Constitution. The document written in 1787 and ratified in 1788 that sets forth the institutional structure of U.S. government and the tasks these institutions perform. It replaced the Articles of Confederation. See also **constitution** and **unwritten constitution.**

V

veto. The constitutional power of the president to send a **bill** back to Congress with reasons for rejecting it. A two-thirds vote in each house can override a veto. See also **legislative veto** and **pocket veto.**

Virginia Plan. The proposal at the Constitutional Convention that called for *representation* of each state in Congress in proportion to that state's share of the U.S. population. Compare **Connecticut Compromise** and **New Jersey Plan.**

voter registration. A system adopted by the states that requires voters to register well in advance of Election Day. A few states permit Election Day registration.

Voting Rights Act of 1965. A law designed to help end formal and informal barriers to African-American **suffrage.** Under the law, federal registrars were sent to Southern states and counties that had long histories of discrimination; as a result, hundreds of thousands of African Americans were registered and the number of African-American elected officials increased dramatically.

W

War Powers Resolution. A law passed in 1973 in reaction to American fighting in Vietnam and Cambodia that requires presidents to consult with Congress whenever possible prior to using military force and to withdraw forces after 60 days unless Congress declares war or grants an extension. Presidents view the resolution as unconstitutional. See also **legislative veto.**

Watergate. The events and scandal surrounding a break-in at the Democratic National Committee headquarters in 1972 and the subsequent cover-up of White House involvement, leading to the eventual resignation of President Nixon under the threat of **impeachment.**

wealth. The amount of funds already owned. Wealth includes stocks, bonds, bank deposits, cars, houses, and so forth. Throughout most of the last generation, wealth has been much less evenly divided than **income.**

whips. Party leaders who work with the **majority leader** or **minority leader** to count votes beforehand and lean on waverers whose votes are crucial to a **bill** favored by the party.

White primary. One of the means used to discourage African-American voting that permitted political parties in the heavily Democratic South to exclude African Americans from primary elections, thus depriving them of a voice in the real contests. The Supreme Court declared White primaries unconstitutional in 1944. See also **grandfather clause** and **poll taxes.**

winner-take-all system. An electoral system in which legislative seats are awarded only to the candidates who come in first in their constituencies. In American presidential elections, the system in which the winner of the popular vote in a state receives all the electoral votes of that state. Compare with **proportional representation.**

World Trade Organization (WTO). International organization that regulates international trade.

writ of certiorari. A formal document issued from the **Supreme Court** to a lower federal or state court that calls up a case.

writ of habeas corpus. A court order requiring jailers to explain to a judge why they are holding a prisoner in custody.

writ of mandamus. A court order forcing action. In the dispute leading to ***Marbury v. Madison,*** Marbury and his associates asked the **Supreme Court** to issue a writ ordering Madison to give them their commissions.

Z

Zelman v. Simmons-Harris. The 2002 Supreme Court decision that upheld a state providing families with vouchers that could be used to pay tuition at religious schools.

Zurcher v. Stanford Daily. A 1978 Supreme Court decision holding that a proper **search warrant** could be applied to a newspaper as well as to anyone else without necessarily violating the **First Amendment** rights to freedom of the press.

Notes

Chapter 1

1. "The Soul of a Senator," *Time*, August 10, 1998.

2. Ganesh Sitaraman and Previn Warren, *Invisible Citizens: Youth Politics After September 11* (New York: iUniverse, Inc., 2003), p ix.

3. Because the level of difficulty of the questions differed somewhat, one should only examine the differences within a year and not necessarily infer that political knowledge as a whole has decreased.

4. Stephen Earl Bennett and Eric W. Rademacher, "The Age of Indifference Revisited: Patterns of Political Interest, Media Exposure, and Knowledge Among Generation X," In Stephen C. Craig and Stephen Earl Bennett, eds., *After the Boom: The Politics of Generation X* (Lanham, MD: Rowman and Littlefield, 1997), 39.

5. Michael X. Delli Carpini and Scott Keeter, *What Americans Know About Politics and Why It Matters* (New Haven, CT: Yale University Press, 1996), chap. 6.

6. Samuel Kernell, *Going Public: New Strategies of Presidential Leadership*, 3rd ed. (Washington, D.C.: Congressional Quarterly Press, 1997), 132.

7. Anthony Corrado, "Elections in Cyberspace: Prospects and Problems," in Anthony Corrado and Charles M. Firestone, eds., *Elections in Cyberspace: Toward a New Era in American Politics* (Washington, D.C.: The Aspen Institute, 1996), 29.

8. Harold D. Lasswell, *Politics: Who Gets What, When, and How* (New York: McGraw-Hill, 1938).

9. Randy Shilts, *And the Band Played On: Politics, People, and the AIDS Epidemic* (New York: Penguin Books, 1987).

10. Robert A. Dahl, *Dilemmas of Pluralist Democracy* (New Haven, CT: Yale University Press, 1982), 6.

11. Robert A. Dahl, *A Preface to Democratic Theory* (Chicago: University of Chicago Press, 1956), 137.

12. Robert Putnam, *Bowling Alone: The Collapse and Revival of American Community* (New York: Simon & Schuster, 2000). Putnam's famous first article on the subject can be found on the Web at *http://muse.jhu.edu/demo/journal_of_democracy/v006/putnam.html*.

13. Kevin Phillips, *The Politics of Rich and Poor: Wealth and the American Electorate in the Reagan Aftermath* (New York: Random House, 1990), 1.

14. Bob Woodward, *The Agenda: Inside the Clinton White House* (New York: Simon & Schuster, 1994).

15. Woodward, *The Agenda*, 145.

16. Dick Armey, *The Freedom Revolution* (Washington, D.C.: Regnery, 1995), 316.

17. Louis Hartz, *The Liberal Tradition in America* (New York: Harcourt, Brace, 1955).

18. Frederick Jackson Turner, *The Significance of the Frontier in American History* (New York: Readex Microprint, 1966), 221.

Chapter 2

1. Gordon S. Wood, *The Radicalism of the American Revolution* (New York: Vintage, 1993), 4.

2. Garry Wills, *Inventing America: Jefferson's Declaration of Independence* (New York: Doubleday, 1978), 13, 77.

3. Clinton Rossiter, *1787: The Grand Convention* (New York: Macmillan, 1966), 60.

4. On the Lockean influence on the Declaration of Independence, see Carl L. Becker, *The Declaration of Independence: A Study in the History of Political Ideas* (New York: Random House, 1942).

5. Seymour Martin Lipset, *The First New Nation* (New York: Basic Books, 1963).

6. Gordon S. Wood, *The Creation of the American Republic, 1776–1787* (Chapel Hill, NC: University of North Carolina Press, 1969), 3.

7. On the Articles of Confederation, see Merrill Jensen, *The Articles of Confederation* (Madison: University of Wisconsin Press, 1940).

8. Wood, *The Radicalism of the American Revolution*, 6–7.

9. "Federalist #10," in Alexander Hamilton, James Madison, and John Jay, *The Federalist Papers*, 2nd ed., Roy P. Fairfield, ed. (Baltimore: Johns Hopkins University Press, 1981), 18.

10. Calvin C. Jillson and Cecil L. Eubanks, "The Political Structure of Constitution-Making: The Federal Convention of 1787," *American Journal of Political Science* 28 (August 1984): 435–458. See also Calvin C. Jillson, *Constitution Making: Conflict and Consensus in the Federal Convention of 1787* (New York: Agathon, 1988).

11. See Arthur Lovejoy, *Reflections on Human Nature* (Baltimore: Johns Hopkins University Press, 1961), 57–63.

12. "Federalist #10," *The Federalist Papers*.

13. This representation may have practical consequences. See Frances E. Lee, "Representation and Public Policy: The Consequences of Senate Apportionment for the Geographic Distribution of Federal Funds," *Journal of Politics* 60 (February 1998): 34–62; and Daniel Wirls, "The Consequences of Equal Representation—The Bicameral Politics of NAFTA in the 103rd Congress," *Congress and the President* 25 (Autumn 1998): 129–145.

14. Cecelia M. Kenyon, ed., *The Antifederalists* (Indianapolis: Bobbs-Merrill, 1966), xxxv.

15. Rossiter, *1787*.

16. See Charles A. Beard, *An Economic Interpretation of the Constitution of the United States* (New York: Macmillan, 1913); Robert E. Brown, *Charles Beard and the Constitution* (Princeton, NJ: Princeton University Press, 1956); Forrest B. McDonald, *We the People: The Economic Origins of the Constitution* (Chicago: University of Chicago Press, 1958); and Forrest B. McDonald, *Novus Ordo Seclorum: The Intellectual Origins of the Constitution* (Lawrence: University Press of Kansas, 1986).

17. A brilliant exposition of the Madisonian model is found in Robert A. Dahl, *A Preface to Democratic Theory* (Chicago: University of Chicago Press, 1956).

18. "Federalist #10," *The Federalist Papers*.

19. "Federalist #51," *The Federalist Papers*.

20. Quoted in Beard, *An Economic Interpretation of the Constitution of the United States*, 299.

21. The three quotations are from Kenyon, *The Antifederalists*, 195, liv, and 1, respectively.

22. Jackson Turner Main, *The Antifederalists* (Chapel Hill: University of North Carolina Press, 1961). For more on the Anti-Federalists, see Herbert J. Storing, *What the Anti-Federalists Were For* (Chicago: University of Chicago Press, 1981).

23. The early attempts at ratification of the ERA are recounted in Janet Boles, *The Politics of the Equal Rights Amendment* (New York: Longman, 1978).

24. Jane J. Mansbridge, *Why We Lost the ERA* (Chicago: University of Chicago Press, 1986).

25. See "Federalist #78," *The Federalist Papers*.

26. James MacGregor Burns, *The Deadlock of Democracy* (Englewood Cliffs, NJ: Prentice-Hall, 1963), 6.

Chapter 3

1. Thomas Anton, *Moving Money* (New York: Oxford University Press, 1982).

2. One useful introduction to federalism and intergovernmental relations is Deil S. Wright, *Understanding Intergovernmental Relations*, 4th ed. (Belmont, CA: Wadsworth, 2003). Another is David B. Walker, *The Rebirth of Federalism*, 2nd ed. (Chatham, NJ: Chatham House, 2000).

3. For a study of how different states enforce federal child support enforcement, see Lael R. Keiser and Joe Soss, "With Good Cause: Bureaucratic Discretion and the Politics of Child Support Enforcement," *American Journal of Political Science* 42 (October 1998): 1133–1156.

4. On the states as innovators, see Jack L. Walker, "The Diffusion of Innovations in the American States," *American Political Science Review* 63 (September 1969): 880–899; Virginia Gray, "Innovation in the States: A Diffusion Study," *American Political Science Review* 67 (December 1973): 1174–1185; and Richard P. Nathan and Fred C. Doolittle, *Reagan and the States* (Princeton, NJ: Princeton University Press, 1987).

5. *Alden v. Maine* (1999). See also *College Savings Bank v. Florida Prepaid Postsecondary Education Expense Board* (1999); and *Florida Prepaid Postsecondary Education Expense Board v. College Savings Bank* (1999).

6. *Federal Maritime Commission v. South Carolina Ports Authority* (2002).

7. The Fourteenth Amendment was passed *after* the Eleventh Amendment.

8. *Monroe v. Pape*, 1961; *Monell v. New York City Department of Social Welfare*, 1978; *Owen v. Independence*, 1980; *Maine v. Thiboutot*, 1980; *Oklahoma City v. Tuttle*, 1985; *Dennis v. Higgins*, 1991.

9. The transformation from dual to cooperative federalism is described in Walker, *The Rebirth of Federalism*, chap. 4.

10. The classic discussion of cooperative federalism is found in Morton Grodzins, *The American System: A New View of Governments in the United States*, Daniel J. Elazar, ed. (Chicago: Rand McNally, 1966).

11. Office of Management and Budget, *Budget of the United States Government, Fiscal Year 2005: Analytical Perspectives* (Washington, D.C.: U.S. Government Printing Office, 2004), Table 8.3.

12. On intergovernmental lobbying, see Donald H. Haider, *When Governments Go to Washington* (New York: Free Press, 1974); and Anne Marie Commisa, *Governments as Interest Groups: Intergovernmental Lobbying and the Federal System* (Westport, CT: Praeger, 1995).

13. Michael A. Bailey and Mark Carl Rom, "A Wider Race? Interstate Competition across Health and Welfare Programs," *Journal of Politics* 66 (May 2004): 326–347; Paul E. Peterson and Mark Rom, "American Federalism, Welfare Policy, and Residential Choices," *American Political Science Review* 83 (September 1989): 711–728; Craig Volden, "The Politics of Competitive Federalism: A Race to the Bottom in Welfare Benefits," *American Journal of Political Science* 46 (April 2002): 352–363. But see William D. Berry, Richard C. Fording, and Russell L. Hanson, "Reassessing the 'Race to the Bottom' in State Welfare Policy," *Journal of Politics* 65 (May 2003): 327–349. Some states limit welfare payments to new residents.

14. Office of Management and Budget, *Budget of the United States Government, Fiscal Year 2005: Historical Tables* (Washington, D.C.: U.S. Government Printing Office, 2004), Table 15.3.

Chapter 4

1. James W. Prothro and Charles M. Grigg, "Fundamental Principles of Democracy: Bases of Agreement and Disagreement," *Journal of Politics* 22 (1960): 276–294; and John L. Sullivan et al., "The Sources of Political Tolerance: A Multivariate Analysis," *American Political Science Review* 75 (1981): 100–115.

2. Darren W. Davis and Brian D. Silver, "Civil Liberties vs. Security: Public Opinion in the Context of the Terrorist Attacks on America," *American Journal of Political Science* 48 (January 2004): 28–46.

3. Samuel Krislov, *The Supreme Court and Political Freedom* (New York: Free Press, 1968), 81.

4. *Widmar v. Vincent* (1981).

5. *Westside Community Schools v. Mergens* (1990).

6. *Good News Club v. Milford Central School* (2001).

7. *Lamb's Chapel v. Center Moriches Union Free School* (1993).

8. *Rosenberger v. University of Virginia* (1995).

9. *Locke v. Davey* (2004).

10. *Illinois ex rel McCollum v. Board of Education* (1948).

11. *Zorach v. Clauson* (1952).

12. *Stone v. Graham* (1980).

13. *Lee v. Weisman* (1992).

14. *Santa Fe School District v. Doe* (2000).

15. *Wallace v. Jaffree* (1985).

16. Kenneth D. Wald, *Religion and Politics in the United States*, 4th ed. (Lanham, MD: Rowman and Littlefield, 2003).

17. *Edwards v. Aguillard* (1987).

18. *Epperson v. Arkansas* (1968).

19. *Lynch v. Donelly* (1984).

20. *County of Allegheny v. American Civil Liberties Union* (1989).

21. *Bob Jones University v. United States* (1983).

22. *Wisconsin v. Yoder* (1972).

23. *Boerne v. Flores* (1997).

24. Charles R. Lawrence III, "If He Hollers Let Him Go: Regulating Racist Speech on Campus," in Mari J. Matsuda, Charles R. Lawrence III, Richard Delgado, and Kimberle Crenshaw, *Words that Wound: Critical Race Theory, Assaultive Speech, and the First Amendment* (Boulder, CO: Westview, 1993), 67–68.

25. Ira Glasser, "Introduction," in Henry Louis Gates, Jr., ed., *Speaking of Race, Speaking of Sex: Hate Speech, Civil Rights, and Civil Liberties* (New York: New York University Press, 1994), 8.

26. *R.A.V. v. St. Paul* (1992). However, states may impose longer prison terms on people convicted of "hate crimes" (crimes motivated by racial, religious, or other prejudice) without violating their rights to free speech.

27. See Fred W. Friendly, *Minnesota Rag* (New York: Random House, 1981).

28. *Hazelwood School District v. Kuhlmeier* (1988).

29. The Supreme Court upheld the government's suit in *United States v. Snepp* (1980).

30. *McIntyre v. Ohio Elections Commission* (1995).

31. *Hudgens v. National Labor Relations Board* (1976).

32. *Pruneyard Shopping Center v. Robins* (1980).

33. *City of Ladue v. Gilleo* (1994).

34. *Nebraska Press Association v. Stuart* (1972).

35. *Richmond Newspapers v. Virginia* (1980).

36. Bob Woodward and Scott Armstrong, *The Brethren* (New York: Avon, 1979), 233.

37. *Jenkins v. Georgia* (1974).

38. *Osborne v. Ohio* (1990).

39. *Reno v. ACLU* (1997).

40. *Ashcroft v. Free Speech Coalition* (2002).

41. *Schad v. Mount Ephraim* (1981).

42. *Barnes v. Glen Theater, Inc.* (1991); *Erie v. Pap's A.M.* (2000).

43. Catherine MacKinnon, *Feminism Unmodified* (Cambridge, MA: Harvard University Press, 1987), 198.

44. The story of this case is told in Anthony Lewis, *Make No Law: The Sullivan Case and the First Amendment* (New York: Random House, 1991).

45. Renata Adler, *Reckless Disregard* (New York: Knopf, 1986).

46. *Tinker v. Des Moines Independent School District* (1969).

47. After Congress passed the Flag Protection Act of 1989 outlawing desecration of the American flag, the Supreme Court also found the act an impermissible infringement on free speech in *United States v. Eichman* (1990).

48. *United States v. O'Brien* (1968).

49. *Virginia v. Black* (2003).

50. *Greater New Orleans Broadcasting, Inc. v. United States* (1999).

51. *Central Hudson Gas & Electric Corporation v. Public Service Commission of N.Y.* (1980).

52. *FCC v. Pacifica Foundation* (1978).

53. *Frisby v. Schultz* (1988).

54. *Michigan v. Sitz* (1990).

55. *Indianapolis v. Edmond* (2000).

56. *Nix v. Williams* (1984).

57. *United States v. Leon* (1984).

58. *Arizona v. Evans* (1995).

59. *United States v. Payner* (1980).

60. *Knowles v. Iowa* (1998).

61. *City of Indianapolis v. Edmond* (2000).

62. *Florida v. J.L.* (2000).

63. *Kyllo v. U.S.* (2001).

64. On the *Miranda* case, see Liva Baker, *Miranda: The Crime, the Law, the Politics* (New York: Atheneum, 1983).

65. *Arizona v. Fulminante* (1991).

66. The story of Gideon is eloquently told by Anthony Lewis, *Gideon's Trumpet* (New York: Random House, 1964).

67. David Brereton and Jonathan D. Casper, "Does It Pay to Plead Guilty? Differential Sentencing and the Function of the Criminal Courts," *Law and Society Review* 16 (1981–1982): 45–70.

68. Joe Soss, Laura Langbein, and Alan R. Metelko, "Why Do White Americans Support the Death Penalty?" *Journal of Politics* 65 (May 2003): 397–421.

69. *Callins v. Callins* (1994).

70. Woodward and Armstrong, *The Brethren*, 271–284.

71. *Madsen v. Women's Health Center* (1994). In 1997, the Court also upheld a 15-foot buffer zone.

72. *Hill v. Colorado* (2000).

73. *National Organization for Women v. Scheidler* (1994).

74. Though, as Chapter 16 on the judiciary will show, there is indirect accountability.

Chapter 5

1. Bland is quoted in Sidney Verba and Gary R. Orren, *Equality in America: The View from the Top* (Cambridge, MA: Harvard University Press, 1985), 25. The Adams' quotes are from Judith A. Baer, *Equality Under the Constitution: Reclaiming the Fourteenth Amendment* (Ithaca, NY: Cornell University Press, 1983), 44–47.

2. For opposing interpretations of the Fourteenth Amendment, see Baer, *Equality Under the Constitution*; and Raoul Berger, *Government by Judiciary: The Transformation of the Fourteenth Amendment* (Cambridge, MA: Harvard University Press, 1977).

3. D. Garth Taylor, Paul B. Sheatsley, and Andrew M. Greeley, "Attitudes Toward Racial Integration," *Scientific American* 238 (June 1978): 42–49; Richard G. Niemi, John Mueller, and John W. Smith, *Trends in Public Opinion* (Westport, CT: Greenwood Press, 1989), 180.

4. There are a few exceptions. Religious institutions such as schools may use religious standards in employment. Gender, age, and disabilities may be considered in the few cases where such occupational qualifications are absolutely essential to the normal operations of a business or enterprise, as in the case of a men's restroom attendant.

5. On the implementation of the Voting Rights Act, see Richard Scher and James Button, "Voting Rights Act: Implementation and Impact," in *Implementation of Civil Rights Policy*, Charles Bullock III and Charles Lamb, ed. (Monterey, CA: Brooks/Cole, 1984); Abigail M. Thernstrom, *Whose Votes Count?* (Cambridge, MA: Harvard University Press, 1987); and Chandler Davidson and Bernard Groffman, eds., *Quiet Revolution in the South: The Impact of the Voting Rights Act, 1965–1990* (Princeton, NJ: Princeton University Press, 1994).

6. U.S. Department of Commerce, *Statistical Abstract of the United States, 2003* (Washington, D.C.: U.S. Government Printing Office, 2004), 268. See David Lublin, *The Paradox of Representation: Racial Gerrymandering and Minority Interests in Congress* (Princeton, NJ: Princeton University Press, 1997) on how racial redistricting helped increase the number of minority representatives in Congress.

7. See Dee Brown, *Bury My Heart at Wounded Knee: An Indian History of the American West* (New York: Holt, Rinehart and Winston, 1970).

8. *Statistical Abstract of the United States, 2003*, 268.

9. *White v. Register* (1973).

10. See Eleanor Flexner, *Century of Struggle* (New York: Atheneum, 1971).

11. See J. Stanley Lemons, *The Woman Citizen: Social Feminism in the 1920s* (Urbana: University of Illinois Press, 1973).

12. *Kirchberg v. Feenstra* (1981).

13. *Arizona Governing Committee for Tax Deferred Annuity and Deferred Compensation Plans v. Norris* (1983).

14. *Michael M. v. Superior Court* (1981).

15. *Kahn v. Shevin* (1974).

16. *Statistical Abstract of the United States, 2003*, 60–61, 386–387, 390–391.

17. *Cleveland Board of Education v. LaFleur* (1974).

18. *United Automobile Workers v. Johnson Controls* (1991).

19. *Roberts v. United States Jaycees* (1984); *Board of Directors of Rotary International v. Rotary Club of Duarte* (1987); and *New York State Club Association v. New York* (1988).

20. *United States v. Virginia et al.* (1996).

21. *Statistical Abstract of the United States, 2003*, 423.

22. *Meritor Savings Bank v. Vinson* (1986).

23. *Massachusetts Board of Retirement v. Murgia* (1976).

24. *Bregdon v. Abbott* (1998).

25. *Sutton v. United Air Lines* (1999), *Albertsons v. Kirkingburg* (1999), and *Murphy v. United Parcel Service* (1999).

26. *Boy Scouts of America v. Dale* (2000).

27. Kenneth D. Wald, James W. Button, and Barbara A. Rienzo, "The Politics of Gay Rights in American Communities: Explaining Antidiscrimination Ordinances and Policies," *American Journal of Political Science* 40 (November 1996):1152–1178, examines why some communities adopt antidiscrimination ordinances and policies that include sexual orientation and others do not.

28. On the affirmative action issues raised by *Bakke* and other cases, see Allan P. Sindler, *Bakke, De Funis and Minority Admissions* (New York: Longman, 1978).

29. *Richmond v. J.A. Croson Co.* (1989).

30. *Fullilove v. Klutznick* (1980).

31. *Metro Broadcasting, Inc. v. Federal Communications Commission* (1990).

32. *Local Number 93 v. Cleveland* (1986), and *United States v. Paradise* (1987).

33. *Local 28 of the Sheet Metal Workers v. EEOC* (1986).

34. *Firefighters v. Stotts* (1984).

35. *Wygant v. Jackson Board of Education* (1986).

36. Harry Holzer and David Newmark, "Assessing Affirmative Action," *Journal of Economic Literature* 38 (September 2000): 483–568.

37. See Barbara S. Gamble, "Putting Civil Rights to a Popular Vote," *American Journal of Political Science* 41 (January 1997): 245–269.

Chapter 6

1. John F. Kennedy, *A Nation of Immigrants* (New York: Harper and Row, 1964).

2. See *Statistical Abstract of the United States, 1999* (Washington, D.C.: U.S. Government Printing Office, 2000), 298.

3. Harold W. Stanley and Richard G. Niemi, *Vital Statistics on American Politics, 2001–2002* (Washington, D.C.: Congressional Quarterly Press, 2001), 61–62.

4. On the details of the 1965 Immigration Act and its unintended consequences, see Steven M. Gillon, *That's Not What We Meant To Do: Reform and Its Unintended Consequences in Twentieth-Century America* (New York: Norton, 2000), chap. 4.

5. Ronald T. Takaki, *Strangers from a Different Shore* (Boston: Little, Brown, 1989), chap. 11.

6. Ellis Cose, *A Nation of Strangers: Prejudice, Politics, and the Populating of America* (New York: William Morrow and Company, 1992), 219.

7. Judith Blake, *Family Size and Achievement* (Berkeley: University of California Press, 1989).

8. Richard Dawson et al., *Political Socialization*, 2nd ed. (Boston: Little, Brown, 1977), 33.

9. See M. Kent Jennings and Richard G. Niemi, *Generations and Politics: A Panel Study of Young Adults and Their Parents* (Princeton, NJ: Princeton University Press, 1981).

10. "The Age of Indifference." Report of the Times Mirror Center for the People and the Press, June 28, 1990.

11. Frank Rich, "The Weight of an Anchor." *New York Times Magazine*, May 19, 2002.

12. Quoted in Sabine Reichel, *What Did You Do in the War Daddy? Growing Up German* (New York: Hill & Wang, 1989), 113.

13. David Easton and Jack Dennis, *Children in the Political System* (New York: McGraw-Hill, 1969), 106–107.

14. Jean M. Converse, *Survey Research in the United States: Roots and Emergence, 1890–1960* (Berkeley: University of California Press, 1987), 116. Converse's work is the definitive study on the origins of public opinion sampling.

15. Herbert Asher, *Polling and the Public: What Every Citizen Should Know* (Washington, D.C.: Congressional Quarterly Press, 1988), 59.

16. Quoted in Norman M. Bradburn and Seymour Sudman, *Polls and Surveys: Under-*

standing What They Tell Us (San Francisco: Jossey-Bass, 1988), 39–40.

17. Lawrence R. Jacobs and Robert Y. Shapiro, *Politicians Don't Pander* (Chicago: University of Chicago Press, 2000), xiii.

18. David W. Moore, *The Superpollsters: How They Measure and Manipulate Public Opinion in America* (New York: Four Walls Eight Windows, 1992), 353–354.

19. W. Lance Bennett, *Public Opinion and American Politics* (New York: Harcourt Brace Jovanovich, 1980), 44.

20. E. D. Hirsch, Jr., *Cultural Literacy* (Boston: Houghton Mifflin, 1986).

21. Michael X. Delli Carpini and Scott Keeter, *What Americans Know About Politics and Why It Matters.* (New Haven, CT: Yale University Press, 1996), chap. 3.

22. W. Russell Neuman, *The Paradox of Mass Politics: Knowledge and Opinion in the American Electorate* (Cambridge, MA: Harvard University Press, 1986).

23. See Ronald Inglehart, *Modernization and Post-modernization* (Princeton, NJ: Princeton University Press, 1997), 254–255. Inglehart also shows that the decline of class voting is a general trend throughout Western democracies.

24. See Seymour Martin Lipset and Earl Raab, *Jews and the New American Political Scene* (Cambridge, MA: Harvard University Press, 1995), chap. 6.

25. Angus Campbell et al., *The American Voter* (New York: John Wiley, 1960), chap. 10.

26. Norman H. Nie, Sidney Verba, and John R. Petrocik, *The Changing American Voter* (Cambridge, MA: Harvard University Press, 1976), chap. 7.

27. See, for example, John L. Sullivan, James E. Pierson, and George E. Marcus, "Ideological Constraint in the Mass Public: A Methodological Critique and Some New Findings," *American Journal of Political Science* 22 (May 1978): 233–249; and Eric R.A.N. Smith, *The Unchanging American Voter* (Berkeley: University of California Press, 1989).

28. This definition is a close paraphrase of that in Sidney Verba and Norman H. Nie, *Participation in America* (New York: Harper & Row, 1972), 2.

29. Tom W. Smith and Lars Jarkko, "National Pride in Cross-National Perspective," April 2001. Posted at *http://www.issp.org/natpride.doc.*

30. See Verba and Nie, *Participation in America;* and Sidney Verba, Kay Lehman Schlozman, and Henry E. Brady, *Voice and Equality: Civic Voluntarism in American Politics* (Cambridge, MA: Harvard University Press, 1995).

31. This letter can be found in Juan Williams, *Eyes on the Prize: America's Civil Rights Years, 1954–1965* (New York: Viking, 1987), 187–189.

32. Verba and Nie, *Participation in America*, 125.

33. On African Americans, see Verba and Nie, *Participation in America*, chap. 10; on Hispanics, see Raymond E. Wolfinger and Steven J. Rosenstone, *Who Votes?* (New Haven, CT: Yale University Press, 1980), 92.

34. Campbell et al., *The American Voter*, 541.

35. Fiorina, *Retrospective Voting*, 5.

Chapter 7

1. See Darrell M. West, *Air Wars: Television Advertising in Election Campaigns, 1952–2000*, 3rd ed. (Washington, D.C.: Congressional Quarterly Press, 2001), 67.

2. Stephen Ansolabehere and Shanto Iyengar, *Going Negative* (New York: Free Press, 1995).

3. December 1, 1969, memo from Nixon to H. R. Haldeman in Bruce Oudes, ed., *From: The President—Richard Nixon's Secret Files* (New York: Harper & Row, 1988), 76–77.

4. Mark Hertsgaard, *On Bended Knee: The Press and the Reagan Presidency* (New York: Farrar, Straus & Giroux, 1988), 34.

5. Bob Woodward, *The Agenda: Inside the Clinton White House* (New York: Simon and Schuster, 1994), 313.

6. Quoted in David Brinkley, *Washington Goes to War* (New York: Knopf, 1988), 171.

7. Theodore H. White, *The Making of the President, 1972* (New York: Atheneum, 1973), 250.

8. Sam Donaldson, *Hold On, Mr. President!* (New York: Random House, 1987), 54.

9. Marvin Kalb, *One Scandalous Story: Clinton, Lewinsky, and Thirteen Days that Tarnished American Journalism* (New York: The Free Press, 2001), 6.

10. *Ibid.*, 20.

11. *Ibid.*, 138.

12. See the classic report by Michael J. Robinson, "Public Affairs Television and the Growth of Political Malaise: The Case of 'The Selling of the Pentagon,'" *American Political Science Review* 70 (June 1976): 409–432. Also see Joseph Cappella and Kathleen Hall Jamieson, *Spiral of Cynicism: The Press and the Public Good* (New York: Oxford, 1997).

13. Quoted in Kathleen Hall Jamieson and Paul Wardman, *Electing the President 2000: The Insider's View* (Philadelphia: University of Pennsylvania Press, 2001), 221.

14. William Manchester, *The Last Lion: Winston Churchill, Visions of Glory, 1874–1932* (Boston: Little, Brown, 1984), 225.

15. See, for example, Michael X. Delli Carpini and Scott Keeter, *What Americans Know About Politics and Why It Matters* (New Haven, CT: Yale University Press, 1996) and Ruy A. Teixeira, *The Disappearing American Voter* (Washington, D.C.: Brookings Institution, 1992).

16. Leonard Downie, Jr. and Robert G. Kaiser, *The News About the News: American Journalism in Peril* (New York: Knopf, 2002), 65.

17. Russell Baker, *The Good Times* (New York: William Morrow, 1989), 326.

18. See Walter Cronkite, *A Reporter's Life* (New York: Knopf, 1996), 257–258.

19. Michael K. Bohn, *Nerve Center: Inside the White House Situation Room* (Dulles, VA: Bassey's, 2003), 59.

20. See Harold W. Stanley and Richard G. Niemi, *Vital Statistics on American Politics*, 5th ed. (Washington, D.C.: Congressional Quarterly Press, 1995), 68.

21. Doris A. Graber, "The 'New' Media and Politics: What Does the Future Hold?" *PS: Political Science and Politics* (March 1996): 34.

22. Doris A. Graber, *Mass Media and American Politics*, 6th ed. (Washington, D.C.: Congressional Quarterly Press, 2002), 44.

23. Cited in Downey and Kaiser, *The News*, 239.

24. Edward J. Epstein, *News from Nowhere: Television and the News* (New York: Random House, 1973).

25. Downie and Kaiser, *The News*, 137.

26. Steven Ansolabehere, Roy Behr, and Shanto Iyengar, *The Media Game: American Politics in the Television Age* (New York: Macmillan, 1993), 53.

27. For example, see Leon V. Sigal, *Reporters and Officials: The Organization and Politics of News Reporting* (Lexington, MA: D.C. Heath, 1973), 122.

28. This letter can be found in Hedrick Smith, ed., *The Media and the Gulf War: The Press and Democracy in Wartime* (Washington, D.C.: Seven Locks Press, 1992), 378–380. Smith's book contains an excellent set of readings on media coverage of the war.

29. Jody Powell, "White House Flackery," in Peter Woll, ed., *Debating American Government*, 2nd ed. (Glenview, IL: Scott, Foresman, 1988), 180.

30. Dan Rather, quoted in Hoyt Purvis, ed., *The Presidency and the Press* (Austin, TX: Lyndon B. Johnson School of Public Affairs, 1976), 56.

31. Kathleen Hall Jamieson and Joseph N. Capella, "The Role of the Press in the Health Care Reform Debate of 1993–1994," in Doris Graber, Denis McQuail, and Pippa Norris, eds., *The Politics of News, the News of Politics* (Washington, D.C.: Congressional Quarterly Press, 1998), 118–119.

32. This point is well argued in Kathleen Hall Jamieson, *Eloquence in an Electronic Age* (New York: Oxford University Press, 1988).

33. For a discussion of CBS's failed attempt to lengthen candidate sound bites in 1992, see S. Robert Lichter and Richard E. Noyes, *Good Intentions Make Bad News*, 2nd ed. (Lanham, MD: Rowman & Littlefield, 1996), 246–250.

34. Quoted in Austin Ranney, *Channels of Power* (New York: Basic Books, 1983), 116.

35. Walter Cronkite, *A Reporter's Life*, 376–377.

36. "Campaign 2000 Final: How TV News Covered the General Election Campaign," *Media Monitor* 14 (November/December 2000).

37. *Ibid.*

38. Michael Waldman, *POTUS Speaks: Finding the Words that Defined the Clinton Presidency* (New York: Simon & Schuster, 2000), 267.

39. Project for Excellence in Journalism, *The First 100 Days: How Bush Versus Clinton Fared in the Press* (Washington, D.C., 2001).

40. William Schneider and I. A. Lewis, "Views on the News," *Public Opinion* 8 (August/September 1985): 6–11.

41. See David Weaver et al., *"The American Journalist in the 21st Century: Key Findings."* Posted at *http://www.knightfdn.org/pulications/americanjournalist/aj_keyfindings.pdf.*

42. See Michael J. Robinson and Margaret A. Sheehan, *Over the Wire and on TV: CBS and UP in Campaign '80* (New York: Russell Sage Foundation, 1983); and C. Richard Hofstetter, *Bias in the News: Network Television Coverage of the 1972 Election Campaign* (Columbus: Ohio State University Press, 1976).

43. Bernard Goldberg, *Bias: A CBS Insider Exposes How the Media Distort the News* (Washington, D.C.: Regnery, 2002), 5.

44. *Ibid.*, 119

45. *Ibid.*, 17.

46. Michael J. Robinson and Margaret Petrella, "Who Won the George Bush-Dan Rather Debate?" *Public Opinion* 10 (March/April 1988): 43.

47. Robinson, "Public Affairs Television," 428.

48. W. Lance Bennett, *News: The Politics of Illusion*, 2nd ed. (New York: Longman, 1988), 46.

49. See Paul F. Lazarsfeld et al., *The People's Choice* (New York: Columbia University Press, 1944).

50. Shanto Iyengar and Donald R. Kinder, *News that Matters* (Chicago: University of Chicago Press, 1987).

51. *Ibid.*, 118–119.

52. Joanne M. Miller and Jon A. Krosnick, "News Media Impact on the Ingredients of Presidential Evaluations: Politically Knowledgeable Citizens Are Guided by a Trusted Source," *American Journal of Political Science* (April 2000): 301–315.

53. Frederick T. Steeper, "Public Response to Gerald Ford's Statements on Eastern Europe in the Second Debate," in George F. Bishop, Robert G. Meadow, and Marilyn Jackson-Beeck, eds., *The Presidential Debates: Media, Electoral, and Public Perspectives* (New York: Praeger, 1978), 81–101.

54. Kathleen Hall Jamieson and Paul Waldman, eds., *Electing the President 2000: The Insiders' View* (Philadelphia: University of Pennsylvania Press, 2001), 5–6.

55. John W. Kingdon, *Agendas, Alternatives, and Public Policies* (Boston: Little, Brown, 1984), 3.

56. *Ibid.*, 3.

57. Henry A. Kissinger, *White House Years* (Boston: Little, Brown, 1979), 757.

58. For an interesting study of how hiring a public relations firm can help a nation's TV image, see Jarol B. Manheim and Robert B. Albitton, "Changing National Images: International Public Relations and Media Agenda Setting," *American Political Science Review* 78 (September 1984): 641–657.

59. Bernard Cohen, *The Press and Foreign Policy* (Princeton, NJ: Princeton University Press, 1963), 13.

60. Ronald W. Berkman and Laura W. Kitch, *Politics in the Media Age* (New York: McGraw-Hill, 1986), 311.

61. *Ibid.*, 313.

62. Matthew Robert Kerbel, *Edited for Television: CNN, ABC, and the 1992 Presidential Campaign* (Boulder, CO: Westview Press, 1994), 196.

Chapter 8

1. E. E. Schattschneider, *Party Government* (New York: Farrar and Rinehart, 1942), 1.

2. Anthony Downs, *An Economic Theory of Democracy* (New York: Harper & Row, 1957).

3. Marjorie Randon Hershey and Paul Allen Beck, *Party Politics in America*, 10th ed. (New York: Longman, 2003), 9.

4. Kay Lawson, ed., *Political Parties and Linkage: A Comparative Perspective* (New Haven, CT: Yale University Press, 1980), 3.

5. The major exception to this rule is nominations for the one-house state legislature in Nebraska, which is officially nonpartisan. In addition, Bernard Sanders has represented Vermont in the House as an Independent since 1990, and in 1994 Angus King was elected governor of Maine as an Independent.

6. Downs, *Economic Theory*.

7. Morris P. Fiorina, *Congress: Keystone of the Washington Establishment*, 2nd ed. (New Haven, CT: Yale University Press, 1989), 101.

8. Martin P. Wattenberg, *The Decline of American Political Parties, 1952–1996* (Cambridge, MA: Harvard University Press, 1998), chap. 10.

9. We wish to thank Anthony Salvanto of the University of California, Irvine for making this finding available to us prior to its publication.

10. See Adam Cohen and Elizabeth Taylor, *American Pharaoh* (Boston: Little, Brown, 2000), 155–163.

11. Kay Lawson, "California: The Uncertainties of Reform," in Gerald Pomper, ed., *Party Renewal in America*, (New Brunswick, NJ: Praeger, 1980), chap. 8.

12. John F. Bibby et al., "Parties in State Politics," in Virginia Gray, Herbert Jacob, and Kenneth Vines, eds., *Politics in the American States*, 4th ed. (Boston: Little, Brown, 1983), 76–79.

13. Hershey and Beck, *Party Politics in America*, 63.

14. John F. Bibby, "State Party Organizations: Coping and Adapting to Candidate-Centered Politics and Nationalization," in L. Sandy Maisel, ed., *The Parties Respond*, 3rd ed. (Boulder, CO: Westview, 1998), 34.

15. Comments of Roy Romer and Jim Nicholson at the Bulen Symposium on American Politics, December 1, 1998, as noted by Martin Wattenberg.

16. Gerald M. Pomper, *Elections in America* (New York: Longman, 1980), 161. Another study of presidential promises from Kennedy through Reagan also reaches the conclusion that campaign pledges are taken seriously. See Jeff Fishel, *Presidents and Promises* (Washington, D.C.: Congressional Quarterly Press, 1985).

17. The term is from V. O. Key. The standard source on critical elections is Walter Dean Burnham, *Critical Elections and the Mainsprings of American Politics* (New York: Norton, 1970).

18. On the origins of the American party system, see William N. Chambers, *Political Parties in a New Nation* (New York: Oxford University Press, 1963).

19. See Richard Hofstader, *The Idea of a Party System: The Rise of Legitimate Opposition in the United States, 1780–1840* (Berkeley: University of California Press, 1969).

20. James W. Ceaser, *Presidential Selection: Theory and Development* (Princeton, NJ: Princeton University Press, 1979), 130.

21. Quoted in James L. Sundquist, *Dynamics of the Party System*, rev. ed. (Washington, D.C.: Brookings Institution, 1983), 88. Sundquist's book is an excellent account of realignments in American party history.

22. *Ibid.*, 1955.

23. On Boston, see Gerald H. Gamm, *The Making of New Deal Democrats: Voting Behavior and Realignment in Boston, 1920–1940* (Chicago: University of Chicago Press, 1989).

24. For a good collection of readings on the causes and consequences of divided party government, see Gary W. Cox and Samuel Kernell, eds., *The Politics of Divided Government* (Boulder, CO: Westview, 1991).

25. See Morris P. Fiorina, *Divided Government* (New York: Macmillan, 1992).

26. Larry Sabato, *The Party's Just Begun: Shaping Political Parties for America's Future* (Glenview, IL: Scott, Foresman/Little, Brown, 1988), 133.

27. Steven J. Rosenstone, Roy L. Behr, and Edward H. Lazarus, *Third Parties in America* (Princeton, NJ: Princeton University Press, 1984).

28. For discussion of political ambiguity as a strategy, see Kenneth A. Shepsle, "The Strategy of Ambiguity: Uncertainty and Electoral Competition," *American Political Science Review* 66 (June 1972): 555–568; and Benjamin I. Page, *Choices and Echoes in Presidential Elections* (Chicago: University of Chicago Press, 1978), chap. 6.

29. The classic statement on responsible parties can be found in "Toward a More Responsible Two-Party System: A Report of the Committee on Political Parties, American Political Science Association," *American Political Science Review* 44 (1950): supplement, number 3, part 2.

30. David R. Mayhew, *Divided We Govern: Party Control, Lawmaking, and Investigations,*

1946–1990 (New Haven: Yale University Press, 1991), 199.

31. *Ibid.*, 126.

32. See Evron M. Kirkpatrick, "Toward a More Responsible Party System: Political Science, Policy Science, or Pseudo-Science?" *American Political Science Review* 65 (1971): 965–990.

33. Leon Epstein, *Political Parties in the American Mold* (Madison: University of Wisconsin Press, 1986), 346.

Chapter 9

1. Anthony King, *Running Scared* (New York: Free Press, 1997).

2. R. W. Apple, Jr., "Foley Assesses Presidential Elections and Tells Why He Wouldn't Run," the *New York Times*, November 4, 1998, A12.

3. Paul Taylor, "Is This Any Way To Pick a President?" *Washington Post National Weekly Edition*, April 13, 1987, 6.

4. See Hugh Winebrenner, *The Iowa Precinct Caucuses: The Making of a Media Event* (Ames: Iowa State University Press, 1987).

5. See Byron Shafer, *Quiet Revolution: The Struggle for the Democratic Party and the Shaping of Post-Reform Politics* (New York: Russell Sage, 1983).

6. Theodore White, *America in Search of Itself: The Making of the President 1956–1980* (New York: Harper & Row, 1982), 285.

7. This tradition extends back to 1916. The early primary date was chosen then to coincide with the already existing town meetings. Town meetings were held in February prior to the thawing of the snow, which in the days of unpaved roads made traveling extremely difficult in the spring. In 1916 no one could have dreamed that by holding the state's primary so early they were creating a mass media extravaganza for New Hampshire.

8. Harold W. Stanley and Richard G. Niemi, *Vital Statistics on American Politics*, 6th ed. (Washington, D.C.: Congressional Quarterly Press, 1998), 173. The same research also showed that New Hampshire received just 3 percent of the TV coverage during the general election—a figure far more in line with its small population size.

9. Robert Farmer, quoted in Clifford W. Brown, Jr., Lynda W. Powell, and Clyde Wilcox, *Serious Money: Fundraising and Contributing in Presidential Nomination Campaigns* (New York: Cambridge University Press, 1995), 1.

10. Frank Bruni, *Ambling into History: The Unlikely Odyssey of George W. Bush* (New York: HarperCollins, 2002), 5.

11. Larry M. Bartels, *Presidential Primaries and the Dynamics of Public Choice* (Princeton, NJ: Princeton University Press, 1988), 269.

12. "Participation Vote Study: Voting on the Run." *CQ Weekly*, January 3, 2004, 22.

13. See Martin P. Wattenberg, "When You Can't Beat Them, Join Them: Shaping the Presidential Nominating Process to the Television Age," *Polity* 21 (Spring 1989): 587–597.

14. R. W. Apple, "No Decisions, No Drama," the *New York Times*, August 1, 2000, A14.

15. Thomas E. Patterson, *The Mass Media Election* (New York: Praeger, 1980), 3.

16. See R. Kenneth Godwin, *One Billion Dollars of Influence: The Direct Marketing of Politics* (Chatham, NJ: Chatham House, 1988).

17. Jonathan S. Krason and Daniel E. Seltz, "Buying Time: Television Advertising in the 1998 Congressional Elections." Posted on the Internet at: *www.brennancenter.org/programs/cmag_temp/download.html.*

18. Patterson, *Mass Media Election*, 22–25. For a more recent study that shows similar results, see Stephen J. Farnsworth and S. Robert Lichter, *The Nightly News Nightmare: Network Television's Coverage of U.S. Presidential Elections, 1988–2000*, (Lanham, MD: Rowman & Littlefield, 2003).

19. David R. Runkel, ed., *Campaign for President: The Managers Look at '88* (Dover, MA: Auburn, 1989), 136.

20. Frank J. Sorauf, *Inside Campaign Finance: Myths and Realities* (New Haven, CT: Yale University Press, 1992), 229.

21. *Ibid.*, 162–163.

22. Archibald Cox and Fred Wertheimer, "The Choice Is Clear: It's People vs. the PACs," in Peter Woll, ed., *Debating American Government*, 2nd ed. (Glenview, IL: Scott, Foresman, 1988), 125.

23. This is discussed in Berry, *The Interest Group Society*, 172.

24. Frank J. Sorauf, *Money in American Elections* (Glenview, IL: Scott, Foresman, 1988), 312.

25. Bradley A. Smith, *Unfree Speech: The Folly of Campaign Finance Reform* (Princeton, NJ: Princeton University Press, 2001), 173.

26. Gary C. Jacobson, "The Effects of Campaign Spending in Congressional Elections," *American Political Science Review* 72 (June 1978): 469. For an updated analysis of this argument, see Gary C. Jacobson, "The Effects of Campaign Spending in House Elections: New Evidence for Old Arguments," *American Journal of Political Science* 34 (May 1990): 334–362.

27. Herbert E. Alexander, *Financing Politics: Money, Elections, and Political Reform*, 4th ed. (Washington, D.C.: Congressional Quarterly Press, 1992), 96.

28. Dan Nimmo, *The Political Persuaders* (Englewood Cliffs, NJ: Prentice-Hall, 1970), 5.

29. Sidney Blumenthal, *The Permanent Campaign* (New York: Simon & Schuster, 1982).

30. See Martin P. Wattenberg, *The Rise of Candidate-Centered Politics: Presidential Elections of the 1980s* (Cambridge, MA: Harvard University Press, 1991).

31. James W. Ceaser, *Presidential Selection: Theory and Development* (Princeton, NJ: Princeton University Press, 1979), 83.

Chapter 10

1. Quoted in Stanley G. Kelley, Jr., *Interpreting Elections* (Princeton, NJ: Princeton University Press, 1983), 3–4.

2. See Thomas E. Cronin, *Direct Democracy* (Cambridge, MA: Harvard University Press, 1989), chap. 7.

3. Daniel A. Smith, *Tax Crusaders and the Politics of Direct Democracy* (New York: Routledge, 1998).

4. Morton Grodzins, "Political Parties and the Crisis of Succession in the United States: The Case of 1800," in Joseph LaPalombara and Myron Weiner, eds., *Political Parties and Political Development* (Princeton, NJ: Princeton University Press, 1966), 319.

5. In 1804, the Twelfth Amendment to the Constitution changed the procedure to the one we know today, in which each elector votes separately for president and vice president.

6. A summary of these survey results can be found at: *http://www.census.gov/population/www/socdemo/voting.html.*

7. See Martin P. Wattenberg, "Should Election Day Be a Holiday?" *The Atlantic Monthly*, October 1998, 42–46.

8. Anthony Downs, *An Economic Theory of Democracy* (New York: Harper & Row, 1957), chap. 14.

9. See *http://www.sos.state.ga.us/elections/race_gender_age.pdf.* Accessed April 3, 2004.

10. See George C. Edwards III, *At the Margins* (New Haven, CT: Yale University Press, 1989), chap. 8.

11. Richard G. Niemi and Herbert F. Weisberg, eds., *Controversies in Voting Behavior*, 2nd ed. (Washington, D.C.: Congressional Quarterly Press, 1984), 164–165.

12. See Martin P. Wattenberg, *The Decline of American Political Parties, 1952–1996* (Cambridge, MA: Harvard University Press, 1998).

13. Shawn W. Rosenberg with Patrick McCafferty, "Image and Voter Preference," *Public Opinion Quarterly* 51 (Spring 1987): 44.

14. Arthur H. Miller, Martin P. Wattenberg, and Oksana Malanchuk, "Schematic Assessments of Presidential Candidates," *American Political Science Review* 80 (1986): 521–540. For more recent data see Martin P. Wattenberg, "Personal Popularity in U.S. Presidential Elections," *Presidential Studies Quarterly* 34 (2004): 119–131.

15. Paul R. Abramson, John H. Aldrich, and David W. Rohde, *Change and Continuity in the 2000 Elections* (Washington, D.C.: Congressional Quarterly Press, 2002), chap. 6.

16. American Bar Association, *Electing the President* (Chicago: American Bar Association, 1967), 3.

17. The Twenty-third Amendment (1961) permits the District of Columbia to have three electors even though it has no representatives in Congress.

18. In both Maine and Nebraska, an elector is allocated for every congressional district won,

and whoever wins the state as a whole wins the two electors allotted to the state for its senators.

19. Benjamin Page, *Choices and Echoes in American Presidential Elections* (Chicago: University of Chicago Press, 1978), 153.

20. See Morris P. Fiorina, *Retrospective Voting in American National Elections* (New Haven, CT: Yale University Press, 1981).

21. V. O. Key, *The Responsible Electorate* (New York: Random House, 1966), 76.

22. Benjamin Ginsberg, *Consequences of Consent* (Reading, MA: Addison-Wesley, 1982), 194.

23. *Ibid.*, 198.

Chapter 11

1. Kay L. Schlozman and John T. Tierney, *Organized Interests and American Democracy* (New York: Harper & Row, 1986), 1.

2. The classic work is David B. Truman, *The Governmental Process*, 2nd ed. (New York: Knopf, 1971).

3. Thomas R. Dye, *Who's Running America?*, 5th ed. (Englewood Cliffs, NJ: Prentice-Hall, 1990), 170.

4. Robert Engler, *The Brotherhood of Oil* (Chicago: University of Chicago Press, 1977).

5. Theodore J. Lowi, *The End of Liberalism*, 2nd ed. (New York: Norton, 1979).

6. See Lee Fritschler, *Smoking and Politics: Policy Making and the Federal Bureaucracy* (Englewood Cliffs, NJ: Prentice-Hall, 1983).

7. Morris P. Fiorina, *Congress: Keystone of the Washington Establishment*, 2nd ed. (New Haven, CT: Yale University Press, 1989), 122.

8. E. E. Schattschneider, *The Semisovereign People* (New York: Holt, Rinehart & Winston, 1960), 35.

9. Truman, *The Governmental Process*, 511.

10. Mancur Olson, *The Logic of Collective Action* (Cambridge, MA: Harvard University Press, 1965), especially 9–36.

11. *Ibid.*, 35.

12. Jeffrey H. Birnbaum and Alan S. Murray, *Showdown at Gucci Gulch: Lawmakers, Lobbyists, and the Unlikely Triumph of Tax Reform* (New York: Vintage, 1987).

13. *Ibid.*, 235.

14. Christine Mauer and Tara E. Sheets, eds., *Encyclopedia of Associations*, 33rd ed. (Detroit: Gale Research Company, 1998).

15. Frank R. Baumgartner and Beth L. Leech, *Basic Interests: The Importance of Groups in Politics and in Political Science* (Princeton, NJ: Princeton University Press, 1998), 109; 2001 data from Burdett A. Loomis and Allan J. Cigler, "Introduction: The Changing Nature of Interest Group Politics," in Loomis and Cigler, eds., *Interest Group Politics*, 6th ed. (Washington, D.C.: Congressional Quarterly Press, 2002), 12.

16. Jack L. Walker, "The Origins and Maintenance of Interest Groups in America,"

American Political Science Review 77 (June 1983): 390–406.

17. Andrew S. McFarland, *Common Cause: Lobbying in the Public Interest* (Chatham, NJ: Chatham House, 1984), 1.

18. Lester W. Milbrath, *The Washington Lobbyists* (Chicago: Rand McNally, 1963), 8.

19. Norman Ornstein and Shirley Elder, *Interest Groups, Lobbying, and Policymaking* (Washington, D.C.: Congressional Quarterly Press, 1978), 59–60.

20. Peter H. Stone, "Friends, After All," *National Journal*, October 22, 1994, 2,440.

21. Raymond A. Bauer, Ithiel de Sola Pool, and Lewis A. Dexter, *American Business and Public Policy* (New York: Atherton, 1963).

22. Milbrath, *The Washington Lobbyists*, 354.

23. For a summary of recent studies on the influence of lobbying, see Baumgartner and Leech, *Basic Interests*, 130.

24. See Laura Langbein and Mark Lotwis, "The Political Efficacy of Lobbying and Money: Gun Control in the U.S. House, 1986," *Legislative Studies Quarterly* 15 (Fall 1990): 413–440.

25. Frederic J. Frommer, "Baseball PAC Gives Thousands to Parties," Associated Press Newswire, May 13, 2003.

26. R. Kenneth Godwin and Barry J. Seldon, "What Corporations Really Want from Government: The Public Provision of Private Goods," in Cigler and Loomis, eds., *Interest Group Politics*, 6th ed., 219.

27. The Sovern story is told in "Taking an Ax to PACs," *Time*, August 20, 1984, 27.

28. Karen Orren, "Standing To Sue: Interest Group Conflict in Federal Courts," *American Political Science Review* 70 (September 1976): 724.

29. Gregory A. Caldeira and John R. Wright, "*Amici Curiae* Before the Supreme Court: Who Participates, When, and How Much," *Journal of Politics* 52 (August 1990): 782–804.

30. Ronald J. Hrebenar and Ruth K. Scott, *Interest Group Politics in America*, 2nd ed. (Englewood Cliffs, NJ: Prentice-Hall, 1990), 201.

31. Ken Kollman, *Outside Lobbying: Public Opinion and Interest Group Strategies* (Princeton, NJ: Princeton University Press, 1998), 33.

32. Quoted in Jeffrey M. Berry, *The Interest Group Society*, 2nd ed. (Glenview, IL: Scott, Foresman, 1989), 103.

33. Paul Edward Johnson, "Organized Labor in an Era of Blue-Collar Decline," in Allan J. Cigler and Burdett A. Loomis, eds., *Interest Group Politics*, 3rd ed. (Washington, D.C.: Congressional Quarterly Press, 1991), 33–62.

34. Schlozman and Tierney, *Organized Interests*, 68.

35. See Pat Choate, *Agents of Influence: How Japan Manipulates America's Political and Economic System* (New York: Simon & Schuster, 1990).

36. Christopher J. Bosso, "The Color of Money: Environmental Groups and the Pathologies of Fund Raising," in Allan J. Cigler and Burdett A. Loomis, *Interest Group Politics*, 4th ed. (Washington, D.C.: Congressional Quarterly Press, 1995), 102.

37. For an interesting analysis of how changes in the regulatory environment, congressional oversight, and public opinion altered the debate on nuclear power, see Frank R. Baumgartner and Bryan D. Jones, *Agendas and Instability in American Politics* (Chicago: University of Chicago Press, 1993).

38. See *http://www.naacp.org/work/economic/economic.shtml*.

39. Dona C. Hamilton and Charles V. Hamilton, *The Dual Agenda: Race and Social Welfare Policies of Civil Rights Organizations* (New York: Columbia University Press, 1997), 2.

40. Jeffrey M. Berry, *Lobbying for the People* (Princeton, NJ: Princeton University Press, 1977), 7.

41. Robert H. Salisbury, "The Paradox of Interest Groups in Washington—More Groups, Less Clout," in Anthony King, ed., *The New American Political System*, 2nd ed. (Washington, D.C.: American Enterprise Institute, 1990), 204.

42. Paul S. Herrnson, *Congressional Elections: Campaigning at Home and in Washington*, 4th ed. (Washington, D.C.: Congressional Quarterly Press, 2004), 133-134.

43. Alexis de Tocqueville, *Democracy in America*, vol. 2 (New York: Vintage, 1945), 114.

44. Hrebenar and Scott, *Interest Group Politics in America*, 2nd ed., 234.

45. Steven V. Roberts, "Angered President Blames Others for the Huge Deficit," the *New York Times*, December 14, 1988, A16.

46. William M. Lunch, *The Nationalization of American Politics* (Berkeley: University of California Press, 1987), 206.

47. Salisbury, "The Paradox of Interest Groups," 229.

Chapter 12

1. David T. Canon, *Race, Redistricting, and Representation: The Unintended Consequences of Black Majority Districts* (Chicago: University of Chicago Press, 1999).

2. Susan A. Banducci, Todd Donovan, and Jeffrey A. Karp, "Minority Representation, Empowerment, and Participation," *Journal of Politics* 66 (May 2004): 534–556.

3. There is some evidence that women state legislators in states with the highest percentage of female representatives are more likely than men to introduce and pass legislation dealing with women, children, and families. See Sue Thomas, "The Impact of Women on State Legislative Policies," *Journal of Politics* 53 (November 1991): 958–976. See also Arturo Vega and Juanita M. Firestone, "The Effects of Gender on Congressional Behavior and the Substantive Representation of Women,"

Legislative Studies Quarterly 20 (May 1995): 213–222; Leslie A. Schwindt-Bayer and Renato Corbetta, "Gender Turnover and Roll-Call Voting in the U.S. House of Representatives," *Legislative Studies Quarterly* 29 (May 2004): 215–229.

4. On various views of representation, see Hanna Pitkin, *The Concept of Representation* (Berkeley: University of California Press, 1967).

5. Sally Friedman, "House Committee Assignments of Women and Minority Newcomers, 1965–1994," *Legislative Studies Quarterly* 21 (February 1996): 73–81; Alan Gerber, "African Americans' Congressional Careers and the Democratic House Delegation," *Journal of Politics* 58 (August 1996): 831–845.

6. An excellent review of congressional campaign costs and spending is Edie N. Goldenberg and Michael W. Traugott, *Campaigning for Congress* (Washington, D.C.: Congressional Quarterly Press, 1984). Another is Paul S. Herrnson, *Congressional Elections: Campaigning at Home and in Washington* (Washington, D.C.: Congressional Quarterly Press, 1995).

7. John L. Sullivan and Eric Uslaner, "Congressional Behavior and Electoral Marginality," *American Journal of Political Science* 22 (August 1978): 536–553.

8. Thomas Mann, *Unsafe at Any Margin* (Washington, D.C.: American Enterprise Institute, 1978).

9. Glenn R. Parker, *Homeward Bound* (Pittsburgh: University of Pittsburgh Press, 1986); and John R. Johannes, *To Serve the People* (Lincoln: University of Nebraska Press, 1984).

10. Patricia Hurley and Kim Q. Hill, "The Prospects for Issue Voting in Contemporary Congressional Elections," *American Politics Quarterly* 8 (October 1980): 446.

11. Mann, *Unsafe at Any Margin*, 37.

12. That presidential elections and congressional elections are not closely related is an argument made in Lyn Ragsdale, "The Fiction of Congressional Elections as Presidential Events," *American Politics Quarterly* 8 (October 1980): 375–398. For evidence that voters' views of the president affect their voting for senators, see Lonna Rae Atkeson and Randall W. Partin, "Economic and Referendum Voting: A Comparison of Gubernatorial and Senatorial Elections," *American Political Science Review* 89 (March 1995): 99–107.

13. John R. Owens and Edward C. Olson, "Economic Fluctuations and Congressional Elections," *American Journal of Political Science* 24 (August 1980): 469–493; Benjamin Radcliff, "Solving a Puzzle: Aggregate Analysis and Economic Voting Revisited," *Journal of Politics* 50 (May 1988): 440–458; Robert S. Erikson, "Economic Conditions and the Congressional Vote: A Review of the Macrolevel Evidence," *American Journal of Political Science* 34 (May 1990): 373–399; James E. Campbell, *The Presidential Pulse of*

Congressional Elections (Lexington: University Press of Kentucky, 1993), 119; and Gary C. Jacobson, "Does the Economy Matter in Midterm Elections?" *American Journal of Political Science* 34 (May 1990): 400–404.

14. David R. Mayhew, *Congress: The Electoral Connection* (New Haven, CT: Yale University Press, 1974).

15. Richard F. Fenno, Jr., *Home Style* (Boston: Little, Brown, 1978), 32.

16. *Ibid.*, 106–107.

17. The "service spells success" argument is made in Morris P. Fiorina, *Congress: Keystone of the Washington Establishment*, 2nd ed. (New Haven, CT: Yale University Press, 1989); and, with a slightly different emphasis, in Glenn R. Parker, "The Advantages of Incumbency in Congressional Elections," *American Politics Quarterly* 8 (October 1980): 449–461.

18. Fiorina, *Congress: Keystone of the Washington Establishment*, 43.

19. Gary C. Jacobson, *The Politics of Congressional Elections*, 6th ed. (New York: Longman, 2004), 122–132; Stephen Ansolabehere, James M. Snyder, Jr., and Charles Stewart III, "Old Voters, New Voters, and the Personal Vote; Using Redistricting To Measure the Incumbency Advantage," *American Journal of Political Science* 44 (January 2000): 17–34.

20. See, for example, Paul Feldman and James Jondrow, "Congressional Elections and Local Federal Spending," *American Journal of Political Science* 28 (February 1984): 147–163; Glenn R. Parker and Suzanne L. Parker, "The Correlates and Effects of Attention to District by U.S. House Members," *Legislative Studies Quarterly* 10 (May 1985): 223–242; and John C. McAdams and John R. Johannes, "Congressmen, Perquisites, and Elections," *Journal of Politics* 50 (May 1988): 412–439.

21. On strategies of challengers, see Gary C. Jacobson and Samuel Kernell, *Strategy and Choice in Congressional Elections*, 2nd ed. (New Haven, CT: Yale University Press, 1983); and Gary C. Jacobson, "Strategic Politicians and the Dynamics of U.S. House Elections, 1946–1986," *American Political Science Review* 83 (September 1989): 773–794. See also Steven D. Levitt and Catherine D. Wolfram, "Decomposing the Sources of Incumbency Advantage in the U.S. House," *Legislative Studies Quarterly* 22 (February 1997): 45–60.

22. See Gary C. Jacobson, *Money in Congressional Elections* (New Haven, CT: Yale University Press, 1980).

23. On the importance of challenger quality and financing, see Alan I. Abramowitz, "Explaining Senate Election Outcomes," *American Political Science Review* 82 (June 1988): 385–403; and Donald Philip Green and Jonathan S. Krasno, "Salvation for the Spendthrift Incumbent," *American Journal of Political Science* 32 (November 1988): 884–907.

24. Jacobson, *The Politics of Congressional Elections*, 41–47, 132–134. See also Gary C. Jacobson, "The Effects of Campaign Spending in House Elections: New Evidence for Old Arguments," *American Journal of Political Science* 34 (May 1990): 334–362; Christopher Kenny and Michael McBurnett, "An Individual-Level Multiequation Model of Expenditure Effects in Contested House Elections," *American Political Science Review* 88 (September 1994): 699–707; Robert S. Erikson and Thomas R. Palfrey, "Campaign Spending and Incumbency: An Alternative Simultaneous Equation Approach," *Journal of Politics* 60 (May 1998): 355–373; and Alan Gerber, "Estimating the Effect of Campaign Spending on Senate Election Outcomes Using Instrumental Variables," *American Political Science Review* 92 (June 1998): 401–412.

25. Federal Election Commission.

26. Gary C. Jacobson and Michael A. Dimock, "Checking Out: The Effects of Bank Overdrafts on the 1992 House Elections," *American Journal of Political Science* 38 (August 1994): 601–624. See also "Checks and Choices: The House Bank Scandal's Impact on Voters in 1992," *Journal of Politics* 57 (November 1995): 1,143–1,159; and Carl McCurley and Jeffrey J. Mondak, "Inspected by #1184063113: The Influence of Incumbents' Competence and Integrity in U.S. House Elections," *American Journal of Political Science* 39 (November 1995): 864–885.

27. John G. Peters and Susan Welch, "The Effects of Corruption on Voting Behavior in Congressional Elections," *American Political Science Review* 74 (September 1980): 697–708; and Susan Welch and John R. Hibbing, "The Effects of Charges of Corruption on Voting Behavior in Congressional Elections, 1982–1990," *Journal of Politics* 59 (February 1997): 226–239.

28. On term limits, see Gerald Benjamin and Michael J. Malbin, eds., *Limiting Our Legislative Terms* (Washington, D.C.: Congressional Quarterly Press, 1992).

29. Said former House Speaker Jim Wright in *You and Your Congressman* (New York: Putnam, 1976), 190. See also Donald R. Matthews and James Stimson, *Yeas and Nays: Normal Decision-Making in the House of Representatives* (New York: Wiley, 1975); and John L. Sullivan et al., "The Dimensions of Cue-Taking in the House of Representatives: Variations by Issue Area," *Journal of Politics* 55 (November 1993): 975–997.

30. Nelson W. Polsby et al., "Institutionalization of the House of Representatives," *American Political Science Review* 62 (1968): 144–168.

31. John R. Hibbing, "Contours of the Modern Congressional Career," *American Political Science Review* 85 (June 1991): 405–428.

32. See Bernard Grofman, Robert Griffin, and Amihai Glazer, "Is the Senate More Liberal than the House? Another Look," *Legislative Studies Quarterly* 16 (May 1991): 281–296.

33. See Sarah A. Binder and Steven S. Smith, *Politics or Principle? Filibustering in the*

United States Senate (Washington, D.C.: Brookings Institution, 1997).

34. Robert L. Peabody, *Leadership in Congress* (Boston: Little, Brown, 1976), 4.

35. On the increasing importance of party leadership in the House, see David W. Rohde, *Parties and Leaders in the Postreform House* (Chicago: University of Chicago Press, 1991); Barbara Sinclair, "The Emergence of Strong Leadership in the 1980s House of Representatives," *Journal of Politics* 54 (August 1992): 657–684; and Gary W. Cox and Matthew D. McCubbins, *Legislative Leviathan* (Berkley: University of California Press, 1993).

36. For more on congressional oversight, see Christopher H. Foreman, Jr., *Signals from the Hill* (New Haven, CT: Yale University Press, 1988); and Diana Evans, "Congressional Oversight and the Diversity of Members' Goals," *Political Science Quarterly* 109 (Fall 1994): 669–687.

37. Joel D. Aberbach, *Keeping a Watchful Eye: The Politics of Congressional Oversight* (Washington, D.C.: Brookings Institution, 1990).

38. Aberbach, *Keeping a Watchful Eye*; Joel D. Aberbach, "What's Happened to the Watchful Eye?" *Congress and the Presidency* 29 (Spring 2002): 3–23.

39. Richard F. Fenno, Jr., *Congressmen in Committees* (Boston: Little, Brown, 1973), 1.

40. Useful studies of committee assignments include Kenneth Shepsle, *The Giant Jigsaw Puzzle* (Chicago: University of Chicago Press, 1978); and Cox and McCubbins, *Legislative Leviathan*, chaps. 1, 7, and 8.

41. Richard F. Fenno, Jr., "If, as Ralph Nader Says, Congress Is the 'Broken Branch,' How Come We Love Our Congressmen So Much?" in Norman Ornstein, ed., *Congress in Change* (New York: Praeger, 1975), 282.

42. For more on congressional reform, see Leroy N. Rieselbach, *Congressional Reform* (Washington, D.C.: Congressional Quarterly Press, 1986).

43. See Susan Webb Hammond, *Congressional Caucuses in National Policy Making* (Baltimore: Johns Hopkins University Press, 1998).

44. Data on staff come from Norman J. Ornstein, Thomas E. Mann, and Michael J. Malbin, *Vital Statistics on Congress, 2001–2002* (Washington D.C.: Congressional Quarterly Press, 2002), 126.

45. For a thorough discussion of rule changes and the impact of procedures, see Steven S. Smith, *Call to Order: Floor Politics in the House and Senate* (Washington, D.C.: Brookings Institution, 1989).

46. Barbara Sinclair, *Unorthodox Lawmaking*, 2nd ed. (Washington, D.C.: Congressional Quarterly Press, 2000).

47. Quoted in Doris Kearns, *Lyndon Johnson and the American Dream* (New York: New American Liberty, 1976), 146.

48. George C. Edwards III, *At the Margins: Presidential Leadership of Congress* (New Haven, CT: Yale University Press, 1989).

49. James M. Snyder, Jr. and Tim Groseclose, "Estimating Party Influence in Congressional Roll-Call Voting," *American Journal of Political Science* 44 (April 2000): 187–205; Aage Clausen, *How Congressmen Decide: A Policy Focus* (New York: St. Martin's, 1973).

50. Quoted in Peter G. Richards, *Honourable Members* (London: Faber and Faber, 1959), 157.

51. See Roger H. Davidson, *The Role of the Congressman* (New York: Pegasus, 1969); and Thomas E. Cavanaugh, "Role Orientations of House Members: The Process of Representation" (paper delivered at the annual meeting of the American Political Science Association, Washington, D.C., August 1979).

52. John L. Sullivan and Robert E. O'Connor, "Electoral Choice and Popular Control of Public Policy: The Case of the 1966 House Elections," *American Political Science Review* 66 (December 1972): 1,256–1,268.

53. The *New York Times*/CBS News Poll cited in "Voters Disgusted With Politicians as Election Nears," the *New York Times*, November 13, 1994, A10.

54. Robert A. Bernstein, *Elections, Representation, and Congressional Voting Behavior* (Englewood Cliffs, NJ: Prentice-Hall, 1989), 99.

55. Patricia A. Hurley and Kim Quaile Hill, "Beyond the Demand-Input Model: A Theory of Representational Linkages," *Journal of Politics* 65 (May 2003): 304–326; Christopher Wlezien, "Patterns of Representation: Dynamics of Public Preferences and Policy," Journal of Politics 66 (February 2004): 1–24.

56. Larry M. Bartels, however, found that members of Congress were responsive to constituency opinion in supporting the Reagan defense buildup. See "Constituency Opinion and Congressional Policy Making: The Reagan Defense Buildup," *American Political Science Review* 85 (June 1991): 457–474.

57. Kim Quaile Hill and Patricia A. Hurley, "Dyadic Representation Reappraised," *American Journal of Political Science* 43 (January 1999): 109–137.

58. On the importance of ideology, see Bernstein, *Elections, Representation, and Congressional Voting Behavior.*

59. *Washington Representatives 2004* (Washington, D.C.: Columbia Books, 2004).

60. Center for Responsive Politics, 2002.

61. John W. Kingdon, *Congressmen's Voting Decisions*, 3rd ed. (Ann Arbor: University of Michigan Press, 1989), 242.

62. See M. Darrell West, *Congress and Economic Policymaking* (Pittsburgh: University of Pittsburgh Press, 1987).

Chapter 13

1. Quoted in Thomas E. Cronin, *The State of the Presidency*, 2nd ed. (Boston: Little, Brown, 1980), 223.

2. Richard E. Neustadt, *Presidential Power and the Modern Presidents* (New York: Free Press, 1990).

3. On the public's expectations of the president, see George C. Edwards III, *The Public Presidency* (New York: St. Martin's Press, 1983), chap. 5.

4. Office of the White House Press Secretary, *Remarks of the President at a Meeting With Non-Washington Editors and Broadcasters*, September 21, 1979, 12.

5. Samuel P. Huntington, *American Politics: The Promises of Disharmony* (Cambridge, MA: Belknap, 1981), 33.

6. On the creation of the presidency, see Donald L. Robertson, *To the Best of My Ability* (New York: Norton, 1987); and Thomas E. Cronin, ed., *Inventing the American Presidency* (Lawrence: University Press of Kansas, 1989).

7. A good example is Clinton Rossiter, *The American Presidency*, rev. ed. (New York: Harcourt, 1960).

8. Arthur Schlesinger, *The Imperial Presidency* (Boston: Houghton Mifflin, 1973).

9. The titles of chaps. 5 and 11 in Thomas E. Cronin, *The State of the Presidency*, 2nd ed. (Boston: Little, Brown, 1980).

10. On the factors important in the presidential nominee's choice of a running mate, see Lee Sigelman and Paul J. Wahlbeck, "The 'Veepstakes': Strategic Choice in Presidential Running Mate Selection," *American Political Science Review* 91 (December 1997): 855–864.

11. See Paul C. Light, *Vice Presidential Power* (Baltimore: Johns Hopkins University Press, 1984).

12. For a study of the backgrounds of cabinet members, see Jeffrey E. Cohen, *The Politics of the U.S. Cabinet* (Pittsburgh: University of Pittsburgh Press, 1988).

13. For background on the Executive Office, see John Hart, *The Presidential Branch*, 2nd ed. (Chatham, NJ: Chatham House, 1995).

14. Two useful books on the history and functions of the White House staff are Hart, *The Presidential Branch*; and Bradley H. Patterson, Jr., *The White House Staff* (Washington, D.C.: Brookings, 2000).

15. For a discussion of presidential party leadership in Congress, see George C. Edwards III, *At the Margins: Presidential Leadership of Congress* (New Haven, CT: Yale University Press, 1989), chaps. 3–5.

16. Jimmy Carter, *Keeping Faith* (New York: Bantam, 1982), 80.

17. For a review of these studies and an analysis showing the limited impact of presidential coattails on congressional election outcomes, see Edwards, *The Public Presidency*, 83–93.

18. For evidence of the impact of the president's campaigning in midterm elections, see Jeffrey E. Cohen, Michael A. Krassa, and John A. Hamman, "The Impact of Presidential Campaigning on Midterm U.S. Senate Elections," *American Political Science Review* 85 (March 1991): 165–178. On the president's

effect on congressional elections more broadly, see James E. Campbell, *The Presidential Pulse of Congressional Elections* (Lexington: University Press of Kentucky, 1993).

19. Quoted in Sidney Blumenthal, "Marketing the President," *New York Times Magazine*, September 13, 1981, 110.

20. Quoted in "Slings and Arrows," *Newsweek*, July 31, 1978, 20.

21. Edwards, *At the Margins*, chaps. 6–7.

22. For an analysis of the factors that affect perceptions of mandates, see Edwards, *At the Margins*, chap. 8.

23. David Stockman, *The Triumph of Politics* (New York: Harper & Row, 1986), 251–265; and William Greider, "The Education of David Stockman," *Atlantic*, December 1981, 51.

24. George C. Edwards III and Andrew Barrett, "Presidential Agenda Setting in Congress," in Jon R. Bond and Richard Fleisher, eds., *Polarized Politics* (Washington, D.C.: Congressional Quarterly Press, 2000).

25. John Kingdon, *Agendas, Alternatives, and Public Policies* (Boston: Little, Brown, 1984), 25. On presidential agenda setting, see Paul C. Light, *The President's Agenda* (Baltimore: Johns Hopkins University Press, 1991); and George C. Edwards III and B. Dan Wood, "Who Influences Whom?" *American Political Science Review* 93 (June 1999): 327–344.

26. Edwards, *At the Margins*, chaps. 9–10; and Jon R. Bond and Richard Fleisher, *The President in the Legislative Arena* (Chicago: University of Chicago Press, 1990), chap. 8.

27. See David Auerswald and Forrest Maltzman, "Policymaking Through Advice and Consent: Treaty Considerations by the United States Senate," *Journal of Politics* 65 (November 2003): 1,097–1,110.

28. For an analysis of war powers and other issues related to separation of powers, see Louis Fisher, *Constitutional Conflicts Between Congress and the President*, 4th ed. rev. (Lawrence: University Press of Kansas, 1997); and Louis Fisher, *Presidential War Power* (Lawrence: University Press of Kansas, 1995).

29. See Barbara Hinckley, *Less than Meets the Eye* (Chicago: University of Chicago Press, 1994).

30. The phrase was originated by Aaron Wildavsky in "The Two Presidencies," *Trans-Action* 4 (December 1966): 7–14. He later determined that the two presidencies applied mostly to the 1950s. See Duane M. Oldfield and Aaron Wildavsky, "Reconsidering the Two Presidencies," in Steven A. Shull, ed., *The Two Presidencies: A Quarter Century Assessment* (Chicago: Nelson-Hall, 1991), 181–190.

31. Edwards, *At the Margins*, chap. 4.

32. See William W. Lammers, "Presidential Attention-Focusing Activities," in Doris A. Graber, ed., in *The President and the Public* (Philadelphia: ISHI, 1982), 145–171; and Samuel Kernell, *Going Public*, 3rd ed. (Washington, D.C.: Congressional Quarterly Press, 1997), chap. 4.

33. Edwards, *The Public Presidency*, chap. 6; and George C. Edwards III, *Presidential Approval* (Baltimore: Johns Hopkins University Press, 1990).

34. Mueller also included the inaugural period of a president's term as a rally event. See John E. Mueller, *War, Presidents and Public Opinion* (New York: Wiley, 1973), 208–213.

35. Kernell, *Going Public*, 169.

36. See Jeffrey K. Tulis, *The Rhetorical Presidency* (Princeton, NJ: Princeton University Press, 1987), on presidents' efforts to build policy support.

37. For a discussion of the social flow of information, see Robert Huckfeldt and John Sprague, "Networks in Context: The Social Flow of Political Information," *American Political Science Review* 81 (December 1987): 1,197–1,216.

38. *Newsweek* Poll, October 28–30, 1994, cited in "The Problem With the President," *Newsweek*, November 7, 1994, 42.

39. George C. Edwards III, "Frustration and Folly: Bill Clinton and the Public Presidency," in Colin Campbell and Bert A. Rockman, eds., *The Clinton Presidency: First Appraisals* (Chatham, NJ: Chatham House, 1995).

40. Useful comparisons over Reagan's and Clinton's tenures can be found in George C. Edwards III, *On Deaf Ears: The Limits of the Bully Pulpit* (New Haven: Yale University Press, 2003), chaps. 2–3.

41. Quoted in "Tax Cut Passed by Solid Margin in House, Senate," *Congressional Quarterly Weekly Report*, August 1, 1981, 1,374.

42. Sam Donaldson, *Hold On, Mr. President!* (New York: Random House, 1987), 196–197.

43. Two of the leading studies are found in Michael J. Robinson and Margaret A. Sheehan, *Over the Wire and on TV* (New York: Russell Sage Foundation, 1983); and Daniel C. Hallin, "The Media, the War in Vietnam, and Political Support," *Journal of Politics* 46 (February 1984): 2–24.

44. Carter, *Keeping Faith*, 179–180.

45. See Mark J. Rozell, *The Press and the Ford Presidency* (Ann Arbor: University of Michigan Press, 1992).

46. Doris A. Graber, *Mass Media and American Politics*, 5th ed. (Washington, D.C.: Congressional Quarterly Press, 1997), 277. On the 1992 presidential campaign, see "Clinton's the One," *Media Monitor* 6 (November 1992): 3–5.

47. Thomas E. Patterson, *Out of Order* (New York: Knopf, 1993), chap. 3.

48. *Ibid.*, 113.

49. *Media Monitor*, May/June 1995, 2–5; Thomas E. Patterson, "Legitimate Beef: The Presidency and a Carnivorous Press," *Media Studies Journal* (Spring 1994): 21–26; "Sex, Lies, and TV News," *Media Monitor* 12 (September/October 1998); "TV News Coverage of the 1998 Midterm Elections," *Media Monitor* 12 (November/December 1998). But see Andras Szanto, "In Our Opinion. . . :

Editorial Page Views of Clinton's First Year," *Media Studies Journal* (Spring 1994): 97–105.

50. Michael Baruch Grossman and Martha Joynt Kumar, *Portraying the President: The White House and the News Media* (Baltimore: Johns Hopkins University Press, 1981), chaps. 10–11.

51. Donaldson, *Hold On, Mr. President!*, 237–238.

52. Quoted in Eleanor Randolph, "Speakes Aims Final Salvo at White House Practices," *Washington Post*, January 31, 1987, A3.

53. George C. Edwards III, Andrew Barrett, and Jeffrey S. Peake, "The Legislative Impact of Divided Government," *American Journal of Political Science* 41 (April 1997): 545–563.

54. David R. Mayhew, *Divided We Govern* (New Haven, CT: Yale University Press, 1991).

Chapter 14

1. Aaron Wildavsky and Naomi Caiden, *The New Politics of the Budgetary Process*, 4th ed. (New York: Longman, 2001), 2.

2. Quoted in Gerald Carson, *The Golden Egg: The Personal Income Tax, Where It Came From, How It Grew* (Boston: Houghton Mifflin, 1977), 12.

3. Statistics on the number of returns and audits come from the U.S. Department of Commerce, *Statistical Abstract of the United States, 2003* (Washington, D.C.: U.S. Government Printing Office, 2004), 330.

4. Tax Foundation, 2004.

5. An exception is Robert Eisner, who argues that if the government counted its debt as families and business firms do—that is, by balancing assets against liabilities—the government would be in pretty good shape. See *How Real Is the Federal Deficit?* (New York: Free Press, 1986).

6. Carson, *The Golden Egg*, 181–182.

7. For some perspectives on the rise of government expenditures, see David Cameron, "The Expansion of the Public Economy: A Comparative Analysis," *American Political Science Review* 72 (December 1978): 1,243–1,261; and William D. Berry and David Lowery, *Understanding United States Government Growth* (New York: Praeger, 1987).

8. E. E. Schattschneider, *Two Hundred Million Americans in Search of a Government* (New York: Holt, Rinehart and Winston, 1969), 29–30.

9. Berry and Lowery, *Understanding United States Government Growth*.

10. Paul Light, *Artful Work: The Politics of Social Security Reform* (New York: HarperCollins, 1992), 82.

11. Aaron Wildavsky and Naomi Caiden, *The New Politics of the Budgetary Process*, 3rd ed. (New York: Longman, 1997), 45.

12. John R. Gist, *Mandatory Expenditures and the Defense Sector* (Beverly Hills, CA: Russell Sage Foundation, 1974).

13. Paul R. Schulman, "Nonincremental Policymaking: Notes Toward an Alternative

Paradigm," *American Political Science Review* 69 (December 1975): 1,354–1,370.

14. A good description of budgetary strategies is in Wildavsky and Caiden, *The New Politics of the Budgetary Process*, chap. 3.

15. *Ibid.*, 2.

16. For a discussion of the ways in which bureaucracies manipulate benefits to gain advantage with members of Congress, see Douglas Arnold, *Congress and the Bureaucracy* (New Haven, CT: Yale University Press, 1979); and the articles in Barry S. Rundquist, ed., *Political Benefits* (Lexington, MA: D.C. Heath, 1980).

17. A good review of the formation of the executive budget is Howard E. Schuman, *Politics and the Budget*, 3rd ed. (Englewood Cliffs, NJ: Prentice-Hall, 1992), chap. 2.

18. An important work on congressional budget making is Wildavsky and Caiden, *The New Politics of the Budgetary Process*.

19. Allen Meltzer and Scott F. Richard, "Why the Government Grows (and Grows) in a Democracy," *The Public Interest* 52 (Summer 1978): 117.

20. See James D. Savage, *Balanced Budgets and American Politics* (Ithaca, NY: Cornell University Press, 1988) for a study of the influence the principle of budget balancing has had on politics and public policy from the earliest days of U.S. history.

Chapter 15

1. This example is based on Allan Freedman, "Battles Over Jurisdiction Likely To Block Merger of Agencies," *Congressional Quarterly Weekly Report* (May 30, 1998), 1,440.

2. H. H. Gerth and C. Wright Mills, *From Max Weber: Essays in Sociology* (New York: Oxford University Press, 1958), chap. 8.

3. See Charles T. Goodsell, *The Case for Bureaucracy*, 4th ed. (Chatham, NJ: Chatham House, 2004), chap. 2. See also Daniel Katz et al., *Bureaucratic Encounters* (Ann Arbor: Institute for Social Research, University of Michigan, 1975).

4. See Paul C. Light, *The True Size of Government* (Washington, D.C.: Brookings Institution, 1999), 1, 44.

5. U.S. Department of Commerce, *Statistical Abstract of the United States, 2003* (Washington, D.C.: U.S. Government Printing Office, 2004), 336; Office of Personnel Management, *The Factbook, 2003 Edition* (Washington, D.C.: U.S. Government Printing Office, 2004), 8.

6. See Herbert Kaufman, *Red Tape* (Washington, D.C.: Brookings Institution, 1977).

7. See Goodsell, *The Case for Bureaucracy*, 48–54.

8. *Ibid.*, chap. 5.

9. Hugh M. Heclo, *A Government of Strangers: Executive Politics in Washington* (Washington, D.C.: Brookings Institution, 1977).

10. On the transient nature of presidential appointees, see G. Calvin Mackenzie, ed., *The In-and-Outers* (Baltimore: Johns Hopkins University Press, 1987).

11. On the independent regulatory agencies, see the classic work by Marver Bernstein, *Regulating Business by Independent Commission* (Princeton, NJ: Princeton University Press, 1955). See also, on regulation, James Q. Wilson, ed., *The Politics of Regulation* (New York: Basic Books, 1980); and A. Lee Fritschler and Bernard H. Ross, *Business Regulation and Government Decision-Making* (Cambridge, MA: Winthrop, 1980).

12. Bernstein, *Regulating Business*, 90. For a partial test of the capture theory that finds the theory not altogether accurate, see John P. Plumlee and Kenneth J. Meier, "Capture and Rigidity in Regulatory Administration," in *The Policy Cycle*, Judith May and Aaron Wildavsky, eds. (Beverly Hills, CA: Russell Sage Foundation, 1978). Another critique of the capture theory is Paul J. Quirk, *Industry Influence in Federal Regulatory Agencies* (Princeton, NJ: Princeton University Press, 1981).

13. George C. Edwards III, *Implementing Public Policy* (Washington, D.C.: Congressional Quarterly Press, 1980), 1.

14. Eugene Bardach, *The Implementation Game* (Cambridge, MA: The M.I.T. Press, 1977), 85; and Robert L. Lineberry, *American Public Policy: What Government Does and What Difference It Makes* (New York: Harper & Row, 1977), 71. Clausewitz called war "the continuation of politics by other means."

15. Lineberry, *American Public Policy*, 70–71.

16. For another dramatic example, see Martha Derthick, *New Towns In-Town* (Washington, D.C.: The Urban Institute Press, 1972).

17. Bardach, *The Implementation Game*, 250–251.

18. A good discussion of how policymakers ignored the administrative capacity of one important agency when assigning it new responsibilities can be found in Martha Derthick, *Agency Under Stress* (Washington, D.C.: Brookings Institution, 1990).

19. The implementation of the athletics policy is well documented in two articles by Cheryl M. Fields in the *Chronicle of Higher Education*, December 11 and 18, 1978, on which this account relies.

20. James Q. Wilson, *Bureaucracy* (New York: Basic Books, 1989), 158.

21. *Report of the DOD Commission on Beirut International Airport Terrorist Act, October 23, 1983*, December 20, 1983, 133.

22. Quoted in M. S. Eccles, *Beckoning Frontiers* (New York: Knopf, 1951), 336.

23. On administrative discretion, see Gary S. Bryner, *Bureaucratic Discretion* (New York: Pergamon Press, 1987).

24. Gerald Carson, *The Golden Egg* (Boston: Houghton Mifflin, 1977), 10. The examples given in this paragraph are from Carson.

25. Michael Lipsky, *Street-Level Bureaucracy* (New York: Russell Sage Foundation, 1980).

26. Quoted in Seymour Hersh, *The Price of Power: Kissinger in the Nixon White House* (New York: Summit, 1983), 235–236.

27. Albert Gore, *From Red Tape to Results: Creating a Government That Works Better and Costs Less* (New York: Times Books, 1993), 11.

28. For a careful analysis of efforts to reorganize the federal bureaucracy, see Peri E. Arnold, *Making the Managerial Presidency*, 2nd ed. (Princeton, NJ: Princeton University Press, 1996).

29. On the implementation and impact of the Voting Rights Act, see Charles S. Bullock III and Harrell R. Rodgers, Jr., *Law and Social Change: Civil Rights Laws and Their Consequences* (New York: McGraw-Hill, 1972), chap. 2; Richard Scher and James Button, "Voting Rights Act: Implementation and Impact," in *Implementation of Civil Rights Policy*, ed. C. S. Bullock and C. M. Lamb (Monterey, CA: Brooks/Cole, 1984), chap. 2; and Abigail M. Thernstrom, *Whose Votes Count?* (Cambridge, MA: Harvard University Press, 1987).

30. Based on a more elaborate account by James Worsham, "A Typical Day Is Full of Rules," *Chicago Tribune*, July 12, 1981, 1ff, with updating by the authors.

31. See Martha Derthick and Paul J. Quirk, *The Politics of Deregulation* (Washington, D.C.: Brookings Institution, 1985).

32. See, for example, Susan J. Tolchin and Martin J. Tolchin, *Dismantling America: The Rush To Deregulate* (New York: Oxford University Press, 1983).

33. Evan J. Ringquist, "Does Regulation Matter? Evaluating the Effects of State Air Pollution Control Programs," *Journal of Politics* 55 (November 1993): 1,022–1,045.

34. Michael Lewis-Beck and John Alford, "Can Government Regulate Safety? The Coal Mine Example," *American Political Science Review* 74 (September 1980): 745–756.

35. Paul Sabatier and Dan Mazmanian, *Can Regulation Work? Implementation of the 1972 California Coastal Initiative* (New York: Plenum, 1983).

36. Gary Copeland and Kenneth J. Meier, "Gaining Ground: The Impact of Medicaid and WIC on Infant Mortality," *American Politics Quarterly* 15 (April 1987): 254–273.

37. See B. Dan Wood and Richard W. Waterman, *Bureaucratic Dynamics: The Role of Bureaucracy in a Democracy* (Boulder, CO: Westview, 1994).

38. A good work on this point is Richard P. Nathan, *The Administrative Presidency* (New York: Wiley, 1983).

39. See Kenneth R. Mayer, *With the Stroke of a Pen, Executive Orders and Presidential Power* (Princeton, NJ: Princeton University Press, 2001); William G. Howell, *Power Without Persuasion* (Princeton, NJ: Princeton University Press, 2003).

40. Andrew B. Whitford and Jeff Yates, "Policy Signals and Executive Governance: Presi-

dential Rhetoric in the War on Drugs," *Journal of Politics* 65 (November 2003): 995–1,012.

41. Morris Fiorina, *Congress: Keystone of the Washington Establishment*, 2nd ed. (New Haven, CT: Yale University Press, 1989).

42. Richard A. Rettig, *Cancer Crusade* (Princeton, NJ: Princeton University Press, 1977).

43. Hugh M. Heclo, "Issue Networks and the Executive Establishment," in *The New American Political System*, Anthony King, ed. (Washington, D.C.: American Enterprise Institute, 1978), 87–124. See also William P. Browne and Won K. Paik, "Beyond the Domain: Recasting Network Politics in the Postreform Congress," *American Journal of Political Science* 37 (November 1993): 1,054–1,078; and John P. Heinz, Edward O. Laumann, Robert L. Nelson, and Robert L. Salisbury, *The Hollow Core: Private Interests in National Policy Making* (Cambridge, MA: Harvard University Press, 1993).

44. Frank R. Baumgartner and Bryan D. Jones, *Agendas and Instability in American Politics* (Chicago: University of Chicago Press, 1993).

45. *Ibid.*

Chapter 16

1. Quoted in Lawrence C. Baum, *The Supreme Court*, 4th ed. (Washington, D.C.: Congressional Quarterly Press, 1992), 72.

2. Administrative Office of the United States Courts.

3. Sarah Binder and Forrest Maltzman, "The Limits of Senatorial Courtesy," *Legislative Studies Quarterly* 29 (February 2004): 5–22.

4. Quoted in J. Woodford Howard, Jr., *Courts of Appeals in the Federal Judicial System: A Study of the Second, Fifth, and District of Columbia Circuits* (Princeton, NJ: Princeton University Press, 1981), 101.

5. Lauren Cohen Bell, "Senatorial Discourtesy: The Senate's Use of Delay To Shape the Federal Judiciary," *Political Research Quarterly* 55 (September 2002): 589–607.

6. See Gary King, "Presidential Appointments to the Supreme Court: Adding Systematic Explanation to Probabilistic Description," *American Politics Quarterly* 15 (July 1987): 373–386.

7. Charles R. Shipan and Megan L. Shannon, "Delaying Justice(s): A Duration Analysis of Supreme Court Confirmations," *American Journal of Political Science* 47 (October 2003): 654–668.

8. Quoted in Nina Totenberg, "Will Judges Be Chosen Rationally?" *Judicature* 60 (August/September 1976): 93.

9. See John Schmidhauser, *Judges and Justices: The Federal Appellate Judiciary* (Boston: Little, Brown, 1978).

10. One study found, however, that judicial experience is not related to the congruence of presidential preferences and the justices' decisions on racial equality cases. See John Gates and Jeffrey Cohen, "Presidents, Supreme Court Justices, and Racial Equality Cases: 1954–1984," *Political Behavior* 10 (November 1, 1988): 22–35.

11. On the importance of ideology and partisanship considerations in judicial retirement and resignation decisions, see Deborah J. Barrow and Gary Zuk, "An Institutional Analysis of Turnover in the Lower Federal Courts, 1900–1987," *Journal of Politics* 52 (May 1990): 457–476.

12. Quoted in Henry J. Abraham, *Justices and Presidents: A Political History of Appointments to the Supreme Court*, 3rd ed. (New York: Oxford University Press, 1992), 266.

13. *Ibid.*, 70.

14. See, for example, the important role that African-American support played in the confirmation of Clarence Thomas even though he was likely to vote against the wishes of leading civil rights organizations. L. Marvin Overby, Beth M. Henschen, Julie Walsh, and Michael H. Strauss, "Courting Constituents: An Analysis of the Senate Confirmation Vote on Justice Clarence Thomas," *American Political Science Review* 86 (December 1992): 997–1,003.

15. On the impact of the background of members of the judiciary, see Robert A. Carp and C. K. Rowland, *Policymaking and Politics in the Federal District Courts* (Knoxville: University of Tennessee Press, 1983); Thomas G. Walker and Deborah J. Barrow, "The Diversification of the Federal Bench: Policy and Process Ramifications," *Journal of Politics* 47 (May 1985): 596–617; and C. Neal Tate, "Personal Attribute Models of the Voting Behavior of United States Supreme Court Justices: Liberalism in Civil Liberties and Economics Decisions, 1946–1978," *American Political Science Review* 75 (June 1981): 355–367.

16. Quoted in Nina Totenberg, "Behind the Marble, Beneath the Robes," *New York Times Magazine*, March 16, 1975, 37.

17. H. W. Perry, Jr., *Deciding To Decide: Agenda Setting in the United States Supreme Court* (Cambridge, MA: Harvard University Press, 1991); Doris Marie Provine, *Case Selection in the United States Supreme Court* (Chicago: University of Chicago Press, 1980); and Stuart H. Teger and Douglas Kosinski, "The Cue Theory of Supreme Court Certiorari Jurisdiction: A Reconsideration," *Journal of Politics* 42 (August 1980): 834–846.

18. Sidney Ulmer, "The Supreme Court's Certiorari Decisions: Conflict as a Predictive Variable," *American Political Science Review* (December 1984): 901–911.

19. On the solicitor general's *amicus* briefs, see Rebecca E. Deen, Joseph Ignagni, and James Meernik, "Executive Influence on the U.S. Supreme Court: Solicitor General *Amicus* Cases, 1953–1997," *American Review of Politics* 22 (Spring 2001): 3–26; and Timothy R. Johnson, "The Supreme Court, the Solicitor General, and the Separation of Powers," *American Politics Research* 31 (July 2001): 426–451.

20. See Rebecca Mae Salokar, *The Solicitor General* (Philadelphia: Temple University Press, 1992).

21. Each year, data on Supreme Court decisions can be found in the November issue of the *Harvard Law Review*.

22. A useful look at attorneys practicing before the Supreme Court is Kevin McGuire, *The Supreme Court Bar: Legal Elites in the Washington Community* (Charlottesville: University Press of Virginia, 1993).

23. See, for example, Forrest Maltzman and Paul J. Wahlbeck, "Strategic Policy Considerations and Voting Fluidity on the Burger Court," *American Political Science Review* 90 (September 1996): 581–592; Paul J. Wahlbeck, James F. Spriggs II, and Forrest Maltzman, "Marshalling the Court: Bargaining and Accommodation on the United States Supreme Court," *American Journal of Political Science* 42 (January 1998): 294–315; James F. Spriggs II, Forrest Maltzman, and Paul J. Wahlbeck, "Bargaining on the U.S. Supreme Court: Justices' Responses to Majority Opinion Drafts," *Journal of Politics* 61 (May 1999): 485–506.

24. A. P. Blaustein and A. H. Field, "Overruling Opinions in the Supreme Court," *Michigan Law Review* 57, no. 2 (1957): 151; David H. O'Brien, *Constitutional Law and Politics*, 3rd ed. (W.W. Norton, 1997), 38.

25. See, for example, Jeffrey A. Segal and Harold J. Spaeth, *The Supreme Court and the Attitudinal Model* (Cambridge: Cambridge University Press, 1993); Jeffrey A. Segal and Albert O. Cover, "Ideological Values and the Votes of U.S. Supreme Court Justices," *American Political Science Review* 83 (June 1989): 557–566; Tracey E. George and Lee Epstein, "On the Nature of Supreme Court Decision Making," *American Political Science Review* 86 (June 1992): 323–337; and Jeffrey A. Segal and Harold J. Spaeth, "The Influence of *Stare Decisis* on the Votes of United States Supreme Court Justices," *American Journal of Political Science* 40 (November 1996): 971–1,003.

26. Doris Graber, *Mass Media and American Politics*, 6th ed. (Washington, D.C.: Congressional Quarterly Press, 2002), 312–313.

27. Charles A. Johnson and Bradley C. Canon, *Judicial Policies: Implementation and Impact*, 2nd ed. (Washington, D.C.: Congressional Quarterly Press, 1999), chap. 1. See also James F. Spriggs II, "The Supreme Court and Federal Administrative Agencies: A Resource-Based Theory and Analysis of Judicial Impact," *American Journal of Political Science* 40 (November 1996): 1,122–1,151.

28. See Richard L. Pacelle, Jr. and Lawrence Baum, "Supreme Court Authority in the Judiciary," *American Politics Quarterly* 20 (April 1992): 169–191; and Donald R. Songer, Jeffrey A. Segal, and Charles M. Cameron, "The Hierarchy of Justice: Testing a Principal-Agent Model of Supreme Court-Circuit Court Interactions," *American Journal of Political Science* 38 (August 1994): 673–696.

29. However, see Gerald N. Rosenberg, *The Hollow Hope: Can Courts Bring About Social Change?* (Chicago: University of Chicago Press, 1991); Rosenberg questions whether courts have brought about much social change.

30. For an excellent overview of the Warren period by former Watergate special prosecutor and Harvard law professor Archibald Cox, see *The Warren Court* (Cambridge, MA: Harvard University Press, 1968).

31. William Rehnquist, "The Notion of a Living Constitution," in *Views from the Bench*, ed. Mark W. Cannon and David M. O'Brien (Chatham, NJ: Chatham House, 1985), 129. One study found, however, that judicial experience is not related to the congruence of presidential preferences and the justices' decisions on racial equality cases. See John Gates and Jeffrey Cohen, "Presidents, Supreme Court Justices, and Racial Equality Cases: 1954–1984," *Political Behavior* 10 (November 1, 1988): 22–35.

32. Richard Funston, "The Supreme Court and Critical Elections," *American Political Science Review* 69 (1975): 810; John B. Gates, *The Supreme Court and Partisan Realignment* (Boulder, CO: Westview, 1992); Thomas R. Marshall, "Public Opinion, Representation, and the Modern Supreme Court," *American Politics Quarterly* 16 (July 1988): 296–316; William Mishler and Reginald S. Sheehan, "The Supreme Court as a Countermajoritarian Institution? The Impact of Public Opinion on Supreme Court Decisions," *American Political Science Review* 87 (March 1993): 87–101; William Mishler and Reginald S. Sheehan, "Public Opinion, the Attitudinal Model, and Supreme Court Decision Making: A Micro-Analytic Perspective," *Journal of Politics* 58 (February 1996): 169–200; Roy B. Flemming and B. Dan Wood, "The Public and the Supreme Court: Individual Justice Responsiveness to American Policy Moods," *American Journal of Political Science* 41 (April 1997): 468–498; Kevin T. McGuire and James A. Stimson, "The Least Dangerous Branch: New Evidence on Supreme Court Responsiveness to Public Preferences," *Journal of Politics* 66 (November 2004): 1018–1035.

33. Mario Bergara, Barak Richman, and Pablo T. Spiller, "Modeling Supreme Court Strategic Decision Making: The Congressional Constraint," *Legislative Studies Quarterly* 28 (May 2003) 247–280.

34. David G. Barnum, "The Supreme Court and Public Opinion: Judicial Decision Making in the Post-New Deal Period," *Journal of Politics* 47 (May 1985): 652–662.

35. Gregory A. Caldeira and John R. Wright, "Organized Interests and Agenda Setting in the U.S. Supreme Court," *American Political Science Review* 82 (December 1988): 1,109–1,128.

36. On group use of the litigation process, see Karen Orren, "Standing To Sue: Interest Group Conflict in the Federal Courts," *American Political Science Review* 70 (September 1976): 723–742; Karen O'Connor and Lee Epstein, "The Rise of Conservative Interest Group Litigation," *Journal of Politics* 45 (May 1983): 479–489; and Lee Epstein and C. K. Rowland, "Debunking the Myth of Interest Group Invincibility in the Courts," *American Political Science Review* 85 (March 1991): 205–217.

37. "Federalist No. 78" in Hamilton, Madison, and Jay, *The Federalist Papers.*

38. Examples of judicial activism are reported in a critical assessment of judicial intervention by Donald Horowitz, *The Courts and Social Policy* (Washington, D.C.: Brookings Institution, 1977).

39. William N. Eskridge, "Overriding Supreme Court Statutory Interpretation Decisions," *Yale Law Journal* 101 (1991): 331–455; and Joseph Ignagni and James Meernik, "Explaining Congressional Attempts To Reverse Supreme Court Decisions," *Political Research Quarterly* 10 (June 1994): 353–372. See also R. Chep Melnick, *Between the Lines: Interpreting Welfare Rights* (Washington, D.C.: Brookings Institution, 1994).

Chapter 17

1. Electrolux press release, "Electrolux Will Close Refrigerator Factory in US," January 16, 2004.

2. "Americans on Globalization, Trade and Farm Subsidies," Program on International Policy Attitudes, University of Maryland, January 22, 2004, 14.

3. "500 Largest U.S. Corporations," *Fortune*, April 14, 2003, F–1.

4. "The World's Billionaires," *Forbes*, March 15, 2004, 91f.

5. "The Wal-Mart You Don't Know," *Fast Company* 77 (December 2003): 68f.

6. Greg Schneider and Din El Boghdady, "Stores Follow Wal-Mart's Lead in Labor," *Washington Post*, November 6, 2003, A1.

7. These data are from C. Fred Bergsten, director of the Institute for International Economics, writing in *Foreign Affairs* (March/April, 2004), 89.

8. "The Long Arm of Bentonville Arkansas," *Business Week*, October 6, 2003, 103.

9. Jeffrey Garten, "Wal-Mart Gives Globalization a Bad Name," *Business Week*, March 8, 2004, 24.

10. "The Wal-Martization of America," the *New York Times*, November 15, 2003, A12.

11. Although political folklore recounts the sign as "It's the economy, stupid," the sign on a white board stuck to a pillar in the middle of the room actually said

    Change vs. More of the Same.
    The economy, stupid.
    Don't forget health care.

    George Stephanopoulos, *All Too Human: A Political Education* (Boston: Little, Brown, 1999), 88.

12. *Ibid.*

13. Brad T. Gomez and J. Matthew Wilson, "Political Sophistication and Economic Voting in the American Electorate: A Theory of Heterogeneous Attribution," *American Journal of Political Science* 45 (October 2001): 899.

14. Robert S. Erikson, Matthew MacKuen, and James L. Stimson, *The Macro Polity* (New York: Cambridge University Press, 2002), 59.

15. Gomez and Wilson, "Political Sophistication and Economic Voting in the American Electorate."

16. For a summary of economic conditions and voting choice, see Michael S. Lewis-Beck and Mary Stegmaier, "Economic Determinants of Electoral Outcomes," *Annual Review of Political Science* (Palo Alto, CA: Annual Reviews, 2000):183–219.

17. Erikson, MacKuen, and Stimson, *The Macro Polity*, 445.

18. Benjamin I. Page and Robert Y. Shapiro, *The Rational Public: Fifty Years of Trends in America's Policy Preferences* (Chicago: University of Chicago Press, 1992), 122.

19. See the Bureau of Labor Statistics, "Frequently Asked Questions" about the CPI at their website, www.bls.gov/cpi.

20. See William Greider, *Secrets of the Temple: How the Federal Reserve Runs the Country* (New York: Simon & Schuster, 1987); Nathaniel Beck, "Elections and the Fed: Is There a Political Monetary Cycle?" *American Journal of Political Science* 31 (February 1987): 194–216; and Manabu Saeki, "Explaining Federal Reserve Monetary Policy," *Review of Policy Research* 19 (Summer 2002): 129–150.

21. *Franklin Delano Roosevelt: Champion of Freedom* (New York: Public Affairs Press, 2003), 1,133–1,134.

22. *The President and the Parties* (New York: Oxford University Press, 1993), 263.

23. *Ibid.*

24. The classic supply-side theory can be found in George Gilder, *Wealth and Poverty* (New York: Basic Books, 1981).

25. John W. Sloan, *The Reagan Effect: Economics and Presidential Leadership* (Lawrence: University Press of Kansas, 1999), 63.

26. "A Phony Jobs Debate," *Washington Post*, February 25, 2004, A25.

27. The most ardent proponent of this view is Edward Tufte. See his *Political Control of the Economy* (Princeton, NJ: Princeton University Press, 1978).

28. In 12 elections studied by Erikson, MacKuen, and Stimson, real income growth grew in a strict linear pattern, rather than in a short spurt, just before the election. *Macro Policy*, 248.

29. The standard and very readable book on globalization is Daniel Yergin and Joseph Stanislaw, *The Commanding Heights* (New York: Touchstone, 2002). See also Benjamin Barber, *Jihad vs. McWorld: How Globalism and Tribalism Are Reshaping the World* (New York: Ballentine, 1996).

30. These items come from Timothy Taylor, "The Truth about Globalization," *The Public Interest* 147 (Spring 2002), 25.

31. Beth A. Simmons and Zachary Elkins, "The Globalization of Liberalization," *American Political Science Review*, 98 (February 2004): 171.

32. Henwood, *After the New Economy*, 159.

33. "Globalization of IT Services and White Collar Jobs: The Next Wave of Productivity Growth," Washington: Institute for International Economics, 2004.

34. Wendy L. Hansen and Neil J. Mitchell, "Disaggregating and Explaining Corporate Political Activity: Domestic and Foreign Corporations in National Politics," *American Political Science Review* 94 (December 2000): 891.

35. Carol Graham, Robert Litan, and Sandip Sukhtankar, "The Bigger They Are, the Harder They Fall: An Estimate of the Costs of the Crisis in Corporate Governance," Washington, D.C.: Brooking Institution Working Papers, August 30, 2002.

Chapter 18

1. Elizabeth Warren and Amelia Warrant Tyagi, *The Two Income Trap: Why Middle Class Mothers and Fathers Are Going Broke* (New York: Basic Books, 2003).

2. David K. Shipler, *The Working Poor: Invisible in America* (New York: Knopf, 2004).

3. On the decline of social insurance in the United States, see Jacob S. Hacker, "Privatizing Risk Without Privatizing the Welfare State: The Hidden Politics of Social Policy Retrenchment in the United States," *American Political Science Review* 98 (May 2004): 243–260.

4. John Leland, "Why America Sees the Silver Lining," The *New York Times*, June 13, 2004.

5. Martin Gilens, *Why Americans Hate Welfare* (Chicago: University of Chicago Press, 2000), 16.

6. Stanley Feldman and Marco R. Steenbergen, "The Humanitarian Foundation of Public Support for Social Welfare," *American Journal of Political Science* 45 (July 2001): 658–677.

7. Alan Weil and Kenneth Finegold, "Introduction," in Weil and Finegold, eds. (Washington, D.C.: The Urban Institute Press, 2002), xiii.

8. Andrew Hacker, *Money: Who Has How Much and Why* (New York: Scribner, 1997), 52.

9. Nolan McCarty, Keith T. Poole, and Howard Rosenthal, *Income Distribution and the Realignment of American Politics* (Washington, D.C.: American Enterprise Institute, 1977), 1.

10. An economic analysis and explanation of the workings of the old adage can be found in Thomas Piketty and Emmanuel Saez, "Income Inequality in the United States 1913–1998," *Quarterly Journal of Economics* 113 (February 2003): 1–39.

11. Arthur Kennickell, "A Rolling Tide; Changes in the Distribution of Wealth in the United States, 1989–2001," Federal Reserve Board, May 3, 2003.

12. *Forbes*, "The World's Richest People," special issue, March 15, 2004.

13. Merrill Lynch, "Merrill Lynch and Cap Gemini Ernst & Young Report Increase in Ranks of Wealthy," press release, June 6, 2004.

14. Mark R. Rank and Thomas A. Hirschl, "Rags or Riches? Estimating the Probabilities of Poverty and Affluence Across the Adult American Life Span," *Social Science Quarterly* 82 (December 2001): 651–669.

15. *Nickel and Dimed: On (Not) Getting By in America* (New York: Owl Books, 2002).

16. See Shipler, *The Working Poor*.

17. Harrell Rodgers, *Poor Women, Poor Children*, 3rd ed. (New York: M. E. Sharpe, 1996).

18. Harrell Rodgers, *American Poverty in a New Era of Reform* (New York: M. E. Sharpe, 2000), 207.

19. Christopher Jencks, *Rethinking Social Policy* (New York: Harper Collins, 1992), 130.

20. "The Real State of the Budget," *Atlantic Magazine* (January/February 2003): 81.

21. Brookings Institution, *Rewarding Work*, June 2001.

22. See, for example, Francis Fox Piven and Richard Cloward, *Regulating the Poor* (New York: Pantheon, 1971). For an empirical analysis of theories of the rise of welfare, which finds some support for the Piven and Cloward thesis, see Richard Fording, "The Political Response to Black Insurgency: A Critical Test of Competing Theories of the State," *American Political Science Review* 95 (March 2001): 115–130.

23. Charles Murray, *Losing Ground: American Social Policy, 1950–1980* (New York: Basic Books, 1984). Marvin Olasky, the guru of "compassionate conservatism," makes a similar argument in his *Tragedy of Human Compassion* (Chicago: Regnery, 1992). Doing good for people, especially through government, Olasky argues, is bad for them. For a contrary argument, see Benjamin Page and James R. Simmons, *What Government Can Do: Dealing With Poverty and Inequality* (Chicago: University of Chicago, 2000).

24. Gilens, *Why Americans Hate Welfare*.

25. Martin Gilens, "Race Coding and White Opposition to Welfare," *American Political Science Review* 90 (December 1996): 593–604.

26. *Why Americans Hate Welfare*, chap. 5

27. These data are from Harrell Rodgers, "Making Work Really Work," paper presented at the Annual Meetings of the American Political Science Association, August 28–September 1, 2002. The Department of Health and Human Services provides annual data on trends in work and welfare at its "TANF" website, the source for the 2002 data.

28. Rebecca Blank, "Fighting Poverty: Lessons from Recent U.S. History," *Journal of Economic Perspectives* 14 (Spring 2000): 3–20.

29. Sylvester J. Schieber and John B. Shoven, *The Real Deal: The History and Future of Social Security* (New Haven. CT: Yale University Press, 1999), chap. 7. The Ida May Fuller story is also from Schieber and Shoven.

29. The math on Social Security is from the President's Commission to Strengthen Social Security, *Interim Report*, August 2001, 13.

30. Worse, President Bush's Commission to Strengthen Social Security argues that in about 2016, the Social Security Commission will have to begin calling in its IOUs from the Federal Treasury, or cashing in its bonds. Social Security funds are not kept in what politicians have come to call a "lockbox." In 2016, Social Security claims would compete for regular budget dollars against national defense, homeland security, school aid, and other federal expenditures. See their *Interim Report*, August 2001.

31. For one rare but dissenting view, which argues that the Social Security "crisis" is exaggerated, partly by people who would profit from more private investment, see Dean Baker and Mark Weisbrot, *Social Security: The Phony Crisis* (Chicago: University of Chicago Press, 2000).

32. Thomas Frank, "The Trillion Dollar Hustle: Hello Wall Street, Goodbye Social Security," *Harper's*, January 2002.

33. Greg Hitt, "Social Security Plan Stalls," *Wall Street Journal*, July 23, 2002, A4.

34. Political scientist Benjamin Radcliff developed some empirical data to show that the extent of government welfare provisions is in fact positively related to people's sense of well-being from country to country. See his "Politics, Markets and Life Satisfaction: The Political Economy of Human Happiness," *American Political Science Review* 95 (December 2001): 939–952.

35. Anne Schneider and Helen Ingram, "The Social Construction of Target Populations," *American Political Science Review* 87 (1993): 334–347.

Chapter 19

1. The background on Carl Moore and the Canadian issue is from *www.businessweekonline.com*. November 17, 2003.

2. The FDA case is *United States of America v. Rx Depot*, November 6, 2003.

3. World Health Organization, "WHO Issues New Healthy Life Expectancy Ranking," press release, June 4, 2000.

4. Douglas Holtz-Eakin, CBO Testimony before the Committee on Health, Education, Labor, and Pensions, United States Senate, January 28, 2004.

5. Gina Kolata, "More May Not Mean Better in Health Care, Studies Find," The *New York Times*, July 21, 2002, 1.

6. *Annual Report of the President's Council of Economic Advisors, 2004,* 202. The CEA reports that 43.6 million people were uninsured *at some point* in 2001—15.2 percent of the population. Only about 21–31 million, though were uninsured *the entire year.*

7. Lucette Lagnado, "Uninsured and Ill, a Woman Is Forced To Ration Her Care," *Wall Street Journal,* November 12, 2002, 1.

8. Daniel Akst, "Why Do Employers Pay Health Insurance Anyway?" The *New York Times,* November 2, 2003, B4.

9. John Budetti et al., *Can't Afford To Get Sick: A Reality for Millions of Working Americans* (New York: Commonwealth Fund, 2000).

10. "Care Without Coverage," Institute of Medicine, May 2002, 6.

11. ABC/*Washington Post* poll, August 10, 2003.

12. On Medicare's future, see Ronald Lee and Jonathan Skinner, "Will Aging Baby Boomers Bust the Federal Budget?" *Journal of Economic Perspectives* 13 (Winter 1999): 117–140.

13. Roland Sturm, "The Effects of Obesity, Smoking and Drinking on Medical Problems and Costs," *Health Affairs* 21 (2002): 245–253.

14. Rob Stein, "Obesity Rivals Tobacco for Most US Deaths," *Washington Post,* March 9, 2004, 1.

15. Andrea Louise Campbell, "Self-Interest, Social Security, and the Distinctive Political Participation Patterns of Senior Citizens," *American Political Science Review* 96 (September 2002): 565–574.

16. The story of the Clinton health care plan is told in Theda Skocpol, *Boomerang: Health Care Reform and the Turn Against Government* (New York: Norton, 1996).

17. These survey data are reported by the Economic Policy Institute in its "Take the Pulse Report" at *www.epinet.org.*

18. Robin Marantz Henig, *Pandora's Baby: How the First Test Tube Babies Sparked the Reproductive Revolution* (New York: Houghton Mifflin, 2004). See also Andrea Bonnickson, *Crafting a Cloning Policy: From Dolly to Stem Cells* (Washington, D.C.: Georgetown University Press, 2002).

19. Robert Blank, *Rationing Medicine* (New York: Columbia University Press, 1988).

20. Howard M. Leichter, "The Poor and Managed Care in the Oregon Experience," *Journal of Health Politics, Policy and Law* 24 (October 1999): 1,172–1,184.

21. Bjorn Lomborg, *The Skeptical Environmentalist: Measuring the Real State of the World* (New York: Cambridge University Press, 2001).

22. See the January 2002 issue, 61f.

23. Robert Stavins, "What Can We Learn from the Grand Policy Experiment? Positive and Normative Lessons from SO2 Allowance Trading," *Journal of Economic Perspectives* 12 (Summer 1998) 69–88; see also A. Denny Ellerman et al., *Markets for Clean Air: The U.S. Acid Rain Program* (Cambridge, MA: Cambridge University Press, 2000).

24. *Economic Report of the President 2004,* chap. 9.

25. Samuel Hays, *Beauty, Health, Permanence* (New York: Cambridge University Press, 1987), 99.

26. On toxic waste and its politics, see John A. Hird, *Superfund: The Politics of Environmental Risk* (Baltimore: Johns Hopkins University Press, 1994).

27. Robert Caro, *The Years of Lyndon Johnson: The Path to Power* (New York: Knopf, 1982), 628–644.

28. A classic study of oil is Daniel Yergin, *The Prize: The Epic Quest for Oil, Money and Power* (New York: Simon and Shuster, 1991).

29. The global warming issue and the politics of climate are discussed in Lamont C. Hemple, "Climate Policy on the Installment Plan," in Norman J. Vig and Michael E. Kraft, eds., *Environmental Policy,* 5th ed. (Washington, D.C.: Congressional Quarterly, 2003), chap. 13.

30. Lomborg, *The Skeptical Environmentalist,* 318.

31. Program on International Policy Attitudes, University of Maryland, "Americans on Climate Change," June 25, 2004.

32. On environmental groups, see Christopher Bosso and Deborah Lynn Guber, "The Boundaries and Contours of American Environmentalism," in Kraft and Vig, eds., *Environmental Policy,* chap. 4. The data on group size are from Bosso and Guber.

33. *Ibid.,* 97.

Chapter 20

1. See, for example, Paul Kennedy, *The Rise and Fall of the Great Powers* (New York: Random House, 1987).

2. Raymond Vernon, *In the Hurricane's Eye: The Troubled Prospects of Multinational Enterprises* (Cambridge, MA: Harvard University Press, 1998); United Nations, *World Investment Report, 2003* (New York: United Nations, 2003).

3. I. M. Destler, "National Security Management: What Presidents Have Wrought," *Political Science Quarterly* 95 (Winter 1980–1981): 573–588.

4. Richard Betts, *Soldiers, Statesmen, and Cold War Crises* (Cambridge, MA: Harvard University Press, 1977), 216, table A.

5. For more on decision-making regarding the Gulf War, see Bob Woodward, *The Commanders* (New York: Simon & Schuster, 1991).

6. See Bob Woodward, *Veil: The Secret Wars of the CIA, 1981–1987* (New York: Simon & Schuster, 1987).

7. A good study of the role of Congress in setting U.S. foreign policy is James M. Lindsay, *Congress and the Politics of U.S. Foreign Policy* (Baltimore: Johns Hopkins University Press, 1994). Congress' role in the defense budget process is discussed in Ralph G. Carter, "Budgeting for Defense," in Paul E. Peterson, ed., *The President, Congress, and the Making of Foreign Policy* (Norman: University of Oklahoma Press, 1994).

8. Louis Fisher, "Executive-Legislative Revelations in Foreign Policy" (paper presented at the United States-Mexico Comparative Constitutional Law Conference, Mexico City, June 17, 1998), 1.

9. An excellent treatment of the origins of the Cold War is Daniel Yergin, *Shattered Peace: The Origins of the Cold War and the National Security State* (Boston: Houghton Mifflin, 1977).

10. The article was titled "Sources of Soviet Conduct" and appeared in *Foreign Affairs* (July 1947), under the pseudonym X.

11. Yergin, *Shattered Peace,* 268.

12. Seymour Melman, *Pentagon Capitalism: The Political Economy of War* (New York: McGraw-Hill, 1970).

13. Stanley Karnow, *Vietnam: A History* (New York: Penguin Books, 1983), 43. Karnow's book is one of the best of many excellent books on Vietnam. See also Frances Fitzgerald, *Fire in the Lake* (Boston: Little, Brown, 1972); and David Halberstam, *The Best and the Brightest* (New York: Random House, 1972).

14. Nicholas Lemann, "The Peacetime War," *Atlantic Monthly,* October 1984, 72.

15. Quoted in Andrew Rosenthal, "Striking a Defensive Tone, Bush Sees Virtue in Caution," the *New York Times,* February 8, 1990, A10.

16. *The National Security Strategy of the United States of America,* September 2002 (Washington, D.C.: Government Printing Office, 2002).

17. See Ivo H. Daalder and James M. Lindsay, *America Unbound: The Bush Revolution in Foreign Policy* (Washington, D.C.: Brookings Institution, 2003).

18. See, for example, Zbigniew Brzezinski, *The Choice: Global Domination or Global Leadership* (New York: Basic Books, 2004).

19. See, for example, Bruce Russett, "Defense Expenditures and National Well-Being," *American Political Science Review* 76 (December 1982): 767–777; William K. Domke, Richard C. Eichenberg, and Catherine M. Kelleher, "The Illusion of Choice: Defense and Welfare in Advanced Industrial Democracies, 1948–78," *American Political Science Review* 77 (March 1983): 19–35; and Alex Mintz, "Guns Versus Butter: A Disaggregated Analysis," *American Political Science Review* 83 (December 1989): 1,285–1,296.

20. Kennedy, *The Rise and Fall of the Great Powers*; and David Calleo, *Beyond American Hegemony: The Future of the Western Alliance* (New York: Basic Books, 1987). For a different view, see Joseph S. Nye, *Bound To Lead* (New York: Basic Books, 1990).

21. On the importance of ideology, see studies discussed in Robert A. Bernstein, *Elections, Representation, and Congressional Voting*

Behavior (Englewood Cliffs, NJ: Prentice-Hall, 1989), 70–76.

22. U.S. Department of Commerce, *Statistical Abstract of the United States, 2003* (Washington, D.C.: U.S. Government Printing Office, 2004), 347.

23. Stephen I. Schwartz, ed., *Atomic Audit: The Costs and Consequences of U.S. Nuclear Weapons Since 1940* (Washington, D.C.: Brookings Institution, 1998).

24. John E. Reilly, ed., *American Public Opinion and U.S. Foreign Policy 1999* (Chicago: Chicago Council on Foreign Relations, 1999).

25. Joseph S. Nye, Jr., *The Paradox of American Power: Why the World's Only Superpower Can't Go It Alone* (New York: Oxford University Press, 2002).

26. Stanley Hoffman, *Gulliver's Troubles, or the Setting of American Foreign Policy* (New York: McGraw-Hill, 1968).

27. Robert O. Keohane and Joseph S. Nye, *Power and Interdependence*, 2nd ed. (New York: HarperCollins, 1989), 27.

28. *Ibid.*, 27–28.

29. Joseph S. Nye, Jr., *Soft Power: The Means to Success in World Politics* (Cambridge, MA: Harvard University Press, 2004).

30. *Ibid.*, 3.

31. U.S. Department of Commerce, Bureau of the Census, 2004.

32. *Ibid.*

33. Carol C. Adelman, "The Privatization of Foreign Aid," *Foreign Affairs* 82 (November/December 2003): 9–14.

34. See Bruce M. Russett, *Controlling the Sword* (Cambridge, MA: Harvard University Press, 1990), chap. 5; Thomas Hartley and Bruce M. Russett, "Public Opinion and the Common Defense: Who Governs Military Spending in the United States?" *American Political Science Review* 86 (December 1992): 905–915; Bruce M. Russett, *Grasping the Democratic Peace* (Princeton, NJ: Princeton University Press, 1993); Spencer R. Weart, *Never at War* (New Haven: Yale University Press, 1998); Michael D. Ward and Kristian S. Gleditsch, "Democratizing Peace," *American Political Science Review* 92 (March 1998): 51–62; and Paul R. Hensel, Gary Foertz, and Paul F. Diehl, "The Democratic Peace and Rivalries," *Journal of Politics* 62 (November 2000): 1,173–1,188.

Chapter 21

1. Laura K. Donohue and Juliette N. Kayyem, "Federalism and the Battle Over Counterterrorist Law: State Sovereignty, Criminal Law Enforcement, and National Security," *Studies in Conflict & Terrorism*, 25 (2002): 1–18.

2. Luther H. Gulick, "Reorganization of the State," *Civil Engineering* (August 1933): 420–421.

3. James N. Miller, "Hamstrung Legislatures," *National Civic Review* (May 1965): 178–187.

4. Ann O' M. Bowman and Richard C. Kearney, *The Resurgence of the States* (Englewood Cliffs, NJ: Prentice-Hall, 1986). For other important statements of the improved capacity of state governments to undertake innovative action, see David Osborne, *Laboratories of Democracy* (Boston: Harvard Business School Press, 1988); David B. Walker, *The Rebirth of Federalism* (Chatham, NJ: Chatham House, 1995); and David M. Hedge, *Governance and the Changing American States* (Boulder, CO: Westview, 1998).

5. See Daniel J. Elazar, "The Principles and Traditions Underlying American State Constitutions," *Publius: The Journal of Federalism* 12 (Winter 1982): 11–25.

6. Mavis Mann Reeves, *The Question of State Government Capability* (Washington, D.C.: Advisory Commission on Intergovernmental Relations, 1985), 38.

7. Christopher W. Hammons, "Was James Madison Wrong? Rethinking the American Preference for Short, Framework-Oriented Constitutions," *American Political Science Review* 93 (December 1999): 837–850.

8. Initiative & Referendum Institute, *I & R Usage, 2000* (Washington, D.C.: Initiative & Referendum Institute, 2000).

9. The Council of State Governments, *The Book of the States, 2003 Edition* (Washington, D.C.: The Council of State Governments, 2004), 235.

10. Thomas M. Carsey, *Campaign Dynamics: The Race for Governor* (Ann Arbor: University of Michigan Press, 1999).

11. The Council of State Governments, *The Book of the States, 2003 Edition*, 176.

12. Thomas M. Carsey and Gerald C. Wright, "State and National Factors in Gubernatorial and Senatorial Elections." *American Journal of Political Science* 42 (July 1998): 994–1002.

13. Data provided by Sue O'Connell of the Institute on Money in State Politics, February 2003 and the Institute website at: *http://www.followthemoney.org/database/NationalOverview/index.p.html* (June 9, 2004).

14. Thomas M. Carsey, *Campaign Dynamics: The Race for Governor*, 1999.

15. Note that not all lower chambers of state legislatures are called the "House of Representatives," although most are; we refer to them as such in this chapter to avoid confusion. The Council of State Governments, *The Book of the States, 2003 Edition*, 108.

16. Alan Rosenthal, *The Decline of Representative Democracy: Process, Participation, and Power in State Legislatures* (Washington, D.C.: Congressional Quarterly Press, 1998).

17. Sarah McCally Morehouse and Malcolm E. Jewell, *State Politics, Parties, & Policy*, 2nd ed. (Lanham, MD: Rowman & Littlefield, 2003), 197–201.

18. Alan Rosenthal, *The Decline of Representative Democracy: Process, Participation, and Power in State Legislatures*, 1998, 179–180. Keith E. Hamm and Gary F. Moncrief, "Legislative Politics in the States," in *Politics in the American States*, 8th ed., Virginia Gray and Russell L. Hanson, eds. (Washington, D.C.: Congressional Quarterly Press, 2004), 168.

19. Sarah McCally Morehouse and Malcolm E. Jewell, *State Politics, Parties, & Policy*, 2nd ed. (2003), 199–200.

20. National Conference of State Legislatures, "NCSLnet: Democratic Share of Legislative Seats," January 21, 2003. Posted at *www.ncsl.org/ncsldb/elect98/partcomp.cfm?yearsel=2003* Denver National Conference of State Legislatures

21. Morris P. Fiorina, "Divided Government in the States," in *The Politics of Divided Government*, Gary Cox and Samuel Kernell, eds. (Boulder, CO: Westview, 1991).

22. John F. Bibby and Thomas M. Holbrook, "Parties and Elections," in *Politics in the American States*, 8th ed., Virginia Gray and Russell L. Hanson, eds. (Washington, D.C.: Congressional Quarterly Press, 2004), 86–92.

23. Keith E. Hamm and Gary F. Moncrief, "Legislative Politics in the States," in *Politics in the American States*, 7th ed., Virginia Gray, Russell L. Hanson, and Herbert Jacob, eds. (Washington, D.C.: Congressional Quarterly Press, 1999), 166.

24. Gary Moncrief, Richard G. Niemi, and Lynda W. Powell, "Time, Turnover and Term Limits: Trends in Membership Turnover in U.S. State Legislatures," Paper presented at the Annual State Politics and Policy Conference, Tucson, AZ, March 2003.

25. Keith E. Hamm and Gary F. Moncrief, "Legislative Politics in the States," in *Politics in the American States*, 8th ed., Denver National Conference of State Legislatures (2004), 172.

26. National Conference of State Legislatures, "Legislative Term Limits: An Overview," June 9, 2004. Posted at *http://www.ncsl.org/programs/legman/ABOUT/Termlimit.htm*

27. Alan Rosenthal, "The Legislature: Unraveling of Institutional Fabric," in *The State of the States*, 3rd ed., Carl E. Van Horn, ed. (Washington, D.C.: Congressional Quarterly Press, 1996), 128.

28. Gary Moncrief, Richard G. Niemi, and Lynda W. Powell, "Time, Turnover and Term Limits: Trends in Membership Turnover in U.S. State Legislatures," 17.

29. Charles E. Menifield, ed. *Representation of Minority Groups in the U.S.: Implications for the Twenty-First Century* (Lanham, MD: Austin & Winfield, 2001).

30. Center for American Women and Politics, "Women in Elected Office 2004: Fact Sheet Summaries," June 14, 2004. Posted at *http://www.cawp.rutgers.edu/Facts/Officeholders/cawpfs.html*

31. National Conference of State Legislatures, "Legislator Demographics," June 14, 2004. *http://www.ncsl.org/Programs/Legman/about/Demographic_Overview.htm*,

32. Nelson C. Dometrius, "Governors: Their Heritage and Future," in *American State and Local Politics: Directions for the 21st Century*,

Ronald E. Weber and Paul Brace, eds. (Chatham, NJ: Chatham House, 1999).

33. Thad Beyle, "The Governors," in Virginia Gray and Russell L. Hanson, eds., 8th ed., *Politics in the American States* (Washington, D.C.: Congressional Quarterly Press, 2004), 210–218.

34. Beyle, "Governors," 215–218.

35. Dennis Farney, "When Wisconsin Governor Wields Partial Veto, the Legislature Might as Well Go Play Scrabble," *Wall Street Journal*, (July 1, 1993).

36. Beyle, "Governors," 205–210.

37. Thomas M. Carsey, *Campaign Dynamics: The Race for Governor*, 1999.

38. Ann O' M. Bowman and Richard C. Kearney, *State and Local Government*, 4th ed. (Boston: Houghton-Mifflin, 1999), 203–204.

39. Associated Press, "Alabama Lt. Governor Finds Nothing To Do," the *New York Times* (February 17, 1999).

40. The Council of State Governments, *The Book of the States, 2003 Edition* (Washington, D.C.: The Council of State Governments, 2004), 199–208.

41. Kenneth J. Meier, "Executive Reorganization of Government: Impact on Employment and Expenditures," *American Journal of Political Science* 24 (1980): 396–412.

42. Hedge, *Governance and the Changing American States*, 111.

43. Alan Rosenthal, "The Legislative Institution: Transformed and At Risk," in *The State of the States*, Carl Van Horn, ed. (Washington, D.C.: Congressional Quarterly Press, 1989), 69.

44. Joel A. Thompson and Gary E. Moncrief, "The Evolution of the State Legislature: Institutional Change and Legislative Careers," in *Changing Patterns in State Legislative Careers*, Gary E. Moncrief and Joel A. Thompson, eds. (Ann Arbor: University of Michigan Press, 1992).

45. Christopher Z. Mooney, "Measuring U.S. State Legislative Professionalism: An Evaluation of Five Indices," *State and Local Government Review* 26 (Spring 1994): 70–71.

46. National Conference of State Legislatures, "Size of State Legislative Staff: 1979, 1988, 1996, and 2003—Permanent Staff (November 2003)," July 7, 2004. Posted at *http://www .ncsl.org/programs/legman/about/staffcount2003.htm*

47. Alan Rosenthal, *The Decline of Representative Democracy* (1998).

48. Peverill Squire, "Legislative Professionalization and Membership Diversity in State Legislatures, *Legislative Studies Quarterly* 17 (February 1992): 69–79.

49. Christopher Z. Mooney, "Citizens, Structures, and Sister States: Influences on State Legislative Professionalism," *Legislative Studies Quarterly* 20 (February 1995): 47–68.

50. Phillip W. Roeder, "State Legislative Reform: Determinants and Policy Consequences," *American Politics Quarterly* 7 (January 1979): 51–70; Morris P. Fiorina "Further Evidence of the Partisan Consequences of Legislative Professionalism," *American Journal of Political Science*, 43 (July 1999): 974–977.

51. James King, "Changes in Professionalism in U.S. State Legislatures," *Legislative Studies Quarterly* 25 (2000): 327–343.

52. Neal Kauder, "National State Court Caseload Trends, 1984–1993," *Caseload Highlights: Examining the Work of State Courts*, 1 (August 1995): 1–4.

53. Paul Brace, Melinda Gann Hall, and Laura Langer. "Placing State Supreme Courts in State Politics," *State Politics and Policy Quarterly* 1 (Spring 2001): 81–108.

54. Delaware, Maine, Mississippi, Montana, Nevada, New Hampshire, North Dakota, Rhode Island, South Dakota, Vermont, West Virginia, and Wyoming.

55. Melinda Gann Hall. "State Supreme Courts in American Democracy: Probing The Myths of Judicial Reform," *American Political Science Review* 95 (June 2001): 315–330.

56. Melinda Gann Hall, "State Supreme Courts in American Democracy: Probing the Myths of Judicial Reform."

57. Initiative & Referendum Institute, *Is the Initiative Process out of Control?* (Washington, D.C.: Initiative & Referendum Institute, 2004), *http://www.iandrinstitute.org/Usage.htm*

58. Elisabeth R. Gerber, "Legislative Response to the Threat of Popular Initiatives," *American Journal of Political Science* 40 (February 1996): 99–128.

59. Edward L. Lascher, Jr., Michael G. Hagen, and Steven A. Rochlin, "Gun Behind the Door?: Ballot Initiatives, State Policies, and Public Opinion," *Journal of Politics* 58 (August 1996): 760–775.

60. Brett Pulley, "The 1998 Campaign: Special Interests; Gambling Proponents Bet $85 Million on Election," the *New York Times* (October 31, 1998).

61. Bowman and Kearney, *State and Local Government*, 125.

62. Thomas E. Cronin, *Direct Democracy* (Cambridge, MA: Harvard University Press, 1989), 143.

63. *City of Clinton v. Cedar Rapids and Missouri RR Co.*, 24 Iowa 475 (1868), as quoted in Richard P. Nathan, "The Role of the States in American Federalism," in *The State of the States*, 2nd ed., Carl E. Van Horn, ed. (Washington, D.C.: Congressional Quarterly Press, 1993).

64. Don AuCoin and William F. Doherty, "House Votes To Pull Plug on Middlesex," *Boston Globe* (June 13, 1997), B12.

65. Clive S. Thomas and Ronald J. Hrebenar, "Interest Groups in the States," in *Politics in the American States*, 8th ed., Virginia Gray and Russell L. Hanson, eds. (Washington, D.C.: Congressional Quarterly Press, 2004), 118.

66. *The Municipal Year Book, 1996* (Washington, D.C.: International City/County Management Association, 1996).

67. David Brockington, Todd Donovan, Shaun Bowler, and Richard Brischetto, "Minority Representation under Cumulative and Limited Voting," *The Journal of Politics* 60 (November 1998): 1,108–1,125.

68. Kenneth J. Meier, Robert D. Wrinkle, and J. L. Polinard "Representative Bureaucracy and Distributional Equity: Addressing the Hard Question," *The Journal of Politics* 61 (November 1999): 1,025–1,039.

69. Kenneth K. Wong. "The Politics of Education," in Virginia Gray and Russell L. Hanson, eds., 8th ed., *Politics in the American States* (Washington, D.C.: Congressional Quarterly Press, 2004), 365–371.

70. Thomas R. Dye, *American Federalism* (Lexington, MA: D.C. Heath, 1990).

71. Paul E. Peterson, *City Limits* (Chicago: University of Chicago Press, 1981).

72. Jeffrey Berry, Kent Portney, and Ken Thomson, *The Rebirth of Urban Democracy* (Washington, D.C.: Brookings Institution, 1993).

73. David Osborne and Ted Gaebler, *Reinventing Government: How the Entrepreneurial Spirit Is Transforming the Public Sector*, (Reading, MA: Addison-Wesley, 1992).

Key Terms in Spanish

A

activation — acción y efecto de activar
actual group — grupo actual
administrative discretion — discreción administrativa
affirmative action — acción afirmativa
Americans with Disabilities Act of 1990 — disposición legal de 1990 para ciudadanos americanos minusválidos
***amicus curiae* briefs** — instrucciones, informes, de la competencia de amigos del senado.
Anti-Federalists — anti-federalistas
antitrust policy — política antimonopolio
appellate jurisdiction — jurisdicción apelatoria
appropriations bill — proyecto de ley de apropiación
arms race — carrera armamentista
Articles of Confederation — Artículos de la Confederación
authorization bill — estatuto de autorización

B

balance of trade — balance de intercambio comercial
beats — v. derrotar; recorrido de vigilancia policiaca
bicameral legislature — legislatura bi-camaral
Bill of Rights — proyecto de ley de derechos
bill — proyecto de ley; moción; cuenta
blanket primaries — cubiertas primarias
block grants — otorgamientos en conjunto
broadcast media — medios de transmisión
budget — presupuesto
budget resolution — resolución de presupuesto
bureaucracy — burocracia

C

cabinet — gabinete
campaign strategy — estrategia de campaña
capitalism — capitalismo
casework — trabajo de asistencia social
categorical grants — concesiones categorizadas
caucus — reunión del comité central o asamblea local de un partido
censorship — censura
census — censo
Central Intelligence Agency (CIA) — Agencia Central de Inteligencia
chains (newspaper chains) — cadena (cadenas periodísticas)
checks and balances — cheques y balances
city manager — aministrador de la ciudad
civic duty — deber cívico
civil disobedience — desobediencia civil
civil liberties — libertades civiles

civil rights — derechos civiles
Civil Rights Act of 1964 — ley de Derechos Humanos de 1964
civil rights movement — movimiento de derechos civiles
civil service — administración pública
class action lawsuits — demanda colectiva
Clean Air Act of 1970 — ley contra la contaminación del aire de 1970
closed primaries — primarias cerradas
coalition — coalición
coalition government — coalición de gobierno
cold war — guerra fría
collective bargaining — negociación colectiva
collective good — bienestar colectivo
command-and-control policy — política de ordenamiento y control
commercial speech — discurso comercial
committee chairs — presidentes de comité
comparable worth — valor comparable
conference committees — comités de conferencias
Congressional Budget and Impoundment Control Act of 1974 — Ley del Presupuesto e Incautación del Congreso de 1974
Congressional Budget Office (CBO) — Oficina de Presupuesto del Congreso
Connecticut Compromise — Compromiso de Connecticut
consent of the governed — consentimiento del gobernado
conservatives — conservadores
Constitution — constitución
consumer price index (CPI) — índice de precios del consumidor
containment doctrine — doctrina o política de contención
continuing resolutions — resoluciones continuas
conversion — conversión
cooperative federalism — federalismo cooperativo
Council of Economic Advisors (CEA) — Consejo de Asesores Económicos
council of governments — consejo de gobiernos
courts of appeal — corte de apelación
crisis — crisis
critical election — elección crítica
cruel and unusual punishment — castigo cruel e inusual
culture of poverty — cultura de pobreza

D

Declaration of Independence — Declaración de Independencia
deficit — déficit
democracy — democracia

demography—demografía
deregulation—desregular, liberalizar
détente—relajación
Dillon's Rule—Regla de Dillon
direct democracy—democracia directa
direct mail—correo directo
district courts—juzgado de distrito
dual federalism—federalismo dual

E

Eighth Amendment—Octava Enmienda (constitucional)
elastic clause—cláusula flexible
electioneering—campaña electoral
electoral college—colegio electoral
elite theory—teoría de la élite
Endangered Species Act of 1973—Ley de Especies en Peligro de Extinción de 1973
entitlements—derechos
enumerated powers—poderes enumerados
Environmental Protection Agency (EPA)—Agencia de Protección al Ambiente
environmental impact statement (EIS)—declaración de impacto sobre el ambiente
Equal Rights Amendment—enmienda de Igualdad de Derechos
equal protection of the laws—igualdad de protección de la ley
establishment clause—cláusula de instauración
European Union (EU)—Unión Europea
exclusionary rule—regla de exclusión
executive orders—órdenes ejecutivas
exit poll—conteo de salida de votación
expenditures—gastos
extradition—extradición

F

factions—facciones
Federal Election Campaign Act—Ley de la Campaña Federal de Elección
Federal Election Commission (FEC)—Comisión Federal Electoral
Federal Reserve System—Sistema Federal de Reserva
Federal Trade Commission (FTC)—Comisión Federal de Comercio
federal debt—deuda federal
federalism—federalismo
Federalist Papers—Documentos Federalistas
Federalists—federalistas
Fifteenth Amendment—Quinceava Enmienda
Fifth Amendment—Enmienda Quinta
filibuster—intervención parlamentaria con objeto de impedir una votación
First Amendment—Enmienda Primera
fiscal federalism—federalismo fiscal

fiscal policy—política fiscal
Food and Drug Administration (FDA)—Departamento Administrativo de Alimentos y Estupefacientes
foreign policy—política extranjera
formula grants—fórmula de concesión
Fourteenth Amendment—Catorceava Enmienda
free exercise clause—cláusula de ejercicio libre
free-rider problem—problema de polizón
frontloading—carga frontal
full faith and credit—fe y crédito completo

G

gender gap—disparidad de género
government—gobierno
government corporations—corporaciones gubernamentales
gross domestic product—producto doméstico bruto
GS (General Schedule) rating—prorrateo programático general

H

Hatch Act—Ley Hatch
health maintenance organization (HMO)—Organización para el Manteniento de la Salud
high-tech politics—política sobre alta tecnología
home rule—regla de casa (local)
House Rules Committee—Comité de Reglas de la Cámara
House Ways and Means Committee—Comité de Formas y Medios de la Cámara
hyperpluralism—hiperpluralismo; pluralismo en exceso

I

impeachment—juicio de impugnación
implied powers—poderes implícitos
incentive system—sistema de incentivos
income—ingresos de enlace
incorporation doctrine—doctrina de incorporación
incrementalism—incrementalismo
incumbents—titular en función
independent executive agencies—agencias ejecutivas independientes
independent regulatory agency—agencia regulatoria independiente
industrial policy—política industrial
inflation—inflación
initiative—iniciativa
initiative petition—iniciativa de petición
interdependency—interdependencia
interest group—grupos de interés
intergovernmental relations—relaciones intergubernamentales
investigative journalism—periodismo de investigación
iron triangles—triángulos de acero
isolationism—aislacionismo
item veto—artículo de veto

J

Joint Chiefs of Staff—Junta de Comandantes de las Fuerzas Armadas (Estado Mayor)
joint committees—comisiones
judicial activisim—activismo judicial
judicial implementation—implementación judicial
judicial restraint—restricción judicial
judicial review—revisión judicial
justiciable disputes—conflictos enjuiciables

K

Keynesian economic theory—teoría económica keynesiana

L

laissez-faire—liberalismo económico
legislative oversight—descuido legislativo
legislative veto—Veto legislativo
legitimacy—legitimidad
libel—difamación, calumnia
liberals—liberales
lieutenant governor—lugarteniente del gobernador
limited government—gobierno limitado
linkage institutions—instituciones de enlace
lobbying—cabildeo
local charter—estatutos locales; fuero local

M

majority leader—líder de la mayoría
majority rule—gobierno de la mayoría
mandate theory of elections—mandato teórico de elecciones
mass media—medios de difusión (comunicación) masiva
McCarthyism—macartismo
McGovern-Fraser Commission—Comisión *McGovern-Fraser*
media event—evento de los medios de difusión (comunicación)
Medicaid—programa de asistencia médica estatal *Medicaid* para personas de bajos ingresos
Medicare—programa de asistencia médica estatal *Medicare* para personas mayores de 65 años
melting pot—crisol
merit plan—plan meritorio (por méritos)
merit principle—principio de mérito
minority leader—líder de la minoría parlamentaria
minority majority—majoria de la minoría
minority rights—derechos de las minorías
mixed economy—economía mixta
monetarism—monetarismo
monetary policy—política monetaria
Motor Voter Act—Ley para promoción del voto

N

narrowcasting—transmisión cerrada; monitoreo cerrado

National Environmental Policy Act (NEPA)—Ley de la Política Ambiental Nacional
National Labor Relations Act—Ley Nacional de Relaciones Laborales
National Security Council (NSC)—Consejo Nacional de Seguridad
national chairperson—director/a de comité nacional
national committee—comité nacional
national convention—convención nacional
national health insurance—seguro de salud nacional
national party convention—convención nacional del partido
national primary—primaria nacional
natural rights—derechos naturales
New Deal coalition—coalición para el Nuevo Tratado
New Jersey Plan—Plan de New Jersey
Nineteenth Amendment—Enmienda Diecinueve
nomination—nominación
North Atlantic Treaty Organization (NATO)—Tratado de las Organizaciones del Atlantico Norte

O

Office of Management and Budget (OMB)—Oficina de Gestión y Presupuesto
Office of Personnel Management (OPM)—Oficina de Gestión de Personal
Olson's law of large groups—ley de Olson de grandes grupos
open primaries—primarias abiertas
opinion—opinión
Organization of Petroleum Exporting Countries (OPEC)—Organización de Países Exportadores de Petróleo
original intent—intento original
original jurisdiction—jurisdicción original

P

party competition—competencia de partido
party dealignment—desalineamiento del partido
party eras—épocas del partido
party identification—identificación partidista
party image—imágen del partido
party machines—maquinaria partidista
party neutrality—neutralidad partidista
party platform—plataforma del partido
party realignment—realinación del partido
patronage—patrocinio
Pendleton Civil Service Act—Ley del Servicio Público de Pendleton
plea bargaining—negociación fiscal-defensa
pluralist theory—teoría pluralista
pocket veto—veto indirecto del presidente al no firmar dentro de los diez días establecidos
policy agenda—agenda política
policy entrepreneurs—política empresarial
policy gridlock—parálisis política

policy implementation—implementación política
policy voting—política de votación
policymaking institutions—instituciones de normatividad política
policymaking system—sistema de normatividad política
political action committees (PACs)—comités de acción política
political culture—cultura política
political efficacy—eficacia política
political ideology—ideología política
political issue—asunto político
political participation—participación política
political party—partido político
political questions—cuestiones políticas
political socialization—socialización política
politics—política
poll taxes—votación para impuestos
pork barrel—asignación de impuestos estatales para el beneficio de una cierta zona o grupo
potential group—grupo potencial
poverty line—límite económico mínimo para sobrevivencia
precedent—precedente
presidential coattails—acción a la sombra presidencial
presidential primaries—elecciones primarias presidenciales
press conferences—conferencias de prensa
print media—medios de comunicación impresos
prior restraint—restricción anterior
privileges and immunities—privilegios e inmunidades
probable cause—causa probable
progressive tax—impuesto progresivo
project grant—proyecto de concesión
proportional representation—representación proporcional
proportional tax—impuesto proporcional
protest—n. protesta; v. protestar
public goods—bienes públicos
public interest lobbies—cabildeo por intereses públicos
public opinion—opinión pública
public policy—política pública

R

random sampling—muestreo aleatorio
random-digit dialing—llamadas con números aleatorios
rational-choice theory—teoría de selección racional
reapportionment—nueva distribución en la representación del congreso
recall—retirar
reconciliation—reconciliación
referendum—referendum
regional primaries—elecciones primarias regionales
regressive tax—impuesto regresivo
regulation—norma, regla
reinforcement—refuerzo
relative deprivation—privación relativa

representation—representación
republic—república
responsible party model—modelo de partido responsable
retrospective voting—votación retrospectiva
revenues—ingresos
right to privacy—derecho a la privacidad
right-to-work laws—leyes del derecho al trabajo

S

sample—muestra
sampling error—error de muestreo
search warrant—orden de cateo
secretary of defense—secretario de la defensa
secretary of state—secretario de estado
select committees—comités seleccionados
selective benefits—beneficios selectivos
selective perception—percepción selectiva
self-incrimination—auto incriminación
Senate Finance Committee—Comité Senatorial de Finanzas
senatorial courtesy—cortesía senatorial
Senior Executive Service—el de más alto rango en el servicio del ejecutivo
seniority system—sistema de antigüedad
separation of powers—separación de poderes
Shays' Rebellion—Rebelion de Shays
single-issue groups—grupos para una sola causa
Sixteenth Amendment—Enmienda Dieciséis
Sixth Amendment—Enmienda Sexta
Social Security Act—Ley de Seguridad Social
social welfare policies—políticas para el bien social
soft money—moneda débil, sin garantía
solicitor general—subsecretario de justicia
sound bites—segmentos de sonido
Speaker of the House—presidente de la cámara
standard operating procedures (SOPs)—procedimientos normales de operación
standing committees—comités permanentes
standing to sue—en posición de entablar demanda
stare decisis—variación de "decisión firme" o "decisión tomada"; la decisión se fundamenta en algo ya decidio.
statutory construction—construcción establecida por ley
Strategic Defense Initiative (SDI)—Iniciativa de Defensa Estratégica
street-level bureaucrats—burócratas de bajo nivel
subnational government—gobierno subnacional
subgovernments—subgobiernos
suffrage—sufragio
Super Tuesday—Super martes: día de votación en varios estados importantes.
superdelegates—superdelegados
Superfund—superfondo; fondo de proporciones mayores
supply-side economics—economía de la oferta
supremacy clause—cláusula de supremacía
Supreme Court—Suprema Corte

symbolic speech—discurso simbólico

T

Taft-Hartley Act—Ley de Taft-Hatley
talking head—busto parlante; presentador, entrevistador
tariff—tarifa
tax expenditures—gastos de impuesto
Tenth Amendment—Enmienda Décima
term limits—periodo límite
third parties—terceras personas
Thirteenth Amendment—Enmienda Treceava
ticket-splitting—votación de candidatos de diferentes partidos para diferentes cargos
town meeting—consejo municipal de vecinos
transfer payments—transferencia de pagos
transnational corporations—corporaciones transnacionales
trial balloons—globo de prueba; proponer algo para conocer la reacción de alguien
Twenty-fifth Amendment—Enmienda veiticincoava
Twenty-fourth Amendment—Enmienda veiticuatrava
Twenty-second Amendment—Enmienda veintidoava

U

U.S. Constitution—Constitución de los Estados Unidos
uncontrollable expenditures—gastos incontrolables
unemployment rate—nivel de desempleo; porcentage de desempleo

union shop—empresa que emplea sólo trabajadores sindicalizados
unitary governments—estados/gobiernos unitarios
United Nations (UN)—Naciones Unidas
unreasonable searches and seizures—cateos y detenciones/ embargos irrazonables
urban underclass—urbanita de clase baja

V

veto—veto
Virginia Plan—Plan Virginia
voter registration—registro de votantes
Voting Rights Act of 1965—Ley de Derechos del Elector de 1965

W

War Powers Resolution—Resolución de Poderes de Guerra
Water Pollution Control Act of 1972—Ley para el Control de la Contaminación de Aguas de 1972
wealth—riqueza
whips—miembro de un cuerpo legislativo encargado de hacer observar las consignas del partido
white primary—primaria blanca/ sin novedad
winner-take-all system—sistema en el que el ganador toma todos los votos
writ of habeas corpus—un recurso de hábeas corpus

Acknowledgments

Text Acknowledgments

9: "Vote Drives Gain Avid Attention of Youth in '04" by Timothy Egan, NYT, 9/15/04. Copyright © 2004 New York Times Company, Inc. Used with permission.

36: "Economic Status of State Legislators Before and After the Revolutionary War," from Jackson Turner Main, "Government by the People: The American Revolution and the Democratization of the Legislatures," *The William and Mary Quarterly*, 3rd ser. 23 (July 1966). Reprinted by permission of the Omohandro Institute of Early American History and culture.

60: "Self-Evident Truths, Now More Evident; National Archives Reopens with New Display of Historic Documents" by James Dao, NYT, 9/17/03. Copyright © 2003 New York Times Company, Inc. Used with permission.

81: "A Pragmatic Federalism," from 1997 public opinion poll, September 25–October 31, 1997. © Pew Research Center for the People and the Press. Used with permission.

86: "Security Grants Still Streaming to Rural States," by Dean E. Murphy, NYT 10/12/04. Copyright © 2004 New York Times Company, Inc. Used with permission.

108: "Hateful Name Calling vs. Calling for Hateful Action" by Edward Rothstein, NYT, 11/23/02. Copyright © 2002 New York Times Company, Inc. Used with permission.

132: "The Abortion Debate," from Gallup Poll, October 24–26, 2003. Copyright © 2003 Gallup, Inc. Used with permission.

147: "Percentage of Black Students Attending School With any Whites in Southern States," from Lawrence Baum, *The Supreme Court*, 7th ed. (Washington, D.C.: Congressional Quarterly, 2001), 229.

165: "Discrimination Against Homosexuals," from Gallup Poll, April 1999, May 2001, May 2003.

168: "What the United States Army Teaches Us About Affirmative Action," by Brent Staples, NYT, 1/6/03. Copyright © 2003 New York Times Company, Inc. Used with permission.

190: "Cellphones and Caller ID are Making Pollsters' Jobs Harder," by Adam Nagourney, NYT, 11/5/02. Copyright © 2002 New York Times Company, Inc. Used with permission.

195: "America in Perspective: Citizens Show Little Knowledge of Geography," from the *New York Times*, 11/9/89.

221: "Young People and Politics: How the Under-30 Crowd Learns from Different Media Sources Compared to Older Americans," from January 2004 survey. Copyright © 2004 Pew Research Center for the People & the Press. Used with permission.

228: "Making of the Digital Press Corps, 2004" by Katharine Seelye, NYT, 01/29/04. Copyright © 2004 New York Times Company, Inc. Used with permission.

248: "The Very, Very Personal is the Political," Jon Gertner, *New York Times Magazine*, February 15, 2004. Copyright © 2004 Jon Gertner. Reprinted by permission.

256: "Party Coalitions Today," Copyright © 2004 Pew Research Center for the People and the Press. Used with permission (from *http://people-press.org/commentary/display.php3?AnalysisID=95*).

272: "California Moves to Reschedule Its Primary from March to June," by Dean E. Murphy, NYT 08/30/04. Copyright © 2004 New York Times Company, Inc. Used with permission.

289: "The Big-Spending PACS," © Center for Responsive Politics, *www.opensecrets.org*.

306: "Immigrants Raise Call for Right to Be Voters," by Rachel L. Swarns, NYT, 08/09/04. Copyright © 2004 New York Times Company, Inc. Used with permission.

329: "The Power 25," © Fortune, Inc. 2001.

331: "The Benefits of Membership in the AARP," © American Association for Retired Persons.

333: "Associations by Type," data from Frank R. Baumgartner and Beth L. Leech, *Basic Interests: The Importance of Groups in Politics and in Political Science* (Princeton, NJ: Princeton University Pres, 1998), 109.

336: "Kerry Releases a List of His Lobbyist Meetings" by Glen Justice, NYT, 04/23/04. Copyright © 2004 New York Times Company, Inc. Used with permission.

355: "A Day in the Life of a Member of Congress," adapted by permission from Craig Schult. Ed., *Setting Course: A Congressional Management Guide*. Copyright © 1994 Congressional Management Foundation, Washington, D.C. and from David E. Price, *The Congressional Experience: A View from the Hill*. Copyright © 1999 Westview Press, a member of Perseus Books, L.L.C.

359: "The Incumbency Factor in Congressional Elections," from Norman J. Ornstein, et al., *Vital Statistics on Congress, 1997–1998* (Washington, D.C.: Congressional Quarterly Press, 1998).

380: "In the House at Least, Moderation is No Virtue," by Robin Toner, NYT, 11/17/02. Copyright © 2002 New York Times Company, Inc. Used with permission.

405: "Principal Offices in the White House," adapted from George C. Edwards III and Stephen J. Wayne, *Presidential Leadership*, 6th ed.

428: "White House Keeps a Grip on Its News," by Jim Rutenberg, NYT, 10/14/02. Copyright © 2002 New York Times Company, Inc. Used with permission.

438: "A Clash of Goals in Bush's Efforts on the Income Tax; Proposals Would Shift Burden from Wealthy to Middle Class," by Ednund Andrews, NYT, 10/06/04. Copyright © 2004 New York Times Company, Inc. Used with permission.

457: "The Congressional Budget Process: Targets and Timetables," from Howard E. Shuman, *Politics and the Budget: The Struggle Between the President and the Congress*, 3rd ed., p. 67. © 1992. Reprinted by permission of Pearson Education, Upper Saddle River, NJ.

Photo Acknowledgments

Index

Numbers preceded by an *n* indicate note numbers.

cue givers, 369
Curley, James Michael, 246
Customs Service, 487–488
Cyprus, 616
Czechoslovakia, 629
Czech Republic, 616, 629

Dahl, Robert, 17–18
Daley, Richard J., 246, 269
Dallek, Robert, 621
Daniels, Mitch, 323
Darrow, Clarence, 392
Darwinian theories of evolution, 103
Daschle, Thomas, 367, 409, 597
Datamart database, 248
data-mining technology, 247–248
Davis, Gray, 273, 673
Davis, Martis J., 581
Davis v. Monroe County Board of Education, 162
Dawes Act (1887), 152
Dawson, Richard, 184
The Day After Tomorrow, 607
Dayton Board of Education v. Brinkman, 149
Dean, Howard
    campaigning and, 268–269, 280
    mass media and, 222, 228–229
    matching funds and, 284
    survey question about, 194
    young voters and, 9
death penalty. *See* capital punishment
debt, federal, 44.440–442
Declaration of Independence, 30–34, 41, 140
de facto segregation, 146
defendants, 504
defendant's rights, 51, 120–129
Defense Nuclear Facilities Safety Board, 477
Defense of Marriage Act, 77, 574
defense policy. *See* national security
defensive medicine, 589
deficit
    annual, 459
    balanced budget and, 442
    balance-of-trade, 643
    Clinton and, 424
    defined, 436
    foreign investors and, 440
    September 11 attacks and, 23
    supply-side economics and, 553
De Jonge v. Oregon, 101
de jure segregation, 146
Delaware
    Articles of Confederation, 37
    balance of power, 658
    counties in, 676
    diversity and, 652
    legislative turnover in, 659
    ratifying Constitution, 52
    representation in, 364
    sales tax, 683
    women as governors, 660
DeLay, Tom, 367, 409
Delli Carpini, Michael, 4
Deloria, Vera, 152
democracy
    budgeting and, 460–463
    bureaucracy and, 494–499
    campaigns and, 291–292
    civil liberties and, 133
    civil rights and, 172
    Congress and, 353, 383–386
    constitutions and, 53, 58–59
    courts and, 531–532
    defined, 16
    early state changes, 36
    in East Europe, 629
    economic policies and, 559–560
    elections and, 317–319
    environment and, 609
    federalism and, 89–91
    federal systems as, 69

government as, 10
Great Britain as, 53
Hamilton on, 38
health care and, 609
interest groups and, 347–348
mass media and, 235–236
national security and, 645–647
nomination and, 291–292
overview, 16–21
political action and, 206
political culture of, 392
political participation and, 201
political parties and, 239, 261–262
polls and, 192–193
presidency and, 430
public debate and, 116
public opinion and, 206
social welfare policy and, 582–583
subnational governments, 674, 686–688
Democratic National Committee, 248, 250, 341, 396
Democratic Party
    on abortion, 241
    African Americans and, 245
    balance of power, 657–659
    blanket primary and, 249
    on committee chairs, 372
    divided party government and, 257
    elections and, 299–302
    employment and, 545
    on free trade, 559
    free trade and, 555
    gender gap and, 199
    gubernatorial elections and, 656
    on illegal immigrants, 182
    Jackson and, 254
    on labor issues, 378
    labor unions and, 343
    mass media and, 227
    membership requirements, 243
    on minimum wage, 558
    on national primary, 276
    New Deal coalition and, 256
    party competition and, 240
    party identification with, 243
    party platform, 252
    political socialization and, 185
    political tides and, 362
    on prescription drugs, 594
    presidential coattails and, 359
    presidential primaries and, 269, 271
    recent presidents from, 393–394
    on right to sue, 592
    on Roosevelt, 552
    on scope of government, 560
    scope of government and, 239
    social group support for, 256
    on social policies, 572
    on Social Security, 577, 583
    states under control of, 258
    superdelegates and, 271
    Supreme Court and, 514, 516
    on tax reform, 446
    on welfare reform, 573
    women as governors and, 660
    young adults and, 259
Democratic Party et al. v. Jones, 249
Democratic-Republicans. *See* Federalists
Democratic Republic of the Congo, 616
demography, 178
Denmark, 308, 445, 448, 645
Dennis, Jack, 186
Dennis v. United States, 107
Department of Agriculture (USDA)
    border security and, 488
    employment at, 470
    fragmentation and, 487
    function, 402
    lack of authority and, 484
    meat and poultry regulation, 466–467

organization of, 477
poverty study, 568
regulation and, 491
tobacco programs and, 328
on trade, 647
Department of Commerce, 402, 470, 476–477, 488, 557, 647
Department of Commerce v. U.S. House of Representatives, 178
Department of Defense (DOD)
    border security and, 488
    employment at, 469–470
    foreign policy and, 618–623
    on homosexual conduct, 165
    national security state and, 449
    organization of, 476–477
    Pentagon papers and, 110
    prescription drugs and, 597
    procurement budget, 462
    secretary of defense and, 619
    troops abroad and, 647
Department of Education, 402, 470, 476–477, 482, 496
Department of Energy
    AEC and, 499
    border security and, 488
    disbanding of, 476
    employment at, 470
    function, 402
    on global warming, 607
    organization of, 477
    Reagan and, 496
Department of Foreign Affairs, 447
Department of Health and Human Services (HHS), 131, 402, 470, 476–477, 487, 587
Department of Health, Education and Welfare (HEW), 483, 496
Department of Homeland Security
    Bush and, 487–488, 473–474
    creation of, 322
    employment at, 470
    function, 402
    job protection and, 475
    organization of, 477
Department of Housing and Urban Development (HUD), 371, 470, 477, 485, 487
Department of Justice
    antitrust legislation and, 556
    border security and, 488
    desegregation and, 148
    employment at, 470
    fragmentation and, 487
    function, 402
    judicial nominees and, 519
    justices and, 518
    Microsoft and, 341
    nominations and, 512
    organization of, 477
    solicitor general, 521
    Voting Rights Act and, 151, 489–490
Department of Labor
    Bureau of Labor Statistics, 546–547
    employment at, 470
    fragmentation and, 487
    function, 402
    offshoring, 643, 647
    organization of, 477
    regulation and, 490
    shared administration and, 80
Department of State, 402, 470, 477, 487–488, 618–619
Department of the Interior, 345, 402, 470, 476–478, 604
Department of the Treasury
    balance of trade, 647
    border security and, 488
    borrowing and, 440
    employment at, 470
    fragmentation and, 487
    function, 402

People's Republic of China. *See* China
per curiam decision, 521
permanent residents, voting and, 306–307
Perot, H. Ross, 241, 259, 261, 285, 314, 442
Persian Gulf War
  Bush and, 423, 621
  censorship and, 107
  coverage of, 223–224
  defense spending and, 633
  emergency order and, 486
  nuclear weapons and, 636
  oil and, 606
  public opinion about, 177
  women and, 160
personal freedoms. *See* individualism
Personal Responsibility and Work Opportunity
    Reconciliation Act (PRWORA), 564, 573
Petrocik, John R., 200
Pew Charitable Trusts, 9
Pew Research Center, 7, 81, 231, 641
Pharmaceutical Research and Manufacturers of
    America, 329
Philadelphia Convention, 38–46, 71, 74, 141
Philip Morris, 289, 341
Philippines, 179, 614, 640
Phillips, Kevin, 18
picketing, 106, 119
Pierce, Franklin, 395
Pinckney, Charles C., 41
Piper Rudnick, 337
plaintiff, 504
Planetary Society, 489
Planned Parenthood v. Casey, 131
Playboy, 217
Playboy Entertainment Group, 118
plea bargaining, 126, 668
Pledge of Allegiance, 11, 186
Plessy, Homer, 144
Plessy v. Ferguson, 144–146, 505, 523
plum book, 475–476, 518
Plunkett, George Washington, 246
pluralist theory, 17–18, 58, 325–328, 347, 531. *See
    also* hyperpluralist theory
pocket veto, 407
Poindexter, John, 622
Pointer v. Texas, 101
Poland, 179, 577, 616, 629
policy. *See* public policy
policy agenda, 13–14, 17, 233–234, 373, 526–530,
    540
policy entrepreneurs, 233–234
policy gridlock, 20, 62
policy implementation, 480
policymaking institutions
  Congress (*See* Congress)
  courts as, 504, 519–526, 536
  defined, 14
  ICC as, 492
  increasing demands on, 57
  policymaking system and, 13
  subgovernments as, 652
policymaking system. *See also* public policy
  congressional caucuses and, 373
  defined, 13
  foreign policy and, 614–623
  governors and, 663
  for health care, 594–600
  interest groups and, 348, 382
  legislative professionalism and, 666
  limiting function, 62
  linkage institutions and, 384
  overview, 13–16
  PACs and, 362
  political parties and, 241
  presidential power and, 400
policy voting, 312, 315–316
political action committees (PACs). *See also* interest
    groups
  business and, 344
  campaign costs and, 20, 204, 362
  defined, 286, 338

electioneering and, 338–339
  eliminating, 340
  elite theory on, 348
  government growth and, 462
  overview, 286–288
  state legislative elections and, 657
political activism, 233–234
"political business cycle," 554
political culture, 183, 392
political efficacy, 305
political ideology, 197–200, 378–382
political issue, 14
political knowledge, 4–5, 7, 194, 379
PoliticalMoneyLine, 336
political participation
  among college students, 4
  challenges for future, 7
  as challenge to democracy, 19–20
  defined, 12, 201
  overview, 200–205
  PACs and, 340
  public policy and, 13
  young people and, 8–9
political parties. *See also* specific parties
  changing political practice and, 56
  decentralized, 262–263
  defined, 240
  democracy and, 239, 261–262
  electorate and, 243–245
  eras in history, 253–258
  factions and, 39
  fiscal policy of, 549–553
  government and, 240, 250–252
  impact of third parties, 258–260
  influence of, 378–379
  meaning of, 240–243
  membership requirements, 243
  nomination and, 268
  organizations and, 245–250
  party platforms, 252, 278
  policy agenda and, 233
  presidential elections and, 59
  scope of government and, 239, 262–263
  weakness of, 369
political questions, 536
political socialization, 184–187
politicians. *See* elected officials
politicos, 379
politics
  of defense policy, 632–636
  defined, 12, 454
  economy and, 542–547
  government and, 12–13
  of health care, 594–600
  high-tech, 212
  impact of third parties on, 258–260
  income and, 565
  international economy and, 554–555
  mass media and, 57, 214–216
  political socialization and, 184–187
  public budgets and, 454–455
Polk, James, 395
Pollock v. Farmer's Loan and Trust Co., 436, 536
polls, 186, 192–190, 379, 421–422
poll taxes, 59, 149–150
pollution, 493, 587, 600–602
Pomper, Gerald, 251
Poole, Keith, 565
poor. *See* poverty
Poor Laws, 572
Poor Women, Poor Children (Rodgers), 569
population
  BLS survey and, 546
  Connecticut Compromise and, 41
  demography and, 178
  environmental interests and, 344
  projections for, 180
  redistricting and, 657
  shifting, 183–184
populism, 621
Populist Party, 259

pork barrel, 360–361, 662
pornography, 115–116, 125
Portugal, 308, 445, 616
position-taking, 361
Postal Rate Commission, 477
Postal Service. *See* U.S. Postal Service
potential group, 330
Potter, Harry, 566
poverty
  African Americans and, 180
  government programs and, 565
  health insurance and, 590
  Hispanic Americans and, 154, 181
  means-tested programs and, 565
  Native Americans and, 152, 183
  other countries and, 579
  party influence and, 378
  public policy and, 565–571
  Social Security Act and, 450
  social welfare policies and, 572–574
  War on Poverty, 256
  welfare programs and, 81
poverty line, 567–568, 594
Powell, Colin, 169, 180, 618–619
Powell, Jody, 225
Powell, Lewis, 513, 518
Powell v. Alabama, 101, 126
power
  balance of, 657–659
  checks on exercise of, 29
  Congress and, 353, 357
  congressional committees and, 371–372
  courts and, 532–537
  division of, 72–74
  elections and, 298
  elite theory on, 325, 327
  factions and, 40
  government exceeding, 74
  of governors, 662–663
  granted by Constitution, 72
  Hamilton on, 39
  Hoover and, 496
  Hussein and, 638
  Johnson on, 371, 376
  Lennon on, 291
  Madisonian model and, 47, 340
  Marshall and, 532
  middle class and, 36
  opposition to, 392
  president and, 371, 391, 397–400, 420–425, 430
  scope of government and, 323
  separation of (*See* separation of power)
  shift of, 37
  of Supreme Court, 503, 529
  transfer of, 10
  U.S. Constitution and, 674
Pratt, Sara, 485
prayer. *See* school prayer
precedents, 522–523
preferential treatment, 167
Pregnancy Discrimination Act (1978), 158
prescription drugs, 450, 586–587, 593–594,
    596–597
president. *See also* executive branch
  amendment process and, 52
  Articles of Confederation on, 35
  bills and, 376–378
  budget and, 454–456
  bureaucracy and, 494–496, 473–474
  checks and balances and, 47
  as chief executive, 400–407
  as chief legislator, 376, 407–408
  Congress and, 353, 391, 399, 407–415, 419–420
  crises and, 620–621
  democracy and, 430
  disability of, 396
  economy and, 554
  executive orders and, 495
  fiscal policy of, 549–553
  government and, 10
  legislative skills of, 413–415

Electoral College Results for 2000 and 2004

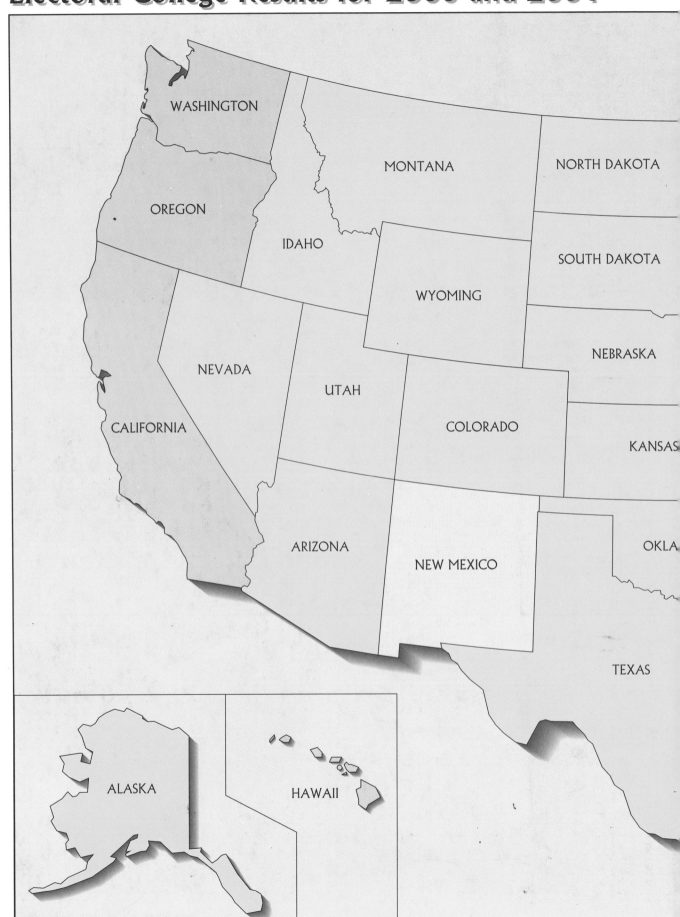